"Brilliant ... always a pleasure to read ... Pauline Kael is the greatest American movie critic."

—Phillip Lopate, in *New York Newsday*

"Sure to please her many fans as well as anyone who just plain loves movies."

—*People*

"She is ferociously funny.... She helps us to believe not only in movies but in criticism."

—*New York Times Book Review*

"Kael is one of the few critics who produce works that will become just as much favorites as the movies they cover."

—*Washington Post Book World*

"Kael showed us what criticism could be.... It was really thrilling to come across writing that was so voracious and so ambitious, that had so much life in it and such a complete absence of pretense."

—*Boston Globe*

"The mother of all critics is back with the mother of all books on film criticism.... Love her or hate her, Kael wrote with more passion, piss and vinegar, longer, harder, and funnier than all those who came before or after her."

—*Film Threat*

"Kael is easily the finest film critic yet to appear and already belongs among those critical writers whose aesthetic principles ... comprise the undeclared philosophical wealth of the last three-quarters of a century."

—Clive James, in *The Listener*

"Today, the best place to find 'the movies,' ... is, alas, in books. And the best books to go to remain those of Pauline Kael."

—*New York*

PAULINE KAEL, during her 25-year tenure as a film critic at *The New Yorker*, established herself as America's most renowned and respected movie reviewer. She is the author of thirteen books on film, inlcuding *Deeper into Movies* (1973), which won a National Book Award. She lives in western Massachusetts.

ALSO BY PAULINE KAEL

I Lost it at the Movies (1965)
Kiss Kiss Bang Bang (1968)
Going Steady (1970)
The Citizen Kane Book (1971)
Deeper Into Movies (1973)
Reeling (1976)
When the Lights Go Down (1980)
5001 Nights at the Movies (1982)
Taking It All In (1984)
State of the Art (1985)
Hooked (1989)
5001 Nights at the Movies, Expanded (1991)
Movie Love (1991)

PAULINE KAEL

· FOR ·
KEEPS

A WILLIAM ABRAHAMS BOOK

PLUME

PLUME

Published by the Penguin Group
Penguin Books USA, Inc., 375 Hudson Street, New York, New York 10014, U.S.A.
Penguin Books Ltd, 27 Wrights Lane London W8 5TZ, England
Penguin Books Australia Ltd Ringwood, Victoria Australia
Penguin Books Canada Ltd, 10 Alcorn Avenue, Toronto, Ontario, Canada M4V 3B2
Penguin Books (N.Z.) Ltd, 182–190 Wairau Road, Auckland 10, New Zealand

Penguin Books Ltd, Registered Offices:
Harmondsworth, Middlesex, England

Published by Plume, an imprint of Dutton Signet
a division of Penguin Books USA Inc.
Previously published in a Dutton edition.

First Plume Printing, September, 1996
10 9 8 7 6 5 4 3 2 1

 REGISTERED TRADEMARK—MARCA REGISTRADA

The Library of Congress has catalogued the Dutton edition as follows:
Kael, Pauline.
For keeps / Pauline Kael.
p. cm.
"A William Abrahams book."
ISBN 0-525-93896-6 (hc.)
ISBN 0-452-27308-0 (pbk.)
1. Motion pictures—Reviews. I. Title.
PN1995.K225 1994
791.43'75—dc20   94-6752
                                               CIP

Printed in the United States of America
Original hardcover design by Steven N. Stathakis

BOOKS ARE AVAILABLE AT QUANTITY DISCOUNTS WHEN USED TO PROMOTE PRODUCTS OR SERVICES. FOR INFORMA-
TION PLEASE WRITE TO PREMIUM MARKETING DIVISION, PENGUIN BOOKS USA INC., 375 HUDSON STREET, NEW YORK,
NEW YORK 10014.

CONTENTS

PART TWO FROM **KISS KISS BANG BANG** 1968

PART SIX FROM **REELING** 1976

PART SEVEN FROM **WHEN THE LIGHTS GO DOWN** 1980

PART EIGHT FROM **TAKING IT ALL IN** 1984

PART NINE FROM **STATE OF THE ART** 1985

PART TEN FROM **HOOKED** 1989

PART ELEVEN FROM **MOVIE LOVE** 1991

INTRODUCTION

I've been lucky: I wrote about movies during a great period, and I wrote about them for a great readership, at *The New Yorker.* It was the best job in the world. But it didn't come about quickly. I had written about movies for almost fifteen years, trying to be true to the spirit of what I loved about movies, trying to develop a voice that would avoid saphead objectivity and let the reader in on what sort of person was responding to the world in this particular way. Writing from the San Francisco area, publishing in a batch of mostly obscure "little" magazines, reviewing on KPFA in Berkeley, and then, in 1965, bringing out *I Lost it at the Movies,* I razzed the East Coast critics and their cultural domination of the country. (We in the West received the movies encumbered with stern punditry.) I was in my mid-thirties when my first review was published in the San Francisco quarterly *City Lights,* in 1953; by the time I wrote about *Bonnie and Clyde* in *The New Yorker,* in 1967, I was close to fifty. But after I'd moved to New York and become a professional (i.e., salaried) reviewer, I had to fight to keep my hard-won voice.

It took a long time for that direct, spoken tone to catch on with *New Yorker* readers. Some of them were real stiffs. If I said I'd walked out on a Fellini extravaganza or a movie of a Pinter play, they informed me that it was my duty to go back and see it all the way through. The hate mail piled up. Then, curiously, some of the readers seemed to begin to enjoy hating me. Maybe my conversational American tone brought them into a closer relationship than they'd been accustomed to; maybe what they had first experienced as a crude invasion from the pop world began to be something they looked forward to. Whatever it was, I can't believe that any other movie critic has had such thoughtful, picky, exuberant readers. They saw aspects of a movie that I had been blind to or hadn't fully perceived. Hyper-intelligent, they were maddeningly eager to catch me out. They said I added to their experience of a movie, and I know they often added to mine.

It was true conviviality—a variation of the intense discussions about the arts that I'd had with friends in high school and college—except that there was never really time to answer the readers' letters properly. By the late sixties, movies had become so political that just about every comment on a movie sparked wider discussion. And readers were arguing with me over last week's movie when I was trying to check this week's galleys and clear my head to get into next week's subjects.

My life was especially hectic during my first years at *The New Yorker,* because I (literally) spent more time and effort restoring what I'd written than writing it. The editors tried to turn me into just what I'd been struggling not to be: a genteel, fuddy-duddy stylist who says, "One assumes that . . ." Sometimes almost every sentence was rearranged. The result was tame and correct; it lost the sound of spoken language. I would scramble for nine or ten hours putting back what I had written, marking the galleys carefully so they wouldn't be misread, and then I would rush to see William Shawn to get the galleys approved. Since he was the person who had instigated the finicky changes, the couple of hours I spent with him were an exhausting series of pleas and negotiations. He had given me a handshake agreement when he hired me that no word would be changed without consultation, and he stuck by his word, but I had to fight for every other contraction, every bit of slang, every description of a scene in a movie that he thought morally offensive—not my description but the scene itself. He didn't see why those things had to be mentioned, he said.

Our sessions were complicated by the fact that he was a loving, dedicated editor and sometimes he was right. But I had to fight him anyway— how else could I keep from turning into one of his pets? He was the most squeamish man I'd ever met. He could hardly ever see all of a film—a hint of blood would send him packing—and so I wrote *Fear of Movies* to spook him. He hero-worshipped Gandhi, and so I made a dumb joke comparing the Gandhi of the 1982 film to the guilt-inducing Jewish mothers that TV comics complained about, and, despite his humble entreaties, refused to remove it. I hardened myself against his disappointed-in-you expression; I had to. Once when I compared the sets of a movie to a banana split, his suggested alternative was a pousse-café. When I quoted Herman J. Mankiewicz's famous line "Imagine—the whole world wired to Harry Cohn's ass," he insisted that it be "Harry Cohn's derrière." (I won out.) For more than twenty years William Shawn and I squared off like two little pit bulls. I was far from being the only writer who fought him, but it took years for me to learn about the others. He told each of us that we were the only ingrates. He brought up the names of all the famous writers who, according to him, had been appreciative of the editing; it was a nightmare listening to that litany. Yet he could also be more responsive to what a writer was trying to do than anyone else I've ever encountered. The man was an enigma. On the day after my review of Mailer's *Marilyn* appeared in the *Sunday Times Book Review,* we ran into each other in a hallway. "Why didn't you give that to us?" he asked. "What for?" I answered. "You wouldn't have printed it." "That's right," he said mournfully.

By the seventies, I'd won some freedom; there were still beefs, but there was no more of that sentence-by-sentence quibbling that can turn your brains to jelly. Maybe partly because of my slangy freedom, reactions to my reviews were startlingly physical. When I was introduced to Tennessee Williams at a New York Film Festival party at Lincoln Center, he crowed my name, scooped me up high above his head and spun about, twirling me in the air. He was short but muscular; I had a flash of news stories I'd read about the strength of the mad. But he was a grinning, happy madman—he was euphoric—and I knew that we were friends. (I also knew that part of his glee was the discovery of how small I was.) I had written enthusiastically of the underground star Holly Woodlawn, the female impersonator who played the wife in *Trash;* when we met, at a New York Film Critics Awards party in Sardi's, Holly, who was usually referred to as "she," was wearing spike heels, a satin gown, and a monkey-fur jacket. He seemed to forget all that as he swung me up to his height to hug me and deliver a big smooch. John Cassavetes, on the opening day of one of his psychodramas, grabbed me as I came out of the theatre and hoisted me, and as I hung there helpless in his grip, my tootsies dangling at least three feet from the sidewalk, his companions, Ben Gazzara and Peter Falk, were chuckling. Cassavetes was saying, "Love ya, Pauline, just love ya," and I felt that he wanted to crush every bone in my body.

The most unlikely men—and women too—suddenly turned macho around me; they didn't all offer to butt heads, as Norman Mailer did, but many confronted me angrily, and my escorts often had to calm them down. Years ago, I went to Elaine's twice, and fights erupted at my table both times. I think that the disjunction between my strong voice as a writer and my five-foot frame somehow got to people: they wanted to take me on—it made them feel big and courageous. I know that I wasn't exactly the innocent party: people who don't like my writing find it both Olympian and smart-alecky. I guess at some level it *is.* But it was hellish to have actors with hurt feelings come gunning for me, demanding to know what right I had not to like a performance of theirs or of a friend of theirs. Gradually, I stopped going to social gatherings in New York.

What began for me as a gregarious activity—talking about movies—

became, at last, almost a monastic pursuit. I lived in a small town in Massachusetts, went into New York City a few days a week to see the new movies, and returned home to write. And as the seventies gave way to the eighties, the excitement I had earlier found in the movies gave way to the pleasure I found in writing.

The pieces in this book belong to the breakneck era before people could rent videos of old movies and before distributors began to supply reviewers with videos of new movies. (Reviewers can use the video as a text.) I wrote at first sight and, when referring to earlier work, from memory. This had an advantage: urgency, excitement. But it also led to my worst flaw as a writer: reckless excess, in both praise and damnation. Writing very fast and trying to distill my experience of a movie, I often got carried away by words. I'd run on (as in *Shampoo* and *Lenny* and *X Y & Zee*), and I'd hit too many high notes. And I'd repeat myself or say things that were only slightly different from what I'd said before (as in *Lumière*). When I look at what I wrote, the adjectives seem fermented, and I long to strike out a word here, a phrase there. I have resisted, because tidying up these reviews would make them false to what I felt then, and false to the period itself. (Did I, as I have read, exaggerate how *Last Tango in Paris* affected me in order to help the film? No. I haven't seen it since its festival showing, yet I retain a clear memory of its emotional nakedness.)

A friend of mine says that he learned from reading me that "content grows from language, not the other way around." That's a generous way of saying that I let it rip, that I don't fully know what I think until I've said it. The reader is in on my thought processes.

It always seemed miraculous to be paid for what I loved doing. I'd still be doing it if age and illness hadn't laid me low. I'd be doing it despite the staleness of American movies. I've heard bright, jaded remarks, such as "I wouldn't mind missing the good movies if I could miss the bad ones" and "The only reason for going to movies now is to see why you're not going to movies." If I could go on, I'd be writing about why people feel that way.

Of the collections of my articles and reviews, the best are, I think, *Deeper Into Movies* (1973), *Reeling* (1976), and *When the Lights Go Down* (1980), because that's when the movies seemed to be about things that mattered. These three and most of the others are out of print in this country; I hope they'll be available again. But I can't expect readers to hang on to a dozen volumes. So here's an anthology, a selection of pieces that may serve as a reminder of the period from 1961 to 1991. (It represents about a fifth of what I published.) The week-by-week flow is gone, but you can still get the sense of how movies interacted with public life, and you can get the critic's first flushes of discovery. I'm frequently asked why I don't write my memoirs. I think I have.

PART ONE

I LOST IT
AT THE
MOVIES

1965

HUD,
DEEP IN THE DIVIDED HEART OF HOLLYWOOD

A s a schoolgirl, my suspiciousness about those who attack American "materialism" was first aroused by the refugees from Hitler who so often contrasted their "culture" with our "vulgar materialism" when I discovered that their "culture" consisted of their having had servants in Europe, and a swooning acquaintance with the poems of Rilke, the novels of Stefan Zweig and Lion Feuchtwanger, the music of Mahler and Bruckner. And as the cultural treasures they brought over with them were likely to be Meissen porcelain, Biedermeier furniture, oriental carpets, wax fruit, and bookcases with glass doors, it wasn't too difficult to reconstruct their "culture" and discover that it was a stuffier, more middle-class materialism and sentimentality than they could afford in the new world.

These suspicions were intensified by later experience: the most grasping Europeans were, almost inevitably, the ones who leveled the charge of American materialism. Just recently, at a film festival, a behind-the-iron-curtain movie director, who interrupted my interview with him to fawn over every Hollywood dignitary (or supposed dignitary) who came in sight, concluded the interview with, "You Americans won't understand this, but I don't make movies just for money."

Americans are so vulnerable, so confused and defensive about prosperity—and nowhere more so than in Hollywood, where they seem to feel they can cleanse it, justify their right to it, by gilding it with "culture,"

3

as if to say, see, we're not materialistic, we appreciate the finer things. ("The hunting scene on the wall of the cabana isn't wallpaper: it's handpainted.") Those who live by making movies showing a luxurious way of life worry over the American "image" abroad. But, the economics of moviemaking being what they are, usually all the producers do about it is worry—which is probably just as well because films made out of social conscience have generally given an even more distorted view of America than those made out of business sense, and are much less amusing.

The most conspicuous recent exception is *Hud*—one of the few entertaining American movies released in 1963 and just possibly the most completely schizoid movie produced anywhere anytime. *Hud* is a commercial Hollywood movie that is ostensibly an indictment of materialism, and it has been accepted as that by most of the critics. But those who made it protected their material interest in the film so well that they turned it into the opposite: a celebration and glorification of materialism—of the man who looks out for himself—which probably appeals to movie audiences just because it confirms their own feelings. This response to *Hud* may be the only time the general audience has understood film makers better than they understood themselves. Audiences ignored the cant of the makers' liberal, serious intentions, and enjoyed the film for its vital element: the nihilistic "heel" who wants the good things of life and doesn't give a damn for the general welfare. The writers' and director's "anti-materialism" turns out to be a lot like the refugees' anti-materialism: they had their Stefan Zweig side—young, tender Lon (Brandon de Wilde) and Melvyn Douglas's Homer, a representative of the "good" as prating and tedious as Polonius; and they had their protection, their solid salable property of Meissen and Biedermeier, in Paul Newman.

Somehow it all reminds one of the old apocryphal story conference— "It's a modern western, see, with this hell-raising, pleasure-loving man who doesn't respect any of the virtues, and, at the end, we'll fool them, he doesn't get the girl and he doesn't change!"

"But who'll want to see *that*?"

"Oh, that's all fixed—we've got Paul Newman for the part."

They could cast him as a mean man and know that the audience would never believe in his meanness. For there are certain actors who have such extraordinary audience rapport that the audience does not believe in their villainy except to relish it, as with Brando; and there are others, like Newman, who in addition to this rapport, project such a traditional heroic frankness and sweetness that the audience dotes on them, seeks to protect them from harm or pain. Casting Newman as a mean materialist is like writing a manifesto against the banking system while juggling your investments so you can break the bank. Hud's shouted last remark, his poor credo, "The world's so full of crap a man's going to get into it sooner or later, whether he's careful or not," has, at least, the ring of *his* truth. The generalized pious principles of the good old codger belong to no body.

■　■　■

The day *Hud* opened in San Francisco the theatre was packed with an audience that laughed and reacted with pleasure to the verve and speed and economy, and (although I can't be sure of this) enjoyed the surprise of the slightly perverse ending as much as I did. It was like the split movies of the war years—with those cynical heel-heroes whom we liked because they expressed contempt for the sanctimonious goody guys and overstuffed family values, and whom we still liked (because they were played by actors who *seemed* contemptuous) even when they reformed.

It's not likely that those earlier commercial writers and directors were self-deceived about what they were doing: they were trying to put something over, and knew they could only go so far. They made the hero a "heel" so that we would identify with his rejection of official values, and then slyly squared everything by having him turn into a conventional hero. And it seems to me that we (my college friends) and perhaps the audience at large didn't take all this very seriously, that we enjoyed it for its obvious hokum and glamour and excitement and romance, and for the wisecracking American idiom, and the tempo and rhythm of slick style. We enjoyed the *pretense* that the world was like this—fast and funny; this pretense which was necessary for its enjoyment separated the good American commercial movie—the good "hack" job like *Casablanca* or *To Have and Have Not*—from film art and other art. This was the best kind of Hollywood *product:* the result of the teamwork of talented, highly paid professional hacks who were making a living; and we enjoyed it as a product, and assumed that those involved in it enjoyed the money they made.

What gave the Hollywood movie its vitality and its distinctive flavor was that despite the melodramatic situations, the absurd triumphs of virtue and the inordinate punishments for trivial vice—perhaps even because of the stale conventions and the necessity to infuse some life that would make the picture seem new within them—the "feel" of the time and place (Hollywood, whatever the locale of the story) came through, and often the attitudes, the problems, the tensions. Sometimes more of American life came through in routine thrillers and prison-break films and even in the yachting-set comedies than in important, "serious" films like *The Best Years of Our Lives* or *A Place in the Sun,* paralyzed, self-conscious imitations of European art, or films like *Gentleman's Agreement,* with the indigenous paralysis of the Hollywood "problem" picture, which is morally solved in advance. And when the commercial film makers had some freedom and leeway, as well as talent, an extraordinary amount came through—the rhythm of American life that give films like *She Done Him Wrong, I'm No Angel,* the Rogers-Astaire musicals, *Bringing Up Baby, The Thin Man, The Lady Eve, Double Indemnity, Strangers on a Train, Pat and Mike, The Crimson Pirate, Singin' in the Rain, The Big Sleep,* or the more recent *The Manchurian Candidate* and *Charade* a freshness and spirit that makes them unlike the films of any other country. Our movies are the best proof that Americans are liveliest and freest when we don't take ourselves too seriously.

Taking *Hud* as a commercial movie, I was interested to see that the audience reacted to Hud as a Stanley Kowalski on the range, laughing with his coarseness and sexual assertiveness, and sharing his contempt for social values. Years before, when I saw the movie version of *A Streetcar Named Desire,* I was shocked and outraged at those in the audience who expressed their delight when Brando as Stanley jeered at Blanche. At the time, I didn't understand it when they laughed their agreement as Stanley exploded in rage and smashed things. It was only later, away from the spell of Vivien Leigh's performance, that I could reflect that Stanley was clinging to his brute's bit of truth, his sense that her gentility and coquetry were intolerably fake. And it seemed to me that this was one of the reasons why *Streetcar* was a great play—that Blanche and Stanley upset us, and complicated our responses. This was no Lillian Hellman melodrama with good and evil clay pigeons. The conflict was genuine and dramatic. But Hud didn't have a dramatic adversary; his adversaries *were* out of Lillian Hellmanland.

The setting, however, wasn't melodramatic, it was comic—not the legendary west of myth-making movies like the sluggish *Shane* but the modern West I grew up in, the ludicrous real West. The comedy was in the realism: the incongruities of Cadillacs and cattle, crickets and transistor radios, jukeboxes, Dr Pepper signs, paperback books—all emphasizing the standardization of culture in the loneliness of vast spaces. My West wasn't Texas; it was northern California, but our Sonoma County ranch was very much like this one—with the frame house, and "the couple's" cabin like the housekeeper's cabin, and the hired hands' bunkhouse, and my father and older brothers charging over dirt roads, not in Cadillacs but in Studebakers, and the Saturday nights in the dead little town with its movie house and ice cream parlor. This was the small-town West I and so many of my friends came out of—escaping from the swaggering small-town hotshots like Hud. But I didn't remember any boys like Brandon de Wilde's Lon: he wasn't born in the West or in anybody's imagination; that seventeen-year-old blank sheet of paper has been handed down from generations of lazy hack writers. His only "reality" is from de Wilde's having played the part before: from *Shane* to *Hud,* he has been our observer, our boy in the West, testing heroes. But in *Hud,* he can't fill even this cardboard role of representing the spectator because Newman's Hud has himself come to represent the audience. And I didn't remember any clean old man like Melvyn Douglas's Homer: his principles and rectitude weren't created either, they were handed down from the authors' mouthpieces of the socially conscious plays and movies of the thirties and forties. Occupied towns in the war movies frequently spawned these righteous, prophetic elder citizens.

Somewhere in the back of my mind, Hud began to stand for the people who would vote for Goldwater, while Homer was clearly an upstanding Stevensonian. And it seemed rather typical of the weakness of the whole message picture idea that the good liberals who made the film made their own spokesman a fuddy-duddy, worse, made him inhuman—except for the brief sequences when he isn't a spokesman for anything, when he follows the bouncing ball and sings "Clementine" at the movies. Hud, the "villain" of the piece, is less phony than Homer.

■   ■   ■

In the next few days I recommended *Hud* to friends (and now "friends" no longer means college students but academic and professional people) and was bewildered when they came back indignant that I'd wasted their time. I was even more bewildered when the reviews started coming out; what were the critics talking about? Unlike the laughing audience, they were taking *Hud* at serious message value as a work of integrity, and, even in some cases, as a tragedy. In the New York *Herald Tribune,* Judith Crist found that "Both the portraits and the people are completely without compromise—and therein is not only the foundation but also the rare achievement of this film." In the *Saturday Review,* Arthur Knight said that "it is the kind of creative collaboration too long absent from our screen . . . by the end of the film, there can be no two thoughts about Hud: he's purely and simply a bastard. And by the end of the film, for all his charm, he has succeeded in alienating everyone, including the audience." According to Bosley Crowther in the *New York Times:*

> Hud is a rancher who is fully and foully diseased with all the germs
> of materialism that are infecting and sickening modern man . . .
> And the place where he lives is not just Texas. It is the whole coun-
> try today. It is the soil in which grows a gimcrack culture that nur-
> tures indulgence and greed. Here is the essence of this picture.
> While it looks like a modern Western, and is an outdoor drama, in-
> deed, *Hud* is as wide and profound a contemplation of the human
> condition as one of the New England plays of Eugene O'Neill. . . .
> The striking, important thing about it is the clarity with which it
> unreels. The sureness and integrity of it are as crystal-clear as the
> plot is spare . . . the great key scene of the film, a scene in which
> [the] entire herd of cattle is deliberately and dutifully destroyed . . .
> helps fill the screen with an emotion that I've seldom felt from any
> film. It brings the theme of infection and destruction into focus
> with dazzling clarity.

As usual, with that reverse acumen that makes him invaluable, Crowther has put his finger on a sore spot. The director carefully builds up the emotion that Crowther and probably audiences in general feel when the cattle, confused and trying to escape, are forced into the mass grave that has been dug by a bulldozer, and are there systematically shot down, covered with lime, and buried. This is the movie's big scene, and it can be no accident that the scene derives some of its emotional power from the Nazis' final solution of the Jewish problem; it's inconceivable that these overtones would not have occurred to the group—predominantly Jewish—who made the film. Within the terms of the story, this emotion that is worked up is wrong, because it is not Hud the bad man who wants to destroy the herd; it is Homer the good man who accedes to what is necessary to stop the spread of infection. And is all this emotion appropriate to the slaughter of animals who were, after all, raised to be slaughtered and would, in the normal course of events, be even more *brutally* slaughtered in a few weeks? What's involved is simply the difference in money between what the government pays for the killing of the animals and their market value. It would not have been difficult for the writers and director to arrange the action so that the audience would feel quick relief at the destruction of the herd. But I would guess that they couldn't resist the opportunity for a big emotional scene, a scene with *impact*, even though the emotions don't support the meaning of the story. They got their big scene: it didn't matter what it meant.

So it's pretty hard to figure out the critical congratulations for clarity and integrity, or such statements as Penelope Gilliatt's in the *Observer*, "*Hud* is the most sober and powerful film from America for a long time. The line of it is very skillfully controlled: the scene when Melvyn Douglas's diseased cattle have to be shot arrives like the descent of a Greek plague." Whose error are the gods punishing? Was Homer, in buying Mexican cattle, merely taking a risk, or committing hubris? One of the things you learn on a ranch, or any other place, is that nobody is responsible for natural catastrophes; one of the things you learn in movies and other dramatic forms is the symbolic use of catastrophe. The locusts descended on Paul Muni in *The Good Earth* because he had gotten rich and *bad:* a farmer in the movies who neglects his humble wife and goes in for high living is sure to lose his crops. *Hud* plays it both ways: the texture of the film is wisecracking naturalism, but when a powerful sequence is needed to jack up the action values, a disaster is used for all the symbolic overtones that can be hit—and without any significant story meaning. I don't think the line of *Hud* is so much "controlled" as adjusted, set by conflicting aims at seriousness and success.

It hardly seems possible but perhaps Crowther thought the *cattle* were symbolically "fully and foully diseased with all the germs of materialism that are infecting and sickening modern man." Those sick cattle must have *something* to do with the language he uses in describing the film. "It is a drama of moral corruption—of the debilitating disease of avaricious self-seeking—that is creeping across the land and infecting the minds of young people in this complex, materialistic age. It is forged in the smoldering confrontation of an aging cattleman and his corrupted son." Scriptwriters have only to toss in a few bitter asides about our expense-account civilization and strew a few platitudes like, "Little by little the country changes because of the men people admire," and the movie becomes "a drama or moral corruption."

The English critics got even more out of it: Derek Prouse experienced a "catharsis" in *The Sunday Times,* as did Peter John Dyer in *Sight and Sound.*

8

Dyer seems to react to cues from his experience at *other* movies; his review, suggesting as it does a super-fan's identification with the film makers' highest aspirations, is worth a little examination. "From the ominous discovery of the first dead heifer, to the massacre of the diseased herd, to Homer's own end and Hud's empty inheritance of a land he passively stood by and watched die, the story methodically unwinds like a python lying sated in the sun." People will be going to *Hud,* as Charles Addams was reported to have gone to *Cleopatra,* "to see the snake." Dyer squeezes out more meaning and lots more symbolism than the film makers could squeeze in. (A) Homer just suddenly up and died, of a broken heart, one supposes. It wasn't prepared for, it was merely convenient. (B) Hud's inheritance isn't empty: he has a large ranch, and the land has oil. Dyer projects the notion of Hud's emptiness as a human being onto his inheritance. (C) Hud didn't passively stand by and watch the land die. The *land* hasn't changed. Nor was Hud passive: he worked the ranch, and he certainly couldn't be held responsible for the cattle becoming infected—unless Dyer wants to go so far as to view that infection as a symbol of or a punishment for Hud's sickness. Even Homer, who blamed Hud for just about everything else, didn't accuse him of infecting the cattle. Dyer would perhaps go that far, because somehow "the aridity of the cattle-less landscape mirrors his own barren future." Why couldn't it equally mirror Homer's barren past? In this scheme of symbolic interpretation, if there was a dog on the ranch, and it had worms, Hud the worm would be the reason. Writing of the "terse and elemental polarity of the film," Dyer says, "The earth is livelihood, freedom and death to Homer; an implacably hostile prison to Hud"—though it would be just as easy, and perhaps more true to the audience's experience of the film, to interpret Hud's opportunism as love of life and Homer's righteousness as rigid and life-destroying—and *unfair.* The scriptwriters give Homer principles (which are hardly likely to move the audience); but they're careful to show that Hud is misunderstood and rejected when he makes affectionate overtures to his father.

Dyer loads meaning onto Hud's actions and behavior: for example, "Instead of bronco-busting he goes in for a (doubtless) metaphorical bout of pig-wrestling." Why "instead of"—as if there were bronco-busting to do and he dodged it—when there is nothing of the kind in the film? And what would the pig-wrestling be a metaphor for? Does Dyer take pigs to represent women, or does he mean that the pig-wrestling shows Hud's swinishness? Having watched my older brothers trying to catch greased pigs in this traditional western small-town sport, I took the sequence as an indication of how boring and empty small-town life is, and how coarse the games in which the boys work off a little steam. I had seen the same boys who wrestled greased pigs and who had fairly crude ideas of sex and sport enter a blazing building to save the lives of panic-stricken horses, and emerge charred but at peace with the world and themselves.

■   ■   ■

Are the reviewers trying to justify having enjoyed the movie, or just looking for an angle, when they interpret the illustrative details *morally*? Any number of them got their tip on Hud's character by his taking advantage of a husband's absence to go to bed with the wife. But he couldn't very well make love to her when her husband was home—although that would be par for the course of "art" movies these days. The summer nights are very long on a western ranch. As a child, I could stretch out on a hammock on the porch and read an Oz book from cover to cover while my grandparents and uncles and aunts and parents didn't stir from their card game. The young men get tired of playing cards. They either think about sex or try to do something about it. There isn't much else to do—the life doesn't exactly stimulate the imagination, though it does stimulate the senses. Dyer takes as proof of Hud's bad character that "his appetites are reserved for married women." What alternatives are there for a young man in a small town? Would it be proof of a *good* character to seduce young girls and wreck their reputations? There are always a few widows, of course, and, sometimes, a divorcee like Alma, the housekeeper. (Perhaps the first female equivalent of the "white Negro" in our films: Patricia Neal plays Alma as the original author Larry McMurtry described the Negro housekeeper, the "chuckling" Halmea with "her rich teasing laugh.") But they can hardly supply the demand from the married men, who are in a better position to give them favors, jobs, presents, houses, and even farms. I remember my father taking me along when he visited our local widow: I played in the new barn which was being constructed by workmen who seemed to take their orders from my father. At six or seven, I was very proud of my father for being the protector of widows.

I assumed the audience enjoyed and responded to Hud's chasing women because this represented a break with western movie conventions and myths, and as the film was flouting these conventions and teasing the audience to enjoy the change, it didn't occur to me that in *this* movie his activity would be construed as "bad." But Crowther finds that the way Hud "indulges himself with his neighbor's wife" is "one of the sure, unmistakable tokens of a dangerous social predator." Is this knowledge derived from the film (where I didn't discover it) or from Crowther's knowledge of life? If the latter, I can only supply evidence against him from my own life. My father who was adulterous, and a Republican who, like Hud, was opposed to any government interference, was in no sense and in no one's eyes a social predator. He was generous and kind, and democratic in the western way that Easterners still don't understand: it was not out of guilty condescension that mealtimes were communal affairs with the Mexican and Indian ranchhands joining the family, it was the way Westerners lived.

If Homer, like my father, had frequented married women or widows, would Dyer interpret that as a symbol of Homer's evil? Or, as Homer voiced sentiments dear to the scriptwriters and critics, would his "transgressions" be interpreted as a touching indication of human frailty? What Dyer and others took for symbols were the clichés of melodrama—where character traits are sorted out and separated, one set of attitudes and behavior for the good characters, another for the bad characters. In melodrama, human desires and drives make a person weak or corrupt: the heroic must be the unblemished good like Homer, whose goodness is not tainted with understanding. Reading the cues this way, these critics missed what audiences were reacting to, just as Richard Whitehall in *Films and Filming* describes Newman's Hud as "the-hair-on-the-chest-male"—although the most exposed movie chest since Valentino's is just as hairless.

I suppose we're all supposed to react on cue to movie rape (or as is usually the case, attempted rape); rape, like a cattle massacre, is a box-office value. No doubt in *Hud* we're really supposed to believe that Alma is, as Stanley Kauffmann says, "driven off by his [Hud's] vicious physical assault." But in terms of the modernity of the settings and the characters, as well as the age of the protagonists (they're at least in their middle thirties), it was more probable that Alma left the ranch because a frustrated rape is just too sordid and embarrassing for all concerned—for the drunken Hud who forced himself upon her, for her for defending herself so titanically, for young Lon the innocent who "saved" her. Alma obviously wants to go to bed with Hud, but she has been rejecting his propositions because she doesn't want to be just another casual dame to him; she wants to be treated differently from the others. If Lon hadn't rushed to protect his idealized view of her, chances are that the next morning Hud would have felt guilty and repentant, and Alma would have been grateful to him for having used the violence necessary to break down her resistance, thus proving that she *was* different. They might have been celebrating ritual rapes annually on their anniversaries.

Rape is a strong word when a man knows that a woman wants him but won't accept him unless he commits himself emotionally. Alma's mixture of provocative camaraderie plus reservations invites "rape." (Just as, in a different way, Blanche DuBois did—though Williams erred in having her go mad: it was enough, it was really *more,* that she was broken, finished.) The scriptwriters for *Hud,* who, I daresay, are as familiar as critics with theories of melodrama, know that heroes and villains both want the same things and that it is their way of trying to get them that separates one from the other. They impart this knowledge to Alma, who tells Hud that she wanted him and he could have had her if he'd gone about it differently. But this kind of knowingness, employed to make the script more clever, more frank, more modern, puts a strain on the credibility of the melodramatic actions it explicates—and embellishes. Similarly, the writers invite a laugh by having Alma, seeing the nudes Lon has on his wall, say, "I'm a girl, they don't do a thing for me." Before the Kinsey report on women, a woman might say, "They don't do a thing for me," but she wouldn't have prefaced it with "I'm a girl" because she wouldn't have known that erotic reactions to pictures are not characteristic of women.

The Ravetches have been highly praised for the screenplay: Penelope

Gilliatt considers it "American writing at its abrasive best"; Brendan Gill says it is "honestly written"; *Time* calls it "a no-compromise script." Dyer expresses a fairly general view when he says it's "on a level of sophistication totally unexpected from their scripts for two of Ritt's least successful, Faulkner-inspired films." This has some special irony because not only is their technique in *Hud* a continuation of the episodic method they used in combining disparate Faulkner stories into *The Long Hot Summer,* but the dialogue quoted most appreciatively by the reviewers to illustrate their new skill (Alma's rebuff of Hud, "No thanks, I've had one cold-hearted bastard in my life, I don't want another") is lifted almost verbatim from that earlier script (when it was Joanne Woodward telling off Paul Newman). They didn't get acclaim for their integrity and honesty that time because, although the movie was entertaining and a box-office hit, the material was resolved as a jolly comedy, the actors and actresses were paired off, and Newman as Ben Quick the barn burner turned out not really to be a barn burner after all. They hadn't yet found the "courage" that keeps Hud what *Time* called him, "an unregenerate heel" and "a cad to the end." It may have taken them several years to learn that with enough close-ups of his blue, blue eyes and his hurt, sensitive mouth, Newman's Ben Quick could have burned barns all right, and audiences would have loved him more for it.

In neither film do the episodes and characters hold together, but Ritt, in the interim having made Hemingway's *Adventures of a Young Man* and failed to find a style appropriate to it, has now, with the aid of James Wong Howe's black and white cinematography, found something like a reasonably clean visual equivalent for Hemingway's prose. Visually *Hud* is so apparently simple and precise and unadorned, so skeletonic, that we may admire the bones without being quite sure of the name of the beast. This Westerner is part gangster, part *Champion,* part rebel-without-a-cause, part the traditional cynic-hero who pretends not to care because he cares so much. (And it is also part *Edge of the City,* at least the part about Hud's having accidentally killed his brother and Homer's blaming him for it. Ritt has plagiarized his first film in true hack style: the episode was integral in *Edge of the City* and the friendship of Cassavetes and Poitier—probably the most beautiful scenes Ritt has directed—drew meaning from it; in *Hud* it's a fancy "traumatic" substitute for explaining why Hud and Homer don't get along.)

When *Time* says *Hud* is "the most brazenly honest picture to be made in the U.S. this season" the key word is brazenly. The film brazens it out. In *The New Yorker* Brendan Gill writes, "It's an attractive irony of the situation that, despite the integrity of its makers, *Hud* is bound to prove a box-office smash. I find this coincidence gratifying. Virtue is said to be its own reward, but money is nice, too, and I'm always pleased to see it flowing toward people who have had other things on their minds." Believing in this coincidence is like believing in Santa Claus. Gill's last sentence lacks another final "too." In Hollywood, a "picture with integrity" is a moneymaking message picture. And that's what Crowther means when he says, "*Hud* is a film that does its makers, the medium and Hollywood proud." He means something similar when he calls his own praise of the film a "daring endorsement"—as if it placed him in some kind of jeopardy to be so forthright.

■   ■   ■

If most of the critics who acclaimed the film appeared as innocent as Lon and as moralistic as Homer, Dwight Macdonald, who perceived that "it is poor Hud who is forced by the script to openly practice the actual as against the mythical American Way of Life" regarded this perception as proof of the stupidity of the film.

But the movie wouldn't necessarily be a good movie if its moral message was dramatically sustained in the story and action, and perhaps it isn't necessarily a bad movie if its moral message is not sustained in the story and action. By all formal theories, a work that is split cannot be a work of art, but leaving the validity of these principles aside, do they hold for lesser works—not works of art but works of commerce and craftsmanship, sometimes fused by artistry? Is a commercial piece of entertainment (which may or may not aspire to be, or pretend to be, a work of art) necessarily a poor one if its material is confused or duplicit, or reveals elements at variance with its stated theme, or shows the divided intentions of the craftsmen who made it? My answer is no, that in some films the more ambivalence that comes through, the more the film may mean to us or the more fun it may be. The process by which an idea for a movie is turned into the product that reaches us is so involved, and so many compromises, cuts, and changes may have taken place, so much hope and disgust and spoilage and waste may be embodied in it or mummified in it, that the tension in the product, or some sense of urgency still left in it, may be our only contact with the life in which the product was processed. Commercial products in which we do not sense or experience divided hopes and aims and ideas may be the dullest—ones in which everything alive was processed out, or perhaps ones that were never alive even at the beginning. *Hud* is so astutely made and yet such a mess that it tells us much more than its message. It is redeemed by its fundamental dishonesty. It is perhaps an archetypal Hollywood movie: split in so many revealing ways that, like *On the Waterfront* or *From Here to Eternity*, it is the movie of its year (even though it's shallow and not nearly so good a film as either of them).

My friends were angry that I'd sent them to *Hud* because, like Macdonald, they "saw through it," they saw that Hud was not the villain, and they knew that though he expressed vulgar notions that offended *them*, these notions might not be unpopular. The film itself flirts with this realization: when Homer is berating Hud, Lon asks, "Why pick on Hud, Grandpa? Nearly everybody around town is like him."

My friends, more or less socialist, detest a crude Hud who doesn't believe in government interference because they believe in more, and more drastic, government action to integrate the schools and end discrimination in housing and employment. However, they are so anti-CIA that at Thanksgiving dinner a respected professor could drunkenly insist that he had positive proof that the CIA had engineered the murder of Kennedy with no voice but mine raised in doubt. They want centralized power when it works for their civil-libertarian aims, but they dread and fear its international policies. They hate cops but call them at the first hint of a prowler: they are split, and it shows in a million ways. I imagine they're very like the people who made *Hud,* and like them they do rather well for themselves. They're so careful to play the game at their jobs that if they hadn't told you that they're *really* screwing the system, you'd never guess it.

Film Quarterly, Summer, 1964

SMILES OF A SUMMER NIGHT

Late in 1955 Ingmar Bergman made a nearly perfect work—the exquisite carnal comedy *Smiles of a Summer Night.* It was the distillation of elements he had worked with for several years in the 1952 *Secrets of Women* (originally called *The Waiting Women*), the 1953 *A Lesson in Love,* and the early 1955 *Dreams;* these episodic comedies of infidelity are like early attempts or drafts. They were all set in the present, and the themes were plainly exposed; the dialogue, full of arch epigrams, was often clumsy, and the ideas, like the settings, were frequently depressingly middle class and novelettish. Structurally, they were sketchy and full of flashbacks. There were scattered lovely moments, as if Bergman's eye were looking ahead to the visual elegance of *Smiles of a Summer Night,* but the plot threads were still woolly. *Smiles of a Summer Night* was made after Bergman directed a stage production of *The Merry Widow,* and he gave the film a turn-of-the-century setting. Perhaps it was this distance that made it possible for him to create a work of art out of what had previously been mere clever ideas. He not only tied up the themes in the intricate plot structure of a love roundelay, but in using the lush period setting, he created an atmosphere that saturated the themes. The film is bathed in beauty, removed from the banalities of short skirts and modern-day streets and shops, and, removed in time, it draws us *closer.*

Bergman found a high style within a set of boudoir farce conventions: in *Smiles of a Summer Night* boudoir farce becomes lyric poetry. The sexual chases and the round dance are romantic, nostalgic: the coy bits of feminine plotting are gossamer threads of intrigue. The film becomes an elegy to transient love: a gust of wind and the whole vision may drift away.

There are four of the most beautiful and talented women ever to appear in one film: as the actress, the great Eva Dahlbeck, appearing on stage, giving a house party and, in one inspired suspended moment, singing "Freut Euch des Lebens"; the impudent love-loving maid, Harriet Andersson—as a blonde, but as opulent and sensuous as in her other great roles; Margit Carlquist as the proud, unhappy countess; Ulla Jacobsson as the eager virgin.

Even Bergman's epigrams are much improved when set in the quotation marks of a stylized period piece. (Though I must admit I can't find justification for such bright exchanges as the man's question, "What can a woman ever see in a man?" and her response, "Women are seldom interested in aesthetics. Besides, we can always turn out the light." I would have thought you couldn't get a laugh on that one unless you tried it in an old folks' home, but Bergman is a man of the theatre—audiences break up on it.) Bergman's sensual scenes are much more charming, more unexpected in the period setting: when they are deliberately unreal they have grace and wit. How different it is to watch the same actor and actress making love in the stuck elevator of *Secrets of Women* and in the golden pavilion of *Smiles of a Summer Night*. Everything is subtly improved in the soft light and delicate, perfumed atmosphere.

In Bergman's modern comedies, marriages are contracts that bind the sexes in banal boredom forever. The female strength lies in convincing the man that he's big enough to act like a man in the world, although secretly he must acknowledge his dependence on her. (J. M. Barrie used to say the same things in the cozy, complacent Victorian terms of plays like *What Every Woman Knows;* it's the same concept that Virginia Woolf raged against— rightly, I think—in *Three Guineas*.) The straying male is just a bad child—but it is the essence of maleness to stray. Bergman's typical comedy heroine, Eva Dahlbeck, is the woman as earth-mother who finds fulfillment in accepting the infantilism of the male. In the modern comedies she is a strapping goddess with teeth big enough to eat you up and a jaw and neck to swallow you down; Bergman himself is said to refer to her as "The Woman Battleship."

But in *Smiles of a Summer Night,* though the roles of the sexes are basically the same, the perspective is different. In this vanished setting, nothing lasts, there are no winners in the game of love; all victories are ultimately defeats— only the game goes on. When Eva Dahlbeck, as the actress, wins back her old lover (Gunnar Bjornstrand), her plot has worked—but she hasn't really won much. She caught him because he gave up; they both know he's defeated. *Smiles* is a tragi-comedy; the man who thought he "was great in guilt and in glory" falls—he's "only a bumpkin." This is a defeat we can all share—for have we not all been forced to face ourselves as less than we hoped to be? There is no lesson, no moral—the women's faces do not tighten with virtuous endurance (the setting is too unreal for endurance to be plausible). The glorious old Mrs. Armfeldt (Naima Wifstrand) tells us that she can teach her daughter nothing, or, as she puts it, "We can never save a single person from a single suffering—and that's what makes us despair."

Smiles of a Summer Night was the culmination of Bergman's "rose" style and he has not returned to it. (*The Seventh Seal,* perhaps his greatest "black" film, was also set in a remote period.) The Swedish critic Rune Waldekranz has written that *Smiles of a Summer Night* "wears the costume of the fin de siècle period for visual emphasis of the erotic comedy's fundamental premise—that the step between the sublime and the ridiculous in love is a short one, but nevertheless one that a lot of people stub their toe on. Although benefiting from several ingenious slapstick situations, *Smiles of a Summer Night* is a comedy in the most important meaning of the word. It is an arabesque on an essentially tragic theme, that of man's insufficiency, at the same time as it wittily illustrates the belief expressed fifty years ago by Hjalmar Söderberg that the only absolutes in life are 'the desire of the flesh and the incurable loneliness of the soul.' "

KPFA broadcast for revival showing, 1961

SHOESHINE

When *Shoeshine* opened in 1947, I went to see it alone after one of those terrible lovers' quarrels that leave one in a state of incomprehensible despair. I came out of the theater, tears streaming, and overheard the petulant voice of a college girl complaining to her boyfriend, "Well I don't see what was so special about that movie." I walked up the street, crying blindly, no longer certain whether my tears were for the tragedy on the screen, the hopelessness I felt for myself, or the alienation I felt from those who could not experience the radiance of *Shoeshine*. For if people cannot feel *Shoeshine*, what *can* they feel? My identification with those two lost boys had become so strong that I did not feel simply a mixture of pity and disgust toward this dissatisfied customer but an intensified hopelessness about everything . . . Later I learned that the man with whom I had quarreled had gone the same night and had also emerged in tears. Yet our tears for each other and for *Shoeshine* did not bring us together. Life, as *Shoeshine* demonstrates, is too complex for facile endings.

Shoeshine was not conceived in the patterns of romance or melodrama; it is one of those rare works of art which seem to emerge from the welter of human experience without smoothing away the raw edges, or losing what most movies lose—the sense of confusion and accident in human affairs. James Agee's immediate response to the film was, "*Shoeshine* is about as beautiful, moving, and heartening a film as you are ever likely to see." A few months later he retracted his evaluation of it as a work of art and wrote that it was not a completed work of art but "the raw or at best the roughed-out materials of art." I think he should have trusted his initial response: the greatness of *Shoeshine* is in that feeling we get of human emotions that have not been worked-over and worked-into something (a pattern? a structure?) and cannot really be comprised in such a structure. We receive something more naked, something that pours out of the screen.

Orson Welles paid tribute to this quality of the film when he said in 1960, "In handling a camera I feel that I have no peer. But what De Sica can do, that I can't do. I ran his *Shoeshine* again recently and the camera disappeared, the screen disappeared; it was just life . . ."

When *Shoeshine* came to this country, *Life* Magazine wrote, "New Italian film will shock the world . . . will act on U.S. audiences like a punch in the stomach." But few Americans felt that punch in the stomach. Perhaps like the college girl they need to be hit by an actual fist before they can feel. Or, perhaps, to take a more charitable view of humanity, they feared the pain of the film. Just about everybody has heard of *Shoeshine*—it is one of the greatest and most famous films of all time—but how many people have actually seen it? They didn't even go to see it in Italy. As De Sica has said, *"Shoeshine* was a disaster for the producer. It cost less than a million lire but in Italy few people saw it as it was released at a time when the first American films were reappearing . . ." Perhaps in the U.S. people stayed away because it was advertised as a social protest picture—which is a little like advertising *Hamlet* as a political study about a struggle for power.

Shoeshine has a sweetness and a simplicity that suggest greatness of feeling, and this is so rare in film works that to cite a comparison one searches beyond the medium—if Mozart had written an opera set in poverty, it might have had this kind of painful beauty. *Shoeshine,* written by Cesare Zavattini, is a social protest film that rises above its purpose. It is a lyric study of how two boys* betrayed by society betray each other and themselves. The two young shoeshine boys who sustain their friendship and dreams amid the apathy of postwar Rome are destroyed by their own weaknesses and desires when sent to prison for black-marketeering. This tragic study of the corruption of innocence is intense, compassionate, and above all, humane.

KPFA broadcast for revival showing, 1961

---

* Rinaldo Smordoni (Giuseppe) became a baker; Franco Interlenghi (Pasquale) became a film star.

THE GOLDEN COACH**

At his greatest, Jean Renoir expresses the beauty in our common humanity—the desires and hopes, the absurdities and follies, that we all, to one degree or another, share. As a man of the theater (using this

** Based on Prosper Merimée's one-act play, *Le Carrosse du Saint Sacrement,* which was derived from the same Peruvian story that served as source material for an episode in Thornton Wilder's *The Bridge of San Luis Rey.*

term in its widest sense to include movies) he has become involved in the ambiguities of illusion and "reality," theater and "life"—the confusions of identity in the role of man as a role-player. The methods and the whole range of ideas that were once associated with Pirandello and are now associated with Jean Genet are generally considered highly theatrical. But perhaps it is when theater becomes the most theatrical—when the theater of surprise and illusion jabs at our dim notions of reality—that we become conscious of the roles we play.

Jean Renoir's *The Golden Coach* (1953) is a comedy of love and appearances. In her greatest screen performance, Anna Magnani, as the actress who is no more of an actress than any of us, tries out a series of love roles in a play within a play within a movie. The artifice has the simplest of results: we become caught up in a chase through the levels of fantasy, finding ourselves at last with the actress, naked in loneliness as the curtain descends, but awed by the wonders of man's artistic creation of himself. Suddenly, the meaning is restored to a line we have heard and idly discounted a thousand times: "All the world's a stage."

The commedia dell'arte players were actors who created their own roles. They could trust in inspiration and the free use of imagination, they could improvise because they had an acting tradition that provided taken-for-granted situations and relationships, and they had the technique that comes out of experience. *The Golden Coach,* Renoir's tribute to the commedia dell'arte, is an improvisation on classic comedy, and it is also his tribute to the fabulous gifts, the inspiration, of Anna Magnani. At her greatest, she, too, expresses the beauty in our common humanity. It is probably not coincident with this that Renoir is the most sensual of great directors, Magnani the most sensual of great actresses. Though he has taken Prosper Merimée's vehicle and shaped it for her, it will be forever debatable whether it contains her or is exploded by her. But as this puzzle is parallel with the theme, it adds another layer to the ironic comedy.

Perhaps only those of us who truly love this film will feel that Magnani, with her deep sense of the ridiculous in herself and others, Magnani with her roots in the earth so strong that she can pull them out, shake them in the face of pretension and convention, and sink them down again stronger than ever—the actress who has come to be the embodiment of human experience, the most "real" of actresses—is the miraculous choice that gives this film its gusto and its piercing beauty. If *this* woman can wonder who she is, then all of us must wonder. Renoir has shaped the material not only for her but out of her and out of other actresses' lives. Talking about the production, he remarked, "Anna Magnani is probably the greatest actress I have ever worked with. She is the complete animal—an animal created completely for the stage and screen . . . Magnani gives so much of herself while acting that between scenes . . . she collapses and the mask falls. Between scenes she goes into a deep state of depression . . ." Like the film itself, the set for the film is an unreal world where people suffer. In *The Golden Coach* we see Magnani in a new dimension: not simply the usual earthy "woman of the people," but the artist who exhausts her resources in creating this illusion of volcanic reality.

The work has been called a masque, a fairy tale, and a fable—each a good try, but none a direct hit: the target shimmers, our aim wavers. *The Golden Coach* is light and serious, cynical and exquisite, a blend of color, wit, and Vivaldi. What could be more unreal than the time and place—a dusty frontier in Renaissance Peru. (You can't even fix the time in the Renaissance—the architecture is already Baroque.) A band of Italian players attempts to bring art to the New World. Magnani is Camilla, the Columbine of the troupe; among her lovers is the Spanish viceroy, who, as the final token of his bondage—the proof of his commitment to love over position and appearances—presents her with the symbol of power in the colony, the golden coach. Through this formal "taken-for-granted" situation, life (that is to say, art) pours out—inventive, preposterous, outrageous, buoyant. And in the midst of all the pleasures of the senses, there is the charging force of Magnani with her rumbling, cosmic laughter, and her exultant cry—"Mama mia!"

The script has its awkward side, and those who don't get the feel of the movie are quick to point out the flaws. Some passages of dialogue are clumsily written, others embarrassingly over-explicit ("Where does the theatre end and life begin?"—which isn't even a respectable question). Much of the strained rhythm in the dialogue may be blamed on the fact that Renoir's writing in English doesn't do justice to Renoir the film artist. And, though Magnani herself, in her first English-speaking role, is vocally magnificent, some of the others speak in dreary tones and some of the minor characters appear to be dubbed. The "international" cast—in this case, largely Italian, English and French—never really seems to work; at the basic level they don't speak the same language. And Renoir allows some of the performers more latitude than their talent warrants; though Duncan Lamont and Ricardo Rioli are marvelous love foils, Paul Campbell is shockingly inept, and the scenes in which he figures go limp. Another defect is in the directorial rhythm. This was Renoir's second color film, and as in his first, *The River,* which was also a collaboration with his great cinematographer-nephew, Claude Renoir, static patches of dialogue deaden the movement; his sense of film rhythm seems to falter when he works in color. Instead of indulging in the fancy fool's game of Freudian speculation that he fails when he tries to compete with his father, it seems simpler to suggest that he gets so bemused by the beauty of color that he carelessly neglects the language of cinema which he himself helped to develop.

But in the glow and warmth of *The Golden Coach*, these defects are trifles. When the singing, tumbling mountebanks transform the courtyard of an inn into a playhouse, the screen is full of joy in creative make-believe. When, at a crucial point in the story, Magnani announces that it is the end of the second act, and the movie suddenly becomes a formalized stage set, we realize that we have been enchanted, that we had forgotten where we were. When the hand of the creator becomes visible, when the actor holds the mask up to view, the sudden revelation that this world we have been absorbed in is not life but theater brings us closer to the actor-characters. So many movies pretend to be life that we are brought up short, brought to consciousness, by this movie that proclaims its theatricality. And the presence of the artists—Renoir and Magnani—is like a great gift. When, in the last scene of *The Golden Coach,* one of the most exquisitely conceived moments on film, the final curtain is down, and Magnani as the actress stands alone on stage, bereft of her lovers, listening to the applause that both confirms and destroys the illusion, the depth of her loneliness seems to be the truth and the pity of all roles played.

KPFA broadcast for revival showing, 1961

THE EARRINGS OF MADAME DE . . .

Madame de, a shallow, narcissistic beauty, has no more feeling for her husband than for his gifts: she sells the diamond earrings he gave her rather than confess her extravagance and debts. Later, when she falls in love with Baron Donati, he presents her with the same pair of earrings and they become a token of life itself. Once she has experienced love she cannot live without it: she sacrifices her pride and honor to wear the jewels, she fondles them as if they were parts of her lover's body. Deprived of the earrings and of the lover, she sickens . . . unto death.

This tragedy of love, which begins in careless flirtation and passes from romance, to passion, to desperation is, ironically, set among an aristocracy that seems too superficial and sophisticated to take love tragically. Yet the passion that develops in this silly, vain, idle society woman not only consumes her but is strong enough to destroy three lives.

The novella and the movie could scarcely be more unlike: the austere, almost mathematical style of Louise de Vilmorin becomes the framework, the logic underneath Max Ophuls's lush, romantic treatment. In *La Ronde* he had used Schnitzler's plot structure but changed the substance from a cynical view of sex as the plane where all social classes are joined and leveled (venereal disease is transmitted from one couple to another in this wry roundelay)—to a more general treatment of the failures of love. For Ophuls *La Ronde* became the world itself—a spinning carousel of romance, beauty, desire, passion, experience, regret. Although he uses the passage of the earrings as a plot motif in the same way that Louise de Vilmorin had, he deepens and enlarges the whole conception by the creation of a world in such flux that the earrings themselves become the only stable, recurrent element—and they, as they move through many hands, mean something different in each pair of hands, and something fatally different for Madame de because of the different hands they have passed through. It may not be accidental that the film suggests de Maupassant: between the 1950 *La Ronde* and the 1953 *Earrings of Madame de . . .* Ophuls had worked (rather unsuccessfully) on three de Maupassant stories which emerged as *Le Plaisir.*

In these earlier films he had also worked with Danielle Darrieux; perhaps he was helping to develop the exquisite sensibility she brings to Madame de—the finest performance of her career. Her deepening powers as an actress (a development rare among screen actresses, and particularly rare among those who began, as she did, as a little sex kitten) make her seem even more beautiful now than in the memorable *Mayerling*—almost twenty years earlier—when, too, she had played with Charles Boyer. The performances by Danielle Darrieux, Charles Boyer, and Vittorio De Sica are impeccable—ensemble playing of the smoothness usually said to be achieved only by years of repertory work.

However, seeing the film, audiences are hardly aware of the performances. A novelist may catch us up in his flow of words; Ophuls catches us up in the restless flow of his images—and because he does not use the abrupt cuts of "montage" so much as the moving camera, the gliding rhythm of his films is romantic, seductive, and, at times, almost hypnotic. James Mason once teased Ophuls with the jingle: "A shot that does not call for tracks is agony for poor dear Max." The virtuosity of his camera technique enables him to present complex, many-layered material so fast that we may be charmed and dazzled by his audacity and hardly aware of how much he is telling us. It is no empty exercise in decor when Madame de and the Baron dance in what appears to be a continuous movement from ball to ball. How much we learn about their luxurious lives, the social forms of their society, and the change in their attitudes toward each other! By the end, they have been caught in the dance; the trappings of romance have become the trap of love.

The director moves so fast that the suggestions, the feelings, must be caught on the wing; Ophuls will not linger, nor will he *tell* us anything. We may see Madame de as a sort of Anna Karenina in reverse; Anna gets her lover but she finds her life shallow and empty; Madame de's life has been so shallow and empty she cannot get her lover. She is destroyed, finally, by the fact that women do not have the same sense of honor that men do, nor the same sense of pride. When, out of love for the Baron, she thoughtlessly lies, how could she know that he would take her lies as proof that she did not really love him? What he thinks dishonorable is merely unimportant to her. She places love before honor (what woman does not?) and neither her husband nor her lover can forgive her. She cannot undo the simple mistakes that have ruined her; life rushes by and the camera moves inexorably.

The very beauty of *The Earrings of Madame de . . .* is often used against it: the sensuous camerawork, the extraordinary romantic atmosphere, the gowns, the balls, the staircases, the chandeliers, the polished, epigrammatic dialogue, the preoccupation with honor are all regarded as evidence of lack of substance. Ophuls's reputation has suffered from the critics' disinclination to accept an artist for what he can do—for what he loves—and their effort to castigate him for not being a different *type* of artist. Style—great personal style—is so rare in moviemaking that critics might be expected to clap their hands when they see it; but, in the modern world, style has become a target, and because Ophuls's style is linked to lovely ladies in glittering costumes in period decor, socially-minded critics have charged him with being trivial and decadent. Lindsay Anderson, not too surprisingly, found him "uncommitted, unconcerned with profundities" (Anderson's *Every Day Except Christmas* is committed all right, but is it really so profound?) and, in his rather condescending review of *The Earrings of Madame de . . .* in *Sight and Sound,* he suggested that "a less sophisticated climate might perhaps help; what a pity he is not, after all, coming to make a film in England." It's a bit like telling Boucher or Watteau or Fragonard that he should abandon his pink chalk and paint real people in real working-class situations.

The evocation of a vanished elegance—the nostalgic fin de siècle grace of Ophuls's work—was perhaps a *necessary* setting for the nuances of love that were his theme. If his characters lived crudely, if their levels of awareness were not so high, their emotions not so refined, they would not be so vulnerable, nor so able to perceive and express their feelings. By removing love from the real world of ugliness and incoherence and vulgarity, Ophuls was able to distill the essences of love. Perhaps he cast this loving look backward to an idealized time when men could concentrate on the refinements of human experience because in his own period such delicate perceptions were as remote as the Greek pursuit of perfection.

Born Max Oppenheimer in Germany in 1902 (he changed his name because of family opposition to his stage career) he worked as an actor and then directed more than 200 plays before he turned to movies in 1930. His first film success, *Liebelei,* came in 1932; because he was Jewish, his name was removed from the credits. The years that might have been his artistic maturity were, instead, a series of projects that didn't materialize or, if started, couldn't be completed. He managed to make a few movies—in Italy, in France, in Holland; he became a French citizen; then, after the fall of France, he went to Switzerland, and from there to the United States, where, after humiliating experiences on such films as *Vendetta* he made *Letter from an Unknown Woman, Caught,* and *The Reckless Moment.* In 1950 in France he finally got back to his own type of material with *La Ronde;* the flight from Hitler and the chaos of the war had lost him eighteen years. Working feverishly, with a bad heart, he had only a few years left—he died in 1957. No wonder the master of ceremonies of *La Ronde* says, "J'adore le passé"; the past of Ophuls's films is the period just before he was born. There was little in his own lifetime for which he could have been expected to feel nostalgia. Perhaps the darting, swirling, tracking camerawork for which he is famous is an expression of the evanescence of all beauty—it must be swooped down on, followed. It will quickly disappear.

KPFA broadcast for revival showing, 1961

BREATHLESS,
AND THE DAISY MILLER DOLL

B*reathless,* the most important New Wave film which has reached the United States, is a frightening little chase comedy with no big speeches and no pretensions. Michel, the young Parisian hood (Jean-Paul Belmondo), steals a car, kills a highway patrolman, chases after some money owed him for past thefts so he and his young American girl friend can get away to Italy. He finances this chase after the money by various other crimes along the way. Meanwhile, the police are chasing him. But both Michel's flight and the police chase are half-hearted. Michel isn't desperate to get away—his life doesn't mean that much to him; and the police (who are reminiscent of Keystone Cops) carry on a routine bumbling manhunt. Part of the stylistic peculiarity of the work—its art—is that while you're watching it, it's light and playful, off-the-cuff, even a little silly. It seems accidental that it embodies more of the modern world than other movies.

What sneaks up on you in *Breathless* is that the engagingly coy young hood with his loose, random grace and the impervious, passively butch American girl are as shallow and empty as the shiny young faces you see in sports cars and in suburban supermarkets, and in newspapers after unmotivated, pointless crimes. And you're left with the horrible suspicion that this is a new race, bred in chaos, accepting chaos as natural, and not caring one way or another about it or anything else. The heroine, who has literary interests, quotes *Wild Palms,* "Between grief and nothing, I will take grief." But that's just an attitude she likes at that moment; at the end she demonstrates that it's false. The hero states the truth for them both: "I'd choose nothing." The characters of *Breathless* are casual, carefree moral idiots. The European critic, Louis Marcorelles, describes their world as "total immorality, lived skin-deep." And possibly because we Americans live among just such people and have come to take them for granted, the film may not, at first, seem quite so startling as it is. And that's what's frightening about *Breathless:* not only are the characters familiar in an exciting, revealing way, they are terribly *attractive.*

If you foolishly depend on the local reviewers to guide you, you may have been put off *Breathless.* To begin with, where did they get the idea that the title refers to the film's fast editing? That's about like suggesting that the title *Two-Way Stretch* refers to the wide screen. The French title, *A Bout de*

Souffle, means "Out of Breath," and it refers to the hero, who keeps going until he's winded. Their confusion is, however, a tribute to the film's fast, improvisatory style, the go go go rhythm. The jazz score, the comic technique are perfectly expressive of the lives of the characters; the jump-cuts convey the tempo and quality of the activities of characters who don't work up to anything but hop from one thing to the next. And as the film seems to explain the people *in their own terms,* the style has the freshness of "objectivity." It does seem breathlessly young, newly created.

If you hold the [San Francisco] *Chronicle*'s review of *Breathless* up to the light, you may see H-E-L-P shining through it.

> Certain scenes are presented with utter candor, lacking in form and impact in their frankness. A long encounter, for instance, in the small room of Jean Seberg, with whom Belmondo claims to be in love, is repetitious—but extremely lifelike. And then young Godard suddenly will present another scene in which a police inspector is tailing Miss Seberg and searching for Belmondo. This is staged so clumsily that one wonders whether parody is what the director intends. But Belmondo's peril is grave and his reaction to his predicament is sensitive. . . . Always energetic and arrogant, he still suggests both a lost quality and a tender humor. This is his facade to shield his small cynical world from all that he does not understand.

The hero of the film understands all that he wants to, but the critic isn't cynical enough to see the basic fact about these characters: they just don't give a damn. And that's what the movie is about. The [San Francisco] *Examiner*'s critic lamented that *Breathless* was a "hodge-podge" and complained that he couldn't "warm up" to the characters—which is a bit like not being able to warm up to the four Mission District kids who went out looking for homosexuals to beat up, and managed to cause the death of a young schoolteacher. For sheer not-getting-the-point, it recalls the remark recently overheard from a well-groomed, blue-rinse-on-the-hair type elderly lady: "That poor Eichmann! I don't think he's got a Chinaman's chance."

How do we connect with people who don't give a damn? Well, is it really so difficult? Even if they weren't all around us, they'd still be (to quote *Double Indemnity*) closer than that.

They are as detached as a foreign colony, as uncommitted as visitors from another planet, yet the youth of several countries seem, to one degree or another, to share the same characteristics. They're not consciously against society: they have no ideologies at all, they're not even rebels without a cause. They're not rebelling against anything—they don't pay that much attention to what doesn't please or amuse them. There is nothing they really want to do, and there's nothing they won't do. Not that they're perverse or deliberately cruel: they have charm and intelligence—but they live on impulse.

The codes of civilized living presuppose that people have an inner life and outer aims, but this new race lives for the moment, because that is all that they care about. And the standards of judgment we might bring to bear on them don't touch them and don't interest them. They have the narcissism of youth, and we are out of it, we are bores. These are the youthful representatives of mass society. They seem giddy and gauche and amusingly individualistic, until you consider that this individualism is not only a reaction to mass conformity, but, more terrifyingly, is the new form that mass society takes: indifference to human values.

Godard has used this, as it were, documentary background for a gangster story. In the traditional American gangster films, we would have been cued for the gangster's fall: he would have shown the one vanity or sentimental weakness or misjudgment that would prove fatal. But *Breathless* has removed the movie gangster from his melodramatic trappings of gangs and power: this gangster is Bogart apotheosized and he is romantic in a modern sense just because he doesn't care about anything but the pleasures of love and fast cars. There is not even the American gangster's hatred of cops and squealers. Michel likes cops because they're cops. This gangster is post-*L'Etranger* and he isn't interested in motives: it's all simple to him, "Killers kill, squealers squeal." Nobody cares if Michel lives or dies, and he doesn't worry about it much either.

Yet Godard has too much affection for Michel to make *him* a squealer: a killer yes, a squealer no. Despite the unrest and anarchy in the moral atmosphere, Michel is as romantic as Pépé Le Moko and as true to love (and his death scene is just as operatic and satisfying). A murderer and a girl with artistic pretensions. She asks him what he thinks of a reproduction she is trying on the wall, and he answers, "Not bad." This doesn't show that he's sufficiently impressed and she reprimands him with, "Renoir was a very great painter." In disgust he replies, "I said 'Not bad.' " There's no doubt which of them responds more. He's honest and likable, though socially classifiable as a psychopath; she's a psychopath, too, but the non-classifiable sort—socially acceptable but a sad, sweet, affectless doll.

There are more ironies than can be sorted out in Patricia—Jean Seberg from Iowa, selected by Otto Preminger from among thousands of American girls to play the French national heroine, Joan of Arc, and now the national heroine of France as the representative American girl abroad. Patricia, a naive, assured, bland and boyish creature, is like a new Daisy Miller—but not quite as envisioned by Henry James. She has the independence, but not the moral qualms or the Puritan conscience or the high aspirations that James saw as the special qualities of the American girl. She is, indeed, the heiress of the ages—but in a more sinister sense than James imagined: she is so free that she has no sense of responsibility or guilt. She seems to be playing at existence, at a career, at "love"; she's "trying them on." But that's all she's capable of in the way of experience. She doesn't want to be bothered; when her lover becomes an inconvenience, she turns him in to the police.

Shot down and dying, the young man gallantly tries to amuse her, and then looks up at her and remarks—without judgment or reproach, but rather, descriptively, as a grudging compliment: "You really are a bitch." (The actual word he uses is considerably stronger.) And in her flat, little-girl, cornbelt voice, she says, "I don't know what the word means." If she does know, she doesn't care to see how it applies to her. More likely, she really doesn't know, and it wouldn't bother her much anyway. The codes of love and loyalty, in which, if you betray a lover you're a bitch, depend on stronger emotions than her idle attachment to this lover—one among many. They depend on *emotions*, and she is innocent of them. As she had observed earlier, "When we look into each other's eyes, we get nowhere." An updated version of the betraying blonde bitches who destroyed so many movie gangsters, she is innocent even of guilt. As Jean Seberg plays her—and that's exquisitely—Patricia is the most terrifyingly *simple* muse-goddess-bitch of modern movies. Next to her, the scheming Stanwyck of *Double Indemnity* is as archaic as Theda Bara in *A Fool There Was.*

Jean-Paul Belmondo, who plays the hood, is probably the most exciting new presence on the screen since the appearance of Brando; nobody holds the screen this way without enormous reserves of talent. At twenty-six, he has already appeared in nine plays and nine movies; he may be, as Peter Brook says, the best young actor in Europe today. In minor parts, the Alfred Hitchcock personal-appearance bit is compounded, and Truffaut *(The 400 Blows)*, Chabrol *(Le Beau Serge, The Cousins)*, and Godard himself flit through. Truffaut supplied the news item on which Godard based the script; Chabrol lent his name as supervising producer. But it is Godard's picture, and he has pointed out how he works: "The cinema is not a trade. It isn't teamwork. One is always alone while shooting, as though facing a blank page." His movie is dedicated to Monogram Pictures—who were, of course, the producers of cheap American gangster-chase movies, generally shot in city locations. (*Breathless* was made for $90,000). Another important director appears in the film—Jean-Pierre Melville—who a few years ago performed one of the most amazing feats on film: he entered into Jean Cocteau's universe and directed, with almost no funds, the brilliant film version of Cocteau's *Les Enfants Terribles,* sometimes known as *The Strange Ones.* He is regarded as a sort of spiritual father to the New Wave; he appears in the movie as a celebrity being interviewed. (The true celebrity and progenitor of the movement is, of course, Cocteau.) Asked by Patricia, "What is your ambition?" the celebrity teases her with a pseudo-profundity: "To become immortal, and then to die."

KPFA broadcast, 1961

KAGI

Among the good films ignored or ludicrously misinterpreted by the critics is, currently, the Japanese film *Kagi*, or *Odd Obsession*, a beautifully stylized and highly original piece of film making—perverse in the best sense of the word, worked out with such finesse that each turn of the screw tightens the whole comic structure. As a treatment of sexual opportunism, it's a bit reminiscent of *Double Indemnity*, but it's infinitely more complex. The opening plunges us into the seat of the material. A young doctor, sensual and handsome, smug with sexual prowess, tells us that his patient, an aging man, is losing his virility. And the old man bends over and bares his buttocks—to take an injection. But the old man doesn't get enough charge from the injection, so he induces the young doctor, who is his daughter's suitor, to make love to his wife. By observing them, by artificially making himself jealous, the old man is able to raise his spirits a bit.

The comedy, of course, and a peculiar kind of black human comedy it is, is that the wife, superbly played by Machiko Kyo, is the traditional, obedient Japanese wife—and she cooperates in her husband's plan. She is so obedient and cooperative that, once aroused by the young doctor, she literally kills her old husband with kindness—she excites him to death. The ambiguities are malicious and ironic: the old man's death is both a perfect suicide and a perfect murder. And all four characters are observed so coldly, so dispassionately that each new evidence of corruption thickens the cream of the jest.

The title *Kagi*—the key—fits the Tanizaki novel, but does not fit the film, which might better be called the keyhole. Everybody is spying on everybody else, and although each conceals his motives and actions, nobody is fooled. The screen is *our* keyhole, and we are the voyeurs who can see them all peeking at each other. When the old man takes obscene pictures of his wife, he gives them to the young man to develop. The young man shows them to his fiancée, the daughter, whose reaction is that she can do anything her mother can do.

But a further layer of irony is that she *can't*. For the film is also a withering satire on the Westernized modern Japanese girl. The mother—mysterious, soft, subtle—uses her traditional obedience for her own purposes. She never says what she thinks about anything—when she starts a diary she puts down romantic hypocrisy worthy of a schoolgirl—and she is infinitely desirable. The daughter, a college student who explains what is going on quite explicitly, is just as corrupt as her mother, but has no interest or appeal to her parents or even to her fiancé. In her sweaters and skirts, and with her forthright speech, she is sexually available but completely unattractive. When she tells her father that nothing so simple as adultery is being practiced by her mother and the young doctor, she seems simply ludicrous; her mother can lower her eyes and murmur distractedly about the terrible things she is asked to do—and excite any man to want to try out a few.

The director, Kon Ichikawa, is probably the most important new young Japanese director. His study of obsessive expiation, *The Burmese Harp*, was subjected to a brutal, hack editing job, and has reached only a small audience in this country; *Enjo* (1958), based on Mishima's novel about a great crime, the young Zen Buddhist burning the Golden Pavilion, has not yet played here. (An earlier film of Ichikawa's—a puppet version of a Kabuki dance—was destroyed by MacArthur's aides because, according to Japanese film historian Donald Richie, they regarded Kabuki as feudalistic. What did they think MacArthur was?)

Kagi, made in 1959, took a special prize at the Cannes Festival in 1960 (the other special prize went to *L'Avventura*). *Kagi* was given "Special commendation for 'audacity of its subject and its plastic qualities.' " I've indicated the audacity of the subject; let me say something about the film's plastic qualities. It is photographed in color, with dark blue tones predominating, and with an especially pale soft pinkish white for flesh tones. I don't think I've ever seen a movie that gave such a feeling of flesh. Machiko Kyo, with her soft, sloping shoulders, her rhythmic little paddling walk, is like some ancient erotic fantasy that is more suggestive than anything Hollywood has ever thought up. In what other movie does one see the delicate little hairs on a woman's legs? In what other movie is flesh itself not merely the surface of desire but totally erotic? By contrast, the daughter, like the exposed, suntanned healthy American girl, is an erotic joke—she is aware, liberated, passionate, and, as in our Hollywood movies, the man's only sexual objective is to get *into* her and have done with it. With Machiko Kyo the *outside* is also erotic substance.

Ichikawa's cold, objective camera observes the calculations and designs, the careful maneuvers in lives that are fundamentally driven and obsessive; and there's deadly humor in the contrast between what the characters pretend they're interested in and what they actually care about.

Kagi is conceived at a level of sophistication that accepts pornography as a fact of life which, like other facts of life, can be treated in art. The subject matter is pornography, but the movie is not pornographic. It's a polite, almost clinical comedy about moral and sexual corruption. It even satirizes the clinical aspects of sex. Modern medicine, with its injections, its pills, its rejuvenating drugs, adds to the macabre side of the comedy. For *Kagi* has nothing to do with love: the characters are concerned with erotic pleasure, and medicine is viewed as the means of prolonging the possibilities of this pleasure. So there is particular humor in having the doctors who have been hastening the old man's death with their hypodermics try to place the blame for his death on the chiropractor who has been working on his muscles. They have all known what they were doing, just as the four principals all know, and even the servant and the nurse. The film has an absurd ending that seems almost tacked on (it isn't in the book); if it ended with the three survivors sitting together, and with Machiko Kyo reading her diary aloud, it could be a perfect no-exit situation, and the movie would have no major defects or even weaknesses.

Reading the reviews, you'd think that no American movie critic had even so much as heard of that combination of increasing lust and diminishing potency which destroys the dignity of old age for almost all men; you'd think they never behaved like silly, dirty old men. Japanese films in modern settings have a hard time with the art-house audience: perhaps the Americans who make up the foreign-film audience are still too bomb-scarred to accept the fact that business goes on as usual in Japan. In *Kagi* the beds— where a good part of the action takes place—are Western-style beds, and when the people ply each other with liquor, it's not saki, it's Hennessy. *Kagi* is the first Japanese comedy that has even had a chance in the art houses: if the judgments of incompetent critics keep people from seeing it, when will we get another? Crowther finds the husband of *Kagi* "a strictly unwholesome type." Let's put it this way: if you've never gotten a bit weary of the classical Western sex position, and if you've never wanted to keep the light on during intercourse, then you probably won't enjoy *Kagi*. But if you caught your breath at the Lady Wakasa sequences in *Ugetsu*, if you gasped when Masayuki Mori looked at Machiki Kyo and cried out, "I never dreamed such pleasures existed!" then make haste for *Kagi*.

KPFA broadcast, October 24, 1961

EXCERPT FROM FANTASIES OF THE ART-HOUSE AUDIENCE
—HIROSHIMA MON AMOUR

For several decades now educated people have been condescending toward the children, the shopgirls, all those with "humdrum" or "impoverished" lives—the mass audience—who turned to movies for "ready-made" dreams. The educated might admit that they sometimes went to the movies designed for the infantile mass audience—the number of famous people who relax with detective fiction makes this admission easy— but presumably they were not "taken in"; they went to get away from the tensions of their complex lives and work. But of course when they really want to enjoy movies as an art, they go to foreign films, or "adult" or unusual or experimental American films.

I would like to suggest that the educated audience often uses "art" films in much the same self-indulgent way as the mass audience uses the Hollywood "product," finding wish fulfillment in the form of cheap and easy congratulation on their sensitivities and their liberalism. (Obviously any of my generalizations are subject to numerous exceptions and infinite qualifications; let's assume that I know this, and that I use large generalizations in order to be suggestive rather than definitive.)

By the time Alain Resnais's *Hiroshima Mon Amour* reached American art houses, expectations were extraordinarily high. Dwight Macdonald in *Esquire* had said: "It is the most original, moving, exciting and important movie I've seen in years, somehow managing to combine a love story with propaganda against war and the atomic bomb without either losing its full force." The rest of the press seemed to concur. The *Saturday Review* considered it "a masterpiece." The New York *Herald Tribune* decided that "it establishes beyond any man's cavilling the potentialities of the film as an art"—something one might have thought already established. *Time* decided that the theme was that "Hiroshima, like God, is love. It is the Calvary of the atomic age. It died for man's sins . . ." I met a couple who had seen the film five nights in a row; a University of California professor informed me that if I didn't like *this* one, he would never speak to me again. Dwight Macdonald wrote more and went further:

> It is as stylised as *Potemkin* or *Ten Days that Shook the World,* as pure and powerful as cinema . . . It is also a novelistic exploration of memory, a *recherche du temps perdu* comparable to Proust. . . . For the first time since Eisenstein—we have a cinematic intelligence so quick, so subtle, so original, so at once passionate and sophisticated that it can be compared with Joyce, with Picasso, with Berg and Bartok and Stravinsky. The audience was extraordinarily quiet—no coughing, whispering, rustling of paper; a hypnotic trance. . . . It was oddly like a religious service, and if someone had made a wisecrack, it would have seemed not an irritation but a blasphemy.

Surely movies—even the greatest movies—are rarely received in such an atmosphere of incense burning. *Breathless* and *L'Avventura* were to be either admired or disliked or ignored, but *Hiroshima Mon Amour* was described in hushed tones; it was some sort of ineffable deep experience. Why?

The picture opened with those intertwined nude bodies—this could be symbolic of true intermingling, but it irresistibly set off some lewd speculations about just *what* was going on. And what was that stuff they were covered with? Beach sand? Gold dust? Ashes? Finally, I accepted it as symbolic bomb ash, but I wasn't happy with it. (Later I discovered that it was supposed to be "sweat, ashes and dew.") Then the French girl said she had seen everything in Hiroshima, and the Japanese man told her she had seen nothing in Hiroshima. Then they said the same things over again, and again, and perhaps again. And I lost patience. I have never understood why writers assume that repetition creates a lyric mood or underlines meaning with profundity. My reaction is simply, "OK, I got it the first time, let's get on with it." Now, this is obviously not how we are supposed to react to Marguerite Duras's dialogue, which is clearly intended to be musical and contrapuntal, and I was going to try to get in the right, passive, receptive mood for a ritual experience, when some outright fraud made me sit up and pay attention. The action—or inaction—in bed was intercut with what purported to be documentary shots of the effect of the bomb on Hiroshima. Only I had seen some of the footage before in a Japanese atrocity movie that was about as documentary as *Peyton Place*. This clumsily staged imposture made me suspect that the Japanese man didn't know Hiroshima either, and I began to look askance at the truth he was supposed to represent. Where did he get this metaphysical identity with Hiroshima? As the film went on, and the heroine recounted her first love for a German soldier, how he had been killed on the last day of fighting, how she had been dragged away and her head shaved, how she had gone mad and been hidden away in the cellar by her shamed parents, I began to think less and less of the movie and more about why so many people were bowled over by it.

Was it possibly an elaborate, masochistic fantasy for intellectuals? Surely both sexes could identify with the girl's sexual desperation, her sensitivity and confusion—and had anyone dreamed up worse punishments for sexuality? Only a few years ago it had looked as if James Dean in *East of Eden* and *Rebel Without a Cause* had gone just about as far as anybody could in being misunderstood. But this heroine not only had her head shaved by people who didn't understand her love and need of the German, but she went *crazy* and was locked in a cellar. You can't go much further in being misunderstood. And, at the risk of giving offense, is this not what sends so many people to analysts—the fear that they'll go crazy if they don't get love?

The Japanese, it may be noted, is rather dull and uninteresting: he says no more than an analyst might; he is simply a sounding board. And if, being Japanese, he is supposed to represent the world's conscience, he brings an unsuitably bland, professionally sympathetic and upper-class manner to the function. But everybody who has suffered sexual deprivation—and who hasn't?—can identify with her and perhaps fantasize brutal parents and cellars. Even her insanity can be equated with those rough nights when a love affair fell apart or that nervous exhaustion at the end of the academic year that sends so many to the hospital or the psychiatric clinic.

It seemed to be a woman's picture—in the most derogatory sense of the term. And still she went on talking: her feelings, her doubts, her memories, kept pouring out. It began to seem like True Confession at the higher levels of spiritual and sexual communion; and I decided the great lesson for us all was to shut up. This woman (beautifully as Emmanuelle Riva interpreted her) was exposing one of the worst faults of intelligent modern women: she was talking all her emotions out—as if bed were the place to demonstrate sensibility. It's unfortunate that what people believe to be the most important things about themselves, their innermost truths and secrets—the real you or me—that we dish up when somebody looks sympathetic, is very likely to be the driveling nonsense that we generally have enough brains to forget about. The real you or me that we conceal because we think people won't accept it is slop—and why *should* anybody want it?

But here was the audience soaking it up—audiences of social workers, scientists, doctors, architects, professors—living and loving and suffering just like the stenographer watching Susan Hayward. Are the experiences involved really so different? Few of us have seen our lovers killed by partisan bullets, but something kills love anyway—something always does—and it's probably highly gratifying for many people to identify with a heroine who isn't responsible: it is the insane world that has punished her for her sexual expression. Emmanuelle Riva's sexual expression is far more forthright than a Hollywood heroine's, which makes it more appealing to an educated audience, and, of course, her character and her manner of indicating her emotional problems have a higher "tone." (It may be relevant to note that the educated audience, which generally ignores Miss Hayward, did turn out for *I Want to Live!*, in which the character of Barbara Graham was turned into a sort of modern Tess of the d'Urbervilles—not only innocent of crime but horribly sinned against and *nobler* than anybody else.)

But what does her sad story have to do with Hiroshima and the bomb? Would not some other psychosexual story of deprivation (say, *Camille* or *Stella Dallas*) be just as relevant to the horrors of war if it were set in Hiroshima? It would seem so. However, the setting itself explains another aspect of the film's strong appeal, particularly to liberal intellectuals. There is a crucial bit of dialogue: "They make movies to sell soap, why not a movie to sell peace?" I don't know how many movies you have gone to lately that were made to sell soap, but American movies *are* like advertisements, and we can certainly assume that indirectly they sell a way of life that includes soap as well as an infinity of other products. But what makes the dialogue crucial is that the audience for *Hiroshima Mon Amour* feels virtuous because they want to buy peace. And the question I want to ask is: who's selling it?

KPFA broadcast, 1961
Sight and Sound, January 1962

VICTIM

It was a bit startling to pick up an English newspaper and see that the review of *Victim* was entitled "Ten-letter word"—but as it turned out, the *Observer* was referring not to Lenny Bruce's much publicized hyphenated word but to the simple term "homosexual," which it appears is startling enough in a movie to make the Johnston office refuse to give *Victim* a seal of approval.

I suppose it's too crude simply to say that *Victim* is *The Mark* in drag but that's not so far from the truth. Like the man who wanted to rape a child but didn't, the hero in *Victim* wants to but doesn't make it with another guy. The lesser characters make out; they don't have the hero's steel will, and they are very pathetic indeed, given to such self-illuminating expressions as "Nature played me a dirty trick." I'm beginning to long for one of those old-fashioned movie stereotypes—the vicious, bitchy old queen who said mean, funny things. We may never again have those Franklin Pangborn roles, now that homosexuals are going to be treated seriously, with sympathy and respect, like Jews and Negroes. It's difficult to judge how far sensitivities will go: *Remembrance of Things Past* may soon be frowned upon like *Huckleberry Finn* and *The Merchant of Venice.* Social progress makes strange bedfellows.

Victim managed to get past other censorial bodies by being basically a thriller, a fairly slick suspense story about a blackmailing ring. But it's a cleverly conceived *moralistic* thriller: as the victims of the ring are homosexuals, various characters are able to point out the viciousness of the English laws, which, by making homosexuality a crime, make homosexuals the victims of ninety percent of the blackmail cases. Just about everyone in the movie has attitudes designed to illuminate the legal problems of homosexuality; without the thriller structure, the moralizing message could get awfully sticky. As it is, the film is moderately amusing.

A number of the reviewers were uneasy about the thesis that consenting adults should be free from legal prosecution for their sex habits; they felt that if homosexuality were not a crime it would spread. (The assumption seems to be that heterosexuality couldn't hold its own in a free market.) *Time*'s attitude to the film is a classic example of *Time*'s capacity for worrying:

> But what seems at first an attack on extortion seems at last a coyly sensational exploitation of homosexuality as a theme—and, what's more offensive, an implicit approval of homosexuality as a practice. Almost all the deviates in the film are fine fellows—well dressed, well spoken, sensitive, kind . . . Nowhere does the film suggest that homosexuality is a serious (but often curable) neurosis that attacks the biological basis of life itself.

On one page *Time* is worried about the population explosion, and on the next it's upset because homosexuals aren't reproducing. (An unwarranted assumption, by the way.)

Time should really be very happy with the movie, because the hero of the film is a man who has never given way to his homosexual impulses; he has fought them—that's part of his heroism. Maybe that's why he seems such a stuffy stock figure of a hero. Oedipus didn't merely want to sleep with Jocasta; he slept with her.

There is, incidentally, a terribly self-conscious and unconvincing attempt to distinguish between the "love" the barrister feels for his wife and the physical desire—presumably some lower order of emotion—that he felt for a boy who is more interesting in every way than the wife. And I find it difficult to accept all the upper-class paraphernalia of stage melodrama; it's hard to believe in people who live at the level on which if you feel insulted by someone's conversation, you show him the door. Generally when I tell someone to leave, that's when he most wants to stay, and I'm stuck for eighteen hours of sordid explanations of how he got so repulsive and how much he hates himself. A minor problem in trying to take *Victim* seriously even as a thriller is that the suspense involves a series of "revelations" that several of the highly placed characters have been concealing their homosexuality; but actors, and especially English actors, generally look so queer anyway, that it's hard to be surprised at what we've always taken for granted—in fact, in this suspense context of who is and who isn't, it's hard to believe in the actors who are supposed to be straight.

Some months ago, reviewing *The Mark,* I discussed the uncomfortable feeling I got that we were supposed to feel sympathetic toward the hero because he was such a pained, unhappy, dull man, and that his sexual problem was the only focus of interest in him. In *Victim* there is so much effort to make us feel sympathetic toward the homosexuals that they are never even allowed to be *gay.* The dreadful irony involved is that Dirk Bogarde looks so pained, so anguished from the self-sacrifice of repressing his homosexuality, that the film seems to give rather a black eye to the heterosexual life.

KPFA broadcast, *Partisan Review,* Fall, 1962

WEST SIDE STORY

Sex is the great leveler, taste the great divider. I have premonitions of the beginning of the end when a man who seems charming or at least remotely possible starts talking about movies. When he says, "I saw a great picture a couple years ago—I wonder what you thought of it?" I start looking for the nearest exit. His great picture generally turns out to be *He Who Must Die* or something else that I detested—frequently a socially conscious problem picture of the Stanley Kramer variety. Boobs on the make always try to impress with their high level of seriousness (wise guys, with their contempt for *all* seriousness).

It's experiences like this that drive women into the arms of truckdrivers—and, as this is America, the truckdrivers all too often come up with the same kind of status-seeking tastes: they want to know what you thought of *Black Orpheus* or *Never on Sunday* or something else you'd much rather forget.

When a really attractive Easterner said to me, "I don't generally like musicals, but have you seen *West Side Story*? It's really great," I felt a kind of gnawing discomfort. I *love* musicals and so I couldn't help being suspicious of the greatness of a musical that would be so overwhelming to somebody who *didn't* like musicals. The gentleman's remark correlated with other expressions of taste—the various encounters in offices and on trains and planes with men who would put on solemn faces as they said, "I don't ordinarily go for poetry but have you read *This is My Beloved*?"

I had an uneasy feeling that maybe it would be better if I *didn't* go to see *West Side Story*—but, if you're driven to seek the truth, you're driven. I had to learn if this man and I were really as close as he suggested or as far apart as I feared. Well, it's a great musical for people who don't like musicals.

You will notice that nobody says *West Side Story* is a good movie; they say it's great—they accept the terms on which it is presented. It aims to be so much more than a "mere" musical like *Singin' in the Rain* (just about the best Hollywood musical of all time) that it is concerned with nothing so basic to the form as lightness, grace, proportion, diversion, comedy. It is not concerned with the musical form as a showcase for star performers in their best routines; it aspires to present the ballet of our times—our conflicts presented in music and dance. And, according to most of the critics, it succeeds. My anxiety as I entered the theatre was not allayed by a huge blow-up of Bosley Crowther's review proclaiming the film a "cinematic masterpiece."

West Side Story begins with a blast of stereophonic music that had me clutching my head. Is the audience so impressed by science and technique, and by the highly advertised new developments that they accept this jolting series of distorted sounds gratefully—on the assumption, perhaps, that because it's so unlike ordinary sound, it must be *better*? Everything about *West Side Story* is supposed to stun you with its newness, its size, the wonders of its photography, editing, choreography, music. It's nothing so simple as a musical, it's a piece of cinematic technology.

Consider the feat: first you take Shakespeare's *Romeo and Juliet* and remove all that cumbersome poetry; then you make the Montagues and Capulets really important and modern by turning them into rival street gangs of native-born and Puerto Ricans. (You get rid of the parents, of course; America is a *young* country—and who wants to be bothered by the squabbles of older people?) There is the choreographer Jerome Robbins (who conceived the stage musical) to convert the street rumbles into modern ballet—though he turns out to be too painstaking for high-powered moviemaking and the co-director Robert Wise takes over. (May I remind you of some of Robert Wise's previous credits—the names may be construed as symbolic. *So Big, Executive Suite, Somebody Up There Likes Me, I Want to Live!*) The writers include Ernest Lehman, who did the script, and Arthur Laurents, who wrote the Broadway show, and, for the lyrics, Stephen Sondheim. The music is by Leonard Bernstein. (Bernstein's father at a recent banquet honoring his seventieth birthday: "You don't expect your child to be a Moses, a Maimonides, a Leonard Bernstein." No, indeed, nor when you criticize Bernstein's music do you expect people to jump in outrage as if you were demeaning Moses or Maimonides.) Surely, only Saul Bass could provide the titles for such a production, as the credits include more consultants and assistants, production designers, sound men, editors, special effects men, and so forth than you might believe possible—until you see the result. Is it his much-vaunted ingeniousness or a hidden streak of cynicism—a neat comment on all this technology—that he turns the credits into graffiti?

The irony of this hyped-up, slam-bang production is that those involved apparently don't really believe that beauty and romance *can* be expressed in modern rhythms, because whenever their Romeo and Juliet enter the scene, the dialogue becomes painfully old-fashioned and mawkish, the dancing turns to simpering, sickly romantic ballet, and sugary old stars hover in the sky. When true love enters the film, Bernstein abandons Gershwin and begins to echo Richard Rodgers, Rudolf Friml, and Victor Herbert. There's even a heavenly choir. When the fruity, toothsome Romeo-Tony meets his Juliet-Maria, everything becomes gauzy and dreamy and he murmurs, "Have we met before?" That's my favorite piece of synthetic mysticism since the great exchange in *Black Orpheus:* "My name is Orpheus." "My name is Eurydice." "Then we must be in love." When Tony, floating on the clouds of romance (Richard Beymer unfortunately doesn't look as if he *could* walk) is asked, "What have you been taking tonight?" he answers, "A trip to the moon." Match *that* for lyric eloquence! (You'd have to go back to Odets.)

When Tony stabs Maria's brother and your mind fills in with "O, I am fortune's fool," the expensive scriptwriters come up with a brilliant exclamation for him. "Maria!" he cries. Do not let this exquisite simplicity mislead you—for they do not call the name "Maria" lightly. She is no mere girl like Juliet—she has the wisdom of all women, she is the mother of us all. And that is why, no doubt, they depart from Shakespeare's plot at the end: suffering Maria survives. And, of course, the appeal to the Catholic audience—which might otherwise become uneasy as both gangs are probably Catholic—is thereby assured. *West Side Story* plays the game in every conceivable way: it makes a strong appeal to youth by expressing the exuberant, frustrated desires of youth in the ugly, constricted city life, but it finally betrays this youth by representing the good characters as innocent and sweet, and making the others seem rather comic and foolish. They're like Dead End kids dancing—and without much improvement in the humor of the Dead End kids.

How can so many critics have fallen for all this frenzied hokum—about as original as, say, *South Pacific* at home—and with a score so derivative that, as we left the theater, and overheard some young man exclaiming "I could listen to that music forever," my little daughter answered "We *have* been listening to it forever." (At his father's banquet, Bernstein recalled that at his debut when he was thirteen he had played variations of a song "in the manner of Chopin, Liszt and Gershwin. Now I will play it in the manner of Bernstein." How, I wonder?) Perhaps the clue is in the bigness, and in the pretensions that are part of the bigness. Arthur Knight in the *Saturday Review* called it "A triumphant work of art"; Stanley Kauffmann in the *New Republic* says:

> The best film musical ever made.... When the film begins, and the Jets move down the streets of the West Side (studio settings faultlessly blended with location shots), as they mold swagger into ballet, we know that we are not seeing dance numbers, we are seeing street gangs for the first time *as they really are*—only we have not been able to perceive it for ourselves.... It is Robbins' vision—of city life expressed in stylized movement that sometimes flowers into dance and song—that lifts this picture high. If a time-capsule is about to be buried anywhere, this film ought to be included, so that possible future generations can know how an artist of ours made our most congenial theatrical form respond to some of the beauty in our time and to the humanity in some of its ugliness.

A candidate for a time-capsule is surely no ordinary multi-million-dollar spectacle. Hasn't Kauffmann, along with a lot of other people, fallen victim to the show of grandeur and importance? If there is anything great in the American musical tradition—and I think there is—it's in the light satire, the high spirits, the giddy romance, the low comedy, and the unpretentiously stylized dancing of men like Fred Astaire and the younger Gene Kelly. There's more beauty there—and a lot more humanity—than in all this jet-propelled ballet. Nothing in *West Side Story* gave me the pleasure of an honest routine like Donald O'Connor's "Make 'Em Laugh" number in *Singin' in the Rain* or almost any old Astaire and Rogers movie.

Despite Kauffmann's feelings that "we are seeing street gangs for the first time *as they really are*," I wonder how actual street gangs feel about the racial composition of the movie's gangs. For, of course, the Puerto Ricans are *not* Puerto Ricans and the only real difference between these two gangs of what I am tempted to call ballerinas—is that one group has faces and hair darkened, and the other group has gone wild for glittering yellow hair dye; and their stale exuberance, though magnified by the camera to epic proportions, suggests no social tensions more world shaking than the desperation of young dancers to get ahead—even at the risk of physical injury. They're about as human as the Munchkins in *The Wizard of Oz*. Maria, the sweet virgin fresh from Puerto Rico, is the most machine-tooled of Hollywood ingenues—clever little Natalie Wood. Like the new Princess telephone, so ingeniously constructed that it transcends its function and makes communication superfluous (it seems to be designed so that teen-agers can read advertising slogans at each other), Natalie Wood is the newly constructed love-goddess—so perfectly banal she destroys all thoughts of love. In his great silent film *Metropolis,* Fritz Lang had a robot woman named the false Maria: she had more spontaneity than Natalie Wood's Maria.

I had a sense of foreboding when I saw that Friar Lawrence had become a kindly old Jewish pharmacist called "Doc," but I was hardly prepared for his ultimate wisdom—"You kids make this world lousy! When will you stop?" These words Bosley Crowther tells us "should be heard by thoughtful people—sympathetic people—all over the land." Why, I wonder? What *is* there in this message that has anything to *do* with thought? These message movies dealing with Negro and white, or Puerto Rican and white, like to get a little extra increment of virtue—unearned—by tossing in a sweet, kindly, harmless old Jew full of prophetic cant. (Presumably, Jews should not be discriminated against because they are so philosophic and impotent.) The film makers wouldn't dream of having a young, pushing, aggressive Jew in the film—just as they don't dare to differentiate or characterize the racial backgrounds of the white gang. (Only sweet, reformed Tony can be identified as a Pole.) Yet this is a movie that pretends to deal with racial tensions. The lyrics keep telling us this is what it's about and the critics seem to accept the authors' word for it.

"But," counter the enthusiasts for the film, "surely you must admit the dancing is great." No, it isn't—it's trying so hard to be great it isn't even good. The impressive, widely admired opening shots of New York from the air overload the story with values and importance—technological and sociological. The Romeo and Juliet story could, of course, be set anywhere, but *West Side Story* wrings the last drop of spurious importance out of the setting, which dominates the enfeebled love story. The dancing is also designed to be urgent and important: it is supposed to be the lyric poetry of the streets, with all the jagged rhythms of modern tensions. The bigger the leap the more, I suppose, the dancer is expressing—on the theory that America is a big, athletic country. Who would have thought that Busby Berkeley's amusing old geometric patterns and aerial views would come back *this* way? Add social ideas to geometry, and you have the new *West Side Story* concept of dance. And just as the American middle classes thought they were being daring and accepting jazz when they listened to the adaptations and arrangements of big orchestras that gave jazz themes the familiar thick, sweet sludge of bad symphonic music, and thought that jazz was being elevated and honored as an art when Louis Armstrong played with the lagging, dragging New York Philharmonic (under Leonard Bernstein), they now think that American dancing is elevated to the status of art by all this arranging and exaggerating—by being turned into the familiar "high" art of ballet. The movements are so huge and sudden, so portentously "alive" they're always near explosion point. The dancing is obviously trying to say something, to *glorify* certain kinds of movement. And looking at all those boys in blue jeans doing their calisthenic choreography, Americans say, "Why it's like ballet . . . it's art, it's really great!" What is lost is not merely the rhythm, the feel, the unpretentious movements of American dancing at its best—but its basic emotion, which, as in jazz music, is the contempt for respectability. The possibilities of dance as an expressive medium are not expanded in *West Side Story;* they're contracted. I would guess that in a few decades the dances in *West Side Story* will look as much like hilariously limited, dated period pieces as Busby Berkeley's "Remember the Forgotten Man" number in *Gold Diggers of 1933.*

After *West Side Story* was deluged with Academy Awards as the best movie of 1961, Murray Schumach reported in the *New York Times* that "there seemed to be general agreement that one reason" it won "was that its choreography, music, and direction were devoted to the serious theme of the brotherhood of man." A few weeks ago, in a talk with a Hollywood director, when I expressed surprise at the historical novel he had undertaken to film, he explained that the "idea" of the book appealed to him because it was really about "the brotherhood of man." I averted my eyes in embarrassment and hoped that my face wasn't breaking into a crooked grin. It's a great conversation closer—the "brotherhood of man." Some suggested new "serious" themes for big movies: the sisterhood of women, "no man is an island," the inevitability of death, the continuity of man and nature, "God Is All."

Sometimes, when I read film critics, I think I can do without brothers.

KPFA broadcast, 1961
Film Quarterly, Summer, 1962

LOLITA

The ads asked "How did they ever make a movie of *Lolita* for persons over 18 years of age?" A few days later the question mark was moved, and the ads asked "How did they ever make a movie of *Lolita?*" and after that, the caution: "for persons over 18 years of age." Either way, the suggestion was planted that the movie had "licked" the book, and that *Lolita* had been turned into the usual kind of sexy movie. The advertising has been slanted to the mass audience, so the art-house audience isn't going. A sizable part of the mass audience doesn't like the movie (their rejection is being interpreted as a vote for "wholesomeness," which according to *Variety* is about to stage a comeback) and the art-house audience is missing out on one of the few American films it might enjoy.

Recommend the film to friends and they reply, "Oh I've *had* it with *Lolita.*" It turns out (now that *Lolita* can be purchased for fifty cents and so is in the category of ordinary popular books) that they never thought much of it; but even though they didn't really like the book, they don't want to see the movie because of all the changes that have been made in the book.

(One person informed me that he wouldn't go to see the movie because he'd heard they'd turned it into a comedy.) Others had heard so much about the book, they thought reading it superfluous (they had as *good* as read it—they were *tired* of it); and if the book was too much talked about to necessitate a reading, surely going to the film was really *de trop?*

Besides, wasn't the girl who played Lolita practically a *matron?* The *New York Times* had said, "She looks to be a good seventeen," and the rest of the press seemed to concur in this peculiarly inexpert judgment. *Time* opened its review with "Wind up the Lolita doll and it goes to Hollywood and commits nymphanticide" and closed with *"Lolita* is the saddest and most important victim of the current reckless adaptation fad . . ." In the *Observer* the premiere of the film was described under the heading "Lolita fiasco" and the writer concluded that the novel had been "turned into a film about this poor English guy who is being given the runaround by this sly young broad." In the *New Republic* Stanley Kauffmann wrote, "It is clear that Nabokov respects the novel. It is equally clear that he does not respect the film—at least as it is used in America . . . He has given to films the *Lolita* that, presumably, he thinks the medium deserves . . ." After all this, who would expect anything from the film?

The surprise of *Lolita* is how enjoyable it is: it's the first *new* American comedy since those great days in the forties when Preston Sturges re-created comedy with verbal slapstick. *Lolita* is black slapstick and at times it's so far out that you gasp as you laugh. An inspired Peter Sellers creates a new comic pattern—a crazy quilt of psychological, sociological commentary so "hip" it's surrealist. It doesn't cover everything: there are structural weaknesses, the film falls apart, and there's even a forced and humiliating attempt to "explain" the plot. But when the wit is galloping who's going to look a gift horse in the mouth? Critics who feel decay in their bones.

The reviews are a comedy of gray matter. Doubts may have remained after Arthur Schlesinger, jr.'s, ex cathedra judgment that *Lolita* is "willful, cynical and repellent . . . It is not only inhuman; it is anti-human. I am reluctantly glad that it was made, but I trust it will have no imitators." Then, "for a learned and independent point of view, *Show* invited Dr. Reinhold Niebuhr, the renowned theologian, to a screening in New York and asked him for an appraisal." The higher primate discovered that "the theme of this triangular relationship exposes the unwholesome attitudes of mother, daughter, and lover to a mature observer." (Ripeness is all . . . but is it enough?) This mature observer does however find some "few saving moral insights"—though he thinks the film "obscures" them—such as "the lesson of Lolita's essential redemption in a happy marriage." (Had any *peripheral* redemptions lately?) If you're still hot on the trail of insights, don't overlook the *New Republic*'s steamy revelation that "the temper of the original might . . . have been tastefully preserved" if Humbert had narrated the film. "The general tone could have been: 'Yes, this is what I did then and thought lovely. Dreadful, wasn't it? Still . . . it has its funny side, no?' " It has its funny side, oui oui.

The movie adaptation tries something so far beyond the simple "narrator" that a number of the reviewers have complained: Bosley Crowther, who can always be counted on to miss the point, writes that "Mr. Kubrick inclines to dwell too long over scenes that have slight purpose, such as scenes in which Mr. Sellers does various comical impersonations as the sneaky villain who dogs Mr. Mason's trail." These scenes "that have slight purpose" are, of course, just what make *Lolita* new, these are the scenes that make it, for all its slackness of pace and clumsy editing, a more exciting comedy than the last American comedy, *Some Like It Hot.* Quilty, the success, the writer of scenarios and school plays, the policeman, the psychologist; Quilty the genius, the man whom Lolita loves, Humbert's brother and tormentor and parodist; Quilty the man of the world is a conception to talk about alongside Melville's *The Confidence Man.* "Are you with someone?" Humbert asks the policeman. And Quilty the policeman replies, "I'm not with someone. I'm with you."

The Quilty monologues are worked out almost like the routines of silent comedy—they not only carry the action forward, they comment on it, and this comment is the *new* action of the film. There has been much critical condescension toward Sellers, who's alleged to be an impersonator rather than an actor, a man with many masks but no character. Now Sellers does a turn with the critics' terms: his Quilty is a character employing masks, an actor with a merciless talent for impersonation. He is indeed "the sneaky villain who dogs Mr. Mason's trail"—and he digs up every bone that "Mr. Mason" ineptly tries to bury, and presents them to him. Humbert can conceal nothing. It is a little like the scene in Victor Sjöström's magnificent *The Wind,* in which Lillian Gish digs a grave for the man she has murdered and then, from her window, watches in horror as the windstorm uncovers the body. But in *Lolita* our horror is split by laughter: Humbert has it coming—*not* because he's having "relations" with a minor, but because, in order to conceal his sexual predilections, he has put on the most obsequious and mealy-minded of masks. Like the homosexual professors who are rising fast in American academia because they are so cautious about protecting their unconventional sex lives that they can be trusted not to be troublesome to the college administrations on any important issues (a convoluted form of blackmail), Humbert is a worm and Quilty knows it.

Peter Sellers works with miserable physical equipment, yet he has somehow managed to turn his lumbering, wide-hipped body into an advantage by *acting* to perfection the man without physical assets. The soft, slow-moving, paper-pushing middle-class man is his special self-effacing type; and though only in his mid-thirties he all too easily incarnates sly, smug middle-aged man. Even his facial muscles are kept flaccid, so that he always looks weary, too tired and cynical for much of a response. The rather frightening strength of his Quilty (who has enormous—almost sinister—reserves of energy) is peculiarly effective just because of his ordinary, "normal" look. He does something that seems impossible: he makes unattractiveness magnetic.

Quilty—rightly, in terms of the film as distinguished from the novel—dominates *Lolita* (which could use much more of him) and James Mason's Humbert, who makes attractiveness tired and exhausted and impotent, is a remarkable counterpart. Quilty who doesn't care, who wins Lolita and throws her out, Quilty the homewrecker is a winner; Humbert, slavishly, painfully in love, absurdly suffering, the lover of the ages who degrades himself, who cares about nothing but Lolita, is the classic loser. Mason is better than (and different from) what almost anyone could have expected. Mason's career has been so mottled: a beautiful *Odd Man Out,* a dull Brutus, an uneven, often brilliant Norman Maine in *A Star Is Born,* a good Captain Nemo, and then in 1960 the beginnings of comic style as the English naval commander who pretends to have gone over to the Russians in *A Touch of Larceny.* And now, in *Lolita* he's really in command of a comic style: the handsome face gloats in a rotting smile. Mason seems to need someone strong to play against. He's very good in the scenes with Charlotte and with her friends, and especially good in the bathtub scene (which Niebuhr thinks "may arouse both the laughter and the distaste of the audience"—imagine being so drained of reactions that you have to be *aroused* to distaste!) but his scenes with Lolita, when he must dominate the action, fall rather flat.

Perhaps the reviewers have been finding so many faults with *Lolita* because this is such an easy way to show off some fake kind of erudition: even newspaper reviewers can demonstrate that they've read a book by complaining about how different the movie is from the novel. The movie *is* different but not *that* different, and if you can get over the reviewers' preoccupation with the sacredness of the novel (they don't complain this much about Hollywood's changes in biblical stories) you'll probably find that even the characters that *are* different (Charlotte Haze, especially, who has become the culture-vulture rampant) are successful in terms of the film. Shelley Winters's Charlotte is a triumphant caricature, so overdone it recalls Blake's "You never know what is enough until you know what is more than enough."

Sue Lyon is perhaps a little less than enough—but not because she looks seventeen. (Have the reviewers looked at the schoolgirls of America lately? The classmates of my fourteen-year-old daughter are not merely nubile: some of them look badly used.) Rather it is because her role is insufficiently written. Sue Lyon herself is good (at times her face is amusingly suggestive of a miniature Elvis Presley) though physically she's too *young* to be convincing in her last scenes. (I don't mean that to sound paradoxical but merely descriptive.) Kubrick and company have been attacked most for the area in which they have been simply accurate: they could have done up Sue Lyon in childish schoolgirl clothes, but the facts of American life are that adolescents and even pre-adolescents wear nylons and make-up and two-piece strapless bathing suits and have *figures.*

Lolita isn't a consistently good movie but that's almost beside the point:

excitement is sustained by a brilliant idea, a new variant on the classic chase theme—Quilty as Humbert's walking paranoia, the madness that chases Humbert and is chased by him, over what should be the delusionary landscape of the actual United States. This panoramic confusion of normal and mad that can be experienced traveling around the country is, unfortunately, lost: the film badly needs the towns and motels and highways of the U.S. It suffers not only from the genteel English landscapes, but possibly also from the photographic style of Oswald Morris—perhaps justly famous, but subtly wrong (and too tasteful) for *Lolita*. It may seem like a dreadfully "uncinematic" idea, but I rather wish that Kubrick, when he realized that he couldn't shoot in the U.S. (the reasons must have been economic) had experimented with stylized sets.

There *is* a paradox involved in the film *Lolita*. Stanley Kubrick shows talents in new areas (theme and dialogue and comedy), and is at his worst at what he's famous for. *The Killing* was a simple-minded suspense film about a racetrack robbery, but he structured it brilliantly with each facet shining in place; *Paths of Glory* was a simple-minded pacifist film, but he gave it nervous rhythm and a sense of urgency. *Lolita* is so clumsily structured that you begin to wonder what was shot and then cut out, why other pieces were left in, and whether the beginning was intended to be the end; and it is edited in so dilatory a fashion that after the first hour, almost every scene seems to go on too long. It's as if Kubrick lost his nerve. If he did, it's no wonder; the wonder is, that with all the pressures on American movie-makers—the pressures to evade, to conceal, to compromise, and to explain everything for the literal-minded—he had the nerve to transform this satire on the myths of love into the medium that has become consecrated to the myths. *Lolita* is a wilder comedy for being, now, family entertainment. Movie theatres belong to the same world as the highways and motels: in first-run theatres, "for persons over 18 years of age" does not mean that children are prohibited but simply that there are no reduced prices for children. In second-run neighborhood theatres, "for persons over 18 years of age" is amended by "unless accompanied by a member of the family." That befits the story of Humbert Humbert.

KPFA broadcast, *Partisan Review*, Fall, 1962

FIRES ON THE PLAIN (NOBI)

Cautious as I am about superlatives, I think the term "masterpiece" must be applied to *Fires on the Plain*. It has the disturbing power of great art: it doesn't leave you quite the same. A few hours after seeing it, or a few days or weeks, it rushes up and overwhelms you.

If Dostoyevsky had been a film maker telling his Grand Inquisitor story with a camera, it might have been much like this great visual demonstration that men are not brothers. *Fires on the Plain* is an obsessive, relentless cry of passion and disgust. The subject is modern man as a cannibal, and after a few minutes of *Fires on the Plain,* this subject does not seem at all strange or bizarre: it seems, rather, to be basic. When violence is carried to the extremes of modern war, cannibalism may appear to be the ultimate truth.

The setting is Leyte. Tamura, the hero, is one of the stragglers of the disintegrating retreating Japanese army—terrified of the Americans, the Filipinos, and each other. Tamura walks across the plain unharmed because he is already a dead man; he is tubercular, no one wants his flesh. In the middle of this desolation, there are bonfires—ambiguous flames in the distance that kindle hope. (Perhaps they are signal fires? Perhaps Filipino farmers are burning corn husks? Perhaps there is still some normal life going on?) At the end Tamura approaches the flames and the last illusion is dispelled.

What can be said of a work so powerfully felt and so intensely expressed that it turns rage into beauty? *Fires on the Plain* is an appalling picture; it is also a work of epic poetry. The director, Kon Ichikawa, and the writer, his wife Natto Wada, are among the foremost screen artists of Japan; their other collaborations include *The Burmese Harp, Enjo,* and *Kagi. Fires on the Plain* is based on the book by Shohei Ooka, the greatest Japanese novel to come out of the war, which, as the translator Ivan Morris says, draws a shocking analogy "between the cannibalism of the starving soldiers . . . and the Christian doctrine of the Mass."

Fires on the Plain is a passion film—and a new vision of hell. The passion that informs the character of Tamura is so intense, so desperate and overwhelming, that he seems both painfully close to us and at the same time remote, detached from what is ordinarily thought of as emotion. The atmosphere of the film is also remote from our normal world: there is nothing banal, nothing extraneous to the single-minded view of man *in extremis.* And what is both shocking and, in some terrible sense, beautiful is the revelation of man's extraordinary passion for life even in an inferno. The soldiers will commit any crime, will kill each other, devour each other, to go on living a few more minutes, a few more hours. Even though there is no future, they are trying to sustain life as if there were; it becomes the new variant of *La Grande Illusion*—that if they can just make it to this forest or that port, they will be saved. Historically, in terms of World War II, some *were* saved; but Ichikawa's film is not, at this level, realistic. It is not merely about World War II, or the experiences on Leyte; it is not an anti-war film in the usual sense. We see no causes, no cures, no enemy; it goes beyond nationalism or patriotism. All men are enemies. It is a post-nuclear-war film—a vision of the end, the final inferno. And oddly, when survival is the only driving force, when men live only to live, survival comes to seem irrelevant.

There is a fiendish irony involved in the physical condition of the hero:

he alone can be a hero—act human—because he can't save his own life anyway. He can be human because he is beyond self-interest; he becomes a Japanese Christ-figure. Tamura, so close to death, is passionately—instinctively and intellectually—committed to the amenities of humanity and civilization. He shares his potatoes with another man because this is how *men* behave; he refuses to eat human flesh because this practice is a destruction of human behavior. It is the only place left to draw the line: Tamura has been degraded in every other way; he has murdered a helpless, terrified girl, but cannibalism is the final degradation. It is the line he will not cross: it becomes the only remaining dividing line, not between man and beast but between beast and beast who clings to the memory, the *idea* of man. Tamura's rejection of cannibalism is the only morality left. Yet, in the circumstances, his behavior—obsessed with the image of man—is what is called "unrealistic"; that is to say, in total war, man preserves himself (if he is lucky) only by destroying his humanity. *Nothing* is left.

Just as Ivan Karamazov is obsessed with the evil in the world that stands in the way of believing in God because he *wants* to believe, Ichikawa's revulsion is the negative image of aspiration and hope. In this film, so harshly realistic, so apparently inevitable that it becomes surrealistic, man is defined as man who cannot forget he is man. As in Céline's novels, there is the poetry of disgust, of catharsis. There is even a black form of humor in a weird Mack Sennett-like sequence—the sudden astonishment of comedy as a succession of soldiers discard their shoes and put on the ones discarded by others.

The film follows the novel very closely except that in the novel Tamura does cross the line: he eats human flesh, or "monkey meat" as the soldiers call it (a term that's like a hideous self-inflicted use of the wartime American expression of contempt for the Japanese). And there is an epilogue to the novel which has not been filmed. At the end of the novel, several years have passed, and Tamura, who has been telling the story, is revealed to be a madman in a mental hospital near Tokyo. Guiltily, he believes that in rejecting the proffered flesh of a dying soldier who had raised his emaciated arm and said, "When I'm dead, you may eat this," he rejected God's flesh. His new formulation is that "all men are cannibals, all women are whores. Each of us must act according to his nature." In his madness, he concludes, ". . . if as a result of hunger human beings were constrained to eat each other, then this world of ours was no more than the result of God's wrath. And if I at this moment, could vomit forth anger, then I, who was no longer human, must be an angel of God, an instrument of God's wrath." Ichikawa (wisely, I think) has infused the whole story with this obsessive angelic wrath, rather than attempting to film the epilogue.

As an ironic aside to the subject of mankind devouring its humanity, man becoming "monkey meat," here is John Coleman's description in the *New Statesman* of an English audience's reaction to the film:

Fires on the Plain is showing to an audience of turnip-headed morons . . . screams of laughter welcoming such acts as the impaling of a mad dog on a bayonet (the spray of blood that hit the ground really rolled them in the aisles), titters as the Japanese hero declines the invitation to cannibalism, bellows of fun as machine guns stuttered and gaunt men ran away.

I have seen just one review in a San Francisco paper: it seems to have been written by one of those turnip-headed morons. I don't know how American audiences—if there are any—will react. If it's anything like the English reaction, perhaps the mad Tamura is right and all men are cannibals.

KPFA broadcast, July 1962

JULES AND JIM

When the Legion of Decency condemned *Jules and Jim,* the statement read: the story has been developed "in a context alien to Christian and traditional natural morality." It certainly has. The Legion went on to say: "If the director has a definite moral viewpoint to express, it is so obscure that the visual amorality and immorality of the film are predominant and consequently pose a serious problem for a mass medium of entertainment." It would be possible to make a fraudulent case for the film's morality by pointing out that the adulterous individuals suffer and die, but this is so specious and so irrelevant to the meanings and qualities of the work that surely the Legion, expert in these matters, would recognize that it was casuistry. The Legion isn't wrong about the visual amorality either, and yet, *Jules and Jim* is not only one of the most beautiful films ever made, and the greatest motion picture of recent years, it is also, viewed as a work of art, exquisitely and impeccably *moral.* Truffaut does not have "a definite moral viewpoint to express" and he does not use the screen for messages or special pleading or to sell sex for money; he uses the film medium to express his love and knowledge of life as completely as he can.

The film is adapted from Henri-Pierre Roché's autobiographical novel, written when he was seventy-four, with some additional material from his even later work, *Deux Anglaises et le Continent.* If some of us have heard of Roché, it's probably just the scrap of information that he was the man who introduced Gertrude Stein to Picasso—but this scrap shouldn't be discarded, because both Stein and Picasso are relevant to the characters and period of *Jules and Jim.* Roché is now dead, but the model for Catherine, the Jeanne Moreau role, is a German literary woman who is still alive; it was she who translated *Lolita* into German. Truffaut has indicated, also, that some of the material which he improvised on location was suggested by Apollinaire's letters to Madeleine—a girl whom he had met for a half-hour on a train.

The film begins in Paris before the First World War. Jules the Austrian (Oskar Werner) and Jim the Frenchman (Henri Serre) are Mutt and Jeff, Sancho Panza and Don Quixote, devoted friends, contentedly arguing about life and letters. Catherine enters their lives, and Jules and Jim try to have both the calm of their friendship and the excitement of her imperious, magical presence. She marries Jules who can't hold her, and in despair he encourages Jim's interest in her—"That way she'll still be *ours.*" But Catherine can't subjugate Jim: he is too independent to be dominated by her whims. Not completely captivated, Jim fails to believe in her love when she most desperately offers it. She kills herself and him.

The music, the camera and editing movement, the rhythm of the film carry us along without pauses for reflection. Truffaut doesn't linger; nothing is held too long, nothing is overstated or even *stated.* Perhaps that's why others besides the Legion of Decency have complained: Stanley Kauffmann in the *New Republic* says that *Jules and Jim* "loses sight of purposes . . . It is a confusion of the sheer happiness of being in the studio . . . with the reason for being there." Truffaut, the most youthfully alive and abundant of all the major film directors, needs a *reason* for making movies about as much as Picasso needs a reason for picking up a brush or a lump of clay. And of what film maker could a reference to a *studio* be less apt? He works everywhere and with anything at hand. Kauffmann says of *Jules and Jim,* "There is a lot less here than meets the eye," and Dwight Macdonald, who considers Kauffmann his only peer, is reassured: "one doesn't want to be the only square," he writes. If it gives him comfort to know there are two of them . . .

What is the film about? It's a celebration of life in a great historical period, a period of ferment and extraordinary achievement in painting and music and literature. Together Jules and Jim have a peaceful friendship (and Jim has a quiet love affair with Gilberte) but when Jules and Jim are with Catherine they feel alive. Anything may happen—she's the catalyst, the troublemaker, the source of despair as well as the source of joy. She is the enchantress who makes art out of life.

At the end, Jules, who has always given in to everything in order to keep Catherine, experiences relief at her death, although he has always delighted in the splendor she conferred on his existence. (Don't we all experience this sort of relief when we say goodbye to a particularly brilliant houseguest?) The dullness in Jules, the bourgeois under the Bohemian, the passivity is made clear from the outset: it is why the girls don't fall in love with him. At the end, the excitements and the humiliations are over. He will have peace, and after a lifetime with Catherine he has earned it.

Catherine is, of course, a little crazy, but that's not too surprising. Pioneers can easily become fanatics, maniacs. And Catherine is part of a new breed—the independent, intellectual modern woman, so determined to live as freely as a man that while claiming equality she uses every feminine wile to gain extra advantages, to demonstrate her superiority, and to increase her power position. She is the emerging twentieth-century woman satirized by Strindberg, who also adored her; she is the woman with rights and responsibilities who entered Western literature after the turn of the century and has almost always been seen by the male authors as demanding the rights but refusing the responsibilities. This is the traditional male view of the feminist, and the film's view is not different. Don't we now hear complaints that Negroes are so sensitive about their rights that you can't treat them casually and equally as you would anybody else, you can't disagree on a job or question their judgment, you have to defer to their sensitivities and treat them as if they were super-whites—always in the right? So it is with Catherine.

Catherine, in her way, compensates for the homage she demands. She has, despite her need to intrude and to dominate, the gift for life. She holds nothing in reserve; she lives out her desires; when she can't control the situation, she destroys it. Catherine may be wrong-headed, as those who aspire to be free spirits often are (and they make this wrongness more visible than pliable, amiable people do), but she is devoid of hypocrisy and she doesn't lie. In one of the most upsetting and odd little scenes in the film she takes out a bottle which she says is "vitriol for lying eyes"—and Jim doesn't react any more than if it were aspirin. Catherine the free spirit has the insanity of many free spirits—she believes that she knows truth from lies, right from wrong. Her absolutism is fascinating, but it is also rather clearly *morally insane*. She punishes Jim because he has not broken with Gilberte, though he has not broken with Jules. Only the relationships *she* sets and dominates are *right*. Catherine suffers from the fatal ambivalence of the "free and equal" woman toward sex: she can leave men, but if they leave her, she is as abandoned and desolate, as destroyed and helpless as any clinging vine (perhaps *more* destroyed—she cannot even ask for sympathy). *Jules and Jim* is about the impossibility of freedom, as it is about the many losses of innocence.

All these elements are elliptical in the film—you catch them out of the corner of your eye and mind. So much happens in the span of an hour and three quarters that even if you don't take more than a fraction of the possible meanings from the material, you still get far more than if you examined almost any other current film, frame by frame, under a microscope. *Jules and Jim* is as full of character and wit and radiance as *Marienbad* is empty, and the performance by Jeanne Moreau is so vivid that the bored, alienated wife of *La Notte* is a faded monochrome. In *Jules and Jim* alienation is just one aspect of her character and we see how Catherine got there: she *becomes* alienated when she can't get her own way, when she is blocked. It is not a universal condition as in *La Notte* (neither Jules nor Jim shares in it): it is her developing insanity as she is cut off from what she wants and no longer takes pleasure in life.

Jules and Jim are portraits of artists as young men, but they are the kind of artists who grow up into something else—they become specialists in some field, or journalists; and the dedication to art of their youth becomes the *civilizing* influence in their lives. The war blasts the images of Bohemian life; both Jules and Jim are changed, but not Catherine. She is the unreconstructed Bohemian who does *not* settle down. She needed more strength, more will than they to live the artist's life—and this determination is the *uncivilizing* factor. Bohemianism has made her, underneath all the graces, a moral barbarian: freedom has come to mean whatever she says it is. And when she loses what she believes to be freedom—when she can no longer dictate the terms on which Jim will live—she is lost, isolated. She no longer makes art out of life: she makes life hell.

She chooses death, and she calls on Jules to observe her choice, the last demonstration of her power over life and death, because Jules by a lifetime of yielding his own freedom to her has become, to her, a witness. He can only observe grand gestures; he cannot *make* them. In the last moment in the car, when self-destruction is completely determined, she smiles the smile of the statue: this was the mystery that drew them to her—the smile that looks so easy and natural but which is self-contained and impenetrable.

Jules and Jim ends after the burning of the books in Germany, the end of an epoch, as Truffaut has said, for intellectual Bohemians like Jules and Jim. The film is, in a way, a tribute to the books that were burned; I can't think of another movie so full of books, and of references to books and of writing and translating books. Books were the blood of these characters: they took their ideas of life from books, and writing books was their idea of living.

Jules and Jim is, among other things, the best movie ever made about what I guess most of us think of as the Scott Fitzgerald period (though it begins much earlier). Catherine jumping into the waters of the Seine to demonstrate her supremacy over Jules and Jim, who are discussing the weaknesses of women, is not unlike Zelda jumping over that balustrade. This film treatment of the period is a work of lyric poetry and a fable of the world as playground, a work of art as complex and suggestive in its way as the paintings and poetry and novels and music of the period that it is based on. It is a tribute to the school of Paris when art and Paris were synonymous; filmically it is a new school of Paris—and the new school of Paris is cinema. You go to movies, you talk movies, and you make movies. The young French painters don't compare with the Americans, and French literature is in a fancy trance, but oh, how the young French artists can make movies!

Several of the critics, among them Kauffmann, have complained that the song Jeanne Moreau sings is irrelevant to the action of the film. It's embarrassing to have to point out the obvious, that the song is the theme and spirit of the film: Jules and Jim and Catherine are the ones who "make their way in life's whirlpool of days—round and round together bound." And, in the film, the song is an epiphany: when Catherine sings, the story is crystallized, and the song, like Jim and the child rolling on the hill, seems to belong to memory almost before it is over. In the same way, the still shots catch for us, as for the characters, the distillation, the beauty of the moment. Throughout the film, Georges Delerue's exquisite music—simple and fragrant, popular without being banal—is part of the atmosphere; it is so evocative that if you put the music on the phonograph, like the little phrase from Vinteuil's sonata, it brings back the images, the emotions, the experience. Though emotionally in the tradition of Jean Renoir, as a work of film craftsmanship *Jules and Jim* is an homage to D. W. Griffith. Truffaut explores the medium, plays with it, overlaps scenes, uses fast cutting in the manner of *Breathless* and leaping continuity in the manner of *Zero for Conduct*, changes the size and shape of the images as Griffith did, and in one glorious act of homage he re-creates a frame out of *Intolerance*, the greatest movie ever made. *Jules and Jim* is the most exciting movie made in the West since *L'Avventura* and *Breathless* and Truffaut's earlier *Shoot the Piano Player;* because of the beauty and warmth of its images, it is a richer, a more satisfying film than any of them. I think it will rank among the great lyric achievements of the screen, right up there with the work of Griffith and Renoir.

KPFA broadcast, 1962
Partisan Review, Fall, 1962

REPLYING TO LISTENERS

I am resolved to start the New Year right; I don't want to carry over any unnecessary rancor from 1962. So let me discharge a few debts. I want to say a few words about a communication from a woman listener. She begins with, "Miss Kael, I assume you aren't married—one loses that nasty, sharp bite in one's voice when one learns to care about others." Isn't it remarkable that women, who used to pride themselves on their chastity, are now just as complacently proud of their married status? They've read Freud and they've not only got the idea that being married is healthier, more "mature," they've also got the illusion that it improves their character. This lady is so concerned that I won't appreciate her full acceptance of femininity that she signs herself with her husband's name preceded by a Mrs. Why, if this Mrs. John Doe just signed herself Jane Doe, I might confuse her with one of those nasty virgins, I might not understand the warmth and depth of connubial experience out of which she writes.

I wonder, Mrs. John Doe, in your reassuring, protected marital state, if you have considered that perhaps caring about others may bring a bite to the voice? And I wonder if you have considered how difficult it is for a woman in this Freudianized age, which turns out to be a new Victorian age in its attitude to women who *do* anything, to show any intelligence without being accused of unnatural aggressivity, hateful vindictiveness, or lesbianism.

50

The latter accusation is generally made by men who have had a rough time in an argument; they like to console themselves with the notion that the woman is semi-masculine. The new Freudianism goes beyond Victorianism in its placid assumption that a woman who uses her mind is trying to compete with men. It was bad enough for women who had brains to be considered freaks like talking dogs; now it's leeringly assumed that they're trying to grow a penis—which any man will tell you is an accomplishment that puts canine conversation in the shadows.

Mrs. John Doe and her sisters who write to me seem to interpret Freud to mean that intelligence, like a penis, is a male attribute. The true woman is supposed to be sweet and passive—she shouldn't argue or emphasize an opinion or get excited about a judgment. Sex—or at least regulated marital sex—is supposed to act as a tranquilizer. In other words, the Freudianized female accepts that whole complex of passivity that the feminists battled against.

Mrs. Doe, you know something, I don't mind sounding sharp—and I'll take my stand with those pre-Freudian feminists; and you know something else, I think you're probably so worried about competing with male egos and those brilliant masculine intellects that you probably bore men to death.

This lady who attacks me for being nasty and sharp goes on to write, "I was extremely disappointed to hear your costic speech on and about the radio station, KPFA. It is unfortunate you were unable to get a liberal education, because that would have enabled you to know that a great many people have many fields of interest, and would have saved you from displaying your ignorance on the matter." She, incidentally, displays her liberal education by spelling caustic c-o-s-t-i-c, and it is with some expense of spirit that I read this kind of communication. Should I try to counter my education—liberal and sexual—against hers, should I explain that Pauline Kael is the name I was given at birth, and that it does not reflect my marital vicissitudes which might over-complicate nomenclature?

It is not really that I prefer to call myself by my own name and hence Miss that bothers her or the other Mrs. Does, it is that I express ideas she doesn't like. If I called myself by three names like those poetesses in the *Saturday Review of Literature,* Mrs. Doe would still hate my guts. But significantly she attacks me for being a Miss. Having become a Mrs., she has gained moral superiority: for the modern woman, officially losing her virginity is a victory comparable to the Victorian woman's officially keeping hers. I'm happy for Mrs. Doe that she's got a husband, but in her defense of KPFA she writes like a virgin mind. And is that really something to be happy about?

Mrs. Doe, the happily, emotionally-secure-mature-liberally-educated-womanly-woman has her opposite number in the mailbag. Here is a letter from a manly man. This is the letter in its entirety: "Dear Miss Kael, Since you know so much about the art of the film, why don't you spend your time making it? But first, you will need a pair of balls." Mr. Dodo (I use the repetition in honor of your two attributes), movies are made and criticism is written by the use of intelligence, talent, taste, emotion, education, imagination and discrimination. I suggest it is time you and your cohorts stop thinking with your genital jewels. There is a standard answer to this old idiocy of if-you-know-so-much-about-the-art-of-the-film-why-don't-you-make-movies. You don't have to lay an egg to know if it tastes good. If it makes you feel better, I have worked making movies, and I wasn't hampered by any biological deficiencies.

Others may wonder why I take the time to answer letters of this sort: the reason is that these two examples, although cruder than most of the mail, simply carry to extremes the kind of thing so many of you write. There are, of course, some letter writers who take a more "constructive" approach. I'd like to read you part of a long letter I received yesterday:

> I haven't been listening to your programs for very long and haven't heard all of them since I began listening ... But I must say that while I have been listening, I have not heard one favorable statement made of any "name" movie made in the last several years. . . . I have heard no movie which received any kind of favorable mention which was not hard to find playing, either because of its lack of popularity or because of its age. In your remarks the other evening about De Sica's earlier movies you praised them all without reservation until you mentioned his "most famous film—*The Bicycle Thief,* a great work, no doubt, though I personally find it too carefully and classically structured." You make me think that the charge that the favorability of your comments on any given movie varies inversely with its popularity, is indeed true even down to the last nuance.

> But even as I write this, I can almost feel you begin to tighten up, to start thinking of something to say to show that I am wrong. I really wish you wouldn't feel that way. I would much rather you leaned back in your chair, looked up at the ceiling and asked yourself, "Well, how about it? Is it true or not? Am I really biased against movies other people like, because they liked them? When I see a popular movie, do I see it as it is or do I really just try to pick it apart?" You see, I'm not like those other people that have been haranguing you. I may be presumptuous, but I am trying sincerely to be of help to you. I think you have a great deal of potential as a reviewer. . . . But I am convinced that great a potential as you have, you will never realize any more of that potential than you have now until you face those questions mentioned before, honestly, seriously, and courageously, no matter how painful it may be. I want you to think of these questions, I don't want you to think of how to convince me of their answers. I don't want you to look

around to find some popular movie to which you can give a good review and thus "prove me wrong." That would be evading the issue of whether the questions were really true or not. Furthermore, I am not "attacking" you and you have no need to defend yourself to me.

May I interrupt? *Please, attack* me instead—it's this kind of "constructive criticism" that misses the point of everything I'm trying to say that drives me mad. It's enough to make one howl with despair, this concern for my potential—as if I were a cow giving thin milk. But back to the letter—

In fact, I would prefer that you make no reply to me at all about the answers to these questions, since I have no need of the answers and because almost any answer given now, without long and thoughtful consideration, would almost surely be an attempt to justify yourself, and that's just what you don't have to do, and shouldn't do. No one needs to know the answers to these questions except you, and you are the only person who must answer. In short, I would not for the world have you silence any voices in you . . . and most certainly not a concerned little voice saying, "Am I really being fair? Do I see the whole movie or just the part I like—or just the part I don't like?"

And so on he goes for another few paragraphs. Halfway through, I thought this man was pulling my leg; as I got further and read "how you missed the child-like charm and innocence of *The Parent Trap* . . . is quite beyond me," I decided it's mass culture that's pulling both legs out from under us all. Dear man, the only real question your letter made me ask myself is, "What's the use?" and I didn't lean back in my chair and look up at the ceiling, I went to the liquor cabinet and poured myself a good stiff drink.

How completely has mass culture subverted even the role of the critic when listeners suggest that because the movies a critic reviews favorably are unpopular and hard to find, that the critic must be playing some snobbish game with himself and the public? Why are you listening to a minority radio station like KPFA? Isn't it because you want something you don't get on commercial radio? I try to direct you to films that, if you search them out, will give you something you won't get from *The Parent Trap*. You consider it rather "suspect" that I don't praise more "name" movies. Well, what makes a "name" movie is simply a saturation advertising campaign, the same kind of campaign that puts samples of liquid detergents at your door. The "name" pictures of Hollywood are made the same way they are sold: by pretesting the various ingredients, removing all possible elements that might affront the mass audience, adding all possible elements that will titillate the largest number of people. As the CBS television advertising slogan put it—"Titillate—and dominate." *South Pacific* is seventh in *Variety*'s list of all-time top grossers. Do you know anybody who thought it was a good movie? Was it popular in any meaningful sense or do we just call it popular because it was sold? The tie-in campaign for Doris Day in *Lover Come Back* included a Doris Day album to be sold for a dollar with a purchase of Imperial margarine. With a schedule of 23 million direct mail pieces, newspaper, radio, TV and store ads, *Lover Come Back* became a "name" picture.

I try not to waste air time discussing obviously bad movies—popular though they may be; and I don't discuss unpopular bad movies because you're not going to see them anyway; and there wouldn't be much point or sport in hitting people who are already down. I do think it's important to take time on movies which are inflated by critical acclaim and which some of you might assume to be the films to see.

There were some extraordinarily unpleasant anonymous letters after the last broadcast on The New American Cinema. Some were obscene; the wittiest called me a snail eating the tender leaves off young artists. I recognize your assumptions: the critic is supposed to be rational, clever, heartless and empty, envious of the creative fire of the artist, and if the critic is a woman, she is supposed to be cold and castrating. The artist is supposed to be delicate and sensitive and in need of tender care and nourishment. Well, this nineteenth-century romanticism is pretty silly in twentieth-century Bohemia.

I regard criticism as an art, and if in this country and in this age it is practiced with honesty, it is no more remunerative than the work of an avant-garde film artist. My dear anonymous letter writers, if you think it so easy to be a critic, so difficult to be a poet or a painter or film experimenter, may I suggest you try both? You may discover why there are so few critics, so many poets.

Some of you write me flattering letters and I'm grateful, but one last request: if you write me, please don't say, "This is the first time I've ever written a fan letter." Don't say it, even if it's true. You make me feel as if I were taking your virginity—and it's just too sordid.

KPFA broadcast, January 1963

BILLY BUDD

Billy *Budd* is not a great motion picture, but it is a very good one—a clean, honest work of intelligence and craftsmanship. It ranks as one of the best films of 1962, and by contrast, it exposes what a slovenly, incoherent production the current *Mutiny on the Bounty* is. *Billy Budd* not only has a strong story line; it has a core of meaning that charges the story, gives it tension and intellectual excitement.

In the film version of *Billy Budd*, Melville's story has been stripped for action; and I think this was probably the right method—the ambiguities of the story probably come through more clearly than if the film were not so straightforward in its narrative line. The very cleanness of the narrative method, Peter Ustinov's efficient direction, Robert Krasker's stylized, controlled photography, help to release the meanings. The film could easily have been clogged by metaphysical speculation and homo-erotic overtones. Instead, it is a good, tense movie that doesn't try to tell us too much—and so gives us a very great deal.

Terence Stamp is a remarkably intelligent casting selection for Billy. If he were a more feminine type—as the role is often filled on the stage—all the overtones would be cheapened and limited. Stamp, fortunately, can wear white pants and suggest angelic splendor without falling into the narcissistic poses that juveniles so often mistake for grace. Robert Ryan gives a fine performance in the difficult role of Claggart. Ryan has had so few chances at anything like characterization in his movie career that each time he comes across, it seems amazing that he could have retained such power and technique. I don't know how many dozens of times I've seen him, but the roles that I remember are his prizefighter in *The Set-Up*, the anti-Semite in *Crossfire*, the vicious millionaire in Max Ophuls's *Caught*, the projectionist in *Clash by Night*, the central figure in *God's Little Acre*. Considering that he is a very specialized physical type—the tall, rangy American of Western mythology—his variety of characterizations is rather extraordinary. Perhaps just because he is the type who looks at home in cowboy movies, critics rarely single out his performances for commendation. The American reviewers of *Billy Budd* seem more concerned to complain that his Claggart doesn't have an English accent than to judge his performance. But it is not at all necessary that Claggart speak with an English accent: his antecedents are deliberately vague in Melville as in the film, and the men on board are drawn from all over. It may even be better that Claggart's accent does not define his background for us.

Ryan's Claggart has the requisite Satanic dignity: he makes evil comprehensible. The evil he defines is the way the world works, but it is also the self-hatred that makes it necessary for him to destroy the image of goodness. In the film Claggart is drawn to Billy but overcomes his momentary weakness. Melville, with all his circumlocutions, makes it overwhelmingly clear that Claggart's "depravity according to nature" is, among other things, homosexual, or as he coyly puts it, "a nut not to be cracked by the tap of a lady's fan." Billy's innocence and goodness are intolerable to Claggart because Billy is so beautiful.

Neither Stamp nor Ryan can be faulted. Unfortunately, the role of Captain Vere as played by Ustinov is a serious misconception that weakens the film, particularly in the last section. Ustinov gives a fine performance but it doesn't belong in the story of *Billy Budd*: it reduces the meanings to something clearcut and banal. Ustinov's physical presence is all wrong; his warm, humane, sensual face turns Melville's Starry Vere into something like a cliché of the man who wants to do the right thing, the liberal. We *believe* him when he presents his arguments about justice and law.

Perhaps it is Ustinov's principles that have prevented him from seeing farther into Melville's equivocations. Ustinov has explained that he was concerned "with a most horrible situation where people are compelled by the letter of the law, which is archaic, to carry out sentences which they don't wish to do. That obviously produces a paradox which is tragic." This is, no doubt, an important subject for Ustinov, but it is not the kind of paradox that interested Melville. Melville, so plagued by *Billy Budd* that he couldn't get it in final form (he was still revising it when he died), had far more unsettling notions of its content. As Ustinov presents the film, the conflict is between the almost abstract forces of good (Billy) and evil (Claggart) with the Captain a human figure tragically torn by the rules and demands of authority. Obviously. But what gives the story its fascination, its greatness, is the ambivalent Captain; and there is nothing in Ustinov's performance, or in his conception of the story, to suggest the unseemly haste with which Vere tries to hang Billy. In Melville's account the other officers can't understand why Vere doesn't simply put Billy in confinement "in a way dictated by usage and postpone further action in so extraordinary a case to such time as they should again join the squadron, and then transfer it to the admiral." The surgeon thinks the Captain must be "suddenly affected in his mind." Melville's Vere, who looks at the dead Claggart and exclaims, "Struck dead by an angel of God. Yet the angel must hang!" is not so much a tragic victim of the law as he is Claggart's master and a distant relative perhaps of the Grand Inquisitor. Sweet Starry Vere is the evil we *can't* detect: the man whose motives and conflicts we can't fathom. Claggart we can spot, but he is merely the underling doing the Captain's work: it is the Captain, Billy's friend, who continues the logic by which saints must be destroyed.

Though it is short, *Billy Budd* is one of the most convoluted, one of the strangest works Melville wrote (in some ways even stranger than *Pierre*). Among its peculiarities is a chapter entitled "A Digression," which is given over to a discussion between the ship's purser and the ship's surgeon after Billy's death. Their subject is why Billy's body during the hanging did not go through the movements which are supposed to be invariable in such cases. The absence of spasm—which is a euphemism for ejaculation—is rather like a variation or a reversal of the famous death stink of Father Zossima in *The Brothers Karamazov*. I don't want to stretch the comparison too far, but it's interesting that Melville and Dostoyevsky, so closely contemporary—Melville born in 1819, Dostoyevsky in 1821—should both have been concerned in works written just before their own deaths with the physical phenomena of death. Billy Budd, by the absence of normal human reactions at the moment of death, turns into a saint, a holy innocent, both more and less than a man. Father Zossima, by the presence of all-too-mortal stench after death, is robbed of his saintliness. Melville's lingering on this singularity about Billy

Budd's death didn't strike me so forcibly the first time I read the story, but reading it again recently, and, as it happened, reading it just after William Burroughs's *The Naked Lunch*, with all its elaborate fantasies of violent deaths and gaudy ejaculations, Melville's treatment seems odder than ever. Billy Budd's goodness is linked with presexuality or nonsexuality; his failure to comprehend evil in the universe is linked with his not being really quite a man. He is, in Melville's view, too pure and beautiful to be subject to the spasms of common musculature.

Before this rereading I had associated the story only with that other work of Dostoyevsky's to which it bears more obvious relationships—*The Idiot*. It is, of course, as a *concept* rather than as a character that Billy resembles Prince Myshkin. It may be worth pointing out that in creating a figure of abnormal goodness and simplicity, both authors found it important for their hero to have an infirmity—Myshkin is epileptic, Billy stammers. In both stories the figure is also both naturally noble and also of aristocratic birth: Myshkin a prince, Billy a bastard found in a silk-lined basket. And in the structure of both, the heroes have their opposite numbers—Myshkin and Rogozhin, Billy and Claggart. For both authors, a good man is not a whole man; there is the other side of the human coin, the dark side. Even with his last words, "God bless Captain Vere," Billy demonstrates that he is not a man: he is unable to comprehend the meaning of Vere's experience, unable to comprehend that he will die just because he is innocent.

What's surprising about the film is how much of all this *is* suggested and comes through. What is missing in the film—the reason it is a very good film but not a great one—is that passion which gives Melville's work its extraordinary beauty and power. I wonder if perhaps the key to this failure is in that warm, humane face of Peter Ustinov, who perhaps, not just as an actor, but also as adaptor and director, is too much the relaxed worldly European to share Melville's American rage—the emotionality that is blocked and held back and still pours through in his work. Melville is not a civilized, European writer; he is our greatest writer because he is the American primitive struggling to say more than he knows how to say, struggling to say more than he knows. He is perhaps the most confused of all great writers; he wrestles with words and feelings. It is probably no accident that Billy's speech is blocked. Dostoyevsky is believed to have shared Myshkin's epilepsy, and when Melville can't articulate, he flails in all directions. Even when we can't understand clearly what he is trying to say, we respond to his Promethean torment, to the unresolved complexities.

The movie does not struggle; it moves carefully and rhythmically through the action to the conclusion. Its precision—which is its greatest virtue—is, when compared with the oblique, disturbing novella, evidence of its limitations. Much of what makes the story great is in Melville's effort to achieve new meanings (and some of the meanings we can only guess at from his retreats and disguises) and it is asking rather too much of the moviemakers to say what he wasn't sure about himself. But as Ustinov interprets

Vere, Billy is just a victim of unfortunate circumstances, and the film is no more than a tragedy of *justice*. There's a good deal in the film, but the grandeur of Melville is not there.

KPFA broadcast, 1962
Film Quarterly, Spring, 1963

YOJIMBO

Kurosawa has made the first great shaggy-man movie. *Yojimbo* (The Bodyguard) is a glorious comedy-satire of force: the story of the bodyguard who kills the bodies he is hired to guard. Our Westerner, the freelance professional gunman, the fastest draw in the West, has become the unemployed samurai; the gun for hire has become the sword for hire. But when our Westerner came into town, although his own past was often shady, he picked the *right* side, the farmers against the gamblers and cattle thieves, the side of advancing law and order and decency and schools and churches. Toshiro Mifune, the samurai without a master, the professional killer looking for employment, walks into a town divided by two rival merchants quarreling over a gambling concession, each supporting a gang of killers. The hero is the Westerner all right, the stranger in town, the disinterested outsider with his special skills and the remnants of a code of behavior, but to whom can he give his allegiance? Nobody represents any principle, the scattered weak are simply weak.

The Westerner has walked into the gangster movie: both sides are treacherous and ruthless (trigger-happy, they would be called in American pictures). He hires out to each and systematically eliminates both. He is the agent of their destruction because they offend his sense of how things should be: he destroys them because they disgust him. This black Robin Hood with his bemused contempt is more treacherous than the gangsters; he can defend his code only by a masterly use of the doublecross, and he enjoys himself with an occasional spree of demolition ("Destruction's our delight"). The excruciating humor of his last line, as he surveys the carnage—"Now there'll be a little quiet in this town"—is that we've heard it so many times before, but not amidst total devastation. His clean-up has been so thorough and so outrageously bloody that it has achieved a hilarious kind of style.

We would expect violence carried to extremity to be sickening; Kurosawa, in a triumph of bravura technique, makes it explosively comic and exhilarating. By taking the soft romantic focus off the Westerner as played by Gary Cooper or Alan Ladd or John Wayne, Kurosawa has made him a comic hero—just because of what he does, which was always incredible. Without his nimbus, he is unbelievably, absurdly larger-than-life. In *Shane,* the rather ponderously "classic" version of the Western, good and evil were white and black. The settlers, morally strong but physically weak, naive and good but not very bright or glamorous, had to be represented in their fight against the rustling-gambling-murderous prince of darkness by a disinterested prince of light. Shane was Galahad. The Western dog, who howled at his master's grave in *Shane,* who crossed the road to frame the action at the beginning and end of *The Ox-Bow Incident,* has a new dimension in *Yojimbo*—he appears with a human hand for a bone. This dog signals us that in this movie the conventions of the form are going to be turned inside out, we'll have to shift expectations, abandon sentiments: in this terrain dog eats man. And if we think that man, having lost his best friend, can still count on his mother, Kurosawa has another shock for us. A boy from one gang, held prisoner by the other, is released; he rushes to his mother, crying "Oka" (ma or mother). She responds by slapping him. Mother isn't sentimental: first things first, and what she cares about is that gambling concession. This Eastern Western isn't merely a confusion in the points of the compass; Kurosawa's control and his sense of film rhythm are so sure that each new dislocation of values produces both surprise and delight, so that when the hero tries to free an old man who has been trussed-up and suspended in air, and the old man protests that he's safer where he is, we giggle in agreement.

Other directors attempt to re-create the pastness of a story, to provide distance, perspective. For Kurosawa, the setting may be feudal or, as in this case, mid-nineteenth century, but we react (as we are supposed to react) as modern men. His time is now, his action so immediate, sensuous, raging, that we are forced to disbelieve, to react with incredulity, to admire. (This is partly the result of using telephoto lenses that put us right into the fighting, into the confusion of bared teeth and gasps and howls.) He shakes spears in our faces. This is more alive than any living we know; this, all our senses tell us, is art, not life. Ironic detachment is our saving grace.

Of all art forms, movies are most in need of having their concepts of heroism undermined. The greatest action pictures have often been satirical: even before Douglas Fairbanks, Sr., mocked the American dreams, our two-reelers used the new techniques of the screen to parody the vacuous heroics of stage melodrama. George Stevens's *Gunga Din,* a model of the action genre, was so exuberant and high-spirited that it both exalted and mocked a schoolboy's version of heroism. But in recent years John Ford, particularly, has turned the Western into an almost static pictorial genre, a devitalized, dehydrated form which is "enriched" with pastoral beauty and evocative nostalgia for a simple, heroic way of life. The clichés we retained from childhood pirate, buccaneer, gangster, and Western movies have been awarded the status of myths, and writers and directors have been making infatuated tributes to the myths of our old movies. If, by now, we dread going to see a "great" Western, it's because "great" has come to mean slow and pictorially composed. We'll be lulled to sleep in the "affectionate," "pure," "authentic" scenery of the West (in "epics" like *My Darling Clementine, She Wore a Yellow Ribbon, Fort Apache*) or, for a change, we'll be clobbered by messages in "mature" Westerns like *The Gunfighter* and *High Noon* (the message is that the myths we never believed in anyway were false). Kurosawa slashes the screen with action, and liberates us from the pretensions of our "serious" Westerns. After all those long, lean-hipped walks across the screen with Cooper or Fonda (the man who knows how to use a gun is, by movie convention, the man without an ass), we are restored to sanity by Mifune's heroic personal characteristic—a titanic shoulder twitch.

The Western has always been a rather hypocritical form. The hero represents a way of life that is becoming antiquated. The solitary defender of justice is the last of the line; the era of lawlessness is over, courts are coming in. But the climax is the demonstration that the old way is the only way that works—though we are told that it is the last triumph of violence. The Westerner, the loner, must take the law into his hands for one last time in order to wipe out the enemies of the new system of justice. *Yojimbo* employs an extraordinary number of the conventions of the form, but takes the hypocrisy for a ride. The samurai is a killer with a code of honor and all that, but no system of justice is supplanting him. He's the last of the line not because law and order will prevail, but because his sword for hire is already anachronistic. Guns are coming in. One of his enemies is a gun-slinger, who looks and acts a parody of American Method actors. That ridiculous little gun means the end of the warrior caste: killing is going to become so easy that it will be democratically available to all. In *Yojimbo* goodness triumphs satirically: the foil at the point of the sword is a huge joke. The samurai is not a man with a poker face, and he's not an executioner who hates his job. He's a man of passion who takes savage satisfaction in his special talents. Violence triumphs whoever wins, and our ideas of courage, chivalry, strength, and honor bite the dust along with the "bad" men. The dogs will have their human fodder.

Yojimbo is not a film that needs much critical analysis; its boisterous power and good spirits are right there on the surface. Lechery, avarice, cowardice, coarseness, animality, are rendered by fire; they become joy in life, in even the lowest forms of human life. (Kurosawa's grotesque variants of the John Ford stock company include a giant—a bit mentally retarded, perhaps.) The whimpering, maimed and cringing are so vivid they seem joyful; what in life might be pathetic, loathsome, offensive is made comic and beautiful. Kurosawa makes us accept even the most brutish of his creatures as more alive than the man who doesn't yield to temptation. There is so much displacement that we don't have time or inclination to ask why we are enjoying the action; we respond kinesthetically. It's hard to believe that others don't share this response. Still, I should remember Bosley Crowther with his "the dramatic penetration is not deep, and the plot complications are many and hard to follow in Japanese." And Dwight Macdonald, who writes, "It is a dark, neurotic, claustrophobic film ..." and, "The Japanese have long been noted for their clever mimicry of the West. *Yojimbo* is the cinematic equivalent of their ten-cent ball-point pens and their ninety-eight-cent mini-cameras. But one expects more of Kurosawa."

More? Kurosawa, one of the few great new masters of the medium, has had one weakness: he has often failed to find themes that were commensurate with the surge and energy of his images. At times he has seemed to be merely a virtuoso stylist, a painter turned director whose visual imagination had outstripped his content. But in at least three films, eye and mind have worked together at the highest levels. His first major international success, *Rashomon* (1950)—despite the longeurs of the opening and closing sequences—is still the classic film statement of the relativism, the unknowability of truth. *The Seven Samurai* (1954) is incomparable as a modern poem of force. It is the Western form carried to apotheosis—a vast celebration of the joys and torments of fighting, seen in new depth and scale, a brutal imaginative ballet on the nature of strength and weakness. Now, in *Yojimbo*, Kurosawa has made a farce of force. And now that he has done it, we can remember how good his comic scenes always were and that he frequently tended toward parody.

Ikiru is often called Kurosawa's masterpiece. (It *does* have one great moment—the old man's song in the swing. *Throne of Blood*, which I much prefer, has at least two great moments—Isuzu Yamada's handwashing scene, and that dazzling filmic achievement of Shakespeare's vision when Birnam Wood does come to Dunsinane.) Movies are, happily, a popular medium (which makes it difficult to understand why Dwight Macdonald with his dedication to high art sacrifices his time to them), but does that mean that people must look to them for confirmation of their soggiest humanitarian sentiments? The prissy liberals who wouldn't give a man with the D.T.'s a quarter for a shot ("He'll waste it on drink") are just the ones who love the message they take out of *Ikiru*, not that one man did manage to triumph over bureaucracy but that the meaning of life is in doing a bit of goody good good for others. I have talked to a number of these people about why they hated *The Manchurian Candidate* and I swear not one of them can remember that when the liberal senator is killed, milk pours out. *Yojimbo* seems so simple, so marvelously obvious, but those who are sentimental don't get it: they think it's a mistake, that it couldn't have been intended as a killing comedy. It's true that even Shakespeare didn't dare give his clowns hot blood to drink. But Kurosawa dares.

KPFA broadcast, 1962
Partisan Review, Summer, 1963

DEVI

The *Apu Trilogy* has been widely acclaimed as a masterpiece, which indeed it is, though I would guess that in the years since its release fewer Americans have seen it than have seen *David and Lisa* in any *week* since its release. Fewer have seen Satyajit Ray's new film, *Devi*, than have seen *David and Lisa* in any *night* since its release. Ingmar Bergman, who was also a slow starter with American audiences, has definitely caught on; why not Ray?

Bergman is sensual and erotic; he provides "stark" beauty and exposed nerves and conventional dramatic conflicts and a theme that passes for contemporary—the coldness of intellectuals. Husbands fail their wives and drive them crazy because they don't understand them and all that. (Really, it's not people who don't understand us who drive us nuts—it's when those who shouldn't, *do*.) But I would guess that what gives his movies their immense appeal is their semi-intellectual, or, to be more rude, "metaphysical" content. His characters are like schoolboys who have just heard the startling new idea that "God is dead"; this sets them off on torments of deep thought. Bergman's greatest "dark" film, *The Seventh Seal,* reminds one of the nightmares of life and death and religion that one had as a child; the sense of mystery and the questions that no one will answer suggest the way religious symbols function in childhood and in fear. Bergman's power over audiences is that he has not developed philosophically beyond the awesome questions: audiences trained in more rational philosophy still respond emotionally to Bergman's kind of mysticism, his searching for "the meaning of life," his fatalism, and the archaic ogres of childhood and religion. Bergman is not a deep thinker, but he is an artist who moves audiences deeply by calling up their buried fears and feelings. People come out of his movies with "something to think about" or, at least, to talk about.

Those who find Bergman profound and sophisticated are very likely to find Satyajit Ray rather too simple. I think that Ray, like Kurosawa, is one of the great new film masters, and that his simplicity is a simplicity arrived at, achieved, a master's distillation from his experience; but it is—and this may be another reason why audiences prefer Bergman—the simplicity to which we must respond with *feeling*. It is not the simplicity of a film like *David and Lisa*—which is simplicity at a pre-art level, the simplicity of those who don't perceive complexities and have not yet begun to explore their medium.

People say that *David and Lisa* is a "heartfelt" experience, but they gobble it up so easily because it appeals to feelings they already had. It's a movie about mental disturbances that couldn't disturb anybody. Similarly, *Sundays and Cybèle,* also a phenomenal box-office success, is gobbled up as "artistic" (it's "artistic" the same way that *Harper's Bazaar* fiction is "beautifully literate"). Bosley Crowther says that *Sundays and Cybèle* is "what *Lolita* might conceivably have been had it been made by a poet and angled to be a rhapsodic song of innocence and not a smirking joke." Surely only a satirist like

Nabokov could have invented this eminent critic whose praise gives the show away—"angled to be a rhapsodic song of innocence."

(One of the delights of life in San Francisco is observing the cultural chauvinism of New York from a safe distance. *Variety* informs us that improvement is expected in West Coast movie tastes now that the Western edition of the *New York Times* brings us Bosley Crowther. And Dwight Macdonald, who calls any place outside New York "the provinces," has a solution for the problems of American movies: they should be made closer to the intellectual life of the nation—in New York. But it's the Eastern banks, not the Western minds, that are destroying our movies.)

The concept of humanity is so strong in Ray's films that a man who functioned as a villain could only be a limitation of vision, a defect, an intrusion of melodrama into a work of art which seeks to illuminate experience and help us feel. There is, for example, a defect of this kind in De Sica's *Umberto D*: the landlady is unsympathetically caricatured so that we do not understand and respond to her as we do to the others in the film. I don't think Ray ever makes a mistake of this kind: his films are so far from the world of melodrama that such a mistake is almost unthinkable. We see his characters not in terms of good or bad, but as we see ourselves, in terms of failures and weaknesses and strength and, above all, as part of a human continuum—fulfilling, altering, and finally accepting ourselves as part of this humanity, recognizing that no matter how much we want to burst the bounds of experience, there is only so much we can do. This larger view of human experience—the simplicity of De Sica at his best, of Renoir at his greatest, is almost miraculously present in every detail of Satyajit Ray's films. Ray's method is perhaps the most direct and least impaired by commercial stratagems in the whole history of film. He does not even invent dramatic devices, shortcuts to feelings. He made no passes at the commercial market; he didn't even reach out toward Western conceptions of drama and construction, although as one of the founders of the Calcutta film society, he must have been familiar with these conceptions. He seems to have had, from the beginning, the intuitive knowledge that this was not what he wanted.

In the background of almost every major new figure in film today we see the same great man—Jean Renoir. In France, the critic André Bazin taught a film-loving juvenile delinquent named François Truffaut "first" as Truffaut says, "to love Renoir and then to know him." The lives of Ray and Renoir intersected in 1950, when Ray, a young painter working as a layout artist for a British advertising firm, was struggling to work out a film treatment for *Pather Panchali*, and Renoir was in Calcutta filming *The River*, a movie that despite its weaknesses is perhaps a genre in itself—the only fictional film shot in a remote culture in which the director had the taste and sensitivity to present an outsider's view without condescension or a perfunctory "documentary" style. Ray has said that "the only kind of professional encouragement I got came from one single man"—Jean Renoir, who "insisted that I shouldn't give up."

There is a common misconception that Ray is a "primitive" artist and although, initially, this probably worked to his advantage in this country (*Pather Panchali* was taken to be autobiographical, and "true" and important because it dealt with rural poverty), it now works to his disadvantage, because his later films are taken to be corrupted by exposure to "art," and thus less "true." *The Apu Trilogy* expresses India in transition, showing the development of the boy Apu's consciousness from the primitive, medieval village life of *Pather Panchali* through the modern city streets and schools of Benares to the University of Calcutta in *Aparajito,* and then, in *The World of Apu,* beyond self-consciousness to the destruction of his egotism, and the rebirth of feeling, the renewal of strength. But Ray himself is not a primitive artist any more than, say, Robert Flaherty was when he chronicled the life of the Eskimos in *Nanook of the North.* Ray was a highly educated man at the beginning of his film career, and he was influenced by a wide variety of films, those of Renoir and De Sica in particular. (Sent by his employers to England for three months in 1950, he went to more than ninety films, and he has reported that the one that helped most to clarify his ideas was *The Bicycle Thief.*) Among his other influences are certainly Dovzhenko's *Earth* and Eisenstein, and probably Von Sternberg. Just as *Nanook,* although a great work, seems primitive compared with a later, more complex Flaherty film like *Man of Aran, Pather Panchali* has a different kind of beauty, a more primitive kind, than later Ray films. But Ray's background is not Apu's: "My grandfather was a painter, a poet, and also a scientist who, in addition to editing the first children's magazine in Bengal, had introduced the half-tone block to India. My father was equally well known. He ... wrote, among other works, Bengal's classic Book of Nonsense—an Englishman might call him India's Edward Lear." After graduating from the University of Calcutta with honors in physics and economics, the nineteen-year-old Ray, at the urging of Rabindranath Tagore, went to study at Tagore's school, Santiniketan. There, he "developed some skill in drawing" and "read widely in the history of art ... studying in particular Chinese calligraphy." After Tagore's death, he left the school ("There were no films there and somehow, I don't know how it happened, but films appealed to me"). In Calcutta he worked as art director for a British advertising firm: "I stayed with them a long while and went through every department. When I was in a position to do so I introduced into their advertisements a fusion of modern western and Bengal tradition, to give it a new look."

In addition, he illustrated books, and it was after he had illustrated an edition of the popular novel *Pather Panchali* that he began to think about visualizing it on the screen.

What I lacked was first-hand acquaintance with the *milieu* of the story. I could, of course, draw upon the book itself, which was a kind of encyclopaedia of Bengali rural life, but I knew that this was not enough. In any case, one had only to drive six miles out of the city to get to the heart of the authentic village. While far from being an adventure in the physical sense, these explorations . . . nevertheless opened up a new and fascinating world. To one born and bred in the city, it had a new flavor, a new texture; and its values were different. It made you want to observe and probe, to catch the revealing details, the telling gestures, the particular turns of speech. You wanted to fathom the mysteries of "atmosphere."

Ray's statements and articles have been widely published, and his English is perfectly clear, but the critics can't resist the chance to play sahib. *Pather Panchali* provided Crowther with an opportunity for a classic example of his style and perception: "Chief among the delicate revelations that emerge from its loosely formed account of the pathetic little joys and sorrows of a poor Indian family in Bengal is the touching indication that poverty does not nullify love and that even the most afflicted people can find some modest pleasures in their worlds . . . Any picture as loose in structure or as listless in tempo as this one is would barely pass as a 'rough cut' in Hollywood." In a review of *Aparajito,* Kingsley Amis, then *Esquire*'s movie critic, thought that "Satyajit Ray, the director, seems to have set out with the idea of photographing without rearrangement the life of a poor Indian family, of reporting reality in as unshaped a form as possible." *The World of Apu,* which died at the box-office, got short shrift from Macdonald: "*Pather* was about a family in a village, *Apu* is about a young writer in a city, a more complex theme, and I'm not sure Ray is up to it." (Somehow he makes us feel that he's more sure than he ought to be; he condescends promiscuously.)

Each of the films of *The Apu Trilogy* represents a change, I think a development, of style. Unfortunately, those who responded to the slow rhythm of *Pather Panchali* felt that this pace was somehow more true to India than the faster pace of the third film, *The World of Apu.* But Ray's rhythm is derived from this subject matter, and for the college students and artists of *The World of Apu,* the leisurely flow of the seasons on which *Pather Panchali* was based would be ludicrous. Even those who prefer *Pather Panchali* to his later work should recognize that an artist cannot retain his first beautiful awkward expressiveness and innocence, and that to attempt to do so would mean redoing consciously what had been beautiful because it was not completely conscious. An artist must either give up art or develop. There are, of course, two ways of giving up: stopping altogether or taking the familiar Hollywood course—making tricks out of what was once done for love.

Ray began his film career with a masterpiece, and a trilogy at that; this makes it easy to shrug off his other films as very fine but not really up to the trilogy (even critics who disparaged each film of the trilogy as it appeared, now use the trilogy as the measure to disparage his other works). It is true that the other films are smaller in scope. But, if there had been no trilogy, I would say of *Devi*, "This is the greatest Indian film ever made." And if there had been no trilogy and no *Devi*, I would say the same of his still later *Two Daughters*, based on Tagore stories, of which the first, *The Postmaster*, is a pure and simple masterpiece of the filmed short story form. (The second has memorable scenes, beauty, and wit, but is rather wearying.) Ray's least successful film that has been imported, *The Music Room* (made early, for respite, between the second and third parts of the trilogy), has such grandeur in its best scenes that we must revise customary dramatic standards. By our usual standards it isn't a good movie: it's often crude and it's poorly constructed; but it's a great experience. It's a study of *noblesse oblige* carried to extremity, to a kind of aesthetic madness. It recalls the film of *The Magnificent Ambersons* and, of course, *The Cherry Orchard* but, more painfully, it calls up hideous memories of our own expansive gestures, our own big-role playing. We are forced to see the recklessness and egomania of our greatest moments—and at the same time we are forced to see the sordid banality of being practical. The hero is great *because* he destroys himself; he is also mad. I was exasperated by the defects of *The Music Room* when I saw it; now, a month later, I realize that I will never forget it. Worrying over its faults as a film is like worrying over whether *King Lear* is well constructed: it doesn't really matter.

Ray is sometimes (for us Westerners, and perhaps for Easterners also?) a little boring, but what major artist outside film and drama isn't? What he has to give is so rich, so contemplative in approach (and this we are completely unused to in the film medium—except perhaps in documentary) that we begin to accept our lapses of attention during the tedious moments with the same kind of relaxation and confidence and affection that we feel for the boring stretches in the great novels, the epic poems.

Although India is second only to Japan in the number of movies it produces, Ray is the *only* Indian director; he is, as yet, in a class by himself. Despite the financial conditions under which he works, despite official disapproval of his themes, despite popular indifference to his work, he is in a position that almost any film maker anywhere in the world might envy. The Indian film industry is so thoroughly corrupt that Ray could start fresh, as if it did not exist. Consider the Americans, looking under stones for some tiny piece of subject matter they can call their own, and then judge the wealth, the prodigious, fabulous heritage that an imaginative Indian can draw upon. Just because there has been almost nothing of value done in films in India, the whole country and its culture is his to explore and express to the limits of his ability; he is the first major artist to draw upon these vast and ancient reserves. The Hollywood director who re-makes biblical spectacles or Fannie Hurst stories for the third or sixth or ninth time is a poor man—no matter how big his budget—compared to the first film artist of India. American directors of talent can still try to beat the system, can still feel that maybe they can do something worth doing, and every once in a while someone almost does. In India, the poverty of the masses, and their desperate *need* for escapist films, cancels out illusions. Ray knows he can't reach a mass audience in India (he can't spend more than $40,000 on a production). Outside of West Bengal, his films are not understood (Bengali is spoken by less than fifteen percent of India's population—of those, only twenty percent can read). In other provinces his films, subtitled, appeal only to the Indian equivalent of the American art-house audience—the urban intellectuals—not only because the masses and the rural audiences want their traditional extravaganzas but because they can't read. Probably India produces so many films just because of the general illiteracy; if Indians could read subtitles, American and European films might be more popular. (India has so many languages, it's impractical to dub for the illiterates—the only justification for dubbing, by the way.)

It's doubtful if Ray could finance his films at all without the international audience that he reaches, even though it's shockingly small and he doesn't reach it easily. Indian bureaucrats, as "image" conscious as our own, and much more powerful in the control of films, prefer to send abroad the vacuous studio productions which they assure us are "technically" superior to Ray's films (everyone and everything in them is so clean and shiny and false that they suggest interminable TV commercials).

Devi, based on a theme from Tagore, is here thanks to the personal intercession of Nehru, who removed the censors' export ban. According to official Indian policy, *Devi* is misleading in its view of Indian life. We can interpret this to mean that, even though the film is set in the nineteenth century, the government is not happy about the world getting the idea that there are or ever were superstitions in India. In the film, the young heroine is believed by her rich father-in-law to be an incarnation of the goddess Kali. I don't know why the Indian government was so concerned about this—anyone who has ever tried to tell children how, for example, saints function in Catholic doctrine may recognize that we have a few things to explain, too. Those who grow up surrounded by Christian symbols and dogmas are hardly in a position to point a finger of shame at Kali worship—particularly as it seems so closely related to prayers to the Virgin Mary, Mother of God. As the film makes clear, Kali is generally called "Ma."

The film has so many Freudian undertones that I was not surprised when the film maker sitting next to me in the empty theater muttered, "Think what Buñuel would do with this." I'm grateful that it's Ray, not Buñuel, and that the undertones stay where they belong—down under. Buñuel would have made it explicit. Ray never tells us that this is the old man's way of taking his son's bride away from him; he doesn't tell us that this is the old man's way of punishing his Westernized, Christianized son; he never says that religion is the last outpost of the old man's sensuality, his return to childhood and "Ma" love. But we experience all this, just as we experience the easy drift of the lovely silly young girl into the auto-intoxication, the narcissism of believing that she *is* a goddess. She is certainly beautiful enough. In one sense the film is about what Christians might call the sin of pride: the girl who finds it not too difficult to believe that she is a goddess, fails to cure the nephew she adores; when the child dies, she goes mad. But that is a Christian oversimplification: what we see is the girl's readiness to believe, her liquid acquiescence; not so much *pride* as a desire to please—the culmination, we suspect, of what the culture expects of a high-born girl. And, surrounded by so much luxury, what is there for the girl to do but try to please? The whole indolent life is centered on pleasure.

Ray creates an atmosphere that intoxicates us as well; the household is so rich and the rich people so overripe. The handsome, soft-eyed men in their silks and brocades are unspeakably fleshly; the half-naked beggars on the steps outside are clothed in their skins, but the rich are eroticized by their garments. And perhaps because of the camera work, which seems to derive from some of the best traditions of the silent screen and the thirties, perhaps because of the Indian faces themselves, the eyes have depths—and a disturbing look of helplessness—that we are unused to. It's almost as if these people were isolated from us and from each other by their eyes. It is not just that they seem exotic to us, but that each is a stranger to the others. Their eyes link them to the painted eyes of the Hindu idols, and, in the film, it is this religion which separates them. They are lost behind their eyes.

Sharmila Tagore (Tagore's great-granddaughter), fourteen when she played Apu's bride, is the seventeen-year-old goddess; she is exquisite, perfect (a word I don't use casually) in both these roles. And the men are wonderfully selected—so that they manage to suggest both the handsomeness of almost mythological figures and the rotting weakness of their way of life. Ray has been developing his own stock company, and anyone who mistook the principal players in the trilogy for people just acting out their own lives for the camera, may be startled now to see them in a nineteenth-century mansion. In the early parts of the trilogy, Ray was able to convince many people that he had simply turned his cameras on life; he performs the same miracle of art on this decadent, vanished period. The setting of *Devi* seems to have been caught by the camera just before it decays. The past is preserved for us, disturbingly, ironically, in its jeweled frame. Are we not perhaps in the position of the "advanced," ineffective young husband who knows that his childish wife can't be Kali because he has "progressed" from Kali worship to the idols of Christianity? (Can we distinguish belief in progress from the sin of pride?)

It is a commentary on the values of *our* society that those who saw truth and greatness in *The Apu Trilogy,* particularly in the opening film with its emphasis on the mother's struggle to feed the family, are not drawn to a film in which Ray shows the landowning class and its collapse of beliefs. It is part of *our* heritage from the thirties that the poor still seem "real" and the rich "trivial." *Devi* should, however, please even Marxists if they would go to see it; it is the most convincing study of upper-class decadence I have ever seen. But it is Ray's feeling for the beauty within this disintegrating way of life that makes it convincing. Eisenstein cartooned the upper classes and made them hateful; they became puppets in the show he was staging. Ray, by giving them the respect and love that he gives the poor and struggling, helps us to understand their demoralization. The rich, deluded father-in-law of *Devi* is as human in his dreamy sensuality as Apu's own poet father. Neither can sustain his way of life or his beliefs against the new pressures; and neither can adapt.

Like Renoir and De Sica, Ray sees that life itself is good no matter how bad it is. It is difficult to discuss art which is an affirmation of life, without fear of becoming maudlin. But is there any other kind of art, on screen or elsewhere? "In cinema," Ray says, "we must select everything for the camera according to the richness of its power to reveal."

KPFA broadcast, 1962
Partisan Review, Summer, 1963

8½:
CONFESSIONS OF A MOVIE DIRECTOR

Some years ago a handsome, narcissistic actor who was entertaining me with stories about his love affairs with various ladies and gentlemen, concluded by smiling seductively as he announced, "Sometimes I have so many ideas I don't know which one to choose." I recall thinking—as I edged him to the door—that he had a strange notion of what an idea was.

The director-hero of *8½* is the center of the film universe, the creator on whose word everything waits, the man sought after by everyone, the one for whom all possibilities are open. Guido can do anything, and so much possibility confuses him. He's like the movies' famous couturier who can't decide what he's going to do for the spring collection. ("I've simply got to get an idea. I'll go mad if I don't. Everybody's depending on me.") I'm afraid that Guido's notion of an "idea" isn't much more highly developed than my silly actor friend's, and it's rather shockingly like the notion of those god-awful boobs who know they could be great writers because they have a great story—they just need someone to put it into words. Indeed the director conforms to the popular notions of a *successful* genius, and our ladies-magazine fiction has always been fond of the "sophisticated" writer or director looking for a story and finding it in romance, or in his own backyard. "Accept me as I am" is Guido's final, and successful, plea to the wife-figure (although that is what she has been rejecting for over two hours).

Just as *La Dolce Vita* confirmed popular suspicions about the depravity of the rich and gifted, *8½* confirms the popular view of a "big" film director's life—the world is his once he finds that important "idea" (it's so important that the boobs will never tell theirs for fear of "giving it away," i.e.,

69

having it stolen—the fewer their "ideas," the greater their fear of plagiarism). Perhaps the irrelevance of what we see (principally his conflicts between his love for his wife, the pleasures of his mistress, his ideal of innocence, and his dreams of a harem) to the composition of a work of art may be indicated by a comparison: can one imagine that Dostoyevsky, say, or Goya or Berlioz or D. W. Griffith or whoever, resolved his personal life before producing a work, or that his personal problems of the moment were even necessarily relevant to the work at hand? This notion of an artist "facing himself" or "coming to grips with himself" as a precondition to "creation" is, however, familiar to us from the popular Freudianized lives of artists (and of everyone else).

It is perhaps easy for educated audiences to see an "advance" in film when a film maker deals with a "creative crisis" or "artist's block," a subject so often dealt with in modern writing; but is it applicable to film? What movie in the half-century history of movies has been held up by the director's having a creative block? No movie with a budget and crew, writers and sets. The irrelevance of what we see to the processes of making a movie can, of course, be explained away with, "He's having a breakdown and all this is his fantasy life." Someone's fantasy life is perfectly good material for a movie *if* it is imaginative and fascinating in itself, or if it illuminates his non-fantasy life in some interesting way. But *8½* is neither; it's surprisingly like the confectionery dreams of Hollywood heroines, transported by a hack's notions of Freudian anxiety and wish fulfillment. *8½* is an incredibly externalized version of an artist's "inner" life—a gorgeous multi-ringed circus that has very little connection with what, even for a movie director, is most likely to be solitary, concentrated hard work. It's more like the fantasy life of someone who wishes he were a movie director, someone who has soaked up those movie versions of an artist's life, in which in the midst of a carnival or ball the hero receives inspiration and dashes away to transmute life into art. "What's the film about? What's on your mind this time?" asks Guido's wife. In *8½* the two questions are one.

Creativity is the new cant—parents are advised not to hit it with a stick, schoolteachers are primed to watch for it, foundations encourage it, colleges and subsidized health farms nourish it in a regulated atmosphere; the government is advised to honor it. We're all supposed to be so in awe of it that when it's in crisis, the screen should be torn asunder by the conflicts. But the creativity con-game, a great subject for comedy, is rather embarrassing when it's treated only semi-satirically. When a satire on big, expensive movies is itself a big, expensive movie, how can we distinguish it from its target? When a man makes himself the butt of his own joke, we may feel too uncomfortable to laugh. Exhibitionism is its own reward.

8½ suggests some of Fellini's problems as a director, but they are not so fantastic nor so psychoanalytic as the ones he parades. A major one is the grubby, disheartening economic problem that probably affects Fellini in an intensified form precisely because of the commercial success of *La Dolce Vita* and the business hopes it raised. A movie director has two "worst" enemies: commercial failure and commercial success. After a failure, he has a difficult time raising money for his next film; after a success, his next must be bigger and "better." In recent years no major Hollywood director with a string of "big" successes has been able to finance a small, inexpensive production—and this is not for want of trying. From the point of view of studios and banks, an expenditure of half a million dollars is a much bigger risk than an investment of several million on a "name" property with big stars, a huge advertising campaign and almost guaranteed bookings. Commenting on the cost of *8½* (and Visconti's *The Leopard*), *Show* reported that "In terms of lire spent, they have nearly been Italian *Cleopatra*s. But what Hollywood bought dearly in *Cleopatra* was a big empty box ... What the Italians got in *8½* was a work of immense visual beauty and impressive philosophy, a sort of spectacle of the spirit that was more than they had paid for. A masterpiece is always a bargain." *Show*'s "philosophy" is the kind you look for, like Fellini's "ideas." *8½* does indeed make a spectacle of the spirit: what else can you do with spirit when you're expected to turn out masterpieces?

According to Fellini, we "need new criteria of judgment to appreciate this film." Yeah. "In my picture everything happens," says Guido, which is intended to mean that he is an artist-magician; but the man who trusts to alchemy is like the man who hopes to create a masterpiece in his sleep and find it miraculously *there* upon awakening. Fellini throws in his disorganized ideas, and lets the audiences sort out the meanings for themselves. *8½* is big, it's "beautiful": but what is it? Is it really a magical work of art? There is an optimum size for a house: if it becomes too big it becomes a mansion or a showplace and we no longer feel the vital connections of family life, or the way the rooms reflect personalities and habits and tastes. When a movie becomes a spectacle, we lose close involvement in the story; we may admire the action and the pageantry or, as in *8½*, the decor, the witty phantasmagoria, the superb "professionalism" ("That Fellini sure can make movies"), but it has become too big and impressive to relate to lives and feelings. Fellini's last home movie was *Nights of Cabiria; 8½* is a madhouse for a movie director who celebrates *La Dolce Vita*, i.e., a funhouse. "What marvelous casting," his admirers exclaim, responding not to the people in his films, but to his cleverness in finding them. That is all one can respond to, because the first appearance of his "characters" tells us all that is to be known about them. They are "set"—embalmed. No acting is necessary: he uses them for a kind of instant caricature. His "magic" is that his casting couch is the world. He uses "real" aristocrats and "real" celebrities as themselves, he turns businessmen into stars, and then he confesses that he's confused about life and art—the confusion which gives his films that special, "professional" chic.

Like those professors of English who boast that they're not interested in what's going on in the world, they're interested only in literature, or critics who say they're not interested in content but in structure, or young poets who tell us they're not interested in anything except their own creativity, Guido announces, "I have nothing to say but I want to say it." The less self, the more need to express it? Or, as the wife said to her drunken husband, "If you had any brains, you'd take them out and play with them."

And the "spa" is just the place to do it, as *Marienbad* demonstrated. Those who honed their wits interpreting what transpired *Last Year at Marienbad* now go to work on *8½*, separating out "memories" and fantasies from "reality." A professor who teaches film told me he had gone to see *8½* several times to test out various theories of how the shifts between the three categories were accomplished, and still hadn't discovered the answer. When I suggested that he had set himself an insoluble problem, because *8½* is all fantasy, he became very angry at what he called my perversity and cited as a clear example of "reality" the sequence of the screen tests for the mistress and wife (one of the most nightmarish episodes in the film) and as an example of "memory" the Saraghina dancing on the beach (which compares as a "memory" with, say, the monster washed up at the end of *La Dolce Vita*).

This is the first (and, predictably, not the last) movie in which the director seems to be primarily interested in glorifying his self-imprisonment. And this failure to reach out imaginatively—which traditionally has been considered artistic suicide—is acclaimed as a milestone in film art by those who accept self-absorption as "creativity."

8½ began as a "sequel" to *La Dolce Vita*—taking up the story of the "Umbrian angel." Now Fellini turns her into Claudia Cardinale, a rather full-bosomed angel with an ambiguous smile. Fluttering about diaphanously, she's not so different from Cyd Charisse or Rita Hayworth in gauze on the ramps of an MGM or Columbia production number. She becomes a showman's ideal of innocence—pulchritudinous purity, the angel-muse as "star" (of the movie and the movie within the movie)—a stalemate endlessly reflected, an infinite regression.

KPFA broadcast, 1963

PART TWO

KISS KISS BANG BANG

1968

BEFORE THE REVOLUTION

There have been few young prodigies in the history of movies: not only must one grasp a complex medium but also perform the more difficult task of finding cash. In 1941 the twenty-five-year-old Orson Welles startled the studios and the moviegoing public with the impious, high-spirited wit of *Citizen Kane*. A few years ago a group of miraculously talented young Frenchmen shook up their country's paralytic film industry. Now from Parma—the most unlikely and yet poetically perfect place, the place where Stendhal set his great, ironic paean to youth, *The Charterhouse of Parma*—has come *Before the Revolution*, written and directed by Bernardo Bertolucci, at the preposterous age of twenty-two.

It is a richly romantic work which makes us realize that most moviemakers are never so far away from youth as when they condescendingly try to deal with those cardboard kids next door—as if youth were a kind of simplicity that will be outgrown. This movie expresses what it means to be young with the lyricism and narcissism and self-consciousness of the intelligent young. (What young artist isn't self-conscious? It's a stage in learning to express yourself.) Bertolucci, a prizewinning poet at twenty-one, deals with the experience of so many young poets and novelists—rebellion against bourgeois life, an egocentric dedication to Communism, disillusion. The movie is set in the 1960s. It is the story of a boy who discovers that he is not singleminded enough to be a revolutionary, that he is too deeply involved in the beauty of life as it is *before* the revolution. He has "a nostalgia for the present."

Not too surprisingly, the love affair between Fabrizio and his young aunt Gina, though the characters are derived from Stendhal, is closer to the seventeen-year-old Raymond Radiguet's *Devil in the Flesh*. However, Bertolucci, trying to discover his feelings and attitudes in movie terms—in image and sound—is much less precise than Radiguet was. This lack of precision, which may be characteristic of modern youth, may also be a factor in their involvement in movies—an art in which so much can be responded to without forming definite attitudes.

I would not insist so much upon Bertolucci's youth if it were not integral to the romantic profusion of this movie, which is most extravagantly beautiful in its excesses—in the manner of supremely gifted children. He has the kind of talent that breaks one's heart: where can it go, what will happen to it? In this country we encourage "creativity" among the mediocre, but real bursting creativity appalls us. We put it down as undisciplined, as somehow "too much." Well, *Before the Revolution is* too much and that is what is great about it. Art doesn't come in measured quantities: it's got to be too much or it's not enough.

When Fabrizio is told that he speaks like a book, it is apparent that Bertolucci is aware that he too is pretentiously literary. But trying to say too much, and saying it too exquisitely, and not always saying it clearly are not the worst crimes in an artist. No doubt the greatest sequences—a Chekhovian lament for the river and forest that the landed gentry are about to lose, and a brilliant night at the opera with the social classes layered in their tiers—stand out "too much"; nevertheless they *are* great.

The worst mechanical defect is that the editing, particularly at the beginning, is too obtrusive, and it takes us a while to get our bearings—to understand, for example, that Fabrizio, who is callowly doctrinaire, is quarreling with his friend Agostino for failing to accept the Communist party as the answer to all human troubles. And the continuity is confusing. We do not always know where or why the action is taking place. But Bertolucci's defects would make the reputation of a dozen lesser directors. And his use of various kinds of music (the most imaginative score since *Jules and Jim*) to fuse the emotions suggests new operatic possibilities in moviemaking.

The greatest achievement is that you come out of the theatre, not dull and depressed the way you feel after movies that insult your intelligence, but *elated*—restored to that youthful ardor when all hopes are raised at once.

Life, August 13, 1965

LAURENCE OLIVIER AS **OTHELLO**

Othello with Laurence Olivier is a filmed record of the theatrical production; it would be our loss if we waited for posterity to discover it. Olivier's Negro Othello—deep voice with a trace of foreign music in it; happy, thick, self-satisfied laugh; rolling buttocks; grand and barbaric and, yes, a little lewd—almost makes this great, impossible play work. It has always made more than sense; now it almost makes sense, too—not only dramatic poetry, but a comprehensible play. Frank Finlay's pale, parched little Iago is not a plotting maniac who's lucky for theatrical convenience, but a man consumed by sexual jealousy and irrational hatred. And because Iago is consumed by sexual jealousy, he infects Othello with the same disease. Maggie Smith's Desdemona is strong and quiet and willful enough to have wanted Othello and gone after him. And Othello, who thought himself almost accepted by these civilized whites, is destroyed by primitive, irrational forces in them that he has no knowledge of. His "civilization" is based on theirs and goes because he believed in theirs.

Olivier is the most physical Othello imaginable. As a lord, this Othello is a little vulgar—too ingratiating, a boaster, an arrogant man. Reduced to barbarism, he shows us a maimed African prince inside the warrior-hero. Iago's irrationality has stripped him bare to a different kind of beauty. We are sorry to see it, and we are not sorry, either. To our eyes, the African prince is more beautiful in his isolation than the fancy courtier in his reflected white glory.

Part of the pleasure of the performance is, of course, the sheer feat of Olivier's transforming himself into a Negro; yet it is not wasted effort, not mere exhibitionism or actor's vanity, for what Negro actor at this stage in the world's history could dare bring to the role the effrontery that Olivier does, and which Negro actor could give it this reading? I saw Paul Robeson and he was not black as Olivier is; Finlay can hate Olivier in a way José Ferrer did not dare—indeed did not have the provocation—to hate Robeson. Possibly Negro actors need to sharpen themselves on white roles before they can *play* a Negro. It is not enough to *be:* for great drama, it is the awareness that is everything.

Every time we single out the feature that makes Olivier a marvel—his lion eyes or the voice and the way it seizes on a phrase—he alters it or casts it off in some new role, and is greater than ever. It is no special asset, it is the devilish audacity and courage of this man. Olivier, who, for Othello, changed his walk, changed his talk, is a man close to sixty who, in an ordinary suit in an ordinary role, looks an ordinary man, and can look even smaller in a role like Archie Rice in *The Entertainer.* What is extraordinary is inside, and what is even more extraordinary is his determination to give it outer form. He has never leveled off; he goes on soaring.

Olivier once said of his interpretation of Henry V: "When you are young, you are too bashful to play a hero; you debunk it. It isn't until you're older that you can understand the pictorial beauty of heroism." And perhaps there is a tendency for people to debunk the kind of heroism necessary to develop your art in a society that offers so many rewards and honors to those who give up and sell out early at the highest market price. One might suspect that in a democratic society the public is on better terms with the mighty after they have fallen. Our mass media are full of the once mighty: they are called "celebrities." Olivier's presence on the screen is the pictorial beauty of heroism. Perhaps that is why we may leave the photographed version of *Othello* with a sense of exaltation and the wonder of sheer admiration.

This *Othello* is history already; it's something to remember. And *Othello* isn't even much of a "movie." Just a reasonably faithful (one assumes) record of a stage interpretation. After thirty-five years in movies and masterpiece upon masterpiece acclaimed in the theatre—every new season seems to bring the tidings that Olivier has exceeded himself as Oedipus, as Lear, in Chekhov—he still could not raise the money to do a real movie version of his Othello. And of his Macbeth, acclaimed as the greatest since—Macbeth, we have not even a record.

Olivier's greatness is in his acting; as a movie director, he is merely excellent and intelligent. Yet his Shakespearean performances deserve—at the minimum—the kind of movie he or other talented directors might do, what he brought to *Henry V, Hamlet, Richard III*. It is a scandal, an indictment of Anglo-American civilization and values, that eight million dollars can go into a spy spoof, twelve into a comic chase, twenty-seven into a spectacle, and for Olivier in *Othello,* we and history must content ourselves with a quickie recording process. And yet the joke is on the spoofs, chases and spectacles. *Othello* lives.

Yes, it's lovely that foundations give all that money to regional theatres, to training ballet students, to raising the pay of symphony orchestras, to encouraging the young and promising and possibly gifted, and that our government is talking about encouraging "standards of excellence"—that eerie schoolteacher's terminology that suggests magical measuring sticks. But do artists have to *aspire* to "excellence" to get help? Where is the help when they have overachieved their promise? Where is the help when Orson Welles botched his great movie version of *Othello* for want of cash, when Olivier can only record a stage production on film? What, then, is the purpose of all the encouragement of "creativity"?

The movies, an art that people don't have to be encouraged, prodded, or "stimulated" to enjoy, which they go to without the path being greased by education and foundations, are still at the mercy of the economics of the mass market, which have broken the heart of almost every artist who has tried to work in the movies.

McCall's, March 1966

MADAME X

There has been much praise of the originality of William Dozier, producer of the new "Batman" television series, in insisting that the performers keep straight faces; but really Ross Hunter pioneered in this field. In his latest production *Madame X* there is little danger of the performers' breaking up, because they are so masked and taped they couldn't laugh if they wanted to. Anyway, I doubt if those connected with this movie will have much to laugh about for a while, though audiences may.

Madame X has one of the "classic" (which, in Hollywood, means perennial) pop-movie themes: a woman is forced to abandon her baby and, years later, having committed a murder, is defended by . . . her very own son, who does not know that . . . she is his very own mother. It jerked tears in silent-movie houses in 1916 and again when Pauline Frederick played the role in 1920; and in 1929, with the great Ruth Chatterton, directed by Lionel Barrymore, it was one of the most celebrated of the early talkie courtroom dramas. In 1937, Gladys George gave it the benefit of her superb technique and her gin-and-tears voice that seemed to have found new lower octaves at the bottom of a glass. These were actresses who knew how to carry a load. And they could get into a broken-down old vehicle and get some mileage out of it.

Lana Turner hasn't the power or the technique.* She's not Madame X, she's Brand X; she's not an actress, she's a commodity. And instead of attempting to update the story so it might make some sense to modern audiences, the Hunter production just buries it under layers of other commodities. The idea is you're supposed to go see it for the gowns, the furs, the jewels and the furnishings, and the sumptuous "production values." That would make sense if, for example, you were going to see Capucine in some breathtaking clothes (that may not be movie art, but it's another kind of art and, in its own way, satisfying). But Miss Turner does not wear clothes well: she wears them as expensively dressed, aging women without much style wear them. Which is not a treat to the eye or the imagination. Her "lavish wardrobe" and the "lush surroundings" are merely gross, and the production values consist of atrocious color and pathetically obvious camera setups.

At the opening of the film, a matronly-looking woman and a man of indefinite age get out of a car in front of a mansion, and we realize they are supposed to be young newlyweds. She seems to be wearing a Lana Turner mask, but before we have time to react, they are greeted by what seems to be a young girl, waiting at the door of the house to welcome them. The groom calls out, "Hello, Mother," and then the youthful apparition comes close, and we see, with horror, that she is wearing a Constance Bennett mask. There were gasps in the audience.

---

* In her alcoholic sequence she projects a lewd, grinning depravity that is the most interesting thing about her, but she does not use it as an actress.

Upper-class mother Bennett and bride Turner are supposed to be a social world apart, but they are alike as two frozen peas in a pod. The dialogue came out of cold storage, too: "Oh, Clay, I don't share your life—I only exist in a cubbyhole of it." The bride and groom are named Holly and Clay. Holly greets Clay with lines like "Oh, Clay, it's so good to have you home." And he musters up the energy to respond, "I'm so happy to *be* here." Holly is lonely when he's away: "I guess I need to feel needed." She doesn't really even want to go to that dinner party that leads to her ruin, and she wouldn't have except that the hostess says, "You'll throw my seating off."

The average age of the cast must be at least fifty. As Turner is supposed to be a ravishing young beauty, the production is designed like a cocoon to protect her. There isn't a *young* actress in the cast, not even among the bit players. This *Madame X* isn't about mother love; it's about mummy love.

It isn't even imitation of life; it's just imitation of movies. This movie is in love with the glamour of old movies. It turns Holly (short for Hollywood?) into a Flying Dutchman, just to get her into more clothes, more décor. To compensate for all those swell clothes, she keeps suffering: not one moment of fun in twenty years. The dialogue begins to comment on the movie itself: "You couldn't cope." "She's worn out in spirit as well as in body. She can't endure much more." "Life has long ceased to have meaning for me."

How can we react to experiences like this film? At the screening where I saw it, some of the same people who were laughing at it also cried in the sad places. Later, I heard that the company was looking for the "instigators" of the laughter: in true paranoid Hollywood style, they can account for it only by a conspiracy.

Madame X presents, in an intensified form, a common problem of movie interpretation. Children sometimes interpret movies in terms of what they actually see on the screen, and the adults with them often try to explain what they are *supposed* to see, so that the children will be able to follow the plot. We would be in the midst of some gigantic confusions if the themes and story lines of all those movies with pouting marshmallows like Lana Turner or iron maidens like Joan Crawford were to be interpreted at the level of what we actually see. No Hollywood plot can really encompass *that* many layers of ambiguity. And so we try to separate out the intentional from the unintentional, what we are supposed to see from what we see. In general, the wider the gap, the less connection the movie has with art or talent or any forms of honesty.

The conventions of the period protect us, to some degree, from seeing what we're not supposed to. It is this lack of protection when we see old movies on television that often makes them seem so absurd: what audiences of the movie's period were willing to ignore is now nakedly exposed.

Madame X is so excruciating not only because the actors and actresses do not embody what they're supposed to, but because the movie depends on the conventions of the MGM style of the forties. It is spiritually dedicated to the worst of old Hollywood—the Hollys and the Clays. How small an aspiration—to want to make a glossy forties' woman's picture—too piddling even to be called decadent; but the clock can't be turned back, even to that. File your regrets at the nearest five-and-dime.

McCall's, April 1966

BAND OF OUTSIDERS

Jean-Luc Godard intended to give the public what it wanted. His next film was going to be about a girl and a gun—"A sure-fire story which will sell a lot of tickets." And so, like Henry James's hero in "The Next Time," he proceeded to make a work of art that sold fewer tickets than ever. What was to be a simple commercial movie about a robbery became *Band of Outsiders.**

The two heroes of *Band of Outsiders* begin by playacting crime and violence movies, then really act them out in their lives. Their girl, wanting to be accepted, tells them there is money in the villa where she lives. And we watch, apprehensive and puzzled, as the three of them act out the robbery they're committing as if it were something going on in a movie—or a fairy tale. The crime does not fit the daydreamers nor their milieu: we half expect to be told it's all a joke, that they can't really be committing an armed robbery. *Band of Outsiders* is like a reverie of a gangster movie as students in an espresso bar might remember it or plan it—a mixture of the gangster film virtues (loyalty, daring) with innocence, amorality, lack of equilibrium.

It's as if a French poet took a banal American crime novel and told it to us in terms of the romance and beauty he read between the lines; that is to say, Godard gives it *his* imagination, re-creating the gangsters and the moll with his world of associations—seeing them as people in a Paris café, mixing them with Rimbaud, Kafka, Alice in Wonderland. Silly? But we know how alien to our lives were those movies that fed our imaginations and have now become part of us. And don't we—as children and perhaps even later—romanticize cheap movie stereotypes, endowing them with the attributes of those figures in the other arts who touch us imaginatively? Don't all our experiences in the arts and popular arts that have more intensity than our ordinary lives tend to merge in another imaginative world? And movies, because they are such an encompassing, eclectic art, are an ideal medium for combining our experiences and fantasies from life, from all the arts, and from our jumbled memories of both. The men who made the stereotypes

* *Band of Outsiders* (with Anna Karina, Sami Frey, Claude Brasseur) opened and closed in New York in a single week of March 1966.

drew them from their own scrambled experience of history and art—as Howard Hawks and Ben Hecht drew *Scarface* from the Capone family "as if they were the Borgias set down in Chicago."

The distancing of Godard's imagination induces feelings of tenderness and despair which bring us closer to the movie-inspired heroes and to the wide-eyed ingenue than to the more naturalistic characters of ordinary movies. They recall so many other movie lives that flickered for us; and the quick rhythms and shifting moods emphasize transience, impermanence. The fragile existence of the characters becomes poignant, upsetting, nostalgic; we care *more*.

This nostalgia that permeates *Band of Outsiders* may also derive from Godard's sense of the lost possibilities in movies. He has said, "As soon as you can make films, you can no longer make films like the ones that made you want to make them." This we may guess is not merely because the possibilities of making big expensive movies on the American model are almost nonexistent for the French but also because as the youthful film enthusiast grows up, if he grows in intelligence, he can see that the big expensive movies now being made are not worth making. And perhaps they never were: the luxury and wastefulness, that when you are young seem as magical as peeping into the world of the Arabian Nights, become ugly and suffocating when you're older and see what a cheat they really were. The tawdry American Nights of gangster movies that were the magic of Godard's childhood formed his style—the urban poetry of speed and no afterthoughts, fast living and quick death, no padding, no explanations—but the meaning had to change.

An artist may regret that he can no longer experience the artistic pleasures of his childhood and youth, the very pleasures that formed him as an artist. Godard is not, like Hollywood's product producers, naïve (or cynical) enough to remake the movies he grew up on. But, loving the movies that formed his tastes, he uses this nostalgia for old movies as an active element in his own movies. He doesn't, like many artists, deny the past he has outgrown; perhaps he is assured enough not to deny it, perhaps he hasn't quite outgrown it. He reintroduces it, giving it a different quality, using it as shared experience, shared joke. He plays with his belief and disbelief, and this playfulness may make his work seem inconsequential and slighter than it is: it is as if the artist himself were deprecating any large intentions and just playing around in the medium. Reviewers often complain that they can't take him seriously; when you consider what they do manage to take seriously, this is not a serious objection.

Because Godard's movies do not let us forget that we're watching a movie, it's easy to think he's just kidding. Yet his reminders serve an opposite purpose. They tell us that his aim is not simple realism, that the lives of his characters are continuously altered by their fantasies. If I may be deliberately fancy: he aims for the poetry of reality and the reality of poetry. I have put it that way to be either irritatingly pretentious or lyrical—depending on your mood and frame of reference—in order to provide a critical equivalent to Godard's phrases. When the narrator in *Band of Outsiders* says, "Franz did not know whether the world was becoming a dream or a dream becoming the world," we may think that that's too self-consciously loaded with mythic fringe benefits and too rich an echo of the narrators of *Orphée* and *Les Enfants Terribles,* or we may catch our breath at the beauty of it. I think those most responsive to Godard's approach probably do both simultaneously. We do something similar when reading Cervantes. Quixote, his mind confused by tales of Knight Errantry, going out to do battle with imaginary villains, is an ancestor of Godard's heroes, dreaming away at American movies, seeing life in terms of cops and robbers. Perhaps a crucial difference between Cervantes's mock romances and Godard's mock melodramas is that Godard may (as in *Alphaville*) share some of his characters' delusions.

It's the tension between his hard, swift, cool style and the romantic meaning that this style has for him that is peculiarly modern and exciting in his work. It's the casual way he omits mechanical scenes that don't interest him so that the movie is all high points and marvelous "little things." Godard's style, with its nonchalance about the fates of the characters—a style drawn from American movies and refined to an intellectual edge in postwar French philosophy and attitudes—is an American teen-ager's ideal. To be hard and cool as a movie gangster yet not stupid or gross like a gangster—that's the cool grace of the privileged, smart young.

It's always been relatively respectable and sometimes fashionable to respond to our own experience in terms drawn from the arts: to relate a circus scene to Picasso, or to describe the people in a Broadway delicatessen as an Ensor. But until recently people were rather shamefaced or terribly arch about relating their reactions in terms of movies. That was more a confession than a description. Godard brought this way of reacting out into the open of *new* movies at the same time that the pop art movement was giving this kind of experience precedence over responsiveness to the traditional arts. By now—so accelerated has cultural history become—we have those students at colleges who when asked what they're interested in say, "I go to a lot of movies." And some of them are so proud of how compulsively they see everything in terms of movies and how many times they've seen certain movies that there is nothing left for them to relate movies *to*. They have been soaked up by the screen.

Godard's sense of the present is dominated by his movie past. This is what makes his movies (and, to a lesser degree, the movies of Jacques Demy) seem so new: for they are movies made by a generation bred on movies. I don't mean that there haven't been earlier generations of directors who grew up on movies, but that it took the peculiar post–World War II atmosphere to make love of movies a new and semi-intellectualized romanticism. To say it flatly, Godard is the Scott Fitzgerald of the movie world, and movies are for the sixties a synthesis of what the arts were for the post–World War I generation—rebellion, romance, a new style of life.

The world of *Band of Outsiders* is both "real"—the protagonists feel, they may even die—and yet "unreal" because they don't take their own feelings or death very seriously, as if they weren't important to anybody, really. Their only identity is in their relationship with each other. This, however we may feel about it, is a contemporary mood; and Godard, who expresses it, is part of it. At times it seems as if the movie had no points of reference outside itself. When this imagined world is as exquisite as in *Band of Outsiders,* we may begin to feel that this indifference or inability to connect with other worlds is a kind of aesthetic expression and a preference. The sadness that pervades the work is romantic regret that you can no longer believe in the kind of movie you once wanted to be enfolded in, becoming part of that marvelous world of beauty and danger with its gangsters who trusted their friends and its whores who never really sold themselves. It's the sadness in frivolity—in the abandonment of efforts to make sense out of life in art. Godard in his films seems to say: only this kind of impossible romance is possible. You play at cops and robbers but the bullets can kill you. His movies themselves become playful gestures, games in which you succeed or fail with a shrug, a smile.

The penalty of Godard's fixation on the movie past is that, as *Alphaville* reveals, old movies may not provide an adequate frame of reference for a view of *this* world. Then we regret that Godard is not the kind of artist who can provide an intellectual structure commensurate with the brilliance of his style and the quality of his details. Because, of course, we think in terms of masterpieces and we feel that here is a man who has the gifts for masterpieces. But maybe he hasn't; maybe he has artistry of a different kind.

The New Republic, September 10, 1966

MOVIE BRUTALISTS

The basic ideas among young American film-makers are simple: the big movies we grew up on are corrupt, obsolete or dead, or are beyond our reach (we can't get a chance to make Hollywood films)—so we'll make films of our own, cheap films that we can make in our own way. For some this is an attempt to break into the "industry"; for others it is a different approach to movies, a view of movies not as a popular art or a mass medium but as an art form to be explored.

Much of the movie style of young American film-makers may be explained as a reaction against the banality and luxuriant wastefulness which are so often called the superior "craftsmanship" of Hollywood. In reaction, the young become movie brutalists.

They, and many in their audiences, may prefer the rough messiness—

the uneven lighting, awkward editing, flat camera work, the undramatic succession of scenes, unexplained actions, and confusion about what, if anything, is going on—because it makes their movies seem so different from Hollywood movies. This inexpensive, inexperienced, untrained look serves as a kind of testimonial to sincerity, poverty, even purity of intentions. It is like the sackcloth of true believers which they wear in moral revulsion against the rich in their fancy garments. The look of poverty is not necessarily a necessity. I once had the experience, as chairman of the jury at an experimental film festival, of getting on the stage, in the black silk dress I had carefully mended and ironed for the occasion, to present the check to the prizewinner, who came forward in patched, faded dungarees. He got an ovation, of course. I had seen him the night before in a good dark suit, but now he had dressed for his role (deserving artist) as I had dressed for mine (distinguished critic).

Although many of the American experimentalists have developed extraordinary kinds of technique, it is no accident that the virtuoso technicians who can apparently do almost anything with drawing board or camera are not taken up as the heroes of youth in the way that brutalists are. Little is heard about Bruce Baillie or Carroll Ballard whose camera skills expose how inept, inefficient, and unimaginative much of Hollywood's self-praised work is, or about the elegance and grandeur of Jordan Belson's short abstract films, like *Allures,* that demonstrate that one man working in a basement can make Hollywood's vaunted special effects departments look archaic. Craftsmanship and skill don't, in themselves, have much appeal to youth. Rough work looks rebellious and sometimes it is: there's anger and frustration and passion, too, in those scratches and stains and multiple superimpositions that make our eyes swim. The movie brutalists, it's all too apparent, are hurting our eyes to save our souls.

They are basically right, of course, in what they're *against.* Aesthetically and morally, disgust with Hollywood's fabled craftsmanship is long overdue. I say fabled because the "craft" claims of Hollywood, and the notion that the expensiveness of studio-produced movies is necessary for some sort of technical perfection or "finish," are just hucksterism. The reverse is closer to the truth: it's becoming almost impossible to produce a decent-looking movie in a Hollywood studio. In addition to the touched-up corpses of old dramatic ideas, big movies carry the dead weight of immobile cameras, all-purpose light, whorehouse décor. The production values are often ludicrously inappropriate to the subject matter, but studio executives, who charge off roughly 30 percent of a film's budget to studio overhead, are very keen on these production values which they frequently remind us are the hallmark of American movies.

In many foreign countries it is this very luxuriousness that is most envied and admired in American movies: the big cars, the fancy food, the opulent bachelor lairs, the gadget-packed family homes, even the loaded freeways and the noisy big cities. What is not so generally understood is the studio executives' implicit assumption that this is also what American audiences like. The story may not involve more than a few spies and counterspies, but the wide screen will be filled. The set decorator will pack the sides of the image with fruit and flowers and furniture.

When Hollywood cameramen and editors want to show their expertise, they imitate the effects of Japanese or European craftsmen, and then the result is pointed to with cries of "See, we can do anything in Hollywood." The principal demonstration of art and ingenuity among these "craftsmen" is likely to be in getting their sons and nephews into the unions and in resisting any attempt to make Hollywood movie-making flexible enough for artists to work there. If there are no cinematographers in modern Hollywood who can be discussed in the same terms as Henri Decae or Raoul Coutard or the late Gianni di Venanzo, it's because the studio methods and the union restrictions and regulations don't make it possible for talent to function. The talent is strangled in the business bureaucracy, and the best of our cinematographers perform safe, sane academic exercises. If the most that a gifted colorist like Lucien Ballard can hope for is to beautify a John Michael Hayes screenplay—giving an old tart a fresh complexion—why not scratch up the image?

The younger generation doesn't seem much interested in the obstacles to art in Hollywood, however. They don't much care about why the older directors do what they do or whether some of the most talented young directors in Hollywood, like Sam Peckinpah (*Ride the High Country, Major Dundee*) or Irvin Kershner (*The Hoodlum Priest, The Luck of Ginger Coffey, A Fine Madness*), will break through and do the work they should be doing. There is little interest in the work of gifted, intelligent men outside the industry, like James Blue (*The Olive Trees of Justice*) or John Korty (*The Crazy Quilt*), who are attempting to make inexpensive feature films as honestly and independently as they can. These men (and their films) are not flamboyant; they don't issue manifestos, and they don't catch the imagination of youth. Probably, like the students in film courses who often do fresh and lively work, they're not surprising enough, not different enough. The new film enthusiasts are, when it comes down to it, not any more interested in simple, small, inexpensive pictures than Hollywood is. The workmen's clothes and crude movie techniques may cry out, "We're poor and honest. They're rich and rotten." But, of course, you can be poor and not so very honest and, although it's harder to believe, you can even be rich and not so very rotten. What the young seem to be interested in is brutalism. In certain groups, automatic writing with a camera has come to be considered the most creative kind of film-making.

Their hero, Jean-Luc Godard—one of the most original talents ever to work in film and one of the most uneven—is not a brutalist at so simple a level, yet he comprises the attitudes of a new generation. Godard is what is meant by a "film-maker." The concept of a "film-maker"—as distinguished from a director (or even writer-directors like Bergman or Fellini)—is a response and reaction to traditional methods of financing as well as shooting, and to traditional concepts of what a movie is. Godard works with a small crew and shifts ideas and attitudes from movie to movie and even within movies. While Hollywood producers straddle huge fences trying to figure out where the action is supposed to be—and never find out—Godard in himself is where the action is.

There is a disturbing quality in Godard's work that perhaps helps to explain why the young are drawn to his films and identify with them, and why so many older people call him a "coterie" artist and don't think his films are important. *His characters don't seem to have any future.* They are most alive (and most appealing) just because they don't conceive of the day after tomorrow; they have no careers, no plans, only fantasies of roles they could play—of careers, thefts, romance, politics, adventure, pleasure, a life like in the movies. Even his world of the future, *Alphaville*, is, photographically, a documentary of Paris in the present. (All of his films are in that sense documentaries—as were also, and also by necessity, the grade B American gangster films that influenced him.) And even before *Alphaville*, the people in *The Married Woman* were already science fiction—so blank and affectless no mad scientist was required to destroy their souls.

His characters are young, unrelated to families and background. Whether deliberately or unconsciously, he makes his characters orphans who, like the students in the theatres, feel only attachments to friends, to lovers attachments that will end with a chance word or the close of the semester. They're orphans, by extension, in a larger sense, too, unconnected with the world, feeling out of relationship to it. They're a generation of familiar strangers.

An elderly gentleman recently wrote me, "Oh, they're such a bore, bore, bore, modern youth! All attitudes and nothing behind the attitudes. When I was in my twenties, I didn't just loaf around, being a rebel, I went places and did things. The reason they all hate the squares is because the squares remind them of the one thing they are trying to forget: there *is* a Future and you must build for it."

He's wrong, I think. The young are not "trying to forget": they just don't think in those terms. Godard's power—and possibly his limitation—as an artist is that he so intensely expresses how they do feel and think. His characters don't plan or worry about careers or responsibilities; they just live. Youth makes them natural aristocrats in their indifference to sustenance, security, hard work; and prosperity has turned a whole generation—or at least the middle-class part of it—into aristocrats. And it's astonishing how many places they do go to and how many things they can do. The difference is in how easily they do it all. Even their notion of creativity—as what comes naturally—is surprisingly similar to the aristocratic artist's condescension toward those middle-class plodders who have to labor for a living, for an education, for "culture."

Here, too, Godard is the symbol, exemplar, and proof. He makes it all seem so effortless, so personal—just one movie after another. Because he is so skillful and so incredibly disciplined that he can make his pictures for under a hundred thousand dollars, and because there is enough of a youthful audience in France to support these pictures, he can do almost anything he wants within those budgetary limits. In this achievement of independence, he is almost alone among movie directors: it is a truly heroic achievement. For a younger generation he is the proof that it is possible to make and go on making films your own way. And yet they don't seem aware of how rare he is or how hard it is to get in that position. Even if colleges and foundations make it easier than it has ever been, they will need not only talent but toughness to be independent.

As Godard has been able to solve the problems of economic freedom, his work now poses the problems of artistic freedom—problems that few artists in the history of movies have been fortunate enough to face. The history of great film directors is a history of economic and political obstacles—of compromises, defeats, despair, even disgrace. Griffith, Eisenstein, von Stroheim, von Sternberg, Cocteau, Renoir, Max Ophuls, Orson Welles—they were defeated because they weren't in a position to do what they wanted to do. If Godard fails, it will be because what he wants to do—which is what he *does*—isn't good enough.

Maybe he is attempting to escape from freedom when he makes a beautiful work and then, to all appearances, just throws it away. There is a self-destructive urgency in his treatment of themes, a drive toward a quick finish. Even if it's suicidal for the hero or the work, Godard is impatient for the ending: the mood of his films is that there's no way for things to work out anyway, something must be done even if it's disastrous, no action is intolerable.

It seems likely that many of the young who don't wait for others to call them artists, but simply announce that they are, don't have the patience to make art. A student's idea of a film-maker isn't someone who has to sit home and study and think and work—as in most of the arts—but someone who goes out with friends and shoots—a social activity. It is an extroverted and egotistic image of the genius-creator. It is the Fellini-Guido figure of *8½*, the movie director as star. Few seem to have noticed that by the time of *Juliet of the Spirits* he had turned into a professional party-giver. Film-making, carried out the way a lot of kids do it, is like having a party. And their movie "ideas" are frequently no more than staging and shooting a wild, weird party.

"Creativity" is a quick route to power and celebrity. The pop singer or composer, the mod designer, says of his work, "It's a creative way to make a living"—meaning it didn't take a dull lot of study and planning, that he was able to use his own inventiveness or ingenuity or talent to get to the top without much sweat. I heard a young film-maker put it this way to a teen-age art student: "What do you go to life class for? Either you can draw or you can't. What you should do is have a show. It's important to get exposure."

One can imagine their faces if they had to listen to those teachers who used to tell us that you had to be able to do things the traditional ways before you earned the right to break loose and do things *your* way. They simply take shortcuts into other art forms or into pop arts where they can "express themselves" now. Like cool Peter Pans, they just take off and fly.

Godard's conception of technique can be taken as a highly intellectualized rationale for these attitudes. "The ideal for me," he says, "is to obtain right away what will work—and without retakes. If they are necessary, it falls short of the mark. The immediate is chance. At the same time it is definitive. What I want is the definitive by chance." Sometimes, almost magically, he seems to get it—as in many scenes of *Breathless* and *Band of Outsiders*—but often, as in *The Married Woman,* he seems to settle for arbitrary effects.

A caricature of this way of talking is common among young American film-makers. Some of them believe that everything they catch on film is definitive, so they do not edit at all. As proof that they do not mar their instinct with pedantry or judgment, they may retain the blank leader to the roll of film. As proof of their creative sincerity they may leave in the blurred shots.

Preposterous as much of this seems, it is theoretically not so far from Godard's way of working. Although his technical control is superb, so complete that one cannot tell improvisation from planning, the ideas and bits of business are often so arbitrary that they appear to be (and probably are) just things that he chanced to think of that day, or that he came across in a book he happened to be reading. At times there is a disarming, an almost ecstatic innocence about the way he uses quotes as if he had just heard of these beautiful ideas and wanted to share his enthusiasm with the world. After smiling with pleasure as we do when a child's discovery of the beauty of a leaf or a poem enables us to re-experience the wonder of responsiveness, we may sink in spirit right down to incredulity. For this is the rapture with "thoughts" of those whose minds aren't much sullied by thought. These are "thoughts" without thought: they don't come out of a line of thought or a process of thinking, they don't arise from the situation. They're "inspirations"—bright illuminations from nowhere—and this is what kids who think of themselves as poetic or artistic or creative think ideas are: noble sentiments. They decorate a movie and it is easy for viewers to feel that they give it depth, that if followed, these clues lead to understanding of the work. But if those who follow the clues come out with odd and disjunctive interpretations, this is because the "clues" are *not* integral to the movie but are clues to what else the artist was involved in while he was making the movie.

Putting into the work whatever just occurred to the artist is its own rationale and needs no justification for young Americans encouraged from childhood to express themselves creatively and to say whatever came into their heads. Good liberal parents didn't want to push their kids in academic subjects but oohed and aahed with false delight when their children presented them with a baked ashtray or a woven doily. Did anyone guess or foresee what narcissistic confidence this generation would develop in its banal "creativity"? Now we're surrounded, inundated by artists. And a staggering number of them wish to be or already call themselves "film-makers."

A few years ago a young man informed me that he was going to "give up" poetry and avant-garde film (which couldn't have been much of a sacrifice as he hadn't done anything more than talk about them) and devote himself to writing "art songs." I remember asking, "Do you read music?" and not being especially surprised to hear that he didn't. I knew from other young men that the term "art" used as an adjective meant that they were bypassing even the most rudimentary knowledge in the field. Those who said they were going to make art movies not only didn't consider it worth their while to go to see ordinary commercial movies, but usually didn't even know anything much about avant-garde film. I did not pursue the subject of "art songs" with this young man because it was perfectly clear that he wasn't going to do anything. But some of the young who say they're going to make "art movies" are actually beginning to make movies. Kids who can't write, who have never developed any competence in photography, who have never acted in nor directed a play, see no deterrent to making movies. And although most of the results are bad beyond our wildest fears, as if to destroy all our powers of prediction a few, even of the most ignorant, pretentious young men and women, are doing some interesting things.

Yet why are the Hollywood movies, even the worst overstuffed ones, often easier to sit through than the short experimental ones? Because they have actors and a story. Through what is almost a technological fluke, 16 mm movie cameras give the experimental film-maker greater flexibility than the "professional" 35 mm camera user, but he cannot get adequate synchronous sound. And so the experimentalists, as if to convert this liability into an advantage, have asserted that their partial use of the capabilities of the medium is the true art of the cinema, which is said to be purely visual. But their visual explorations of their states of consciousness (with the usual implicit social protest) get boring, the mind begins to wander, and though this lapse in attention can be explained to us as a new kind of experience, as even the purpose of cinema, our desire to see a movie hasn't been satisfied. (There are, of course, some young film-makers who are not interested in movies as we ordinarily think of them, but in film as an art medium like painting or music, and this kind of work must be looked at a different way—without the expectation of story content or meaning.) They probably won't be able to make satisfying *movies* until the problems of sound are solved not only technically but in terms of drama, structure, meaning, relevance.

It is not an answer to toss on a spoofing semi-synchronous sound track as a number of young film-makers do. It can be funny in a cheap sort of way—as in Robert Downey's *Chafed Elbows* where the images and sound are, at least, in the same style; but this isn't fundamentally different from the way George Axelrod works in *Lord Love a Duck* or Blake Edwards in *What Did You*

Do in the War, Daddy?, and there's no special reason to congratulate people for doing underground what is driving us down there. Total satire is opportunistic and easy; what's difficult is to make a movie in which something is taken seriously without making a fool of yourself.

Is Hollywood interested in the young movement? If it attracts customers, Hollywood will eat it up, the way *The Wild Angels* has already fed upon *Scorpio Rising*. At a party combining the commercial and noncommercial worlds of film, a Hollywood screenwriter watched as an underground filmmaker and his wife entered. The wife was wearing one of those classic filmmakers' wives' outfits: a simple sack of burlap in natural brown, with scarecrow sleeves. The screenwriter greeted her enthusiastically, "I really dig your dress, honey," he said, "I used to have a dress like that once."

The New Republic, September 24, 1966

FROM EPICS—**THE BIBLE**

When the announcement was made that Norman Mailer's *An American Dream* was to be made into a movie, my reaction was that John Huston was the only man who could do it. And what a script it could be for him! But Huston was working on *The Bible*. A quarter of a century had passed since *The Maltese Falcon*, it was a long time since *San Pietro* and *The Treasure of the Sierra Madre* and *The Red Badge of Courage* and *The African Queen*. It was a decade since the stirring, often brilliant, but misconceived *Moby Dick*, and Huston had gone a different route—away from the immediacy of men testing themselves and the feel and smell of American experience. He had become a director of spectacles. Possibly, because of the way that big movie stars and directors live in a world of their own, insulated and out of touch, he might not even recognize that *An American Dream* was the spectacle of our time; was, even, his spectacle.

It turns out he was, at least, testing himself—as, earlier, he had attempted to do in *Moby Dick*, and, even after that, in parts of *The Roots of Heaven*. If, in making *The Treasure of the Sierra Madre* he risked comparison with *Greed*, and if with *The Red Badge of Courage*, he risked comparison with *The Birth of a Nation*, *The Bible* risks comparison with *Intolerance*. It is a huge sprawling epic—an attempt to use the medium to its fullest, to overwhelm the senses and feelings, for gigantic mythmaking, for a poetry of size and scope.

In recent years the spectacle form has become so vulgarized that probably most educated moviegoers have just about given it up. They don't think of movies in those terms anymore because in general the only way for artists to work in the medium is frugally. Though there might occasionally be great sequences in big pictures, like the retreat from Russia in King Vidor's *War and Peace,* those who knew the novel had probably left by then. If, however, you will admit that you went to see *Lawrence of Arabia* under the delusion that it was going to be about T. E. Lawrence, but you stayed to enjoy the vastness of the desert and the pleasures of the senses that a huge movie epic can provide—the pleasures of largeness and distances—then you may be willing to override your prejudices and too-narrow theories about what the art of the film is, and go to see *The Bible.*

For John Huston is an infinitely more complex screen artist than David Lean. He can be far worse than Lean because he's careless and sloppy and doesn't have all those safety nets of solid craftsmanship spread under him. What makes a David Lean spectacle uninteresting finally is that it's in such goddamn good taste. It's all so ploddingly intelligent and controlled, so "distinguished." The hero may stick his arm in blood up to the elbow but you can be assured that the composition will be academically, impeccably composed. Lean plays the mad game of superspectacles like a sane man. Huston (like Mailer) tests himself, plays the crazy game crazy—to beat it, to win.

The worst problem of recent movie epics is that they usually start with an epic in another form and so the director must try to make a masterpiece to compete with an already existing one. This is enough to petrify most directors but it probably delights Huston. What more perverse challenge than to test himself against the Book? It's a flashy demonic gesture, like Nimrod shooting his arrow into God's heaven.

Huston shoots arrows all over the place; he pushes himself too hard, he tries to do too many different things. The movie is episodic not merely because the original material is episodic but also because, like Griffith in *Intolerance,* he can find no way to rhythm together everything that he's trying to do. Yet the grandeur of this kind of crazy, sinfully extravagant movie-making is in trying to do too much. We tend, now, to think of the art of the film in terms of depth, but there has always been something about the eclectic medium of movies that, like opera, attracts artists of Promethean temperament who want to use the medium for scale, and for a scale that will appeal to multitudes. I don't mean men like De Mille who made small-minded pictures on a big scale—they're about as Promethean as a cash register. I mean men like Griffith and von Stroheim and Abel Gance and Eisenstein and Fritz Lang and Orson Welles who thought *big,* men whose prodigious failures could make other people's successes look puny. This is the tradition in which Huston's *The Bible* belongs. Huston's triumph is that despite the insanity of the attempt and the grandiosity of the project, the technology doesn't dominate the material: when you respond to the beauty of such scenes in *The Bible* as the dispersal of the animals after the landing of the Ark, it is not merely the beauty of photography but the beauty of conception.

The stories of Genesis are, of course, free of that wretched masochistic piety that makes movies about Christ so sickly. Pasolini's *The Gospel According to St. Matthew* was so static that I could hardly wait for that loathsome prissy young man to get crucified. Why do movie-makers think that's such a good story, anyway? The only thing that gives it plausibility is, psychologically, not very attractive. And whether it's told the De Mille way, loaded with hypocritic sanctity, or the Pasolini way, drabness supposedly guaranteeing purity and truth, it's got a bad ending that doesn't make sense after those neat miracles.

The legends that Huston uses are, fortunately, more remote in time, are, indeed, all "miracles," and we are spared sanctity. The God who orders these events is so primitive and inexplicable that we may indeed wonder and perhaps be appalled. From Eve, whose crime scarcely seems commensurate with her punishment, on through to Hagar cast into the wilderness, and the cruel proof of obedience demanded of Abraham, it is a series of horror stories, alleviated only by the sweet and hopeful story of the Ark, where, for once, God seems to be smiling—no doubt, because we are taken inside the boat rather than left outside to suffer in the Flood. Huston retains that angry God, and Eve as the source of mischief, and phrases disquieting to modern ears, like "Fair are the angels of God." He hasn't taken the fashionable way out of trying to turn it all into charming metaphors and he hasn't "modernized" it into something comfortable and comforting. He doesn't, in the standard show business way, twist the story to make the hero sympathetic. Only with Peter O'Toole's three angels do we get the stale breath of the New Testament with the familiar skinny figure and that suffering-for-our-sins look.

The movie may present a problem for religious people who have learned not to think of the Bible stories like this: it is commonly understood now that although the childish take the stories for truth, they are then educated to know that the stories are "metaphorical." The movie undercuts this liberal view by showing the power (and terror) of these cryptic, primitive tribal tales and fantasies of the origins of life on earth and why we are as we are. This God of wrath who frightens men to worship ain't no pretty metaphor.

One of the worst failures of the movie is, implicitly, a rather comic modern predicament. Huston obviously can't make anything acceptable out of the Bible's accounts of sinfulness and he falls back upon the silliest stereotypes of evil: the barbaric monsters who jeer at Noah's preparations for the Flood look like leftovers from a Steve Reeves Hercules epic, and the posing, prancing faggots of Sodom seem as negligible as in *La Dolce Vita*. God couldn't have had much sense of humor if He went to the trouble of destroying them. Even their worship of the Golden Calf seems like a nightclub act, absurd all right, but not nearly as horrible as the animal sacrifices that God accepts of Abel and orders of Abraham. It is a measure of the strength of Huston's vision that we are constantly shocked by the barbarism of this primitive religion with its self-serving myths; it is a measure of weakness that he goes along with its strange notions of evil without either making them believable or treating them as barbaric. Only in the rare moments when the Bible's ideas of wrong and our ideas of wrong coincide—as in Cain's murder of his brother—can Huston make sin convincing.

This movie has more things wrong with it than his *Moby Dick,* but they're not so catastrophic. Though Huston might conceivably have made a great Ahab himself, Gregory Peck could not: that nice man did not belong in the whirling center of Melville's vision. In *The Bible* it's questionable if that Ahab-character Huston belongs in Noah's homespun on the Ark. He plays it in the crowd-pleasing vein of his cute, shrewd Archbishop in *The Cardinal:* his Noah is a puckish, weathered old innocent, a wise fool. He indulged his father Walter Huston in one scene of *The Treasure of the Sierra Madre,* when the grizzled, toothless old prospector, tended by native lovelies, cocked an eye at the audience. Huston's Noah keeps asking the audience's indulgence, and Huston as director extends it. What was a momentary weakness in Huston Senior is the whole acting style of Huston Junior. His air of humility and wonder isn't so much acted as assumed, like a trick of personality—a double-take that has taken over the man.

The early part of the Abraham and Sarah story is poor: it looks and sounds like acted-out Bible stories on television. But then it begins to unfold, and we see Abraham raised to nobility by suffering. George C. Scott has the look of a prophet, and he gives the character an Old Testament fervor. It's a subdued, magnificent performance.

Probably the most seriously flawed sequence is the Tower of Babel, and as it is one of the most brilliant conceptions in the work, it is difficult to know why it is so badly structured and edited. The ideas remain latent: we can see what was intended, but the sequence is over before the dramatic point has been developed. And in this sequence, as in several others, Huston seems unable to maneuver the groups of people in the foreground; this clumsiness of staging and the dubbing of many of the actors in minor roles produce occasional dead scenes and dead sounds. It would be better if the musical score *were* dead: it is obtrusively alive, and at war with the imagery.

And what of *An American Dream?* It has been written and directed by some fellows from television. The first fifteen minutes of Eleanor Parker in and out of bed can be recommended to connoisseurs of the tawdry, though the movie as a whole doesn't rank with *The Oscar. The Oscar* is the modern classic of the genre. The Joseph E. Levine beds and draperies were already deluxe in *The Carpetbaggers* and *Harlow.* In *The Oscar* he added Harlan Ellison's incomparable bedroom conversations, and it's such a perfect commingling the words might have sprouted from the coverlets.

The New Republic, October 22, 1966

GEORGY GIRL, MORGAN!, THE RED DESERT

Like just about everything else at the moment, movies seem to be out of control. Is it possible that, as we increasingly hear suggested in discussions of civil rights or air pollution or Vietnam or education, "nobody's minding the store"? At *Georgy Girl* you may find yourself laughing, but intermittently, in discomfort or even stupefaction, asking yourself "What are they doing in this movie? Do they know what they're doing?" They're obviously very clever, very talented, but what's going on? To get at the peculiar nature of *Georgy Girl*, let me go back a bit to *Morgan!*, which probably just because of the way it's out of control has touched a nerve for this generation.

Thirty years ago in *My Man Godfrey*, when Mischa Auer, as the parasitic left-wing artist, imitated a gorilla to entertain the rich family who kept him as a pet, the meaning and relations were so clear no one had to signal us that it was symbolic. In *Morgan!* David Warner isn't nearly as good at the gorilla act, which is plastered with so many tags and labels that all we can be sure of is that it's meant to be symbolic. He's not just a parasitic left-wing artist with a gorilla act, he's the misfit as hero, and a childlike romantic rebel, anarchist, outsider, nonconformist, etc.; he's also crazy, and in his pop fantasy life he's King Kong. *Morgan!* is Ionesco's *Rhinoceros* turned inside out: the method of *Rhinoceros* may have been absurd but its meaning was the conventional liberal theme—the danger of people becoming conformist-animals. *Morgan!* is a modernized version of an earlier, romantic primitivist notion that people are conformists, animals are instinctively "true" and happy and, of course, "free."

Morgan! was maddening to many older people because of its kids' notion of nonconformity as crazy fun, its way of giving adolescent confusion the borrowed significance of symbols, its maudlin, schizoid mixture of comedy and whimsy and psychopathology and tragedy and pathos. It seemed the ultimate in grotesque pop homogenization: Trotsky's death acted out in farce with a smashed eggshell went even farther than Edward Albee turning a great writer's name into a stupid joke.

I haven't bothered to say that *Morgan!* is a bad movie because although that's implicit in what I'm saying, it's a minor matter. The point is that it's not an ordinary movie and whether it's good or bad is of less interest than why so many young people respond to it the way they do, especially as, in this case, they are probably responding to exactly what we think makes it bad. Sometimes bad movies are more important than good ones just because of those unresolved elements that make them such a mess. They may get at something going on around us that the movie-makers felt or shared and expressed in a confused way. *Rebel Without a Cause* was a pretty terrible movie but it reflected (and possibly caused) more cultural changes than many a good one. And conceivably it's part of the function of a movie critic

95

to know and indicate the difference between a bad movie that doesn't much matter because it's so much like other bad movies and a bad movie that matters (like *The Chase* or *The Wild Angels*) because it affects people strongly in new, different ways. And if it be said that this is sociology, not aesthetics, the answer is that an aesthetician who gave his time to criticism of current movies would have to be an awful fool. Movie criticism to be of any use whatever must go beyond formal analysis—which in movies is generally a disguised form of subjective reaction to meanings and implications, anyway.

Those who made *Morgan!* probably not only share in the confusion of the material but, like the college audience, *accept* the confusion. This indifference to artistic control is new. I think *Morgan!* is so appealing to college students because it shares their self-view: they accept this mess of cute infantilism and obsessions and aberrations without expecting the writer and director to straighten it out or resolve it and without themselves feeling a necessity to sort it out. They didn't squirm as we did: they accepted the grotesque and discordant elements without embarrassment. I'd guess that to varying degrees they felt they *were* Morgan. And that suited them just fine.

They may be shocked when they see that he really is crazy and in pain, but they can quickly accept that, too, because he's mad in a pop way they respond to—madness as the ultimate irresponsibility for the rebel, the only sanity for those who see what the "responsible" people supposedly did to this world, and all that. If flipness is all (as it is in so many of the new movies) the flip-out is just an accepted part of life. Students liberally educated not to regard analysis and breakdowns and treatment as anything shameful refer to their own crack-ups casually, even a little proudly, like battle scars, proof that they've had *experience*. They even talk about breakdowns as "opting-out"—as if it were a preference and a moral choice. And of course to flip out and then flip back again, that makes you a hero because you've *been* there. It also takes the fear away.

Georgy is a misfit heroine: it isn't that she doesn't want to conform but that she can't because she just about *is* a gorilla. She's a brontosaurus of a girl, with the bizarre problems of a girl who's too big to be treated as a girl, and she's childlike and "natural" and artistic and all the rest of the paraphernalia which now decorate characters designed to be appealing to young audiences. *Georgy Girl* is so shrewdly designed it will probably appeal to older audiences as well. The out-of-control thing is so bad you take it for granted from the beginning. What's offensive about it is that *Georgy Girl* is already a commercialization of what in *Morgan!* seemed a genuine split and confusion. Lack of control is made grotesquely *cute*. Although it's funny, it's tricky and anarchistically chic and on the side of youth (like *The Knack*)—as if the most important thing that the writers and director could imagine was to be "larky."

Georgy Girl is so glib, so clever, so determinedly "kinky" that everything seems to be devalued. It's the cleverness of advertising art, of commercials, of fancy titles—it's as if nothing really meant anything and nothing simple could work any more. It's "touching" one moment and weird the next, and like *The Knack*, it has evaporated before you're outside the theatre.

Even the sense of discomfort, of puzzlement, evaporates, because it is all made trivial—Georgy's pain as well as her bright remarks. For example, without any preparation or explanation, there is a horrifying sequence in which she makes a monstrous fool of herself at a party, and then everything goes on as if it never happened. Will the episode or the lack of reactions to it be upsetting to a younger audience? I doubt it. I recently saw a famous professor make such a spectacle of himself on a public platform that I had one of those great feminine intuitions—a premonition that he would go home and kill himself. As it turned out, he gave a big party for his students later that night, and his students didn't think anything special about how he'd behaved on the platform, because he did it all the time. Maybe they liked him for it; it made him more colorful, more of a character. His lack of control brought him closer to them. And I assume that we're supposed to like Georgy more because she acts out her ludicrous and self-pitying impulses and doesn't think too much about it afterward. She has all the blessings of affect and of affectlessness.

Is *Georgy Girl* a good movie or a bad one? It just isn't that simple. To discuss the cast (Lynn Redgrave, Alan Bates, James Mason) or Narizzano's direction wouldn't help. It's a less important movie than *Morgan!* because it isn't so seriously confused; it doesn't touch a nerve, it only comes teasingly close. It's more enjoyable partly because it doesn't get at anything so fundamental.

These movies are not just symptoms that will go away. I think a pretty good case could be made for including *Lord Love a Duck* and *Who's Afraid of Virginia Woolf?* among the American works that are out of control, and this may suggest that here, as in England, some of the most talented people don't really quite know what they're doing. At best, we may get something that makes a new kind of art out of embarrassment; at worst, lack of control may become what art is taken to mean. There is already a generation for whom art is the domain of the irrational, of whatever can't be clearly expressed or clearly understood, and they have adopted film as their medium, their "religion."

The general public probably cares less about artistic control than has been assumed, or the public is also changing. One of the most surprising box-office successes of last year, *A Thousand Clowns,* laid some claims to being about nonconformity and it, too, went more and more out of control, becoming redundant and embarrassing and gross in that same they-don't-know-what-they're-doing way. It didn't take its hero as far as Morgan's romantic insanity but only to romantic crackpotism—harmless American nonconformity. The hero's idea of freedom was to wander in Central Park with a kid and make TV-style jokes about TV before going back to do it for money. Basically, it was about as nonconformist as Mom's apple pie, and it even fudged on that much daring by giving the Madison Avenue spokesman the audience-pulling speech, which the Motion Picture Academy promptly and gratefully honored with an Academy Award.

These movies are full of contradictions. Is part of their appeal the ancient, wheezing plot devices which crank them in motion? The kid is being forcibly taken away from the TV gag-writer; the gorilla is being separated from his mate; Georgy gets a baby to mother only to have the authorities take it away. Underneath all the nonconformity gear are the crooked little skeletons of old Shirley Temple pictures. Heartwarming. *Georgy Girl,* like *The Knack,* is the story of the ugly duckling, and by beating *Funny Girl* to the screen it jumps the gun on the new exploitation of comic pathos. Somehow those who made *Morgan!* managed (instinctively maybe but certainly shrewdly) to alter the original TV play hero from a tired adulterer to a monogamous free spirit—probably the purest-in-heart hero of recent years. The director Karel Reisz's method is so eclectic, in the most blatant sense of that word, that he has taken what he feels will "go" together; the last sequence, which so many people have tried to interpret, is borrowed from the end of Buñuel's *El,* where it made perfect sense. Here it supplies a "larky" finish. The obscenely "happy ending" of *Georgy Girl* is so off-beat we lose the beat.

Because these movies all use and manipulate pop, it's easy for serious critics to attack them for their mixture of conventions, for the infantilism of a Morgan, etc. Yet I think that, for example, the meanings of *The Red Desert* were basically just as confused and uncontrolled.

Those who tried to make sense out of *The Red Desert* as an attack on industrialism had their best efforts quashed by word from the source that nothing of the sort was intended. What *was* intended? No one could be sure, yet the movie did express certain modern emotional states with which we're probably all familiar. I once visited a woman in Beverly Hills who sat in a settee backed by a huge inlaid table covered with a marvelous collection of art books, but when I referred to one of them, her face was blank and confused, as if to say, what are you talking about? She almost quivered with terror whenever anyone came into the room, although God knows the butler had screened them carefully. Her conversation, or rather the phrases she dropped from nowhere into nothing, were about whether she should open an art gallery or give up her marriage or take a trip, but to where? I think she would have been perfectly likely to take a sandwich out of someone's mouth if the idea of food suddenly occurred to her.

Obviously, she couldn't think of anything to do with her life so she did nothing for herself, her husband, or anyone else—and made herself "interesting" by her desolation. Is she fascinating? Well in a way, if you like to observe this kind of post-analytic destroyed consciousness. These ladies who are taken care of and give nothing may be the new heiresses of the ages. They're taken care of presumably because they're so sensitive, so vulnerable. But, of course, who with money and nothing to do can't be sensitive and vulnerable? They're not vulnerable to what the rest of us are; they're indifferent to all that. At worst, they're patronizingly envious of us—of our exhausting jobs, our household chores, our struggle to find time to read and see and think. Their male equivalent is the handsome, rich young man who says, "Sometimes I wish I were Negro or Jewish or something . . ."

Knowing there are people like this, I can understand that *The Red Desert* relates to something. But the title and Ravenna and industrialism, that's all a red herring, and so, I think, is the use of color in the movie. The bored, indolent ladies of Beverly Hills and elsewhere are much more likely to feel that their *clothes* have suddenly gone gray and to rush out to buy others. Their lovers go gray, too, and they try on others. Despite this relationship to the world around us, I found the movie deadly: a hazy poetic illustration of emotional chaos—which was made peculiarly attractive. If I've got to be driven up a wall, I'd rather do it at my own pace—which is considerably faster than Antonioni's. I thought it qualified as the definitive example of art cinema: a movie becomes cinema when it can bore you as much as your worst experiences at lectures, concerts, and ballet; i.e., when it becomes something you feel you shouldn't walk out on. Those who loved the movie, the TV producers' and architects' wives who feel that their lives are wasted and who are too "gifted" to do good, useful work, were likely to say things like, "I loved looking at it, I didn't care what the content was," which probably means not just that they found it visually pleasurable but that they enjoyed drifting away into vague, stylish emotional states—which is about the only way one *can* respond to the frozen rhythms. I think they thought it was the story of their lives: they identified with that crazy sensitive broad the way college students do with Morgan. And as reacting to the movie meant for these women not an interpretation which could be validated by checking it against the meanings and connections in the work, but anything that happened to occur to them as they saw it or thought about it afterward, they didn't necessarily care that it didn't make sense. What it comes down to is which of these bad movies is their movie, or which fantasy of themselves do they adore?

You can wait to see if the high arts will put us in touch with these distortions of experience, or if the social sciences will deal with them in the "fullness of time," or you can go to the key bad movies now.

The New Republic, November 5, 1966

MASCULINE FEMININE

Masculine Feminine is that rare movie achievement: a work of grace and beauty in a contemporary setting. Godard has liberated his feeling for modern youth from the American gangster-movie framework which limited his expressiveness and his relevance to the non-movie centered world. He has taken up the strands of what was most original in his best films—the life of the uncomprehending heroine, the blank-eyed career-happy little opportunist-betrayer from *Breathless,* and thc hully-gully, the dance of sexual isolation, from *Band of Outsiders.* Using neither crime nor the romance of crime but a simple romance for a kind of interwoven story line, Godard has, at last, created the form he needed. It is a combination of essay, journalistic sketches, news and portraiture, love lyric and satire.

What fuses it? The line "This film could be called The Children of Marx and Coca-Cola." The theme is the fresh beauty of youth amidst the flimsiness of pop culture and pop politics. The boy (Jean-Pierre Léaud) is full of doubts and questions, but a pop revolutionary; the girl (Chantal Goya) is a yé-yé singer making her way.

It is fused by the differing attitudes of the sexes to love and war even in this atmosphere of total and easy disbelief, of government policies accepted with the same contempt as TV commercials. The romance is punctuated with aimless acts of aggression and martyrdom: this is young love in a time of irreverence and hopelessness. These lovers and their friends, united by indifference and disdain toward the adult world, have a new kind of community in their shared disbelief. Politically they are anti-American enough to be American.

They are also Americanized. This community of unbelievers has a style of life by which they recognize each other; it is made up of everything adults attack as the worst and shoddiest forms of Americanization and dehumanization. It is the variety of forms of "Coca-Cola"—the synthetic life they were born to and which they love, and which they make human, and more beautiful and more "real" than the old just-barely-hanging-on adult culture. Membership is automatic and natural for the creatures from inner space. The signals are jukebox songs, forms of dress, and, above all, what they do with their hair. Americanization makes them an international society; they have the beauty of youth which can endow pop with poetry, and they have their feeling for each other and all those shared products and responses by which they know each other.

There are all sorts of episodes and details and jokes in the film that may be extraneous, but they seem to fit, to be part of the climate, the mood, the journalistic approach to this new breed between teen-agers and people. Even if you don't really like some pieces or can't understand why they're there, even if you think they're not well done (the episode out of LeRoi Jones, or the German boy and prostitute bit, or the brief appearance of Bardot, or the parody of *The Silence* which isn't as ludicrously pretentious as *The Silence* itself, or the ambiguous death of the hero—the end of him like a form of syntax marking the end of the movie), they're not too jarring. The rhythms, and the general sense, and the emotion that builds up can carry you past what you don't understand: you don't need to understand every detail in order to experience the beauty of the work as it's going on. An

Elizabethan love song is no less beautiful because we don't catch all the words; and when we look up the words, some of the meanings, the references, the idiom may still elude us. Perhaps the ache of painful, transient beauty is that we never can completely understand, and that, emotionally, we more than understand. *Masculine Feminine* has that ache, and its subject is a modern young lover's lament at the separateness of the sexes.

Godard has caught the girl now in demand (and in full supply) as no one else has. Chantal Goya, like Sylvie Vartan (whose face on a billboard dominates some of the scenes), is incredibly pretty but not beautiful, because there is nothing behind the eyes. Chantal Goya's face is haunting just because it's so empty: she doesn't look back. Her face becomes alive only when she's looking in the mirror, toying with her hair. Her thin, reedy little singing voice is just as pleasantly, perfectly empty, and it is the new sound. There's nothing behind it musically or emotionally. The young girls in the movie are soulless—as pretty and lost and soulless as girls appear to a lover who can make physical contact and yet cannot make the full contact he longs for, the contact that would heal. The girl he loves sleeps with him and is forever lost to him. She is the ideal—the girl in the fashion magazine she buys.

Possibly what flawed the conception of Godard's *My Life to Live* was the notion of the prostitute giving her body but keeping her soul to herself, because there was no evidence of what she was said to be holding back. Now, in *Masculine Feminine*, Godard is no longer trying to tell just the girl's story but the story of how a lover may feel about his girl, and we can see that it's not because she's a prostitute that he gets the sense that she isn't giving everything but because she's a girl and (as the camera of *My Life to Live* revealed though it wasn't the story being told) a love object. A lover may penetrate her body but there is still an opaque, impenetrable surface that he can never get through. He can have her and have her and she is never his.

The attraction of this little singer is that she isn't known, can't be known, and worst of all, probably there's nothing to know (which is what we may have suspected in *My Life to Live*). The ache of love is reaching out to a blank, which in this case smiles back. This male view of the eternal feminine mystery is set in the childlike simplicity of modern relations: before they go out on their first date, the boy and girl discuss going to bed. Easy sex is like a new idiom, but their talk of the pill is not the same as having it, and the spectre of pregnancy hovers over them. The old sexual morality is gone, but the mysteries of love and isolation remain; availability cancels out the pleasurable torments of anticipation, but not the sadness afterward.

With the new breed, Godard is able to define the romantic problem precisely and essentially. This approachable girl who adores Pepsi—the French cousin of Jean Seberg in *Breathless*—is as mysterious as a princess seen from afar, *more* mysterious because the princess might change if we got close. The boy's friend says, what's in "masculine"—mask and ass, what's in "feminine"—nothing. And that's what defeats the boy. Worse than losing a love is holding it in your arms and not finding it. At the close of the movie the word the boys failed to see in "feminine" is revealed—*fin.*

In *Masculine Feminine* Godard asks questions of youth and sketches a portrait in a series of question-answer episodes that are the dramatic substance of the movie. The method was prefigured by the psychiatric interview in Truffaut's *The 400 Blows* (Léaud, now the questioning hero, was the child-hero who was quizzed), the celebrity interview in *Breathless,* and cinema vérité movies by Jean Rouch and Chris Marker. It is most like Chris Marker's rapturous inquiry of the young Japanese girl in *The Koumiko Mystery.* There are informal boy-to-boy conversations about women and politics; there is a phenomenal six-minute single-take parody-interview conducted by the hero with a Miss Nineteen, who might be talking while posing for the cover of *Glamour;* and there are two boy-girl sessions which define the contemporary meaning of masculine and feminine. These dialogues are dating talk as a form of preliminary sex play—verbal courtship rites. The boy thrusts with leading questions, the girl parries, backs away, touches her hair. Godard captures the awkwardnesses that reveal, the pauses, the pretensions, the mannerisms—the rhythms of the dance—as no one has before. *Masculine Feminine* is the dance of the sexes drawing together and remaining separate. He gets the little things that people who have to follow scripts can't get: the differences in the way girls are with each other and with boys, and boys with each other and with girls. Not just what they do but how they smile or look away.

What can a boy believe that a girl says, what can she believe of what he says? We watch them telling lies and half truths to each other and we can't tell which are which. But, smiling in the darkness because we know we've all been there, we recognize the truth of Godard's art. He must have discovered his subject as he worked on it (as a man working on a big-budget movie with a fixed shooting schedule cannot). And because he did, we do, too. We can read all those special fat issues of magazines devoted to youth and not know any more than we do after watching big TV specials on youth. But even in the ladies' lounge right after the movie, there were the girls, so pretty they hardly seemed real, standing in a reverie at the mirror, toying with their shiny hair. And because Godard uses people (as he uses ideas) for suggestiveness, echoes, romantic overtones—for resonance—we see them differently now.

There is a question that remains, however: why haven't more people responded to this movie? Maybe because *Masculine Feminine* is not only partial to youth but partial as a view, and movie hucksterism has accustomed people to big claims (and movie experience to big flops). Maybe because Godard has made so many films and critics have often urged the worst upon the public. I would not recommend *The Married Woman:* Godard loves the games and style of youth but does not have the same warm feeling for older characters. He presents them as failed youth: they don't grow up, they just deteriorate, and those movies in which they figure become cold and empty. But there's life in *Masculine Feminine,* which shows the most dazzlingly inventive and audacious artist in movies today at a new peak.

The New Republic, November 19, 1966

ABOUT COMIC-STRIP STYLE, FROM
A Sense of Disproportion

There are not—and there never were—any formal principles that can be used to judge movies but there are concepts that are serviceable for a while and so pass for, or are mistaken for, "objective" rules until it becomes obvious that the new work that we respond to violates them. One serviceable notion was the distinction between comedy and mere gag-writing. In comedy, the humor was supposed to be integral, to grow out of a situation and to contribute to a mood or idea and to the development of the structure; in gag-writing, the joke was just brought in for a laugh—and we probably felt mildly contemptuous even when we did laugh. Now we're more likely to respond to surreal suddenness, to the surprises of an "inspired" gag-writer and to be impatient of the too-tame comedic situation with its neat preparations and its air of expectation. The decisive factor, then, is not—or is not any longer—structural preparation but the style of the work and/or the quality of the joke itself.

Good construction used to be considered a formal necessity, but twenty years ago an accident split the seams of the well-constructed Hollywood movie. William Faulkner, Jules Furthman, and their co-writers employed to whip up a screenplay for Howard Hawks out of Raymond Chandler's *The Big Sleep* couldn't figure out the plot, and, probably on the basis that nobody gave a damn anyway, they went ahead with the screenplay. As if determined to blow the plot, somebody even threw in a swatch of "suggestive" dialogue from an old horse-racing comedy, *Straight, Place, and Show,* which hadn't attracted much attention when spoken by Ethel Merman and Richard Arlen but which, out of context, was all innuendo—and with a new high voltage not only because of the Bacall and Bogart delivery but *because* it didn't relate to anything in the movie. Sophisticated sex talk became the link for the movie, and the incidents and talk were so entertaining that audiences didn't care about the solution of the murder plot. More than that, as audience, we enjoyed the joke that (probably partly inadvertently) had been played on us: *The Big Sleep* made us aware how little we often *had* cared about the ridiculously complicated plots of detective thrillers, how fed up with them we were—that we had been going for the riffs for a long time without being aware of it.

Part of the fun of movies is in not believing, and it's often a relief to see a movie that doesn't go through all the clumsy motions of trying to make a situation seem believable. The wits who worked in the movies in the thirties had known it then. In the early Marx Brothers comedies like *Duck Soup,* in the great W. C. Fields–Jack Oakie *Million Dollar Legs,* even in the Crosby–Hope *Road* pictures, part of the pleasure was in the *absence* of solemn preparation. The construction that wasn't there was our referent when we saw these films: we enjoyed its absence as a nose-thumbing at the tediously constructed conventional movies. But those writers had been pressured to pin their wit down in situation comedy and family entertainment.

There was a clue right at the beginning of movies that perhaps dramatic structure wasn't so important: the serials, which were even more primitive—and more flexible—in construction than the simplest stage dramas. They were constructed *serially,* just one incident after another without regard to logic or dramatic coherence. But not even the Hollywood merchants thought that they could get by with that kind of construction in feature films made for metropolitan audiences. The triumph of virtue over vice had to be constructed dramatically: if something was introduced, it had to be related to the whole, if a character appeared we knew there was a reason for his coming on and we waited to find out how he was related to the events. Everything that happened had to be prepared for. The heroine couldn't suddenly be killed in a car accident: we would have to see first that the driver wasn't in condition to drive, that something awful was going to happen. Or as even fairly recently in *Lonely Are the Brave,* the whole movie could be preparation for the final collision. In life there were accidents; in art, it was assumed, there had to be reasons, and fates were explained by character and circumstance. Hack writers and directors showed their hand, forcing each piece of plot creakingly in place; but when a good writer and director were at work, the smooth unfolding was an aesthetic pleasure. Now, this kind of construction can still give pleasure but of a different nature: it appears to be such an *unnecessary* formalism that it is freakishly entertaining—an aesthetic game played for its own sake. In its older form, it can still be viewed weekly on the television series "Peyton Place," which is so full of anxious preparation for each new terrible revelation or calamity that nothing that happens can ever fulfill the dreadful expectations.

When, in the past, movies didn't create expectations, didn't build and prepare for their climaxes, people often referred to them contemptuously as comic strips because they had that dead, flat, one-dimensional quality of narrative without dramatic structure, just one thing after another. That's how we used to be able to tell when a movie director was an amateur who didn't understand the medium. It's only recently, with the success of the James Bond pictures and in the general enthusiasm for pop, that there has been the discovery that for certain kinds of one-dimensional material, this comic-strip style (developed, after all, on one-dimensional material), used intentionally, has a kind of nonreflective immediacy that people enjoy. One of the pleasures of the Bond pictures is in getting away from the mechanics of dramatic construction back to the one-damn-thing-after-another serial; and it's a liberation. The audience doesn't have to watch the characters drag their feet through all those boring, unconvincing motions that used to get them into tricky situations: they start right off in one, and go on to the next.

The New Republic, January 14, 1967

BLOW-UP
TOURIST IN THE CITY OF YOUTH

Some years ago I attended an evening of mime by Marcel Marceau, an elaborate exercise in aesthetic purification during which the audience kept applauding its own appreciation of culture and beauty, i.e., every time they thought they recognized what was supposed to be going on. It had been bad enough when Chaplin or Harpo Marx pulled this beauty-of-pathos stuff, and a whole evening of it was truly intolerable. But afterwards, when friends were acclaiming Marceau's artistry, it just wouldn't do to say something like "I prefer the Ritz Brothers" (though I do, I passionately do). They would think I was being deliberately lowbrow, and if I tried to talk in terms of Marceau's artistry versus Harry Ritz's artistry, it would be stupid, because "artist" is already too pretentious a term for Harry Ritz and so I would be falsifying what I love him for. I don't want to push this quite so far as to say that Marceau is to comedians I like as Antonioni's *Blow-Up* is to movies I like, but the comparison may be suggestive. And it may also be relevant that Antonioni pulls a Marceau-like expressionist finale in this picture, one of those fancy finishes that seem to say so much (but what?) and reminds one of so many naïvely bad experimental films.

Will *Blow-Up* be taken seriously in 1968 only by the same sort of cultural diehards who are still sending out five-page single-spaced letters on their interpretation of *Marienbad*? (No two are alike, no one interesting.) It has some of the *Marienbad* appeal: a friend phones for your opinion and when you tell him you didn't much care for it, he says, "You'd better see it again. I was at a swinging party the other night and it's all anybody talked about!" (Was there ever a good movie that everybody was talking about?) It probably won't blow over because it also has the *Morgan!–Georgy Girl* appeal; people identify with it so strongly, they get *upset* if you don't like it—as if you were rejecting not just the movie but *them*. And in a way they're right, because if you don't accept the peculiarly slugged consciousness of *Blow-Up*, you *are* rejecting something in them. Antonioni's new mixture of suspense with vagueness and confusion seems to have a kind of numbing fascination for them that they associate with art and intellectuality, and they are responding to it as *their* film—and hence as a masterpiece.

Antonioni's off-screen conversation, as reported to us, is full of impeccable literary references, but the white-faced clowns who open and close *Blow-Up* suggest that inside his beautifully fitted dinner jacket he carries—next to his heart—a gilt-edged gift edition of Kahlil Gibran. From the way people talk about the profundity of *Blow-Up*, that's probably what they're responding to. What would we think of a man who stopped at a newsstand to cluck at the cover girls of *Vogue* and *Harper's Bazaar* as tragic symbols of emptiness and sterility, as evidence that modern life isn't "real," and then went ahead and bought the magazines? Or, to be more exact, what would we think of a man who conducted a leisurely tour of "swinging" London, lingering along the flashiest routes and dawdling over a pot party and mini-orgy, while ponderously explaining that although the mod scene appears to be hip and sexy, it represents a condition of spiritual malaise in which people live only for the sensations of the moment? Is he a foolish old hypocrite or is he, despite his tiresome moralizing, a man who knows he's hooked?

It's obvious that there's a new kind of noninvolvement among youth, but we can't get at what that's all about by Antonioni's terms. He is apparently unable to respond to or to convey the new sense of community among youth, or the humor and fervor and astonishing speed in their rejections of older values; he sees only the emptiness of pop culture.

Those who enjoy seeing this turned-on city of youth, those who say of *Blow-Up* that it's the trip, it's where we are now in consciousness and that Antonioni is in it, part of it, ahead of it like Warhol, may have a better sense of what Antonioni is about than the laudatory critics. Despite Antonioni's negativism, the world he presents looks harmless, and for many in the audience, and not just the youthful ones, sex without "connecting" doesn't really seem so bad—naughty, maybe, but nice. Even the smoke at the pot party is enough to turn on some of the audience. And there's all that pretty color which delights the critics, though it undercuts their reasons for praising the movie because it's that bright, cleaned-up big-city color of I-have-seen-the-future-and-it's-fun. Antonioni, like his fashion-photographer hero, is more interested in getting pretty pictures than in what they mean. But for reasons I can't quite fathom, what is taken to be shallow in his hero is taken to be profound in him. Maybe it's because of the symbols: do pretty pictures plus symbols equal art?

There are the revelers who won't make room on the sidewalk for the nuns (spirit? soul? God? love?) and jostle them aside; an old airplane propeller is found in an antique shop; the hero considers buying the antique shop; two homosexuals walk their poodle, etc. Antonioni could point out that the poodle is castrated, and he'd probably be acclaimed for that, too—one more bitter detail of modern existential agony. There is a mock copulation with camera and subject that made me laugh (as the planes fornicating at the beginning of *Strangelove* did). But from the reviews of

Blow-Up I learn that this was "tragic" and "a superbly realized comment on the values of our time" and all that. People seem awfully eager to abandon sense and perspective and humor and put on the newest fashion in hair shirts; New York critics who are just settling into their upper East Side apartments write as if they're leaving for a monastery in the morning.

Hecht and MacArthur used to write light satirical comedies about shallow people living venal lives that said most of what Antonioni does and more, and were entertaining besides; they even managed to convey that they were in love with the corrupt milieu and were part of it without getting bogged down. And Odets, even in late work like his dialogue for *Sweet Smell of Success,* also managed to convey both hate and infatuation. Love-hate is what makes drama not only exciting but possible, and it certainly isn't necessary for Antonioni to resolve his conflicting feelings. But in *Blow-Up* he smothers this conflict in the kind of platitudes the press loves to designate as proper to "mature," "adult," "sober" art. Who the hell goes to movies for mature, adult, sober art, anyway? Yes, we want more from movies than we get from the usual commercial entertainments, but would anybody use terms like mature, adult, and sober for *The Rules of the Game* or *Breathless* or *Citizen Kane* or *Jules and Jim?*

The best part of *Blow-Up* is a well-conceived and ingeniously edited sequence in which the hero blows up a series of photographs and discovers that he has inadvertently photographed a murder. It's a good murder mystery sequence. But does it symbolize (as one reviewer says) "the futility of seeking the hidden meanings of life through purely technological means"? I thought the hero did rather well in uncovering the murder. But this kind of symbolic interpretation is not irrelevant to the appeal of the picture: Antonioni loads his atmosphere with so much confused symbolism and such a heavy sense of importance that the viewers use the movie as a Disposall for intellectual refuse. We get the stock phrases about "the cold death of the heart," "the eroticism is chilling in its bleakness," a "world so cluttered with synthetic stimulations that natural feelings are overwhelmed," etc., because Antonioni *inspires* this jargon.

When the photographer loses the photographic record of the murder, he loses interest in it. According to *Time,* "Antonioni's anti-hero"—who is said to be a "little snake" and "a grincingly accurate portrait of the sort of squiggly little fungus that is apt to grow in a decaying society"—"holds in his possession, if only for an instant, the alexin of his cure: the saving grace of the spirit." (My Webster doesn't yield a clue to "grincingly"; an "alexin" is "a defensive substance, found normally in the body, capable of destroying bacteria.") In other words, if he did something about the murder, like going to the police, he would be accepting an involvement with the life or death of others, and he would find his humanity and become an OK guy to *Time.* (Would he then not be a representative of a decaying society, or would the society not then decay? Only *Time* can tell.)

This review, and many others, turn the murder into something like what the press and TV did with the Kitty Genovese case: use it as an excuse for another of those what-are-we-coming-to editorials about alienation and indifference to human suffering. What was upsetting about the Genovese case was not those among the "witnesses" who didn't want to get involved even to the degree of calling the police (cowardice is not a new phenomenon), but our recognition that in a big city we don't know when our help is needed, and others may not know when we need help. This isn't a new phenomenon, either; what is new is that it goes against the grain of modern social consciousness, i.e., we feel responsible even though we don't know how to act responsibly. The press turned it into one more chance to cluck, and people went around feeling very superior to those thirty-eight witnesses because they were sure *they* would have called the police.

The moral satisfaction of feeling indignant that people take away from these cases (though I'm not sure that *Time*'s moral is what Antonioni intended; probably not) is simple and offensive. Do all the times that the police are called when they are or aren't needed prove how humanly involved with each other we are? The editorial writers don't tell us. And they couldn't do much with the West Coast case of the young academic beaten, tied to his bed, moaning and crying for help for days before he died. His friends and neighbors heard him all right, but as that's how he customarily took his pleasure, they smiled sympathetically and went about their own affairs, not knowing that this time the rough trade he had picked up to beat him had been insanely earnest.

The quick rise to celebrity status of young fashion photographers, like the quick success of pop singers, makes them ideal "cool" heroes, because they don't come up the slow, backbreaking Horatio Alger route. And the glamour of the rich and famous and beautiful rubs off on the photographer who shoots them, making him one of them. Antonioni uses David Hemmings in the role very prettily—with his Billy Budd hair-do, he's like a Pre-Raphaelite Paul McCartney. But if we're supposed to get upset because this young man got rich quick—the way some people get morally outraged at the salaries movie stars make—that's the moral outrage television personalities specialize in and it's hardly worth the consideration of art-house audiences. Yet a surprising lot of people seem willing to accept assumptions such as: the fashion photographer is symbolic of life in our society and time; he turns to easy sex because his life and ours are empty, etc. Mightn't people like easy sex even if their lives were reasonably full? And is sex necessarily empty just because the people are strangers to each other, or is it just different? And what's so terrible about fast, easy success? Don't most of the people who cluck their condemnation wish they'd had it?

Vanessa Redgrave, despite an odd mod outfit, has a tense and lovely presence, and because she has been allowed to act in this film (in which almost no one else is allowed to project) she stands out. However, someone has arranged her in a wholly gratuitous mood—laughing with her head back and teeth showing in a blatant imitation of Garbo. It's almost a subliminal trailer for *Camelot* in which, according to advance publicity, she will be "the Garbo of the sixties." This little deformation does not stick out as it might in another movie because this movie is so ill-formed anyway. The exigencies of the plot force Antonioni to alter his typical "open" construction (famous partly because it was the most painstakingly planned openness in movie history). In *Blow-Up* he prepares for events and plants characters for reappearances when they will be needed, but limply, clumsily; and he finds poor excuses for getting into places like the discotheque and the pot party, which "use" London to tell us about dehumanization. In some terrible way that I suppose could be called Antonioni's genius, he complains of dehumanization in a dehumanized way, and it becomes part of noninvolvement to accept a movie like this as "a chronicle of our time."

Just as *Marienbad* was said to be about "time" and/or "memory," *Blow-Up* is said (by Antonioni and the critics following his lead) to be about "illusion and reality." They seem to think they are really saying something, and something impressive at that, though the same thing can be said about almost any movie. In what sense is a movie "about" an abstract concept? Probably what Antonioni and the approving critics mean is that high fashion, mod celebrity, rock and roll, and drugs are part of a sterile or frenetic existence, and they take this to mean that the life represented in the film is not "real" but illusory. What seems to be implicit in the prattle about illusion and reality is the notion that the photographer's life is based on "illusion" and that when he discovers the murder, he is somehow face to face with "reality." Of course this notion that murder is more real than, say, driving in a Rolls-Royce convertible, is nonsensical (it's more shocking, though, and when combined with a Rolls-Royce it gives a movie a bit of box office— it's practical). They're not talking about a concept of reality but what used to be called "the real things in life," the solid values they approve of versus the "false values" of "the young people today."

Antonioni is the kind of thinker who can say that there are "no social or moral judgments in the picture"; he is merely showing us the people who have discarded "all discipline," for whom freedom means "marijuana, sexual perversion, anything," and who live in "decadence without any visible future." I'd hate to be around when he's making judgments. Yet in some sense Antonioni is right: because he doesn't *connect* what he's showing to judgment. And that dislocation of sensibility is probably why kids don't notice the moralizing, why they say *Blow-Up* is hip.

The cultural ambience of a film like this becomes mixed with the experience of the film: one critic says Antonioni's "vision" is that "the further we draw away from reality, the closer we get to the truth," another that Antonioni means "we must learn to live with the invisible." All this can sound great to those who don't mind not knowing what it's about, for whom the ineffable seems most important. "It's about the limits of visual experience. The photographer can't go beyond make-believe," a lady lawyer who loved the movie explained to me. "But," I protested, "visual experience is hardly make-believe any more than your practice is—perhaps less." Without pausing for breath she shifted to, "Why does it have to mean anything?" That's the game that's being played at parties this year at Marienbad. They feel they understand *Blow-Up,* but when they can't explain it, or why they feel as they do, they use that as the grounds for saying the movie is a work of art. *Blow-Up* is the perfect movie for the kind of people who say, "now that films have become an art form . . ." and don't expect to understand art.

Because the hero is a *photographer* and the blow-up sequence tells a story in pictures, the movie is also said to be about Antonioni's view of himself as an artist (though even his worst enemies could hardly accuse him of "telling stories" in pictures). Possibly it is, but those who see *Blow-Up* as Antonioni's version of *8½*—as making a movie about making a movie—seem to value that much more than just making a movie, probably because it puts the film in a class with the self-conscious autobiographical material so many young novelists struggle with (the story that ends with their becoming writers . . .) and is thus easy to mistake for the highest point of the artistic process.

There is the usual post-*Marienbad* arguing about whether the murder is "real" or "hallucinatory." There seems to be an assumption that if a movie can be interpreted as wholly or partially a dream or fantasy, it is more artistic, and I have been hearing that there is no murder, it's all in the photographer's head. But then the movie makes even less sense because there are no indications of anything in his character that relate to such fantasies. Bosley Crowther has come up with the marvelously involuted suggestion that as the little teeny-bopper orgy wasn't "real" but just the hero's "juvenile fantasy," the Production Code people shouldn't have thought they were seeing real tidbits on the screen.

What is it about the symbolic use of characters and details that impresses so many educated people? It's not very hard to do: almost any detail or person or event in our lives can be pressed into symbolic service, but to what end? I take my dogs for a walk in New York City in January and see examples of "alienation." An old Negro woman is crooning, "The world out here is lonely and cold." A shuffling old man mutters, "Never did and never will, never again and never will." And there's a crazy lady who glowers at my dogs and shouts, "They're not fit to shine my canary's shoes!" Do they tell us anything about a "decaying society"? No, but if you had some banal polemical, social, or moral point to make, you could turn them into cardboard figures marked with arrows. In so doing I think you would diminish their individuality and their range of meaning, but you would probably increase your chances of being acclaimed as a deep thinker.

When journalistic details are used symbolically—and that is how Antonioni uses "swinging" London—the artist does not create a frame of reference that gives meaning to the details; he simply exploits the ready-made symbolic meanings people attach to certain details and leaves us in a profound mess. (The middlebrow moralists think it's profound and the hippies enjoy the mess.) And when he tosses in a theatrical convention like a mimed tennis game without a ball—which connects with the journalistic data only in that it, too, is symbolic—he throws the movie game away. It becomes ah-sweet-mystery-of-life we-are-all-fools, which, pitched too high for human ears, might seem like great music beyond our grasp.

The New Republic, February 11, 1967

FROM REVIEW OF JEAN RENOIR'S
BOUDU SAVED FROM DROWNING*

Boudu is a more leisurely film than we are used to now, not that it is long, or slow, but that the camera isn't in a rush, the action isn't overemphatic, shots linger on the screen for an extra split second—we have time to look at them, to take them in. Renoir is an unobtrusive, unselfconscious storyteller: he doesn't "make points," he doesn't rub our noses in "meaning." He seems to find his story as he tells it; sometimes the improvisation falters, the movie gets a little untidy. He is not a director to force things. *Boudu* is a simple shaggy-man story told in an open way, and it is the openness to the beauty of landscape and weather and to the varieties of human folly which is Renoir's artistry. He lets a movie breathe.

Boudu is a tramp saved from suicide by a bookseller who takes him into his home and tries to do for him what decent, generous people *would* try to do—make him over in their own solid-bourgeois image, make him one of them. But *Boudu* is not a lovable tramp like Chaplin nor a Harry Langdon innocent nor a precursor of the artist-in-rebellion tramp like Alec Guinness's Gulley Jimson or Sean Connery's Samson Shillitoe. Boudu, bearded and long-haired like a premature Hell's Angel, is a dropout who just wants to be left alone. And this may help to explain why the movie wasn't imported earlier: he doesn't want romance or a job or a place in society (like the forlorn little hero of *À Nous La Liberté*), he isn't one of the deserving poor. There's no "redeeming" political message in *Boudu* and no fancy Shavian double-talk either.

Boudu is the underside of middle-class life, what's given up for respectability. We agree to be clean and orderly and responsible, but there is something satisfying about his *refusal*. There's a kind of inevitability—like someone acting out our dream—about the way he spills wine on the table, leaves the water running in the sink, wipes his shoes on the bedspread. There's some disorderly malice in him. He's like a bad pet that can't be

---

* Made in France in 1931, but not released in the U.S. until 1967.

trained: he makes messes. If Boudu's character were reformed, that would be defeat. The bookseller, despite his mistress-maid, is unmanned by the female household—and by being a householder. Boudu is, at least, his own dog.

Michel Simon, who plays Boudu, is better known for his masochistic roles, as, earlier, in Renoir's *La Chienne,* and, later, in Duvivier's *Panique* and *La Fin du jour.* But his Boudu, like his tattooed Père Jules of *L'Atalante,* which Agee described as "a premental old man . . . a twentieth-century Caliban," is a misfit loner. The loose walk, the eyes that don't communicate, the Margaret Rutherford jaw and the Charles Laughton sneaky self-satisfaction are not those of a man who rejects society: rejection is built into him, he merely acts it out. One of the New York reviewers complained that Michel Simon "misses completely. . . . He is gross where he should be droll. He does wrong all the things that Fernandel later was to do right." That's rather like complaining that Olivier in *The Entertainer* is no Tony Bennett.

Renoir's camera reveals the actors as if they were there naturally or inadvertently—not arranged for a shot but found by the camera on the streets, in the shop, on the banks of the Seine. The camera doesn't overdramatize their presence, it just—rather reticently—picks them up, and occasionally lets them disappear from the frame, to be picked up again at a later point in their lives.

Despite the problems of sound recording in 1931, Renoir went out of the studio, and so *Boudu* provides not only a fresh encounter with the movie past but also a photographic record of an earlier France, which moved in a different rhythm, and because of the photographic equipment and style of the period, in a softly different light. The shop fronts look like Atget; the houses might have modeled for Bonnard. It is a nostalgic work, not in the deliberate, embarrassing way we have become inured to, but in spite of itself—through the accidents of distribution. And because Renoir is free of the public-courting sentimentality of most movie directors, our nostalgia is—well—clean.

The New Republic, April 15, 1967

NOTES ON **THE RULES OF THE GAME (LA RÈGLE DU JEU)**

Jean Renoir's *The Rules of the Game* is a love roundelay that accelerates and intensifies until it becomes a rare mingling of lyric poetry and macabre farce. The lyric and the macabre turn out to be different aspects of the same love game.

What is, at one level, simply a large house party is, at another level, a tragi-comic world in motion. Ironically, the man who begins at the center of it all, the romantic aviator-hero, becomes irrelevant and expendable. He is odd man out on a carousel: when the whole mechanism is spinning he is flicked off. After observing his courtship rites, we can only accede to his quick demise: in this whirl, who has patience for his outmoded sense of honor?

The chase is a combination of two shooting parties. The hunt, the ostensible reason for the weekend gathering, serves as a relief from moneyed boredom. Who cares what you shoot? The beaters precede the guests who shoot at animals, birds—any living thing that can be shot at. The second shooting party is not planned: the jealous gamekeeper, a rigid man with an antique morality, runs amuck among the guests who confuse his passion with play-acting. They accept as divertissement the chase of servants and master among them (a later generation would call this "total theatre"). Mechanical toys are in motion, shots are fired; the targets are random—a toy, and then the romantic hero, as surprised by the shot as the rabbit.

In *La Grande Illusion,* made in 1937 but set during World War I, Renoir had dealt with a trio of heroes—the French aristocrat De Boeldieu, the German aristocrat von Rauffenstein, and the French plebeian Maréchal. A fourth character, Rosenthal, played by Dalio, was a rich young Jew from the merchant class. *The Rules of the Game,* Renoir's last prewar French film, is set at the time it was made—in 1939, at the eve of the outbreak of World War II—and Dalio has become a marquis. But he has not really changed: he is still Rosenthal, or rather Rosenthal's descendant, though socially he has moved into the château and the grounds of a De Boeldieu. The old military aristocracy is dead, as De Boeldieu and von Rauffenstein had predicted it would be; the new aristocracy is based on money and celebrity.

What are "the rules of the game" in this society? They are in flux—nobody knows what they are. The mores are just convenient manners. The aviator and the gamekeeper who *do* live by rules (the rules of an older, more stable society) cannot play the "game"; they upset everything because they can't just relax and adapt to the graceful decay of morals. What are the distinctions that have disappeared or become confused among the house guests? Love is indistinguishable from sexual activity; adultery is an escape from idleness. The concept of honor has disappeared (the honor that meant so much to a von Rauffenstein, a De Boeldieu); dishonor is just another term for indiscretion. Charm is more important than feeling. The marquis and his guests at the château still have some energy and some feeling, but they are becoming enervated; they foreshadow the guests at the big hotel parties in later movies—*La Dolce Vita, L'Avventura,* and *Last Year at Marienbad.* The house party suggests comparison with the house party in Ingmar Bergman's *Smiles of a Summer Night,* which is, however, far less complicated. The way the animals die calls up other film images of death (some, no doubt, inspired by *The Rules of the Game*)—particularly the opening sequence of *Forbidden Games* and Magnani's death in *Open City.* The look of the animals about to die recalls an image from another Renoir film—the frightened eye of the girl in *A Day in the Country* as she is seduced, looking trapped, almost wounded.

Images and ideas that tease the imagination: The marquis's sense of fellowship with the poacher—they're both men of the world, rogues and sly weaklings, and there isn't even much class distinction between them . . . The poacher who poaches rabbits, or with equal ease, the gamekeeper's wife . . . The marquis's distaste for the gamekeeper—who can't keep his own wife from being poached . . . The marquis, who is incapable of conscious cruelty, organizes the slaughter of wild life for the entertainment of his guests; he collects and treasures rare, old mechanical toys . . . It seems right that Renoir himself should be one of the characters. He has never, even in his lesser movies, saved himself from total immersion in the work; here his role, that of Octave, the friendly observer, "the friend of the family" who is suddenly caught up in the game, suggests a parody of the artist as observer. No one in the film—not even its creator—remains aloof from the frenzy. Renoir dresses as a bear for the masquerade—and can't quite shed his animal skin. Is he aligned with the animals hunted down—and with the big shaggy dog-man of *Boudu?*

It would be possible to discuss the film simply in terms of its craftsmanship and the extraordinary editing (particularly in the last sequence); technically, it is breathtaking. But it seems almost an insult to worry over *how* it is done—what is far more exciting is to explore what is in it. Renoir, the great master of French naturalism, and the source of so much of the neorealist movement, is revealed in *The Rules of the Game* as the progenitor also of the trends in film associated with Bergman, Antonioni, Resnais, and others.

With Roland Toutain as the aviator, Carette as the poacher, Gaston Modot as the gamekeeper, Nora Gregor as Christine, Mila Parely as Genevieve, Paulette Dubost as Lisette. The script, by Renoir, assisted by Carl Koch, was derived from Alfred de Musset's *Les Caprices de Marianne.* Costumes by Chanel. Cinematography by Jean Bachelet and J. P. Alphen; Cartier-Bresson served as an assistant director. Released in Paris in 1939 after being cut by the distributors, cut again after violent audience reactions, then banned as demoralizing by the Vichy government and then by the Nazis. The original negative was destroyed when the Allies bombed the studios at Boulogne. Reassembled (from two hundred cans of film and bits of sound track) and restored in the late fifties. Selected in the 1962 international poll of critics as third among the greatest motion pictures of all time. I set that down only for the record: a numbered honor is an insult to the greatest living film artist.

Notes for a showing at U.C.L.A., Spring, 1962

ACCIDENT
THE COMEDY OF DEPRAVITY

"**I**sn't the moonlight *terrible!*" cried the young girl in *Our Town,* and we in the audience laughed at the comedy of sensual innocence, at the desires that made her fear the excitement of beauty. The images say it in *Accident*: the sunlight is terrible, it's *rotten,* because it makes the characters feel sexy. Joseph Losey uses sexual desperation and the beauty of Oxford in summertime to make our flesh crawl. It's a comedy of depravity, and we laugh all right, maybe not out loud but at least to ourselves. It's hard not to: Losey and his scenarist, Harold Pinter, are so knowingly sensual and we are so alerted to look for their knowingness. We laugh, also, at Pinter's barbed, mannered dialogue as a sign of recognition, a demonstration of our knowingness. We see how clever it all is. And I mean "clever" pejoratively—meaning *limited, thin,* meaning without the imagination of innocence. We're all "in the know" and corrupt together in the sheer physicality of it all—the triangular compositions of legs and crotch, the lines of dialogue that ooze out of sweating faces. But, at least, it *is* clever. *Accident* is nasty fun—a fascinating, rather preposterous movie, uneven, unsatisfying, but with virtuoso passages of calculated meanness.

Separately, Pinter and Losey have similar weaknesses (of organization, purpose, dramatic clarity) and they share an inability to achieve a dramatic climax. They have almost the same specialty: Pinter can create scenes that are loaded with unspecified anxieties and emotions; Losey is a master of sloth, and he can make the atmosphere of a scene thick with loathsome erotic overtones. As Losey's target is often the middle or upper classes, his erotophobia is often taken to be an expression of social consciousness, but his purposes are often so opaque that, for example, in *King and Country* the homoeroticism took over and the military argument got lost. The union of Pinter and Losey is almost incestuous: it produces a doubling of their defects and their specialties. *Accident* is so full of ambience and the director and writer seem to have so little sense of what to do with it that they just use it for its own sake. Their work is full of "suggestions" and "implications" about marriage and class and education and violence; they use malice and cruelty as if to speak volumes of truth. The movie is saturated with "meaning," it drips attitudes.

Accident is effective because it's almost all set within their specialty, but although what they do is a formidable accomplishment in terms of current movies (and *Accident* is the best new movie around), it's too easy for art. It's too easy to get audience response by pointing up the enervation and bestiality of educated and/or rich people. Are they muckraking for us or for themselves? Maybe they really dig that muck.

Albee gave us Maggie and Jiggs at the old U; Losey and Pinter give us a black sudser—Oxford as Peyton Place, full of lust, hatred, promiscuity

("Three men in love with the same girl . . . who is this strange seductress who has disrupted the peaceful lives of the respected citizens of Peyton Place? Can Stephen and Rosalind go on as before? Will Charley's wife Laura recover her wits and come in out of the rain?"). It's good theatrical gimmickry—not, however, to be confused with a masterpiece, as the mixed media of reviews and advertising might suggest. We now have generations of moviegoers who have never been to a burlesque show and who react to jokes about age and potency as if they were the latest invention of art movies. And as they didn't go to the theatre much either, they don't know that the comedy of manners was almost always the comedy of bad manners, and that dirty gamesmanship is the staple of melodrama. But critics are supposed to have been born at least the day before yesterday and be able to sort out what's new in a work from what's old. And to know that schtik is an anagram of kitsch.

The protagonist of *Accident* is the nothing-heart, not-much-of-a-man at work and play. As the philosophy-don husband, Dirk Bogarde is just about perfect: he acts like a man who's had a spinal tap. He's a virtuoso at this civilized, stifled anguish racket, better even than Ralph Richardson used to be at suppressed emotion because he's so much more ambiguous that we can't even be sure what he's suppressing. He aches all the time all over, like an all-purpose sufferer for a television commercial—locked in, with a claustrophobia of his own body and sensibility. Bogarde looks rather marvelous going through his middle-aged frustration routines, gripping his jaw to stop a stutter or folding his arms to keep his hands out of trouble. The Ralph Richardson civilized sufferer was trying to spare others pain, but Bogarde isn't noble: he goes through the decent motions because of training and because of an image of himself, but he's exquisitely guilty in thought—a mouse with the soul of a rat. He compulsively tells little half-lies that he intends to make true and hesitates before each bit of truth he calculatingly parts with. If only Losey and Pinter would let him out now and then! A man can stay in a continual, acute state of suppression and humiliation only so long. If Bogarde plays this role again, he may wind up his career touring backwaters of the Commonwealth countries in *The Browning Version*.

So often men like Pinter and Losey who are acclaimed on the "less is more" principle are really giving us much too much—but all of the same kind. Pinter is indirect and Losey provides treatises on how rolling green fields and beautiful buildings can be made ominous. They sustain interest by portent, but portent without any clear intent. In this, too, *Accident* resembles sudsers, as it does in its manufactured incidents (the visit to the television studio), the worked-up parallels (Laura with Rosalind).

It also has many resemblances to Pinter's play *The Homecoming:* each has its philosophy professor; each has its enigmatic female—the respectable whore to whom all the important male characters are attracted. Each is a satire of home, and in both movie and play Pinter's peculiar talent for dislocating family life and social and sexual relations to a kind of banal horror

has some recognizable truth in it, and his cadences are funny and reverberating. He's a new—hideously sophisticated—kind of cliché expert. He deals with characters who give each other nothing willingly, who defend their privacy against attack with evasions, repetitions, silences. And we laugh to show that we appreciate what is unsaid—the underside of what is said. The focus in *Accident* is on the men, who are trying to get one up on each other; the women (Jacqueline Sassard as the love object, Anna, and Vivien Merchant as the wife, Rosalind) are passive and sly. (We must partly guess at this from Miss Sassard's inept performance.) We laugh because of the absence of goodwill. In the theatre and movies, truly dedicated selfishness is amusing; and it is somehow liberating to laugh at a family of monsters. Isn't that the secret of the success of plays like *Tobacco Road* and *The Little Foxes* and the comic mechanism of the recent *A Lion in Winter*? The monsters of a melodramatist like Lillian Hellman are rich and decadent white Southerners or Nazis, and these people who *lust* are contrasted with the good, straight, affirmative people who are for civil rights and Life and who have healthy, decent impulses.

Pinter (in *The Servant,* in his play *The Homecoming,* and now in *Accident*) carries this traditional device further by omitting any sympathetic characters. What makes for all the lust in his works is that his people have no tender or compassionate feelings; if they're not decent enough for love, then any sex impulses they feel can only be lust. Elizabeth Hardwick has written that in *The Homecoming* Pinter "avoids exposition in the ordinary sense and is not seduced by affection for pieties." True enough, but perhaps we are seduced by his disaffection for pieties? Pinter is so consistent that there's not a single likable character in any of these three works: what happens, on screen as on stage, is that in a competition of monsters the most fiendish and obscene are the most amusingly theatrical and become the favorites of the audience—the belligerent, lecherous father and his son, the pimp, in *The Homecoming;* Stanley Baker's swinish Charley in *Accident.* Charley's best line is the vile (in context), "What room is everybody in?" This is fine with me. I enjoy it because I enjoy fancy kitsch. But I don't think Pinter's device—which is ingeniously theatrical but nothing more—should be overrated or confused with an *artistic* solution. (I don't mean to suggest that Pinter has claimed to discover new forms; but that claim has been made for him.) We are so aware of the absence of goodness and of the usual melodramatic conflict that we wait eagerly to see what he will provide in its place. So far he hasn't come up with anything, and that's why one leaves *Accident* as one left *The Homecoming*—dissatisfied and perhaps a little indignant. Like Albee, Pinter is good at dialogue with a sense of drama in it. For the rest of what makes drama, Albee provides explanations which don't explain the charge of the dialogue; Pinter is cagier. But though he's smart enough to avoid the adversary approach to good and evil, he rattles some very dry bones from the theatre basement: woman as eternal, mysterious whore-wife-

mother; the man of thought who is cut off from the instinctual; etc. Those old bones aren't going to grow any meat.

In movies Pinter doesn't avoid exposition—he's just no good at it. His talent is for cryptic, "suggestive" dialogue and for ghastly scenes; in *Accident,* as in *The Pumpkin Eater* and *The Servant,* when he tries to use dramatic narrative methods, he uses them so badly that the movies fall apart. In *Accident,* it shouldn't be that difficult to make at least the accident itself relate to the characters and plot. Nothing in the movie would be much changed if there were no accident (the only revelation—that the philosophy don would "take advantage" of a girl in shock—isn't convincing anyway).

Off screen Losey and Pinter, perhaps following a course set for them by the enthusiasts for *The Homecoming,* have taken the position that (as Pinter said when queried about the movie) "I have no explanation for anything I do at all." This might give the impression that the movie has been written out of the unconscious, but it is so carefully plotted that you can watch the preparations being made and chart how each event or reaction was led up to. And in some cases—as when the don is raping the girl while the phone is ringing to tell him his wife is having a baby—even those construction men who lay out Sodom and Gomorrah in weekly segments might be ashamed to be so crude. But although it can be charted by a viewer (and, no doubt, was cunningly planned), the plotting often doesn't work dramatically—the viewer can only piece it together *afterward.* (For example, when Stephen returns from London and finds Charley and Anna in his home, it takes too long to figure out what's going on, and the obfuscation of Anna's face and her appearance in Rosalind's clothes are merely chic.)

Losey and Pinter work best close-in, and their smaller version of the Antonioni-Fellini terrible party—the long, drunken Sunday house party, with people sitting down to supper when they're too drunk to eat—is perhaps the most shocking of movie parties because it's so exactly, familiarly horrible. They're less successful at show pieces—like the affectation of their reprise of *Marienbad,* with Delphine Seyrig as a dumb blonde (with what sounds like Vivien Merchant on the voice-over dialogue). And the big exhibition piece—"aristocrats" playing some nasty game in the great hall of a castle—tells less than a flushed face in close-up. The final crash—a fancy, ambiguous finish—is a cheat.

I enjoyed *Accident,* but I don't really *like* it. It has an archness which I associate with a kind of well-written but fundamentally empty novel. *Accident* is, despite what Losey and Pinter say in it, for and of "the upper classes." They use a lot of craftsmanship and technique to pave the old dirt roads.

The New Republic, June 3, 1967

A few years ago, a jet on which I was returning to California after a trip to New York was instructed to delay landing for a half hour. The plane circled above the San Francisco area, and spread out under me were the farm where I was born, the little town where my grandparents were buried, the city where I had gone to school, the cemetery where my parents were, the homes of my brothers and sisters, Berkeley, where I had gone to college, and the house where at that moment, while I hovered high above, my little daughter and my dogs were awaiting my return. It was as though my whole life were suspended in time—as though no matter where you'd gone, what you'd done, the past were all still there, present, if you just got up high enough to attain the proper perspective.

Sometimes I get a comparable sensation when I turn from the news programs or the discussion shows on television to the old movies. So much of what formed our tastes and shaped our experiences, and so much of the garbage of our youth that we never thought we'd see again—preserved and exposed to eyes and minds that might well want not to believe that this was an important part of our past. Now these movies are there for new generations, to whom they cannot possibly have the same impact or meaning, because they are all jumbled together, out of historical sequence. Even what may deserve an honorable position in movie history is somehow dishonored by being so available, so meaninglessly present. Everything is in hopeless disorder, and that is the way new generations experience our movie past. In the other arts, something like natural selection takes place: only the best or the most significant or influential or successful works compete for our attention. Moreover, those from the past are likely to be touched up to accord with the taste of the present. In popular music, old tunes are newly orchestrated. A small repertory of plays is continually reinterpreted for contemporary meanings—the great ones for new relevance, the not so great rewritten, tackily "brought up to date," or deliberately treated as period pieces. By contrast, movies, through the accidents of commerce, are sold in blocks or packages to television, the worst with the mediocre and the best, the successes with the failures, the forgotten with the half forgotten, the ones so dreary you don't know whether you ever saw them or just others like them with some so famous you can't be sure whether you actually saw them or only imagined what they were like. A lot of this stuff never really made it with any audience; it played in small towns or it was used to soak up the time just the way TV in bars does.

There are so many things that we, having lived through them, or passed over them, never want to think about again. But in movies nothing is cleaned away, sorted out, purposefully discarded. (The destruction of negatives in studio fires or deliberately, to save space, was as indiscriminate as the preservation and resale.) There's a kind of hopelessness about it: what does not deserve to last lasts, and so it all begins to seem one big pile of junk, and some people say, "Movies never really were any good—except maybe the Bogarts." If the same thing had happened in literature or music or painting—if we were constantly surrounded by the piled-up inventory of the past—it's conceivable that modern man's notion of culture and civilization would be very different. Movies, most of them produced as fodder to satisfy the appetite for pleasure and relaxation, turned out to have magical properties—indeed, to *be* magical properties. This fodder can be fed to people over and over again. Yet, not altogether strangely, as the years wear on it doesn't please their palates, though many will go on swallowing it, just because nothing tastier is easily accessible. Watching old movies is like spending an evening with those people next door. They bore us, and we wouldn't go out of our way to see them; we drop in on them because they're so close. If it took some effort to see old movies, we might try to find out which were the good ones, and if people saw only the good ones maybe they would still respect old movies. As it is, people sit and watch movies that audiences walked out on thirty years ago. Like Lot's wife, we are tempted to take another look, attracted not by evil but by something that seems much more shameful—our own innocence. We don't try to reread the girls' and boys' "series" books of our adolescence—the very look of them is dismaying. The textbooks we studied in grammar school are probably more "dated" than the movies we saw then, but we never look at the old schoolbooks, whereas we keep seeing on TV the movies that represent the same stage in our lives and played much the same part in them—as things we learned from and, in spite of, went beyond.

Not all old movies look bad now, of course; the good ones are still good—surprisingly good, often, if you consider how much of the detail is lost on television. Not only the size but the shape of the image is changed, and, indeed, almost all the specifically visual elements are so distorted as to be all but completely destroyed. On television, a cattle drive or a cavalry charge or a chase—the climax of so many a big movie—loses the dimensions of space and distance that made it exciting, that sometimes made it great. And since the structural elements—the rhythm, the buildup, the suspense—are also partly destroyed by deletions and commercial breaks and the interruptions incidental to home viewing, it's amazing that the bare bones of performance, dialogue, story, good directing, and (especially important for close-range viewing) good editing can still make an old movie more entertaining than almost anything new on television. (That's why old movies are taking over television—or, more accurately, vice versa.) The verbal slapstick of the newspaper-life comedies—*Blessed Event, Roxie Hart, His Girl Friday*—may no longer be fresh (partly because it has been so widely imitated), but it's still funny. Movies with good, fast, energetic talk seem better than ever on television—still not great but, on television, better than what *is* great. (And as we listen to the tabloid journalists insulting the corrupt politicians, we respond once again to the happy effrontery of that period when the targets of popular satire were still small enough for us to laugh at without choking.) The wit of dialogue comedies like Preston Sturges's *Unfaithfully Yours* isn't much diminished, nor does a tight melodrama like *Double Indemnity* lose a great deal. Movies like Joseph L. Mankiewicz's *A Letter to Three Wives* and *All About Eve* look practically the same on television as in theatres, because they have almost no visual dimensions to lose. In them the camera serves primarily to show us the person who is going to speak the next presumably bright line—a scheme that on television, as in theatres, is acceptable only when the line *is* bright. Horror and fantasy films like Karl Freund's *The Mummy* or Robert Florey's *The Murders in the Rue Morgue*—even with the loss, through miniaturization, of imaginative special effects—are surprisingly effective, perhaps because they are so primitive in their appeal that the qualities of the imagery matter less than the basic suggestions. Fear counts for more than finesse, and viewing horror films is far more frightening at home than in the shared comfort of an audience that breaks the tension with derision.

Other kinds of movies lose much of what made them worth looking at—the films of von Sternberg, for example, designed in light and shadow, or the subtleties of Max Ophuls, or the lyricism of Satyajit Ray. In the box the work of these men is not as lively or as satisfying as the plain good movies of lesser directors. Reduced to the dead grays of a cheap television print, Orson Welles's *The Magnificent Ambersons*—an uneven work that is nevertheless a triumphant conquest of the movie medium—is as lifelessly dull as a newspaper Wirephoto of a great painting. But when people say of a "big" movie like *High Noon* that it has dated or that it doesn't hold up, what they are really saying is that their judgment was faulty or has changed. They may have overresponded to its publicity and reputation or to its attempt to deal with a social problem or an idea, and may have ignored the banalities surrounding that attempt; now that the idea doesn't seem so daring, they notice the rest. Perhaps it was a traditional drama that was new to them and that they thought was new to the world; everyone's "golden age of movies" is the period of his first moviegoing and just before—what he just missed or wasn't allowed to see. (The Bogart films came out just before today's college kids started going.)

Sometimes we suspect, and sometimes rightly, that our memory has improved a picture—that imaginatively we made it what we knew it could have been or should have been—and, fearing this, we may prefer memory to new contact. We'll remember it better if we don't see it again—we'll remember what it meant to us. The nostalgia we may have poured over a performer or over our recollections of a movie has a way of congealing when we try to renew the contact. But sometimes the experience of reseeing is wonderful—a confirmation of the general feeling that was all that remained with us from childhood. And we enjoy the fresh proof of the rightness of our responses that reseeing the film gives us. We re-experience what we once felt, and memories flood back. Then movies seem magical—all those *madeleines* waiting to be dipped in tea. What looks bad in old movies is the culture of which they were part and which they expressed—a tone of American life that we have forgotten. When we see First World War posters, we are far enough away from their patriotic primitivism to be amused at the emotions and sentiments to which they appealed. We can feel charmed but superior. It's not so easy to cut ourselves off from old movies and the old selves who responded to them, because they're not an isolated part of the past held up for derision and amusement and wonder. Although they belong to the same world as stories in *Liberty*, old radio shows, old phonograph records, an America still divided between hayseeds and city slickers, and although they may seem archaic, their pastness isn't so very past. It includes the last decade, last year, yesterday.

Though in advertising movies for TV the recentness is the lure, for many of us what constitutes the attraction is the datedness, and the earlier movies are more compelling than the ones of the fifties or the early sixties. Also, of course, the movies of the thirties and forties look better technically, because, ironically, the competition with television that made movies of the fifties and sixties enlarge their scope and their subject matter has resulted in their looking like a mess in the box—the sides of the image lopped off, the crowds and vistas a boring blur, the color altered, the epic themes incongruous and absurd on the little home screen. In a movie like *The Robe*, the large-scale production values that were depended on to attract TV viewers away from their sets become a negative factor. But even if the quality of the image were improved, these movies are too much like the ones we can see in theatres to be interesting at home. At home, we like to look at those stiff, carefully groomed actors of the thirties, with their clipped, Anglophile stage speech and their regular, clean-cut features—walking profiles, like the figures on Etruscan vases and almost as remote. And there is the faithless wife—how will she decide between her lover and her husband, when they seem as alike as two wax grooms on a wedding cake? For us, all three are doomed not by sin and disgrace but by history. Audiences of the period may have enjoyed these movies for their action, their story, their thrills, their wit, and all this high living. But through our window on the past we see the actors acting out other dramas as well. The Middle European immigrants had children who didn't speak the king's English and, after the Second World War, didn't even respect it so much. A flick of the dial and we are in the fifties amid the slouchers, with their thick lips, shapeless noses, and shaggy haircuts, waiting to say their lines until they think them out, then mumbling something that is barely speech. How long, O Warren Beatty, must we wait before we turn back to beautiful stick figures like Phillips Holmes?

We can take a shortcut through the hell of many lives, turning the dial from the social protest of the thirties to the films of the same writers and directors in the fifties—full of justifications for blabbing, which they shifted onto characters in oddly unrelated situations. We can see in the films of the forties the displaced artists of Europe—the anti-Nazi exiles like Conrad Veidt, the refugees like Peter Lorre, Fritz Kortner, and Alexander Granach.

And what are they playing? Nazis, of course, because they have accents, and so for Americans—for the whole world—they become images of Nazi brutes. Or we can look at the patriotic sentiments of the Second World War years and those actresses, in their orgies of ersatz nobility, giving their lives—or, at the very least, their bodies—to save their country. It was sickening at the time; it's perversely amusing now—part of the spectacle of our common culture.

Probably in a few years some kid watching *The Sandpiper* on television will say what I recently heard a kid say about *Mrs. Miniver:* "And to think they really believed it in those days." Of course, we didn't. We didn't accept nearly as much in old movies as we may now fear we did. Many of us went to see big-name pictures just as we went to *The Night of the Iguana,* without believing a minute of it. The James Bond pictures are not to be "believed," but they tell us a lot about the conventions that audiences now accept, just as the confessional films of the thirties dealing with sin and illegitimacy and motherhood tell us about the sickly-sentimental tone of American entertainment in the midst of the Depression. Movies indicate what the producers thought people would pay to see—which was not always the same as what they *would* pay to see. Even what they enjoyed seeing does not tell us directly what they believed but only indirectly hints at the tone and style of a culture. There is no reason to assume that people twenty or thirty years ago were stupider than they are now. (Consider how *we* may be judged by people twenty years from now looking at today's movies.) Though it may not seem obvious to us now, part of the original appeal of old movies—which we certainly understood and responded to as children—was that, despite their sentimental tone, they helped to form the liberalized modern consciousness. This trash—and most of it was, and is, trash—probably taught us more about the world, and even about values, than our "education" did. Movies broke down barriers of all kinds, opened up the world, helped to make us aware. And they were almost always on the side of the mistreated, the socially despised. Almost all drama is. And, because movies were a mass medium, they had to be on the side of the poor.

Nor does it necessarily go without saying that the glimpses of something really good even in mediocre movies—the quickening of excitement at a great performance, the discovery of beauty in a gesture or a phrase or an image—made us understand the meaning of art as our teachers in appreciation courses never could. And—what is more difficult for those who are not movie lovers to grasp—even after this sense of the greater and the higher is developed, we still do not want to live only on the heights. We still want the pleasure of discovering things for ourselves; we need the sustenance of the ordinary, the commonplace, the almost-good as part of the anticipatory atmosphere. And though it all helps us to respond to the moments of greatness, it is not only for this that we want it. The educated person who became interested in cinema as an art form through Bergman or Fellini or Resnais is an alien to me (and my mind goes blank with hostility and indifference when he begins to talk). There isn't much for the art-cinema person on television; to look at a great movie, or even a poor movie carefully designed in terms of textures and contrasts, on television is, in general, maddening, because those movies lose too much. (Educational television, though, persists in this misguided effort to bring the television viewer movie classics.) There are few such movies anyway. But there are all the not-great movies, which we probably wouldn't bother going to see in museums or in theatre revivals—they're just not that important. Seeing them on television is a different kind of experience, with different values—partly because the movie past hasn't been filtered to conform to anyone's convenient favorite notions of film art. We make our own, admittedly small, discoveries or rediscoveries. There's Dan Dailey doing his advertising-wise number in *It's Always Fair Weather,* or Gene Kelly and Fred Astaire singing and dancing "The Babbitt and the Bromide" in *Ziegfeld Follies.* And it's like putting on a record of Ray Charles singing "Georgia on My Mind" or Frank Sinatra singing "Bim Bam Baby" or Elisabeth Schwarzkopf singing operetta, and feeling again the elation we felt the first time. Why should we deny these pleasures because there are other, more complex kinds of pleasure possible? It's true that these pleasures don't deepen, and that they don't change *us,* but maybe that is part of what makes them seem our own—we realize that we have some emotions and responses that *don't* change as we get older.

People who see a movie for the first time on television don't remember it the same way that people do who saw it in a theatre. Even without the specific visual loss that results from the transfer to another medium, it's doubtful whether a movie could have as intense an impact as it had in its own time. Probably by definition, works that are not truly great cannot be as compelling out of their time. Sinclair Lewis's and Hemingway's novels were becoming archaic while their authors lived. Can *On the Waterfront* have the impact now that it had in 1954? Not quite. And revivals in movie theatres don't have the same kind of charge, either. There's something a little stale in the air, there's a different kind of audience. At a revival, we must allow for the period, or care because of the period. Television viewers seeing old movies for the first time can have very little sense of how and why new stars moved us when they appeared, of the excitement of new themes, of what these movies meant to us. They don't even know which were important in their time, which were "hits."

But they can discover *something* in old movies, and there are few discoveries to be made on dramatic shows produced for television. In comedies, the nervous tic of canned laughter neutralizes everything; the laughter is as false for the funny as for the unfunny and prevents us from responding to either. In general, performances in old movies don't suffer horribly on television except from cuts, and what kindles something like the early flash fire is the power of personality that comes through in those roles that made a star. Today's high school and college students seeing *East of Eden* and *Rebel Without a Cause* for the first time are almost as caught up in James Dean as the first generation of adolescent viewers was, experiencing that tender, romantic, marvelously masochistic identification with the boy who does everything wrong because he cares so much. And because Dean died young and hard, he is not just another actor who outlived his myth and became ordinary in stale roles—he is the symbol of misunderstood youth. He is inside the skin of moviegoing and television-watching youth—even educated youth—in a way that Keats and Shelley or John Cornford and Julian Bell are not. Youth can respond—though not so strongly—to many of our old heroes and heroines: to Gary Cooper, say, as the elegant, lean, amusingly silent romantic loner of his early Western and aviation films. (And they can more easily ignore the actor who sacrificed that character for blubbering righteous bathos.) Bogart found his myth late, and Dean fulfilled the romantic myth of self-destructiveness, so they look good on television. More often, television, by showing us actors before and after their key starring roles, is a myth-killer. But it keeps acting ability alive.

There is a kind of young television watcher seeing old movies for the first time who is surprisingly sensitive to their values and responds almost with the intensity of a moviegoer. But he's different from the moviegoer. For one thing, he's housebound, inactive, solitary. Unlike a moviegoer, he seems to have no need to discuss what he sees. The kind of television watcher I mean (and the ones I've met are all boys) seems to have extreme empathy with the material in the box (new TV shows as well as old movies, though rarely news), but he may not know how to enter into a conversation, or even how to come into a room or go out of it. He fell in love with his baby-sitter, so he remains a baby. He's unusually polite and intelligent, but in a mechanical way—just going through the motions, without interest. He gives the impression that he wants to withdraw from this human interference and get back to his real life—the box. He is like a prisoner who has everything he wants in prison and is content to stay there. Yet, oddly, he and his fellows seem to be tuned in to each other; just as it sometimes seems that even a teen-ager locked in a closet would pick up the new dance steps at the same moment as other teen-agers, these television watchers react to the same things at the same time. If they can find more intensity in this box than in their own living, then this box can provide *constantly* what we got at the movies only a few times a week. Why should they move away from it, or talk, or go out of the house, when they will only experience that as a loss? Of course, we can see why they should, and their inability to make connections outside is frighteningly suggestive of ways in which we, too, are cut off. It's a matter of degree. If we stay up half the night to watch old movies and can't face the next day, it's partly, at least, because of the fascination of our own movie past; *they* live in a past they never had, like people who become obsessed by places they have only imaginative connections with—Brazil, Venezuela, Arabia Deserta. Either way, there is always something a little shameful about living in the past; we feel guilty, stupid—as if the pleasure we get needed some justification that we can't provide.

For some moviegoers, movies probably contribute to that self-defeating romanticizing of expectations which makes life a series of disappointments. They watch the same movies over and over on television, as if they were constantly returning to the scene of the crime—the life they were so busy dreaming about that they never lived it. They are paralyzed by longing, while those less romantic can leap the hurdle. I heard a story the other day about a man who ever since his school days had been worshipfully "in love with" a famous movie star, talking about her, fantasizing about her, following her career, with its ups and downs and its stormy romances and marriages to producers and agents and wealthy sportsmen and rich businessmen. Though he became successful himself, it never occurred to him that he could enter her terrain—she was so glamorously above him. Last week, he got a letter from an old classmate, to whom, years before, he had confided his adoration of the star; the classmate—an unattractive guy who had never done anything with his life and had a crummy job in a crummy business— had just married her.

Movies are a combination of art and mass medium, but television is so single in its purpose—selling—that it operates without that painful, poignant mixture of aspiration and effort and compromise. We almost never think of calling a television show "beautiful," or even of complaining about the absence of beauty, because we take it for granted that television operates without beauty. When we see on television photographic records of the past, like the pictures of Scott's Antarctic expedition or those series on the First World War, they seem almost too strong for the box, too pure for it. The past has a terror and a fascination and a beauty beyond almost anything else. We are looking at the dead, and they move and grin and wave at us; it's an almost unbearable experience. When our wonder and our grief are interrupted or followed by a commercial, we want to destroy the ugly box. Old movies don't tear us apart like that. They do something else, which we can take more of and take more easily: they give us a sense of the passage of life. Here is Elizabeth Taylor as a plump matron and here, an hour later, as an exquisite child. That charmingly petulant little gigolo with the skinny face and the mustache that seems the most substantial part of him—can he have developed into the great Laurence Olivier? Here is Orson Welles as a young man, playing a handsome old man, and here is Orson Welles as he has really aged. Here are Bette Davis and Charles Boyer traversing the course of their lives from ingenue and juvenile, through major roles, into character parts— back and forth, endlessly, embodying the good and bad characters of many styles, many periods. We see the old character actors put out to pasture in television serials, playing gossipy neighbors or grumpy grandpas, and then we see them in their youth or middle age, in the roles that made them famous—and it's startling to find how good they were, how vital, after we've encountered them caricaturing themselves, feeding off their old roles. They have almost nothing left of that young actor we responded to—and still find ourselves responding to—except the distinctive voice and a few crotchets. There are those of us who, when we watch old movies, sit there murmuring the names as the actors appear (Florence Bates, Henry Daniell, Ernest Thesiger, Constance Collier, Edna May Oliver, Douglas Fowley), or we recognize them but can't remember their names, yet know how well we once knew them, experiencing the failure of memory as a loss of our own past until we can supply it (Maude Eburne or Porter Hall)—with great relief. After a few seconds, I can always remember them, though I cannot remember the names of my childhood companions or of the prizefighter I once dated, or even of the boy who took me to the senior prom. We are eager to hear again that line we know is coming. We hate to miss anything. Our memories are jarred by cuts. We want to see the movie to the end.

The graveyard of *Our Town* affords such a tiny perspective compared to this. Old movies on television are a gigantic, panoramic novel that we can tune in to and out of. People watch avidly for a few weeks or months or years and then give up; others tune in when they're away from home in lonely hotel rooms, or regularly, at home, a few nights a week or every night. The rest of the family may ignore the passing show, may often interrupt, because individual lines of dialogue or details of plot hardly seem to matter as they did originally. A movie on television is no longer just a drama in itself; it is part of a huge ongoing parade. To a new generation, what does it matter if a few gestures and a nuance are lost, when they know they can't watch the parade on all the channels at all hours anyway? It's like traffic on the street. The television generation knows there is no end; it all just goes on. When television watchers are surveyed and asked what kind of programming they want or how they feel television can be improved, some of them not only have no answers but can't understand the questions. What they get on their sets is television—that's it.

The New Yorker, June 3, 1967

ORSON WELLES: THERE AIN'T NO WAY
FALSTAFF (CHIMES AT MIDNIGHT)

What makes movies a great popular art form is that certain artists can, at moments in their lives, reach out and unify the audience—educated and uneducated—in a shared response. The tragedy in the history of movies is that those who have this capacity are usually prevented from doing so. The mass audience gets its big empty movies full of meaningless action; the art-house audience gets its studies of small action and large inaction loaded with meaning.

Almost everyone who cares about movies knows that Orson Welles is such an artist. Even audiences who don't know that Welles is a great *director* sense his largeness of talent from his presence as an actor. Audiences are alert to him, as they often were to John Barrymore, and later to Charles Laughton, as they sometimes are to Bette Davis, as they almost always are to Brando—actors too big for their roles, who play the clown, and not always in comedy but in roles that for an artist of intelligence can only be comedy. Like Brando, Welles is always being attacked for not having fulfilled his prodigious promise; but who has ever beaten the mass culture fly-by-night system of economics for long? What else could Welles do with his roles in *Black Magic* or *Prince of Foxes* or *The Black Rose* or *Trent's Last Case* but play them as comedy? Could one take such work seriously? The mediocre directors and the cynical hacks got money when he couldn't. His ironic playing is all that one remembers from those movies anyway; like Brando, he has the greatness to make effrontery a communicated, shared experience—which lesser artists had better not attempt. It takes large *latent* talent to tell the audience that you know that what you're doing isn't worth doing and still do it better than anyone else in the movie.

Waiting for a train in Grand Central station recently, I was standing next to a group of Negroes. To everything that they talked about, one of them—a young girl—said, "There ain't no way"; and it fit perfectly each time.

■　■　■

Orson Welles's *Falstaff* came and went so fast there was hardly time to tell people about it, but it should be back (it should be around forever) and it should be seen. It's blighted by economics and it will never reach the audience Welles might have and should have reached, because there just ain't no way. So many people—and with such complacent satisfaction, almost, one would say, delight—talk of how Welles has disappointed them, as if he had willfully thrown away his talent through that "lack of discipline" which is always brought in to explain failure. There is a widespread notion that a man who accomplishes a great deal is thus a "genius" who should be able to cut through all obstacles; and if he can't (and who can?), what he does is too far beneath what he should have done to be worth consideration. On the contrary, I think that the more gifted and imaginative a director, the greater the obstacles. It is the less imaginative director who has always flourished in the business world of movies—the "adaptable," reliable fellow who is more concerned to get the movie done than to do it his way, who, indeed, after a while has no way of his own, who is as anonymous as the director of *Prince of Foxes*. And the more determined a man is to do it his way or a new way, the more likelihood that this man (quickly labeled a "troublemaker" or "a difficult person" or "self-destructive" or "a man who makes problems for himself"—standard Hollywoodese for an artist and, of course, always true at some level, and the greater the artist, the more true it's likely to become) won't get the support he needs to complete the work his way. In the atmosphere of anxiety surrounding him, the producers may decide to "save" the project by removing him or adding to or subtracting from his work, or finally dumping the film without publicity or press screenings, consigning it to the lower half of double bills.

All these things have happened to Welles (*Citizen Kane* was not big enough at the box office and it caused trouble; he was not allowed to finish his next picture, *The Magnificent Ambersons*). Treatment of this sort, which usually marks the end of great movie careers, was for Welles the beginning. Most of these things have happened to men as pacific as Jean Renoir, whom few could accuse of being "undisciplined." (Renoir turned to writing a novel, his first, in 1966, when he could not raise money to make a movie, though the budget he required was less than half that allotted to movies made to be premiered on television.) And they are still happening to men in Hollywood like Sam Peckinpah. Such men are always blamed for the eventual failure of whatever remains of their work, while men who try for less have the successes (and are forgiven their routine failures because they didn't attempt anything the producers didn't understand). Joseph L. Mankiewicz's *Julius Caesar* was considered a success and Orson Welles's *Othello* a failure. The daring of doing Shakespeare at all was enough for Mankiewicz and his producer, John Houseman, who was to be ritualistically referred to as "the distinguished producer John Houseman" because of this film—not from his early theatre work with Orson Welles—much as George Schaefer is referred to as "the distinguished director" because of his specialty of embalming old war horses for television. Mankiewicz's luck held good on *Julius Caesar*: it's perfectly suited to the small screen, where it recently appeared, while Welles's *Othello*—with its disastrous, imperfectly synchronized soundtrack—isn't even intelligible. How could it be? A movie shot over a period of four years with Welles dashing off periodically to act in movies like *The Black Rose* to earn the money to continue; and then, his cast scattered, trying to make a soundtrack, reading half the roles himself (not only Roderigo, but if my ear is to be trusted, parts of Iago, too), selecting long shots and shots with the actors' backs to the camera to conceal the sound problem. This, of course, looked like "affectation." And his splendid, flawed production—visually and emotionally a near-masterpiece—was a "failure." Earlier, working on a Republic Pictures budget (for Republic Pictures), Welles had shot his barbaric *Macbeth*—marred most by his own performance—in twenty-three days because "no one would give me any money for a further day's shooting."

In the early fifties, Welles as an actor was in top flamboyant form. Nobody seemed to enjoy the sheer physical delight of acting as much as he in roles like his Lord Mountdrago in *Three Cases of Murder*. Still very young, he played like a great ham of the old school—which was marvelous to watch in his Father Mapple in *Moby Dick* and in *The Roots of Heaven*. This lesser talent that he could live on was a corollary to his great talent. It was a demonstration of his love of (and prowess in) traditional theatre—like the way Vittorio De Sica (also an actor from adolescence) could go from being the romantic singing star of Italian musical comedy to make *Shoeshine* and then back again (he, too, to raise money for his own films) to playing in an ornate style, Gina's lawyer or Sophia's papa, a whole Barzini gallery of glory-ridden, mustachioed Italians. But Welles was beginning to turn into America's favorite grotesque. Like Barrymore and Laughton and Brando, he seemed to be developing an obsession with false noses, false faces. He had once, at least, played a role in his own face, Harry Lime in *The Third Man;* by the sixties he was encased in makeup and his own fat—like a huge operatic version of W. C. Fields. Audiences laughed when he appeared on the screen. He didn't need to choose the role of Falstaff: it chose him.

■ ■ ■

When Welles went to Europe, he lost his single greatest asset as a movie director: his sound. (He had already lost the company that *talked* together, the Mercury players he had brought to Hollywood—Joseph Cotten, Agnes Moorehead, Everett Sloane, et al.—who were now working separately.) Welles had first skyrocketed to public attention on radio, and what he had brought to movies that was distinctively new was the radio sound—with an innovative use of overlapping dialogue—which was used for trick shock purposes, almost playfully, in *Citizen Kane.* But by the time of *The Magnificent Ambersons* he was using this technique for something deeper (the family bickering was startling in its almost surreal accuracy; the sound was of arguments overheard from childhood, with so many overtones they were almost mythic). Welles himself had a voice that seemed to carry its own echo chamber; somehow, in becoming the whiz kid of vocal effects, in simulating so many deep, impersonal voices, he had emptied his own voice of emotion, and when he spoke his credit at the end of *The Ambersons,* audiences laughed at the hollow voice (and perhaps at the comic justice of the *spoken* credit). Ironically, sound—the area of his greatest mastery—became his worst problem as he began to work with actors who didn't speak English and actors who did but weren't around when he needed them (for the post-synchronization which is standard practice in Europe, because the actors don't speak the same language, and is becoming standard here, too, because it saves shooting time). Welles compensated by developing greater visual virtuosity.

Yeats said "Rhetoric is heard, poetry overheard," and though I don't agree, I think I see what he means, and I think this assumption is involved in much of the rejection of a talent like Welles's. His work is often referred to as flashy and spectacular as if this also meant cheap and counterfeit. Welles is unabashedly theatrical in a period when much of the educated audience thinks theatrical flair vulgar, artistry intellectually respectable only when subtle, hidden. Welles has the approach of a *popular* artist: he glories in both verbal and visual rhetoric. He uses film *theatrically*—not stagily, but with theatrical bravado. He makes a show of the mechanics of film. He doesn't, if I may be forgiven the pun, hide his tracks. Movies gave him the world for a stage, and his is not the art that conceals art, but the showman's delight in the flourishes with which he pulls the rabbit from the hat. (This is why he was the wrong director for *The Trial,* where the poetry needed to be overheard.) I think that many people who enjoy those flourishes, who really love them—as I do—are so fearfully educated that they feel they must put them down. It's as if people said he's a mountebank, an actor showing off. But there's life in that kind of display: it's part of an earlier theatrical tradition that Welles carries over into film, it's what the theatre has lost, and it's what brought people to the movies.

Welles might have done for American talkies what D. W. Griffith did for the silent film. But when he lost his sound and his original, verbal wit, he seemed to lose his brashness, his youth, and some of his vitality. And he lost his American-ness; in Europe he had to learn a different, more exclusively visual language of film. An *enfant terrible* defeated ages fast. At fifty-one, Welles seems already the grand old master of film, because, of course, everybody knows that he'll never get in the position to do what he might have done. Governments and foundations will prattle on about excellence and American film companies will rush to sign up Englishmen and Europeans who have had a hit, hoping to snare that magic moneymaking gift. And tired transplanted Europeans will go on making big, lousy American movies, getting financed because they once had a hit and maybe the magic will come back. And Welles—the one great creative force in American films in our time, the man who might have redeemed our movies from the general contempt in which they are (and for the most part, rightly) held—is, ironically, an expatriate director whose work thus reaches only the art-house audience. And he has been so crippled by the problems of working as he does, he's lucky to reach that. The distributors of *Falstaff* tested it out of town before risking Bosley Crowther's displeasure in New York.

■ ■ ■

You may want to walk out during the first twenty minutes of *Falstaff.* Although the words on the soundtrack are intelligible, the sound doesn't match the images. We hear the voices as if the speakers were close, but on the screen the figures may be a half mile away or turned from us at some angle that doesn't jibe with the voice. In the middle of a sentence an actor may walk away from us while the voice goes on. Often, for a second, we can't be sure who is supposed to be talking. And the cutting is maddening, designed as it is for camouflage—to keep us from seeing faces closely or from registering that mouths which should be open and moving are closed. Long shots and Shakespearean dialogue are a crazy mix. It's especially jarring because the casting is superb and the performance beautiful. It's not hard to take Shakespeare adapted and transformed by other cultures—like Kurosawa's *Throne of Blood,* a *Macbeth* almost as much related to Welles's as to Shakespeare's—but the words of Shakespeare slightly out of synch! This is as intolerable as those old prints of *Henry V* that the miserly distributors circulate—chewed up by generations of projection machines, crucial syllables lost in the splices. The editing rhythm of *Falstaff* is at war with the rhythm and comprehension of the language. Welles, avoiding the naturalis-tic use of the outdoors in which Shakespeare's dialogue sounds more stagey than on stage, has photographically stylized the Spanish locations, creating a theatrically darkened, slightly unrealistic world of angles and low beams and silhouettes. When this photographic style is shattered by the cuts neces-sary to conceal the dialogue problems, the camera angles seem unnecessar-ily exaggerated and pretentious. But then despite everything—the angles, the doubles in long shots, the editing that distracts us when we need to con-centrate on the dialogue—the movie begins to be great. The readings in *Fal-staff* are great even if they don't always go with the images, which are often great, too.

Welles has brought together the pieces of Falstaff that Shakespeare had strewn over the two parts of *Henry IV* and *The Merry Wives of Windsor,* with cuttings from *Henry V* and *Richard II,* and fastened them into place with nar-ration from Holinshed's Chronicles (read by Ralph Richardson). Those of us who resisted our schoolteachers' best efforts to make us appreciate the comic genius of Shakespeare's fools and buffoons will not be surprised that Welles wasn't able to make Falstaff very funny: he's a great conception of a character, but the charades and practical jokes seem meant to be funnier than they are. This movie does, however, provide the best Shakespearean comic moment I can recall: garrulous Falstaff sitting with Shallow (Alan Webb) and Silence (Walter Chiari), rolling his eyes in irritation and impa-tience at Silence's stammer. But Welles's Falstaff isn't essentially comic; W. C. Fields's Micawber wasn't either: these actors, so funny when they're playing with their own personae in roles too small for them, are not so funny when they're trying to measure up. The carousing and roistering in the tavern doesn't seem like such great fun either, though Welles and the cast work very hard to convince us it is. Oddly, we never really see the friendship of Prince Hal—played extraordinarily well by Keith Baxter—and Falstaff; the lighter side in *Henry IV, Part I* is lost—probably well lost, though we must take it for granted in the film. What we see are the premonitions of the end: Hal taking part in games that have gone stale for him, preparing himself for his final rejection of his adopted father Falstaff in order to turn into a worthy successor of his father the king. And we see what this does to Falstaff, the braggart with the heart of a child who expects to be forgiven ev-erything, even what he knows to be unforgivable—his taking the credit away from Hal for the combat with Hotspur (Norman Rodway). Falstaff lacks judgment, which kings must have.

John Gielgud's Henry IV is the perfect contrast to Welles; Gielgud has never been so monkishly perfect in a movie. Welles could only get him for two weeks of the shooting and the makeshift of some of his scenes is obvi-ous, but his performance gives the film the austerity it needs for the conflict in Hal to be dramatized. Gielgud's king is so refined—a skeleton too digni-fied for any flesh to cling to it, inhabited by a voice so modulated it is an exquisite spiritual whine. Merrie England? Falstaff at least provides a carcass to mourn over.

Welles as an actor had always been betrayed by his voice. It was too much and it was inexpressive; there was no warmth in it, no sense of a life lived. It was just an instrument that he played, and it seemed to be the key to something shallow and unfelt even in his best performances, and most fraudulent when he tried to make it tender. I remember that once, in *King Lear* on television, he hit a phrase and I thought his voice was emotionally right; it had beauty—and what a change it made in his acting! In *Falstaff* Welles seems to have grown into his voice; he's not too young for it anymore, and he's certainly big enough. And his emotions don't seem fake anymore; he's grown into them, too. He has the eyes for the role. Though his Falstaff is short on comedy, it's very rich, very full.

He has directed a sequence, the battle of Shrewsbury, which is unlike anything he has ever done, indeed unlike any battle ever done on the screen before. It ranks with the best of Griffith, John Ford, Eisenstein, Kurosawa—that is, with the best ever done. How can one sequence in this movie be so good? It has no dialogue and so he isn't handicapped: for the only time in the movie he can edit, not to cover gaps and defects but as an artist. The compositions suggest Uccello and the chilling ironic music is a death knell for all men in battle. The soldiers, plastered by the mud they fall in, are already monuments. It's the most brutally somber battle ever filmed. It does justice to Hotspur's great "O, Harry, thou hast robbed me of my youth."

Welles has filled the cast with box-office stars. Margaret Rutherford, Jeanne Moreau, Marina Vlady are all in it (though the girl I like best was little Beatrice Welles as the pageboy). And Falstaff is the most popular crowd-pleasing character in the work of the most enduringly popular writer who ever lived. Yet, because of technical defects due to poverty, Welles's finest Shakespearean production to date—another near-masterpiece, and this time so very close—cannot reach a large public. There ain't no way.

The New Republic, June 24, 1967

EL DORADO, THE WAR WAGON, THE WAY WEST

Recently a young film enthusiast from abroad said, "Someday I'm going to cause a revolution in American movies. I'm going to make a Western that's fair to the Indians." I groaned, because just about every writer and director and star about to make a big Western has explained it that way. And just about every Western one can think of has tried to be "fair" in the sense that the Indians were represented as noble and decent people who were pushed to violence by betrayal—by broken treaties that deprived them of land and food, or, in the usual melodrama, by the treachery of "renegade" whites who sold them guns and whiskey or cheated and manipulated them. In the plot structure, the Indians are almost always the victims, the white men the villains.

Yet that is not how audiences, abroad or here, experience the genre; and each new group of film-makers that sets out to right the movie wrongs done to the Indians probably thinks that they're going to correct a grave injustice—"cause a revolution"—as they make the Western that audiences will experience in the same old way. The mechanism is so simple: King Kong is a lovable creature who, chained and goaded beyond endurance, breaks out into a rampage of indiscriminate destruction; the people in the audience, who are like the people being slaughtered in the movie (Kong even starts his rampage on the theatre audience gathered to look at him), are terrified by the big murderous ape. The fact that they felt sympathy for him only a few minutes before adds to the drama, but does not make them fear him the less. The same mechanism was at work with Karloff as the monster in the original *Frankenstein*—yet producers announce that they're going to make a new kind of monster movie in which the monster will be sympathetic. These moviemakers, too, talking about earlier movies, think only of their fear of the monster; they forget the sympathy built up for him early in the pictures. Yet when they talk about the movies they are going to make, they emphasize the sympathy they are going to build up as if they did not know that this was necessary dramatic preparation for the fear and carnage to follow, which is what dominates their own memories and will dominate memories of their films, too.

As a child, I saw the 1932 movie *Freaks,* in which the circus sideshow attractions—the dwarfs, pinheads, idiots, and maimed creatures—fall upon the beautiful trapeze artist, mutilate her and make her one of themselves; and the sight of any deformity used to bring the movie back to me in nightmares. A few years ago I saw the movie again and was amazed to discover that the freaks were meant to be sympathetic and the trapeze artist was a bitch. But I don't think that the director, Tod Browning, who also directed some of the best of the Lon Chaney pictures—and his horribly maimed phantoms and hunchbacks were also meant-to-be-sympathetic—can have been so naïve. When tiny, deformed creatures are swarming all over the screen on a mission of mutilation, surely the intention is to terrify us. They are good people who have been mistreated and driven to take direct action only in the preparatory dramatic stages, until they are needed for the climactic fearful images.

In the Western, once we are in danger—huddled in the wagon train with the stars and young lovers and old comics, the arrows coming at us, piercing flesh and starting fires that are burning us alive—the Indians circling us are no longer noble victims. Painted, half-naked men who do not speak our language, who do not know that we mean them no harm, might as well be another species. And decent liberal movie-makers will go on congratulating themselves on their sympathetic treatment of the Indians; and new movie-makers will arrive to show us how to do it all over again.

■   ■   ■

In some Westerns, cruel and mercenary white men torture and kill Indians—as in *Nevada Smith*, where the hero, Steve McQueen, is half Indian. White men raised as Indians *(Hombre)*, white men who have married Indians *(Duel at Diablo, The Way West)*, and half-Indian heroes may become almost as popular in our Westerns as the half-Jewish heroes of recent American novels, and for the same reason: the authors hope for extra perspective by playing it both ways. (Traditionally, second- and third-generation Jews acted cowboys, first-generation Jews acted Indians; now half-Jews can be half-Indians.) Split in his loyalties, the half-and-half hero can observe the cruelties and misunderstandings of both sides; he's a double loner—an ideally alienated, masochistic modern hero (like Paul Newman in *Hombre*). Typically, his sympathies are with the Indians, though he generally comes through and acts for the whites. In this, the Western has not changed.

But the mechanism of the movie and how we react to it is very different when it is white men torturing Indians. When the murderers are white men, the movie-makers don't feel the guilty necessity to make them sympathetic or to explain them at all; they are simply moral monsters, as in *Nevada Smith*, where the young hero's Indian mother is mutilated—skinned alive—by white degenerates. (This episode is not staged to pleasure the audience or for wanton excitement but rather to make the audience understand the boy's helpless rage. It is violence used to make us hate violence.) And yet their images don't carry the kind of fear that the most meant-to-be-sympathetic Indians do when they turn warlike. We hate the act, but we don't fear the men in the same way. If Hollywood made a movie in which we as audience were involved in the lives of an Indian village which was then attacked by villainous white men, I doubt if we would feel the terror we do when we are attacked by Indians. In general, Wilhelm Reich was probably right when he said that "a horror story has the same effect whether it deals with Ali Baba and the Forty Thieves or with the execution of white spies. The important thing to the reader is the gooseflesh and not whether it is forty thieves or forty counter-revolutionaries who get decapitated." But suppose it is forty frightening men from some strange tribe whose language and customs we don't understand, or forty Dead End Kids. One raises more gooseflesh than the other. It involves primitive fears—of what we don't know.

■   ■   ■

There is a fairly widespread assumption that no matter how bad American movies in general are, the Westerns are still great. The people who take this for granted probably don't go to them, but they have an idea that Westerns are authentic movie-making—the *real* movies—and are somehow pure (as

Western heroes used to be), exempt from the general corruption. They assume that the Westerns are still there, as pristine and "great" as ever for their kids, as if the air of the wide open spaces would have kept the genre clean.

I don't believe that there ever were the great works in this genre that so many people claim for it. There were some good Westerns, of course, and there was a beautiful kind of purity in some of them, and later even the ritual plots and dull action were, at least, set outdoors, and the horses were often good to look at. But all that was a long time ago. The last good Western that had this ritual purity was Sam Peckinpah's *Ride the High Country,* which came out in 1962. (I am not forgetting David Miller's *Lonely Are the Brave,* which came out at the same time: despite the ingenious and entertaining performance by Walter Matthau and the excellent performance by Kirk Douglas, the Dalton Trumbo script gives the film that awful messagey self-righteousness of *High Noon* and *The Gunfighter* and a fake ironic tragedy, an O. Henry finish—the "last" cowboy is run down by a truck loaded with toilets.) Kids may read the same novel by Robert Louis Stevenson that their parents did, but in movies parents think in terms of the old *Stagecoach* and the kids are going to the new *Stagecoach.* Probably in no art except movies can new practitioners legally eliminate competition from the past. A full-page notice in *Variety* gave warning that Twentieth Century-Fox, which released the 1966 *Stagecoach,* featuring Bing Crosby and Ann-Margret, would "vigorously" prosecute the exhibition of the 1939 original—John Ford's classic Western, one of the most highly regarded and influential movies ever made.

Surely the public should have the right to see the old as well as the new? And not just for its own sake but because that is how we learn about an art. How else do we develop a critical sense about new novels, new paintings, new music, new poetry? If the old is legally retired, we become barbarians (movie barbarians, at least) without a past. The producer of the new version, Martin Rackin, said, "In the process of updating, we can improve on the old films by learning from their mistakes." With equal cynicism, one may reply, "Then why do you remove the old films so that new generations cannot appreciate how much you've improved on them?"

Just about every good Western made since 1939 has imitated *Stagecoach* or has learned something from it. Ironically, the 1966 version merely took the plot and the character stereotypes; and without the simple, clear, epic vision with which John Ford informed them, they are just standard Western equipment. The original *Stagecoach* had a mixture of reverie and reverence about the American past that made the picture seem almost folk art; we *wanted* to believe in it even if we didn't. That is what *Ride the High Country* had, too.

The 1966 *Stagecoach* was undistinguished—a big, brawling action picture that gets audience reactions by brutal fights and narrow escapes photographed right on top of you. The director, Gordon Douglas, doesn't trust you to project yourself imaginatively into his stagecoach; he tries to force you into it—which may make you want to escape to the farthest row in the balcony. Kurosawa (who acknowledges his debt to John Ford) can plunge you into action to make you experience the meaning of action. When the Gordon Douglas crew does it, all it means is they don't want you to get bored. And probably the most that can be said about their movie is that it isn't boring—but then, that could be said of most visits to the dentist.

No one mistakes the 1966 *Stagecoach* for folk art. And though Rackin and company cast Ann-Margret as the prostitute-with-a-heart-of-gold, nobody misunderstands, because Ann-Margret comes through dirty no matter what she plays. She does most of her acting inside her mouth. Julie Andrews could play a promiscuous girl in *The Americanization of Emily* and shine with virtue; Ann-Margret gleams with built-in innuendo. She's like Natalie Wood with sex, a lewd mechanical doll. Men seem to have direct-action responses to Ann-Margret: they want to give her what she seems to be asking for. (A new variation on "star quality"?) This may represent a new polarization of screen types—the good Julie Andrews, the bad Ann-Margret. They're both willing, but for one it's "natural," for the other it's "dirty." Or, as they used to say, it ain't what you do but the way that you do it.

■   ■   ■

John Ford himself doesn't bother going outdoors much anymore. A few years back I dragged a painter-friend to see *The Man Who Shot Liberty Valance;* it was a John Ford Western, and though I dreaded an evening with James Stewart and John Wayne, I felt I *should* see it. My friend agreed because "the landscapes are always great"; but after about ten minutes of ugly studio sets, he wanted to leave. By the time Edmond O'Brien, as a drunken newspaper editor, was getting beaten up in the offices of the *Star,* which we saw from inside the glass, my friend was fed up: "Star is rats spelled backward; let's get the hell out of here." What those who believe in the perennial greatness of the Western may not have caught on to is that the new big Western is, likely as not, a studio-set job. What makes it a "Western" is no longer the wide open spaces but the presence of men like John Wayne, James Stewart, Henry Fonda, Robert Mitchum, Kirk Douglas, and Burt Lancaster, grinning with their big new choppers, sucking their guts up into their chests, and hauling themselves onto horses. They are the heroes of a new Western mythology: stars who have aged in the business, who have survived and who go on dragging their world-famous, expensive carcasses through the same old motions. That is the essence of their heroism and their legend. The new Western is a joke and the stars play it for laughs, and the young film enthusiasts react to the heroes not because they represent the mythological heroes of the Old West but because they are mythological movie stars. An actor in his forties would be a mere stripling in a Western these days. Nor would he *belong* in these movies which derive their small, broad humor from the fact that the actors have been doing what they're doing so long that they're pro-

fessional Westerners. Like Queen Victoria, John Wayne has become lovable
because he's stayed in the saddle into a new era.

The world has changed since audiences first responded to John Wayne
as a simple cowboy thirty-seven years ago; now, when he does the same
things and represents the same simple values, he's so archaic it's funny. We
used to be frightened of a reactionary becoming "a man on horseback";
now that seems the best place for him.

■　　■　　■

My father went to a Western just about every night of his life that I remember. He didn't care if it was a good one or a bad one or if he'd seen it before. He said it didn't matter. I have just seen three new Westerns—*The Way
West, The War Wagon,* and *El Dorado*—and I think I understand what my father meant. If you're going for *a* Western (the same way you'd sit down to
watch *a* television show), it doesn't much matter which one you see. And if
you're going for something else, even the best one of these three isn't good
enough. The differences between them aren't, finally, very significant—
which is what the mass audience probably understands better than film enthusiasts.

The Way West is about as bad an epic Western as I've ever seen. Students
in college film departments sometimes say they can learn more from bad
movies than from good ones, because they can examine what the director
did wrong: to them *The Way West* should serve as a textbook. Everything essential to explain what's going on seems missing. It's a jerk's idea of an epic:
big stars, big landscapes, bad jokes, folksy-heroic music by Bronislau Kaper
to plug up the holes, and messy hang-ups. In the neurotic-Western mode,
the leader of this 1843 caravan of pioneers, Kirk Douglas, goes in for self-
flagellation. (He arranges for his Negro servant to whip him; the darkies
have the best rhythm?) Richard Widmark's desire to go West seems to be
some sort of compulsive behavior; and Robert Mitchum—the scout!—must
be cozened out of irrational mourning for his Indian wife. And to make
sure that 1967 audiences won't find this pioneering too old-fashioned, the
villainess is a frightened virgin and the heroine is a teen-ager so grotesquely
avid for sex that at one point her lusty parents tease that if she doesn't get
a husband pretty soon they'll have to mate her with an ox—a line which gets
a big laugh. (Maybe it should, because oxen don't mate.) Crude as this
movie is, audiences seem to enjoy it; it has that stage-Irish comic sentimentality that used to destroy one's pleasure in many of the John Ford epics and
was possibly responsible for their box-office success. *The Way West* was
directed by Andrew V. McLaglen, a chip off the old block.

Burt Kennedy's *The War Wagon* is classy Western camp with John Wayne,
and Kirk Douglas in a black leather shirt, wearing a ring on his black glove.
There are pretty little visual divertissements out of von Sternberg's *Shanghai
Gesture* and Buñuel's *L'Age d'Or* and Cocteau's *Orpheus,* and hard-edge cinematography (by William H. Clothier, who also did the more conventional
shooting of *The Way West*) that makes the actors look like pop cutouts. The

delicate decorator colors include fancy salmon pinks; and there's real bougainvillea growing in the sets. There's even a camp version of backlash when the Indians tell John Wayne that they're not asking him to dinner because having a white man at table offends them. Howard Keel turns up playing an Indian named Levi Walking Bear, and old Bruce Cabot (who saved Fay Wray from King Kong) turns up looking like Maurice Chevalier. And *The War Wagon* has an opening song by Dimitri Tiomkin to tell us it's going to be tough and hardheaded—"All men are fightin' for a wagon full of gold. . . ." In Hollywood that's realistic philosophy.

What does all the chic amount to and who is it for? It's a kind of sophisticated exhibitionism. I received a publicity release from the company that represents *The War Wagon* that puts the movie in more accurate perspective. It's entitled "Suggestions for a Feature" and it reads:

> John Wayne's Western movies are always made in color. In two colors, to be exact: greenback green and glittering gold.
>
> Not a single one of more than 200 films of the great-outdoorsy genre he's made since 1929 has ever lost money. It's a fact of Hollywood life that John Wayne Westerns always show a profit.
>
> For let's face it: John Wayne *is* the Western movie today. Westerns are a folk phenomenon, the one kind of film which has never really fallen from favor, even temporarily. The cinematic years since *The Great Train Robbery* have seen thousands of Western movies, and hundreds of Western heroes. There are scores of them fully and gainfully occupied right this minute, both on theatre and TV screens.
>
> But among them all, there's only one John Wayne. He looms above the others the way the heroes' heads on Mount Rushmore dominate the surrounding pebbles. He may be a homely, middle-aged, battered, unpretentious, non-Actors Studio guy, but he is *the* Western star. And he is undoubtedly going to remain *the* Western star until he's so old he falls off his horse—which will likely be never.
>
> Big John's next big one, *The War Wagon,* is likely to be an especially lucrative lollapalooza. It has the kind of rugged, roisterous script which is the perfect setting for this human diamond-in-the-rough. . . .
>
> We suggest a story on those three phenomenal W's: Westerns, Wayne and *War Wagon.*
>
> It could turn out to be WWWonderful.

That drool contains the awful germy truth: Westerns are money in the bank. When the big studios were breaking up in the fifties and the big box-office stars were forming their own production companies, the Westerns were the safest investment. The studios tried to get whatever money was left in big-name contract stars like Clark Gable and Robert Taylor; and other stars, like Wayne and Douglas and Lancaster, going into business on their own, wanted to protect their investments. That's how the modern Western with the big old stars took over the genre. Others who went into the "safe" genre in the fifties, like Gregory Peck and Frank Sinatra, dropped out (not, I am afraid, from disgust but from financial failure); but Douglas and Lancaster persisted and were joined later by Robert Mitchum. Soon, because they were so well known anyway and people don't know much about film history, they could pass for real old-time Western heroes, like Wayne.

The structure of this Western-movie business is becoming as feudalistic as the movies themselves: Kirk Douglas has a production company named for his mother (Bryna), another for his son (Joel), yet another for himself and a partner (Douglas-Lewis), etc.; *The War Wagon* is produced by John Wayne's company, Batjac. These corporate-head Westerners appear in each other's films; there are jobs for their sons and their old buddies and the sons of their old buddies. The next big Batjac production is *The Green Berets,* which Wayne himself will direct and one of his sons will produce.

And so we have Kirk Douglas exposing his fat overmuscled chest in *The War Wagon* and doing a series of parodied leaps onto a horse. And for all the aestheticism of dust and hooves and flowers, after a while it might just as well be *The Way West:* when it's the tired comic spectacle of rich old men degrading themselves for more money and fame and power, does it much matter if it's done poorly or with chic? In some ways the chic is more offensive.

The classic Western theme is the doomed hero—the man without a future because the way of life is changing, the frontier is vanishing, and the sheriff and the schoolteacher are representatives of progress and a new order. The hero is the living antique who represents the best of the old order just as it is disappearing. But star-centered movies and TV gave the Westerner a new future: he's got to keep going to keep the series alive. The toilets won't run him down because that would be flushing away good money. Douglas in *The War Wagon* has metamorphosed back into his post–World War II character—the heel. He's now the too smart Westerner, mercenary and untrustworthy in a way the audience is supposed to like. His Westerner is a swinger—a wisecracking fancy talker with intentionally anachronistic modern attitudes.

El Dorado combines Wayne and Mitchum, both looking exhausted. The director, Howard Hawks, is also tired, and like Ford, he doesn't want to go out on location. The theory of why Westerns are such a great form is that directors can show what they can really do in the framework of a ritualized genre and the beauty of the West. But the directors are old and rich, too. (Ford was born in 1895 and directed his first movie in 1917; Hawks was born in 1896 and has been in films since 1918, directing them since the mid-twenties.) Their recent movies look as if they were made for television. Except for a few opening shots, *El Dorado* is a studio job—and it has the second-worst lighting of any movie in recent years (the worst: *A Countess from Hong Kong*). When the movie starts, you have the sense of having come in on a late episode of a TV serial. Mitchum plays a drunken old sheriff (like Charles Winninger in *Destry Rides Again*), and there are home remedies for alcoholism, vomiting scenes that are supposed to be hilarious, and one of those girls who hide their curls under cowboy hats and are mistaken for boys until the heroes start to wrestle with them. Wayne has a beautiful horse in this one—but when he's hoisted onto it and you hear the thud, you don't know whether to feel sorrier for man or beast.

The Old West was a dream landscape with simple masculine values; the code of the old Western heroes probably wouldn't have much to say to audiences today. But the old stars, battling through stories that have lost their ritual meaning, are part of a new ritual that does have meaning. There's nothing dreamy about it: these men have made themselves movie stars—which impresses audiences all over the world. The fact that they can draw audiences to a genre as empty as the contemporary Western is proof of their power. Writers and painters now act out their fantasies by becoming the superstars of their own movies (and of the mass media); Wayne and Douglas and Mitchum and the rest of them do it on a bigger scale. When it makes money, it's not just their fantasy. The heroes nobody believes in—except as movie stars—are the result of a corrupted art form. Going to a Western these days for simplicity or heroism or grandeur or meaning is about like trying to mate with an ox.

The New Republic, August 5, 1967

BONNIE AND CLYDE

How do you make a good movie in this country without being jumped on? *Bonnie and Clyde* is the most excitingly American American movie since *The Manchurian Candidate*. The audience is alive to it. Our experience as we watch it has some connection with the way we reacted to movies in childhood: with how we came to love them and to feel they were ours—not an art that we learned over the years to appreciate but simply and immediately ours. When an American movie is contemporary in feeling, like this one, it makes a different kind of contact with an American audience from the kind that is made by European films, however contemporary. Yet any movie that is contemporary in feeling is likely to go further than other movies—go too far for some tastes—and *Bonnie and Clyde* divides audiences, as *The Manchurian Candidate* did, and it is being jumped on almost as hard. Though we may dismiss the attacks with "What good movie doesn't give some offense?," the fact that it is generally *only* good movies that provoke attacks by many people suggests that the innocuousness of most of our movies is accepted with such complacence that when an American movie reaches people, when it makes them react, some of them think there must be something the matter with it—perhaps a law should be passed against it. *Bonnie and Clyde* brings into the almost frighteningly public world of movies things that people have been feeling and saying and writing about. And once something is said or done on the screens of the world, once it has entered mass art, it can never again belong to a minority, never again be the private possession of an educated, or "knowing," group. But even for that group there is an excitement in hearing its own private thoughts expressed out loud and in seeing something of its own sensibility become part of our common culture.

Our best movies have always made entertainment out of the anti-heroism of American life; they bring to the surface what, in its newest forms and fashions, is always just below the surface. The romanticism in American movies lies in the cynical tough guy's independence; the sentimentality lies, traditionally, in the falsified finish when the anti-hero turns hero. In 1967, this kind of sentimentality wouldn't work with the audience, and *Bonnie and Clyde* substitutes sexual fulfillment for a change of heart. (This doesn't quite work, either; audiences sophisticated enough to enjoy a movie like this one are too sophisticated for the dramatic uplift of the triumph over impotence.)

Structurally, *Bonnie and Clyde* is a story of love on the run, like the old Clark Gable–Claudette Colbert *It Happened One Night* but turned inside out; the walls of Jericho are psychological this time, but they fall anyway. If the story of Bonnie Parker and Clyde Barrow seemed almost from the start, and even to them while they were living it, to be the material of legend, it's because robbers who are loyal to each other—like the James brothers—are a grade up from garden-variety robbers, and if they're male and female partners in crime and young and attractive they're a rare breed. The Barrow gang had both family loyalty and sex appeal working for their legend. David Newman and Robert Benton, who wrote the script for *Bonnie and Clyde,* were able to use the knowledge that, like many of our other famous outlaws and gangsters, the real Bonnie and Clyde seemed to others to be acting out forbidden roles and to relish their roles. In contrast with secret criminals—the furtive embezzlers and other crooks who lead seemingly honest lives—the known outlaws capture the public imagination, because they take chances, and because, often, they enjoy dramatizing their lives. They know that newspaper readers want all the details they can get about the criminals who do the terrible things they themselves don't dare to do, and also want the satisfaction of reading about the punishment after feasting on the crimes. Outlaws play to this public; they show off their big guns and fancy clothes and their defiance of the law. Bonnie and Clyde established the images for their own legend in the photographs they posed for: the gunman and the gun moll. The naïve, touching doggerel ballad that Bonnie Parker wrote and had published in newspapers is about the roles they play for other people contrasted with the coming end for them. It concludes:

> Someday they'll go down together;
> They'll bury them side by side;
> To few it'll be grief—
> To the law a relief—
> But it's death for Bonnie and Clyde.

That they did capture the public imagination is evidenced by the many movies based on their lives. In the late forties, there were *They Live by Night,* with Farley Granger and Cathy O'Donnell, and *Gun Crazy,* with John Dall and Peggy Cummins. (Alfred Hitchcock, in the same period, cast these two Clyde Barrows, Dall and Granger, as Loeb and Leopold, in *Rope.*) And there was a cheap—in every sense—1958 exploitation film, *The Bonnie Parker Story,* starring Dorothy Provine. But the most important earlier version was Fritz Lang's *You Only Live Once,* starring Sylvia Sidney as "Joan" and Henry Fonda as "Eddie," which was made in 1937; this version, which was one of the best American films of the thirties, as *Bonnie and Clyde* is of the sixties, expressed certain feelings of its time, as this film expresses certain feelings of ours. (*They Live by Night,* produced by John Houseman under the aegis of Dore Schary, and directed by Nicholas Ray, was a very serious and socially significant tragic melodrama, but its attitudes were already dated thirties attitudes: the lovers were very young and pure and frightened and underprivileged; the hardened criminals were sordid; the settings were committedly grim. It made no impact on the postwar audience, though it was a great success in England, where our moldy socially significant movies could pass for courageous.)

Just how contemporary in feeling *Bonnie and Clyde* is may be indicated by contrasting it with *You Only Live Once,* which, though almost totally false to the historical facts, was *told* straight. It is a peculiarity of our times—perhaps it's one of the few specifically modern characteristics—that we don't take our stories straight any more. This isn't necessarily bad. *Bonnie and Clyde* is the first film demonstration that the put-on can be used for the purposes of art. *The Manchurian Candidate almost* succeeded in that, but what was implicitly wild and far-out in the material was nevertheless presented on screen as a straight thriller. *Bonnie and Clyde* keeps the audience in a kind of eager, nervous imbalance—holds our attention by throwing our disbelief back in our faces. To be put on is to be put on the spot, put on the stage, made the stooge in a comedy act. People in the audience at *Bonnie and Clyde* are laughing, demonstrating that they're not stooges—that they appreciate the joke—when they catch the first bullet right in the face. The movie keeps them off balance to the end. During the first part of the picture, a woman in my row was gleefully assuring her companions, "It's a comedy. It's a comedy." After a while, she didn't say anything. Instead of the movie spoof, which tells the audience that it doesn't need to feel or care, that it's all just in fun, that "we were only kidding," *Bonnie and Clyde* disrupts us with "And you thought we were only kidding."

This is the way the story was told in 1937. Eddie (Clyde) is a three-time loser who wants to work for a living, but nobody will give him a chance. Once you get on the wrong side of the law, "they" won't let you get back. Eddie knows it's hopeless—once a loser, always a loser. But his girl, Joan (Bonnie)—the only person who believes in him—thinks that an innocent man has nothing to fear. She marries him, and learns better. Arrested again and sentenced to death for a crime he didn't commit, Eddie asks her to smuggle a gun to him in prison, and she protests, "If I get you a gun, you'll kill somebody." He stares at her sullenly and asks, "What do you think they're going to do to me?" He becomes a murderer while escaping from prison; "society" has made him what it thought he was all along. *You Only Live Once* was an indictment of "society," of the forces of order that will not give Eddie the outcast a chance. "We have a right to live," Joan says as they set out across the country. During the time they are on the run, they become notorious outlaws; they are blamed for a series of crimes they didn't commit. (They do commit holdups, but only to get gas or groceries or medicine.) While the press pictures them as desperadoes robbing and killing and living high on the proceeds of crime, she is having a baby in a shack in a hobo jungle, and Eddie brings her a bouquet of wild flowers. Caught in a police trap, they die in each other's arms; they have been denied the right to live.

Because *You Only Live Once* was so well done, and because the audience in the thirties shared this view of the indifference and cruelty of "society," there were no protests against the sympathetic way the outlaws were pictured—and, indeed, there was no reason for any. In 1958, in *I Want to Live!* (a very popular, though not very good, movie), Barbara Graham, a drug-addict prostitute who had been executed for her share in the bludgeoning to death of an elderly woman, was presented as gallant, wronged, morally superior to everybody else in the movie, in order to strengthen the argument against capital punishment, and the director, Robert Wise, and his associates weren't accused of glorifying criminals, because the "criminals," as in *You Only Live Once*, weren't criminals but innocent victims. Why the protests, why are so many people upset (and not just the people who enjoy indignation), about *Bonnie and Clyde*, in which the criminals *are* criminals—Clyde an ignorant, sly near psychopath who thinks his crimes are accomplishments, and Bonnie a bored, restless waitress-slut who robs for excitement? And why so many accusations of historical inaccuracy, particularly against a work that is far more accurate historically than most and in which historical accuracy hardly matters anyway? There is always an issue of historical accuracy involved in any dramatic or literary work set in the past; indeed, it's fun to read about Richard III vs. Shakespeare's Richard III. The issue is always with us, and will always be with us as long as artists find stimulus in historical figures and want to present their versions of them. But why didn't movie critics attack, for example, *A Man for All Seasons*—which involves material of much more historical importance—for being historically inaccurate? Why attack *Bonnie and Clyde* more than the other movies based on the same pair, or more than the movie treatments of Jesse James or Billy the Kid or Dillinger or Capone or any of our other fictionalized outlaws? I would suggest that when a movie so clearly conceived as a new version of a legend is attacked as historically inaccurate, it's because it shakes people a little. I know this is based on some pretty sneaky psychological suppositions, but I don't see how else to account for the use only against a *good* movie of arguments that could be used against almost all movies. When I asked a nineteen-year-old boy who was raging against the movie as "a cliché-ridden fraud" if he got so worked up about other movies, he informed me that that was an argument *ad hominem*. And it is indeed. To ask why people react so angrily to the best movies and have so little negative reaction to poor ones is to imply that they are so unused to the experience of art in movies that they fight it.

Audiences at *Bonnie and Clyde* are not given a simple, secure basis for identification; they are made to feel but are not told *how* to feel. *Bonnie and Clyde* is not a serious melodrama involving us in the plight of the innocent but a movie that assumes—as William Wellman did in 1931 when he made *The Public Enemy*, with James Cagney as a smart, cocky, mean little crook— that we don't need to pretend we're interested only in the falsely accused, as if real criminals had no connection with us. There wouldn't be the popular excitement there is about outlaws if we didn't all suspect that—in some cases, at least—gangsters must take pleasure in the profits and glory of a life of crime. Outlaws wouldn't become legendary figures if we didn't suspect that there's more to crime than the social workers' case studies may show. And though what we've always been told will happen to them—that they'll come to a bad end—does seem to happen, some part of us wants to believe in the tiny possibility that they can get away with it. Is that really so terrible? Yet when it comes to movies people get nervous about acknowledging that there must be some fun in crime (though the gleam in Cagney's eye told its own story). *Bonnie and Clyde* shows the fun but uses it, too, making comedy out of the banality and conventionality of that fun. What looks ludicrous in this movie isn't *merely* ludicrous, and after we have laughed at ignorance and helplessness and emptiness and stupidity and idiotic deviltry, the laughs keep sticking in our throats, because what's funny isn't only funny.

In 1937, the movie-makers knew that the audience wanted to believe in the innocence of Joan and Eddie, because these two were lovers, and innocent lovers hunted down like animals made a tragic love story. In 1967, the movie-makers know that the audience wants to believe—maybe even prefers to believe—that Bonnie and Clyde were guilty of crimes, all right, but that they were innocent in general; that is, naïve and ignorant *compared with us*. The distancing of the sixties version shows the gangsters in an already legendary period, and part of what makes a legend for Americans is viewing anything that happened in the past as much simpler than what we are involved in now. We tend to find the past funny and the recent past campy-funny. The getaway cars of the early thirties are made to seem hilarious. (Imagine anyone getting away from a bank holdup in a tin lizzie like that!) In *You Only Live Once*, the outlaws existed in the same present as the audience, and there was (and still is, I'm sure) nothing funny about them; in *Bonnie and Clyde* that audience is in the movie, transformed into the poor people, the Depression people, of legend—with faces and poses out of Dorothea Lange and Walker Evans and *Let Us Now Praise Famous Men*. In 1937, the audience felt sympathy for the fugitives because they weren't allowed to lead normal lives; in 1967, the "normality" of the Barrow gang and their individual aspirations toward respectability are the craziest things about them—not just because they're killers but because thirties "normality" is in itself funny to us. The writers and the director of *Bonnie and Clyde* play upon our attitudes toward the American past by making the hats and guns and holdups look as dated as two-reel comedy; emphasizing the absurdity with banjo music, they make the period seem even farther away than it is. The Depression reminiscences are not used for purposes of social consciousness; hard times are not the reason for the Barrows' crimes, just the excuse. "We" didn't make Clyde a killer; the movie deliberately avoids easy sympathy by picking up Clyde when he is already a cheap crook. But Clyde is not the urban sharpster of *The Public Enemy;* he is the hick as bank robber—a countrified gangster, a hillbilly killer who doesn't mean any harm. People so simple that they are alienated from the results of their actions—like the primitives who don't connect babies with copulation—provide a kind of archetypal comedy for us. It may seem like a minor point that Bonnie and Clyde are presented as not mean and sadistic, as having killed only when cornered; but in terms of legend, and particularly movie legend, it's a major one. The "classic" gangster films showed gang members betraying each other and viciously murdering the renegade who left to join another gang; the gang-leader hero no sooner got to the top than he was betrayed by someone he had trusted or someone he had double-crossed. In contrast, the Barrow gang represent family-style crime. And Newman and Benton have been acute in emphasizing this—not making them victims of society (they are never that, despite Penn's cloudy efforts along these lines) but making them absurdly "just-folks" ordinary. When Bonnie tells Clyde to pull off the road—"I want to talk to you"—they are in a getaway car, leaving the scene of a robbery, with the police right behind them, but they are absorbed in family bickering: the traditional all-American use of the family automobile. In a sense, it is the absence of sadism—it is the violence without sadism—that throws the audience off balance at *Bonnie and Clyde*. The brutality that comes out of this innocence is far more shocking than the calculated brutalities of mean killers.

Playfully posing with their guns, the real Bonnie and Clyde mocked the

"Bloody Barrows" of the Hearst press. One photograph shows slim, pretty Bonnie, smiling and impeccably dressed, pointing a huge gun at Clyde's chest as he, a dimpled dude with a cigar, smiles back. The famous picture of Bonnie in the same clothes but looking ugly squinting into the sun, with a foot on the car, a gun on her hip, and a cigar in her mouth, is obviously a joke—her caricature of herself as a gun moll. Probably, since they never meant to kill, they thought the "Bloody Barrows" were a joke—a creation of the lying newspapers.

There's something new working for the Bonnie-and-Clyde legend now: our nostalgia for the thirties—the unpredictable, contrary affection of the prosperous for poverty, or at least for the artifacts, the tokens, of poverty, for Pop culture seen in the dreariest rural settings, where it truly seems to belong. Did people in the cities listen to the Eddie Cantor show? No doubt they did, but the sound of his voice, like the sound of Ed Sullivan now, evokes a primordial, pre-urban existence—the childhood of the race. Our comic-melancholic affection for thirties Pop has become sixties Pop, and those who made *Bonnie and Clyde* are smart enough to use it that way. Being knowing is not an artist's highest gift, but it can make a hell of a lot of difference in a movie. In the American experience, the miseries of the Depression are funny in the way that the Army is funny to draftees—a shared catastrophe, a leveling, forming part of our common background. Those too young to remember the Depression have heard about it from their parents. (When I was at college, we used to top each other's stories about how our families had survived: the fathers who had committed suicide so that their wives and children could live off the insurance; the mothers trying to make a game out of the meals of potatoes cooked on an open fire.) Though the American derision of the past has many offensive aspects, it has some good ones, too, because it's a way of making fun not only of our forebears but of ourselves and our pretensions. The toughness about what we've come out of and what we've been through—the honesty to see ourselves as the Yahoo children of yokels—is a good part of American popular art. There is a kind of American poetry in a stickup gang seen chasing across the bedraggled backdrop of the Depression (as true in its way as Nabokov's vision of Humbert Humbert and Lolita in the cross-country world of motels)—as if crime were the only activity in a country stupefied by poverty. But Arthur Penn doesn't quite have the toughness of mind to know it; it's not what he means by poetry. His squatters'-jungle scene is too "eloquent," like a poster making an appeal, and the Parker-family-reunion sequence is poetic in the gauzy mode. He makes the sequence a fancy lyric interlude, like a number in a musical (*Funny Face*, to be exact); it's too "imaginative"—a literal dust bowl, as thoroughly becalmed as Sleeping Beauty's garden. The movie becomes dreamy-soft where it should be hard (and hard-edged).

If there is such a thing as an American tragedy, it must be funny. O'Neill undoubtedly felt this when he had James Tyrone get up to turn off the lights in *Long Day's Journey Into Night*. We are bumpkins, haunted by the bottle of ketchup on the dining table at San Simeon. We garble our foreign words and phrases and hope that at least we've used them right. Our heroes pick up the wrong fork, and the basic figure of fun in the American theatre and American movies is the man who puts on airs. Children of peddlers and hod carriers don't feel at home in tragedy; we are used to failure. But, because of the quality of American life at the present time, perhaps there can be no real comedy—nothing more than stupidity and "spoof"—without true horror in it. Bonnie and Clyde and their partners in crime are comically bad bank robbers, and the backdrop of poverty makes their holdups seem pathetically tacky, yet they rob banks and kill people; Clyde and his good-natured brother are so shallow they never think much about anything, yet they suffer and die.

If this way of holding more than one attitude toward life is already familiar to us—if we recognize the make-believe robbers whose toy guns produce real blood, and the Keystone cops who shoot them dead, from Truffaut's *Shoot the Piano Player* and Godard's gangster pictures, *Breathless* and *Band of Outsiders*—it's because the young French directors discovered the poetry of crime in American life (from our movies) and showed the Americans how to put it on the screen in a new, "existential" way. Melodramas and gangster movies and comedies were always more our speed than "prestigious," "distinguished" pictures; the French directors who grew up on American pictures found poetry in our fast action, laconic speech, plain gestures. And because they understood that you don't express your love of life by denying the comedy or the horror of it, they brought out the poetry in our tawdry subjects. Now Arthur Penn, working with a script heavily influenced—one might almost say inspired—by Truffaut's *Shoot the Piano Player*, unfortunately imitates Truffaut's artistry instead of going back to its tough American sources. The French may tenderize their American material, but we shouldn't. That turns into another way of making "prestigious," "distinguished" pictures.

■   ■   ■

Probably part of the discomfort that people feel about *Bonnie and Clyde* grows out of its compromises and its failures. I wish the script hadn't provided the upbeat of the hero's sexual success as a kind of sop to the audience. I think what makes us not believe in it is that it isn't consistent with the intelligence of the rest of the writing—that it isn't on the same level, because it's too manipulatively clever, too much of a gimmick. (The scene that shows the gnomish gang member called C.W. sleeping in the same room with Bonnie and Clyde suggests other possibilities, perhaps discarded, as does C.W.'s reference to Bonnie's liking his tattoo.) Compromises are not new to the Bonnie-and-Clyde story; *You Only Live Once* had a tacked-on coda featuring a Heavenly choir and William Gargan as a dead priest, patronizing Eddie even in the afterlife, welcoming him to Heaven with "You're free, Eddie!" The kind of people who make a movie like *You Only Live Once* are not the kind who write endings like that, and, by the same sort of internal evidence, I'd guess that Newman and Benton, whose Bonnie seems to owe so much to Catherine in *Jules and Jim,* had more interesting ideas originally about Bonnie's and Clyde's (and maybe C.W.'s) sex lives.

But people also feel uncomfortable about the violence, and here I think they're wrong. That is to say, they *should* feel uncomfortable, but this isn't an argument *against* the movie. Only a few years ago, a good director would have suggested the violence obliquely, with reaction shots (like the famous one in *The Golden Coach,* when we see a whole bullfight reflected in Anna Magnani's face), and death might have been symbolized by a light going out, or stylized, with blood and wounds kept to a minimum. In many ways, this method is more effective; we feel the violence more because so much is left to our imaginations. But the whole point of *Bonnie and Clyde* is to rub our noses in it, to make us pay our dues for laughing. The dirty reality of death—not suggestions but blood and holes—is necessary. Though I generally respect a director's skill and intelligence in inverse ratio to the violence he shows on the screen, and though I questioned even the Annie Sullivan–Helen Keller fight scenes in Arthur Penn's *The Miracle Worker,* I think that this time Penn is right. (I think he was also right when he showed violence in his first film, *The Left Handed Gun,* in 1958.) Suddenly, in the last few years, our view of the world has gone beyond "good taste." Tasteful suggestions of violence would at this point be a more grotesque form of comedy than *Bonnie and Clyde* attempts. *Bonnie and Clyde* needs violence; violence is its meaning. When, during a comically botched-up getaway, a man is shot in the face, the image is obviously based on one of the most famous sequences in Eisenstein's *Potemkin*—to convey in an instant how someone who just happens to be in the wrong place at the wrong time, the irrelevant "innocent" bystander, can get it full in the face. And at that instant the meaning of Clyde Barrow's character changes; he's still a clown, but *we've* become the butt of the joke.

It is a kind of violence that says something to us; it is something that movies must be free to use. And it is just because artists must be free to use violence—a legal right that is beginning to come under attack—that we must also defend the legal rights of those film-makers who use violence to sell tickets, for it is not the province of the law to decide that one man is an artist and another man a no-talent. The no-talent has as much right to produce works as the artist has, and not only because he has a surprising way of shifting from one category to the other but also because men have an inalienable right to be untalented, and the law should not discriminate against lousy "artists." I am not saying that the violence in *Bonnie and Clyde* is legally acceptable because the film is a work of art; I think that *Bonnie and Clyde,* though flawed, is a work of art, but I think that the violence in *The Dirty Dozen,* which isn't a work of art, and whose violence offends me *personally,* should also be legally defensible, however morally questionable. Too many people—including some movie reviewers—want the law to take over the job of movie criticism; perhaps what they really want is for their own criticisms to have the force of law. Such people see *Bonnie and Clyde* as a danger to public morality; they think an audience goes to a play or a movie and takes the actions in it as examples for imitation. They look at the world and blame the movies. But if women who are angry with their husbands take it out on the kids, I don't think we can blame *Medea* for it; if, as has been said, we are a nation of mother-lovers, I don't think we can place the blame on *Oedipus Rex*. Part of the power of art lies in showing us what we are *not* capable of. We see that killers are not a different breed but are *us* without the insight or understanding or self-control that works of art strengthen. The tragedy of *Macbeth* is in the fall from nobility to horror; the comic tragedy of *Bonnie and Clyde* is that although you can't fall from the bottom you can reach the same horror. The movies may set styles in dress- or love-making, they may advertise cars or beverages, but art is not examples for imitation— that is not what a work of art does for us—though that is what guardians of morality *think* art is and what they want it to be and why they think a good movie is one that sets "healthy," "cheerful" examples of behavior, like a giant all-purpose commercial for the American way of life. But people don't "buy" what they see in a movie quite so simply; Louis B. Mayer did not turn us into a nation of Andy Hardys, and if, in a film, we see a frightened man wantonly take the life of another, it does not encourage us to do the same, any more than seeing an ivory hunter shoot an elephant makes us want to shoot one. It may, on the contrary, so sensitize us that we get a pang in the gut if we accidentally step on a moth.

Will we, as some people have suggested, be lured into imitating the violent crimes of Clyde and Bonnie because Warren Beatty and Faye Dunaway are "glamorous"? Do they, as some people have charged, confer glamour on violence? It's difficult to see how, since the characters they play are horrified by it and ultimately destroyed by it. Nobody in the movie gets pleasure from violence. Is the charge based on the notion that simply by their presence in the movie Warren Beatty and Faye Dunaway make crime attractive? If movie stars can't play criminals without our all wanting to be criminals, then maybe the only safe roles for them to play are movie stars—which, in this assumption, everybody wants to be anyway. After all, if they played factory workers, the economy might be dislocated by everybody's trying to become a factory worker. (Would having criminals played by dwarfs or fatties discourage crime? It seems rather doubtful.) The accusation that the beauty of movie stars makes the anti-social acts of their characters dangerously attractive is the kind of contrived argument we get from people who are bothered by something and are clutching at straws. Actors and actresses are *usually* more beautiful than ordinary people. And why not? Garbo's beauty notwithstanding, her Anna Christie did not turn us into whores, her Mata Hari did not turn us into spies, her Anna Karenina did not make us suicides. We did not want her to be ordinary looking. Why should we be deprived of the pleasure of beauty? Garbo could be all women in love because, being more beautiful than life, she could more beautifully express emotions. It is a supreme asset for actors and actresses to be beautiful; it gives them greater range and greater possibilities for expressiveness. The handsomer they are, the more roles they can play; Olivier can be anything, but who would want to see Ralph Richardson, great as he is, play Antony? Actors and actresses who are beautiful start with an enormous advantage, because we love to look at them. The joke in the glamour charge is that Faye Dunaway has the magazine-illustration look of countless uninterestingly pretty girls, and Warren Beatty has the kind of high-school good looks that are generally lost fast. It's the roles that make *them* seem glamorous. Good roles do that for actors.

There is a story told against Beatty in a recent *Esquire*—how during the shooting of *Lilith* he "delayed a scene for three days demanding the line 'I've read *Crime and Punishment* and *The Brothers Karamazov*' be changed to 'I've read *Crime and Punishment* and *half* of *The Brothers Karamazov.*' " Considerations of professional conduct aside, what is odd is why his adversaries waited three days to give in, because, of course, he was right. That's what the character he played *should* say; the other way, the line has no point at all. But this kind of intuition isn't enough to make an actor, and in a number of roles Beatty, probably because he doesn't have the technique to make the most of his lines in the least possible time, has depended too much on intuitive non-acting—holding the screen far too long as he acted out self-preoccupied characters in a lifelike, boringly self-conscious way. He has a gift for slyness, though, as he showed in *The Roman Spring of Mrs. Stone,* and in most of his films he could hold the screen—maybe because there seemed to be something going on in his mind, some kind of calculation. There was something smart about him—something shrewdly private in juvenile roles. Beatty was the producer of *Bonnie and Clyde,* responsible for keeping the company on schedule, and he has been quoted as saying, "There's not a scene that we have done that we couldn't do better by taking another day." This is the hell of the expensive way of making movies, but it probably helps to explain why Beatty is more intense than he has been before and why he has picked up his pace. His business sense may have improved his timing. The role of Clyde Barrow seems to have released something in him. As Clyde, Beatty is good with his eyes and mouth and his hat, but his body is still inexpressive; he doesn't have a trained actor's use of his body, and, watching him move, one is never for a minute convinced he's impotent. It is, however, a tribute to his performance that one singles this failure out. His slow timing works perfectly in the sequence in which he offers the dispossessed farmer his gun; there may not be another actor who would have dared to prolong the scene that way, and the prolongation until the final "We rob banks" gives the sequence its comic force. I have suggested elsewhere that one of the reasons that rules are impossible in the arts is that in movies (and in the other arts, too) the new "genius"—the genuine as well as the fraudulent or the dubious—is often the man who has enough audacity, or is simpleminded enough, to do what others had the good taste not to do. Actors before Brando did not mumble and scratch and show their sweat;

dramatists before Tennessee Williams did not make explicit a particular sub-stratum of American erotic fantasy; movie directors before Orson Welles did not dramatize the techniques of film-making; directors before Richard Lester did not lay out the whole movie as cleverly as the opening credits; actresses before Marilyn Monroe did not make an asset of their ineptitude by turning faltering misreadings into an appealing style. Each, in a large way, did something that people had always enjoyed and were often embarrassed or ashamed about enjoying. Their "bad taste" shaped a new accepted taste. Beatty's non-actor's "bad" timing may be this kind of "genius"; we seem to be watching him *think out* his next move.

It's difficult to know how Bonnie should have been played, because the character isn't worked out. Here the script seems weak. She is made too warmly sympathetic—and sympathetic in a style that antedates the style of the movie. Being frustrated and moody, she's not funny enough—neither ordinary, which, in the circumstances, would be comic, nor perverse, which might be rather funny, too. Her attitude toward her mother is too loving. There could be something funny about her wanting to run home to her mama, but, as it has been done, her heading home, running off through the fields, is unconvincing—incompletely motivated. And because the element of the ridiculous that makes the others so individual has been left out of her character she doesn't seem to belong to the period as the others do. Faye Dunaway has a sixties look anyway—not just because her eyes are made up in a sixties way and her hair is wrong but because her personal style and her acting are sixties. (This may help to make her popular; she can seem prettier to those who don't recognize prettiness except in the latest styles.) Furthermore, in some difficult-to-define way, Faye Dunaway as Bonnie doesn't keep her distance—that is to say, an *actor's* distance—either from the role or from the audience. She doesn't hold a characterization; she's in and out of emotions all the time, and though she often hits effective ones, the emotions seem *hers*, not the character's. She has some talent, but she comes on too strong; she makes one conscious that she's a willing worker, but she doesn't seem to know what she's doing—rather like Bonnie in her attempts to overcome Clyde's sexual difficulties.

■　　■　　■

Although many daily movie reviewers judge a movie in isolation, as if the people who made it had no previous history, more serious critics now commonly attempt to judge a movie as an expressive vehicle of the director, and a working out of his personal themes. Auden has written, "Our judgment of an established author is never simply an aesthetic judgment. In addition to any literary merit it may have, a new book by him has a historic interest for us as the act of a person in whom we have long been interested. He is not only a poet . . . he is also a character in our biography." For a while, people went to the newest Bergman and the newest Fellini that way; these movies were greeted like the latest novels of a favorite author. But Arthur Penn is not a writer-director like Bergman or Fellini, both of whom began as writers, and who (even though Fellini employs several collaborators) compose their spiritual autobiographies step by step on film. Penn is far more dependent on the talents of others, and his primary material—what he starts with—does not come out of his own experience. If the popular audience is generally uninterested in the director (unless he is heavily publicized, like De Mille or Hitchcock), the audience that is interested in the art of movies has begun, with many of the critics, to think of movies as a directors' medium to the point where they tend to ignore the contribution of the writers—and the directors may be almost obscenely content to omit mention of the writers. The history of the movies is being rewritten to disregard facts in favor of celebrating the director as the sole "creative" force. One can read Josef von Sternberg's autobiography and the text of the latest books on his movies without ever finding the name of Jules Furthman, the writer who worked on nine of his most famous movies (including *Morocco* and *Shanghai Express*). Yet the appearance of Furthman's name in the credits of such Howard Hawks films as *Only Angels Have Wings, To Have and Have Not, The Big Sleep,* and *Rio Bravo* suggests the reason for the similar qualities of good-bad-girl glamour in the roles played by Dietrich and Bacall and in other von Sternberg and Hawks heroines, and also in the Jean Harlow and Constance Bennett roles in the movies he wrote for *them.* Furthman, who has written about half of the most entertaining movies to come out of Hollywood (Ben Hecht wrote most of the other half), isn't even listed in new encyclopedias of the film. David Newman and Robert Benton may be good enough to join this category of unmentionable men who do what the directors are glorified for. The Hollywood writer is becoming a ghostwriter. The writers who succeed in the struggle to protect their identity and their material by becoming writer-directors or writer-producers soon become too rich and powerful to bother doing their own writing. And they rarely have the visual sense or the training to make good movie directors.

Anyone who goes to big American movies like *Grand Prix* and *The Sand Pebbles* recognizes that movies with scripts like those don't have a chance to be anything more than exercises in technology, and that this is what is meant by the decadence of American movies. In the past, directors used to say that they were no better than their material. (Sometimes they said it when they weren't even up to their material.) A good director can attempt to camouflage poor writing with craftsmanship and style, but ultimately no amount of director's skill can conceal a writer's failure; a poor script, even well directed, results in a stupid movie—as, unfortunately, does a good script poorly directed. Despite the new notion that the direction is everything, Penn can't redeem bad material, nor, as one may surmise from his *Mickey One,* does he necessarily know when it's bad. It is not fair to judge Penn by a film like *The Chase,* because he evidently did not have artistic control over the production, but what happens when he does have control and is working with a poor, pretentious mess of a script is painfully apparent in *Mickey One*—an art film in the worst sense of that term. Though one cannot say of *Bonnie and Clyde* to what degree it shows the work of Newman and Benton and to what degree they merely enabled Penn to "express himself," there are ways of making guesses. As we hear the lines, we can detect the intentions even when the intentions are not quite carried out. Penn is a little clumsy and rather too fancy; he's too much interested in being cinematically creative and artistic to know when to trust the script. *Bonnie and Clyde* could be better if it were simpler. Nevertheless, Penn is a remarkable director when he has something to work with. His most interesting previous work was in his first film, *The Left Handed Gun* (and a few bits of *The Miracle Worker*, a good movie version of the William Gibson play, which he had also directed on the stage and on television). *The Left Handed Gun,* with Paul Newman as an ignorant Billy the Kid in the sex-starved, male-dominated Old West, has the same kind of violent, legendary, nostalgic material as *Bonnie and Clyde;* its script, a rather startling one, was adapted by Leslie Stevens from a Gore Vidal television play. In interviews, Penn makes high, dull sounds—more like a politician than a movie director. But he has a gift for violence, and, despite all the violence in movies, a gift for it is rare. (Eisenstein had it, and Dovzhenko, and Buñuel, but not many others.) There are few memorable violent moments in American movies, but there is one in Penn's first film: Billy's shotgun blasts a man right out of one of his boots; the man falls in the street, but his boot remains upright; a little girl's giggle at the boot is interrupted by her mother's slapping her. The mother's slap—the seal of the awareness of horror—says that even children must learn that some things that look funny are not only funny. That slap, saying that only idiots would laugh at pain and death, that a child must develop sensibility, is the same slap that *Bonnie and Clyde* delivers to the woman saying "It's a comedy." In *The Left Handed Gun,* the slap is itself funny, and yet we suck in our breath; we do not dare to laugh.

Some of the best American movies show the seams of cuts and the confusions of compromises and still hold together, because there is enough energy and spirit to carry the audience over each of the weak episodes to the next good one. The solid intelligence of the writing and Penn's aura of sensitivity help *Bonnie and Clyde* triumph over many poorly directed scenes: Bonnie posing for the photograph with the Texas Ranger, or—the worst sequence—the Ranger getting information out of Blanche Barrow in the hospital. The attempt to make the Texas Ranger an old-time villain doesn't work. He's in the tradition of the mustachioed heavy who foreclosed mortgages and pursued heroines in turn-of-the-century plays, and this one-dimensional villainy belongs, glaringly, to spoof. In some cases, I think, the writing and the conception of the scenes are better (potentially, that is) than the way the scenes have been directed and acted. If Gene Hackman's Buck Barrow is a beautifully controlled performance, the best in the film, several of the other players—though they are very good—needed a tighter rein. They act too much. But it is in other ways that Penn's limitations show—in his excessive reliance on meaning-laden closeups, for one. And it's no wonder he wasn't able to bring out the character of Bonnie in scenes like the one showing her appreciation of the fingernails on the figurine, for in other scenes his own sense of beauty appears to be only a few rungs farther up that same cultural ladder.

The showpiece sequence, Bonnie's visit to her mother (which is a bit reminiscent of Humphrey Bogart's confrontation with his mother, Marjorie Main, in the movie version of *Dead End*), aims for an effect of alienation, but that effect is confused by all the other things attempted in the sequence: the poetic echoes of childhood (which also echo the child sliding down the hill in *Jules and Jim*) and a general attempt to create a frieze from our national past—a poetry of poverty. Penn isn't quite up to it, though he is at least good enough to communicate what he is trying to do, and it is an attempt that one can respect. In 1939, John Ford attempted a similar poetic evocation of the legendary American past in *Young Mr. Lincoln*; this kind of evocation, by getting at how we *feel* about the past, moves us far more than attempts at historical re-creation. When Ford's Western evocations fail, they become languorous; when they succeed, they are the West of our dreams, and his Lincoln, the man so humane and so smart that he can outwit the unjust and save the innocent, is the Lincoln of our dreams, as the Depression of *Bonnie and Clyde* is the Depression of our dreams—the nation in a kind of trance, as in a dim memory. In this sense, the effect of blur is justified, is "right." Our memories *have* become hazy; this is what the Depression has faded into. But we are too conscious of the technical means used to achieve this blur, of the *attempt* at poetry. We are aware that the filtered effects already include our responses, and it's too easy; the lines are good enough so that the stylization wouldn't have been necessary if the scene had been played right. A simple frozen frame might have been more appropriate.

The editing of this movie is, however, the best editing in an American movie in a long time, and one may assume that Penn deserves credit for it along with the editor, Dede Allen. It's particularly inventive in the robberies and in the comedy sequence of Blanche running through the police barricades with her kitchen spatula in her hand. (There is, however, one bad bit of editing: the end of the hospital scene, when Blanche's voice makes an emotional shift without a corresponding change in her facial position.) The quick panic of Bonnie and Clyde looking at each other's face for the last time is a stunning example of the art of editing.

The end of the picture, the rag-doll dance of death as the gun blasts keep the bodies of Bonnie and Clyde in motion, is brilliant. It is a horror that seems to go on for eternity, and yet it doesn't last a second beyond what it should. The audience leaving the theatre is the quietest audience imaginable.

■   ■   ■

Still, that woman near me was saying "It's a comedy" for a little too long, and although this could have been, and probably was, a demonstration of

155

plain old-fashioned insensitivity, it suggests that those who have attuned themselves to the "total" comedy of the last few years may not know when to stop laughing. Movie audiences have been getting a steady diet of "black" comedy since 1964 and *Dr. Strangelove, Or: How I Learned to Stop Worrying and Love the Bomb*. Spoof and satire have been entertaining audiences since the two-reelers; because it is so easy to do on film things that are difficult or impossible in nature, movies are ideally suited to exaggerations of heroic prowess and to the kind of lighthearted nonsense we used to get when even the newsreels couldn't resist the kidding finish of the speeded-up athletic competition or the diver flying up from the water. The targets have usually been social and political fads and abuses, together with the heroes and the clichés of the just preceding period of film-making. *Dr. Strangelove* opened a new movie era. It ridiculed *everything* and *everybody* it showed, but concealed its own liberal pieties, thus protecting itself from ridicule. A professor who had told me that *The Manchurian Candidate* was "irresponsible," adding, "I didn't like it—I can suspend disbelief only so far," was overwhelmed by *Dr. Strangelove:* "I've never been so involved. I had to keep reminding myself it was only a movie." *Dr. Strangelove* was clearly intended as a cautionary movie; it meant to jolt us awake to the dangers of the bomb by showing us the insanity of the course we were pursuing. But artists' warnings about war and the dangers of total annihilation never tell us how we are supposed to regain control, and *Dr. Strangelove,* chortling over madness, did not indicate any possibilities for sanity. It was experienced not as satire but as a confirmation of fears. Total laughter carried the day. A new generation enjoyed seeing the world as insane; they *literally* learned to stop worrying and love the bomb. Conceptually, we had already been living with the bomb; now the mass audience of the movies—which is the youth of America—grasped the idea that the threat of extinction can be used to devaluate everything, to turn it all into a joke. And the members of this audience do love the bomb; they love feeling that the worst has happened and the irrational are the sane, because there is the bomb as the proof that the rational are insane. They love the bomb because it intensifies their feelings of hopelessness and powerlessness and innocence. It's only three years since Lewis Mumford was widely acclaimed for saying about *Dr. Strangelove* that "unless the spectator was purged by laughter he would be paralyzed by the unendurable anxiety this policy, once it were honestly appraised, would produce." Far from being purged, the spectators are paralyzed, but they're still laughing. And how odd it is now to read, *"Dr. Strangelove* would be a silly, ineffective picture if its purpose were to ridicule the characters of our military and political leaders by showing them as clownish monsters—stupid, psychotic, obsessed." From *Dr. Strangelove* it's a quick leap to *MacBird* and to a belief in exactly what it was said we weren't meant to find in *Dr. Strangelove*. It is not war that has been laughed to scorn but the possibility of sane action.

Once something enters mass culture, it travels fast. In the spoofs of the last few years, everything is gross, ridiculous, insane; to make sense would be

to risk being square. This is the context in which *Bonnie and Clyde,* an entertaining movie that has some feeling in it, upsets people—people who didn't
get upset even by *Mondo Cane.* Maybe it's because *Bonnie and Clyde,* by making us care about the robber lovers, has put the sting back into death.

The New Yorker, October 21, 1967

PART THREE

GOING STEADY

1970

CHINA IS NEAR
MOVIES AS OPERA

Movies have been doing so much of the same thing—in slightly different ways—for so long that few of the possibilities of this great hybrid art have yet been explored. At the beginning, movies served many of the functions of primitive theatre; they were Punch-and-Judy shows. But by bringing simple forms of theatre and great actors and dancers and singers to the small towns of the world, they helped to create a taste for more complex theatre, and by bringing the world to people who couldn't travel they helped to develop more advanced audiences. When Méliès photographed his magic shows, when D. W. Griffith re-created the Civil War or imagined the fall of Babylon, when Pabst made a movie with Chaliapin, when Flaherty went to photograph life in the Aran Islands or the South Seas, they were just beginning to tap the infinite possibilities of movies to explore, to record, to dramatize. Shipped in tins, movies could go anywhere in the world, taking a synthesis of almost all the known art forms to rich and poor. In terms of the number of people they could reach, movies were so inexpensive that they could be hailed as the great democratic art form. Then, as businessmen gained control of the medium, it became almost impossibly difficult for the artists to try anything new. Movies became in one way or another remakes of earlier movies, and until inexpensive pictures from abroad began to attract large audiences the general public probably believed what the big studios advertised—that great movies meant big stars, best-seller stories, expensive production. The infinite variety of what was possible on film was almost forgotten, along with the pioneers, and many of those who loved movies lost some of their own vision. They began to ask what cinema "really" was, as if ideal cinema were some preexistent entity that had to be discovered; like Platonists turned archeologists, they tried to unearth the true essence of cinema. Instead of celebrating the multiplicity of things that movies can do better or more easily than the other arts, and in new ways and combinations, they looked for the true nature of cinema in what cinema can do that the other arts can't—in artistic apartheid. Some decided on "montage," others on "purely visual imagery." (There was even a period when true cinema was said to be "the chase," and for a while audiences were being chased right out of the theatres.) They wanted to prove that cinema was a real art, like the other arts, when the whole world instinctively preferred it because it was a bastard, cross-fertilized super-art.

"Cinema" in a pure state is not to be found, but movies in the sixties began to expand again, and so quickly it's hard to keep up with them. In France men like Jean Rouch and Chris Marker are extending movies into what were previously thought to be the domains of anthropologists, sociologists, and journalists, while in *Masculine Feminine* Jean-Luc Godard made a modern love lyric out of journalism and essays and interviews, demonstrating that there are no boundaries in the arts that talent can't cross. Not even the grave. In *China Is Near* the young Italian director Marco Bellocchio now brings back to startling life a form that had been laid to rest with modern ceremony—that is, with a few regrets, kicks, and jeers. The new, great talent—perhaps the genius—of Godard brought chance into the art of movies. Bellocchio's talent—so distinctive that already it resembles genius—flourishes within the confines of intricate plot. *China Is Near* has the boudoir complications of a classic comic opera.

Among the five principals in *China Is Near,* who use each other in every way they can, are a pair of working-class lovers—a secretary and an accountant who scheme to marry into the rich landed gentry. Their targets are a professor, Vittorio (Glauco Mauri), who is running for municipal office on the Socialist ticket, and his sister, Elena, a great lady who lets every man in town climb on top of her but won't marry because socially they're all beneath her. Vittorio, the rich Socialist candidate, is that role so essential to comic opera—the ridiculous lover, the man whose mission in life is to be deceived—and Bellocchio, who wrote the film (with Elda Tattoli, who plays Elena) as well as directed it, has produced a classic modern specimen of the species: a man who's out of it, who doesn't get anything while it's going on. The fifth principal is their little brother, Camillo, who is a prissy, sneering despot—a seventeen-year-old seminary student turned Maoist who looks the way Edward Albee might look in a drawing by David Levine. Camillo provides the title when he scrawls "China Is Near" on the walls of the Socialist Party building—his brother's campaign headquarters.

Bellocchio uses the underside of family life—the inbred family atmosphere—for borderline horror and humor. His people are so awful they're funny. One might say that Bellocchio, though he is only twenty-eight, sees sex and family and politics as a dirty old man would, except that his movie is so peculiarly exuberant; perhaps only a very young (or a very old) director can focus on such graceless, mean-spirited people with so much enjoyment. As the pairs of lovers combine and recombine and the five become one big, ghastly family (with a yapping little house pet as an emblem of domesticity), Bellocchio makes it all rhyme. He provides the grace of formal design. The grand manner of the movie is hilarious. I found myself smiling at the wit of his technique; it was pleasurable just to see the quick way doors open and close, or how when the scene shifts to a larger, more public area, there's always something unexpected going on—surprises that explode what has seemed serious. Bellocchio's visual style is almost incredibly smooth; the camera glides in and out and around the action. He uses it as if there were no obstructions, as if he could do anything he wanted with it; it moves as simply and with as much apparent ease as if it were attached to the director's forehead. In *China Is Near,* as in his first film (*I Pugni in Tasca,* or *Fists in the Pocket,* which was made in 1965 and is soon to open in this country), he probably exhibits the most fluid directorial technique since Max Ophuls, and I don't know where it came from—that is, how he developed it so fast.

Fists in the Pocket must surely be one of the most astonishing directorial débuts in the history of movies, yet it is hard to know how to react to the movie itself. The material is wild, the direction cool and assured. *Fists in the Pocket,* which Bellocchio made fresh from film schools in Italy and England, is also about a prosperous family, but a family of diseased monsters. And as epileptic fits multiply between bouts of matricide, fratricide, and incest, one is too busy gasping at the director's technique and the performances of a cast of unknown actors (Lou Castel, with his pug-dog manner, and Paola Pitagora, looking like a debauched gazelle, are the best strange brother-and-sister act since Edouard Dermithe and Nicole Stéphane in *Les Enfants Terribles*) to doubt his directorial genius. But the movie is a portrait of the genius as a very young man. It is so savage it often seems intended to be funny, but *why* it was so intended isn't clear. Though *Fists in the Pocket* is exhilarating because it reveals a new talent, not everybody cares about movies enough to want to see a movie—no matter how brilliant—about a family cage of beasts, and to a casual moviegoer *Fists in the Pocket* may seem as heavily charged with misguided energy as one of those epileptic seizures. But in a few years people will probably be going to see it as, after seeing Ingmar Bergman's later films, they went to see his early ones. After only two films, Bellocchio's characters already seem his, in the way that the characters of certain novelists seem theirs—a way uncommon in movies except in the movies of writer-directors of especially individual temperaments. Bellocchio's characters are as much a private zoo as Buñuel's.

It was not just coincidence when, a few years ago, first one young

French director broke through, then another and another; it was obvious not only that they took encouragement from each other but that they literally inspired each other. Bellocchio was preceded in this way by another young Italian, Bernardo Bertolucci, who at twenty-one directed *La Commare Secca* and at twenty-two wrote and directed the sweepingly romantic *Before the Revolution,* which also dealt with a provincial family and sex and politics, and which suggested a new, operatic approach to movie-making. Both these young directors refer to opera the way the French refer to American movies; they not only use operatic structure and themes but actually introduce performances and recordings of operas—especially Verdi operas—into their work. (The bit of opera performed in *China Is Near* is the damnedest thing since "Salammbô" in *Citizen Kane.*) In the analogy they draw with opera, they seem to glory in the hybrid nature of movies, and to Italians movies may seem almost an outgrowth of the hybrid art of opera. If Verdi wrote a larger number of enduring operas than any other composer (perhaps a fifth of the total standard repertory), it's not only because he wrote great music but also because he filled the stage with action and passion and a variety of good roles for different kinds of voice—which is how these two directors make their movies. Maybe, too, these directors are saying that sex and family and politics in modern Italy are still out of Verdi. Both these young Italians are different from the older Italian directors—even those just a little older, like Pasolini—in the way that their movies move. Men like Fellini and Antonioni developed their techniques over the years, laboriously, and their early movies attest to how long it took them to become Fellini and Antonioni. This is not to put them down—most of us take a long time and never become anything—but to contrast them with Bertolucci and Bellocchio, who started their movie careers with masterly techniques, proving that it doesn't take decades of apprenticeship or millions of dollars to tell planned and acted stories, and that there is still joy in this kind of movie-making. I think Godard is the most exciting director working in movies today, and it's easy to see how and why he is influencing movie-makers all over the world. But chance and spontaneity and improvisation and the documentary look are only one way to go—not, as some have begun to think, the only way. The clear triumph of *China Is Near* is that it demonstrates how good other ways can be.

The New Yorker, January 13, 1968

THE FOX

I f you're going to see a movie based on a book you think is worth reading, read the book first. You can never read the book with the same imaginative responsiveness to the author once you have seen the movie. The great French film critic André Bazin believed that even if movies vulgarized and distorted books they served a useful purpose, because they led people to read the books on which the movies were based. But when you read the book after seeing the movie, your mind is saturated with the actors and the images, and you tend to read in terms of the movie, ignoring characters and complexities that were not included in it, because they are not as vivid to you. At worst, the book becomes a souvenir of the movie, an extended reminiscence. (Girls read *Doctor Zhivago* so they can "see more" of Omar Sharif.) Bazin didn't live to find out that reading the book after seeing the movie would become such a mass-audience phenomenon that movies not based on novels would be "novelized" for additional revenue, nor to find out that college students, taking up "film as film," would increasingly reject the whole reading experience as passé. There is a new generation of moviegoers which believes that a movie is *sui generis* and that a critic is betraying a literary bias—and thus an incompetence at dealing with film as film—in bringing up a movie's literary origins. Last year Brendan Gill discussed this problem in relation to *Reflections in a Golden Eye,* and it recently came up in a symposium on movies at the New School for Social Research, where the participating critics were dumbfounded to discover that some of the younger members of the audience did not believe that even Albert Camus's *The Stranger* was relevant to a discussion of Visconti's film version.

Even if one hadn't read D. H. Lawrence's *The Fox,* it would enter into a discussion of the movie version, because from the movie one would almost inevitably assume that Lawrence was to blame for what seems dated. There are moments in *The Fox,* as there are in *Reflections in a Golden Eye,* when one is likely to smile a little patronizingly at dear old D. H. Lawrence, as at poor little Carson McCullers. As the creaking Freudian wheels turn, one is tempted to say that nothing dates faster than the sex revelations of yesteryear. It wasn't until these movies were over that my head cleared and I realized that what had seemed so ploddingly literary that I had automatically blamed it on the original authors wasn't in the books at all. It seemed so "literary" just because it wasn't the author—wasn't Lawrence or McCullers—but an attempt to modernize or clarify the author and to "fill out" the author's material. Lawrence's 1923 novella, like McCullers's short novel of 1941, is still too subtle to be made into a movie aimed at a large audience without "bringing it up to date," which means bringing in the sexual platitudes that—in movies—are considered Freudian modernism. This has the odd result of making both these movies seem novelistic when they depart most from the novels.

The movie *The Fox* is about two young women—sickly, chattering, ultra-feminine Jill (Sandy Dennis) and dark, quiet, strong March (Anne Heywood)—who are trying, rather hopelessly, to run a chicken farm in Canada. A gentle but powerful man (Keir Dullea, in a fantasy portrait of Everywoman's dream) who used to live on their farm returns and puts things in order (thus demonstrating that farming is really man's work). But his proposal of marriage to March awakens the lesbianism dormant in the girls: Jill uses her weakness to make March feel protective, and the women become active (at least, kissing-in-bed) lesbians. Though he and March go out to a convenient little shack and shack up, Jill is still dependent on March; he eliminates Jill, in a scene of implausible and clumsy contrivance, by chopping down a tree so that it hits her. There is also some symbolism about a fox that March has somehow been unable to shoot, although it has been wrecking the girls' farming plans by raiding the hen coop; the man kills the fox and, of course, raids the hen coop himself. The symbolism seems rather quaint and rather extraneous to this triangle—which is pretty much *The Children's Hour* in a woodsy setting—and rather confusing; the ads therefore explain that the fox is the "symbol of the male," and the trade press "clarifies" things even more by explaining that the "shotgun, axe, carving knife, tree, pitchfork, etc." are "phallic symbology." The movie (again like *Reflections*) has a solemnly measured manner, which one might assume is the result of following a "classic" in an honorably respectful but too literal-minded way; one seems to wait for the next development rather than enjoy what's going on.

But D. H. Lawrence's *The Fox* is a story about two spinsterish, educated, and refined English ladies, approaching thirty, in the year 1918; the ladies are, as people used to say, attached to each other. The fox of the story does indeed represent the male to March—but to a sexually repressed March. And the male who comes into their lives, and whom March immediately identifies with the fox, because of his smell and look, is a boy of twenty and, instead of a nice big farmer, primarily a hunter. And it's because he is a hunter—in that same mystic sense of willing the death of his prey which reappears in Norman Mailer's recent novel *Why Are We in Vietnam?*—that he is able to kill the inconvenient Jill, doing so right in front of the poor girl's parents. (The parents are one of those "details" that movies eliminate when they want to keep certain characters sympathetic—in the same way that Perry and Dick in the movie of *In Cold Blood* still kill four people but no longer deliberately swerve their car to smash a dog.) This hunter-boy, far from giving March a sexual sample of what she has been missing, is rather afraid of so-much-woman, and at the end of the story D. H. Lawrence undercuts the simple, "Lawrentian" male-female stuff with some impassioned second thoughts about the whole thing. Married to the boy, March is not the submissive female he had hoped for; she is independent and unsettled and unhappy. The fox may have outfoxed himself; he wishes he had left the two women "to kill one another."

The central problem of *The Fox* as a movie is the problem of adaptation. The adapters (Lewis John Carlino and Howard Koch) are neither incompetent nor stupid, but is there a mass market for a story about repressed spinsters in 1918? That being highly questionable, they have made *The Fox* a modern story. But you can hardly make it modern without making it more explicit, and if it's all spelled out, if everyone is sexually aware, if March is the kind of girl who sings a bawdy song like "Roll Me Over" and proceeds to roll around and thrash about in an experienced, if bewildering, way in that shack, you no longer need symbolism. The sex sequence not only makes the symbolism superfluous but disintegrates the characters, because if March is a swinger like this, if she isn't afraid of sex with men, what's she doing in the woods playing house with that frumpy little Jill? The force of the novella is in what Lawrence treats symbolically—the hidden power of sex in the women and the ambivalence of the male. The movie not only brings the hidden to the surface but resolves the male ambivalence in banal male strength. One kind of schoolgirl crush gives way to another. I wonder whether we could watch *The Fox* feeling so relaxed and patronizing about the author who used to be considered sensational if the man were still Lawrence's *boy*.

To take this a step further: My guess is that *The Fox* will meet with less critical opposition than *Reflections in a Golden Eye,* just because it is so sexually explicit that it is tame and "healthy," whereas the stifled homosexuality of Marlon Brando's duty-bound Major Penderton is grotesque and painful. Although Brando's character could hardly be taken as a cue to go and do likewise, *Reflections* was condemned; the ban became an embarrassment, because where but in the seminaries are there still any considerable number of *repressed* homosexuals? The scenes of Elizabeth Taylor and Brian Keith making love in the berry patch could hardly shock a modern audience, but the fat, ugly Major putting cold cream on his face, or preening himself at the mirror, or patting his hair nervously when he thinks he has a gentleman caller, is so ghastly that some members of the audience invariably cut themselves off from him by laughter. Lawrence's scared boy with a latent-lesbian bride might have made them laugh, too. Both these movies are about homosexual drives and how they lead to murder, and I think it's fair to say that neither of them would have been made even just a few years ago. And yet it's already too late to make these movies the way they have been done. *Reflections* has been furbished with *additional* fetishes, as if the original weren't Southern and Gothic enough. The horsewhipping that Elizabeth Taylor gives Brando—which doesn't appear in the book—is a new antique, and so is the conversation that follows, in which she explains that the whipping cleared the air and that he is more agreeable now, so that we are cued to crank out the Freudian explanation "Oh, yes, he wanted to be beaten," as we crank out "He hit the horse because . . ." There is much heavy cranking to do in both these movies. Is there any reason, then, to see them instead of just reading the slender little books, with their glimpses of character, and an author's distinctive voice, and prose that carries one along? Despite everything that is laboriously wrong with *Reflections,* the visual style—like paintings made from photographs—is interesting, and the director, John Huston, and the actors were able to do some extraordinary things with Carson McCullers's conceptions. One cannot imagine earlier reigning idols of the screen (Gable? Tracy?) playing the Brando role, and though his performance doesn't completely come to life—maybe because the Major doesn't have much life in him, and Brando subdued is Brando partly wasted—it nevertheless shows our greatest actor in a serious, complex role, and there are moments when the performance *does* work and Brando shows how good he is. And when Brian Keith does, too. And Elizabeth Taylor is charming as a silly, sensual Southern "lady"—a relief from the movies in which Burton ostentatiously plays down to her and she valiantly tries to act up to him and they're both awful. *The Fox* doesn't have such striking performances, and although it is probable that not very many rising young stars would care to risk the whining Sandy Dennis role, one might uncharitably point out that she had already made an acting style out of postnasal drip. *The Fox* is monumentally unimaginative, but it certainly has been mounted; the color photography is banally handsome, and there's a tricky Lalo Schifrin score to supply excitement. Maybe it is because the adapters and the director, Mark Rydell, are so plainly wrestling with Lawrence in terms of their commercial idea of honesty—making Lawrence more Lawrentian—that the movie has a simple-minded fascination. It's easy to sink into and soak up, and it may be a popular success, because many people will enjoy the sexy romance, which is pretentious enough to pass for a serious treatment of a classic. This would be no more foolish than to take a detective thriller like *In the Heat of the Night*—which is entertaining because it's a good racial joke about a black Sherlock Holmes and a shuffling, redneck Watson—and inflate it to the status of important drama, as if that inflation was necessary for one to enjoy the picture. Lawrence once sent his Frieda a picture of Jonah and the whale, with the caption, "Who is going to swallow whom?" This may have some small relevance to his unresolved novella. There's no doubt about the movie's swallowing the book; will moviegoers who then read the book be able to see Lawrence through the blubber?

No matter *how* a movie like *The Fox* might be done—even if it should be done with artistry, and even if Lawrence's conceptions should be retained—it would be unlikely to have the kind of impact that Lawrence's writing had when his books appeared. The movie of *The Stranger* is set in the correct period, the thirties, but that doesn't help to relate it to what Camus's great modern statement of the concept of alienation meant in its period—which, conceptually, was the forties. The picture might be more imaginative, the hero better cast, and so on, but how can the historical impact and importance of the novel be communicated when the idea of alienation has already become conventional—has been reduced to the cut-rate *Cool Hand Luke?* *The Stranger* is a beautiful movie, but it is not an "important" one; it functions on the screen not as a definitive new vision but as a simple story with intelligent overtones—a factual account of Meursault's last days, which, because of the impact the book was to have, now seems almost prealienation, a precursor of Camus. By the time *The Stranger* or a book by D. H. Lawrence is *filmed,* the book has already changed our lives, and the movie is just a famous story. Only if you know the book and what it meant, only if you have a sense of history, does the movie version suggest more, and help to bring back to you what the book represents. To be "important," a movie must deal with characters and situations, whether historical or modern, in terms of the greatest honesty possible in its time—what Lawrence and Camus did in their novels, and Carson McCullers did, on her own scale.

The New Yorker, February 10, 1968

SWEET NOVEMBER

Sandy Dennis, the hapless heroine of *Sweet November,* is wasting away. Queried about the nameless disease, her friend Theodore Bikel explains, "It's quite rare, but it's incurable." The movie is also afflicted with an incurable disease. *Sweet November* is the kind of squishy whimsey that is always referred to as "a woman's picture." This means not that it was written or directed by a woman but that, as the trade press says, it will "undoubtedly appeal to femme audiences." Doubt might give us hope. It's a story about a kook who is also a "doomed" girl—a synthesis of the "smart," Broadway-style repartee of *Barefoot in the Park* and *Any Wednesday* and *A Thousand Clowns,* with the worst of Robert Nathan and Margaret (*The Constant Nymph*) Kennedy. Each month, our gallant, forlorn heroine takes into her life and her bed a different man with a problem, for therapeutic purposes—his, not hers. Impotents presumably need not apply. The nature of the therapy is not disclosed, but the man seems to be considered cured when he falls in love with her. Jennifer Jones was the forties specialist in this kind of swill, and before that, in the thirties, the genre had already become so depleted that only a superlatively gifted technician like Elisabeth Bergner had the otherworldly grace to make these frail child-women halfway tolerable. Here we are in the sixties, and box manufacturer Anthony Newley is liberated by love; he releases the poet in himself with this breakthrough composition (which also serves as the advertising copy for the movie):

> *A girl I know,*
> *she is partly mad.*

Yet beyond that smile,
she is partly sad.

She is partly calm,
she is partly wild.

But she is mostly woman—

No.

She is mostly child.

This movie, like so many others lately, assumes that characters are liberated and healthy when they behave like kids—flying model airplanes, and so on. There seems to be almost no way for a sixties movie to suggest that adults might take pride and pleasure in their work, or might need to find work in which they can take pride and pleasure. The gamine characters in early movies were often pathetically unable to survive. Now they have become innocent kooks who triumph. *Sweet November* plays it both ways. A doomed kook. It's the kind of terrible idea that just might make money. Sandy Dennis, however, has exhausted her bag of tics. Yes, her beautiful, rabbity smile is still touching, and she looks sweet in her little pinafores that might have been designed by Beatrix Potter. As a crazy lady, junior division, she has a certain authenticity, and she could be very amusing in small parts. But she doesn't have the range and variety for starring roles.

The direction, by Robert Ellis Miller, is flat—as if neither he nor anyone else had any confidence in the material. He and the rest were right, of course. Let's suppose that Sandy Dennis had little choice and that Miller was stuck with the assignment—that still doesn't explain how Michel Legrand could have composed and conducted the maudlin score, which could be self-parody if it had any wit. Newley's poem is called "Enigma," but the only enigma posed by *Sweet November* is: Who is responsible? That is to say: Who is guilty? The producers, Jerry Gershwin and Elliott Kastner? Did they encourage Herman Raucher, the author of this "original"? There still seems to be an attraction for movie audiences in a kind of subnormal philosophizing issuing from the smiling mouths of unfortunates—Irene Dunne, paralyzed in a wheelchair, singing "Wishing will make it so," or Sidney Poitier, in *To Sir, with Love,* hiding his sorrow at the racial discrimination he suffers while encouraging the young to go out and conquer the world with good manners. This is the miserable tradition in which dying Sandy Dennis spews out such wisdom as "People must be remembered, Charlie. Otherwise, they were never here at all. All we are are the people who remember us." She's an icky little rabbit Babbitt. If you're wondering why *Sweet November* opened in February, the answer is that it's Radio City Music Hall's valentine to the public. I'm sure pictures like this give people pimples.

The New Yorker, February 17, 1968

INTOLERANCE
A GREAT FOLLY

"She is madonna in an art as wild and young as her sweet eyes," Vachel Lindsay wrote of Mae Marsh, who died on Tuesday of last week. She is the heroine of D. W. Griffith's *Intolerance,* which came out in 1916 and which will soon have its annual showing at the Museum of Modern Art. *Intolerance* is one of the two or three most influential movies ever made, and I think it is also the greatest. Yet many of those who are interested in movies have never seen it. *The Birth of a Nation,* which Griffith brought out in 1915 (with Mae Marsh as the little sister who throws herself off a cliff through "the opal gates of death"), still draws audiences, because of its scandalous success. But those who see it projected at the wrong speed, so that it becomes a "flick," and in mutilated form—cut and in black-and-white or faded color—are not likely to develop enough interest in Griffith's art to go to see his other films. *Intolerance* was a commercial failure in 1916, and it has never had much popular reputation. After the reactions to *The Birth of a Nation,* Griffith was so shocked that people could think he was anti-Negro that he decided to expand some material he had been working on and make it an attack on bigotry throughout the ages. *Intolerance* was intended to be virtuous and uplifting. It turned out to be a great, desperate, innovative, ruinous film—perhaps the classic example of what later came to be known as *cinéma maudit.* Griffith had already, in the over four hundred movies he had made—from the one-reelers on up to *The Birth of a Nation*—founded the art of screen narrative; now he wanted to try something more than simply telling the story of bigotry in historical sequence. He had developed crosscutting in his earlier films, using discontinuity as Dickens did in his novels. In *Intolerance,* he attempted to tell four stories taking place in different historical periods, crosscutting back and forth to ancient Babylon, sixteenth-century France, the modern American slums, and Calvary. He was living in an era of experiments with time in the other arts, and although he worked in a popular medium, the old dramatic concepts of time and unity seemed too limiting; in his own way he attempted what Pound and Eliot, Proust and Virginia Woolf and Joyce were also attempting, and what he did in movies may have influenced literary form as much as they did. He certainly influenced them. The events of *Intolerance* were, he said, set forth "as they might flash across a mind seeking to parallel the life of the different ages." It doesn't work. *Intolerance* almost becomes a film symphony, but four stories intercut and rushing toward simultaneous climaxes is, at a basic level, too naïve a conception to be anything more than four melodramas told at once. The titles of *Intolerance* state the theme more than the action shows it, and the four parallel stories were probably just too much and too bewildering for audiences. Also, the idealistic attack on hypocrisy, cruelty, and persecution may have seemed uncomfortably pacifistic in 1916.

No simple framework could contain the richness of what Griffith tried to do in this movie. He tried to force his stories together, and pushed them into ridiculous patterns to illustrate his theme. But his excitement—his madness—binds together what his arbitrarily imposed theme does not. *Intolerance* is like an enormous, extravagantly printed collection of fairy tales. The book is too thick to handle, too richly imaginative to take in, yet a child who loves stories will know that this is the treasure of treasures. The movie is the greatest extravaganza and the greatest folly in movie history, an epic celebration of the potentialities of the new medium—lyrical, passionate, and grandiose. No one will ever again be able to make last-minute rescues so suspenseful, so beautiful, or so absurd. In movies, a masterpiece is of course a folly. *Intolerance* is charged with visionary excitement about the power of movies to combine music, dance, narrative, drama, painting, and photography—to do alone what all the other arts together had done. And to do what they had failed to. Griffith's dream was not only to reach the vast audience but to express it, to make of the young movie art a true democratic art.

Griffith's movies are great not because he developed the whole range of film techniques—the editing, the moving camera, the closeup, the flexible use of the frame so that it becomes a pinpoint of light or a CinemaScope shape at will—but because he invented or pioneered those techniques out of an expressive need for them. When Griffith is at his best, you are hardly aware of how short the shots are, how brilliantly they are edited, how varied the camera angles are. Reaching for color, he not only had the prints of his movies dyed in different hues selected to convey the mood of the sequences but had crews of girls adding extra color by hand, frame by frame. Still dissatisfied, he had the projectionists throw beams of red or blue light to intensify the effects. Reaching for sound, he had scores specially prepared and orchestras playing in the pit. In *Intolerance,* he overstretched. There is hardly anything that has been attempted in movies since (except for sound effects, of course) that was not tried in *Intolerance. The Birth of a Nation,* the longest American film up to that date, was rehearsed for six weeks, shot in nine weeks, and edited in three months; it cost a hundred thousand dollars—a record-breaking budget in those days. *Intolerance* cost several times as much. The huge statue-cluttered Babylonian set, which is the most famous of all movie sets, is big in the way De Mille's sets were to be big later on—a picture-postcard set—and neither the camera nor any of the players seems to know what to do with it. The steps on this set undoubtedly inspired Eisenstein's Odessa Steps sequence, but the action that Griffith staged on them looks mechanical and confused. The movie had got too big, and even Griffith was crushed by the weight of it. Yet the enormous project released his imagination, and there are incomparable images—for example, the death of the young mountain girl, with the toy chariot drawn by doves at her feet—and miraculously successful sequences: the prison scenes, later imitated in the Warner Brothers social-protest films of the thirties, and almost reproduced in *I Am a Fugitive from a Chain Gang;* the strike scenes, which influenced the Russians; the great night-fighting scenes, originally in red, which are imitated in practically every spectacle.

One can trace almost every major tradition and most of the genres, and even many of the metaphors, in movies to their sources in Griffith. The Ku Klux Klan riders of *The Birth of a Nation* became the knights of Eisenstein's *Alexander Nevsky;* the battle scenes, derived from Mathew Brady, influenced almost all subsequent war films, and especially *Gone with the Wind.* A history of Russian movies could be based on the ice breaking up in Griffith's *Way Down East,* taking that ice through Pudovkin's epic *Mother* up to Chukhrai's *Clear Skies,* where the thaw after Stalin's death is represented literally by the breaking up of ice. One can also trace the acting styles. Mae Marsh returned to us via the young Garbo and other Scandinavian actresses, and Lillian Gish returned to us via Brigitte Helm of *Metropolis,* Dorothea Wieck of *Mädchen in Uniform,* and *most* of the European actresses of the twenties. Griffith's stylized lyric tragedy *Broken Blossoms* (which will also be shown at the Museum of Modern Art), though smaller in scope than *The Birth* or *Intolerance,* is, I think, the third of a trio of great works. It is the source of much of the poignancy of Fellini's *La Strada.* Donald Crisp's brutal prizefighter became Anthony Quinn's Zampano, and Lillian Gish's childish waif must have strongly influenced the conception of Giulietta Masina's role as well as her performance.

Griffith used Lillian Gish and Mae Marsh contrastingly. In his films, Lillian Gish is a frail, floating heroine from romantic novels and poems—a maiden. She is the least coarse of American screen actresses; her grace is pure and fluid and lilylike. She is idealized femininity, and her purity can seem rather neurotic and frightening. Mae Marsh is less ethereal, somehow less actressy, more solid and "normal," and yet, in her own way, as exquisite and intuitive. She is our dream not of heavenly beauty, like Gish, but of earthly beauty, and sunlight makes her youth more entrancing. She looks as if she could be a happy, sensual, ordinary woman. The tragedies that befall her are accidents that could happen to any of us, for she has never wanted more than common pleasures. There is a passage in *Intolerance* in which Mae Marsh, as a young mother who has had her baby taken away from her, grows so distraught that she becomes a voyeur, peeping in at windows to simper and smile at other people's babies. It's horrible to watch, because she has always seemed such a sane sort of girl. When Lillian Gish, trapped in the closet in *Broken Blossoms,* spins around in terror, we feel terror for all helpless, delicate beauty, but when Mae Marsh is buffeted by fate every ordinary person is in danger. Mae Marsh died at seventy-two, but the girl who twists her hands in the courtroom scene of *Intolerance* is the image of youth-in-trouble forever.

It took Griffith years to pay off the disaster of *Intolerance,* and though he later made box-office successes, like *Way Down East,* he wasn't financially strong enough to keep his independence. By 1925, he was forced to go to work for Paramount as a contract director, which meant doing the scripts they handed him, and doing them *their* way. By the thirties, he had sunk even further; he was called in to fix films that other directors had messed up, and he didn't receive screen credits anymore. There was so much emphasis in Hollywood on the newest product that it was feared his name would make people think a picture old-fashioned. Eventually, alcoholic and embittered, he could get no work at all. Until his death, in 1948, Griffith lived in a hotel room in near obscurity in the Hollywood he had created—which was filled with famous directors he had trained and famous stars he had discovered. They could not really help him. Motion pictures had become too big a business for sentiment, or for art.

The New Yorker, February 24, 1968

THE TWO OF US
THAT CLEAN OLD PEASANT AGAIN

The *Two of Us* is a simple, decent story, told in a simple, direct, unaffected way. The late James Agee might perhaps have brought out his full panoply of loving terms for it, because it is bare and plain and true and honest and, of course, tender and disciplined, and it isn't artificial or corrupt, and it doesn't exploit or overdramatize its subject, and I suppose one could even say it is vigorous and healthy and masculine. It is a film that one can—indeed, must—respect, and I wish I liked it better, because not liking such an unspoiled film lays one open to the charge of not being good enough, not being pure in heart. But this was a side of Agee's criticism I never could fully accept; I always wondered if he really liked *Farrebique* (the life cycle on a French farm) as much as he said, or if he only thought he *should.* I come from a farm, and even *Sunset Boulevard* is closer to my experience than *Farrebique.* Cocteau's magnificent Beast with the smoking claws seems closer than the cattle of *Farrebique,* because it's exciting in a way that those cattle will never be. Was Agee's moviegoing so virtuous, or did he, perhaps, now and then, like the rest of us, enjoy decadent, sleazy, slick commercial pictures? We ought to be able to see a reasonably lousy picture without feeling we've been violated. Agee always seemed to feel personally betrayed by synthetic elements in a movie, by "sophistication."

Because Agee was so great a critic, there is a tendency to take over his terms, but his excessive virtue may have been his worst critical vice. Agee's demands were, in some ways, both impossibly high for the movie medium and peculiarly childlike. As a result, we may need to be liberated from guilt both for enjoying irresponsible movies and for failing to respond to works of such impeccable moral character as *The Two of Us,* but a movie that, to use Agee's language, is tender and full of "reverence for reality" and all can still seem pretty thin, and there's so little going on in *The Two of Us* that one has to begin thinking of it as an idyll-fable, which has never been my idea of a good time. I don't think we would be expected to respond to this sort of thing in literature, but, possibly because of Agee's influence, we are expected to have very simple tastes when it comes to movies. Yet simple people in simple stories made some of us yawn even as children—which is probably why we started going to the movies. The place for goodness is in life, not on the screen. I realize that Agee used words like "love" and "purity" in order to get away from clever language and professional jargon—that he wanted language as well as movies cleansed—but though movies need cleansing more than ever, we mustn't throw the whore out with the bath water. Do we want to be left with the "gentle irony" of a galumphingly lovable old anti-Semitic peasant romping around with a child in Vichy France and never realizing that the child is Jewish? The child thus becomes a living O. Henry twist, like Sidney Poitier in *The Slender Thread.*

To be half chaste is an abomination. For the kind of movie it is, *The Two of Us* should be *more* chaste; its simple artlessness is clean and good, but its director, Claude Berri, may be getting credit for purity because he doesn't (yet) know how to be corrupt. When he tries for comic situations, he's a clumsy amateur. When I saw the old man (Michel Simon) play ball with the boy and break a window, I closed my eyes in remembrance of all the movie generations of infantile adults who had done the same; the first time the Georges Delerue music commented on the simple joys of life, I forced a smile, but the same music kept coming back with the same comment. There was that arch stuff between the old man and his wife about vegetarianism, and then there was that damned dog. I believe that my own dogs are prescient, but I can't stand prescience in other people's dogs, and Simon's spoon-fed mutt who wears a bib at table is a bit much. The big problem is, of course, Simon. If ever there was an actor qualified by appearance and style to be the essence of dirty old man, it is Michel Simon (and that is how Jean Vigo and Jean Renoir used him, even when he was young). As a mischievous, dear old peasant, he's a fraudulent old actor, and he gives an impure and unconvincing performance.

There are some beautiful moments in *The Two of Us,* but they don't involve the adult actors, whose roles are as one-dimensional as the grownups in a second-grade reader. But Berri, who has probably drawn much of the character of the child, Claude, played by Alain Cohen, from himself, has endowed the child with a wonderfully complex nature, so that he is both baby and shrewed adult, lovingly dependent and resourcefully tough. And Alain Cohen is marvellous-*looking* for the role; there is a moment when this plump and happy child has his head shaved, and suddenly the horrors of the concentration camps and what happened to children just like him open before us. That, I think, is the one moment of great artistry in the movie—though there is also, for a few seconds, a memorable image of a little girl holding a goose. This is quite a lot to get from a movie, but I don't think that in order to take this away with us we should have to pretend about the quality of the rest. There's no point in overvaluing one's lost innocence, artistically speaking. Once it's lost, it's lost. Pretending it isn't is sentimentality.

The New Yorker, March 2, 1968

LA CHINOISE
A MINORITY MOVIE

A few weeks ago, I was startled to see a big Pop poster of Che Guevara—startled not because students of earlier generations didn't have comparable martyrs and heroes but because they didn't consider their heroes part of popular culture, though their little brothers and sisters might have been expected to conceive of them in comic-strip terms. Jean-Luc Godard, who said on the sound track of a recent film, "One might almost say that to live in society today is something like living inside an enormous comic strip," has already made a movie about the incorporation of revolutionary heroes and ideas into Pop—*La Chinoise*. In the narration of an earlier movie, Godard defined his field as "the present, where the future is more present than the present." In *Masculine Feminine*, which was about "the children of Marx and Coca-Cola," a man about to burn himself up needed to borrow a match, and many people were irritated by the levity and absurdity of it—but the *Times* reported just such an incident this month. In the further adventures of those children, in *La Chinoise*, the heroine wants to blow up the Louvre; someone threw a stink bomb into a party at the Museum of Modern Art last week. We don't have time to catch up with the future that is here, and Godard is already making movie critiques of it—documentaries of the future in the present. His movies have become a volatile mixture of fictional narrative, reporting, essay, and absurdist interludes. His tempo is so fast that it is often difficult to keep up with the dialogue, let alone the punctuation of advertising art and allusions to history, literature, movies, and current events. There is little doubt that many of us react to movies in terms of how the tempo suits our own tempo (as a child, I could never sit still through a Laurel-and-Hardy feature, and I have something of the same problem with most of Antonioni's recent work). Since Godard's tempo is too fast for many people—perhaps most people—they have some ground for anger and confusion. But I think he is driven to ignore the difficulties that audiences may experience—not because he wants to assault them or to be deliberately "uncommercial," not out of pretentiousness or arrogance, but out of the nature of his material and his talent.

Though Godard is a social critic, using largely documentary material, he does not work in the expository manner of television documentaries but intuitively seizes new, rapidly changing elements and dramatizes them as directly as possible, projecting his feelings and interpretations into the material. He assumes in his audience an Americanized sensibility—that is, a quick comprehension of devices and conventions derived from American film style—and his temperamental affinity with American popular art probably seems particularly disreputable and trivial to those educated Americans who go to art-film houses for the European cultural ambiance. Antonioni's ponderously serious manner serves as a guarantee of quality; Godard is so restless and inquiring that he hardly develops his ideas at all. In a new picture he may leap back to rework a theme when he sees how to develop what was only partly clear before. His style is a form of shorthand, and this irritates even some people who one might assume are perfectly able to read it. We all know that an artist can't discover anything for himself—can't function as an *artist*—if he must make everything explicit in terms accessible to the widest possible audience. This is one of the big hurdles that defeat artists in Hollywood: they aren't allowed to assume that anybody knows anything, and they become discouraged and corrupt when they discover that studio thinking is not necessarily wrong in its estimate of the mass audience. Godard, like many American novelists, works in terms of an audience that is assumed to have the same background he has. And, of course, many people do—perhaps a majority of the people in the art-house audiences, though they're not used to making connections among fast references at the movies. No one complains about the quotation from Kafka's *Metamorphosis* in *The Producers,* or about Gene Wilder's being named Leo Bloom in the same film, or even about another character's being called Carmen Giya; this is considered cute "inside humor" when it's obviously done just for a laugh. But if, as in *La Chinoise,* some of the names are used as a shortcut to the characters' roles—Kirilov, for example, for the most desperately confused of the revolutionaries—people are sure to object, though this is done in novels all the time. There are many references that may be incomprehensible to some in the audience, but should Godard stop to explain who Rosa Luxembourg was or what Malraux stands for or why he brings in Sartre and Aragon or Artaud or Theatre Year Zero or Daniel and Sinyavsky? Can't he assume that those who care about the kind of film he's making—those who are involved with the issues of his art—already share most of his frame of reference and are prepared to respond to someone's using it in movies, that they are no longer much involved with movies in the same old frame of reference, which doesn't permit dealing with the attitudes of, as in this case, radical youth? This is minority art not by desire but by necessity. Most innovative artists working in movies have tried to reach the mass audience and failed—failed to reach it as artists. Godard, who is perhaps a symptom of the abandonment of hope for a great popular art, works as artists do in less popular media—at his own highest level.

Inventive and visually gifted, Godard is also, and perhaps even primarily, literary in his approach, and his verbal humor presupposes an educated audience. In *La Chinoise* he uses words in more ways than any other filmmaker: they're in the dialogue and on the walls, on book jackets and in headlines; they're recited, chanted, shouted, written, broken down; they're in commentaries, quotations, interviews, narration; they're in slogans and emblems and signs. Those who dislike verbal allusions will be irritated constantly, and those who want only straightforward action on the screen may be driven wild by his neo-Brechtian displacement devices (his voice on the sound track, a cut to Raoul Coutard at the camera) and by his almost novelistic love of digression—his inclusion of anecdotes and of speculations about movie art and of direct-to-the-camera interviews. And his doubts can be irritating in a medium that is customarily used for banal certainties. Not many movie directors regard their movies as a place to raise the questions that are troubling them. Sometimes Godard's questioning essays come apart like hasty puddings, and then his whole method falls open to question. He is also prone to the use of the *acte gratuit,* so common in philosophical French fiction of this century but rather maddening in films because such acts violate the basic premise of dramatic construction—that the author will show us what led to the crimes or deaths. Godard gives us quick finishes that are not resolutions of what has gone before.

Some of these factors are genuine deterrents to moviegoing, but Godard is, at the moment, the most important single force keeping the art of the film alive—that is to say, responsive to the modern world, moving, reaching out for new themes. The last year has been a relatively good year for American movies—there have been more pictures fit to look at than there were in the preceding few years, when Hollywood seemed to have become a desert, but, with the exception of *Bonnie and Clyde,* if you missed any or all of them you would hardly have missed a thing, because they are merely genre pieces brought up to date: thrillers, Westerns, or "strikingly new" films, which is to say films about adolescent rebellion that take over material, attitudes, and sensibility already commonplace to anybody who reads books or goes to plays. We can go to foreign films, and a romantic tragedy set in another period and culture, like *Elvira Madigan,* may be highly satisfying when we want to dream away and weep a little and look at lovely pictures—as we did at *Mayerling* in the thirties. And a slick thriller or a Western may still be entertaining enough and basically, crudely satisfying when we are tired and just want to go sit and see some action. But what these late-sixties versions of standard movies don't have is the excitement of contemporaneity, of using movies in new ways. Going to the movies, we sometimes forget—because it so rarely happens—that when movies are used in new ways there's an excitement about them much sharper than there is about the limited-entertainment genres. Godard's films—the good ones, that is—are funny, and they're funny in a new way: *La Chinoise* is a comic elegy on a group of modern revolutionary youth—naïve, forlorn little ideologues who live out a Pop version of *The Possessed*.

Godard once wrote, "I want to be able sometimes to make you feel far from the person when I do a closeup." We feel far from Véronique, the teen-age philosophy student of *La Chinoise,* all the time, and it's a scary sensation, because she is so much like every other girl on campus these days. As embodied by Anne Wiazemsky, the granddaughter of Mauriac who made her début in Bresson's *Balthazar* and is now married to Godard, Véronique may be more of a representative of the new radical youth than any other movie has come up with. She is an engaged nihilist, an activist who wants to close the universities by acts of terrorism; she thinks that this will open the way for a new educational system, and that a few deaths don't matter. She is politically engaged, and yet this condition seems to go hand in hand with a peculiar, and possibly new, kind of detachment. She and the four other members of her Maoist group who share the apartment where most of the movie takes place seem detached from the life around them, from how they live, from feelings of any kind. In her soft, small voice, and with the unself-conscious, frightened, yet assured face of so many American college girls, Véronique makes rigid formulations about morals and philosophy; she has no resonance. The group live in a political wonderland of slogans lifted out of historical continuity; they prattle about correct programs and objective conditions and just, progressive wars and the Treaty of Brest Litovsk. They have none of the strength or the doubts that come from experience. They are disparately together in their communal life; they could just as easily re-combine in another grouping. Véronique is a new version of Godard's un-reachable, perfidious girl, but this unreachable ideologue, though as blankly affectless as the heroines of *Breathless* and *Masculine Feminine,* is not treach-erous, nor is there any deep enough emotional involvement between the boys and the girls for deceit to be necessary or for betrayal or victimization to be possible. Sex is taken for granted, is so divorced from emotion that the members of the group seem almost post-sexual, which may be just about the same as pre-sexual. They study Marxism-Leninism, and chant Chairman Mao's sayings from the little red book like nursery rhymes; they play with lethal toys, and—in that bizarre parroting of the Red Guard which is so common here, too—they attack not the economic system and the advertising culture that has produced them but the culture of the past and its institutions, and bourgeois "compromisers," and Russian-style Communists. Véronique wants to bomb the Sorbonne, the Louvre, the Comédie-Française; she murders a Soviet cultural emissary visiting Paris, a representa-tive of the culture stifling the universities, who is selected almost at random to be the first in a series. The group's political life in the flat is a contained universe that almost seems to dematerialize the more familiar world, because it is such a separate, paper-thin universe. Their conspiratorial plots seem like games; they are too open and naïve to hide anything. They expel a member for "revisionism," and the little bespectacled boy goes to the foot of the table and consoles himself with bread and jam. Yet from the flat where they play-act revolution they go out and commit terrorist acts with the same affectless determination. Véronique kills the wrong man and is not fazed by it; she goes back and gets "the right one" as unemotionally as she might correct a mistake in an examination. Godard shows the horror, the beauty, and the absurdity of their thinking and their living, all at the same time.

La Chinoise is a satire of new political youth, but a satire from within, based on observation, and a satire that loves its targets more than it loves anything else—that, perhaps, can see beauty and hope only in its targets. But not much hope. In a section toward the end, the movie goes outside comedy. Godard introduces Francis Jeanson, an older man with political experience, a humane radical who *connects*. Jeanson tries to explain to Véronique that her terrorist actions will not have the consequences she envisions. She describes her tactics for closing the universities, and, gently but persistently, he raises the question "What next?" There is no question whose side Godard is on—that of the revolutionary children—but in showing their styles of action and of thought he has used his doubts, and his fears for them. Though his purpose is didactic, the movie is so playful and quick-witted and affectionate that it's possible—indeed, likely—that audiences will be confused about Godard's "attitude."

How can the modern "possessed" be *funny*? The fusion of attitudes—seeing characters as charming and poetic and, at the same time, preposterous and absurd—is one of Godard's contributions to modern film. (Truffaut worked in almost the same mode in *Shoot the Piano Player*—the mode that in America led to *Bonnie and Clyde*.) Godard's attitude toward his characters is similar to Scott Fitzgerald's in that he loves beautiful, doomed youth, but his style is late-sixties. If one examines books on modern movies, the stills generally look terrible—shlocky, dated, cluttered, and artificially lighted. Stills from Godard's films provide such a contrast that they can be spotted at once. In natural light, his figures are isolated and clearly defined in space against impersonal modern buildings with advertising posters or in rooms against white walls with unframed pictures from magazines. The look is of modern graphics, and that, of course, is why the stills reproduce so well. The ironic elegance of his hard-edge photographic compositions on screen is derived from graphics, comic strips, modern décor, and the two-dimensional television image. The frames in a Godard film are perfectly suited to fast comprehension—one can see everything in them at a glance—and to quick cutting. They can move with the speed of a comic strip, in which we also read the whole picture and the words at once. This visual style, which enables him to make a comedy out of politics and despair, has, however, often been misinterpreted as an attempt to achieve "pure form" on screen. Godard is not trying to create a separate world of abstract film that might be analogous to the arts of music and abstract painting, and it is a way not of explaining his movies but of explaining them away to say that they are works of art because they are going in the same direction as painting—as if every art reached its culmination when it was emptied of verbal meaning and of references to this world. Godard uses abstract design because he responds to the future in the present and because he is trying to show how human relationships are changing in this new world of advertising art, dehumanized housing, multiple forms of prostitution. He does not work in a studio; he selects locations that reveal how abstract modern urban living already is. He fills the screen with a picture of Brecht and the definition "Theatre is a commentary on reality." He uses words as words—for what they mean (and he satirizes the characters in *La Chinoise* for using words abstractly). He is no more an abstractionist than the comic strip artist, who also uses simplified compositions and bright primary colors as a visual-verbal shorthand technique. If the meaning is conveyed by a balloon containing the word "Splat!" you don't need to paint in the leaves on the branches of the trees or the herringbone design on the pants. And if modern life is seen in terms of the future, the leaves and the weave are already gone. It's folly to view Godard's stripped-down-for-speed-and-wit visual style as if he were moving away from the impurities of meaning; that's a way of cancelling out everything that goes on in a movie like *La Chinoise*—of "appreciating" everything the "artist" does and not reacting to or understanding anything the person says.

For a movie-maker, Godard is almost incredibly intransigent. At this point, it would be easy for him to court popularity with the young audience (which is the only audience he has ever had, and he has had little of that one) by making his revolutionaries romantic, like the gangster in *Breathless*. Romantic revolutionaries could act out political plots instead of robberies. But he does not invest the political activists of *La Chinoise* with glamour or mystery, or even passion. His romantic heroes and heroines were old-fashioned enough to believe in people, and hence to be victimized; the members of Véronique's group believe love is impossible, and for them it is. Godard does just what will be hardest to take: he makes them infantile and funny—victims of Pop culture. And though he likes them because they are ready to convert their slogans into action, because they want to do something, the movie asks, "And after you've closed the universities, what next?"

The New Yorker, April 6, 1968

FUNNY GIRL
BRAVO!

B arbra Streisand arrives on the screen, in *Funny Girl*, when the movies are in desperate need of her. The timing is perfect. There's hardly a star in American movies today, and if we've got so used to the absence of stars that we no longer think about it much, we've also lost one of the great pleasures of moviegoing: watching incandescent people up there, more intense and dazzling than people we ordinarily encounter in life, and far more charming than the extraordinary people we encounter, because the ones on the screen are objects of pure contemplation—like athletes all wound up in the stress of competition—and we don't have to undergo the frenzy or the risks of being involved with them. In life, fantastically gifted people, people who are driven, can be too much to handle; they can be a pain. In plays, in opera, they're divine, and on the screen, where they can be seen in their perfection, and where we're even safer from them, they're *more* divine.

Let's dispose at once of the ugly-duckling myth. It has been commonly said that the musical *Funny Girl* was a comfort to people because it carried the message that you do not need to be pretty to succeed. That is nonsense; the "message" of Barbra Streisand in *Funny Girl* is that talent is beauty. And this isn't some comforting message for plain people; it's what show business is all about. Barbra Streisand is much more beautiful than "pretty" people. This has not always been as true for the movies as for the stage; not handled carefully, some stage stars looked awful on the screen, so the legend developed that movie actors and actresses had to have "perfect" little features, and studio practices kept the legend going. But the banality of mere prettiness is a blight on American movies: Who can tell those faces apart? The Italian actresses, with their big, irregular features, became so popular here because we were starved for a trace of life after all those (usually fake) Wasp stereotypes. It's unfortunate that in this case the (I assume unintentional) demonstration of how uninteresting prettiness is should be at the expense of Omar Sharif, who goes as far as to demonstrate that good looks can be nothing.

Most Broadway musicals are dead before they reach the movies—the routines are so worked out they're stiff, and the jokes are embalmed in old applause. But Streisand has the gift of making old written dialogue sound like inspired improvisation; almost every line she says seems to have just sprung to mind and out. Her inflections are witty and surprising, and, more surprisingly, delicate; she can probably do more for a line than any screen comedienne since Jean Arthur, in the thirties. There hasn't been a funny girl on the screen for so long now that moviegoers have probably also got used to doing without one of the minor, once staple pleasures of moviegoing: the wisecracking heroines, the clever funny girls—Jean Arthur, of course, and Claudette Colbert, and Carole Lombard, and Ginger Rogers, and Rosalind Russell, and Myrna Loy, and all the others who could be counted on to be sassy and sane. They performed a basic comic function— they weren't taken in by sham; they had the restorative good sense of impudence—and in the pre-bunny period they made American women distinctive and marvellous. The story and the situations of *Funny Girl* are even drearier than those of most big musicals, but we know the form is corrupt and we're used to the conventions of rags-to-riches-to-price-of-fame, and it's easy to take all that for granted and ignore it when a performer knows how to deliver a line. The form is corrupt but the spirit of the performer isn't— that's why a big, heavy, silly musical like this can still have some brute force in it. The comedy is the comedy of cutting through the bull, of saying what's really on your mind. Such comedy was usually derived from urban Jewish humor, even in the thirties; now the Midwestern mask has been removed. Though this comedy is often self-deprecating (not hostile or paranoid), it's *lightly* self-mocking, in a way that seems admirably suited to the genre. Here one can see the experience and tact of a good, solid director like William Wyler. Younger, less capable, more anxious directors will permit anything for a laugh, and material like this could easily become raucous and embarrassing; we're never in danger in Wyler's hands, and that sense of security puts us in the right mood for laughter.

It is Streisand's peculiar triumph that in the second half, when the routine heartbreak comes, as it apparently must in all musical biographies, she shows an aptitude for suffering that those clever actresses didn't. Where they became sanctimonious and noble, thereby violating everything we had loved them for, she simply drips as unself-consciously and impersonally as a true tragic muse. And the tears belong to her face; they seem to complete it, as Garbo's suffering in *Camille* seemed to complete her beauty. Much stronger and more dominating than the earlier comediennes, she skirts pathos because her emotions are so openly expressed. She doesn't "touch" us for sympathy in the Chaplinesque way by trying to conceal her hurt. She conceals nothing; she's fiercely, almost frighteningly direct.

Whenever Streisand is not on the screen, the movie is stodgy, advancing the plot and telegraphing information in tedious little scenes of Sharif with servants, Sharif gambling, etc. We know that he's playing Nicky Arnstein, Fanny Brice's husband, but we can't make any sense of him. If shady gamblers are not going to be flashy and entertaining, what good are they as musical-comedy heroes? This Arnstein is too phlegmatic for a playboy and too proper for a gambler, and he seems not only devoid of humor but almost unaware of it. So what is supposed to draw him and a funny girl together? Sharif appears to be some sort of visiting royalty, with a pained professional smile to put the common people at their ease. The result is that no one seems to know how to talk to him. But then there's no one in the movie but Streisand anyway; the world of the movie is a stage full of stooges (with Walter Pidgeon stuck playing Ziegfeld like Mr. Miniver). In all these ways it's a terrible movie, and though Streisand's makeup and costumes are beautiful and sumptuous (she sometimes resembles Monica Vitti), the other girls are not well served—partly, it appears, through a failure to decide whether the Ziegfeld girls should be glorified or parodied. (No definite tone is taken.) And the sets are not elegant and stylized; they're just bad period reconstructions. Sometimes all this gets in the way of enjoyment: the visual affront of square photography and a studio "alley" help to kill the "People" number (it's also strategically ill placed), and the shipboard sequences are damaged by their unappealing look. But one can fault everything else in the movie, too, and it doesn't really matter—not even the fact that the second half has to coast on the good will built up in the first. The crucial thing is that Wyler never makes the kind of mistake that Tony Richardson made in *The Entertainer* when he cut away from Laurence Olivier's great number to give us backstage business. We do not ask of a musical like *Funny Girl* that it give us the life story of Fanny Brice; we know that her story is simply the pretext for a show, a convention of our realistically rooted musical theatre, which seeks protection in great names or big properties from the past. What we do ask is that an actress who plays a star like Fanny Brice be able to live up to the image of a great star; if she isn't, we cannot accept the pretext, and the show is exposed as just an attempt to cash in on past glories. There is no such difficulty with *Funny Girl*. The end of the movie, in a long single take, is a bravura stroke, a gorgeous piece of showing off, that makes one intensely, brilliantly aware of the star as performer and of the star's pride in herself as performer. The pride is justified.

The New Yorker, September 28, 1968

WEEKEND
WEEKEND IN HELL

Only the title of Jean-Luc Godard's new film is casual and innocent; *Weekend* is the most powerful mystical movie since *The Seventh Seal* and *Fires on the Plain* and passages of Kurosawa. We are hardly aware of the magnitude of the author-director's conception until after we are caught up in the comedy of horror, which keeps going further and becoming more nearly inescapable, like *Journey to the End of the Night.* The danger for satirists (and perhaps especially for visionary satirists) is that they don't always trust their art. They don't know how brilliantly they're making their points; they become mad with impatience and disgust, and throw off their art as if it were a hindrance to direct communication, and they begin to preach. When Godard is viciously funny, he's on top of things, and he scores and scores, and illuminates as he scores. When he becomes didactic, we can see that he really doesn't know any more about what should be done than the rest of us. But then he goes beyond didacticism into areas where, though he is as confused and divided as we are, his fervor and rage are so imaginatively justified that they are truly apocalyptic. It is in the further reaches—in the appalling, ambivalent revolutionary vision—that *Weekend* is a great, original work.

Weekend begins with a callous disrespect for life which is just a slight stylization of civilized living now; it's as if the consumers of *The Married Woman* had become more adulterous, more nakedly mercenary, and touchier. The people in *Weekend* have weapons and use them at the slightest provocation, and it seems perfectly logical that they should get into their cars and bang into each other and start piling up on the roads. By the time the bourgeois couple (Mireille Darc and Jean Yanne) start off on their weekend trip—to get money out of her mother—we have been prepared for almost anything by the wife's description of a sex orgy that moved from bedroom to kitchen and went so far she doesn't know for sure if it really happened, and by a couple of car collisions and the violence with which people responded to having their cars injured. And then the larger orgy begins, with a traffic jam that is a prelude to highways littered with burning cars and corpses. As long as Godard stays with cars as the symbol of bourgeois materialism, the movie is superbly controlled; the barbarousness of these bourgeois—their greed and the self-love they project onto their possessions—is exact and funny. But the movie goes much further—sometimes majestically, sometimes with brilliantly surreal details that suggest a closer affinity between Godard (who is of Swiss Protestant background) and Buñuel than might have been expected, sometimes with methods and ideas that miss, even though the intentions are interesting. The couple wreck their car, and as they wander the highways, lost among battered cars and bleeding dead, they have a series of picaresque adventures, encountering figures from literature and from films, until they meet a new race of hippie guerrillas—revolutionary cannibals raping and feeding on the bourgeoisie. It is both the next step and a new beginning.

The movie has extraordinary sections: the sequence of the wife's erotic confession, with only very small camera adjustments slightly changing what we see; a long virtuoso sequence that is all one or two tracking shots of the cars stalled on the highway and the activities of the motorists, with the car horns sounding triumphantly, like trumpets in Purcell—a masterly demonstration of how film technique can itself become the source of wit—until we get to the accident that is the start of the congestion, and the principals drive by and out of frame; a discussion seen through the windshield of a moving car when the couple are grilled by an "exterminating angel" who promises them miracles but refuses to give them anything when he finds out what they want (a big sports Mercedes, naturally blond hair, a weekend with James Bond).

But not all the big scenes work. There is respite in the story, a musicale sequence (which might be one of the cultural programs outlined in *La Chinoise*) in which a pianist plays Mozart in a farmyard while a few peasants and farm laborers listen or walk by. We are so alerted to the technical feat of this sequence (another long single shot, this one a three-hundred-and-sixty-degree tracking pan around the pianist, taking in the action in the area, and then returning to the pianist and circling *again,* catching the same actions at their next stage) that the actions caught seem too mechanical. And the meaning of the sequence is too ideological and too ambiguous (like much of *Les Carabiniers*); Godard may possibly believe in that musicale—that is to say, Godard may believe that art must be taken to the peasants—but more likely he's satirizing the function and the place of art, of himself along with Mozart. This might be clearer if it were not for another and worse, ideological sequence—a big symbolic garbage truck manned by a Negro and an Algerian, who empty the refuse of our civilization and make speeches directly at us. The more "direct" Godard is, the more fuzzy and obscure he is. Who can assimilate and evaluate this chunk of theory thrown at us in the middle of a movie? Probably most of us blank out on it. And there is the embarrassment of the thirties again because artists are not as well equipped to instruct us in political decisions as, in the intensity of their concern, they may suppose. Though the movie slackens during this agitprop, the horrors soon begin to rise again, and they get higher and higher. Some of this doesn't work, either: Godard has been showing us life going wild and depraved into nightmare, beyond totem and taboo, but his method has been comic and Brechtian. Characters become corpses and the actors reappear as new characters. We are reminded that the two principals are moving through the landscape of a movie; the fields are unrealistically green, and the blood on faces and bodies is thinly painted and patterned (like the blood on the peasant-prostitute's face in *La Chinoise*), and when the heroine kills her mother, the mother's blood splashes over a skinned rabbit like cans of paint being spilled. But then Godard shoves at our unwilling eyes the throat-cutting of a pig and the decapitation of a goose. Now, when people are killed in a movie, even when the killing is *not* stylized, it's generally O.K., because we know it's a fake, but when animals are slaughtered we are watching life being taken away. No doubt Godard intends this to shock us out of "aesthetic" responses, just as his agitprop preaching is intended to affect us directly, but I think he miscalculates. I look away from scenes like this, as I assume many others do. Is he forcing us to confront the knowledge that there are things we don't want to look at? But we knew that. Instead of drawing us into his conception, he throws us out of the movie. And, because we know how movies are made, we instinctively recognize that his method of jolting us is fraudulent; he, the movie director, has ordered that slaughter to get a reaction from us, and so we have a right to be angry with him. Whatever our civilization is responsible for, that sow up there is his, not ours.

The excellent score, by Antoine Duhamel, is ominous and dramatic; the pulse of the music helps to carry us through some of the weaker passages (such as the witless movie jokes, and the prattling of the figures from literature, who are feeble and seem fairly arch—rather like the book people in

Truffaut's *Fahrenheit 451*—though Emily Brontë has a good, flaming finish). The astonishing thing is that, with all these weaknesses, the nightmarish anger that seems to cry out for a revolution of total destruction and the visionary lyricism are so strong they hold the movie together; they transcend the perfectly achieved satire. The most hideously flawed of all Godard's movies, it has more depth than anything he's done before. Although by the end his conscious meanings and attitudes are not at all clear, the vision that rises in the course of the film is so surreally powerful that one accepts it, as one accepts a lunar landscape by Bosch or a torment by Grünewald. *Weekend* is Godard's vision of Hell, and it ranks with the visions of the greatest.

■   ■   ■

Weekend is the fifteenth of Godard's feature films, which began with *Breathless* in 1959, and he has also made sections of several omnibus films. At thirty-seven, he is in something of the position in the world of film that James Joyce was at a considerably later age in the world of literature; that is, he has paralyzed other filmmakers by shaking their confidence (as Joyce did to writers), without ever reaching a large public. He will probably never have a popular, international success; he packs film-festival halls, but there is hardly enough audience left over to fill small theatres for a few weeks. His experimentation irritates casual moviegoers, but those who are more than casual can see that what may have appeared to be experimentation for its own sake in a movie like *Contempt* is validated by the way he uses the techniques in *Weekend*. It's possible to hate half or two-thirds of what Godard does—or find it incomprehensible—and still be shattered by his brilliance.

Again like Joyce, Godard seems to be a great but terminal figure. The most gifted younger directors and student filmmakers all over the world recognize his liberation of the movies; they know that he has opened up a new kind of movie-making, that he has brought a new sensibility into film, that, like Joyce, he is both kinds of master—both innovator and artist. But when they try to follow him they can't beat him at his own game, and they can't (it appears) take what he has done into something else; he's so incredibly fast he always gets there first. He has obviously opened doors, but when others try to go through they're trapped. He has already made the best use of his innovations, which come out of his need for them and may be integral only to his material. It's the strength of his own sensibility that gives his techniques excitement. In other hands, his techniques are just mannerisms; other directors who try them resemble a schoolboy walking like his father. Godard has already imposed his way of seeing on us—we look at cities, at billboards and brand names, at a girl's hair differently because of him. And when others pick up the artifacts of his way of seeing, we murmur "Godard" and they are sunk. At each new film festival, one can see the different things that are lifted from him; sometimes one can almost hear the directors saying to themselves, "I know I shouldn't do that, it's too much like Godard, but I've just got to try it." They can't resist, and so they do what Godard himself has already gone past, and the young filmmakers look out-of-date before they've got started; and their corpses are beginning to litter the festivals. For if Godard can't save himself how can he save them? If he is driven, like his self-destructive heroes, to go to the limits and beyond, to pursue a non-reflective art as though fearful of a pause, to take all risks and burn himself out, it's partly because his imitators are without this drive—this monomaniac's logic that carries him beyond logic to mysticism—that his liberation of film technique and content becomes mere facility when they attempt to follow him. Michelangelo is said to have observed, "He who walks behind others will never advance." Jean Renoir has been a different kind of movie influence; with his masterly simplicity and unobtrusive visual style, he has helped people to find their own way. You don't have to walk behind Renoir, because he opens an infinite number of ways to go. But when it comes to Godard you can only follow and be destroyed. Other filmmakers see the rashness and speed and flamboyance of his complexity; they're conscious of it all the time, and they love it, and, of course, they're right to love it. But they can't walk behind him. They've got to find other ways, because he's burned up the ground.

The New Yorker, October 5, 1968

ABOUT JANE FONDA IN **BARBARELLA**

Jane Fonda having sex on the wilted feathers and rough, scroungy furs of *Barbarella* is more charming and fresh and bouncy than ever—the American girl triumphing by her innocence over a lewd comic-strip world of the future. She's the only comedienne I can think of who is sexiest when she is funniest. (Shirley MacLaine is a sweet and sexy funny girl, but she has never quite combined her gifts as Jane Fonda does.) Jane Fonda is accomplished at a distinctive kind of double take: she registers comic disbelief that such naughty things can be happening to her, and then her disbelief changes into an even more comic delight.

The New Yorker, November 2, 1968

THE LION IN WINTER
LIONESS IN WINTER

Many things can go wrong with a movie; what goes wrong with *The Lion in Winter* is so unusual that it may be some weird sort of first. The movie has been done with too much "integrity"—with inappropriate "integrity." Plays are customarily coarsened when they're filmed, but James Goldman's play has been elevated—with serious emotions, more or less authentic costumes and settings, pseudo-Stravinsky music, and historical pomp. And it just won't do to have actors carrying on as if this were a genuine, "deep" historical play, on the order of *A Man for All Seasons*. What made *The Lion in Winter* entertaining on the stage was Goldman's reduction of the first Plantagenet, Henry II, and his queen, Eleanor of Aquitaine, and their three sons to a family of monsters playing Freudian games of sex and power. They were the jolliest collection of bad seeds since *The Little Foxes,* and the notion that diplomatic maneuvers and historical issues were determined by *their* characters seemed no more than an elaborate theatrical conceit. On the screen, when their games are played out in a real castle, and played not for laughs and melodrama but emotionally, with impressive dramatic performances and real tears for defeats, it all seems hysterical. One begins to wonder why the actors are getting so overwrought; the point of view is too limited and anachronistic to justify all this howling and sobbing and carrying on. They're playing a camp historical play as if it were the real thing—delivering commercial near-poetry as if it were Shakespeare.

This melodrama for two pros and some young semi-pros to horse around in is now full of the pitiful desperation of weak, weepy people trapped by need and greed, and there are sage, important thoughts for us to take away. And the quick transitions from feigned emotion to cunning, which on the stage were so shallow and silly that they were amusing, are exhausting when the actors try to make them convincing. Goldman has a facile but not very high-grade wit, and although his screen adaptation omits some of his cheaper epigrams (it was embarrassing in the Broadway version to hear the twelfth-century rulers of England and France tossing off quips that had been popular in one's high school), what's left is still rather sophomoric. Peter O'Toole, I thought, looked a little unhappy as he disposed of the line "Well, what shall we hang? The holly or each other?" O'Toole, as Henry II, is the brightest thing in the movie. He gives the most robust performance I've seen from him; he isn't that pale-eyed O'Toole, and he keeps his pink flesh covered. He's loud and, fortunately, histrionic; underacting would *really* expose this material, by making it pretentious, whereas O'Toole, by shouting and having a good time, almost carries it off. (Not a small feat when you have to deliver lines like "The sky is pocked with stars." Goldman has the Maxwell Anderson pox.) The sons and the minor characters are good enough in their way; Anthony Hopkins as Richard the Lionhearted has urgency and weight, and Timothy Dalton as young King Philip of France is a pretty playing-card King. The sons are even fairly convincing as belonging to one family; at least, they and O'Toole all speak with some kind of English accent. Katharine Hepburn is their mother, and her accent is so peculiarly hers that we just accept it as the way she talks. And it seems proper for a queen to sound like Hepburn. I don't know what the actors *could* have done with this material that is written for clowns but would be gruesome if it were played clownishly in realistic settings; I don't know what the director, Anthony Harvey—starting with this material—could have done, either (though he might have overcome his affection for moving the camera in quickly from a great distance). The color and the photography are not especially interesting, but they're not offensive. Everybody seems to have worked hard, yet the delusion that this conception and this dialogue could bear the weight of aspirations to grandeur is crippling. Nor is that quite all that is the matter with *The Lion in Winter.*

Seven years ago, in *Pocketful of Miracles,* when Bette Davis became lovable and said "God bless" to Glenn Ford with heartfelt emotion in her voice, I muttered an obscenity as I slumped down in my seat. I slumped again during *Guess Who's Coming to Dinner,* because Katharine Hepburn had become sweet and lovable, too. The two great heroines of American talkies, the two who dared to play smart women (who *had* to), the two most specifically modern of women stars—the tough, embattled Davis and the headstrong, noble Hepburn—have both gone soft on us, have become everything we admired them for not being. They had been independent enough to fight the studios, but they have given in to themselves. The public has got them at last as it always wanted them. They have become old dears—a little crotchety, maybe, but that only makes them more harmlessly lovable. And though, of course, we can't help prizing them still—because what they once meant to us is too important a part of our lives to be relinquished—there's a feeling of dismay, and even of betrayal, when we watch them now. They make us fearful that they will humiliate us by turning piteous, and they *mustn't;* we've got to have a few people who know how to age gracefully in public, who don't go flabby with the joy of being loved every time there's a fan or a reporter around.

There were occasions in the past when Hepburn had poor roles and was tremulous and affected—almost a caricature of quivering sensitivity. But at her best—in the archetypal Hepburn role as the tomboy Linda in *Holiday,* in 1938—her wit and nonconformity made ordinary heroines seem mushy, and her angular beauty made the round-faced ingénues look piggy and stupid. She was hard where they were soft—in both head and body. (As Spencer Tracy said, in the Brooklyn accent he used in *Pat and Mike,* "There's not much meat on her, but what's there is cherce.") Other actresses could be weak and helpless, but Davis and Hepburn had too much vitality. Unlike Davis, Hepburn was limited to mandarin roles, although some of her finest performances were as poor girls who were mandarins by nature, as in *Little*

Women and *Alice Adams,* rather than by birth or wealth, as in *Bringing Up Baby* and in the movie that the public liked her best in, *The Philadelphia Story* (even if her dedicated admirers, including me, tended to be less wild about it). Hepburn has always been inconceivable as a coarse-minded character; her bones are too fine, her diction is too crisp, she wears clothes too elegantly. And she has always been too individualistic, too singular, for common emotions. Other actresses who played career girls, like Crawford, could cop out in their roles by getting pregnant, or just by turning emotional—all womanly and ghastly. Hepburn was too hard for that, and so one could go to see her knowing that she wouldn't deteriorate into a conventional heroine; that didn't suit her style. As Rosemary Harris played the role on Broadway, Eleanor of Aquitaine was hard and funny—a tough cat who enjoyed scratching and fighting—and it might have been a good role for the brittle high priestess of modernism if she had still held her own. But Hepburn plays Eleanor as a gallant great lady. She's about as tough as Helen Hayes.

When an actress has been a star for a long time, we know too much about her; for years we have been hearing about her romances or heartbreaks, or whatever the case may be, and all this carries over into her presence on the screen. And if she *uses* this in a role, she's sunk. When actresses begin to use our knowledge about them and of how young and beautiful they used to be—when they offer themselves up as ruins of their former selves—they may get praise and awards (and they generally do), but it's not really for their acting, it's for capitulating and giving the public what it wants: a chance to see how the mighty have fallen. Only a few years ago, in *Long Day's Journey Into Night,* the crowning achievement of her career, Katharine Hepburn kept her emotions within the role, and she was truly great—ravaged and magnificent. But in *Guess Who's Coming to Dinner* and much more in *The Lion in Winter* she draws upon our feelings for *her,* not for the character she's playing. When Hepburn, the most regal of them all, contemplates her blotches and wrinkles with tears in her anxious eyes, it's self-exploitation, and it's horrible.

The New Yorker, November 9, 1968

FACES

Although I am far from being an enthusiast of John Cassavetes's kind of movie-making, after seeing something like *Joanna* one may think back on the glum, naïve realism of *Faces* with respect, if not quite affection. When his *Shadows* came out, almost a decade ago, it was generally thought of as a group improvisation rather than as a first film by John Cassavetes. But from bits of his two intervening, commercially produced films (*Too Late*

Blues and *A Child Is Waiting*), and now from *Faces,* in which he apparently had full control, it is clear that either he made *Shadows* or working on *Shadows* made his style. Cassavetes's method is peculiar in that its triumphs and its failures are not merely inseparable from the method but often truly hard to separate from each other. The acting that is so bad it's embarrassing sometimes seems also to have revealed something, so we're forced to reconsider our notions of good and bad acting. In 1961, I commented on *Shadows,* "As the creative effort of a group, it has the rawness and insistence of a form of psychodrama, but it has a special fascination—it reveals a good deal about what actors think is the content of drama (and what they think life is)." In *Faces,* the people are older and richer, and the milieu is southern California rather than New York, yet not only is the method the same (though the technique is infinitely smoother and the *cinéma-vérité*-style photography is generally handsome and effective) but the attitudes are the same. The heroine, after a night of extramarital sex, experiences the very same pathos and guilt and disgust that the virgin in *Shadows* experienced when she was seduced. In fact, nobody seems to have got very far, except downhill. *Faces* is going to be a big success and it doesn't need critical generosity, so, still awarding Cassavetes high marks for doing something "interesting," I would like to point out some of the limitations and implications of the method.

Cassavetes's approach to making a film is not unlike Andy Warhol's in *The Chelsea Girls* and Norman Mailer's in *Wild 90* and *Beyond the Law;* by depending on the inspiration of the amateurs and professionals in their casts, they attempt to get at something more truthful than ordinary movies do. And the actors act away. The movie equivalent of primitive painters may be movie-makers like these, who expect the movie to happen when the camera is on. Their movies become the games actors play (and this can be true even when there is a conventional script, as in *Rachel, Rachel*). They are likely to go for material that they feel is being left out of commercial films, but they make their movies in terms of what impressed them in their childhood—the stars—and ignore the other elements of movies. In Warhol and in Mailer, the best moments may be when the actors have a good time performing for the camera. Cassavetes has a good, clear sense of structure; he uses a script and allows improvisation only within strict limits, and, as a result, *Faces*—which is like an upper-middle-class, straight version of *The Chelsea Girls*—has the unified style of an agonizing honesty. Many professional and nonprofessional actors have something they're particularly good at, and in this kind of movie they may get a chance to show it: in *Shadows,* the heroine's flirtatiousness, the quarreling of the two men in the train station; in *Faces,* Lynn Carlin's comic rapport with John Marley in her first scene. And there are nuances and inventions we get from such scenes which in context seem remarkable—seem to be unlike what we get in ordinary movies. But these actors may be inadequate or awful in the rest of the film, because, working out of themselves this way, they can't create a character. Their performances don't have enough range, so one tends to tire of them before the movie is finished. It's my feeling that nothing makes one so aware of acting as this self-conscious kind of willed realism, and I think we may overreact to the occasional small victories because we sit there waiting for the actors to think up something to say and do. The actors dominate, as they do on a stage, and they can bring something like the tedium of dull people on the stage to the screen. But what actors think is true to life, and what, given the impetus to be sincere and the opportunity to improvise, they come up with, is very much like what the public thinks is true to life.

Glowering with integrity, determined not to pander to commercial tastes, Cassavetes has stumbled on a very commercial idea. His great commercial asset is that he thinks not like a director but like an actor. His deliberately raw material about affluence and apathy, loneliness and middle age, the importance of sex and the miseries of marriage may not say any more about the subject than glossy movies on the same themes, and the faces with blemishes may not be much more revealing than faces with a little makeup, but the unrelieved effort at honesty is, for some people, intensely convincing. When it's done as psychodrama rather than as entertainment, they seem to accept all this bruising-searing stuff, the sad whore and the tender hustler, and the false-laughter bit, and the-lies-people-live-by, etc. Watching the kind of drunken salesmen one would have sense enough to avoid in life can, I suppose, seem an illumination. Watching a fat, drunken old woman fall on top of a man she has just begged for a kiss can seem an epiphany. There are scenes in *Faces* so dumb, so crudely conceived, and so badly performed that the audience practically burns incense. I think embarrassment is not a quality of art but our reaction to failed art, yet many members of the audience apparently feel that embarrassment is a sign of flinching before the painful truth, and hence they accept what is going on as deeper and truer because they have been embarrassed by it. Cassavetes's people are empty, lecherous middle-aged failures, like Benjamin's parents and their friends in *The Graduate,* seen not in terms of comedy but in terms of bitterness and despair—a confirmation of the audience's anxieties. The theme of *Faces* is exactly the same theme as that of many now fashionable films—sex as the last quest for meaning in this meaningless, godless, etc., life, or "We who are about to die want to try everything." But the aging people and the Los Angeles setting (which, of course, makes it all seem suburban) have the ghastliness and monotonousness of the commonplace. The heroine is the most banal of all statistical entities—"housewife." And no matter how much is written on aesthetics people think something is good because "I've known people just like that. It's so true to life."

Artists use their technique in order to express themselves more fully; the actors in *Faces* strip away technique as if it were a falsehood that stood between them and "reality." This idea has great popular appeal; it's like the theory of character in *The Boys in the Band*—that when you peel away the protective layers of personality you get to the real person inside. *Faces* has the kind of seriousness that a serious artist couldn't take seriously—the kind of seriousness that rejects art as lies and superficiality. And this lumpen-artists' anti-intellectualism, this actors' unformulated attack on art may be what much of the public also believes—that there is a real thing that "art" hides. The audience comes out shaken and in no mood for levity—as I discovered when I attempted to cheer someone up by remarking that if people's lives were so empty, wasn't it lucky that they had a little money to ease the pain? I was reprimanded with "The pain is due to America and money." (A) I don't believe it, and (B) just about every "serious" movie lately has been saying it. But audiences really seem to want to hear it. I have tried to describe the audience reaction rather than just my own because that reaction may be important to the future of movies. A movie like *Joanna* makes one want to throw up, but *Faces* makes a sacrament of throwing up modern life and American society. Like a number of new forms of theatre, *Faces* is being taken as a religious experience. It's almost a form of self-flagellation to go to a movie like this—"to see yourself," which, of course, means to see how awful you are. And the hushed seriousness with which people respond (to what is really not much more than the routine sorrows of middle age or a bad office party) seems almost hysterical. They come out chanting the liberal forms of "Mea culpa."

The New Yorker, December 7, 1968

THE SEA GULL
FILMED THEATRE

There is something about the way a character who has discharged his dramatic function exits just before the character who is now dramatically necessary enters that, though perfectly logical on the stage, seems farcical or archaic on the screen. The novel form is more readily adaptable to movies than the play, because the conventions are usually more fluidly naturalistic. A character who is left behind in an early chapter to reappear later on can come and go with ease in a movie, but that poor stage character who exits and waits in the wings for his logical, structured reappearance is likely, in a movie, to convey precisely the impression that he has been waiting in the wings. The revelations and conflicts and climaxes of stage drama present problems, too, and the dialogue is likely to seem mechanical and artificial on the screen. These problems are sometimes, though rarely, solved by the adapters and directors (for example, by Cocteau in *Les Parents Terribles* and by Howard Hawks in *His Girl Friday*—movies that retain the limited settings of the stage originals and yet are, triumphantly, movies). Usually, they're not solved. The movie breaks the back of the play by "opening it up," and then makes a halfhearted gesture toward transforming it. Because the movie lacks action or dialogue for the new locales, the characters merely take walks or go to discothèques or do something equally (and nonsensically) "cinematic." The movie is like a dog with the broken bones of a cat sticking out. (What's lovable about the beast is the part that purrs.) The stage conventions are generally still present in some form and can be felt (as in *Who's Afraid of Virginia Woolf?* or *A Streetcar Named Desire*), but we may enjoy filmed plays anyway—even mediocre plays not very well filmed—because we enjoy hearing the "literate" dialogue of the theatre and seeing stylish "theatrical" performances.

Movies made from plays give actors the kind of roles they have been trained to play; they are actors, delivering their goods to us. It is *their* show, as on a stage, and although this may cause the movie to seem clumsy and may undermine it as a possible work of movie art, the power of personality often succeeds in making that clumsy movie more lively and more satisfying than a movie in which the actors are subdued and controlled for the sake of the director's conception. A play gives an actor a role he can work up and make his own, and this is usually still the case when the play is filmed— something that is rarely possible in movies derived from other material. When a play is filmed, if most of a stage-version company is retained but its star is replaced by a film actor, the movie version often goes flat, just because the film actor does not work up his role and dominate the material in the way that it was dominated on the stage, and though subjugating oneself to the material may *seem* like better film acting, the vitality that made the play effective on the stage is missing. The problem for the movie director with a stage cast is to tone down the stage performance and work it into the production so that it doesn't seem grotesque on the screen, without losing the drive and individuality that make actors exciting—and that movies need as badly as the theatre does. (A major reason for the decline of interest in theatregoing may be that so few of the great magnetic personalities are still working in the theatre. The stars have left the stage for the movies.) Most of us—particularly those of us who grew up outside major theatrical capitals—probably got our experience of the theatre from the movies more than from plays; seeing famous stage personalities repeat their roles on the screen was often our only way of seeing them. Plays on film gave us a kind of sophistication—a knowledge of what it means to turn a phrase or time a gesture—that kept alive a civilized tradition in the dispersed culture of a big country, and those of us who walked home from the movie house on dirt roads needed it. But, beyond that, I think play adaptations are one of the many *kinds* of movies and should simply be accepted as such. Some of the most enjoyable movies ever made—such as George Cukor's *Dinner at Eight*— seem appalling if they are thought of in purist terms as cinema, but they are well-made movie adaptations of plays. I *like* filmed theatre; I think there is a charge and a glamour about filmed plays and revues and vaudeville and music hall that one rarely gets from adaptations of novels or from those few screen "originals." Filmed plays are often denigrated, somewhat dishonestly, by people who learn a little cant about what is said to be proper to the film medium and forget about the pleasure they've been getting from filmed plays all their lives. Some of them don't realize (though early movie audiences did) that, for example, the Marx Brothers comedies came direct from the stage, and that W. C. Fields was doing his stage routines on the screen, just as Chaplin and others before him had done. Reviewers sometimes complain about filmed plays' not being movies—as if they'd got on the screen illegally—but most people, I think (except for the men who like only Westerns and who have probably never developed an appreciation of the delights of repartee or performance), enjoy theatre on film.

The movie version of Chekhov's *The Sea Gull* is a disaster, not because it is a filmed play but because it is a badly filmed play. And it's a disaster in spite of the fact that Chekhov might seem to offer fewer problems for screen adaptation than most dramatists, since his plays are not rigidly structured in terms of stage conventions. They're already open: the characters drift in and out casually—gather for lunch, break away, wander off. The drama is not concentrated in dialogue that builds up tensions; the drama develops indirectly—one might say undramatically—through the rhythm of glimpses and details. We don't see the beginning of a dramatic action and follow it through. Rather, we are among people whose patterns of relationship have long since been formed, and how they behave on this day is how they always behave. Unlike dramatists who try to show us what is inside their characters (and is customarily hidden), Chekhov lets the weaknesses and follies of his characters and the things that defeat them appear right on the surface—a surface that the camera could record easily and admirably. In *The Sea Gull* we observe a group of people who feel sorry for themselves, regretting their positions in life and their lost opportunities. It opens with a classic demonstration of self-pity and self-dramatization: a young man asks a young girl, "Why do you always wear black?" and the girl replies, "I am in mourning for my life." The milieu is that of educated middle-class and professional people—mixed with bohemians—just before the turn of the century. They're beset by financial problems, unrequited love, unrealized aspirations; they indulge in unhappiness and nostalgia and despair. It's a slightly stylized milieu, in which they speak their thoughts aloud, but each character knows the others too well to listen to or care about what the others say—though each is miserable at times because the others don't care enough about him to listen to him. This dramatic device (a naturalistic form of soliloquy that does not require either clearing the stage or having an actor turn aside to the audience) is also a slightly stylized psychological device, suggesting the self-absorption and isolation that are part of the texture of the characters' lives. They have poured out their hearts too many times, and nobody is listening. It takes subtle direction to orchestrate the weariness of lovers who have been dallying together adulterously for decades, the boredom of people who play cards together every night and have heard each other's anecdotes over and over, the modulations of familiarity and indifference of those who know each other's limitations. The play should be lyrical and delicately comic, and, finally, melancholy and forlorn, when, after observing the trivial daily concerns of superficial people who keep complaining that they have wasted their lives, we begin to see that what they've been saying is true and that we've been watching them make it true. The play is a graceful comic elegy on human weakness; they're almost all like that absurd girl in mourning for her life.

The Sea Gull is a strange, not fully achieved drama that proceeds by gentle understatement in such a relaxed way that it already seems "cinematic," but under Sidney Lumet's coarse and careless direction it's somber and ridiculously stagy. In the movie, people come and go more rigidly than on a stage; they're practically swept away when they have spoken their lines. Lumet brought one great play, perhaps our greatest—Long Day's Journey Into Night—to screen with marvellous success, but the driving energy and determination that worked for O'Neill are not what is needed for Chekhov. One must have a feeling for the beauty in comedy. Chekhov makes the ordinary melodrama of our lives poignant and comic; Lumet turns Chekhov's poetic conception back into ordinary melodrama—which makes it seem inadvertently funny. Lumet's virtues as a director are hardly put to use—except for his gift for casting. There are marvellous actors here, and now and then almost all of them demonstrate how good they can be, but they can't sustain their roles or blend them without help from the director, because in a movie—with shooting spread over weeks—only the director, finally, can be responsible for the coming together of the pieces. We must see how separate the characters feel yet how closely bound they are by ties of inertia and frustration, and in Chekhov this is all accomplished by subtlety, refined humor, attention to detail—by just what Lumet notoriously lacks as a director. His method is simply to shoot the play as if it were a film script, and, given the kind of informal scenes-of-country-life play it is, this might have worked if he had had patience and if he had really paid attention. But he treats Chekhov the way the characters treat each other. Technically, the movie is slovenly. The color and the grain don't match from shot to shot, and the sound level varies. There are totally dead spots in the direction. The actors' vocal inflections aren't properly modulated, and sometimes their faulty enunciation stops the show; for example, the director permits Simone Signoret to say she's always on the "qui vive" so that people in the audience can be heard asking, "TV?" (It's not such a glowing example of the translator's art that it's indispensable.) And the translation has Trigorin say to Nina that he'd like to be inside her for an hour, when all he means is that he'd like to see things through her eyes for an hour. Details, only details—but in Chekhov the details are everything. Mess them up, neglect them, and the musical conception falls apart. On the other hand, Chekhov himself is responsible for the rather vacuous and conventional symbolism of the title; it was hardly a master stroke to have the characters drag that damned stuffed bird around the stage. One might have hoped that the movie would dump some of the repetitive obviousness of the symbolism and would improve on the appearance of the customary prop bird—which looks as if it had never flown except when the prop man threw it into the theatre basement. The audience laughs when Lumet makes the transition from Act III to Act IV with a title announcing that two years have passed, and it does seem ludicrous. Here he has run afoul of a new movie problem. Nobody else has solved this problem, either, which is an even worse problem in movies derived from novels. In *Far from the Madding Crowd*, as events years apart followed one another like the events in a day, the passions and obsessions appeared to come out of nowhere and were melodramatic and meaningless. The old movie shorthand of dissolves and montages, devised to impart the news of a lapse of time, has been eliminated as "corny," but there is as yet no substitute. Partly as a result of this mechanical problem, audiences at *Far from the Madding Crowd* didn't get involved in the story, and so people said, "Nobody's interested in that kind of novel anymore." When the audience laughs at the time-passing title in *The Sea Gull,* it may think it's laughing at an old-fashioned device, but probably it's laughing because of an unsolved mechanical problem.

I think that if one is prepared for the disgraceful production, one may be able to go to the movie and enjoy it. There are several reasons for doing so, the most spectacular being Vanessa Redgrave. Chekhov should be played by ensemble actors, but in consequence of Lumet's banal direction the actors seize their roles and play them separately, as in more conventional drama. Lumet has the wrong thing going for him in this movie—the interest we have in seeing actors show what they can do—but at least that gives him *something* going for him. Vanessa Redgrave is extraordinary-looking, and she is an extraordinary actress. As Nina, the young, inexperienced, somewhat pretentious country girl who wants to go on the stage, she is grave and girlish. It's a great role, which she has also played on the stage, and, if anything, she's almost too brilliant in it; she's so inventive she does too much. Beautiful and electrifying—like the young Katharine Hepburn, whom she sometimes resembles here—she has everything to make a great actress, and, of course, with her physical appearance and her height, she must play great heroines or great eccentrics or she cannot be used at all. But perhaps she doesn't yet have the simplicity of soul that would unify her talents. She does so many marvellous things that at times they cancel each other out; she cannot yet make each gesture count, the way Duse (on film) could and Garbo could—the way that said their whole being was expressed in that gesture. But already she seems able to do just about everything else. Her spotty performance gives one a painful sense of the missed opportunity, because it should be one of the great filmed performances (like Vivien Leigh's Blanche DuBois) and it's probably not her fault that it isn't.

James Mason, who is unusual among movie actors in that he seems to get better all the time, is remarkably fine as Trigorin, the "minor" novelist in the Russia of giants, and because he is such a quiet, almost passive actor, he seems more at home in Chekhov country than the rest of the cast does. David Warner takes the gauche young romantic hero, Konstantin, perhaps too seriously, and makes him so gauche he's no longer romantic. His performance lacks irony. Gangling and quizzical, he proves monotonous, possibly because his role as the callow, unstable young writer who wears the guise of unappreciated genius is not really well conceived in the original, and partly because he is photographed in such exhausting closeup that after a while one may begin to wonder if he's supposed to be desperately earnest or just nearsighted. Harry Andrews has a great moment or two, initially, in the role of the crotchety old Sorin, but then he overdoes it. Sorin is one of those deathtrap roles that are too easy to play and hence impossible to play; it's the archetype of all those Lionel Barrymore old codgers that made one groan. Denholm Elliott, Kathleen Widdoes, and Eileen Herlie all have some moments, but Simone Signoret is miscast in the pivotal role of Arkadina. There are no rules to guide one in cross-culture casting, and sometimes an actor who has another language background can be brilliantly effective (as Max von Sydow was in *Hawaii*); one can't tell for certain whether it will work until afterward. Still, it does seem that one could have predicted that in a play so dependent on vocal nuances a French mother with an English son and brother would disrupt the extended-family ambiance and that Signoret's accent would give her lines the wrong shadings and emphases. What has actually happened is even worse. Because Signoret's style isn't in tune with the others' and because her lines sound heavy, Arkadina loses her charm and becomes the villainess of the piece—a selfish, stingy, son-devouring Freudian mother. And every time this monster speaks she stomps on the remnants of the fragile play. But it's interesting to see actors wrestling with real roles, even when the actors are wrong for them. Simone Signoret is bad, but she is still Simone Signoret. And *The Sea Gull* is a terrible movie, but it is a movie of *The Sea Gull*.

The New Yorker, January 11, 1969

THE SCALPHUNTERS
WILD IN THE STREETS
THE MANCHURIAN CANDIDATE
SEVEN DAYS IN MAY
IN THE HEAT OF THE NIGHT
THE THOMAS CROWN AFFAIR
PETULIA
2001
THE GRADUATE

TRASH, ART, AND THE MOVIES

I

Like those cynical heroes who were idealists before they discovered that the world was more rotten than they had been led to expect, we're just about all of us displaced persons, "a long way from home." When we feel defeated, when we imagine we could now perhaps settle for home and what it represents, that home no longer exists. But there are movie houses. In whatever city we find ourselves we can duck into a theatre and see on the screen our familiars—our old "ideals" aging as we are and no longer looking so ideal. Where could we better stoke the fires of our masochism than at rotten movies in gaudy seedy picture palaces in cities that run together, movies and anonymity a common denominator. Movies—a tawdry corrupt art for a tawdry corrupt world—fit the way we feel. The world doesn't work the way the schoolbooks said it did and we are different from what our parents and teachers expected us to be. Movies are our cheap and easy expression, the sullen art of displaced persons. Because we feel low we sink in the boredom, relax in the irresponsibility, and maybe grin for a minute when the gunman lines up three men and kills them with a single bullet, which is no more "real" to us than the nursery-school story of the brave little tailor.

We don't have to be told those are photographs of actors impersonating characters. We know, and we often know much more about both the actors and the characters they're impersonating and about how and why the movie has been made than is consistent with theatrical illusion. Hitchcock teased us by killing off the one marquee-name star early in *Psycho*, a gambit which startled us not just because of the suddenness of the murder or how it was committed but because it broke a box-office convention and so it was a joke played on what audiences have learned to expect. He broke the rules of the movie game and our response demonstrated how aware we are of commercial considerations. When movies are bad (and in the bad parts of good movies) our awareness of the mechanics and our cynicism about the aims and values is peculiarly alienating. The audience talks right back to the phony "outspoken" condescending *The Detective;* there are groans of dejection at *The Legend of Lylah Clare,* with, now and then, a desperate little titter. How well we all know that cheap depression that settles on us when our hopes and expectations are disappointed *again.* Alienation is the most common state of the knowledgeable movie audience, and though it has the peculiar rewards of low connoisseurship, a miser's delight in small favors, we long to be surprised out of it—not to suspension of disbelief nor to a Brechtian kind of alienation, but to pleasure, something a man can call good without self-disgust.

A good movie can take you out of your dull funk and the hopelessness that so often goes with slipping into a theatre; a good movie can make you feel alive again, in contact, not just lost in another city. Good movies make you care, make you believe in possibilities again. If somewhere in the Hollywood-entertainment world someone has managed to break through with something that speaks to you, then it isn't *all* corruption. The movie doesn't have to be great; it can be stupid and empty and you can still have the joy of a good performance, or the joy in just a good line. An actor's scowl, a small subversive gesture, a dirty remark that someone tosses off with a mock-innocent face, and the world makes a little bit of sense. Sitting there alone or painfully alone because those with you do not react as you do, you know there must be others perhaps in this very theatre or in this city, surely in other theatres in other cities, now, in the past or future, who react as you do. And because movies are the most total and encompassing art form we have, these reactions can seem the most personal and, maybe the most important, imaginable. The romance of movies is not just in those stories and those people on the screen but in the adolescent dream of meeting others who feel as you do about what you've seen. You do meet them, of course, and you know each other at once because you talk less about good movies than about what you love in bad movies.

II

There is so much talk now about the art of the film that we may be in danger of forgetting that most of the movies we enjoy are not works of art. *The Scalphunters,* for example, was one of the few entertaining American movies this past year, but skillful though it was, one could hardly call it a work of art—if such terms are to have any useful meaning. Or, to take a really gross example, a movie that is as crudely made as *Wild in the Streets*—slammed together with spit and hysteria and opportunism—can nevertheless be enjoyable, though it is almost a classic example of an unartistic movie. What makes these movies—that are not works of art—enjoyable? *The Scalphunters* was more entertaining than most Westerns largely because Burt Lancaster and Ossie Davis were peculiarly funny together; part of the pleasure of the movie was trying to figure out what made them so funny. Burt Lancaster is an odd kind of comedian: what's distinctive about him is that his comedy seems to come out of his physicality. In serious roles an undistinguished and too obviously hard-working actor, he has an apparently effortless flair for comedy and nothing is more infectious than an actor who can relax in front of the camera as if he were having a good time. (George Segal sometimes seems to have this gift of a wonderful amiability, and Brigitte Bardot was radiant with it in *Viva Maria!*) Somehow the alchemy of personality in the pairing of Lancaster and Ossie Davis—another powerfully funny actor of tremendous physical presence—worked, and the director Sydney Pollack kept tight control so that it wasn't overdone.

And *Wild in the Streets*? It's a blatantly crummy-looking picture, but that somehow works for it instead of against it because it's smart in a lot of ways that better-made pictures aren't. It looks like other recent products from American International Pictures but it's as if one were reading a comic strip that looked just like the strip of the day before, and yet on this new one there are surprising expressions on the faces and some of the balloons are really witty. There's not a trace of sensitivity in the drawing or in the ideas, and there's something rather specially funny about wit without *any* grace at all; it can be enjoyed in a particularly crude way—as Pop wit. The basic idea is corny—*It Can't Happen Here* with the freaked-out young as a new breed of fascists—but it's treated in the paranoid style of editorials about youth (it even begins by blaming everything on the parents). And a cheap idea that is this current and widespread has an almost lunatic charm, a nightmare gaiety. There's a relish that people have for the idea of drug-taking kids as monsters threatening them—the daily papers merging into *Village of the Damned*. Tapping and exploiting this kind of hysteria for a satirical fantasy, the writer Robert Thom has used what is available and obvious but he's done it with just enough mockery and style to make it funny. He throws in touches of characterization and occasional lines that are not there just to further the plot, and these throwaways make odd connections so that the movie becomes almost frolicsome in its paranoia (and in its delight in its own cleverness).

If you went to *Wild in the Streets* expecting a good movie, you'd probably be appalled because the directing is unskilled and the music is banal and many of the ideas in the script are scarcely even carried out, and almost every detail is messed up (the casting director has used bit players and extras who are decades too old for their roles). It's a paste-up job of cheap moviemaking, but it has genuinely funny performers who seize their opportunities and throw their good lines like boomerangs—Diane Varsi (like an even more zonked-out Geraldine Page) doing a perfectly quietly convincing freak-out as if it were truly a put-on of the whole straight world; Hal Holbrook with his inexpressive actorish face that is opaque and uninteresting in long shot but in closeup reveals tiny little shifts of expression, slight tightenings of the features that are like the movement of thought; and Shelley Winters, of course, and Christopher Jones. It's not so terrible—it may even be a relief—for a movie to be without the look of art; there are much worse things aesthetically than the crude good-natured crumminess, the undisguised reach for a fast buck, of movies without art. From *I Was a Teen-Age Werewolf* through the beach parties to *Wild in the Streets* and *The Savage Seven,* American International Pictures has sold a cheap commodity, which in its lack of artistry and in its blatant and sometimes funny way of delivering action serves to remind us that one of the great appeals of movies is that we don't have to take them too seriously.

Wild in the Streets is a fluke—a borderline, special case of a movie that is entertaining because some talented people got a chance to do something at American International that the more respectable companies were too nervous to try. But though I don't enjoy a movie so obvious and badly done as the big American International hit, *The Wild Angels,* it's easy to see why kids do and why many people in other countries do. Their reasons are basically why we all started going to the movies. After a time, we may want more, but audiences who have been forced to wade through the thick middle-class padding of more expensively made movies to get to the action enjoy the nose-thumbing at "good taste" of cheap movies that stick to the raw materials. At some basic level they *like* the pictures to be cheaply done, they enjoy the crudeness; it's a breather, a vacation from proper behavior and good taste and required responses. Patrons of burlesque applaud politely for the graceful erotic dancer but go wild for the lewd lummox who bangs her big hips around. That's what they go to burlesque for. Personally, I hope for a reasonable minimum of finesse, and movies like *Planet of the Apes* or *The Scalphunters* or *The Thomas Crown Affair* seem to me minimal entertainment for a relaxed evening's pleasure. These are, to use traditional common-sense language, "good movies" or "good bad movies"—slick, reasonably inventive, well-crafted. They are not art. But they are almost the maximum of what we're now getting from American movies, and not only these but much worse movies are talked about as "art"—and are beginning to be taken seriously in our schools.

It's preposterously egocentric to call anything we enjoy art—as if we could not be entertained by it if it were not; it's just as preposterous to let prestigious, expensive advertising snow us into thinking we're getting art for our money when we haven't even had a good time. I did have a good time at *Wild in the Streets,* which is more than I can say for *Petulia* or *2001* or a lot of other highly praised pictures. *Wild in the Streets* is not a work of art, but then I don't think *Petulia* or *2001* is either, though *Petulia* has that kaleidoscopic hip look and *2001* that new-techniques look which combined with "swinging" or "serious" ideas often pass for motion picture art.

III

Let's clear away a few misconceptions. Movies make hash of the schoolmarm's approach of how well the artist fulfilled his intentions. Whatever the original intention of the writers and director, it is usually supplanted, as the production gets under way, by the intention to make money—and the industry judges the film by how well it fulfills that intention. But if you could see the "artist's intentions" you'd probably wish you couldn't anyway. Nothing is so deathly to enjoyment as the relentless march of a movie to fulfill its obvious purpose. This is, indeed, almost a defining characteristic of the hack director, as distinguished from an artist.

The intention to make money is generally all too obvious. One of the excruciating comedies of our time is attending the new classes in cinema at the high schools where the students may quite shrewdly and accurately interpret the plot developments in a mediocre movie in terms of manipulation for a desired response while the teacher tries to explain everything in terms of the creative artist working out his theme—as if the conditions under which a movie is made and the market for which it is designed were irrelevant, as if the latest product from Warners or Universal should be analyzed like a lyric poem.

People who are just getting "seriously interested" in film always ask a critic, "Why don't you talk about technique and 'the visuals' more?" The answer is that American movie technique is generally more like technology and it usually isn't very interesting. Hollywood movies often have the look of the studio that produced them—they have a studio style. Many current Warner films are noisy and have a bright look of cheerful ugliness, Universal films the cheap blur of money-saving processes, and so forth. Sometimes there is even a *spirit* that seems to belong to the studio. We can speak of the Paramount comedies of the thirties or the Twentieth-Century Fox family entertainment of the forties and CinemaScope comedies of the fifties or the old MGM gloss, pretty much as we speak of Chevvies or Studebakers. These movies look alike, they move the same way, they have just about the same engines because of the studio policies and the *kind* of material the studio heads bought, the ideas they imposed, the way they had the films written, directed, photographed, and the labs where the prints were processed, and, of course, because of the presence of the studio stable of stars for whom the material was often purchased and shaped and who dominated the output of the studio. In some cases, as at Paramount in the thirties, studio style was plain and rather tacky and the output—those comedies with Mary Boland and Mae West and Alison Skipworth and W. C. Fields—looks the better for it now. Those economical comedies weren't slowed down by a lot of fancy lighting or the adornments of "production values." Simply to be enjoyable, movies don't need a very high level of craftsmanship: wit, imagination, fresh subject matter, skillful performers, a good idea—either alone or in any combination—can more than compensate for lack of technical knowledge or a big budget.

The craftsmanship that Hollywood has always used as a selling point not only doesn't have much to do with art—the expressive use of techniques—it probably doesn't have very much to do with actual box-office appeal, either.

A dull movie like Sidney Furie's *The Naked Runner* is technically competent. The appalling *Half a Sixpence* is technically astonishing. Though the large popular audience has generally been respectful of expenditure (so much so that a critic who wasn't impressed by the money and effort that went into a *Dr. Zhivago* might be sharply reprimanded by readers), people who like *The President's Analyst* or *The Producers* or *The Odd Couple* don't seem to be bothered by their technical ineptitude and visual ugliness. And on the other hand, the expensive slick techniques of ornately empty movies like *A Dandy in Aspic* can actually work against one's enjoyment, because such extravagance and waste are morally ugly. If one compares movies one likes to movies one doesn't like, craftsmanship of the big-studio variety is hardly a decisive factor. And if one compares a movie one likes by a competent director such as John Sturges or Franklin Schaffner or John Frankenheimer to a movie one doesn't much like by the same director, his technique is probably not the decisive factor. After directing *The Manchurian Candidate* Frankenheimer directed another political thriller, *Seven Days in May*, which, considered just as a piece of direction, was considerably more confident. While seeing it, one could take pleasure in Frankenheimer's smooth showmanship. But the material (Rod Serling out of Fletcher Knebel and Charles W. Bailey II) was like a straight (i.e., square) version of *The Manchurian Candidate*. I have to chase around the corridors of memory to summon up images from *Seven Days in May;* despite the brilliant technique, all that is clear to mind is the touchingly, desperately anxious face of Ava Gardner—how when she smiled you couldn't be sure if you were seeing dimples or tics. But *The Manchurian Candidate,* despite Frankenheimer's uneven, often barely adequate, staging, is still vivid because of the script. It took off from a political double entendre that everybody had been thinking of ("Why, if Joe McCarthy were working for the Communists, he couldn't be doing them more good!") and carried it to startling absurdity, and the extravagances and conceits and conversational non sequiturs (by George Axelrod out of Richard Condon) were ambivalent and funny in a way that was trashy yet liberating.

Technique is hardly worth talking about unless it's used for something worth doing: that's why most of the theorizing about the new art of television commercials is such nonsense. The effects are impersonal—dexterous, sometimes clever, but empty of art. It's because of their emptiness that commercials call so much attention to their camera angles and quick cutting— which is why people get impressed by "the art" of it. Movies are now often made in terms of what television viewers have learned to settle for. Despite a great deal that is spoken and written about young people responding visually, the influence of TV is to make movies visually less imaginative and complex. Television is a very noisy medium and viewers listen, while getting used to a poor quality of visual reproduction, to the absence of visual detail, to visual obviousness and overemphasis on simple compositions, and to atrociously simplified and distorted color systems. The shifting camera styles, the movement, and the fast cutting of a film like *Finian's Rainbow*—one of the better big productions—are like the "visuals" of TV commercials, a disguise for static material, expressive of nothing so much as the need to keep you from getting bored and leaving. Men are now beginning their careers as directors by working on commercials—which, if one cares to speculate on it, may be almost a one-sentence résumé of the future of American motion pictures.

I don't mean to suggest that there is not such a thing as movie technique or that craftsmanship doesn't contribute to the pleasures of movies, but simply that most audiences, if they enjoy the acting and the "story" or the theme or the funny lines, don't notice or care about how well or how badly the movie is made, and because they don't care, a hit makes a director a "genius" and everybody talks about his brilliant technique (i.e., the technique of grabbing an audience). In the brief history of movies there has probably never been so astonishingly gifted a large group of directors as the current Italians, and not just the famous ones or Pontecorvo (*The Battle of Algiers*) or Francesco Rosi (*The Moment of Truth*) or the young prodigies, Bertolucci and Bellocchio, but dozens of others, men like Elio Petri (*We Still Kill the Old Way*) and Carlo Lizzani (*The Violent Four*). *The Violent Four* shows more understanding of visual movement and more talent for movie-making than anything that's been made in America this year. But could one tell people who are not crazy, dedicated moviegoers to go see it? I'm not sure, although I enjoyed the film enormously, because *The Violent Four* is a gangster genre picture. And it may be a form of aestheticism—losing sight of what people go to movies for, and particularly what they go to foreign movies for—for a critic to say, "His handling of crowds and street scenes is superb," or, "It has a great semi-documentary chase sequence." It does, but the movie is basically derived from our old gangster movies, and beautifully made as it is, one would have a hard time convincing educated people to go see a movie that features a stunning performance by Gian Maria Volonte which is based on Paul Muni and James Cagney. Presumably they want something different from movies than a genre picture that offers images of modern urban decay and is smashingly directed. If a movie is interesting primarily in terms of technique then it isn't worth talking about except to students who can learn from seeing how a good director works. And to talk about a movie like *The Graduate* in terms of movie technique is really a bad joke. Technique at this level is not of any aesthetic importance; it's not the ability to achieve what you're after but the skill to find something acceptable. One must talk about a film like this in terms of what audiences enjoy it for or one is talking gibberish—and might as well be analyzing the "art" of commercials. And for the greatest movie artists where there is a unity of technique and subject, one doesn't need to talk about technique much because it has been subsumed in the art. One doesn't want to talk about how Tolstoi got his effects but about the work itself. One doesn't want to talk about how Jean Renoir does it; one wants to talk about what he has done. One can try to separate it all out, of course, distinguish form and content for purposes of analysis. But that is a secondary, analytic function, a scholarly function, and hardly needs to be done explicitly in criticism. Taking it apart is far less important than trying to see it whole. The critic shouldn't need to tear a work apart to demonstrate that he knows how it was put together. The important thing is to convey what is new and beautiful in the work, not how it was made—which is more or less implicit.

Just as there are good actors—possibly potentially great actors—who have never become big stars because they've just never been lucky enough to get the roles they needed (Brian Keith is a striking example) there are good directors who never got the scripts and the casts that could make their reputations. The question people ask when they consider going to a movie is not "How's it made?" but "What's it about?" and that's a perfectly legitimate question. (The next question—sometimes the first—is generally, "Who's in it?" and that's a good, honest question, too.) When you're at a movie, you don't have to believe in it to enjoy it but you do have to be interested. (Just as you have to be interested in the human material, too. Why should you go see *another* picture with James Stewart?) I don't want to see another samurai epic in exactly the same way I never want to read *Kristin Lavransdatter.* Though it's conceivable that a truly great movie director could make any subject interesting, there are few such artists working in movies and if they did work on unpromising subjects I'm not sure we'd really enjoy the results even if we did *admire* their artistry. (I recognize the greatness of sequences in several films by Eisenstein but it's a rather cold admiration.) The many brilliant Italian directors who are working within a commercial framework on crime and action movies are obviously not going to be of any great interest unless they get a chance to work on a subject we care about. Ironically the Czech successes here (*The Shop on Main Street, Loves of a Blonde, Closely Watched Trains*) are acclaimed for their techniques, which are fairly simple and rather limited, when it's obviously their human concern and the basic modesty and decency of their attitudes plus a little barnyard humor which audiences respond to. They may even respond partly because of the *simplicity* of the techniques.

IV

When we are children, though there are categories of films we don't like—documentaries generally (they're too much like education) and, of course, movies especially designed for children—by the time we can go on our own we have learned to avoid them. Children are often put down by adults when the children say they enjoyed a particular movie; adults who are short on empathy are quick to point out aspects of the plot or theme that the child didn't understand, and it's easy to humiliate a child in this way. But it is one of the glories of eclectic arts like opera and movies that they include so many possible kinds and combinations of pleasure. One may be enthralled by Leontyne Price in *La Forza del Destino* even if one hasn't boned up on the libretto, or entranced by *The Magic Flute* even if one has boned up on the libretto, and a movie may be enjoyed for many reasons that have little to do with the story or the subtleties (if any) of theme or character. Unlike "pure" arts which are often defined in terms of what only they can do, movies are open and unlimited. Probably everything that can be done in movies can be done some other way, but—and this is what's so miraculous and so expedient about them—they can do almost anything any other art can do (alone or in combination) and they can take on some of the functions of exploration, of journalism, of anthropology, of almost any branch of knowledge as well. We go to the movies for the variety of what they can provide, and for their marvellous ability to give us easily and inexpensively (and usually painlessly) what we can get from other arts also. They are a wonderfully *convenient* art.

Movies are used by cultures where they are foreign films in a much more primitive way than in their own; they may be enjoyed as travelogues or as initiations into how others live or in ways we might not even guess. The sophisticated and knowledgeable moviegoer is likely to forget how new and how amazing the different worlds up there once seemed to him, and to forget how much a child reacts to, how many elements he is taking in, often for the first time. And even adults who have seen many movies may think a movie is "great" if it introduces them to unfamiliar subject matter; thus many moviegoers react as naïvely as children to *Portrait of Jason* or *The Queen*. They think they're wonderful. The oldest plots and corniest comedy bits can be full of wonder for a child, just as the freeway traffic in a grade Z melodrama can be magical to a villager who has never seen a car. A child may enjoy even a movie like *Jules and Jim* for its sense of fun, without comprehending it as his parents do, just as we may enjoy an Italian movie as a sex comedy although in Italy it is considered social criticism or political satire. Jean-Luc Godard liked the movie of *Pal Joey,* and I suppose that a miserable American movie musical like *Pal Joey* might look good in France because I can't think of a single good dance number performed by French dancers in a French movie. The French enjoy what they're unable to do and we enjoy the French studies of the pangs of adolescent love that would be corny if made in Hollywood. A movie like *The Young Girls of Rochefort* demonstrates how even a gifted Frenchman who adores American musicals misunderstands their conventions. Yet it would be as stupid to say that the director Jacques Demy couldn't love American musicals because he doesn't understand their conventions as to tell a child he couldn't have liked *Planet of the Apes* because he didn't get the jokey references to the Scopes trial.

Every once in a while I see an anthropologist's report on how some preliterate tribe reacts to movies; they may, for example, be disturbed about where the actor has gone when he leaves the movie frame, or they may respond with enthusiasm to the noise and congestions of big-city life which in the film story are meant to show the depths of depersonalization to which we are sinking, but which they find funny or very jolly indeed. Different cultures have their own ways of enjoying movies. A few years ago the new "tribalists" here responded to the gaudy fantasies of *Juliet of the Spirits* by using the movie to turn on. A few had already made a trip of *8½*, but *Juliet,* which was, conveniently and perhaps not entirely accidentally, in electric, psychedelic color, caught on because of it. (The color was awful, like in bad MGM musicals—so one may wonder about the quality of the trips.)

The new tribalism in the age of the media is not necessarily the enemy of commercialism; it is a direct outgrowth of commercialism and its ally, perhaps even its instrument. If a movie has enough clout, reviewers and columnists who were bored are likely to give it another chance, until on the second or third viewing, they discover that it affects them "viscerally"—and a big expensive movie is likely to do just that. *2001* is said to have caught on with youth (which can make it happen); and it's said that the movie will stone you—which is meant to be a recommendation. Despite a few dissident voices—I've heard it said, for example, that *2001* "gives you a bad trip because the visuals don't go with the music"—the promotion has been remarkably effective with students. "The tribes" tune in so fast that college students thousands of miles apart "have heard" what a great trip *2001* is before it has even reached their city.

Using movies to go on a trip has about as much connection with the art of the film as using one of those Doris Day–Rock Hudson jobs for ideas on how to redecorate your home—an earlier way of stoning yourself. But it is relevant to an understanding of movies to try to separate out, for purposes of discussion at least, how we may personally *use* a film—to learn how to dress or how to speak more elegantly or how to make a grand entrance or even what kind of coffee maker we wish to purchase, or to take off from the movie into a romantic fantasy or a trip—from what makes it a good movie or a poor one, because, of course, we can *use* poor films as easily as good ones, perhaps *more* easily for such non-aesthetic purposes as shopping guides or aids to tripping.

V

We generally become interested in movies because we *enjoy* them and what we enjoy them for has little to do with what we think of as art. The movies we respond to, even in childhood, don't have the same values as the official culture supported at school and in the middle-class home. At the movies we get low life and high life, while David Susskind and the moralistic reviewers chastise us for not patronizing what they think we should, "realistic" movies that would be good for us—like *A Raisin in the Sun,* where we could learn the lesson that a Negro family can be as dreary as a white family. Movie audiences will take a lot of garbage, but it's pretty hard to make us queue up for pedagogy. At the movies we want a different kind of truth, something that surprises us and registers with us as funny or accurate or maybe amazing, maybe even amazingly beautiful. We get little things even in mediocre and terrible movies—José Ferrer sipping his booze through a straw in *Enter Laughing*, Scott Wilson's hard scary all-American-boy-you-can't-reach face cutting through the pretensions of *In Cold Blood* with all its fancy bleak cinematography. We got, and still have embedded in memory, Tony Randall's surprising depth of feeling in *The Seven Faces of Dr. Lao*, Keenan Wynn and Moyna MacGill in the lunch-counter sequence of *The Clock*, John W. Bubbles on the dance floor in *Cabin in the Sky*, the inflection Gene Kelly gave to the line, "I'm a rising young man" in *DuBarry Was a Lady*, Tony Curtis saying "avidly" in *Sweet Smell of Success*. Though the director may have been responsible for releasing it, it's the human material we react to most and remember longest. The art of the performers stays fresh for us, their beauty as beautiful as ever. There are so many kinds of things we get—the hangover sequence wittily designed for the CinemaScope screen in *The Tender Trap*, the atmosphere of the newspaper offices in *The Luck of Ginger Coffey*, the Automat gone mad in *Easy Living*. Do we need to lie and shift things to false terms—like those who have to say Sophia Loren is a great actress as if her *acting* had made her a star? Wouldn't we rather watch her than better actresses because she's so incredibly charming and because she's probably the greatest model the world has ever known? There are great moments—Angela Lansbury singing "Little Yellow Bird" in *Dorian Gray*. (I don't think I've ever had a friend who didn't also treasure that girl and that song.) And there are absurdly right little moments—in *Saratoga Trunk* when Curt Bois says to Ingrid Bergman, "You're very beautiful," and she says, "Yes, isn't it lucky?" And those things have closer relationships to art than what the schoolteachers told us was true and beautiful. Not that the works we studied in school weren't often great (as we discovered *later*) but that what the teachers told us to admire them for (and if current texts are any indication, are still telling students to admire them for) was generally so false and prettified and moralistic that what might have been moments of pleasure in them, and what might have been cleansing in them, and subversive, too, had been coated over.

Because of the photographic nature of the medium and the cheap admission prices, movies took their impetus not from the desiccated imitation European high culture, but from the peep show, the Wild West show, the music hall, the comic strip—from what was coarse and common. The early Chaplin two-reelers still look surprisingly lewd, with bathroom jokes and drunkenness and hatred of work and proprieties. And the Western shoot-'em-ups certainly weren't the schoolteachers' notions of art—which in my school days, ran more to didactic poetry and "perfectly proportioned" statues and which over the years have progressed through nice stories to "good taste" and "excellence"—which may be more poisonous than homilies and dainty figurines because then you had a clearer idea of what you were up against and it was easier to fight. And this, of course, is what we were running away from when we went to the movies. All week we longed for Saturday afternoon and sanctuary—the anonymity and impersonality of sitting in a theatre, just enjoying ourselves, not having to be responsible, not having to be "good." Maybe you just want to look at people on the screen and know they're not looking back at you, that they're not going to turn on you and criticize you.

Perhaps the single most intense pleasure of moviegoing is this non-aesthetic one of escaping from the responsibilities of having the proper responses required of us in our official (school) culture. And yet this is probably the best and most common basis for developing an aesthetic sense because responsibility to pay attention and to appreciate is anti-art, it makes us too anxious for pleasure, too bored for response. Far from supervision and official culture, in the darkness at the movies where nothing is asked of us and we are left alone, the liberation from duty and constraint allows us to develop our own aesthetic responses. Unsupervised enjoyment is probably not the only kind there is but it may feel like the only kind. Irresponsibility is part of the pleasure of all art; it is the part the schools cannot recognize. I don't like to buy "hard tickets" for a "road show" movie because I hate treating a movie as an occasion. I don't want to be pinned down days in advance; I enjoy the casualness of moviegoing—of going in when I feel like it, when I'm in the mood for a movie. It's the feeling of freedom from respectability we have always enjoyed at the movies that is carried to an extreme by American International Pictures and the Clint Eastwood Italian Westerns; they are stripped of cultural values. We may want more from movies than this negative virtue but we know the feeling from childhood moviegoing when we loved the gamblers and pimps and the cons' suggestions of muttered obscenities as the guards walked by. The appeal of movies was in the details of crime and high living and wicked cities and in the language of toughs and urchins; it was in the dirty smile of the city girl who lured the hero away from Janet Gaynor. What draws us to movies in the first place, the opening into other, forbidden or surprising, kinds of experience, and the vitality and corruption and irreverence of that experience are so direct and immediate and have so little connection with what we have been taught is art that many people feel more secure, feel that their tastes are becoming more cultivated when they begin to *appreciate* foreign films. One foundation executive told me that he was quite upset that his teen-agers had chosen to go to *Bonnie and Clyde* rather than with him to *Closely Watched Trains*. He took it as a sign of lack of maturity. I think his kids made an honest choice, and not only because *Bonnie and Clyde* is a good movie, but because it is closer to us, it has some of the qualities of direct involvement that make us care about movies. But it's understandable that it's easier for us, as Americans, to see *art* in foreign films than in our own, because of how we, as Americans, think of art. Art is still what teachers and ladies and foundations believe in, it's civilized and refined, cultivated and serious, cultural, beautiful, European, Oriental: it's what America isn't, and it's especially what American movies are not. Still, if those kids had chosen

Wild in the Streets over *Closely Watched Trains* I would think that was a sound and honest choice, too, even though *Wild in the Streets* is in most ways a terrible picture. It connects with their lives in an immediate even if a grossly frivolous way, and if we don't go to movies for excitement, if, even as children, we accept the cultural standards of refined adults, if we have so little drive that we accept "good taste," then we will probably never really begin to care about movies at all. We will become like those people who "may go to American movies sometimes to relax" but when they want "a little more" from a movie, are delighted by how colorful and artistic Franco Zeffirelli's *The Taming of the Shrew* is, just as a couple of decades ago they were impressed by *The Red Shoes,* made by Powell and Pressburger, the Zeffirellis of their day. Or, if they like the cozy feeling of uplift to be had from mildly whimsical movies about timid people, there's generally a *Hot Millions* or something musty and faintly boring from Eastern Europe—one of those movies set in World War II but so remote from our ways of thinking that it seems to be set in World War I. Afterward, the moviegoer can feel as decent and virtuous as if he'd spent an evening visiting a deaf old friend of the family. It's a way of taking movies back into the approved culture of the schoolroom—into gentility—and the voices of schoolteachers and reviewers rise up to ask why America can't make such movies.

VI

Movie art is not the opposite of what we have always enjoyed in movies, it is not to be found in a return to that official high culture, it is what we have always found good in movies only more so. It's the subversive gesture carried further, the moments of excitement sustained longer and extended into new meanings. At best, the movie is totally informed by the kind of pleasure we have been taking from bits and pieces of movies. But we are so used to reaching out to the few good bits in a movie that we don't need formal perfection to be dazzled. There are so many arts and crafts that go into movies and there are so many things that can go wrong that they're not an art for purists. We want to experience that elation we feel when a movie (or even a performer in a movie) goes farther than we had expected and makes the leap successfully. Even a film like Godard's *Les Carabiniers,* hell to watch for the first hour, is exciting to think about after because its one good sequence, the long picture-postcard sequence near the end, is so incredible and so brilliantly prolonged. The picture has been crawling and stumbling along and then it climbs a high wire and walks it and keeps walking it until we're almost dizzy from admiration. The tightrope is rarely stretched so high in movies, but there must be a sense of tension somewhere in the movie, if only in a bit player's face, not just mechanical suspense, or the movie is just more hours down the drain. It's the rare movie we really *go* with, the movie that keeps us tense and attentive. We learn to dread Hollywood "realism" and all that it implies. When, in the dark, we concentrate our attention, we are driven frantic by events on the level of ordinary life that pass at the rhythm of ordinary life. That's the self-conscious striving for integrity of humorless, untalented people. When we go to a play we expect a heightened, stylized language; the dull realism of the streets is unendurably boring, though we may escape from the play to the nearest bar to listen to the same language with relief. Better life than art imitating life.

If we go back and think over the movies we've enjoyed—even the ones we knew were terrible movies while we enjoyed them—what we enjoyed in them, the little part that was good, had, in some rudimentary way, some freshness, some hint of style, some trace of beauty, some audacity, some craziness. It's there in the interplay between Burt Lancaster and Ossie Davis, or, in *Wild in the Streets,* in Diane Varsi rattling her tambourine, in Hal Holbrook's faint twitch when he smells trouble, in a few of Robert Thom's lines; and they have some relation to art though they don't look like what we've been taught is "quality." They have the joy of playfulness. In a mediocre or rotten movie, the good things may give the impression that they come out of nowhere; the better the movie, the more they seem to belong to the world of the movie. Without this kind of playfulness and the pleasure we take from it, art isn't art at all, it's something punishing, as it so often is in school where even artists' little *jokes* become leaden from explanation.

Keeping in mind that simple, good distinction that all art is entertainment but not all entertainment is art, it might be a good idea to keep in mind also that if a movie is said to be a work of art and you don't enjoy it, the fault may be in you, but it's probably in the movie. Because of the money and advertising pressures involved, many reviewers discover a fresh masterpiece every week, and there's that cultural snobbery, that hunger for respectability that determines the selection of the even bigger annual masterpieces. In foreign movies what is most often mistaken for "quality" is an imitation of earlier movie art or a derivation from respectable, approved work in the other arts—like the demented, suffering painter-hero of *Hour of the Wolf* smearing his lipstick in a facsimile of expressionist anguish. Kicked in the ribs, the press says "art" when "ouch" would be more appropriate. When a director is said to be an artist (generally on the basis of earlier work which the press failed to recognize) and especially when he picks artistic subjects like the pain of creation, there is a tendency to acclaim his new bad work. This way the press, in trying to make up for its past mistakes, manages to be wrong all the time. And so a revenge-of-a-sour-virgin movie like Truffaut's *The Bride Wore Black* is treated respectfully as if it somehow revealed an artist's sensibility in every frame. Reviewers who would laugh at Lana Turner going through her *femme fatale* act in another Ross Hunter movie swoon when Jeanne Moreau casts significant blank looks for Truffaut.

In American movies what is most often mistaken for artistic quality is box-office success, especially if it's combined with a genuflection to importance; then you have "a movie the industry can be proud of" like *To Kill a Mockingbird* or such Academy Award winners as *West Side Story, My Fair Lady,* or *A Man for All Seasons.* Fred Zinnemann made a fine modern variant of a Western, *The Sundowners,* and hardly anybody saw it until it got on television; but *A Man for All Seasons* had the look of prestige and the press felt honored to praise it. I'm not sure most movie reviewers consider what they honestly enjoy as being central to criticism. Some at least appear to think that that would be relying too much on their own tastes, being too personal instead of being "objective"—relying on the ready-made terms of cultural respectability and on consensus judgment (which, to a rather shocking degree, can be arranged by publicists creating a climate of importance around a movie). Just as movie directors, as they age, hunger for what was meant by respectability in their youth, and aspire to prestigious cultural properties, so, too, the movie press longs to be elevated in terms of the cultural values of their old high schools. And so they, along with the industry, applaud ghastly "tour-de-force" performances, movies based on "distinguished" stage successes or prize-winning novels, or movies that are "worthwhile," that make a "contribution"—"serious" messagy movies. This often involves praise of bad movies, of dull movies, or even the praise in good movies of what was worst in them.

This last mechanism can be seen in the honors bestowed on *In the Heat of the Night.* The best thing in the movie is that high comic moment when Poitier says, "I'm a police officer," because it's a reversal of audience expectations and we laugh in delighted relief that the movie is not going to be another self-righteous, self-congratulatory exercise in the gloomy old Stanley Kramer tradition. At that point the audience sparks to life. The movie is fun largely because of the amusing central idea of a black Sherlock Holmes in a Tom and Jerry cartoon of reversals. Poitier's color is used for comedy instead of for that extra dimension of irony and pathos that made movies like *To Sir, with Love* unbearably sentimental. He doesn't really play the super sleuth very well: he's much too straight even when spouting the kind of higher scientific nonsense about right-handedness and left-handedness that would have kept Basil Rathbone in an ecstasy of clipped diction, blinking eyes and raised eyebrows. Like Bogart in *Beat the Devil* Poitier doesn't seem to be in on the joke. But Rod Steiger compensated with a comic performance that was even funnier for being so unexpected—not only from Steiger's career which had been going in other directions, but after the apparently serious opening of the film. The movie was, however, praised by the press as if it had been exactly the kind of picture that the audience was so relieved to discover it wasn't going to be (except in its routine melodramatic sequences full of fake courage and the climaxes such as Poitier slapping a rich white Southerner or being attacked by white thugs; except that is, in its worst parts). When I saw it, the audience, both black and white, enjoyed the joke of the fast-witted, hyper-educated black detective explaining matters to the backward, blundering Southern-chief-of-police slob. This racial joke is far more open and inoffensive than the usual "irony" of Poitier being so good and so black. For once it's *funny* (instead of embarrassing) that he's so superior to everybody.

In the Heat of the Night isn't in itself a particularly important movie; amazingly alive photographically, it's an entertaining, somewhat messed-up comedy-thriller. The director Norman Jewison destroys the final joke when Steiger plays redcap to Poitier by infusing it with tender feeling, so it comes out sickly sweet, and it's too bad that a whodunit in which the whole point is the demonstration of the Negro detective's ability to unravel what the white man can't, is never clearly unraveled. Maybe it needed a Negro super director. (The picture might have been more than just a lively whodunit if the detective had proceeded to solve the crime not by "scientific" means but by an understanding of relationships in the South that the white chief of police didn't have.) What makes it interesting for my purposes here is that the audience enjoyed the movie for the vitality of its surprising playfulness, while the industry congratulated itself because the film was "hard-hitting"— that is to say, it flirted with seriousness and spouted warm, worthwhile ideas.

Those who can accept *In the Heat of the Night* as the socially conscious movie that the industry pointed to with pride can probably also go along with the way the press attacked Jewison's subsequent film, *The Thomas Crown Affair,* as trash and a failure. One could even play the same game that was played on *In the Heat of the Night* and convert the *Crown* trifle into a subfascist exercise because, of course, Crown, the superman, who turns to crime out of boredom, is the crooked son of *The Fountainhead,* out of Raffles. But that's taking glossy summer-evening fantasies much too seriously: we haven't had a junior executive's fantasy-life movie for a long time and to attack this return of the worldly gentlemen-thieves genre of Ronald Colman and William Powell *politically* is to fail to have a sense of humor about the little romantic-adolescent fascist lurking in most of us. Part of the fun of movies is that they allow us to see how silly many of our fantasies are and how widely they're shared. A light romantic entertainment like *The Thomas Crown Affair,* trash undisguised, is the kind of chic crappy movie which (one would have thought) nobody could be fooled into thinking was art. Seeing it is like lying in the sun flicking through fashion magazines and, as we used to say, feeling rich and beautiful beyond your wildest dreams.

But it isn't easy to come to terms with what one enjoys in films, and if an older generation was persuaded to *dismiss* trash, now a younger generation, with the press and the schools in hot pursuit, has begun to talk about trash as if it were really very serious art. College newspapers and the new press all across the country are full of a hilarious new form of scholasticism, with students using their education to cook up impressive reasons for enjoying very simple, traditional dishes. Here is a communication from Cambridge to a Boston paper:

> To the Editor:
> *The Thomas Crown Affair* is fundamentally a film about faith between people. In many ways, it reminds me of a kind of updated old fable, or tale, about an ultimate test of faith. It is a film about

a love affair (note the title), with a subplot of a bank robbery, rather than the reverse. The subtlety of the film is in the way the external plot is used as a matrix to develop serious motifs, much in the same way that the *Heat of the Night* functioned.

Although Thomas Crown is an attractive and fascinating character, Vicki is the protagonist. Crown is consistent, predictable: he courts personal danger to feel superior to the system of which he is a part, and to make his otherwise overly comfortable life more interesting. Vicki is caught between two opposing elements within her, which, for convenience, I would call masculine and feminine. In spite of her glamour, at the outset she is basically masculine, in a man's type of job, ruthless, after prestige and wealth. But Crown looses the female in her. His test is a test of her femininity. The masculine responds to the challenge. Therein lies the pathos of her final revelation. Her egocentrism had not yielded to his.

In this psychic context, the possibility of establishing faith is explored. The movement of the film is towards Vicki's final enigma. Her ambivalence is commensurate with the increasing danger to Crown. The suspense lies in how she will respond to her dilemma, rather than whether Crown will escape.

I find *The Thomas Crown Affair* to be a unique and haunting film, superb in its visual and technical design, and fascinating for the allegorical problem of human faith.

The Thomas Crown Affair is pretty good trash, but we shouldn't convert what we enjoy it for into false terms derived from our study of the other arts. That's being false to what we enjoy. If it was priggish for an older generation of reviewers to be ashamed of what they enjoyed and to feel they had to be contemptuous of popular entertainment, it's even more priggish for a new movie generation to be so proud of what they enjoy that they use their education to try to place trash within the acceptable academic tradition. What the Cambridge boy is doing is a more devious form of that elevating and falsifying of people who talk about Loren as a great actress instead of as a gorgeous, funny woman. Trash doesn't belong to the academic tradition, and that's part of the *fun* of trash—that you know (or *should* know) that you don't have to take it seriously, that it was never meant to be any more than frivolous and trifling and entertaining.

It's appalling to read solemn academic studies of Hitchcock or von Sternberg by people who seem to have lost sight of the primary reason for seeing films like *Notorious* or *Morocco*—which is that they were not intended solemnly, that they were playful and inventive and faintly (often deliberately) absurd. And what's good in them, what relates them to art, is that playfulness and absence of solemnity. There is talk now about von Sternberg's technique—his use of light and décor and detail—and he is, of course, a kitsch master in these areas, a master of studied artfulness and pretty excess. Unfortunately, some students take this technique as proof that his films are works of art, once again, I think, falsifying what they really respond to—the satisfying romantic glamour of his very pretty trash. *Morocco* is great trash, and movies are so rarely great art, that if we cannot appreciate great *trash*, we have very little reason to be interested in them. The kitsch of an earlier era—even the best kitsch—does not become art, though it may become camp. Von Sternberg's movies became camp even while he was still making them, because as the romantic feeling went out of his trash—when he became so enamored of his own pretty effects that he turned his human material into blank, affectless pieces of décor—his absurd trashy style was all there was. We are now told in respectable museum publications that in 1932 a movie like *Shanghai Express* "was completely misunderstood as a mindless adventure" when indeed it was completely *understood* as a mindless adventure. And enjoyed as a mindless adventure. It's a peculiar form of movie madness crossed with academicism, this lowbrowism masquerading as highbrowism, eating a candy bar and cleaning an "allegorical problem of human faith" out of your teeth. If we always wanted works of complexity and depth we wouldn't be going to movies about glamorous thieves and seductive women who sing in cheap cafés, and if we loved *Shanghai Express* it wasn't for its mind but for the glorious sinfulness of Dietrich informing Clive Brook that, "It took more than one man to change my name to Shanghai Lily" and for the villainous Oriental chieftain (Warner Oland!) delivering the classic howler, "The white woman stays with me."

If we don't deny the pleasures to be had from certain kinds of trash and accept *The Thomas Crown Affair* as a pretty fair example of entertaining trash, then we may ask if a piece of trash like this has any relationship to art. And I think it does. Steve McQueen gives probably his most glamorous, fashionable performance yet, but even enjoying him as much as I do, I wouldn't call his performance art. It's artful, though, which is exactly what is required in this kind of vehicle. If he had been luckier, if the script had provided what it so embarrassingly lacks, the kind of sophisticated dialogue—the sexy shoptalk—that such writers as Jules Furthman and William Faulkner provided for Bogart, and if the director Norman Jewison had Lubitsch's lightness of touch, McQueen might be acclaimed as a suave, "polished" artist. Even in this flawed setting, there's a self-awareness in his performance that makes his elegance funny. And Haskell Wexler, the cinematographer, lets go with a whole bag of tricks, flooding the screen with his delight in beauty, shooting all over the place, and sending up the material. And Pablo Ferro's games with the split screen at the beginning are such conscious, clever games designed to draw us in to watch intently what is of no great interest. What gives this trash a lift, what makes it entertaining is clearly that some of those involved, knowing of course that they were working on a silly shallow script and a movie that wasn't about anything of consequence, used the chance to have a good time with it. If the director, Norman Jewison, could have built a movie instead of putting together a patchwork of sequences, *Crown* might have had a chance to be considered a movie in the class and genre of Lubitsch's *Trouble in Paradise*. It doesn't come near that because to transform this kind of kitsch, to make art of it, one needs that unifying grace, that formality and charm that a Lubitsch could sometimes provide. Still, even in this movie we get a few grace notes in McQueen's playfulness, and from Wexler and Ferro. Working on trash, feeling free to play, can loosen up the actors and craftsmen just as seeing trash can liberate the spectator. And as we don't get this playful quality of art much in movies except in trash, we might as well relax and enjoy it freely for what it is. I don't trust anyone who doesn't admit having at some time in his life enjoyed trashy American movies; I don't trust *any* of the tastes of people who were born with such good taste that they didn't need to find their way through trash.

There is a moment in *Children of Paradise* when the rich nobleman (Louis Salou) turns on his mistress, the pearly plebeian Garance (Arletty). He complains that in all their years together he has never had her love, and she replies, "You've got to leave something for the poor." We don't ask much from movies, just a little something that we can call our own. Who at some point hasn't set out dutifully for that fine foreign film and then ducked into the nearest piece of American trash? We're not only educated people of taste, we're also common people with common feelings. And our common feelings are not all *bad*. You hoped for some aliveness in that trash that you were pretty sure you wouldn't get from the respected "art film." You had long since discovered that you wouldn't get it from certain kinds of American movies, either. The industry now is taking a neo-Victorian tone, priding itself on its (few) "good, clean" movies—which are always its worst movies because almost nothing can break through the smug surfaces, and even performers' talents become cute and cloying. The lowest action trash is preferable to wholesome family entertainment. When you clean them up, when you make movies respectable, you kill them. The wellspring of their *art*, their greatness, is in not being respectable.

VII

Does trash corrupt? A nutty Puritanism still flourishes in the arts, not just in the schoolteachers' approach of wanting art to be "worthwhile," but in the higher reaches of the academic life with those ideologues who denounce us for enjoying trash as if this enjoyment took us away from the really disturbing, angry new art of our time and somehow destroyed us. If we had to *justify* our trivial silly pleasures, we'd have a hard time. How could we possibly *justify* the fun of getting to know some people in movie after movie, like Joan Blondell, the brassy blonde with the heart of gold, or waiting for the virtuous, tiny, tiny-featured heroine to say her line so we could hear the riposte of her tough, wisecracking girlfriend (Iris Adrian was my favorite). Or, when the picture got too monotonous, there would be the song interlude, introduced "atmospherically" when the cops and crooks were both in the same never-neverland nightclub and everything stopped while a girl sang. Sometimes it would be the most charming thing in the movie, like Dolores Del Rio singing "You Make Me That Way" in *International Settlement;* sometimes it would drip with maudlin meaning, like "Oh Give Me Time for Tenderness" in *Dark Victory* with the dying Bette Davis singing along with the chanteuse. The pleasures of this kind of trash are not intellectually defensible. But why should pleasure need justification? Can one demonstrate that trash desensitizes us, that it prevents people from enjoying something better, that it limits our range of aesthetic response? Nobody I know of has provided such a demonstration. Do even Disney movies or Doris Day movies do us lasting harm? I've never known a person I thought had been harmed by them, though it does seem to me that they affect the tone of a culture, that perhaps—and I don't mean to be facetious—they may poison us collectively though they don't injure us individually. There are women who want to see a world in which everything is pretty and cheerful and in which romance triumphs (*Barefoot in the Park, Any Wednesday*); families who want movies to be an innocuous inspiration, a good example for the children (*The Sound of Music, The Singing Nun*); couples who want the kind of folksy blue humor (*A Guide for the Married Man*) that they still go to Broadway shows for. These people are the reason slick, stale, rotting pictures make money; they're the reason so few pictures are any good. And in that way, this terrible conformist culture does affect us all. It certainly cramps and limits opportunities for artists. But that isn't what generally gets attacked as trash, anyway. I've avoided using the term "harmless trash" for movies like *The Thomas Crown Affair,* because that would put me on the side of the angels—against "harmful trash," and I don't honestly know what that is. It's common for the press to call cheaply made, violent action movies "brutalizing" but that tells us less about any actual demonstrable effects than about the finicky tastes of the reviewers—who are often highly appreciative of violence in more expensive and "artistic" settings such as *Petulia.* It's almost a class prejudice, this assumption that crudely made movies, movies without the look of art, are bad for people.

If there's a little art in good trash and sometimes even in poor trash, there may be more trash than is generally recognized in some of the most acclaimed "art" movies. Such movies as *Petulia* and *2001* may be no more than trash in the latest, up-to-the-minute guises, using "artistic techniques" to give trash the look of art. The serious art look may be the latest fashion in *expensive trash.* All that "art" may be what prevents pictures like these from being *enjoyable* trash; they're not honestly crummy, they're very fancy and they take their crummy ideas seriously.

I have rarely seen a more disagreeable, a more dislikable (or a bloodier) movie than *Petulia* and I would guess that its commercial success represents a triumph of publicity—and not the simple kind of just taking ads. It's a very strange movie and people may, of course, like it for all sorts of reasons, but I think many may dislike it as I do and still feel they should be impressed by it; the educated and privileged may now be more susceptible to the mass media than the larger public—they're certainly easier to reach. The publicity about Richard Lester as an artist has been gaining extraordinary momentum ever since *A Hard Day's Night.* A critical success that is also a hit makes the director a genius; he's a magician who made money out of art. The media are in ravenous competition for ever bigger stories, for "trend" pieces and editorial essays, because once the process starts it's considered news. If Lester is "making the scene" a magazine that hasn't helped to build him up feels it's been scooped. *Petulia* is the come-dressed-as-the-sick-soul-of-America-party and in the opening sequence the guests arrive— rich victims of highway accidents in their casts and wheel chairs, like the spirit of '76 coming to opening night at the opera. It's science-horror fiction—a garish new world with charity balls at which you're invited to "Shake for Highway Safety."

Lester picked San Francisco for his attack on America just as in *How I Won the War* he picked World War II to attack war. That is, it looks like a real frontal attack on war itself if you attack the war that many people consider a just war. But then he concentrated not on the issues of that war but on the class hatreds of British officers and men—who were not engaged in defending London or bombing Germany but in building a cricket pitch in Africa. In *Petulia,* his hate letter to America, he relocates the novel, shifting the locale from Los Angeles to San Francisco, presumably, again, to face the big challenge by showing that even the best the country has to offer is rotten. But then he ducks the challenge he sets for himself by making San Francisco look like Los Angeles. And if he must put carnival barkers in Golden Gate Park and invent Sunday excursions for children to Alcatraz, if he must invent such caricatures of epicene expenditure and commercialism as bizarrely automated motels and dummy television sets, if he must provide his own ugliness and hysteria and lunacy and use filters to destroy the city's beautiful light, if, in short, he must falsify America in order to make it appear hateful, what is it he really hates? He's like a crooked cop framing a suspect with trumped-up evidence. We never find out *why:* he's too interested in making a flashy case to examine what he's doing. And reviewers seem unwilling to ask questions which might expose them to the charge that they're *still* looking for meaning instead of, in the new cant, just reacting to images—such questions as why does the movie keep juxtaposing shots of bloody surgery with shots of rock groups like the Grateful Dead or Big Brother and the Holding Company and shots of the war in Vietnam. What are these little montages supposed to do to us—make us feel that even the hero (a hardworking life-saving surgeon) is implicated in the war and that somehow contemporary popular music is also allied to destruction and death? (I thought only the moralists of the Soviet Union believed that.) The images of *Petulia* don't make valid connections, they're joined together for shock and excitement, and I don't believe in the brilliance of a method which equates hippies, war, surgery, wealth, Southern decadents, bullfights, etc. Lester's mix is almost as fraudulent as *Mondo Cane; Petulia* exploits any shocking material it can throw together to give false importance to a story about Holly Golightly and The Man in the Gray Flannel Suit. The jagged glittering mosaic style of *Petulia* is an armor protecting Lester from an artist's task; this kind of "style" no longer fools people so much in writing but it knocks them silly in films.

Movie directors in trouble fall back on what they love to call "personal style"—though how impersonal it often is can be illustrated by *Petulia*—which is not edited in the rhythmic, modulations-of-graphics style associated with Lester (and seen most distinctively in his best-edited, though not necessarily best film, *Help!*) but in the style of the movie surgeon, Anthony Gibbs, who acted as chopper on it, and who gave it the same kind of scissoring which he had used on *The Loneliness of the Long Distance Runner* and in his rescue operation on *Tom Jones*. This is, in much of *Petulia,* the most insanely obvious method of cutting film ever devised; keep the audience jumping with cuts, juxtapose startling images, anything for effectiveness, just make it *brilliant*—with the director taking, apparently, no responsibility for the *implied* connections. (The editing style is derived from Alain Resnais, and though it's a debatable style in his films, he uses it responsibly not just opportunistically.)

Richard Lester, the director of *Petulia,* is a shrill scold in Mod clothes. Consider a sequence like the one in which the beaten-to-a-gruesome-pulp heroine is taken out to an ambulance, to the accompaniment of hippies making stupid, unfeeling remarks. It is embarrassingly reminiscent of the older people's comments about the youthful sub-pre-hippies of *The Knack.* Lester has simply shifted villains. Is he saying that America is so rotten that even our hippies are malignant? I rather suspect he is, but why? Lester has taken a fashionably easy way to attack America, and because of the war in Vietnam some people are willing to accept the bloody montages that make them feel we're all guilty, we're rich, we're violent, we're spoiled, we can't relate to each other, etc. Probably the director who made three celebrations of youth and freedom (*A Hard Day's Night, The Knack,* and *Help!*) is now desperate to expand his range and become a "serious" director, and this is the new look in seriousness.

It's easy to make fun of the familiar ingredients of trash—the kook heroine who steals a tuba (that's not like the best of Carole Lombard but like the worst of Irene Dunne), the vaguely impotent, meaninglessly handsome rotter husband, Richard Chamberlain (back to the rich, spineless weaklings of David Manners), and Joseph Cotten as one more insanely vicious decadent Southerner spewing out villainous lines. (Even Victor Jory in *The Fugitive Kind* wasn't much meaner.) What's terrible is not so much this feeble conventional trash as the director's attempts to turn it all into scintillating art and burning comment; what is really awful is the trash of his ideas and artistic effects.

Is there any art in this obscenely self-important movie? Yes, but in a format like this the few good ideas don't really shine as they do in simpler trash; we have to go through so much unpleasantness and showing-off to get to them. Lester should trust himself more as a director and stop the cinemagician stuff because there's good, tense direction in a few sequences. He got a good performance from George C. Scott and a sequence of post-marital discord between Scott and Shirley Knight that, although overwrought, is not so glaringly overwrought as the rest of the picture. It begins to suggest something interesting that the picture might have been about. (Shirley Knight should, however, stop fondling her hair like a miser with a golden hoard; it's time for her to get another prop.) And Julie Christie is extraordinary just to look at—lewd and anxious, expressive and empty, brilliantly faceted but with something central missing, almost as if there's no woman inside.

VIII

2001 is a movie that might have been made by the hero of *Blow-Up*, and it's fun to think about Kubrick really doing every dumb thing he wanted to do, building enormous science-fiction sets and equipment, never even bothering to figure out what he was going to do with them. Fellini, too, had gotten carried away with the Erector Set approach to movie-making, but his big science-fiction construction, exposed to view at the end of *8½*, was abandoned. Kubrick never really made his movie either but he doesn't seem to know it. Some people like the American International Pictures stuff because it's rather idiotic and maybe some people love *2001* just because Kubrick did all that stupid stuff, acted out a kind of super sci-fi nut's fantasy. In some ways it's the biggest amateur movie of them all, complete even to the amateur-movie obligatory scene—the director's little daughter (in curls) telling daddy what kind of present she wants.

There was a little pre-title sequence in *You Only Live Twice* with an astronaut out in space that was in a looser, more free style than *2001*—a daring little moment that I think was more fun than all of *2001*. It had an element of the unexpected, of the shock of finding death in space lyrical. Kubrick is carried away by the idea. The secondary title of *Dr. Stragelove*, which we took to be satiric, *How I learned to stop worrying and love the bomb*, was not, it now appears, altogether satiric for Kubrick. *2001* celebrates the invention of tools of death, as an evolutionary route to a higher order of *non-human* life. Kubrick literally learned to stop worrying and love the bomb; he's become his own butt—the Herman Kahn of extraterrestrial games theory. The ponderous blurry appeal of the picture may be that it takes its stoned audience out of this world to a consoling vision of a graceful world of space, controlled by superior godlike minds, where the hero is reborn as an angelic baby. It has the dreamy somewhere-over-the-rainbow appeal of a new vision of heaven. *2001* is a celebration of cop-out. It says man is just a tiny nothing on the stairway to paradise, something better is coming, and it's all out of your hands anyway. There's an intelligence out there in space controlling your destiny from ape to angel, so just follow the slab. Drop up.

It's a bad, bad sign when a movie director begins to think of himself as a myth-maker, and this limp myth of a grand plan that justifies slaughter and ends with resurrection has been around before. Kubrick's story line—accounting for evolution by an extraterrestrial intelligence—is probably the most gloriously redundant plot of all time. And although his intentions may have been different, *2001* celebrates the *end of man;* those beautiful mushroom clouds at the end of *Strangelove* were no accident. In *2001, A Space Odyssey*, death and life are all the same: no point is made in the movie of Gary Lockwood's death—the moment isn't even defined—and the hero doesn't discover that the hibernating scientists have become corpses. That's unimportant in a movie about the beauties of resurrection. Trip off to join the cosmic intelligence and come back a better mind. And as the trip in the movie is the usual psychedelic light show, the audience doesn't even have to worry about getting to Jupiter. They can go to heaven in Cinerama.

It isn't accidental that we don't care if the characters live or die; if Kubrick has made his people so uninteresting, it is partly because characters and individual fates just aren't big enough for certain kinds of big movie directors. Big movie directors become generals in the arts; and they want subjects to match their new importance. Kubrick has announced that his next project is *Napoleon*—which, for a movie director, is the equivalent of Joan of Arc for an actress. Lester's "savage" comments about affluence and malaise, Kubrick's inspirational banality about how we will become as gods through machinery, are big-shot show-business deep thinking. This isn't a new show-business phenomenon; it belongs to the genius tradition of the theatre. Big entrepreneurs, producers, and directors who stage big spectacular shows, even designers of large sets have traditionally begun to play the role of visionaries and thinkers and men with answers. They get too big for art. Is a work of art possible if pseudoscience and the technology of movie-making become more important to the "artist" than man? This is central to the failure of *2001*. It's a monumentally unimaginative movie: Kubrick, with his $750,000 centrifuge, and in love with gigantic hardware and control panels, is the Belasco of science fiction. The special effects—though straight from the drawing board—are good and big and awesomely, expensively detailed. There's a little more that's good in the movie, when Kubrick doesn't take himself too seriously—like the comic moment when the gliding space vehicles begin their Johann Strauss waltz; that is to say, when the director shows a bit of a sense of proportion about what he's doing, and sees things momentarily as comic—when the movie doesn't take itself with such idiot solemnity. The light-show trip is of no great distinction; compared to the work of experimental filmmakers like Jordan Belson, it's third-rate. If big film directors are to get credit for doing badly what others have been doing brilliantly for years with no money, just because they've put it on a big screen, then businessmen are greater than poets and theft is art.

IX

Part of the fun of movies is in seeing "what everybody's talking about," and if people are flocking to a movie, or if the press can con us into thinking that they are, then ironically, there is a sense in which we want to see it, even if we suspect we won't enjoy it, because we want to know what's going on. Even if it's the worst inflated pompous trash that is the most talked about (and it usually is) and even if that talk is manufactured, we want to see the movies because so many people fall for whatever is talked about that they make the advertisers' lies true. Movies absorb material from the culture and the other arts so fast that some films that have been widely *sold* become culturally and sociologically important whether they are good movies or not. Movies like *Morgan!* or *Georgy Girl* or *The Graduate*—aesthetically trivial movies which, however, because of the ways some people react to them, enter into the national bloodstream—become cultural and psychological equivalents of watching a political convention, to observe what's going on. And though this has little to do with the art of movies, it has a great deal to do with the appeal of movies.

An analyst tells me that when his patients are not talking about their personal hangups and their immediate problems they talk about the situations and characters in movies like *The Graduate* or *Belle de Jour* and they talk about them with as much personal involvement as about their immediate problems. I have elsewhere suggested that this way of reacting to movies as psychodrama used to be considered a pre-literate way of reacting but that now those considered "post-literate" are reacting like pre-literates. The high school and college students identifying with Georgy Girl or Dustin Hoffman's Benjamin are not that different from the stenographer who used to live and breathe with the Joan Crawford-working girl and worry about whether that rich boy would really make her happy—and considered her pictures "great." They don't see the movie as a movie but as part of the soap opera of their lives. The fan magazines used to encourage this kind of identification; now the *advanced* mass media encourage it, and those who want to sell to youth use the language of "just let it flow over you." The person who responds this way does not respond more freely but less freely and less fully than the person who is aware of what is well done and what badly done in a movie, who can accept some things in it and reject others, who uses all his senses in reacting, not just his emotional vulnerabilities.

Still, we care about what other people care about—sometimes because we want to know how far we've gotten from common responses—and if a movie is important to other people we're interested in it because of what it means to them, even if it doesn't mean much to us. The small triumph of *The Graduate* was to have domesticated alienation and the difficulty of communication, by making what Benjamin is alienated from a middle-class comic strip and making it absurdly evident that he has nothing to communicate—which is just what makes him an acceptable hero for the large movie audience. If he said anything or had any ideas, the audience would probably hate him. *The Graduate* isn't a *bad* movie, it's entertaining, though in a fairly slick way (the audience is just about programmed for laughs). What's surprising is that so many people take it so seriously. What's funny about the movie are the laughs on that dumb sincere boy who wants to talk about art in bed when the woman just wants to fornicate. But then the movie begins to pander to youthful narcissism, glorifying his innocence, and making the predatory (and now crazy) woman the villainess. Commercially this works: the inarticulate dull boy becomes a romantic hero for the audience to project into with all those squishy and now conventional feelings of look, his parents don't communicate with him; look, he wants truth not sham, and so on. But the movie betrays itself and its own expertise, sells out its comic moments that click along with the rhythm of a hit Broadway show, to make the oldest movie pitch of them all— asking the audience to identify with the simpleton who is the latest version of the misunderstood teen-ager and the pure-in-heart boy next door. It's almost painful to tell kids who have gone to see *The Graduate* eight times that once was enough for you because you've already seen it eighty times with Charles Ray and Robert Harron and Richard Barthelmess and Richard Cromwell and Charles Farrell. How could you convince them that a movie that sells innocence is a very commercial piece of work when they're so clearly in the market to buy innocence? When *The Graduate* shifts to the tender awakenings of love, it's just the latest version of *David and Lisa*. *The Graduate* only wants to succeed and that's fundamentally what's the matter with it. There is a pause for a laugh after the mention of "Berkeley" that is an unmistakable sign of hunger for success; this kind of movie-making shifts values, shifts focus, shifts emphasis, shifts everything for a sure-fire response. Mike Nichols's "gift" is that he lets the audience direct him; this is demagoguery in the arts.

Even the cross-generation fornication is standard for the genre. It goes back to Pauline Frederick in *Smouldering Fires,* and Clara Bow was at it with mama Alice Joyce's boyfriend in *Our Dancing Mothers,* and in the forties it was *Mildred Pierce.* Even the terms are not different: in these movies the seducing adults are customarily sophisticated, worldly, and corrupt, the kids basically innocent, though not so humorless and blank as Benjamin. In its basic attitudes *The Graduate* is corny American; it takes us back to before *The Game of Love* with Edwige Feuillère as the sympathetic older woman and *A Cold Wind in August* with the sympathetic Lola Albright performance.

What's interesting about the success of *The Graduate* is sociological: the revelation of how emotionally accessible modern youth is to the same old manipulation. The recurrence of certain themes in movies suggests that each generation wants romance restated in slightly new terms, and of course it's one of the pleasures of movies as a popular art that they can answer this need. And yet, and yet—one doesn't expect an *educated* generation to be so soft on itself, much softer than the factory workers of the past who didn't go back over and over to the same movies, mooning away in fixation on themselves and thinking this fixation meant movies had suddenly become an art, and *their* art.

<h1 style="text-align:center">X</h1>

When you're young the odds are very good that you'll find something to enjoy in almost any movie. But as you grow more experienced, the odds change. I saw a picture a few years ago that was the sixth version of material that wasn't much to start with. Unless you're feebleminded, the odds get worse and worse. We don't go on reading the same kind of manufactured novels—pulp Westerns or detective thrillers, say—all of our lives, and we don't want to go on and on looking at movies about cute heists by comically assorted gangs. The problem with a popular art form is that those who want something more are in a hopeless minority compared with the millions who are always seeing it for the first time, or for the reassurance and gratification of seeing the conventions fulfilled again. Probably a large part of the older audience gives up movies for this reason—simply that they've seen it before. And probably this is why so many of the best movie critics quit. They're wrong when they blame it on the movies going bad; it's the odds becoming so bad, and they can no longer bear the many tedious movies for the few good moments and the tiny shocks of recognition. Some become too tired, too frozen in fatigue, to respond to what *is* new. Others who *do* stay awake may become too demanding for the young who are seeing it all for the first hundred times. The critical task is necessarily comparative, and younger people do not truly know what is new. And despite all the chatter about the media and how smart the young are, they're incredibly naïve about mass culture—perhaps *more* naïve than earlier generations (though I don't know why). Maybe watching all that television hasn't done so much for them as they seem to think; and when I read a young intellectual's appreciation of *Rachel, Rachel* and come to "the mother's passion for chocolate bars is a superb symbol for the second coming of childhood" I know the writer is still in his first childhood, and I wonder if he's going to come out of it.

One's moviegoing tastes and habits change—I still like in movies what I always liked but now, for example, I really want documentaries. After all the years of stale stupid acted-out stories, with less and less for me in them, I am desperate to know something, desperate for facts, for information, for faces of non-actors and for knowledge of how people live—for revelations, not for the little bits of show-business detail worked up for us by show-business minds who got them from the same movies we're tired of.

But the big change is in our *habits*. If we make any kind of decent, useful life for ourselves we have less need to run from it to those diminishing pleasures of the movies. When we go to the movies we want something good, something sustained, we don't want to settle for just a bit of something, because we have other things to do. If life at home is more interesting, why go to the movies? And the theatres frequented by true moviegoers—those perennial displaced persons in each city, the loners and the losers—depress us. Listening to them—and they are often more audible than the sound track—as they cheer the cons and jeer the cops, we may still share their disaffection, but it's not enough to keep us interested in cops and robbers. A little nose-thumbing isn't enough. If we've grown up at the movies we know that good work is continuous not with the academic, respectable tradition but with the glimpses of something good in trash, yet we want the subversive gesture carried to the domain of discovery. Trash has given us an appetite for art.

Harper's, February 1969

SIMON OF THE DESERT
SAINTLINESS

We are so often bathed in emotion at the movies by all those directors whose highest ambition is to make us feel feelings that aren't worth feeling that the cool detachment of Luis Buñuel has a surprising edge. Buñuel doesn't make full contact with us, and the distance can be fun; it can result in the pleasure of irony, though it can also result in the dissatisfaction of feeling excluded. His indifference to whether we understand him or not can seem insolent, and yet this is part of what makes him fascinating. Indifference can be tantalizing in art, as in romance, and by keeping us at a distance in a medium with which most directors try to involve us he deliberately undermines certain concepts that are almost axiomatic in drama and movies—especially drama and movies in their mass-culture form. Buñuel, who regards all that tender involvement as "bourgeois morality," deliberately assaults us for being so emotional. His most distinctive quality as a movie-maker is the lack of certainty he inflicts on us about how we should feel toward his characters. Buñuel shoots a story simply and directly, to make just the points he wants to make, though if he fails to make them or doesn't make them clearly he doesn't seem to give a damn. He leaves in miscalculations, and fragments that don't work—like the wheelchair on the sidewalk in *Belle de Jour*. He's a remarkably fast, economical, and careless movie-maker, and the carelessness no doubt accounts for some of the ambiguity in the films, such as the unresolved trick endings that leave us dangling. From the casting and the listless acting in many of his movies, one can conclude only that he's unconcerned about such matters; often he doesn't seem to bother even to cast for type, and one can't easily tell if the characters are meant to be what they appear to be. He uses actors in such an indifferent way that they scarcely even stand for the characters. Rather than allow the bad Mexican actors that he generally works with to act, he seems to dispense with acting by just rushing them through their roles without giving them time to understand what they're doing. Clearly, he prefers no acting to bad acting. The mixture of calculation and carelessness in his ambiguity can be maddening, as in some of *Viridiana* (1961) and in most of the slackly directed *The Exterminating Angel* (1962). But sometimes what makes an artist great and original is that in his lack of interest in (or lack of talent for) what other artists have been concerned with he helps us see things differently and develops the medium in new ways. Like Borges, who won't even bother to write a book, Buñuel probably doesn't think casting or acting is important enough to bother about. And casting without worrying about whether the actors suit the role—casting almost *against* type—and not allowing the actors to work up characterizations can give movies a new kind of tone. Without the conventional emotional resonances that actors acting provide, his movies have a thinner texture that begins to become a new kind of integrity, and they affect us as fables. Most movies are full of actors trying to appeal to us, and the movies themselves try so hard to win us over that the screen is practically kissing us. When Buñuel is at his most indifferent, he is sometimes at his best and most original, as in parts of *Nazarin* (1958), which opened here last summer, and in almost all of his newly released— and peculiarly exhilarating—*Simon of the Desert.*

Other movie directors tell us how we should feel; they want our approval for being such good guys, and most of them are proudest when they can demonstrate their commitment to humanitarian principles. Buñuel makes the charitable the butt of humor and shows the lechery and mendacity of the poor and misbegotten. As a movie-making comedian, he is a critic of mankind. One can generally define even a critic's position, but there is no way to get a hold on what Buñuel believes in. There is no characteristic Buñuel hero or heroine, and there is no kind of behavior that escapes his ridicule. His movies are full of little sadistic jokes that we can't quite tell how to take. The movie director most influenced by de Sade, and the only one still at work who had close ties to the Surrealist movement, Buñuel has gone on using the techniques of the Surrealists in the medium that once seemed their natural habitat. We may not really like his jokes, yet they make us laugh. A perturbing example that comes all too readily to mind: When Jorge, in *Viridiana,* frees a mistreated dog that has been tied to a cart and then we see another cart coming from the opposite direction with another dog tied to it, is Buñuel saying that Jorge is a realist who does what he can, or does Buñuel really mean what the audience, by its laughter, clearly takes the scene to mean—that Jorge's action was useless, since there are so many mistreated dogs? This "joke" could be extended to the "comedy" of saving one Jew from the ovens or one Biafran baby from starvation, and I think we are aware of the obscenity in the humor even as we laugh—we laugh at the recognition that we are capable of participating in the obscenity. His jokes are perverse and irrational and blasphemous, and it may feel liberating to laugh at them just because they are a return to a kind of primitive folk comedy—the earliest form of black comedy, enjoyed by those who laugh at deformity and guffaw when a man kicks a goat or squeezes an udder too hard. Buñuel reminds us of the cruelty that he feels sentimental art tries to hide, and we respond by laughing at horrors. This is partly, I think, because we are conscious of the anti-sentimentality of his technique—of his toughness and his willingness to look things in the eye.

Some of his recurrent jokes are really rather private jokes—the udders and little torture kits and objects turned into fetishes—and Buñuel throwing his whammies can seem no more than a gigantic, Spanish Terry Southern. Bad Buñuel is like good Terry Southern—a putdown and a cackle. Sometimes when we laugh at a Buñuel film we probably want to sound more knowledgeable than we are; we just know it's "dirty." Yet this is the vindication of the Surrealist idea of the power of subjective images: we *do* feel certain things to be "dirty" and some kinds of violence to be funny, and we laugh at them without being able to explain why. Buñuel gets at material we've buried, and it's a release to laugh this impolite laughter, which is like laughter from out of nowhere, at jokes we didn't know we knew.

Once, in Berkeley, after a lecture by LeRoi Jones, as the audience got up to leave, I asked an elderly white couple next to me how they could applaud when Jones said that all whites should be killed. And the little gray-haired woman replied, "But that was just a metaphor. He's a wonderful speaker." I think we're inclined to react similarly to Buñuel—who once referred to some of those who praised *Un Chien Andalou* as "that crowd of imbeciles who find the film beautiful or poetic when it is fundamentally a desperate and passionate call to murder." To be blind to Buñuel's meanings as a way of being open to "art" is a variant of the very sentimentality that he satirizes. The moviegoers apply the same piousness to "art" that his mock saints do to humanity: both groups would rather swallow insults than be tough-minded. Buñuel is the opposite of a flower child.

Simon of the Desert, a short (forty-five-minute) feature made in Mexico in 1965, just before he made *Belle de Jour*, is a playful little travesty on the temptations of St. Simeon Stylites, the fifth-century desert anchorite who spent thirty-seven years preaching to pilgrims from his perch on top of a column. It is, in both a literal and a figurative sense, a shaggy-saint story, and (unlike much of Buñuel's work) it is charming. The narrative style of *Simon* is so straightforward and ascetically simple that it may be easier to see what he is saying in this film than in his more elaborate divertissements about saintliness turning into foolishness—*Nazarin* and the complicated, allusive *Viridiana*, which was cluttered with Freudian symbols. Buñuel seems to have a grudging respect for Nazarin and Simon that he didn't show for Viridiana, whom he made sickly, chaste, and priggish.

Viridiana seemed dramatically out of focus because Buñuel didn't even dignify her desire to do good, and so the film had to depend on the pleasures and shocks of blasphemy—probably not inconsiderable for insiders, but insufficient for others. The tone of *Simon* is almost jovial, though the style is direct—just one incident after another—and as bare and objective as if he were documenting a scientific demonstration; even the Surreal details (like a coffin skittering over the ground) are presented in a matter-of-fact way. Buñuel has himself in the past given in to temptation: with more money than he was accustomed to, he fell for the fanciness of all that French *mise-en-scène* that made his *Diary of a Chambermaid* so revoltingly "beautiful." But there's very little money in *Simon,* and there was, apparently, none to finish it; the bummer of an ending was just a way to wind it up.

Simon (Claudio Brook) performs his miracles, and the crowds evaluate them like a bunch of New York cabdrivers discussing a parade: whatever it was, it wasn't much. He restores hands to a thief whose hands have been chopped off; the crowds rate the miracle "not bad," and the thief's first act with his new hands is to slap his own child. The Devil, in the female form of Silvia Pinal (much more amusing as the Devil than she was in her guises in other Buñuel films), tempts him, and, at one point, frames him in front of the local priests, who are more than willing to believe the worst of him. Simon is a saint, and yet not only are his miracles worthless—they can't change men's natures—but even he is dragged down by his instincts. Buñuel is saying that saintliness is sentimentality, that, as the platitude has it, human nature doesn't change. This is not, God knows, a very interesting point; nor do I think it has the slightest validity; the theme is an odd mixture—a Spanish schoolboy's view of life joined to an adult atheist's disbelief in redemption. This outlook creates some problems when it comes to responding to Buñuel's work.

There are probably many lapsed Catholics who still believe in sin though they no longer believe in redemption, who have the disease though they have lost faith in the cure. In this they are not much different from the Socialists who still accept the general Socialist analysis of capitalism without having much confidence in the Socialist solutions. But psychologically there is an enormous difference between those who regard man as the victim of violent instinctual drives and those who live by a belief in justice and decency, even without any real conviction that society will ever be better. The pessimistic view can be so offensive to our ameliorative, reforming disposition that it's almost inconceivable to us that an artist whose work we respond to on many levels can disagree with us at such a fundamental level. And so with Luis Buñuel in films, as, in literature, with D. H. Lawrence and T. S. Eliot and Pound, we often contrive to overlook what the artist is saying that is alien to us. Because Buñuel is anti-Church and is a Spaniard at odds with Franco, because he satirizes bourgeois hypocrisy, there is, I think, a tendency to applaud his work as if this were all it encompassed. At the movies, when we see horrors we expect the reformer's zeal; that is the convention in democratic art, and perhaps we project some of our outraged virtue onto Buñuel's films. We feel free to enjoy his anarchic humor—which is often funniest when it is cruelest—because we can feel we're laughing at Fascism and at the human stupidity that reinforces Fascism. But though his work is a series of arguments against the Grand Inquisitor's policies, his basic view of man is the Grand Inquisitor's. Buñuel attacks the Church as the perverter and frustrater of man—

the power trying to hold down sexuality, animality, irrationality, man's "instinctual nature." He sees bourgeois hypocrisy as the deceptions that men practice to deny the truth of their urges. His movies satirize the blindness of the spiritual; his would-be saints are fools—denying the instinctive demands not only in others but in themselves. Surrealism is both a belief in the irrationality of man and a technique for demonstrating it. In his *Land Without Bread*, Spain itself—that country that seems to be left over from something we don't understand—was a Surreal joke, a country where the only smiling faces were those of cretins. Like other passionate artists who fling horrors at us, Buñuel is an outraged lover of man, a disenchanted idealist; being a Spaniard, he makes comedy of his own disgust. He can't let go of the Church; he's an anti-Catholic the way Bogart was an anti-hero. He wants man to be purged of inhibitions, yet the people in his movies become grotesque when they're uninhibited. And when his saintly characters wise up and lose their faith, he can't show us that they're useful or better off, or even happier. He is overtly anti-romantic and anti-religious, yet he is obsessed with romantic, religious fools. He has never made a movie of *Don Quixote*, but he keeps pecking away at the theme of *Don Quixote*, and gets himself so enraged by the unfulfillment of ideals that he despises dreamers who can't make their dreams come true. In *Viridiana*, he twisted the theme into knots—turning in on himself so far that he came out the other end.

How can Buñuel in *Simon of the Desert* make a comedy out of a demonstration of what liberals have always denied and yet make liberals (rather than conservatives) laugh at it? It's as if someone made a comedy demonstrating that if you divided the world's wealth equally, it would all be back in the hands of the same people in a year, and this comedy became a big hit in Communist countries—which, however, it might very well do if the style of the comedy and the characters and details were the kind that the Communists responded to. And it might become an underground hit if it had jokes that brought something hidden out into the open: Buñuel's Freudian symbols and blasphemous gags alienate the conservatives and, of course, please the liberals. And then there is the matter of style. Buñuel doesn't pour on the prettiness, he doesn't turn a movie into a catered affair. There is such a thing as mass bourgeois movie sentimentality; we are surrounded by it, inundated by it, sinking in it, and Buñuel pulls us out of this muck. *Simon* is so palpably clean that it's an aesthetic assault on conservative taste. It's hard to love man; Hollywood movies pretend it's easy, but every detail gives the show away. Buñuel's style tells the truth of his feelings; the Spanish stance is too strong for soft emotions like pity. Though, as in *Diary of a Chambermaid*, he can be so coldly unpleasant that we are repelled (and happy to be excluded), he never makes people pitiable lumps. And though he may turn Quixote into a cold green girl or a dithering man, in his films the quixotic gestures of the simple peasants are the only truly human gestures. A dwarf gives his inamorata an apple and his total love; a woman offers Nazarin a pineapple and her blessing. Nazarin is so stubbornly proud that it's a struggle for him to accept, and Buñuel himself is so proud that he will hardly give in to the gesture. Humility is so difficult for him that he just tosses in the pineapple ambiguously—he's so determined not to give in to the folly of tenderness that he cops out.

At the end of *Simon of the Desert* Simon is transported to the modern world, and we see him, a lost soul, in a Greenwich Village discothèque full of dancing teen-agers. This is a disastrous finish for the movie—a finish of the careless kind that Buñuel is prone to. The primitive Mexican desert setting situates the story plausibly, but New York is outside the movie's frame of reference, nor does this discothèque conceivably represent what Simon's temptation might be. What Buñuel intended as another little joke is instead a joke on his gloomy view. "It's the last dance," the Devil says, though what is presented to us as a vision of a mad, decaying world in its final orgy looks like a nice little platter party.

The New Yorker, February 15, 1969

PART FOUR

RAISING KANE

FROM THE CITIZEN KANE BOOK

1971

RAISING KANE

Citizen Kane is perhaps the one American talking picture that seems as fresh now as the day it opened. It may seem even fresher. A great deal in the movie that was conventional and almost banal in 1941 is so far in the past as to have been forgotten and become new. The Pop characterizations look modern, and rather better than they did at the time. New audiences may enjoy Orson Welles's theatrical flamboyance even more than earlier generations did, because they're so unfamiliar with the traditions it came out of. When Welles was young—he was twenty-five when the film opened—he used to be accused of "excessive showmanship," but the same young audiences who now reject "theatre" respond innocently and wholeheartedly to the most unabashed tricks of theatre—and of early radio plays—in Citizen Kane. At some campus showings, they react so gullibly that when Kane makes a demagogic speech about "the underprivileged," stray students will applaud enthusiastically, and a shout of "Right on!" may be heard. Though the political ironies are not clear to young audiences, and though young audiences don't know much about the subject—William Randolph Hearst, the master jingo journalist, being to them a stock villain, like Joe McCarthy; that is, a villain without the contours of his particular villainy—they nevertheless respond to the effrontery, the audacity, and the risks. Hearst's career and his power provided a dangerous subject that stimulated and energized all those connected with the picture—they felt they were *doing* something instead of just working on one more cooked-up story that didn't relate to anything that mattered. And to the particular kinds of people who shaped this enterprise the dangers involved made the subject irresistible.

Citizen Kane, the film that, as Truffaut said, is "probably the one that has started the largest number of filmmakers on their careers," was not an ordinary assignment. It is one of the few films ever made inside a major studio in the United States *in freedom*—not merely in freedom from interference but freedom from the routine methods of experienced directors. George J. Schaefer, who, with the help of Nelson Rockefeller, had become president of R.K.O. late in 1938, when it was struggling to avert bankruptcy, needed a miracle to save the company, and after the national uproar over Orson Welles's *The War of the Worlds* broadcast Rockefeller apparently thought that Welles—"the wonder boy"—might come up with one, and urged Schaefer to get him. But Welles, who was committed to the theatre and wasn't especially enthusiastic about making movies, rejected the first offers; he held out until Schaefer offered him complete control over his productions. Then Welles brought out to Hollywood from New York his own production unit—the Mercury Theatre company, a group of actors and associates he could count on—and, because he was inexperienced in movies and was smart and had freedom, he was able to find in Hollywood people who had been waiting all their lives to try out new ideas. So a miracle did come about, though it was not the kind of miracle R.K.O. needed.

Kane does something so well, and with such spirit, that the fullness and completeness of it continue to satisfy us. The formal elements themselves produce elation; we are kept aware of how marvellously worked out the ideas are. It would be high-toned to call this method of keeping the audience aware "Brechtian," and it would be wrong. It comes out of a different tradition—the same commercial-comedy tradition that Walter Kerr analyzed so beautifully in his review of the 1969 Broadway revival of *The Front Page,* the 1928 play by Ben Hecht and Charles MacArthur, when he said, "A play was held to be something of a machine in those days. . . . It was a machine for surprising and delighting the audience, regularly, logically, insanely, but accountably. A play was like a watch that laughed." The mechanics of movies are rarely as entertaining as they are in *Citizen Kane,* as cleverly designed to be the kind of fun that keeps one alert and conscious of the enjoyment of the artifices themselves.

Walter Kerr goes on to describe the second-act entrance prepared for Walter Burns, the scheming, ruthless managing editor of *The Front Page:*

He can't just come on and declare himself. . . . He's got to walk into a tough situation in order to be brutally nonchalant, which is what we think is funny about him. The machinery has not only given him and the play the right punctuation, the change of pace that refreshes even as it moves on. It has also covered him, kept him from being obvious while exploiting the one most obvious thing about him. You might say that the machinery has covered itself, perfectly squared itself. We are delighted to have the man on, we are delighted to have him on at this time, we are aware that it is sleight-of-hand that has got him on, and we are as delighted by the sleight-of-hand as by the man.

Citizen Kane is made up of an astonishing number of such bits of technique, and of sequences built to make their points and get their laughs and hit climax just before a fast cut takes us to the next. It is practically a collection of blackout sketches, but blackout sketches arranged to comment on each other, and it was planned that way right in the shooting script.

It is difficult to explain what makes any great work great, and particularly difficult with movies, and maybe more so with *Citizen Kane* than with other great movies, because it isn't a work of special depth or a work of subtle beauty. It is a shallow work, a *shallow* masterpiece. Those who try to account for its stature as a film by claiming it to be profound are simply dodging the problem—or maybe they don't recognize that there is one. Like most of the films of the sound era that are called masterpieces, *Citizen Kane* has reached its audience gradually over the years rather than at the time of release. Yet, unlike the others, it is conceived and acted as entertainment in a popular style (unlike, say, *Rules of the Game* or *Rashomon* or *Man of Aran*, which one does not think of in crowd-pleasing terms). Apparently, the easiest thing for people to do when they recognize that something is a work of art is to trot out the proper schoolbook terms for works of art, and there are articles on *Citizen Kane* that call it a tragedy in fugal form and articles that explain that the hero of *Citizen Kane* is time—time being a proper sort of modern hero for an important picture. But to use the conventional schoolbook explanations for greatness, and pretend that it's profound, is to miss what makes it such an American triumph—that it manages to create something aesthetically exciting and durable out of the playfulness of American muckraking satire. *Kane* is closer to comedy than to tragedy, though so overwrought in style as to be almost a Gothic comedy. What might possibly be considered tragic in it has such a Daddy Warbucks quality that if it's tragic at all it's comic-strip tragic. The mystery in *Kane* is largely fake, and the Gothic-thriller atmosphere and the Rosebud gimmickry (though fun) are such obvious penny-dreadful popular theatrics that they're not so very different from the fake mysteries that Hearst's *American Weekly* used to whip up—the haunted castles and the curses fulfilled. *Citizen Kane* is a "popular" masterpiece—not in terms of actual popularity but in terms of its conceptions and the way it gets its laughs and makes its points. Possibly it was too complexly told to be one of the greatest commercial successes, but we can't really tell whether it might have become even a modest success, because it didn't get a fair chance.

237

Orson Welles brought forth a miracle, but he couldn't get by with it. Though Hearst made some direct attempts to interfere with the film, it wasn't so much what he did that hurt the film commercially as what others feared he might do, to them and to the movie industry. They knew he was contemplating action, so they did the picture in for him; it was as if they decided whom the king might want killed, and, eager to oblige, performed the murder without waiting to be asked. Before *Kane* opened, George J. Schaefer was summoned to New York by Nicholas Schenck, the chairman of the board of Loew's International, the M-G-M affiliate that controlled the distribution of M-G-M pictures. Schaefer had staked just about everything on Welles, and the picture looked like a winner, but now Schenck made Schaefer a cash offer from Louis B. Mayer, the head of production at M-G-M, of $842,000 if Schaefer would destroy the negative and all the prints. The picture had actually cost only $686,033; the offer handsomely included a fair amount for the post-production costs.

Mayer's motive may have been partly friendship and loyalty to Hearst, even though Hearst, who had formerly been associated with M-G-M, had, some years earlier, after a dispute with Irving Thalberg, taken his investment out of M-G-M and moved his star, Marion Davies, and his money to Warner Brothers. M-G-M had lost money on a string of costume clinkers starring Miss Davies (*Beverly of Graustark*, et al.), and had even lost money on some of her good pictures, but Mayer had got free publicity for M-G-M releases out of the connection with Hearst, and had also got what might be called deep personal satisfaction. In 1929, when Herbert Hoover invited the Mayers to the White House—they were the first "informal" guests after his inauguration—Hearst's *New York American* gave the visit a full column. Mayer enjoyed fraternizing with Hearst and his eminent guests; photographs show Mayer with Hearst and Lindbergh, Mayer with Hearst and Winston Churchill, Mayer at lunch with Bernard Shaw and Marion Davies—but they never, of course, show Mayer with both Hearst and Miss Davies. Candid cameramen sometimes caught the two together, but Hearst, presumably out of respect for his wife, did not pose in groups that included Miss Davies. Despite the publicity showered on her in the Hearst papers, the forms were carefully observed. She quietly packed and left for her own house on the rare occasions when Mrs. Hearst, who lived in the East, was expected to be in residence at San Simeon. Kane's infatuation for the singer Susan Alexander in the movie was thus a public flaunting of matters that Hearst was careful and considerate about. Because of this, Mayer's longtime friendship for Hearst was probably a lesser factor than the fear that the Hearst press would reveal some sordid stories about the movie moguls and join in one of those recurrent crusades against movie immorality, like the one that had destroyed Fatty Arbuckle's career. The movie industry was frightened of reprisals. (The movie industry is always frightened, and is always proudest of films that celebrate courage.) As one of the trade papers phrased it in those nervous weeks when no one knew whether the picture would be released, "the industry could ill afford to be made the object of counterattack by the Hearst newspapers."

There were rumors that Hearst was mounting a general campaign; his legal staff had seen the script, and Louella Parsons, the Hearst movie columnist, who had attended a screening of the film flanked by lawyers, was agitated and had swung into action. The whole industry, it was feared, would take the rap for R.K.O.'s indiscretion, and, according to the trade press at the time (and Schaefer confirms this report), Mayer was not putting up the $842,000 all by himself. It was a joint offer from the top movie magnates, who were combining for common protection. The offer was presented to Schaefer on the ground that it was in the best interests of everybody concerned—which was considered to be the entire, threatened industry— for *Citizen Kane* to be destroyed. Rather astonishingly, Schaefer refused. He didn't confer with his board of directors, because, he says, he had good reason to think they would tell him to accept. He refused even though R.K.O., having few theatres of its own, was dependent on the other companies and he had been warned that the big theatre circuits—controlled by the men who wanted the picture destroyed—would refuse to show it.

Schaefer knew the spot he was in. The premiere had been tentatively set for February 14th at the Radio City Music Hall—usually the showcase for big R.K.O. pictures, because R.K.O. was partly owned by the Rockefellers and the Chase National Bank, who owned the Music Hall. The manager of the theatre had been enthusiastic about the picture. Then, suddenly, the Music Hall turned it down. Schaefer phoned Nelson Rockefeller to find out why, and, he says, "Rockefeller told me that Louella Parsons had warned him off it, that she had asked him, 'How would you like to have the *American Weekly* magazine section run a double-page spread on John D. Rockefeller?' " According to Schaefer, she had also called David Sarnoff, another large investor in R.K.O., and similarly threatened him. In mid-February, with a minor contract dispute serving as pretext, the Hearst papers blasted R.K.O. and Schaefer in front-page stories; it was an unmistakable public warning. Schaefer was stranded; he had to scrounge for theatres, and, amid the general fear that Hearst might sue and would almost certainly remove advertising for any houses that showed *Citizen Kane*, he couldn't get bookings. The solution was for R.K.O. to take the risks of any lawsuits, but when the company leased an independent theatre in Los Angeles and refurbished the Palace (then a vaudeville house), which R.K.O. owned, for the New York opening, and did the same for a theatre R.K.O. owned in Chicago, Schaefer had trouble launching an advertising campaign. (Schenck, not surprisingly, owned a piece of the biggest movie-advertising agency.) Even after the early rave reviews and the initial enthusiasm, Schaefer couldn't get bookings except in the theatres that R.K.O. itself owned and in a few small art houses that were willing to take the risk. Eventually, in order to get the picture into theatres,

Schaefer threatened to sue Warners', Fox, Paramount, and Loew's on a charge of conspiracy. (There was reason to believe the company heads had promised Hearst they wouldn't show it in their theatres.) Warners' (perhaps afraid of exposure and the troubles with their stockholders that might result from a lawsuit) gave in and booked the picture, and the others followed, halfheartedly—in some cases, theatres paid for the picture but didn't play it.

By then, just about everybody in the industry was scared, or mad, or tired of the whole thing, and though the feared general reprisals against the industry did not take place, R.K.O. was getting bruised. The Hearst papers banned publicity on R.K.O. pictures and dropped an announced serialization of the novel *Kitty Foyle* which had been timed for the release of the R.K.O. film version. Some R.K.O. films didn't get reviewed and others got bad publicity. It was all petty harassment, of a kind that could be blamed on the overzealous Miss Parsons and other Hearst employees, but it was obviously sanctioned by Hearst, and it was steady enough to keep the industry uneasy.

By the time *Citizen Kane* got into Warners' theatres, the picture had acquired such an odd reputation that people seemed to distrust it, and it didn't do very well. It was subsequently withdrawn from circulation, perhaps because of the vicissitudes of R.K.O., and until the late fifties, when it was reissued and began to play in the art houses and to attract a new audience, it was seen only in pirated versions in 16 mm. Even after Mayer had succeeded in destroying the picture commercially, he went on planning vengeance on Schaefer for refusing his offer. Stockholders in R.K.O. began to hear that the company wasn't prospering because Schaefer was anti-Semitic and was therefore having trouble getting proper distribution for R.K.O. pictures. Schaefer says that Mayer wanted to get control of R.K.O. and that the rumor was created to drive down the price of the stock—that Mayer hoped to scare out Floyd Odlum, a major stockholder, and buy his shares. Instead, Odlum, who had opposed Nelson Rockefeller's choice of Schaefer to run the company, bought enough of Sarnoff's stock to have a controlling interest, and by mid-1942 Schaefer was finished at R.K.O. Two weeks after he left, Welles's unit was evicted from its offices on the lot and given a few hours to move out, and the R.K.O. employees who had worked with Welles were punished with degrading assignments on B pictures. Mayer's friendship with Hearst was not ruffled. A few years later, when Mayer left his wife of forty years, he rented Marion Davies's Beverly Hills mansion. Eventually, he was one of Hearst's honorary pallbearers. *Citizen Kane* didn't actually lose money, but in Hollywood bookkeeping it wasn't a big enough moneymaker to balance the scandal.

III

Welles was recently quoted as saying, "Theatre is a collective experience; cinema is the work of one single person." This is an extraordinary remark from the man who brought his own Mercury Theatre players to Hollywood (fifteen of them appeared in *Citizen Kane*), and also the Mercury coproducer John Houseman, the Mercury composer Bernard Herrmann, and various assistants, such as Richard Wilson, William Alland, and Richard Barr. He not only brought his whole supportive group—his family, he called them then—but found people in Hollywood, such as the cinematographer Gregg Toland, to contribute their knowledge and gifts to *Citizen Kane*. Orson Welles has done some marvellous things in his later movies—some great things—and there is more depth in the somewhat botched *The Magnificent Ambersons*, of 1942 (which also used many of the Mercury players), than in *Citizen Kane*, but his principal career in the movies has been in adaptation, as it was earlier on the stage. He has never again worked on a subject with the immediacy and impact of *Kane*. His later films—even those he has so painfully struggled to finance out of his earnings as an actor—haven't been *conceived* in terms of daring modern subjects that excite us, as the very idea of *Kane* excited us. This particular kind of journalist's sense of what would be a scandal as well as a great subject, and the ability to write it, belonged not to Welles but to his now almost forgotten associate Herman J. Mankiewicz, who wrote the script, and who inadvertently destroyed the picture's chances. There is a theme that is submerged in much of *Citizen Kane* but that comes to the surface now and then, and it's the linking life story of Hearst and of Mankiewicz and of Welles—the story of how brilliantly gifted men who seem to have everything it takes to do what they want to do are defeated. It's the story of how heroes become comedians and con artists.

The Hearst papers ignored Welles—Hearst may have considered this a fit punishment for an actor—though they attacked him indirectly with sneak attacks on those associated with him, and Hearst would frequently activate his secular arm, the American Legion, against him. But the Hearst papers worked Mankiewicz over in headlines; they persecuted him so long that he finally appealed to the American Civil Liberties Union for help. There was some primitive justice in this. Hearst had never met Welles, and, besides, Welles was a kid, a twenty-five-year-old prodigy (whose daughter Marion Davies's nephew was bringing up)—hardly the sort of person one held responsible. But Mankiewicz was a friend of both Marion Davies and Hearst, and had been a frequent guest at her beach house and at San Simeon. There, in the great baronial banquet hall, Hearst liked to seat Mankiewicz on his left, so that Mankiewicz, with all his worldliness and wit (the Central Park West Voltaire, Ben Hecht had called him a few years earlier), could entertain the guest of honor and Hearst wouldn't miss any of it. Mankiewicz betrayed their hospitality, even though he liked them both. They must have presented an irresistible target. And so Hearst, the yellow-press lord who had trained Mankiewicz's generation of reporters to betray *anyone* for a story, became at last the victim of his own style of journalism.

IV

In the first Academy Award ceremony, for 1927–28, Warner Brothers, which had just produced *The Jazz Singer,* was honored for "Marking an Epoch in Motion Picture History." If the first decade of talkies—roughly, the thirties—has never been rivalled in wit and exuberance, this is very largely because there was already in Hollywood in the late silent period a nucleus of the best American writers, and they either lured their friends West or were joined by them. Unlike the novelists who were drawn to Hollywood later, most of the best Hollywood writers of the thirties had a shared background; they had been reporters and critics, and they knew each other from their early days on newspapers and magazines.

In his autobiography, Ben Hecht tells of being broke in New York—it was probably the winter of 1926—and of getting a telegram from Herman Mankiewicz in Hollywood:

WILL YOU ACCEPT THREE HUNDRED PER WEEK TO WORK FOR PARAMOUNT PICTURES? ALL EXPENSES PAID. THE THREE HUNDRED IS PEANUTS. MILLIONS ARE TO BE GRABBED OUT HERE AND YOUR ONLY COMPETITION IS IDIOTS. DON'T LET THIS GET AROUND.

A newspaper photograph shows Mankiewicz greeting Hecht, "noted author, dramatist, and former newspaperman," upon his arrival. After Hecht had begun work at Paramount, he discovered that the studio chief, B. P. Schulberg—who at that time considered writers a waste of money—had been persuaded to hire him by a gambler's ploy: Mankiewicz had offered to tear up his own two-year contract if Hecht failed to write a successful movie. Hecht, that phenomenal fast hack who was to become one of the most prolific of all motion-picture writers (and one of the most frivolously cynical about the results), worked for a week and turned out the script that became Josef von Sternberg's great hit *Underworld.* That script brought Hecht the first Academy Award for an original story, and a few years later he initiated the practice of using Oscars as doorstops. The studio heads knew what they had in Hecht as soon as they read the script, and they showed their gratitude. Hecht has recorded:

I was given a ten-thousand-dollar check as a bonus for the week's work, a check which my sponsor Mankiewicz snatched out of my hand as I was bowing my thanks.

"You'll have it back in a week," Manky said. "I just want it for a few days to get me out of a little hole."

He gambled valiantly, tossing a coin in the air with Eddie Cantor and calling heads or tails for a thousand dollars. He lost constantly. He tried to get himself secretly insured behind his good wife Sara's back, planning to hock the policy and thus meet his obligation. This plan collapsed when the insurance-company doctor refused to accept him as a risk.

I finally solved the situation by taking Manky into the Front Office and informing the studio bosses of our joint dilemma. I asked that my talented friend be given a five-hundred-a-week raise. The studio could then deduct this raise from his salary. . . .

I left . . . with another full bonus check in my hand; and Manky, with his new raise, became the highest paid writer for Paramount Pictures, Inc.

The bait that brought the writers in was money, but those writers who, like Mankiewicz, helped set the traps had their own reason: conviviality. Mankiewicz's small joke "Don't let this get around" came from a man who lived for talk, a man who saw moviemaking as too crazy, too profitable, and too *easy* not to share with one's friends. By the early thirties, the writers who lived in Hollywood or commuted there included not only Mankiewicz and Hecht and Charles MacArthur but George S. Kaufman and Marc Connelly, and Nathanael West and his brother-in-law S. J. Perelman, and Preston Sturges, Dorothy Parker, Arthur Kober, Alice Duer Miller, John O'Hara, Donald Ogden Stewart, Samson Raphaelson (the *New York Times* reporter who wrote the play *The Jazz Singer*), Gene Fowler, and Nunnally Johnson, and such already famous playwrights as Philip Barry, S. N. Behrman, Maxwell Anderson, Robert E. Sherwood, and Sidney Howard. Scott Fitzgerald had already been there for his first stretch, in 1927, along with Edwin Justus Mayer, and by 1932 William Faulkner began coming and going, and from time to time Ring Lardner and Moss Hart would turn up. In earlier periods, American writers made a living on newspapers and magazines; in the forties and fifties, they went into the academies (or, once they got to college, never left). But in the late twenties and the thirties they went to Hollywood. And though, apparently, they one and all experienced it as prostitution of their talents—joyous prostitution in some cases—and though more than one fell in love with movies and thus suffered not only from personal frustration but from the corruption of the great, still new art, they nonetheless as a group were responsible for that sustained feat of careless magic we call "thirties comedy." *Citizen Kane* was, I think, its culmination.

V

Herman J. Mankiewicz, born in New York City in 1897, was the first son of a professor of education, who then took a teaching position in Wilkes-Barre, where his second son, Joseph L. Mankiewicz, was born in 1909, and where the boys and a sister grew up. Herman Mankiewicz graduated from Columbia in 1916, and after a period as managing editor of the *American Jewish Chronicle* he became a flying cadet with the United States Army in 1917 and, in 1918, a private first class with the Fifth Marines, 2nd Division, A.E.F. In 1919 and 1920, he was the director of the American Red Cross News Service in Paris, and after returning to this country to marry a great beauty, Miss Sara Aaronson, of Baltimore, he took his bride overseas with him while he worked as a foreign correspondent in Berlin from 1920 to 1922, doing political reporting for George Seldes on the *Chicago Tribune*. During that time, he also sent pieces on drama and books to the *New York Times* and *Women's Wear*. Hired in Berlin by Isadora Duncan, he became her publicity man for her return to America. At home again, he took a job as a reporter for the *New York World*. He was a gifted, prodigious writer, who contributed to *Vanity Fair,* the *Saturday Evening Post,* and many other magazines, and, while still in his twenties, collaborated with Heywood Broun, Dorothy Parker, Robert E. Sherwood, and others on a revue (*Round the Town*), and collaborated with George S. Kaufman on a play (*The Good Fellow*) and with Marc Connelly on another play (*The Wild Man of Borneo*). From 1923 to 1926, he was at the *Times,* backing up George S. Kaufman in the drama department; while he was there, he also became the first regular theatre critic for *The New Yorker,* writing weekly from June, 1925, until January, 1926, when Walter Wanger offered him a motion-picture contract and he left for Hollywood. The first picture he wrote was the Lon Chaney success *The Road to Mandalay*. In all, he worked on over seventy movies. He went on living and working in Los Angeles until his death, in 1953. He left three children: Don, born in Berlin in 1922, who is a novelist (*Trial*) and a writer for the movies (co-scenarist of *I Want to Live!*) and television ("Marcus Welby, M.D."); Frank, born in New York in 1924, who became a lawyer, a journalist, a Peace Corps worker, and Robert Kennedy's press assistant, and is now a columnist and television commentator; and Johanna, born in Los Angeles in 1937, who is a journalist (on *Time*) and is married to Peter Davis, the writer-producer of "The Selling of the Pentagon."

Told this way, Herman Mankiewicz's career sounds exemplary, but these are just the bare bones of the truth. Even though it would be easy to document this official life of the apparently rising young man with photographs of Mankiewicz in his Berlin days dining with the Chancellor, Mankiewicz in his newspaperman days outside the *Chicago Tribune* with Jack Dempsey, and so on, it would be hard to explain his sudden, early aging and the thickening of his features and the transparently cynical look on his face in later photographs.

It was a lucky thing for Mankiewicz that he got the movie job when he did, because he would never have risen at the *Times,* and though he wrote regularly for *The New Yorker* (and remarked of those of the Algonquin group who didn't, "The part-time help of wits is no better than the full-time help of half-wits"), *The New Yorker,* despite his pleas for cash, was paying him partly in stock, which wasn't worth much at the time. Mankiewicz drank heavily, and the drinking newspaperman was in the style of the *World* but not in the style of the *Times*. In October, 1925, he was almost fired. The drama critic then was Brooks Atkinson, and the drama editor was George S. Kaufman, with Mankiewicz second in line and Sam Zolotow third. Mankiewicz was sent to cover the performance of Gladys Wallis, who was the wife of the utilities magnate Samuel Insull, as Lady Teazle in *School for Scandal*. Mrs. Insull, who had abandoned her theatrical career over a quarter of a century before, was, according to biographers, bored with being a nobody when her husband was such a big somebody. She was fifty-six when she resumed her career, as Lady Teazle, who is meant to be about eighteen. The play had opened in Chicago, where, perhaps astutely, she performed for charity (St. Luke's Hospital), and the press had described her as brilliant. The night of the New York opening, Mankiewicz came back to the office drunk, started panning Mrs. Insull's performance, and then fell asleep over his typewriter. As Zolotow recalls it, "Kaufman began to read the review, and it was so venomous he was outraged. That was the only time I ever saw Kaufman lose his temper." The review wasn't printed. The *Times* suffered the humiliation of running this item on October 23, 1925:

A NEW SCHOOL FOR SCANDAL

The *School for Scandal,* with Mrs. Insull as Lady Teazle, was produced at the Little Theatre last night. It will be reviewed in tomorrow's *Times.*

Mankiewicz was in such bad shape that night that Kaufman told Zolotow to call Sara Mankiewicz and have her come get him and take him home. Mrs. Mankiewicz recalls that he still had his head down on his typewriter when she arrived, with a friend, to remove him. She says he took it for granted that he was fired, but nevertheless went to work promptly the next day. Zolotow recalls, "In the morning, Herman came down to the office and asked me to talk to Mr. Birchall, the assistant managing editor, on his behalf. Herman had brought a peace offering of a bottle of Scotch and I took it to Birchall. He had a red beard, and he tugged at it and he stabbed the air a few times with his index finger and said, 'Herman is a bad boy, a bad boy.' But he took the bottle and Herman kept his job until he got the movie offer."

The review—unsigned—that the *Times* printed on October 24, 1925, was a small masterpiece of tact:

As Lady Teazle, Mrs. Insull is as pretty as she is diminutive, with a clear smile and dainty gestures. There is a charming grace in her bearing that makes for excellent deportment. But this Lady Teazle seems much too innocent, too thoroughly the country lass that Joseph terms her, to lend credit to her part in the play.

245

■ ■ ■

Scattered through various books, and in the stories that are still told of him in Hollywood, are clues that begin to give one a picture of Herman Mankiewicz, a giant of a man who mongered his own talent, a man who got a head start in the race to "sell out" to Hollywood. The pay was fantastic. After a month in the movie business, Mankiewicz—though his Broadway shows had not been hits, and though this was in 1926, when movies were still silent—signed a year's contract giving him $400 a week and a bonus of $5,000 for each story that was accepted, with an option for a second year at $500 a week and $7,500 per accepted story, the company guaranteeing to accept at least four stories per year. In other words, his base pay was $40,800 his first year and $56,000 his second; actually, he wrote so many stories that he made much more. By the end of 1927, he was head of Paramount's scenario department, and in January, 1928, there was a newspaper item reporting that he was in New York "lining up a new set of newspaper feature writers and playwrights to bring to Hollywood," and that "most of the newer writers on Paramount's staff who contributed the most successful stories of the past year were selected by 'Mank.' " One reason that Herman Mankiewicz is so little known today is, ironically, that he went to Hollywood so early, before he had gained a big enough reputation in the literary and theatrical worlds. Screenwriters don't make names for themselves; the most famous ones are the ones whose names were famous before they went to Hollywood, or who made names later in the theatre or from books, or who, like Preston Sturges, became directors.

Mankiewicz and other *New Yorker* writers in the twenties and the early thirties were very close to the world of the theatre; many of them were writing plays, writing about theatre people, reviewing plays. It's not surprising that within a few years the magazine's most celebrated contributors were in Hollywood writing movies. Of the ten friends of the editor Harold Ross who were in the original prospectus as advisory editors, six became screenwriters. When Mankiewicz gave up the drama critic's spot, in 1926, he was replaced by Charles Brackett, and when Brackett headed West, Robert Benchley filled it while commuting, and then followed. Dorothy Parker, the book reviewer Constant Reader, went West, too. Nunnally Johnson, who was to work on over a hundred movies, was a close friend of Harold Ross's and had volunteered to do the movie reviewing in 1926 but had been told that that job was for "old ladies and fairies." Others in the group didn't agree: Benchley had written on movies for the old *Life* as early as 1920, and John O'Hara later took time out from screenwriting to become the movie critic for *Newsweek*—where he was to review *Citizen Kane*. The whole group were interested in the theatre and the movies, and they were fast, witty writers, used to regarding their work not as deathless prose but as stories written to order for the market, used also to the newspaperman's pretense of putting a light value on what they did—the "Look, no hands" attitude. Thus, they were well prepared to become the scenarists and gag writers of the talkies.

VI

The comic muse of the most popular "daring" late silents was a carefree, wisecracking flapper. Beginning in 1926, Herman Mankiewicz worked on an astounding number of films in that spirit. In 1927 and 1928, he did the titles (the printed dialogue and explanations) for at least twenty-five films that starred Clara Bow, Bebe Daniels, Nancy Carroll, Esther Ralston, George Bancroft, Thomas Meighan, Jack Holt, Richard Dix, Wallace Beery, and other public favorites. He worked on the titles for Jules Furthman's script of *Abie's Irish Rose,* collaborated with Anita Loos on the wisecracks for *Gentlemen Prefer Blondes,* and did the immensely successful *The Barker* and *The Canary Murder Case,* with William Powell, Louise Brooks, James Hall, and Jean Arthur. By then, sound had come in, and in 1929 he did the script as well as the dialogue for *The Dummy,* with Ruth Chatterton and Fredric March (making his screen début), wrote William Wellman's *The Man I Love,* with Richard Arlen, Pat O'Brien, and Mary Brian, and worked for Josef von Sternberg and many other directors.

Other screenwriters made large contributions, too, but probably none larger than Mankiewicz's at the beginning of the sound era, and if he was at that time one of the highest-paid writers in the world, it was because he wrote the kind of movies that were disapproved of as "fast" and immoral. His heroes weren't soft-eyed and bucolic; he brought good-humored toughness to the movies, and energy and astringency. And the public responded, because it was eager for modern American subjects. Even those of us who were children at the time loved the fast-moving modern-city stories. The commonplaceness—even tawdriness—of the imagery was such a relief from all that silent "poetry." The talkies were a great step down. It's hard to make clear to people who didn't live through the transition how sickly and unpleasant many of those "artistic" silent pictures were—how you wanted to scrape off all that mist and sentiment.

Almost from the time the motion-picture camera was invented, there had been experiments with sound and attempts at synchronization, and the public was more than ready for talking pictures. Many of the late silents, if one looks at them now, seem to be trying to talk to us, crying out for sound. Despite the legend of paralysis of the medium when sound first came in, there was a burst of inventiveness. In musicals, directors like René Clair and, over here, Ernst Lubitsch and, to a lesser degree, Rouben Mamoulian didn't use sound just for lip synchronization; they played with sound as they had played with images, and they tried to use sound without losing the movement of silents or the daring of silent editing. Some of the early talkies were static and inept; newly imported stage directors literally staged the action, as if the space were stage space, and the technicians had to learn to handle the microphones. But movies didn't suddenly become stagebound because of the microphone. Many of the silents had always been stagebound, for the sufficient reason that they had been adapted from

247

plays—from the war-horses of the repertory, because they had proved their popularity, and from the latest Broadway hits, because the whole country wanted to see them. The silent adaptations were frequently deadly, not just because of construction based on the classical unities, with all those entrances and exits and that painful emptiness on the screen of plays worked out in terms of absolutely essential characters only, but because everything kept stopping for the explanatory titles and the dialogue titles.

Even in the movies adapted from novels or written directly for the screen, the action rarely went on for long; silents were choked with titles, which were perhaps, on the average, between ten and twenty times as frequent as the interruptions for TV commercials. The printed dialogue was often witty, and often it was essential to an understanding of the action, but it broke up the rhythm of performances and the visual flow, and the titles were generally held for the slowest readers, so that one lost the mood of the film while staring at the dialogue for the third scanning. (It seems to me, thinking back on it, that we were so eager for the movie to go on that we gulped the words down and then were always left with them for what, to our impatience, seemed an eternity, and that the better the movie, the more quickly we tried to absorb and leap past the printed words, and the more frustrating the delays became.) The plain fact that many silent movies were plays without the spoken dialogue, plays deprived of their very substance, was what made the theatre-going audience—and the Broadway crowd of writers—so contemptuous of them. Filmed plays without the actors' voices, and with the deadening delays for the heterogeneous audience to read the dialogue, were an abomination. Many of the journalists and playwrights and wits of the Algonquin Round Table had written perceptively about motion pictures (Alexander Woollcott, who managed to pan some of the greatest films, was an exception); they had, in general, been cynical only about the slop and the silent filmed plays. But though they had been active in the theatre, there had been no real place for them in movies; now, with the introduction of sound, they could bring to the screen the impudence that had given Broadway its flavor in the twenties—and bring it there before the satirical references were out of date. Sound made it possible for them to liberate movies into a new kind of contemporaneity.

VII

There is an elaborate body of theory that treats film as "the nocturnal voyage into the unconscious," as Luis Buñuel called it, and for a director such as Buñuel "the cinema seems to have been invented to express the life of the subconscious." Some of the greatest work of D. W. Griffith and other masters of the silent film has a magical, fairy-tale appeal, and certainly Surrealists like Buñuel, and other experimental and avant-garde filmmakers as well, have drawn upon this dreamlike vein of film. But these artists were the exceptions; much of the dreamy appeal to the "subconscious" and to "universal" or "primitive" fantasies was an appeal to the most backward, not to say reactionary, elements of illiterate and semiliterate mass society. There was a steady load of calendar-art guck that patronized "the deserving poor" and idealized "purity" (i.e., virginity) and "morality" (i.e., virginity plus charity). And all that is only one kind of movie anyway. Most of the dream theory of film, which takes the audience for passive dreamers, doesn't apply to the way one responded to silent comedies—which, when they were good, kept the audience in a heightened state of consciousness. When we join in laughter, it's as if the lights were on in the theatre. And not just the Mack Sennett comedies and Keaton and Chaplin kept us fully awake but the spirited, bouncy comediennes, like Colleen Moore and Marion Davies, and the romantic comedy "teams," and the suave, "polished" villains, like William Powell. My favorite movies as a child were the Bebe Daniels comedies—I suppose they were the movie equivalent of the series books one reads at that age. During 1927 and 1928, Paramount brought a new one out every few months; Bebe, the athletic madcap, would fence like Douglas Fairbanks, or she would parody Valentino by kidnapping and taming a man, or she might be a daredevil newsreel camerawoman or a cub reporter.

I did not know until I started to look into the writing of *Citizen Kane* that the man who wrote *Kane* had worked on some of those pictures, too—that Mankiewicz had, in fact, written (alone or with others) about forty of the films I remember best from the twenties and thirties (as well as many I didn't see or don't remember). Mankiewicz didn't work on *every* kind of picture, though. He didn't do Westerns, and once, when a studio attempted to punish him for his customary misbehavior by assigning him to a Rin Tin Tin picture, he turned in a script that began with the craven Rin Tin Tin frightened by a mouse and reached its climax with a house on fire and the dog taking a baby *into* the flames. I had known about Mankiewicz's contribution to *Kane* and a few other films, but I hadn't realized how extensive his career was. I had known that he was the producer of *Million Dollar Legs* (with W. C. Fields and Jack Oakie and Lyda Roberti) and *Laughter* (with Fredric March and Nancy Carroll), but I hadn't known, for example, that he had produced two of the Marx Brothers films that I've always especially liked, the first two made in Hollywood and written directly for the screen—*Monkey Business* and *Horse Feathers*—and part of *Duck Soup* as well. A few years ago, some college students asked me what films I would like to see again just for my own pleasure, and without a second's thought I replied *Duck Soup* and *Million Dollar Legs,* though at that time I had no idea there was any connection between them. Yet surely there is a comic spirit that links them—even the settings, Freedonia and Klopstokia, with Groucho as Prime Minister of one and Fields as President of the other—and now that I have looked into Herman Mankiewicz's career it's apparent that he was a key linking figure in just the kind of movies my friends and I loved best.

When the period of the great silent comedians, with their international audience, was over, a new style of American comedy developed. One couldn't really call a colloquial, skeptical comedy a "masterpiece," as one could sometimes call a silent comedy a masterpiece, especially if the talkie looked quite banal and was so topical it felt transient. But I think that many of us enjoyed these comedies more, even though we may not have felt very secure about the aesthetic grounds for our enjoyment. The talking comedies weren't as aesthetically pure as the silents, yet they felt liberating in a way that even great silents didn't. The elements to which we could respond were multiplied; now there were vocal nuances, new kinds of timing, and wonderful new tricks, like the infectious way Claudette Colbert used to break up while listening to someone. It's easy to see why Europeans, who couldn't follow the slang and the jokes and didn't understand the whole satirical frame of reference, should prefer our action films and Westerns. But it's a bad joke on our good jokes that film enthusiasts here often take their cues on the American movie past from Europe, and so they ignore the tradition of comic irreverence and become connoisseurs of the "visuals" and "mises en scène" of action pictures, which are usually too silly even to be called reactionary. They're sub-reactionary—the antique melodramas of silent days with noise added—a mass art better suited, one might think, to Fascism, or even feudalism, than to democracy.

There is another reason the American talking comedies, despite their popularity, are so seldom valued highly by film aestheticians. The dream-art kind of film, which lends itself to beautiful visual imagery, is generally the creation of the "artist" director, while the astringent film is more often directed by a competent, unpretentious craftsman who can be made to look very good by a good script and can be turned into a bum by a bad script. And this competent craftsman may be too worldly and too practical to do the "imaginative" bits that sometimes helped make the reputations of "artist" directors. Ben Hecht said he shuddered at the touches von Sternberg introduced into *Underworld:* "My head villain, Bull Weed, after robbing a bank, emerged with a suitcase full of money and paused in the crowded street to notice a blind beggar and give him a coin—before making his getaway." That's exactly the sort of thing that quantities of people react to emotionally as "deep" and as "art," and that many film enthusiasts treasure—the inflated sentimental with a mystical drip. The thirties, though they had their own load of sentimentality, were the hardest-headed period of American movies, and their plainness of style, with its absence of false "cultural" overtones, has never got its due aesthetically. Film students—and their teachers—often become interested in movies just because they are the kind of people who are emotionally affected by the blind-beggar bits, and they are indifferent by temperament to the emancipation of American movies in the thirties and the role that writers played in it.

I once jotted down the names of some movies that I didn't associate with any celebrated director but that had nevertheless stayed in my memory over the years, because something in them had especially delighted me— such rather obscure movies as *The Moon's Our Home* (Margaret Sullavan and

Henry Fonda) and *He Married His Wife* (Nancy Kelly, Joel McCrea, and Mary Boland). When I looked them up, I discovered that Dorothy Parker's name was in the credits of *The Moon's Our Home* and John O'Hara's in the credits of *He Married His Wife*. Other writers worked on those films, too, and perhaps they were the ones who were responsible for what I responded to, but the recurrence of the names of that group of writers, not just on rather obscure remembered films but on almost *all* the films that are generally cited as proof of the vision and style of the most highly acclaimed directors of that period, suggests that the writers—and a particular group of them, at that—may for a brief period, a little more than a decade, have given American talkies their character.

VIII

There is always a time lag in the way movies take over (and broaden and emasculate) material from the other arts—whether it is last season's stage success or the novels of the preceding decade or a style or an idea that has run its course in its original medium. (This does not apply to a man like Jean-Luc Godard, who is not a mass-medium movie director.) In most productions of the big studios, the time lag is enormous. In the thirties, after the great age of musical comedy and burlesque, Hollywood, except for Paramount, was just discovering huge operettas. After the Broadway days of Clifton Webb, Fred Astaire, the Marx Brothers, Fanny Brice, W. C. Fields, and all the rest, M-G-M gave us Nelson Eddy and Jeanette MacDonald, and Universal gave us Deanna Durbin. This is the history of movies. J. D. Salinger has finally come to the screen through his imitators, and Philip Roth's fifties romance arrived at the end of the sixties. It may be that for new ideas to be successful in movies, the way must be prepared by success in other media, and the audience must have grown tired of what it's been getting and be ready for something new. There are always a few people in Hollywood who are considered mad dreamers for trying to do in movies things that have already been done in the other arts. But once one of them breaks through and has a hit, he's called a genius and everybody starts copying him.

The new spirit of the talkies was the twenties moved West in the thirties. George S. Kaufman was writing the Marx Brothers stage shows when he and Mankiewicz worked together at the *Times*; a little later, Kaufman directed the first Broadway production of *The Front Page*. Kaufman's collaborators on Broadway plays in the twenties and the early thirties included Marc Connelly, Edna Ferber, Ring Lardner, Morrie Ryskind, and Moss Hart as well as Mankiewicz—the nucleus of the Algonquin-to-Hollywood group. Nunnally Johnson says that the two most brilliant men he has ever known were George S. Kaufman and Herman Mankiewicz, and that, on the whole, Mankiewicz was the more brilliant of the two. I think that what Mankiewicz did in movies was an offshoot of the gag comedy that Kaufman had initiated on Broadway; Mankiewicz spearheaded the movement of that whole Broadway style of wisecracking, fast-talking, cynical-sentimental entertainment onto the national scene. Kaufman's kind of impersonal, visionless comedy, with its single goal of getting the audience to laugh, led to the degeneration of the Broadway theatre, to its play doctors and gimmickry and scattershot jokes at defenseless targets, and so it would be easy to look down on the movie style that came out of it. But I don't think the results were the same when this type of comedy was transplanted to movies; the only bad long-range consequences were to the writers themselves.

Kaufman fathered a movement that is so unmistakably the bastard child of the arts as to seem fatherless; the gag comedy was perfectly suited to the commercial mass art of the movies, so that it appears to be an almost inevitable development. It suited the low common denominator of the movies even better than it suited the needs of the relatively selective theatre audience, and the basic irresponsibility of this kind of theatre combined with the screenwriters' lack of control over their own writing to produce what one might call the brothel period of American letters. It was a gold rush, and Mankiewicz and his friends had exactly the skills to turn a trick. The journalists' style of working fast and easy and working to order and not caring too much how it was butchered was the best kind of apprenticeship for a Hollywood hack, and they had loved to gather, to joke and play games, to lead the histrionic forms of the glamorous literary life. Now they were gathered in cribs on each studio lot, working in teams side by side, meeting for lunch at the commissary and for dinner at Chasen's, which their old friend and editor Harold Ross had helped finance, and all over town for drinks. They adapted each other's out-of-date plays and novels, and rewrote each other's scripts. Even in their youth in New York, most of them had indulged in what for them proved a vice: they were "collaborators"—dependent on the fun and companionship of joint authorship, which usually means a shared shallowness. Now they collaborated all over the place and backward in time; they collaborated promiscuously, and within a few years were rewriting the remakes of their own or somebody else's rewrites. Mankiewicz adapted Kaufman and Ferber's *The Royal Family* and *Dinner at Eight,* turned Alice Duer Miller's *Come Out of the Kitchen* into *Honey,* and adapted George Kelly's *The Show-Off* and James Thurber's *My Life and Hard Times* and works by Laurence Stallings and other old friends while Ben Hecht or Preston Sturges or Arthur Kober was working over something of his. They escaped the cold, and they didn't suffer from the Depression. They were a colony—expatriates without leaving the country—and their individual contributions to the scripts that emerged after the various rewrites were almost impossible to assess, because their attitudes were so similar; they made the same kind of jokes, because they had been making them to each other for so long. In Hollywood, they sat around building on to each other's gags, covering up implausibilities and dull spots, throwing new wisecracks on top of jokes they had laughed at in New York. Screenwriting was an extension of what they used to do for fun, and now they got paid for it. They had liked to talk more than to write, and this weakness became their way of life. As far as the official literary culture was concerned, they dropped from sight. To quote a classic bit of dialogue from Budd Schulberg's *The Disenchanted:*

> "Bane had two hits running on Broadway at the same time. Even Nathan liked 'em. Popular 'n satirical. Like Barry, only better. The critics kept waiting for him to write that great American play."
> "What happened to him?"
> "Hollywood."

Hollywood destroyed them, but they did wonders for the movies. In New York, they may have valued their own urbanity too highly; faced with the target Hollywood presented, they became cruder and tougher, less tidy, less stylistically elegant, and more iconoclastic, and in the eyes of Hollywood they were slaphappy cynics, they were "crazies." They were too talented and too sophisticated to put a high value on what they did, too amused at the spectacle of what they were doing and what they were part of to be respected the way a writer of "integrity," like Lillian Hellman, was later to be respected—or, still later, Arthur Miller. Though their style was often flippant and their attitude toward form casual to the point of contempt, they brought movies the subversive gift of sanity. They changed movies by raking the old moralistic muck with derision. Those sickly Graustarkian romances with beautiful, pure high-born girls and pathetic lame girls and dashing princes in love with commoners, and all the Dumas and Sabatini and Blasco-Ibáñez, now had to compete with the freedom and wildness of American comedy. Once American films had their voice and the Algonquin group was turned loose on the scripts, the revolting worship of European aristocracy faded so fast that movie stars even stopped bringing home Georgian princes. In the silents, the heroes were often simpletons. In the talkies, the heroes were to be the men who weren't fooled, who were smart and learned their way around. The new heroes of the screen were created in the image of their authors: they were fast-talking newspaper reporters.

That Walter Burns whose entrance in *The Front Page* Kerr described was based on Walter Howey, who was the city editor of the *Chicago Tribune,* at $8,000 a year, until Hearst lured him away by an offer of $35,000 a year. Howey is generally considered the "greatest" of all Hearst editors—by those who mean one thing by it, and by those who mean the other. He edited Hearst's *New York Mirror* at a time when it *claimed* to be ten percent news and ninety percent entertainment. The epitome of Hearstian journalism, and a favorite of Hearst's until the end, he was one of the executors of Hearst's will. At one time or another, just about all the Hollywood writers had worked for Walter Howey and/or spent their drinking hours with friends who did. He was the legend: the classic model of the amoral, irresponsible, irrepressible newsman who cares about nothing but scoops and circulation. He had lost an eye (supposedly in actual fighting of circulation wars), and Ben Hecht is quoted as saying you could tell which was the glass eye because it was the warmer one. Hecht used him again in *Nothing Sacred,* as Fredric March's editor—"a cross between a Ferris wheel and a werewolf"—and he turns up under other names in other plays and movies. In a sense, all those newspaper plays and movies were already about Hearst's kind of corrupt, manic journalism.

The toughest-minded, the most satirical of the thirties pictures often featured newspaper settings, or, at least, reporters—especially the "screwball" comedies, which had some resemblances to later "black" comedy and current "freaky" comedy but had a very different spirit. A newspaper picture meant a contemporary picture in an American setting, usually a melodrama with crime and political corruption and suspense and comedy and romance. In 1931, a title like *Five Star Final* or *Scandal Sheet* signalled the public that the movie would be a tough modern talkie, not a tearjerker with sound. Just to touch a few bases, there was *The Front Page* itself, in 1931, with Pat O'Brien as the reporter and Adolphe Menjou as Walter Burns; Lee Tracy as the gossip columnist in *Blessed Event* and as the press agent in *Bombshell;* Clark Gable as the reporter in *It Happened One Night;* Paul Muni giving advice to the lovelorn in *Hi, Nellie;* Spencer Tracy as the editor in *Libeled Lady;* Stuart Erwin as the correspondent in *Viva Villa!;* Jean Harlow stealing the affections of a newspaperman from girl reporter Loretta Young in *Platinum Blonde;* Jean Arthur as the girl reporter in *Mr. Deeds Goes to Town;* a dozen pictures, at least, with George Bancroft as a Walter Howey–style bullying editor; all those half-forgotten pictures with reporter "teams"—Fredric March and Virginia Bruce, or Joel McCrea and Jean Arthur, or Loretta Young and Tyrone Power (*Love Is News*); Cary Grant as the editor and Joan Bennett as the reporter in *Wedding Present;* and then Cary Grant as Walter Burns in *His Girl Friday,* with Rosalind Russell as the reporter; and then Cary Grant and James Stewart (who had been a foreign correspondent in *Next Time We Love*) both involved with a newsmagazine in *The Philadelphia Story,* in 1940. Which takes us right up to *Citizen Kane,* the biggest newspaper picture of them all— the picture that ends with the introduction of the cast and a reprise of the line "I think it would be fun to run a newspaper."

IX

After years of swapping stories about Howey and the other werewolves and the crooked, dirty press, Mankiewicz found himself on story-swapping terms with the power behind it all, Hearst himself. When he had been in Hollywood only a short time, he met Marion Davies and Hearst through his friendship with Charles Lederer, a writer, then in his early twenties, whom Ben Hecht had met and greatly admired in New York when Lederer was still in his teens. Lederer, a child prodigy, who had entered college at thirteen, got to know Mankiewicz, the MacArthurs, Moss Hart, Benchley, and their friends at about the same time or shortly after he met Hecht, and was immediately accepted into a group considerably older than he was. Lederer was Marion Davies's nephew—the son of her sister Reine, who had been in operetta and musical comedy. In Hollywood, Charles Lederer's life seems to have revolved around his aunt, whom he adored. (Many others adored her also, though *Citizen Kane* was to give the world a different—and false—impression.) She was childless, and Lederer was very close to her; he spent a great deal of his time at her various dwelling places, and took his friends to meet both her and Hearst. The world of letters being small and surprising, Charles Lederer was among those who worked on the adaptation of *The Front Page* to the screen in 1931 and again when it was remade as *His Girl Friday* in 1940, and, the world being even smaller than that, Lederer married Orson Welles's ex-wife, Virginia Nicholson Welles, in 1940, at San Simeon. (She married two prodigies in succession; the marriage to Welles had lasted five years and produced a daughter.)

Hearst was so fond of Lederer that on the evening of the nuptials he broke his rule of one cocktail to guests before dinner and no hard liquor thereafter. A guest who gulped the cocktail down was sometimes able to swindle another, but this is the only occasion that I can find recorded on which Hearst dropped the rule—a rule that Marion Davies customarily eased by slipping drinks to desperate guests before Hearst joined them but that nevertheless made it possible for Hearst to receive, and see at their best, some of the most talented alcoholics this country has ever produced. Not all writers are attracted to the rich and powerful, but it's a defining characteristic of journalists to be drawn to those who live at the center of power. Even compulsive drinkers like Mankiewicz and Dorothy Parker were so fascinated by the great ménage of Hearst and his consort—and the guest lists of the world-famous—that they managed to stay relatively sober for the evenings at Marion Davies's beach house (Colleen Moore described it as "the largest house on the beach—and I mean the beach from San Diego to the Canadian border") and the weekends at San Simeon.

If *Kane* has the same love-hate as *The Front Page,* the same joyous infatuation with the antics of the unprincipled press, it's because Mankiewicz, like Hecht and MacArthur, revelled in the complexities of corruption. And Hearst's life was a *spectacle.* For short periods, this was intoxication enough. A man like Hearst seems to embody more history than other people do; in his company a writer may feel that he has been living in the past and on the outskirts and now he's living in the dangerous present, right where the decisions are really made.

Hearst represented a new type of power. He got his first newspaper in 1887, when he was twenty-four, by asking his father for it, and, in the next three decades, when, for the first time, great masses of people became literate, he added more and more papers, until, with his empire of thirty newspapers and fifteen magazines, he was the most powerful journalist and publisher in the world. He had brought the first comic strips to America in

1892, and his battling with Pulitzer a few years later over a cartoon character named the Yellow Kid revived the term "yellow journalism." Because there was no tradition of responsibility in this new kind of popular journalism, which was almost a branch of show business, Hearst knew no restraints; perhaps fortunately, he was unguided. Ultimately, he was as purposeless about his power as the craziest of the Roman emperors. His looting of the treasures of the world for his castle at San Simeon symbolized his imperial status. Being at his table was being at court, and the activities of the notables who were invited there were slavishly chronicled in the Hearst papers.

The new social eminence of the Mankiewiczes, who sometimes visited San Simeon for as long as ten days at a time, can be charted from Louella Parsons's columns. By the end of 1928, Louella was announcing Mankiewicz's writing assignments with a big bold headline at the top of the column, and was printing such items as:

> One of the few scenario writers in Hollywood who didn't have
> to unlearn much that he had learned is Herman Mankiewicz.
> Herman came to Paramount directly from the stage, and naturally
> he knows the technique just as well as if he hadn't written movies
> in the interval.

It was worth another item in the same column that Herman Mankiewicz had been observed "taking his son down Hollywood Boulevard to see the lighted Christmas trees." In 1931, the Mankiewiczes were so prominent that they were among those who gave Marion Davies a homecoming party at the Hotel Ambassador; the other hosts were Mr. and Mrs. Irving Thalberg, Mr. and Mrs. King Vidor, Mr. and Mrs. Samuel Goldwyn, John Gilbert, Lewis Milestone, Hedda Hopper, and so on. Hedda Hopper, who worked as a movie columnist for a rival newspaper chain but was a close friend of Marion Davies (to whom, it is said, she owed her job), was also an enthusiastic reporter of Mankiewicz's activities during the years when he and his ravishing Sara were part of the Hearst-Davies social set.

When writers begin to see the powerful men operating in terms of available alternatives, while they have been judging them in terms of ideals, they often develop "personal" admiration for the great bastards whom they have always condemned and still condemn. Hearst was to Mankiewicz, I suspect, what Welles was to be to him a little later—a dangerous new toy. And he needed new toys constantly to keep off the booze. Mankiewicz could control himself at San Simeon in the late twenties and the very early thirties, as, in those days, he could control himself when he was in charge of a movie. Producing the Marx Brothers comedies kept him busy and entertained for a while. With the title of "supervisor" (a term for the actual working producer, as distinguished from the studio executive whose name might appear above or below the name of the movie), he worked on their pictures from the inception of the ideas through the months of writing and then the shooting. But he got bored easily, and when he started cutting up in the middle of preparing *Duck Soup,* in 1933, he was taken off the picture. When the Marx Brothers left Paramount and went to M-G-M, he joined them again, in the preparation of *A Night at the Opera,* in 1935, and the same thing happened; he was replaced as supervisor by his old boss George S. Kaufman.

His credits began to taper off after 1933, and in 1936 Mankiewicz didn't get a single credit. That year, he published an article called "On Approaching Forty," a brief satirical account of what had happened to him as a writer. It began:

> Right before me, as I write, is a folder in which my wife keeps the blotters from Mr. Eschner, the insurance man, Don's first report card, the letter from the income tax people about the gambling loss at Tia Juana, the press photograph of me greeting Helen Kane (in behalf of the studio) at the Pasadena Station and my literary output. There are four separate pieces of this output and they are all excellent. I hope some friend will gather them into a little book after my death. There is plenty of ninety point Marathon in the world, and wide margins can't be hard to find.

He includes those tiny pieces in their entirety, and after one of them—the first three sentences of a short story—he comments:

> I moved to Hollywood soon after I had made this notation and was kept so busy with one thing and another—getting the pool filled, playing the Cadillac and Buick salesmen against each other, only to compromise on a Cadillac and a Buick, after all, and locating the finance company's downtown office—that the first thing I knew, a story, a good deal like the one I had in mind, appeared in the *Saturday Evening Post,* and in *Collier's,* too.

This is the end of his article:

> The fourth note looks rather naked now, all by itself on the desk. It says, simply:
> "Write piece for *New Yorker* on reaching thirty-fifth birthday. No central idea. Just flit from paragraph to paragraph."
> People who complain that my work is slipshod would be a little surprised to find that I just am *not* always satisfied with the first thing I put down. I'm changing that thirty-fifth to fortieth right now.

"On Approaching Forty" didn't come out in *The New Yorker;* it appeared in the *Hollywood Reporter.*

Ambivalence was the most common "literary" emotion of the screen-writers of the thirties, as alienation was to become the most common "liter-ary" emotion of the screenwriters of the sixties. The thirties writers were ambivalently nostalgic about their youth as reporters, journalists, critics, or playwrights, and they glorified the hard-drinking, cynical newspaperman. They were ambivalent about Hollywood, which they savaged and satirized whenever possible. Hollywood paid them so much more money than they had ever earned before, and the movies reached so many more people than they had ever reached before, that they were contemptuous of those who hadn't made it on their scale at the same time that they hated themselves for selling out. They had gone to Hollywood as a paid vacation from their playwriting or journalism, and screenwriting became their only writing. The vacation became an extended drunken party, and while they were there in the debris of the long morning after, American letters passed them by. They were never to catch up; nor were American movies ever again to have in their midst a whole school of the richest talents of a generation.

We in the audience didn't have to wake up *afterward* to how good those films of the thirties were; in common with millions of people, I enjoyed them while they were coming out. They were immensely popular. But I did take them for granted. There was such a steady flow of bright comedy that it appeared to be a Hollywood staple, and it didn't occur to me that those films wouldn't go on being made. It didn't occur to me that it required a special gathering of people in a special atmosphere to produce that flow, and that when those people stopped enjoying themselves those pictures couldn't be made. And I guess it didn't occur to older, more experienced people, either, because for decades everybody went on asking why Holly-wood wasn't turning out those good, entertaining comedies anymore.

By the end of the thirties, the jokes had soured. The comedies of the forties were heavy and pushy, straining for humor, and the comic impulse was misplaced or lost; they came out of a different atmosphere, a different *feeling*. The comic spirit of the thirties had been happily self-critical about America, the happiness born of the knowledge that in no other country were movies so free to be self-critical. It was the comedy of a country that didn't yet hate itself. Though it wasn't until the sixties that the self-hatred became overt in American life and American movies, it started to show, I think, in the phony, excessive, duplicit use of patriotism by the rich, guilty liberals of Hollywood in the war years.

X

In the forties, a socially conscious film historian said to me, "You know, Par-amount never made a good movie," and I brought up the names of some Paramount movies—*Easy Living* and *Trouble in Paradise* and lovely trifles like *Midnight*—and, of course, I couldn't make my point, because those movies weren't what was thought of in the forties as a good movie. I knew I wouldn't get anywhere at all if I tried to cite *Million Dollar Legs* or *Mississippi*, or pictures with the Marx Brothers or Mae West; I would be told they weren't even movies. Though Paramount made some elegant comedies in the "Continental" style, many of the best Paramount pictures were like revues—which was pretty much the style of the Broadway theatre they'd come out of, and was what I liked about them. They entertained you without trying to change your life, yet didn't congratulate you for being a slobbering bag of mush, either. But by the forties these were considered "escapist entertainment," and that was supposed to be *bad*. Many of the thirties comedies, especially the Paramount ones, weren't even "artistic" or "visual" movies—which is why they look so good on television now. They also sound good, because what that historian thought of as their irresponsibility is so much more modern than the sentimentalities of the war years. What was believed in was implicit in the styles of the heroes and heroines and in the comedy targets; the writers had an almost aristocratic disdain for putting beliefs into words. In the forties, the writers convinced themselves that they believed in everything, and they kept putting it all into so many bad words. It's no wonder the movies had no further use for a Groucho or a Mae West; one can imagine what either of them might have done to those words.

It's common to blame the McCarthyism of the fifties and the removal of blacklisted writers for the terrible, flat writing in American movies of recent years, but the writers might have recovered from McCarthyism (they might even have stood up to it) if they hadn't been destroyed as writers long before. The writing that had given American talkies their special flavor died in the war, killed not in battle but in the politics of Stalinist "anti-Fascism." For the writers, Hollywood was just one big crackup, and for most of them it took a political turn. The lost-in-Hollywood generation of writers, trying to clean themselves of guilt for their wasted years and their irresponsibility as *writers*, became political in the worst way—became a special breed of anti-Fascists. The talented writers, the major ones as well as the lightweight yet entertaining ones, went down the same drain as the clods—drawn into it, often, by bored wives, less successful brothers. They became naïvely, hysterically pro-Soviet; they ignored Stalin's actual policies, because they so badly needed to believe in something. They had been so smart, so gifted, and yet they hadn't been able to beat Hollywood's contempt for the writer. (Walter Wanger had put twenty-seven of them to work in groups in succession on the script of Vincent Sheean's *Personal History*.) They lived in the city where Irving Thalberg was enshrined; Thalberg, the saint of M-G-M, had rationalized Mayer's system of putting teams of writers to work simultaneously and in relays on the same project. It had been lunatic before, but Thalberg made it seem mature and responsible to fit writers into an assembly-line method that totally alienated them and took away their last shreds of pride. And most of the Algonquin group had been in Hollywood so long they weren't even famous anymore.

Talented people have rarely had the self-control to flourish in the Hollywood atmosphere of big money and conflicting pressures. The talented—especially those who weren't using their talents to full capacity—have become desperate, impatient, unreliable, self-destructive, and also destructive, and so there has always been some validity in the businessman's argument that he couldn't afford to take chances on "geniuses." Thalberg didn't play around with a man like Mankiewicz; after throwing him off *A Night at the Opera*, he didn't use him again.

The writers who had become accustomed to being assembly-line workers were ready to believe it when, in the forties, they were told that, like factory workers, they were "part of the team on the assembly line" and needed "that strengthening of the spirit which comes from identity with the labor of others." Like the producers, the Screen Writers Guild respected discipline and responsibility, but though the businessmen had never been able to organize people of talent—producers like Thalberg just kept discarding them—the union ideologues knew how. The talented rarely become bureaucrats, but the mediocre had put down roots in Hollywood—it doesn't take long in Los Angeles, the only great city that is purely modern, that hasn't even an architectural past in the nineteenth century. In the forties, the talented merged with the untalented and became almost indistinguishable from them, and the mediocre have been writing movies ever since. When the good writers tried to regain their self-respect by becoming political activists in the Stalinist style, it was calamitous to talent; the Algonquin group's own style was lost as their voice blended into the preachy, self-righteous chorus.

The comedy writers who had laughed at cant now learned to write it and were rehabilitated as useful citizens of the community of mediocrity. It was just what the newly political congratulated themselves on—their constructive, uplifting approach—that killed comedy. When they had written frivolously, knowing that they had no control over how their writing would be used, or buried, or rewritten, they may have failed their own gifts and the dreams of their youth, but the work they turned out had human dimensions; they were working at less than full capacity, but they were still honest entertainers. Their humor was the humor of those trapped by human weakness as well as by "the system," and this was basic comedy—like the jokes and camaraderie of Army men. But when they became political in that morally superior way of people who are doing something for themselves but pretending it's for others, their self-righteousness was insufferable. They may have told lies in the themes and plots of the thirties comedies, but they didn't take their own lies seriously, they didn't *believe* their own lies, the way they did in the forties. In the forties, the Screen Writers Guild and the Hollywood Writers Mobilization (for wartime morale-building) held conferences at which "responsible" writers brought the irresponsibles into line. The irresponsibles were told they were part of an army and must "dedicate their creative abilities to the winning of the war." And, in case they failed to understand the necessity for didactic, "positive" humor, there were panels and seminars that analyzed jokes and pointed out which ones might do harm. It was explained to the writers that "catch-as-catch-can," "no-holds-barred" comedy was a thing of the past. "A very funny line may make black-market dealings seem innocent and attractive," they were told, and "Respect for officers must be maintained at all times, in any scene, in any situation."

Show-business people are both giddy and desperately, sincerely intense. When Stalinism was fashionable, movie people became Stalinists, the way they later became witches and warlocks. Apparently, many of the Hollywood Stalinists didn't realize they were taking any risks; they performed propaganda services for the various shifts in Russia's foreign policy and, as long as the needs of American and Russian policy coincided, this took the form of super-patriotism. When the war was over and the Cold War began, history left them stranded, and McCarthy moved in on them. The shame of McCarthyism was not only "the shame of America" but the shame of a bunch of newly rich people who were eager to advise the world on moral and political matters and who, faced with a test, informed on their friends—and, as Orson Welles put it, not even to save their lives but to save their swimming pools. One might think that whatever they had gained emotionally from their activity they would have lost when they informed on each other, but it doesn't seem to have always worked that way. They didn't change their ideas when they recanted before the House Un-American Activities Committee; they merely gave in and then were restored to themselves. And they often seem to regard it not as their weakness but as their martyrdom. Show-business-Stalinism is basically not political but psychological; it's a fashionable form of hysteria and guilt that is by now not so much pro-Soviet as just abusively anti-American. America is their image of Hell (once again, because of Vietnam, they're in a popular position), and they go on being "political" in the same way, holding the same faith, and for the same reasons, as in the late thirties and the forties. The restoration there is fairly general. In Hollywood recently, a man who used to be "involved" told me he wanted to become more active again, and added, "But, you know, I'm scared. The people who are urging me to do more are the same ones who ratted on me last time."

Mankiewicz was too well informed politically to become a Communist Partyliner. Because he didn't support this line, he was—and only in part jokingly—considered a "reactionary" by the activists of the Screen Writers Guild. Yet he went on to write the movie they point to with pride in Hollywood, the movie they all seem to feel demonstrates what *can* be done and what movies should be doing, and it's their all-time favorite because they understand it—and correctly—as a leftist film. Its leftism is, however, the leftism of the twenties and early thirties, before the left became moralistic. There were other expressions of the tough spirit of the thirties that came after the thirties were over. There may be a little of it in the newspaper film of the fifties *Sweet Smell of Success,* but the ambivalence there is harsher, grimmer, more artistically "serious"' than it was in the thirties; there's some in the happy mockery of Hollywood in *Singin' in the Rain,* which takes off from Kaufman and Hart's *Once in a Lifetime,* and in the films of Preston Sturges, who alone somehow managed to stay funny and tart. The only writer of this whole group who became a director with an individual style, Sturges kept American comedy alive singlehanded through the mawkish forties. Maybe he was able to because he was a cynic and so politically baroque that he wasn't torn by doubts and guilts. The political show in Hollywood in the forties was just one more crazy scene to him; he'd grown up rich and eccentric in Europe, the son of that expatriate lady (called Mary in *The Loves of Isadora*) who gave Isadora Duncan the fatal scarf.

But Mankiewicz climaxed an era in *Kane.* He wrote a big movie that is untarnished by sentimentality, and it may be the only big biographical movie ever made in this country of which that can be said. *Kane* is unsanctimonious; it is without scenes of piety, masochism, or remorse, without "truths"—in that period when the screenwriters were becoming so politically "responsible" that they were using all the primitive devices to sell their messages, and movies once again became full of blind beggars, and omens of doom, and accidental death as punishment for moral and sexual infractions, and, of course, Maria Ouspenskaya seeing into people's hearts—the crone as guru.

XI

Orson Welles wasn't around when *Citizen Kane* was written, early in 1940. Mankiewicz, hobbling about on a broken leg in a huge cast, was packed off—away from temptation—to Mrs. Campbell's Guest Ranch, in Victorville, California, sixty-five miles from Los Angeles, to do the script. He had a nurse and a secretary to watch over him and John Houseman to keep him working, and they all lived there for about three months—in a combination dude ranch and rest home, where liquor was forbidden and unavailable—until the first draft of *Citizen Kane,* called simply and formidably *American,* was completed.

That insurance-company doctor who refused to accept Mankiewicz as a risk back in 1927 had no need to be prophetic. Ben Hecht once described a summer earlier in the twenties when he and his wife and Charles MacArthur were living in a borrowed house near Woodstock, New York, with no money, and Harpo, Groucho, Chico, and Zeppo Marx and their wives, sweethearts, and children came to stay, and then Herman Mankiewicz arrived, carrying two suitcases. "He had decided to spend his vacation from the *New York Times* drama section with us," Hecht wrote. "He had not been allowed to bring any money with him because of Sara's certainty that he would spend it on liquor, and thus impair the influence of country air and sunshine. . . . Herman's larger suitcase contained sixteen bottles of Scotch and nothing else." A few weeks later, Hecht and MacArthur went in to New York to try to sell a play they'd just written, and encountered Mankiewicz, who, having sent his wife and children out of town to escape the heat, was "occupying Prince Bibesco's grand suite in the Plaza Hotel while His Highness capered in Long Island."

Hecht went on, "We moved in with him, there being no rent to pay. We discovered, while helping Herman to undress the first night, that his torso was bound with yards of adhesive tape. He had slipped while trying to get out of the bathtub and lamed his back. When Herman was asleep, MacArthur and I rolled him on his stomach and with an indelible pencil wrote ardent and obscene love messages on his taping. We signed them Gladys and chuckled over the impending moment in Far Rockaway when Herman would undress before his keen-eyed Sara."

Not only was Mankiewicz alcoholic and maniacally accident-prone; he was a gambler, constantly in debt. There was a sequence in a thirties movie about a gambling newspaperman that was based on the way the other writers at Paramount used to line up with him when he got his check on Friday afternoon and walk with him to the bank so they could get back some of the money he'd borrowed from them during the week. His old friends say that he would bet from sheer boredom; when he ran out of big sporting events, he would bet on anything—on high-school football games or whether it would rain. He got to the point where he was bored with just betting; he wanted the stakes to be dangerously high. He once explained, "It's not fun gambling if I lose two thousand and just write a check for it. What's thrilling is to make out a check for fifteen thousand dollars knowing there's not a penny in the bank." James Thurber referred to him as an "incurable compulsive gambler." He described how Mankiewicz went to a psychiatrist to see if anything could be done about it. "I can't cure you of gambling," the analyst told him on his last visit, "but I can tell you why you do it."

By the late thirties, Mankiewicz had just about run out of studios to get fired from. Scott Fitzgerald described him in those years as "a ruined man." His friends would get him jobs and he would lose them—sometimes in spectacular ways that became part of Hollywood legend. Perhaps the best-known is his exit from Columbia Pictures. In his biography of Harry Cohn, who was then the head of the studio, Bob Thomas describes it this way:

> The most famous incident in the Columbia dining room concerned an erratic genius named Herman J. Mankiewicz.... The freewheeling world of journalism seemed better suited to his temperament than did Hollywood. He possessed two failings that were inimical to the autocratic studio domains: he drank, and he was scornful of his bosses.
>
> Theses faculties tumbled him from the position of a major screenwriter, and he had difficulty finding jobs. His agent, Charles Feldman, proposed a post at Columbia. Cohn was interested, since he enjoyed hiring bargain talent discarded by the major studios.... Cohn agreed to employ him at $750 a week.

263

"I want to make good," said Mankiewicz when he reported to William Perlberg, then Columbia's executive producer.

"Fine," said the producer. . . . "But . . . don't go in the executive dining room. You know what will happen if you tangle with Cohn."

Mankiewicz concurred. . . . His work habits were exemplary, and he produced many pages a day. But . . . his office was on the third floor, near the door to the executive dining room. As Riskin, Swerling, and other fellow-writers emerged after lunch, he could hear them laughing over wisecracks and jokes that had been told inside. Mankiewicz himself was considered one of Hollywood's premier wits and raconteurs, and he rankled over his banishment.

One day Perlberg entered the dining room and was startled to find Mankiewicz sitting at the end of the table. The writer held a napkin to his mouth and promised, "I won't say a word."

When Cohn entered the room, he gave Mankiewicz a warm greeting, then assumed his monarchial position at the head of the table.

Cohn began the conversation: "Last night I saw the lousiest picture I've seen in years."

He mentioned the title, and one of the more courageous of his producers spoke up: "Why, I saw that picture at the Downtown Paramount, and the audience howled over it. Maybe you should have seen it with an audience."

"That doesn't make any difference," Cohn replied. "When I'm alone in a projection room, I have a foolproof device for judging whether a picture is good or bad. If my fanny squirms, it's bad. If my fanny doesn't squirm, it's good. It's as simple as that."

There was a momentary silence, which was filled by Mankiewicz at the end of the table: "Imagine—the whole world wired to Harry Cohn's ass!"

Mankiewicz's attitude toward himself and his work is summed up in one very short, very famous story. A friend who hadn't seen him for a while asked, "How's Sara?"

Mankiewicz, puzzled: "Who?"

"Sara. Your wife, Sara."

"Oh, you mean Poor Sara."

The only evidence of an instinct for self-preservation in the life of Herman Mankiewicz is his choice of keen-eyed Sara. He was in bad shape by 1939, but Mayer kept him on the payroll—some said so that top people at M-G-M could collect their gambling winnings from him. But Mayer also seems to have had some affection for him, and Sara had become a close friend of Mayer's daughter Irene. Mayer became concerned about Mankiewicz's gambling debts, and, assuming that Mankiewicz was also concerned about them, he concluded that if he got the debts straightened out, Mankiewicz would pull himself together. Mayer called him in and asked him how much money he needed to get financially clear. Mankiewicz came up with the figure of $30,000, and Mayer offered to advance him that sum on a new contract if he would swear a solemn vow never to gamble again. Mankiewicz went through an elaborate ritual of giving Mayer his sacred word, and walked out with the $30,000. The very next day, it is said, Mankiewicz was playing poker on the lot, and he had just raised the stakes to $10,000 when he looked up and saw Mayer standing there. Mankiewicz left the studio and didn't return. A few days after that—early in September of 1939—Thomas Phipps, a nephew of Lady Astor's, who was also employed as a writer at M-G-M, was driving to New York to court a lady there, and, with nothing better to do, Mankiewicz decided to go along. As Mankiewicz described the trip some months later, in a guest column he wrote, filling in for Hedda Hopper on vacation, it was fairly giddy right from the start. Mankiewicz said that each song on the car radio sent Phipps swooning, because either he had heard it while he was with his lady or he had heard it while he was not with her. On the outskirts of Albuquerque, the car skidded and turned over. Mankiewicz's jocular account included as the climax "thirty-four weeks in a cast in bed and thirty-two weeks in a brace." Phipps had a broken collarbone; when it healed, he proceeded on his romantic way to New York. Mankiewicz had a compound fracture of the left leg, which, together with further injuries suffered while the fracture was healing, left him with a limp for the rest of his life.

During the long recuperation—very long, because on his first night out on the town after his cast was removed, he went on crutches to Chasen's, got drunk, slipped and broke more bones, and had to be put in another cast—Mankiewicz, bedridden and in exile from the studios, began to write the Mercury Theatre's "Campbell Playhouse" radio shows, and the actors often gathered around his bed for story conferences, and even rehearsals. Welles, having come to Hollywood in July to fulfill his contract with Schaefer, had been flying to and from New York for the series; in October he arranged to have the shows originate in Los Angeles, and in November he hired Mankiewicz to write five of them. Welles had met Mankiewicz sometime earlier in New York. This is John Houseman's recollection of those events, set down in a letter to Sara Mankiewicz after her husband's death:

> I remember so well the day Orson came back to the theatre from 21, telling me he had met this amazingly civilized and charming man. I can just see them there at lunch together—magicians and highbinders at work on each other, vying with each other in wit and savoir-faire and mutual appreciation. Both came away enchanted and convinced that, between them, they were the two most dashing and gallantly intelligent gentlemen in the Western world. And they were not so far wrong! Soon after that I met

Herman myself, but I didn't get to know him until . . . he lay in bed at Tower Road, his leg in a monstrous plaster cast . . . and we started to do those peculiar collaborative radio shows in the beginning of our long conspiracy of love and hate for Maestro, the Dog-Faced Boy. Then came *Kane* and Victorville and those enchanted months of inhabiting Mrs. Campbell's ranch with our retinue of nurse and secretary and our store of Mickey Finns!

Tower Road was where the Mankiewiczes lived and the Mercury group gathered. The Dog-Faced Boy is, of course, Orson Welles (Cocteau once described him as "a dog who has broken loose from his chain and gone to sleep on the flower bed"), and the Mickey Finns were a medical concoction that was supposed to make Mankiewicz hate alcohol. It failed. The secretary, Mrs. Rita Alexander (she lent her name to the character of Susan Alexander), recalls that during her first week, before Sara Mankiewicz had had a chance to give her a briefing, Mankiewicz persuaded her to take him in to the town of Victorville, where he could get a drink. She withstood his wiles after that. He really wasn't in condition to do much drinking; the broken bones included a hip break, and he was in such poor condition that even eating presented problems. Mrs. Alexander recalls spoon-feeding him bicarbonate of soda, and recalls his courtly, formal apologies for the belches that rocked the room.

XII

There are monsters, and there are also sacred monsters; both Welles and Mankiewicz deserve places in the sacred-monster category. Some writers on film—particularly in England—blithely say that Kane wasn't based on Hearst, using as evidence statements that Welles made to the press in early 1941, when he was trying to get the picture released. But those who think Louella Parsons got the *mistaken* idea that the picture was about Hearst don't understand what kind of man the young Welles was. Welles and Mankiewicz wanted to do something startling, something that would cap the invasion of the Martians—which had, after all, panicked only the boobs, and inadvertently at that, though Welles now makes it sound deliberate. This time, he and Mankiewicz *meant* to raise Cain. The pun is surely theirs, and Hearst had walked right into it; he was so fond of a story called *Cain and Mabel,* which he'd bought and produced as a Cosmopolitan Picture back in 1924, that he remade it late in 1936, at Warners', starring Clark Gable and Marion Davies. It had been one of her last pictures before her retirement. Cain and Mabel—it was a perfect description of Hearst and Marion. In 1960, when Welles was interviewed on British television, he said, "Kane isn't really founded on Hearst in particular." I suppose he was feeling rather expansive at that moment, and it may have seemed to limit his importance if his Kane had been based on anyone "in particular." In the same interview, he said, "You asked me did Mr. Hearst try to stop it. *He* didn't. . . . He was like Kane in that he wouldn't have stooped to such a thing." This was rather droll, but Welles seemed to mean it. He didn't seem to know much about Hearst anymore; probably he'd forgotten. One may also fairly conclude that Welles, with that grandeur which he seems to have taken over from the theatre into his personal life, was elevating Hearst, lending Hearst some of his own magnitude. More characteristically, however, his grandeur is double-edged, as in this typical statement on Gregg Toland:

> I had a great advantage not only in the real genius of my cameraman but in the fact that he, like all men who are masters of a craft, told me at the outset that there was nothing about camerawork that any intelligent being couldn't learn in half a day. And he was right.

Welles was thus telling us that he learned all there was to know about camerawork in half a day. What, one wonders, was the craft that Toland needed to master? Welles, like Hearst, and like most very big men, is capable of some very small gestures. And so was Mankiewicz, who brought his younger, more stable brother, Joe, out to Hollywood and helped him get started, but, as soon as Joe had some success, began behaving atrociously, referring to him as "my idiot brother."

Mankiewicz's ambivalence was generally on a higher level, however. There are many different kinds of senses of humor, and the one that sometimes comes through Mankiewicz anecdotes is the perverse soul of Kane himself. There is, for example, the story that Ezra Goodman tells in *The Fifty Year Decline and Fall of Hollywood*. Hollywood was not often elegant and correct, but the producer Arthur Hornblow, Jr., was known for the punctiliousness of his social functions. At a dinner party that he gave for Hollywood notables, Herman Mankiewicz drank too much and threw up on the table. "A deadly hush descended over the assembled guests. . . . Mankiewicz broke the silence himself: 'It's all right, Arthur; the white wine came up with the fish.' "

The man who in those circumstances could put his host down was a fit companion for Welles. They were big eaters, big talkers, big spenders, big talents; they were not men of what is ordinarily called "good character." They were out to get not only Hearst but each other. The only religious remark that has ever been attributed to Mankiewicz was recorded on the set of *Citizen Kane:* Welles walked by, and Mankiewicz muttered, "There, but for the grace of God, goes God."

XIII

Herman Mankiewicz didn't—to be exact—write *Citizen Kane;* he dictated it. The screenwriters may have felt like whores and they may have been justified in that feeling, but they were certainly well-paid whores. In New York, they hadn't had secretaries, but the movie business was mass culture's great joke on talent. The affectation of "Look, no hands" became the literal truth. Mankiewicz dictated the script while the nurse watched over him and John Houseman stood by in attendance. This was a cut-rate job—Mankiewicz was getting $500 a week for his ghostly labors—but it was still in the royal tradition of screenwriting. Outside the movie business, there has probably never been a writer in the history of the world who got this kind of treatment. There was an urgency about it: Welles and most of the Mercury Theatre company were in Hollywood doing their weekly radio shows and waiting while this odd little group spent the spring of 1940 in Victorville preparing the script for Orson Welles's début in films.

Welles had come to Hollywood the previous July in a burst of publicity, but his first two film projects hadn't got under way. Within a few months of his arrival, he was being jeered at because nothing had happened. Although his contract with R.K.O. gave him freedom from interference, Schaefer and his legal staff had to approve the project and clear the shooting script and, of course, the budget. It had been agreed that his first project would be Conrad's *Heart of Darkness,* which he had already done as a radio drama. He was to play both Marlow and Kurtz, the two leading roles, and it was reported in the trade press that he was working on the script with John Houseman and Herbert Drake, who was the Mercury's press agent. In the latter part of 1939, Welles brought actors out from New York and shot long test sequences, but the budget looked too high to the poverty-stricken studio, and the production was repeatedly postponed. He decided to do something while he was waiting—something that he could start on right away, to get the Mercury actors on the R.K.O. payroll—and he hit on a spy thriller with a political theme: *The Smiler with the Knife,* from the novel by Nicholas Blake (C. Day-Lewis). Welles adapted the book himself—"in seven days," according to the trade press—but this project was abandoned almost at once because of differences with Schaefer over casting. (Welles wanted to use Lucille Ball, then a contract player at R.K.O., in the lead, and Schaefer didn't think she could carry the picture. As the whole world knows, she wound up owning the studio, but Schaefer wasn't necessarily wrong; she never did carry a picture.) There was still hope for *Heart of Darkness*—and a lot of money had already been spent on it—but things seemed to be falling apart for the Mercury group. By the end of 1939, Welles was desperate for a subject that would be acceptable to R.K.O. The movie plans were up in the air, and there was dissension within the Mercury group about staying on in Hollywood with nothing definite in sight to work on. Some of the actors left to take jobs elsewhere, and some were beginning to get film roles—a development that upset Welles, because he wanted them to be "new faces" in his first film.

A policy meeting was arranged to discuss the failing fortunes of the group and to decide whether to keep them all in Los Angeles or send some of them back to New York. The more or less administrative heads of the

Mercury Theatre met for dinner in an upper room at Chasen's. The group included Welles; Houseman, who had founded the Mercury Theatre with him; two all-purpose assistants, Richard Wilson and William Alland; the press agent, Drake; and several others. Houseman argued that the actors should return to New York, but nothing had been settled by the time the coffee and brandy arrived, and then Welles, in a sudden access of rage, shouted that Houseman had always been against him, and he threw the coffee warmers—full of Sterno canned heat—at Houseman. He did not throw them very precisely, it seems; he threw not so much with intent to hit as in Houseman's general direction. Dave Chasen, having been summoned by a waiter, opened the door, and, with the aplomb he had used back in the thirties in vaudeville, when he was the stooge of the comedian Joe Cook, he took one look—a curtain was on fire by then—and closed the door. The men in the room stamped out the fire, and Houseman went home and sent Welles a letter of resignation. The partnership was ended, and a week later Houseman left for New York.

Welles's tantrum and how it ended the partnership that had created the Mercury Theatre was the talk of the actors who gathered around Mankiewicz's bed, and it must have registered on Mankiewicz in a special way: it must have practically thrust on him the recognition of an emotional link between Welles and William Randolph Hearst, whose tantrums had been the stuff of legend among newspapermen for half a century, and whose occasional demonstrations of childishness were the gossip of guests at San Simeon. A week or two after the Chasen's dinner party, Mankiewicz proposed to Welles that they make a "prismatic" movie about the life of a man seen from several different points of view. Even before he went to work in Hollywood and met Hearst, when he was still at the *New York Times,* Mankiewicz was already caught up in the idea of a movie about Hearst. Marion Fisher, the Mankiewicz baby-sitter, whose family lived in the same Central Park West building, was learning to type in high school and Mankiewicz offered to "test her typing." He dictated a screenplay, organized in flashbacks. She recalls that he had barely started on the dictation, which went on for several weeks, when she remarked that it seemed to be about William Randolph Hearst, and he said, "You're a smart girl." Mankiewicz couldn't pay her but she and her parents saw about fifty shows on the theatre tickets he gave them, and it was a great year for Broadway—1925. Although in the intervening years Mankiewicz had often talked to friends about what a movie Hearst's life would make, his first suggestions to Welles for the "prismatic" movie were Dillinger and, when Welles was cool to that, Aimee Semple McPherson. Only after Welles had rejected that, too, and after they had discussed the possibilities in the life of Dumas, did he propose Hearst. Mankiewicz must have been stalling and playing games to lead Welles on, because although he was interested in both Dillinger and Aimee Semple McPherson, and subsequently did prepare scripts on them, this movie had to be a starring vehicle for Welles, and what major role could

Welles play in the life of either Dillinger or Aimee? From what Mankiewicz told friends at the time, when he sprang the name Hearst, Welles leaped at it.

Welles had grown up hearing stories about Hearst from Dr. Maurice Bernstein, who was his guardian after his parents died. Dr. Bernstein was a good friend of Ashton Stevens, who had originally been the drama critic on Hearst's flagship paper, the *San Francisco Examiner,* and had gone on to work for Hearst in Chicago. Welles himself was a Hearst-press "discovery"; it was Ashton Stevens, whom Dr. Bernstein got in touch with, who had publicized the nineteen-year-old Orson Welles when he produced *Hamlet* on a vacant second floor in Illinois. But Welles, being a knowledgeable young man, would have known a great deal about Hearst even without this personal connection, for Hearst was the unifying hatred of all liberals and leftists. Welles, with his sense of the dramatic, would have known at once what a sensational idea a movie about Hearst was. Aimee and Dillinger just didn't have the dimensions that Hearst had; Hearst was even right for Welles *physically.* Welles and Mankiewicz must have enjoyed thinking what a scandal a movie about him would make. Mankiewicz didn't need to have misgivings about repercussions, because the risks would all be Welles's. Schaefer had signed Welles up to a widely publicized four-way contract as producer, director, writer, and actor. It was understood that he would take the credit for the script, just as he did for the scripts of the radio plays. His R.K.O. contract stated that "the screenplay for each picture shall be written by Mr. Orson Welles," and Welles probably took this stipulation as no more than his due—a necessity of his station. He probably accepted the work that others did for him the way modern Presidents accept the work of speech-writers.

The title *American* suggests how Mankiewicz felt about the project. Several years before, in 1933, his friend and drinking companion Preston Sturges had written a big one, an original called *The Power and the Glory,* which, when it was produced, with Spencer Tracy and Colleen Moore in the leading roles, made Tracy a star. *The Power and the Glory* was about a ruthless railroad tycoon who fails in his personal life, and it was told in flashbacks and narration from his funeral. It was an impressive picture, and it was lauded in terms similar to those later used about *Kane.* "Its subject," William Troy wrote in the *Nation,* "is the great American Myth, and its theme is futility." The ballyhoo included putting a bronze tablet in the New York theatre where it opened to commemorate "the first motion picture in which narratage was used as a method of telling a dramatic story." (Hollywood, big on ballyhoo but short on real self-respect, failed to transfer the nitrate negative to safety stock, and modern prints of *The Power and the Glory* are tattered remnants.) Not only is the tycoon treated ambivalently by Sturges but in the boyhood sequence he is injured through his own arrogance, so that he acquires a jagged, lightninglike scar on his hand—the mark of Cain. The idea of the big-businessman as a Cain figure was basic to this genre, which had become popular in the Depression thirties, when many business giants of the twenties were revealed to be swindlers, or, at the very least, ruthless. In another 1933 film, *I Loved a Woman,* a tycoon's mistress sang at the Chicago Opera House. (It was where the tycoons' mistresses did sing in the twenties.) In 1937, Mankiewicz himself had done a trial run on the tycoon theme (with Edward Arnold as a lumber baron) in *John Meade's Woman.* To do Hearst, a much more dangerous man—the only tycoon who was also a demagogue—in a technique similar to Sturges's but from several different points of view would make a really big picture.

But there was a sizable hurdle: How could they get R.K.O. to approve this project? Welles and Mankiewicz went on talking about it for a couple of weeks, while Mankiewicz continued writing the weekly radio shows. When they decided to go ahead and try to slip it over on the studio somehow, Welles still had to find a way to get Mankiewicz to do the writing; the Mercury company couldn't be kept waiting in Los Angeles indefinitely while Mankiewicz wandered loose. Mankiewicz had had to be hauled off to sanatoriums to be dried out too many times for Welles to take chances, and the screenwriters who had worked with Mankiewicz at Metro told too many stories about his losing interest in the scripts he was assigned to and drinking so much during working hours that the other writers would load him into a studio car in midafternoon and have the driver haul him home, where Sara would unload him and put him to bed, and he would sleep it off before dinner and be ready for the night's drinking. He had just injured himself again, in his fall at Chasen's, and his bones were being reset, but soon he would be off on the town once more, despite cast or crutches, and there would be no way to hold him down to work. Welles hit on the scheme of packing Mankiewicz off to the country to recuperate. In early January, 1940, Welles flew to New York, and over lunch at "21" the young magician prevailed on Houseman to return to the Coast and do him and the Mercury one last service by running herd on Mankiewicz; only a month had passed since the fiery scene at Chasen's. (It was to be not the last but the next-to-last collaborative project of Welles and Houseman. A week after *American* was done and the troupe had left Victorville, Houseman and Welles were on bad terms again, but Mankiewicz, who was said to have read every new book by publication date, even when he was in the worst possible shape, told them that they'd be crazy if they didn't buy a new book that was just coming out, and dramatize it. Houseman went to work on it, and as a result Richard Wright's *Native Son* was adapted for the stage and produced so quickly that Welles had it playing in New York by the time *Citizen Kane* opened.)

Both Houseman and Mankiewicz unquestionably had mixed feelings about Welles by the time they found themselves at the guest ranch. Houseman admits that right from the beginning, when Mankiewicz started on the script, they planned to have Welles re-enact his tantrum. It was set for the scene in which Susan leaves Kane (Welles's wife, Virginia, had brought suit for divorce during the month Welles had his tantrum), and Mankiewicz wrote it up rather floridly and with explicit directions, in a passage begin-

271

ning, "Kane, in a truly terrible and absolutely silent rage . . ." When it was time to shoot the scene, the various members of the group who had been at Chasen's—or had heard about what happened there, and everybody *had*—encouraged Welles to do what he had done that night. Last year, William Alland, describing the making of the film in an interview printed in the magazine of the Directors Guild of America, said:

> There was one scene which stands out above all others in my memory; that was the one in which Orson broke up the roomful of furniture in a rage. Orson never liked himself as an actor. He had the idea that he should have been feeling more, that he intellectualized too much and never achieved the emotion of losing himself in a part.
>
> When he came to the furniture-breaking scene, he set up four cameras, because he obviously couldn't do the scene many times. He did the scene just twice, and each time he threw himself into the action with a fervor I had never seen in him. It was absolutely electric; you felt as if you were in the presence of a man coming apart.
>
> Orson staggered out of the set with his hands bleeding and his face flushed. He almost swooned, yet he was exultant. "I really felt it," he exclaimed. "I really felt it!"
>
> Strangely, that scene didn't have the same power when it appeared on the screen. It might have been how it was cut, or because there hadn't been close-in shots to depict his rage. The scene in the picture was only a mild reflection of what I had witnessed on that movie stage.

Writing that scene into the movie was a cruel trick on Welles, designed to make him squirm. He had been built up so much that he was by then the white hope (as it used to be called) of the theatre. In 1938, even George S. Kaufman and Moss Hart had taken him to be that; they had written one of their worst maudlin "serious" plays (and a flop)—*The Fabulous Invalid,* a cavalcade-of-the-American-theatre sort of play—and had modelled its hero on Welles. The hero—the leader of a new acting company—made a classic final curtain speech to his actors:

> We haven't got very much money, but we've got youth and, I think, talent. They'll tell you the theatre is dying. I don't believe it. Anything that can bring us together like this, and hold us to this one ideal in spite of everything, isn't going to die. They'll tell you it isn't important, putting makeup on your face and playacting. I don't believe it. It's important to keep alive a thing that can lift men's spirits above the everyday reality of their lives. We mustn't let that die. Remember—you're going to be kicked around, and a

lot of the time you're not going to have enough to eat, but you're going to get one thing in return. The chance to write, and act, say the things you want to say, and do the things you want to do. And I think that's enough.

For the people who did much of the work on Welles's projects, the temptation must have been strong to expose what they considered this savior's feet of clay.

The menagerie at Mrs. Campbell's being scarcely a secret, they had many visitors (Welles himself came to dinner once or twice), and several of these visitors, as well as Houseman and Mrs. Alexander, describe how Herman Mankiewicz turned out the script that became *Citizen Kane*. Mankiewicz couldn't go anywhere without help; he sat up, in the cast that covered one leg and went up to his middle, and played cribbage with Mrs. Alexander during the day, while telling her stories about Hearst and Marion Davies and San Simeon. Then, at night, from about eight-thirty to eleven-thirty or twelve, he dictated, and she would type it out so he could have it the next day. Mrs. Alexander recalls that during the first days on the job, when she was fascinated by the romantic significance of "Rosebud" and asked him how the story would turn out, he said, "My dear Mrs. Alexander, I don't know. I'm making it up as I go along." Welles was so deeply entangled in the radio shows and other activities and a romance with Dolores Del Rio at the time the script was being prepared that even when he came to dinner at Victorville, it was mainly a social visit; the secretary didn't meet him until after Mankiewicz had finished dictating the long first draft. Welles probably made suggestions in his early conversations with Mankiewicz and since he received copies of the work weekly while it was in progress at Victorville, he may have given advice by phone or letter. Later, he almost certainly made suggestions for cuts that helped Mankiewicz hammer the script into tighter form, and he is known to have made a few changes on the set. But Mrs. Alexander, who took the dictation from Mankiewicz, from the first paragraph to the last, and then, when the first draft was completed and they all went back to Los Angeles, did the secretarial work at Mankiewicz's house on the rewriting and the cuts, and who then handled the script at the studio until after the film was shot, says that Welles didn't write (or dictate) one line of the shooting script of *Citizen Kane*.

Toward the end of the period at the ranch, Mankiewicz began to realize that he'd made a very bad financial deal, and that the credit might be more important than he'd anticipated. After talks with Mrs. Alexander and the Mercury people who visited on weekends, he decided he was going to get screen credit, no matter what his bargain with Welles had been. Meanwhile, Houseman, who says that according to his original agreement to go off to the ranch he was supposed to get some kind of credit, discovered once again, and as so many others had, that it wasn't easy to get your name on anything Orson Welles was involved in. Houseman was apparently fed up with arguments, and he says he waived his claim when he saw how determined Welles was; he left for New York and got started on the preparations for *Native Son*. But Mankiewicz was an experienced Hollywood hand and veteran of credit brawls who kept all his drafts and materials, and a man who relished trouble. He had ample proof of his authorship, and he took his evidence to the Screen Writers Guild and raised so much hell that Welles was forced to split the credit and take second place in the listing.

At the time the movie came out, Mankiewicz's contribution to the film was generally known. The screen credit was to Herman J. Mankiewicz and Orson Welles. The *Hollywood Reporter* simplified the credit to "Written by Herman Mankiewicz"; Burns Mantle, in his newspaper column, referred to Mankiewicz's having written it; and, of course, Ben Hecht explained to the readers of *PM,* "This movie was not written by Orson Welles. It is the work of Herman J. Mankiewicz." In that period, it was well known that if the producer of a film wanted a screenplay credit it was almost impossible to prevent him from getting it. So many producers took a writing credit as a *droit du seigneur* for a few consultations or suggestions that the Screen Writers Guild later instituted a rule calling for compulsory arbitration whenever a producer sought a credit. Under the present rules of the Guild, Welles's name would probably not have appeared. And so it was by an awful fluke of justice that when Academy Awards night came, and Welles should have got the awards he deserved as director and actor, the award he got (the only Academy Award he has ever got) was as co-author of the Best Original Screenplay.*

XIV

The Mercury group wasn't surprised at Welles's taking a script credit; they'd had experience with this foible of his. Very early in his life as a prodigy, Welles seems to have fallen into the trap that has caught so many lesser men—believing his own publicity, believing that he really was the whole creative works, producer-director-writer-actor. Because he *could* do all these things, he imagined that he *did* do them. (A Profile of him that appeared in *The New Yorker* two years before *Citizen Kane* was made said that "outside the theatre ... Welles is exactly twenty-three years old.") In the days before the Mercury Theatre's weekly radio shows got a sponsor, it was considered a good publicity technique to build up public identification with Welles's name, so he was credited with just about everything, and was named on the air as the writer of the Mercury shows. Probably no one but Welles believed it. He had written some of the shows when the program first started, and had also worked on some with Houseman, but soon he had become much too busy even to collaborate; for a while Houseman wrote them, and then they were farmed out. By the time of the *War of the Worlds* broadcast, on Hal-

---

* Shortly after this article appeared, Welles was voted a special Academy Award for "superlative artistry and versatility in the creation of motion pictures."

loween, 1938, Welles wasn't doing any of the writing. He was so busy with his various other activities that he didn't always direct the rehearsals himself, either—William Alland or Richard Wilson or one of the other Mercury assistants did it. Welles might not come in until the last day, but somehow, all agree, he would pull the show together "with a magic touch." Yet when the Martian broadcast became accidentally famous, Welles seemed to forget that Howard Koch had written it. (In all the furor over the broadcast, with front-page stories everywhere, the name of the author of the radio play wasn't mentioned.) Koch had been writing the shows for some time. He lasted for six months, writing about twenty-five shows altogether—working six and a half days a week, and frantically, on each one, he says, with no more than half a day off to see his family. The weekly broadcasts were a "studio presentation" until after the *War of the Worlds* (Campbell's Soup picked them up then), and Koch, a young writer, who was to make his name with the film *The Letter* in 1940 and win an Academy Award for his share in the script of the 1942 *Casablanca,* was writing them for $75 apiece. Koch's understanding of the agreement was that Welles would get the writing credit on the air for publicity purposes but that Koch would have any later benefit, and the copyright was in Koch's name. (He says that it was, however, Welles's idea that he do the Martian show in the form of radio bulletins.) Some years later, when C.B.S. did a program about the broadcast and the panic it had caused, the network re-created parts of the original broadcast and paid Koch $300 for the use of his material. Welles sued C.B.S. for $375,000, claiming that he was the author and that the material had been used without his permission. He lost, of course, but he may still think he wrote it. (He frequently indicates as much in interviews and on television.)

"Foible" is the word that Welles's former associates tend to apply to his assertions of authorship. Welles could do so many different things in those days that it must have seemed almost accidental when he didn't do things he claimed to. Directors, in the theatre and in movies, are by function (and often by character, or, at least, disposition) cavalier toward other people's work, and Welles was so much more talented and magnetic than most directors—and so much younger, too—that people he robbed of credit went on working with him for years, as Koch went on writing more of the radio programs after Welles failed to mention him during the national publicity about the panic. Welles was dedicated to the company, and he was exciting to work with, so the company stuck together, working for love, and even a little bit more money (Koch was raised to $125 a show) when they got a sponsor and, also as a result of the *War of the Worlds* broadcast, the movie contract that took them to Hollywood.

If there was ever a young man who didn't need unearned credits, it was Orson Welles, yet though he was already too big, he must have felt he needed to dazzle the world. Welles was hated in Hollywood long before he'd made a movie; he was hated almost upon his arrival. From time to time, Hollywood used to work up considerable puerile resentment against "out-

275

siders" who dared to make movies. The scope of Welles's reputation seems to have infuriated Hollywood; it was a cultural reproach from the East, and the Hollywood people tried to protect themselves by closing ranks and making Welles a butt of their humor. Gene Lockhart composed a stupid, nasty ditty called "Little Orson Annie," which was sung at Hollywood parties; the name stuck and was used by the columnists, though Hedda Hopper supported him and suggested that Hollywood reserve judgment, and Louella Parsons, on December 31st, selected him as "the most discussed personality to come to the films in 1939." Yet for Welles, with his beard (he was growing it for the Shakespearean production he intended to stage as soon as he could pick up his Hollywood loot), to be ensconced in the Mary Pickford–Buddy Rogers estate, right next door to Shirley Temple, was too much for Hollywood. Welles became the victim of practical jokers. One night when he was dining at Chasen's, an actor cut off his tie with a table knife. Not all the jokes were so Freudian, but they were mostly ugly. Welles had come with an unprecedented contract. Probably the old Hollywoodians not only expected him to fall on his face but hoped he would, so that their mediocrity and prosperity would be vindicated. But Welles was the braggart who makes good. And, despite their resentment, they *were* dazzled by *Citizen Kane*.

XV

The picture got a thunderous reception, even in the Hollywood press. In recent years, the rumor has spread that *Citizen Kane* opened to bad reviews—presumably on the theory that it was so far ahead of its time that it wasn't understood—and this is now recorded in many film histories. But it was very well understood by the press (who would understand a newspaper picture better?), and it got smashing reviews. It isn't, after all, a difficult picture. In some ways, it was probably better understood then than it is now, and, as far as I can determine, it was more highly praised by the American press than any other movie in history. The New York opening of *Citizen Kane*, which had been scheduled for February 14, 1941, finally took place on May 1st, and a week later it opened in Los Angeles. In January, Hedda Hopper had "doubted" whether the picture would ever be released, and some of the trade press had predicted that it wouldn't be. Possibly it wouldn't have been except for the screenings that Welles arranged and the publicity that he got.

The whole industry was already involved in the picture. Although technically Welles had the right of final cut, the editor, Robert Wise, was instructed by the studio, with Welles's consent, to take a print to New York in January. Wise ran it for the heads of all the major companies and their lawyers, and for six weeks he and his then assistant, Mark Robson, who was on the Coast, fussed over the movie, making tiny, nervous changes—mostly a word here or there—that the executives and lawyers hoped would render the picture less objectionable to Hearst. Meanwhile, Schaefer had engaged Time, Inc.'s legal specialist on invasion-of-privacy suits; the lawyer instructed

Schaefer that if he made one small cut in the film, no one could win such a suit. The dangerous section was a bit of dialogue by Raymond, the butler, suggesting that the old man was senile. Schaefer says he had no difficulty persuading Welles to agree to the cut. However, at the beginning of March, Hearst sent for Walter Howey, and no one was sure what they might be poking into. "Nor are private lives to be overlooked," Hedda Hopper predicted; and her predictions were the same as threats. Hearst's maneuvers were in the true Kane spirit: In January, Hedda Hopper had warned that "the refugee situation would be looked into," which meant that there would be pressure for a legal review of whether various imported stars and directors should be allowed to remain in the country, and the industry would be attacked for employing foreigners; that is, refugees from Hitler. Three days after the press previews, the Hearst newspapers, the American Legion, the Veterans of Foreign Wars, and other patriotic organizations went into action to rid radio of "subversives." The "subversives" they were after were William Saroyan, Maxwell Anderson, Marc Connelly, Robert E. Sherwood, Stephen Vincent Benét, Paul Green, Sherwood Anderson, and James Boyd, who were involved with Welles in a series of C.B.S. radio plays on the general theme of freedom, which, although it had been encouraged by the Justice Department, was now condemned as un-American and as tending to promote Communism. Before *Citizen Kane* was released, *PM* reported that Hearst photographers were following Welles "in G-man style," trying to get something on him, while *Variety* reported "persistent inquiries at the draft board as to why Welles hadn't been drafted." It was along about this time that Hearst himself saw the picture. Schaefer says, "Hearst personally sent to me at the studio and asked to see a print, and we let him have it. This was before it opened. There was no response, no comment. Orson knew this." Welles may have feared that Schaefer would buckle unless he squeezed him from the other side, or, as Schaefer claims, it may have been Welles's way of getting more publicity, but, for whatever reason, Welles began to issue threats: he gave R.K.O. the deadline of March 30th for releasing the picture or facing a lawsuit. On March 11th, Welles called a press conference to alert the press to the danger that the film might be suppressed, and gave out this statement:

> I believe that the public is entitled to see *Citizen Kane*. For me to stand by while this picture was being suppressed would constitute a breach of faith with the public on my part as producer. I have at this moment sufficient financial backing to buy *Citizen Kane* from R.K.O. and to release it myself. Under my contract with R.K.O. I have the right to demand that the picture be released and to bring legal action to force its release. R.K.O. must release *Citizen Kane*. If it does not do so immediately, I have instructed my attorney to commence proceedings.
>
> I have been advised that strong pressure is being brought to

bear in certain quarters to cause the withdrawal of my picture *Citizen Kane* because of an alleged resemblance between incidents in the picture and incidents in the life of Mr. William Randolph Hearst.

Any such attempts at suppression would involve a serious interference with freedom of speech and with the integrity of the moving picture industry as the foremost medium of artistic expression in the country.

There is nothing in the facts to warrant the situation that has arisen. *Citizen Kane* was not intended to have nor has it any reference to Mr. Hearst or to any other living person. No statement to the contrary has ever been authorized by me. *Citizen Kane* is the story of a wholly fictitious character.

The script for *Citizen Kane* was scrutinized and approved by both R.K.O. Radio Pictures and the Hays office. No one in those organizations nor anyone associated with me in the production of the picture believed that it represented anything but psychological analysis of an imaginary individual. I regret exceedingly that anyone should interpret *Citizen Kane* to have a bearing upon any living person, or should impugn the artistic purposes of its producers.

Several of the magazines responded to his plea for the pressure of publicity by reviewing the picture before it opened, obviously with the intention of helping to get it released. A review in *Time* on March 17, 1941, began:

As in some grotesque fable, it appeared last week that Hollywood was about to turn upon and destroy its greatest creation.

It continued:

To most of the several hundred people who have seen the film at private showings, *Citizen Kane* is the most sensational product of the U.S. movie industry. It has found important new techniques in picture-making and story telling. . . . It is as psychiatrically sound as a fine novel. . . . It is a work of art created by grown people for grown people.

In *Newsweek,* also on March 17, 1941, John O'Hara began his review with

It is with exceeding regret that your faithful bystander reports that he has just seen a picture which he thinks must be the best picture he ever saw.

With no less regret he reports that he has just seen the best actor in the history of acting.

278

Name of picture: *Citizen Kane.*

Name of actor: Orson Welles.

Reason for regret: you, my dear, may never see the picture.

I saw *Citizen Kane* the other night. I am told that my name was crossed off a list of persons who were invited to look at the picture, my name being crossed off because some big shot remembered I had been a newspaperman. So, for the first time in my life, I indignantly denied I was a newspaperman. Nevertheless, I had to be snuck into the showing of *Citizen Kane* under a phony name. That's what's going on about this wonderful picture. Intrigue.

Why intrigue? Well, because. A few obsequious and/or bulbous middle-aged ladies think the picture ought not to be shown, owing to the fact that the picture is rumored to have something to do with a certain publisher, who, for the first time in his life, or maybe the second, shall be nameless. That the nameless publisher might be astute enough to realize that for the first time in his rowdy life he had been made a human being did not worry the loyal ladies. Sycophancy of that kind, like curtseying, is deliberate. The ladies merely wait for a chance to show they can still do it, even if it means cracking a femur. This time I think they may have cracked off more than they can chew. I hope.

Along the way, O'Hara said such things as

My intention is to make you want to see the picture; if possible, to make you wonder why you are not seeing what I think is as good a picture as was ever made. . . . And aside from what it does not lack, *Citizen Kane* has Orson Welles. It is traditional that if you are a great artist, no one gives a damn about you while you're still alive. Welles has had plenty of that. He got a tag put to his name through the Mars thing, just as Scott Fitzgerald, who wrote better than any man in our time, got a Jazz Age tag put to his name. I say, if you plan to have any grandchildren to see and to bore, see Orson Welles so that you can bore your grandchildren with some honesty. There never has been a better actor than Orson Welles. I just got finished saying there never has been a better actor than Orson Welles, and I don't want any of your lip.

Do yourself a favor. Go to your neighborhood exhibitor and ask him why he isn't showing *Citizen Kane.*

The same day—March 17, 1941—*Life*, which was to run several more features on the movie in the following months, came out with four pages of pictures and a review:

Few movies have ever come from Hollywood with such powerful narrative, such original technique, such exciting photography. Director Welles and Cameraman Gregg Toland do brilliantly with a camera everything Hollywood has always said you couldn't do. They shoot into bright lights, they shoot into the dark and against low ceilings, till every scene comes with the impact of something never seen before. Even the sound track is new. And for narrative Welles has tapped a segment of life fearfully skirted by the U.S. cinema: the swift and brutal biography of a power-mad newspaper tycoon, a man of twisted greatness who buys or bullies his way into everything but friends' love and his nation's respect. To a film industry floundering in a rut, *Citizen Kane* offers enough new channels to explore for five years to come.

Hearst must have known he would be in for a bad time if the picture should be withheld; the Luce magazines—*Time* and *Life*—had always been eager to embarrass him, and certainly wouldn't let the subject drop. (The financial backing that Welles said he had to buy the picture was probably from Henry Luce.) One surmises that Hearst decided not to try to block its release—though the petty harassment of R.K.O. and others involved went on, like a reflex to a blow.

Here is a representative selection from the reviews:

Variety: A film possessing the sure dollar mark.

Times (Bosley Crowther): Suppression of this film would have been a crime. . . . *Citizen Kane* is far and away the most surprising and cinematically exciting motion picture to be seen here in many a moon. . . . It comes close to being the most sensational film ever made in Hollywood.

Herald Tribune (Howard Barnes): A young man named Orson Welles has shaken the medium wide-awake with his magnificent film, *Citizen Kane.* His biography of an American dynast is not only a great picture; it is something of a revolutionary screen achievement. . . . From any standpoint *Citizen Kane* is truly a great motion picture.

Post (Archer Winsten): It goes without saying this is the picture that wins the majority of 1941's movie prizes in a walk, for it is inconceivable that another will come along to challenge it. . . . Orson Welles with this one film establishes himself as the most exciting director now working. . . . Technically the result marks a new epoch.

PM (Cecelia Ager): Before *Citizen Kane,* it's as if the motion picture was a slumbering monster, a mighty force stupidly sleeping, lying there sleek, torpid, complacent—awaiting a fierce young man to come kick it to life, to rouse it, shake it, awaken it to its potentialities, to show it what it's got. Seeing it, it's as if you never really saw a movie before: no movie has ever grabbed you, pummelled you, socked you on the button with the vitality, the accuracy, the impact, the professional aim, that this one does.

Esquire (Gilbert Seldes): Welles has shown Hollywood how to make movies. . . . He has made the movies young again, by filling them with life.

Cue (Jesse Zunser): It is an astounding experience to watch Orson Welles, 25-year-old Boy Genius of the Western World, in the process of creating on the screen one of the awesome products of his fertile imagination. You come away limp, much as if you had turned into Broadway and suddenly beheld Niagara Falls towering behind the Paramount Building, the Matterhorn looming over Bryant Park, and the Grand Canyon yawning down the middle of Times Square.

Hollywood Reporter: A great motion picture. . . . A few steps ahead of anything that has been made in pictures before.

Chicago Journal of Commerce (Claudia Cassidy): Anyone who has eyes in his head and ears to hear with will enjoy *Citizen Kane* for the unleashed power of its stature on the screen.

Even Kate Cameron, in the *Daily News,* gave it four stars, and on Sunday, May 4th, Bosley Crowther (though he had some second thoughts of his own) wrote in the *Times,* "The returns are in from most of the local journalistic precincts and Orson Welles' *Citizen Kane* has been overwhelmingly selected as one of the great (if not the greatest) motion pictures of all time. . . ." The *Film Daily* said, "Welles can prepare his mantel for a couple of Oscars."

XVI

Had it not been for the delays and the nervous atmosphere that made the picture *seem* unpopular and so *become* unpopular, it might have swept the Academy Awards. It had taken the New York Film Critics Award with ease, but early in 1942, when the 1941 Academy Awards were given, the picture had the aroma of box-office failure—an aroma that frightens off awards in Hollywood. The picture had been nominated in nine categories, and at the ceremony, each time the title or Orson Welles's name was read, there were hisses and loud boos. The prize for the Original Screenplay was perhaps partly a love gesture to Herman Mankiewicz, one of their own; the film community had closed ranks against Orson Welles.

While the picture was being shot, Welles, like a good showman, had done his best to preserve the element of surprise, and he had been smart about keeping a tight, closed set. He didn't want interference from anybody, and even though the R.K.O. executives had read the script, when one of them "dropped in" once to see what was going on, Welles coolly called a halt in the shooting, and the Mercury players went outside and played baseball until he left. There were visitors, of course. Invitations to attend the first official day of shooting were sent to the press, and Welles was simply careful about what he shot that day. And the crew didn't go out to play baseball when Louella Parsons visited the set a few weeks later; they were just very careful, so that even though she had heard rumors that the picture was about Hearst, everything looked so innocent and Welles denied the rumors so disarmingly that she went on giving him an enthusiastic press. (She later described his outfoxing her on this occasion as "one of the classic double crosses of Hollywood.") But Mankiewicz with his "Don't let this get around," was practically incapable of keeping a secret. He was so proud of his script that he lent a copy to Charles Lederer. In some crazily naïve way, Mankiewicz seems to have imagined that Lederer would be pleased by how good it was. But Lederer, apparently, was deeply upset and took the script to his aunt and Hearst. It went from them to Hearst's lawyers (who marked various passages) before it was returned to Mankiewicz, and thus Hearst and his associates were alerted early to the content of the film. It was probably as a result of Mankiewicz's idiotic indiscretion that the various forces were set in motion that resulted in the cancellation of the première at the Radio City Music Hall, the commercial failure of *Citizen Kane,* and the subsequent failure of Orson Welles. This was how, even before the film was finished, Hearst's minions were in action, and how there was time for Mayer and his people to set about their attempt to suppress the film, and, having failed in that, to destroy it commercially.

In the aftermath of the pressures, and of the disappointing returns on the film, the members of the Academy could feel very courageous about the writing award. Mankiewicz had become a foolhardy hero in taking on Hearst; *Kane* was Mankiewicz's finest moment. They wanted him to have a prize; he deserved it and he needed it. Hollywood loves the luxury of show-business sentimentality, and Hollywood loves a comeback. The members of the Academy destroyed Orson Welles that night, but they probably felt good because their hearts had gone out to crazy, reckless Mank, their own resident loser-genius, the has-been who was washed up in the big studios, who was so far down he had been reduced to writing Welles's radio shows. At the beginning of the thirties, he had been earning $4,000 a week; at the end of the thirties, he was a ghost. What they couldn't know was that *Kane* was Welles's finest moment, too; the reason they couldn't know it was that their failure to back him that night was the turning point. Welles had made *Citizen Kane* at twenty-five, and he seemed to have the world before him. They'd had time to get used to Mank's self-destructiveness, and he'd been down on his luck so long he was easy to love; besides, they admired the pranks that had got him thrown out of one studio after another. Welles was self-destructive in a style they weren't yet accustomed to.

One may speculate that if the members of the Academy had supported Welles and voted *Citizen Kane* Best Picture of the Year, if they had backed the nation's press and their own honest judgment, the picture might have got into the big theatrical showcases despite the pressures against it. If they had, *Kane* might have made money, and things might have gone differently for Welles—and for American movies. The Academy had plenty of sentiment but not enough guts. And so Orson Welles peaked early. Later, as his situation changed and his fortunes sank and *Kane* became the golden opportunity of his youth, his one great chance of freedom to accomplish something, then, when he looked back, he may really have needed to believe what he was quoted as saying in France: "Le seul film que j'aie jamais écrit du premier du dernier mot et pu mener à bien est *Citizen Kane*." The literal translation is "The only film that I ever wrote from first word to last and was able to bring to a successful issue is *Citizen Kane*," but I think that what it means is "The picture came out well." What else can it mean when one considers the contributions of Mankiewicz and Toland and all the rest? Men cheated of their due are notoriously given to claiming more than their due. The Academy members had made their token gesture to *Citizen Kane* with the screenplay award. They failed what they believed in; they gave in to the scandal and to the business pressures. They couldn't yet know how much guilt they *should* feel: guilt that by their failure to support *Citizen Kane* at this crucial time—the last chance to make *Kane* a financial success—they had started the downward spiral of Orson Welles, who was to become perhaps the greatest loser in Hollywood history.

XVII

Like D. W. Griffith, Orson Welles came into the movies in order to make money so that he could continue in the theatre, and, like Griffith, he discovered that movies were the medium in which he could do what he had barely dreamed of doing in the theatre. Soon—even before he started on *Citizen Kane*—Welles was desperate for money to make movies. It took guile to get *Kane* approved. Robert Wise, whom the head of the R.K.O. editing department had assigned to the picture because he was close to Welles's age, says, "Orson sneaked the project onto R.K.O. He told the studio that he was merely shooting tests." Sets were built, and shooting began on June 29, 1940; the "test shots" were fully produced. The Mercury actors and associates were there anyway, most of them under personal contract to Welles, as Mankiewicz was. But Dorothy Comingore, not a member of the Mercury Theatre but a Hollywood bit player (who, as Linda Winters, had worked in Westerns and with the Three Stooges and in Blondie and Charlie Chan pictures), says that she lived on unemployment checks of $18 a week while she "tested for one month" for the role of Susan Alexander. She adds, "All these tests were incorporated into the film; they were never retaken." After a month, with the studio buzzing about how brilliant the footage was, the movie was practically a *fait accompli*, and Welles was able to bulldoze Schaefer into approving the project. All the people who were already at work on

Citizen Kane—the cameraman, the grips, the composer, the assistants, and the actors—met at Herman Mankiewicz's house for breakfast, and Welles announced that the picture had been approved and could formally begin. They officially started on July 30, 1940, and they finished "principal photography" eighty-two shooting days later, on October 23, 1940, even though Welles—almost as accident-prone as Mankiewicz—broke his ankle during the scene when he ran down the stairs from Susan's room while yelling that he'd get Boss Gettys.

Yet it took more than guile to function in the motion-picture business at that time. It helped to be mercenary, of course, but what really counted then was not to care *too* much about your work. After *Citizen Kane,* the contract that gave Welles the right of final cut was cancelled, so he did not have control of *The Magnificent Ambersons,* and it was shortened and mangled. The industry was suspicious of him, and not just because of the scandal of *Kane,* and the general fear of Hearst, and *Kane's* unsatisfactory financial returns. Alva Johnston described the Hollywood attitude toward Welles in an article in the *Saturday Evening Post* in 1942, the year after *Kane* came out:

> Big agents soon lost interest in the boy genius. They learned that he wasn't interested in money. Welles became known as a dangerous Red because, when his first picture project was shelved after the studio had wasted a good deal of money on it, he offered to make another picture for nothing.
>
> Genius got a bad name on account of Welles. It was brought into complete disrepute by Saroyan. The gifted Armenian came to Hollywood with a small agent and insisted on working without a salary, leaving it to M-G-M to set a value on his services after his work was completed. He said, "I'll trust the studio." The $10,000,000-a-year agency business is wholly based on the motto "Don't trust the studio." Since the Welles and Saroyan affairs, it has been practically impossible to interest a big agent in an intellectual giant.

When you write straight reporting about the motion-picture business, you're writing satire. Motion-picture executives prefer to do business with men whose values they understand. It's very easy for these executives—businessmen running an art—to begin to fancy that they are creative artists themselves, because they are indeed very much like the "artists" who work for them, because the "artists" who work for them are, or have become, businessmen. Those who aren't businessmen are the Hollywood unreliables—the ones whom, it is always explained to you, the studios can't hire, because they're crazy. As soon as movies became Welles's passion, and he was willing to work on any terms, he was finished in the big studios—they didn't trust him. And so, somehow, Welles aged before he matured—and not just physically. He went from child prodigy to defeated old man, though today, at fifty-five, he is younger by a decade or two than most of the big American directors.

In later years, Welles, a brilliant talker, was to give many interviews, and as his power in the studios diminished, his role in past movies grew larger. Sometimes it seems that his only power is over the interviewers who believe him. He is a masterful subject. The new generation of film historians have their own version of "Look, no hands": they tape-record interviews. Young interviewers, particularly, don't bother to check the statements of their subjects—they seem to regard that as outside their province—and thus leave the impression that the self-aggrandizing stories they record are history. And so, as the years go on, if one trusts what appears in print, Welles wrote not only *Kane* but just about everything halfway good in any picture he ever acted in, and in interviews he's beginning to have directed anything good in them, too. Directors are now the most interviewed group of people since the stars in the forties, and they have told the same stories so many times that not only they believe them, whether they're true or false, but everybody is beginning to.

This worship of the director is cyclical—Welles or Fellini is probably adored no more than von Stroheim or von Sternberg or De Mille was in his heyday—but such worship generally doesn't help in sorting out what went into the making of good pictures and bad pictures. The directors try to please the interviewers by telling them the anecdotes that have got a good response before. The anecdotes are sometimes charming and superficial, like the famous one—now taken for motion-picture history—about how Howard Hawks supposedly discovered that *The Front Page* would be better if a girl played the reporter Hildy, and thus transformed the play into *His Girl Friday* in 1940. ("I was going to prove to somebody that *The Front Page* had the finest modern dialogue that had been written, and I asked a girl to read Hildy's part and I read the editor, and I stopped and I said, 'Hell, it's better between a girl and a man than between two men.' ") Now, a charming story is not nothing. Still, this is nothing but a charming and superficial story. *His Girl Friday* turned out joyously, but if such an accident did cause Hawks to see how easy it was to alter the play, he still must have done it rather cynically, in order to make it conform to the box-office patterns then current. By the mid-thirties—after the surprise success of *It Happened One Night*—the new independent, wisecracking girl was very popular, especially in a whole cycle of newspaper pictures with rival girl and boy reporters. Newspaper pictures were now "romantic comedies," and, just as the movies about lady fliers were almost all based on Amelia Earhart, the criminal-mouthpiece movies on William Fallon, and the gossip-column movies on Walter Winchell, the movies about girl reporters were almost all based on the most highly publicized girl reporter—Hearst's Adela Rogers St. Johns. Everybody had already been stealing from and unofficially adapting *The Front Page* in the "wacky" romantic newspaper comedies, and one of these rewrites, *Wedding Present*, in 1936 (by Adela Rogers St. Johns's then son-in-law Paul

Gallico), had tough editor (Cary Grant) and smart girl reporter (Joan Bennet) with square fiancé (Conrad Nagel). This was the mold that *The Front Page* was then squeezed into to become *His Girl Friday,* with Cary Grant, Rosalind Russell, and Ralph Bellamy (already a favorite square from *The Awful Truth*) in the same roles, and Rosalind Russell was so obviously playing Adela Rogers St. Johns that she was dressed in an imitation of the St. Johns girl-reporter striped suit.

Some things that students now, seeing films out of the context of the cycles they were part of, may take to be brilliant inventions were fairly standard; in fact, the public at the time was so familiar with the conventions of the popular comedies that the clichés were frequently spoofed within the pictures. But today, because of the problems peculiar to writing the history of modern mass-art forms, and because of the jumbled circumstances in which movies survive, with knowledge of them acquired in haphazard fashion from television, and from screenings here and there, film enthusiasts find it simpler to explain movies in terms of the genius-artist-director, the schoolbook hero—the man who did it all. Those who admire *Citizen Kane,* which is constructed to present different perspectives on a man's life, seem naïvely willing to accept Welles's view of its making; namely, that it is his sole creation.

Howard Hawks must wonder what the admiration of the young is worth when he learns from them that he invented overlapping dialogue in *His Girl Friday,* since it means that they have never bothered to look at the text of the original Hecht and MacArthur play. Welles, too, has been said to have invented overlapping dialogue, and just about everything else in *Kane.* But unearned praise is insulting, and a burden; Welles sometimes says, "I drag my myth around with me." His true achievements are heavy enough to weigh him down. Welles is a great figure in motion-picture history: he directed what is almost universally acclaimed as the greatest American film of the sound era; he might have become the greatest all-around American director of that era; and in his inability to realize all his artistic potentialities he is the greatest symbolic figure in American film history since Griffith.

XVIII

In the past few years, I have heard two famous "artist" directors, after showings of their early films, explain how it happened that in the screen credits there was someone else listed for the script. It seems there was this poor guy on the lot who needed a credit desperately, and the company asked the director if he'd give the stumblebum a break; the incompetent turned in some material, but the director couldn't use any of it. Some listeners must swallow this, because in the latest incense-burning book on Josef von Sternberg the screen credits are simply ignored, and he, rather than Ben Hecht, is listed as the author of *Underworld.* Herman J. Mankiewicz has been similarly dropped from one film after another. The directors' generosity to those poor credit-hungry guys seems to have cutoff points in time (the directors' creative roles get bigger when the writers are dead) and in space (when the directors are interviewed abroad). Orson Welles, however, didn't need time or distance; he omitted any mention of his writer right from the start. (This custom is now being followed by many directors.) In later years, when he has been specifically asked by interviewers whether Mankiewicz wrote the scenario for *Citizen Kane,* he has had a set reply. "Everything concerning Rosebud belongs to him," he has said. Rosebud is what was most frequently criticized in the movie, and Gilbert Seldes, in one of the most solid and intelligent reviews of *Kane* (in *Esquire*), called it "a phony" and "the only bit of stale stuff in the picture." Welles himself has said, "The Rosebud gimmick is what I like least about the movie. It's a gimmick, really, and rather dollar-book Freud."

Welles may have been goaded into malice; he had probably never come up against a man so well equipped to deal with him as Mankiewicz. Welles, who used to tell stories about how when he was seventeen he became a *torero* in Seville and entered several *corridas* and was billed on the posters as "The American," may have got a few welts, starting with Mankiewicz's original title—*American.* When Welles read the script, he must certainly have recognized what he was caught in. There's no doubt that Welles—the fabulous Orson Welles—wasn't accustomed to sharing credit. However, his persistent lack of generosity toward Mankiewicz started at the time the movie came out, and it may have its basis in a very specific grievance. Mankiewicz may have outsmarted Welles on the credits more than once. Nunnally Johnson says that while *Citizen Kane* was being shot, Mankiewicz told him that he had received an offer of a ten-thousand-dollar bonus from Welles (through Welles's "chums") to hold to the original understanding and keep his name off the picture. Mankiewicz said that Welles had been brooding over the credits, that he could see how beautiful they would be: "Produced by Orson Welles. Directed by Orson Welles. Starring Orson Welles." It was perfect until he got to "Herman J. Mankiewicz" in the writing credit, which spoiled everything. Mankiewicz said he was tempted by Welles's offer. As usual, he needed money, and, besides, he was fearful of what would happen when the picture came out—he might be blackballed forever. William Randolph Hearst, like Stalin, was known to be fairly Byzantine in his punishments. At the same time, Mankiewicz knew that *Citizen Kane* was his best work, and he was proud of it. He told Johnson that he went to Ben Hecht with his dilemma, and that Hecht, as prompt with advice as with scripts, said, "Take the ten grand and double-cross the son of a bitch."

I asked Nunnally Johnson if he thought Mankiewicz's story was true, and Mankiewicz actually had got the offer and had taken Hecht's advice. Johnson replied, "I like to believe he did." It's not unlikely. Mankiewicz wrote the first draft in about three months and tightened and polished it into the final shooting script of *Citizen Kane* in a few more weeks, and he probably didn't get more than eight or nine thousand dollars for the whole job; according to the cost sheets for the movie, the screenplay cost was $34,195.24, which wasn't much, even for that day, and the figure probably includes the salary and expenses of John Houseman and the others at Victorville. Mankiewicz may easily have felt he deserved an extra ten thousand. "An Irish bum," Johnson calls him—and if that makes him sound lovable, the operative word is still "bum." If Mankiewicz made up the story he told Johnson—and he was probably capable of such juicy slander—this kind of invention may be a clue to why Welles tries to turn the credit into blame. And if Mankiewicz did get the offer, did take the money, and did double-cross Welles, this might equally well explain why Welles doesn't want Mankiewicz to get any honor.

But Welles needed Mankiewicz. Since sound came in, almost every time an actor has scored in a role and become a "star," it has been because the role provided a realistic base for contradictory elements. Welles has never been able to write this kind of vehicle for himself. *Kane* may be a study of egotism and a movie about money and love, but it isn't just another movie about a rich man who isn't loved; it's a scandalously unauthorized, muckraking biography of a man who was still alive and—though past his peak influence—still powerful, so it conveyed shock and danger, and it drew its strength from its reverberations in the life of the period. Mankiewicz brought to the film the force of journalism. The thirties had been full of movie biographies of tycoons and robber barons, and some, like *The Power and the Glory,* were complexly told, but even Preston Sturges, as if in awe of the material, had taken a solemn, almost lachrymose approach to the money-doesn't-bring-happiness theme. Mankiewicz did it better: the prismatic technique turned into a masterly juggling act. There's an almost palpable sense of enjoyment in the script itself; Mankiewicz was skillful at making his points through comedy, and frequently it's higher, blacker comedy than was customary in the thirties pictures. Welles is a different kind of writer—theatrical and Gothic, not journalistic, and not *organized.* His later thrillers are portentous, sensational in a void, entertaining thrillers, often, but *mere* thrillers.

Lacking the realistic base and the beautifully engineered structure that Mankiewicz provided, Welles has never again been able to release that charming, wicked rapport with the audience that he brought to *Kane* both as actor and as director (or has been able to release it only in distorted form, in self-satire and self-humiliation). He has brought many qualities to film—and there was perhaps a new, mellowed vitality in his work in the flawed *Falstaff* of a few years ago—but he has brought no more great original characters. In his movies, he can create an atmosphere but not a base. And without that the spirit that makes Kane so likable a bastard is missing. Kane, that mass of living contradictions, was conceived by Mankiewicz, an atheist who was proud of his kosher home, a man who was ambivalent about *both* Hearst and Welles.

However, things that get printed often enough begin to seep into the general consciousness of the past, so there is a widespread impression that Welles wrote *Citizen Kane*. And even if one hadn't heard that he wrote it, and despite the presence in the film of so many elements and interests that are unrelated to Welles's other work (mundane activities and social content are not his forte), Kane and Welles are identified in our minds. This is not only a tribute to Welles as an actor but a backhanded tribute to Mankiewicz who wrote the role for Welles the actor and wrote Welles the capricious, talented, domineering prodigy into the role, combining Welles's personality and character traits with Hearst's life in publishing and politics and acquisition.

If one asks how it is that Herman J. Mankiewicz, who wrote the film that many people think is the greatest film they've ever seen, is almost unknown, the answer must surely be not just that he died too soon but that he outsmarted himself. As a result of his wicked sense of humor in drawing upon Welles's character for Kane's, his own authorship was obscured. Sensing the unity of Kane and Welles, audiences assume that Kane is Welles's creation, that Welles is playing "the role he was born to play," while film scholars, seeing the material from Welles's life in the movie, interpret the film as Welles working out autobiographical themes. It is a commonplace in theatre talk to say that Olivier *is* Archie Rice or Olivier *is* Macbeth without assuming that the actor has conceived the role, but in movies we don't see other actors in the same role (except in remakes, which are usually very different in style), and film is so vivid and the actor so large and so close that it is a common primitive response to assume that the actor invented his lines. In this case, the primitive response is combined with the circumstances that Welles's name had been heavily featured for years, that the role was a new creation, that the movie audience's image of Welles was set by this overpowering role, in which they saw him for the first time, and that not only was the role partly based on him but he began to live up to it. Herman Mankiewicz died, and his share faded from knowledge, but Welles carries on in a baronial style that always reminds us of Kane. Kane seems an emanation of Welles, and if Mankiewicz didn't take the ten thousand, he might just as well have, because he helped stamp Welles all over the film.

XIX

James Agee, who didn't begin reviewing until later in 1941, wrote several years afterward that Welles had been "fatuously overrated as a 'genius,' " and that he himself, annoyed by all the talk, had for a while underrated him. At the time the film was released, the most perceptive movie critic in the United States was Otis Ferguson (an early volunteer and early casualty in the Second World War), on *The New Republic*. Ferguson saw more clearly than anybody else what was specifically good and bad in *Kane,* and though he was wrong, I think, in maintaining that unobtrusive technique is the only good technique, he did perceive that *Citizen Kane* challenged this concept.

One of the games that film students sometimes play is to judge a director on whether you have the illusion that the people on the screen will go on doing what they're doing after the camera leaves them. Directors are rated by how much time you think elapsed before the actors grabbed their coats or ordered a sandwich. The longer the time, the more of a film man the director is said to be; when a director is stage-oriented, you can practically see the actors walking off the set. This game doesn't help in judging a film's content, but it's a fairly reliable test of a director's film technique; one could call it a test of movie believability. However, it isn't applicable to *Citizen Kane.* You're perfectly well aware that the people won't go on doing what they're doing—that they have, indeed, completed their actions on the screen. *Kane* depends not on naturalistic believability but on our enjoyment of the very fact that those actions *are* completed, and that they all fit into place. This bravura is, I think, the picture's only true originality, and it wasn't an intentional challenge to the concept of unobtrusive technique but was (mainly) the result of Welles's discovery of—and his delight in—the fun of making movies.

The best American directors in the thirties had been developing an unpretentious American naturalism; modern subjects and the advent of sound had freed them from the heavy dead hand of Germanic stage lighting and design. And so Ferguson was dismayed to see this all come back, and it *was* depressing that the critics who had always fallen for the synthetic serious were bowing and scraping and calling the picture "deep" and "realistic." Probably so many people called it realistic because the social satire made contact with what they felt about Hearst and the country; when they used the term, they were referring to the content rather than the style. But it was the "retrogressive" style that upset Ferguson—because it was when Orson Welles, an "artist" director, joined the toughness and cynicism and the verbal skills of the thirties to that incomparable, faintly absurd, wonderfully overblown style of his that people said "art." Where Ferguson went wrong was in not recognizing one crucial element: that the unconcealed—even flaunted—pleasure that Welles took in all that claptrap made it new.

And it has kept it new. Even a number of those who worked on *Kane,* such as Houseman and Dorothy Comingore, have observed that the film seems to improve with the years. At the time, I got more simple, frivolous pleasure from Preston Sturges's *The Lady Eve,* which had come out a few months earlier, and I found more excitement in John Huston's *The Maltese Falcon,* which came out a few months later. At the time (I was twenty-one), I enjoyed *Kane* for the performances and the wit, but I was very conscious of how shallow the iconoclasm was. I don't think I was wrong, exactly, but now the movie seems marvellous to me. It's an *exuberant* shallow iconoclasm, and that youthful zest for shock and for the Expressionist theatricality seems to transform the shallowness. Now the movie sums up and preserves a period, and the youthful iconoclasm is preserved in all its freshness—even the freshness of its callowness. Now that the political theme (in its specific form, that is) is part of the past, the naïveté and obviousness fade, and what remains is a great American archetype and a popular legend—and so it has a strength that makes the artificially created comic world of a movie like *The Lady Eve* disappear by comparison. *Citizen Kane* has such energy it drives the viewer along. Though Mankiewicz provided the basic apparatus for it, that magical exuberance which fused the whole scandalous enterprise was Welles's. Works of art are enjoyed for different reasons in different periods; it may even be one the defining characteristics of a lasting work of art that it yields up different qualities for admiration at different times. Welles's "magic," his extraordinary pleasure in playacting and illusion and in impressing an audience—what seems so charming about the movie now—was what seemed silly to me then. It was bouncy Pop Gothic in a period when the term "comic strip" applied to works of art was still a term of abuse. Now Welles's discovery of movie-making—and the boyishness and excitement of that discovery—is preserved in *Kane* the way the snow scene is preserved in the glass ball.

Seeing the movie again recently, I liked the way it looked; now that the style no longer boded a return to the aestheticism of sets and the rigidly arranged figures of the German silents, I could enjoy it without misgivings. In the thirties, Jean Renoir had been using deep focus (that is, keeping the middle range and the background as clear as the foreground) in a naturalistic way. The light seemed (and often was) "natural." You looked at a scene, and the drama that you saw going on in it was just part of that scene, and so you had the sense of discovering it for yourself, of seeing drama in the midst of life. This was a tremendous relief from the usual studio lighting, which forced your attention to the dramatic action in the frame, blurred the rest, and rarely gave you a chance to feel that the action was part of anything larger or anything continuous. In Welles's far more extreme use of deep focus, and in his arrangement of the actors in the compositions, he swung back to the most coercive use of artificial, theatrical lighting. He used light like a spotlight on the stage, darkening or blacking out the irrelevant. He used deep focus not for a naturalistic effect but for the startling dramatic effect of having crucial action going on in the background (as when Kane appears in a distant doorway). The difference between Renoir's style and Welles's style seems almost literally the difference between day and night. Welles didn't have (nor did he, at that time, need) the kind of freedom Renoir needed and couldn't get in Hollywood—the freedom to shoot outside the studio and to depart from the script and improvise. *Kane* is a studio-made film—much of it was shot in that large room at R.K.O. where, a few years earlier, Ginger Rogers and Fred Astaire had danced their big numbers. However, Welles had the freedom to try out new solutions to technical problems, and he made his theatrical technique work spectacularly. Probably it was the first time in American movies that Expressionism had ever worked for comic and satiric effects (except in bits of some of the early spoof horror films), and probably it would have been impossible to tell the *Kane* story another way without spending a fortune on crowds and set construction. Welles's method is a triumph of ingenuity in that the pinpoints of light in the darkness conceal the absence of detailed sets (a chair or two and a huge fireplace, and one thinks one is seeing a great room), and the almost treacherously brilliant use of sound conceals the absence of crowds. We see Susan at the *deserted* cabaret; we see her from the back on the opera-house stage and we imagine that she is facing an audience; we get a sense of crowds at the political rally without seeing them. It was Welles's experience both in the theatre and in radio that enabled him to produce a huge historical film on a shoestring; he produced the *illusion* of a huge historical film.

But, seeing *Kane* now, I winced, as I did the first time, at the empty virtuosity of the shot near the beginning when Kane, dying, drops the glass ball and we see the nurse's entrance reflected in the glass. I noticed once again, though without being bothered by it this time, either, that there was no one in the room to hear the dying Kane say "Rosebud." I was much more disturbed by little picky defects, like the obtrusive shot up to the bridge before the reporter goes into the hospital. What is strange about re-seeing a movie that one reacted to fairly intensely many years ago is that one may respond exactly the same way to so many details and *be aware* each time of having responded that way before. I was disappointed once again by the clumsily staged "cute" meeting of Kane and Susan, which seemed to belong to a routine comedy, and I thought the early scenes with Susan were weak not just because while listening to her dull, sentimental singing Welles is in a passive position and so can't animate the scenes but—and mainly—because the man of simple pleasures who would find a dumb girl deeply appealing does not tie in with the personality projected by Orson Welles. (And as Welles doesn't project any sexual interest in either Kane's first wife, Emily, or in Susan, his second wife, we don't know how to interpret Susan's claim that he just likes her voice.) Most of the newspaper-office scenes looked as clumsily staged as ever, and the first appearance of Bernstein, Kane's business manager, arriving with a load of furniture, was still confusing. (He seems to be a junk dealer—probably because an earlier scene in *American* introducing him was eliminated.) I disliked again the attempt to wring humor out of the sputtering confusion of Carter, the old Dickensian editor. It's a scene like the ones Mankiewicz helped prepare for the Marx Brothers, but what was probably intended to make fun of a stuffed shirt turned into making fun of a helpless old man trying to keep his dignity, which is mean and barbarous. I still thought Susan became too thin a conception, and more shrill and shrewish than necessary, and, as Emily, Ruth Warrick was all pursed lips—a stereotype of refinement. I was still uncomfortable during the visit to Jed Leland in the hospital; Leland's character throughout is dependent on Joseph Cotten's obvious charm, and the sentimental-old-codger bit in this sequence is really a disgrace. The sequence plays all too well at a low conventional level—pulling out easy stops. I still didn't see the function of the sequence about Kane's being broke and losing control of his empire, since nothing followed from it. (I subsequently discovered that things weren't going well on the set at one point, and Welles decided to go back to this scene, which had been in an earlier draft and had then been eliminated. What it coördinated with was, unfortunately, not restored.) This sequence also has the most grating bad line in the movie, when Kane says, "You know, Mr. Bernstein, if I hadn't been very rich, I might have been a really great man."

What's still surprising is how well a novice movie director handled so many of the standard thirties tricks and caricatures—the device of the alternative newspaper headlines, for example, and the stock explosive, hand-waving Italian opera coach (well played by Fortunio Bonanova). The engineering—the way the sequences are prepared for and commented on by preceding sequences, the way the five accounts tie together to tell the story—seems as ingenious as ever; though one is aware that the narrators are telling things they couldn't have witnessed, one accepts this as part of the convention. The cutting (which a reading of the script reveals to have been carried out almost exactly as it was planned) is elegantly precise, and some sequences have a good, sophomoric musical-comedy buoyancy.

What had changed for me—what I had once enjoyed but now found almost mysteriously *beautiful*—was Orson Welles's performance. An additional quality that old movies acquire is that people can be seen as they once were. It is a pleasure we can't get in theatre; we can only hear and read descriptions of past fabulous performances. But here in *Kane* is the young Welles, and he seems almost embarrassed to be exposed as so young. Perhaps he *was* embarrassed, and that's why he so often hid in extravagant roles and behind those old-man false faces. He seems unsure of himself as the young Kane, and there's something very engaging (and surprisingly *human*) about Welles unsure of himself; he's a big, overgrown, heavy boy, and rather sheepish, one suspects, at being seen as he is. Many years later, Welles remarked, "Like most performers, I naturally prefer a live audience to that lie-detector full of celluloid." Maybe his spoiled-baby face was just too nearly perfect for the role, and he knew it, and knew the hostile humor that lay behind Mankiewicz's putting so much of him in the role of Hearst the braggart self-publicist and making Kane so infantile. That statement of principles that Jed sends back to Kane and that Kane then tears up must surely refer to the principles behind the co-founding of the Mercury Theatre by Welles and Houseman. Lines like Susan's "You're not a professional magician are you?" may have made Welles flinch. And it wasn't just the writer who played games on him. There's the scene of Welles eating in the newspaper office, which was obviously caught by the camera crew, and which, to be "a good sport," he had to use. Welles is one of the most self-conscious of actors—it's part of his rapport with the audience—and this is what is so nakedly revealed in this role, in which he's playing a young man his own age and he's insecure (and with some reason) about what's coming through. Something of the young, unmasked man is revealed in these scenes—to be closed off forever after.

Welles picks up assurance and flair as Kane in his thirties, and he's also good when Kane is just a little older and jowly. I think there's no doubt that he's more sure of himself when he's playing this somewhat older Kane, and this is the Kane we remember best from the first viewing—the brash, confident Kane of the pre-election-disaster period. He's so fully—classically—American a showoff one almost regrets the change of title. But when I saw the movie again it was the younger Kane who stayed with me—as if I had been looking through a photograph album and had come upon a group of pictures of an old friend, long dead, as he had been when I first met him. I had almost forgotten Welles in his youth, and here he is, smiling, eager, looking forward to the magnificent career that everyone expected him to have.

XX

Just as Welles suggested the radio-bulletin approach to the H. G. Wells landing-of-the-Martians material to Howard Koch, he may very well have suggested the "March of Time" summary of Hearst's career in his early talks with Mankiewicz. Welles had worked as an actor for the "March of Time" radio program in 1934 and 1935, and he had worked steadily as a narrator and radio actor (his most famous role was the lead in the popular weekly mystery show "The Shadow") until he went to Hollywood. The "March of Time" is exactly the kind of idea the young Welles *would* have suggested. It's the sort of technique that was being used in the experimental theatre of the late thirties—when the Federal Theatre Project (in which Welles and Houseman had worked together) staged the documentary series "The Living Newspaper," and when members of the Group Theatre and other actors were performing anti-Fascist political cabaret. The imitation "March of Time" was not a new device, even in movies; it had already been used, though humorlessly, to convey the fact that a theme was current, part of "today's news," and to provide background information—as in *Confessions of a Nazi Spy,* of 1939. What was needed to transform that device and make it the basis for the memorable parody in *Citizen Kane* was not only Welles's experience and not only his "touch" but the great sense of mischief that he and Mankiewicz shared. The smug manner of the "March of Time" was already a joke to many people; when I was a student at Berkeley in the late thirties, there was always laughter in the theatres when the "March of Time" came on, with its racy neo-conservatism and its ritual pomposity—with that impersonal tone, as if God above were narrating. There was an element of unconscious self-parody in the important tone of the "March of Time," as in all the Luce enterprises, and, in his script, Mankiewicz pushed it further. He used consciously those elements which part of the public already found funny, bringing into a mass medium what was already a subject for satire among the knowledgeable.

Mankiewicz's "On Approaching Forty" had not appeared in *The New Yorker,* but a few weeks after it was printed in 1936, Wolcott Gibbs, who was to take Mankiewicz's old chair as *The New Yorker*'s drama critic (and who was the first occupant of that chair not to emigrate to Hollywood), published the celebrated Profile "Time—Fortune—Life—Luce," which was written in mock Timese ("Backward ran sentences until reeled the mind," and so on, concluding with "Where it all will end, knows God!"), and this was probably not merely the spur to Mankiewicz but the competition. Mankiewicz's pastiche was fully worked out in the first long draft of the script, the processed prose and epigrams already honed to perfection ("For forty years appeared in Kane newsprint no public issue on which Kane papers took no stand. No public man whom Kane himself did not support or denounce—often support, then denounce"). And even on paper—without Welles's realization of the plan—the section is good enough to invite the comparison that I suspect Mankiewicz sought with the Gibbs parody. (Mankiewicz's widow keeps the Oscar statuette for *Citizen Kane* on the mantel, along with the latest *Who's Who in America* with the marker set at her sons' listings, and on the shelf next to the mantel are the bound volumes of *The New Yorker* in which her husband's reviews appeared.)

Part of the fun of the "March of Time" parody for the audiences back in 1941 was that, of course, we kept *recognizing* things about Hearst in it, and its daring meant great suspense about what was to follow in the picture. But Mankiewicz tried to do more with this parody than is completely evident either in the final script or in the film itself. He tried to use the "March of Time" as a historical framing device to close one era and open the next, with Hearstian journalism giving way to the new Luce empire. In the movie, it seems a structural gimmick—though a very cleverly *used* gimmick, which is enjoyable in itself. In Mankiewicz's original conception, in the long first-draft *American,* which ran three hundred and twenty-five pages, that device is more clearly integral to the theme. In Mankiewicz's conception, the Hearst-Kane empire is doomed: Kane's own death is being "sent" to the world by the filmed "March of Time" (called "News on the March" in the movie), which means the end of the newspaper business as Hearst knew it. The funny thing is that Mankiewicz, in commenting on Hearst's lack of vision, overestimated Luce's vision. After Luce took news coverage from newspapers into newsmagazines, he moved into photo-journalism and then into news documentaries, but he didn't follow through on what he had started, and he failed to get into television production. Now, after *his* death, the Luce organization is trying to get back into film activities.

In Mankiewicz's original conception, the historical line of succession was laid out as in a chronicle play. Hearst supplanted the old-style quiet upper-class journalism with his penny-dreadful treatment of crime and sex and disasters, his attacks on the rich, his phony lawsuits against the big corporations that he called "predators," his screaming patriotism, his faked photographs, and his exploitation of superstition, plus puzzles, comics, contests, sheet music, and medical quackery. His youthful dedication to the cause of the common people declined into the cheap chauvinism that infected everything and helped to turn the readers into a political mob. The irony built into the structure was that his own demise should be treated in the new, lofty style of Luce.

And it was in terms of this framework that the elements of admiration in the ambivalent portrait of Kane made sense. Hearst represented a colorful kind of journalism that was already going out. Mankiewicz was summing up the era of *The Front Page* at the end of it, and was treating it right at its source in the American system that made it possible for a rich boy to inherit the power to control public opinion as his own personal plaything. *American* (and, to a lesser degree, *Citizen Kane*) was a there-were-giants-in-those-days valedictory to the old-style big scoundrels. The word had been used straight by Mrs. Fremont Older in 1936 when she published the authorized biography, *William Randolph Hearst, American.* "American" was Hearst's shibboleth; his Sunday magazine section was the *American Weekly,* and he had been changing his newspaper titles to include the word "American" whenever possible ever since Senator Henry Cabot Lodge accused him of being un-American in those days after the McKinley assassination when Hearst was hanged in effigy. Hearst's attacks on McKinley as "the most despised and hated creature in the hemisphere" had culminated in an editorial that said "Killing must be done" shortly before it was. When the storm died down, Hearst became super-American. For Mankiewicz, Hearst's Americanism was the refuge of a scoundrel, though by no means his last refuge; *that,* in the first draft, was clearly blackmail. What the title was meant to signify was indicated by Kane in the "News on the March" segment when he said, "I am, have been, and will be only one thing—an American." That was pure flag-waving Pop before we had a name for it: "American" as it was used by the American Legion and the Daughters of the American Revolution. In addition, Mankiewicz may have wanted to score off his movie friends who since the middle thirties—the period of the Popular Front—had also been draping themselves in the flag. In that period, the Communist left had become insistent about its Americanism, in its rather embarrassing effort to tout American democracy, which it had called "imperialism" until the U.S.S.R. sought the United States as an ally against Hitler. In the later title, "Citizen" is similarly ironic: Hearst, the offspring of an economic baron, and himself a press lord and the master of San Simeon, was a "citizen" the way Louis XIV at Versailles was a citizen. And joining the word to "Kane" (Cain) made its own point.

Both the parodistic use of Timese and the facelessness of Luce's company men served a historical purpose in the first script. But *American* was much too long and inclusive and loose, and much too ambitious, and Mankiewicz rapidly cut it down (copies of these gradually shorter drafts were saved) until it reached the hundred and fifty-six pages of the final shooting script—which still made for a then unusually long picture, of a hundred and nineteen minutes. In the trimming, dialogue that was crucial to the original dramatic conception of the Hearst-Luce succession was cut.

(In terms of the final conception, though, it's perfectly clear why.) This deleted exchange between Thompson, the investigating reporter for the Rawlston (Luce) organization, and Raymond, Kane's butler, makes the point about the line of succession from Hearst to Luce all too explicitly:

THOMPSON

Well, if you get around to your memoirs—don't forget, Mr. Rawlston wants to be sure of getting first chance. We pay awful well for long excerpts.

RAYMOND

Maybe he'd like to buy the excerpts of what Mr. Kane said about him.

THOMPSON

Huh?

RAYMOND

IIc thought Rawlston would break his neck sooner or later. He gave that weekly magazine of yours three years.

THOMPSON

(Smugly) He made a bit of a mistake.

RAYMOND

He made a lot of mistakes.

Welles, who did such memorable casting in the rest of the movie, used a number of his own faceless executive assistants in the vapid roles of the Luce men. They are the performers in *Citizen Kane* that nobody remembers, and they didn't go on to become actors. William Alland, whose voice was fine as the voice of "News on the March" but who was a vacuum as Thompson, the reporter, became a producer and investment broker; another of Welles's assistants, Richard Wilson, who also played a reporter, is now a director (*Three in the Attic*); still another, Richard Barr, is the well-known New York theatrical producer. Among the "News on the March" men, there were some bit players who did have potential faces (Alan Ladd was one of them), but they weren't presented as personalities. Nevertheless, in a movie as verbally explicit as *Citizen Kane* the faceless idea doesn't really come across. You probably don't get the intention behind it in *Kane* unless you start thinking about the unusual feebleness of the scenes with the "News on the March" people and about the fact that though Thompson is a principal in the movie in terms of how much he appears, there isn't a shred of characterization in his lines or in his performance; he is such a shadowy presence that you may even have a hard time remembering whether you ever saw his face, though this movie introduced to the screen a large group of performers who made strong, astonishingly distinct impressions, sometimes in very brief roles. Perhaps the acting and the group movement of the faceless men needed to be more stylized, the dialogue more satirical; as it was done, it's just dull rather than purposefully blank. Welles probably thought it didn't matter how bad these actors were, because they should be colorless anyway; after R.K.O. gave him the go-ahead on the project, he didn't reshoot the test scene he had made of the projection-room sequence. But the movie misses on the attitudes *behind* Luce's new journalism. It's true that for the practitioners of Timese impersonality becomes their personal style and reporters become bureaucrats, but there's also a particular aura of programmed self-importance and of awareness of power—the ambitiousness of colorless people.

Among the minor absurdities of the script is that the "News on the March" men never think of sending a cameraman along with the inquiring reporter, though Gable had just played a newsreel cameraman in *Too Hot to Handle,* in 1938, and though in *The Philadelphia Story,* which had opened on Broadway in 1939, and which Mankiewicz's brother Joe produced for the screen in 1940, while *Kane* was being shot, the magazine team, also obviously from Luce, includes a photographer. There's something rather pathetic—almost as if *Kane* were a Grade B movie that didn't have a big enough budget for a few extra players—about that one lonely sleuthing reporter travelling around the country while a big organization delays the release of an important newsreel documentary on the head of a rival news chain. Maybe Mankiewicz, despite his attempt to place Hearst historically through the "March of Time" framework, still thought in terms of the older journalism and of all the gimmicky movies about detective-reporters. And Mankiewicz was by temperament a reckless, colorful newspaperman. That deleted material about the Luce organization's wanting Raymond's memoirs, with Raymond's teaser "He made a lot of mistakes," is part of an elaborate series of scandalous subplots, closely paralleling scandals in Hearst's life, that were cut out in the final script. In the movie, Susan says to Thompson, "Look, if you're smart, you'll get in touch with Raymond. He's the butler. You'll learn a lot from him. He knows where all the bodies are buried." It's an odd, cryptic speech. In the first draft, Raymond *literally* knew where the bodies were buried: Mankiewicz had dished up a nasty version of the scandal sometimes referred to as the Strange Death of Thomas Ince. Even with this kind of material cut down to the barest allusions, Mankiewicz, in *Citizen Kane,* treated the material of Hearst's life in Hearstian yellow-journalism style.

XXI

Welles is right, of course, about Rosebud—it *is* dollar-book Freud. But it is such a primitive kind of Freudianism that, like some of the movie derivations from Freud later in the forties—in *The Seventh Veil*, for instance—it hardly seems Freudian at all now. Looking for "the secret" of a famous man's last words is about as phony as the blind-beggar-for-luck bit, yet it does "work" for some people; they go for the idea that Rosebud represents lost maternal bliss and somehow symbolizes Kane's loss of the power to love or be loved. The one significant change from Hearst's life—Kane's separation from his parents—seems to be used to explain Kane, though there is an explicit disavowal of any such intention toward the end. Someone says to Thompson, "If you could have found out what Rosebud meant, I bet that would've explained everything." Thompson replies, "No, I don't think so. No. Mr. Kane was a man who got everything he wanted, and then lost it. Maybe Rosebud was something he couldn't get or something he lost. Anyway, it wouldn't have explained anything. I don't think any word can explain a man's life. No. I guess Rosebud is just a piece in a jigsaw puzzle, a missing piece."

Nevertheless, the structure of the picture—searching for the solution to a mystery—and the exaggerated style make it appear that Rosebud *is* the key to Kane's life, and the public responds to what is presented dramatically, not to the reservations of the moviemakers. Rosebud has become part of popular. culture, and people remember it who have forgotten just about everything else in *Citizen Kane;* the jokes started a week before the movie opened, with a child's sled marked "Rosebud" dragged onstage in the first act of *Native Son,* and a couple of years ago, in *Peanuts,* Snoopy walked in the snow pulling a sled and Charlie Brown said, "Rosebud?" The Rosebud of Rosebud is as banal as Rosebud itself. It seems that as a child Herman Mankiewicz had had a sled, which may or may not have carried the label "Rosebud" (his family doesn't remember); he wasn't dramatically parted from the sled, but he once had a bicycle that was stolen, and he mourned that all his life. He simply put the emotion of the one onto the other.

Though Rosebud was in the long first draft, it didn't carry the same weight there, because the newspaper business itself undermined Kane's idealism. In that draft, Kane, like Hearst, in order to reach the masses he thought he wanted to serve and protect, built circulation by turning the newspapers into pulp magazines, and, in order to stay in business and expand, squeezed nonadvertisers. The long script went as far as to show that, in the process of becoming one of the mighty, Kane-Hearst, like Louis B. Mayer and so many other tycoons, developed close ties to the underworld. Mankiewicz was trying to give a comprehensive view of the contradictions that emerge when an idealist attempts to succeed in business and politics. Fragments of this are left, but their meaning is no longer clear. For example, the point of the sequence of Kane's buying up the staff of the *Chronicle,* the paper that was outselling his *Inquirer* by featuring crime and sex, was that the *Chronicle*'s staff would change him by deflecting him from an idealistic course (and Jed tries to point this out to Bernstein), but as it appears in the film it almost seems that in buying the *Chronicle*'s staff Kane is corrupting *them*.

It is just a fragment, too, that Kane's first wife, Emily, is the niece of the President of the United States. Hearst's only wife, Millicent, the daughter of a vaudeville hoofer, was a teen-age member of a group called The Merry Maidens when he met her. Emily was probably made the niece of the President in order to link Kane with the rich and to make a breach in the marriage when Kane was held responsible for the assassination of the President (as Hearst was accused of having incited the death of President McKinley).

In the condensation, the whole direction was, for commercial reasons, away from the newspaper business that dominated the early script, and, for obvious reasons, away from factual resemblances to Hearst's life. This was generally accomplished by making things funny. For example, Hearst had actually been cheated out of the office of mayor of New York by fraud at the polls, and this incident was included in *American*. In *Citizen Kane* it became, instead, a joke: when Kane loses the election for governor, the Kane papers automatically claim "FRAUD AT POLLS." This version is, of course, a quick way of dramatizing the spirit of yellow journalism, and it's useful and comic, but the tendency of this change, as of many others, was, whether deliberately or unconsciously, to make things easier for the audience by playing down material on how wealth and the power it buys can also buy the love of the voters. Hearst (the son of a senator whose money had got him into the Senate) did buy his way into public office; as a young man, he was twice elected to Congress, and he had tried to get the Democratic nomination for President just before he decided to run for mayor of New York. The movie flatters the audience by saying that Kane couldn't buy the people's love—that he "was never granted elective office by the voters of his country."

Actually, it wasn't the voters but crooked politicians who defeated Hearst. When the Tammany boss Charles F. Murphy refused to help Hearst get the Democratic nomination for mayor, he ran as an independent, campaigning against the corrupt Tammany "boodlers," and he printed a cartoon of Murphy in prison stripes. Kane gives Boss Jim Gettys this treatment. Murphy was so deeply wounded by the cartoon that he arranged for Hearst's ballots to be stolen, and, it is said, even managed to rig the recount. That reckless cartoon was the turning point in Hearst's political career. The movie gives Gettys a different revenge; namely, exposing Kane's "love nest"—which was something that also happened to Hearst, but on another occasion, long after he had abandoned his political ambitions, when his *Los Angeles Examiner* was attacking the *Los Angeles Times*, and the *Times* used his own tactics against him by bringing up his "double life" and his "love nest" with Marion Davies. The movie ultimately plays the same game. *Citizen Kane* becomes a movie about the private life of a public figure—the scandals and tidbits and splashy sensations that the Hearst press always preferred to issues. The assumption of the movie was much like that of the yellow press: that the mass audience wasn't interested in issues, that all it wanted was to get "behind the scenes" and find out the dirt.

XXII

As the newspaper business and the political maneuvering were pared away, the personal material took on the weight and the shape of the solution to a mystery. Even so, if the movie had been directed in a more matter-of-fact, naturalistic style, Thompson's explanation that Rosebud was just a piece in a jigsaw puzzle would have seemed quite sensible. Instead, Welles's heavily theatrical style overemphasized the psychological explanation to such a point that when we finally glimpse the name on the sled we in the audience are made to feel that we're in on a big secret—a revelation that the world missed out on. However, Rosebud is so cleverly worked into the structure that, like the entrance that Hecht and MacArthur prepared for Walter Burns, it is enjoyable as beautiful tomfoolery even while we are conscious of it as "commercial" mechanics. I think what makes Welles's directorial style so satisfying in this movie is that we are constantly aware of the mechanics— that the pleasure *Kane* gives doesn't come from illusion but comes from our enjoyment of the dexterity of the illusionists and the working of the machinery. *Kane,* too, is a clock that laughs. *Citizen Kane* is a film made by a very young man of enormous spirit; he took the Mankiewicz material and he played with it, he turned it into a magic show. It is Welles's distinctive quality as a movie director—I think it is his genius—that he never hides his cleverness, that he makes it possible for us not only to enjoy what he does but to share his enjoyment in doing it. Welles's showmanship is right there on the surface, just as it was when, as a stage director, he set *Julius Caesar* among the Nazis, and set *Macbeth* in Haiti with a black cast and, during the banquet scene, blasted the audience with a recording of the "Blue Danube Waltz"—an effect that Kubrick was to echo (perhaps unknowingly?) in *2001.* There is something childlike—and great, too—about his pleasure in the magic of theatre and movies. No other director in the history of movies has been so open in his delight, so eager to share with us the game of pretending, and Welles's silly pretense of having done everything himself is just another part of the game.

Welles's magic as a director (at this time) was that he could put his finger right on the dramatic fun of each scene. Mankiewicz had built the scenes to end at ironic, dramatic high points, and Welles probably had a more innocently brazen sense of melodramatic timing than any other movie director. Welles also had a special magic beyond this: he could give *élan* to scenes that were confused in intention, so that the movie seems to go from dramatic highlight to highlight without lagging in between. There doesn't appear to be any waste material in *Kane,* because he charges right through the weak spots as if they were bright, and he almost convinces you (or *does*

301

convince you) that they're shining jewels. Perhaps these different kinds of magic can be suggested by two examples. There's the famous sequence in which Kane's first marriage is summarized by a series of breakfasts, with overlapping dialogue. The method was not new, and it's used here on a standard marriage joke, but the joke is a basic good joke, and the method is honestly used to sum up as speedily as possible the banality of what goes wrong with the marriage. This sequence is adroit, and Welles brings out the fun in the material, but there's no *special* Wellesian magic in it—except, perhaps, in his own acting. But in the cutting from the sequence of Kane's first meeting with Susan (where the writing supplies almost no clue to why he's drawn to this particular twerp of a girl beyond his finding her relaxing) to the political rally, Welles's special talent comes into play. Welles directs the individual scenes with such flourish and such *enjoyment of flourish* that the audience reacts as if the leap into the rally were clever and funny and logical, too, although the connection between the scenes isn't established until later, when Boss Jim Gettys uses Susan to wreck Kane's political career. As a director, Welles is so ebullient that we go along with the way he wants us to feel; we're happy to let him "put it over on us." Given the subject of Hearst and the witty script, the effect is of complicity, of a shared knowingness between Welles and the audience about what the movie is about. Kane's big smile at the rally seals the pact between him and us. Until Kane's later years, Welles, in the role, has an almost total empathy with the audience. It's the same kind of empathy we're likely to feel for smart kids who grin at us when they're showing off in the school play. It's a beautiful kind of emotional nakedness—ingenuously exposing the sheer love of playacting—that most actors lose long before they become "professional." If an older actor—even a very good one—had played the role, faking youth for the young Kane the way Edward Arnold, say, sometimes faked it, I think the picture might have been routine. Some people used to say that Welles might be a great director but he was a bad actor, and his performances wrecked his pictures. I think just the opposite—that his directing style is such an emanation of his adolescent love of theatre that his films lack a vital unifying element when he's not in them or when he plays only a small part in them. He needs to be at the center. *The Magnificent Ambersons* is a work of feeling and imagination and of obvious effort—and the milieu is much closer to Welles's own background than the milieu of *Kane* is—but Welles isn't in it, and it's too bland. It feels empty, uninhabited. Without Orson Welles's physical presence—the pudgy, big prodigy who incarnates egotism—*Citizen Kane* might (as Otis Ferguson suggested) have disintegrated into vignettes. We feel that he's making it all happen. Like the actor-managers of the old theatre, he's the man onstage running the show, pulling it all together.

XXIII

Mankiewicz's script, though nominally an "original"—and in the best sense original—was in large part an adaptation of the material (much of it published) of Hearst's life. Hearst's life was so full of knavery and perversity that Mankiewicz simply sorted out the plums. Mankiewicz had been a reporter on the *New York World,* the Pulitzer paper, where Hearst himself had worked for a time before he persuaded his father to give him the *San Francisco Examiner.* When Hearst got the *Examiner,* he changed it in imitation of the *World,* and then expanded to New York, where he bought a paper and started raiding and decimating the *World*'s staff. One of his favorite tactics was to hire away men he didn't actually want at double or treble what Pulitzer was paying them, then fire them, leaving them stranded (a tactic memorialized in *The Front Page* when Walter Burns hires and fires the poetic reporter Bensinger). Kane's business practices are so closely patterned on Hearst's that in reading about Hearst one seems to be reading the script. Descriptions—like the one in the *Atlantic Monthly* in 1931—of how Hearst cynically bought away the whole of Pulitzer's Sunday staff might be descriptions of Kane's maneuver. In 1935, *Fortune* described Hearst's warehouse in the Bronx in terms that might have been the specifications for the warehouse in the film, and by 1938 even the *Reader's Digest* was reprinting, from the *Saturday Evening Post,* a description of Hearst's empire in phrases that might be part of the script:

> All his life, Mr. Hearst bought, bought, bought—whatever touched his fancy. He purchased newspapers, Egyptian mummies, a California mountain range, herds of Tibetan yaks. He picked up a Spanish abbey, had it knocked down, crated, shipped to New York, and never has seen it since.
>
> To his shares in the Homestake, largest gold producer in the United States, his Peruvian copper mines, his 900,000 acre Mexican cattle ranch, and his other inherited properties, he added 28 daily newspapers, 14 magazines here and in England, eight radio stations, wire services, a Hollywood producing unit, a newsreel, a castle in Wales, and one of the world's largest collections of objects d'art, gathered at a toll of $40,000,000.

Kane's dialogue is often almost Hearst verbatim; in the margin of the script that Mankiewicz lent to Charles Lederer one of Hearst's lawyers annotated Kane's speech beginning, "Young man, there'll be no war. I have talked with the responsible leaders," with the words "This happens to be the gist of an authentic interview with WRH—occasion, his last trip from Europe." Some of the dialogue was legendary long before the movie was made. When Hearst was spending a fortune in his circulation war with Pulitzer, someone told his mother that Willie was losing money at the rate of a million dollars a year, and she equally replied, "Is he? Then he will only last about thirty years." This is no more than slightly transposed in the film, though it's really milked:

THATCHER

Tell me, honestly, my boy, don't you think it's rather unwise to continue this philanthropic enterprise . . . this "Inquirer" that is costing you a million dollars a year?

KANE

You're right, Mr. Thatcher. I did lose a million dollars this year. I expect to lose a million dollars next year. You know, Mr. Thatcher, at the rate of a million dollars a year . . . I'll have to close this place in sixty years.

(To audiences in 1941, Thatcher, appearing at the congressional-committee hearing, was obviously J. P. Morgan the younger, and the Thatcher Library was, of course, the Pierpont Morgan Library.)

Mankiewicz could hardly improve on the most famous of all Hearst stories, so he merely touched it up a trifle. According to many accounts, Hearst, trying to foment war with Spain, had sent Richard Harding Davis to Havana to write about the Spanish atrocities and Frederic Remington to sketch them. Remington grew restless there and sent Hearst a telegram:

EVERYTHING IS QUIET, THERE IS NO TROUBLE HERE. THERE WILL BE NO WAR. I WISH TO RETURN.—REMINGTON.

Hearst replied,

PLEASE REMAIN. YOU FURNISH THE PICTURES AND I'LL FURNISH THE WAR.—W.R. HEARST.

In the movie, Bernstein reads Kane a telegram from a reporter named Wheeler:

GIRLS DELIGHTFUL IN CUBA, STOP. COULD SEND YOU PROSE POEMS ABOUT SCENERY BUT DON'T FEEL RIGHT SPENDING YOUR MONEY, STOP. THERE IS NO WAR IN CUBA. SIGNED WHEELER.

And Bernstein asks, "Any answer?"
Kane replies:

DEAR WHEELER, YOU PROVIDE THE PROSE POEMS, I'LL PROVIDE THE WAR.

304

These stories were so well known at the time of the movie's release that in the picture spread on the movie in *Life* (with captions in the very style that Mankiewicz had parodied in his "News on the March") the magazine—unconsciously, no doubt—returned to the Hearst original, and flubbed even that:

> Kane buys a newspaper in New York and sets out to be a great social reformer. But even at 25 he is unscrupulous and wangles the U.S. into war by fake news dispatches. To a cartoonist in Cuba he wires: "You get the pictures and I'll make the war."

One passage of dialogue that is bad because it sounds slanted to make an ideological point is almost a straight steal (and that's probably why Mankiewicz didn't realize how fraudulent it would sound), and was especially familiar because John Dos Passos had quoted it in *U.S.A.,* in his section on Hearst, "Poor Little Rich Boy." (That title might be the theme of the movie.) Dos Passos quotes Hearst's answer to fellow-millionaires who thought he was a traitor to his class:

> You know I believe in property, and you know where I stand on personal fortunes, but isn't it better that I should represent in this country the dissatisfied than have somebody else do it who might not have the same real property relations that I may have?

Hearst apparently did say it, but even though it's made more conversational in the movie, it's unconvincing—it sounds like left-wing paranoia.

KANE

> I'll let you in on another little secret, Mr. Thatcher. I think I'm the man to do it. You see, I have money and property. If I don't look after the interests of the underprivileged maybe somebody else will . . . maybe somebody without any money or property.

Despite the fake childhood events, Kane's life story follows Hearst's much more closely than most movie biographies follow acknowledged and named subjects. Kane is burned in effigy, as Hearst was, and there is even a reference to Kane's expulsion from Harvard; one of the best-known stories in America was how young Willie Hearst had been expelled from Harvard after sending each of his instructors a chamber pot with the recipient's name handsomely lettered on the inside bottom. Even many of the subsidiary characters are replicas of Hearst's associates. For example, Bernstein (given the name of Welles's old guardian) is obviously Solomon S. Carvalho, the business manager of Pulitzer's *World,* whom Hearst hired away, and who became the watchdog of the *Journal*'s exchequer and Hearst's devoted business manager. There was no special significance in the use of Mankiewicz's secretary's last name for Susan Alexander, or in naming Jed Leland for Leland Hayward (Mankiewicz's agent, whose wife, Margaret Sullavan, spent a weekend visiting at Victorville), just as there was no significance in the fact that the actor Whitford Kane had been part of the nucleus of the Mercury Theatre, but the use of the name Bernstein for Kane's devoted, uncritical friend had some significance in relation not only to Welles but to Hearst, and it was Mankiewicz's way of giving Hearst points (he did it in the breakfast scene when Emily is snobbish about Bernstein) because, whatever else Hearst was, he was not a snob or an anti-Semite. (For one thing, Marion's brother-in-law—Charles Lederer's father—was Jewish.) No doubt Mankiewicz also meant to give Kane points when he had him finish Jed's negative review of Susan's singing in the same negative spirit—which was more than George S. Kaufman had done for Mankiewicz's review back at the *New York Times*. This episode is perversely entertaining but not convincing. *Kane* used so much of Hearst's already legendary life that for liberals it was like a new kind of folk art; we knew all this about Hearst from books and magazines but gasped when we saw it on the big movie screen, and so defiantly—almost contemptuously—undisguised.

The departure from Hearst's life represented by Susan Alexander's opera career, which is a composite of the loves and scandals of several Chicago tycoons, didn't weaken the attack on Hearst—it strengthened it. Attaching the other scandals to him made him seem the epitome of the powerful and spoiled, and thus stand for them all. Opera—which used to be called "grand opera"—was a ritual target of American comedy. It was an easier target for the public to respond to than Hearst's own folly—motion pictures—because the public already connected opera with wealth and temperament, tycoons in opera hats and women in jewels, imported prima donnas, and all the affectations of "culture." It was a world the movie public didn't share, and it was already absurd in American movies—the way valets and effete English butlers and the high-toned Americans putting on airs who kept them were absurd. George S. Kaufman and Morrie Ryskind had worked opera over in two of the Marx Brothers pictures; Mankiewicz had been taken off *A Night at the Opera,* but what he and Welles—with the assistance of Bernard Herrmann—did to opera in *Citizen Kane* was in almost exactly the same style, and as funny.

Mankiewicz was working overseas for the *Chicago Tribune* when Harold McCormick and his wife, Edith Rockefeller McCormick, were divorced, in 1921. The McCormicks had been the leading patrons of opera in Chicago; they had made up the Chicago Opera Company's deficits, which were awe-inspiring during the time the company was under the management of Mary Garden (she chose to be called the "directa"), rising to a million dollars one great, lavish season. After the divorce, McCormick married Ganna Walska, the preëminent temperamental mediocre soprano of her day. Mankiewicz combined this scandal with a far more widely publicized event that occurred

306

a few years later, replacing Hearst and Cosmopolitan Pictures with Samuel Insull and his building of the Chicago Civic Opera House. Insull didn't build the opera house for his wife (dainty little Gladys Wallis didn't sing), but there was a story to it, and it was the biggest opera story of the decade. After the McCormick–Rockefeller divorce, their joint largesse to opera ended, and the deficits were a big problem. Insull, "the Czar of Commonwealth Edison," who also loved opera (and dallied with divas), wanted to put it on a self-supporting business basis. He concluded that if an opera house should be built in a skyscraper, the rental of the upper regions would eventually cover the opera's deficits. The building was started in 1928; it had forty-five stories, with the opera company occupying the first six, and with Insull's office-lair on top. The structure was known as "Insull's throne," and it cost twenty million dollars. The opening of the new opera house was scheduled for November 4, 1929; six days before, on October 29th, the stock market crashed. The opening took place during the panic, with plainclothesmen and eight detective-bureau squads guarding the bejewelled patrons against robbers, rioters, and the mobsters who more or less ran the city. (The former Mrs. McCormick attended, wearing, according to one newspaper report, "her gorgeous diamond necklace, almost an inch wide and reaching practically to her waist"; Mrs. Insull wore pearls and "a wide diamond bracelet.") Mankiewicz must have placed the episode of the opera house in Chicago in order to give it roots—to make it connect with what the public already knew about Chicago and robber barons and opera. (Chicago was big on opera; it was there that the infant Orson Welles played Madame Butterfly's love child.) Insull's opera house never really had a chance to prove or disprove his financial theories. Mary Garden quit after one year there, calling it "that long black hole," and in 1932, when Insull's mammoth interlocking directorate of power plants collapsed and he fled to Greece, the opera house was closed. Insull was extradited, and in the mid-thirties he stood trial for fraud and embezzlement; he died two years before *Citizen Kane* was written.

The fretful banality of Susan Alexander is clearly derived from Mankiewicz's hated old adversary Mrs. Insull—notorious for her "discordant twitter" and her petty dissatisfaction with everything. The Insulls had been called the least popular couple who had ever lived in Chicago, and there was ample evidence that they hadn't even liked each other. Opera and the Insulls provided cover for Mankiewicz and Welles. George J. Schaefer, who is quite open about this, says that when he couldn't get an opening for *Kane*, because the theatres were frightened off by the stories in the Hearst press about injunctions and lawsuits, he went to see Hearst's lawyers in Los Angeles and took the position that Kane could be Insull. No one was expected to be fooled; it was simply a legal maneuver.

There was also an actual (and malicious) scrap of Hearst's past in the opera idea in the first draft. As Mankiewicz planned it, Susan was to make her début in Massenet's *Thaïs*. As a very young man, Hearst had been briefly engaged to the San Francisco singer Sybil Sanderson. In order to break the engagement, Miss Sanderson's parents had sent her to study in Paris, where she became well known in opera and as the "constant companion" of Massenet, who wrote *Thaïs* for her. But to use *Thaïs* would have cost a fee, so Bernard Herrmann wrote choice excerpts of a fake French-Oriental opera—*Salammbô*. (Dorothy Comingore did her own singing in the movie except for the opera-house sequence; that was dubbed by a professional singer who deliberately sang badly.) The Kane amalgam may also contain a dab or two from the lives of other magnates, such as Frank Munsey and Pulitzer, and more than a dab from the life of Jules Brulatour, who got his start in business by selling Eastman Kodak film. Hope Hampton, his blond protégée and later his wife, had a career even more ridiculous than Susan Alexander's. After she failed as a movie actress, Brulatour financed her career at the Chicago Opera Company at the end of the twenties, and then, using his power to extend credit to movie companies for film stock, he pushed the near-bankrupt Universal to star her in a 1937 disaster, in which she sang eight songs.

The only other major addition to Hearst's actual history comes near the beginning of the movie. The latter days of Susan Alexander as a tawdry-looking drunken singer at El Rancho in Atlantic City, where she is billed as "Susan Alexander Kane"—which tells us at once that she is so poor an entertainer that she must resort to this cheap attempt to exploit her connection with Kane—may have been lifted from the frayed end of Evelyn Nesbit's life. After her divorce from Harry K. Thaw—the rich socialite who murdered Stanford White on her account—she drifted down to appearing in honky-tonks, and was periodically denounced in the press for "capitalizing her shame."

XXIV

Dorothy Comingore says, "When I read for Orson, Herman was in the room, with a broken leg and a crutch, and Orson turned to him and said, 'What do you think?' and Herman said, 'Yes, she looks precisely like the image of a kitten we've been looking for.' "

The handling of Susan Alexander is a classic of duplicity. By diversifying the material and combining several careers, Mankiewicz could protect himself. He could claim that Susan wasn't meant to be Marion Davies—that she was nothing at all like Marion, whom he called a darling and a minx. He could point out that Marion wasn't a singer and that Hearst had never built an opera house for her—and it was true, she wasn't and he hadn't, but she was an actress and he did run Cosmopolitan Pictures for her. Right at the beginning of the movie, Kane was said to be the greatest newspaper tycoon of this or any other generation, so he was obviously Hearst; Xanadu was transparently San Simeon; and Susan's fake stardom and the role she played in Kane's life spelled Marion Davies to practically everybody in the Western world. And even though Mankiewicz *liked* Marion Davies, he was the same Mankiewicz who couldn't resist the disastrous "Imagine—the whole world wired to Harry Cohn's ass!" He skewered her with certain identifying details that were just too good to resist, such as her love of jigsaw puzzles. They were a feature of San Simeon; the puzzles, which sometimes took two weeks to complete, were set out on tables in the salon, and the guests would work at them before lunch. And when Kane destroys Susan's room in a rage after she leaves him, he turns up a hidden bottle of booze, which was a vicious touch, coming from Mankiewicz, who had often been the beneficiary of Marion's secret cache. He provided bits that had a special *frisson* for those in the know.

One can sometimes hurt one's enemies, but that's nothing compared to what one can do to one's friends. Marion Davies, living in the style of the royal courtesans with a man who couldn't marry her without messes and scandal (his wife, Millicent, had become a Catholic, and she had also given him five sons), was an easy target. Hearst and Louella Parsons had set her up for it, and she became the victim of *Citizen Kane*. In her best roles, Marion Davies was a spunky, funny, beautiful girl, and that's apparently what she *was* and why Hearst adored her. But, in his adoration, he insisted that the Hearst press overpublicize her and overpraise her constantly, and the public in general got wise. A typical Davies film would open with the theatre ventilating system pouring attar of roses at the audience, or the theatre would be specially redecorated, sometimes featuring posters that famous popular artists had done of her in the costumes of the picture. Charity functions of which she was the queen would be splashed all over the society pages, and the movie would be reviewed under eight-column headlines. In the news section, Mayor Hylan of New York would be saying, *"When Knighthood Was in Flower* is unquestionably the greatest picture I have ever seen. . . . No person can afford to miss this great screen masterpiece," or *"Little Old New York* is unquestionably the greatest screen epic I have ever looked upon, and Marion Davies is the most versatile screen star ever cast in any part. The wide range of her stellar acting is something to marvel at. . . . Every man, woman and child in New York City ought to see this splendid picture. . . . I must pay my tribute to the geniuses in all lines who created such a masterpiece."

When the toadying and praise were already sickening, Hearst fell for one of the dumbest smart con tricks of all time: A movie reviewer named Louella O. Parsons, working for the *New York Telegraph* for $110 a week, wrote a column saying that although Marion Davies's movies were properly publicized, the star herself wasn't publicized *enough*. Hearst fell for it and hired Parsons at $250 a week, and she began her profitable lifework of praising (and destroying) Marion Davies. Some of Davies's costume spectacles weren't bad—and she was generally charming in them—but the pictures didn't have to be bad for all the corrupt drumbeaters to turn the public's stomach. Other actresses were pushed to stardom and were accepted. (The flapper heroine Colleen Moore was Walter Howey's niece, and she was started on her career when she was fifteen. D. W. Griffith owed Howey a favor for getting *The Birth of a Nation* and *Intolerance* past the Chicago censors, and her movie contract was the payoff. She says that many of the Griffith stars were "payoffs.") Marion Davies had more talent than most of the reigning queens, but Hearst and Louella were too ostentatious, and they never let up. There was a steady march of headlines ("Marion Davies' Greatest Film Opens Tonight"); there were too many charity balls. The public can swallow just so much: her seventy-five-thousand-dollar fourteen-room mobile "bungalow" on the M-G-M lot, O.K.; the special carpet for alighting, no. Her pictures had to be forced on exhibitors, and Hearst spent so much on them that even when they did well, the cost frequently couldn't be recovered. One of his biographers reports a friend's saying to Hearst, "There's money in the movies," and Hearst's replying, "Yes. Mine."

Marion Davies was born in 1897, and, as a teen-ager, went right from the convent to the musical-comedy stage, where she put in two years as a dancer before Ziegfeld "glorified" her in the "Ziegfeld Follies of 1916." That was where William Randolph Hearst, already in his mid-fifties, spotted her. It is said, and may even be true, that he attended the "Follies" every night for eight weeks, buying two tickets—one for himself and the other for his hat—just "to gaze upon her." It is almost certainly true that from then "to the day of his death," as Adela Rogers St. Johns put it, "he wanted to know every minute where she was." Marion Davies entered movies in 1917, with *Runaway Romany,* which she also wrote, and then she began that really strange, unparalleled movie career. She had starred in about fifty pictures by the time she retired, in 1937—all under Hearst's aegis, and under his close personal supervision. (Leading men were afraid to kiss her; Hearst was always watching.) The pictures were all expensively produced, and most of them were financial failures. Marion Davies was a mimic and a parodist and a very original sort of comedienne, but though Hearst liked her to make him laugh at home, he wanted her to be a romantic maiden in the movies, and—what was irreconcilable with her talent—dignified. Like Susan, she was tutored, and he spent incredible sums on movies that would be the perfect setting for her. He appears to have been sincerely infatuated with her in old-fashioned, sentimental, ladylike roles; he loved to see her in ruffles on garden swings. But actresses didn't become public favorites in roles like those, and even if they could get by with them sometimes, they needed startling changes of pace to stay in public favor, and Hearst wouldn't let Marion Davies do anything "sordid."

To judge by what those who worked with her have said, she was thoroughly unpretentious and was depressed by Hearst's taste in roles for her. She finally broke out of the costume cycle in the late twenties and did some funny pictures: *The Red Mill* (which Fatty Arbuckle, whom Hearst the moralizer had helped ruin, directed, under his new, satirical pseudonym, Will B. Goodrich), *The Fair Coed,* my childhood favorite *The Patsy,* and others. But even when she played in a slapstick parody of Gloria Swanson's career (*Show*

People, in 1928), Hearst wouldn't let her do a custard-pie sequence, despite her own pleas and those of the director, King Vidor, and the writer, Laurence Stallings. (King Vidor has described the conference that Louis B. Mayer called so that Vidor could make his case to Hearst for the plot necessity of the pie. "Presently, the great man rose and in a high-pitched voice said, 'King's right. But I'm right, too—because I'm not going to let Marion be hit in the face with a pie.' ") She wanted to play Sadie Thompson in *Rain,* but he wouldn't hear of it, and the role went to Gloria Swanson (and made her a star all over again). When Marion Davies should have been playing hard-boiled, good-hearted blondes, Hearst's idea of a role for her was Elizabeth Barrett Browning in *The Barretts of Wimpole Street,* and when Thalberg reserved that one for *his* lady, Norma Shearer, Hearst, in 1934, indignantly left M-G-M and took his money and his "Cosmopolitan Pictures" label over to Warner Brothers. (The editors of his newspapers were instructed never again to mention Norma Shearer in print.) It was a long blighted career for an actress who might very well have become a big star on her own, and she finally recognized that with Hearst's help it was hopeless. By the time *Citizen Kane* came out, she had been in retirement for four years, but the sickening publicity had gone grinding on relentlessly, and, among the audiences at *Kane,* probably even those who remembered her as the charming, giddy comedienne of the late twenties no longer trusted their memories.

Mankiewicz, catering to the public, gave it the empty, stupid, no-talent blonde it wanted—the "confidential" backstairs view of the great gracious lady featured in the Hearst press. It was, though perhaps partly inadvertently, a much worse betrayal than if he'd made Susan more like Davies, because movie audiences assumed that Davies was a pathetic whiner like Susan Alexander, and Marion Davies was nailed to the cross of harmless stupidity and nothingness, which in high places is the worst joke of all.

XXV

Right from the start of movies, it was a convention that the rich were vulgarly acquisitive but were lonely and miserable and incapable of giving or receiving love. As a mass medium, movies have always soothed and consoled the public with the theme that the rich can buy everything except what counts—love. (The convention remains, having absorbed the *Dolce Vita* variation that the rich use each other sexually because they are incapable of love.) It was consistent with this popular view of the emptiness of the lives of the rich to make Susan Alexander a cartoon character; the movie reduces Hearst's love affair to an infatuation for a silly, ordinary nothing of a girl, as if everything in his life were synthetic, his passion vacuous, and the object of it a cipher. What happened in Hearst's life was far more interesting: he took a beautiful, warm-hearted girl and made her the best-known kept woman in America and the butt of an infinity of dirty jokes, and he did it out of love and the blindness of love.

Citizen Kane, however, employs the simplification, so convenient to melodrama, that there is a unity between a man's private life and his public one. This simplification has enabled ambitious bad writers to make reputations as thinkers, and in the movies of the forties it was given a superficial plausibility by popular Freudianism. Hideous character defects traceable to childhood traumas explained just about anything the authors disapproved of. Mankiewicz certainly knew better, but as a screenwriter he dealt in ideas that had popular appeal. Hearst was a notorious anti-union, pro-Nazi Red-baiter, so Kane must have a miserable, deformed childhood. He must be *wrecked* in infancy. It was a movie convention going back to silents that when you did a bio or a thesis picture you started with the principal characters as children and showed them to be miniature versions of their later characters. This convention almost invariably pleased audiences, because it also demonstrated the magic of movies—the kids so extraordinarily resembled the adult actors they would turn into. And it wasn't just makeup—they really did, having been searched out for that resemblance. (This is *possible* in theatre, but it's rarely feasible.) That rather old-fashioned view of the predestination of character from childhood needed only a small injection of popular Freudianism to pass for new, and if you tucked in a trauma, you took care of the motivation for the later events. Since nothing very bad had happened to Hearst, Mankiewicz drew upon Little Orson Annie. He *orphaned* Kane, and used that to explain Hearst's career. (And, as Welles directed it, there's more real emotion and pain in the childhood separation sequence than in all the rest of the movie.)

Thus Kane was emotionally stunted. Offering personal emptiness as the explanation of Hearst's career really doesn't do much but feed the complacency of those liberals who are eager to believe that conservatives are "sick" (which is also how conservatives tend to see liberals). Liberals were willing to see this hollow-man explanation of Hearst as something much deeper than a cliché of popular melodrama, though the film's explaining his attempts to win public office and his empire-building and his art collecting by the childhood loss of maternal love is as unilluminating as the conservative conceit that Marx was a revolutionary because he hated his father. The point of the film becomes the cliché irony that although Hearst has everything materially, he has nothing humanly.

Quite by chance, I saw William Randolph Hearst once, when I was about nineteen. It was Father's Day, which sometimes falls on my birthday, and my escort bumped me into him on the dance floor. I can't remember whether it was at the Palace Hotel in San Francisco or at the St. Francis, and I can't remember the year, though it was probably 1938. But I remember Hearst in almost terrifying detail, with the kind of memory I generally have only for movies. He was dinner-dancing, just like us, except that his table was a large one. He was seated with Marion Davies and his sons with their

wives or dates; obviously, it was a kind of family celebration. I had read the
then current *Hearst, Lord of San Simeon* and Ferdinand Lundberg's *Imperial
Hearst,* and probably almost everything else that was available about him,
and I remember thinking, as I watched him, of Charles A. Beard's preface
to the Lundberg book—that deliberately cruel premature "Farewell to William Randolph Hearst," with its tone of "He will depart loved by few and respected by none whose respect is worthy of respect. . . . None will be proud
to do honor to his memory," and so on. You don't expect to bump into a
man on the dance floor after you've been reading that sort of thing about
him. It was like stumbling onto Caligula, and Hearst looked like a Roman
emperor mixing with the commoners on a night out. He was a huge man—
six feet four or five—and he was old and heavy, and he moved slowly about
the dance floor with *her.* He seemed like some prehistoric monster gliding
among the couples, quietly majestic, towering over everyone; he had little,
odd eyes, like a whale's, and they looked pulled down, sinking into his
cheeks. Maybe I had just never seen anybody so massive and dignified and
old *dancing,* and maybe it was that plus who he was, but I've never seen anyone else who seemed to incarnate power and solemnity as he did; he was
frightening and he was impressive, almost as if he were wearing ceremonial
robes of office. When he danced with Marion Davies, he was indifferent to
everything else. They looked isolated and entranced together; this slow,
huge dinosaur clung to the frowzy-looking aging blonde in what seemed to
be a ritual performance. Joined together, they were as alone as the young
dancing couple in the sky with diamonds in *Yellow Submarine.* Maybe they
were that couple a few decades later, for they had an extraordinary
romance—one that lasted thirty-two years—and they certainly had the diamonds (or *had* had them). He seemed unbelievably old to me that night,
when he was probably about seventy-five; they were still together when he
died, in 1951, at the age of eighty-eight.

The private pattern that was devised as a correlative (and possible explanation) of Hearst's public role was false. Hearst didn't have any (recorded) early traumas, Marion Davies did have talent, and they were an
extraordinarily devoted pair; far from leaving him, when he faced bankruptcy she gave him her money and jewels and real estate, and even borrowed money to enable him to keep his newspapers. He was well loved, and
still he was a dangerous demagogue. And, despite what Charles A. Beard
said and what Dos Passos said, and despite the way Mankiewicz presented
him in *Citizen Kane,* and all the rest, Hearst and his consort were hardly
lonely, with all those writers around, and movie stars and directors, and
Shaw, and Winston Churchill, and weekend parties with Marion Davies spik-
ing teetotaller Calvin Coolidge's fruit punch (though only with liquor that
came from fruit). Even Mrs. Luce came; the pictures of Hearst on the walls
at Time-Life might show him as an octopus, but who could resist an invitation? Nor did Hearst lose his attraction or his friends after he lost his *big*
money. After San Simeon was stripped of its silver treasures, which were sold

at auction in the thirties, the regal-party weekends were finished, but he still entertained, if less lavishly, at his smaller houses. Dos Passos played the same game as *Citizen Kane* when he wrote of Hearst "amid the relaxing adulations of screenstars, admen, screenwriters, publicitymen, columnists, millionaire editors"—suggesting that Hearst was surrounded by third-raters and syco-phantic hirelings. But the lists and the photographs of Hearst's guests tell another story. He had the one great, dazzling court of the first half of the twentieth century, and the statesmen and kings, the queens and duchesses at his table were as authentic as the writers and wits and great movie stars and directors. When one considers who even those screenwriters were, it's not surprising that Hearst wanted their company. Harold Ross must have wondered what drew his old friends there, for he came, too, escorted by Robert Benchley.

It is both a limitation and *in the nature of the appeal* of popular art that it constructs false, easy patterns. Like the blind-beggar-for-luck, *Kane* has a primitive appeal that is implicit in the conception. It tells the audience that fate or destiny or God or childhood trauma has already taken revenge on the wicked—that if the rich man had a good time he has suffered remorse, or, better still, that he hasn't really enjoyed himself at all. Before Mankiewicz began writing the script, he talked about what a great love story it would be—but who would buy tickets for a movie about a rich, powerful tycoon who also found true love? In popular art, riches and power destroy people, and so the secret of Kane is that he longs for the simple pleasures of his childhood before wealth tore him away from his mother—he longs for what is available to the mass audience.

XXVI

Even when Hearst's speeches, or facsimiles of them, were used in *Kane*, their character was transformed. If one looks at his actual remarks on property and then at Mankiewicz's adaptation of them, one can see how. Hearst's remarks are tight and slightly oblique, and it takes one an instant to realize what he's saying. Mankiewicz makes them easier to grasp (and rather florid) but kills some of their almost sinister double edge by making them consciously flip. He turns them into a joke. And when Mankiewicz didn't make the speeches flip, Welles's delivery did. When you hear Kane dictate the telegram to Cuba, you don't really think for a minute that it's *acted* on. And so the movie be-comes a comic strip about Hearst, without much resonance, and certainly without much tragic resonance. Hearst, who compared himself to an ele-phant, *looked* like a great man. I don't think he actually was great in any sense, but he was *extraordinary,* and his power and wealth, plus his enormous size, made him a phenomenally commanding presence. Mankiewicz, like Dos Passos, may have believed that Hearst fell from greatness, or (as I suspect) Mankiewicz may have liked the facile dramatic possibilities of that approach. But he couldn't carry it out. He couldn't write the character as a tragic fallen hero, because he couldn't resist making him funny. Mankiewicz had been hacking out popular comedies and melodramas for too long to write drama; one does not *dictate* tragedy to a stenotypist. He automatically, because of his own temperament and his writing habits, turned out a bitchy satirical melodrama. Inside the three hundred and twenty-five pages of his long, ambitious first draft was the crowd-pleasing material waiting to be carved out. When one reads the long version, it's obvious what must go; if I had been doing the cutting I might have cut just about the same material. *And yet* that fat to be cut away is everything that tends to make it a political and historical drama, and what is left is the private scandals of a poor little rich boy. The scandals in the long draft—some of it, set in Italy during Kane's youth, startlingly like material that came to the screen twenty years later in *La Dolce Vita*—served a purpose beyond crowd pleasing: to show what a powerful man could cover up and get away with. Yet this, of course, went out, for reasons similar to the ones that kept Kane, unlike Hearst, from winning elected office—to reassure the public that the rich *don't* get away with it.

Welles now has a lumbering grace and a gliding, whalelike motion not unlike Hearst's, but when he played the role he became stiff and crusty as the older Kane, and something went blank in the aging process—not just because the makeup was erratic and waxy (especially in the bald-headed scenes, such as the one in the picnic tent) but because the character lost his connection with business and politics and became a fancy theatrical notion, an Expressionist puppet. Also, there are times when the magic of movies fails. The camera comes so close that it can reveal too much: Kane as an old man was an actor trying to look old, and Welles had as yet only a school-boy's perception of how age weighs one down. On a popular level, however, his limitations worked to his advantage; they tied in with the myth of the soulless rich.

The conceptions are basically *kitsch;* basically, *Kane* is popular melodrama—Freud plus scandal, a comic strip about Hearst. Yet, partly because of the resonance of what was left of the historical context, partly because of the juiciness of Welles's young talent and of the varied gifts and personalities others brought to the film, partly because of the daring of the attack on the most powerful and dangerous press lord known to that time, the picture has great richness and flair: it's *kitsch* redeemed. I would argue that this is what is remarkable about movies—that shallow conceptions in one area can be offset by elements playing against them or altering them or affecting the texture. If a movie is good, there is a general tendency to believe that everything in it was conceived and worked out according to a beautiful master plan, or that it is the result of the creative imagination of the director, but in movies things rarely happen that way—even more rarely than they do in opera or the theatre. There are so many variables; imagine how different the whole feeling of *Kane* would be if the film had been shot in a naturalistic style, or even if it had been made at M-G-M instead of at R.K.O. Extraordinary movies are the result of the "right" people's getting together on the "right" project at the "right" time—in their lives and in history. I don't mean to suggest that a good movie is just a mess that happens to work (although there have been such cases)—only that a good movie is not always the result of a single artistic intelligence. It can be the result of a fortunate collaboration, of cross-fertilizing accidents. And I would argue that what redeems movies in general, what makes them so much easier to take than other arts, is that many talents in interaction in a work can produce something more enjoyable than one talent that is not of the highest. Because of the collaborative nature of most movies, masterpieces are rare, and even masterpieces may, like *Kane,* be full of flaws, but the interaction frequently results in special pleasures and surprises.

XXVII

The director should be in control not because he is the sole creative intelligence but because only if he is in control can he liberate and utilize the talents of his co-workers, who languish (as directors do) in studio-factory productions. The best interpretation to put on it when a director says that a movie is totally his is not that he did it all himself but that he wasn't interfered with, that he made the choices and the ultimate decisions, that the whole thing isn't an unhappy compromise for which no one is responsible; not that he was the sole creator but almost the reverse—that he was free to use all the best ideas offered him.

Welles had a vitalizing, spellbinding talent; he was the man who brought out the best in others and knew how to use it. What keeps *Citizen Kane* alive is that Welles wasn't prevented (as so many directors are) from trying things out. He was young and *open,* and, as the members of that crew tell it—and they remember it very well, because it was the only time it ever happened for many of them—they could always talk to him and make suggestions, as long as they didn't make the suggestions publicly. Most big-studio movies were made in such a restrictive way that the crews were hostile and bored and the atmosphere was oppressive. The worst aspect of the factory system was that almost everyone worked beneath his capacity. Working on *Kane,* in an atmosphere of freedom, the designers and technicians came forth with ideas they'd been bottling up for years; they were all in on the creative process. Welles was so eager to try out new ideas that even the tough, hardened studio craftsmen were caught up by his spirit, just as his co-workers in the theatre and in radio had been. *Citizen Kane* is not a great work that suddenly burst out of a young prodigy's head. There are such works in the arts (though few, if any, in movies), but this is not one of them. It is a superb example of collaboration; everyone connected with it seems to have had the time of his life because he was able to contribute something.

Welles had just the right background for the sound era. He used sound not just as an inexpensive method of creating the illusion of halls and crowds but to create an American environment. He knew how to convey the

way people feel about each other by the way they sound; he knew how they sounded in different rooms, in different situations. The directors who had been most imaginative in the use of sound in the early talkies were not Americans, and when they worked in America, as Ernst Lubitsch did, they didn't have the ear for American life that Welles had. And the good American movie directors in that period (men like Howard Hawks and John Ford and William Wellman) didn't have the background in theatre or—that key element—the background in radio. Hawks handled the dialogue expertly in *His Girl Friday,* but the other sounds are not much more imaginative than those in a first-rate stage production. When Welles came to Hollywood, at the age of twenty-four, his previous movie experience had not been on a professional level, but he already knew more about the dramatic possibilities of sound than most veteran directors, and the sound engineers responded to his inventiveness by giving him extraordinary new effects. At every point along the way, the studio craftsmen tried something out. Nearly all the thirty-five members of the R.K.O. special-effects department worked on *Kane;* roughly eighty percent of the film was not merely printed but reprinted, in order to add trick effects and blend in painted sets and bits of stock footage. The view up from Susan singing on the opera stage to the stagehands high above on the catwalk, as one of them puts two fingers to his nose—which looks like a tilt (or vertical pan)—is actually made up of three shots, the middle one a miniature. When the camera seems to pass through a rooftop skylight into the El Rancho night club where Susan works, the sign, the rooftop, and the skylight are miniatures, with a flash of lightning to conceal the cut to the full-scale interior. The craftsmen were so ingenious about giving Welles the effects he wanted that even now audiences aren't aware of how cheaply made *Citizen Kane* was.

In the case of the cinematographer, Gregg Toland, the contribution goes far beyond suggestions and technical solutions. I think he not only provided much of the visual style of *Citizen Kane* but was responsible for affecting the conception, and even for introducing a few elements that are not in the script. It's always a little risky to assign credit for ideas in movies; somebody is bound to turn up a film that used whatever it is—a detail, a device, a technique—earlier. The most one can hope for, generally, is to catch on to a few late links in the chain. It was clear that *Kane* had visual links to James Wong Howe's cinematography in *Transatlantic* (Howe, coincidentally, had also shot *The Power and the Glory*), but I had always been puzzled by the fact that *Kane* seemed to draw not only on the Expressionist theatrical style of Welles's stage productions but on the German Expressionist and Gothic movies of the silent period. In *Kane,* as in the German silents, depth was used like stage depth, and attention was frequently moved from one figure to another within a fixed frame by essentially the same techniques as on the stage—by the actors' moving into light or by a shift of the light to other actors (rather than by the fluid camera of a Renoir, which follows the actors or the fragmentation and quick cutting of the early Russians). There were

frames in *Kane* that seemed so close to the exaggerations in German films like *Pandora's Box* and *The Last Laugh* and *Secrets of a Soul* that I wondered what Welles was talking about when he said he had prepared for *Kane* by running John Ford's *Stagecoach* forty times. Even allowing for the hyperbole of the forty times, why should Orson Welles have studied *Stagecoach* and come up with a film that looked more like *The Cabinet of Dr. Caligari?* I wondered if there might be a link between Gregg Toland and the German tradition, though most of Toland's other films didn't suggest much German influence. When I looked up his credits as a cameraman, the name *Mad Love* rang a bell; I closed my eyes and visualized it, and there was the Gothic atmosphere, and the huge, dark rooms with lighted figures, and Peter Lorre, bald, with a spoiled-baby face, looking astoundingly like a miniature Orson Welles.

Mad Love, made in Hollywood in 1935, was a dismal, static horror movie—an American version of a German film directed by the same man who had directed *The Cabinet of Dr. Caligari.* The American remake, remarkable only for its photography, was directed by Karl Freund, who had been head cinematographer at Ufa, in Germany. He had worked with such great directors as Fritz Lang and F. W. Murnau and G. W. Pabst, and, by his technical innovations, had helped create their styles; he had shot many of the German silent classics (*The Last Laugh, Variety, Metropolis, Tartuffe*). I recently looked at a print of *Mad Love,* and the resemblances to *Citizen Kane* are even greater than my memories of it suggested. Not only is the large room with the fireplace at Xanadu similar to Lorre's domain as a mad doctor, with similar lighting and similar placement of figures, but Kane's appearance and makeup in some sequences might be a facsimile of Lorre's. Lorre, who had come out of the German theatre and German films, played in a stylized manner that is visually imitated in *Kane.* And, amusingly, that screeching white cockatoo, which isn't in the script of *Kane* but appeared out of nowhere in the movie to provide an extra "touch," is a regular member of Lorre's household.

Gregg Toland was the "hottest" photographer in Hollywood at the time he called Welles and asked to work with him; in March he had won the Academy Award for *Wuthering Heights,* and his other recent credits included *The Grapes of Wrath* and the film in which he had experimented with deep focus, *The Long Voyage Home.* He brought along his own four-man camera crew, who had recently celebrated their fifteenth year of working together. This picture was made with love; the year before his death, in 1948, Toland said that he had wanted to work with Welles because he was miserable and felt like a whore when he was on run-of-the-mill assignments, and that "photographing *Citizen Kane* was the most exciting professional adventure of my career." I surmise that part of the adventure was his finding a way to use and develop what the great Karl Freund had taught him.

Like the German cinematographers in the silent period, Toland took a more active role than the usual Hollywood cinematographer. For some

years, whenever it was possible, he had been supervising the set construction of his films, so that he could plan the lighting. He probably responded to Welles's penchant for tales of terror and his desire for a portentous, mythic look, and since Welles didn't have enough financing for full-scale sets and was more than willing to try the unconventional, Toland suggested many of the Expressionist solutions. When a director is new to films, he is, of course, extremely dependent on his cameraman, and he is particularly so if he is also the star of the film, and is thus in front of the camera. Toland was a disciplined man, and those who worked on the set say he was a steadying influence on Welles; it is generally agreed that the two planned and discussed every shot together. With Welles, Toland was free to make suggestions that went beyond lighting techniques. Seeing Welles's facial resemblance to the tiny Lorre—even to the bulging eyes and the dimpled, sad expression—Toland probably suggested the makeup and the doll-like, jerky use of the body for Kane in his rage and as a lonely old man, and, having enjoyed the flamboyant photographic effect of the cockatoo in *Mad Love,* suggested that, too. When Toland provided Welles with the silent-picture setups that had been moribund under Karl Freund's direction, Welles used them in a child-like spirit that made them playful and witty. There's nothing static or Germanic in Welles's *direction,* and he had such unifying energy that just a couple of years ago an eminent movie critic cited the cockatoo in *Citizen Kane* as "an unforced metaphor arising naturally out of the action."

It's the Gothic atmosphere, partly derived from Toland's work on *Mad Love,* that inflates *Citizen Kane* and puts it in a different tradition from the newspaper comedies and the big bios of the thirties. *Citizen Kane* is, in some ways, a freak of art. Toland, although he used deep focus again later, reverted to a more conventional look for the films following *Kane,* directed by men who rejected technique "for its own sake," but he had passed on Freund's techniques to Welles. The dark, Gothic horror style, with looming figures, and with vast interiors that suggested castles rather than houses, formed the basis for much of Welles's later visual style. It suited Welles; it was the visual equivalent of The Shadow's voice—a gigantic echo chamber. Welles, too big for ordinary roles, too overpowering for normal characters, is stylized by nature—is by nature an Expressionist actor.

XXVIII

Two years after the release of *Citizen Kane,* when Herman Mankiewicz had become respectable—his career had taken a leap after *Kane,* and he had had several major credits later in 1941, and had just won another Academy nomination, for his work on *Pride of the Yankees*—he stumbled right into Hearst's waiting arms. He managed to have an accident that involved so many of the elements of his life that it sounds like a made-up surreal joke. Though some of his other calamities are lost in an alcoholic fog—people remember only the bandages and Mankiewicz's stories about how he got them, and maybe even he didn't always know the facts—this one is all too well documented.

Driving home after a few drinks at Romanoff's, he was only a block and a half from his house when he hit a tiny car right at the gates of the Marion Davies residence. And it wasn't just any little car he hit; it was one driven by Lee Gershwin—Ira Gershwin's wife, Lenore, a woman Mankiewicz had known for years. He had adapted the Gershwins' musical *Girl Crazy* to the screen in 1932, and he had known the Gershwins before that, in the twenties, in New York; they were part of the same group. It was a gruesomely comic accident: Hearst was living on the grounds of the Marion Davies estate at the time, in that bungalow that Marion had used at M-G-M and then at Warners, and he was conferring with the publisher of his *New York Journal-American* when he heard the crash. Hearst sent the publisher down to investigate, and as soon as the man reported who was involved, Hearst went into action. Lee Gershwin had had two passengers—her secretary, who wasn't hurt, and her laundress, whom she was taking home, and who just got a bump. Mrs. Gershwin herself wasn't badly hurt, though she had a head injury that required some stitches. It was a minor accident, but Mankiewicz was taken to the police station, and he apparently behaved noisily and badly there. When he got home, a few hours later, his wife, Sara, sobered him up, and, having ascertained that Lee Gershwin had been treated at the hospital and had already been discharged, she sent him over to the Gershwins' with a couple of dozen roses. Marc Connelly, who was at the Gershwins' that night, says that when Mankiewicz arrived the house was full of reporters, and Ira Gershwin was serving them drinks and trying to keep things affable. Mankiewicz went upstairs to see Lee, who was lying in bed with her head bandaged. Amiable madman that he was, he noticed a painting on the bedroom wall, and his first remark was that he had a picture by the same artist. He apparently didn't have any idea that he was in serious trouble.

Hearst's persistent vindictiveness was one of his least attractive traits. Mankiewicz was charged with a felony, and the minor accident became a major front-page story in the Hearst papers across the country for four successive days, with headlines more appropriate to a declaration of war. It became the excuse for another Hearst campaign against the orgies and dissolute lives of the movie colony, and Hearst dragged it on for months. By then, the Hearst press was on its way to becoming the crank press, and Hearst had so many enemies that Mankiewicz had many friends. When Mankiewicz appealed to the American Civil Liberties Union, there had already been stories in *Time, Newsweek, Variety,* and elsewhere pointing out that the persecution in the Hearst papers was a reprisal for his having written the script of *Citizen Kane*. Mankiewicz, however, had to stand trial on a felony charge. And although he got through the mess of the trial all right, the hounding by the Hearst papers took its toll, and his reputation was permanently damaged.

In a letter to Harold Ross after the trial, Mankiewicz asked to write a

Profile of Hearst that Ross was considering. "Honestly," he wrote, "I know more about Hearst than any other man alive. (There are a couple of deaders before their time who knew more, I think.) I studied his career like a scholar before I wrote *Citizen Kane.*" And then, in a paragraph that suggests his admiration, despite everything, for both Hearst and Welles, he wrote, "Shortly after I had been dragged from the obscurity of the police blotter and—a middle-aged, flat-footed, stylish-stout scenario writer—been promoted by the International News Service into Gary Grant, who, with a tank, had just drunkenly ploughed into a baby carriage occupied by the Dionne quintuplets, the Duchess of Kent, Mrs. Franklin D. Roosevelt (the President's wife), and the favorite niece of the Pope, with retouched art combining the more unflattering features of Goering and Dillinger, I happened to be discussing Our Hero with Orson. With the fair-mindedness that I have always recognized as my outstanding trait, I said to Orson that, despite this and that, Mr. Hearst was, in many ways, a great man. He was, and is, said Orson, a horse's ass, no more nor less, who has been wrong, without exception, on everything he's ever touched. For instance, for fifty years, said Orson, Hearst did nothing but scream about the Yellow Peril, and then he gave up his seat and hopped off two months before Pearl Harbor."

XXIX

In 1947, Ferdinand Lundberg sued Orson Welles, Herman J. Mankiewicz, and R.K.O. Radio Pictures, Inc., for two hundred and fifty thousand dollars for copyright infringement, charging that *Citizen Kane* had plagiarized his book *Imperial Hearst*. On the face of it, the suit looked ridiculous. No doubt (as Houseman admits) Mankiewicz had drawn upon everything available about Hearst, in addition to his own knowledge, and no doubt the Lundberg book, which brought a great deal of Hearst material together and printed some things that had not been printed before, was especially useful, but John Dos Passos might have sued on similar grounds, since material that was in *U.S.A.* was also in the movie, and so might dozens of magazine writers. Hearst himself might have sued, on the basis that he hadn't been credited with the dialogue. The defense would obviously be that the material was in the public domain, and the suit looked like the usual nuisance-value suit that Hollywood is plagued by—especially since Lundberg offered to settle for a flat payment of $18,000. But R.K.O. had become one of Howard Hughes's toys in the late forties, and a crew of expensive lawyers was hired. When the suit came to trial, in 1950, Welles was out of the country; he had given his testimony earlier, in the form of a deposition taken before the American vice-consul at Casablanca, Morocco. This deposition is a curious document, full of pontification and evasion and some bluffing so outrageous that one wonders whether the legal stenographer was able to keep a straight face. *Citizen Kane* had already begun to take over and change the public image of Hearst; Hearst and Kane had become inseparable, as Welles and Kane were, but Welles possibly didn't really know in detail—or, more likely, simply didn't remember—how close the movie was to Hearst's life. He seemed more concerned with continuing the old pretense that the movie was not about Hearst than with refuting Lundberg's charge of plagiarism, and his attempts to explain specific incidents in the movie as if their relationship to Hearst were a mere coincidence are fairly funny. He stated that "I have done no research into the life of William Randolph Hearst at any time," and that "in writing the screenplay of *Citizen Kane* I drew entirely upon my own observations of life," and then was helpless to explain how there were so many episodes from Hearst's life in the movie. When he was cornered with specific details, such as the picture of Jim Gettys in prison clothes, he gave up and said, "The dialogue for the scene in question was written in its first and second draftings exclusively by my colleague Mr. Mankiewicz. I worked on the third draft." When he was read a long list of events in the film that parallel Hearst's life as it is recorded in *Imperial Hearst,* he tried to use the Insull cover story and came up with the surprising information that the film dealt "quite as fully with the world of grand opera as with the world of newspaper publishing."

Mankiewicz, in a preparatory statement, freely admitted that many of the incidents and details came from Hearst's life but said that he knew them from personal acquaintance and from a lifetime of reading. He was called to testify at the trial, and John Houseman was called as a witness to Mankiewicz's labor on the script. Mankiewicz was indignant that anyone could suggest that a man of his knowledge would need to crib, and he paraded his credentials. It was pointed out that John Gunther had said Mankiewicz made better sense than all the politicians and diplomats put together, and that he was widely known to have a passionate interest in contemporary history, particularly as it related to power, and to have an enormous library. And, of course, he had known Hearst in the years of his full imperial glory, and his friends knew of his absorption in everything to do with Hearst. According to Houseman, he and Mankiewicz thought they were both brilliant in court; they treated the whole suit as an insult, and enjoyed themselves so much while testifying that they spent the time between appearances on the stand congratulating each other. Mankiewicz, in a final gesture of contempt for the charge, brought an inventory of his library and tossed it to the R.K.O. lawyers to demonstrate the width and depth of his culture. It was an inventory that Sara had prepared some years before, when (during a stretch of hard times) they had rented out their house on Tower Road; no one had bothered to look at the inventory—not even the R.K.O. attorneys before they put it into evidence. But Lundberg's lawyers did; they turned to "L," and there, neatly listed under "Lundberg," were three copies of *Imperial Hearst*. During Mankiewicz's long recuperation, his friends had sent him many books, and since his friends knew of his admiration for many sides of the man he called "the outstanding whirling pagoda of our times," he had been showered with copies of this particular book. The inventory apparently made quite an impression in court, and the tide turned. The jury had been cordial to Mankiewicz's explanation of how it was that he knew details that were in the Lundberg book and were unpublished elsewhere, but now the width and depth of his culture became suspect. After thirty days, the trial resulted in a hung jury, and rather than go through another trial, R.K.O. settled for $15,000—and also paid an estimated couple of hundred thousand dollars in lawyers' fees and court costs.

Mankiewicz went on writing scripts, but his work in the middle and late forties is not in the same spirit as *Kane*. It's rather embarrassing to look at his later credits, because they are yea-saying movies—decrepit "family pictures" like *The Enchanted Cottage*. The booze and the accidents finally added up, and he declined into the forties sentimental slop. He tried to rise above it. He wrote the script he had proposed earlier on Aimee Semple McPherson, and he started the one on Dillinger, but he had squandered his health as well as his talents. I have read the McPherson script; it is called *Woman of the Rock,* and it's a tired, persevering-to-the-end, burned-out script. He uses a bit of newspaper atmosphere, and Jed again, this time as a reporter, and relies on a flashback structure from Aimee's death to her childhood; there are "modern" touches—a semi-lesbian lady who manages the evangelist, for instance—and the script comes to life whenever he introduces sophisticated characters, but he can't write simple people, and even the central character is out of his best range. The one device that is interesting is the heroine's love of bright scarves, starting in childhood with one her father gives her and ending with one that strangles her when it catches on a car wheel, but this is stolen from Isadora Duncan's death, and to give the death of one world-famous lady to another is depressingly poverty-stricken. Mankiewicz's character hadn't changed. He had written friends that he bore the scars of his mistake with Charlie Lederer, but just as he had lent the script of *Kane* to Lederer, Marion Davies's nephew, he proudly showed *Woman of the Rock* to Aimee Semple McPherson's daughter, Roberta Semple, and that ended the project. His behavior probably wasn't deliberately self-destructive as much as it was a form of innocence inside the worldly, cynical man—I visualize him as so *pleased* with what he was doing that he wanted to share his delight with others. I haven't read the unfinished Dillinger; the title, *As the Twig Is Bent,* tells too hoary much.

In his drama column in *The New Yorker* in 1925, Mankiewicz parodied those who thought the Marx Brothers had invented all their own material in *The Cocoanuts* and who failed to recognize George S. Kaufman's contribution. It has been Mankiewicz's fate to be totally ignored in the books on the Marx Brothers movies; though his name is large in the original ads, and though Groucho Marx and Harry Ruby and S. J. Perelman all confirm the fact that he functioned as the producer of *Monkey Business* and *Horse Feathers,* the last reference I can find to this in print is in *Who's Who in America* for 1953, the year of his death. Many of the thirties movies he wrote are popular on television and at college showings, but when they have been discussed in film books his name has never, to my knowledge, appeared. He is never mentioned in connection with *Duck Soup,* though Groucho confirms the fact that he worked on it. He is now all but ignored even in many accounts of *Citizen Kane.* By the fifties, his brother Joe—with *A Letter to Three Wives* and *All About Eve*—had become the famous wit in Hollywood, and there wasn't room for two Mankiewiczes in movie history; Herman became a parentheses in the listings for Joe.

XXX

Welles has offered his semi-defiant apologia for his own notoriously self-destructive conduct in the form of the old fable that he tells as Arkadin in *Confidential Report,* of 1955—an "original screenplay" that, from internal evidence, he may very well have written. A scorpion wants to get across a lake and asks a frog to carry him on his back. The frog obliges, but midway the scorpion stings him. As they both sink, the frog asks the scorpion why he did it, pointing out that now he, too, will die, and the scorpion answers, "I know, but I can't help it; it's my character." The fable is inserted conspicuously, as a personal statement, almost as if it were a confession, and it's a bad story for a man to use as a parable of his life, since it's a disclaimer of responsibility. It's as if Welles believed in predestination and were saying that he was helpless. Yet Welles's characterization of himself seems rather odd. Whom, after all, has he fatally stung? He was the catalyst for the only moments of triumph that most of his associates ever achieved.

Every time someone in the theatre or in movies breaks through and does something good, people expect the moon of him and hold it against him personally when he doesn't deliver it. That windy speech Kaufman and Hart gave their hero in *The Fabulous Invalid* indicates the enormous burden of people's hopes that Welles carried. He has a long history of disappointing people. In the *Saturday Evening Post* of January 20, 1940, Alva Johnston and Fred Smith wrote:

> Orson was an old war horse in the infant prodigy line by the time he was ten. He had already seen eight years' service as a child genius. . . . Some of the oldest acquaintances of Welles have been disappointed in his career. They see the twenty-four-year-old boy of today as a mere shadow of the two-year-old man they used to know.

A decade after *Citizen Kane,* the gibes were no longer so good-natured; the terms "wonder boy" and "boy genius" were thrown in Welles's face. When Welles was only thirty-six, the normally gracious Walter Kerr referred to him as "an international joke, and possibly the youngest living has-been." Welles had the special problems of fame without commercial success. Because of the moderate financial returns on *Kane,* he lost the freedom to control his own productions; after *Kane,* he never had complete control of a movie in

America. And he lost the collaborative partnerships that he needed. For whatever reasons, neither Mankiewicz nor Houseman nor Toland ever worked on another Welles movie. He had been advertised as a one-man show; it was not altogether his own fault when he became one. He was alone, trying to be "Orson Welles," though "Orson Welles" had stood for the activities of a group. But he needed the family to hold him together on a project and to take over for him when his energies became scattered. With them, he was a prodigy of accomplishments; without them, he flew apart, became disorderly. Welles lost his magic touch, and as his films began to be diffuse he acquired the reputation of being an intellectual, difficult-to-understand artist. When he appears on television to recite from Shakespeare or the Bible, he is introduced as if he were the epitome of the highbrow; it's television's more polite way of cutting off his necktie.

The Mercury players had scored their separate successes in *Kane*, and they went on to conventional careers; they had hoped to revolutionize theatre and films, and they became part of the industry. Turn on the TV and there they are, dispersed, each in old movies or his new series or his reruns. Away from Welles and each other, they were neither revolutionaries nor great originals, and so Welles became a scapegoat—the man who "let everyone down." He has lived all his life in a cloud of failure because he hasn't lived up to what was unrealistically expected of him. No one has ever been able to do what was expected of Welles—to create a new radical theatre and to make one movie masterpiece after another—but Welles's "figurehead" publicity had snowballed to the point where all his actual and considerable achievements looked puny compared to what his destiny was supposed to be. In a less confused world, his glory would be greater than his guilt.

The New Yorker, February 20, 1971 and February 27, 1971

PART FIVE

DEEPER INTO MOVIES

1973

BUTCH CASSIDY AND THE SUNDANCE KID
THE BOTTOM OF THE PIT
(ALSO **EASY RIDER, MIDNIGHT COWBOY, ALICE'S RESTAURANT**)

A college-professor friend of mine in San Francisco who has always tried to stay in tune with his students looked at his class recently and realized it was time to take off his beads. There he was, a superannuated flower child wearing last year's talismans, and the young had become austere, even puritanical. Movies and, even more, movie audiences have been changing. The art houses are now (for the first time) dominated by American movies, and the young audiences waiting outside, sitting on the sidewalk or standing in line, are no longer waiting just for entertainment. The waiting together may itself be part of the feeling of community, and they go inside almost for sacramental purposes. For all the talk (and fear) of ritual participation in the "new" theatre, it is really taking place on a national scale in the movie houses, at certain American films that might be called cult films, though they have probably become cult films because they are the most interesting films around. What is new about *Easy Rider* is not necessarily that one finds its attitudes appealing but that the movie conveys the mood of the drug culture with such skill and in such full belief that these simplicities are the truth that one can understand why these attitudes are appealing to others. *Easy Rider* is an expression and a confirmation of how this audience feels;

the movie attracts a new kind of "inside" audience, whose members enjoy tuning in together to a whole complex of shared signals and attitudes. And although one may be uneasy over the satisfaction the audience seems to receive from responding to the general masochism and to the murder of Captain America, the movie obviously rings true to the audience's vision. It's cool to feel that you can't win, that it's all rigged and hopeless. It's even cool to believe in purity and sacrifice. Those of us who reject the heroic central character and the statements of *Easy Rider* may still be caught by something edgy and ominous in it—the acceptance of the constant danger of sudden violence. We're not sure how much of this paranoia isn't paranoia.

Some of the other cult films *try* to frighten us but are too clumsy to, though they succeed in doing something else. One has only to talk with some of the people who have seen *Midnight Cowboy*, for example, to be aware that what they care about is not the camera and editing pyrotechnics; they are indifferent to all that by now routine filler. John Schlesinger in *Midnight Cowboy* and, at a less skillful level, Larry Peerce in *Goodbye, Columbus* hedge their bets by using cutting and camera techniques to provide a satirical background as a kind of enrichment of the narrative and theme. But it really cheapens and impoverishes their themes. Peerce's satire is just cheesy, like his lyricism, and Schlesinger's (like Richard Lester's in *Petulia*) is offensively inhuman and inaccurate. If Schlesinger could extend the same sympathy to the other Americans that he extends to Joe Buck and Ratso, the picture might make better sense; the point of the picture must surely be to give us some insight into these derelicts—two of the many kinds of dreamers and failures in the city. Schlesinger keeps pounding away at America, determined to expose how horrible the people are, to dehumanize the people these two are part of. The spray of venom in these pictures is so obviously the directors' way of showing off that we begin to discount it. To varying degrees, these films share the paranoid view of America of *Easy Rider*—and they certainly reinforce it for the audience—but what the audience really reacts to in *Midnight Cowboy* is the two lost, lonely men finding friendship. The actors save the picture, as the actors almost saved parts of *Petulia;* the leading actors become more important because the flamboyantly "visual" exhibitionism doesn't hold one's interest. Despite the recurrent assertions that the star system is dead, the audience is probably more interested than ever in the human material on the screen (though the new stars don't always resemble the old ones). At *Midnight Cowboy*, in the midst of all the grotesque shock effects and the brutality of the hysterical, superficial satire of America, the audiences, wiser, perhaps, than the director, are looking for the human feelings—the simple, *Of Mice and Men* kind of relationship at the heart of it. Maybe they wouldn't accept the simple theme so readily in a simpler setting, because it might look square, but it's what they're taking from the movie. They're looking for "truth"—for some signs of emotion, some evidence of what keeps people together. The difference between the old audiences and the new ones is that the old audiences wanted immediate gratification and used to get restless and bored when a picture didn't click along; these new pictures don't all click along, yet the young audiences stay attentive. They're eager to respond, to love it—eager to *feel*.

Although young movie audiences are far more sentimental now than they were a few years ago (Frank Capra, whose softheaded populism was hooted at in college film societies in the fifties, has become a new favorite at U.C.L.A.), there is this new and good side to the sentimentality. They are going to movies looking for feelings that will help synthesize their experience, and they appear to be willing to feel their way along with a movie like Arthur Penn's *Alice's Restaurant*, which is also trying to feel its way. I think we (from this point I include myself, because I share these attitudes) are desperate for some sensibility in movies, and that's why we're so moved by the struggle toward discovery in *Alice's Restaurant*, despite how badly done the film is. I think one would have to lie to say *Alice's Restaurant* is formally superior to the big new Western *Butch Cassidy and the Sundance Kid*. In formal terms, neither is very good. But *Alice's Restaurant* is a groping attempt to express something, and *Butch Cassidy* is a glorified vacuum. Movies can be enjoyed for the *quality* of their confusions and failures, and that's the only way you can enjoy some of them now. Emotionally, I stayed with Penn during the movie, even though I thought that many of the scenes in it were inept or awful, and that several of the big set pieces were expendable (to put it delicately). But we're *for* him, and that's what carries the movie. Conceptually, it's unformed, with the director trying to discover his subject as well as its meaning and his own attitudes. And, maybe for the first time, there's an audience for American pictures which is willing to accept this.

Not every movie has to matter; generally we go hoping just to be relaxed and refreshed. But because most of the time we come out slugged and depressed, I think we care far more now about the reach for something. We've simply spent too much time at movies made by people who didn't enjoy themselves and who didn't respect themselves or us, and we rarely enjoy ourselves at their movies anymore. They're big catered affairs, and we're humiliated to be there among the guests. I look at the list of movies playing, and most of them I genuinely just can't face, because the odds are so strong that they're going to be the same old insulting failed entertainment, and, even though I may have had more of a bellyful than most people, I'm sure this isn't just my own reaction. Practically everybody I know feels the same way. This may seem an awfully moral approach, but it comes out of surfeit and aesthetic disgust. There's something vital to enjoyment which we haven't been getting much of. Playfulness? Joy? Perhaps even honest cynicism? What's missing isn't anything as simple as talent; there's lots of talent, even on TV. But the business conditions of moviemaking have soured the spirit of most big movies. That's why we may be willing to go along with something as strained and self-conscious as *Alice's Restaurant*. And it's an immensely hopeful sign that the audience isn't derisive, that it wishes the movie well.

■   ■   ■

All this is, in a way, part of the background of why, after a few minutes of *Butch Cassidy and the Sundance Kid,* I began to get that depressed feeling, and, after a half hour, felt rather offended. We all know how the industry men think: they're going to try to make "now" movies when now is already then, they're going to give us orgy movies and plush skinflicks, and they'll be trying to feed youth's paranoia when youth will, one hopes, have cast it off like last year's beads. This Western is a spinoff from *Bonnie and Clyde;* it's about two badmen (Paul Newman and Robert Redford) at the turn of the century, and the script, by William Goldman, which has been published, has the prefatory note "Not that it matters, but most of what follows is true." Yet everything that follows rings false, as that note does.

It's a facetious Western, and everybody in it talks comical. The director, George Roy Hill, doesn't have the style for it. (He doesn't really seem to have the style for anything, yet there is a basic decency and intelligence in his work.) The tone becomes embarrassing. Maybe we're supposed to be charmed when this affable, loquacious outlaw Butch and his silent, "dangerous" buddy Sundance blow up trains, but how are we supposed to feel when they go off to Bolivia, sneer at the country, and start shooting up poor Bolivians? George Roy Hill is a "sincere" director, but Goldman's script is jocose; though it reads as if it might play, it doesn't, and probably this isn't just Hill's fault. What can one do with dialogue like Paul Newman's Butch saying, "Boy, I got vision. The rest of the world wears bifocals"? It must be meant to be sportive, because it isn't witty and it isn't dramatic. The dialogue is all banter, all throwaways, and that's how it's delivered; each line comes out of nowhere, coyly, in a murmur, in the dead sound of the studio. (There is scarcely even an effort to supply plausible outdoor resonances or to use sound to evoke a sense of place.) It's impossible to tell whose consciousness the characters are supposed to have. Here's a key passage from the script—the big scene when Sundance's girl, the schoolteacher Etta (Katharine Ross), decides to go to Bolivia with the outlaws:

> ETTA (*For a moment, she says nothing. Then, starting soft, building as she goes*): I'm twenty-six, and I'm single, and I teach school, and that's the bottom of the pit. And the only excitement I've ever known is sitting in the room with me now. So I'll go with you, and I won't whine, and I'll sew your socks and stitch you when you're wounded, and anything you ask of me I'll do, except one thing: I won't watch you die. I'll miss that scene if you don't mind . . . (*Hold on Etta's lovely face a moment—*)

It's clear who is at the bottom of the pit, and it isn't those frontier schoolteachers, whose work was honest.

Being interested in good movies doesn't preclude enjoying many kinds of crummy movies, but maybe it does preclude acceptance of this enervated, sophisticated business venture—a movie made by those whose talents are a little high for mere commercial movies but who don't break out of the mold. They're trying for something more clever than is attempted in most commercial jobs, and it's all so archly empty—Conrad Hall's virtuoso cinematography providing constant in-and-out-of-focus distraction, Goldman's decorative little conceits passing for dialogue. It's all posh and josh, without any redeeming energy or crudeness. Much as I dislike the smugness of puritanism in the arts, after watching a put-on rape and Conrad Hall's *Elvira Madigan* lyric interlude (and to our own Mozart—Burt Bacharach) I began to long for something simple and halfway *felt*. If you can't manage genuine sophistication, you may be better off simple. And when you're as talented as these fellows, perhaps it's necessary to descend into yourself sometime and try to find out what you're doing—maybe, even, to risk banality, which is less objectionable than this damned waggishness.

Butch Cassidy will probably be a hit; it has a great title, and it has star appeal for a wide audience. Redford, who is personable and can act, is overdue for stardom, though it will be rather a joke if he gets it out of this nonacting role. Newman throws the ball to him often—that's really exactly what one feels he's doing—and is content to be his infectiously good-humored (one assumes) self. He plays the public image of himself (as an aging good guy), just as Arlo Guthrie plays himself as a moonchild. Yet, hit or no, I think what this picture represents is finished. Butch and Sundance will probably be fine for a TV series, which is what I mean by finished.

■   ■   ■

One can't just take the new cult movies head on and relax, because they're too confused. Intentions stick out, as in the thirties message movies, and you may be so aware of what's wrong with the movies while you're seeing them that you're pulled in different directions, but if you reject them because of the confusions, you're rejecting the most hopeful symptoms of change. Just when there are audiences who may be ready for something, the studios seem to be backing away, because they don't understand what these audiences want. The audiences themselves don't know, but they're looking for *something* at the movies. This transition into the seventies is maybe the most interesting as well as the most confusing period in American movie history, yet there's a real possibility that, because the tastes of the young audience are changing so fast, the already tottering studios will decide to minimize risks and gear production straight to the square audience and the networks. That square audience is far more alienated than the young one—so alienated that it isn't looking for *anything* at the movies.

The New Yorker, September 27, 1969

BOB & CAROL & TED & ALICE
WAITING FOR ORGY

Bob & Carol & Ted & Alice has been widely attacked in advance: it opened the New York Film Festival, and the *Times* has had at it three times already, calling it a "sniggery" movie, and the news magazines have been jumping on it, too. *Time* was outraged that it was chosen to open "a presumably serious film festival." If one laughs at it, as I did (and I didn't snigger), one may suspect either (a) that even as good an American commercial comedy as this is *too* American and *too* commercial for the kind of fusty film-festival thinking that splits movies into art versus entertainment or (b) that there is something about the film that bugs people. It's both, I think.

When I see those ads with the quote "You'll have to see this picture twice," I know it's the kind of picture I don't want to see once. It's practically a penance to sit through some of these movies, and a new Pasolini or a "late" Bresson lasts one a long time. The movie press has not suddenly become avant-garde; it's just embracing the European cultural values it feels safe with. European films have not struck out in any major new directions this year; they've been rather dull—which can hardly be said of American movies at this time. When one considers some of what has been urged on us as "art" this last year—all those films that *look* like art (*Teorema*)—it's clear that a commercial comedy doesn't fit into this framework of austere mortification of the audience. If you ever wanted to go see *Bob & Carol & Ted & Alice* again, it would be because it was funny, not because you didn't get it the first time. It's true it's not a work of depth that would yield up more with subsequent viewings, but it's almost schizophrenic for the movie critics to attack a movie for having just those entertaining qualities that drew them to movies in the first place. It's so damned easy to be cultured.

Bob & Carol & Ted & Alice is a slick, whorey movie, and the liveliest American comedy so far this year. It's unabashedly commercial, and in some ways it's the kind of commercial picture that succeeds with audiences by going just a little farther than they expect, but titillation is no longer easy, and this particular kind of titillation is so unconcealed that maybe it has earned the right to be called honestly comic. There is nothing hidden in this movie—the acrid commercial flavor is right there, out front. Because it's funny, and because it's marital-situation comedy and it's set in the middle-class southern California of so much tawdry Americana, it's easy to say this is DorisDayland, and those bothered by the acridity may use that as a way of putting the film down. Superficially, the picture looks like a Day, and the people live in the same style (they did in *The Graduate* also), but this movie is made up of what was left out of the optimistic Doris Day comedies. (What a perfect name. *Sui generis.*) This is the far side of middle-class marriage, after Doris Day fades out. The period is late 1969, when the concept of legal marriage is being undermined and the members of the middle class who are trying to be swingers are nervous—culturally uneasy about clinging to something square, and personally tantalized by thoughts of the sex possibilities they're missing. The movie works its way through cuteness and "sophistication" and out the other end of nowhere. It's tawdry, all right, but the tawdriness is *used*. This is the kind of movie in which a modern husband who has just had an affair comes home unexpectedly to find another man in bed with his wife and decides that the sensible new behavior is to have a friendly drink. This solution is hardly satisfactory; the tension is unresolved. The scene is badly played, but still it nags at one: Is there a better solution?

A sophisticated popular comedy isn't Hollywood's stock-in-trade anymore; the times are too volatile. This picture is a bit more unusual than it may seem, and it raises some of the problems that may plague actors in the next few years. Paul Mazursky and Larry Tucker who wrote *Bob & Carol & Ted & Alice,* also wrote last year's *I Love You, Alice B. Toklas!,* which had some very funny dialogue but was directed (by Hy Averback) in a loose scat style that didn't give the movie much distinction. Mazursky has directed this time, and the material takes on a far more self-aware aspect. The occasional attempts at visual effects (such as a sex fantasy on a plane) are disastrously shoddy, but Mazursky, directing his first picture, has done something very ingenious. He has developed a style from satiric improvisational revue theatre—he and Tucker were part of the Second City troupe—and from TV situation comedy, and, with skill and wit, has made this mixture work.

During the past three or four years, many directors have tried to put revue humor on film, and, except for some of the early comedy sequences in *The Graduate,* it has failed, painfully—as in *Luv, The Tiger Makes Out,* the Eleanor Bron-William Daniels bits of *Two for the Road,* parts of *Bedazzled,* the Elaine May role in *Enter Laughing, The President's Analyst,* and so on. Revue theatre is a form of actors' theatre; even when the material isn't worked up by the actors—even when it is written by a Murray Schisgal (or in England, transformed into more serious drama by Harold Pinter)—the meaning comes from the rhythm of clichés, defenses, and little verbal aggressions, and this depends on the pulse and the intuition of the performers. It would be as difficult to write down as dance notation. Typically, as in the Nichols-and-May routines, the satire is thin and the thinness is the essence of the joke. We laugh at the tiny, almost imperceptible hostilities that suddenly explode, because we recognize that we're tied up in knots about small issues more than about big ones, and that we don't lose our pretensions even when (or especially when) we are concerned about the big ones.

This style developed here (and in England) in the fifties, when college actors went on working together in cabarets, continuing and developing sophomoric humor. That word isn't used pejoratively; I *like* sophomoric college-revue humor, and one has only to contrast its topicality and freshness with the Joe Miller Jokebook world to understand why it swept the country. In revue, the very latest in interpersonal relations—the newest clichés and courtship rites and seduction techniques—could be polished to the point of satire almost overnight. Mort Sahl and the stand-up comics might satirize the political *them*, but cabaret, with its interacting couples, satirized *us*. We laugh at being nailed by these actors who are cartoons of us, all too easy to understand, and though there's a comic discomfort in listening to what our personal and social rituals might sound like if they were overheard, it's a comfortable form of theatre—the dishevelled American's form of light domestic comedy.

But it didn't work in the movies. A skit builds by the smallest of inflections, and each inflection becomes important because we construct the whole ambience from the performers—mainly from their voices. And that's what, in the past, killed this kind of acting on the screen: the performers did too much with voices and pauses, and when the director interrupted them with camera shifts and cuts, the performers lost their own rhythm and rapport. In relation to how it was being used, their acting was overdeveloped in a specialized way, and the result was, oddly, that they seemed ugly and rather grotesque and terribly stagy. And the milieu always felt wrong, because we didn't need it; instead of getting our bearings from the performers we looked at the sets and lost our bearings. This is still a problem in *Bob & Carol & Ted & Alice*—the houses the couples live in get in the way of our accepting the situations—but some of the other problems have been solved.

Mazursky has designed most of the picture in a series of sequences focussing on the actors, letting the rhythm of their interplay develop, and he has taken the series of revue sketches on the subject of modern marital stress and built them into a movie by using the format of situation comedy, with its recurrent synthetic crises. What is so surprising—and yet it should have been obvious—is that he has found useful dramatic elements in situation comedy. It's pleasant to stick to the same people throughout a movie, instead of wandering around and having the continuity broken into all the time, and it's relaxing to be in a form with controlled expectations. This TV format is probably the best and most straightforward way to make revue material work on film, and it gives Mazursky a few small miracles (largely from Elliott Gould and Dyan Cannon), but, as a result of the long scenes, there's almost no way to conceal the failures.

Revue theatre has attracted actors of a different kind from ordinary theatre; frequently they are actor-writer-directors, literary satirists as well as satirical actors, and since their acting is so close to directing, they frequently become directors or comedians, but few of them have really become big *actors*. The kind of acting they've learned to do—which is both more demanding and, in some areas, less demanding than conventional acting—is *different*, and a basic trouble with *Bob & Carol & Ted & Alice* is that Natalie Wood can't do it. The design of the film is for two contrasting marriages—one a "good" marriage (Robert Culp, as a documentary filmmaker, and Natalie Wood), the other a mismatch (Elliott Gould, as a lawyer, and Dyan

336

Cannon), yet a mismatch so recognizably common (she's bored and he's bewildered) that it's almost the typical perfect match. But there's no possibility of our believing in the good marriage. Natalie Wood doesn't seem to have any substance as a human being, so there's nothing at stake, as there would be with a fuller-dimensioned woman in the role. Her resources as an actress are skinny; she has nothing to draw upon but that same desperate anxiety and forced smile and agitation she's always drawn upon.

The whole area of screen acting is probably going to be a big can of worms in the next few years. We are already looking for closer identity between actor and role in many movies; we have become too acute about nuances (partly because of revue) to accept the iron-butterfly kind of star acting anymore. We never had the slightest illusion we were seeing Doris Day as she was offscreen, and that hardly concerned us. In the kind of acting now being required, it *does* concern us, partly because of nudity and sex scenes, the influence of non-actors in *cinéma-vérité* roles, and the effect of TV news and talk shows, but mainly because of a new interest in less structured and less stereotyped approaches to character than in past movies. I think it's almost impossible to watch *Bob & Carol & Ted & Alice* without wondering how much the actors are playing themselves. Natalie Wood is still doing what she was doing as a child—still telegraphing us that she's being cute and funny—and she's wrong. When she tries hard, she just becomes an agitated iron butterfly. An actress's armor becomes embarrassing when character armor is the subject of the movie—and it's the subject of this movie, as it has always been the basic subject of revue.

With this material—concerning how much people are hiding from themselves—we begin to ask questions about the actors, to wonder whether they are what they appear to be. The performances that work best force us to a speculative invasion of the privacy of the actors; what would have once seemed gossip is now central not only to the performance but to the conception itself. With the camera coming in closer and closer, the inescapable question is: Can you act it if you're *not* it? Playing the bitch who sets the mechanism of "Let's have an orgy" in motion, Dyan Cannon—who looks a bit like Lauren Bacall and a bit like Jeanne Moreau, but the wrong bits—is most effective (really brilliant), I think, just because you don't like her, and I don't mean simply the character she plays; we react to her in the way untutored people used to react to actors, identifying them with their roles. We don't think she's just playing a bitch. And, on the same basis, we *like* Gould—not just because of his performance but because of an assumption, which is probably false, but which this kind of acting imposes, that he is what he's playing. Culp, who has the most difficult role, is solidly competent, and yet he fails somewhat, because he is too much the conventional actor *type*—Robert Cummings crossed with Timothy Leary.

But there is something else in this movie that bothers people. I don't think it's because it's *conventional* that they're somewhat unnerved by it; it's because, though it *looks* conventional, it *isn't*, and it doesn't quite give them what they want. The press loved Woody Allen's *Take the Money and Run*—a limply good-natured little nothing of a comedy, soft as sneakers. And it would probably feel more comfortable with this if it were soft or if it *were* "sniggery"; then it could be put down more easily as just another commercial picture. Maybe, like Dyan Cannon in the movie, the press and the audience want an orgy—and think it's a cop-out when they don't get one. An orgy would be the simplest thing in the movie world to give us right now, but it wouldn't be consistent with the idea of this movie, which, as in revue, is the comedy of recognizing that we (those on the screen and we in the audience) are not earth-shakers or sexual new frontiersmen. This light domestic comedy no longer takes domesticity for granted, but after the characters begin to experiment sexually, they return for cover. Near the end, when the two couples go into one bedroom together, it's obvious that the movie could take a different turn—that if they went into two bedrooms instead of one, the cross-coupling would probably occur without any difficulty. But that would only *postpone* the return, or the movie would descend into romp and farce. The return makes perfect sense: they realize that they are about to go farther than they can handle, and they retreat to save something they still care about. Though the ending might have been better served by wit than by a "thoughtful" neo-Fellini walk, the point is clear. They need some home base and the safety of the old bourgeois traps. Forced to choose between decaying DorisDayland and Warhol Nowheresville, they go back to what is for them, if not the good life, at least the not-bad life.

Many people in the audience have probably done just what the people in the movie do (either before or after a little wife-swapping and a small orgy or two). Why, then, do they resent it in the film? I'll make the guess that the situations are so comically close to the people in the audience that they may reject the characters for doing what they themselves have done, because that retreat cuts them off from what they want to believe in. At the beginning, the film has some satirical passages on Esalen "encounter" techniques (satire that backfired because Natalie Wood looks as if the treatment might help her), and people around me became rather hostile—not just the young, who might be expected to, because the touching is very important to them (it's a form of "truth," of approaching without being afraid, of making non-aggressive, non-hostile, "human" contact), but older people, too, because they, too, are looking for healers. The atmosphere around me was as if the Church were being satirized before an audience of early Christians. In commercial terms, the opening, with its easy targets, may be a miscalculation, and it's loosely ambivalent—as if Mazursky and Tucker were unsure and were trying to play it safe. The audience reaction to the opening may be a clue to the later discomfort: People may be so desperate to be other than what they are that they resent a movie for dealing with bourgeois values even in disruption. They may consider these characters (so like themselves) not worthy even of comic attention. And they may resent still more the suggestion that an orgy *won't* expand their consciousness, and that they might risk losing something if they try everything. They don't believe they've *got anything.* The audience is still waiting for Godot, which in this context is salvation by orgy.

The New Yorker, October 4, 1969

HIGH SCHOOL

Movies sometimes connect with our memories in surprising ways. My vocabulary loosened up during my freshman year at Berkeley, and I was quite pleased when my mother remarked that the more educated I got the more I sounded like a truck driver. When I was a sophomore, a group of us went on a trip to Los Angeles, and our car broke down in Oxnard; we were huddled there in the garage at night when two garage mechanics got into an argument and started swearing at each other. As the rhythm of their fury and venom built up, those words that I had been so free with sounded hideous. I hadn't understood their function as swearwords—hadn't understood that they were meant to insult the person receiving them, that they were a way of degrading another person. That night at Oxnard came back when I saw Frederick Wiseman's *Law and Order* on N.E.T.: the police were cursed constantly by thieves and drunks. I had assumed that the police, coming from stricter and more religious backgrounds, didn't understand that college kids use the words in that liberated way that empties them of degradation or any real power; I hadn't considered that they hear that kind of talk so much they probably just can't stand it anymore. They're drowning in obscenity. College students are sometimes contemptuous of the cops for fearing *words,* but in the film those words really *are* weapons—often the *only* weapons of angry, frustrated people—and they're directed against the police all the time. *Law and Order* was the most powerful hour and a half of television that I've seen all year, and, since it won an Emmy, one might suppose that it would stir up interest in Wiseman's other films, but the New York Film Festival, which featured so many mindless forms of "artistic" moviemaking in the main auditorium, tossed some of the best new American pictures into the two-hundred-seat hall, and among them was Wiseman's *High School,* in its first New York showing.

There's a good deal to be said for finding your way to moviemaking—as most of the early directors did—after living for some years in the world and gaining some knowledge of life outside show business. We are beginning to spawn teen-age filmmakers who at twenty-five may have a brilliant technique but are as empty-headed as a Hollywood hack, and they will become the next generation of hacks, because they don't know anything except moviemaking. Wiseman is a law professor and urban planner turned film-maker, a muckraking investigative journalist who looks into American institutions with a camera and a tape recorder, and because he doesn't go in with naïve and limiting concepts, what he finds ties in with one's own experience.

Many of us grow to hate documentaries in school, because the use of movies to teach us something seems a cheat—a pill disguised as candy—and documentaries always seem to be about something we're not interested in. But Wiseman's documentaries show what is left out of both fictional movies and standard documentaries that simplify for a purpose, and his films deal with the primary institutions of our lives: *Titicut Follies* (Bridgewater, an institution in which we lock away the criminally insane), *High School* (a high school in a large Eastern city), and *Law and Order* (the Kansas City police force). Television has been accustoming us to a horrible false kind of "involvement"; sometimes it seems that the only thing the news shows can think of is to get close to emotion. They shove a camera and a microphone in front of people in moments of stress and disaster and grief, and ram their equipment into any pores and cavities they can reach. Wiseman made comparable mistakes in *Titicut Follies,* but he learned better fast.

High School is so familiar and so extraordinarily evocative that a feeling of empathy with the students floods over us. How did we live through it? How did we keep any spirit? When you see a kid trying to make a phone call and being interrupted with "Do you have a pass to use the phone?" it all floods back—the low ceilings and pale-green walls of the basement where the lockers were, the constant defensiveness, that sense of always being in danger of breaking some pointless, petty rule. When since that time has one ever needed a pass to make a phone call? This movie takes one back to where, one discovers, time has stood still. Here is the girl humiliated for having worn a short dress to the Senior Prom, being told it was "offensive" to the whole class. Here it is all over again—the insistence that you be "respectful," and the teachers' incredible instinct for "disrespect," their antennae always extended for that little bit of reservation or irony in your tone, the tiny spark that you desperately need to preserve your *self*-respect. One can barely hear it in the way a boy says "Yes, sir" to the dean, but the dean, ever on the alert, snaps, "Don't give me that 'Yes, sir' business! . . . There's no sincereness behind it." Here, all over again, is the dullness of high-school education:

TEACHER: What on the horizon or what existed that forced labor to turn to collective bargaining? What was there a lack of?
GIRL: Communications?
TEACHER: Security, yes, communications, lack of security, concern for the job. The important thing is this, let's get to the beginning. First of all, there was the lack of security; second of all, there was a lack of communication. . . .

The same old pseudo-knowledge is used to support what the schools think is moral. The visiting gynecologist in a sex-education class lectures the boys:

> The more a fellow gets into bed with more different girls, the more insecure he is, and this shows up actually later in all the divorce statistics in America. . . . You can graph right on a graph, the more girls fellows got into bed with or vice-versa the higher the divorce rate, the greater the sexual inadequacy. . . .

And there's the beautiful military doubletalk when it's a question of a teacher's incompetence or unfairness. A boy protests a disciplinary action against him by a teacher, and after he has explained his innocence, the dean talks him into accepting the punishment "to establish that you can be a man and that you can take orders." The teachers are masters here; they're in a superior position for the only time in their lives, probably, and most of the petty tyrannies—like laying on the homework—aren't fully conscious. They justify each other's actions as a matter of course, and put the students in the wrong in the same indifferent way. They put a student down with "It's nice to be individualistic, but there are certain places to be individualistic," yet they never tell you where. How can one stand up against such bland authoritarianism? The teachers, crushing and processing, are the most insidious kind of enemy, the enemy with corrupt values who means well. The counsellor advising on college plans who says "You can have all your dream schools, but at the bottom you ought to have some college of last resort where you could be sure that you would go, if none of your dreams came through" certainly means to be realistic and helpful. But one can imagine what it must feel like to be a kid trudging off to that bottom college of last resort. There's a jolly good Joe of a teacher staging a fashion show who tells the girls, "Your legs are all too heavy. . . . Don't wear it too short; it looks miserable." And she's not wrong. But, given the beauty norms set up in this society, what are they to do? Cut off their legs? Emigrate? They're defeated from the legs up. Mediocrity and defeat sit in the offices and classrooms, and in those oppressive monitored halls.

We went through it all in order to graduate and be rid of passes forever, and once it was over we put it out of our minds, and here are the students still serving time until graduation, still sitting in class staring out the windows or watching the crawling hands of those ugly school clocks. So much of this education is part of an obsolete system of authority that broke down long ago, yet the teachers and administrators are still out there, persevering, "building character." *High School* seems an obvious kind of film to make, but as far as I know no one before has gone into an ordinary, middle-class, "good" (most of the students go to college) high school with a camera and looked around to see what it's like. The students are even more apathetic than we were. Probably the conflicts over the restrictions come earlier now—in junior high—and by high school the kids either are trying to cool it and get through to college or are just beaten down and sitting it out. We may have had a few teachers who really got us interested in something—it was one of the disappointments of the movie *Up the Down Staircase* that, treating this theme, it failed to be convincing—and, remembering our good luck, we could always say that even if a school was rotten, there were bound to be a few great teachers in it. This movie shows competent teachers and teachers who are trying their best but not one teacher who really makes contact in the way that means a difference in your life. The students are as apathetic toward the young English teacher playing and analyzing a Simon & Garfunkel record as toward the English teacher reciting "Casey at the Bat," and, even granted that as poetry there might not be much to choose between them—and perhaps Casey has the edge—still, one might think the students would, just as a *courtesy,* respond to the young teacher's attempt, the way one always gave the ingénue in the stock company a special round of applause. But it's very likely that high schools no longer *are* saved by live teachers, if hostility and cynicism and apathy set in right after children learn their basic skills. The students here sit on their hands even when a teacher tries. That's the only visible difference between this school and mine. I think we would have responded appreciatively to obvious effort, even if we thought the teacher was a jerk; these kids are beyond that. So the teachers are trapped, too. The teachers come off much worse than the police do in *Law and Order. High School* is a revelation because now that we see school from the outside, the teachers seem to give themselves away every time they open their mouths—and to be unaware of it.

At the end, the principal—a fine-looking woman—holds up a letter from a former student, on stationery marked "U.S.S. Okinawa," and reads it to the faculty:

> I have only a few hours before I go. Today I will take a plane trip from this ship. I pray that I'll make it back but it's all in God's hands now. You see, I am going with three other men. We are going to be dropped behind the D.M.Z. (the Demilitarized Zone). The reason for telling you this is that all my insurance money will be given for that scholarship I once started but never finished, if I don't make it back. I am only insured for $10,000. Maybe it could help someone. I have been trying to become a Big Brother in Vietnam, but it is very hard to do. I have to write back and forth to San Diego, California, and that takes time. I only hope that I am good enough to become one. God only knows. My personal family usually doesn't understand me.... They say: "Don't you value life? Are you crazy?" My answer is: "Yes. But I value all the lives of South Vietnam and the free world so that they and all of us can live in peace." Am I wrong? If I do my best and believe in what I do, believe that what I do is right—that is all I can do.... Please don't

say anything to Mrs. C. She would only worry over me. I am not worth it. I am only a body doing a job. In closing I thank everyone for what they all have done for me.

And the principal comments, "Now, when you get a letter like this, to me it means that we are very successful at [this] high school. I think you will agree with me."

It's a great scene—a consummation of the educational process we've been watching: They are successful at turning out bodies to do a job. Yet it's also painfully clear that the school must have given this soldier more kindness and affection than he'd ever had before. There must be other students who respond to the genuine benevolence behind the cant and who are grateful to those who labor to turn them into men. For those students, this schooling in conformity is successful.

Wiseman extends our understanding of our common life the way novelists used to—a way largely abandoned by the modern novel and left to the journalists but not often picked up by them. What he's doing is so simple and so basic that it's like a rediscovery of what we knew, or should know. We often want more information about the people and their predicaments than he gives, but this is perhaps less a criticism of Wiseman's method than it is a testimonial to his success in making us care about his subjects. With fictional movies using so little of our shared experience, and with the big TV news "specials" increasingly using that idiot "McLuhanite" fragmentation technique that scrambles all experience—as if the deliberate purpose were to make us indifferent to the life around us—it's a good sign when a movie sends us out wanting to know more and feeling that there is more to know. Wiseman is probably the most sophisticated intelligence to enter the documentary field in recent years.

The New Yorker, October 18, 1969

Z

Z is almost intolerably exciting—a political thriller that builds up so much tension that you'll probably feel all knotted up by the time it's over. The young director Costa-Gavras, using everything he knows to drive home his points as effectively as possible, has made something very unusual in European films—a political film with a purpose and, at the same time, a thoroughly commercial film. Z is undoubtedly intended as a political act, but it never loses emotional contact with the audience. It derives not from the traditions of the French film but from American gangster movies and prison pictures and anti-Fascist melodramas of the forties (*Cornered, Crossfire, Brute*

Force, All the King's Men, Edge of Darkness, The Cross of Lorraine, et al.), and, like those pictures, it has a basically simple point of view. America stopped making this kind of melodrama (melodrama was always the chief vehicle for political thought in our films) during the McCarthy era, so Costa-Gavras has the advantage of bringing back a popular kind of movie and of bringing it back in modern movie style. *Z* has been photographed by Raoul Coutard, Godard's cameraman, in Eastmancolor used in a very strong, almost robust way, and although the photography is perhaps a little too self-consciously dynamic and, at times, not as hard-focussed as it might be, the searching, active style doesn't allow you to get away. Remember when the movie ads used to say, "It will knock you out of your seat"? Well, *Z* damn near does.

There hasn't been an exciting anti-Fascist suspense film around for a long time, and the subject of *Z* is so good that the audience is not likely to resent the use of melodramatic excitement the way it would now if the film were anti-Communist, like those Hollywood films of the early fifties in which our boy Gregory Peck was ferreting out Communist rats. *Z* is based on the novel by the Greek exile Vassili Vassilikos about the assassination of Gregorios Lambrakis, in Salonika, in May, 1963. Lambrakis, it may be recalled, was a professor of medicine at the University of Athens who was also a legislator and a spokesman for peace. He was struck down by a delivery truck as he left a peace meeting—a murder planned to look like an accident. The investigation of his death uncovered such a scandalous network of corruption and illegality in the police and in the government that the leader of the opposition party, George Papandreou, became Premier. But in April, 1967, the military coup d'état overturned the legal government. *Z* reënacts the murder and the investigation in an attempt to demonstrate how the mechanics of Fascist corruption may be hidden under the mask of law and order; it is a brief on the illegality of the present Greek government.

Jorge Semprun, the Spanish writer, who worked on the screenplay and wrote the dialogue, has said, "Let's not try to reassure ourselves: this type of thing doesn't only happen elsewhere, it happens everywhere." Maybe, but not necessarily in the same way, though some Americans are sure to take the conspiracy of *Z* as applying to our political assassinations, too. This movie has enough layers of reference without anyone's trying to fit the American political assassinations into it; our freaky loners, on the loose in a large, heterogeneous country, are part of a less tightly structured, more volatile situation. It's ironic that what apparently did happen in the Lambrakis affair should resemble the conspiracy fantasies of Mark Lane and other Americans about the death of President Kennedy. And to see how the network of crime and politics works to conceal the assassination in *Z* is aesthetically satisfying. One can easily recognize the psychological attraction, for both left and right, of spinning conspiratorial systems that make things grand and orderly. (*Z* opens with a witty treatment of right-wing paranoia.)

Z could not, of course, be made in Salonika; it was shot in Algeria, in

French, as a French-Algerian co-production. The director, Costa-Gavras, is a Greek exile. (He was a teen-age ballet dancer in Greece before going to France, where he studied filmmaking and made his first picture, *The Sleeping Car Murder.*) The score, by Mikis Theodorakis, who is now under house arrest in Greece (where his music is banned), is said to have been smuggled out. Yves Montand, who is the Lambrakis figure here, was recently seen as the Spanish hero of *La Guerre Est Finie,* which Semprun, an exile from Spain, also wrote, and other actors from the Spanish setting turn up here, too. The Algerian locations, being the sites of actual tortures and demonstrations, add their own resonances; the hospital where injured men may be mistreated instead of treated plays its former role. The atmosphere is thus full of echoes, and the movie—consciously, I think—reactivates them. The subject touches off our recollections of Greece, of Algeria, of Spain, which combine to make us feel, "Yes—this is the way it happens," and to evoke images of and fears about all rightist terrorism.

On the one hand, there are the weak and corrupt and degenerate, the bullies and criminals—in a word, the Fascists. On the other, there are the gentle, intelligent, honorable pacifists—in a word, humanitarians. But Costa-Gavras gets by with most of this, because, despite our knowledge that he's leaning on us, he has cast the actors so astutely and kept them so busy that they miraculously escape being stereotypes. Some of them—particularly those who play the right-wing leaders, such as Pierre Dux in the role of a general—manage to suggest more than one notorious political figure. The cast of famous names and faces from the confused, combined past of many other movies forms a familiar, living background. I'm not sure exactly how Costa-Gavras has accomplished it, but in this movie—in contrast to so many other movies—the fact that we vaguely know these people works to his advantage, and enables him to tell the story very swiftly. It does not surprise us that François Périer, as the public prosecutor, is weak; that Renato Salvatori enjoys hitting people; that the magnificent Irene Papas is a suffering widow; that Charles Denner is half-Jewish; that Jean-Louis Trintignant is civilized and intelligent; and so on. All their earlier make-believe characters have merged in our memories; by now, when we see these actors they seem like people we actually used to know. I have sometimes found myself nodding at someone on the street before I realized that that was no old friend, it was David Susskind. There is the same sort of acquaintance with these actors, whom we have come to take for granted, and the ambience of known people seems to authenticate the case.

Not all the elements are convincing. The staging of the crowd at the peace rally and of the police lines surrounding it doesn't feel right; it's confusing that the leader who dies appears to be beaten less than a man who survives; the motives of one of the assassins, who turns himself in, are obscure. Marcel Bozzufi, the actor playing this assassin, gives the most flamboyant performance in the film; it's enjoyable, because the movie needs to be lifted out of its documentary style from time to time, yet you are as much aware of Bozzufi's performance—even though it's a good one—as you were in *Open City* when the Gestapo chief came on faggy. There are scenes, such as Georges Geret acting a shade too comic with an ice pack, and Magali Noel being excessively vicious as his vicious sister, that are too much in the standard Jules Dassin-Edward Dmytryk tradition. And, as in the Hollywood forties, the martyred man is such a perfect non-denominational Good Man—like Victor in *Casablanca*—that one never really understands his politics or why the police and the military want to get rid of him. This is an ironic element in the book, where a possible explanation is offered—that the Fascists were afraid not of the left but of liberals, like this man, who were beginning to coöperate with the Communists. In the movie, though, we get the impression that this pure peacenik-liberal and his friends *are* the left and that they are mistaken for Communists (who probably don't exist at all) by the paranoid right.

But the pace, the staccato editing, the strong sense of forward movement in the storytelling, and that old but almost unfailingly effective melodramatic technique of using loud music to build up the suspense for the violent sequences put so much pressure on you that these details don't detract much. There is a serious flaw at the end, however, where the wrap-up comes too fast. All the way through, *Z* stays so close to the action that it doesn't explain the larger context, and by the end we have been battered so much that we want to understand more, so that we won't have been riding this roller coaster just for the thrills. The explanations of what happened to whom and how this incident precipitated the change in government, and then the reversals of fortune after the military coup, go by at dizzying speed, and this is a psychological miscalculation. We have an almost physical need for synthesis from a movie as powerful as this. We want to know who was protected by the new rightist regime and who was sacrificed; we want to see the larger political meaning of the events. We don't want just to use the film masochistically, to feed our worst fears or to congratulate ourselves for being emotionally exhausted.

In a thriller, the director's job is to hold you in his grip and keep squeezing you to react the way he wants you to, and Costa-Gavras does his job efficiently—in fact, sensationally. Is it valid, morally, to turn actual political drama—in this case, political tragedy—into political melodrama, like *Z*? I honestly don't know. The techniques of melodrama are not those of art, but if we accept them when they're used on trivial, fabricated stories (robberies, spy rings, etc.) merely to excite us, how can we reject them when the filmmakers attempt to use them to expose social evils and to dramatize political issues? Yet there is an aesthetic discrepancy when the methods are not worthy of the subject; when coercive, manipulative methods are used on serious subjects, we feel a discomfort that we don't feel when the subjects are trivial. It's one of the deep contradictions in movies that in what should be a great popular, democratic art form ideas of any kind seem to reach the mass audience only by squeezing it. I anticipate that some people may ask,

"What's the problem? The movie is telling the truth." And others may say, "Whether it's accurate or not, it's convincing, and that's all a critic need fret about." Neither of these arguments clears away my basic uneasiness about the use of loaded melodramatic techniques, particularly now, when they can be so effectively blended with new semi-documentary methods to produce the illusion of current history caught by the camera. Given the genre, however, the men who made this film have been intelligent and restrained. I don't think Costa-Gavras ever uses violence except to make you hate violence, and such humanitarianism in filmmaking is becoming rare.

Melodrama works so well on the screen, and when it works against the present Greek military government it's hard to think ill of it. People will say of the moviemakers not that they're "laying it on" but that they're "laying it on the line." The truth is, they're doing both. Z is a hell of an exciting movie, and it carries you along, though when it's over and you've caught your breath you know perfectly well that its techniques of excitation could as easily be used by a smart Fascist filmmaker, if there were one (fortunately, there isn't), against the left or the center.

The New Yorker, December 13, 1969

M*A*S*H
BLESSED PROFANITY

M*A*S*H is a marvellously unstable comedy, a tough, funny, and sophisticated burlesque of military attitudes that is at the same time a tale of chivalry. It's a sick joke, but it's also generous and romantic—an erratic, episodic film, full of the pleasures of the unexpected. I think it's the closest an American movie has come to the kind of constantly surprising mixture in *Shoot the Piano Player*, though M*A*S*H moves so fast that it's over before you have time to think of comparisons. While it's going on, you're busy listening to some of the best overlapping comic dialogue ever recorded. The picture has so much spirit that you keep laughing—and without discomfort, because all the targets *should* be laughed at. The laughter is at the horrors and absurdities of war, and, specifically, at people who flourish in the military bureaucracy. The title letters stand for Mobile Army Surgical Hospital; the heroes, played by Donald Sutherland and Elliott Gould, are combat surgeons patching up casualties a few miles from the front during the Korean war. They do their surgery in style, with humor; they're hip Galahads, saving lives while ragging the military bureaucracy. They are so quick to react to bull—and in startling, unpredictable ways—that the comedy is, at times, almost a poetic fantasy. There's a surreal innocence about the movie; though the setting makes it seem a "black" comedy, it's a cheery

347

"black" comedy. The heroes win at everything. It's a modern kid's dream of glory: Holden Caulfield would, I think, approve of them. They're great surgeons, athletes, dashing men of the world, sexy, full of noblesse oblige, but ruthless to those with pretensions and lethal to hypocrites. They're so good at what they do that even the military brass admires them. They're winners in the war with the Army.

War comedies in the past have usually been about the little guys who foul things up and become heroes by accident (Chaplin in *Shoulder Arms,* Danny Kaye in *Up in Arms*). In that comedy tradition, the sad-sack recruit is too stupid to comprehend military ritual. These heroes are too smart to put up with it. Sutherland and Gould are more like an updated version of Edmund Lowe's and Victor McLaglen's Sergeant Quirt and Captain Flagg from *What Price Glory* and *The Cockeyed World*—movies in which the heroes retain their personal style and their camaraderie in the midst of blood and muck and the general insanity of war. One knows that though what goes on at this surgical station seems utterly crazy, it's only a small distortion of actual wartime situations. The pretty little helicopters delivering the bloody casualties are a surreal image, all right, but part of the authentic surrealism of modern warfare. The jokes the surgeons make about their butchershop work are a form of plain talk. The movie isn't naïve, but it isn't nihilistic, either. The surgery room looks insane and is presented as insane, but as the insanity in which we must preserve the values of sanity and function as sane men. An incompetent doctor is treated as a foul object; competence is one of the values the movie respects—even when it is demonstrated by a nurse (Sally Kellerman) who is a pompous fool. The heroes are always on the side of decency and sanity—that's why they're contemptuous of the bureaucracy. They are heroes *because* they're competent and sane and gallant, and in this insane situation their gallantry takes the form of scabrous comedy. The Quirt and Flagg films were considered highly profane in their day, and I am happy to say that *M*A*S*H,* taking full advantage of the new permissive rating system, is blessedly profane. I've rarely heard four-letter words used so exquisitely well in a movie, used with such efficacy and glee. I salute *M*A*S*H* for its contribution to the art of talking dirty.

The profanity, which is an extension of adolescent humor, is central to the idea of the movie. The silliness of adolescents—compulsively making jokes, seeing the ridiculous in everything—is what makes sanity possible here. The doctor who rejects adolescent behavior flips out. Adolescent pride in skills and games—in mixing a Martini or in devising a fishing lure or in golfing—keeps the men from becoming maniacs. Sutherland and Gould, and Tom Skerritt, as a third surgeon, and a lot of freakishly talented new-to-movies actors are relaxed and loose in their roles. Their style of acting underscores the point of the picture, which is that people who aren't hung up by pretensions, people who are loose and profane and have some empathy—people who can joke about anything—can function, and maybe even do something useful, in what may appear to be insane circumstances.

There's also a lot of slapstick in the movie, some of it a little like *Operation Mad Ball,* a fifties service comedy that had some great moments but was still tied to a sanctimonious approach to life and love. What holds the disparate elements of *M*A*S*H* together in the precarious balance that is the movie's chief charm is a free-for-all, throwaway attitude. The picture looks as if the people who made it had a good time, as if they played with it and improvised and took some chances. It's elegantly made, and yet it doesn't have that overplanned rigidity of so many Hollywood movies. The cinematography, by Harold E. Stine, is very fine—full of dust and muddy olive-green tones; it has immediacy and the clarity possible in Panavision. The editing and the sound engineering are surprisingly quick-witted. When the dialogue overlaps, you hear just what you should, but it doesn't seem all worked out and set; the sound seems to bounce off things so that the words just catch your ear. The throwaway stuff isn't really thrown away; it all helps to create the free, graceful atmosphere that sustains the movie and keeps it consistently funny. The director, Robert Altman, has a great feel for low-keyed American humor. With the help of Ring Lardner, Jr.'s, script (from a novel by a combat surgeon), Altman has made a real sport of a movie which combines traditional roustabout comedy with modern attitudes. As in other good comedies, there's often a mixture of what seems perfectly straight stuff and what seems incredible fantasy, and yet when we try to say which is which we can't. *M*A*S*H* affects us on a bewildering number of levels, like the Radio Tokyo versions of American songs on the camp loudspeaker system. All this may sound more like a testimonial than a review, but I don't know when I've had such a good time at a movie. Many of the best recent American movies leave you feeling that there's nothing to do but get stoned and die, that that's your proper fate as an American. This movie heals a breach in American movies; it's hip but it isn't hopeless. A surgical hospital where the doctors' hands are lost in chests and guts is certainly an unlikely subject for a comedy, but I think *M*A*S*H* is the best American war comedy since sound came in, and the sanest American movie of recent years.

The New Yorker, January 24, 1970

TROPIC OF CANCER

Joseph Strick's movie version of Henry Miller's *Tropic of Cancer* is an entertaining little sex comedy—a trifling series of vignettes and sex fantasies about Americans abroad, with bits of Miller's language rolling out, happy and bawdy. The movie is so much less than the book that it almost seems deliberately intended to reduce Henry Miller—probably the funniest American writer since Mark Twain—to pipsqueak size. I'm sure this isn't deliberate, however. Having seen several Strick adaptations by now (Genet's *The Balcony* and Joyce's *Ulysses* preceded *Tropic of Cancer* to the block), I think the diminution is an all but inevitable result of Strick's methods. He adapts "daring" literary classics the way a Broadway playwright adapts a successful Parisian farce; that is, he picks out the scenes and lines and characters he thinks will travel (to the movie medium). Since he gives no evidence of independent imagination and doesn't invent, his adaptations can be called "faithful" to their sources. Though Strick's approach hasn't changed, his *Tropic of Cancer* doesn't have the respectful library worminess of his flat, unfunny *Ulysses;* that was really a sobering experience. At least, this movie of *Tropic of Cancer*—careless and slipshod though it is—makes one laugh, and, unlike his *Ulysses,* it won't be mistaken for a classic. (I have already heard *Tropic of Cancer* panned by a television reviewer as a "filthy picture." That probably means he had a good time at it.) I enjoyed the movie and I think others will, too, though there's something rather tacky and second-hand about it that prevents us from laughing very deeply. One could hardly guess from this thin trickle of jokes that Henry Miller is the closest an American has come to Rabelais. It's rather discouraging to read in *Variety,* "The fault, however, may not be Strick's at all, because, stripping away the once-shocking dialogue which formerly made 'criminals' out of many a returning American tourist, what is there left? A few philosophical truisms, little more. This wouldn't be the first film to show up an established book writer." I have an uncomfortable feeling that the movie may have come out at a time when some members of the press are eager to prove that they draw the line *somewhere,* so this harmlessly amusing movie (and the sublimely funny book it derives from) may take an unjustified trouncing.

The movie doesn't begin to suggest the American tradition that Miller belongs to—or, more exactly, belonged to, because it is by discounting his work after the thirties that one can clearly see him as the link between *Leaves of Grass* and the beats, and, of course, as the precursor of Mailer. Since the movie doesn't bother to keep the book in its period, Miller loses his place in history and, with it, his originality. We lamented the time change in *Ulysses,* yet had to forgive it, because we recognized the difficulty and expense of re-creating Dublin as it was in 1904, but there's no good excuse in this case. Moviemakers who modernize books usually say that the period doesn't matter, that the work is "universal," but what makes Miller's book "universal" is that it is the story of the bum as writer at a particular period, which made him a particular kind of bum. Earlier or later, he might have been a thief or a professor; in his time, he was the Joe Gould who wrote. Taken out of the bohemian Depression milieu of rootless Russian and American expatriates scrounging around Paris in the early thirties, the anecdotes are no longer parts of life stories. They don't connect with anything; they're just small jokes. Because American moochers abroad are younger now, the characters all seem tired and over-age, and we never really know what these people are doing there. When the story is made timeless, the characters are out of nowhere, and the author-hero is not discovering a new kind of literary freedom in self-exposure, he's just a dirty not-so-young man hanging around the tourist spots of Paris. Strick tosses in so many starts of parades and tourist views that at times the movie feels like a travelogue (and one that isn't particularly well shot, either); luckily, the fast edit keeps the action from sagging.

George Orwell said that Miller treated English as "a spoken language, but spoken *without fear,*" and Orwell was referring not just to the fact that Miller's language rode right over the taboos but to the fact that it was "without fear of rhetoric or of the unusual or poetical word" and was "a flowing, swelling prose, a prose with rhythms in it." One hears Miller's prose as one reads him; in the early forties, when a friend of mine got hold of a smuggled-in copy of *Tropic of Cancer,* our immediate impulse was to read him aloud. But when that same prose is used in the film as a voice-over narration, it doesn't have the drive of common speech, it has the static fake poetry of cultivated literary language. Somehow, Strick has performed a reverse miracle—a feat like turning bread into stones.

When I saw the movie and started to think about the book again, I realized that I remembered it filtered through the Orwell essay "Inside the Whale." Orwell clarified the feelings we had about Miller; in a sense, he authenticated our excitement, not just by agreeing with us but by helping us to understand why we felt as we did. *Tropic of Cancer* is now easily available for ninety-five cents, but it comes with an introduction explaining enthusiastically, "If one had to type him [Miller] one might call him a Wisdom writer, Wisdom literature being a type of literature which lies between literature and scripture; it is poetry only because it rises above literature and because it sometimes ends up in bibles." This was not what drew us to Miller—Wisdom literature is what I can do without. Miller's later writing, full of boozy mysticism about his creativity and lyrical bulling about his sexual prowess, is what Orwell anticipated in 1940 (there was already plenty of evidence) when he said Miller might "descend into unintelligibility, or into charlatanism." *Tropic of Cancer* had a liberating spirit, because it seemed *totally* without hypocrisy. This basic appeal of the book doesn't emerge in the movie, owing to something so obvious one might not think of it. In the book, Miller sees friends in terms of the possible meal or bed he can cadge from them, women in terms of their sexual possibilities. Miller seems to bring us closer to "reality," seems to bring art closer to truth. But when we're reading him we don't think of his sexual hyperbole as objective description; we don't assume, for example, that all the women Miller meets are sexy sluts visibly panting for what he can give them. In the movie, however, Strick has made the outer circumstances correspond to the inner vision. This disintegrates the meanings; the levels of comedy collapse, and the narrator-hero's character collapses, too. In the book, the hero is amazing because he takes such joy in the diversity of possible pleasures; one imagines him as a mild little man with all-embracing tastes, a man eager to try whatever he can get, being excited by even the most unlikely ladies. In the movie, no eye for hidden possibilities is necessary. Joseph Strick's fantasy life being more limited than Henry Miller's, the women are the same bundles of lust that they are in the dull porny pix all over town. Not only are they the same easily available and badly used type, they're nearly all around the same age.

The whole movie lacks contrasts, depth, surprises. It succeeds best with two characters, Fillmore (James Callahan), whose essential American innocence is really lovely, and Carl (David Bauer), who has a sizable discrepancy between his surface character and what we see of his self-deceptions and lies. But Miller, one of the great characters in American literature—Huck Finn as a starving expatriate—is just a straight man for Fillmore and Carl. Considering that Rip Torn is almost completely wrong for the role of Miller—that he's cast against his usual type, and even against his own physical tensions—he does quite well. Miller the hero of the book is a joyful coward who will always sneak away rather than face an unpleasant scene. Torn is a tight actor whose face can split in a mean grin or a satyr's crooked smile. Miller needs not a satyr's smile but the satyr's soul of an ordinary man. Torn manages to kill the hostility that had become his stock in trade, and he's quite amiable, but he is never really loose or passive or relaxed, never the hero whose heroism is his acceptance of whatever comes his way, never really *friendly*. And that may be another reason the narration—which is about openness to experience—sounds so phony.

With the actual Henry Miller available, the director couldn't think of anything to do with him but to plunk him into a shot, just standing in front of a church. The poverty of imagination represented by that shot haunts me. I've been torturing myself thinking of the ways that Strick would probably use other authors if they were around. If he made a film of *Hamlet,* he might stuff Shakespeare into a seat at the Globe watching the performance; in his *Don Quixote,* Cervantes could be planted among the guests dining at an inn; and so on.

The New Yorker, March 7, 1970

FELLINI SATYRICON
FELLINI'S "MONDO TRASHO"

Fellini Satyricon uses the pre-Christian Roman world of debauchery during the time of Nero as an analogue of the modern post-Christian period. Like Cecil B. De Mille, who was also fond of pagan infernos, Fellini equates sexual "vice" with apocalypse; in *La Dolce Vita* he used the orgies of modern Rome as a parallel to ancient Rome, and now he reverses the analogy to make the same point. The idea that sticks out in every direction from Fellini Satyricon is that man without a belief in God is a lecherous beast. I think it's a really bad movie—a terrible movie—but Fellini has such intuitive rapport with the superstitious child in the adult viewer that I imagine it will be a considerable success. If it were put to members of the foreign-film audience rationally, probably few of them would identify the problems in the world today with fornication and licentiousness, or with the loss of faith in a divine authority. But when people at the movies are shown an orgiastic world of human beasts and monsters it's easy for them to fall back upon the persistent cliché that godlessness is lawlessness. De Mille, whose specialty was also the photogenic demonstration that modern immorality resembles the hedonism of declining Rome, used to satisfy the voyeuristic needs of the God-abiding by showing them what they were missing by being good and then soothe them by showing them the terrible punishments they escaped by being good. Fellini is not a sanctimonious manipulator of that kind; he makes fantasy extravaganzas out of tabloid sensationalism, but he appears to do it from emotional conviction, or, perhaps more exactly, from a master entertainer's feeling for the daydreams of the audience. He seems to draw upon something in himself that many people respond to as being profound, possibly because it has been long buried in them. When he brings it out, they think he is a great artist.

Fellini's pagans are freaks—bloated or deformed, or just simulated freaks with painted faces and protruding tongues. This is not the first time Fellini has used freaks in a movie; he has been using them, though in smaller numbers, to represent mystery and depravity all along, and especially since La Dolce Vita. Often they were people made up freakishly, as if in his oddly sophisticated-naïve eyes decadence were a wig and a heavy makeup job. His homosexual boys with gold dust in their hair were the "painted women" of naughty novels. It's the most simple-minded and widespread of all attitudes toward sin—identical with De Mille's. And so it wasn't surprising that some enthusiasts of La Dolce Vita took it as "a lesson to us"—a lesson that Rome fell because of high living and promiscuity, and we would, too. The labors of Gibbon and other historians never really permeated people's minds the way banalities about retribution for sin did. The freak show of Fellini Satyricon is a grotesque interpretation of paganism, yet I think many people in the audience will accept it without question. When we were children, we may have feared people with physical defects, assuming that they were frightening to look at because they were bad. In our fairy tales, it was the ugly witches who did wicked deeds, and didn't we pick up the idea that if we were good we would be beautiful but if we did forbidden things it would show in our faces? Some of us probably thought that depravity caused deformity; at the most superstitious level, ugliness was God's punishment for disobedience. Many of us have painfully learned to overcome these superstitions, and yet the buried feelings can be easily touched. Fellini's popular strength probably comes from primitive elements such as these in a modern style that enables audiences to respond as if the content were highly sophisticated. Perhaps the style enables some viewers to think that the primitive fantasies are Jungian, or whatever, and so are somehow raised to the status of art. But there is no evidence that Fellini is using them consciously, or using them *against* their original impact; they're not even fully brought to light. In Fellini's films, buried material isn't jabbed at and released in obscene jokes, as in Buñuel's films. Our primitive fears are tapped and used just as they are by a punishing parent or an opportunistic schoolteacher who's unaware of what he's doing—except that Fellini does it more playfully.

Like a naughty Christian child, Fellini thinks it's a ball to be a pagan, but a naughty ball, a *bad* one, which can't really be enjoyed. In *La Dolce Vita,* Fellini's hero was a society reporter who got caught up in the life of the jaded rich international party set; in *8½,* the hero was a movie director who lived out the public fantasy of what a big movie director's life is like—a big, swirling party; in *Juliet of the Spirits,* the hero was some sort of official greeter and partygiver whose wife dreamed of fruity, balletistic parties. In *Fellini Satyricon* the party scenes are no longer orgiastic climaxes. Fellini uses Petronius and other classic sources as the basis for a movie that is one long orgy of eating, drinking, cruelty, and copulation, and he goes all the way with his infatuation with transvestism, nymphomania, homosexuality, monsters.

Fellini Satyricon is *all* phantasmagoria, and though from time to time one may register a face or a set or an episode, for most of the film one has the feeling of a camera following people walking along walls. The fresco effect becomes monotonous and rather oppressive. It's almost as if the movie were a theatrically staged panorama, set on a treadmill. At first, while we're waiting for Fellini to get into the material and involve us, there's a sequence on an ancient stage which seems to promise that the movie will be a theatrical spectacle in the modern theatre-of-cruelty sense. But Fellini never does involve us: we seem to be at a stoned circus, where the performers go on and on whether we care or not. And though there's a story, we anticipate the end a dozen times—a clear sign that his episodic structuring has failed. Afterward, one recalls astonishingly little; there are many episodes and anecdotes, but, for a work that is visual if it is anything, it leaves disappointingly few visual impressions. Giton, the adolescent boy whom the two heroes battle over *is* memorable, because Max Born makes him a soft, smiling coquette full of sly promise; he's the complete whore, who takes pleasure in being used. The one charming episode is a sweetly amoral Garden of Eden sexual romp of the two heroes with a beautiful slave girl in a deserted house. Except for Giton's scenes and the slave girl's, and perhaps a shipboard-rape-and-marriage sequence, the picture isn't particularly sensual—though one assumes that carnality is part of its subject matter, and though Fellini has previously shown a special gift for carnal fantasies, as in the harem sequence of *8½.* Some of the set designs (by Danilo Donati) have a hypnotic quality—a ship like a sea serpent, a building with many stories and no front wall, so that we look into it as if it were a many-layered stage set—but the photography isn't very distinguished. It's a tired movie; during much of it, we seem to be moving past clumsily arranged groups and looking at people exhibiting their grossness or their abnormalities and sticking their tongues out at us. If you have ever been at a high-school play in which the children trying to look evil stuck their tongues out, you'll know exactly why there's so little magic in Fellini's apocalyptic extravaganza. It's full of people making faces, the way people do in home movies, and full of people staring at the camera and laughing and prancing around, the way they often do in 16-millimeter parodies of sex epics, like *Mondo Trasho*. Fellini's early films had a forlorn atmosphere, and there were bits of melancholy still drifting through *La Dolce Vita* and *8½;* if the people were lost, at least their sorrow gave them poetic suggestions of depth. There was little depth in *Juliet of the Spirits,* and there is none in this *Satyricon.* Perhaps Fellini thinks Christ had to come before people could have souls, but, lacking emotional depth, the movie is so transient that elaborate episodes like Trimalchio's banquet barely leave a trace in the memory.

Somewhere along the line—I think it happened in *La Dolce Vita*—Fellini gave in to the luxurious basking in sin that has always had such extraordinary public appeal. He became the new De Mille—a purveyor of the glamour of wickedness. And, though he doesn't appear in them, he became the star of his movies, which are presented as emanations of his imagination, his genius; he functioned as if the creative process had no relation to experience, to thought, or to other art. As this process has developed, the actors, and the characters, in his movies have become less and less important, so at *Fellini Satyricon* one hardly notices the familiar people in it—it's all a masquerade anyway, and they are made up to be hideous, and they come and go so fast—and one hardly knows or cares who the leads are, or which actor is Encolpius, which Ascyltus. (Encolpius, the blond Botticelli-angel face, is an English stage and TV actor named Martin Potter; Ascyltus, the goatish brunet, is Hiram Keller, an American who was in *Hair.* Encolpius and Ascyltus look as if they might be found among the boys cruising the Spanish Steps, and that is certainly right for the ancient-modern parallel Fellini makes, but Potter appears uncomfortable in his role.) I feel that what has come over Fellini is a movie director's megalomania, which has not gone so far with anyone else, and that part of the basis for his reputation is that his narcissistic conception of his role is exactly what celebrity worshipers have always thought a movie director to be. His idea of a movie seems to be to gather and exhibit all the weird people he can find, and one gets the feeling that more excitement and energy go into casting than into what he does with his cast, because, after the first sight of them, the faces don't yield up anything further to the camera. People coming out of *La Dolce Vita* and *8½* could be heard asking, "Where do you suppose he found them?"—as if he were a magician of a zookeeper who had turned up fabulous specimens. This increasingly strange human zoo into which he thrusts us is what people refer to when they say that there is a Fellini world. The partygoers of *La Dolce Vita,* with their masklike faces of dissatisfaction and perversity, have given way to this parade of leering, grinning cripples. And these primitive caricatures of what depravity supposedly does to us are used as cautionary images. In interviews, Fellini frequently talks of the need to believe in miracles, and of how "we have not the strength" to do without religion or myth. My guess would be that Fellini, as a Catholic, and a notably emotional one, has small knowledge of or interest in any forms of control outside the Church. As an artist, he draws upon the imagination of a Catholic schoolboy and presents us with a juvenile version of the Grand Inquisitor's argument.

Fellini's work has an eerie, spellbinding quality for some people which must be not unlike the powerful effect the first movies were said to have. Perhaps the opulence and the dreamlike movement of his films and the grotesques who populate them are what some people want from the movies—a return to frightening fairy tales. Following the Kubrick line in selling pictures, Fellini, in an interview, says, "Even the young ones not smoking, not with drugs—they grasp the picture, they feel the picture, eat the picture, breathe it, without asking, 'What does it mean?' This film—I don't want to sound presumptuous, but it is a very good test just to choose friends with, a test if people are free or not. The young kids, they pass the test." I should say that emotionally his *Satyricon* is just about the opposite of "free"; emotionally, it's a hip version of *The Sign of the Cross.* There's a certain amount of confusion in it about what's going on and where, so some people may take it "psychedelically" and swallow it whole, though the audience at *Fellini Satyricon* is already on to part of the con: there was a big laugh when Encolpius identifies himself as a student. But this new selling technique of congratulating youth for not thinking—which is also a scare selling technique to reviewers who are afraid of being left behind "free" youth—puts the audience at the mercy of shrewd promotion. "The young, they just love and feel," says Fellini, "and if there is a new cinema, pictures such as *2001*—and, yes, *Satyricon*—it is for them." Sure it's for them, because they constitute about fifty percent of the paid admissions, and so poor old *Fantasia* has now been reissued as a trip movie, and the ads for *Zabriskie Point* say "It blows your mind," and so on. When Susan Kohner, sobbing, clutched the flowers on her black mother's casket in *Imitation of Life,* you might have felt the anguish in your chest even as you laughed at yourself for reacting. Maybe if Fellini personally didn't impress people so much as a virtuoso they'd become as conscious of the emotional and intellectual shoddiness they're responding to in *his* films. The usual refrain is "With Fellini, I'm so captivated by the images I don't ask what it means." But suppose it's not the "beauty" of the images they're reacting to so much as that step-by-step intuitive linkage between Fellini's emotions and their own almost forgotten ones? I'm sure there are people who will say that it doesn't matter if Fellini's movies are based on shallow thinking, or even ignorance, because he uses popular superstitions for a poetic vision, and makes art out of them. The large question in all this is: *Can* movie art be made out of shallow thinking and superstitions? The answer may, I think, be no. But even if it's yes, I don't think Fellini transformed anything in *Fellini Satyricon*.

The New Yorker, March 14, 1970

WOMEN IN LOVE
LUST FOR "ART"

Ken Russell's movie of *Women in Love* could perhaps be described as a Gothic sex fantasy on themes from D. H. Lawrence's novel. Visually and emotionally, it's extravagant and, from time to time, impressive; Russell is no ordinary, uncertain-of-himself filmmaker. He goes for what you've never seen anything quite like before; he pours on the décor and startling camera positions. Russell has a purple style of filmmaking, and by that I mean just what we mean when we say an author writes purple prose: he goes for grand effects, but his meanings are wildly imprecise. The picture practically wallows in "style," which is to say, in excess; he overreaches so consistently that one comes out without any clear idea of what was supposed to be going on among the characters. Because Lawrence was one of the most (perhaps the most, though rivalled by Conrad) purple of all great writers, Russell's style might deceive one into imagining that he was providing a film equivalent to Lawrence's prose. But Lawrence's passionate imprecision is what's bad in his writing. It's unforgivable in a pulpy novel like *The Plumed Serpent,* but the overwriting is easy to pass right through in *Women in Love,* because Lawrence was reaching for clarity; he might make a fool of himself groping around his characters' psychosexual insides like a messianic explorer, but he *was* opening up new terrain. Russell, on the other hand, heads right for the purple, and does it not for character revelation, or for clarity about how sexual relations are affected by character, but for virtuoso tableaux "inspired" by Lawrence: the domineering Gerald (Oliver Reed) forcing his terrified horse toward a roaring train, whipping and kicking the bleeding animal; Gerald and Rupert Birkin (Alan Bates) wrestling nude by firelight in a gloomy mansion; the discovery of the entwined bodies of a drowned newlywed couple; Gudrun (Glenda Jackson) dancing defiantly in front of a herd of bullocks, their long horns swaying rhythmically to her movements; and so on. Russell's baroque, romantic period evocations are never static—he treats period material with the speed of *cinéma-vérité* techniques—but the overheated scenes are piled on for our admiration, not for our understanding. The movie is a series of lavish caricatures, bursting

357

with intensity that isn't really grounded in anything. It might seem that Russell confuses being gorgeously lurid with capturing the essence of the novel. More likely, however, this is not confusion as much as it is the drive of Russell's temperament; he takes off from Lawrence's novel in the way that Kurosawa in *Throne of Blood* takes off from *Macbeth*, and he does it with great assurance, even though *Women in Love* does not have the kind of structure that is intelligible when it's treated this way. Russell, I think, is after a highly colored swirl of emotional impressions that is more Brontë sisters than Lawrence. He makes Lawrence's period romantically *exotic*, the way a movie like *Black Narcissus* was exotic, so even when he's most effective it's a fruity falsification of Lawrence's work. Vulgarisms like "With Ken Russell for a friend, Lawrence doesn't need an enemy" come to mind. Yet some instinct tells one that Russell is indifferent to all that—that he sees himself not as an interpreter of Lawrence but as a free artist, using past art as material to make something new. And he has not merely a lust for art but a lust for "art"—for visual effects that are strikingly "artistic." His movie is purple because his idea of art is purple pastiche.

Superficially, in its use of words and scenes from the text, the movie stays close to Lawrence, but in a way that makes little sense—and certainly doesn't make *Lawrence's* sense—unless you know the book. Richard Aldington wrote, "The less you know about Lawrence the more baffling and irritating you will find *Women in Love*. . . . Was it his knowledge that he put so much of his mysterious self into it which made him so often claim it as his best?" To extend this, the less you know of the book the less you'll understand of the movie, and I think maybe to see the movie before reading this particular book is desecration. The novel is a staggering accomplishment—the sort of book that leaves one dumbfounded at how far its author got—and since there are few English novels of this stature, we shouldn't jeopardize our vision of it by reading it in terms of the actors and images of the movie. Movies affect us so powerfully that if you pick up the book afterward Lawrence seems to be lying or to have got things all wrong. There's an even worse danger. The movie is full of "big scenes," which churn up a lot of emotion, but they're not great scenes; they're not fun, and not good to watch. If one tries to view this movie as *sui generis* in what one assumes are Ken Russell's terms—as one big violently sensuous experience—it's disturbing and unresolved and anti-erotic. One feels uneasy when it's over; it's an opaque, unsatisfactory movie—the experience of it is rather like Lawrence's accounts of bad sex. You feel so confused you don't even want to talk about it. Those who don't know the book (and there are many) might take being overpowered by Russell's knockabout passion as the equivalent of reading *Women in Love*, and, since the after-emotions of the movie are so turgidly unpleasant, never open the book. They not only will never know what the movie is about but will have lost out on something much bigger.

In the movie, there's so much rumbling from the unconscious that we begin to feel we need seismograph readings on the people. That, of course, was what Lawrence—investigating our "subterranean selves"—provided: he showed us the hidden mechanisms of the characters that explained what they said and did. The script—by Larry Kramer, who is also the co-producer—retains some of Lawrence's dialogue, but without supplying clues to the motives behind it. Kramer has an aberrant gift for selecting the dialogue in which Lawrence sounds like a prizewinning television dramatist and changing it slightly to make it even worse.

BIRKIN: You can't bear anything to be spontaneous, can you? Because then it's no longer in your power. You must clutch things and have them in your power. And why? Because you haven't got any real body—any dark sensual body of life! All you've got is your will and your lust for power.

And there are serious pre-coital conversations that make one squirm:

GUDRUN: Try to love me a little more and want me a little less.
GERALD: You mean you don't want me?
GUDRUN: You're so insistent. You have so little grace. So little finesse. You are crude. You break me and waste me and it is horrible to me.

In the novel, we are told *why* the characters talk such drivel. Since the movie doesn't tell why, it's hardly surprising that reviewers are praising Russell but commiserating with him for being stuck with poor old Lawrence's "dated" material. According to one, the film is *too* faithful, and "The trouble with *Women in Love* is D. H. Lawrence." Since various movie reviewers also blamed what they didn't like about *Far from the Madding Crowd* on dated old Thomas Hardy, one wonders who is hip enough for them to read, or if they're catering to "the film generation," for whom, they believe, all books are dated. But it's a gross deception to pretend that you can get the same things out of a movie that you can get out of a great novel, and the movie of *Women in Love* isn't even *interested* in the same things.

The women in love are sisters, educated women trying to be free women—the unimaginative Ursula, based on Frieda Lawrence (though Jennie Linden in the role suggests Debbie Reynolds), and Gudrun, Lawrence's glittering, poisonous portrait of Katherine Mansfield. Glenda Jackson is an odd, tense, compelling actress, and her Gudrun dominates the movie. However, except for occasional glimmers of humor, Miss Jackson isn't—so far, at least—a very likable actress; she's not someone an audience is likely to identify with or feel with. She interests us, but she puts us off; if you know the book, you can see that her interpretation of an unyielding, castrating woman is original and bold and a considerable feat, but her Gudrun is so self-contained and remote from the audience that without that knowledge of the book you can't figure out what she is meant to be. Russell is flamboyantly gifted, but where human beings are concerned he may be a little obtuse. Either he takes too much for granted or he's indifferent to meaning;

he doesn't compensate for what is left out or for his casting. Miss Jackson has a stony, artificial quality that is like an Expressionist study of Gudrun's soul. In Lawrence's portrait, this was on the inside of a soft, desirable woman; now that it's outside, any man could spot it and beware.

Birkin, Lawrence's autobiographical hero, marries Ursula, while the destructive Gudrun torments to death his friend Gerald. The movie doesn't enable us to understand the contrasting chemistries of these two couples. Oliver Reed isn't bad as Gerald, but nothing clues us in on what sort of man he is, and there isn't enough shading in the portrait. He just seems to be rather glum and bilious—a masochistic Rochester—and we don't see why this suffering lump is drawn to Gudrun. The worst failures are with subsidiary characters—especially Eleanor Bron's disastrous Hermione, a character so repulsively misconceived and satirized that one feels sorry for the actress. Russell gives us effects without causes: a flashy scene showing Gerald's mother's hatred of beggars, but without Lawrence's brilliant, Dostoyevskian analysis of why. As a human observer, Russell fails all along. In a schoolroom sequence, with Birkin explaining about the long danglers that produce pollen to fertilize the little seed-producing flowers, the kids in the class don't burst out laughing—they don't respond at all. And however we are meant to react to the nude-wrestling sequence, what we do react to is the fact that Oliver Reed's genitals are clearly visible, while the lighting and the photographic angles obscure Bates's; we are thrown right out of the movie, to consider the actors, not the characters.

Despite the visual sophistication of this film, in some ways its techniques are primitive. We know more about the sex lives of the characters played by Trevor Howard and Wendy Hiller in *Sons and Lovers,* because as performers they had mastered ways to represent emotions that included sexuality. The movies don't really have any iconography for a direct representation of what goes right or wrong in sexual relations. For actors, trying to stay in character and to act sexual abandonment and unselfconsciousness is like trying to swim on land—they go through the motions, but it's a dry run. The movies used to use symbolic substitutes for sex acts—a blazing fire or the embers dying, trains and tunnels, exploding fireworks, and so on—or else indicate how the act had gone by a pussycat smile of satisfaction (Scarlett O'Hara) or a hostile look of frustration or just a bored expression. Now, when the performers are naked and are either simulating or actually having intercourse, the directors clue us in by the same old methods. And it becomes ludicrous to watch two people thrashing around if, in addition to that, we have to wait for acted closeups or some symbolic action to tell us how it is. Sometimes the heightened realism in *Women in Love* is grotesque: when Gerald and Gudrun are together and the activity is bed-bangingly violent, Russell seems to be staging a love match and a boxing match simultaneously. There was one marvellous bed scene in *Room at the Top,* in which Simone Signoret talked to Laurence Harvey and one got a sense of sexual passion—one believed in her pleasure in sex, and her fears. There is nothing comparable in *Women in Love*—we never believe that either girl is in love. Lawrence's fervor was for knowledge of what love and sex mean in our lives; Birkin said it for him in the novel: "I only want us to *know* what we are." Ken Russell wants merely to excite the senses—to make a bash of a movie. A great movie artist must, I think, care about both; and perhaps a movie director can't excite the senses pleasurably and satisfyingly unless he does care about both.

The New Yorker, March 28, 1970

BURN!
MYTHMAKING

Gillo Pontecorvo's *Burn!* is an attempt to tell the story of a mid-nineteenth-century slave uprising on a fictitious Caribbean island from a neo-Marxist, Frantz Fanonian point of view, so that it will become *the* story of black revolution and a call to action. No one, with the possible exception of Eisenstein, has ever before attempted a political interpretation of history on this epic scale, or attempted to plant an insurrectionary fuse within a historical adventure film. The 1952 *Viva Zapata!*, which also starred Marlon Brando, and which *Burn!* somewhat resembles, merely imposed the then current American liberalism on the Mexican revolutionaries. If Pontecorvo's film is flawed throughout, it is nevertheless an amazing film, intensely controversial even in its failures. The audience seems to be grooving to the emotionally charged imagery (which has some of that quality that Buffy Sainte-Marie and the Missa Luba and classic blues have of hurting while giving pleasure) and yet, at times, arguing about political points, and I think this mixed reaction is a valid one. *Burn!* is primarily a celebration not of Black Is Beautiful but of Black Is Strong, and the strength Pontecorvo celebrates has a far deeper beauty than we are accustomed to at the movies. Nevertheless, the movie goes wrong. Maybe it was one of those ambitious ideas that look great until you try to carry them out; if there was a way to make it work, Pontecorvo didn't find it.

Pontecorvo can show brutality without giving the audience cheap shocks, and he doesn't arrange suffering in pretty compositions. He has a true gift for epic filmmaking: he can keep masses of people in movement on the screen so that we care about what happens to them. They're not just crowds of extras; they're the protagonist. And *Burn!* is perhaps the least condescending film that has ever dealt with slavery. No doubt the dignity of the slave victims is ideological, but, clearly, Pontecorvo is not distorting his vision to fit his ideology; when he endows them with nobility, it rings aesthetically true.

The film is large-spirited, and sometimes it really soars with the imaginative force of art. Movie imagery rarely overwhelms us with such a mixture of sorrow and anger as the sequence near the opening in which the widow of an executed insurgent pulls a cart bearing her husband's decapitated body. The film, though political, is by no means Spartan; it's luxuriant and ecstatic. When black rebels ride white horses that prance to what sounds like a syncopated Gregorian chant, the sequence is so shimmering and showy that one knows that Pontecorvo and his cinematographer, Marcello Gatti, couldn't resist it. Wasn't it this kind of thing that drew the director to the theme? *Burn!* shows the violation of rapturous beauty, and this is the emotional basis for whites to believe that blacks should destroy white civilization. (It may be a tragedy for whites that their culture and traditions are not so photogenic.) In his feeling for crowds and battles, for color and imagery, and for visual rhythms, Pontecorvo is a sensuous, intoxicating director, and he gives his island (which has been synthesized from locations in Colombia, Africa, and the Caribbean) physical unity and, by the use of moving figures in the background of the compositions, a volatile, teeming population. In the last two years, Pontecorvo's *The Battle of Algiers,* a reconstruction of the violent death of a colonial regime, has become known as the black militants' training film. Pontecorvo appears fully committed to the idea of killing and being killed for your principles; in *Burn!,* however, the whites have no principles. *Burn!* is unquestionably intended to arouse revolutionary passions, but the racist-Marxist plot is too schematic to structure the heroic fall and rise of a people.

Some of the flaws in the film are not the director's fault. *Burn!* was originally called *Quemada,* which means "burned" in Spanish, and which was the name that Pontecorvo and his scriptwriters (Franco Solinas and Georgio Arlorio) gave to their sugar-producing island. They also gave it a history of having been burned by the Spaniards in the sixteenth century, because the Indians were rebellious, and then repopulated with African slaves. The movie was to show how, in the 1840s, the English fomented a new rebellion to wrest power from the Spanish. However, the current Spanish government, sensitive about Spaniards' being cast as heavies even in a period piece, applied severe economic pressures against the producers, who, remembering what the Spanish government had done when it was displeased by Fred Zinnemann's *Behold a Pale Horse* (the losses from the Spanish boycott of Columbia Pictures ran to several millions), capitulated. Parts of the film were deleted, others reshot, and the Spaniards who had historically dominated the Antilles were replaced by the Portuguese, who hadn't, but aren't a big movie market. The European title was changed to *Queimada*—the Portuguese for "burned." After the delays and extra expenses, the picture has still not been released widely; United Artists, which has probably been financially burned in the deal, has rather touchingly altered the American title to the opportunistic *Burn!* In addition, the American version has lost twenty-odd minutes at the hands of a New York "film doctor" whose previous experience was in editing movie trailers. These cuts are, I assume, responsible for some of the non sequiturs in the action and some of the lacunae. Finally, the movie was "dumped"—opened without the usual publicity and advance screenings. This ordinarily means that a company doesn't expect a movie to do well, and such a lack of faith usually insures that it won't do well, because magazine reviews will come out two or three months late, and even reviewers who might have been enthusiastic have their spirits dampened by the general feeling that it's a bomb and will close before they get into print. I'm reasonably certain that this film has been dumped not because of its incendiary potential but because of the company's evaluation of its box-office potential. I think that the company miscalculated and that *Burn!* could have been a hit, because it plays right into the current feelings of the young movie audience. But now we'll never know, though the picture may do well in revivals. Such are the business conditions in the background of a revolutionary movie, but the larger irony is that white men made this movie that says black men should never trust white men.

Despite its visual sophistication, *Burn!* has an unmistakable tang of the old heart-stirring swashbucklers in which Errol Flynn risked all for liberty, or Tyrone Power (*Son of Fury*) abandoned the corrupt life of the English nobility for an island, a dream, and a native girl (Gene Tierney). Although Pontecorvo's feeling for the slaves is that of an artist, his treatment of the vacillating, cowardly white colonial officials and their mulatto accomplices is exactly that of the more conventional seafaring adventure films. In scenes involving these officials, one might as well be at *Lydia Bailey* or *Anthony Adverse,* and Marlon Brando's cynical, daredevil Sir William Walker seems a direct development from his foppish Fletcher Christian in *Mutiny on the Bounty.*

Considered politically (rather than dramatically), the plot is an ingenious synthesis. (You don't appreciate *how* ingenious until you think over what has been left out.) Sir William is an *agent provocateur* sent by the British Admiralty to instigate a revolt of the slaves against their Portuguese masters. He tricks a band of slaves into committing a robbery in order to make them outlaws, arms them, turns them into killers, and trains a black leader, José Dolores (Evaristo Marquez), who defeats the Portuguese and tries to seize power for the slaves. Sir William is reluctantly preparing to eliminate him when José Dolores, unable to run the government without advisers, relinquishes power to the British and their mulatto puppet ruler. Having accomplished his mission and obtained sugar for a nation of tea drinkers, Sir William leaves the island. So far, he appears to be a super-cool C.I.A.-type mastermind crossed with Lawrence of Arabia. Brando's impersonation of a languid British gentleman is amusing and decorated with linguistic conceits, and since Sir William helped to liberate the slaves and tried to convince the businessmen of the economic advantages of free workers, one assumes he is personally on the slaves' side, and so does José Dolores, still his friend, who accompanies him to the ship to say goodbye. When José asks him where he's going, he replies, "I don't suppose you've ever heard of a place called Indo-China? Well, they're sending me there."

Ten years pass offscreen. José Dolores has been fighting the British all these years, and he has organized a new rebellion. Sir William has left the Admiralty and (like Lawrence?) has sought obscurity. The sugar company's agents go to look for Sir William in London, find him brawling in a cheap dive, and report that he is "like another man," but they make him a lucrative offer to return to Queimada to deal with José Dolores, and he accepts. His hopes are gone, he says, and the ten years have revealed the century's contradictions. He tries to establish contact with José Dolores but is rebuffed. Then, although he gives evidence of believing in what the rebels are doing and despising the whites, he organizes the slaughter of the blacks, burns native villages that help the guerrillas hiding in the mountains, and, when the puppet tries to regain control in order to end the suffering, has him executed. Sir William explains why the blacks will eventually win—a guerrilla can do fifty times as much as an ordinary soldier, because the guerrilla "has nothing to lose," and so on. Yet Sir William brings in British troops and destroys the island. It is shelled and shelled and then burned again, so that the British businessmen are left asking what good his actions have done them, since now there's no sugar for anybody. He says that he doesn't really know what he's doing but that he must do it. And so he comes to represent the murderous, self-destructive folly of colonialism—the whites' irrational determination to destroy everything rather than share with the blacks—and when he's killed there's a happy heavenly choir.

There's a contradiction between Brando's role as the personification of colonial manipulative policies (as well as, by implication, of the American involvement in Vietnam) and Brando's style, because, the way he plays his role, he's the comic relief in a tragedy. The oppressor as cynical clown is an entertaining idea, and perhaps the audience needs his foppish foolery, the contempt with which he addresses the English businessmen, his sophistic explanation that he's merely an instrument of government policy and if he didn't carry it out the Admiralty would send someone else, but he seems to have wandered into the wrong movie. He causes starvation and death, yet he's also slapping his horse and drawling "Giddyap, you fool." If Sir William were played impersonally as a historical force, the movie would be heavy and didactic; a more conventionally villainous interpretation would probably turn it into Grade B melodrama. But when the role is played with Brando's bravura, so that Sir William becomes a daring white loner who loved and betrayed the blacks, it's a muddle, because we simply don't understand his motives or why he is so zealous in crushing the rebellion, or why no one else understands anything.

When you personify a deterministic theory of history and don't stylize it but, rather, do it in natural settings, the leaders seem to be all that matter, so the method distorts the theory. It seems as if history were a melodrama made solely by heroes and adventurers. This movie really becomes a swashbuckler—a romantic, glamorized view of black struggle—but a swash-buckler engaged in a cute game of slipping in historical parallels and of scoring textbook points. Almost every line jogs us to fit it into the scheme. "Ah, yes," we say to ourselves, "Sir William is a liberator of the blacks only when the English interests and theirs coincide," and so on. When Brando warns the English of the danger of making José Dolores a martyr—"Think of his ghost running through the Antilles!"—we see it as another point racked up, and when Brando thinks it's madness for José Dolores to sacrifice his life, we know we're being prodded to see that whites are incapable of understanding the blacks' true passion for freedom, and we're being prodded to see that it is this passion that makes the blacks superior, and will make them win.

The end is clearly meant to be only the beginning. The spirit of the film is one of triumph, for José Dolores, who preferred death to compromise, has set an example for the survivors and for the slaves on other islands. "Ideas travel," Sir William has explained, and dead heroes become myths. The message of the film is that freedom is worth all the suffering it takes. After we have seen the blacks tricked and maneuvered and crushed over and over again, this simplistic encouragement to die for your principles seems rather cavalier, as if the film had been made by a new incarnation of Sir William, who still doesn't know what he's doing. José Dolores's visionary speeches about lighting the flames for whites to burn in are fashionably modern, and his last words are "Civilization belongs to whites. But what civilization? Until when?"

There's something painful and disturbing about movies that fail on as high a level as *Burn!*, but mixing art and politics has always had its difficulties. Still, if you can't force human suffering into an ideological diagram without having it all look phony, that could be a blessing.

The New Yorker, November 7, 1970

ABOUT BARBRA STREISAND, FROM REVIEW OF
THE OWL AND THE PUSSYCAT

Barbra Streisand's delicate snarl is the voice of New York tuned to a parodist's sensibility. It's the sound of urban character armor; she rattles it for a finely modulated raucousness. In *The Owl and the Pussycat,* her clipped diction is so full of controlled tension that her lines never go slack; the words come out impetuously fast and hit such surprising notes that she creates her own suspense. She's a living, talking cliff-hanger; we're kept alert catching the inflections, hoping that the laughter in the theatre won't make us lose anything. Though she doesn't sing in this picture, she's still a singing actress; she makes her lines funny musically, and she can ring more changes on a line than anybody since W. C. Fields, who was also a master of inflection. (I'm not forgetting Mae West; her specialty was innuendo—a more limited comic field.)

The New Yorker, November 14, 1970

HUSBANDS

If you resist the aggression of a certain kind of loudmouth, he is quick to tell you that you're afraid of life. And no matter how dispassionately you analyze what's the matter with *Husbands*—which is just about everything— those who made it and those who love it will insist that if you didn't like it, you're hung up or uptight, or some other "up" or "tight" construction. I think I gave my all by sitting through it. The film, which ran two hours and eighteen minutes when I saw it, had already lost sixteen minutes; if I were cutting it, I don't think there would be much left except one shot of Ben Gazzara coughing, a sequence of an actor named John Kullers singing "Brother, Can You Spare a Dime?," a short scene of John Cassavetes's little daughter crying when he comes home, and a few scenes involving two charming English actresses—a tall blonde named Jenny Runacre and a medium-sized blonde named Jenny Lee Wright. Maybe twenty minutes in all, and that's stretching it.

Husbands, directed by Cassavetes, extends the faults of his last film, *Faces;* one might even say that *Husbands* takes those faults into a new dimension. It is, as *Faces* was, semi-written by Cassavetes and semi-improvised by the actors. This time, the film is about three suburban husbands—Cassavetes (a dentist), Gazzara (a Peter Max sort of commercial artist), and Peter Falk (profession unspecified)—who go on a bender after attending the funeral of a fourth. The three buddies are boy-boy American males taking flight from their marriages and responsibilities, and, for the period in which we observe them, more emotionally involved with sports and each other than with their professions or their families. One assumes they are meant to be searching for themselves, their lost freedom, and their lost potentialities— and one can guess that Cassavetes believes that their boyishness is creative. But the boyishness he shows us isn't remotely creative; it's just infantile and offensive.

The three leads are like performers in a Norman Mailer movie, role-playing at being lowlifes. Despite the suburban-commuter roles they have chosen, they punch and poke each other like buffoonish hardhats. When one cries, "Harry, you're a phony," the riposte is "Nobody calls me a phony"—and this sort of exchange may be followed by gales of laughter. In fact, they act very much like Gazzara, Falk, and Cassavetes doing their buddy-buddy thing on the *Dick Cavett Show*. They horse around, encouraging each other to come up with dialogue like "The man is right. When the man is right, he's right." Cassavetes replaces the exhausted artifices of conventional movies with a new set of pseudo-realistic ones, which are mostly instantaneous clichés. As a writer-director, he's so dedicated to revealing the pain under the laughter he's a regular Pagliacci. To put it in the puerile terms in which it is conceived, Cassavetes thinks that in *Husbands* he has stripped people of their pretenses and laid bare their souls.

Cassavetes's method was originally, back in the *Shadows* days, to combine a group of actors' improvisations into a loose story; now he writes and stages sequences to look improvised. *Husbands,* which went considerably over its initial million-dollar budget, is a fairly elaborate shot-in-color production that was planned to look like grainy caught "reality." The dialogue—written to sound unwritten—is deliberately banal; the timing is agonizingly slow, to simulate spontaneity; and there are inexplicable sequences (such as one involving a Chinese girl) that are staged to look crazily accidental.

His approach to filmmaking is an actor's approach, and when it's effective it has certain resemblances to Harold Pinter's approach to theatre. The three men interacting onscreen are like the basic Pinter stage situation. We don't know anything about the supposed characters or their connections to the world—when they're throwing up their past lives we don't know what they're throwing up—but the actors have occasional intense and affecting moments, going through emotions that they set off in each other. We're glued to the acting in this movie, because that's really all there is, and maybe the best clue to the chaos of Cassavetes's method comes from the subsidiary players. The three leads are, after all, successful actors who have chosen to do what they're doing; they seem to be having a good time, and it's their psychodrama and their picture. But there are a couple of dozen New York and London professionals in the cast, and it's troubling to watch them. There is a long sequence in a New York bar in which a bunch of drinkers are sitting around a table, and the three men tell each in turn to sing, and proceed to torment the person singing. And all we can see are actors and actresses trying their damnedest to do what is wanted because they need the work. When a middle-aged woman (who looks as if she'd be a wonderful movie mother for Tuesday Weld) sings a song beginning "It was just a little love affair" over and over—at their insistence—while they bait her and tell her they hate her and then kiss her, we're acutely conscious of discomfort. She isn't playing a role, she's being *used,* and yet she's also coöperating as an actress. Are Cassavetes and his buddies aware of how hostile their role-playing is, how much of it is just a form of picking on people on camera?

Husbands is a messy synthesis—a staged film with a documentary-style use of professional performers. We don't know what to react to: we can't sort out what we're meant to see from what we see. We know that the people around the table in the bar wouldn't sit there while these clowns bully them unless they were paid for it, but we also know that the sequence is supposed to reveal something that "ordinary" movies don't. But what does it reveal except the paralysis and humiliation of the bit players? Kullers and the two English girls triumph over *Husbands* by their talent and looks and style, but characteristically the camera gloats on hysteria or dismay or aging flesh. Cassavetes's camera style is to move in for the kill, like those TV newsmen who ask people in distress the questions that push them to break down while the camera moves in on the suffering eyes and choking mouth. In the past, Cassavetes has given some erratic evidence of being a compassionate director; I think he forfeits all claims to compassion in *Husbands.* A long closeup scene in a London gambling club in which an elderly woman is approached by Peter Falk and coyly propositions him is perhaps the most grotesquely insensitive movie sequence of the year. It's hideous not because this is truth that the spectator seeks to evade but because this is bad acting and a gross conception. It reveals nothing more than a sensitive director would reveal by a look or a gesture, and at a discreet distance. Since Cassavetes conveys no sense of illusion—since he's after the naked "reality"—we don't think about the role, we think about the actress, and we wonder if she could ever get enough money to compensate for what is being done to her.

The New Yorker, January 2, 1971

FROM NOTES ON HEART AND MIND

When movies were bad a decade ago, it wasn't such a serious matter; despite the greatness of some films, movies in general weren't expected to be more than casual, light entertainment. You weren't expected to get your ideas of artistic possibilities from movies. I remember seeing *To Have and Have Not* the night it opened, in 1944, and I remember how everyone loved it, but if anyone I knew had said that it was a masterpiece comparable to the greatest works of literature or drama, he would have been laughed at as a fool who obviously didn't know literature or drama. Now, by and large, even the college-educated moviegoer isn't expected to, and the media constantly apply superlatives to works that lack even the spirit and energy of a *To Have and Have Not.*

■　■　■

What must it be like for those who know and love only movies, and not literature as well? Even if they don't consciously miss it, surely the loss of the imaginative ranging over experience is irreparable.

There's been almost no fight for it. Fiction has been abandoned casually and quickly. There haven't even been journalists to defend it. On TV talk shows, the hosts have generally given up even the pretense of having read the books that are being plugged. There are several cooking celebrities on TV but no TV personality who discusses books. If you ask college students to name half a dozen movie critics, they have no trouble supplying names. If you ask them to name three book critics, they flounder, and finally one of them may triumphantly recall the name of a critic who abandoned regular reviewing before they were born.

■　　■　　■

If a movie is a bowdlerization of a book and the movie's director is acclaimed for his artistry, surely something has gone askew. In some cases, directors add virtually nothing, and diminish and cheapen what was in the original, and yet the fraction of the original they managed to reproduce is sufficient to make their reputations.

■　　■　　■

Film theorists often say that film art is, "by its nature," closest to painting and music, but all these years movie companies haven't been buying paintings and symphonies to adapt, they've been buying plays and novels. And although the movies based on those plays and novels have visual and rhythmic qualities, their basic material has nevertheless come from the theatre and from books.

When a movie based on a book goes wrong but one isn't sure exactly how or why, one of the best ways to find out is to go to the book. The changes that have been made in the course of the adaptation frequently upset the structure, the characterizations, and the theme itself.

Generally speaking, when people become angry if you refer to the original novel or play while you're discussing a movie, it means they haven't read it. Twenty years ago, they hadn't always, either, but they didn't feel they didn't need to. McLuhanism and the media have broken the back of the book business; they've freed people from the shame of not reading. They've rationalized becoming stupid and watching television.

And television has become the principal advertising medium for movies. Even the few talk shows that held out against the show-biz personalities for a while are now loaded with movie people plugging away and often inflicting pain and embarrassment by trying to sing. Talk shows are becoming amateur hours for professionals.

■　　■　　■

American fiction seems to have reached a fairly high plateau at the very time when college students were deciding movies were more interesting. They didn't make that decision without encouragement from the media. *Would* they have made it without encouragement? I don't know. But the new dominance of Pop is the culmination of processes that have been at work in the mass media for many years. Gradually, as the things people used to fear would happen happened, ways were found to refer to the changes positively instead of negatively, and so "the herd instinct" that mass culture was expected to lead to became "the new tribalism."

■   ■   ■

If some people would rather see the movie than read the book, this may be a fact of life that we must allow for, but let's not pretend that people get the same things out of both, or that nothing is lost. The media-hype encourages the sacrifice of literature.

Movies are good at action; they're not good at reflective thought or conceptual thinking. They're good for immediate stimulus, but they're not a good means of involving people in the other arts or in learning about a subject. The film techniques themselves seem to stand in the way of the development of curiosity.

Movies don't help you to develop independence of mind. They don't give you much to mull over, and they don't give you the data you need in order to consider the issues they raise.

■   ■   ■

A young film critic recently told me that he needed to read more books than he did before he got the job—that he felt empty after seeing films daily. I don't have any doubts about movies' being a great art form, and what makes film criticism so peculiarly absorbing is observing—and becoming involved in—the ongoing battle of art and commerce. But movies alone are not enough: a steady diet of mass culture is a form of deprivation. Most movies are shaped by calculations about what will sell; the question they're asking about new projects in Hollywood is "In what way is it like *Love Story?*"

A teacher writes that "literature students are getting into the terms of film and the history of film in the same way that they have always got into the terms of literature, for example, and the history and evolution of that art form." If movies had become what they might be, this would make sense, but to study mass culture in the same terms as traditional art forms is to accept the shallowness of mass culture. It could mean that the schools are beginning to accept the advertisers' evaluations; the teachers don't want to be left behind, either.

■   ■   ■

The Faulkner who collaborated on the screenplay for *To Have and Have Not* is not commensurate with the Faulkner of the novels. Faulkner's work for hire is fun, but it's not his major work (though, as things are going, he and many other writers may remain known only for the hackwork they did to support the work they cared about). Yet until writers as well as directors can bring their full powers to American movies, American movies are not going to be the works of imagination and daring that the media claim they are already.

The New Yorker, January 23, 1971

THE CONFORMIST
THE POETRY OF IMAGES

What makes Bernardo Bertolucci's films different from the work of older directors is an extraordinary combination of visual richness and visual freedom. In a Hollywood movie, the big scenes usually look pre-arranged; in a film by David Lean, one is practically wired to react to the hard work that went into gathering a crowd or dressing a set. Bertolucci has been working on a big scale since his first films—*La Commare Secca,* made when he was twenty, and *Before the Revolution,* a modern story derived from *The Charterhouse of Parma,* made when he was twenty-two—and his films just seem to flow, as if the life he photographs had not been set up for the camera but were all there and he were moving in and out of it at will. Most young filmmakers now don't attempt period stories—the past is not in good repute, and period pictures cost more and tend to congeal—but Bertolucci, because of the phenomenal ease of his sweeping romanticism, is ideally suited to them; he moves into the past, as he works in the present, with a lyrical freedom almost unknown in the history of movies. He was a prize-winning poet at twenty-one, and he has a poet's gift for using objects, land-scapes, and people expressively, so that they all become part of his vision. It is this gift, I think, that makes *The Conformist* a sumptuous, emotionally charged experience.

Bertolucci's adaptation of the Alberto Moravia novel about the psychology of an upper-class follower of Mussolini is set principally in 1938 (Bertolucci was born in 1941), and I think it's not unfair to say that except for Jean-Louis Trintignant's grasp of the central character—it's an extraordinarily prehensile performance—the major interest is in the way everything is imbued with a sense of the past. It's not the past we get from films that survive from the thirties but Bertolucci's evocation of the past—the thirties made expressive through the poetry of images.

Trintignant, who has quietly come to be the key French actor that so many others (such as Belmondo) were expected to be, digs into the character of the intelligent coward who sacrifices everything he cares about because he wants the safety of normality. Trintignant has an almost incredible intuitive understanding of screen presence; his face is never too full of emotion, never completely empty. In this role, as an indecisive intellectual, he conveys the mechanisms of thought through tension, the way Bogart did, and he has the grinning, teeth-baring reflexes of Bogart—cynicism and humor erupt in savagery. And, playing an Italian, he has an odd, ferrety resemblance to Sinatra. Everything around him seems an emanation of the director's velvet style—especially the two beautiful women: Stefania Sandrelli, an irresistible comedienne, as Trintignant's deliciously corrupt middle-class wife, and Dominique Sanda, with her swollen lips and tiger eyes, as the lesbian wife of an anti-Fascist professor he is ordered to kill.

(She's rather like a prowling, predatory stage lesbian, but she's such an ecstatic erotic image that she becomes a surreal figure, and Bertolucci uses
her as an embodiment of repressed desires. She also appears, only slightly
disguised, in two other roles—conceived to be almost subliminal.) The film
succeeds least with its ideas, which are centered on Trintignant's Fascist. I
think we may all be a little weary—and properly suspicious—of psychosexual
explanations of political behavior; we can make up for ourselves these textbook cases of how it is that frightened, repressed individuals become Fascists. In an imaginative work, one might hope for greater illumination—for
a Fascist seen from inside, not just a left view of his insides. Yet though the
ideas aren't convincing, the director makes the story itself seem organic in
the baroque environment he has created, and the color is so soft and deep
and toned down, and the texture so lived in, that the work is, by its nature,
ambiguous—not in the tedious sense of confusing us but in the good sense
of touching the imagination. The character Trintignant plays is by no means
simple; when he says "I want to build a normal life," it's clear that he needs
to *build* it because it's not normal for him. He shows a streak of bravura enjoyment as he watches himself acting normal.

Bertolucci's view isn't so much a reconstruction of the past as an infusion from it; *The Conformist* cost only seven hundred and fifty thousand
dollars—he brought together the décor and architecture surviving from that
modernistic period and gave it all a unity of style (even with the opening titles). Visconti used the thirties-*in-extremis* in *The Damned*—as a form of estrangement. Bertolucci brings the period close, and we enter into it. His
nostalgia is open; it's a generalized sort of empathy, which the viewer begins
to share. You don't think in terms of watching a story being acted out, because he provides a consciousness of what's going on under the scenes;
they're fully orchestrated. Bertolucci is perhaps the most operatic of movie
directors. I don't mean simply that he stages movies operatically, in the way
that other Italians—notably Zeffirelli—do, but that he conceives a movie operatically; the distinction is something like that between an opera director
and an opera composer. Visconti in *The Damned* was somewhere in the
middle—composing, all right, but in a single, high-pitched scale, as if the
music were to be howled by wolves. *The Damned* was hysterical; *The Conformist*
is lyrical. You come away with sequences in your head like arias: a party of
the blind that opens with the cry of *"Musica!"*; an insane asylum situated in
a stadium—a theatre-of-the-absurd spectacle of madness; a confession-box
satirical duet between priest and non-believer; a wedding-night scherzo, the
bride describing her sins, to the groom's amusement; the two women on a
late-afternoon shopping expedition in Paris; a French working-class dance
hall (a *Bal Populaire*) where the women dance a parody of passion that is
one of the most romantic screen dances since Rogers and Astaire, and
where the crowd join hands in a farandole. The political assassination in the
forest—an operatic love-death—is the emotional climax of the film;

Trintignant sits in his car, impotent—paralyzed by conflicting impulses—while the woman he loves is murdered.

Two years ago, Bertolucci made *Partner,* an inventive but bewildering modernization of Dostoyevsky's *The Double,* in which the hero, a young drama teacher (Pierre Clémenti), had fantasies of extending the theatre of cruelty into political revolution. This basic idea is shared by many young filmmakers, including, probably, Bertolucci, but Clémenti never conveyed enough intellectuality for us to understand the character, who seemed to be a comic-strip Artaud. Despite the fascination of *Partner* (I recall one image in particular, in which books were piled up in heaps on the floor of a room like the Roman ruins outside), the film was shown here only at the 1968 New York Film Festival. It was a political vaudeville for the movie generation bred on Godard's *La Chinoise;* the meanings were lost in the profusion of images and tricks of his original, daring high style. Bertolucci seemed to have forgotten the story of his own *Before the Revolution,* in which his Fabrizio discovered that he was not single-minded enough to be a Communist—that he was too deeply involved in the beauty of life as it was *before* the revolution. Bertolucci, like Fabrizio, has "a nostalgia for the present." This may seem a bourgeois weakness to him (and to some others), but to be deeply involved in the beauty of life as it is is perhaps the first requisite for a great movie director. (And, far from precluding activity for social change, it is, in a sense, the only sane basis for such activity.) It's a bit ironic that the young director who has the greatest natural gifts of his generation for making movies as sensual celebrations should have sought refuge for this talent in the Fascist period.

After *Partner,* Bertolucci made a television film about a plot to murder Mussolini during a performance of *Rigoletto*—*The Spider's Stratagem.* Based on a Borges story, it was attenuated—it didn't have enough content to justify the atmosphere of mystification. *The Conformist* is his most accessible, least difficult film from an audience point of view. I don't put that accessibility down; despite the intermittent brilliance of *Partner,* it *is* a failure, and trying to figure out what a director has in mind is maddening when it's apparent he hasn't worked it out himself. *The Conformist,* though in some ways less audacious, is infinitely more satisfying. One may wish that Bertolucci had been able to integrate some of the Godard influence, but no one has been able to do that; Bertolucci has simply thrown the discordant notes out of his system and gone back to his own natural flowing film rhythm. (Is it perhaps an in-joke that the saintly bespectacled professor who is murdered faintly resembles Godard?) In this film, one knows that Bertolucci knows who he is and what he's doing; young as he is, he's a master director. Except for the unconvincing and poorly staged concluding sequence, the flaws in *The Conformist* are niggling. It's very tempting for young filmmakers, through cutting, to make their films difficult; the filmmakers look at their own footage so many times that they assume an audience can apprehend connections that are barely visible. Bertolucci uses an organizing idea that puts an unnecessary strain on the viewer: the film begins with the dawn of the assassination day, and the events that led up to it unfold while Trintignant and a Fascist agent are driving to the forest. The editing at the outset is so fast anyway that cutting to and from that car is slightly confusing, but as one gets caught up in the imagery that slight confusion no longer matters. In a Bertolucci film, in any case, there are occasional images that have no logical explanation but that work on an instinctive level—as surreal poetry, like the piles of books in *Partner* or the desk here, in a Fascist's office, that is covered with neatly arranged walnuts. However, I don't think *The Conformist* is a great movie. It's the best movie this year by far, and it's a film by a prodigy who—if we're all lucky—is going to make great films. But it's a triumph of style; the substance is not sufficiently liberated, and one may begin to feel a little queasy about the way the movie left luxuriates in Fascist decadence.

One of the peculiarities of movies as a mass medium is that what the directors luxuriate in—and what we love to look at—has so often been held up as an example of vice. Except for the sophisticated comedies of the past and occasional thrillers about classy crooks, we get most of our views of elegance under the guise of condemnation. Our desire for grace and seductive opulence is innocent, I think, except to prigs, so when it's satisfied by movies about Fascism or decadence we get uncomfortable, because our own enjoyment is turned against us. One wants modern directors to be able to use the extravagant emotional possibilities of the screen without falling into the De Mille–Fellini moralistic bag. There are some sequences in *The Conformist* that suggest the moralistic extremism of *The Damned*—that party of the blind, for example, and the blue light on Trintignant's and Sanda's faces in the cloakroom of a ballet school.

The old puritanism imposed on moviemakers is now compounded by the puritanism of the left which coerces filmmakers into a basically hypocritical position: they begin to deny the very feelings that brought them to movies in the first place. The democratic impulse that informed the earliest screen masterpieces was to use the new medium to make available to all what had been available, through previous art forms, only to the rich and aristocratic. It was the dream of a universalization of the best work that could be done. As this dream became corrupted by mass culture produced for the lowest common denominator, the young filmmakers had to fight to free themselves from mass culture, and the fervor of the earlier democratic spirit was lost. Most young American filmmakers, in college and after, now think of themselves as artists in the same way American poets or painters do—and the poets have long since abandoned Whitman's dream of the great American audience. Filmmakers often talk as if it were proof of their virtue that they think in terms of a minority art. American movies have now reached just about the place the American theatre did a decade or so back, when, except for the rare big hits, it had dwindled into a medium for the few.

The radicalized young are often the most antidemocratic culturally, and they push radical filmmakers to the point where no one can enjoy their work. Any work that is enjoyable is said to be counter-revolutionary. The effect may be to destroy the most gifted filmmakers (who are also—not altogether coincidentally—mostly left) unless the young left develops some tolerance for what the pleasures of art can mean to people. These issues become central when one considers a Bertolucci film, because his feeling for the sensuous surfaces of life suggests the revelatory abandon of the Russian film poet Dovzhenko. If anyone can be called a born moviemaker, it's Bertolucci. Thus far, he is the only young moviemaker who suggests that he may have the ability of a Griffith to transport us imaginatively into other periods of history—and without this talent movies would be even more impoverished than they are. The words that come to mind in connection with his work—sweeping, operatic, and so on—describe the talents of the kind of moviemaker who has the potential for widening out the appeal of movies once again. But movies—the great sensual medium—are still stuck with the idea that sensuality is decadent.

The New Yorker, March 27, 1971

McCABE & MRS. MILLER
PIPE DREAM

McCabe & Mrs. Miller is a beautiful pipe dream of a movie—a fleeting, almost diaphanous vision of what frontier life might have been. The film, directed by Robert Altman, and starring Warren Beatty as a small-time gambler and Julie Christie as an ambitious madam in the turn-of-the-century Northwest, is so indirect in method that it throws one off base. It's not much like other Westerns; it's not really much like other movies. We are used to movie romances, but this movie is a figment of the romantic imagination. Altman builds a Western town as one might build a castle in the air—and it's inhabited. His stock company of actors turn up quietly in the new location, as if they were part of a floating crap game. Altman's most distinctive quality as a director here, as in *M*A*S*H*, is his gift for creating an atmosphere of living interrelationships and doing it so obliquely that the viewer can't quite believe it—it seems almost a form of effrontery. He has abandoned the theatrical convention that movies have generally clung to of introducing the characters and putting tags on them. Though Altman's method is a step toward a new kind of movie naturalism, the technique may seem mannered to those who are put off by the violation of custom—as if he simply didn't want to be straightforward about his storytelling. There are slight losses in his method—holes that don't get filled and loose ends that we're used to having tied up—but these losses (more like temporary inconveniences, really) are, I think, inseparable from Altman's best qualities and from his innovative style.

There's a classical-enough story, and it's almost (though not quite) all there, yet without the usual emphasis. The fact is that Altman is dumping square conventions that don't work anymore: the spelled-out explanations of motive and character, the rhymed plots, and so on—all those threadbare remnants of the "well-made" play which American movies have clung to. He can't be straightforward in the old way, because he's improvising meanings and connections, trying to find his movie in the course of making it—an incredibly risky procedure under modern union conditions. But when a director has a collaborative team he can count on, and when his instinct and his luck both hold good, the result can be a *McCabe & Mrs. Miller.* The classical story is only a thread in the story that Altman is telling. Like the wartime medical base in *M*A*S*H,* the West here is the life that the characters are part of. The people who drop in and out and the place—a primitive mining town—are not just background for McCabe and Mrs. Miller; McCabe and Mrs. Miller are simply the two most interesting people in the town, and we catch their stories, in glimpses, as they interact with the other characters and each other. But it isn't a slice-of-life method, it's a peculiarly personal one—delicate, elliptical. The picture seems to move in its own quiet time, and the faded beauty of the imagery works a spell. Lives are picked up and let go, and the sense of how little we know about them becomes part of the texture; we generally know little about the characters in movies, but since we're assured that that little is all we need to know and thus all there is to know, we're not bothered by it. Here we seem to be witnesses to a vision of the past—overhearing bits of anecdotes, seeing the irrational start of a fight, recognizing the saloon and the whorehouse as the centers of social life. The movie is so affecting it leaves one rather dazed. At one point, cursing himself for his inability to make Mrs. Miller understand the fullness of his love for her, McCabe mutters, "I got poetry in me. I do. I got poetry in me. Ain't gonna try to put it down on paper . . . got sense enough not to try." What this movie reveals is that there's poetry in Robert Altman and he *is* able to put it on the screen. Emotionally far more complex than *M*A*S*H, McCabe & Mrs. Miller* is the work of a more subtle, more deeply gifted—more mysterious—intelligence than might have been guessed at from *M*A*S*H.*

The picture is testimony to the power of stars. Warren Beatty and Julie Christie have never been better, and they *are* the two most interesting people in the town. They seem to take over the screen by natural right—because we want to look at them longer and more closely. Altman brings them into focus so unobtrusively that it's almost as if we had sorted them out from the others by ourselves. Without rigid guidelines, we observe them differently, and as the story unfolds, Beatty and Christie reveal more facets of their personalities than are apparent in those star vehicles that sell selected aspects of the stars to us. Julie Christie is no longer the androgynous starlet of *Darling,* the girl one wanted to see on the screen not for her performances but because she was so great-looking that she was compelling on her own, as an original. She had the profile of a Cocteau drawing—tawdry-classical—and that seemed enough: who could expect her to act? I think this is the first time (except, perhaps, for some of the early scenes in *Doctor Zhivago*) that I've believed in her as an *actress*—a warm and intense one—and become involved in the role she was playing, instead of merely admiring her extraordinary opaque mask. In this movie, the Cocteau girl has her opium. She's a weird, hounded beauty as the junky madam Mrs. Miller—that great, fat underlip the only flesh on her, and her gaunt, emaciated face surrounded by frizzy ringlets. She's like an animal hiding in its own fur. Julie Christie has that gift that beautiful actresses sometimes have of suddenly turning ugly and of being even more fascinating because of the crossover. When her nose practically meets her strong chin and she gets the look of a harpy, the demonstration of the thin line between harpy and beauty makes the beauty more dazzling—it's always threatened. The latent qualities of the one in the other take the character of Mrs. Miller out of the realm of ordinary movie madams. It is the depth in her that makes her too much for the cocky, gullible McCabe; his inexpressible poetry is charming but too simple. An actor probably has to be very smart to play a showoff so sensitively; Beatty never overdoes McCabe's foolishness, the way a foolish actor would. It's hard to know what makes Beatty such a magnetic presence; he was that even early in his screen career, when he used to frown and loiter over a line of dialogue as if he hoped to find his character during the pauses. Now that he has developed pace and control, he has become just about as attractive a screen star as any of the romantic heroes of the past. He has an unusually comic romantic presence; there's a gleefulness in Beatty, a light that comes on when he's onscreen that says "Watch this—it's fun." McCabe pantomimes and talks to himself through much of this movie, complaining of himself to himself; his best lines are between him and us. Beatty carries off this tricky yokel form of soliloquy casually, with good-humored self-mockery. It's a fresh, ingenious performance; we believe McCabe when he says that Mrs. Miller is freezing his soul.

A slightly dazed reaction to the film is, I think, an appropriate one. Right from the start, events don't wait for the viewers' comprehension, as they do in most movies, and it takes a while to realize that if you didn't quite hear someone's words it's all right—that the exact words are often expendable, it's the feeling tone that matters. The movie is inviting, it draws you in, but at the opening it may seem unnecessarily obscure, perhaps too "dark" (at times it suggests a dark version of Sam Peckinpah's genial miss *The Ballad of Cable Hogue*), and later on it may seem insubstantial (the way Max Ophuls's *The Earrings of Madame de . . .* seemed—to some—insubstantial, or Godard's *Band of Outsiders*). One doesn't quite know what to think of an American movie that doesn't pretend to give more than a partial view of events. The gaslight, the subdued, restful color, and Mrs. Miller's golden opium glow, Leonard Cohen's lovely, fragile, ambiguous songs, and the drifting snow all make the movie hazy and evanescent. Everything is in motion, and yet there is a stillness about the film, as if every element in it were conspiring to tell the same incredibly sad story: that the characters are lost in their separate dreams.

The pipe dreamer is, of course, Robert Altman. *McCabe & Mrs. Miller* seems so strange because, despite a great deal of noise about the art of film, we are unaccustomed to an intuitive, quixotic, essentially impractical approach to moviemaking, and to an exploratory approach to a subject, particularly when the subject is the American past. Improvising as the most gifted Europeans do has been the dream of many American directors, but few have been able to beat the economics of it. In the past few years, there have been breakthroughs, but only on sensational current subjects. Can an American director get by with a movie as personal as this—personal not as in "personal statement" but in the sense of giving form to his own feelings, some not quite defined, just barely suggested? A movie like this isn't made by winging it; to improvise in a period setting takes phenomenal discipline, but *McCabe & Mrs. Miller* doesn't look "disciplined," as movies that lay everything out for the audience do. Will a large enough American public accept American movies that are delicate and understated and searching—movies that don't resolve all the feelings they touch, that don't aim at leaving us *satisfied,* the way a three-ring circus satisfies? Or do we accept such movies only from abroad, and then only a small group of us—enough to make a foreign film a hit but not enough to make an American film, which costs more, a hit? A modest picture like *Claire's Knee* would probably have been a financial disaster if it had been made in this country, because it might have cost more than five times as much and the audience for it is relatively small. Nobody knows whether this is changing—whether we're ready to let American moviemakers grow up to become artists or whether we're doomed to more of those "hard-hitting, ruthlessly honest" American movies that are themselves illustrations of the crudeness they attack. The question is always asked, "Why aren't there American Bergmans and Fellinis?" Here is an American artist who has made a beautiful film. The question now is "Will enough people buy tickets?"

The New Yorker, July 3, 1971

KLUTE

Jane Fonda's motor runs a little fast. As an actress, she has a special kind of smartness that takes the form of speed; she's always a little ahead of everybody, and this quicker beat—this quicker responsiveness—makes her more exciting to watch. This quality works to great advantage in her full-scale, definitive portrait of a call girl in *Klute*. It's a good, big role for her, and she disappears into Bree, the call girl, so totally that her performance is very pure—unadorned by "acting." As with her defiantly self-destructive Gloria in *They Shoot Horses, Don't They?*, she never stands outside Bree, she gives herself over to the role, and yet she isn't *lost* in it—she's fully in control, and her means are extraordinarily economical. She has somehow got to a plane of acting at which even the closest closeup never reveals a false thought and, seen on the movie streets a block away, she's Bree, not Jane Fonda, walking toward us.

The center of the movie is the study of the temperament and the drives of this intelligent, tough high-bracket call girl who wants to quit; she tries to get modelling jobs, she wants to be an actress, she is in analysis, yet she enjoys her power over her customers. It is the life surrounding her profession that frightens her; the work itself has peculiar compensations. Though there have been countless movie prostitutes, this is perhaps the first major attempt to transform modern clinical understanding into human understanding and dramatic meaning. The conception may owe some debt to the Anna Karina whore in *My Life to Live,* but Bree is a much more ambivalent character. She's maternal and provocative with her customers, confident and contemptuously cool; she's a different girl alone—huddled in bed in her disorderly room. The suspense plot involves the ways in which prostitutes attract the forces that destroy them. Bree's knowledge that as a prostitute she has nowhere to go but down and her mixed-up efforts to escape make her one of the strongest feminine characters to reach the screen. It's hard to remember that this is the same actress who was the wide-eyed, bare-bottomed Barbarella and the anxious blond bride of *Period of Adjustment* and the brittle, skittish girl in the broad-brimmed hat of *The Chapman Report;* I wish Jane Fonda could divide herself in two, so we could have new movies with that naughty-innocent comedienne as well as with this brilliant, no-nonsense dramatic actress. Her Gloria invited comparison with Bette Davis in her great days, but the character of Gloria lacked softer tones, shading, variety. Her Bree transcends the comparison; there isn't another young dramatic actress in American films who can touch her.

Klute is far from a work of art, but it's a superior thriller-melodrama, well written, by Andy and Dave Lewis, and directed tactfully and intelligently, by Alan J. Pakula, so that it provides a framework for the pivotal character. Donald Sutherland's Klute, a straight, country-town policeman who has come to Manhattan to investigate the disappearance of a man said to have been one of Bree's Johns, is a supporting role, and Sutherland plays him with becoming modesty. The movie founders, however, on the conventions of the murder-mystery genre. Of course, everyone longs to see a good murder mystery, like the ones of the forties, but how can you make one now? Pakula is as much aware of the problem of square conventions as Altman, but, unlike Altman, who throws out as many as he can, Pakula compromises by trying to soft-pedal them. However, the mechanics of suspense—the lurking figures, the withheld information, the standard gimmick of getting the heroine to go off alone so she can be menaced by the big-shot sadistic sex fiend, the improbable confessions and last-minute rescues—are just claptrap, overused and inevitably associated in our minds with B pictures and TV fodder. That doesn't prevent us from being scared, but we're aware of what a synthetic sort of reaction we're having. There's no conviction in these devices anymore; they're hokum, and the movie's awful, repetitive horror-tingle music emphasizes the fancy excesses of the photography; the shadows and angles are as silly as a fright wig. Would a simpler, more documentary approach to the look of the film have worked better? A little, perhaps, but simplicity is far more difficult, and probably somewhat more hazardous commercially, and it wouldn't really solve the basic problem of fraudulent suspense. Nevertheless, *Klute* is a powerful, scary melodrama, and only once does the discreet director intrude on Miss Fonda's performance. In a scene between Bree and a customer, there is a cut to her looking at her wristwatch while feigning passion. A businesslike look at the watch *before* her ecstatic cries, or even after, might possibly be consistent with the character—Jane Fonda is just naturally in a hurry—but this is a crummy, cute nod to the audience for a laugh. The bit sticks out, because Miss Fonda has moved beyond working the audience.

The New Yorker, July 3, 1971

THE TROJAN WOMEN
HELEN OF TROY, SEXUAL WARRIOR

The flaws in the Michael Cacoyannis film of Euripides's *The Trojan Women* seem unimportant compared to the simple fact that here is a movie of one of the supreme works of the theatre, and not a disgraceful movie, either. The play is not just the first but the one great anti-war play. What Euripides did was to look at war's other side, and the view from the losing side was not pomp and glory but cruelty and pain. The Trojan women are powerless, defenseless. As Andromache, Hector's widow, says, "I cannot save my child from death. Oh, hide my head for shame . . ." The shame of these captive women is that they can do nothing but yield to the victors. When the play opens, their children have been taken from them and sent to unknown destinations, and the women are waiting to be shipped into slavery; it closes when they have all been consigned and the city is burned. *The Trojan Women* is the greatest lament for the loss of freedom ever written, the greatest lament for the suffering of the victims of war. An Athenian, Euripides staged this profoundly radical play in Athens in 416 B.C., during a long war, only a few months after Athens had conquered a small island in the Aegean that was trying to stay neutral, killing the men and enslaving the women and children. The play might be called *Woman's Fate.* The dramatist's vision of the women whose husbands and sons have been slaughtered is austere and controlled and complete, so that, in a way, he said it all, and for all time. And because he said it all, and yet said it simply, the play is inexorable; we go from step to step until it is all there and the full effect has us by the throat. We knew about the miseries of war before. The play does more than confirm what we knew; it lays it out so clearly that we feel a deeper and higher understanding. Euripides has put it into words for us; he distills the worst that can happen. ("The gods—I prayed, they never listened." "Count no one happy, however fortunate, before he dies.") Despite the makeshift style of the film, one may come out grateful for this clarity, grateful to be caught by the throat, because it has been achieved by the most legitimate of all means—by a drama that states its case, and achieves nobility, through simplicity.

Katharine Hepburn, always forthright, starts as a fine, tough Hecuba, plainspoken and direct, but she comes to seem pitiful and mummified. Too many "O sorrow"s and references to her old gray head, and your mind begins to wander, asking vagrant questions such as "Why are all the women listening to the Queen—don't they have troubles enough of their own?" That is to say, you stop accepting the classical stage convention of the chorus and ask the questions you normally ask at movies. Actually, Euripides was so acutely sensible that within the convention of the chorus he provided the answers to one's natural questions. But in the movie the chorus, instead of going through their own hells, appear to be passive witnesses to Hecuba's, and she, instead of expressing the emotions of all of them, seems to be speaking of her own grief only, and her voice begins to seem thin and querulous. Hepburn is splendid when she's angry—when she has an antagonist. Perhaps our awareness of her as Hepburn makes us a little impatient with the weak, resigned side of the character.

A false nose (a trifle pale but very becoming) gives Genevieve Bujold's mad seeress Cassandra a classical look, and Bujold is becoming a daring and fascinating actress. She stretches the traditional sensitive-young-actress effects with a bursting conviction that they are good effects, and by strength of will, makes some of them work. That her performance doesn't come off is probably not entirely her fault. The role is the least modern, and the hokiest, in the play—Cassandra's virginal oaths and her prophecies don't mean much to us—and Cacoyannis has staged it with Ophelia-like flutters and with so much camera and chorus commotion that the narrative line goes out of whack. Bujold makes a stunning try, however, especially in her final fit. This performance is a leap in her career; her ambitiousness in tackling a role like this suggests prodigies ahead.

As Andromache, Vanessa Redgrave—that great goosey swan of the screen—fares better. Andromache is not as showy a role as Cassandra; it is written in a no-frills, clear-purpose style that pushes the narrative forward, and Redgrave's Andromache is magnificently uncomplicated. There are those who think that Vanessa Redgrave is a bad screen actress—that she jumps out of the screen at you, that she's always acting and does not allow you to *discover* anything in her performances. I think she *is* always acting, always "on." Though many moviegoers would probably be happy just to bask in her goddess image, she insists on doing something for them, on giving them the most imaginative performance she can. It's true one could look into Garbo, whereas Redgrave often seems to be staring one down, but there's a marvellous romantic excitement about this woman, because one never knows what audacity she will attempt, what heights she'll scale. This may prevent unconscious involvement, because we are always conscious of a *performance,* but our conscious involvement in the tension she creates has its own kind of excitement. She seems to act with her whole soul: you don't see her as a woman trying to play a role—the woman has been consumed by the determination to give the role all she has. Vanessa Redgrave never does the expected, and is never sloppy or overexpressive. Her Andromache is being freshly thought out while we watch—a dazed, pale-golden matron, unflirtatious, enough like Hepburn to suggest that Hector chose her because she was as free from guile and as naturally regal as his mother. Redgrave holds us by the quiet power of her concentration; she does odd little things—a tiny half sob gurgles from her throat. As an actress, she is such an embodiment of the idealistic, romantic spirit that I find myself rooting for her when she reaches for something new and difficult. There is a long meant-to-sound-wild cry when she is told that her child is to be slaughtered. She brings the cry to a sensational screaming finish; I realized I was hoping that others hadn't noticed how carefully it had begun. (Only once have I stopped rooting for her; I thought her dancing in *The Loves of Isadora* unforgivable, because she lacked the fluidity and lyricism to transform calisthenics into dance.)

Vanessa Redgrave gives the finest performance in the movie, but Cacoyannis demonstrates his love of the material, and his right to film it, in casting her as Andromache, and not in the obvious role for her—Helen. Because it is Irene Papas as Helen of Troy who cancels out the clichés of the legend and lifts the movie right out of the women's-college virtuous cultural ambience that plagues stage productions. *The Trojan Women* is not just a plainsong elegy disguised as a play. Euripides gave it one great melodramatic stroke. Helen, the adulterous wife of King Menelaus of Sparta, she whose flight with Paris, Prince of Troy, precipitated the war, is among the Trojan women survivors. The women would kill her if she were not protected from them by guards. Papas's Helen is a force of nature—a greedy woman who wants what she wants and who means to live. She has the vitality of a natural aggressor. She is first introduced prowling behind the slats of the stockade that protects her, and all we see are her brown-black eyes, as fiercely alive as a wolf's. While the other women mourn their dead, Helen uses all her animal cunning to survive. Cacoyannis makes the point that she is not defenseless—that the ruthless have weapons that the righteous don't have. Irene Papas is on her own turf in this play, and her Helen is a great winner—right there in the flesh. This Helen breathes sexuality; she is not merely a beauty but the strongest woman one has ever seen, and the more seductive because of her strength. You can *believe* that men would kill for her. She is not merely the cause of war, she is the spirit of war. When Hecuba says, "Fires comes from her to burn homes," it is perfectly plausible. The words of Andromache that seem like rhetoric on the page are given body:

> O Helen,
> many the fathers you were born of,
> Madness, Hatred, Red Death,
>   whatever poison
> the earth brings forth—God curse
>   you,
> with those beautiful eyes that
>   brought to shame and ruin
> Troy's far-famed plains.

The phrasing of the speeches is not always satisfying, however, and ends of phrases get swallowed when the characters are especially upset or are in motion. These variations in audibility may make the play superficially lifelike on the screen, but we regret not hearing all the words. And why oh why was the movie shot in the kind of muted dark color that dummies think is right for tragedy? The drained, gloomy spectrum looks like stage lighting. An even more fundamental problem is Cacoyannis's sense of movement and place. In a movie, before characters enter a room we are customarily shown their arrival on the street and at the house and sometimes in the foyer or a passageway. This isn't mere filler. In the live theatre, we know exactly where the characters are—they're on that stage right in front of us. But at movies we seem to need to get our bearings—to know where people are coming from and where they're going and where things are happening. Most of the time, movies provide this information and we take it in unconsciously. When we don't get it, the movie appears to be impoverished and *stagy*. When people enter and leave an area that we cannot locate in terms of surrounding areas, the area is, inescapably, stage space, and we become even more aware of this when the area is outdoors—and therefore unconfined—than when it's indoors. Everything in *The Trojan Women* is outdoors, and yet the movie is claustrophobic, because the locations—the harbor, Cassandra's cave, a field of corpses, and so on—have no more connection with each other than if they were stage sets replacing each other. I would guess that Cacoyannis was working on a relatively small budget and had to piece his Troy together from bits of Spain. But, with all consideration made for the problem, the fact is that he didn't solve it. And he doesn't seem to know how to use the ground he's got. You're not sure where the people are in relation to each other even when they're in the same shot.

It obviously took extraordinary dedication and talent to make this movie—to inspire the actresses to test themselves, and to coach them and blend their voices so that an American, a French-Canadian, and an English-woman become acceptable as a family. Yet I question whether a director with so little feeling for the most basic elements of moviemaking can ever be a good movie director. A director with a "film sense" knows where to put the camera so that you don't question the shot; for others every setup looks arbitrary. This play demands a plain, consistent cinematic style, with no flourishes—a style as supremely matter-of-fact as Euripides's language. Cacoyannis tries to make the movie impressive—there's embalming fluid in the images—and the tragic line breaks down into sequences. Some are derivative, such as the whirling camera when Cassandra spins about, the cacophonous music and fast cuts when the chorus is distraught; some are effective in an overly prestigious way, such as the freeze frames in the opening sequence while the narrator speaks—like the breaks for words in Stravinsky's *Oedipus Rex*. These are the attempts of a man without a film sense to make a drama cinematic; it winds up an anthology of second-rate film styles.

One may long for the ideal—for a great play transformed by a great movie artist into a great movie. But great movie artists are not often tempted to tackle great plays, and when they do, it sometimes turns out that they don't have the right skills. Short of the ideal, what it comes down to is whether in seeing a movie version one can still respond to what makes the play great. By that standard, I count the Cacoyannis film a success. Even if one is aware of everything the matter with it, the emotion of the play gets to you, and the emotion of Greek tragedy has a purity that you *can't get from anything else.* That's a very good reason to make a movie—to bring people the emotions that only a few in our time have experienced in the theatre. (And the productions they see are flawed and stilted, too—though, of course, in different ways.) Beautiful as the Edith Hamilton translation is, the movie has something you can't get from a reading: Irene Papas's Helen is a demonic illumination of the text. I think one would have to be maybe a little foolish to let aesthetic scruples about the movie's mediocrity as cinema deprive one of seeing *The Trojan Women* with a cast that one could never hope to see on the stage. The actresses come from different cultures, but they bring intensity of life to the screen; that's what makes them stars. If a movie releases that intensity, it hasn't bungled what matters most.

The New Yorker, October 16, 1971

MURMUR OF THE HEART
LOUIS MALLE'S PORTRAIT OF THE ARTIST AS A YOUNG DOG

Murmur of the Heart is mellow and smooth, like a fine old jazz record, but when it's over it has the kick of a mule—a *funny* kick, which sends you out doubled over grinning. Assured and unflamboyant in technique, it is yet an exhilarating film—an irresistible film, one might say if one had not heard word of some resistance, especially by the jury at Cannes, which chose to ignore it, managing even to pass over Lea Massari's full-scale portrait of the carelessly sensual mother of a bourgeois brood of sons in favor of Kitty Winn's drab, meagre-spirited performance in *The Panic in Needle Park*. Massari's Clara is a woman without discretion or calculation; she's shamelessly loose and free, and she's loved by her sons because of her indifference to the bourgeois forms, which they nevertheless accept—on the surface, that is. What makes this movie so different from other movies about bourgeois life is that the director, Louis Malle, sees not only the prudent, punctilious surface but the volatile and slovenly life underneath. He looks at this bourgeois bestiary and sees it as funny and appalling and also—surprisingly— hardy and happy. It is perhaps the first time on film that anyone has shown us the bourgeoisie *enjoying* its privileges.

From the way Malle observes the sex education of the youngest, brightest son of the family, fourteen-year-old Laurent (Benoit Ferreux), one knows that the movie is a portrait of the artist as a young dog. It comes after a succession of Malle films, but in its subject, and in the originality and the special sure-footedness that the director (who also wrote the script) brings to the material, it is, clearly, the obligatory first film. The picture is set in Dijon—also the setting for Malle's *The Lovers*—in 1954, at the time of Dien Bien Phu (which must have been only a few years after the director's schoolboy days), and before the children of the bourgeoisie became radicalized. Though the film itself reveals the sources of Malle's humor, this story probably wouldn't have been nearly so funny or, perhaps, so affectionate if Malle had told it fifteen years ago. It is a film by someone who doesn't have to simplify in order to take a stand, who no longer needs to rebel; he has come a distance, and the story is additionally distanced by the changes in French student life that Godard recorded in *Masculine Feminine* and *La Chinoise*. In 1954, the sons of the successful gynecologist (Daniel Gélin) and the Italian-born Clara could still enjoy their wealth as their due. Seen with the vivacity of fresh intelligence, they're a family of monsters, all right, but normal monsters—no more monstrous than other close-knit families—and they're happy hypocrites.

I'm not sure how the picture was sustained and brought off so that we see the stuffiness and snobbery of the privileged class on the outside and the energetic amorality underneath, but the story moves toward its supremely logical yet witty and imaginative conclusion so stealthily that the kicker joke is perfect. Advance word had suggested that the picture was a serious, shocking view of incest, but the only shock is the joke that, for all the repressions these bourgeois practice and the conventions they pretend to believe in, they are such amoral, instinct-satisfying creatures that incest doesn't mean any more to them than to healthy animals. The shock is that in this context incest *isn't* serious—and that, I guess, may really upset some people, so they won't be able to laugh.

I can't remember another movie in which family life and adolescence have been used for such high comedy. The details are as singular, as deeply rooted in the period and the place, as the details in Truffaut's *The 400 Blows,* and the picture has that kind of candor. But no one in the film requires sympathy. Malle's approach has some of Buñuel's supple objectivity and aberrant humor. Malle satirizes the family from inside as Buñuel satirizes Catholicism from inside. The boys casually loot their own home, turn the dining room into a tennis court with a ball of spinach. Members of the family tease and squabble, but they enjoy the squabbling, because it is part of their intimacy and their security. Home is chaos; the three boys are not subdued even when there are guests. The vinegar-face father, severe and disgusted, though in a sort of ineffectual, ritualistic way, is tolerant—perhaps even, like the old family servant, proud that his boys are such irresponsible, uncontrollable *boys.* They're expensive pets, expected to commit outrages, and also expected to shape up eventually. In a poor environment, the boys would be brats, or even punks and delinquents; here they're the young masters. Papa's distaste is amusing, and the boys goad him; the grumblings of a put-upon father are a reassuring sound. And when you're furious with a brother, he's still a brother, and you have the pride and safety in that that you can never feel when you quarrel with those outside the family. This movie catches the way people care about each other in a family, and the feeling of a household in which there's no discipline. Which I think is probably generally the case but is something that movies like to lie about. The mixture of contempt and affection that the boys feel toward the old servant is so accurate—even if one has never been near a fuddy-duddy family retainer—that it sweeps away all those false, properly respected movie servants.

The only quality common to the films of Louis Malle is the restless intelligence one senses in them, and it must be this very quality that has led Malle to try such different subjects and styles. A new Chabrol or a Losey is as easily recognizable as a Magritte, but even film enthusiasts have only a vague idea of Malle's work. Had Malle gone on making variations of almost any one of his films, it is practically certain he would have been acclaimed long ago, but a director who is impatient and dissatisfied and never tackles the same problem twice gives reviewers trouble and is likely to be dismissed as a dilettante. Malle, though he is still under forty, predates the New Wave, and has made amazingly good films in several styles. Born in 1932, he was co-director with Cousteau of *The Silent World,* then assistant to Bresson on *A*

Man Escaped, and then, in 1957, at twenty-five, he made his first film, the ingenious, slippery thriller *Lift to the Scaffold* (also called *Frantic*), with Maurice Ronet and Jeanne Moreau, and a Miles Davis score. The following year, he had his biggest American success—*The Lovers,* with its flowing rhythms and its Brahms, the message of woman's desire for sexual fulfillment and the wind rippling through Moreau's white chiffon. It was facile movie-poetry but erotic and beautifully made. In 1960, he did a flipover to *Zazie dans le Métro,* from the Queneau novel—a fiendishly inventive slapstick comedy about a foulmouthed little girl, which was too fast and too freakish for American tastes, so that Americans did not credit Malle with the innovative editing, and later gave the credit instead to Tony Richardson's *Tom Jones* and to Richard Lester and others. *Zazie,* a comedy that owed a debt to Tati but carried Tati's dry, quick style to nightmarish anxiety, included satirical allusions to *La Dolce Vita* and *The Lovers.* After the wild *Zazie* came *Vie Privée,* with Brigitte Bardot and about her life as a sex-symbol star. *Le Feu Follet,* in 1963, the film that first convinced me that Malle was a superb director, shows the influence of Bresson but is without the inhuman pride that I think poisons so much of Bresson's later work. *Le Feu Follet* (sometimes called *The Fire Within*) has been seen by few people in this country. It received some generous reviews (especially in *The New Yorker*), and no one appears to be very clear about the reasons for its commercial failure—whether it got snarled in distribution problems or whether the film was simply "not commercial" in American terms. An elegy for a wasted life, adapted by Malle from a thirties novel, it dealt with the forty-eight hours before the suicide of a dissolute playboy (Maurice Ronet again) who, at thirty, has outlived his boyish charm and his social credit. It is a study of despair with no possibility of relief; the man has used up his slim resources and knows it. He does not want to live as what he has become; his taste is too good. It was directed in a clean, deliberate style, with a lone piano playing Satie in the background. Genêt wrote of the director, "He has effected something phenomenal this time, having turned literature into film, photographed the meaning of an unsubstantial, touching, and rather famous book, and given its tragic intention a clarity it never achieved in print." And Brendan Gill said, "Between them, Malle and Ronet have composed a work as small and vast, as affecting, and, I think, as permanent as Fitzgerald's *Babylon Revisited.*" It was a masterly film, and it seemed almost inconceivable that a director still so young could produce a work about such anguish with such control. *Le Feu Follet* should have made Malle's reputation here—in the way that *L'Avventura* made Antonioni's. After that painful, claustrophobic film, Malle did another flip, to the outdoors and the New World—to the frivolous, picaresque *Viva Maria!,* set in the Latin America of La Belle Epoque, with Moreau and Bardot. At the opening, the child who will become Bardot helps her imperialist-hating father dynamite a British fortress in Ireland, and the contrast between the father's act and the child's blooming, innocent happiness as she plays in the fields planting explosives is rapturously comic. *Viva Maria!* was lavish and visually beautiful, but the subsequent bombings and shootings weren't so funny; the central conceit involved in the pairing of Bardot and Moreau didn't work out, so the slapstick facetiousness was just left there, with nothing under it. But Bardot—not because of any *acting*—has never been more enchanting than in parts of this movie. When Malle put her into boys' clothes, with a cap and a smudge on her cheek, she was a tomboy looking for fun: Zazie grown up but still polymorphously amoral. After *The Thief of Paris*, with Jean-Paul Belmondo, Malle went to India, where he shot documentaries, the most famous of which, *Calcutta*, has never opened in New York.*

The director travelled a long road before looking into his own back yard; now, when he goes back to it in *Murmur of the Heart*, we can see in that gleeful, chaotic household the origins of the radiant prankishness of *Zazie* and *Viva Maria!* and of those riffs that don't stop for breath, and we can see the sources of the studied, overblown romanticism of *The Lovers*, and also of the caustic view of romanticism in the great *Le Feu Follet*. I don't think *Murmur of the Heart* is a greater film than *Le Feu Follet*, but in excluding all joy that film was a very special sort of film: getting so far inside a suicide's attitude toward himself can really wipe viewers out. This is a joyous and accessible work, and so the anguish of *Le Feu Follet* begins to seem youthful—like an early spiritual crisis that has been resolved. Although *Murmur of the Heart* is obviously semi-autobiographical, it's a movie not about how one has been scarred but about how one was formed. You can see that Malle is off the hook by the justice he does to the other characters. (The only character that seems to me a failure and no more than a stereotype is the lecherous priest, played by Michel Lonsdale.)

Lea Massari (she was the girl who disappeared in *L'Avventura*) has, as Clara, the background of a libertarian father—reminiscent of Bardot's background in *Viva Maria!* Clara says she grew up "like a savage," and when she smiles her irregular teeth show her to be a spiritual relative of the impudent Zazie. Malle's films have swung back and forth between the eroticism of the Moreau characters and the anarchic, childish humor of the Zazies; Massari's ravishing Clara combines them. Her relaxed sensuality is the essence of impropriety. There is a moment when Clara, who has blithely remarked to her sons as they watch her changing clothes, "I simply have no modesty," catches Laurent peeping at her in her bath. She instinctively slaps him; he is deeply offended, and she apologizes and says he should have slapped her back. This many-layered confusion of principle and hypocrisy and instinct and injustice is one of the rare occasions when a movie has shown how knotted the ties of family life really are for most of us. Clara comes alive because of that freak bit of Zazie in her; she will never grow up and become the

---

*Calcutta was shown on Channel 13 in New York early in December 1971, followed by *The Impossible Camera*—the first in a series of seven films that make up *Phantom India*. All eight later opened in a theatre.

mature mother of simplified fiction. She is not one of those Fay Bainter mothers, born at forty full of wisdom and christened "Mother."

As for Laurent—or Renzino, as Clara calls him—Benoit Ferreux probably is only about fourteen, but, without being fey, he looks enough like the Lauren Bacall of an earlier era to hold the camera in a vise, and he appears to have an impeccable sense of what's wanted. You're never quite sure how you feel about Laurent. His musical tastes—Charlie Parker and the other jazz greats we hear on the track—are irreproachable, and, in their irreproachability, marks of fashion and caste. He's extraordinarily clever, but he's also an arrogant, precocious little snot who thinks that people were put in the world to serve him; he despises a snob Fascist boy because the boob hasn't mastered the right tone—the acceptable amount of snobbery. The movie is about the childhood and growing into manhood of those who are pampered from birth, and at every step it shows what they take for granted. It defines the ways in which the rich are not like you and me, and the ways in which they are. Malle resembles Fitzgerald, but a Fitzgerald with a vision formed from the inside, and with the intelligence for perspective. His is a deeply realistic comic view—free of Fitzgerald's romantic ruined dreams. In pulling his different styles together in *Murmur of the Heart,* Malle finds a new ripe vein of comedy; believable comedy: that is to say, life seen in its comic aspects. There's a sequence in which smart Laurent outsmarts himself: he attempts to disrupt a meeting that his mother is having with her lover, and his intrusion results in her going off with the lover for a few days. When it comes to family ties and basic affections and how to lose one's virginity, even the smart and the dumb aren't so very far apart.

The New Yorker, October 23, 1971

THE FRENCH CONNECTION
URBAN GOTHIC

When New York's Mayor Lindsay began his efforts to attract the movie-production business, it probably didn't occur to him or his associates that they were ushering in a new movie age of nightmare realism. The Los Angeles area was selected originally for the sunshine and so that the movie-business hustlers—patent-violators who were pirating inventions as well as anything else they could get hold of—could slip over the border fast. As it turned out, however, California had such varied vegetation that it could be used to stand in for most of the world, and there was space to build whatever couldn't be found. But New York City is always New York City; it can't be anything else, and, with practically no studios for fakery, the movie companies use what's really here, so the New York–made movies have been set in Horror City. Although recent conflicts between the producers and the New York unions seem to have ended this Urban Gothic period,* the New York–made movies have provided a permanent record of the city in breakdown. I doubt if at any other time in American movie history there has been such a close relationship between the life on the screen and the life of a portion of the audience. Los Angeles–made movies were not *about* Los Angeles; often they were not about any recognizable world. But these recent movies are about New York, and the old sentimentalities are almost impossible here—physically impossible, because the city gives them the lie. (I'm thinking of such movies as *Klute, Little Murders, The Anderson Tapes, Greetings, The Landlord, Where's Poppa?, Midnight Cowboy, Harry Kellerman, Diary of a Mad Housewife, No Way to Treat a Lady, Shaft, Cotton Comes to Harlem, The Steagle, Cry Uncle, The Owl and the Pussycat, The Panic in Needle Park, Bananas,* and the forthcoming *Born to Win.*) The city of New York has helped American movies grow up; it has also given movies a new spirit of nervous, anxious hopelessness, which is the true spirit of New York. It is literally true that when you live in New York you no longer believe that the garbage will ever be gone from the streets or that life will ever be sane and orderly.

The movies have captured the soul of this city in a way that goes beyond simple notions of realism. The panhandler in the movie who jostles the hero looks just like the one who jostles you as you leave the movie theatre; the police sirens in the movie are screaming outside; the hookers and junkies in the freak show on the screen are indistinguishable from the ones in the freak show on the streets. Famous New York put-on artists and well-known street people are incorporated in the movies; sometimes they are in the movie theatre, dressed as they are in the movie, and sometimes you leave the theatre and see them a few blocks away, just where they were photographed. There's a sense of carnival about this urban-crisis city; everyone seems to be dressed for a mad ball. Screams in the theatre at Halloween movies used to be a joke, signals for laughter and applause, because nobody believed in the terror on the screen. The midnight showings of horror films now go on all year round, and the screams are no longer pranks. Horror stories and brutal melodramas concocted for profit are apparently felt on a deeper level than might have been supposed. People don't laugh or applaud when there's a scream; they try to ignore the sound. It is assumed that the person yelling is stoned and out of control, or crazy and not to be trifled with—he may want an excuse to blow off steam, he may have a knife or a gun. It is not uncommon now for fights and semi-psychotic episodes to take place in the theatres, especially when the movies being played are shockers. Audiences for these movies in the Times Square area and in the Village are highly volatile. Probably the unstable, often dazed members of the audience are particularly susceptible to the violence and tension on the screen; maybe crowds now include a certain

*After two and a half months, the five major companies signed an agreement with the unions and production in New York was resumed.

number of people who simply can't stay calm for two hours. But whether the movies bring it out in the audience or whether the particular audiences that are attracted bring it into the theatre, it's *there* in the theatre, particularly at late shows, and you feel that the violence on the screen may at any moment touch off violence in the theatre. The audience is explosively *live*. It's like being at a prizefight or a miniature Altamont.

Horror is very popular in Horror City—old horror films and new ones. The critics were turned off by the madness of *The Devils;* the audiences were turned on by it. They wanted the benefits of the sexual pathology of religious hysteria: bloody tortures, burning flesh, nuns violated on altars, lewd nuns stripping and orgying, and so on. Almost all the major movie companies are now, like the smaller ones, marginal businesses. The losses of the American film industry since 1968 are calculated at about five hundred and twenty-five million dollars. Besides Disney, the only company that shows profits is A.I.P.—the producers of ghouls-on-wheels schlock pictures, who are now also turning out movies based on Gothic "classics." I don't believe that people are going to shock and horror films because of a need to exorcise their fears; that's probably a fable. I think they're going for entertainment, and I don't see how one can ignore the fact that the kind of entertainment that attracts them now is often irrational and horrifyingly brutal. A few years ago, *The Dirty Dozen* turned the audience on so high that there was yelling in the theatre and kicking at the seats. And now an extraordinarily well-made new thriller gets the audience sky-high and keeps it up there—*The French Connection,* directed by William Friedkin, which is one of the most "New York" of all the recent New York movies. It's also probably the best-made example of what trade reporters sometimes refer to as "the cinema du zap."

How's this for openers? A peaceful day in Marseille. A *flic* strolls into a boulangerie, comes out carrying a long French bread, and strolls home. As he walks into his own entranceway, a waiting figure in a leather coat sticks out an arm with a .45 and shoots him in the face and then in the torso. The assassin picks up the bread, breaks off a piece to munch, and tosses the remainder back onto the corpse. That's the first minute of *The French Connection.* The film then jumps to New York and proceeds through chases, pistol-whippings, slashings, beatings, murders, snipings, and more chases for close to two hours. The script, by Ernest Tidyman (who wrote *Shaft*), is based on the factual account by Robin Moore (of *The Green Berets*) of the largest narcotics haul in New York police history until the recent Jaguar case. The producer, Philip D'Antoni, also produced *Bullitt,* and the executive producer was G. David Schine, of Cohn and Schine. That's not a creative team, it's a consortium. The movie itself is pretty businesslike. There are no good guys in this harsh new variant of cops-and-robbers; *The French Connection* features the latest-model sadistic cop, Popeye (Gene Hackman). It's undeniably gripping, slam-bang, fast, charged with suspense, and so on—a mixture of *Razzia* and *Z,* and hyped up additionally with a television-thriller-style score that practically lays you out all by itself. At one point, just in case we might lose interest if we didn't have our minute-to-minute injections of excitement, the camera cuts from the street conversation of a few cops to show us the automobile smashup that brought them to the scene, and we are treated to two views of the bloody faces of fresh corpses. At first, we're confused as to who the victims are, and we stare at them thinking they must be characters in the movie. It takes a few seconds to realize that they bear no relation whatsoever to the plot.

It's no wonder that *The French Connection* is a hit, but what in hell is it? It uses eighty-six separate locations in New York City—so many that it has no time for carnival atmosphere: it crashes right through. I suppose the answer we're meant to give is that it's an image of the modern big city as Inferno, and that Popeye is an Existential hero, but the movie keeps zapping us. Though *The French Connection* achieves one effect through timing and humor (when the French Mr. Big, played by Fernando Rey, outwits Popeye in the subway station by using his silver-handled umbrella to open the train doors) most of its effects are of the *Psycho*-derived blast-in-the-face variety. Even the expert pacing is achieved by somewhat questionable means; the ominous music keeps tightening the screws and heating things up. The noise of New York already has us tense. The movie is like an aggravated case of New York: it raises this noise level to produce the kind of painful tension that is usually described as almost unbearable suspense. But it's the same kind of suspense you feel when someone outside your window keeps pushing down on the car horn and you think the blaring sound is going to drive you out of your skull. This horn routine is, in fact, what the cop does throughout the longest chase sequence. The movie's suspense is magnified by the sheer pounding abrasiveness of its means; you don't have to be an artist or be original or ingenious to work on the raw nerves of an audience this way—you just have to be smart and brutal. The high-pressure methods that one could possibly accept in *Z* because they were tools used to try to show the audience how a Fascist conspiracy works are used as ends in themselves. Despite the dubious methods, the purpose of the brutality in *Z* was moral—it was to make you hate brutality. Here you love it, you wait for it—that's all there is. I know that there are many people—and very intelligent people, too—who love this kind of fast-action movie, who say that this is what movies do best and that this is what they really want when they go to a movie. Probably many of them would agree with everything I've said but will still love the movie. Well, it's not what I want, and the fact that Friedkin has done a sensational job of direction just makes that clearer. It's not what I want not because it fails (it doesn't fail) but because of what it is. It is, I think, what we once feared mass entertainment might become: jolts for jocks. There's nothing in the movie that you enjoy thinking over afterward—nothing especially clever except the timing of the subway-door-and-umbrella sequence. Every other effect in the movie—even the climactic car-versus-runaway-elevated-train chase—is achieved by noise, speed, and brutality.

On its own terms, the picture makes few mistakes, though there is one small but conspicuous one. A good comic contrast of drug dealers dining at their ease in a splendid restaurant while the freezing, hungry cops who are tailing them curse in a cold doorway and finally eat a hunk of pizza is spoiled because, for the sake of a composition with the two groups in the same shot, the police have been put where the diners could obviously see them. It is also a mistake, I think, that at the end the picture just stops instead of coming to a full period. The sloppy plotting, on the other hand, doesn't seem to matter; it's amazing how much implausibility speed and brutality can conceal. Hitchcock's thrillers were full of holes, but you were having too good a time to worry about them; *The French Connection* is full of holes, but mostly you're too stunned to notice them. There's no logic in having the Lincoln Continental that has been shipped from France with the heroin inside abandoned on a back street at night rather than parked snugly in the garage of its owner's hotel; it appears to be on the street just so the narcotics agents can spot it and grab it. There's an elaborate sequence of an auction at an automobile graveyard which serves no clear purpose. And if you ever think about it you'll realize that you have no idea who that poor devil was who got shot in the overture, or why. For all the movie tells you, it may have been for his French bread. But you really know what it's all in there for. It's the same reason you get those juicy pictures of the corpses: zaps.

Listen to Popeye's lines and you can learn the secrets of zap realism. A crude writer can give his crummy, cheap jokes to a crude character, and the jokes really pay off. The rotten jokes get laughs and also show how ugly the character's idea of humor is. Popeye risks his life repeatedly and performs fabulously dangerous actions, yet the movie debases him in every possible way. Hackman has turned himself into a modern Ted Healy type—porkpie hat, sneaky-piggy eyes, and a gut-first walk, like Robert Morley preceded by his belly coming toward us in those BOAC "Visit Britain" commercials. Popeye (the name is out of Faulkner, I assume) has a filthy mouth and a complete catalogue of race prejudices, plus some "cute" fetishes; e.g., he cases girls who wear boots. He is the anti-hero carried to a new lumpenprole low—the mean cop who used to figure on the fringes of melodrama (as in *Sweet Smell of Success*) moved to the center. Sam Spade might play dirty, but he had a code and he had personal style; even Bullitt, a character contrived to hold the chases and bloodshed together, was a super-cop with style and feelings. This movie turns old clichés into new clichés by depriving the central figure of *any* attractive qualities. Popeye is insanely callous, a shrewd bully who enjoys terrorizing black junkies, and the film includes raids on bars that are gratuitous to the story line just to show what a subhuman son of a bitch he is. The information is planted early that his methods have already cost the life of a police officer, and at the end this plant has its pat payoff when he accidentally shoots an F.B.I. agent, and the movie makes the point that he doesn't show the slightest remorse. The movie presents him as the most ruthlessly lawless of characters and yet—here is where the basic amorality comes through—shows that this is the kind of man it takes to get the job done. It's the vicious bastard who gets the results. Popeye, the lowlifer who makes Joe or Archie sound like Daniel Ellsberg, is a cop the way the movie Patton was a general. When Popeye walks into a bar and harasses blacks, part of the audience can say, "That's a real pig," and another part of the audience can say, "That's the only way to deal with those people. Waltz around with them and you get nowhere."

I imagine that the people who put this movie together just naturally think in this commercially convenient double way. This right-wing, left-wing, take-your-choice cynicism is total commercial opportunism passing itself off as an Existential view. And maybe that's why Popeye's determination to find the heroin is not treated unequivocally as socially useful but is made obsessive. Popeye's low character is used to make the cops-and-robbers melodrama superficially modern by making it *meaningless;* his brutality serves to demonstrate that the cops are no better than the crooks. In personal style and behavior, he is, in fact, deliberately shown as worse than the crooks, yet since he's the cop with the hunches that pay off, the only cop who gets results, the movie can be seen as a way of justifying police brutality. At the end, a Z-style series of titles comes on to inform us that the dealers who were caught got light sentences or none at all. The purpose of giving us this information is also probably double: to tell us to get tougher judges and to make tougher laws, and to provide an ironic coda showing that Popeye's efforts were really futile. A huge haul of heroin was destroyed, but the movie doesn't bother to show us that—to give a man points for anything is unfashionable. The series of titles is window-dressing anyway. The only thing that this movie believes in is giving the audience jolts, and you can feel the raw, primitive response in the theatre. This picture says Popeye is a brutal son of a bitch who gets the dirty job done. So is the picture.

The New Yorker, October 30, 1971

FIDDLER ON THE ROOF
A BAGEL WITH A BITE OUT OF IT

I can't talk about Hollywood. It was a horror to me when I was there and it's a horror to look back on. I can't imagine how I did it. When I got away from it I couldn't even refer to the place by name. "Out there," I called it. You want to know what "out there" means to me? Once I was coming down a street in Beverly Hills and I saw a Cadillac about a block long, and out of the side window was a wonderfully slinky mink, and an arm, and at the end of the arm a hand in a white suède glove wrinkled around the wrist, and in the hand was a bagel with a bite out of it.

—DOROTHY PARKER, IN 1956,
IN AN INTERVIEW IN THE *PARIS REVIEW*

Everyone may have a different view of what that bagel represents, but if it is the symbolic ordinary Jewish food that the show-business *nouveaux riches* cling to, it may also symbolize a vulgar strength that repelled Dorothy Parker—and in which she did not share. Hollywood Jews overdressed like gypsies who had to carry it all on their backs, and they clung to a bit of solid, heavy food even when they were no longer hungry, because it seemed like reality. Vulgarity is not as destructive to an artist as snobbery, and in the world of movies vulgar strength has been a great redemptive force, cancelling out niggling questions of taste. I think *Fiddler on the Roof*, directed by Norman Jewison, is an absolutely smashing movie; it is not especially sensitive, it is far from delicate, and it isn't even particularly imaginative, but it seems to me the most *powerful* movie musical ever made.

Musical comedy is one of the American contributions to world theatre; it is also primarily an American Jewish contribution. There would be a theatre in America without Jews, and perhaps it would be not much worse than it is—though it would certainly be different—but, as William Goldman has pointed out, "Without Jews, there simply would have been no musical comedy to speak of in America. . . . In the last half century, the only major Gentile composer to come along was Cole Porter." What separates *Fiddler on the Roof*, which is set in Czarist Russia, from other Broadway shows and from such movie musicals as *West Side Story* and *The Sound of Music* and *My Fair Lady* and *Hello, Dolly!* and *Camelot* and *Paint Your Wagon* and *Star!* and *Doctor Dolittle* is that it is probably the only successful attempt to use this theatrical form on the subject of its own sources—that is, on the heritage that the Jewish immigrants brought to this country. The only other big movie musical of recent years with any explicit Jewish material was *Funny Girl*, and although essentially a blown-up show-business bio, it also got some of its drive from that explicitness. *Fiddler on the Roof* finds its theme in the energy and gusto and the few remnants of moldy traditions—the religion of the bagel—that have resulted in such wonders as the American musical theatre as well as in the horrors of a pandering theatre full of Jewish-mother jokes. But *Fiddler on the Roof* is a celebration of a Jewish *father*, and Tevye, the dairyman pulling his wagon, is a male Mother Courage, not a male Molly Goldberg. Maybe because its means are utterly square and plain, the movie succeeds in doing what Elia Kazan, for all his gifts and despite some fine scenes, failed to do in *America America* (which dealt with the persecution of his Greek ancestors in Turkey and the dream of the new country). Though it is a musical, *Fiddler on the Roof* succeeds in telling one of the root stories of American life: as Tevye's daughters marry and disperse and the broken family is driven off its land and starts the long trek to America, Tevye's story becomes the story of the Jewish people who came to America at the turn of the century—what they left behind and what they brought with them.

It is not a movie about "little people," though it seems so in the first five minutes—a "hearty" pre-title sequence featuring the song "Tradition," which is show-business Jewish-Americana, a gruesome romp that makes one wince in expectation of more of the same. But then the credits come on, and Isaac Stern plays the theme (as he does in the solo parts throughout the movie) with startling *brio* and attack; Isaac Stern's energy and style carry us into a different realm. His harshly sweet music clears away the sticky folk stuff, and the movie takes off. It never again sinks to the little-people-at-their-simple-tasks level, because Topol's Tevye has the same vitality and sweetness and gaiety as Isaac Stern's music; he's a rough presence, masculine, with burly, raw strength, but also sensual and warm. He's a poor man but he's not a little man, he's a big man brought low—a man of Old Testament size brought down by the circumstances of oppression. The crooked, ironic grin when he gestures to God and the light in his eyes after a love song with his wife tell the story of a dogged man who can be crushed again and again and still come back.

Topol is a broad actor, but not in the bad sense of broad; Clark Gable, though incapable of registering much suffering, was a broad actor, and so is Sean Connery. I mean not an actor who lacks finer shades (although Gable certainly did, and it may turn out that Topol does, too) but, rather, an actor with a heroic presence, a man's man, an actor with *male* authority—a Raimu, a Jean Gabin. Typically, these actors play earthy, working-with-their-hands roles and look out of place when they are cast in the upper class. They are almost totally physical actors—deep-voiced men who dominate the stage or screen by energy and power, actors with a gift for projecting common emotions and projecting them to the gallery. Anna Magnani is the last woman star of this type—the actors and actresses of the people. Anthony Quinn's Zorba was a comparable large-spirited role. It's easy for small-spirited people to put down this kind of acting, but when a director has enough taste and control to keep an outsize performer within limits, the emotional effects can be satisfying and rich in a way that other kinds of acting never are. Topol (rather too broad for his role in *Before Winter Comes*) was a superb choice for the movie Tevye, because his brute vitality makes Tevye a force of nature—living proof of the power to endure. Tevye is the soul of *Fiddler on the Roof;* Topol, a giant dancing bear of a man, embodies the theme, and, big as the movie is—and it's *huge*—he carries it on his back.

Topol has a fine speaking voice, low and resonant but also cracked and playful; he can twist a word right up to a high register. The humor in Tevye's role is not only in the jokes themselves but in the playing; they don't stale, because a good performer reactivates them. Such folk humor as a man talking about a girl while the man he's talking to thinks the conversation is about a cow is so primitive one watches it ritualistically; it's the beginning of vaudeville. Perhaps because Topol is an Israeli, not an American Jew, he plays with a strength that is closer to peasant strength than to an American urban Jewish image. If his heroic strength overpowers the original qualities of the character, his backbone is what this big musical-comedy movie needs. His is a Sabra Tevye, and I suppose this may disconcert those who saw the first Broadway Tevye, Zero Mostel, who I understand was much funnier. Mostel is a brilliant, baleful, sad-eyed buffoon, weirdly inventive, and with his freak specialty—the surprise of how light he is on his toes—but on the screen he could no more embody the Jewish Everyman than W. C. Fields or Jonathan Winters could be the Wasp Everyman. He is a clown, and, like many great clowns, he creates his own atmosphere. Topol is handsome, which is a blessing in movies, and, though bigger than life, he's still in the normal human range—his bigness is an intensification of normal emotions.

Norman Jewison's movie is astonishingly square—astonishing not only in how square his approach is but in how joyously square the results are. Never having seen *Fiddler* on the stage, I can't judge what has been lost, but, on its own terms, the movie has an over-all, ongoing vitality that is overwhelming. It is a show that reveals not what made Jewish writers or thinkers but what has made American Jewish show business. It is an attempt to bring joy out of basic experience; the hero is a myth-size version of a limited, slightly stupid common man. Jewison has a sound instinct for robust, masculine low comedy; he showed it in the way he handled Rod Steiger in *In the Heat of the Night* and Alan Arkin in *The Russians Are Coming, The Russians Are Coming.* (On a small scale, Arkin's Russian was a warm-up for Tevye.) The producers were probably wise—or maybe lucky—when they selected a Gentile director, because Jewison (an exotic name for a Methodist) doesn't let the movie slip into chummy Jewish sentimentality. In the movie, to be chosen for suffering is a joke that Tevye and the other Jews in the Ukrainian village are in on. The Jews are a chosen people the way blacks are beautiful. Those who suffer may need to believe there is a higher meaning in their suffering, just as those whose beauty has not been sufficiently recognized may need to rediscover it and emphasize it. The irony that the chosen of God seem to have less access to Him than others do is, in fact, the source of Tevye's comedy in the movie, as it is in the Sholom Aleichem stories on which the musical is based. Tevye is a religious man but also a realist— because he can't get God's ear. Younger members of the audience— particularly if they are Jewish—may be put off the movie if their parents and grandparents have gone on believing in a special status with God long after the oppression was over, and have tried to prop up their authority over their children with boring stories about early toil and hardship (as the superpatriot judge in *Little Murders* does). Too many people have *used* their early suffering as a platitudinous weapon and so have made it all seem fake. And I suppose that *Fiddler on the Roof* has been such a phenomenal stage success partly because it can be used in this same self-congratulatory way—as a public certificate of past suffering. And perhaps the movie can be, too. But this movie is far from a Jewish *The Sound of Music* and is infinitely less sentimental than the youth rock musicals.

Jewison treats the Jews as an oppressed people—no better, no worse than others—and this sensible attitude, full of essential good will, and yet not self-conscious, as a Jewish movie director's attitude might easily have been, keeps the movie sane and balanced, and allows it to be powerful. The movie is not a celebration of Jewishness; it is a celebration of the sensual pleasures of staying alive, and of trying to hang on to a bit of ceremony, too—a little soul food, Jewison does not permit the Jewish performers to be too "Jewish"; that is, to become familiar with the audience with that degrading mixture of self-hatred and self-infatuation that corrupts so much Jewish comedy. Only one of the leads—Molly Picon, as Yente, the matchmaker— gets away from him and carries on like a stage Jew, with a comic accent. Why do Jewish performers like Molly Picon have to overdo being Jewish when they play Jews? What do they think they are the rest of the time? They're like those Hollywood actresses who, when they got past forty and the time came for them to play the parents of teen-age children, did themselves up like Whistler's mother. It is an anomaly of American entertainment, in which Jews have played so major a role, that it is not the Gentiles but the Jews who have created the Jewish stereotypes, and not to satisfy any need in the Gentiles but to satisfy the mixed-up masochism of Jewish audiences. (Black performers put on comic black masks for black audiences, too; it could conceivably be argued that the comedy is in showing their own people the masks they wear for whites, but this argument certainly doesn't carry over to the Jews.) It's this kind of cheap courting of favor with the Jewish audience that one may fear when one goes to see *Fiddler on the Roof,* and Jewison keeps the movie about ninety-nine percent pure.

As the timid tailor who loves Tzeitel, Tevye's oldest daughter, Leonard Frey is as innocent of heart and tangled in his limbs as a young Ben Blue, and as the daughter Rosalind Harris, a tall, slender young actress, looks just enough like Frey for the marriage to have been made in Heaven; they're a lunatically sweet pair of Shakespearean lovers—funny, pastoral, perfect. Paul Mann, with his winged eyebrows and ruddy, button-nose face, is a marvellous camera image—a true St. Nick. His wealthy butcher, like his rug merchant in *America America,* is a lived-in character. You look at him and you see a whole way of life—groaning boards loaded with meat, the pleasures of materialism. The butcher's and Tevye's explosions of temper at Tzeitel's wedding are possibly the truest moments of folk humor. (The movie is most false, I think, in the reaction shots of the constable when he and Tevye talk; these shots seem to come out of a Second World War movie—they make dignity-of-man points.) Michele Marsh is a bit too conventional an ingénue as the second daughter but redeems the performance with her farewell song; the third daughter, Neva Small, very young and with long red hair, has a special comic spark in her early scenes. The Golde (Tevye's wife) of Norma Crane is physically suitable, but the character, regrettably, never emerges.

The movie is highly theatrical, but it isn't stagy. Joseph Stein, who wrote the stage show, also did the movie script, and it's a serviceable adaptation. Jewison has managed to keep the whole production, including the out-of-doors scenes, somewhat stylized, so that the simple transitions in and out of the songs and dances are not jarring but just a further step in stylization. And since, as the stage show was conceived (mostly by Jerome Robbins, from all accounts), the songs and dances are meant to be not "professional" but heightened expressions of emotion by the characters, the numbers are in any case not so different from the somewhat formalized theatrical scenes they grow out of. Jewison's devices to get from one scene to the next are so naïve that they can easily be accepted, because they serve the material. The vastness of fields with only a few figures is a simple conversion from a bare stage. These fields may then be dissolved into an abstraction to end a scene, or the camera may move from the figures in a field to a landscape. Some of the devices don't serve good purposes. Though the picture seems to ride right over its own faults, it *is* irritating that the direction and editing so often go for obvious effects—a shift, say, from the candles' being lighted in one home to the candles' being lighted all over the village. Jewison fails at certain scenes because of a kind of nondenominational blandness: the revolutionary from Kiev (Michael Glaser) becomes just an attractive juvenile, and the scene in which he tries to teach radical ideas to Tevye's daughters is insipid. The third daughter's Gentile suitor (Raymond Lovelock) is a walking example of Hitler-youth-movement calendar art. However, the worst flaw in the film except for the unrealized Golde is that the best dance scenes are all but wrecked by the whirlybird attempt to create dazzle and speed with a camera amidst the figures instead of letting the dances build by choreographic means. You want to see the whole figures and the steps, not blurred faces and bits of bodies. Dance has greater power than filmmakers may realize, and the wedding dance of four men with wine bottles on their heads is the high point of the film. I don't know if it's traditional or a Jerome Robbins contribution—perhaps it's a blend of both—but it's a beautiful ritual dance, and beautifully performed. It comes as a gift of art, like Isaac Stern's violin songs.

I fear that people of taste have been so indoctrinated now with a narrow conception of cinematic values that a movie in a broad popular style will be subject to a snobbish reaction. But square can be beautiful, too. It can be strong in a very direct way, and the theme of *Fiddler on the Roof* justifies this large-scale (nine-million-dollar) production. One doesn't go to a big American movie musical expecting impeccable ethnic nuances or fine brushwork; that's not what this particular genre provides. What it does offer is the pleasure of big, bold strokes—and spirit. *Fiddler on the Roof* is American folk opera, commercial style. So was *Porgy and Bess*. And though the score, by Jerry Bock (the music) and Sheldon Harnick (the lyrics, functional but uninspired), isn't in the Gershwin class, it isn't *bad*. No other American folk opera (certainly not *Porgy and Bess,* which has a rather unfortunate libretto) has ever been so successfully brought to the screen as *Fiddler on the Roof.* Its great advantage on the screen is its narrative strength; the material builds and accumulates meaning, until, at the end, when the Jews who have left their homes huddle on a raft, Tevye's story becomes part of the larger story, and the full scope of the movie is achieved. Though the techniques and simplifications are those of musical comedy, when they are put to work on a large emotional theme that is consonant with the very nature of American musical comedy—is, in fact, at its heart—the effect on the large screen is of a musical epic. The music is certainly not operatic, but the movie of *Fiddler on the Roof* has operatic power. It's not a soft experience; you come out shaken.

Dorothy Parker, so apt and so funny, was also so *wrong.* She was right, of course, in seeing Hollywood as a mink-and-bagel story; that's what anyone researching movie history comes up against, and it must be what anyone researching the musical theatre comes up against, too. And it's the easiest thing to patronize. But that bagel with the bite out of it should have cheered her. Imagine that arm without the bagel and you have cold money. Didn't it tell her that the woman in the mink in the Cadillac didn't quite believe in the mink or the Cadillac? Didn't it tell her that movies, like musical comedies, were made by gypsies who didn't know how to act as masters, because they were still on the road being chased? Couldn't Miss Parker, split down the middle herself—a Jewish father and a Gentile mother—see that that bagel was a piece of the raft, a comic holy wafer?

The New Yorker, November 13, 1971

EL TOPO
EL POTO——HEAD COMICS

The atmosphere in the theatre is enough to inform you that *El Topo* is a head film, but while I was watching Alexandro Jodorowsky's horror circus I was nevertheless puzzled about why the mostly young audience sat there quietly—occasionally laughing at a particularly garish murder or mutilation—while the few older people staggered out in disgust. At one point, I drew in my breath sharply at the prospect of another slaughter scene, and a pretty, blank-faced girl sitting in front of me with her boyfriend's arm on her shoulder turned her head slightly toward me, as if to say, "What's the matter with her? Is she taking it seriously, or something?" And I realized that I and those older people who left—I would have joined them if I had not had a professional interest in seeing the film—were responding on a different level from the rest of the audience, part of which had probably already seen the film before its official opening last week, during the six months it played at midnight screenings, like a Black Mass. This film that they return to over and over doesn't need reviews (not in the overground press, anyway) to lure an audience, but maybe it's up to reviewers to try to explain why that audience is being lured.

Jodorowsky, born in Chile in 1930 of Polish-Russian-Jewish parentage, was once a member of Marcel Marceau's company and composed some of Marceau's pantomimes; he is now a theatre director in Mexico, and a cartoonist as well, whose weekly comic strip "Fabulas Panicas" (or "Panic Fables") appears in a major Mexico City newspaper. *El Topo* (it means "The Mole") was made in Mexico, and it resembles the spaghetti Westerns. It begins with a bearded stranger in black leather (Jodorowsky) riding on a sandy plain; the color looks cheap and overbright, unreal in that gaudy way that unsophisticated attempts at realism often produce—it's like Kodacolor, with aquamarine skies. But the stranger rides with his naked son sitting behind him, and it is immediately apparent that the nakedness is symbolic—the more so when the father says, "Now you are a man. You are seven years old. Bury your first toy and your mother's picture," and the burial ceremony consists of propping the symbols up in the sand. And when the father and son come to a town, the town is a scene of more than usual spaghetti-Western carnage. It is a town of corpses and entrails; animals, children—everyone has been butchered, and the waters literally flow red. The bearded man in black becomes the gunfighter, the avenger; he tracks down the murderous bandits and castrates their warlord. Then, with the words "Destroy me. Depend on no one," he leaves his son with a group of young monks whom he has liberated, and takes up with the warlord's mistress. Up to this point, the carnage has been steady, and with quantities of fetishism and perversion. (As captives of the brigands, used for sexual sport, the young monks had bloodstained bare bottoms.)

In the next section, the picture becomes more occult, and more like a fairy tale, as the man in black and the woman, whom he christens Mara, go into the desert, where she persuades him that he must conquer the four masters who dwell there. The masters being different varieties of holy men, each of the four contests is enigmatic, and in this section the characters converse in high-flown riddles—a sort of Zen, Confucius-say talk ("The desert is a circle"). The hero wins his contests by trickery and realizes too late that he has truly lost, and cries out to ask why God has forsaken him. Meanwhile, Mara has been joined by a sadistic lesbian in butch black couture, and as he thrashes about in guilt for his crimes, battering himself against walls that crumble, the lesbian comes at him, like Mercedes McCambridge in *Johnny Guitar*, and pumps lead into him; he keeps walking, arms outstretched and with stigmata on his hands and feet, until Mara shoots him down. The women kiss—tongues extended—and leave him for dead. A group of dwarfs and cripples lug his body off. Can it be the end? No, there is a third section.

Years have passed—perhaps twenty. He sits as a holy man in a cave in a mountain, tended by a worshipful dwarf woman. Spiritually reborn, with his beard and head shaved in penitence, he pledges himself to liberate the tiny, shrivelled cave people, who are now trapped in the mountain, imprisoned there by the people of a nearby town, so that the townspeople will not have to see the deformed results of their generations of incest. The holy man begins work on a tunnel; because of his height, he himself can scale the walls of the cave, and he comes and goes, taking the woman dwarf with him. When they go into the town, we are once more back in a Western. The town is a synthesis of the gambling, whoring saloon towns of American movies, with a cartoon catalogue of evils: blacks are sold as slaves and branded, accused of rape by lecherous women, lynched, and so on. The penitent cleans toilets in the town jail and becomes a clown—God's fool—in order to buy dynamite to blast the mountain open. When he and his little woman (the only good woman in the entire film, and good by virtue of her total selfless devotion to him) go to the church (where the parishioners normally play Russian roulette) and ask to be married, the priest turns out to be the abandoned son. The three of them go back to the mountain to free the cave people; once free, however, the crippled, helpless little monstrosities—they're like deformed Munchkins—rush to see the wonders of the town, and the townspeople meet them with rifles and shoot them down. The holy man arrives too late; they have all been massacred. He yells and is shot, and is shot again and again, but he keeps coming toward the townspeople, like a Golem. Full of holes (like Toshiro Mifune's porcupine Macbeth full of spears in *Throne of Blood*), he picks up a gun and, once more the avenger, retaliates by slaughtering the townspeople. Seated then, cross-legged, he soaks himself in kerosene from a Western lamp and immolates himself (successfully). A new holy family—his son, bearded and dressed in black, and his dwarf widow, carrying his newborn baby, ride away into the whatever the movie began from.

Blood-soaked and piled high with deformity, the film is commercialized Surrealism. *El Topo* has been called a Zen Buddhist Western, but in terms of its derivations it's a spaghetti Western in the style of Luis Buñuel, and tinsel all the way. The avant-garde devices that once fascinated a small bohemian group because they seemed a direct pipeline to the occult and "the marvellous" now reach the new mass bohemianism of youth. But the marvellous has become a bag of old Surrealist tricks: the acid-Western style is snythesized from devices of the once avant-garde—especially *L'Age d'Or* and the whole lifework of Buñuel, with choice lifts from Cocteau's *The Blood of a Poet,* too. In *El Topo,* a brigand out on a rocky terrain sucks a woman's pink slipper, and then a collection of women's slippers are set up on the rocks as targets for shooting practice. An armless man and a legless man he carries on his shoulders function as one person—stumps exposed, of course; when shot apart, the helpless sections writhe on the ground. A man cuts a banana with a sabre. Crowds in the Western town applaud murders as if they were theatrical events. The lesbian lashes Mara's back, licks and kisses the wounds, and then offers her blood-smeared face for Mara to kiss. Even the dwarf woman is forced into a sex show by the lewd townspeople, and must remove her blouse and expose her pathetic little body. And not just to them but to us.

Bizarrely complicated though it is, one can follow the story without difficulty. The movie may seem bewildering, however, because the narrative is overlaid with a clutter of symbols and ideas. Jodorowsky employs anything that can give the audience a charge, even if the charges are drawn from different systems of thought that are—*as thought*—incompatible. For example, he gets a lot of mileage out of the viciousness of lecherous, sex-starved fat old women gloating over murders, pawing a young black boy to the accompaniment of pig noises on the track, and taking up rifles to mow down helpless, stunted children on crutches; it's a further distortion of the conventional distortions of Freudianism in American movies. But the movie is not a Freudian movie; if it were, the saintly love between the hero and the selfless, crippled dwarf might look pretty funny, but for *that* Jodorowsky shifts gears to penitential piety. One enthusiast of the film, who characterized it in an article in the Sunday *Times* as "a monumental work of filmic art," described Jodorowsky as "a man of passionate erudition in matters religious and philosophical, which he draws on with the zest of the instinctual thinker for whom ideas are sensuous entities." Well, of course, you don't need erudition to draw on matters religious and philosophical that way— any dabbler can do it. All you need is a theatrical instinct and a talent for (a word I once promised myself never to use) *frisson.* Jodorowsky is, it is true, a director for whom ideas are sensuous entities—sensuous toys, really, to be played with. By piling onto the Western man-with-no-name righteous-avenger form elements from Eastern fables, Catholic symbolism, and so on, Jodorowsky achieves a kind of comic-strip mythology. And when you play with ideas this way, promiscuously—with thoughts and enigmas and with symbols of human suffering—the resonances get so thick and confused that the game may seem not just theatre but labyrinthine, "deep": a masterpiece. I used the term "enthusiast" deliberately; the same writer describes the worshipful audiences and is himself among the worshipful, who treat *El Topo* as if it were the movie equivalent of a holy book. It is taken to be deep in the same sense that *The Prophet* used to be; "a work of incomprehensible depth," another enthusiast called it, and, still another, "an indescribable masterpiece." *El Topo* is really "The Bloody Prophet."

At the beginning, when the gunfighter in black is asked, "Who are you to judge me?" he replied, "I am God," and after punishing those who are not good enough to live he immolates himself because of the evil in the world. Unlike Buñuel, whose Surrealist techniques cracked open conventional pieties, Jodorowsky uses those techniques to support a sanctimonious view: Man-God tempted by evil, power-hungry woman abandons righteous ways and then, with the love of a good woman, becomes spiritual man, only to learn that the world is not ready for his spirituality. The movie uses Catholic symbols for "depth" much the way symbols were used to deepen *On the Waterfront,* or the way the directors of American-made Westerns hang a cross around the neck of a poor Mexican whore. Catholics may be losing belief in the magical power of artifacts, but moviemakers still squeeze crosses for the last drops of superstitious thrill. Titles flash on the screen—"Genesis," "Prophets," "Psalm," "Apocalypse"—like "Powie!" in a cartoon. They inflate the meaning of what you actually get. The Eastern riddles and prophetic utterances are used the same way, only they're cute—lisping profundities. But, of course, those who are drawn to the movie can say, "What's the matter with putting it all together? Everything is Everything." Or, as someone actually wrote, *"El Topo* is the all-inclusive myth, the Jungian archetypical dream of love/death, power and glory, body and spirit."

What makes it a head hit? Jodorowsky is not totally untalented; he has some feeling for pace and for sadistic comedy, and he seems to get the performances he wants. But he wouldn't be called a great master if he were being judged simply as a film director; enthusiasts think of him as a visionary, and even as a saint. Jodorowsky doesn't treat horror seriously as horror but, rather, treats it as both commonplace and somewhat funny—and, in a way, reversible. People in cruel comics who have their heads cut off sometimes put them right back on. The movie has a comparable buffoonishness about death—as, indeed, the spaghetti Westerns often have, but there is more of it here. It's a death romp, and the young audience appears to accept the film as no more "real" than the experiences they have in their skulls on drugs. That's why the blood doesn't bother them; that's why they don't gasp at knife thrusts or castrations, and why they're not repelled, either. I don't mean to suggest that this film appeals only to heads, or only to the pot generation (roughly, those who use marijuana frequently and trip out occasionally); there are others—probably some of the parents of the pot generation—who share in the sensibility, and still others who try to in order to feel in touch with youth. But *El Topo* has the right properties for a head film—the glaring color, the excesses and anomalies, the comic-strip jumble of periods and places, cacophonous music alternating with camp music and screeching bird sounds, women who speak with men's voices, primitive settings, nameless universal characters, porno eroticism, prophecies, transformations, rituals, miracles, and a sacrificial, somewhat paranoid vision. *El Topo* is all freaked out on love and mystery. And it's *violent*.

The confusion in talking about this film with someone who thinks it's a masterpiece comes from the fact that many heads consider their actual drug trips to be aesthetic experiences, and their only criterion for judging certain movies—head movies, especially, but some others, too—has become the intensity with which the movies hit them. I do not believe they would flock to *El Topo* and return to it if it were not for the violence. And, although I'm certainly not an authority on marijuana or on drugs, it seems obvious why: If the intensity of your sensations is what you judge a movie by, then the more shocks and dislocations and bloody thrills the better. On the one hand, the violence doesn't bother the heads, because they don't take it for real—it's a trip, a fantasy experience, separate from day-to-day living. On the other hand, the violence is what blows their minds. Devices from the theatre of cruelty are used to set off kicky fantasies. The cruelty becomes delectable, like the gore. I look at the screen and I know that the animals being slaughtered aren't plaster—not in Mexico, they're not—and I look at the cripples exhibiting their sores and shrunken limbs, which aren't plaster, either. And I react to the brutality, because I still associate violence with pain. But my guess is that for the head-movie audiences violence is dissociated from pain and is the richest ingredient of fantasy. It's the violence that turns them on.

I would not presume to guess whether there are dangers in this; I just don't know enough. But I do think this is at the core of why some of us want to walk out while others are having a big experience. One enthusiast wrote that the audience was "intoxicated" by the blood, another that "*El Topo* runs RED, with castrations, beheadings, shootings, and mass murders which make the Sharon Tate scene look like kindergarten fare." Jodorowsky uses violence, just as he uses the collection of cripples, to excite the audience, to help it fantasize, and I don't imagine that the young audience drawn to this film sees anything wrong with that, since indeed it does excite fantasies in them, and that is basically their criterion for a great movie. But I do see something wrong with it, and I feel it the more strongly because Jodorowsky's fundamental amorality isn't even honest amorality. He's an exploitation filmmaker, but he glazes everything with a useful piety. It's the violence plus the unctuous prophetic tone that makes *El Topo* a *heavy* trip. The filmmaker-star says, I am God and I sacrifice Myself for your sins; I am Christ-turned-killer for your sins. The whole movie is an act of self-worship, a narcissist's Mass, and it sells mystical violence at just the moment when the counter-culture is buying mystical violence. Who would have thought that in the twentieth century Americans would become Spaniards?

Exploitation filmmakers have always specialized in sex or shock (or a combo), and their greatest virtue—their only virtue, really—has been how nakedly they sold it. Hollywood might titillate and pour on the sentimentality, but the exploitation men weren't such hypocrites; besides, they didn't have the means to pour on sentimentality. Jodorowsky has come up with something new: exploitation filmmaking joined to sentimentality—the sentimentality of the counter-culture. They mix frighteningly well: for the counter-culture violence is romantic and shock is beautiful, because extremes of feeling and lack of control are what one takes drugs *for.* What has been happening, I think, is that the counter-culture has begun to look for the equivalent of a drug trip in its theatrical experiences. I think it still responds to non-head movies if there's a possibility of direct identification with the characters, but increasingly movies appear to be valued only for their intensity. In the Arts and Leisure section of the Sunday *Times,* which has become a gathering place for euphoric critics, one can see that even the critical prose attempts to evoke psychedelic experience: "At moments [Ken] Russell achieves a kind of cinematic synesthesia, a dizzying, disorienting experience in which all senses—visual, aural, even tactile—seem to blur," and so on. The worst blows to the art of motion pictures in the past have come from the businessmen who primed everything for the tastes of the conformist mass audience; the worst blows now (and maybe not just to films) could come from the businessmen priming everything for the counter-culture—if the biggest successes turn out to be head movies. (*El Topo* is being distributed by the manager of three of the Beatles.) Head movies don't have to be works of art—they just have to be sensational. For heads, there appears to be no difference.

The New Yorker, November 20, 1971

BILLY JACK
WINGING IT

There was an unusual sequence in *Christopher Strong,* an arch, high-strung, sickeningly noble Katharine Hepburn movie back in 1933. Hepburn played a famous record-breaking aviatrix, obviously modelled on Amelia Earhart, who fell in love with a distinguished political figure, a married man (Colin Clive). He was drawn to her because, unlike his conventionally feminine wife (Billie Burke), she had audacity and independence; he said that that was what he loved her for. But as soon as they went to bed together, he insisted, late on the very first night, that she not fly in the match she was entered in. There were many movies in the thirties in which women were professionals and the equals of men, but I don't know of any other scene that was so immediately recognizable to women of a certain kind as *their* truth. It was clear that the man wasn't a bastard, and that he was doing this out of anxiety and tenderness—out of love, in his terms. Nevertheless, the heroine's acquiescence destroyed her. There are probably few women who have ever accomplished anything beyond the care of a family who haven't in one way or another played that scene. Even those who were young girls at the time recognized it, I think, if only in a premonitory sense. It is the intelligent woman's primal post-coital scene, and it's on film; probably it got there because the movie was written by a woman, Zoë Akins, and directed by a woman, Dorothy Arzner.

I thought of it when I saw *Billy Jack* last week, because after the heroine (Delores Taylor), a Southwestern woman who runs an experimental "freedom school" on an Indian reservation, is raped by the son of a right-wing bully, she describes her emotions in terms of a specific feminine anger at the violation of her person. She may appear to be making too much of what happened; certainly the boring insistence of her tone is, by normal dramatic standards, a drag. Yet her reactions have some truth to women's feelings and to women's difficulties in articulating these feelings. The sequence doesn't have the high gloss of the crucial scene in *Christopher Strong*, which was accomplished in a few seconds—a line or two of dialogue, and that was it. The specifically feminine material in *Billy Jack* isn't slick at all; the movie just stops and lets the woman try to analyze her feelings. She speaks haltingly in a singsong monotone—as if she were working it out—and the scene is more affecting when you think about it afterward than when she's talking.

Movies have featured rapes and attempted rapes from the beginning of movies; rapes, after all, have both sex and violence. But I can't remember another movie in which the rape victim explained what the invasion of her body meant to her or how profound the insult and humiliation were. This woman isn't young—a woman of indeterminate age, she looks like a Dorothea Lange photograph of a hungry mountain woman; it's never suggested that she's a virgin, and she hasn't been beaten or injured. This kind of rape might be treated jeeringly, as of no consequence. Yet the film pauses for these emotions, which were perhaps improvised by Delores Taylor, who also narrates the story in her plain, non-actressy voice. Squinting, and talking out of the side of her mouth, she really looks like what she plays—a hard, dedicated pacifist. The schoolmistress is a heroine by virtue of what she does and how she thinks, not how glamorous she looks. Throughout the film, the girls in her charge—even the young beauties—are non-flirtatious, straight-talking girls, and as independent as the boys. One girl wears false eyelashes and comes on, but she's treated as a case.

The credits read, "Directed by T. C. Frank. Screenplay by Teresa Cristina and Mr. Frank. Produced by Mary Rose Solti." Those credits are as fake as they sound. Actually, there is no Mary Rose Solti, nor is there a

T. C. Frank, and Teresa Cristina (T.C.) is the name of one of the children of Tom Laughlin, who plays Billy Jack, and his wife, Delores Taylor, who made the picture together. They wrote it and produced it jointly; he was the director. I don't know the reason for the pseudonyms (perhaps simply to augment the size of the team?), but the Laughlins played the same game in their first picture—a wheeler, *Born Losers,* released by A.I.P. in 1967—though in that one the fake names they threw in were masculine. That film, which they began on their own and then sold to A.I.P., is one of the three or four most profitable A.I.P. films. The character of Billy Jack, the half-Indian war veteran who has become a loner, has been carried over from *Born Losers,* in which he came to the aid of a boy beaten by an outlaw motorcycle gang. The Laughlins started *Billy Jack* on their own again, inadequately financed; they began shooting in Prescott, Arizona, then had to close down for three months, and finally finished the film in New Mexico with a different cinematographer. (The changes show.) Then they sold it to Warner Brothers. Despite initial bad luck (and poor handling) in the big cities this summer, it has turned into a huge success, especially with teen-agers in the "heartland," but not only with them; I saw it on Forty-second Street with a very happy audience. It's one of Warner's top-grossing films of the year.

In plot and structure, *Billy Jack* is a shapeless mess. You feel as if the movie could expand or contract at any point, or add another theme or drop a couple; this is frequently the way one feels when moviemakers have shot a lot of footage without thinking it out and then tried to pare it down in the editing room. The story is about how the long-haired, racially mixed students of the workshop school are persecuted by the vicious bigots of the neighboring town. The movie sets this situation up like a Grade B melodrama, and you find yourself smiling at a lot of it, yet the smile is a sympathetic one, because even when the Laughlins' writing is terrible, their instincts are mostly very good. There's a sweet, naïve feeling to *Billy Jack* even when it's atrocious, and in the funny scenes and those involving the hip children of the school (the students appear to be of all ages, and the school is like a big encounter group) it's good in an unorthodox, improvisatory style. As a director, Laughlin shows an ingenuous, romantic talent in these scenes. I'd never before seen comic improvisations turn a movie audience on like this. The audience on Forty-second Street laughed at a street-theatre mock robbery and cheered at one sequence, involving the children's attendance at a Town Council meeting, which they break up. Though the setting is Southwestern and the hero out of a Western, the picture rather resembles *To Sir, with Love,* which was also a surprise success. But *Billy Jack,* a mongrel movie, isn't cloyingly simple like *To Sir, with Love.* When *Billy Jack* moves by feeling—when the scenes keep going because everybody's winging it together—it's like a good jazz session. The trouble with this approach is that you need a freshly thought-out core story to take off from and go back to. That's where the movie fails—at its center. But in movies this isn't necessarily fatal. The good things in *Billy Jack* create an atmosphere that helps blot out the dumb plot about a deputy sheriff's teen-age daughter who gets pregnant, takes refuge in the school, and falls in love with an Indian boy. Some of the appeal is very basic. On Forty-second Street, when Billy Jack said there was no place people could get a square deal—not in this country, not in the world—a voice bellowed "New York!" and the theatre shook with laughter, and with solidarity.

Very young audiences, who are becoming repeaters, may like the picture because it has a hero, rather than the now customary anti-hero. Laughlin wears his cowboy hat flat across his forehead, like William S. Hart, and, except for a comic slow burn of disgust at examples of revolting behavior, and an occasional smile, his acting is similar, and it's not bad. I'm not sure how the tradition got started of the Westerner's having a poker face (was it carried over from the card table?), but Billy Jack, a folk hero who rights social injustices, is a throwback to this mode. He personifies the good, and he doesn't need to be expressive. And for the very young he not only is a hero, the idealist armed, but is armed on *their* behalf, since he protects Indians, children, and horses. You don't even have to go looking for him: he has mystic powers—he's in touch all the time and is there when you need him. It sounds silly, it *is* silly, but it's also innocent. The Laughlins seem, partly through their inexperience as writers, to have stumbled on a winning combination. For several years now, the heroes of hip American movies have been heroes not by virtue of anything they attempted or accomplished but by virtue of having rejected the possibility that anything could be done and of turning inward. In the pop arts, those who were *first* to start searching for themselves became culture heroes. To be hip has meant to feel that nothing external could be changed, and the movies have been ending in violence or failure or death. The character of Billy Jack combines the good man of action with the soul-searching mystic. He appears to be armed, rather than disarmed, by his studies with an Indian holy man. (In a ceremony in which a rattler strikes him repeatedly, he becomes "brother-to-the-snake.") He doesn't need weapons; in one sequence he K.O.'s a gang of toughs by karate. Also, the movie restores the—by now welcome—tradition of the (relatively) happy ending. And in a new way: unlike the Westerns in which the hero shoots the villains and thus demonstrates to the schoolteacher that her pacifism won't work, it is the schoolmistress and her principles of nonviolence that carry the day.

Billy Jack gets by with most of its nonsense (even the new cliché of the director-star as savior) because the kids (a mixture of professionals and non-professionals) and some of the hip comics (from San Francisco's The Committee) are so loose and charming that they really do inspire hope. You can believe that the world isn't all gloom and corruption, because, despite the rigged polarity of adult psychopathic fools versus the free, happy, loving kids, the acting of the kids really is so free, happy, and loving—and so funny. The kids' fast, offhand semi-improvisations incarnate the hopeful theme and give the fairy-tale picture a surprising validity. The happy ending isn't the family-picture seal of approval that it is on Disney products or on a newly made antiquity like *Kotch*, because, in a primitive and original way, *Billy Jack* is hip. It's probably the first hip movie for teen-agers (and sub-teen-agers) since the Beatles' films, which were also hopeful. I don't mean that it was intended for children; I mean that it's so naïve that they respond to it as a hip fairy tale. ("How do you find Billy?" "We just want him and he shows up.") The school is the sub-teen Con III, where baby rock composers sing their condemnations of prejudice and war, and where there are no ambiguities, only right and wrong. We may have learned to resist the adorableness of Disney-style kids, but this infant counter-culture is harder to resist, because the kids are *like our own*—they scatter tough phrases and four-letter words, and their fresh faces take all the obscenity out. This infant idealism is widespread in the country; the Laughlins have put it on the screen, and the kids must be overjoyed to see themselves there.

Considering the material, there's one rather strange and implausible detail. The town's leading citizen and chief bigot, played by beefy Bert Freed, seems to be Jewish and is given a Jewish name; he and his son, the rapist, appear to be the only Jews in the town. I would guess that this is an expression not of anti-Semitism but of the frustrations and anger that build up when moviemakers are torn to shreds while trying to make deals with tough producers—who often physically resemble Bert Freed. The same sort of thing happens in *The Ski Bum:* the character of the hero's employer, a rich, big-time bore, is a blatant caricature of Joe Levine, who financed the movie. *The Ski Bum* (which is being released in New York this week) might seem wildly anti-Semitic if one failed to consider that one of the young filmmaking team is Jewish, and so are several members of the cast; probably, while doing the picture, they got so high on rage—or audacity—that things went a little out of control.

Though the audience I saw *Billy Jack* with was almost all male, it responded happily to the independent, tough-talking girls. It is a curious fact of movie history (and one that may be lost sight of) that, in general, the men always did like the independent women. It was the women who liked the sobbing and suffering ladies. (My father's favorite actresses were Joan Blondell and Barbara Stanwyck; my mother's were Helen Hayes and Ruth Chatterton.) The movie businessmen recognized what the female preferences were when they called certain pictures "women's pictures"; that meant not that they were made by women (though frequently women wrote them, and Dorothy Arzner directed a batch of them) but that they were shaped for women's tastes. They were lachrymose, masochistic, supposedly *realistic* stories about noble dames sacrificing everything for their children, or for their lovers or husbands, or sometimes even for their lover's children by his wife. And though men usually hated them, a lot of women did like them. Those sacrificial tearjerkers were often highly refined in tone, and they could seem serious and worthwhile, whereas it was very difficult to know what to do with tart, independent women except in wisecracking comedies or in men's action films, in which the shady ladies could be tough.

Though the only word for what the man did to Hepburn's aviatrix in *Christopher Strong* is "emasculation," it was perfectly well understood in 1933 that her full possibilities as a woman, as a person, were being destroyed. By the forties, however, it was standard Broadway and Hollywood practice to show that a woman of any achievement must give up whatever she was good at in order to get a man and become a real woman, which meant marriage and family *only*. At worst, there was something sick about a woman if she was successful—like Ginger Rogers as a neurotic magazine editor looking for a dominating male, in the poisonous movie of *Lady in the Dark*. The contrived, often sour endings of the Claudette Colbert and Rosalind Russell pictures were never, I think, felt as satisfactory by anybody. Those slapped-on endings in which sophisticated women had to humble themselves became more and more frequent as the men returning from the war wanted the jobs the women had been filling, but they always felt phony. The movies fell apart at the end because nobody really knew how to resolve those battles of the sexes. By the end of the sixties, there was practically nothing for women on the screen to *be* but prosties or bitches or bunnies, and, as a result, there are at present almost no women movie stars, while the male stars double up in buddy-buddy pictures. How many different kinds of prostitute could Shirley MacLaine play?

In movies, the primal scene of *Christopher Strong* has never been played out satisfactorily—at least, not from the woman's point of view. She always gives in, whether fatally, as in *Christopher Strong* or in the paste-up screwball style that provided the fake resolutions in the forties. And not solving this problem is a major factor in the gradual impoverishment of human relations on the screen since the war years. *Billy Jack*, hopeful as it is, and even though it was made by a husband-and-wife team, ducks the problem. There is no sexual relationship between Billy Jack and the teacher; they are both loners, and though they love each other, they appear to be only spiritual lovers. I suppose this is better than having them enemies, but if it's any reflection of a new mood, it's dispiriting. Movies are full of depersonalized sex, but in terms of sexual love between equals nobody's flying, both sexes are grounded.

The New Yorker, November 27, 1971

EXCERPTS FROM "NOTES ON NEW ACTORS, NEW MOVIES"

Frank Capra destroyed Gary Cooper's early sex appeal when he made him childish as Mr. Deeds; Cooper, once devastatingly lean and charming, the man Tallulah and Marlene had swooned over, began to act like an old woman and went on to a long sexless career—fumbling, homey, mealy-mouthed. Can this process be reversed? It's easy to see why Richard Benjamin has been working so much. He's a gifted light romantic comedian (on the order of Robert Montgomery in the thirties), and he's physically well suited to the urban Jewish heroes who dominated American fiction for over a decade and have now moved onto the screen. Benjamin is good at miming frustration and wild fantasies, and he's giggly and boyishly apologetic in a way that probably pleases men, because it reminds them of their adolescent silliness, but he doesn't quite appeal to women. What's missing seems to be that little bit of male fascism that makes an actor like Robert Redford or Jack Nicholson dangerous and hence attractive. Benjamin needs some sexual menace, some threat; without that there's no romantic charge to his presence. There's a distinctive nervous emotionalism in his voice (there is in Deborah Kerr's, too); one isn't quite sure how to react to it, because, although his sensitivity is sometimes rich (like Miss Kerr's), it's also on the borderline of weakness. He uses his voice for tricky comic effects: he cackles when one least expects it, or lets the sound break on a word, as if his voice were still changing. (That's a borderline device, too, although Melvyn Douglas always got by with it—but only within limits. Douglas was a leading man, never a star.) When Benjamin slips into nasality—even when it's for humor—there's the danger that he'll slide down into the Arnold Stang range and be sexually hopeless. Can Benjamin get by in the movies without that bit of coarseness or aggression which seems so essential to sex appeal? Fredric March did, but I can't think of many others. And now there's a new question: Can Benjamin get by if he *develops* sex appeal?

Richard Benjamin has, of course, been in demand for some roles just *because* he can project lack of confidence and suggest sexual inadequacy; he can impersonate the new movie stereotype of the American male as perennial adolescent. The Tony Perkins boyish juveniles of the late fifties are now exposed, like Art Garfunkel in *Carnal Knowledge,* in terms of their failure to become men. The new trend is to show the women as abused, deprived, and depersonalized, and an actor with sexual assurance wouldn't function right in these movies, because then there might seem to be something the matter with the woman if she wasn't having a good time. In *Diary of a Mad House-wife,* the mopey heroine is meant to be superior to her tormentors; she's given a nagging, social-climbing fool of a husband (Benjamin), and her self-ish lover is played by Frank Langella, the new chief contender for the acting-in-a-mirror (or Hermann Hesse) award. The period coming up may not be the best period for actors who project sexual competence. In Paula Fox's fine novel, *Desperate Characters,* the husband is civilized and fastidious, a rather elegant man, who deeply loves his wife; in the movie version, the director, Frank Gilroy, cast an actor best known for his mad Nazi in *The Producers,* and so the reason for the woman's isolation becomes largely the brutish man she is married to, who at one point in the movie is so sexually excited by the vandalism of their home that he is moved to rape her.

Though directors become fairly knowledgeable about the chemistry of performers, even the greatest directors are not always in control of the effects the performers produce. I was offended for Bibi Andersson in Ingmar Bergman's *The Touch* when Elliott Gould, playing a lout, but also playing loutishly, was nuzzling her—offended that she should have to be touched by him. Gould's performance threw me out of the framework of the movie, since what was happening on the screen made me react for the actress, and not in terms of the role she was playing. Most of the women I know felt Gould's touching Bibi Andersson as a physical affront to her and recoiled in the same kinesthetic, emphatic way that I did. Some men have said they felt it, too, and were embarrassed for the women they were with. At *Waterloo,* the audience broke into laughter when Rod Steiger, as Napoleon, spoke his first line, simply because he was so unmistakably Rod Steiger. Second-generation actors and actresses may throw us out of the movie because of a line reading or a camera angle that recalls their parents. Peter Fonda can't move or talk without creating an echo chamber, and he looks as if somehow, on the set of *The Grapes of Wrath,* John Carradine and Henry Fonda had mated.

In *Doc,* Stacy Keach presents so obdurate a face that you feel he has to consider when to let a flicker of expression through. Those who fight easy expressiveness may be actors of integrity, but they're likely to be repellent screen actors. In movies, one can accept non-actors and mediocrities, one can accept stone-faced dummies, but deliberately masked, intellectualized acting—acting by a theory—is intolerable. Keach doesn't offer himself to the camera; he fights it, and in so doing he limits the meaning of his roles and sharply limits our pleasures. Such pleasures may have as much to do with what we see in an actor as in what he consciously projects. We care more for a trace of personality than for all of Keach's serious intentions. If Richard Benjamin is too lightweight, and maybe even too *loose,* Keach turns himself into a heavyweight and is much too tight. He's so determined to give us the constricted performance he has worked out that he gives us less than most Hollywood bums do just by not caring.

If an actor has any screen presence at all, his ego usually shows: you know he thinks well of himself. (When he pushes his luck, we call it conceit.) For a while in the thirties, juvenile leads did the passive-vulnerable bit, like some of the ingénues, but that was when there were strong women to overpower them—Garbo swooping down over them and exposing her throat, and Hepburn playing tomboy to fey young men—and it doesn't work anymore. Even a juvenile like Ryan O'Neal comes on cocky-vulnerable, and when you see a non-egocentric performer, like Timothy Bottoms in *The Last Picture Show,* you know that he requires a director to bring him out—that, like the European actors who often fail over here, he doesn't have the strength of the actors who bust through no matter what. Richard Benjamin's comic persona is based on his self-confidence as an *actor*. George Segal has this cockiness, Spencer Tracy carried it to monotonous extremes, Gable wore it as his crown. It's what gives Warren Beatty his comic edge—he uses it ironically; so did Burt Lancaster and Kirk Douglas. A dull actor like Rock Hudson lacks it, and so does Gregory Peck—competent but always a little boring, a leading man disguised as a star. It's a quality that is usually described unflatteringly in women, though the only recently arrived woman star, Barbra Streisand, has got it, and I doubt if a new woman star could come up without it.

Robert Mitchum has that assurance in such huge amounts that he seems almost a lawless actor. He does it all out of himself. He doesn't use the tricks and stratagems of clever, trained actors. Mitchum is *sui generis*. There have been other good movie actors who invented for themselves without falling back on stage techniques—Joel McCrea, for one, a talented romantic comedian who became a fine, quiet, and much underrated actor. But there's no other powerhouse like Mitchum. This great bullfrog with the puffy eyes and the gut that becomes an honorary chest has been in movies for almost thirty years, and he's still so strong a masculine presence that he knocks younger men off the screen. His strength seems to come precisely from his avoidance of conventional acting, from his dependence on himself; his whole style is a put-on, in the sense that it's based on our shared understanding that he's a man acting in material conceived for puppets.

The New Yorker, December 4, 1971

A CLOCKWORK ORANGE
STANLEY STRANGELOVE

Literal-minded in its sex and brutality, Teutonic in its humor, Stanley Kubrick's *A Clockwork Orange* might be the work of a strict and exacting German professor who set out to make a porno-violent sci-fi comedy. Is there anything sadder—and ultimately more repellent—than a clean-minded pornographer? The numerous rapes and beatings have no ferocity and no sensuality; they're frigidly, pedantically calculated, and because there is no motivating emotion, the viewer may experience them as an indignity and wish to leave. The movie follows the Anthony Burgess novel so closely that the book might have served as the script, yet that thick-skulled German professor may be Dr. Strangelove himself, because the meanings are turned around.

Burgess's 1962 novel is set in a vaguely Socialist future (roughly, the late seventies or early eighties)—in a dreary, routinized England that roving gangs of teen-age thugs terrorize at night. In perceiving the amoral destructive potential of youth gangs, Burgess's ironic fable differs from Orwell's *1984* in a way that already seems prophetically accurate. The novel is narrated by the leader of one of these gangs—Alex, a conscienceless schoolboy sadist—and, in a witty, extraordinarily sustained literary conceit, narrated in his own slang (Nadsat, the teen-agers' special dialect). The book is a fast read; Burgess, a composer turned novelist, has an ebullient, musical sense of language, and you pick up the meanings of the strange words as the prose rhythms speed you along. Alex enjoys stealing, stomping, raping, and destroying until he kills a woman and is sent to prison for fourteen years. After serving two, he arranges to get out by submitting to an experiment on conditioning, and he is turned into a moral robot who becomes nauseated at thoughts of sex and violence. Released when he is harmless, he falls prey to his former victims, who beat him and torment him until he attempts suicide. This leads to criticism of the government that robotized him—turned him into a clockwork orange—and he is deconditioned, becoming once again a thug, and now at loose and triumphant. The ironies are protean, but Burgess is clearly a humanist; his point of view is that of a Christian horrified by the possibilities of a society turned clockwork orange, in which life is so mechanized that men lose their capacity for moral choice. There seems to be no way in this boring, dehumanizing society for the boys to release their energies except in vandalism and crime; they do what they do as a matter of course. Alex the sadist is as mechanized a creature as Alex the good.

Stanley Kubrick's Alex (Malcolm McDowell) is not so much an expression of how this society has lost its soul as he is a force pitted against the society, and by making the victims of the thugs more repulsive and contemptible than the thugs Kubrick has learned to love the punk sadist. The end is no longer the ironic triumph of a mechanized punk but a real triumph. Alex is the only likable person we see—his cynical bravado suggests a broad-nosed, working-class Olivier—and the movie puts us on his side. Alex, who gets kicks out of violence, is more alive than anybody else in the movie, and younger and more attractive, and McDowell plays him exuberantly, with the power and slyness of a young Cagney. Despite what Alex does at the beginning, McDowell makes you root for his foxiness, for his crookedness. For most of the movie, we see him tortured and beaten and humiliated, so when his bold, aggressive punk's nature is restored to him it seems not a joke on all of us but, rather, a victory in which we share, and Kubrick takes an exultant tone. The look in Alex's eyes at the end tells us that he isn't just a mechanized, choiceless sadist but prefers sadism and knows he can get by with it. Far from being a little parable about the dangers of soullessness and the horrors of force, whether employed by individuals against each other or by society in "conditioning," the movie becomes a vindication of Alex, saying that the punk was a free human being and only the good Alex was a robot.

The trick of making the attacked less human than their attackers, so you feel no sympathy for them, is, I think, symptomatic of a new attitude in movies. This attitude says there's no moral difference. Stanley Kubrick has assumed the deformed, self-righteous perspective of a vicious young punk who says, "Everything's rotten. Why shouldn't I do what I want? They're worse than I am." In the new mood (perhaps movies in their cumulative effect are partly responsible for it), people want to believe the hyperbolic worst, want to believe in the degradation of the victims—that they are dupes and phonies and weaklings. I can't accept that Kubrick is merely reflecting this post-assassinations, post-Manson mood; I think he's catering to it. I think he wants to dig it.

This picture plays with violence in an intellectually seductive way. And though it has no depth, it's done in such a slow, heavy style that those prepared to like it can treat its puzzling aspects as oracular. It can easily be construed as an ambiguous mystery play, a visionary warning against "the Establishment." There are a million ways to justify identifying with Alex: Alex is fighting repression; he's alone against the system. What he does isn't nearly as bad as what the government does (both in the movie and in the United States now). Why shouldn't he be violent? That's all the Establishment has ever taught him (and us) to be. The point of the book was that we must be as men, that we must be able to take responsibility for what we are. The point of the movie is much more *au courant*. Kubrick has removed many of the obstacles to our identifying with Alex; the Alex of the book has had his personal habits cleaned up a bit—his fondness for squishing small animals under his tires, his taste for ten-year-old girls, his beating up of other prisoners, and so on. And Kubrick aids the identification with Alex by small directorial choices throughout. The writer whom Alex cripples (Patrick Magee) and the woman he kills are cartoon nasties with upper-class accents a mile wide. (Magee has been encouraged to act like a bathetic madman; he seems to be preparing for a career in horror movies.) Burgess gave us society through Alex's eyes, and so the vision was deformed, and Kubrick, carrying over from *Dr. Strangelove* his joky adolescent view of hypocritical, sexually dirty authority figures and extending it to all adults, has added an extra layer of deformity. The "straight" people are far more twisted than Alex; they seem inhuman and incapable of suffering. He alone suffers. And how he suffers! He's a male Little Nell—screaming in a straitjacket during the brainwashing; sweet and helpless when rejected by his parents; alone, weeping, on a bridge; beaten, bleeding, lost in a rainstorm; pounding his head on a floor and crying for death. Kubrick pours on the hearts and flowers; what is done to Alex is far worse than what Alex has done, so society itself can be felt to justify Alex's hoodlumism.

The movie's confusing—and, finally, corrupt—morality is not, however, what makes it such an abhorrent viewing experience. It is offensive long before one perceives where it is heading, because it has no shadings. Kubrick, a director with an arctic spirit, is determined to be pornographic, and he has no talent for it. In *Los Olvidados*, Buñuel showed teen-agers committing horrible brutalities, and even though you had no illusions about their

416

victims—one, in particular, was a foul old lecher—you were appalled. Buñuel makes you understand the pornography of brutality: the pornography is in what human beings are capable of doing to other human beings. Kubrick has always been one of the least sensual and least erotic of directors, and his attempts here at phallic humor are like a professor's lead balloons. He tries to work up kicky violent scenes, carefully estranging you from the victims so that you can *enjoy* the rapes and beatings. But I think one is more likely to feel cold antipathy toward the movie than horror at the violence—or enjoyment of it, either.

Kubrick's martinet control is obvious in the terrible performances he gets from everybody but McDowell, and in the inexorable pacing. The film has a distinctive style of estrangement: gloating closeups, bright, hard-edge, third-degree lighting, and abnormally loud voices. It's a style, all right—the movie doesn't look like other movies, or sound like them—but it's a leering, portentous style. After the balletic brawling of the teen-age gangs, with bodies flying as in a Western saloon fight, and after the gang-bang of the writer's wife and an orgy in speeded-up motion, you're primed for more action, but you're left stranded in the prison sections, trying to find some humor in tired schoolboy jokes about a Hitlerian guard. The movie retains a little of the slangy Nadsat but none of the fast rhythms of Burgess's prose, and so the dialect seems much more arch than it does in the book. Many of the dialogue sequences go on and on, into a stupor of inactivity. Kubrick seems infatuated with the hypnotic possibilities of static setups; at times you feel as if you were trapped in front of the frames of a comic strip for a numbing ten minutes per frame. When Alex's correctional officer visits his home and he and Alex sit on a bed, the camera sits on the two of them. When Alex comes home from prison, his parents and the lodger who has displaced him are in the living room; Alex appeals to his seated, unloving parents for an inert eternity. Long after we've got the point, the composition is still telling us to appreciate its cleverness. This ponderous technique is hardly leavened by the structural use of classical music to characterize the sequences; each sequence is scored to Purcell (synthesized on a Moog), Rossini, or Beethoven, while Elgar and others are used for brief satiric effects. In the book, the doctor who has devised the conditioning treatment explains why the horror images used in it are set to music: "It's a useful emotional heightener." But the whole damned movie is heightened this way; yes, the music is effective, but the effect is self-important.

When I pass a newsstand and see the saintly, bearded, intellectual Kubrick on the cover of *Saturday Review,* I wonder: Do people notice things like the way Kubrick cuts to the rival teen-age gang before Alex and his hoods arrive to fight them, just so we can have the pleasure of watching that gang strip the struggling girl they mean to rape? Alex's voice is on the track announcing his arrival, but Kubrick can't wait for Alex to arrive, because then he couldn't show us as much. That girl is stripped for our benefit; it's the purest exploitation. Yet this film lusts for greatness, and I'm not sure that Kubrick knows how to make simple movies anymore, or that he cares to, either. I don't know how consciously he has thrown this film to youth; maybe he's more of a showman than he lets on—a lucky showman with opportunism built into the cells of his body. The film can work at a pop-fantasy level for a young audience already prepared to accept Alex's view of the society, ready to believe that that's how it is.

At the movies, we are gradually being conditioned to accept violence as a sensual pleasure. The directors used to say they were showing us its real face and how ugly it was in order to sensitize us to its horrors. You don't have to be very keen to see that they are now in fact desensitizing us. They are saying that everyone is brutal, and the heroes must be as brutal as the villains or they turn into fools. There seems to be an assumption that if you're offended by movie brutality, you are somehow playing into the hands of the people who want censorship. But this would deny those of us who don't believe in censorship the use of the only counterbalance: the freedom of the press to say that there's anything conceivably damaging in these films—the freedom to analyze their implications. If we don't use this critical freedom, we are implicitly saying that no brutality is too much for us—that only squares and people who believe in censorship are concerned with brutality. Actually, those who believe in censorship are primarily concerned with sex, and they generally worry about violence only when it's eroticized. This means that practically no one raises the issue of the possible cumulative effects of movie brutality. Yet surely, when night after night atrocities are served up to us as entertainment, it's worth some anxiety. We become clockwork oranges if we accept all this pop culture without asking what's in it. How can people go on talking about the dazzling brilliance of movies and not notice that the directors are sucking up to the thugs in the audience?

The New Yorker, January 1, 1972

DIRTY HARRY
SAINT COP

The movie opens on a memorial plaque in the lobby of the San Francisco Hall of Justice, and we read the words "In Tribute to the Police Officers of San Francisco Who Gave Their Lives in the Line of Duty," and then the beginning of a list of names. This is a rather strange opening for *Dirty Harry* since it isn't about the death of a police officer. The tribute, however, puts the viewer in a respectful frame of mind; we all know that many police are losing their lives. The movie then proceeds to offer a magically simple culprit for their deaths: the liberals. Actually, the opening is strange for other reasons, too. I grew up in San Francisco, and one of the soundest pieces of folk wisdom my mother gave me was "If you're ever in trouble, don't go to the cops." I remember a high-school teacher telling me that it never ceased to amaze him that his worst students—the sadists and the bullies—landed not in jail but on the police force, though sometimes on the police force and then in jail. Even as children, San Franciscans were deeply aware of the corruption of the police—something totally ignored in this movie. *Dirty Harry* is not about the actual San Francisco police force; it's about a right-wing fantasy of that police force as a group helplessly emasculated by unrealistic liberals. The conceit of this movie is that for one brief, glorious period the police have a realist in their midst—and drive him out.

Dirty Harry is not one of those ambivalent, you-can-read-it-either-way jobs, like *The French Connection;* Inspector Harry Callahan is not a Popeye—porkpie-hatted and lewd and boorish. He's soft-spoken Clint Eastwood—six feet four of lean, tough saint, blue-eyed and shaggy-haired, with a rugged, creased, careworn face that occasionally breaks into a mischief-filled Shirley MacLaine grin. He's the best there is—a Camelot cop, courageous and incorruptible, and the protector of women and children. Or at least he would be, if the law allowed him to be. But the law coddles criminals; it gives them legal rights that cripple the police. And so the only way that Dirty Harry—the dedicated trouble-shooter who gets the dirtiest assignments—can protect the women and children of the city is to disobey orders.

As suspense craftsmanship, *Dirty Harry* is smooth and trim; based on an original screenplay by Harry Fink and his wife, R.M. Fink (formerly a TV writing team, now operating out of Switzerland), with some additional writing by Dean Riesner, it was directed in the sleekest style by the veteran urban-action director Don Siegel, and Lalo Schifrin's pulsating, jazzy electronic trickery drives the picture forward. Lalo Schifrin doesn't compose music—he works on you. It would be stupid to deny that *Dirty Harry* is a stunningly well-made genre piece, and it certainly turns an audience on. But turning on an audience is a function of motor excitation that is not identical with art (though there is an overlap); if it were, the greatest artists would be those who gave us heart attacks. Don Siegel is an accomplished exciter; once considered a liberal, he has now put his skills to work in a remarkably single-minded attack on liberal values, with each prejudicial detail in place. *Dirty Harry* is a kind of hardhat *The Fountainhead;* Callahan, a free individual, afraid of no one and bowing to no man, is pitted against a hippie maniac (loosely based on San Francisco's Zodiac Killer) who is a compendium of criminal types. The variety of his perversions is impressive—one might say that no depravity is foreign to him. He is pure evil: sniper, rapist, kidnapper, torturer, defiler of all human values. Paradisiacal San Francisco supports this vision. In New York, where crime is so obviously a social outgrowth, the dregs belong to the city, and a criminal could not be viewed as a snake in paradise. But, as everyone knows, the San Francisco light and the beauty of the natural setting transform and unify the architectural chaos; even poverty looks picturesque, as in other tourist traps, and crime can be treated as a defiler from outside the society. This criminal is not one for whom we need feel any responsibility or sympathy, yet he stands for everything the audience fears and loathes. And Harry cannot destroy this walking rot, because of the legal protections, such as the court rulings on Miranda and Escobedo, that a weak, liberal society gives its criminals. Those are the terms of the film. The dirtiness on Harry is the moral stain of recognition that evil must be dealt with; he is our martyr—stained on our behalf. The content fits the form, and beautifully—hand in glove. In the action genre, it's easier—and more fun—to treat crime in this medieval way, as evil, without specific causes or background. What produces a killer might be a subject for an artist, but it's a nuisance to an exciter, who doesn't want to slow the action down. When you're making a picture with Clint Eastwood, you naturally want things to be simple, and the basic contest between good and evil is as simple as you can get. It makes this genre piece more archetypal than most movies, more primitive and dreamlike; fascist medievalism has a fairy-tale appeal.

The movie was cheered and applauded by Puerto Ricans in the audience, and they jeered—as they were meant to—when the maniac whined and pleaded for his legal rights. Puerto Ricans could applaud Harry because in the movie laws protecting the rights of the accused are seen not as remedies for the mistreatment of the poor by the police and the courts but as protection for evil abstracted from all social conditions—metaphysical evil, classless criminality. The movie shrewdly makes the maniac smart, well-spoken, and white, and in order to clear Harry of any charge of prejudice or racism he is given a Mexican partner (Reni Santoni). The audience is led to identify totally with Harry and to feel victorious because the liberals don't succeed in stopping him. He saves us this time; he slaughters the maniac who has grabbed a busload of terrified children and is slapping them around. But Harry Callahan has to defy the mayor and the police department to do it. And, in a final gesture of contempt for the unrealistic legal system, Harry throws his badge into the same waters that the killer's corpse is floating in. Harry has dirtied himself for the last time; there is no one now to save us from evil, because the liberals are running the city.

The gesture at the end is a reprise of Gary Cooper's gesture at the end of *High Noon,* but with a difference; in high-minded *High Noon,* phony in its own way, Cooper, the marshal, singlehandedly cleaned up the outlaw gang and then threw his badge on the ground in contempt for the cowardice of the townspeople, who didn't live up to the principles of the law and wouldn't help him defend it. *Dirty Harry* says that the laws were written by dupes who protect criminal rats and let women and children be tortured, and Eastwood throws his badge away because he doesn't respect the law; he stands for vigilante justice.

If you go along with the movie—and it's hard to resist, because the most skillful suspense techniques are used on very primitive emotional levels—you have but one desire: to see the maniac get it so it hurts. The movie lacks the zing and brute vitality of *The French Connection,* but it has such sustained drive toward this righteous conclusion that it is an almost perfect piece of propaganda for para-legal police power. The evil monster represents urban violence, and the audience gets to see him kicked and knifed and shot, and finally triumphantly drowned. Violence has rarely been presented with such righteous relish.

At one point, Harry catches the mass murderer, but the police—in an implausible scene that really pushes its political point—decide they can't bring him to trial, because of legal technicalities, and so they blithely release him. Although they know he has already killed several people, they don't even bother to put a tail on him. And whom do they consult before releasing him? A Berkeley law professor, of course. Such a perfect touch for the audience. Anyone who knows San Francisco knows that in the highly un-likely circumstance that a law professor were to be consulted, he would be from the University of San Francisco, a Catholic institution closer in loca-tion and nearer in heart to the S. F. Police Department—or, if not from there, from Hastings College of the Law, a branch of the University of Cal-ifornia that is situated in San Francisco. But Berkeley has push-button ap-peal as the red center of bleeding-heart liberalism; it has replaced Harvard as the joke butt and unifying hatred of reactionaries. The movie is just as as-tute in what it leaves out: in his guise as sniper, the many-sided evil one has an impressive arsenal that includes a high-powered rifle and a machine gun. But the movie raises no question about how he was able to purchase these weapons. There is one virtuoso plot development: the maniac arranges to get himself beaten to a garish pulp, so that he can scream police brutality and pin the blame on Callahan. The San Francisco police, with their unen-viable record of free-style use of the billy, should contribute to a memorial plaque for *Dirty Harry.*

On the way out, a pink-cheeked little girl was saying "That was a *good* picture" to her father. Of course; the dragon had been slain. *Dirty Harry* is obviously just a genre movie, but this action genre has always had a fascist potential, and it has finally surfaced. If crime were caused by super-evil drag-ons, there would be no Miranda, no Escobedo; we could all be licensed to kill, like Dirty Harry. But since crime is caused by deprivation, misery, psy-chopathology, and social injustice, *Dirty Harry* is a deeply immoral movie.

To excite an audience, you don't really need to believe in anything but manipulative skills—and success. If you're intelligent and work this way, you become a cynic; if you're not very intelligent, you can point with pride to the millions of people buying tickets.

The New Yorker, January 15, 1972

STRAW DOGS
PECKINPAH'S OBSESSION

am Peckinpah is the youngest legendary American director. When you see his Western movies, you feel that he's tearing himself apart, split between a compulsion to show that people are messing up their lives and an overwhelming love of the look and feel of those people rattling around in the grandeur and apparent freedom of the landscape. He is so passionate and sensual a film artist that you may experience his romantic perversity kinesthetically, and get quite giddy from feeling trapped and yet liberated. He's an artist in conflict with himself, but unmistakably and prodigally an artist, who uses images of great subtlety and emotional sophistication—the blown-up bridge of *The Wild Bunch*, with the horses and riders falling to the water in an instant extended to eternity; the exhilaration of space in *Major Dundee;* the visual tribute to the old Westerner of *Ride the High Country*, who sinks to the bottom of the frame to die; the vulture in *The Wild Bunch* sitting on a dead man's chest and turning his squalid, naked head to stare at the camera.

Peckinpah has finally made the movie he's been working his way toward: though small in scale, and not nearly as rich or varied as parts of his earlier films, *Straw Dogs* is a complete work—a structured vision of life on film. I think Peckinpah has been honest in terms of his convictions, and in terms of those convictions it's a work of integrity, but it's not a work of major intelligence. It represents—superficially, at least—a resolution of his conflicts, but in a spiritually ugly way. His earlier films were recklessly high on beauty and excess; this time he brings everyone down. The vision of *Straw Dogs* is narrow and puny, as obsessions with masculinity so often are; Peckinpah's view of human experience seems to be no more than the sort of anecdote that drunks tell in bars. The story is a male fantasy about a mathematics professor's hot young wife (Susan George) who wants to be raped and gets sodomized, which is more than she bargained for, and the timid cuckold-mathematician (Dustin Hoffman), who turns into a man when he learns to fight like an animal. The subject of *Straw Dogs* is machismo. It has been the obsession behind most of Peckinpah's other films; now that it's out in the open, his strengths and follies are clearly visible. His intuitions as a director are infinitely superior to his thinking.

From the opening shot, of ambiguous children's games in a church cemetery, through to the close, there is no suggestion of human happiness, no frolicking animal, nothing blooming anywhere. The actors are not allowed their usual freedom to become characters, because they're pawns in the overall scheme. The director doesn't cut loose, either; he sacrifices the flow and spontaneity and the euphoria of spaciousness that have made him a legend—but not the savagery. For the first time, he has left the West, and for the first time he has a statement to make. The film is constructed like a demonstration—a misanthropic one. Working from a script that he wrote with David Z. Goodman, he carefully plants the prejudicial details that will later pay off; there are menacing closeups and more than one superfluous reaction shot. The preparations are not in themselves pleasurable; the atmosphere is ominous and oppressive, but you're drawn in and you're held, because you can feel that it is building purposefully. The setting is a Cornish village and a lonely farmhouse on the moor that the American mathematician—he has a grant to work on celestial navigation—and his English wife have moved into. The farmhouse is singularly uninviting; no objects have been placed to catch the light or give off a glow. The landscape is barren and alien—not exactly desolate but neutral. Peckinpah is famous for the love that makes his Western landscapes expressive, but no love informs this landscape with feeling. The townspeople, who are creepy enough for a horror thriller, include a collection of stud louts who jeer at Hoffman while they snigger and smack their lips over his wife's braless sweaters. One look at her provocative walk and you know that her husband is in trouble—that he can't handle her.

The setting, the music, and the people are deliberately disquieting. It *is* a thriller—a machine headed for destruction. Hoffman, the victim of the villagers' (and the director's) contempt, is that stock figure of fun—the priggish, cowardly intellectual. It's embarrassing that a man of Peckinpah's gifts should offer such stale anti-intellectualism, but one can't avoid the conclusion that Hoffman's David is meant to be a symbolic "uncommitted" intellectual who is escaping the turmoil of America. "You left because you didn't want to take a stand," his wife taunts him, while we squirm and wish she didn't represent the film's point of view. Inevitably, David discovers that he can't hide in his study, and that in the peaceful countryside nature is red in tooth and claw. The casting, however, is impeccable. Hoffman, notoriously a cerebral actor, projects thought before movement; he's already a cartoon of an intellectual. There's a split second of blank indecision before the face lights up with purpose. He never looks as if he just naturally lived in the places he's stuck into for the camera; he always seems slightly the outsider anyway, and his duck walk and physical movements are a shade clumsy. Whatever he does seems a bit of a feat—and that, I think, is why we're drawn to him. This role might almost be a continuation of his Benjamin in *The Graduate.*

The movie never explains how he and his Lolita-wife got together, and one's mind strays from the action to ask this question. We can't believe in this marriage; we feel it to be a marriage for Peckinpah's convenience. Susan George, with her smudged, pouty mouth and her smile that's also a snarl, is superlatively cast and can act, besides; she's a sex kitten here—an unsatisfied little tart, a child-wife who wants to be played with. David is even more of an ingenuous jerk than Benjamin. We don't believe it when he interrupts his wife's passionate lovemaking to wind the alarm clock; we just take it as a point being racked up. Peckinpah treats him so prejudicially that it isn't even meant to be funny when he stares in bewilderment at the joshing of the locals—as if no one in America ever indulged in coarse, dumb badinage—and it isn't played for comedy when he goes out hunting with local yokels, who leave him sitting in the brush while they go back to get at his wife. David allows himself to be humiliated for an unpleasantly long time—for so long that he becomes quite unappetizing. We're just about ready to give up on him when his car hits a half-wit (David Warner) who is trying to escape these same bullies, who are after him for molesting a teen-age girl. David shelters the half-wit in the farmhouse, and, while waiting for a doctor to arrive, is confronted by them—a childish, crazed, indiscriminately violent gang (like the most wanton degenerates among the Wild Bunch) led by a grizzle-bearded old horror who fills the screen with repulsiveness. David knows that this gang will beat the simpleton to death, and he feels he can't turn him over. And that's when the ferocity we've been dreading, and waiting for, erupts.

He announces, "This is where I live," and he refuses to let the men come into his home; as they lay siege to the farmhouse, he destroys each of them—with grisly ingenuity—until the last one, whom his wife shoots. When he takes a knife to the first, his action comes faster than you expect, and it's startling; you're better prepared for the frenzies that follow, and although the tension mounts, you're not caught off guard again. Not surprisingly, the audience cheers David's kills; it is, after all, a classic example of the worm turning. It's mild-mannered Destry putting on his guns, it's the triumph of a superior man who is fighting for basic civilized principles over men who are presented as mindless human garbage. It's David versus Goliath, and so, of course, the audience roots for David. When the last of the louts has him pinned down, and his terrified wife, with her finger on the trigger, panics and delays, it's unbearable; your whole primitive moviegoer's soul cries out for her to fire—and then she does. You just about can't help feeling that way. You know that the response has been pulled out of you, but you're trapped in that besieged house and you want the terror to be over, and if you believe in civilization at all you want David to win. As the situation has been set up, every possibility for nonviolent behavior has been eliminated.

If all that *Straw Dogs* set out to say was that certain situations may be posited in which fighting is a moral decision, few besides total pacifists would disagree. In a sense, what the movie does is play a variation on the old question asked of conscientious objectors: "What would you do if someone tried to rape your sister?" The question asked here is "What would you do if someone tried to invade your house to kill an innocent person?" In such extreme circumstances, probably most of us would use whatever means came to hand and brain, and if we won by violence we would be glad to have won but be sickened and disgusted at the choice forced on us. We would feel robbed of part of our humanity—as soldiers even in "just" wars are said to feel. And here is where we can part company with Peckinpah, for the movie intends to demonstrate not merely that there is a point at which a man will fight but that he is a better man for it—a real man at last. The goal of the movie is to demonstrate that David *enjoys* the killing, and achieves his manhood in that self-recognition. David experiences no shock, no horror at what he has done but only a new self-assurance and pleasure. And Peckinpah wants us to dig the sexiness of violence. There is even the faint smile of satisfaction on the tarty wife's face that says she will have a new sexual respect for her husband. The movie takes not merely a non-pacifist position but a rabidly anti-pacifist position; it confirms the old militarists' view that pacifism is unmanly, is pussyfooting, is false to "nature."

And this is the stupidity and moral corruption of *Straw Dogs*. It may be necessary to be violent in order to defend your home and your principles, but Peckinpah-Patton thinks that's what makes a man a man. Yet there is also—one senses—a slight condescension on Peckinpah's part, and this relates to his anti-intellectualism: David has become as other men, has lost his intellectual's separation from the beasts, and Peckinpah's victory is in bringing him down. Another ambivalence in Peckinpah is his contempt for the brute yokels and his respect for David for using brains to kill them. In the view of the movie, the yokels deserve their deaths. Peckinpah appears to despise them for their ignorance and inefficiency, just as he despises David as unnatural and dishonest when he is pacific. The corollary of David's becoming a man is that the slutty, baby-doll wife becomes a woman when her husband learns to be man and master—which is what she wanted all along. As a woman, she is not expected to have any principles; she was perfectly willing to yield the half-wit to the mob—she doesn't have an idea in her head but sex and self-preservation. The movie is tight, and it all adds up; the male clichés come together in a coherent fantasy.

Peckinpah is a spartan director this time, but with an aesthetic of cruelty. The only beauty he allows himself is in eroticism and violence—which he links by an extraordinary aestheticizing technique. The rape is one of the few truly erotic sequences on film, and the punches that subdue the wife have the exquisite languor of slightly slowed-down motion. This same languor is present in the later slaughters; the editing is superb in these sequences, with the slowing-down never prolonged but just long enough to fix the images of violence in your imagination, to make them seem already classic and archaic—like something you remember—while they're happening. The rape has heat to it—there can be little doubt of that—but what goes into that heat is the old male barroom attitude: we can see that she's asking for it, she's begging for it, that her every no means yes. The rape scene says that women really want the rough stuff, that deep down they're little beasts asking to be made submissive. I think it's clear from the structuring of the film and the use of the mathematician to represent intellectuals out of touch with their own natures that his wife is intended to be representative of woman's nature, and that the louts understand her better than her husband does. The first rapist understands what she needs; the sodomist (this has been slightly trimmed, so that the film could get an R rating, rather than an X) terrorizes her. Another girl in the movie—the teen-ager who gets the gentle simpleton in trouble by making advances to him after David, the only other gentle person in town, rejects her—sustains the image of Eve the troublemaker. We know as we watch the teen-ager luring the simpleton that girls her age are not so hard up for boys to fondle them that they are going to play around with the village half-wit; we realize it's a plot device to get him pursued by the louts. But implicit in this recognition is that the movie is a series of stratagems to get the characters into the positions that are wanted for a symbolic confrontation. The siege is not simply the climax but the proof, and it has the kick of a mule. What I am saying, I fear, is that Sam Peckinpah, who is an artist, has, with *Straw Dogs,* made the first American film that is a fascist work of art.

It has an impact far beyond the greedy, opportunistic, fascist *Dirty Harry* or the stupid, reactionary *The Cowboys,* because—and here, as a woman, I must guess—it gets at the roots of the fantasies that men carry from earliest childhood. It confirms their secret fears and prejudices that women respect only brutes; it confirms the male insanity that there is no such thing as rape. The movie taps a sexual fascism—that is what machismo is—that is so much a part of folklore that it's on the underside of many an educated consciousness and is rampant among the uneducated. It's what comes out in David's character—what gives him that faintly smug expression at the end. Violence is erotic in the movie because a man's prowess is in fighting and loving. The one earns him the right to the other. You can see why Peckinpah loaded the dice against David at the beginning: he had to make David such a weakling that only killing could rouse him to manhood.

I realize that it's a terrible thing to say of someone whose gifts you admire that he has made a fascist classic. And in some ways Peckinpah's attitudes are not that different from those of Norman Mailer, who is also afflicted with machismo. But Mailer isn't so single-minded about it; he worries it and pokes at it and tries to dig into it. Despite Peckinpah's artistry, there's something basically grim and crude in *Straw Dogs.* It's no news that men are capable of violence, but while most of us want to find ways to control that violence, Sam Peckinpah wants us to know that that's all hypocrisy. He's discovered the territorial imperative and wants to spread the Neanderthal word. At its sanest level, the movie says no more than that a man should defend his home, but Peckinpah has not only pushed this to a sexual test but turned the defense of the home into a destruction orgy, as if determined to trash everything and everyone on the screen. The fury goes way beyond making his point; it almost seems a fury against the flesh. The title has been extracted from a gnomic passage in Lao-tse: "Heaven and earth are ruthless and treat the myriad creatures as straw dogs; the sage is ruthless and treats the people as straw dogs." That's no sage, it's a demon.

The New Yorker, January 29, 1972

X Y & ZEE
THE MESSINESS OF LOVE

Love knows no honor; people in love do things that they never thought they'd do and that they've always despised other people for doing. They violate not only their own scruples but their own *style*. The shocking messiness of love, which is the subtext of so much great literature, rises to the surface in Edna O'Brien's writing, and in her original screenplay for *X Y & Zee* it has become the text. *X Y & Zee* resembles *Who's Afraid of Virginia Woolf?* but the revelations and emotional convulsions are not so dramatically structured, or so decisive; *X Y & Zee* is more like a long short story. A hollering, brawling marriage, based on the same sort of cast-iron dependencies, is picked up at a time of crisis, when the husband considers leaving the wife—Zee—for another woman, and it ends when the crisis is more or less resolved. The crisis is never *explained*. We never quite discover what brought this couple (Elizabeth Taylor and Michael Caine) together or how the marriage works or why it stops working the night the film begins, when they go to a party and the husband—a veteran philanderer—sees Stella (Susannah York) in a silvery gown. In the past, his affairs didn't disrupt the marriage; inexplicably, this one becomes more than an affair. The way nothing makes sense in love and everything gets loused up is part of Edna O'Brien's subject, and of her method. Characters aren't "worked out" to behave a certain way; the evaporation of love isn't necessarily explainable, or its renewal, either. Things change unpredictably. What is less satisfactory in the movie—and this may be the failure of the director, Brian G. Hutton—is that we must take the dependency of Zee and her husband for granted, though we don't really feel the bondage.

Reading Edna O'Brien's fiction, I've been surprised by perceptions of what I thought no one else knew—and I wasn't telling. Probably other readers react exactly the same way; she makes private shames public. But I've also been disappointed that, knowing so much, she didn't know more—that she didn't move outside the magic circle of women's emotional problems. Maybe that's why this movie seems like M-G-M forties heightened—because, essentially, it deals with the wife's fierce determination to hold on to her husband by any means. It deals, that is, with a willfully spoiled woman's living on her rapacious impulses—and this is only a few steps up from the old Joan Crawford–Rosalind Russell bitches. The gloss and corruption of this kind of "women's picture" is that love, knowing no honor, is treated not as a sloppy fact but as a triumphal statement—a battle cry in the war of the sexes. The prize defines the genre: the prize is not losing your man. It's a specialized, limited view, commercial and rubbishy, but the contestants here are entertainingly polarized—Zee the sun lover, the overdressed wife in her millionaire gypsy couture, versus the cool, restful mistress. And the dialogue has a sardonic tickle to it. There's some wildness in Edna O'Brien's playfulness and love of words; her writing isn't merely clever—it's delicate in odd, indelicate

427

ways. Indelicacy in women artists can be like the stripping off of corsets. Edna O'Brien likes to reveal, and even though her revelations don't go deep, they're loose and free; she's so full of the wicked zest of being unfettered that there's something almost rapturous about her naughtiness. For her, writing seems another way of sowing her wild oats. Her dialogue, which is one trespass after another, is so good because there's no sense of strain: it flows. The performers in this movie—they must be greedy for lines like this—know what to do with it. The dialogue isn't hollow, like Broadway wisecracks. It sounds likely, because the wit belongs to the subject; rich, smart women who have never needed to develop their intelligence, who use their brains only to climb and to hang on to money and men, do become high-pitched and clever in this combative way. This honed edge of glitzy bitchery isn't an accomplishment, it's a dysfunctional weapon—the tic of wasted minds.

At the beginning of *X Y & Zee*, Elizabeth Taylor, peering out of blue lamé eyeshadow like a raccoon, seemed ridiculous and—well, monstrous. But as the picture went on, I found myself missing her whenever she wasn't onscreen (when Michael Caine and Susannah York were acting immaculately), and I'm forced to conclude that, monstrous though she is, her jangling performance is what gives this movie its energy. She has grown into the raucous-demanding-woman role she faked in *Who's Afraid of Virginia Woolf?* When she goes too far, she's like the blowziest scarlet woman in a Mexican movie, but she's still funny. She wears her hair like upholstery, to balance the upholstery of flesh. The weight she has put on in these last years has not made her gracefully voluptuous; she's too hardboiled to be Rubensesque. The weight seems to have brought out this coarseness, and now she basks in vulgarity. She uses it as a form of assault in *X Y & Zee*, and I don't think she's ever before been as strong a star personality.

Elizabeth Taylor has changed before our eyes from the fragile child with a woman's face to the fabled beauty to this great bawd. Maybe child actresses don't quite grow up if they stay in the movies; maybe that's why, from ingénue-goddess, she went right over the hill. (The change in her is not unlike the change in Judy Garland.) Her Zee is a gross sensualist beyond shame or fear; possibly Zee is not really written to be as down-to-earth honest as Taylor plays her, but Taylor's all-out, let-it-bleed performance is a phenomenon—a world-famous woman changing status and, I think, maybe getting in touch with the audience in a new, egalitarian way. Her range has become even smaller. She's worst in some subdued scenes that take place in a hospital, when she droops and tries to call up that early demure beauty; she becomes flaccid—a fallen-angel-face. And she's not enough of an actress to get by with the bruised-and-hurting bit. She's got to be active and brassy and bold; she's best when she lets her gift for mimicry and for movie-colony sluttiness roll out. What she does may not be acting, exactly—I can't think of any tradition or school it fits into—but this isn't like her moldy performances in *Boom!* and *Secret Ceremony* or the anachronistic girlishness of her sweet young thing in *The Only Game in Town*. She responds to the zest in Edna O'Brien's material; you can feel her willingness to go all the way with it, and her delight at letting it all spill out. Though her voice is stronger now, she still gets shrill, and she starts so whoopingly high that the performance can't build and the viewer needs to recover. But Taylor has a talent for comic toughness; what she needs is a director to rein her in a little, to keep her from toppling over into the ridiculous and turning into a heavyweight Susan Hayward.

Brian Hutton plunges us straight into this *haut*-forties bedlam of domestic crisis. He aims each shot for the jugular. Nothing is implied, nothing suggested; everything belts you. Hutton isn't incompetent—he keeps things going by staying with the performers—but he can't redeem the hokey scenes toward the end, and he doesn't have much skill at modulation or atmosphere. We need to feel the contagion of Zee's messiness, feel how it works on her husband, driving him berserk, and how it infects Stella, but the picture doesn't develop. It has nowhere to go, anyway, because its emotional logic has been jiggled. Had Edna O'Brien's screenplay (published in England as *Zee & Co*) been followed, the movie might have got at the insanity of passion and might have broken through the fancy "women's-picture" format by sheer sensuous force. The author pushed what's implicit in the triangle to a classic climax: the couple jointly possess Stella. The movie substitutes a makeshift ending (Zee seducing Stella and thus winning out and keeping her husband) that has no strength. Photographed in Billy Williams's ripest palette, the production is mod-harem—a cushiony London version of old studio style. I don't suppose anyone in his right mind would call *X Y & Zee* a good movie; it's more like a plush circus, and it's even got slurpy theme music. But one may remember bits of old "women's pictures"—or even a relatively recent one, like *The Chapman Report*—for a surprisingly long time; in their gaudy way, they deal with a familiar inferno.

This one has a script that enabled Elizabeth Taylor to come out. The aging beauty has discovered in herself a gutsy, unrestrained spirit that knocks two very fine performers right off the screen—and, for the first time that I can recall, she appears to be having a roaring good time on camera. Susannah York, with her corn-silk hair and her round blue eyes, seems lovely, if a bit pallid. She has a harlequin voice—she rings wonderful low notes on it—and she carries her own quiet, vulnerable atmosphere, but the character she plays is slightly withdrawn, and that is Taylor's opportunity. After Zee, in a nasty snit, describes her as soulful and always a little out of breath, Stella looks like a narcissistic moonbeam. Even Susannah York's subtle, lapidary acting begins to seem overrefined when this rowdy broad is working up one of her rages. The corn-silk Stella is no match for Zee, and York, the polished actress, is unfairly matched against Taylor, an uncontrolled actress but a cunning force of nature. One can take pleasure in Taylor's brute triumph, especially since she's working with two of the best screen performers of our time. (Michael Caine does all he can with a role that requires him to be mostly exasperated, infuriated, and exhausted.) Perhaps a loud, uncontrolled performer can always dominate a controlled performer, because the element of accident and risk, the possibility that something grotesque may be revealed, adds danger and excitement—and there is something of this in Taylor's performance here. But there is also the excitement of seeing a woman who has vast reserves of personality and who wants to come forward, who wants to make contact. There's a documentary going on inside this movie—part of it may be parallel to Edna O'Brien's theme, but part of it isn't. It's of a woman declaring herself to be what she has become. Like everyone else, I adored the child Elizabeth Taylor, but I have never liked her as much since as in this bizarre exhibition. She's Beverly Hills Chaucerian, and that's as high and low as you can get.

The New Yorker, February 12, 1972

CABARET
GRINNING

Cabaret is a great movie musical, made, miraculously, without compromises. It's miraculous because the material is hard and unsentimental, and until now there has never been a diamond-hard big American movie musical. The people involved must have said something like "Let's do it right—let's use the right people, let's not wreck it the way *Pal Joey* was wrecked, and *The Boys from Syracuse* and *Guys and Dolls* and *Gypsy* and *Sweet Charity* and all the rest. Maybe it won't work at the box office, maybe the movie moguls have basically been shrewd when they insisted on all the softening and spoiling and the big names in the leads, but let's do it right for once anyway." And so *Cabaret* was made, with Joel Grey as our devil-doll host—the master of ceremonies—and Liza Minnelli, in her first singing role on the screen, as Sally Bowles. And it is everything one hopes for and more; if it doesn't make money, it will still make movie history.

After *Cabaret,* it should be a while before performers once again climb hills singing or a chorus breaks into song on a hayride; it is not merely that *Cabaret* violates the wholesome approach of big musicals but that it violates the pseudo-naturalistic tradition—the *Oklahoma!–South Pacific–West Side Story* tradition, which requires that the songs appear to grow organically out of the story. That pretense used to be charming in the light musical comedies with a French-farce base, like the Ginger Rogers and Fred Astaire series, but the "organic" big show has become the white elephant of Broadway, and by the time the elephants reached the screen nothing seemed more theatrical—in the worst sense—than the clumping attempts to go into a number "naturally." It was as if there were something the matter with song and dance, as if they had to be excused by being worked into "a life situation"—or one of those damn dream ballets.

Cabaret turns the conventions of recent big-musical movies inside out: the floor show at the Kit Kat Klub is used as a prism through which we see the characters' lives. The formalized numbers are at the center of the movie—are its essence. The songs comment on the lives of Sally Bowles and the other characters from the Christopher Isherwood "Goodbye to Berlin" stories, and they interpret the period—the end of an era (Weimar) and the beginning of Nazism. With this prismatic approach, *Cabaret* totally escapes grandiosity; it's a big musical that doesn't feel like one, and the first really innovative movie musical in many years. Not only is the subject not wholesome but the tone is detached and objective.

The usual movie approach to decadent periods of history is to condemn decadence while attempting to give us vicarious thrills. Here, in a prodigious balancing act, Bob Fosse, the choreographer-director, keeps this period—Berlin, 1931—at a cool distance. We see the decadence as garish and sleazy, and yet we see the animal energy in it, and the people driven to endure. The movie does not exploit decadence; rather, it gives it its due. The reminiscences of Brecht and Kurt Weill in Joel Grey's opening "Willkommen" and of *The Blue Angel* in Liza Minnelli's first song, "Mein Herr," help us get our bearings; reminiscence is part of the texture. The whory chorus girls displaying the piquant flesh around their garters, the Max Beckmann angles and the Edvard Munch hollows are part of the texture, too. The movie is never cynical (it may be one of the least cynical big movies ever made); it is, on the contrary, so clear-eyed that it winks at nothing. Though it uses camp material, it carries camp to its ultimate vileness—in the m.c.'s mockery of all things human, including himself. His lewd smirks, like Sally's broad, fatuous, flirtatious grins, are emblems of corruption. *Cabaret* does not merely suggest Egon Schiele's moribund, erotic figures and the rictus smiles and rotting flesh in the paintings and graphics of artists such as James Ensor and George Grosz but captures the same macabre spirit—and *sustains* it. What makes the art of such men powerful is that they help us recognize the sensual strength of decadence. When there is nothing to believe in but survival and pleasure, gaiety has a ghastly, desperate edge, but the way people still seek pleasure is testimony to something both base and fascinating. Everything seems to become sexualized. The grotesque amorality in *Cabaret* is frightening, not because it's weak but because it's intensely, obscenely alive.

The method of the movie is to embrace this life and to show us the appeal of its horror, and by this satiric embrace to put us at a distance. The detached tone makes it possible for us to observe the decay, consciously—with full awareness. You never get lost in it; you're aware of every detail—and you're also aware of the intelligence at work, keeping you aware. Fosse never slips tongue into cheek or lets the performers get moist; the movie doesn't lose its chilling tone. When the apocalyptic chill deepens, it deepens because of the precise, unhysterical direction. It's this masterly control that makes the movie biting and aesthetically exciting—so that it gets better as it goes along.

The metallic songs by John Kander, who wrote the music, and Fred

Ebb, who did the lyrics, have a distinctive, acrid flavor—a taste of death on the tongue. In the smoky atmosphere, the little m.c. is both ringmaster and marionette. His professional, insidious complicity with us, the audience—his slyness and malice—makes us draw back to objectivity. He looks as if he had been born in a night club. With his rouged cheeks, yellow-stained teeth, and smeared-down patent-leather hair, Joel Grey is every tantalizingly disgusting show-biz creep one has ever seen—all the cheap comics and night-club entertainers rolled into one. He's the essence of show-biz tawdriness, and the pure-tin evil heart of the period.

Joel Grey, Bob Fosse, and Liza Minnelli are all children of show-business families, and that may be why they understand these musical numbers so shatteringly well. Liza Minnelli's exuberant, corruptible Sally, going after fame and stardom no matter what, has that persistent spark—the amoral soul of theatre. Her emerald-green fingernails are no longer just the mark of a girl who wants to be shockingly original; Sally is no longer just an innocently and adorably mad gamine, older sister to Holly Golightly. This Sally has grown claws. The m.c. has burnt out his hopes, but she has youth and drive. He presides over a sinking ship and enjoys the spiteful knowledge of how tacky it is. But Sally, at the end, beckoning us with those emerald nails, has real force. Liza Minnelli makes you believe in the cabaret as "life" because she comes fully to life only when she sings. The features that seemed too large for her face suddenly fit. Her cherry lips and unnaturally bright eyes are no longer wild makeup; they belong to her performer's face. And her movements have speed and tension. Her desperation and Sally's are fused together; when a singer is belting it out, how can one separate the performer from the role? Liza Minnelli is a fine, if slightly overeager, actress and an inventive, appealing comedienne, but only when she sings is she a star: she's charged to give all she's got.

The material has come a long way from the Isherwood stories—through the play and movie of *I Am a Camera* to the Broadway musical *Cabaret* and this version, adapted for the screen by Jay Allen, with the assistance of Hugh Wheeler. The heightened powers of song and dance dominate the naturalistic characters (Michael York in the Isherwood-as-a-young-writer role, Marisa Berenson as a beautiful Jewish heiress, Fritz Wepper as her penniless suitor, Helmut Griem as a baron who courts both Sally and the writer) and subtly alter the meanings of the original material. When theatrical rot becomes a metaphor for a rotting period, it may also illuminate rotting theatre. If the cabaret numbers are the frame through which we see the themes and the story, the themes are also mirrored in the cabaret. And what these three children of show business may know in their bones is how true that mirror is.

There are a few minor imperfections: I could have done without the montage that involves a child, a ball, and some shrieking can-can dancers. Michael York's creamy-smooth glaze-of-youth skin looks too much like the baron's creamy-smooth skin—they seem to have come out of the same jar. (On the other hand, York's makeup after a street fight is a hilarious success.) Though York acts more simply and attractively than usual, his phrasing sounds uncannily as if he were being dubbed by James Mason. The first use of dialogue as a bridge between two sequences sticks out as a device, and a few lines are too pat. But this is nit-picking; I can see no major faults. My ideal musical would include far more dancing, but this conception doesn't allow for it, and that is hardly a fault. What dancing there is—which is mostly movement during songs—is marvellous, particularly that of Liza Minnelli and Joel Grey in the "Money" number, and of Grey and the shy gorilla lady dressed in flesh-pink tulle in the romantic soft-shoe "If You Could See Her." And there's a brief goose-stepping dance performed by helmeted chorus girls, with Grey among them in drag, that has prurient images worthy of Lautrec; Liza Minnelli, too, when she sings takes positions—the way she leads with her truculent shoulders, her small flapper-head like a predatory bird's—that suggest Lautrec's posters.

Cabaret is the only expensive American movie musical (actually, it was shot in West Germany) that takes its form from political cabaret. The political satire here might be thought to have too easy and obvious a target, but, as it works out, the associations we have with this target—from art and literature and journalism—enable the satire to function at a higher level of ironic obscenity than would be possible with a more topical subject. And the picture goes way beyond topical satire into a satire of temptations. The only number that doesn't take place in the Kit Kat Klub is a song in the open air. In a country-inn beer garden, a golden-haired, fresh-faced young boy begins to sing with the lilting sweetness of an Irish tenor. He's everything the movies have taught us to idolize—his teeth are the prettiest white teeth in the world—and as his stirring Nazi song, "Tomorrow Belongs to Me," builds relentlessly his radiant fervor transforms itself before our eyes. More typically, the movie intercuts between a slapdance on the stage inside the Klub and a beating in the street outside. The counterpoint may be a facile idea, but it is not carried out facilely. Decadence comprises so much more than any specific satirical target that the movie's cold embrace of decadence is a richly suggestive form of satire.

No one has ever made a musical that looked better than this one—photographed by Geoffrey Unsworth, and the first film produced by the Broadway producer Cy Feuer. The design and the lighting and the color are superb; the picture has the distortions and the exaggerations and the grinning vividness of Expressionist art. *Cabaret* demonstrates that when you revolt against the organic *Oklahoma!* conception of musicals you can create a new organic whole by style and imagination—if you have enough faith in the audience to do it right.

The New Yorker, February 19, 1972

THE GODFATHER
ALCHEMY

If ever there was a great example of how the best popular movies come out of a merger of commerce and art, *The Godfather* is it. The movie starts from a trash novel that is generally considered gripping and compulsively readable, though (maybe because movies more than satisfy my appetite for trash) I found it unreadable. You're told who and what the characters are in a few pungent, punchy sentences, and that's all they are. You're briefed on their backgrounds and sex lives in a flashy anecdote or two, and the author moves on, from nugget to nugget. Mario Puzo has a reputation as a good writer, so his potboiler was treated as if it were special, and not in the Irving Wallace–Harold Robbins class, to which, by its itch and hype and juicy *roman-à-clef* treatment, it plainly belongs. What would this school of fiction do without Porfirio Rubirosa, Judy Garland, James Aubrey, Howard Hughes, and Frank Sinatra? The novel *The Godfather*, financed by Paramount during its writing, features a Sinatra stereotype, and sex and slaughter, and little gobbets of trouble and heartbreak. It's gripping, maybe, in the same sense that Spiro Agnew's speeches were a few years back. Francis Ford Coppola, who directed the film, and wrote the script with Puzo, has stayed very close to the book's greased-lightning sensationalism and yet has made a movie with the spaciousness and strength that popular novels such as Dickens's used to have. With the slop and sex reduced and the whoremongering guess-who material minimized ("Nino," who sings with a highball in his hand, has been weeded out), the movie bears little relationship to other adaptations of books of this kind, such as *The Carpetbaggers* and *The Adventurers*. Puzo provided what Coppola needed: a storyteller's outpouring of incidents and details to choose from, the folklore behind the headlines, heat and immediacy, the richly familiar. And Puzo's shameless turn-on probably left Coppola looser than if he had been dealing with a better book; he could not have been cramped by worries about how best to convey its style. Puzo, who admits he was out to make money, wrote "below my gifts," as he puts it, and one must agree. Coppola uses his gifts to reverse the process—to give the public the best a moviemaker can do with this very raw material. Coppola, a young director who has never had a big hit, may have done the movie for money, as *he* claims—in order to make the pictures he really wants to make, he says—but this picture was made at peak capacity. He has salvaged Puzo's energy and lent the narrative dignity. Given the circumstances and the rush to complete the film and bring it to market, Coppola has not only done his best but pushed himself farther than he may realize. The movie is on the heroic scale of earlier pictures on broad themes, such as *On the Waterfront, From Here to Eternity,* and *The Nun's Story.* It offers a wide, startlingly vivid view of a Mafia dynasty. The abundance is from the book; the quality of feeling is Coppola's.

The beginning is set late in the summer of 1945; the film's roots, however, are in the gangster films of the early thirties. The plot is still about rival gangs murdering each other, but now we see the system of patronage and terror, in which killing is a way of dealing with the competition. We see how the racketeering tribes encroach on each other and why this form of illegal business inevitably erupts in violence. We see the ethnic subculture, based on a split between the men's conception of their responsibilities—all that they keep dark—and the sunny false Eden in which they try to shelter the women and children. The thirties films indicated some of this, but *The Godfather* gets into it at the primary level; the willingness to be basic and the attempt to understand the basic, to look at it without the usual preconceptions, are what give this picture its epic strength.

The visual scheme is based on the most obvious life-and-death contrasts; the men meet and conduct their business in deep-toned, shuttered rooms, lighted by lamps even in the daytime, and the story moves back and forth between this hidden, nocturnal world and the sunshine that they share with the women and children. The tension is in the meetings in the underworld darkness; one gets the sense that this secret life has its own poetry of fear, more real to the men (and perhaps to the excluded women also) than the sunlight world outside. The dark-and-light contrast is so operatic and so openly symbolic that it perfectly expresses the basic nature of the material. The contrast is integral to the Catholic background of the characters: innocence versus knowledge—knowledge in this sense being the same as guilt. It works as a visual style, because the Goyaesque shadings of dark brown into black in the interiors suggest (no matter how irrationally) an earlier period of history, while the sunny, soft-edge garden scenes have their own calendar-pretty pastness. Nino Rota's score uses old popular songs to cue the varying moods, and at one climactic point swells in a crescendo that is both Italian opera and pure-forties movie music. There are rash, foolish acts in the movie but no acts of individual bravery. The killing, connived at in the darkness, is the secret horror, and it surfaces in one bloody outburst after another. It surfaces so often that after awhile it doesn't surprise us, and the recognition that the killing is an integral part of business policy takes us a long way from the fantasy outlaws of old movies. These gangsters don't satisfy our adventurous fantasies of disobeying the law; they're not defiant, they're furtive and submissive. They are required to be more obedient than we are; they live by taking orders. There is no one on the screen we can identify with—unless we take a fancy to the pearly teeth of one shark in a pool of sharks.

Even when the plot strands go slack about two-thirds of the way through, and the passage of a few years leaves us in doubt whether certain actions have been concluded or postponed, the picture doesn't become soft-headed. The direction is tenaciously intelligent. Coppola holds on and pulls it all together. The trash novel is there underneath, but he attempts to draw the patterns out of the particulars. It's amazing how encompassing the view seems to be—what a sense you get of a broad historical perspective, considering that the span is only from 1945 to the mid-fifties, at which time the Corleone family, already forced by competitive pressures into dealing in narcotics, is moving its base of operations to Las Vegas.

The enormous cast is headed by Marlon Brando as Don Vito Corleone, the "godfather" of a powerful Sicilian-American clan, with James Caan as his hothead son, Sonny, and Al Pacino as the thoughtful, educated son, Michael. Is Brando marvellous? Yes, he is, but then he often is; he was marvellous a few years ago in *Reflections in a Golden Eye,* and he's shockingly effective as a working-class sadist in a current film, *The Nightcomers,* though the film itself isn't worth seeing. The role of Don Vito—a patriarch in his early sixties—allows him to release more of the gentleness that was so seductive and unsettling in his braggart roles. Don Vito could be played as a magnificent old warrior, a noble killer, a handsome bull-patriarch, but Brando manages to debanalize him. It's typical of Brando's daring that he doesn't capitalize on his broken-prow profile and the massive, sculptural head that has become the head of Rodin's Balzac—he doesn't play for statuesque nobility. The light, cracked voice comes out of a twisted mouth and clenched teeth; he has the battered face of a devious, combative old man, and a pugnacious thrust to his jaw. The rasp in his voice is particularly effective after Don Vito has been wounded; one almost feels that the bullets cracked it, and wishes it hadn't been cracked before. Brando interiorizes Don Vito's power, makes him less physically threatening and *deeper,* hidden within himself.

Brando's acting has mellowed in recent years; it is less immediately exciting than it used to be, because there's not the sudden, violent discharge of emotion. His effects are subtler, less showy, and he gives himself over to the material. He appears to have worked his way beyond the self-parody that was turning him into a comic, and that sometimes left the other performers dangling and laid bare the script. He has not acquired the polish of most famous actors; just the opposite—less mannered as he grows older, he seems to draw directly from life, and from himself. His Don is a primitive sacred monster, and the more powerful because he suggests not the strapping sacred monsters of movies (like Anthony Quinn) but actual ones—those old men who carry never-ending grudges and ancient hatreds inside a frail frame, those monsters who remember minute details of old business deals when they can no longer tie their shoelaces. No one has aged better on camera than Brando; he gradually takes Don Vito to the close of his life, when he moves into the sunshine world, a sleepy monster, near to innocence again. The character is all echoes and shadings, and no noise; his strength is in that armor of quiet. Brando has lent Don Vito some of his own mysterious, courtly reserve: the character is not explained; we simply assent to him and believe that, yes, he could become a king of the underworld. Brando doesn't dominate the movie, yet he gives the story the legendary presence needed to raise it above gang warfare to archetypal tribal warfare.

Brando isn't the whole show; James Caan is very fine, and so are Robert Duvall and many others in lesser roles. Don Vito's sons suggest different aspects of Brando—Caan's Sonny looks like the muscular young Brando but without the redeeming intuitiveness, while as the heir, Michael, Al Pacino comes to resemble him in manner and voice. Pacino creates a quiet, ominous space around himself; his performance—which is marvellous, too, big yet without ostentation—complements Brando's. Like Brando in this film, Pacino is simple; you don't catch him acting, yet he manages to change from a small, fresh-faced, darkly handsome college boy into an underworld lord, becoming more intense, smaller, and more isolated at every step. Coppola doesn't stress the father-and-son links; they are simply there for us to notice when we will. Michael becomes like his father mostly from the inside, but we also get to see how his father's face was formed (Michael's mouth gets crooked and his cheeks jowly, like his father's, after his jaw has been smashed). Pacino has an unusual gift for conveying the divided spirit of a man whose calculations often go against his inclinations. When Michael, warned that at a certain point he must come out shooting, delays, we are left to sense his mixed feelings. As his calculations will always win out, we can see that he will never be at peace. The director levels with almost everybody in the movie. The women's complicity in their husbands' activities is kept ambiguous, but it's naggingly there—you can't quite ignore it. And Coppola doesn't make the subsidiary characters lovable; we look at Clemenza (Richard Castellano) as objectively when he is cooking spaghetti as we do when he is garotting a former associate. Many of the actors (and the incidents) carry the resonances of earlier gangster pictures, so that we almost unconsciously place them in the prehistory of this movie. Castellano, with his resemblance to Al Capone and Edward G. Robinson (plus a vagrant streak of Oscar Levant), belongs in this atmosphere; so does Richard Conte (as Barzini), who appeared in many of the predecessors of this movie, including *House of Strangers,* though perhaps Al Lettieri (as Sollozzo) acts too much like a B-picture hood. And perhaps the director goes off key when Sonny is blasted and blood-splattered at a toll booth; the effect is too garish.

The people dress in character and live in character—with just the gewgaws that seem right for them. The period details are there—a satin pillow, a modernistic apartment-house lobby, a child's pasted-together greeting to Grandpa—but Coppola doesn't turn the viewer into a guided tourist, told what to see. Nor does he go in for a lot of closeups, which are the simplest tool for fixing a director's attitude. Diane Keaton (who plays Michael's girl friend) is seen casually; her attractiveness isn't labored. The only character who is held in frame for us to see exactly as the character looking at her sees her is Apollonia (played by Simonetta Stefanelli), whom Michael falls in love with in Sicily. She is fixed by the camera as a ripe erotic image, because that is what she means to him, and Coppola, not having wasted his resources, can do it in a few frames. In general, he tries not to fix the images. In *Sunday Bloody Sunday*, John Schlesinger showed a messy knocked-over ashtray being picked up in closeup, so that there was nothing to perceive in the shot but the significance of the messiness. Coppola, I think, would have kept the camera on the room in which the woman bent over to retrieve the ashtray, and the messiness would have been just one element among many to be observed—perhaps the curve of her body could have told us much more than the actual picking-up motion. *The Godfather* keeps so much in front of us all the time that we're never bored (though the picture runs just two minutes short of three hours)—we keep taking things in. This is a heritage from Jean Renoir—this uncoercive, "open" approach to the movie frame. Like Renoir, Coppola lets the spectator roam around in the images, lets a movie breathe, and this is extremely difficult in a period film, in which every detail must be carefully planted. But the details never look planted: you're a few minutes into the movie before you're fully conscious that it's set in the past.

When one considers the different rates at which people read, it's miraculous that films can ever solve the problem of a pace at which audiences can "read" a film together. A hack director solves the problem of pacing by making only a few points and making those so emphatically that the audience can hardly help getting them (this is why many of the movies from the studio-system days are unspeakably insulting); the tendency of a clever, careless director is to go too fast, assuming that he's made everything clear when he hasn't, and leaving the audience behind. When a film has as much novelistic detail as this one, the problem might seem to be almost insuperable. Yet, full as it is, *The Godfather* goes by evenly, so we don't feel rushed, or restless, either; there's classic grandeur to the narrative flow. But Coppola's attitudes are specifically modern—more so than in many films with a more jagged surface. Renoir's openness is an expression of an almost pagan love of people and landscape; his style is an embrace. Coppola's openness is a reflection of an exploratory sense of complexity; he doesn't feel the need to comment on what he shows us, and he doesn't want to reduce the meanings in a shot by pushing us this way or that. The assumption behind this film is that complexity will engage the audience.

These gangsters *like* their life style, while we—seeing it from the outside—are appalled. If the movie gangster once did represent, as Robert Warshow suggested in the late forties, "what we want to be and what we are afraid we may become," if he expressed "that part of the American psyche which rejects the qualities and the demands of modern life, which rejects 'Americanism' itself," that was the attitude of another era. In *The Godfather* we see organized crime as an obscene symbolic extension of free enterprise and government policy, an extension of the worst in America—its feudal ruthlessness. Organized crime is not a rejection of Americanism, it's what we fear Americanism to be. It's our nightmare of the American system. When "Americanism" was a form of cheerful, bland official optimism, the gangster used to be destroyed at the end of the movie and our feelings resolved. Now the mood of the whole country has darkened, guiltily; nothing is resolved at the end of *The Godfather,* because the family business goes on. Terry Malloy didn't clean up the docks at the end of *On the Waterfront;* that was a lie. *The Godfather* is popular melodrama, but it expresses a new tragic realism.

The New Yorker, March 18, 1972

THE SORROW AND THE PITY
COLLABORATION AND RESISTANCE

Inexplicably, despite everything—the suicidal practices of the film industry, the defeat of many people of talent, the financial squeeze here and abroad—this has been a legendary period in movies. Just since last March: *The Conformist, McCabe & Mrs. Miller, Sunday Bloody Sunday, The Last Picture Show, Fiddler on the Roof, Murmur of the Heart, The Garden of the Finzi-Continis, Cabaret, The Godfather,* and, of course, the films one may have major reservations about—the smash-bang cops-and-robbers. *The French Connection* and the controversial *A Clockwork Orange* and *Straw Dogs.* In addition: Jane Fonda's portrait of a call girl in *Klute,* George Segal's wild, comic hustling junkie in *Born to Win,* George C. Scott's bravura hamminess in *The Hospital,* the documentary-style *Derby,* the childishly primitive, touching, messed-up *Billy Jack,* the casually diverting *Skin Game,* and the comedies *Bananas* and *Made for Each Other.* A reviewer could hardly ask for more from any art, high or popular, and that list shows how far movies have gone in blurring the distinction. And now *The Sorrow and the Pity,* a documentary epic on the themes of collaboration and resistance.

The Hollywood war movies were propaganda for our side, and put us in the comfortable position of identifying with the heroic anti-Nazis. *The Sorrow and the Pity* makes us ask what we and our friends and families would actually have done if our country had been invaded, like France. Wartime France presents one of the most intricately balanced moral dilemmas imaginable, since, of all the countries occupied by the Nazis, the French were the only people to cave in and support a regime (the Pétain government, with its capital in Vichy) that actively collaborated with Hitler. That fact has been buried from sight in France, and a legend of national heroism has been officially encouraged; the government decided that the public was "not yet mature enough" to see this film on television. "Myths," according to the Gaullist official who made the decision, "are important in the life of a people. Certain myths must not be destroyed."

The Sorrow and the Pity is both oral history and essay: people who lived through the German occupation tell us what they did during that catastrophic period, and we see and hear evidence that corroborates or corrects or sometimes flatly contradicts them. A good portion of the material is no more than informed, intelligent television interviewing; what makes the film innovative is the immediate annotation of what has just been said, and the steady accumulation of perspectives and information. As the perspectives ramify—when we see the people as they are now and, in old snapshots and newsreel footage, as they were then—we begin to get a sense of living in history: a fuller sense of what it was like to participate in the moral drama of an occupied nation than we have ever before had. When history literally becomes the story of people's lives, we can't help but feel the continuity of those lives and our own. There's nothing comparable to *The Sorrow and the Pity*. Yet the director, Marcel Ophuls, didn't need to invent a new kind of mirror to hold up to us; all he needed to do was to hold up the old mirrors at different angles.

The Second World War was heavily recorded on film, and Ophuls draws upon newsreels from several countries and also upon propaganda shorts designed to educate and inspire the citizenry. The bits are fresh—selected, it might almost seem at first, to make marginal points; even those of us who know that period on film haven't seen much of this material. A piece of Nazi newsreel shows captured black troops from the French Army as evidence of France's racial decadence; another bit, on how to recognize a Jew, shows a collection of photos, including a glimpse of an infamous poster of Ernst Lubitsch—which, it is said, broke his heart when he realized he was being used as the model of Jewish bestiality. Pétain, visiting a schoolroom, talking high-mindedly, is the model of rectitude. There are fragments that in context gain a new meaning: the viciousness of shaving the heads of the women who had slept with Germans is horrible enough without the added recognition that probably those who did the shaving had spiritually slept with the Germans themselves. Ophuls sustains a constant ironic interplay between the old film clips and the interviews with those who gave orders, those who took orders, those who suffered and survived, and those who went on as before. The period (1940–44) is so recently past that it's still possible to delve into the psychology of history: *The Sorrow and the Pity* is about the effects of character upon political action.

It's one of the most demanding movies ever made—four hours and twenty minutes of concentrated attention. Narration, titles, voice-over translations that finish quickly so you can hear the actual voices in their own languages—Ophuls employs a variety of devices to get the data to the audience, and he tries to be aboveboard, as in the matter of the voices. (You can decide for yourself whether the dubber misrepresents the person's character.) You really process information, and doing so makes you aware of how falsely the phrase is applied to the unconscious soaking up of TV commercials and banalities. You experience the elation of using your mind—of evaluating the material, and perceiving how it's all developing, while you're storing it up. There's a point of view, but judgments are left to you, and you know that Ophuls is reasonable and fairminded, and trying to do justice to a great subject: how and why the French accepted Nazism, and then rejected what they had done, so that it was lost even from public memory. The Occupation has long been demythologized in print, and this film does not attempt to replace the printed studies; it does something different. On film it's possible to incorporate the historian's process of research—to show us the witnesses and the participants, so that we are put in the position of the investigators, seeing what they see and trying to frame some conclusions. Inevitably, the picture gets better as it goes along: the more we have to work with, the more complex our own reactions become. There's grace in Ophuls's method; he helps us to see that the issues go way beyond conventional ideas of assessing guilt—that the mysteries of human behavior in the film are true mysteries.

The cast is made up of the known, such as Pierre Mendès-France, George Bidault, Anthony Eden, and Albert Speer, and the unknown, who are principally from the small industrial city of Clermont-Ferrand, which the movie focuses on. Clermont-Ferrand is near Vichy and was the home base of Pierre Laval, and it is in the Auvergne, which was one of the centers of the Resistance. Those interviewed are, in their own terms, articulate and clearheaded, and are at their ease; *no one* appears to feel any guilt about past conduct. Whatever they did, they have, from what we can see, made their peace with themselves, though an upper-class Frenchman who fought alongside the Nazis in Russia appears to be almost in mourning for his duped and wasted youth. Some are less reflective and more open than we could have expected: Pétain's Minister of Youth discusses his morale-building among French children; a former Wehrmacht captain who was stationed in Clermont-Ferrand defends his right to wear his war decorations. From England, Anthony Eden, who used to look weak and foolish, suggests that anyone who did not live under the Occupation cannot judge the French. He comments on those days with great dignity and humanity: who would have expected him to age so intelligently? The heroes of the Resistance are the most unlikely people—stubborn, rebellious "misfits": a genial, though formidable, farmer, a bohemian aristocrat who at one time smoked opium, a diffident homosexual who became a British agent in France in order, he says, to prove that he was as brave as other men. They're not like the fake heroes in Hollywood's anti-Nazi movies, and they're impossible for us to project onto: we would be diminishing them if we tried. People who suffered tell stories of iniquities that we can scarcely bear to hear; others remember nothing, selectively. One man saw no Nazis and doesn't believe Clermont-Ferrand was occupied.

Were the French perhaps so passive in the Second World War because they were still depleted by their courage and sacrifices in the First World War? All sorts of speculative questions come to mind, and there are aspects of what happened in France in the early forties that I wish the film had clarified; for example, that the Germans had taken two million French prisoners of war, and that the promise of liberating these prisoners was a factor in encouraging France to fill its industrial quotas. Still . . . the French coöperation was peerless. The picture neglects to point out that the French Communists, serving the interests of Russian foreign policy (it was during the period of the Hitler-Soviet pact), were collaborationists until Hitler invaded Russia. But then the movie doesn't go into the close ties between the Catholic Church and the Vichy government, either. There are probably countless areas in which specialists would ask for more emphasis or greater detail, but that is true of almost any written work of history, and such works do not provide the psychological understanding that this film does.

We see that those who were inactive were not necessarily indifferent to the suffering of others: a sane, prosperous pharmacist sits, surrounded by his handsome children, and, without attempting to deny knowledge of what was going on, tells his reasons for remaining apolitical. They're not bad reasons—and who could call a man a coward for not having the crazy, aberrant nobility it takes to risk his life (and maybe his family)? (It's especially difficult for a woman to pass judgment, since women are traditionally exempted from accusations of cowardice. For most women, the risk of being separated from their children is a sufficient deterrent from any dangerous political acts, and who considers them immoral for that, even though they constitute a huge body of the docile and fearful?) It's only when you think of a country full of decent, reasonable people with such good reasons that you experience revulsion. The inactive, like the pharmacist, and the actual collaborators are easily accessible to the camera—perhaps more so than the resisters, because there is something special about the nature of intransigence, and maybe for that we need a literary or dramatic artist rather than a documentarian. But this film goes very far in bringing those approaches together. There may be a streak of romanticism in the way Ophuls leads us to the theory that only loners and black sheep—and workers and youth— are free enough to resist authority; I wasn't convinced, but I was charmed. I would like to know more of Louis Grave, the Maquis farmer who was betrayed by a neighbor and sent to Buchenwald: what formed this man that makes him so solid and contained, so beautifully rooted? When he tells about an old German's slipping him an apple when he was starving, you know that "documentary" has no boundaries. Louis Grave and his apple might be out of *Grand Illusion,* while Maurice Chevalier singing away becomes a little like the m.c. in *Cabaret.* We enjoy him, yet his entertainer's soul is perplexing; there's an element of the macabre in his good cheer. A German comedian entertaining troops and straining for laughs has that same macabre gaiety—the emblem of show business—but he's coarser (and German), and so less troubling. Chevalier's recurrent presence gives the film a lilt of satirical ambiguity.

It was in France during the Occupation that Simone Weil wrote, "Nothing is so rare as to see misfortune fairly portrayed. The tendency is either

442

to treat the unfortunate person as though catastrophe were his natural vocation or to ignore the effects of misfortune on the soul; to assume, that is, that the soul can suffer and remain unmarked by it—can fail, in fact, to be recast in misfortune's image." She was writing about the *Iliad*, but she was writing about it because the Nazis, like the Greek and Trojan warriors, were modifying the human spirit by the use of force. It is the highest praise I can offer *The Sorrow and the Pity* to say that in it misfortune *is* fairly portrayed. One is left with the question of whether (and how much) the French really have been marked—in the long run—by the Nazi experience.

The New Yorker, March 25, 1972

PART SIX

REELING

1976

FROM THE FOREWORD TO
REELING*

Movies—which arouse special, private, hidden feelings—have always had an erotic potential that was stronger than that of the live theater. Enlarged so that they seem totally ours, movie actors are more purely objects of contemplation than people who are physically present. Since they're not actually there on the stage, speaking, rushing off to change a costume, we can fantasize about them with impunity; by etherealizing the actors, film removes the contraints on our imaginations. This was obviously a factor in the early disapproval of movies, even if it wasn't consciously formulated. Probably movies weren't culturally respectable for a long time because they are so sheerly enjoyable; in a country with a Puritan background, the sensuality of movies was bound to be suspect. Even now, it's common for older educated people to insist on the superiority of live theater. This may mean that they prefer the feeling of control which they can generally maintain at a play.

Movies can overwhelm us, as no other art form, except, perhaps, opera does—although folk and rock music can do it, too. For some people being carried away by a movie is very frightening: not everyone wants to have many senses affected at once. Some people feel that they're on the receiving end, being attacked. The appeal of movies seems to go against the grain of

*Which covers the years 1972–1975.

447

everything they've been told during the processes of education—how they should learn to discriminate, learn to think for themselves, learn not to be led blindly.

No doubt movies attract us from earliest childhood because they excite us and work on us, and perhaps movies came to the fore in the sixties because, unlike books but like rock music, movies could be experienced tribally, yet they also provide aesthetic experiences of a sensual complexity that it's merely priggish to deny. People bred on TV and weaned on movies often feel sensually starved at a play—and they experience that starvation as boredom. When they are used to movies, live theater no longer works for them on a fantasy level. There aren't enough elements going for them in a play; they miss the constant flow of imagery, the quick shifts of place, the sudden rush of feeling. They miss all the compensatory elements which can sustain them during even a bad movie.

There's a reason for that "Wow!" which often seems all that a person can say after coming out of a movie house. So many images, sounds, and awakened memories may contribute to the film's effect on us that often we can't quite sort out what we think about the way we've been moved. We're not even sure sometimes if we liked it, but we certainly *felt* it. I think many people experience a sense of danger as part of the attraction of movies—they're going to be swept up in they know not what. Unstable people, people with a record of nervous disorders, leap to see a hyped-up Gothic, such as *The Exorcist,* knowing they may flip out on it. That, maybe, is the extreme of what we all sometimes want from the movies—sensations we can't control, an excitement that is a great high. Preferably a high without a sullen hangover, but sometimes moviegoers, particularly the generations of the counter-culture and after, want sensations so much that they don't really mind the downers. Those who go to the documentary-musical *Janis* may alternate between an exploding high and a nervous discomfort, yet that masochistic element can be what they want, too. It makes them feel closer to the subject of the film: it makes them feel that Janis Joplin went through what they're going through, just as the young audiences of earlier generations did when they watched James Dean in *Rebel Without a Cause* or the heroes of *Easy Rider.* However, *Janis,* with the raw erotic charge of the musical numbers one after another, affects them far more overpoweringly than those earlier films. And some, of course, go to it stoned to intensify the sensations of losing control. That's what Janis Joplin, losing triumphantly, in a spirit of comic defiance, celebrates.

It says something about the nature of movies that people don't say they like them, they say they love them—yet even those who love movies may feel that they can't always handle the emotions that a film heats up. They need to talk to friends, to read critics, in order to understand why they're reacting as they are, and whether it's an aberration or others feel the same way. People didn't have this same need when the movies they went to were on the order of *Going My Way, The Greatest Show on Earth,* or *My Fair Lady.*

The greater sensory impact of films in recent years—the acceleration in violence and in shock-editing—makes a critic's job tougher than before. Moviegoers have very different thresholds of response and of gullibility; some are almost unbelievably susceptible to suspense devices. And large numbers of them—educated and uneducated alike—react to the incineration of characters in *The Towering Inferno* as marvellous entertainment. That indicates one of the problems of movies: they can be effective on shameless levels. Who isn't terrified of burning to death? You don't have to be an artist to frighten audiences by fire. Yet when a movie has startled people, like *The Towering Inferno,* or enlisted their sympathies and made them weep, like *Walking Tall,* or made them feel vindictive and sadistic, like the Charles Bronson film *Death Wish,* the hardest thing for a critic to do is convince them that it isn't necessarily a great picture. It's almost impossible to persuade people that a shallow, primitive work can give them a terrific kick.

Movies operate in a maze of borderlines; criticism is a balancing act, trying to suggest perspectives on the emotions viewers feel, trying to increase their enjoyment of movies without insulting their susceptibilities to simple, crude pop. I know that I've failed in some of these reviews—dismissing big, bludgeoning movies without realizing how much they might mean to people, rejecting humid sentiment and imagining that no one could be affected by it. I still can't quite get it through my head that tricks that I laugh at are being played on some moviegoers for the first time—and may trigger strong, anxious responses.

But if dealing with some of the thickset films has been a chore (and my crowbar writing shows it), there were also the opportunities that a reviewer dreams of. Film artists have the capacity to give us more than they consciously know, more than they could commit to paper. They can reach out beyond themselves; that is what the greatest film masters—highrollers, all of them—have tried to do. The artists who seem natural filmmakers—D. W. Griffith, Jean Renoir, Satyajit Ray, Bernardo Bertolucci—accept the simple pleasures of moviegoing and extend them. They use everything at hand, and yet imbue their films with their own emotion. That is what is beginning to happen once again among American directors: they're trying to go all the way with movies. Expansionist personalities such as Robert Altman, Francis Ford Coppola, and Martin Scorsese allow for the surprises an actor may come up with; they seize whatever delights them and put it to fresh uses. They don't simplify for a mass audience. They work in movies for the same reason we go to movies: because movies can give us almost anything, almost everything. There are moments in recent films when we get the mind-swaying sensation of experiencing several arts—at their highest—combined. We come out reeling.

When you think back on the movies of the past, or when you watch them on television, they're like samples—swatches of cloth—of the period in which they were made: *In The Heat of the Night* belongs to the Lyndon Johnson age as clearly as *Dirty Harry* belongs to the heyday of the Nixon era.

New pictures such as *Mean Streets, The Godfather, Part II,* and *Nashville* don't supply reassuring smiles or self-righteous messages, but they have something in common (and it's something they share with films from abroad such as *Last Tango in Paris* and Jan Troell's *The Emigrants* and *The New Land*)—a new openminded interest in examining American experience. This interest is at once skeptical, disenchanted, despairing, and lyrical. Our filmmakers seem to be on a quest—looking to understand what has been shaping our lives. A few decades hence, these years may appear to be the closest our movies have come to the tangled, bitter flowering of American letters in the early 1850s.

LAST TANGO IN PARIS

Bernardo Bertolucci's *Last Tango in Paris* was presented for the first time on the closing night of the New York Film Festival, October 14, 1972; that date should become a landmark in movie history comparable to May 29, 1913—the night *Le Sacre du Printemps* was first performed—in music history. There was no riot, and no one threw anything at the screen, but I think it's fair to say that the audience was in a state of shock, because *Last Tango in Paris* has the same kind of hypnotic excitement as the *Sacre*, the same primitive force, and the same thrusting, jabbing eroticism. The movie breakthrough has finally come. Exploitation films have been supplying mechanized sex—sex as physical stimulant but without any passion or emotional violence. The sex in *Last Tango in Paris* expresses the characters' drives. Marlon Brando, as Paul, is working out his aggression on Jeanne (Maria Schneider), and the physical menace of sexuality that is emotionally charged is such a departure from everything we've come to expect at the movies that there was something almost like fear in the atmosphere of the party in the lobby that followed the screening. Carried along by the sustained excitement of the movie, the audience had given Bertolucci an ovation, but afterward, as individuals, they were quiet. This must be the most powerfully erotic movie ever made, and it may turn out to be the most liberating movie ever made, and so it's probably only natural that an audience, anticipating a voluptuous feast from the man who made *The Conformist,* and confronted with this unexpected sexuality and the new realism it requires of the actors, should go into shock. Bertolucci and Brando have altered the face of an art form. Who was prepared for that?

Many of us had expected eroticism to come to the movies, and some of us had even guessed that it might come from Bertolucci, because he seemed to have the elegance and the richness and the sensuality to make lushly erotic movies. But I think those of us who had speculated about erotic movies had tended to think of them in terms of Terry Southern's deliriously comic novel on the subject, *Blue Movie;* we had expected *artistic* blue movies, talented directors taking over from the *Shlockmeisters* and making sophisticated voyeuristic fantasies that would be gorgeous fun—a real turn-on. What nobody had talked about was a sex film that would churn up everybody's emotions. Bertolucci shows his masterly elegance in *Last Tango in Paris,* but he also reveals a master's substance.

The script (which Bertolucci wrote with Franco Arcalli) is in French and English; it centers on a man's attempt to separate sex from everything else. When his wife commits suicide, Paul, an American living in Paris, tries to get away from his life. He goes to look at an empty flat and meets Jeanne, who is also looking at it. They have sex in an empty room, without knowing anything about each other—not even first names. He rents the flat, and for three days they meet there. She wants to know who he is, but he insists that sex is all that matters. We see both of them (as they don't see each other) in their normal lives—Paul back at the flophouse-hotel his wife owned, Jeanne with her mother, the widow of a colonel, and with her adoring fiancé (Jean-Pierre Léaud), a TV director, who is relentlessly shooting a sixteen-millimeter film about her, a film that is to end in a week with their wedding. Mostly, we see Paul and Jeanne together in the flat as they act out his fantasy of ignorant armies clashing by night, and it *is* warfare—sexual aggression and retreat and battles joined.

The necessity for isolation from the world is, of course, his, not hers. But his life floods in. He brings into this isolation chamber his sexual anger, his glorying in his prowess, and his need to debase her and himself. He demands total subservience to his sexual wishes; this enslavement is for him the sexual truth, the real thing, sex without phoniness. And she is so erotically sensitized by the rounds of lovemaking that she believes him. He goads her and tests her until when he asks if she's ready to eat vomit as a proof of love, she is, and gratefully. He plays out the American male tough-guy sex role—insisting on his power in bed, because that is all the "truth" he knows.

What they go through together in their pressure cooker is an intensified, speeded-up history of the sex relationships of the dominating men and the adoring women who have provided the key sex model of the past few decades—the model that is collapsing. They don't know each other, but their sex isn't "primitive" or "pure"; Paul is the same old Paul, and Jeanne, we gradually see, is also Jeanne, the colonel's daughter. They bring their cultural hangups into sex, so it's the same poisoned sex Strindberg wrote about: a battle of unequally matched partners, asserting whatever dominance they can, seizing any advantage. Inside the flat, his male physical strength and the mythology he has built on it are the primary facts. He pushes his morose, romantic insanity to its limits; he burns through the sickness that his wife's suicide has brought on—the self-doubts, the need to prove himself and torment himself. After three days, his wife is laid out for burial, and he is ready to resume his identity. He gives up the flat: he wants to live normally again, and he wants to love Jeanne as a *person*. But Paul is forty-five, Jeanne is twenty. She lends herself to an orgiastic madness, shares it, and then tries to shake it off—as many another woman has, after a night or a twenty years' night. When they meet in the outside world, Jeanne sees Paul as a washed-up middle-aged man—a man who runs a flophouse.

Much of the movie is American in spirit. Brando's Paul (a former actor and journalist who has been living off his French wife) is like a drunk with a literary turn of mind. He bellows his contempt for hypocrisies and orthodoxies; he keeps trying to shove them all back down other people's throats. His profane humor and self-loathing self-centeredness and street "wisdom" are in the style of the American hardboiled fiction aimed at the masculine-fantasy market, sometimes by writers (often good ones, too) who believe in more than a little of it. Bertolucci has a remarkably unbiased intelligence. Part of the convulsive effect of *Last Tango in Paris* is that we are drawn to Paul's view of society and yet we can't help seeing him as a self-dramatizing, self-pitying clown. Paul believes that his animal noises are more honest than words, and that his obscene vision of things is the way things really are; he's often convincing. After Paul and Jeanne have left the flat, he chases her and persuades her to have a drink at a ballroom holding a tango contest. When we see him drunkenly sprawling on the floor among the bitch-chic mannequin-dancers and then baring his bottom to the woman official who asks him to leave, our mixed emotions may be like those some of us experienced when we watched Norman Mailer put himself in an indefensible position against Gore Vidal on the Dick Cavett show, justifying all the people who were fed up with him. Brando's Paul carries a yoke of masculine pride and aggression across his broad back; he's weighed down by it and hung on it. When Paul is on all fours barking like a crazy man-dog to scare off a Bible salesman who has come to the flat,* he may—to the few who saw Mailer's *Wild 90*—be highly reminiscent of Mailer on his hands and knees barking at a German shepherd to provoke it. But Brando's barking extends the terms of his character and the movie, while we are disgusted with Mailer for needing to prove himself by teasing an unwilling accomplice, and his barking throws us outside the terms of his movie.

Realism with the terror of actual experience still alive on the screen— that's what Bertolucci and Brando achieve. It's what Mailer has been trying to get at in his disastrous, ruinously expensive films. He was right about what was needed but hopelessly wrong in how he went about getting it. He tried to pull a new realism out of himself onto film, without a script, depending wholly on improvisation, and he sought to bypass the self-consciousness and fakery of a man acting himself by improvising within a fictional construct—as a gangster in *Wild 90,* as an Irish cop in *Beyond the Law* (the best of them), and as a famous director who is also a possible Presidential candidate in *Maidstone.* In movies, Mailer tried to will a work of art into existence without going through the steps of making it, and his theory

*This scene was deleted by the director after the New York Film Festival showing.

of film, a rationale for this willing, sounds plausible until you see the movies, which are like Mailer's shambling bouts of public misbehavior, such as that Cavett show. His movies trusted to inspiration and were stranded when it didn't come. Bertolucci builds a structure that supports improvisation. Everything is prepared, but everything is subject to change, and the whole film is alive with a sense of discovery. Bertolucci builds the characters "on what the actors are in themselves. I never ask them to interpret something preëxistent, except for dialogue—and even that changes a lot." For Bertolucci, the actors "make the characters." And Brando knows how to improvise: it isn't just Brando improvising, it's Brando improvising as Paul. This is certainly similar to what Mailer was trying to do as the gangster and the cop and the movie director, but when Mailer improvises, he expresses only a bit of himself. When Brando improvises within Bertolucci's structure, his full art is realized. His performance is not like Mailer's acting but like Mailer's best writing: intuitive, rapt, princely. On the screen, Brando is our genius as Mailer is our genius in literature. Paul is Rojack's expatriate-failure brother, and Brando goes all the way with him.

We all know that movie actors often merge with their roles in a way that stage actors don't, quite, but Brando did it even on the stage. I was in New York when he played his famous small role in *Truckline Café* in 1946; arriving late at a performance, and seated in the center of the second row, I looked up and saw what I thought was an actor having a seizure onstage. Embarrassed for him, I lowered my eyes, and it wasn't until the young man who'd brought me grabbed my arm and said "Watch this guy!" that I realized he was *acting*. I think a lot of people will make my old mistake when they see Brando's performance as Paul; I think some may prefer to make this mistake, so they won't have to recognize how deep down he goes and what he dredges up. Expressing a character's sexuality makes new demands on an actor, and Brando has no trick accent to play with this time, and no putty on his face. It's perfectly apparent that the role was conceived for Brando, using elements of his past as integral parts of the character. Bertolucci wasn't surprised by what Brando did; he was ready to use what Brando brought to the role. And when Brando is a full creative presence on the screen, the realism transcends the simulated actuality of any known style of *cinéma vérité*, because his surface accuracy expresses what's going on underneath. He's an actor: when he shows you something, he lets you know what it means. The torture of seeing Brando—at his worst—in *A Countess from Hong Kong* was that it was a *reductio ad absurdum* of the wastefulness and emasculation (for both sexes) of Hollywood acting; Chaplin, the director, obviously allowed no participation, and Brando was like a miserably obedient soldier going through drill. When you're nothing but an inductee, you have no choice. The excitement of Brando's performance here is in the revelation of how creative screen acting can be. At the simplest level, Brando, by his inflections and rhythms, the right American obscenities, and perhaps an improvised monologue, makes the dialogue his own and makes Paul an authentic

American abroad, in a way that an Italian writer-director simply couldn't do without the actor's help. At a more complex level, he helps Bertolucci discover the movie in the process of shooting it, and that's what makes moviemaking an art. What Mailer never understood was that his *macho* thing prevented flexibility and that in terms of his own personality he *couldn't* improvise—he was consciously acting. And he couldn't allow others to improvise, because he was always challenging them to come up with something. Using the tactics he himself compared to "a commando raid on the nature of reality," he was putting a gun to their heads. Lacking the background of a director, he reduced the art of film to the one element of acting, and in his confusion of "existential" acting with improvisation he expected "danger" to be a spur. But acting involves the joy of self-discovery, and to improvise, as actors mean it, is the most instinctive, creative part of acting—to bring out and give form to what you didn't know you had in you; it's the surprise, the "magic" in acting. A director has to be supportive for an actor to feel both secure enough and free enough to reach into himself. Brando here, always listening to an inner voice, must have a direct pipeline to the mystery of character.

Bertolucci has an extravagant gift for sequences that are like arias, and he has given Brando some scenes that really sing. In one, Paul visits his dead wife's lover (Massimo Girotti), who also lives in the run-down hotel, and the two men, in identical bathrobes (gifts from the dead woman), sit side by side and talk. The scene is miraculously basic—a primal scene that has just been discovered. In another, Brando rages at his dead wife, laid out in a bed of flowers, and then, in an excess of tenderness, tries to wipe away the cosmetic mask that defaces her. He has become the least fussy actor. There is nothing extra, no flourishes in these scenes. He purifies the characterization beyond all that: he brings the character a unity of soul. Paul feels so "real" and the character is brought so close that a new dimension in screen acting has been reached. I think that if the actor were anyone but Brando many of us would lower our eyes in confusion.

His first sex act has a boldness that had the audience gasping, and the gasp was caused—in part—by our awareness that this was Marlon Brando doing it, not an unknown actor. In the flat, he wears the white T-shirt of Stanley Kowalski, and he still has the big shoulders and thick-muscled arms. Photographed looking down, he is still tender and poetic; photographed looking up, he is ravaged, like the man in the Francis Bacon painting under the film's opening titles. We are watching *Brando* throughout this movie, with all the feedback that that implies, and his willingness to run the full course with a study of the aggression in masculine sexuality and how the physical strength of men lends credence to the insanity that grows out of it gives the film a larger, tragic dignity. If Brando knows this hell, why should we pretend we don't?

The colors in this movie are late-afternoon orange-beige-browns and pink—the pink of flesh drained of blood, corpse pink. They are so delicately modulated (Vittorio Storaro was the cinematographer, as he was on *The Conformist*) that romance and rot are one; the lyric extravagance of the music (by Gato Barbieri) heightens this effect. Outside the flat, the gray buildings and the noise are certainly modern Paris, and yet the city seems muted. Bertolucci uses a feedback of his own—the feedback of old movies to enrich the imagery and associations. In substance, this is his most American film, yet the shadow of Michel Simon seems to hover over Brando, and the ambience is a tribute to the early crime-of-passion films of Jean Renoir, especially *La Chienne* and *La Bête Humaine*. Léaud, as Tom, the young director, is used as an affectionate takeoff on Godard, and the movie that Tom is shooting about Jeanne, his runaway bride, echoes Jean Vigo's *L'Atalante*. Bertolucci's soft focus recalls the thirties films, with their lyrically kind eye for every variety of passion; Marcel Carné comes to mind, as well as the masters who influenced Bertolucci's technique—von Sternberg (the controlled lighting) and Max Ophuls (the tracking camera). The film is utterly beautiful to look at. The virtuosity of Bertolucci's gliding camera style is such that he can show you the hype of the tango-contest scene (with its own echo of *The Conformist*) by stylizing it (the automaton-dancers do wildly fake head turns) and still make it work. He uses the other actors for their associations, too—Girotti, of course, the star of so many Italian films, including *Senso* and *Ossessione*, Visconti's version of *The Postman Always Rings Twice*, and, as Paul's mother-in-law, Maria Michi, the young girl who betrays her lover in *Open City*. As a maid in the hotel (part of a weak, diversionary subplot that is soon dispensed with), Catherine Allégret, with her heart-shaped mouth in a full, childishly beautiful face, is an aching, sweet reminder of her mother, Simone Signoret, in her *Casque d'Or* days. Bertolucci draws upon the movie background of this movie because movies are as active in him as direct experience—perhaps more active, since they may color everything else. Movies are a past we share, and, whether we recognize them or not, the copious associations are at work in the film and we feel them. As Jeanne, Maria Schneider, who has never had a major role before, is like a bouquet of Renoir's screen heroines and his father's models. She carries the whole history of movie passion in her long legs and baby face.

Maria Schneider's freshness—Jeanne's ingenuous corrupt innocence—gives the film a special radiance. When she lifts her wedding dress to her waist, smiling coquettishly as she exposes her pubic hair, she's in a great film tradition of irresistibly naughty girls. She has a movie face—open to the camera, and yet no more concerned about it than a plant or a kitten. When she speaks in English, she sounds like Leslie Caron in *An American in Paris,* and she often looks like a plump-cheeked Jane Fonda in her *Barbarella* days. The role is said to have been conceived for Dominique Sanda, who couldn't play it, because she was pregnant, but surely it has been reconceived. With Sanda, a tigress, this sexual battle might have ended in a draw. But the pliable, softly unprincipled Jeanne of Maria Schneider must be the winner: it is the soft ones who defeat men and walk away, consciencelessly. A

Strindberg heroine would still be in that flat, battling, or in another flat, battling. But Jeanne is like the adorably sensual bitch-heroines of French films of the twenties and thirties—both shallow and wise. These girls know how to take care of themselves; they know who No. 1 is. Brando's Paul, the essentially naïve outsider, the romantic, is no match for a French bourgeois girl.

Because of legal technicalities, the film must open in Italy before it opens in this country, and so *Last Tango in Paris* is not scheduled to play here until January. There are certain to be detractors, for this movie represents too much of a change for people to accept it easily or gracefully. They'll grab at aesthetic flaws—a florid speech or an oddball scene—in order to dismiss it. Though Americans seem to have lost the capacity for being scandalized, and the Festival audience has probably lost the cultural confidence to admit to being scandalized, it might have been easier on some if they could have thrown things. I've tried to describe the impact of a film that has made the strongest impression on me in almost twenty years of reviewing. This is a movie people will be arguing about, I think, for as long as there are movies. They'll argue about how it is intended, as they argue again now about *The Dance of Death*. It is a movie you can't get out of your system, and I think it will make some people very angry and disgust others. I don't believe that there's *anyone* whose feelings can be totally resolved about the sex scenes and the social attitudes in this film. For the very young, it could be as antipathetic as *L'Avventura* was at first—more so, because it's closer, more realistic, and more emotionally violent. It could embarrass them, and even frighten them. For adults, it's like seeing pieces of your life, and so, of course, you can't resolve your feelings about it—our feelings about life are never resolved. Besides, the biology that is the basis of the "tango" remains.

The New Yorker, October 28, 1972

LADY SINGS THE BLUES
POP VERSUS JAZZ

L*ady Sings the Blues* fails to do justice to the musical life of which Billie Holiday was a part, and it never shows what made her a star, much less what made her an artist. The sad truth is that there is no indication that those who made the picture understand that jazz is any different from pop corruptions of jazz. And yet when the movie was over I wrote "I love it" on my pad of paper and closed it and stuffed it back in my pocket. In certain kinds of movies, the chemistry of pop vulgarization is all-powerful. You don't want to resist the pull of it, because it has a celebrity-star temperament you don't get from anything else; this kitsch has its own kind of authenticity. It's a compliment to the brand of tarnished-lady realism Motown has produced that one thinks of Warners and such Bette Davis vehicles as *Dark Victory* and *Dangerous* rather than of M-G-M. This movie isn't heavy and glazed. Factually it's a fraud, but emotionally it delivers. It has what makes movies work for a mass audience: easy pleasure, tawdry electricity, personality—great quantities of personality. Pop music provides immediate emotional gratifications that the subtler and deeper and more lasting pleasures of jazz can't prevail against. Pop drives jazz back underground. And that's what this pop movie does to the career of a great jazz singer.

How can you trash an artist's life and come up with a movie as effective as *Lady Sings the Blues?* Well, at one level Billie Holiday trashed her own life, and so her morbid legend works for the picture. Movie-trade reporters say that movies with "lose" or "loser" in the title always make money; a movie about Billie Holiday hardly needs the word in the title. Who could be a more natural subject for a flamboyant downer than Billie Holiday, whose singing can send the cheeriest extroverts into a funk? Good Morning, Heartache. Billie Holiday expressed herself in her bantering with lachrymose lyrics, making them ironic and biting, or else exploiting them for their full measure of misery, giving in so deeply to cheap emotions that she wrung a truth of her own out of them. Maybe not quite a truth but an essence. How many masochists have sated themselves on her "Gloomy Sunday"? And the defiance of her "Ain't Nobody's Business If I Do" was always borderline self-pity: the subtext was "I don't need any of you, I'm so miserable." We've all got a lot of slop in us, and she glorified it, so she was irresistible. She lived so close to those self-destructive suffering-star myths epitomized by the term "a Susan Hayward picture" that only by suggesting the Billie Holiday who was an intuitive innovator and played her oboe voice like a jazz instrument, the artist who was fully happy only when she was singing, could the movie have transcended the old gallant-victim-paying-the-price-of-fame routine. Instead, it stays snugly within commercial confines, relying on the variation of the black sufferer to make it new. This bio-melodrama wasn't made with love for Billie Holiday, exactly (except perhaps from Diana Ross, who plays the role), but *I'll Cry Tomorrow* and *Love Me or Leave Me* (which we think of as "forties" but which were actually mid-fifties—not very far in the past) didn't show much love, either, and they were made with much less energy and spirit.

Still, it's shocking to see a great black artist's experience poured into the same Hollywood mold, and to see that it works—and works far better than it did on the white singers' lives. There's an obvious, external cause for the torments Billie Holiday goes through, and black experience is still new and exotic on the screen—a fresh setting with a new cast of characters, a new vernacular, and a different kind of interplay. And since you can show almost anything in movies now, you don't have to find euphemisms and substitutions. A whore is no longer a "hostess." But this freedom in language and atmosphere isn't to be confused with freedom from commercialism. The movie prefers invented horrors to the known (and much worse) horrors of Billie Holiday's actual life. Her promiscuity has been jettisoned; the lovers and domestic messes and quick affairs all disappear, and her third husband, Louis McKay (Billy Dee Williams), becomes the only man she loves and wants. It's when they're separated (because of her career) that she's so lonely and unhappy she tries drugs; and she falls back on them again later on when he must be away for a few months. Billie Holiday's music certainly doesn't send us messages about a good man who's always there when she needs him; her torch blues express the disorder and dissatisfaction of her human relations. How could anybody listen to her highwire singing and write this monogamous script? Well, that's not what the troop of writers were listening to.

When this Billie Holiday announces that she is giving up singing to marry Louis and spend her time in the kitchen, audiences cheer. The way they have been conditioned by movies and TV, how else can they react? In terms of the movie, they're reacting *appropriately;* the movie itself can't deal with why Billie wants to go on singing after she has married her fairy-tale prince. The picture is solidly aimed at a mass audience that knows a junkie is damned lucky to get a fine, substantial husband to take care of her, and Louis McKay has been made such a deep-voiced, sexy Mr. Right that the audience's sympathies tend to go to him rather than to her. At times, the movie seems deliberately shaped to make Billy Dee Williams a star. One can almost feel the calculation that swooning teenagers will say to themselves, "*I* wouldn't take dope if I had a man like that waiting for me." McKay is black, but he's an early-model Clark Gable dreamboat. This ridiculously suave, couth man (who is involved in some unspecified business that permits him to be a hot-shot big spender) belongs in another sort of movie altogether. Since he doesn't save her, what's he here for? For black popular romance, of course, and maybe it's only a commercial dividend that he embodies the stability against which Billie Holiday is then judged.

The assumption is that the basic audience will be black, and so the movie plays a few get-Whitey games: you never see Billie with any of her *white* lovers, or in her quarrels with blacks (including her own mother), and she's turned onto dope by a smiling white dude (platinum-blond Paul Hampton, who overdoes the white sliminess). Operating on a scrambled calendar of events, the movie avoids the complexity of the race issues in her life, making her strictly a victim. Her tour with Artie Shaw's band has been turned into the road to ruin for a little black girl who should have stayed with her own people. And with this approach Billie Holiday seems so weak a person that we can't see how she ever made it to the peak of her profession. For reasons that are obscure—possibly in order to sustain the victim image—her records, by which the whole world came to know her, are omitted. One would never suspect that she began to record at the age of eighteen and that by her early twenties she was an important figure in the world of jazz. How shrewd it is, consciously or unconsciously, to show us not the woman who had made over a hundred recordings by the time she was twenty-five, not the embattled woman who broke down racial barriers while creating a new musical style, but a junkie girl who makes it to the top—the stage of Carnegie Hall—yet at too great a price. A loser. A movie that dealt with Billie Holiday's *achievements* wouldn't be hip; what's hip is the zingy romanticism of failure. *Lady Sings the Blues* is about a junkie who has it made but keeps pulling herself down.

Diana Ross, a tall, skinny goblin of a girl, intensely likable, always in motion, seemed an irrational choice for the sultry, still Billie Holiday, yet she's like a beautiful bonfire: there's nothing to question—you just react with everything you've got. You react in kind, because she has given herself to the role with an all-out physicality, not holding anything back. At times, she reminded me a little of the way Carole Lombard used to throw herself into a role; Lombard wasn't a great comedienne, but she had such zest and vitality that you liked her better than mere comediennes. She was striking and special—an original. So is Diana Ross, and with gifts that can't be defined yet. She couldn't have won us over so fast if the director hadn't shaped and built our interest in her from the childhood scenes. She's knockabout, tomboy angular as an adolescent, and a little later she has a harlequin beauty: huge eyes and a pointed chin and an impishly pretty smile. When she wears ruby lipstick, it's so absolutely right it looks like part of her. She's made up to look uncannily like Billie Holiday in flashes in the latter part of the film, but she's most appealing in the early scenes, when she's least like Billie. The elements of camp and self-parody in Diana Ross's performances with the Supremes and in her TV solo appearances are gone, but, in her whore's orange dress with ruffles at the shoulders and a snug fit over her wriggly, teasing little bottom, she still has her impudence. She's scat-fast with a funny line, she's inventive when she delivers her dialogue like lyrics, and she has a sneaky face for the times when Billie is trying to put something over on Louis. The drugs act like a dimmer: the lights in her voice go down. She differentiates the stoned singing from the "clean" singing by a slight slippery uncertainty (though there's a kitchen scene when she's clean but depressed and she sings—inappropriately, I thought—in this desultory way).

In the established Hollywood tradition, Billie Holiday doesn't have to become Billie Holiday, musically speaking; the first time she sings in public, she has the full Holiday style. But, of course, Diana Ross doesn't pierce us the way Holiday does. She's strong in everything but her singing; as a singer, she's caught in the trap of this bio-melodrama form. *Funny Girl* was a stylized musical comedy, and so no one expected Streisand to sing like Fanny Brice; besides, Fanny Brice isn't on many jukeboxes. But the star of *Lady Sings the Blues* is expected to sound like Billie Holiday. And the key problem for me with the movie is that Diana Ross's singing is *too* close. Her voice is similar—small and thin and reedy, and suspended in air, like a little girl's—and when she sings the songs that Holiday's phrasing fixed in our minds and imitates that phrasing, our memories are blurred. I felt as if I were losing something. I could hear Billie Holiday in my head perfectly clearly as

Ross sang each number, but by the time she had finished it, I could no longer be certain of the exact Holiday sounds. What's involved here isn't quite like the vandalism that Stokowski and Disney committed in *Fantasia,* with cupids and winged horses cavorting to the "Pastoral" and volcanoes erupting to Stravinsky—wrecking music for us by forcing us to hear it forever after with incongruous images welded to it—or like the way Kubrick played droog to Beethoven, and even to "Singin' in the Rain." But something similar is at work: Kubrick left Moog-synthesized versions of classics echoing in our skulls, and I think *Lady Sings the Blues,* by its pop versions of Billie Holiday's numbers, will deprive people of the originals. Yes, of course, they still exist, just as the originals of the Benny Goodman and Duke Ellington records that Time-Life has had imitated by modern bands still exist, but new generations are effectively deprived of them just the same. Movies never use the original records in these bios, because the contemporary sound always sells better, and so movies use art as grist.

With Holiday, it was as if everything extra—the padding, all the resonances—had been pared away by troubles: just this thin, wounded sound was left. She made her limited voice yield pure emotion—what jazz horn players sought to do. And her plaintiveness made even her vivacious numbers hurt. There's no pain in Diana Ross's voice, and none of that lazy, sullen sexiness that was a form of effrontery and a turn-on. In song after song in *Lady Sings the Blues,* the phrasing has been split off from its emotional meaning. Diana Ross's "Them There Eyes" comes at the happiest moment in the movie and she's charming on it, but it works on a simple, pop level. She sings the showpiece number, "Strange Fruit," very well, and it's pretty, but it lacks Holiday's chilling tautness that keeps you silent until the final word, "crop," flicks you like a whip. Holiday's acrid edge is missing, and her authority. Ross gives you the phrasing without the intensity that makes it dramatic and memorable, and fresh each time you hear it.

What one always knew, with Billie Holiday, was that there was one thing her voice could never do: heal, the way a rich, full voice can—as Bessie Smith could and Aretha Franklin can. Maybe Billie Holiday willed that effect of being a lone, small voice in the wilderness—isolation rooted in the sound—because that was the only way she could make a great instrument out of her limited voice, and because she meant to wound, not to heal. She wasn't hiding anything: her voice was a direct line from her to us, hurting us (exquisitely, of course) because she'd been hurt (and not exquisitely at all). She was a jazz singer; Ross is a pop singer singing in the Holiday manner. It's imitation soul. That was the letdown of Billie Holiday's later singing—her creativity gave out and she was imitating her own style. Diana Ross's imitation may be an act of homage as much as a requirement of the role, but what she had with the Supremes—which was freaky and as commercial as hell—was recognizably hers. Singing in the style of someone else kills her spark, though she has it here as an actress. Perhaps the decision to spare us the dregs of Billie Holiday's life—the club appearances when her voice was shot and she could barely be heard and the scattering of audience was mostly narcotics agents anyway—was based on a recognition that it wouldn't jibe with Diana Ross's lively, quick spirit. She doesn't have the punishing personality of Billie Holiday; she wants to give pure, crazy, hip pleasure.

So, in his own way, does the director, Sidney J. Furie, the young Canadian with a mottled career of hits and flops *(The Leather Boys, The Ipcress File, The Appaloosa, The Naked Runner, The Lawyer, Little Fauss and Big Halsy)*. Furie is wily and talented in small ways that count, but sometimes in his pictures it's *only* the small ways that count—the marginal details and minor characters. He hammers out the heavy stuff, such as the hokey-powerful opening scene, under the titles, with Holiday being hauled into jail and tied in a straitjacket while Michel Legrand's hyperactive crime-suspense music cues us in to the overwrought genre, but he also disposes of a lot of second-rate dialogue by fast throwaway delivery and overlaps, and his best sequences are unusually loose. In one, a scene of gruesome comic confusion, Billie and Richard Pryor, as her accompanist, Piano Man, are backstage at a club, with her connection waiting to give her a shot, when she learns of her mother's death; they're in no shape to deal with the situation, and the talk dribbles on in a painfully lifelike way. Pryor, a West Coast coffeehouse comic, has such audience rapport that a shot of him in Los Angeles in fancy clothes and a beret is enough to bring down the house. Billie and Piano Man have a sequence that feels improvised, on a California beach, when she asks him to get her some dope, and then a long unstructured "high" scene together, when they're like two innocently obscene junkie babies. Elsewhere, Furie's direction is often crude (as with the Smilin' Jack villain, and Black Beauty Billy Dee Williams), but he has a sense of pace and a knack for letting the audience know that he wants us to have a good time. The bad side of his hardboiled expertise—the insistence on being modern and tough by not showing too much compassion—is that though Diana Ross wins you and holds you, your feelings about Billie Holiday become uncertain and muddy as the film progresses. The keys to her life are in her art, and that's not in the movie. (It almost never is in movies, because how do you re-create the processes of artistic creation?) *Lady Sings the Blues* is as good as one can expect from the genre—better, at times—and I enjoyed it hugely, yet I don't want Billie Holiday's hard, melancholic sound buried under this avalanche of pop. When you get home, you have to retrieve her at the phonograph; you have to do restoration work on your own past.

The New Yorker, November 4, 1972

THE DISCREET CHARM OF THE BOURGEOISIE
ANARCHIST'S LAUGHTER

The Discreet Charm of the Bourgeoisie is a cosmic vaudeville show—an Old
Master's mischief. Now seventy-two, Luis Buñuel is no longer savage
about the hypocrisy and the inanity of the privileged classes. They don't
change, and since they have become a persistent bad joke to him, he has
grown almost fond of their follies—the way one can grow fond of the snarls
and the silliness of vicious pets. He looks at them now and they're such perfectly amoral little beasts they amuse him; he enjoys their skin-deep proprieties, their faith in appearances, their sublime confidence. At the same time,
this Spanish exile-expatriate may have come to a point in life when the hell
he has gone through to make movies is receding into the past, like an old
obscene story; he is so relaxed about his medium now that he enjoys pinching its nose, pulling its tail. He has become a majestic light prankster—not
a bad way for a man full of disgust and pity to age. The movie is slight, but
it has a special enchantment: it's a development—more like an
emanation—of Buñuel's movies which couldn't have been expected but
which seems <i>right;</i> that is, the best thing that could have happened. Buñuel's
cruelty and mockery were often startlingly funny, but they were also sadistic;
that was the power of his work and part of what made his films scandalous.
He was diabolically antibourgeois, and he wasn't just anticlerical—he was hilariously, murderously anticlerical. Here his old rages have become buoyant
jokes. (Might Swift without his disease have ended up like this?) The movie
comes close to serenity, and it's a deep pleasure to see that the unregenerate anarchist-atheist has found his own path to grace. Buñuel has never
given in, never embraced the enemy, and maybe that's why the tone of this
spontaneous chamber music is so happy.

In *The Exterminating Angel,* which was about guests who came to a dinner and couldn't leave, the jest grew heavy and allegorical. We were stuck
there waiting to leave, too. He has turned that situation upside down here.
A group of six friends—three men and three women—have trouble getting
together for dinner, but they're not trapped: the series of interrupted din-
ners spans an indefinite period while food, that ritual center of bourgeois
well-being, keeps eluding them. And Buñuel has left himself free: this is his
most frivolously witty movie, and it's open in time and place. It's a divertimento on themes from his past movies—the incidental pleasures of twists
and dream logic for their own sake. It's all for fun—the fun of observing
how elegantly these civilized monsters disport themselves in preposterous
situations. This offhand, trickster approach to the medium is very like that
of the comedy *Assassins et Voleurs* (called *Lovers and Thieves* here), which
Sacha Guitry wrote and directed, also at the age of seventy-two. That film,
too, looked unbelievably easy, the technique imperceptible. It's as if they
both just sat on a sunny balcony with a bottle of good wine and waved a

hand to direct the company. (Actually, Guitry worked from a wheelchair.) But there's a different atmosphere in the Buñuel film—there's a strong sense of timelessness, stronger than in his genial but antiquarian and rather innocuous *The Milky Way*, in which the characters travel through many eras. Here it is achieved in modern clothes and modern settings; one is simply aware of having lost a sense of time, and that this timelessness, which is tonic, is somehow linked to Buñuel's ironic detachment. The characters hit the road of life here, too; we don't know where they're heading, but they're such energetic travellers they seem to be going to a picnic. Their heads are stuffed with clichés, and they're indifferent to anything except their own self-interest, but they were there when Buñuel began making movies, and they'll survive him. Why not be playful, when all your rage and cruelty have hardly dented their armor?

The three men—Fernando Rey, as the bachelor Ambassador to France from Miranda (in South America), and his respectable married friends Jean-Pierre Cassel and Paul Frankeur—are secret business associates with a thriving trade in dope, brought in via diplomatic pouch. (Fernando Rey also played the suave gentleman with the silver-handled umbrella who sold the cache of heroin in *The French Connection*—the man who got away.) His friends' wives are Stéphane Audran and Delphine Seyrig (with whom he is dallying); the sixth member of the group is Delphine Seyrig's sister, played by Bulle Ogier. The other principals are representatives of the Church (Julien Bertheau as a bishop) and of the Army (Claude Piéplu), and Michel Piccoli does a small turn as a government minister. There is not, however, as much acting as this list of eminent names may suggest. Bertheau plays with supreme finesse, but most of the others don't really act characters; they represent something more like "humors." Buñuel works fast; he obviously prefers casual performances (and even the awkward performances he gets from the minor players) to sentimentality. He uses the actors matter-of-factly to make his points, and this unemotional approach results in such a clean, thin-textured style that the merest anecdote begins to resemble a fable. In comedy, underdirected acting often dampens the jokes; here it becomes part of the exhilarating ease of the film, and of its simplicity. The principals—especially Stéphane Audran—embody their roles with professional awareness: they have that discreet charm, and they do nicely judged turns in a polished drawing-room style, as if they were doing charades at a party.

American novelists sometimes parody the processes of artistic creation too early in their own lives, when their parody means little to us except a demonstration of cleverness, but when Buñuel parodies the methods by which a movie director can lead you into story structures, and into dreams, and dreams within dreams, and tales of the supernatural, the joke is how easy it has become for him. The charm of the film is that the old magician can show off his skills and make fun of them at the same time. He can say, "Look, there's nothing to it. Just take the rabbit out of the hat." (The first shot in the movie looks like a black cat's face, yellow eyes glowing, but turns out to be a car coming toward us with its headlights on.) There is nothing else in the movie—just the surprises, and the pleasures of his dexterity as he springs them. You have no idea what's coming from minute to minute; he keeps leading you down garden paths that disappear. (Only once, I found his dream logic faulty: when the bishop gives a dying man—the murderer of the bishop's parents—absolution and then shoots him, the idea is perhaps too cutely paradoxical to go with the ugliness of the act. The gunshot— definite and resonant, like nothing else in the film—violates the light, un- premeditated style.) The movie proceeds by interruptions: just as you have been gulled into getting interested in a situation he pulls the rug out from under you, and goes on to something else. And, in the same way that he par- odies bourgeois instincts and manners in the day-to-day episodes, he paro- dies bourgeois fears and superstitions in the supernatural-fantasy episodes. He hokes up these scary death jokes with fancy lighting and cutting that he disdains in the rest of the movie, demonstrating how easy it is to draw an au- dience into childish ghost stories, demonstrating how primitive audience re- sponses are. He says, "If you want cheap mysteries, this is how simple it is." Then each time the interruption comes one can almost hear the director laughing. The old anarchist has planted his bombs under bourgeois moviemaking.

The New Yorker, November 11, 1972

PLAY IT AS IT LAYS

The ultimate princess fantasy is to be so glamorously sensitive and beauti- ful that you have to be taken care of; you are simply too sensitive for this world—you see the truth, and so you suffer more than ordinary people, and can't function. *Play It As It Lays* is set in the *Red Desert* region of Holly- wood, which means it's about empty lives, acute anguish, Hollywood and Hell. The beautiful and damned heroine—Maria Wyeth, a onetime model and sometime screen star, played by Tuesday Weld—walks the tree-lined paths of a sanatorium and tells the story of her disintegration. Needless to say, it is the world that is having the breakdown, not Maria. I know I have a lower tolerance for this sort of thing than many people; but should it be tolerated? I found the Joan Didion novel ridiculously swank, and I read it between bouts of disbelieving giggles. I whooped at the first line:

What makes Iago evil? some people ask. I never ask.

I whooped at the ending:

> One thing in my defense, not that it matters: I know some-
> thing Carter never knew, or Helene, or maybe you. I know what
> "nothing" means, and keep on playing.
> Why, BZ would say.
> Why not, I say.

I even whooped when I saw an article about Joan Didion and read the epigraph:

> I am haunted by the cannibalism of the Donner Party.
> —*Joan Didion in conversation.*

Certainly I recognize that Miss Didion can write: the smoke of creation rises
from those dry-ice sentences. You know at once that you're in the fast company of *Butterfield 8* and *Miss Lonelyhearts* and *The Day of the Locust* and Fitzgerald and Zelda herself. But you also know that this is what movies have
done to the novel. What's missing from these books is the morally tough
common sense that has been called the strongest tradition in English letters.
As a novel, *Play It As It Lays* is a creature of the movies, celebrating the glamour abyss, transferring Fitzgerald's spoiled-rotten rich to the movie-colony
locale—a perfect mass-culture home for them, their spiritual home all along.

The book itself was already show business—a writer's performance, with
every word screwed tight, and a designer's feat, the sparse words placed in
the spiritual emptiness of white pages. Reading the book was, in fact, like
going to the movies. And it drew upon many films—especially, I thought,
upon Bergman's *Through a Glass Darkly,* in which the racked, misunderstood
heroine who sees God as a spider is also hauled away. But the waif sensibility
in a Hollywood novel—that was an inspiration. The novel was a touchstone
of a sort, and I imagine the movie will be, too. Joan Didion wanted Frank
Perry to direct—possibly because he had already glorified the suffering
little-girl-woman in *Diary of a Mad Housewife*—and he has been extremely
faithful to her book. She and her husband, John Gregory Dunne, did the
adaptation,* and her brother-in-law Dominick Dunne co-produced with
Perry. The adaptation is a novelist's wish fulfillment: narration that retains
the most "eloquent" passages in the book, dialogue virtually intact, and a
transfer to the screen of the shattered-sensibility style by means of quick
scenes that form a mosaic. Even the coiled rattler that decorated the book
jacket turns up signalling evil throughout the movie (and perhaps inspiring
those dissidents, like me, who hissed when the picture was over). For what
it is, the movie is well done: posh, narcissistic, flashy. Image by image, it's

---

*Their *first* choice for director was Sam Peckinpah, who wanted to do it but wasn't acceptable
to the studios, except on "men's pictures."

handsome. Perry hasn't found a "visual equivalent" for the famished prose, but maybe this high-class-whorehouse style of moviemaking is the *true* equivalent.

The movie doesn't have that glittering austerity that made me giggle, but the emotional content is basically the same. It's all there: the romance of suicidal despair and the gloriously bleak lives of the lucky people. Maria, throwing herself away on men she doesn't like, is different from the crowd of decadent, calculating studs and stars and witches who surround her. (Tammy Grimes, Adam Roarke, Ruth Ford, Richard Anderson, and Paul Lambert are among them.) She's superior because she can't adjust to the "sick arrangements" they accept, even though—and here is the real cheat of this genre—in the movie there is no other way to live. This soulless high life represents the moral corruption of our time, and the apocalypse. Maria, separated and then divorced, comes equipped with a brain-damaged child she can't communicate with, and in the course of the movie she has an abortion; the fetus in the garbage is—like the snake—a recurrent motif. Maria herself has lost interest in communicating, and her success-satisfied movie-director husband accuses her of playing at catatonia, but his producer—a homosexual, BZ (Tony Perkins)—understands her all right. Because BZ, too, has discovered the nothingness of life. "Tell me what matters," he says to her, but she has no answer, and he commits suicide while she cradles him in her arms. The cotton-candy misery of all this might have been dreamed up by a Catholic schoolgirl who loses her God and thinks that if she doesn't find something to put in His place the world will come to an end. If you use Hollywood as the test tissue for mankind, what could the prognosis be? Brimstone, of course, brought on by the fornication and bitchery that audiences enjoy.

The movie feels like a remake of the book. But it has lost the book's accumulating sense of dread—possibly because the splintered opening doesn't help you get your bearings the way the splintering in the book did. And what Frank Perry misses out on is that Maria is meant not just to be numb but to be numb because she hurts. That never comes across in Tuesday Weld's limited, mannered performance. She doesn't use her body anymore; as in last year's *A Safe Place,* she does everything with her face, mainly with her mouth—there are a lot of puckers. With her Alice in Wonderland forehead and her calm, wide eyes, she's like a great pumpkin-headed doll, and she doesn't express pain—just a beautiful blobby numbness that suggests childlike abstraction as much as suffering. Tony Perkins uses his contrasting skinny tightness, in his supporting role, very well; when his lines are dry, he's the best thing in the picture. But who could deliver lines like, "We've been out there where nothing is"? Tuesday Weld is onscreen steadily. Maria drives the freeways in search of the reasons that they're there; she shoots at highway signs; and she broods. "Maybe I was holding all the aces, but what was the game?" she says to us—a line that echoes the Mickey Spillane parody in *The Band Wagon.* But Maria is the twin sister of the Jack Nicholson character in *Five Easy Pieces*, and this is classy—plastic L.A. and the freeways, sin and loss. Poor Maria keeps asking the meaning of it all, and because she's thinking this heavy question she can't do anything for herself or anyone else. And the movie cuddles her and cuddles her *Cosmopolitan*-girl questions.

The New Yorker, November 11, 1972

FROM REVIEW OF
SAVAGE MESSIAH

Ken Russell's admirers say they experience sensual intoxication from his highly theatrical, whirling lives of celebrated, scandalous artists. And those who are intoxicated are willing to accept his passionate, compulsively ambivalent romanticism—in which tumult and rapture are carried to madhouse pitch and everything is a joke, nothing is a joke. They find the extremities exciting; they get stoned on his excesses. But what if his visions of artists' lives—it's Henri Gaudier-Brzeska's turn this time—that are sometimes acclaimed as too shocking for Philistines are camp fantasies derived from Hollywood's wildest kitsch? What does it then mean if you're swept up by it? It doesn't necessarily mean that the picture that does it is art; it could just mean you've been softened. As a picture of bohemian life in Paris and London, *Savage Messiah* is about as convincing as *The Subterraneans* was about the Beats in San Francisco; but you understood the commercial pressures that shaped that, while with *Savage Messiah* the pressures are from Russell's insides. He's a one-man marketplace, a compulsive Hollywoodizer, and his images of the artist's suffering are frantic versions of Hollywood's. This movie is like a continuation of *The Music Lovers*, but now it's all random buffoonery. Russell seems almost cursed by his subjects; he seems to want something from them, but each time he gets close to them he dances away. His movies are charged with sex, but it's androgynous sex, and sterile. There's a giddy violence to the sensations of dislocation that this new film produces. The abrupt contrasts score points against the characters. Russell celebrates the pandemonium and senselessness of art and life. Yet in the middle of this lurid debauchery the virginal hero seems to be saving himself for something: he's like Alice Faye singing "No Love, No Nothin'."

The actual Henri Gaudier, a gifted sculptor, born near Orléans in 1891, had been helped by scholarships as a boy, but he was proud and frail and starving in Paris, and, worst of all, desperately lonely, when he met Sophie Brzeska, a Polish woman, even more lonely than he—she'd been lonely all her life. Weakened by years of near-starvation, she was studying languages and trying to become a writer. He was eighteen and she was thirty-eight. For the next five years—until he died in battle in 1915, at twenty-three—they were platonic lovers, joining their names into Gaudier-Brzeska and living as brother and sister. Had he survived, Henri Gaudier-Brzeska might have become a major sculptor, but he is known to us as a minor artist and, of course, a legend. Considering the age difference between him and Sophie, and Sophie's background, her fear and reluctance to change the terms of their relationship from intellectual and artistic comradeship to the full, consummated, and legal marriage that he eventually wanted is perhaps not so strange; but their relationship—more mother and son than sister and brother—was painful and stormy. Sophie was a woman of passionate ideals who had had a bitter life; of middle-class background, she had been deserted by her suitors because she had no dowry, and her determination to be independent had gone sour in a series of jobs as a governess, including a long stint in the United States, where she had been stranded. Failure and deprivation had left her a high-strung, near-mad woman, and an angry woman. When Henri's work began to sell and he began to make friends—Roger Fry, Frank Harris, Enid Bagnold, Wyndham Lewis, Katherine Mansfield and Middleton Murry, Ezra Pound (who was a friend until Henri's death, and who wrote a small book about him)—her assertiveness often drove them away. Many people tried to help them, though they concealed their extreme poverty. Gaudier-Brzeska is known not only through his sculpture and drawings but also through his letters, which form a large part of the book that H. S. Ede put together in 1931 under the dubious but selling title *Savage Messiah.*

The title seems so appropriate to Ken Russell, however, that some people have thought the film—written by Christopher Logue, from Ede's book—to be autobiographical. And in a sense it is, because Russell has wrested Gaudier-Brzeska's story from its place in art history and made it one more of his unstable satires on romanticism. Gentle, delicate-looking Gaudier, who was so embarrassed not to be sleeping with Sophie that he used to lie to people and say he was, and who once went to a prostitute but fled in disgust, becomes Russell's strutting, phallic artist assaulting society. His whole life builds up to the final Hollywood-style irony: he is taken up after death by the fashionable world, for its amusement. In a musical-comedy finale, Russell concocts a parade of rich and vapid young people with pink parasols who attend a posthumous exhibition of Gaudier-Brzeska's work and flirt and politely smile their approval. Russell seems drawn to the old movie story of the unappreciated "immortal" artist recognized after his death. But Gaudier-Brzeska never did become a major figure—he's hardly a household word now—and to suggest that his art was immediately taken up by smart young society people is to miss out on the meaning of his dedication to the avant-garde movement of his time, which was what kept him poor.

In Hollywood bios, the consummation of the artist's life was, of course, the romanticizing movie itself; Russell seems to be tormented by this convention—he keeps jabbing at it, angrily demonstrating that artists are not the ethereal dreamers those silly movies said they were, yet accepting the Hollywood myths of genius and "inspiration." This movie doesn't have the deliberate shocks and horrors of *The Music Lovers* or *The Devils*—the sores and the burning, bubbling flesh, and the Rube Goldberg machines inserted into women. This time, Russell's full energy—a kind of mad zip—goes into parodies that burst out where they don't belong. The most inventive sequence is a freakily decadent erotic entertainment in a Vorticist night club in London, with red lips protruding through the mouth hole of a painted nude, and singing. The canvas is then slashed by a suffragette; she proceeds to strip and do a number about votes for women. To anyone who knows anything about the Vorticist movement or the Bloomsbury group—or, for that matter, the suffragettes—Russell's jokes don't work, because they're so maniacally off target. The points aren't satirically valid; they're simply for kicks (though I imagine that Russell himself would defend them as valid, and would *also* say it's all meant to be a joke on us). Russell has his actors declaiming in a way that makes everything unbelievable, and we can't always judge whether this is intentional (he seems to have a very bad ear for speech); but he sometimes deliberately uses Christopher Logue's stylish, overwritten dialogue as rant, flinging literary epigrams at the audience. His hyperbolic method—going from climax to climax—is itself a form of ridicule, and it's orgiastic. And I think this is a large part of his fascination: some people can't resist his movies, because they can hardly wait to see what mad thing he'll do next. His films are preceded by puffery about the biographical research and the authentic incidents. But he removes those incidents from their human context: the attraction for him and for the audience is the porn of fame. He's not trying to deal with the age any of his artist subjects lived in, or the appetites and satisfactions of that age, or the vision of a particular artist, but is always turning something from the artists' lives into something else—a whopping irony, a phallic joke, a plushy big scene.

A famous anecdote about how Gaudier-Brzeska boasted to Epstein that he had worked directly in stone, and then, when Epstein said he would come visit his studio the next day, stayed up all night and produced three small pieces of sculpture, which were casually lying about when Epstein arrived, is turned here into a promise to visit by a malicious, epicene art dealer named Shaw (played by John Justin, in 1940 the Thief of Bagdad), who fails to show up, enraging the young sculptor, who hurls the statue he has worked on all night through Shaw's gallery window. Russell is as crazed in his hatred of art lovers as some reactionary fantasists are about liberals. The world of the movie is made up of repulsive desiccated poseurs like Shaw (and Mme. von Meck in *The Music Lovers*), who are mocked for the sensuality in their love of art. To Russell, love of art is an affectation: these ghoulish art lovers really want the artist's flesh.

While his heroes posture and suffer, the emotional tensions are in the female performances. Dorothy Tutin's Sophie Brzeska is the only reason to consider going to this movie, even though her Sophie exists only in bits. Perhaps Dorothy Tutin *had* to play the role so bracingly in order to survive, yet without the very special psychosexual dynamics that are at work for her here—as they were at work for Glenda Jackson's Gudrun in *Women in Love* and for some parts of Glenda Jackson's Nina in *The Music Lovers*—she wouldn't have this ambivalent force. Opposite her, Scott Antony is like a young, *less* talented Rock Hudson or Stewart Granger; he doesn't appear to be an actor at all—he acts young by jumping around—and his husky, almost buxom Gaudier is merely an embarrassment. But Dorothy Tutin makes something theatrical yet original and witty and psychologically stupefying out of the distraught Sophie's rant. Her long monologues and songs are witchlike, but Shakespearean-witchlike in their ferocious lilt. (Women have rarely delivered complex monologues from the screen, and, whether we think of that or not, probably her feat here startles us more than an actor's monologues would.) Sophie talks to herself and harangues everyone; her rhythmic tirades on the horrors of her past life and the treatment she has had as a woman are delivered at a mad speed and at a constant, loud, high pitch—and, for once in the film, the speed and the pitch are justified. Russell's fevered style doesn't allow her great scenes to grow out of anything; he even cuts away from her most extraordinary diatribe (while she's chopping half-rotten vegetables) to show us vacuous reaction shots of Scott Antony listening. Yet Russell's antipathy for and fascination with strong, hard-edged women makes her intermittent triumphs possible. When, in an idyll at the sea, she and Antony celebrate being together, dancing symbolically separate dances, she on the sand, he on the cliffs high above, her little jigging mazurka is so compelling that she wipes poor Antony off the screen.

There is a link between Russell's two authentic, flawed creations: Gudrun and Sophie. Katherine Mansfield (on whom D. H. Lawrence based his Gudrun) not only knew Sophie Brzeska but was so repelled by her that she had to break off her friendship with Henri Gaudier. In *Women in Love,* Glenda Jackson was photographed and made up to look extraordinarily like Katherine Mansfield (the photograph of Mansfield in the new Quentin Bell biography of Virginia Woolf could be a study for the movie), and Dorothy Tutin exactly fits Ede's description of Sophie: "She was small, flat-chested, with a pointed chin, thin lips, tilted nose, sensitive nostrils, and high cheekbones, which rose up to meet the large eyelids sheltering strange tired eyes, eyes that often stared big and vacant, and then of a sudden melted into roguish intimacy. Her movements were rapid, abrupt, and angular." Gudrun and Sophie are alike, of course, and on the screen they're both shrews, comic, high-powered, and erotically nasty—Gudrun a strident, castrating female who drives Gerald Crich to suicide, and Sophie, who by her neurotic hatred of sex drives Gaudier to death in battle. (Russell seems to have no interest in the fact that Gudrun was an artist herself, and Sophie a failed artist.) Both are without a core and without any soft spots at all, yet both are glittering portraits. But what are we to make of them? Russell doesn't tell us, doesn't show us. You never get to see what brought Henri Gaudier and Sophie Brzeska together, and you never get to understand why he needed the woman who called him her little son. There's one quiet moment in a shelter on the beach when Henri and Sophie talk together and you actually begin to feel something; but Russell doesn't trust it, and he throws it away. He's in his full show-off glory with Scott Antony leaping on the huge stone blocks above the sea, trying to act like a genius.

The New Yorker, November 18, 1972

THE FRED ASTAIRE AND GINGER ROGERS BOOK

The Fred Astaire & Ginger Rogers Book, by Arlene Croce, has verve and wit, like the series of musicals it covers. Movie criticism suffered a loss when, in the mid-sixties, Miss Croce abandoned the field and gave most of her energies to dance criticism; now she has joined her two major talents. No one has ever described dance in movies the way she does: she's a slangy, elegant writer; her compressed descriptions are evocative and analytic at the same time, and so precise and fresh that while bringing the pleasure of the dances back she adds to it. There is a sense of pressure in her style that has something like the tension and pull of the dances themselves. Her descriptions are original and imperially brusque in a way that keeps the reader alert; one responds to her writing kinesthetically, as if it were dance. This small book, published this week by Outerbridge & Lazard, and about half text, half photographs (with two flip-page dances, of which one is effective, the other badly cropped), is a history of the team and an assessment of its place in dance and movie history, and also an acute examination of how movies were made in the factory-system days. We learn who did what on those musicals and how they "happened," and yet, just as Astaire never lets you see the hard work, so that his dances appear to be spontaneous, Miss Croce doesn't present the history as history; she lets it come in casually, jauntily, as she covers the series of films, fitting the background material to the illustrated section on each movie. There are times when one may want her to expand on a point or explain, but the reward of her brevity is the same achieved nonchalance that she prizes in these movies; it comes out of her controlled ecstatic response to the dances. Here is a sentence of Miss Croce's on Astaire in the "I Won't Dance" number from *Roberta:*

Two big Cossacks have to carry him protesting onto the dance floor, and there he does his longest and most absorbing solo of the series so far, full of stork-legged steps on toe, wheeling pirouettes in which he seems to be winding one leg around the other, and those ratcheting tap clusters that fall like loose change from his pockets.

And here a fragment on Astaire's singles:

> With him, a dance impulse and a dramatic motive seem to be
> indivisible and spontaneous, so that we get that little kick of imag-
> inative sympathy every time he changes the rhythm or the speed or
> the pressure of a step. And though we don't perceive the dance as
> "drama," the undertone of motivation continually sharpens and re-
> freshes our interest in what we do see.

And, on the pair in "Let's Face the Music and Dance," from *Follow the Fleet:*

> The mood is awesomely grave. The dance is one of their sim-
> plest and most daring, the steps mostly walking steps done with a
> slight retard. The withheld impetus makes the dance look dragged
> by destiny, all the quick little circling steps pulled as if on a single
> thread.

Every few sentences, you're stopped by the audacity of a description or by
some new piece of information; we learn what that mysterious name Van
Nest Polglase in the credits actually meant, and of the writing contribution
of Laurette Taylor's son, Dwight Taylor, and we get such footnotes to social
history as this, from the section on *Top Hat:*

> The most quoted line in the film is the motto of the House of
> Beddini, delivered with supreme flourish by Erik Rhodes: "For the
> women the kiss, for the men the sword." This was originally writ-
> ten, "For the men the sword, for the women the whip," and was
> changed when the Hays office objected.

I doubt if anyone else will ever love Astaire the dancer and creator as fully
as this author: the book is a homage to him and the simplicity and mastery
he represents. Miss Croce documents how he choreographed the dances—
improvising them with Hermes Pan, with Pan doing Rogers's steps and later
training her to do them. ("With Fred I'd be Ginger," Pan says, "and with
Ginger I'd be Fred." After the dances were photographed, Hermes Pan usually dubbed in the taps for her as well.) It was Astaire himself who controlled the shooting, and he insisted that each dance be recorded in a single
shot, without fakery, and without the usual cuts to the reactions of onlookers. But sometimes the ideal of "perfection within a single shot"—the dance
just as it would be done for a live audience, so that moviegoers would see
it as if from the best seats in a theater—wasn't attained. There is a cut toward the close of the "Never Gonna Dance" number, in *Swing Time;* Miss
Croce explains that it "may have been one of the few Astaire-Rogers dances
that couldn't be filmed entirely in one continuous shot, for its climax, a

spine-chilling series of pirouettes by Rogers, took forty takes to accomplish, and in the middle of shooting Rogers' feet began to bleed."

For Miss Croce, in the best Astaire-and-Rogers films *(The Gay Divorcée, Roberta, Top Hat, Follow the Fleet, Swing Time)* something happened that "never happened in movies again"—"dancing was transformed into a vehicle of serious emotion between a man and a woman." And from this, I think, flow my disagreements with her. We have had many happy arguments about dance and movies; I suspect that they hinge on temperament. Miss Croce (she is the editor of *Ballet Review*) is a perfectionist—a romantic perfectionist. I, too, find Astaire and Rogers rapturous together, but Miss Croce's romanticism about the two leads her to ascribe a *dance* perfection to them. I think that Astaire's dry buoyancy comes through best in his solos, which are more exciting dances than the romantic ballroom numbers with Rogers. Miss Croce says Rogers's "technique became exactly what she needed in order to dance with Fred Astaire, and, as no other woman in movies ever did, she created the feeling that stirs us so deeply when we see them together: Fred need not be alone." Well, that's maybe a bit much. Of Rogers in a rare tap solo (on "Let Yourself Go," in *Follow the Fleet*), she writes, "It's easy to underrate Rogers' dancing because she never appeared to be working hard. . . . She avoided any suggestion of toil or inadequacy. She was physically incapable of ugliness." But she was certainly capable of *clumsiness* when she danced with Astaire, and you can see that she *is* working hard. She doesn't always look comfortable doing the steps—her arms are out of kilter, or she's off balance. And, from Miss Croce's own account of how the dances were devised, you can see why: If Astaire had improvised the choreography with Rogers instead of with Hermes Pan, Rogers would probably have worked out things that came more easily and naturally to her, and you wouldn't have the sense you often get—that it's too difficult for her and she's doing her damnedest just to get the steps right. Rogers, of course, who was making three pictures to each one of Astaire's, was too valuable a property of R.K.O.'s to be spared for these sessions (even if the men had wanted her, which is doubtful). A ballet dancer, whose technique is set in training, can accept the choreography of others far more easily than a pop dancer. In the case of this team, Astaire, with his winged body, his weightless, essentially bodiless style, devised his own personal balletistic jazz form of dance, and then Ginger Rogers had to try to fit into it. But her clumsiness is rather ingratiating; it isn't *bad*, and the choreography and the whole feeling of their dances is so romantically appealing that you don't *mind* Ginger's dancing. We don't care if Ginger Rogers isn't a *superb* dancer. (The team might be boringly ethereal if she were.) It's part of Ginger's personality that she's a tiny bit klutzy. Yes, she has that beautiful figure, which Miss Croce rightly admires, but there is also the slight grossness of her face and her uncultivated voice. What makes Ginger Rogers so unsettling, so *alive*, on the screen is the element of insensitivity and the happy, wide streak of commonness in a person of so much talent. Maybe it's her greatest asset that she always seems to have a wad of gum in her mouth. I don't mean to suggest that Miss Croce is unaware of this side of Ginger Rogers (she's at her satirical best on Rogers as an actress, and there really isn't much that Arlene Croce is unaware of)—only that she and I view it differently. Miss Croce sees it as what was *overcome* in the dance—"Astaire would turn her into a goddess"; she believes Rogers was transformed, that she "turned from brass to gold under his touch." Sure, she was Cinderella at the ball, but we still thought of her as the spunky, funny, slightly pie-faced chorus girl trying to keep up with him. Rogers seems most fully herself to me in the comic hoofing showing-off numbers, and that's when I love her dancing best; in the more decorous simulated passion of the dramatic dances with Astaire, she's not that different from other fancy ballroom dancers—she's not quite Ginger.

Miss Croce takes their dancing perhaps a bit too seriously, seeing it not just as heavenly romance or—as perhaps many of us did—as a dream of a date but as something more: "Astaire in his flying tails, the pliant Rogers in one of her less-is-more gowns, were an erotic vision that audiences beheld in the electric silence of the dance. Everyone knew what was happening in these dances." But how could Fred Astaire be erotic? Fred Astaire has no flesh, and I think the only conceivable "eroticism" in their dances is a sort of transfigured view of courtship and romance, a fantasy of being swept off one's feet.

I suspect it is this *Camelot* view that leads Miss Croce to be rather unfair to Gene Kelly. She says, "The major difference between Astaire and Kelly is a difference, not of talent or technique, but of levels of sophistication." I should say the difference starts with their bodies. If you compare Kelly to Astaire, accepting Astaire's debonaire style as perfection, then, of course, Kelly looks bad. But in popular dance forms, in which movement is not rigidly codified, as it is in ballet, perfection is a romantic myth or a figure of speech, nothing more. Kelly isn't a winged dancer; he's a hoofer, and more earthbound. But he has warmth and range as an actor. Kelly's "natural," unaffected line readings, in a gentle, unactorish voice, probably come from the same basic sense of timing that leads Astaire to the clocked, tapped-out readings. Kelly's inflections are subtle and delicate, while his acting is slightly larger than life. He leaps into a simple scene, always "on" (as "on" as Cagney), distinctively eager and with a chesty, athletic, overdramatic exuberance that makes audiences feel good. Though there was something moist and too exposed in the young Judy Garland, Kelly and Garland, both emotional performers, had a special rapport based on tenderness. They could bring conviction to banal love scenes (as in *Summer Stock*) and make them naïvely fresh. They balanced each other's talents: she joined her odd and undervalued cakewalker's prance to his large-spirited hoofing, and he joined his odd, light, high voice to her sweet, good, deep one. Their duets (such as "You Wonderful You," in *Summer Stock*, and the title song in *For Me and My Gal*) have a plaintive richness unlike anything in the Astaire-Rogers pictures. They could really sing together; Astaire and Rogers couldn't despite Astaire's skill and charm when he sang alone. Astaire's grasshopper lightness was his limitation as an actor—confining him to perennial gosh-oh-gee adolescence; he was always and only a light comedian and could function only in fairy-tale vehicles. Miss Croce, for whom ballet is the highest form of dance, sees the highest, subtlest emotional resonances in the most stylized forms. I don't think she's wrong in her basic valuation of Astaire and Rogers, but she's too exclusive about it: she has set up an ideal based on Astaire which denies the value of whatever he didn't have.

What it comes down to is that Miss Croce, as in her discussion of Astaire and Rogers in *Swing Time,* sees "the dance as love, the lovers as dancers"; in a funny way, Astaire and Rogers are both too likable for that, and it's the wrong kind of glorification of their frivolous mixture of romance and comedy—a fan's deification. Astaire and Rogers were fortunate: they embodied the swing-music, white-telephone, streamlined era before the Second World War, when frivolousness wasn't decadent and when adolescents dreamed that "going out" was dressing up and becoming part of a beautiful world of top hats and silver lamé. It was a lovely dream, and perhaps Miss Croce still dreams it. A possible indication of the degenerative effects of movies on our good sense is that a writer with a first-class mind can say of Astaire, after the partnership ended, "He never ceased to dance wonderfully and he has had some good dancing partners. But it is a world of sun without a moon." However, it is also because of such swoony romanticism that this writer has brought her full resources to bear on the kind of subject that generally attracts pinheads. I think it's perfectly safe to say that this is the best book that will ever be written about Astaire and Rogers.

The New Yorker, November 25, 1972

THE POSEIDON ADVENTURE

The Poseidon Adventure is about an ocean liner that turns turtle. The suspense is in the method of escape and the narrowing number of survivors; you watch as fate ticks them off in photogenically horrible ways—engulfing water, flames, scalding liquids, falling chandeliers. In order to lend a movie cataclysm some spiritual importance, it is customary to clue us in on who will perish and who will survive by making the former cowardly, life-denying types and the latter courageous and life-enhancing, and so the hero, Gene Hackman, is a robust, forward-looking radical clergyman. This hallowed, wheezing formula can be hilariously inappropriate, but here it's just a drag, since it makes the picture lofty when we want it to get right to the vulgar bravado inherent in its *Grand Hotel* approach to the romance of catastrophe. The movie is advertised in terms of Oscars ("In the cast and staff there is a total of fifteen of these precious golden statuettes"), but it's a lackluster bunch we see. The picture would be more fun if we cared about who got killed and who survived; there's a lot of Red Buttons (one Oscar, but not my candidate for survival). The only loss I regretted for an instant was Roddy McDowall; on the other hand, it was a wise decision to dump Arthur O'Connell early. We could certainly do with less of the antique feminine hysteria that slows down the action, especially since we can see perfectly well that the girls (Stella Stevens, Carol Lynley, and Pamela Sue Martin) are there for the splendor of their rear ends as the camera follows them climbing ladders toward safety. Shelley Winters (two Oscars) yearns to see her grandson in Israel and makes endless jokes about her bloated appearance. (She's so enormously fat she goes way beyond the intention to create a warm, sympathetic Jewish character. It's like having a whale tell you you should love her because she's Jewish.) The script is the true cataclysm. The writers, Stirling Silliphant and Wendell Mayes, don't do anything for the actors, and they don't provide a speck of originality. Their attempt to turn Stella Stevens, as a former prostitute, and Ernest Borgnine, as her police-lieutenant husband, into the Jean Harlow-Wallace Beery pair of *Dinner at Eight* merely exposes how mangy their writing is. Only once do they achieve true camp: just before the ship capsizes, a crewman says to the captain (Leslie Nielsen), "I never saw anything like it—an enormous wall of water coming toward us." Ronald Neame directs about the same way Leslie Nielsen acts—stalwart, dull—and the special effects, literal and mostly full-scale, have none of the eerie beauty of early-movie catastrophes designed in miniature and employing illusions (as they were by the UFA technicians). There's no beauty anywhere in this movie, but as a dumb, square adventure story—expensive pop primitivism manufactured for the *Airport* market—it is honestly what it is, and the logistics of getting out of an upside-down ship are fairly entertaining. That enormous wall of water hits while the characters are celebrating New Year's Eve. Ah, movie men and their exquisite calculations! How much does it add to the TV sale if a picture can be shown on holidays from here unto eternity?

The New Yorker, December 16, 1972

IMAGES

Robert Altman is almost frighteningly nonrepetitive. He goes out in a new direction each time, and he scores an astonishing fifty percent—one on, one off. *M*A*S*H* was followed by *Brewster McCloud,* and *McCabe & Mrs. Miller* has now been followed by *Images.* I can hardly wait for his next movie.

The New Yorker, December 23, 1972

ABOUT BARBRA STREISAND, FROM REVIEW OF

UP THE SANDBOX

As Streisand's pictures multiply, it becomes apparent that she is not about to master an actress's craft but, rather, is discovering a craft of her own, out of the timing and emotionality that make her a phenomenon as a singer. You admire her not for her acting—or singing—but for herself, which is what you feel she gives you in both. She has the class to be herself, and the impudent music of her speaking voice is proof that she knows it. The audacity of her self-creation is something we've had time to adjust to; we already know her mettle, and the dramatic urgency she can bring to roles. In *Up the Sandbox,* she shows a much deeper and warmer presence and a freely yielding quality. And a skittering good humor—as if, at last, she had come to accept her triumph, to believe in it. That faint weasellike look of apprehensiveness is gone—and that was what made her seem a little frightening. She is a great undeveloped actress—undeveloped in the sense that you feel the natural richness in her but can see that she's idiosyncratic and that she hasn't the training to play the classical roles that still define how an actress's greatness is expressed. But in movies new ways may be found.

The New Yorker, December 30, 1972

CRIES AND WHISPERS
FLESH

Cries and Whispers is set in a manor house at the turn of the century where Agnes (Harriet Andersson), a spinster in her late thirties, is dying of cancer. Her two married sisters have come to attend her in her final agony—the older, the severe, tense Karin (Ingrid Thulin), and the shallow, ripe, adulterous Maria (Liv Ullmann)—and they watch and wait, along with the peasant servant Anna (Kari Sylwan). We see their interrelations, and the visions triggered by their being together waiting for death and, when it comes, by death itself. But the gliding memories, the slow rhythm of the women's movements, the hands that search and touch, the large faces that fill the screen have the hypnotic style of a single dream. It is all one enveloping death fantasy; the invisible protagonist, Ingmar Bergman, is the presence we feel throughout, and he is the narrator. He is dreaming these fleshly images of women that loom in front of us, and dreaming of their dreams and memories.

Bergman is not a playful dreamer, as we already know from nightmarish films like *The Silence*, which seems to take place in a trance. He apparently thinks in images and links them together to make a film. Sometimes we may feel that we intuit the eroticism or the fears that lie behind the overwhelming moments in a Bergman movie, but he makes no effort to clarify. In a considerable portion of his work, the imagery derives its power from unconscious or not fully understood associations; that's why, when he is asked to explain a scene, he may reply, "It's just my poetry." Bergman doesn't always find ways to integrate this intense poetry with his themes. Even when he attempts to solve the problem by using the theme of a mental breakdown or a spiritual or artistic crisis, his intensity of feeling may explode the story elements, leaving the audience moved but bewildered. In a rare film such as *Shame*, the wartime setting provides roots for the anguish of the characters, and his ordering intelligence is in full control; more often the intensity appears to have a life of its own, apart from the situations, which don't account for it and can't fully express it. We come out of the theater wondering about Bergman himself and what he was trying to do.

Like Bergman, his countryman Strindberg lacked a sovereign sense of reality, and he experimented with a technique that would allow him to abandon the forms that he, too, kept exploding. In his author's note to the Expressionist *A Dream Play* (which Ingmar Bergman staged with great success in 1970), Strindberg wrote:

The author has sought to reproduce the disconnected but apparently logical form of a dream. Anything can happen; everything is possible and probable. Time and space do not exist; on a slight groundwork of reality, imagination spins and weaves new patterns made up of memories, experiences, unfettered fancies, absurdities, and improvisations.

The characters are split, double, and multiply; they evaporate, crystallize, scatter, and converge. But a single consciousness holds sway over them all—that of the dreamer. For him there are no secrets, no incongruities, no scruples, and no law.

That is Bergman's method here. *Cries and Whispers* has oracular power, and many people feel that when something grips them strongly it must be realistic; they may not want to recognize that being led into a dreamworld can move them so much. But I think it's the stylized-dream-play atmosphere of *Cries and Whispers* that has made it possible for Bergman to achieve such strength. The detached imaginary world of the manor house becomes a heightened form of reality—more literal and solid, closer than the actual world. The film is emotionally saturated in female flesh—flesh as temptation and mystery. In almost every scene you're aware of bodies and parts of bodies, of the quality of Liv Ullmann's skin and the miniature worlds in the dying woman's brilliant eyes. The almost empty rooms are stylized, and these female bodies inhabit them overpoweringly. The effect—a culmination of the visual emphasis on women's faces in recent Bergman films—is intimate and hypnotic. We are put in the position of the little boy at the beginning of *Persona,* staring up at the giant women's faces on the screen.

In the opening shots, the house is located in a series of autumnal landscapes of a formal park with twisted, writhing trees, and the entire film has a supernal quality. The incomparable cinematographer Sven Nykvist achieves the look of the paintings of the Norwegian Edvard Munch, as if the neurotic and the unconscious had become real enough to be photographed. But, unhappily, the freedom of the dream has sent Bergman back to Expressionism, which he had a heavy fling with in several of his very early films and in *The Naked Night,* some twenty years ago, and he returns to imagery drawn from the *fin de siècle,* when passion and decadence were one.

Bergman has often said that he likes to use women as his chief characters because women are more expressive. They have more talent for acting, he explained on the Dick Cavett show; they're not ashamed of looking in the mirror, as men are, he said, and the camera is a kind of mirror. It would be easy to pass over this simplistic separation of the sexes as just TV-interview chitchat if Bergman were still dealing with modern women as characters (as in *Törst, Summer Interlude, Monika*), but the four women of *Cries and Whispers* are used as obsessive male visions of women. They are women as the Other, women as the mysterious, sensual goddesses of male fantasy. Each sister represents a different aspect of woman, as in Munch's "The Dance of Life," in which a man dances with a woman in red (passion) while a woman in white (innocence) and a woman in black (corruption, death) look on. Bergman divides woman into three and dresses the three sisters for their schematic roles: Harriet Andersson's Agnes is the pure-white sister with innocent thoughts; Liv Ullmann's Maria, with her red-gold hair, wears soft, alluring colors and scarlet-woman dresses with tantalizing plunging necklines; and Ingrid Thulin's death-seeking Karin is in dark colors or black. The film itself is predominantly in black and white and red—red draperies, red wine, red carpets and walls, and frequent dissolves into a blank red screen, just as Munch frequently returned to red for his backgrounds, or even to cover a house (as in his famous "Red Virginia

Creeper"). The young actress who plays Agnes as a child resembles Munch's wasted, sick young girls, and the film draws upon the positioning and look of Munch's figures, especially in Munch's sickroom scenes and in his studies of the laying out of a corpse. *Cries and Whispers* seems to be part of the art from the age of syphilis, when the erotic was charged with peril—when pleasure was represented by an enticing woman who turned into a grinning figure of death. "All our interiors are red, of various shades," Bergman wrote in the story (published in *The New Yorker*) that was also the working script. "Don't ask me why it must be so, because I don't know," he went on. "Ever since my childhood I have pictured the inside of the soul as a moist membrane in shades of red."

The movie is built out of a series of emotionally charged images that express psychic impulses, and Bergman handles them with the fluidity of a master. Yet these images are not discoveries, as they were for Munch, but a vocabulary of shock and panic to draw upon. Munch convinces us that he has captured the inner stress; Bergman doesn't quite convince, though we're impressed and we're held by the smoothness of the dreamy progression of events. The film moves with such eerie slow grace that it almost smothers its own faults and absurdities. I had the divided awareness that almost nothing in it quite works and, at the same time, that the fleshiness of those big bodies up there and the pull of the dream were strong and, in a sense, did make everything work—even the hopeless musical interludes (a Chopin mazurka, and a Bach suite for unaccompanied cello played romantically) and the robotized performances of all but Harriet Andersson. Still, there's a dullness at the heart of the movie, and the allegorical scheme leads to scenes that recall the conventions of silent films and the clichés of second-rate movie acting. The dying Agnes is devout as well as innocent. Liv Ullmann's Maria seduces a visiting doctor with the telegraphic leering of a Warner Brothers dance-hall hostess. Her conversation with him is a variant of the old "You're dirt, but so am I; we deserve each other," and the picture supports the doctor's view of her—that her physical desires and flirtatiousness are signs of laziness and vacuity. And that peasant Anna—the selfless, almost mute servant, close to nature, happy to do anything for the three sisters—has the proud-slave cast of mind that is honored in barrelfuls of old fiction. When Anna bares her breast to make a soft pillow for the dying Agnes, and, later, when she gets into bed, with her thighs up, supporting the dead Agnes in a sculptural pose that suggests both a "Pietà" and "The Rape of Europa," these are Bergman's visions of the inner life of a peasant mindlessly in harmony with the earth. The latter pose is altogether extraordinary, yet the very concept of Anna as a massive mound of comforting flesh takes one back (beyond childhood) to an earlier era. *Cries and Whispers* feels like a nineteenth-century European masterwork in a twentieth-century art form.

The words, which are often enigmatic, are unsuccessful attempts to support the effects achieved by the images. Most of Ingrid Thulin's acting as Karin belongs in a frieze of melodrama, alongside such other practitioners of the stately-stony dragon lady in torment as Gale Sondergaard and Cornelia Otis Skinner. Karin shuts her eyes to blot out her own despair and expresses herself in such dialogue as "I can't breathe anymore because of the guilt" and "Don't touch me!" and "It's all a tissue of lies." Most of her lines can be reduced to "Oh, the torment of it all!"—which actually isn't much of a reduction. That's how she talks when she isn't prowling the halls suffering. The suicidal, hate-filled Karin represents Bergman's worst failure in the movie. She escapes from the stereotype only twice—in a moment of manic humor when she complains of her disobedient big hands while wiggling them, and when she acts out a startling Expressionist fantasy of self-mutilation (followed by more lip-licking pleasure than the fantasy can quite accommodate). It is the advantage of the dream-play form that these two scenes appear to belong here, and people don't have to puzzle about them afterward, as they did with comparable passages in, say, *The Silence*. If Bergman can't make us accept the all-purpose complaints about guilt and suffering that are scattered through his films, his greatest single feat as a movie craftsman is that he can prepare an atmosphere that leads us to accept episodes brimming with hysteria in almost any makeshift context. Here, as Strindberg formulated, the dream context itself makes everything probable; the dreamer leads, the viewer follows. In *Cries and Whispers* Bergman is a wizard at building up a scene to a memorable image and then quickly dissolving into the red that acts as a fixative. The movie is structured as a series of red-outs. We know as we see these images disintegrate before our eyes that we will be taking them home with us. But Bergman doesn't have Strindberg's deviltry and dash; he uses a dreamlike atmosphere but not the language of dreams. He stays with his obsessional images, and his repressed, grave temperament infects even his technical surrender to the dream. (Strindberg, by contrast, was making twentieth-century masterworks in a nineteenth-century art form.)

Who knows how we would react if someone came back from the dead? But here, as in an old Hollywood movie, everyone reacts as scheduled. When Agnes's decaying corpse speaks, pleading for Karin to comfort her, Karin says she won't, because she doesn't love her; Agnes calls next for Maria, who also fails the test, fleeing in horror when the dead woman tries to kiss her. It is, of course, as we knew it would be, the peasant-lump Anna who is not afraid of holding the dead woman. This gothic-fairy-tale test of love is shown as Anna's dream, but it is also integral to the vision of the film, which is about the sick souls of the landed-gentry bourgeoisie. I think it is *because* Bergman lacks the gift for bringing order out of his experiences that he falls back on this schematism. It would be ludicrous if he similarly divided "man." The men in the movie are a shade small—so narrowly realistic they're less than life-size—while the women are more than a shade too splendidly large and strange: allegorical goddesses to be kept in the realm of mystery; never women, always facets of "woman."

Death dreams that come equipped with ticking clocks and uncanny silences and the racked wheezes of the dying are not really very classy, and Bergman's earnest use of gothic effects seems particularly questionable now, arriving just after Buñuel, in *The Discreet Charm of the Bourgeoisie,* has turned them on and off, switching to the spooky nocturnal as a movie joke. But even when Bergman employs sophisticated versions of primitive gothic-horror devices, he is so serious that his dream play is cued to be some sort of morality play as well. Other chaotic artists (Lorca, for example, in his dream play *If Five Years Pass*) haven't been respected in the same way as Bergman, because their temperaments weren't moralistic. But Bergman has a winning combination here: moral + gothic = medieval. And when medieval devices are used in the atmosphere of bourgeois decadence, adults may become as vulnerable as superstitious children.

Bergman is unusual among film artists in that he is an artist in precisely those terms drawn from the other arts which some of us have been trying to free movie aesthetics from. He is the movie director that those who are not generally interested in movies can recognize as an artist, because of the persistent gloom and weight of his work. It is his lack of an entertaining common touch—a lack that is extremely unusual among theatrical artists and movie artists—that has put him on a particular pinnacle. His didact's temperament has obtained this position for him, and although he is a major film artist, it's an absurd position, since he is a didact of the inscrutable. He *programs* mystery. *Cries and Whispers* features long scenes in which the camera scans the faces of Liv Ullmann and Ingrid Thulin as they talk and touch and kiss (scenes similar to the ones that led some people to assume that the sisters in *The Silence* were meant to be lesbians); the camera itself may be part of the inspiration for these scenes, and perhaps some male fantasy of Sisterhood Is Powerful. The eroticism of this vision of sisterly love is unmistakable, yet the vision also seems to represent what Bergman takes to be natural to women. The dreamer, fascinated, is excluded from what he observes, like the staring, obsessed boy in *Persona.* This film is practically a ballet of touching, with hands, like the hands of the blind, always reaching for faces, feeling the flesh and bones. Maria's husband touches her face after she has committed adultery, and feels her guilt. Touching becomes a ritual of soul-searching, and Karin, whose soul has been rotted away, is, of course, the one who fears contact, and the one who violates the graceful ballet by—unforgivably—slapping Anna. Even the dead Agnes's hands reach up to touch and to hold. Didacticism and erotic mystery are mingled—this is Bergman as a northern Fellini. Strindberg's dream plays do not have the great tensions of the plays in which he struggled to express his ferocity, and this movie, compellingly beautiful as it is, comes too easily to Bergman. The viewer can sink back and bask in flesh, but to keep scanning woman as the Other doesn't get any of us anywhere.

The New Yorker, January 6, 1973

CÉSAR AND ROSALIE

The genteel quotes in the ads for *César and Rosalie* ("A movie to see with someone you love," "An enchanting story of what love is all about," etc.) are somewhat misleading. It's not all that bad. The movie looks like those mistily expensive love potions the French have been exporting, and it's certainly loaded with the appurtenances of the pleasurable whirl of the beautiful rich, but it's really a jazzier version of a Marcel Pagnol film, with Yves Montand in the Raimu role. César (Montand) is a tycoon in scrap metal, a self-made man who enjoys being No. 1 in work and in play, and he adores Rosalie (Romy Schneider) and loves to amuse her child by a marriage now dissolved. There are no obstacles to their happiness and their eventual marriage; they have everything—yet almost inexplicably, before our eyes, it evaporates. Nobody's fault—just bad luck. An old love of Rosalie's—David, an eminent cartoonist (Sami Frey)—returns to France after an absence of five years, and when Rosalie sees him again, her feelings about César change. She still loves him, but she begins to look at him differently, and the love goes flat. It's as if César were cuckolded by a moonbeam.

The action skitters back and forth as Rosalie leaves César, then returns to him, and as César tries to help her get over her attraction to David, and that fails, and so on, but whenever you think the relationships are going to be stabilized into formulas, the picture wiggles free. And just when you think the picture is on the skids, the director, Claude Sautet, picks everything up for the end, and it becomes apparent that the irresolute behavior was a way of demonstrating an unresolvable unstable situation. It's a silly movie—a fluky, wry ode on the imperfect, haphazard nature of romantic love. What sustains it is that it never takes its three subjects too solemnly—never makes too big a deal out of their happiness or unhappiness. The movie's essential frivolousness makes its melancholy tone acceptable: we can laugh at the characters' self-centered sorrows.

Romy Schneider, a ripe *Fräulein* now, her kittenish face larger but also more luscious, so that she occasionally suggests the sensual beauty of Simone Signoret in the postwar films, is perfectly convincing as the one woman César wants. The contrasting character sketches of the men are, however, what give the film its wit: as the loud, blatantly materialistic, what-makes-Sammy-run tycoon, Montand provides the confident super-male energy that draws us into the situation (and it's César's whipping around in fast cars that sets the film in motion). He's playing a likable maniac, the kind of part an actor can sink his teeth in, and Montand chomps on everything in sight, overdoing the character in a jovial parodistic style. César's sudden violent squalls are in the earthy, whole-souled Raimu tradition, and when he bluffs his way through something or tries to ingratiate himself, his thinking processes are so childlike and easy to read we might be seeing them above his head in comic-strip balloons. (It's the sort of role Anthony Quinn thinks he can play.) Sautet has a very delicate sense of tone: we get to know César so well that when he comes up against the challenge he can't fight—Rosalie's changed feelings—we recognize that his collapse isn't pathetic, it's funny. And Sami Frey's wan elegance is just right for the man who hoodoos César's and Rosalie's happiness, since Frey's romantic appeal comes from what he is; he has what you can't get if you don't have it—the right blend of nuances. It's impossible to dislike César after you've heard him performing Bach without the aid of an instrument; you enjoy him so much that you're implicated in his foolishness. But you can also see that he looks like a hyperactive clown when Rosalie watches him while she is talking to the exquisitely modulated David, and the energy of clowns isn't very sexy. Rosalie begins to feel protective toward him, which is fatal to romance (though it may sometimes be the substance of marriage). It can't be held against César that he has the tiresomeness of the self-made man who can't just relax and take things for granted, the way the unobtrusively tasteful David can. And it can't really be held against David that he doesn't make much of an effort to hang on to Rosalie, and that losing her adds only the teeniest bit to his permanent air of despondency. The piquancy of the movie is that it reveals the two men's deadlocked characters without the usual pretense that a man's love turns him into just what a woman wants. The movie isn't quite as satisfying once César begins to unravel—it loses some of its charge—but the disconsolate confusion that sets in is integral to the theme. The film is a situation comedy about a love triangle, but it's also a *chanson*, saying ever so softly (why make a big noise about it?) that life is unfair. It's a movie not to be taken any more seriously than a tune one hums for a season—a little tedious, faintly absurd, but really quite pleasant.

The New Yorker, January 13, 1973

PAYDAY
THE RIDDLES OF POP

Rip Torn, with his smirking satyr grin, will probably never have a role that suits him better than Maury Dann, the country singer of *Payday*. Torn projects the magnetism of unstable personalities. He is so volatile and charged he really does have the pop charisma the role demands; you don't necessarily think Torn is a good actor, but you don't look away from the screen when he's up there. He can do split-second seizures of rage and pain, and he can flip in an instant from his usual nakedly appraising look to a fiend-pixie smile that is so broad it's hardly human. He is one of the few actors who are convincingly goaty; nobody else does rancidly unromantic sex scenes with the dippy arrogance—the near-madness—he brings to them. Always a little meaner and more self-sufficient than his roles seem to require, he is also freakishly, slyly funny. Torn has life to him, no matter what, and here his terrifying, sneaky smartness *fits*. Maury Dann has been touring in the Deep South for months, doing one-night stands. In the back of his Cadillac, between two girls, he's a sweating rajah, drinking Coke and beer and bourbon, smoking pot and popping pills. In the thirty-six hours that the film spans, just about everything goes wrong for him, and, already tense and exhausted, he is wound up so tight he's ready to explode.

The people who made *Payday* knew what they were doing. From the opening shots of a couple going in to a country-music concert through to Maury Dann's ultimate explosion, the film lays open his scrambling, chiseling life. An exceptionally functional script, by the novelist Don Carpenter (the first he has had produced), makes it possible for the film to cover the grimy pop scene of a small-time recording "star"—the barnstorming life of deals and motels and restaurants, of groupies, quarrels, blackmailing disc jockeys, and payoffs. Maury, a third-rate Johnny Cash, travels in a two-car caravan with his entourage: his manager, McGinty (Michael C. Gwynne); his driver, cook, and "chief bottle washer," the fat, loyal Chicago (Cliff Emmich); and his musicians and girls. They are rootless refugees from poverty, out of nowhere and rushing to a more affluent nowhere. A teen-age groupie with the slow smile of a Southern belle (Elayne Heilveil) works in a dime store and doesn't know what an omelet is; all her life she's eaten at counters and at McDonald's—"maybe three thousand hamburgers," she says. Being taken along by Maury is like being drawn into orbit. The people in the small towns idolize Maury, because he's somebody; he may be the only kind of somebody they feel is theirs.

Payday was made by an independent company, with Ralph J. Gleason, the veteran writer on jazz, who is vice-president of Fantasy Records, as executive producer. Financed by Fantasy Records and completed last year, it was brought in for under seven hundred and eighty thousand dollars. Universal, Warner Brothers, Twentieth Century-Fox, and Columbia all turned it down for distribution—though it's doubtful if they could bring in a film that looked this professional for three times that amount. To direct, Gleason and Carpenter picked Daryl Duke, who worked for the National Film Board of Canada before moving into Canadian and American television; he had not directed a theatrical feature before, but he knew the music scene. He's maybe too professional a director—too businesslike and slick—but he never lets your attention falter. *Payday* was shot entirely on location in Alabama, and with a cast partly of professionals and partly of local people, who play the drifters and the small-town characters without any false notes that I could detect. *Payday* isn't designed to be conventionally gripping or to have the usual melodramatic suspense; even halfway through, we're not quite conscious of where it's heading. Everything that happens is prepared for, yet in such an unforced way that we don't feel shoved. The editing (by Richard Halsey) seems to carry us along on the undercurrents; when from time to time the plot surfaces, we receive small hair-trigger shocks.

We get to know Maury Dann in different relationships, and we see what he came out of. On the way to a date in Birmingham, he visits his wreck of a mother, who bore him at sixteen, and now, fifty-one and a pill head, looks eighty; he goes out on a quail shoot, has a fight about his hunting dog, stops in on his ex-wife but doesn't stick around to see his three kids. After each contact with the past, his frustrations need release, and when his blond mistress (Ahna Capri, doing an Ann-Margret role, and very well) goads him at the wrong moment, he throws her out of the car. Carpenter's writing is skillful; each person is given his due—no one is put down or treated condescendingly. Yet this very awareness, this intelligence that informs and controls every detail, shuts us out. The conception precludes Hollywood "heart," as it precludes "poetry"—yet, perhaps irrationally, we want more than accuracy and slice-of-life understanding. We want an illumination, a sense of discovery—*something*.

Rip Torn seems perfect in the role, but there is a disadvantage to him: who could have empathy with Rip Torn? He's always on his own malevolent wavelength. And the movie keeps its distance at all times; we observe what the characters feel, but we are never invited to feel with them. When we stay on the outside like this, there's no mystery. We don't sense other possibilities in the people; we never intuit what else they might have been, never feel anything larger in them than the life they're caught in. It's part of the picture's realistic integrity to show them for what they are, without sentimentality; yet to view stunted lives is not altogether satisfactory—as I think *Fat City* also demonstrated. This picture is much tougher-minded, and it's up-to-date—it has none of the blurring, softening (and antiquing) effect of a tragic tone. I don't know *how* it would be possible to present this life as acridly and faithfully as *Payday* does and infuse into it the beauty of some redeeming illumination without falsifying and destroying it. But this realism is close to the realism of hardboiled fiction; the astuteness is self-protective, and it prevents *Payday* from rising above craft.

When you hear people in the pop-music business swapping stories, you may think that someone should make a movie and show how it really is, and that's what these moviemakers have done. But to lay out what you know is a limited approach to realism. We grasp exactly what we are meant to think and feel about each detail of these dissolute, messy lives. And it frustrates the imagination when a world is so clearly defined—more clearly than is possible, I think, for an artist.

A clue to what's missing may be found by making a comparison with, say, Francesco Rosi's extraordinary 1965 film *The Moment of Truth*—socially a comparable story, dealing with a poor Spanish boy's road out of rural poverty and his barnstorming life as a matador. It, too, is about poverty, dislocation, and corruption, and the movie's method is also apparently objective and impersonal. The difference is that *The Moment of Truth* raises emotions that neither its moviemaking team nor we can fully comprehend, and so the material draws us in and stays with us. It does so, I think, because Rosi's

486

style expresses a larger vision of life than that of his characters—his art is in itself a cry of rage about what the poor are deprived of. The largeness of his vision is proof of the human possibilities that his hero, living in a circle of corruption, is cut off from. *Payday* doesn't have an expressive style that says there's something more than Maury Dann's corruption. There's no rage in the film, and no sensibility that goes beyond awareness, except in a few flashes. There are brief memorable moments: the blowsy blonde's face when she wakes from a nap in the car to see her lover making out with the little groupie belle right next to her; the driver Chicago's mixture of emotions when he hands the car keys over to Maury Dann before being hauled off by the police. And they're memorable just because something larger and not easy to define is going on in them—because they transcend programmed realism. They have what a work of film art has in its *approach*—a sense of wonder.

In *Payday* we see only the crudiness of the pop scene; the music itself is largely neglected. But country music has links to the past, and if we could feel that there was love for this music in Maury Dann himself, and in his followers and audiences, the movie might have that transforming quality we miss. Because when a people's folk art is corrupted—and they're still trying to find some joy in it, since it's still the only art that's theirs—there is deprivation, all right, and rage isn't far away. To show corruption as it is is the honest reporter's way, and although it's a great deal for a movie to do, it's not enough. (It may even imply assent—though I don't think that happens here.) To show corruption as it is and by your style to reveal why it shouldn't be—that's the honest artist-reporter's way.

The New Yorker, February 24, 1973

FROM "A GENERATION'S CLOWN"—REVIEW OF
TEN FROM YOUR SHOW OF SHOWS

Sid Caesar rose to stardom faster than any other comedian who comes to mind, and he was flung into the pressure-cooker existence of live TV. Without underestimating the burning-out effect of eight seasons of live TV (ten if one includes the *Admiral Broadway Revue* series, done in 1949, and the final series, *Sid Caesar Invites You,* in 1958, in which he and Carl Reiner reunited with Imogene Coca, but which ran only a half season), I think that he might have come back—been restored, after a period of rest, the way Jonathan Winters bounces back, punchy but game—if he were a madman at heart, maybe with or without the early experience, though possibly only with. The training of a lifetime shows. Even if you couldn't take Milton Berle years ago, when you see him on TV now you're staggered by his knowledge of the mechanics of his craft, and the spark in him seems to have taken over the whole man. George Burns can do his dotty but charming patter songs with the ease of a master. Groucho, barely audible, still sings and engages in repartee. They are all simply older versions of themselves. The shock of seeing Sid Caesar when he first appeared on TV looking thinner, in the sixties, was that his funnyman's fat moon face was burned away. The comic drive seemed to be gone, too; the thinner Sid Caesar was no longer the mighty Caesar. His energy had made his size seem unlimited; now the energy was apparently gone, along with the exaggerated grief of the heavy-set man, which was often his dominant expression—as it was with Herman Bing, too. Can one imagine a thin Herman Bing or, say, a frail Sig Rumann? Their entire personality and style grew out of their size, just as, at the opposite end, Keaton's and Chaplin's did. Sid Caesar is an ordinary man now, and it's strangely upsetting. It's as if what his ten years on TV did to him were symbolized by his loss of flesh. When he does funny faces, they're not funny; the abnormality has gone out of them. Sid Caesar isn't Sid Caesar.

The New Yorker, March 3, 1973

DAYS AND NIGHTS IN THE FOREST

"It adds years to your life," the young men from Calcutta in Satyajit Ray's *Days and Nights in the Forest* say of the country quiet, and it's easy to believe. Ray's images are so emotionally saturated that they become suspended in time and, in some cases, fixed forever. Satyajit Ray's films can give rise to a more complex feeling of happiness in me than the work of any other director. I think it must be because our involvement with his characters is so direct that we are caught up in a blend of the fully accessible and the inexplicable, the redolent, the mysterious. We accept the resolutions he effects not merely as resolutions of the stories but as truths of human experience. Yet it isn't only a matter of thinking, Yes, this is the way it is. What we assent to is only a component of the pattern of associations in his films; to tell the stories does not begin to suggest what the films call to mind or why they're so moving. There is always a residue of feeling that isn't resolved. Two young men sprawled on a porch after a hot journey, a drunken group doing the Twist in the dark on a country road, Sharmila Tagore's face lit by a cigarette lighter, her undulating walk in a sari—the images are suffused with feeling and become overwhelmingly, sometimes unbearably beautiful. The emotions that are imminent may never develop, but we're left with the sense of a limitless yet perhaps harmonious natural drama that the characters are part of. There are always larger, deeper associations impend-

488

ing; we recognize the presence of the mythic in the ordinary. And it's the mythic we're left with after the ordinary has been (temporarily) resolved.

When *Days and Nights in the Forest*, which was made in 1969, was shown at the New York Film Festival in 1970, it received a standing ovation, and it seemed so obvious that a film of this quality—and one more immediate in its appeal than many of Ray's works—would be snapped up by a distributor that I waited to review it upon its theater opening. But distributors are often lazy men who don't bother much with festivals, least of all with films that are shown at the dinner hour (it went on at six-thirty); they wait for the *Times*. The review was condescendingly kindly and brief—a mere five and a half inches, and not by the first-string critic—and *Days and Nights in the Forest*, which is a major film by a major artist, is finally opening, two and a half years later, for a week's run at a small theater. On the surface, it is a lyrical romantic comedy about four educated young men from Calcutta driving together for a few days in the country, their interrelations, and what happens to them in the forest, which is both actual and metaphorical. As the men rag each other and bicker, we quickly sort them out. Ashim is a rising executive and the natural leader of the group. Lordly and disdainful to underlings, he is the worst-behaved; the most intelligent, he is also the most dissatisfied with his life and himself—he feels degraded. He and Sanjoy, who is more polite and reticent, used to slave on a literary magazine they edited, but they have settled down. Ashim is much like what Apu might have turned into if he had been corrupted, and he is played by Soumitra Chatterjee, who was Apu in *The World of Apu*. On this holiday in the forest, Ashim meets Aparna, played by the incomparably graceful Sharmila Tagore (who ten years before, when she was fourteen, played Aparna, Apu's exquisite bride). In his fine book on the Apu Trilogy, Robin Wood wrote that the physical and spiritual beauty of Soumitra Chatterjee and Sharmila Tagore seems "the ideal incarnation of Ray's belief in human potentialities." And I think they represent that to Ray, and inspire him to some of his finest work (he used them also in *Devi*) because they are modern figures with overtones of ancient deities. Unlike the other characters in *Days and Nights in the Forest*, they bridge the past and the future and—to some degree—India and the West. As Ray uses them, they embody more than we can consciously grasp. But we feel it: when Sharmila Tagore in her sunglasses and white slacks stands still for a second, she's a creature of fable—the image carries eternity. Even her melodious voice seems old and pure, as if it had come through fire.

Ashim has been strangling in the business bureaucracy of Calcutta; frustrated, he has become an egotist, and confidently condescending to women. Aparna, a city girl vacationing at her father's house in the forest along with her widowed sister-in-law, is not impressed by his big-city line. Her irony and good sense cut through his arrogance, and, made to feel foolish, he rediscovers his humanity. Underneath their love story, and the stories of Ashim's companions, there's the melancholy and corruption of their class and country. In a quiet way, the subtext is perhaps the subtlest, most plangent study of the cultural tragedy of imperialism the screen has ever had. It is the trag-edy of the bright young generation who have internalized the master race (like many of the refugees from Hitler who came to America); their status identity is so British that they treat all non-Anglicized Indians as non-persons. The caste system and the British attitudes seem to have conspired to turn them into self-parodies—clowns who ape the worst snobberies of the British. The highest compliment the quartet can bestow on Aparna's fa-ther's cottage is to say, "The place looks absolutely English." We don't laugh at them, though, because they're achingly conscious of being anachronistic and slightly ridiculous. When we see them playing tennis in the forest, the image is so ambiguous that our responses come in waves.

Ray not only directed but did the screenplay (from a novel by Sunil Ganguly), drew the credit titles, and wrote the music. His means as a direc-tor are among the most intuitively right in all moviemaking: he knows when to shift the camera from one face to another to reveal the utmost, and he knows how to group figures in a frame more expressively than anyone else. He doesn't butt into a scene; he seems to let it play itself out. His under-statement makes most of what is thought of as film technique seem unnec-essary, and even decadent, because he does more without it. (No Western director has been able to imitate him.) The story is told with great precision at the same time that the meanings and associations multiply. Ray seems to add something specifically Eastern to the "natural" style of Jean Renoir. Renoir, too, put us in unquestioning and total—yet discreet—contact with his people, and everything seemed fluid and easy, and open in form. But Renoir's time sense is different. What is distinctive in Ray's work (and it may be linked to Bengali traditions in the arts, and perhaps to Sanskrit) is that sense of imminence—the suspension of the images in a larger context. The rhythm of his films seems not slow but, rather, meditative, as if the viewer could see the present as part of the past and could already reflect on what is going on. There is a rapt, contemplative quality in the beautiful intelli-gence of his ideal lovers. We're not at all surprised in this film that both Ashim and Aparna have phenomenal memories; we knew that from looking at them.

Ray takes a risk when he contrasts his poetic sense of time against the hasty Western melodramatic tradition. One of the four young men is a fig-ure in the sporting world—Hari, who is quick-tempered and rash. He has just been jilted by a dazzler of a girl for his insensitivity. (He answered a six-page letter from her in a single curt sentence.) Hari picks up a local "tribal" girl in the forest for some fast sex, and he is also attacked and almost killed by a servant he has wrongly accused of stealing. The scenes relating to Hari (especially those dealing with the equally thoughtless local girl) feel very thin and unconvincing, because they are conventional. They have no mys-tery, no resonance, and though this is surely deliberate, the contrast doesn't succeed; the scenes seem more contrived than they would in an American movie. In a scene by a river, Sharmila Tagore's glance brings Hari back into the film's harmony, but he goes out again. The fourth young man, Sekhar, has no subplot; he's a plump buffoon, a fawning hanger-on, who drops pidgin-English phrases into his conversation as if they were golden wit. Like Joyce Cary's Mr. Johnson in Africa, he's a joke the British left behind. Nothing happens to him; spinelessly affable, he behaves in the country as he does in the city.

It is the shy Sanjoy who has the worst experience. Aparna's sister-in-law, the young, heavily sensual widow, makes a physical overture to him. She has been flirting with him for days, and we have observed the ordinariness of her middle-class character, listened to the coyness in her slightly disagreeable voice; we know that he is flattered by her attention and oblivious of the import of her broad smiles and provocative, teasing manner. When she lures him in at night with an offer of real coffee and puts her hand on his chest, we see his stricken face, and we are torn in half. She hadn't seen in him what we had, or he in her. Ray, without our full awareness, has prepared us, and now we are brought closer to them both than we had ever anticipated. This desperately lonely woman might be too much for most men, and this man is less secure than most. The moment of his petrified indecision about how to retreat and her realization of the rejection is a fully tragic experience. Ray is a master psychologist: the pain for us is the deeper because Ray had made her so coarse-grained that we hadn't cared for her; now her humiliation illuminates what was going on in her while we were dismissing her for her middle-classness and the tension in her voice. No artist has done more than Satyajit Ray to make us reëvaluate the commonplace. And only one or two other film artists of his generation—he's just past fifty—can make a masterpiece that is so lucid and so inexhaustibly rich. At one point, the four young blades and the two women sit in a circle on picnic blankets and play a memory game that might be called Let Us Now Praise Famous Men; it's a pity that James Agee didn't live to see the films of Satyajit Ray, which fulfill Agee's dreams.

The New Yorker, March 17, 1973

MARILYN A BIOGRAPHY BY NORMAN MAILER

It's the glossiest of glossy books—the sexy waif-goddess spread out in over 100 photographs by two dozen photographers plus the Mailer text and all on shiny coated paper. It's a rich and creamy book, an offensive physical object, perhaps even a little sordid. On the jacket, her moist lips parted, in a color photograph by Bert Stern taken just before her death in 1962, Marilyn Monroe has that blurry, slugged look of her later years; fleshy but pasty. A sacrificial woman—*Marilyn* to put beside *Zelda.* This glassy-eyed goddess is not the funny bunny the public wanted, it's Lolita become Medusa. The book was "produced" by the same Lawrence Schiller who packaged the 1962 Hedda Hopper story congratulating 20th Century-Fox for firing Monroe from her last picture; now there are new ways to take her. The cover-girl face on *Marilyn* is disintegrating; and the astuteness of the entrepreneurs in exploiting even her disintegration, using it as a Pop icon, gets to one. Who knows what to think about Marilyn Monroe or about those who turn her sickness to metaphor? I wish they'd let her die.

In his opening, Mailer describes Marilyn Monroe as "one of the last of cinema's aristocrats" and recalls that the sixties, which "began with Hemingway as the monarch of American arts, ended with Andy Warhol as its regent." Surely he's got it all wrong? He can't even believe it; it's just a conceit. Hemingway wasn't the monarch of American arts but our official literary celebrity—our big writer—and by the end of the sixties, after *An American Dream* and *Cannibals and Christians* and *The Armies of the Night* and *Miami and the Siege of Chicago,* the title had passed to Mailer. And Marilyn Monroe wasn't a cinema aristocrat (whatever nostalgic reverie of the "old stars" is implied); a good case could be made for her as the first of the Warhol superstars (funky caricatures of sexpot glamour, impersonators of stars). Jean Harlow with that voice of tin may have beat her to it, but it was Monroe who used her lack of an actress's skills to amuse the public. She had the wit or crassness or desperation to turn cheesecake into acting—and vice versa; she did what others had the "good taste" not to do, like Mailer, who puts in what other writers have been educated to leave out. She would bat her Bambi eyelashes, lick her messy suggestive open mouth, wiggle that pert and tempting bottom, and use her hushed voice to caress us with dizzying innuendos. Her extravagantly ripe body bulging and spilling out of her clothes, she threw herself at us with the off-color innocence of a baby whore. She wasn't the girl men dreamed of or wanted to know but the girl they wanted to go to bed with. She was Betty Grable without the coy modesty, the starlet *in flagrante delicto* forever because that's where everybody thought she belonged.

Her mixture of wide-eyed wonder and cuddly drugged sexiness seemed to get to just about every male; she turned on even homosexual men. And women couldn't take her seriously enough to be indignant; she was funny and impulsive in a way that made people feel protective. She was a little knocked out; her face looked as if, when nobody was paying attention to her, it would go utterly slack—as if she died between wolf calls.

She seemed to have become a camp siren out of confusion and ineptitude; her comedy was self-satire, and apologetic—conscious parody that had begun unconsciously. She was not the first sex goddess with a trace of somnambulism; Garbo was often a little out-of-it, Dietrich was numb most of the time, and Hedy Lamarr was fairly zonked. But they were exotic and had accents, so maybe audiences didn't wonder why they were in a daze; Monroe's slow reaction time made her seem daffy, and she tricked it up into a comedy style. The mystique of Monroe—which accounts for the book *Marilyn*—is that she became spiritual as she fell apart. But as an actress she had no way of expressing what was deeper in her except in moodiness and weakness. When she was "sensitive" she was drab.

Norman Mailer inflates her career to cosmic proportions. She becomes "a proud, inviolate artist," and he suggests that "one might literally have to invent the idea of a soul in order to approach her." He pumps so much wind into his subject that the reader may suspect that he's trying to make Marilyn Monroe worthy of him, a subject to compare with the Pentagon and the moon. Laying his career calibrations before us, he speculates that "a great biography might be constructed some day" upon the foundation of Fred Lawrence Guiles's *Norma Jean* and proceeds to think upon himself as the candidate for the job: "By the logic of transcendence, it was exactly in the secret scheme of things that a man should be able to write about a beautiful woman, or a woman to write about a great novelist—that would be transcendence, indeed!" Has he somehow forgotten that even on the sternest reckonings the "great" novelists include Jane Austen and George Eliot?

But no he decides that he cannot give the years needed for the task; he will write, instead, a "novel biography." "Set a thief to catch a thief and put an artist on an artist," he hums, and seeing the work already in terms to give Capote shivers, he describes it as "a *species* of novel ready to play by the rules of biography." The man is intolerable; he works out the flourishes of the feat he's going to bring off before allowing his heroine to be born. After all this capework and the strain of the expanding chest on the buttons of his vest, the reader has every right to expect this blowhard to take a belly flop, and every reason to want him to. But though it's easy—in fact, natural—to speak of Mailer as crazy (and only half in admiration) nobody says dumb. *Marilyn* is a rip-off all right but a rip-off with genius.

Up to now we've had mostly contradictory views of Monroe. Those who have taken a hard line on her (most recently Walter Bernstein in the July *Esquire*) never accounted for the childlike tenderness, and those who have seen her as shy and loving (like the Strasbergs or Diana Trilling or Norman Rosten) didn't account for the shrill sluttiness. Arthur Miller had split her into *The Misfits* and the scandalous *After the Fall,* and since each was only a side of her, neither was believable. With his fox's ingenuity, Mailer puts her together and shows how she might have been torn apart, from the inside by her inheritance and her childhood, by the outside pressures of the movie business. But it's all conjecture and sometimes pretty wild conjecture; he's a long way from readiness "to play by the rules of biography" since his principal technique—how could the project interest him otherwise?—is to jump inside everyone's head and read thoughts.

He acknowledges his dependence for the putative facts on the standard biographies—principally Guiles's *Norma Jean,* and also Maurice Zolotow's *Marilyn Monroe*—but deciding to interpret the data researched and already presented by others is a whopping putdown of them; their work thus becomes grist for his literary-star mill. Some of his milling is not so stellar. He quotes trashy passages (with a half-smile) and uses them for their same trashy charge. And his psychoanalytic detective work is fairly mawkish; we don't need Norman Mailer to tell us about Marilyn Monroe's search for parent figures—even fan magazines have become adept at this two-bit stuff about her claiming to her schoolmates that Clark Gable was her father and then winding up in Gable's arms in *The Misfits*.

Mailer explains her insomnia and her supposed attraction to death by her own account of someone's attempt to suffocate her when she was thirteen months old. But since there's no evidence for her account (except hindwise, in her insomnia) and since she apparently didn't start telling the story until the mid-fifties, when she was embroidering that raped and abused Little Nell legend that *Time* sent out to the world in a cover story, isn't it possible that before building a house of cards on the murderous incident one should consider if it wasn't linked to her having played (in *Don't Bother to Knock* in 1952) a psychopathic babysitter who blandly attacks a little girl? (The faintly anesthetized vagueness of her babysitter prefigured the ethereal vacuity of the face in the last photos.)

When the author says that it was his "prejudice that a study of Marilyn's movies might offer more penetration into her early working years in film than a series of interviews. . . ." one may guess that his model is Freud's book on Leonardo da Vinci, which is also an ecstasy of hypothesis. But surprisingly, Mailer makes only perfunctory use of her movies. He can't be much interested: he doesn't even bother to discuss the tawdriness of *Niagara* (made in 1953, just before she won Hollywood over with *Gentlemen Prefer Blondes*), in which her amoral destructive tramp—carnal as hell—must surely have represented Hollywood's lowest estimate of her.

Nor is he very astute about her career possibilities: He accepts the pious view that she should have worked with Chaplin and he says, complaining of Twentieth Century-Fox's lack of comprehension of her film art, that she could "have done *Nana, The Brothers Karamazov, Anna Christie* or *Rain* to much profit, but they gave her *Let's Make Love*." Who would quarrel with his judgment of *Let's Make Love,* but do the other titles represent his idea of what she should have done? (To *her* profit, he must mean, surely not the studio's.) Yes, probably she could have played a Grushenka (though not a Russian one), but does Mailer want to look at a Hollywood *Karamazov* or new versions of those other clumping war-horses? (Not a single one of those girls is American, and how could Monroe play anything else?)

Monroe might have "grown" as an actress but she would have died as a star. (Isn't the vision of the Reverend Davidson kneeling to her Sadie Thompson the purest camp?) The pity is that she didn't get more of the entertaining roles that were in her range; she hardly had the stability to play a mother or even a secretary and she was a shade too whorey for Daisy Miller or her descendants, but she was the heroine of every porny-spooflike *Candy* come to life, and she might have been right for *Sweet Charity* or for

Lord Love a Duck or *Born Yesterday* or a remake of the Harlow comedy *Bomb-shell* or another *Red Dust*. She might have had a triumph in *Breakfast at Tif-fany's* and she probably could have toned down for Tennessee Williams's *Pe-riod of Adjustment* and maybe even *Bonnie and Clyde*. Plain awful when she suffered, she was best at demi-whores who enjoyed the tease, and she was too obviously a product of the movie age to appear in a period picture.

It isn't enough for Mailer that people enjoyed her; he cranks her up as great and an "angel of sex" and, yes, "Napoleonic was her capture of the at-tention of the world." Monroe the movie star with sexual clout overpowers Norman Mailer. But most of her late pictures (such as *The Prince and the Showgirl, Let's Make Love* and *The Misfits*) didn't capture the public. Audi-ences didn't want the nervous, soulful Monroe—never so dim as when she was being "luminous"; they wanted her to be a mock-dumb snuggly blonde and to have some snap. When Mailer writes about her "artist's intelligence" and "superb taste" and about the sort of work she did in *The Misfits* as "the fulfillment of her art," he just seems to be getting carried away by the im-portance of his subject. Back in 1962, he wrote that "she was bad in *The Mis-fits,* she was finally too vague, and when emotion showed, it was unattractive and small," and he was right. It was already the Marilyn legend in that role—the baffled, vulnerable child-woman; she didn't have the double-edged defenselessness of her comedy hits, she looked unawakened yet sick—anguished.

But Mailer understands how Hollywood uses its starlets and how Marilyn Monroe the star might have reacted to that usage, and that is the key understanding that most commentators on her have lacked (though Clifford Odets's obit of her had it, also the story Ezra Goodman wrote for *Time* in 1956, which *Time* didn't print but which appears in his *The Fifty Year Decline and Fall of Hollywood*). And who but Norman Mailer could have pro-vided the analysis (that starts on page 35, the real beginning of the book) of the effect on Monroe of the torpor of her twenty-one months in an or-phanage and why it probably confirmed her into a liar and reinforced "ev erything in her character that was secretive"? And who else, writing about a Pop figure, would even have thought about the relation of narcissism to in-stitutional care? His strength—when he gets rolling—isn't in Freudian guesses but in his fusing his knowledge of how people behave with his worst suspicions of where they really live.

His best stuff derives from his having been on the scene, or close enough to smell it out. When it comes to reporting the way American rituals and institutions operate, Mailer's low cunning is maybe the best tool anyone ever had. He grasps the psychological and sexual rewards the studio system offered executives. He can describe why Zanuck, who had Monroe under contract, didn't like her; how she became "a protagonist in the great Amer-ican soap opera" when her nude calendar was "discovered"—i.e., leaked to the press by Jerry Wald to publicize *Clash by Night;* and what it may have meant to her to date DiMaggio, "an American king—her first. The others have been merely Hollywood kings." He's elegantly cogent on the Method and his paragraphs on Lee Strasberg as a critic of acting are a classic.

About half of *Marilyn* is great as only a great writer, using his brains and feelers could make it. Just when you get fed up with his flab and slop, he'll come through with a runaway string of perceptions and you have to recognize that, though it's a bumpy ride, the book still goes like a streak. His writing is close to the pleasures of movies; his immediacy makes him more accessible to those brought up with the media than, say, Bellow. You read him with a heightened consciousness because his performance has zing. It's the star system in literature; you can feel him bucking for the big time, and when he starts flying it's so exhilarating you want to applaud. But it's a good-bad book. When Mailer tries to elevate his intuitions into theories, the result is usually verbiage. (His theory that men impart their substance and qualities into women along with their semen is a typical macho Mailerism; he sees it as a one-way process, of course. Has no woman slipped a little something onto his privates?) There are countless bits of literary diddling: "—she had been alive for twenty years but not yet named!—"; the exclamation points are like sprinkles. Mailer the soothsayer with his rheumy metaphysics and huckster's magick is a carny quack, and this Hollywood milieu seems to bring out his fondness for the slacker reaches of the occult—reincarnation and sob-sister omens ("a bowl of tomato sauce dropped on her groom's white jacket the day of her first wedding"). We know his act already and those words (dread, existential, ontology, the imperatives) that he pours on like wella balsam to tone up the prose. And there's his familiar invocation of God, i.e., mystery. But it's less mysterious now because it has become a weapon: the club he holds over the villain of the book—respectable, agnostic Arthur Miller, a writer of Mailer's own generation (and closer than that) who won Marilyn Monroe. Set a thief to catch a thief, an artist on an artist, and one nice Jewish boy from Brooklyn on another.

It's not just a book about Monroe, it's Mailer's show. "Feedback has become the condition of our lives," he said in an interview in 1972. "It's the movies. We've passed the point in civilization where we can ever look at anything as an art work. There is always our knowledge of it and of the making of it." Whether true or false, this applies to Mailer, and he has made us more aware than we may want to be of his titles and campaigns, his aspiration to be more than a writer, to conquer the media and be monarch of American arts—a straight Jean Cocteau who'd meet anybody at high noon. Something has been withheld from Norman Mailer: his crown lacks a few jewels, a star. He has never triumphed in the theater, never been looked up to as a Jewish Lincoln, and never been married to a famous movie queen—a sex symbol. (He's also not a funny writer; to be funny you have to be totally unfettered, and he's too ambitious.) Mailer's waddle and crouch may look like a put-on, but he means it when he butts heads. *Marilyn* is his whammy to Arthur Miller.

In 1967, in an article written to promote the off-Broadway version of

The Deer Park, Mailer said of himself, "There were too many years when he dreamed of *The Deer Park* on Broadway and the greatest first night of the decade, too many hours of rage when he declaimed to himself that his play was as good as *Death of a Salesman*, or even, and here he gulped hard, *A Streetcar Named Desire.*" The sly sonuvabitch coveted Miller's success and cut him down in the same sentence. (*The Deer Park* wasn't Mailer's *Salesman*; based on Mailer's own second marriage and dealing with integrity and the McCarthy period and sex and love, it was more like Mailer's *After the Fall*.) In his warm-up in *Marilyn* Mailer points out that though he'd never met Marilyn Monroe, she had for a time lived with Miller in Connecticut "not five miles away from the younger author, who [was] not yet aware of what his final relation to Marilyn Monroe would be. . . ." It appears to be destiny's decree that he should take her over. Mailer isn't the protagonist of this book; Marilyn is. But Mailer and God are waiting in the wings.

How can we readers limit ourselves to the subject when he offers us this name-play: "it was fair to engraved coincidence that the letters in Marilyn Monroe (if the 'a' were used twice and 'o' but once) would spell his own name leaving only the 'y' for excess, a trifling discrepancy, no more calculated to upset the heavens than the most minuscule diffraction of the red shift"? (What would happen to any other serious writer trying to foist his giddy acrostics on us?) He fails to record that both Miller and Mailer probably derive from Mähler. Siblings. He had said in *The Armies of the Night* that he dreaded winding up "the nice Jewish boy from Brooklyn," that that was the one personality he considered "absolutely insupportable," but it was clearly a love-hate game—or why dread it? Actually he's in no danger. He's cut off from respectability, like our country; the greatest American writer is a bum, and a bum who's starting not to mind it. The time to begin worrying is when both he and the U.S. start finding virtues in this condition, we could all wind up like drunks doing a music-hall turn.

He can't get Arthur Miller's long bones, but he's busy trying to take off his skin; he wouldn't do it to Robert Lowell. But Miller and Mailer try for the same things: he's catching Miller's hand in the gentile cookie jar. Mailer doesn't get into confessional self-analysis on Miller as he did with Lowell; he writes as if with lordly objectivity—but the reader can feel what's going on. He says of Miller's possible fear of the marriage's failing, "a man who has lost confidence in his creative power sees ridicule as the broom that can sweep him to extinction" and then proceeds to make every kind of fool of him, attributing to him the impulses and motives that Mailer considers most contemptible. Ultimately what he's saying is that Miller wasn't smart enough to get any more out of Monroe than *After the Fall*. With Mailer, if you're going to use, use big. The second half of the book is supremely cruel to Miller—and it infects and destroys one's pleasure in the good parts. The "novel biography" becomes Mailer's way to perform character assassination with the freedom of a novelist who has created fictional characters. He's so cold-blooded in imputing motives to others that he can say of Yves Montand, for example, that Marilyn Monroe was "his best ticket to notoriety." Is this how Mailer maneuvers—is Marilyn Monroe Norman Mailer's sure-fire subject after a few box-office flops? Is that why he shoots the works in his final orgies of gossipy conjecture and turns her death into another Chappaquiddick—safe in the knowledge no one is left to call him a liar?

He uses his gifts meanly this time—and that's not what we expect of Mailer, who is always billed as generous. This brilliant book gives off bad vibes—and vibes are what Mailer is supposed to be the master of. *Marilyn* is a feat all right: matchstick by matchstick, he's built a whole damned armada inside a bottle. (Surely he's getting ready to do *Norman?* Why leave it to someone who may care less?) But can we honor him for this book when it doesn't sit well on the stomach? It's a metaphysical cocktail-table book, and probably not many will be able to resist looking for the vicious digs and the wrap-up on the accumulated apocrypha of many years, many parties. To be king of the bums isn't really much. What are we actually getting out of *Marilyn?* Good as the best parts of it are, there's also malevolence that needs to be recognized. Is the great reporter's arrogance so limitless that he now feels free to report on matters to which he's never been exposed? Neither the world nor Marilyn Monroe's life should be seen in Norman Mailer's image.

The New York Times Book Review, July 22, 1973

THE LAST AMERICAN HERO
AFTER INNOCENCE

The Watergate hearings have overshadowed the movies this summer, yet the corruption that Watergate has come to stand for can be seen as the culmination of what American movies have been saying for almost a decade. The movies of the thirties said that things would get better. The post-Second World War movies said that villainy would be punished and goodness would triumph; the decencies would be respected. But movies don't say that anymore; the Vietnamization of American movies is nearly complete. Today, movies say that the system is corrupt, that the whole thing stinks, and they've been saying this steadily since the mid-sixties. The Vietnam war has barely been mentioned on the screen, but you could feel it in *Bonnie and Clyde* and *Bullitt* and *Joe,* in *Easy Rider* and *Midnight Cowboy* and *The Last Picture Show,* in *They Shoot Horses, Don't They?* and *The Candidate* and *Carnal Knowledge* and *The French Connection* and *The Godfather.* It was in good movies and bad, flops and hits, especially hits—in the convictionless atmosphere, the absence of shared values, the brutalities taken for granted, the glorification of loser-heroes. It was in the harshness of the attitudes, the abrasiveness that made you wince—until, after years of it, maybe you stopped wincing. It had become normal.

In earlier action and adventure films, strength—what the strapping American hero was physically and what he embodied as the representative of the most powerful nation on earth—had to triumph. The American in those movies was the natural leader of men; he had to show the natives of any other country how to defend themselves. Even little Alan Ladd used to show them how to fight. Of course, it was a fantasy world, but this set of fantasies must have satisfied something deep down in the audience; it didn't come out of nowhere. Now the American man of action has become the enemy of all men—a man out for his own good only, and, very likely, a psychotic racist. In recent films, if a character spoke of principles or ideals the odds were he would turn out to be a ruthless killer, or at least a con artist; the heroes didn't believe in anything and didn't pretend they did. American history was raked over and the myths of the Old West were turned upside down; massacre scenes, indicting our past as well as our present, left us with nothing. Just jokes and horror. Whatever the period—in *Little Big Man* or *Butch Cassidy and the Sundance Kid* or *The Wild Bunch*—you could be sure nobody was going to amount to much. The air wasn't right for achievement.

In action pictures, there was no virtuous side to identify with and nobody you really felt very good about cheering for. Both sides were unprincipled; only their styles were different, and it was a matter of preferring the less gross and despicable characters to the total monsters. In cops-and-robbers movies, the cops were likely to be no better than the crooks; sometimes they'd be worse crooks. The freshest, most contemporary element in the current movie *Cops and Robbers* is that the cops commit a robbery to get away from the hell and hopelessness of trying to keep law and order. There was a cycle of movies about drugs, and, of all those addicts sinking down and down, was there one who got himself together? In some of the most popular films, the heroes were helpless losers, self-destructive, or drifters, mysteriously defeated. Defeated just in the nature of things. Sometimes, as in *Five Easy Pieces,* the hero was so defeated he was morally superior. There were few happy endings; when a comedy such as *The Owl and the Pussycat* or *Made for Each Other* wound up with a matched pair, the characters were so knocked out that if they didn't want each other who would? It wasn't exactly as if they'd taken first place in a contest; it was more like the last stand of bedraggled survivors. And it was emotionally satisfying just because it wasn't the sort of upbeat finish that you'd have to put down as a Hollywood ending.

Though it was exhilarating to see the old mock innocence cleared away, a depressive uncertainty has settled over the movies. They're seldom enjoyable at a simple level, and that may be one of the reasons older people no longer go; they watch TV shows, which are mostly reprocessed versions of old movies—the same old plots, characters, and techniques, endlessly recombined. The enjoyment has been squeezed out, but not the reassuring simplicity. Almost three-fourths (73 percent) of the movie audience is under twenty-nine; it's an audience of people who grew up with TV and began going out to theaters when they became restless and started dating. Chances are that when they have children of their own they'll be back with the box. But while they're going out to the movies they want something different, and this demand—in the decade of Vietnam—has created a fertile chaos, an opportunity for artists as well as for the bums who pile on the meat-cleaver brawls, and for those proud of not giving a damn. Maybe the effects of the years of guilt can be seen in the press's inability to be disgusted by the witless, desiccated *The Last of Sheila,* with its pinched little dregs of chic, its yearning for Weimar. Often even the fairy-tale films are indecisive and not quite satisfying, as if the writers and directors were afraid of showing any feeling. If *Paper Moon* had been made in an earlier decade, the con man (Ryan O'Neal) would have embraced the child (Tatum O'Neal) at the end and maybe he'd have told her he was her father (whether he was or not), and the audience would have had some emotional release. The way Peter Bogdanovich did it, it's pleasant while you're watching, but you're waiting for something that never comes; it's finally a little flat and unfulfilled. But if the story had been carried to the classic tearful father-daughter embrace, mightn't the audience—or, at least, part of it—have been turned off by the unabashed sweetness? By the hope for a better future? (In movies now, people don't talk about the future; they don't make plans; they don't expect much.) Possibly the very flatness makes it easier for audiences to accept the movie.

American movies didn't "grow up"; they did a flipover from their prolonged age of innocence to this age of corruption. When Vietnam finished off the American hero as righter of wrongs, the movie industry embraced corruption greedily; formula movies could be energized by infusions of brutality, cynicism, and Naked Apism, which could all be explained by Vietnam and called realism. Moviemakers could celebrate violence and pretend, even to themselves, that they were doing the public a service. Even though some writers and directors have probably been conscientious in their attempts to shock the audience by exposing the evils of the past, the effect has not been like that of Costa-Gavras's *State of Siege,* which is literally an SOS, and makes one want to find out what's going on and do something about it. And not like the effects of *I Am a Fugitive from a Chain Gang,* which outraged people, or Fred Wiseman's *Titicut Follies* and *High School,* which shook things up and led to reforms. Outrage isn't the aim of our most violent films; outrage isn't expected. When movie after movie tells audiences that they should be against themselves, it's hardly surprising that people go out of the theaters drained, numbly convinced that, with so much savagery and cruelty everywhere, nothing can be done. The movies have shown us the injustice of American actions throughout our history, and if we have always been rotten, the effect is not to make us feel we have the power to change but, rather, to rub our noses in it and make us accept it. In this climate, Watergate seems the most natural thing that could happen. If one were to believe recent movies, it was never any different in this country: Vietnam and Watergate are not merely where we got to but where we always were. The acceptance of corruption and the sentimentalization of defeat—that's the prevailing atmosphere in American movies, and producers, writers, and directors now make their choices in terms of a set of defeatist conventions.

■　■　■

When Tom Wolfe wrote about stock-car racing in *Esquire* in March, 1965 ("The Last American Hero Is Junior Johnson. *Yes!*"), he tried to evoke the physical sensations of this motor-age sport, with its rural speed-demon kings. Wolfe used the youth culture for excitement just as the movies did. Movies hit us in more ways than we can ever quite add up, and that's the kind of experience that Tom Wolfe tried to convey in prose. He described the sensations without attempting to add them up or theorize about them, and, because he had a remarkable gift for hyperactive, evocative writing, the effect was an impassioned turn-on. And, because in this article and others he didn't make his obeisances to the higherness of the traditional arts, he ran into the sort of disapproval that movies get. It was a compliment, of course—recognition from the enemy, because he had set up a great polemical target: the genteel, condescending press, which had ignored the new sports or treated them marginally. When Wolfe reprinted the racing article, which became the largest section of *The Kandy-Kolored Tangerine-Flake Streamline Baby,* he shortened the title to "The Last American Hero," and that's the name of the film based on it.

As journalism, Wolfe's charged-up pieces had the impact of an explorer's excited report on new terrain. But the youth culture that he brought into star journalism was already in the movies (just as the movies were in it). That culture was partly created by the movies, and his surfers and rockers and racers had been the lifeblood of the Grade B pop-genre films of the fifties. The car and the movie came along together, and chases, usually involving cars, have been surefire for so long that there was a time when the chase used to be called "pure movie"; there's barely a male star who hasn't served his days as a racer. The first demolition derby wasn't held until 1961, but moviemakers had always known about people's loving to see cars bashed. Demolition scenes were the primeval laugh-getters of silent pictures, and smashed cars and planes still get the biggest laughs in a new primeval picture like *Live and Let Die.* (Geoffrey Holder's leering wickedness as the impresario of the revels in the picture is kiddie camp.)

In the introduction to his book, Wolfe recorded the discovery that a builder of baroque custom cars he talked with "had been living like the *complete artist* for years," and went on, "He had starved, suffered—the whole thing—so he could sit inside a garage and create these cars which more than 99 percent of the American people would consider ridiculous, vulgar and lower-class-awful beyond comment almost." That's a strange overestimate of the number of people with good taste arrayed against the car builder; racing pictures were made for audiences to whom such a man had been an artist all along. So when you make a movie out of Tom Wolfe's reports on the world outside the class biases of Eastern-establishment prudery, you're taking the material back where it came from, and there's no occasion for whoops of revelation. The movie of "The Last American Hero" isn't startling, the way Wolfe's pieces were; but, with a script that uses Wolfe as the source for most of the story elements, Lamont Johnson, who directed, has done the Southern racing scene and the character of the people caught up in it better, perhaps, than they've ever been done before. The movie has everything *but* originality.

The title (which is a tired one anyway) no longer means what it did for Tom Wolfe. The Junior Johnson that Wolfe wrote about beat the system and won on his own terms; that was what made him a hero and a legend. Driving whatever he could stick together, he won out over the cars sponsored and specially built by the motor industry. He won even when his own car couldn't go as fast, by tricks such as catching free rides—by tailgating and being sucked along by the vacuum of the faster cars. A Southern country boy who became a hot-rod genius by running his father's moonshine whiskey in the middle of the night, he beat the big pros by ingenuity, skill, and blind impudence, and he beat them over and over—seven times, even though he was out for a couple of seasons when he was sent to federal prison for helping his daddy with some of the heavy labor at the still. (The agents were gunning for him, because he'd made them look ridiculous on the back roads years before.) That's the stuff of legend, all right. By the time Junior Johnson made his peace with Detroit and started to drive the factory-built racing cars, he was too much of a hero to be judged a sellout. He had already proved himself and then some, so it was all right for him to settle down, like a man of sense.

But between the publication of the Wolfe article and the making of the movie there was Vietnam. The hero of the movie—called Junior Jackson—starts out by cheating to win a demolition derby, and when he moves on to racing he can't make it with his own car. He wins his first big race *after* he starts driving as a hired hand for a big-money man, Colt (Ed Lauter). Even the steady girl the real Junior had gone with since high school, and later married, is replaced by a track follower (Valerie Perrine), who floats along with the winners. So there's sex without romance, sex without a future. The movie also avoids the easy possibilities for sympathy; it doesn't make Junior's path as hard as it was. He doesn't go to prison in the movie—it's his father who is busted as a result of Junior's bravado at the wheel. Colt, rather like George C. Scott in *The Hustler,* suggests a personification of the power of money, rather than just a representative of Detroit. Colt is almost lascivious about winning, and his winning is evil (but we never learn what winning gets him, or what it did for the diabolical Scott character). In *The Last American Hero,* corruption seems to be inescapable: if you want to win, you learn to take orders even from people whose idea of winning you don't understand. And at the end Junior Jackson is growing up—which is to say, learning the price of success in the real world. He is forced to sacrifice his friendships and his principles. The film says that to win you give up everything you care about except winning. It tells the story not of a man who fights for his independence but of a man who is smart enough not to sell himself too cheap.

Who would believe the actual story of Junior Johnson now—how hard it really was for him, and that he made it? This version will seem far more honest to movie audiences, because the new conventions are that you can't win and that everybody's a sellout. Even the absence of romance makes the movie more convincing—tougher, cool. And since Junior, played by Jeff Bridges, has a visible capacity for tenderness, the absence of romance is cruelly felt by the audience. By turning Junior Johnson's story around, the director, Lamont Johnson (and his writer, William Roberts, with a sizable, though uncredited, assist from William Kerby, who wrote the best scenes), has been able to make a hip, modern movie. It is, ironically, the most honest and gifted and tough-minded people in Hollywood who are fighting for defeat. The picture has total fidelity to its own scrupulous, hard-edged vision: the hero pays a price. It costs Junior Jackson something to win races; you can see that in Jeff Bridges's face.

Lamont Johnson doesn't exploit the backwoods people for the folksy touches that can make urban audiences laugh; he perceives the values in Junior Jackson's family life—in his affection for his mother (Geraldine Fitzgerald) and his vacuously grinning brother (Gary Busey), and, especially, in his bond to his father (Art Lund, in a towering performance). The picture was shot in Virginia and the Carolinas, using footage from actual races and derbies, and the crowds and details, the excited Southern faces at the stockcar tracks—everything feels right. Lamont Johnson has the feel for the South that John Boorman (who is English) couldn't get in *Deliverance*. Boorman is such an aestheticizing director—alienated, inhuman, yet the more gripping for the distance he keeps—that *Deliverance* held audiences by its mannered, ghastly-lovely cumulative power. It had the formality of a nightmare. (There was a hush in the theater when it was over.) *Deliverance* demonstrated that a movie can be effective even if you are always aware of the actors' acting and don't really believe in a single character, down to the bit players (except maybe James Dickey as the sheriff). But there is a special elation about a movie when the casting and the acting and the milieu seem effortlessly, inexplicably right. Paul Mazursky can get Los Angeles (*Alex in Wonderland, Blume in Love*) but can't get Venice (*Blume in Love*). Lamont Johnson's feeling for the milieu here amounts to an unusual sensibility: a gift for bringing all the elements of film together so that the people breathe right for where they live. He isn't an original—not in the way that, say, Mazursky, manic poet of middle-class quirk, is. (Has there ever been another self-satirist like Mazursky—humanly understanding and utterly freaked out?) But Lamont Johnson's work is attentive and satisfying. He's a far better movie man than many of the more original talents, and this film, if one sees the version he made, has everything going for it. (Twentieth Century-Fox tampered with the film, cutting a couple of the best scenes and then opening it in the South as an action racing picture. Since it isn't, it bombed out. And then the Fox executives decided it was a dog that wouldn't go in the big cities, because they knew that sophisticated people don't go to racing pictures. It opened in New York for a week in the summer as a "Showcase" presentation—that is to say, it got a second run without a first run—and its failure was the movie company's self-fulfilling prophecy. Though the reviews were excellent, they came out too late to attract an audience; Fox hadn't bothered with advance press screenings for a racing picture. But this movie transcends its genre; *The Last American Hero,* which is coming back next week, isn't just about stock-car racing, any more than *The Hustler* was only about shooting pool, and in terms of presenting the background of a sports hero it goes far beyond anything in *Downhill Racer.* If *The Last American Hero* finds a fraction of its rightful audience now, perhaps someone in the head office at Fox could do the sane, decent thing and restore the cuts?)

Sometimes, just on his own, Jeff Bridges is enough to make a picture worth seeing, and he's never before been used so fully, or in a way so integral to a film's conception. Only twenty-two when this picture was shot, he may be the most natural and least self-conscious screen actor who ever lived; physically, it's as if he had spent his life in the occupation of each character. He's the most American—the loosest—of all the young actors, unencumbered by stage diction and the stiff, emasculated poses of most juveniles. If he has a profile, we're not aware of it. He probably can't do the outrageous explosive scenes that Robert De Niro brings off in *Mean Streets* or the giddy-charming romantic clowning that De Niro did in the otherwise forgettable *The Gang That Couldn't Shoot Straight,* but De Niro—a real winner—is best when he's coming on and showing off. Jeff Bridges just moves into a role and lives in it—so deep in it that the little things seem to come straight from the character's soul. His brother Beau shares this infallible instinct, but Beau's effects don't seem to come from as far down; Beau Bridges has a lighter presence, an easier smile. Jeff Bridges's Junior Jackson is a cocky Huck Finn in the age of Detroit: impulsive, dogged, and self-sufficient; sure enough of himself to show his rank, shrewd enough to know where he's outranked. In a monologue scene (possibly suggested by Godard's *Masculine Feminine*), Junior, away from home for a race and feeling sentimental, uses a make-your-own-record machine to tell his family he's thinking of them and loves them; then, realizing he's beyond this kind of kid stuff, he throws the record away. The quality of Bridges's acting in this scene enlarges the meaning of the movie, yet he doesn't seem to be using anything more than a few shrugs and half-smothered words.

■   ■   ■

The Last American Hero never goes soft, and maybe that's why the picture felt so realistic to me; it wasn't until I reread the Wolfe piece that I realized what a turnaround it was. But we believe the worst now—maybe *only* the worst.

When we see a picture from the age of happy endings, the conventions may stick out as antiquated and ludicrous (and often they did when the picture was new), but the conventions that flow from the acceptance of corruption are insidiously believable, because they seem smart, while the older ones seem dumb. We will never know the extent of the damage movies are doing to us, but movie art, it appears, thrives on moral chaos. When the country is paralyzed, the popular culture may tell us why. After innocence, winners become losers. Movies are probably inuring us to corruption; the sellout is the hero-survivor for our times.

The New Yorker, October 1, 1973

MEAN STREETS
EVERYDAY INFERNO

Martin Scorsese's *Mean Streets* is a true original of our period, a triumph of personal filmmaking. It has its own hallucinatory look; the characters live in the darkness of bars, with lighting and color just this side of lurid. It has its own unsettling, episodic rhythm and a high-charged emotional range that is dizzyingly sensual. At the beginning, there's a long, fluid sequence as the central character, Charlie, comes into a bar and greets his friends; there's the laying on of hands, and we know that he is doing what he always does. And when the camera glides along with him as he's drawn toward the topless dancers on the barroom stage, we share his trance. At the end of the scene, when he's up on the stage, entering into the dance, he's not some guy who's taken leave of his senses but a man going through his nightly ritual. Movies generally work you up to expect the sensual intensities, but here you may be pulled into high without warning. Violence erupts crazily, too, the way it does in life—so unexpectedly fast that you can't believe it, and over before you've been able to take it in. The whole movie has this effect; it psychs you up to accept everything it shows you. And since the story deepens as it goes along, by the end you're likely to be openmouthed, trying to rethink what you've seen. Though the street language and the operatic style may be too much for those with conventional tastes, if this picture isn't a runaway success the reason could be that it's so original that some people will be dumbfounded—too struck to respond. It's about American life here and now, and it doesn't look like an American movie, or feel like one. If it were subtitled, we could hail a new European or South American talent—a new Buñuel steeped in Verdi, perhaps—and go home easier at heart. Because what Scorsese, who is thirty, has done with the experience of growing up in New York's Little Italy has a thicker-textured rot and violence than we have ever had in an American movie, and a riper sense of evil.

The zinger in the movie—and it's this, I think, that begins to come together in one's head when the picture is over—is the way it gets at the psychological connections between Italian Catholicism and crime, between sin and crime. Some editorial writers like to pretend this is all a matter of prejudice; they try to tell us that there is no basis for the popular ethnic stereotypes—as if crime among Italians didn't have a different tone from crime among Irish or Jews or blacks. Editorial writers think they're serving the interests of democracy when they ask us to deny the evidence of our senses. But all crime is not alike, and different ethnic groups have different styles of lawlessness. These Mafiosi loafers hang around differently from loafing blacks; in some ways, the small-time hoods of *Mean Streets* (good Catholics who live at home with their parents) have more in common with the provincial wolf pack of Fellini's *I Vitelloni* (cadging, indulged sons of middle-class families) than with the other ethnic groups in New York City. And these hoods live in such an insulated world that anyone outside it—the stray Jew or black they encounter—is as foreign and funny to them as a little man from Mars.

Many people interpreted the success of *The Godfather* to mean that the film glorified the gangsters' lives. During the Second World War, a documentary showing the noise and congestion of New York City was cheered by nostalgic American soldiers overseas; if audiences were indeed attracted to the life of the Corleone family (and I think some probably were), the reaction may be just as aberrant to the intentions of *The Godfather,* the best gangster film ever made in this country. It's likely that Italian, or Sicilian, Catholicism has a special, somewhat romantic appeal to Americans at this time. Italians appear to others to accept the fact that they're doomed; they learn to be comfortable with it—it's what gives them that warm, almost tactile glow. Their voluptuous, vacant-eyed smiles tell us that they want to get the best out of this life: they know they're going to burn in eternity, so why should they think about things that are depressing? It's as if they were totally carnal: everything is for their pleasure. Maybe it is this relaxed attitude that gave the Mafiosi of *The Godfather* their charm for the American audience. Was the audience envying them their close family ties and the vitality of their lawlessness? Was it envying their having got used to a sense of sin? It's almost as if the non-Catholic part of America wanted to say that *mea culpa* is *nostra culpa.*

Before *Mean Streets* is over, that glow gets very hot and any glamour is sweated off. The clearest fact about Charlie (Harvey Keitel), junior member of a Mafia family—and, in a non-literal sense, the autobiographical central figure—is that whatever he does in his life, he's a sinner. Behind the titles you see him smiling his edgy, jocular smile and shaking hands with a priest, as if sealing a pact, while the words appear: "Directed by Martin Scorsese." Charlie, you can see in his tense ferret's face, feels he was born to be punished. Like his friends, round-faced, jovial Tony the barkeep (David Proval) and pompous Michael (Richard Romanus), a chiseling dude, he basks in the life. Running numbers, gambling, two-bit swindles: they grew up in this squalor and it's all they've ever known or wanted. To them, this is living it up. But Charlie isn't a relaxed sinner; he torments himself, like a fanatic seminarian. He's so frightened of burning he's burning already. Afraid of everything, he's everybody's friend, always trying to keep the peace. He's a dutiful toady to his Uncle Giovanni (Cesare Danova), the big man in the Mafia, and he fails those he really cares about: his girl, Teresa (Amy Robinson), and his friend Johnny Boy (Robert De Niro), a compulsive gambler—more than compulsive, irrational, a gambler with no sense of money. Charlie is too vain and sycophantic not to give in to social pressure. Teresa isn't rated high enough by his uncle; and his uncle, his king, the source of the restaurant he hopes to get, has told him not to be involved with Johnny Boy. Johnny Boy was named after Giovanni, but the family protects you only if you truckle to the elder statesmen and behave yourself—if you're a good timeserver.

Johnny Boy isn't; he flouts all the rules, he just won't "behave." He's fearless, gleefully self-destructive, cracked—moonstruck but not really crazy. His madness isn't explained (fortunately, since explaining madness is the most limiting and generally least convincing thing a movie can do). When you're growing up, if you know someone crazy-daring and half-admirable (and maybe most of us do), you don't wonder how the beautiful nut got that way; he seems to spring up full-blown and whirling, and you watch the fireworks and feel crummily cautious in your sanity. That's how it is here. Charlie digs Johnny Boy's recklessness. De Niro's Johnny Boy is the only one of the group of grifters and scummy racketeers who is his own man; he is the true hero, while Charlie, through whose mind we see the action, is the director's worst vision of himself.

The story emerges from the incidents without dominating them; it's more like a thread running through. The audience isn't propelled by suspense devices, nor is the cataclysmic finish really an end—it's only a stop. Johnny Boy needs help. He owes Michael, the dude, a lot of money, and it hurts Michael's self-esteem that he can't collect; nagging and spiteful, he threatens violence. But Charlie doesn't save Johnny Boy by going to his big-shot uncle for help, because he just can't risk taking a problem to his uncle. A good Mafia boy is not only subservient; unless something important is happening to him, he maintains his visibility as near to invisibility as possible. Uncle Giovanni, a dignified, dull, dull man, doesn't really see Charlie—doesn't register his existence—and that's what keeps Charlie in his good graces. But if Charlie asks for help for a crazy friend in trouble, he loses his low visibility. So Charlie talks a lot to Johnny Boy about friendship and does nothing. He's Judas the betrayer because of his careful angling to move up the next rung of the ladder. How can a man show his soul to be pettier than that? Charlie, the surrogate for the director, is nobody's friend, and—as the movie itself proves—least of all his own. Charlie knows from the beginning that he pays for everything. Scorsese isn't asking for expiation of Charlie's sins in the movie; sins aren't expiated in this movie. (The director has cast himself in the bit part of Michael's helper; when Johnny Boy makes Michael look so bad that Michael decides to get satisfaction, it is Scorsese who, as the gunman, pulls the trigger.)

It's twenty years since Fellini's *I Vitelloni* planted the autobiographical hero on the screen. Fellini did it in a fairly conventional way: his Moraldo (Franco Interlenghi) was the sensitive, handsome observer who looked at the limitations of small-town life and, at the end, said goodbye to all that. In *La Dolce Vita,* the Fellini figure was the seduced, disillusioned journalist (Marcello Mastroianni) to whom everything happened, and in *8½* Mastroianni, again standing in for Fellini, was the movie director at the center of a multi-ring circus, the man sought after by everyone. In *Roma,* Fellini threw in new versions of several of his earlier representatives, and himself to boot. No other movie director, except among the "underground" filmmakers, has been so explicitly autobiographical. But in *I Vitelloni* we never caught a glimpse of the actual Fellini who emerged later; we never saw the fantasist as a young man, or the energy and will that drove him on. Movie directors have not yet learned the novelists' trick of throwing themselves into the third person, into the action, as Norman Mailer does even in his reporting; directors tend to make their own representatives passive, reflective figures, with things happening to them and around them, like Curt (Richard Dreyfuss) in George Lucas's nice (though overrated) little picture *American Graffiti.* Scorsese does something far more complex, because Charlie's wormy, guilt-ridden consciousness is made abhorrent to us at the same time that we're seeing life through it. Charlie is so agitated because he is aware of his smallness.

Scorsese's method is more like that of the Montreal filmmaker Claude Jutra, who, playing himself in *À Tout Prendre,* masochistically made himself weak, like those chinless self-portraits with traumatic stares which painters put at the edges of their canvases. Jutra left out the mind and energies that made him a movie director, and apparently put on the screen everything in himself he loathed, and this is what Scorsese does, but Scorsese also puts in the tensions of a man in conflict, and a harlequin externalization of those tensions. He's got that dervish Johnny Boy dancing around Charlie's fears, needling Charlie and exposing him to danger despite all his conciliatory nice-guyism. Johnny Boy's careless, contemptuous explosions seem a direct response to Charlie's trying to keep the lid on everything—it's as if Charlie's id were throwing bombs and laughing at him. When Johnny Boy has finally loused everything up, he can say to Charlie, "You got what you wanted."

While an actor like Jeff Bridges in *The Last American Hero* hits the true note, De Niro here hits the far-out, flamboyant one and makes his own truth. He's a bravura actor, and those who have registered him only as the grinning, tobacco-chewing dolt of that hunk of inept whimsey *Bang the Drum*

Slowly will be unprepared for his volatile performance. De Niro does something like what Dustin Hoffman was doing in *Midnight Cowboy,* but wilder; this kid doesn't just act—he takes off into the vapors. De Niro is so intensely appealing that it might be easy to overlook Harvey Keitel's work as Charlie. But Keitel makes De Niro's triumph possible; Johnny Boy can bounce off Charlie's anxious, furious admiration. Keitel, cramped in his stiff clothes (these Mafiosi dress respectable—in the long, dark overcoats of businessmen of an earlier era), looks like a more compact Richard Conte or Dane Clark, and speaks in the rhythms of a lighter-voiced John Garfield, Charlie's idol; it's his control that holds the story together. The whole world of the movie—Catholicism as it's actually practiced among these people, what it means on the street—is in Charlie's mingy-minded face.

The picture is stylized without seeming in any way artificial; it is the only movie I've ever seen that achieves the effects of Expressionism without the use of distortion. *Mean Streets* never loses touch with the ordinary look of things or with common experience; rather, it puts us in closer touch with the ordinary, the common, by turning a different light on them. The ethnic material is comparable to James T. Farrell's Studs Lonigan trilogy and to what minor novelists like Louis Golding did in the street-and-tenement novels of the thirties, but when this material is written on the screen the result is infinitely more powerful. (In a film review in 1935, Graham Greene—a Catholic—said that "the camera . . . can note with more exactitude and vividness than the prose of most living playwrights the atmosphere of mean streets and cheap lodgings.") And though *Mean Streets* has links to all those Richard Conte Italian-family movies, like *House of Strangers,* and to the urban-feudal life of *The Godfather,* the incidents and details are far more personal. Scorsese, who did the writing with Mardik Martin, knows the scene and knows how it all fits together; it's his, and he has the ability to put his feelings about it on the screen. All this is what the Boston Irish world of *The Friends of Eddie Coyle* lacked; the picture was shallow and tedious, because although we could see how the gangsters victimized each other, the police and the gangsters had no roots—and intertwined roots were what it was meant to be about. It was a milieu picture without milieu. In *Mean Streets,* every character, every sound is rooted in those streets. The back-and-forth talk of Charlie and Johnny Boy isn't little-people empty-funny (as it was in *Marty*); it's a tangle of jeering and joshing, of mutual goading and nerves getting frayed. These boys understand each other too well. Charlie's love for Johnny Boy is his hate for himself, and Johnny Boy knows Charlie's flaw. No other American gangster-milieu film has had this element of personal obsession; there has never before been a gangster film in which you felt that the director himself was saying, "This is my story." Not that we come away thinking that Martin Scorsese is or ever was a gangster, but we're so affected because we know in our bones that he has walked these streets and has felt what his characters feel. He knows how natural crime is to them.

There is something of the Carol Reed film *The Third Man* in the way the atmosphere imposes itself, and, like Reed, Scorsese was best known as an editor (on *Woodstock, Medicine Ball Caravan, Elvis on Tour,* C.B.S. documentaries, etc.) before he became a director *(Who's That Knocking at My Door?, Boxcar Bertha).* Graham Greene, the screenwriter of *The Third Man,* wrote a prescription for movies that fits this one almost perfectly. "The cinema," Greene said, "has always developed by means of a certain low cunning.... We are driven back to the 'blood,' the thriller.... We have to ... dive below the polite level, to something nearer to the common life.... And when we have attained to a more popular drama, even if it is in the simplest terms of blood on a garage floor ('There lay Duncan laced in his golden blood'), the scream of cars in flight, all the old excitements at their simplest and most sure-fire, then we can begin—secretly, with low cunning—to develop our poetic drama." And, again, "If you excite your audience first, you can put over what you will of horror, suffering, truth." However, Scorsese's atmosphere is without the baroque glamour of evil that makes *The Third Man* so ambiguous in its appeal. There's nothing hokey here; it is a low, malign world Scorsese sees. But it's seen to the beat of an exuberant, satiric score. Scorsese has an operatic visual style (the swarthy, imaginative cinematography is by Kent Wakeford), and, with Jonathan T. Taplin, the twenty-six-year-old rock-record impresario, as producer, he has used a mixture of records to more duplicit effect than anyone since Kenneth Anger in *Scorpio Rising.* It's similar to Bertolucci's use of a motley score in *Before the Revolution* and *The Conformist* and to the score in parts of *The Godfather,* but here the music is a more active participant. The score is the background music of the characters' lives—and not only the background, because it enters in. It's as if these characters were just naturally part of an opera with pop themes. The music is the electricity in the air of this movie; the music is like an engine that the characters move to. Johnny Boy, the most susceptible, half dances through the movie, and when he's trying to escape from Michael he does a jerky frug before hopping into the getaway car. He *enjoys* being out of control—he revels in it—and we can feel the music turning him on. But *Mean Streets* doesn't use music, as *Easy Rider* sometimes did, to do the movie's work for it. (In *American Graffiti,* the old-rock nostalgia catches the audience up before the movie even gets going.) The music here isn't our music, meant to put us in the mood of the movie, but the characters' music. And bits of old movies become part of the opera, too, because what the characters know of passion and death, and even of big-time gangsterism, comes from the movies. In Scorsese's vision, music and the movies work within us and set the terms in which we perceive ourselves. Music and the movies and the Church. A witches' brew.

Scorsese could make poetic drama, rather than melodrama laced with decadence, out of the schlock of shabby experience because he didn't have to "dive below the polite level, to something nearer to the common life" but had to do something much tougher—descend into himself and bring up what neither he nor anyone else could have known was there. Though he must have suspected. This is a blood thriller in the truest sense.

The New Yorker, October 8, 1973

THE WAY WE WERE

he Way We Were is a fluke—a torpedoed ship full of gaping holes which comes snugly into port. There is just about every reason for this film to be a disaster: the cinematography is ugly; several scenes serve no purpose, and the big dramatic sequences come butting in, like production numbers, out of nowhere; the decisive change in the characters' lives which the story hinges on takes place suddenly and hardly makes sense; a whining title-tune ballad embarrasses the picture in advance, and it has the excruciating score of a bad forties movie. Yet the damned thing is enjoyable. It stays afloat because of the chemistry of Barbra Streisand and Robert Redford. The movie is about two people who are wrong for each other, and Streisand and Redford are an ideal match to play this mismatch: Katie Morosky, always in a rush, a frizzy-haired Jewish girl from New York with a chip on her shoulder; and Hubbell Gardiner, a Wasp jock from Virginia with straw hair and the grin of a well-fed conquistador. She's a hyper-emotional Communist who's always sure she's right; he is incapable of any kind of commitment. The movie, directed by Sydney Pollack—from Arthur Laurents's novel, which reads like a screenplay—deals with their collision course. Theirs isn't a Bridget-loves-Bernie type of marriage. He tells her she pushes too hard, and she answers that she'll push him to be what he should be—which she thinks is a great writer. A hideous basis for a marriage—and she can't stand his friends. We can see what draws them to each other: she's attracted to the fairy-tale prince in him, and he can't tear himself away from her emotionality, from her wistfulness and drive. And we can certainly see what creates the tension between them; Katie and Hubbell have been breaking up since they got together.

The picture opens in New York in 1944, goes back to their college days (Class of 1937), and then returns to 1944 and goes on to their married life in Hollywood, where he becomes a screenwriter and she a reader for a studio; it continues through the onset of the blacklisting troubles, breaking off in 1948, with a coda in New York in the early fifties. I offer this chronology as a libretto, because the movie has the sweat stains of interfering hands and is so bewildering about the passage of time that you can't tell how long Katie and Hubbell have been married before she gets pregnant, and, once she is, she seems to stay that way for years. The climactic Hollywood section, which should have been played for high irony, is so botched and overwrought that

511

the picture becomes more hysterical than Katie. The changes she goes through are, however, psychologically accurate: the quicksilver gaucheness as an undergraduate in the thirties; the wavy long bob and the carefully groomed attempt to emulate a woman of the world in the forties; the more relaxed Los Angeles style; and then the recovery of the earlier look, but accepted by her now, in the fifties. Her changes are attempts to get closer to Hubbell's style, whereas he stays much the same—very much the same, since Redford doesn't pass for college-student age as easily as Streisand does.

The movie doesn't overtly take sides in the characters' political arguments, but its simplifications put the past in a phony perspective. This is worth noting, I think, because movies seep through the consciousness of audiences. We laugh now at the old story about Clark Gable's destroying the undershirt industry when the whole country discovered he wasn't wearing one in *It Happened One Night,* but applications for admission to Radcliffe skyrocketed after the movie of *Love Story* came out. And a lot of people get their knowledge of history from movies. (In some schools, history is now being taught with the aid of movies set in the past.) Because of the sordid injustices to the black-listed, and their suffering, it's easy for new generations to get the idea that what they stood for politically was an intelligent and moral position. This movie doesn't actually say that, but it's the impression that the audience may come away with, because there appears to be nothing between Communist commitment and smug indifference. Hubbell makes valid points against Katie's blind faith in Stalin's policies, but since he represents polite cynicism and defeatism, her allegiance to those policies seems to be the only form of activism. (Implicitly, the movie accepts the line the Communist Party took—that it was the only group doing anything, so if you cared about peace or social injustice you had to join up.) Hubbell is reasonable when he tries to calm Katie down so they can have an evening together without her screaming at his Beekman Place spoiled rich friends, but in a movie a person who stands back and does nothing is likely to come out even worse than he should, in contrast to someone who is full of fervor and does something, however misguided and ineffective. Katie, who has no common sense, cares so much about everything, and cares so much for Hubbell, that our feelings go out to her, even when her outbursts are offensive—perhaps most when they're offensive, because we can see that she's destroying Hubbell's tolerance of both her and her politics.

There's another factor that puts the audience on Katie's side: Streisand. She has caught the spirit of the hysterical Stalinist workhorses of the thirties and forties—both the ghastly desperation of their self-righteousness and the warmth of their enthusiasm. Katie hangs on to her man as monomaniacally as she hangs on to the Party's shifting positions, but she's a painfully vulnerable woman, a woman of great sweetness, and Hubbell drowns in that sweetness. Redford's role is necessarily less colorful, but that doesn't do him a disservice. It's good to see Redford with a woman again after all that flirting with Paul Newman, and he has the glamour that is needed for the young Hubbell, and the opacity, the reserve. He gives a good performance whenever he can (in the college-classroom scene in which Hubbell's story is read aloud, and in the scene when Hubbell tells Katie that he's sold a story), though he's betrayed toward the end by the film editor, who allows him to be caught staring at her wonderingly a few too many times. (When Redford hasn't anything special to register, his blankly anguished look can get very stony.) At the end, Katie is a believer still, and still radiant, while Hubbell, a man with so many doubts he had nothing to sell out, remains tentative and tormented, but he's older, and drained. Streisand has her miraculous audience empathy, while Redford loses touch with us, but this is just as much what his personality and appeal are all about as that self-deprecating empathy of Streisand's is what her appeal is all about. The roles and the temperaments of the stars are inseparable here. That's what makes the movie so effective a throwback (with a political difference) to the romantic star vehicles of an earlier era. But when Redford's glamour is overdone and his white teeth glitter, the movie seems to share Katie's infatuation, and you have to laugh at yourself for what you're enjoying.

We've had time now to get used to Streisand. (A friend of mine who "couldn't stand her" in *Funny Girl* confessed that she had capitulated totally when she saw the film again, on television.) The tricky thing about the role of Katie Morosky is that Streisand must emphasize just that element in her own persona which repelled some people initially: her fast sass is defensive and aggressive in the same breath. But it's part of her gradual conquest of the movie public that this won't put people off now. Even the unflattering photography and the forties makeup (the bright-red lipstick is hideous on her large, expressive mouth—her finest, most sensitive feature) don't damage her.

At the moment, there are so few women stars in American movies: Streisand, Minnelli, Fonda, that charming, ultrafeminine survivor-waif Mia Farrow—anybody else? Shirley MacLaine hasn't been crinkling and twinkling lately; it's too soon to know if Liv Ullmann or Blythe Danner will get good enough parts; and that waxed blonde Faye Dunaway won't stir much interest unless somebody renovates her. A movie with a woman star or co-star has become a rarity, and the male-female story of *The Way We Were* gives it a vital connection to people's lives that the spoofy male-dominated odd-couple movies have often lacked; besides, the humor doesn't have to be so coy. It's hit entertainment, and maybe even memorable entertainment; it's a terrible movie because of that ugly glossy superstructure and the crushed midsection, but it's got Streisand and Redford, and some very well-written (Alvin Sargent was among the uncredited writers) and well-directed moments. I'm not sure it's going to be possible for people who know Sydney Pollack to look him in the eye after they watch Streisand and Redford making love in front of a sexy fire while the plaintive schlock music rises up in the general direction of paradise, but at least there are no sexy storms.

The New Yorker, October 15, 1973

THE LONG GOODBYE

Edmund Wilson summed up Raymond Chandler convincingly in 1945 when he said of *Farewell, My Lovely,* "It is not simply a question here of a puzzle which has been put together but of a malaise conveyed to the reader, the horror of a hidden conspiracy which is continually turning up in the most varied and unlikely forms. . . . It is only when I get to the end that I feel my old crime-story depression descending upon me again—because here again, as is so often the case, the explanation of the mysteries, when it comes, is neither interesting nor plausible enough. It fails to justify the excitement produced by the picturesque and sinister happenings, and I cannot help feeling cheated." Locked in the conventions of pulp writing, Raymond Chandler never found a way of dealing with that malaise. But Robert Altman does, in *The Long Goodbye,* based on Chandler's 1953 Los Angeles-set novel. The movie is set in the same city twenty years later; this isn't just a matter of the private-detective hero's prices going from twenty-five dollars a day to fifty—it's a matter of rethinking the book and the genre. Altman, who probably works closer to his unconscious than any other American director, tells a detective story, all right, but he does it through a spree—a high-flying rap on Chandler and the movies and that Los Angeles sickness. The movie isn't just Altman's private-eye movie—it's his Hollywood movie, set in the mixed-up world of movie-influenced life that is L.A.

In Los Angeles, you can live any way you want (except the urban way); it's the fantasy-brothel, where you can live the fantasy of your choice. You can also live well without being rich, which is the basic and best reason people swarm there. In that city—the pop amusement park of the shifty and the uprooted, the city famed as the place where you go to sell out—Raymond Chandler situated his incorruptible knight Philip Marlowe, the private detective firmly grounded in high principles. Answering a letter in 1951, Chandler wrote, "If being in revolt against a corrupt society constitutes being immature, then Philip Marlowe is extremely immature. If seeing dirt where there is dirt constitutes an inadequate social adjustment, then Philip Marlowe has inadequate social adjustment. Of course Marlowe is a failure, and he knows it. He is a failure because he hasn't any money. . . . A lot of very good men have been failures because their particular talents did not suit their time and place." And he cautioned, "But you must remember that Marlowe is not a real person. He is a creature of fantasy. He is in a false position because I put him there. In real life, a man of his type would no more be a private detective than he would be a university don." Six months later, when his rough draft of *The Long Goodbye* was criticized by his agent, Chandler wrote back, "I didn't care whether the mystery was fairly obvious, but I cared about the people, about this strange corrupt world we live in, and how any man who tried to be honest looks in the end either sentimental or plain foolish."

Chandler's sentimental foolishness is the taking-off place for Altman's film. Marlowe (Elliott Gould) is a wryly forlorn knight, just slogging along. Chauffeur, punching bag, errand boy, he's used, lied to, double-crossed. He's the gallant fool in a corrupt world—the innocent eye. He isn't stupid and he's immensely likable, but the pulp pretense that his chivalrous code was armor has collapsed, and the romantic machismo of Bogart's Marlowe in *The Big Sleep* has evaporated. The one-lone-idealist-in-the-city-crawling-with-rats becomes a schlemiel who thinks he's tough and wise. (He's still driving a 1948 Lincoln Continental and trying to behave like Bogart.) He doesn't know the facts of life that everybody else knows; even the police know more about the case he's involved in than he does. Yet he's the only one who *cares*. That's his true innocence, and it's his slack-jawed crazy sweetness that keeps the movie from being harsh or scabrous.

Altman's goodbye to the private-eye hero is comic and melancholy and full of regrets. It's like cleaning house and throwing out things that you know you're going to miss—there comes a time when junk dreams get in your way. *The Long Goodbye* reaches a satirical dead end that kisses off the private-eye form as gracefully as *Beat the Devil* finished off the cycle of the international-intrigue thriller. Altman does variations on Chandler's theme the way the John Williams score does variations on the title song, which is a tender ballad in one scene, a funeral dirge in another. Williams's music is a parody of the movies' frequent overuse of a theme, and a demonstration of how adaptable a theme can be. This picture, less accidental than *Beat the Devil*, is just about as funny, though quicker-witted, and dreamier, in soft, mellow color and volatile images—a reverie on the lies of old movies. It's a knockout of a movie that has taken eight months to arrive in New York because after opening in Los Angeles last March and being badly received (perfect irony) it folded out of town. It's probably the best American movie ever made that almost didn't open in New York. Audiences may have felt they'd already had it with Elliott Gould; the young men who looked like him in 1971 have got cleaned up and barbered and turned into Mark Spitz. But it actually adds poignancy to the film that Gould himself is already an anachronism.

Thinner and more lithe than in his brief fling as a superstar (his success in *Bob & Carol & Ted & Alice* and *M*A*S*H* led to such speedy exploitation of his box-office value that he appeared in seven films between 1969 and 1971), Gould comes back with his best performance yet. It's his movie. The rubber-legged slouch, the sheepish, bony-faced angularity have their grace; drooping-eyed, squinting, with more blue stubble on his face than any other hero on record, he's a loose and woolly, jazzy Job. There's a skip and bounce in his shamble. Chandler's arch, spiky dialogue—so hardboiled it can make a reader's teeth grate—gives way to this Marlowe's muttered, befuddled throwaways, his self-sendups. Gould's Marlowe is a man who is had by everybody—a male pushover, reminiscent of Fred MacMurray in *Double*

Indemnity. He's Marlowe as Miss Lonelyhearts. Yet this softhearted honest loser is so logical a modernization, so "right," that when you think about Marlowe afterward you can't imagine any other way of playing him now that wouldn't be just fatuous. (Think of Mark Spitz as Marlowe if you want fatuity pure.) The good-guys-finish-last conception was implicit in Chandler's L.A. all along, and Marlowe was only one step from being a clown, but Chandler pulped his own surrogate and made Marlowe, the Victorian relic, a winner. Chandler has a basic phoniness that it would have been a cinch to exploit. He wears his conscience right up front; the con trick is that it's not a writer's conscience. Offered the chance to break free of the straitjacket of the detective novel, Chandler declined. He clung to the limiting stereotypes of pop writing and blamed "an age whose dominant note is an efficient vulgarity, an unscrupulous scramble for the dollar." Style, he said, "can exist in a savage and dirty age, but it cannot exist in the Coca-Cola age . . . the Book of the Month, and the Hearst Press." It was Marlowe, the independent man, dedicated to autonomy—his needs never rising above that twenty-five dollars a day—who actually lived like an artist. Change Marlowe's few possessions, "a coat, a hat, and a gun," to "a coat, a hat, and a typewriter," and the cracks in Chandler's myth of the hero become a hopeless split.

Robert Altman is all of a piece, but he's complicated. You can't predict what's coming next in the movie; his plenitude comes from somewhere beyond reason. An Altman picture doesn't have to be great to be richly pleasurable. He tosses in more than we can keep track of, maybe more than *he* bothers to keep track of; he nips us in surprising ways. In *The Long Goodbye,* as in *M*A*S*H,* there are climaxes, but you don't have the sense of waiting for them, because what's in between is so satisfying. He underplays the plot and concentrates on the people, so it's almost all of equal interest, and you feel as if it could go on indefinitely and you'd be absorbed in it. Altman may have the most glancing touch since Lubitsch, and his ear for comedy is better than anybody else's. In this period of movies, it isn't necessary (or shouldn't be) to punch the nuances home; he just glides over them casually, in the freest possible way. Gould doesn't propel the action as Bogart did; the story unravels around the private eye—the corrupt milieu wins. Maybe the reason some people have difficulty getting onto Altman's wavelength is that he's just about incapable of overdramatizing. He's not a pusher. Even in this film, he doesn't push decadence. He doesn't heat up angst the way it was heated in *Midnight Cowboy* and *They Shoot Horses, Don't They?*

■ ■ ■

Pop culture takes some nourishment from the "high" arts, but it feeds mainly on itself. *The Long Goodbye* had not been filmed before, because the book came out too late, after the private-eye-movie cycle had peaked. Marlowe had already become Bogart, and you could see him in it when you read the book. You weren't likely to have kept the other Marlowes of the forties (Dick Powell, Robert Montgomery, George Montgomery) in your mind, and you had to see somebody in it. The novel reads almost like a parody of pungent writing—like a semi-literate's idea of great writing. The detective-novel genre always verged on self-parody, because it gave you nothing under the surface. Hemingway didn't need to state what his characters felt, because his external descriptions implied all that, but the pulp writers who imitated Hemingway followed the hardboiled-detective pattern that Hammett had invented; they externalized everything and implied nothing. Their gaudy terseness demonstrates how the novel and the comic strip can merge. They described actions and behavior from the outside, as if they were writing a script that would be given some inner life by the actors and the director; the most famous practitioners of the genre were, in fact, moonlighting screenwriters. *The Long Goodbye* may have good descriptions of a jail or a police lineup, but the prose is alternately taut and lumpy with lessons in corruption, and most of the great observations you're supposed to get from it are just existentialism with oil slick. With its classy dames, a Marlowe influenced by Marlowe, the obligatory tension between Marlowe and the cops, and the sentimental bar scenes, *The Long Goodbye* was a product of the private-eye films of the decade before. Chandler's corrupt milieu—what Auden called "The Great Wrong Place"—was the new-style capital of sin, the city that made the movies and was made by them.

In Chandler's period (he died in 1959), movies and novels interacted; they still do, but now the key interaction may be between movies and movies—and between movies and us. We can no longer view ourselves—the way Nathanael West did—as different from the Middle Westerners in L.A. lost in their movie-fed daydreams, and the L.A. world founded on pop is no longer the world *out there,* as it was for Edmund Wilson. Altman's *The Long Goodbye* (like Paul Mazursky's *Blume in Love*) is about people who live in L.A. because they like the style of life, which comes from the movies. It's not about people who work in movies but about people whose lives have been shaped by them; it's set in the modern L.A. of the stoned sensibility, where people have given in to the beauty that always looks unreal. The inhabitants are an updated gallery of California freaks, with one character who links this world to Nathanael West's—the Malibu Colony gatekeeper (Ken Sansom), who does ludicrous, pitiful impressions of Barbara Stanwyck in *Double Indemnity* (which was Chandler's first screenwriting job), and of James Stewart, Walter Brennan, and Cary Grant (the actor Chandler said he had in mind for Marlowe). In a sense, Altman here has already made *Day of the Locust*. (To do it as West intended it, and to have it make contemporary sense, it would now have to be set in Las Vegas.) Altman's references to movies don't stick out—they're just part of the texture, as they are in L.A.—but there are enough so that a movie pedant could do his own weirdo version of *A Skeleton Key to Finnegans Wake.*

The one startlingly violent action in the movie is performed by a syndicate boss who is as rapt in the glory of his success as a movie mogul. Prefigured in Chandler's description of movie producers in his famous essay "Writers in Hollywood," Marty Augustine (Mark Rydell) is the next step up in paranoid self-congratulation from the Harry Cohn-like figure that Rod Steiger played in *The Big Knife;* he's freaked out on success, L.A.-Las Vegas style. His big brown eyes with their big brown bags preside over the decaying pretty-boy face of an Eddie Fisher, and when he flashes his ingenuous Paul Anka smile he's so appalling he's comic. His violent act is outrageously gratuitous (he smashes a Coke bottle in the fresh young face of his unoffending mistress), yet his very next line of dialogue is so comic-tough that we can't help laughing while we're still gasping, horrified—much as we did when Cagney shoved that half grapefruit in Mae Clarke's nagging kisser. This little Jewish gangster-boss is a mod imp—offspring of the movies, as much a creature of show business as Joel Grey's m.c. in *Cabaret.* Marty Augustine's bumbling goon squad (ethnically balanced) are the illegitimate sons of Warner Brothers. In the Chandler milieu, what could be better casting than the aristocratic Nina van Pallandt as the rich dish—the duplicitous blonde, Mrs. Wade? And, as her husband, the blocked famous writer Roger Wade, Sterling Hayden, bearded like Neptune, and as full of the old mach as the progenitor of tough-guy writing himself. The most movieish bit of dialogue is from the book: when the police come to question Marlowe about his friend Terry Lennox, Marlowe says, "This is where I say, 'What's this all about?' and you say, 'We ask the questions.'" But the resolution of Marlowe's friendship with Terry isn't from Chandler, and its logic is probably too brutally sound for Bogart-lovers to stomach. Terry Lennox (smiling Jim Bouton, the baseball player turned broadcaster) becomes the Harry Lime in Marlowe's life, and the final sequence is a variation on *The Third Man,* with the very last shot a riff on the leave-taking scenes of the movies' most famous clown.

The movie achieves a self-mocking fairy-tale poetry. The slippery shifts within the frames of Vilmos Zsigmond's imagery are part of it, and so are the offbeat casting (Henry Gibson as the sinister quack Dr. Verringer; Jack Riley, of the Bob Newhart show, as the piano player) and the dialogue. (The script is officially credited to the venerable pulp author Leigh Brackett; she also worked on *The Big Sleep* and many other good movies, but when you hear the improvised dialogue you can't take this credit literally.) There are some conceits that are fairly precarious (the invisible-man stunt in the hospital sequence) and others that are waywardly funny (Marlowe trying to lie to his cat) or suggestive and beautiful (the Wades' Doberman coming out of the Pacific with his dead master's cane in his teeth). When Nina van Pallandt thrashes in the ocean at night, her pale-orange butterfly sleeves rising above the surf, the movie becomes a rhapsody on romance and death. What separates Altman from other directors is that time after time he can attain crowning visual effects like this and they're so elusive they're never precious. They're like ribbons tying up the whole history of movies. It seems unbelievable that people who looked at this picture could have given it the reviews they did.

■　■　■

The out-of-town failure of *The Long Goodbye* and the anger of many of the reviewers, who reacted as if Robert Altman were a destroyer, suggest that the picture may be on to something bigger than is at first apparent. Some speculations may be in order. Marlowe was always a bit of a joke, but did people take him that way? His cynical exterior may have made it possible for them to accept him in Chandler's romantic terms, and really—below the joke level—believe in him. We've all read Chandler on his hero: "But down these mean streets a man must go who is not himself mean, who is neither tarnished nor afraid." He goes, apparently, in our stead. And as long as he's there—the walking conscience of the world—we're safe. We could easily reject sticky saviors, but a cynical savior satisfies the Holden Caulfield in us. It's an adolescent's dream of heroism—someone to look after you, a protector like Billy Jack. And people cleave to the fantasies they form while watching movies.

After reading *The Maltese Falcon,* Edmund Wilson said of Dashiell Hammett that he "lacked the ability to bring the story to imaginative life." Wilson was right, of course, but this may be the basis of Hammett's appeal; when Wilson said of the detective story that "as a department of imaginative writing, it looks to me completely dead," he was (probably intentionally) putting it in the wrong department. It's precisely the fact that the detective novel is engrossing but does not impinge on its readers' lives or thoughts that enables it to give a pleasure to some which is distinct from the pleasures of literature. It has no afterlife when they have closed the covers; it's completely digested, like a game of casino. It's a structured time killer that gives you the illusion of being speedy; *The Long Goodbye* isn't a fast read, like Hammett, but when I finished it I had no idea whether I'd read it before. Essentially, we've all read it before.

But when these same stories were transferred to the screen, the mechanisms of suspense could strike fear in the viewer, and the tensions could grow almost unbearable. The detective story on the screen became a thriller in a much fuller sense than it had been on the page, and the ending of the movie wasn't like shutting a book. The physical sensations that were stirred up weren't settled; even if we felt cheated, we were still turned on. We left the theater in a state of mixed exhilaration and excitement, and the fear and guilt went with us. In our dreams, we were menaced, and perhaps became furtive murderers. It is said that in periods of rampant horrors readers and moviegoers like to experience imaginary horrors, which can be resolved and neatly put away. I think it's more likely that in the current craze for horror films like *Night of the Living Dead* and *Sisters* the audience wants an intensive dose of the fear sickness—not to confront fear and have it conquered but to feel that crazy, inexplicable delight that children get out of terrifying stories that give them bad dreams. A flesh-crawler that affects as many senses as a horror movie can doesn't end with the neat fake solution. We are always aware that the solution will not really explain the terror we've felt; the forces of madness are never laid to rest.

Suppose that through the medium of the movies pulp, with its five-and-dime myths, can take a stronger hold on people's imaginations than art, because it doesn't affect the conscious imagination, the way a great novel does, but the private, hidden imagination, the primitive fantasy life—and with an immediacy that leaves no room for thought. I have had more mail from adolescents (and post-adolescents) who were badly upset because of a passing derogatory remark I made about *Rosemary's Baby* than I would ever get if I mocked Tolstoy. Those adolescents think *Rosemary's Baby* is great because it upsets them. And I suspect that people are reluctant to say goodbye to the old sweet bull of the Bogart Marlowe because it satisfies a deep need. They've been accepting the I-look-out-for-No.1 tough guys of recent films, but maybe they're scared to laugh at Gould's out-of-it Marlowe because that would lose them their Bogart icon. At the moment, the shared pop culture of the audience may be all that people feel they have left. The negative reviews kept insisting that Altman's movie had nothing to do with Chandler's novel and that Elliott Gould wasn't Marlowe. People still want to believe that Galahad is alive and well in Los Angeles—biding his time, perhaps, until movies are once again "like they used to be."

■ ■ ■

The jacked-up romanticism of movies like those featuring Shaft, the black Marlowe, may be so exciting it makes what we've always considered the imaginative artists seem dull and boring. Yet there is another process at work, too: the executive producers and their hacks are still trying to find ways to make the old formulas work, but the gifted filmmakers are driven to go beyond pulp and to bring into movies the qualities of imagination that have gone into the other arts. Sometimes, like Robert Altman, they do it even when they're working on pulp material. Altman's isn't a pulp sensibility. Chandler's, for all his talent, was.

The New Yorker, October 22, 1973

THE ICEMAN COMETH
MOMENTS OF TRUTH

The Iceman Cometh is a great, heavy, simplistic, mechanical, beautiful play. It is not the Eugene O'Neill masterpiece that *Long Day's Journey Into Night*, the finest work of the American theater, is, but it is masterpiece enough—perhaps the greatest thesis play of the American theater—and it has been given a straightforward, faithful production in handsome dark-toned color in the subscription series called the American Film Theatre. A filmed play like this doesn't offer the sensual excitement that movies *can* offer, but you don't go to it for that. You go to it for O'Neill's crude, prosaic virtuosity, which is also pure American poetry, and, as with most filmed dramas, if you miss the "presence" of the actors, you gain from seeing it performed by the sort of cast that rarely gathers in a theater. John Frankenheimer directed fluently and unobtrusively, without destroying the conventions of the play. The dialogue is like a ball being passed from one actor to the next; whenever possible (when the speakers are not too far apart), the camera pans smoothly from one to another. We lose some of the ensemble work we'd get from a live performance, but we gain a closeup view that allows us to see and grasp each detail. The play here is less broad than it would be on the stage, and Frankenheimer wisely doesn't aim for laughs at the characters' expense (even those that O'Neill may have intended), because the people are so close to us. The actors become close to us in another way. Actors who have been starved for a good part get a chance to stretch and renew themselves. In some cases, we've been seeing them for years doing the little thing that passes for acting on TV and in bad movies, and their performances here are a revelation; in a sense, the actors who go straight for the occasion give the lie to the play's demonstration that bums who live on guilt for what they don't do can't go back and do it.

Set in 1912 in a waterfront saloon, much like the one in which O'Neill had attempted suicide that year, the play was written in the late thirties and was first produced in 1946, on Broadway, under his supervision, but it achieved its present eminence from the Circle in the Square revival in 1956, starring Jason Robards, who then appeared in the celebrated television version of 1960, directed by Sidney Lumet. The characters are drunken bums and whores who have found sanctuary in Harry Hope's flophouse saloon; each has a "pipe dream" that sustains him until Hickey the salesman, the "iceman," who attempts to free them all by stripping them of their lies and guilt, takes the life out of them. It is both a pre-Freudian play and a post-Freudian one, and that may be the source of the trouble people have "placing" it; you can't call this play dated, and you can't quite call it modern, either. The thesis is implicitly anti-Freudian: the play says that the truth destroys people—that it wipes them out. Like most thesis plays, this one rigs the situation to make its points. There are no planned surprises in O'Neill's world—no freak characters who go out and make good. The people forced by Hickey to rid themselves of illusions are such ruins that they can live only on false hopes; without illusions they have nothing. O'Neill has rather cruelly—and comically (which is the most cruel, I think, though others may say the most human)—designed the play to demonstrate that they're better off as lying, cadging bums. With his stageproof craft, O'Neill sets in motion a giant game of ten little Indians. Each of the many characters has his lie, and each in turn has it removed and must face his truth, and we look to see who's next. It's as if illusion were a veil, and under it lay truth. This simplistic view of illusion and reality is the limiting thesis device of the play, and O'Neill's demonstration that mankind is too weak to live without the protective veil is—well, maudlin. But O'Neill was too powerful and too instinctual a dramatist to stay locked within the thesis structure. Not quite all of mankind is reconciled to wearing the veil that protects the weak, and that's where the ambiguities burst through the mechanics of *The Iceman Cometh*.

The play is essentially an argument between Larry, an aging anarchist (Robert Ryan), and Hickey (Lee Marvin); they speak to each other as equals, and everything else is orchestrated around them. Larry speaks for pity and the necessity of illusions, Hickey for the curative power of truth. They're the two poles of consciousness that O'Neill himself is split between. Larry, a self-hating alcoholic, is a weak man and a windbag, but Robert Ryan brings so much understanding to Larry's weakness that the play achieves new dimensions. In the most difficult role he ever played on the screen, Ryan is superb. Larry's dirty "truth" is hidden under a pile of philosophizing, and the actor is stuck with delivering that philosophizing, which rings like the fakery it's meant to be but which we know O'Neill half believes. Ryan becomes O'Neill for us, I think. George Jean Nathan said that O'Neill carefully selected the photographs of himself that were to be published, and "always made sure that the photographs were not lacking in that impressive look of tragic handsomeness which was his." Ryan has that tragic handsomeness here and O'Neill's broken-man jowls, too, and at the end, when Larry is permanently "iced"—that is, stripped of illusion—we can see that this is the author's fantasy of himself: he alone is above the illusions that the others fall back on; he is tragic, while the others, with their restored illusions, have become comic. Yes, it's sophomoric to see yourself as the one who is doomed to live without illusions, but then so is the idea of the play sophomoric, and yet what O'Neill does with that sophomoric idea is masterly. And Ryan gets right to the boozy, gnarled soul of it. According to his associates, Ryan did not know he was dying until after the picture was finished, but he brought to this role the craft that he had perfected in his fifty-nine years and that he certainly knew he might never be able to exercise to its fullest again. The man who had tested himself against such uncompromisingly difficult roles on the stage as Coriolanus and the father in *Long Day's Journey* and on the screen as the depraved Claggart of *Billy Budd* got a last chance to show his stature, and he was ready. Ryan is so subtle he seems to have penetrated to the mystery of O'Neill's gaunt grandeur—to the artist's egotism and that Catholic Cassandra's pride in tragedy which goes along with the fond pity for the foolish clowns lapping up their booze.

Lee Marvin's Hickey is another matter. The characters have been waiting for Hickey, as for Godot, and his entrance is preceded by a whore who acts as herald; it's an unparalleled opportunity for an actor, as Jason Robards demonstrated so memorably in the TV version. I remember that during his long, scarily self-lacerating monologue I felt as if I couldn't breathe until it was finished. Suddenly, you knew that Hickey had been punishing the others for what he had been trying to live with, and that he was totally indifferent to them as people, and the play rose to heights you hadn't anticipated. But Hickey, with his edgy, untrustworthy affability, is a part for a certain kind of actor, and Lee Marvin isn't it. Marvin has a jokester's flair for vocal tricks and flip gestures; he can project the tough guy's impassive strength that is needed for the films he's generally in, and I don't think I've ever seen him give a bad performance in an action film. Here it's a matter not just of his not being up to it but of his being all wrong for it. We need to see the man under the salesman's exterior, and instead we realize how little interior life Marvin's action-film characters have had and how few expressive resources he has had besides a gleam in the eye. With his snub nose and long upper lip, he has a great camera face, but he's been acting for a long time now on star presence, and though that may be what you attract backers with, it's not what you play O'Neill with. What Marvin does is all on one level. At first, he's like a pudgy, complacent actor having a go at Mr. Scratch in *The Devil and Daniel Webster,* and then he just seems to coast. Hickey needs an element of irony and an awareness of horror; Marvin's Hickey exudes hostile, stupid arrogance—the impatience of the prosperous, well-fed, insensitive man with the sick. Marvin is so poorly equipped for the kind of acting required for Hickey that as the monologue approached I began to dread it. As it turns out, the monologue goes by without really being experienced by the viewer. Marvin's best recourse is to shout, because when he doesn't shout there's nothing going on. We don't seem to see this Hickey's eyes; Marvin offers us a blank face. He's thick, somehow, and irrelevantly vigorous. Marvin doesn't appear to have found anything in himself to draw on for the role. The film isn't destroyed by this performance, but it's certainly marred; yet who knows whether we will ever get a definitive version on film? We're lucky to get as much as we get here, even though the film never rises to the intensity that O'Neill put into the play. Frankenheimer has directed tactfully but not very probingly.

O'Neill is such an orderly madman: he neatly constructs a massive play around a weird conceit—the sexual wordplay on "come" in the title, which refers to Hickey's murderous explosion when he kills his wife. What we don't get, because of Marvin's one-level performance, are the terrifying intimations in this Strindbergian monologue that O'Neill is talking about himself and his wife—that he is giving Hickey the kind of raging emotion that is in *Long Day's Journey Into Night,* the kind that transcended O'Neill's ideas, yet that in this play he used to fuel his thesis. The intensity of the monologue should blow the play sky-high. Maybe O'Neill's conscious plan had become too easy to fulfill, and, as sometimes happened in Ibsen's greatest thesis plays, what was underneath the choice of subject suddenly boiled up. How, one may wonder, did Carlotta O'Neill take it as Hickey talked about the peace he found after he killed his wife? The play has a subtext that fuses with the thesis at this point, and the subtext is the hell and horror of marriage. Every character in the saloon who has talked about marriage has given us a variation on Hickey's murderous solution, and his monologue awakens Harry Hope (Fredric March) to expose his own loathing of the dead wife he's been sentimentalizing about for twenty years. O'Neill twists this male-female hatred in and out of his they-need-their-illusions thesis. It is he as dramatist who furiously, yet icily, tears away the sentimental illusions; that's what gives his kind of playwriting its power. It's not polite entertainment—not a show—but an exploration; he digs down as far as he can go. That he is the worst sentimentalist—the man who needs his illusions the most—is what makes him, like Tennessee Williams, so greatly to be felt for, and respected.

What this play seems to say, in the end, is that O'Neill the man of pity is the illusion, and that the only man he respects is the man without illusions. (I think one could say that it is just the opposite for Williams—that he abandons the man without illusions.) It's Larry, the man too full of self-loathing even to get drunk—Larry the man of pity—who refuses to offer the eighteen-year-old Parritt (Jeff Bridges) any comfort or hope, who judges him pitilessly and sends him to his death. Parritt has come to see Larry, the one person who was ever kind to him, asking to be helped. And Larry, the kindly spokesman for the necessity of illusion, doesn't want to help Parritt lie to himself; he wants him dead. It's a cruel, ambiguous kicker in the neat-looking finish. Larry's compassion, it seems, extends only to those he's not emotionally involved with. O'Neill makes Larry a hard man, finally, and desolate and unyielding, like himself. And though the bums are restored to their illusions, it's a fools' paradise regained; there's a streak of contempt in O'Neill's final view of them. O'Neill gives the lie to his own thesis: the bums need illusions not in order to be fully human (as would be the case in Tennessee Williams) but because they're weak. Those who find life without illusions insupportable are poor slobs—not strong enough to face truth and be broken by it. Hickey deceived himself about why he killed his wife; Larry, the self-hater, the only man Hickey succeeded in stripping of illusions, is, at the end, the iceman. He's stone sober, like the O'Neill of the photographs. How could anyone look at O'Neill's face and believe that he's telling people to be happy with their illusions? Sure, O'Neill is destroyed by "the truth," but he thinks he lives with "truth"; that's the secret in that haunted, sunken-jawed, angry face. And if he didn't linger on the implications of Larry's position at the end, maybe it's because he didn't dare to examine the false glory in it. It's hubris if ever there was hubris in an American play; it's also a common delusion of the mad.

It was only when, in *Long Day's Journey Into Night*, O'Neill abandoned the mechanistic dualisms (such as illusion and truth here) which he used as the underpinnings of his plays—and which make them look dated yet give them structural clarity and easy-to-take-home "serious" themes—that he could see people whole. But though the characters in *Iceman* are devised for a thesis, and we never lose our consciousness of that, they are nevertheless marvellously playable. Fredric March, like Ryan, can let the muscles in his face sag to hell to show a character falling apart. He interprets Harry Hope (who could be a dismal bore) with so much quiet tenderness and skill that when Harry regains his illusions and we see March's muscles tone up we don't know whether to smile for the character or for the actor. March is such an honorable actor; he's had a long and distinguished career. On the stage since 1920, in movies since 1929, and at seventy-six he goes on taking difficult roles; he's not out doing TV commercials or grabbing a series. At a press conference just before the 1946 opening of *The Iceman Cometh*, Eugene O'Neill said that the secret of happiness was contained in one simple sentence: "For what shall it profit a man if he shall gain the whole world and lose his own soul?" I think that once again he was being simplistic (O'Neill didn't sell his own soul, and I seriously doubt he was a happy man), but what he said has a basic truth in terms of the life of theater people. Taking on a role in *The Iceman Cometh* is a moment of truth for an actor. One of the pleasures is the way Bradford Dillman (a hole in the screen in *The Way We Were*) passes the test here. As Willie, singing his Harvard drinking song and shaking from the DTs, Dillman is funny and lively—like a Rip Torn without pent-up aggression. It's a small but flawless performance; you can almost taste the actor's joy in the role—in *working* again. Jeff Bridges has been working all along; he's one of the lucky ones in Hollywood—so fresh and talented that just about every movie director with a good role wants him for it. But he has been cast as a country boy *(The Last Picture Show, Fat City, Bad Company, The Last American Hero)* and used for his "natural" ease on the screen—used, that is, for almost the opposite of what a stage actor needs. What he does here as the kid Parritt (it's the role that Robert Redford played in the TV version) is a complete change from the improvisational style he has developed, and initially it is a thankless role, a pain, really—one of those hideously-obvious-guilty-secret roles that you wish weren't in the play. Every line Parritt utters tells of his guilt. But, of course, O'Neill knew what he was doing; the obviousness turns out to be necessary, and when it pays off in Parritt's big scenes with Larry, Bridges, looking as young as the role requires, and so powerfully built that his misery has physical force, comes through. He is convincing-looking as a boy of that period, and he makes an almost impossibly schematic role believable. Toward the end, there is an instant while he's looking at Larry when his face is childishly soft and vulnerable; it's this instant that reminds us to be grateful for what a camera can add to the experience of a play.

We may think we could do without the irritating repetition of the term "pipe dream," and I know that at times I felt I could do without the three painted whores and maybe without the captain and the general who are still fighting the Boer War (though not without the actors who play them—Martyn Green and George Voskovec). But in O'Neill the laborious and the mysterious are peculiarly inextricable, and, with actors like Sorrell Booke as Hugo (which he played in the 1960 TV version), and Moses Gunn as Joe, and Tom Pedi as Rocky (which he played on Broadway in 1946 and again on TV in 1960), and John McLiam as a lyrically sad Jimmy Tomorrow, the four hours less a minute have a special grace. It was O'Neill's genius to discover what no other dramatist has—that banality in depth can let loose our common demons.

The New Yorker, November 5, 1973

ABOUT
THE BATTLE OF ALGIERS,
FROM POLITICS AND THRILLS

The first wave of revolutionary politics on film came from the newly formed Soviet Union; its masters were Eisenstein, Dovzhenko, and Pudovkin. The second wave broke in 1966, with Gillo Pontecorvo and *The Battle of Algiers*, probably the most emotionally stirring revolutionary epic since Eisenstein's *Potemkin* (1925) and Pudovkin's *Mother* (1926). After him have come Costa-Gavras—with the modern classic political thriller *Z*, in 1969, and then *The Confession*, and *State of Siege*, all three starring Yves Montand—and Pontecorvo again, with *Burn!*, in 1970, and Francesco Rosi, with *The Mattei Affair*, in 1973. Approaching filmmaking as a political act and trying to reach a large audience by putting political material into popular forms, the writers and directors have found themselves sacrificing meaning to thrills, or thrills to meaning. Yet their work has had a potency that ordinary films haven't; their subjects were new to the screen and made restorative contact with the actual world. And even though most of the films weren't imaginatively satisfying, they raised political and aesthetic questions, and showed the intelligence of directors aware of the problems they'd got into.

Like *Potemkin*, *The Battle of Algiers* is an epic in the form of a "created documentary," with the oppressed, angry masses as the hero. The imperialist enemy and class enemy of the Algerian National Liberation Front—the hyperintelligent French colonel played by Jean Martin—isn't really a character; he represents the cool, inhuman manipulative power of imperialism versus the animal heat of the multitudes rushing toward us as they rise against their oppressors. Pontecorvo and his writer, Franco Solinas, were almost too clever in their use of this device of the colonel—yet it works, and brilliantly. The revolutionaries forming their pyramid of cells didn't need to express revolutionary consciousness, because the French colonel was given such a full counter-revolutionary consciousness that he said it all for them. He even expressed the knowledge that history was on the side of the oppressed colonial peoples, who would win; he himself was merely part of a holding action, preserving imperialism a little longer but bound to fail. To put it satirically but, in terms of the movie, accurately, the Algerian people were spontaneously turned into revolutionaries by historical events, and if they hadn't studied Marx, the counter-revolutionaries had, and knew they were on the wrong side and were doomed by history. In Eisenstein's revolutionary "documentaries," his technique—the formal design of the images, the dynamics of their interaction—had visceral impact, but the films were like giant posters in motion, and the harshly simplified contrasts (the inhumanity of the officers versus the generous camaraderie of the common sailors and soldiers) made one completely aware of the loaded message. In *The Battle of Algiers,* the movie hardly seems to be "saying" anything, yet the historical-determinist message seeps right into your bones. As a propaganda film, it ranks with Leni Riefenstahl's big-game rally, the 1935 *Triumph of the Will,* and it's the one great revolutionary "sell" of modern times.

The Battle of Algiers has a firebrand's fervor; it carries you with it, and doesn't give you time to think. Since the colonel provides the Marxist ideology of the picture, the revolutionaries are spared any taint of ideology (even though you observe how the N.L.F. leadership serves as a spearhead), and the inevitability of the ultimate victory of revolution is established to your—almost ecstatic—emotional relief. You may even accept the movie's implicit message that the N.L.F.'s violent methods are the only way to freedom. Pontecorvo's inflammatory passion works directly on your feelings, saying that both sides kill in a revolution and that it's unavoidable, saying that the bombs set in a city by revolutionaries—resulting in the death of men and women and children—are regrettable but justified, because this movement toward freedom is natural and unstoppable and good. The special genius of Pontecorvo as a Marxist filmmaker is that, though the masses are the hero, he has a feeling for the beauty and primitive terror in faces, and you're made to care for the oppressed people—to think of them not as masses but as people. Pontecorvo—the most dangerous kind of Marxist, a Marxist poet—shows us the raw strength of the oppressed, and the birth pangs of freedom. He gives us a portrait of a revolution that explains it and justifies whatever is done in its name, and serves as the most impassioned, most astute call to revolution ever. (The film, an Italian and Algerian co-production, is said to be the first feature ever made in Algeria; born in Italy, Gillo Pontecorvo is a younger brother of the famous Bruno Pontecorvo, the atomic physicist, part of Fermi's team, who worked in this country and then at Harwell, and disappeared into Russia in 1950, subsequently winning the Lenin Prize.)

No one has carried "immediacy" farther than Pontecorvo—neither Rossellini, from whose post-Second World War films, such as *Open City* (1945) and *Paisan* (1946), he learned so much, nor Francesco Rosi, who had experimented in a similar direction in *Salvatore Giuliano,* a 1962 political "created documentary" that Franco Solinas worked on. *The Battle of Algiers* is probably the only film that has ever made middle-class audiences believe in the necessity of bombing innocent people—perhaps because Pontecorvo made it a *tragic* necessity. In none of the political melodramas that were to follow from his epic is there any sequence that comes near to the complex overtones of the sorrowful acceptance with which each of the three bomb-planting women looks to see who will be killed by her bomb. Pontecorvo produces these mixed emotions in us and *still* is able to carry most of us with him. I think people's senses are so overwhelmed by the surging inevitability of the action that they are prepared to support what in another context—such as newsprint—they would reject. It's practically rape of the doubting intelligence. In *The Battle of Algiers,* music becomes a form of agitation: at times, the strange percussive sound is like an engine that can't quite start; pounding music gives the audience a sense of impending horror at each critical point; the shrill, rhythmic, birdlike cries from the Casbah tell us that all life is trilling and screaming for freedom.

The New Yorker, November 19, 1973

DON'T LOOK NOW
LABYRINTHS

Nicolas Roeg employs fast, almost subliminal imagery in the new English film *Don't Look Now,* and his entire splintering style affects one subliminally. The unnerving cold ominousness that he imparts to the environment says that things are not what they seem, and one may come out of the theater still seeing shock cuts and feeling slightly dissociated. The environment may briefly be fractured; for me ten minutes or so passed before it assembled itself and lost that trace of hostile objectivity. I don't recall having had this sort of residue of visual displacement from a movie before, but it's reasonable if one has been looking at a splintered universe for almost two hours. And one looks at this picture with intense concentration, because here life is treated as a puzzle, and the clues are in visual cross-references that go by in split seconds. Afterward, the environment one moves into holds the danger of discontinuity, as if at any moment something frightening might be intercut. Roeg has an elegant, edgy style that speaks to us of the broken universe and our broken connections, of modern man's inability to order his experience and to find meaning and coherence in it. The style speaks of the lesions in our view of the world; everything on the screen is vaguely incongruous and unnatural. A child outdoors on his bicycle runs over a pane of glass; wherever one turns, there are cracks and spreading stains. But Roeg's modernist style is too good for the use he puts it to.

Taken from a Daphne du Maurier story of the occult, adapted by Alan Scott and Chris Bryant, *Don't Look Now* is about a young English couple (Donald Sutherland and Julie Christie) whose drowned daughter may or may not be sending them messages. The bereaved parents leave their surviving child in school and go to Venice—deserted at the end of the season—where the husband, an art restorer, works at repairing eroded church mosaics. The film, too, is a mosaic, organized on the basis of premonitions. (The present is visually interrupted by glimpses of the future.) The husband is psychic but refuses to admit it; he fails to give credence to the omens that appear to him, and so, misinterpreting them, is destroyed. The material is Daphne du Maurier, but it's treated in the intricate manner of Borges, whose face filled the screen and crowned the murderous climax of *Performance,* the first film Roeg directed (with Donald Cammell as co-director). The atmosphere has too much class for the Gothic paraphernalia: the warnings unheeded, the city plagued by a mass murderer, the worrying bishop (Massimo Serato) with uncanny intuitions, and the ambiguous, dumpy, sub-Hitchcock sisters—one (Hilary Mason)blind and claiming to be psychic, the other (Clelia Matania) a chesty Helen Hokinson woman—who laugh together as if they were swindlers. We've seen all that before—with less style, it's true, but also with more vitality when it wasn't so convoluted and veneered with art. In a less refined picture, one mightn't be so critical of the way Roeg pulls out all the stops in the sisters' creaking, stagy scenes.

When you join the modernist sense of disorder to this canned Gothic mystery, you may satisfy only those who can accept the titillating otherworldly, but you can intrigue the more demanding, too. All that the movie really says to one is that Nicolas Roeg has a modern sensibility without having a modern mind—or, to put it another way, he has the style without the consciousness. And so the lesions are a form of high-fashion chic. It's a great commercial advantage to him not to have a fuller consciousness. Roeg doesn't examine the jaggedness, or ask the why of it, or try to find order within it; he uses this shattered vision to bring a Gothic story up to date. Put them together and you have the new international-celebrity look: the boy or girl looking like Bianca Jagger and talking about psychic phenomena. Unisex and ghosts in one smart, high-style package. And there they are on the screen—the modern couple, Julie Christie and Donald Sutherland, with matching curly hairdos.

The movie has a special ambience: the dislocation is eroticized, and rotting Venice, the labyrinthine city of pleasure, with its crumbling, leering gargoyles, is obscurely, frighteningly sensual. It's a Borgesian setting—the ruins tokens of a mysteriously indifferent universe; Venice might be a reptile-infested Mayan city discovered in a jungle. Roeg, drawn to Borges's tone—the controlled, systematic way in which Borges turns life into a mystical, malevolent nightmare—brings out the sensuality that is hidden in our response to the Borges cool. In *Don't Look Now,* the romanticism isn't of the traditional Gothic variety but a coolly enigmatic sexiness, and though it isn't strong enough to be a turn-on for a large popular audience, it gives the film a reticent, insinuating quality. Nothing in Roeg's style appears to be spontaneous or free-flowing; it's all artifice and technique. And yet the essence of the style is languor. *Don't Look Now* is the newest form of the trip movie. The young couple are at home in this jagged universe; they belong to it, and so does Roeg. He digs it, the way Joseph Losey dug the sunny rot and corruption in *Accident* and *The Go-Between,* but Roeg doesn't feel Losey's need to condemn the decadence that attracts him. *Don't Look Now* particularly recalls Losey's nutty *Secret Ceremony,* but Roeg isn't confused by a sense of shame. He thinks with his eyes, and puffs up what he sees. Roeg has taken Losey's luxuriant, richly ornamental style into a new domain; he may be the genius of chic that, in movies, Warhol and Morrissey only prefigured. Detached and psychedelic, *Don't Look Now* never touches our sympathies, never arouses any feeling for its characters. Roeg's vision is as impersonal and noncommittal as Warhol's, but with the gloss and craftsmanship of Losey. If the elliptical style says that things are not what they seem, it also says that though they're not as simple as people used to think they were, we don't have to worry about it, because they've all gone out of our grasp. We can relax and accept everything. To tie this together with a du Maurier story of the supernatural is to return to a pre-modernist account of why they're not what they seem. How blissfully, commercially acute to join our anxieties to superstition. And not even honest superstition but superstition used to relieve boredom— superstition as a deadpan camp. Believed in only as much as anything else is; that is, not believed in at all. This new Gothic of Roeg's is baby talk joined to dislocation. And isn't that just what Warhol was doing? Only Roeg joins the cool indifference to rich elegance. Maybe it's from the tension between the two that we get that faint, erotic vertigo. Roeg seems to say what Losey never dared to but what the audience for Losey was always responding to: that decay among the rich and beautiful is sexy. Actually, Losey's films and this one of Roeg's tantalize audiences in exactly the way that sad stories of the jazz age do; whatever Losey claimed to be doing, he was giving us the beautiful and damned in a fantasy playground for a daydreaming audience. Roeg, I suspect, knows what he's doing (though I imagine people will cook up the usual elaborate deep meanings for this film, just as they do for Losey's moralizing erotic fantasies).

Julie Christie and Donald Sutherland work together wonderfully here— maybe because their sexual differences are so muted. The other actors are merely exploited for sinister effects, and Roeg is crudely derivative in his handling of them, but his treatment of Christie and Sutherland has a highly original awareness. Psychologically, the film barely exists, but Roeg does so much with the two stars' faces—Sutherland's long and thin, Christie's desperately frail—that they become not characters but an archetype of the new couple: sophisticated, gallant, frightened. Sutherland gives a soft, fine-toned performance, and Christie is lovely—with that delicately rapacious jaw and the poignant eyes. She has the anxious face of a modern tragic muse. A key sex scene, with the two nude in bed, intercut with flash-forwards to their postcoital mood as they dress to go out together, is almost the reverse of a striptease. The images of their getting dressed—their bemused, distant expressions, their isolation from each other, and their movements getting into their perfect clothes—have an erotic glitter that displaces interest from their quiet, playfully tender coupling to its aftermath. (To avoid an X rating for the picture, this sequence has been slightly reëdited, but Roeg himself made the changes—substituting a few frames from the outtakes—and they are said to be so slight that someone seeing the English and American versions might not notice the difference.) The sequence is consistent with the whole premonitory scheme of the film, and it also relates to the way eroticism is displaced throughout; dressing is splintered and sensualized, like fear and death—death most of all, with splashes of red.

Roeg, who used to be a writer and director for British TV besides being a famous cinematographer, did the celebrated second-unit work on *Lawrence of Arabia* and was the cinematographer for *A Funny Thing Happened on the Way to the Forum* as well as for a number of Julie Christie's films—*Fahrenheit 451, Far from the Madding Crowd, Petulia*—which have, I think, a close relationship to his work here. It is the assumption in this film that the juxtaposition of images provides instant meaning. Roeg uses the technique, out of Alain Resnais, more effectively than Richard Lester did in *Petulia;* since Roeg doesn't get into complicated feelings or social attitudes, you don't question what he's saying. Despite the surreal portentousness of the atmosphere, the meanings are very simple, very much on a Hitchcock level, and are often organized with that same mechanical precision. But the deliberate mystification is a problem for Roeg that it wasn't for Hitchcock, because Roeg's systematic trickery doesn't quite jibe with the otherworldly. The discrepancy involved in a tightly planned, interlocking *mystery* made me impatient; the preordained can be experienced as the mechanically delayed. (Borges always keeps it short.) The final kicker is predictable, and strangely flat, because it hasn't been made to matter to us; fear is decorative, and there's nothing to care about in this worldly, artificial movie. Yet at a mystery level the movie can still affect the viewer; even the silliest ghost stories can. It's not that I'm not impressionable; I'm just not as proud of it as some people are. *Don't Look Now* gets fairly moldy when the hero confronts his red-hooded fate (seen rather too clearly). The non-believer hero destroyed by his refusal to trust his second sight (that old, old shtick—the agnostic punished because he refuses to believe in the supernatural) gives one such a strong whiff of Hollywood. But the picture is the fanciest, most carefully assembled Gothic enigma yet put on the screen; it's emblazoned in chic, and compared to such Gothics as *Seance on a Wet Afternoon* it's a masterwork. It's also trash.

In Borges, mystery and decadence come close together, and at the picture's consummation the perfect, beautiful couple are split by a hideous joke of nature—their own child become a dwarf monstrosity. Using du Maurier as a base, Roeg comes closer to getting Borges on the screen than those who have tried it directly, but there's a distasteful clamminess about the picture—not because Venice is dying (though this sure is a counter-commercial for Venice) but because Roeg's style is in love with disintegration. A little boy can look at his dead sister with no emotion in his face, but terror and decay are made radiant. Julie Christie is the perfect actress for Roeg, because her feelings are so exquisitely modulated and so small; she doesn't project with enough force to disturb the visual surface with rage or pain. Her jagged face—so extraordinarily beautiful yet not adding up right for ordinary beauty—might be the emblem of his style. She gives the picture a soul—but a soul in a body that's trembling on the verge of breakdown. Roeg is a chillingly chic director. *Don't Look Now* is shallow in a way that I think people are looking for right now; I can practically hear someone asking, "What's the matter with shallow?" This could be Warhol's legacy. *Don't Look Now* is going to be a great success, because it represents the new, high-fashion Gothic sensibility—what the movie audience is just getting into. But it's like an entertainment for bomb victims: nobody expects any real pleasure from it.

The New Yorker, December 24, 1973

SLEEPER

Woody Allen appears before us as the battered adolescent, scarred forever, a little too nice and much too threatened to allow himself to be aggressive. He has the city-wise effrontery of a shrimp who began by using language to protect himself and then discovered that language has a life of its own. The running war between the tame and the surreal—between Woody Allen the frightened nice guy trying to keep the peace and Woody Allen the wiseacre whose subversive fantasies keep jumping out of his mouth—has been the source of the comedy in his films. Messy, tasteless, and crazily uneven (as the best talking comedies have often been), the last two pictures he directed—*Bananas* and *Everything You Always Wanted to Know About Sex*—had wild highs that suggested an erratic comic genius. The tension between his insecurity and his wit makes us empathize with him; we, too, are scared to show how smart we feel. And he has found a nonaggressive way of dealing with urban pressures. He stays nice; he's not insulting, like most New York comedians, and he delivers his zingers without turning into a cynic. We enjoy his show of defenselessness, and even the I-don't-mean-any-harm ploy, because we see the essential sanity in him. We respect that sanity—it's the base from which he takes flight. At his top, in parts of *Bananas* and *Sex*, the inexplicably funny took over; it might be grotesque, it almost always had the flippant, corny bawdiness of a frustrated sophomore running amok, but it seemed to burst out—as the most inspired comedy does—as if we had all been repressing it. We laughed as if he had let out what we couldn't hold in any longer.

The surreal is itself tamed in Woody Allen's *Sleeper*, the most stable and most sustained of his films. (It also has the best title.) Easily the slapstick comedy of the year—there hasn't been any other—*Sleeper* holds together, as his sharpest earlier films failed to do; it doesn't sputter and blow fuses, like *Bananas* and *Sex*. It's charming—a very even work, with almost no thudding bad lines and with no low stretches. I can't think of anything much the matter with it; it's a small classic. But it doesn't have the loose, manic highs of those other films. You come out smiling and perfectly happy, but not driven crazy, not really turned on, the way his messier movies and some musicals *(Singin' in the Rain, Cabaret)* and some comic movies *(M*A*S*H, The Long Goodbye)* and parts of Paul Mazursky's movies can turn one on. I had a wonderful time at *Sleeper*, and I laughed all the way through, but it wasn't exhilarating. Allen's new sense of control over the medium and over his own material seems to level out the abrasive energy. You can be with it all the way, and yet it doesn't impose itself on your imagination—it dissolves when it's finished. If it sounds like a contradiction to say that *Sleeper* is a small classic and yet not exhilarating—well, I can't completely explain that. Comedy is impossibly mysterious; this is a beautiful little piece of work—it shows a development of skills in our finest comedy-maker—and yet it's mild, and doesn't quite take off.

Woody Allen plays a Rip Van Winkle who wakes up in 2173—and that's all I'm going to say about the story, because I don't want to squeeze the freshness out of the jokes. His girl is Diane Keaton (who was practically the only good thing in *Play It Again, Sam*), and she has a plucky, almost Jean Arthur quality. She's very appealing, and in *Sleeper* you want to like her; I always felt right on the verge of responding to her (as a broad-faced, Slavic-looking poet of the future), but she isn't quite funny enough. She has good bits (like her Brando parody), but her timing is indefinite, and so is the character she plays. She's really just there to be Woody's girl, and there's nobody else—other than Allen himself—you remember from the movie. *Sleeper* could really use a *cast*. In a Preston Sturges comedy, the various characters' madnesses and obsessions bounced off each other and got all scrambled up; Chaplin and Keaton had their big fellows to contend with; the Marx Brothers had each other, plus Margaret Dumont and Walter Woolf King and Sig Rumann and those blondes wriggling in satin. But Woody Allen has no set characters to respond to. He needs a great stock company, like Carol Burnett's (Who wants to be a crazy alone? That leads to melancholy), but so far in his movies he's the only character, because his conception of himself keeps him alone.

The Woody Allen character suffers, in all his films, from sex in the head which he figures his body can't get for him. It's the comedy of sexual inadequacy; what makes it hip rather than masochistic and awful is that he thinks women want the media macho ideal, and we in the audience are cued to suspect, as he secretly does, that that's the real inadequacy (social even more than sexual). Woody Allen is a closet case of potency; he knows he's potent, but he's afraid to tell the world—and adolescents and post-adolescents can certainly identify with that. His shrimp-hero's worst fear may be that he would be attractive only to women who feel sorry for him (or want to dominate him). The latter is parenthetical because Allen hasn't explored that possibility; the thought of him with, say, Anne Bancroft suggests the sort of gambit he hasn't tried. When we see his films, all our emotions attach to him; his fear and his frailty are what everything revolves around. No one else in his pictures has a vivid presence, or any particular quality except being a threat to him, and even that quality isn't really characterized. Maybe the reason he doesn't invest others with comic character (or even villainous character) is that he's so hung up that he has no interest in other people's hangups; that could be why his stories never really build to the big climactic finish one expects from a comedy. His plots don't tie a gigantic knot and then explode it, because the other characters aren't strong enough to carry the threads. The end of *Sleeper* is just a mild cutoff point—not bad but unexciting. The movie has a more conventional slapstick-comedy structure than *Bananas,* and slapstick isn't something you can do with a pickup cast. The comedy isn't forced, it looks relaxed and easy, but the routines don't gather momentum—they slide off somewhere. Woody Allen loses his supporting players along the way, and one hardly notices. It's likely that he sees his function as being all of us, and since he's all of us, nobody else can be anything.

But, being all of us, he can get too evenly balanced, he can lose his edge. Nobody else could have made *Bananas* or parts of *Sex,* but others could conceivably make a movie like *Sleeper,* just as others are beginning to write in the Woody Allen manner—and one of the most gifted of them, Marshall Brickman, is co-author of the *Sleeper* script. The humor here doesn't tap the mother lode; it's strip-mining. The movie is in the Woody Allen style, but it doesn't have the disruptive inspiration that is the unbalanced soul of Woody Allen. In interviews, Allen has often been quoted as saying that he wants to stay rough in his movie technique; I used to enjoy reading those quotes, because I thought he was right, and in *Bananas* his instinct to let the jokes run shapelessly loose instead of trimming them and making them tidy paid off. The effect was berserk, in an original way. But he tailored his play *Play It Again, Sam* in the smooth George S. Kaufman-Broadway style, and the movie version, which Herbert Ross directed even more smoothly (I hated it), turned out to be Woody Allen's biggest box-office success up to that time, and made him a mass-audience star. How could a man who really trusted the free and messy take up the clarinet, an instrument that appeals to controlled, precise people? You can't really goof around with a clarinet. (The group he plays with, the New Orleans Funeral and Ragtime Orchestra, can be heard on the *Sleeper* track, along with the Preservation Hall Jazz Band.) I think he knows that the free and messy is the right, great direction for his comedy, but he's very well organized, and, like most comedians, he really trusts success. He trusts laughs, and how can a comedian tell when they're not earned? He's a romantic comedian—he goes on believing in love and the simple, good things in life. He's also a very practical-man comedian—he's the harried, bespectacled nice guy who just wants to stay nice and be a success and get the girl. In terms of his aspirations, he's rather like Truffaut's Antoine Doinel—the unpretentious, hopeful joiner of the bourgeoisie—as a jester. In American terms, he's Harold Lloyd with Groucho's tongue.

To have found a clean visual style for a modern slapstick comedy in color is a major victory; Woody Allen learns with the speed of a wizard. *Sleeper* has a real look to it, and simple, elegant design. (The robot servants of the future, in their tuxedos, might be windup dandies by Elie Nadelman.) Physically, Woody Allen is much more graceful in *Sleeper;* he's turning into that rarity, a verbal comedian who also knows how to use his body. And his acting has developed; he can register more emotions now, and his new silly beatific look—the look of a foolish sage—goes with the wonderful infantile jokes that don't make sense. But one might say that *Sleeper* is a sober comedy; it doesn't unhinge us, we never feel that our reason is being shredded. It has a businesslike, nine-to-five look about it, and a faint nine-to-five lethargy. For a comedian, the price of stability may be the loss of inspiration. (Our most inspired comedian, Jonathan Winters, has never found his forms. But then he doesn't have that base of sanity, either.) What's missing is the wild man's indifference to everything but the joke. In Woody Allen's case, this out-of-control edge went way past Groucho's effrontery and W. C. Fields's malice into a metaphysical outrageousness, but the impulse was similar: finally, the pleasure in the joke was all that mattered. That's what put him among the great ones.

Woody Allen has become our folk hero because we felt that if we stuck with him failure could succeed; this was, in a sense, his pact with us to get our loyalty, and it worked. We don't want to have to go through failure; we want to watch him go through it—and come out the other side. I always thought the danger for him was that he wanted to be a universal little fellow—a Chaplin—and that he might linger too long on the depressive, misfit side of his character and let the schleppy pathos take over (as he did in *Take the Money and Run*). And I thought that if he ever convinced us that he was really failing he'd lose us—who wants to watch a wispy schlep? He may not fully know it, but he doesn't need our sympathy; he's got much more than that already. What Woody Allen probably doesn't realize is that when he uses his wit he becomes our D'Artagnan. He isn't a little fellow for college students; he's a *hero*. They want to be funny, like him.

What I had underestimated was another danger. Woody Allen tips the scales toward winning in *Sleeper*, all right, but he overvalues normality; the battered adolescent still thinks that that's the secret of happiness. He hasn't come to terms with what his wit is telling him. He's dumped Chaplin (blessings) and devised a Buster Keaton-style story, but Keaton's refined physical movements were a clown's poetry, while when Allen does physical comedy—even when he's good at it—he's a very ordinary person. His gift is upstairs. It's really lucky that he cares about himself as much as he does, or he might get so balanced out that his jokes would become monotonous, like those of his imitators. If only he can begin to take control for granted, now that he's improving as a physical comedian and gaining infinitely greater skill as a director. Surreal comedy is chaos; to be really funny, you have to be willing to let your unconscious take over. That's what doesn't happen in *Sleeper.*

The New Yorker, December 31, 1973

THE EXORCIST

S hallowness that asks to be taken seriously—shallowness like William Peter Blatty's—is an embarrassment. When you hear him on TV talking about communicating with his dead mother, your heart doesn't bleed for him, your stomach turns for him. Some people have impenetrable defense systems. You can't kid around with a man who says that he wrote *The Exorcist* because "as I went along writing my funny books and screenplays, I felt I wasn't making a contribution to the welfare of the world." He says that he looks upon it "quite frankly as an apostolic work." That the work has made him a millionaire doesn't make him a liar. Blatty is apostle to the *National Enquirer,* and to *Cosmopolitan,* in which the novel was condensed—so those Cosmopolitan Girls could make conversation without looking tired around the eyes. The crushing blunt-wittedness of the movie version, which he produced, tends to bear out Blatty's apostolic claims. Directed by William Friedkin, who won the Academy Award as Best Director of 1971 for *The French Connection,* the film is a faithful adaptation of the Blatty book—and that's not a compliment. Blatty did the intractable screenplay, so Friedkin may have been faithful in spite of himself. The picture isn't a gothic horror comedy, like *Psycho* or *Rosemary's Baby;* it has been made as a heavy, expensive *family* picture. It's faithful not to the way many people read the book—as a fast turn-on entertainment—but to Blatty's claims about what the book was intended to be. It's an obtuse movie, without a trace of playfulness in it. A viewer can become glumly anesthetized by the brackish color and the senseless ugliness of the conception.

Following on the success of *Rosemary's Baby* (Rosemary gave birth to a cloven-hoofed infant, her actor-husband having mated her with Satan in exchange for a Broadway hit), Blatty, a veteran screenwriter, developed an outline for a novel about the demonic possession of a child, and Marc Jaffe, of Bantam Books, subsidized the effort. Harper & Row picked up the hardcover rights, and the movie deal (stipulating that Blatty was to produce) was made even before publication. Blatty, who once hoaxed people by impersonating a Saudi Arabian prince, and whose screen credits include a hand in *Darling Lili, The Great Bank Robbery, What Did You Do in the War, Daddy?, Promise Her Anything, John Goldfarb, Please Come Home,* etc., is not an austere writer. The key personnel in *The Exorcist* are (a) Chris MacNeil (Ellen Burstyn), a beautiful movie-star mother, divorced, agnostic; (b) her twelve-year-old daughter, Regan (Linda Blair), who becomes a foul-mouthed, sex-obsessed, blaspheming, church-desecrating murderess; (c) Father Damien Karras (Jason Miller), a tormented Jesuit psychiatrist who is losing his faith; (d) a jokey, warmhearted Jewish police lieutenant (Lee J. Cobb); (3) a distinguished, ascetic priest, Father Merrin (Max von Sydow), whose archeological work has somehow—it's not made clear how, in either the book or the movie—released the demon that takes over Regan.

The book features a murder victim—a British movie director—whose "head was turned completely around, facing backward"; little Regan rotating her head; little Regan masturbating with a crucifix and grabbing her mother and forcing her mother's face against her bloody vagina; vomit propelled from Regan's mouth into people's faces. And what Blatty didn't manage to have his characters do he had them talk about, so there were fresh atrocities every few hundred words. Like the pulp authors who provide flip-page sex, he provided flip-page torture, infanticide, cannibalism, sexual hysteria, werewolves. The book is a manual of lurid crimes, written in an easy-to-read tough-guy style yet with a grating heightening word here and there, supposedly to tone it up. ("When the Mass was over, he polished the chalice and carefully placed it in his bag. He rushed for the seven-ten train back to Washington, carrying pain in a black valise.") The book turns up on high-school reading lists now, and the Bantam edition carries such quotes as "Deeply religious . . . a parable for our times" and "*The Exorcist* should be read twice; the first time for the passion and horrifying intensity of the story, with a second reading to savor the subtleties of language and phrasing overlooked in the mounting excitement of the first perusal."

For the movie, Blatty had to dispense with a subplot about the butler's daughter, and, of course, he couldn't retain all the gory anecdotes, but the basic story is told, and the movie—religiously literal-minded—shows you a heaping amount of blood and horror. This explicitness must be what William Friedkin has in mind when he talks publicly about the picture's "documentary quality." The movie also has the most ferocious language yet heard in a picture that is rated R, and is thus open to children (to those whose parents are insane enough to take them, or are merely uninformed). *The Exorcist* was budgeted at four million dollars, but, what with swiveling heads, and levitations, and vomit being spewed on target, the cost kept rising, and the picture came in somewhere around ten million. If *The Exorcist* had cost under a million, or had been made abroad, it would almost certainly be an X film, but when a movie is as expensive as this one, the

M.P.A.A. rating board doesn't dare to give it an X. Will people complain? I doubt it; the possible complainers have become accessories. Two Jesuits appear in the cast and served, with a third, as "technical advisers," along with a batch of doctors. Besides, the Catholic Church is hardly likely to be upset by the language or actions in a film that says that the Catholic Church is the true faith, feared by the Devil, and that its rituals can exorcise demons. The two heroes of the film are von Sydow and Jason Miller, both playing Jesuits; Georgetown University coöperated with the production, which was shot partly in Georgetown; and one of the Jesuit actor-advisers enriched us, even before the film was finished, with information about its high moral character ("It shows that obscenity is ugly ... vicious ugly, like the Vietnamese news"). The movie may be in the worst imaginable taste—that is, an utterly unfeeling movie about miracles—but it's also the biggest recruiting poster the Catholic Church has had since the sunnier days of *Going My Way* and *The Bells of St. Mary's.*

Whatever Blatty's claims, if *The Exorcist* scares people that's probably all it has to do, in box-office terms, and basically that's all the whole unpleasant movie is designed to do. "People only go to movies for three reasons, to laugh, cry, or be frightened," Friedkin has said. And "There are only three reasons to make a movie, to make people laugh, to make them cry, or to frighten them." The scaring here is a matter of special effects and sound and editing—the roaring-animal noises from the attic coming at the right instant, Regan's bed shaking just enough, the objects in her room flying about without looking silly, and so on. If the audience ever started giggling at the sounds and tricks, the picture might collapse, because it's entirely mechanical and impersonal. Von Sydow brings some elegance to his role, and the makeup that ages him is one of the most convincing aging jobs I've ever seen, but once you perceive that his Father Merrin is saintly and infirm, that's it. As Father Karras, the most active character, Jason Miller does the gloomy, tormented John Garfield bit—and it's a wheeze by now. All the performances are; there's nothing the actors can do with the juiceless stock roles.

The book's success may relate to its utter shallowness; the reader can go at a fast clip, following the plot and not paying any attention to the characters. But in the movie version the psychology, which is tiresomely moralistic (as in a fifties TV drama), is dead center. There we are with the freethinking mother feeling guilty about her divorce and its effects on Regan; we may not know why the demon picked on Regan, but we're tipped that that broken home—the first step to Hell—gave the Devil his chance. And there we are with the creaking goodness of the Jewish cop, and the jocular bonhomie of the Jesuits. It's all so tired that we can keep going only on fresh atrocities. Apart from the demonic special effects, which are done in staccato quick cuts, the picture is in a slugging, coercive style. It piles up points, like a demonstration. Friedkin, beloved of studio heads for such statements as "I'm not a thinker. . . . If it's a film *by* somebody instead of *for* somebody, I smell art," is not a director given to depth or mystery. Nor is he a man with a light touch—a failing that appears to have been exacerbated by the influence of *El Topo*. He has himself said that Blatty's book took hold of him and made him physically ill. That's the problem with moviemakers who aren't thinkers: they're mentally unprotected. A book like Blatty's makes them sick, and they think this means they should make everybody sick. Probably Friedkin really believes he is communicating an important idea to us. And the only way he knows how to do it is by surface punch; he's a true commercial director—he confuses blatancy with power.

As a movie, *The Exorcist* is too ugly a phenomenon to take lightly. Its gothic seriousness belongs to the class of those old Hearst Sunday-supplement stories about archeologists defiling tombs and the curses that befall them, and it soaks into people's lives. A critic can't fight it, because it functions below the conscious level. How does one exorcise the effects of a movie like this? There is no way. The movie industry is such that men of no taste and no imagination can have an incalculable influence. Blatty and Friedkin can't muster up any feeling, even when Father Karras sacrifices himself—a modern Christ who dies to save mankind. We in the audience don't feel bad when the saintly Father Merrin dies; we don't even feel a pang of sympathy when the words "Help Me" appear on Regan's body. From the mechanical-scare way that the movie works on an audience, there is no indication that Blatty or Friedkin has any feeling for the little girl's helplessness and suffering, or her mother's, any feeling for God or terror of Satan. Surely it is the religious people who should be most offended by this movie. Others can laugh it off as garbage, but are American Catholics willing to see their faith turned into a horror show? Are they willing to accept *anything* just as long as their Church comes out in a good light? Aren't those who accept this picture getting their heads screwed on backward?

Somewhere in the publicity for the film there was an item about William Friedkin's having looked at five hundred little girls before he chose his Regan, and, indeed, Linda Blair is a sparkling, snub-nosed, happy-looking little girl, who matches up perfectly with Ellen Burstyn. I wonder about those four hundred and ninety-nine mothers of the rejected little girls—or about the hundred and ninety-nine, if that's a more reasonable figure. They must have read the novel; they must have known what they were having their beautiful little daughters tested for. When they see *The Exorcist* and watch Linda Blair urinating on the fancy carpet and screaming and jabbing at herself with the crucifix, are they envious? Do they feel, "That might have been my little Susie—famous forever"?

The New Yorker, January 7, 1974

MAGNUM FORCE
KILLING TIME

Clint Eastwood isn't offensive; he isn't an actor, so one could hardly call him a bad actor. He'd have to *do* something before we could consider him bad at it. And acting isn't required of him in *Magnum Force*, which takes its name from the giant's phallus—the long-barreled Magnum 44—that Eastwood flourishes. Acting might even get in the way of what the movie is about—what a big man and a big gun can do. Eastwood's wooden impassivity makes it possible for the brutality in his pictures to be *ordinary*, a matter of routine. He may try to save a buddy from getting killed, but when the buddy gets hit no time is wasted on grief; Eastwood couldn't express grief any more than he could express tenderness. With a Clint Eastwood, the action film can—indeed, must—drop the pretense that human life has any value. At the same time, Eastwood's lack of reaction makes the whole show of killing seem so unreal that the viewer takes it on a different level from a movie in which the hero responds to suffering. In *Magnum Force*, killing is dissociated from pain; it's even dissociated from life. The killing is totally realistic—hideously, graphically so—yet since it's without emotion it has no impact on us. We feel nothing toward the victims; we have no empathy when they get it, and no memory of them afterward. As soon as one person gets it, we're ready for the next. The scenes of carnage are big blowouts—parties for the audience to gasp at in surprise and pleasure.

At an action film now, it just doesn't make much difference whether it's a good guy or a bad guy who dies, or a radiant young girl or a double-dealing chippie. Although the plots still draw this distinction, the writers and the directors no longer create different emotional tones for the deaths of good and bad characters. The fundamental mechanism of melodrama has broken down, I think: the audience at action pictures reacts to the killing scenes simply as spectacle. A tall, cold cod like Eastwood removes the last pretensions to humane feelings from the action melodrama, making it an impersonal, almost abstract exercise in brutalization. Eastwood isn't very different from many of the traditional inexpressive, stalwart heroes of Westerns and cops-and-robbers films—actors notoriously devoid of personality—but the change in action films can be seen in its purest form in him. He walks right through the mayhem without being affected by it—and we are not cued to be affected, either. The difference is a matter of degree, but it's possible that this difference of degree has changed the nature of the beast—or, to put it more accurately, the beast can now run wild. The audiences used to go mainly for the action but also to hate the ruthless villains, sympathize with the helpless victims, and cheer on the protector-of-the-weak heroes. It was the spaghetti Westerns (which made Clint Eastwood a star) that first eliminated the morality-play dimension and turned the Western into pure violent reverie. Apart from their aesthetic qualities (and they did have some), what made these Italian-produced Westerns popular was that they stripped the Western form of its cultural burden of morality. They discarded its civility along with its hypocrisy. In a sense, they liberated the form: what the Western hero stood for was left out, and what he embodied (strength and gun power) was retained. Abroad, that was probably what he had represented all along. In the figure of Clint Eastwood, the Western morality play and the myth of the Westerner were split. Now American movies treat even the American city the way the Italians treated the Old West; our cops-and-robbers pictures are like urban spaghetti Westerns. With our ethical fabric torn to shreds in this last decade, American action films such as *Magnum Force* and *The Laughing Policeman* are becoming daydream-nightmares of indiscriminate mayhem and slaughter.

The John Wayne figure—the man who stood for the right (in both senses, I fear, and in both senses within the movies themselves)—has been replaced by a man who essentially stands for nothing but violence. Eastwood has to deliver death, because he has no other appeal. He can barely speak a line of dialogue without making an American audience smile in disbelief, but his big gun speaks for him. The concept of the good guy has collapsed simultaneously in our society and in our movies. Eastwood isn't really a good guy; you don't *like* him, the way you liked Wayne. You don't even enjoy him in the way you could enjoy a scoundrel. He's simply *there*, with his Magnum force. For a hero who can't express himself in words or by showing emotion, shooting first and asking questions later has got to be the ultimate salvation. In *Dirty Harry,* Eastwood said to the hippie psychotic, "This is the most powerful handgun in the world, punk. It can blow your head off." The strong, quiet man of the action film has been replaced by the emotionally indifferent man. He's the opposite of Bogart, who knew pain. Perhaps the top box-office star in the movie business, Eastwood is also the first truly stoned hero in the history of movies. There's an odd disparity between his deliberate, rather graceful physical movements and his practically timbreless voice. Only his hands seem fully alive. In Italian movies, the character he played was known as the Man with No Name, and he speaks in a small, dead, non-actor's voice that drops off to nowhere at the end of a line and that doesn't tell us a thing about him. While actors who are expressive may have far more appeal to educated people, Eastwood's inexpressiveness travels preposterously well. What he does is unmistakable in any culture. He's utterly unbelievable in his movies—inhumanly tranquil, controlled, and assured—and yet he seems to represent something that isn't so unbelievable. He once said of his first Italian Western, *A Fistful of Dollars,* that it "established the pattern," that it was "the first film in which the protagonist initiated the action—he shot first." Eastwood stands melodrama on its head: in his world nice guys finish last. This is no longer the romantic world in which the hero is, fortunately, the best shot; instead, the best shot is the hero. And that could be what the American audience for action films, grown derisive about the triumph of the good, was waiting for. Eastwood's gun power makes him the hero of a totally nihilistic dream world.

■   ■   ■

Hollywood's flirtation with the ideology of the law-and-order advocates reached its peak two years ago with the release of *Dirty Harry,* a Warner Brothers picture directed by Don Siegel and starring Eastwood as the saintly tough cop Harry Callahan. A right-wing fantasy about the San Francisco police force as a helpless group, emasculated by the liberals, the picture propagandized for para-legal police power and vigilante justice. The only way Harry could protect the city against the mad hippie killer who was terrorizing women and children was by taking the law into his own hands; the laws on the books were the object of his contempt, because he knew what justice was and how to carry it out. The political climate of the country has changed, of course, and, besides, Hollywood is, in its own cheaply Machiavellian way, responsive to criticism. In *Magnum Force,* the sequel to *Dirty Harry,* and also from Warner Brothers, Clint Eastwood, again playing Harry Callahan, is just as contemptuous of the laws on the books, but he believes in enforcing them. John Milius, who had an uncredited paw in *Dirty Harry,* and who gets the screenwriting credit here, along with Michael Cimino, twists the criticism of the earlier film to his own purposes: he takes his plot gimmick from those of us who attacked *Dirty Harry* for its fascist medievalism. The villains now are a Nazi-style élite cadre of clean-cut, dedicated cops who have taken the law into their own hands and are cleaning out the scum of the city—assassinating the labor racketeers, the drug dealers, the gangsters and their groupies. They are explicit versions of what we accused Harry of being; they might be the earlier Harry's disciples, and the new Harry wipes them all out. "I hate the goddam system," he says, "but I'll stick with it until something better comes along." *Magnum Force* disarms political criticism and still delivers the thrills of brutality. Harry doesn't bring anyone to court; the audience understands that Harry *is* the court. The picture is so sure it can get away with its political switch that before it allows Harry to spout his new defender-of-the-system line it actually tweaks the audience (and the movie press) by implying that he is the assassin who's mowing down the gangsters. But the movie—and this is what is distinctively new about it—uses the same tone for the Storm Troopers' assassination orgies that is used for Harry's killing of the Storm Troopers. At no point are we asked to be appalled by homicide. We get the shocks without any fears for the characters' safety or any sadness or horror at their gory deaths. The characters aren't characters in any traditional sense; they're not meant to be cared about.

Studio-machine-made action pictures have the speedy, superficial adaptability of journalism. One can measure some of the past two years' changes in the society by comparing the two films. In *Dirty Harry,* the sniper villain (wearing a peace symbol on his belt) idly picked off an innocent girl in a bikini while she was swimming, and the pool filled with her blood. In *Mag-*

num Force, one of the young Storm Troopers machine-guns everyone at a gangland swimming-pool party, and you get the impression that the girls prove their corruption and earn their deaths by being bra-less. Generally speaking, the victims now are all guilty of something, even if only of taking drugs, so you're exonerated—you don't have to feel anything. You can walk out and pretend you didn't see what went on. If the élite cadre and their prim Führer (Hal Holbrook) represent what Harry the hero represented the first time around, and if it's now right for Harry the hero to kill them, what of the writers who confect one position and then the next? Do they believe in anything? I think they do. Despite the superficial obeisance to the rule of law, the underlying content of *Magnum Force*—the buildup of excitement and pleasure in brutality—is the same as that of *Dirty Harry,* and the strong man is still the dispenser of justice, which comes out of his gun. Harry says it: "Nothing's wrong with shooting as long as the right people get shot." He's basically Paul Newman's Judge Roy Bean—another Milius concoction—all over again. Although Ted Post's direction of *Magnum Force* is mediocre, the picture isn't as numbing as *The Life and Times of Judge Roy Bean,* because it stays on its own coarse, formula-entertainment level, trying to turn on the audience to the garish killings and sustaining a certain amount of suspense about what's coming next. It sticks to its rationale. In *Magnum Force,* Dirty Harry is still the urban garbage man, cleaning up after us. His implicit justification is "You in the audience don't have the guts to do what I do, so don't criticize me." He says he does our dirty work for us, and so he invokes our guilt, and we in the audience don't raise the question "Who asked you to?" If Milius were a real writer instead of a hero-idolater, he might begin to raise questions about whether Harry unconsciously manipulates himself into these situations because he likes to kill, and about whether he keeps his face stony so as not to reveal this. But *Magnum Force,* the new city Western, has no mind and no class; the moviemakers seem unaware that their hero lives and kills as affectlessly as a psychopathic personality.

"A man's got to know his limitations," Harry keeps saying, and it's a comment not on himself but on his enemies' failure to recognize that he's the better man. Harry is tougher than the élite cadre, just as he was tougher than the mad hippie killer. The Nazis look like a troupe of juveniles in training for stardom in the old studio days, and are suspected by other cops of being homosexual, so Harry's weathered face and stud reputation (which is all hearsay as far as the audience goes) are like additional equipment for destroying them. But Eastwood is not a lover: women flock to him, but he makes no moves toward them. From what we see, they have to do all the work; he accepts one as dispassionately as he declines another. In one sequence, a woman bares her feelings and tells Harry of her desire for him while he just sits there, as unconcerned as ever; he's not going to get involved. Like the Western loner, he's almost surreally proper—lunatically so, considering what he does with his gun and fists. The only real sex scene in

Magnum Force is a black pimp's murder of a black whore, which is staged for a turn-on erotic effect that I found genuinely shocking and disgusting. But the movie is full of what in a moral landscape would be sickening scenes of death: a huge metal girder smashes right into a man's face, and the audience is meant not to empathize and to hide from the sight but to say "Wow!"

The right-wing ideology functioned in *Dirty Harry;* here the liberalized ideology is just window dressing. What makes Harry the sharpshooter a great cop is that he knows the guilty from the innocent, and in this action world there's only one thing to be done with the guilty—kill them. Alternatives to violence are automatically excluded. If we talk to Harry, if after he dispatches his thirty-fifth or eightieth criminal one of us says "Harry, could you maybe ask the guy's name before you shoot, to make sure you've got the right man?" Harry's answer *has* to be "All criminals are liars anyway," as he pulls the trigger. Because that's what he wants to do: pull the trigger. What keeps the audience watching is one round of killings after another. *Magnum Force* is a far less skillful fantasy than *Dirty Harry,* and so is less involving, and it isn't likely to be as big a hit, yet my hunch is that the audience, after these last couple of years, rather likes its fantasies to be uninvolving.

■ ■ ■

It's the emotionlessness of so many violent movies that I'm becoming anxious about, not the rare violent movies *(Bonnie and Clyde, The Godfather, Mean Streets)* that make us care about the characters and what happens to them. A violent movie that intensifies our experience of violence is very different from a movie in which acts of violence are perfunctory. I'm only guessing, and maybe this emotionlessness means little, but, if I can trust my instincts at all, there's something deeply wrong about anyone's taking for granted the dissociation that this carnage without emotion represents. Sitting in the theater, you feel you're being drawn into a spreading nervous breakdown. It's as if pain and pleasure, belief and disbelief had got all smudged together, and the movies had become some schizzy form of put-on.

The New Yorker, January 14, 1974

THIEVES LIKE US

In *McCabe & Mrs. Miller,* a rangy, buck-toothed young boy discovered undreamed-of pleasures at a snowbound brothel and met a scrawny, scared girl, a widowed bride who had just turned whore. She had teeth and a grin to match his own, and when he left they said goodbye, like the affectionate innocents they were, and he called out that he'd be back the next year. A minute later, still harmlessly affable, he was shot down from a bridge, and his body slowly crushed the ice before disappearing in the water. Robert Altman has reunited the pair, Keith Carradine and Shelley Duvall, in *Thieves Like Us;* he's Bowie, one of three escaped convicts, and she is Keechie, whose drunken father runs the gas station the convicts hide in. Bowie has been in prison for seven years, since he took part in a holdup when he was sixteen; Keechie has never had a boyfriend—not even one to walk her to church. They fall in love; it's two-sided, equal, and perfect—the sort of romantic love that people in movies don't fall into anymore. Keith Carradine takes the screen the way a star does, by talent and by natural right. In his bit role in *McCabe,* he made the audience yield to him so completely that his sequence almost threw the movie out of whack; he makes us yield here for the entire film. He has the rawboned, open-faced look of a young Henry Fonda or Gary Cooper; he's a beautiful camera subject, and the rawness saves him from the too-handsome-juvenile look of earlier stars. There has never been an ingénue like Shelley Duvall, with her matter-of-fact manner and her asymmetrical, rag-doll face; if it weren't for her goofy, self-conscious smile, she could be the child of Grant Wood's "American Gothic" parents. Her Keechie carries candor to the point of eccentricity: she's so natural that she seems bizarrely original. Whatever it was that Altman saw in her when he put the twenty-year-old Houston girl, who had never acted professionally, into *Brewster McCloud* didn't quite come through that time, but it certainly peeped out in her small role in *McCabe,* and here she melts indifference. You're unable to repress your response; you go right to her in delight, saying "I'm yours." She looks like no one else and she acts like no one else. Shelley Duvall may not be an actress, exactly, but she seems able to be herself on the screen in a way that nobody has ever been before. She doesn't appear to project—she's just *there.* Yet you feel as if you read her every thought; she convinces you that she has no veils and nothing hidden. Her charm appears to be totally without affectation. Altman must have sensed in that inexperienced twenty-year-old girl some of the same qualities that separate him from other directors: a gambler's euphoria about playing the game his own way, assurance without a trace of imitativeness.

In other Altman films, there is always something that people can complain about; they ask, "What's that there for?" In *Thieves Like Us,* there's nothing to stumble over. It's a serenely simple film—contained and complete. You feel elated by the chasteness of the technique, and the film engages your senses and stays with you, like a single vision. It's beautiful right from the first, pearly-green long shot. Robert Altman finds a sureness of tone and never loses it; *Thieves Like Us* has the pensive, delicate romanticism of *McCabe,* but it isn't hesitant or precarious. It isn't a heady, whirling sideshow of a movie, like *The Long Goodbye;* it has perfect clarity. I wouldn't say that I respond to it more than to *McCabe* or that I enjoy it more than the loony *The Long Goodbye,* but *Thieves Like Us* seems to achieve beauty without artifice. It's the closest to flawless of Altman's films—a masterpiece.

Altman breaks the pattern of what American directors are commonly supposed to be good at; this picture has the relaxed awareness that we honor Europeans for and that still mystifies Hollywood. Like *Mean Streets,* it didn't cost enough for Hollywood people to understand it. *Thieves Like Us* is based on a neglected, long-out-of-print 1937 novel by Edward Anderson—the novel that Nicholas Ray's 1948 picture *They Live by Night* was derived from. (Edward Anderson won a literary prize with his first novel, *Hungry Men,* in 1935, and then, as far as I can determine, published *Thieves Like Us* and disappeared from the writing world. It is said that he was living in Texas when *They Live by Night* was made, but the novel, according to Avon Books, which is putting out a new edition, is in the public domain, and the publishers have had no contact with the author.*) The Ray film, produced by John Houseman and starring Cathy O'Donnell and Farley Granger as Bonnie-and-Clyde figures, retained Anderson's plot but strayed far from the book's tone; the Altman film stays very close to that tone, while moving the action from Oklahoma and Texas to Mississippi. The picture was shot in sequence in forty-three days, at a cost of $1,250,000. Altman didn't build thirties sets; he found the vegetating old towns that he needed. He took his crew to Mississippi and made the picture in the sort of freedom that Jean Renoir had when, as a young man, he took his family and friends out to make *A Day in the Country.* Before Altman was hired to direct, the producer, Jerry Bick, had commissioned a script by Calder Willingham. Although Willingham gets a screen credit, his script didn't have the approach Altman wanted, and Altman's former script girl, Joan Tewkesbury, then devised another script, in collaboration with the director, which stays on Edward Anderson's narrative line, retaining much of his dialogue. (He was a considerable writer.) The movie has the ambience of a novel; it is the most literary of all Altman's films, yet the most freely intuitive. *Thieves Like Us* is so sensuous and lucid that it is as if William Faulkner and the young Jean Renoir had collaborated.

Robert Altman spoils other directors' films for me; Hollywood's paste-up, slammed-together jobs come off a faulty conveyor belt and are half chewed up in the process. I think I know where just about all the elements come from in most American movies (and in most foreign movies, too), and how the mechanisms work, but I don't understand how Robert Altman gets his effects, any more than I understand how Renoir did (or, for that matter, how Godard did from *Breathless* through *Weekend,* or how Bertolucci does). When an artist works right on the edge of his unconscious, like Altman, not asking himself why he's doing what he's doing but trusting to instinct (which in Altman's case is the same as taste), a movie is a special kind of gamble. If Altman fails, his picture won't have the usual mechanical story elements to carry it, or the impersonal excitement of a standard film. And if he succeeds aesthetically, audiences still may not respond, because the light, prodigal way in which he succeeds is alien

*His son and people who worked with him provide the information that he was a screenwriter at M-G-M in 1941, but mostly he supported his family by one crummy newspaper job or another. He died in 1963.

to them. Three-quarters of a century of slick movies have conditioned audiences' expectations. But *Thieves Like Us* might win him the audience that was put off by the elliptical poetry of *McCabe & Mrs. Miller* and the offhand pyrotechnics of *The Long Goodbye*. There's no predicting what he'll do next; *Thieves Like Us*, with its soft, unassuming grace, may be the only fully accessible movie he'll ever make. Its vision is just as singular as that of his other films, but the masterly above-board method could put him in touch with a popular audience; Griffith used to reach that audience (less corrupted then, of course) with comparable pastoral romances, such as *True Heart Susie*. *Thieves Like Us* is not just the easiest-to-like picture Altman has ever made—I think one would have to fight hard to resist it.

The scope is small, but *Thieves Like Us* is a native work in the same way that *The Godfather* is; we know the genre (Depression, bank robbers, Bonnie and Clyde), and the characters are as archetypal as one's next-door neighbors. Altman didn't have his usual cinematographer and production designer with him this time; working with Jean Boffety, a French cinematographer who had never done a picture in this country, and with a newcomer, Jackson De Govia, as production designer, he seems to have changed his style of improvisation—to have become calmer, more fluid. Everything in the Anderson book is refined in the movie, instead of what usually happens to novels—the coarsening that results from trying to make things fit a preordained plan, and settling for the approximate. The milky, semi-transparent cinematography makes the story seem newborn. Altman uses the novel as his base, but he finds his story through the actors, and, as Renoir did, through accidents of weather and discoveries along the way. He finds spontaneous comedy; the novel isn't funny, but the movie is. The lovers are far less conventional in the movie than in the book. (With Shelley Duvall, you couldn't be conventional even if you wanted to.) Bowie isn't a psychopath or a crazed dreamer, like his two robber friends; he's still a kid, and his essential healthiness becomes the core of the picture. He wants what Keechie represents, but he's caught, living a life that doesn't make sense to him. When he says to a wandering dog "Do you belong to someone, or are you a thief like me?" we know that for him "thief" means "stray." Identifying with Bowie, we react to each eruption of violence as he does—with a moral chill. Anderson, too, had basically seen him as gentle and straight, but the picture takes its cue from the rapport of Carradine and Duvall, omitting other elements in his character and moving away from the links to *Bonnie and Clyde*.

At first, the two convicts who escape with Bowie—T-Dub and Chicamaw—sit around giggling, high on freedom, but then their characters start to take shape. Bert Remsen, who had given up acting, was working as casting director on *Brewster McCloud* when Altman put him into the picture; he appeared again, memorably, in *McCabe*, and now he's T-Dub, a veteran bank robber. T-Dub is a cheery, likable fool who becomes flushed with success and gets reckless; Remsen plays the role so warmly that T-Dub's careless idiocy is fully believable. John Schuck, who was Painless in *M*A*S*H*, has also turned up in two other Altman films, but there was nothing in his earlier work to prepare one for his major performance here, in the pivotal role of the heavy-drinking, half-mad Chicamaw. Schuck has always had a suggestion of a bulldog in his face, and now, grown corpulent and more powerful-looking, he gives a performance that in some scenes rivals the intensity that Bogart brought to his Fred C. Dobbs in *The Treasure of the Sierra Madre.* Schuck's comic, terrifying big scene, when he insists on play-acting a robbery at home with small children and explodes in a murderous rage when they lose interest, and his last scene, in which he's deserted, yelling in torment on a country road, are classic moments. Altman often picks up part of his cast on location, or puts members of the crew to work; the writer Joan Tewkesbury turns up here as the woman in the train-station sequence. Louise Fletcher, who is Mattie, T-Dub's sister-in-law, had been a TV actress in the early sixties and had retired, but she is married to the film's producer and was on location in Mississippi. Altman asked her to play the small part of Mattie, and then, when he saw the presence she brought to it, he enlarged the role. Louise Fletcher has a full, strong body and great rounded arms; her Mattie is a no-nonsense woman who looks as if she had lived through what women in soap operas prattle about. She's a tough-broad earth mother with a coating of banal respectability—an authentic American-woman character.

You can see that Altman doesn't have to prove to anybody that he can re-create the thirties. The movie isn't a work of nostalgia; it's not a glorification of the past. It's localized in an era, and the people can be understood only in terms of that era. They are part of the age of radio, and Altman uses radio programs of the thirties for his score, and Coca-Cola for his motif. Everyone swigs Coca-Cola. Keechie is always reaching for a bottle; the old truck advertising Coca-Cola makes an appearance; and on the prison sign at the Mississippi State Penitentiary, at Parchman, there are Coca-Cola ads. I inquired, to find out if this was on the level, and was told that the crew was denied permission to film at actual prisons, where these ads are indeed on the signs, but that the reproduction is faithful. The prison at Parchman is, of course, a landmark in several Faulkner novels. For the last two years now, friends of mine have been shouting that Altman must do *The Wild Palms* or *As I Lay Dying;* they've been convinced that he is the man to bring Faulkner to the screen. Maybe he knew it all along, and maybe he was smart enough to know that he could do it best by using someone else's material for his text. (Perhaps this is also how someday someone will put Fitzgerald on film.) *Thieves Like Us* comes closer to the vision and sensibility of Faulkner's novels than any of the movie adaptations of them do. Altman didn't start from Faulkner, but he wound up there. If he did a Faulkner novel, he might not be able to achieve what people want him to. But *Thieves Like Us* is *his* Faulkner novel.

The New Yorker, February 4, 1974

WALKING TALL
THE STREET WESTERN

In the landscape of the traditional Western, the simple, masculine values that the Westerner stood for were ancient and noble. He was the hero of our mass-culture folk art; for the whole world, this mythic hero symbolized American democracy and virtue and justice. If he was part of a reverie, it was a reverie about what was best in this country, and Westerns made us nostalgic for the imagined simplicities of our country's past, and for the naïveté of our own childhood, when we had innocently believed in faultless protector-heroes. Riding to the rescue, the cowboy hero fought fair and punished the guilty. The hero might himself be an outlaw (as in John Ford's *Stagecoach*), but he was a good man. The theme was always good against evil, and the iconography—the horses, the hats, the spurs and leather vests, the sunsets and cactus and cattle—was a reminder of an unspoiled country that the hero was fighting to keep from being destroyed. The villains were spoilers of the American dream. Between the villains and the hero were the farmers or townspeople—ordinary people, who stood up to the villains and lost, or who accommodated to evil because they were defenseless or too scared to fight. They were in the same position as most of us in the audience, but we were not asked to identify with their ineffectiveness, or with their partial victories, either. In the midst of a legend, why consider the actual world? Our hearts rode with the protector. The hero was a natural leader—the American knight. He won because he was physically stronger than the villains; his fists and his gun represented Justice. We didn't worry about his assumption of authority or about his use of force. The story was formal and remote, a ritualized dream of the past that we clung to. It had no direct application; the Westerner's ability to outfight the spoilers was part of our inspirational mythology. The landscape itself—the immensity of deserts and plains that the hero rode through—distanced the Westerns; and horses, with their patrician beauty, were natural carriers of deities.

A few more Westerns may still straggle in, but the Western is dead. Nobody's making even those last-grasp Westerns anymore—the ones about the lonely last cowboy, or the semi-spoofs featuring heavy old movie stars falling off their horses or kinky cowboys going to Mexico or farther south (*Butch Cassidy and the Sundance Kid*). There's been nothing since *Jeremiah Johnson* and *The Life and Times of Judge Roy Bean*, in 1972, and nothing appears to be scheduled. It's the end of a movie era. But the Western cowboy hero hasn't disappeared; he's moved from the mythological purity of the wide-open spaces into the corrupt modern cities and towns (*Dirty Harry*), and on paved streets he's an inflammatory figure. When Buford Pusser (Joe Don Baker), the hero of *Walking Tall,* trims the bark off a stout hickory limb and starts swinging this skull-breaking club against the spoilers who are operating a wide-open Sin City strip near his birthplace in Tennessee, mythology and realism are joined.

Walking Tall is a volcano of a movie—and in full eruption—loosely based on the life of a man who has become a legendary figure through ballads celebrating his exploits. (Johnny Mathis sings an excruciating *Walking Tall* ballad at the close.) From *Bonnie and Clyde* on, our recent powerful, big-box-office hits have mostly questioned the old movie myths, turning them inside out and indicating that the bad guys often win. *Walking Tall* goes right back to *Beowulf* and stays on course. The actual Buford Pusser is a six-foot-six-inch former professional wrestler. As the movie tells it, he returns to Tennessee after several years on the road, and when he complains because a friend of his has been cheated in a dice game at a state-line gambling casino he is beaten, slashed, and left to die. A man of prodigious strength, Pusser recovers, and since the sheriff refuses to prosecute his assailants, he take a club, goes back to the casino, and fractures the crooked gamblers' arms. On trial, he defends his act of revenge as a man's natural right, tearing off his shirt and showing his knife-scarred chest as evidence. Acquitted, he enters the race for sheriff against the incumbent, Al Thurman (Gene Evans), who had refused to help him, and Thurman, trying to run him off a bridge, is killed—though Pusser tries valiantly to save him and does succeed in rescuing Thurman's deputy. Elected sheriff, Pusser proceeds to clean up the area, though at terrible cost to himself and his family. Buford Pusser's inspirational ordeal is like a small-town version of *Dirty Harry,* but it isn't snide or deliberately right-wing, like *Dirty Harry. Walking Tall* appears to be pre-political, as the traditional Westerns were. It is solemnly, unself-consciously square—a celebration of the same virtues that the Westerns always stood for, but, unlike those Westerns, not distanced. Those Westerns weren't rabble-rousing; *Walking Tall* is.

Maybe, during all those years of watching Westerns, though we didn't believe in them we wanted to. The child in us wanted to, and maybe the Westerns softened us up for primitivism in the guise of realism. *Walking Tall* appeals to a deep-seated belief in a simple kind of justice—perfect, swift, Biblical justice. It returns us to the moral landscape of the Western, yet the picture is more crude in its appeal than the Westerns, because it works almost totally on the blood-and-guts level of emotionally charged violence. Buford's union of force and righteous wrath has the drive of a crusade against corruption—a crusade for a fundamentalist politics. When Buford began to clobber the bad guys, people in the audience cried out, "Get 'em, get 'em!"—and they weren't kidding. *Walking Tall* has just opened in New York, but it has been playing around the country for the past year, and is said to have already grossed close to thirty-five million dollars. I'm told that in parts of the South it is a ritual that at the end audiences stand in homage and cheer; in New York, audiences scream and shout their assent to each act of vengeance that the towering hero takes upon his enemies. I've heard of people who have already seen it twice and are going back.

Born in 1908, the director, Phil Karlson, has been working in Hollywood since 1932. He made low-budget Westerns and routine pictures until the mid-fifties, when he made the sleeper *Tight Spot* and won recognition for the Alabama-set *The Phenix City Story,* about a crusading candidate for Attorney General and his son who did battle against an earlier Sin City vice operation. Later, Karlson directed the intelligent action melodrama *Hell to Eternity,* and such films as *The Young Doctors, Rampage,* the popular Matt Helm *The Silencers* and *The Wrecking Crew,* and, recently, *Ben.* He was a veteran low-budget action director's skills, and these are what he brings to bear on *Walking Tall:* he doesn't overprepare a scene; he makes his points and moves on. Karlson pushes and punches, but he's good at it. He can dredge up emotion; he can make the battle of virtuous force against organized evil seem primordial. He has a tawdry streak (there's an exploitation sequence with a nude prostitute being whipped), and he's careless (a scene involving a jewelry salesman is a decrepit mess), but in the onrush of the story the viewer is overwhelmed. *Walking Tall* isn't afraid to pull out all the stops of classical cheapie melodrama, right down to the murder of the Pusser family dog and the weeping face of a bereaved child. One would be tempted to echo Thelma Ritter in *All About Eve*—"Everything but the bloodhounds snappin' at her rear end"—but some of the suffering has a basis in fact. Mrs. Pusser, played by Elizabeth Hartman, was actually ambushed and killed in 1967. The film is a heartbreaker as well as a gut-cruncher. Elizabeth Hartman is a gifted actress who appears too seldom; a delicate-featured redhead with a beautifully modeled brow, she has the appealing quality that the young Janet Gaynor had. You want to reach right out to her; she's huggable. Karlson uses her for as much tearjerking potential as he dares. Brenda Benet (she has lazy, hot eyes, like Gail Russell's) plays a Vietnam widow turned whore, a good-bad temptress who makes overtures to Buford; Rosemary Murphy is a lively dragonlady whore-mistress; and Ed Call, as Lutic, Buford's old high-school chum, practically oozes Southernness—which is right for his role. The cast is frowzily passable; that is, the frowziness passes for authentic (although, as Buford's father, Noah Beery appears to think that he can be Southern by acting Hollywood-cornpone sweet). The pink, freckled faces without makeup carry a message of "truth," the same way the run-down bars do. (The film was shot in Tennessee, partly in McNairy County, where the actual Pusser served three two-year terms as sheriff, from 1964 to 1970.) Even the crummy cinematography gets by, because the picture's very crudeness makes it seem innocently honest. *Walking Tall* doesn't seem a sell, as a movie with a slicker surface might. All of it works to give the audience an exultant sense of the triumph of the heroic common man—his victory over "the system."

In the movie, Pusser as a wrestler is known as Buford the Wild Bull; this name must have been the key for Joe Don Baker's performance. Baker plays Buford as a soft-drawling, peace-loving man who, enraged by injustice, becomes a maddened fighting bull. Astonishingly, even when pummeling an adversary with body blows that are amplified so that they sound as if a tractor were being driven into flesh, he has the dignity of a wounded bull. At six feet two, Baker is a good deal smaller than the actual Pusser, but he looks enormous enough; he comes from Texas via the Actors Studio and TV (*Mongo's Back in Town, That Certain Summer*) and films (*Junior Bonner*), and he seems Southern redneck—a common man who works outdoors in the sun—to the soul. He has that heavy, flaccid look that Southern white men often get early in life; it goes with a physical relaxation that can fool Northerners like me, who don't always recognize the power hidden in the flab. As Baker plays him, Buford is a nonreflective hero who, when angered, tramples on his enemies uncontrollably. This brute obsessiveness may easily be the result of the moviemakers' desire to show plenty of beatings, but Baker almost makes us believe that Buford fights back because he has to. Baker's Buford has the mighty stature of a classic hero; he seems like a giant from the earth. This Buford is a primitive folk hero worthy of the tales of an earlier era—though actually he's the hero of a modern tall tale.

When Baker, as Buford, says to his little son, "There's nothing wrong with a gun in the right hands," and promises him a rifle when he's nine, the bit of dialogue comes from the same homiletic Hollywood as Clint Eastwood's speeches in *Magnum Force.* Actually, although Mrs. Pusser had two children by a previous marriage, Pusser has only one child—a daughter—but you can see why the fictional son has been added; so that later, when he comes to the hospital to see his injured father, the child can walk down the corridor crying but clutching his rifle. It's the little prince taking up his fallen king's mission, and the audience gasps at the raw power of a device that pre-dates D. W. Griffith. The script, by the producer, Mort Briskin, who first heard of Pusser's heroic ordeal when Roger Mudd did a ten-minute report on him on C.B.S. in 1969, may appear authentic just because it's so shameless and tacky. Briskin's previous credits as a writer are strictly small-time (*A Man Alone, The Magic Face*), but this script didn't require literary talent. Briskin, the producer of such TV series as "Sheriff of Cochise," "U.S. Marshal," and "The Texan," is also a producer for Bing Crosby Productions,* for whom he has done *Willard, Ben,* and *Walking Tall.* In Buford Pusser, Briskin found a hero whose story embodied the values of the conventional Westerns; Briskin embroidered it, but basically the pattern was already there, shaped by Pusser himself (he had made a deputy sheriff of the man who wrote the first ballad about him), and Karlson knew just how to bring it out. The street Western is a corruption of the Western, an attempt to apply the Western's mythology to actual problems—and since it doesn't apply, the movies (and other forms of pop culture, and politics, too) fabricate situations that are just like those in Westerns so that the mythology *will* apply.

The actual Buford Pusser (not known as Buford the Wild Bull) was

* Except for the name, the company no longer has any ties to Bing Crosby.

beaten up in 1957 in a brawl in a casino over money he himself had lost. Almost three years later, the casino operator was robbed and beaten, and Pusser and two of his friends were charged with armed robbery. At the trial, Pusser didn't defend his right to assault the gambler; he and the two others were acquitted because they had an airtight alibi. Pusser got into police work in 1962, when his father, who was chief of police in Adamsville, retired, having arranged for his son to succeed him. When Pusser ran for sheriff in 1964, the incumbent sheriff *was* killed in an auto crash, but there was no connection between that crash and Pusser, who in fact defeated the dead man, whose name was still on the ballot, by only three hundred votes. Aside from Mrs. Pusser's murder in 1967—which was what really started the legend of Buford Pusser—and the extraordinary amount of physical punishment that Pusser took and also dished out, there doesn't seem to be a great deal of factual support for the movie. The first new deputy he appointed was not a black buddy, as in the film, but his father. And as for the amazing incident, in the movie, of Buford's magically quick apprehensions of the murderers of eight civil-rights workers (only to have the case dismissed on a technicality), I can find no mention of it even in Buford's romantic authorized biography of 1971. As for the powerhouse scenes when Buford rises from his hospital bed, his head swathed in bandages (like the Invisible Man), to attend his wife's funeral and to wreak vengeance once again, and then, Job-like, rests upon his great hickory stick, using it as a cane—pure invention, of course. As sheriff, Pusser had in fact become partial to the less photogenic head cracker the gun. He has boasted that in his first term he "wore out more pistol barrels banging mean drunks over the head than the county would pay for." The movie's basic premise—that Buford Pusser became sheriff so that he could rid the community of vice and corruption—seems shaky. And although he piled up a big number of arrests by busting drunks and raiding moonshiners, the state-line dives operate as usual, and when Pusser ran for sheriff again in 1972—while the movie was being shot—he was defeated. The man who won explained his victory (in an interview in the *Nashville Tennessean Sunday Magazine*) by saying, "If either man had to arrest your son, which would you prefer? I just don't think the people here cared for killing and beating up on people. They just didn't think that was necessary to enforce the law." The brutalities and killings, including the murder of Mrs. Pusser, seem to have been a chain of reprisals. Pusser, who now does promotional work for supermarkets, Jaycee gatherings, mobile homes, and automobile dealers (he gives away autographed sticks to those who buy cars), has authorized a glorifying industry about himself, as well as this movie (he owns seven percent). The only complaint he has been known to make about the film is that it isn't violent enough. There is some talk of his running for governor or for Congress. How does one define corruption?

The moral setup in this street Western is a direct carry-over from the myths of the wide-open spaces. No matter how high the odds against him, the virtuous man wins out. And the virtuous man always knows whom to clobber. He can be trusted with his fists, his stick, and his gun because he has absolute knowledge of innocence and guilt. In *Walking Tall*, the forces of corruption are just as easily recognizable as in any early Western; they're basically the same forces—mean crooks. Buford says that he quit wrestling because of the system and he's not going to let the system wreck his town. To put it in the way the audience at *Walking Tall* perceives it: because of the system, the honest small guy doesn't stand a chance, but Buford—the man who cares about what's right—bucks the system. The movie's simplistic outlook is commercial genius: the only serious problems in the community are the problems created by the vice lords—the system is represented by the prostitutes and crooked gamblers and their confederates in the police department and on the bench. The solution is the same as in a Western: kill them or drive them out of town. In *Walking Tall*, as in *Dirty Harry*, the hero could never mistakenly injure an innocent person, or the whole structure of the morality play would collapse. He's a one-man lynch mob, but with the judgment of a god. Buford's sad, sick look in the eyes after he's forced to shoot an evil woman is knightly chivalry modern style.

After a decade of hip but often numbingly cynical movies, the country is on a regression trip—watching the Waltons and the Apples and cheering *Walking Tall*. Breaking a few arms has a basic demagogic appeal; it makes audiences feel that there is a direct, fast way to solve problems. There's a deliberate appeal to the vigilante spirit at the (miserably staged) end: the townspeople make a bonfire of the gamblers' equipment. But vigilantes need to be on horses; vigilantes who arrive in a procession of cars don't jibe with the picture's brute power. It's no accident that the director lingers on those tractor punches that Buford delivers. When the nostalgic dream morality of cowboy movies is imposed on an actual modern town, it becomes a demand for bloodletting. Early on, Karlson showed us the bloody Buford, a red mass of wounds, lying in the road; in the movie's terms, there is only one answer to that. His enemies' blood must flow. And the audience is worked up to believe that bloodletting is necessary, that that is what does the job. In a sense, this is also what *Dirty Harry* said, and the same message is embedded in the new police thrillers that feature cops who are really cowboy heroes. The blood-pounding excitement that most of the street Westerns aim for is simply box-office excitement, but in *Walking Tall* it is integral to the fundamentalist politics that probably all of us carry inside us at some primitive level—even those of us who watch this picture appalled. Buford has a galvanic effect on the audience because he incarnates the blood rage that can so easily be worked up in frustrated people. The visceral impact of this shrewd, humble film makes one know how crowds must feel when they're being swayed by demagogues.

The New Yorker, February 25, 1974

THE MOTHER AND THE WHORE
THE USED MADONNA

The *Mother and the Whore* is made from inside the state of mind that is thought of as Village or Berkeley-graduate-school or, as in this case, Left Bank. It's about the attitudes of educated people who use their education as a way of making contact with each other rather than with the larger world. Their manner of dress and behavior is a set of signals: they're telling each other that they're illusionless. Their way of life is a group courtship rite, though they court each other not in order to find someone to love but in order to be loved—that is, admired. They live in an atmosphere of apocalyptic narcissism. The characters in *The Mother and the Whore* belong to the café life of St.-Germain-des-Prés, and so does the film, which can be said to represent the dead hopes of a decade and a generation. The Don Juans of this group hardly need to be ambulatory; they cruise from their coffeehouse chairs. The hero, Alexandre (Jean-Pierre Léaud), is a thirty-year-old puppy; in his milieu the less you do the cooler you appear. Alexandre has the glib, attitudinizing male-intellectual vanity that is the educated bum's form of machismo. He's a harmless, lightweight liar; he cultivates his whims; he lies for the fun of it. He's an amusing put-on artist, with no visible convictions or depth of feeling. When he sees an old girl friend who's about to be married (Isabelle Weingarten), he makes a declaration of undying passion merely for the pleasure of hearing himself sound passionate. She's smart enough not to take him any more seriously than he takes himself.

Alexandre has no interest in a profession; he's just a professional charmer. He's able to live without working because he has found a "mother"—a mistress who takes care of him. Tough, good-natured Marie (Bernadette Lafont) runs a dress shop, but she's far from being a bourgeoise. She's a coarse, unpretentious working-class woman trying to enjoy herself; she's the solid world that Alexandre returns to from the hours of preening at the café. All his energy goes into his poses and paradoxes, and the strategies of coolness. But when he plots a little campaign to make himself important to Veronika—a new girl he spots—it's wasted effort. Veronika (Françoise Lebrun), a young, bone-poor nurse, has a tired, solid madonna face, but she's so whorishly available that, as she says, "it turns a lot of people off." The movie is a fugal series of monologues and dialogues among Alexandre, Marie, and Veronika, almost entirely on the subject of sex. It was shot in grainy black-and-white that's deliberately dark and streaked; there's no musical score—only "natural" sounds and an occasional scratchy record played on a phonograph—and it's three hours and thirty-five minutes long. A viewer's response to this debauch of talk will be determined by whether he can accept the whorish madonna Veronika's monologues as revealing the truth or thinks they're the familiar rant of Catholic women on the sauce. If the former, the film, which was written and directed by Jean Eustache, may seem a depressive-generation masterpiece; if the latter, a sour conceit. I think it's part one and part the other—but the parts are inseparable.

The rough-and-tumble Marie is warmly played. Bernadette Lafont, whose large, generous features make her a natural for working-class women, is open-hearted in the role—crass and likable. The filmmaker goes in for paradoxes, too: Marie, the "mother," resembles the traditional understanding whore of French films (such as Arletty in *Le Jour Se Lève*), and her relationship with Alexandre is an updating of the whore-pimp relationship. Alexandre (and the graduate-school little bohemias of the world are full of Alexandres, though generally they sponge off their parents as well as friends and girl friends) is, in fact, a spoiled-infant pimp, who lives off Marie and doesn't even provide a pimp's protection. He has nothing to offer but his taste, his classy prattle, and some body warmth. He considers that his presence—when he's around—is gift enough. Léaud doesn't just walk through his role (as he sometimes does); he projects the shallow Alexandre's emotional states, and he gives what is probably his most deeply felt performance as an adult. Alexandre is onscreen throughout, reacting to the women, cajoling them, trying on attitudes—so infatuated with his own pranks he hardly cares what effect they have on others. Alexandre likes to perform, and his dry facetiousness is often funny (probably considerably funnier if one knows French well enough to get the slang). Though Jean Eustache has said that he wrote the roles specifically for the performers, Léaud's performance is nevertheless a feat of giving oneself over to a role. He never drops the mask, he never slips away from Alexandre.

However, the picture stands or falls with the character of Veronika (and she's a very creepy, dolorous character), because it's Veronika who carries the burden of Eustache's emotionalism. She looks Slavic (she says she is of Polish origin), and she appears to be Eustache's holy-whory Sonia, an updated version of the heroine of *Crime and Punishment;* she's there to awaken silly Alexandre's soul, though he's no Raskolnikov. The only thing that keeps Alexandre from being the Léaud specialty—a pet—is that he's forced to listen to Veronika's recital of her ugly, seamy deprivations and her nausea. She's drunken and insistent; once Alexandre has gone to bed with her, he can't get rid of her. She hounds him; she comes to Marie's apartment and climbs into bed with them. Veronika, who wears her hair saint-style, braided around her head, is a sexually abused character; her tiny garret room in the nurses' quarters of a hospital is like a penitential chamber. She volunteers for abuse; she seeks sex and feels humiliated by it. She's the biggest bundle of guilt ever to be hurled on the screen, and once she stops listening to Alexandre and starts talking she never shuts up—except to vomit up all the sex-without-love that she has subjected herself to.

Bernadette Lafont, who made her first screen appearance in the leading role of Truffaut's short *Les Mistons* (1957), and Léaud, whose long scarves here stretch back to his appearance as the twelve-year-old boy in *The 400 Blows* (1959), have been the emblematic New Wave performers; and the characters they play here are further extensions of the characters they've developed over the intervening years. (Even Isabelle Weingarten, who played the lead in Bresson's *Four Nights of a Dreamer,* carries that credential.) But Françoise Lebrun, a graduate student in modern literature who has never acted on the screen before, is completely Eustache's; she gives the picture its sullen, scratched soul. One may guess that her sad, deceptively placid face, with its suggestion of a badly used madonna, inspired Eustache. She has the sort of young-old face that a moviemaker could easily project onto; she's like a beat-out version of the young Dietrich, with her pale-gold braid around her head, as the innocent peasant, soon to be a fallen woman, in *The Song of Songs,* the hokey old Mamoulian-Sudermann film of innocence betrayed. Lebrun's wide-eyed face is blankly opaque—the face of a woman locked in her miseries. She keeps a sullen, suffering deadpan, and as the torrent of obscenities and complaints pours out, we can all project onto that face. *The Mother and the Whore* is a psychodrama that keeps shifting and redefining its terms; those terms are ironic until the last hour, when Veronika is exempted from irony and we are asked to identify with her and to see her as an icon of modern loneliness and suffering and degradation. She's a martyr to callous sex.

Eustache has no distance from Veronika. That's why the movie seems so arbitrary—you may feel that you've been a good sport to sit through it, that it's been an endurance contest—but it's also what gives the film its distinction. Eustache is right in there. His method is rather like that of a French Cassavetes; he's trying to put raw truth on the screen, and this film might be his *Lovers* to set next to Cassavetes's *Husbands.* Cassavetes tries to give acted material the look and sound of *cinéma vérité;* Eustache goes even further. He puts in dead stretches and trivia, building in boredom so that the material will seem lifelike; he prolongs the movie after one thinks it's finished—the prolongation seems almost like a director's joke. Eustache's method resembles the static randomness of the Warhol-Morrissey pictures, yet the randomness here is not a matter of indifference but a conscious goal. Chance is the illusion that Eustache seeks. He didn't allow the actors to deviate from the three-hundred-page script, but he keeps the framing a little rough and insecure, as if the cameraman were looking for the action, and it took three months of editing to make this film seem unedited. Eustache wants the look of chance because he's determined not to be ingratiating. It's as if he felt that only by pushing us beyond patience, only by taking us away from the surface pleasures of cinematographic elegance and a full score, only by rubbing our noses in his view of reality, can he make us *feel.* (He may equate us with the infantile, pleasure-seeking Alexandre.)

It's true that films tend to look too rich and that they're often rotten with meaningless "production values"—and sometimes rotten with "beauty." But those who try to strip them down to naked fundamentals usually seem to be puritan aesthetes—and a pain. *The Mother and the Whore* proclaims its honesty and its purity in a way I can't stomach—as if its messiness and its characters' messy lives were holy. The religiously inspired polarity of the title suggests that Eustache sees himself as Alexandre, divided, torn between the mother and the whore. And it's part of the emotional tone of this period to reject the mother and to identify with the whore. Like Veronika, Eustache is saying, "I'm going to show you more of the tormented soul than anybody has ever shown you," and, like Veronika, he confuses rag-chewing and revulsion with holy revelation.

Art and disgust are closely related in the thinking of a number of modern filmmakers of religious background. Paul Morrissey's films seem to be made by a dirty-minded altar boy, and the concept that messy anguish sanctifies is at the very heart of Cassavetes's films. *The Mother and the Whore* is not a negligible film: it's unmistakably a personal expression, and it does achieve moments of intensity. No doubt some people will say more than moments, and some will consider Veronika's ultimate monologue cathartic, though the fact that it signals reprieve for the exhausted viewer may contribute to that feeling. (The three hours and thirty-five minutes feel so long that you want to think you've had something to show for it, and catharsis is big stuff—worth squirming for.) But is Alexandre ultimately moved to ask Veronika to marry him because he's a fool who loves grand gestures, or are we really meant to believe in the authenticity of what she represents? For me, it was as if Alexandre were pressured into confessing a crime he hadn't committed. Veronika rants so much that finally he assumes the guilt for all the men whom this obsessive woman has landed in bed with and then felt lacerated by. He assumes the guilt for the whole world's failure to love. Alexandre may be just trying on his new deep feelings, but she, I'm afraid, is intended to be the real thing. It turns out that Eustache is a sin-ridden bohemian of an earlier school and that the movie is about the penance that must be done for sex-without-love. He has welded together the disaffection of a generation and his own sexual disgust. Isn't that really what Veronika's diatribe is all about? Isn't she really saying, "I want to be loved"? I suspect that that's why the movie will appeal to people who feel stranded in a confusion of personal freedom and social hopelessness. Antonioni explored the theme of sex without love, but he placed it among the affluent; in placing this theme among the students and those who go on living like students, Eustache makes direct contact with the movie audience. Antonioni's bleak atmosphere spoke of spiritual emptiness; Eustache's atmosphere is like a spiritual mange, and probably many people in the aging-young movie audience feel mangy and lost and degraded, and have had their share of miserable sex experiences. They may be willing to embrace Veronika's loathing of her life, and perhaps willing to look to the healing power of Christian love. The film is designed to be a religious experience, but the musty answer it offers to the perils of sexual freedom is actually a denial of sexual freedom. In *The Mother and the Whore*, the New Wave meets the Old Wave.

The New Yorker, March 4, 1974

THE SUGARLAND EXPRESS

The Sugarland Express is like some of the entertaining studio-factory films of the past (it's as commercial and shallow and impersonal), yet is has so much eagerness and flash and talent that it just about transforms its scrubby ingredients. The director, Steven Spielberg, is twenty-six; I can't tell if he has any mind, or even a strong personality, but then a lot of good moviemakers have got by without being profound. He isn't saying anything special in The Sugarland Express, but he has a knack for bringing out young actors, and a sense of composition and movement that almost any director might envy. Composition seems to come naturally to him, as it does to some of the young Italians; Spielberg uses his gift in a very free-and-easy, American way—for humor, and for a physical response to action. He could be that rarity among directors—a born entertainer—perhaps a new generation's Howard Hawks. In terms of the pleasure that technical assurance gives an audience, this film is one of the most phenomenal début films in the history of movies. If there is such a thing as a movie sense—and I think there is (I know fruit venders and cabdrivers who have it and some movie critics who don't)—Spielberg really has it. But he may be so full of it that he doesn't have much else. There's no sign of the emergence of a new film artist (such as Martin Scorsese) in The Sugarland Express, but it marks the début of a new-style, new-generation Hollywood hand.

The story—based on an occurrence in Texas in 1969—is about Lou Jean (Goldie Hawn) and her husband, Clovis (William Atherton), petty thieves who lost custody of their infant son while they were in jail, and their attempt to get him back, which involves taking a highway-patrol officer, Slide (Michael Sacks), hostage. The child is with his adoptive parents in the town of Sugarland, and as Lou Jean and Clovis drive there in the patrol car they've commandeered, with a stream of police behind, other cars follow, and crowds gather to wish them well. Spielberg, young as he is, is already a graduate of TV, having caused a stir by his direction of an episode of Columbo, and a sensation with a terrifying made-for-TV movie called Duel, which was mostly about a truck. The Sugarland Express is mostly about cars; Spielberg is a choreographic virtuoso with cars. He patterns them; he makes them dance and crash and bounce back. He handles enormous configurations of vehicles; sometimes they move so sweetly you think he must be wooing them. These sequences are as unforced and effortless-looking as if the cars themselves—mesmerized—had just waltzed into their idiot formations. It's implicit in the movie's whole scheme that vast numbers of cops are pursuing the kidnapped patrolman, and that people are joining the procession and encouraging the young parents to retrieve their child, because that gives them all an opportunity to get in their cars and whiz across Texas. Photographed by Vilmos Zsigmond, the cars shimmer in the hot sunlight; in the dark, the red lights of the police cars are like eerie night-blooming flowers. The cars have tiffs, wrangle, get confused. And so do the people, who are also erratic and—in certain lights—eerily beautiful. There's a suggestion of a Robert Altman influence in the fast and loose conversations, but they're not really so loose. The flurries of talk aren't casual; these aren't Altman's people, whose talk overlaps, as in life, but rabid people all talking at once—to heat the movie. These huffy characters, riled up and yelling at each other, are in the combustible comedy style of Preston Sturges (of his *Hail the Conquering Hero* and *The Miracle of Morgan's Creek*, especially). This movie enjoys orneriness and collision courses, as the Sturges movies did; it sees the characters' fitful, moody nuttiness as the American's inalienable right to make a fool of himself. It merges Sturges's love of comic confusion with the action world of cars to create a jamboree. We wind up feeling affectionate toward some highly unlikely people—particularly toward the Goldie Hawn character, Lou Jean, who started it all.

Probably everybody knows how talented Goldie Hawn is, and that has made her screen performances the more disappointing. She's done darting, fidgety little bits of business in several roles, but she was stymied; she was thrashing around in tightly blocked pictures. Here you don't see her yanking the director's sleeve and asking "Now?" She just does it. Spielberg's youth and speed release her; she stays in character, and the character grows. Lou Jean has more gumption than brains; she's the American go-getter gone haywire. Right at the opening, Lou Jean gets off a bus and her bouncy, determined walk spells trouble. She could have a sign engraved on her forehead: "I want it now." Whatever it is, Lou Jean can't wait for it. When she goes to the prison farm to visit her husband and starts to scream at him, you know poor Clovis is sunk. In some ways, the world divides into the hysterics—the screamers and scene-makers and weepers—and those who want to keep the peace. Clovis is a pushover for his wife's tantrummy demands; he loves peace, and he loves her, too. He has only four more months to serve, but he'll break out of prison when she tells him to, because he's more scared of her than of the authorities. Lou Jean can't think ahead, and Clovis tries not to. It takes awhile before we recognize that, in her own flighty, screwed-up way, she loves him, too, and that she really does want her baby back. Nothing in the movie which involves Lou Jean or Clovis or Slide (or the cars) looks rehearsed or tired. William Atherton (he appeared on the stage in *The House of Blue Leaves, The Basic Training of Pavlo Hummel,* and *Suggs in the City*) has the most difficult role; Clovis knows (intermittently, anyway) what his wife is too easily distracted to grasp—that they're over their heads in trouble. Atherton's performance gives the picture solidity. Without him, it would be a giddy new-style screwball comedy, but he's the sparrow who falls. With the director's help but without a great deal of help from the script, Atherton—he looks like the skinny offspring of Robert Redford and Paul Newman—deepens the picture; we begin to share Clovis's apprehensiveness.

The script, by Hal Barwood and Matthew Robbins, who are also young, is satisfying and full of incident, but it's made up of swipes from other movies; one routine from *Roxie Hart* turns up twice; two crabbed, mean fathers—each decades older than is called for—make dour pronouncements about their own kids. There's a difference in quality between the writing and the direction. You get the feeling that the director grew up with TV and wheels (My Mother the Car?), and that he has a new temperament. Maybe Spielberg loves action and comedy and speed so much that he really doesn't care if a movie has anything else in it. But he doesn't copy old stuff. He isn't deep, but he isn't derivative, either. The scriptwriters are living off the past. I think it's likely that being part of the TV-and-young-moviemaker generation affects a director—changes his perceptions—much more basically than it affects writers. It may turn writers on so that they want to work in movies, but they tend to draw upon old movies for their ideas, and this is particularly true of the film-school and American Film Institute troops (which Barwood and Robbins belong to), whose education has been sitting around and looking at movies, and who are now selling scripts to the major studios. They're not really writers, any more than most of the other Hollywood writers are. They're synthesizers of other people's ideas, even when they write an "original" like *The Sugarland Express.*

Spielberg is a bit leaden with some of the older actors, and can't always redeem the low-comedy effects—the sort of squalls and antic outrage that got laughs in *The Russians Are Coming, The Russians Are Coming.* There are hero-worshipful views of Ben Johnson, who plays the captain who leads the pursuit; the camera regards him as if he were a diva and his face the big aria. The captain's excesses (breaking the weapons of a pair of right-wing nuts, shooting the tires of a TV-crew truck) are in a too cute old-movie style. I'm not a great fan of Ben Johnson's acting in general; he holds positions like a pointer—imparting an air of deliberation and importance to every move he makes. Some of the comic touches that pull down Spielberg's style are probably the result of the editors' leaving a nudging extra beat; their work is mostly split-second right, but they leave a beat on an art effect, too—on the Teddy bear in the road near the end of the picture (the shot featured in the ad campaign). Spielberg can't redeem it all, but he gets away with it; he's one of those wizard directors who can make trash entertaining. That's what *The Sting,* for example, tries to do, and though I may be lonely in this, I think it fails. Spielberg savors film, and you respond to that. *The Sugarland Express* has life to it. Not the kind of life that informs a young film like *Mean Streets*—probably the best American movie of 1973—but the vitality that a director with great instincts can bring to commercial entertainment.

The New Yorker, March 18, 1974

There is no way to estimate the full effect of Vietnam and Watergate on popular culture, but earlier films were predicated on an implied system of values which is gone now, except in the corrupt, vigilante form of a *Dirty Harry* or a *Walking Tall*. Almost all the current hits are jokes on the past, and especially on old films—a mixture of nostalgia and parody, laid on with a trowel. The pictures reach back in time, spoofing the past, jabbing at it. Nobody understands what contemporary heroes or heroines should be, or how they should relate to each other, and it's safer not to risk the box-office embarrassment of seriousness. I often come out of a movie now feeling wiped out, desolate—and often it's a movie that the audience around me has reacted to noisily, as if it were having a high, great time—and I think I feel that way because of the nihilism in the atmosphere. It isn't intentional or philosophical nihilism; it's the kind one sometimes feels at a porn show—the way everything is turned to dung, oneself included. A couple of years ago, I went with another film critic, a young man, to see a hard-core movie in the Broadway area, and there was a live stage show with it. A young black girl—she looked about seventeen but must have been older—did a strip and then danced naked. The theater was small, and the girl's eyes, full of hatred, kept raking the customers' faces. I was the only other woman there, and each time her eyes came toward me, I had to look down; finally, I couldn't look up at all. The young critic and I sat in misery, unable to leave, since that would look like a put-down of her performance. We had to take the contempt with which she hid her sense of being degraded, and we shared in her degradation, too.

■ ■ ■

There are a few exceptions, but in general it can be said that the public no longer discovers movies, the public no longer makes a picture a hit. If the advertising for a movie doesn't build up an overwhelming desire to be part of the event, people just don't go. They don't listen to their own instincts, they don't listen to the critics—they listen to the advertising. Or, to put it more precisely, they do listen to their instincts, but their instincts are now controlled by advertising. It seeps through everything—talk shows, game shows, magazine and newspaper stories. Museums organize retrospectives of a movie director's work to coördinate with the opening of his latest film, and publish monographs paid for by the movie companies. College editors travel at a movie company's expense to see its big new film and to meet the director, and directors preview their new pictures at colleges. The public-relations event becomes part of the national consciousness. You don't hear anybody say, "I saw the most wonderful movie you never heard of"; when you hear people talking, it's about the same blasted movie that everybody's going to—the one that's flooding the media. Yet even the worst cynics still like to think that "word of mouth" makes hits. And the executives who set up the machinery of manipulation love to believe that the public—the public that's sitting stone-dead in front of its TV sets—spontaneously discovered their wonderful movie. If it's a winner, they say it's the people's choice. But, in the TV age, when people say they're going to see *Walking Tall* because they've "heard" it's terrific, that rarely means a friend has told them; it means they've picked up signals from the atmosphere. It means *Walking Tall* has been plugged so much that every cell in a person's body tells him he's got to see it. Advertising is a form of psychological warfare that in popular culture, as in politics, is becoming harder to fight with aboveboard weapons. It's becoming damned near invincible. If Hollywood executives still believe in word of mouth, it's because the words come out of their own mouths. These men were shaken for a few years; they didn't understand what made a film a counterculture hit. They're happy to be back on firm ground with *The Sting*. Harmless, inoffensive. Plenty of plot but no meanings. Not even any sex to worry about.

Much—perhaps most—of the students' and educated moviegoers' unresponsiveness to recent fine work can be traced to the decisions of the movie companies about what will sell and what won't. With their overweening campaign budgets for *The Great Gatsby* and *Chinatown,* the Paramount executives didn't even take a full-page ad in the *Times* to announce that *The Conversation* had won the Grand Prize at Cannes. They didn't *plan* on *The Conversation* being a success, and nothing is going to make them help it become one. *Gatsby* and *Chinatown* were their pictures, but *The Conversation* was Francis Ford Coppola's, and they're incensed at his being in a position (after directing *The Godfather*) to do what he wanted to do; they're *hurt* that he flouts their authority, working out of San Francisco instead of Los Angeles. And they don't really have any respect for *The Conversation,* because it's an idea film. It's the story of a compulsive loner (Gene Hackman), a wizard at electronic surveillance who is so afraid others will spy on him that he empties his life; he's a cipher—a cipher in torment. There's nothing to discover about him, and *still* he's in terror of being bugged. (Hackman is a superlative actor, but his peculiarity, his limitation, like Ralph Richardson's when he was younger, is his quality of anonymity: just what is right for this role.) *The Conversation* is driven by an inner logic. It's a little thin, because the logic is the working out of one character's obsession, but it's a buggy movie that can get to you so that when it's over you really feel you're being bugged. Maybe the reason the promotion people didn't try to exploit the Watergate tie-in was that they suspected the picture might also be saying something about movie companies. If a film isn't promoted, it's often because something about it—the idea itself, or the director's obstinate determination to make it—needles the bosses.

Executives show a gambler's ardor in arranging the financing of a picture. Sometimes they buy into one when it's finished or almost finished, in what appears to be the absolute conviction that it's a winner. But almost any straw in the wind can make them lose confidence. They'll try out a tricky, subtle movie on a Friday-night preview audience that has come to see *Walking Tall* or John Wayne in *McQ,* and decide that the movie has no public appeal. They pull away from what they fear will be a failure; within the fiefdom of their company they don't want to be associated with a risky venture. They all snuggle deep into the company's hits; a picture like *The Sting* becomes a soft fur collar that they caress themselves with. The company that has *The Sting* doesn't worry about a real sendoff for *The Sugarland Express:* where are the big stars? The company with *The Exorcist* doesn't give much thought to a campaign for *Mean Streets:* some of the executives don't find it "satisfying," so they're sure the public won't. The movie companies used to give all their pictures a chance, but now they'll put two or three million, or even five, into selling something they consider surefire, and a token—a pittance—into the others. And when an unpublicized picture fails they can always cover their tracks by blaming the director. "There was nothing we could do for it," the executives in charge of advertising always say, and once they have doomed a picture, who can prove them wrong?

What isn't generally understood is that the top men don't want to be proved wrong and the lower-echelon executives have a jobholder's interest in proving their bosses right. For all the publicity the companies get from giving a picture "a second chance"—never really having given it a first—I can think of only one or two cases when they honestly did provide a fresh chance, and there's a whole morgueful of movies that were killed despite indications of public response; for example, Gillo Pontecorvo's only picture after *The Battle of Algiers—Burn!,* starring Marlon Brando, which came and went so fast that hardly anybody knows it exists.

If the company men don't like a picture, or are nervous about its chances, or just resent the director's wanting to do something he cares about (instead of taking the big assignments they believe in), they do minimal advertising, telling him, "Let's wait for the reviews," or "We'll see how the reviewers like it," and then, even if the reviews are great, they say, "But the picture isn't doing business. Why should we throw away money on it?" And if he mentions the reviews, they say, "Listen, the critics have never meant anything. You know that. Why waste money? If people don't want to go, you can't force them to buy tickets."

■　■　■

There's a natural war in Hollywood between the businessmen and the artists. It's based on drives that may go deeper than politics or religion: on the need for status, and warring dreams. The entrepreneur class in the arts is a relatively late social development; there were impresarios earlier, but it was roughly a hundred years ago, when the arts began to be commercialized for a large audience, that the mass-culture middleman was born. He functions as a book publisher, as a theatrical producer, as a concert manager, as a rock promoter, but the middleman in the movie world is probably more filled with hatred for the arts he traffics in than the middleman in any other area. The movie entrepreneur is even more of a self-made man than the others; he came out of nowhere. He has to raise—and risk—more money, and he stands to gain more. In a field with no traditions, he is more of a gambler and less of an aesthete than entrepreneurs in the other arts. He's a street fighter, his specialty low cunning. Even if he's a second- or third-generation movie executive with a college education, or a Harvard-educated lawyer turned agent turned producer, he's learned to be a street fighter if he wasn't born to it, and he has the same hatred of the artist. The artist, with his expressive needs—the artist, who, by definition, cares about something besides money—denigrates the only talent that the entrepreneur has: raising money. Nobody respects the entrepreneur's dream of glory, and nobody respects his singular talent—least of all the artist who needs him, and is often at his mercy.

The entrepreneur has no class, no status; and, whether he was a scrambling junk dealer or a scheming agent or a poor little rich boy who managed to survive his mogul father's ruthless bullying, he knows that. A director or an actor doesn't even have to be an artist—only to identify himself as an artist—to get the cachet, while the moneyman is likely to be treated as a moneygrubbing clown. Some few—Joe Levine, and Sam Goldwyn before him—have been able to make celebrities of themselves by acquiring a comic status, the status of a shrewd, amusing vulgarian. In no other field is the entrepreneur so naked a status-seeker. Underlings are kept busy arranging awards and medals and honorary degrees for the producer, whose name looms so large in the ads that the public—and often the producer himself—comes to think he actually made the pictures. Ross Hunter, Robert Radnitz, even Hal Wallis in recent years hardly have room in their advertising for the writers' and directors' names. The packagers offer themselves as the stars, and in many cases their pictures fail because they insist on employing nonentity directors who don't assert any authority.

The hatred of the moneyman for the ungovernable artist is based on a degradation that isn't far from that stripper's hatred of the audience—furious resentment of the privileged people who, as he sees it, have never had to stoop to do the things he has done. As in Mordecai Richler's exultant novel *The Apprenticeship of Duddy Kravitz* (which really enables one to understand what makes Sammy run), and the teeming, energetic Canadian film based on it, the entrepreneur is, typically, a man who has always been treated like dirt. And even after he's fought his way up, finagling like crazy every step of the way, a profligate director with the world at his feet may not only threaten that solvency but still treat him like dirt, as in Peter Viertel's thinly disguised account, in the novel *White Hunter, Black Heart,* of the relations of John Huston and Sam Spiegel during the making of *The African Queen.* There are few directors who feel such disdain, fewer still who would express it so nakedly, but the moneymen keep looking for signs of it: they tap phones, they turn employees into sneaks and spies—all to get proof of the disloyalty of those ingrate artists. It doesn't help if the artists like the tough bosses personally—if they prize the unconcealed wiliness or the manic, rude drive. In Richler's later novel *St. Urbain's Horseman,* the now rich Duddy Kravitz appears as a minor character. When someone assures

Duddy that his blond actress wife loves him, Duddy is exasperated: "What are you talking, she loves me? Who in the hell could love Duddy Kravitz?" Duddy's view of himself doesn't leave much of a basis for friendship, and any affection the artist may feel disintegrates as soon as the businessman uses his power to control the artist's work. The war of the businessmen against the artists is the war of the powerful against the powerless, based on the hatred of those who can't for those who can, and in return the hatred of those who can for those who won't let them.

The producers' complaint about the hothead director who puts up a fight to try something different is "He's self-destructive. He's irresponsible. You can't do business with him." And they make him suffer for it. The artists in Hollywood are objects of ridicule because they're trying to work as artists. When a gifted director is broke and needs to work, the producers stick him on a project that is compromised from the start, and then the picture is one more failure to be held against him. They frustrate him at every turn because he doesn't respect them, and he is humiliated by men he doesn't even respect. The producers feel secure with the directors and actors who don't have ideas of their own, who will take jobs because they need to work and don't really care what they do. Those are the ones the producers call "artists with discipline."

■　　■　　■

An actor or a director can become an "artist with discipline" when he has a huge box-office hit, and his reputation for discipline will soar if, like Paul Newman or Robert Redford, he has a string of hits. Actually, to the money-men discipline means success plus a belief in success. The moneymen want a director who won't surprise them. They're scared of a man like Altman, because they just don't know what he'll do on a picture; they can't trust him to make it resemble the latest big hit. They want solid imitations, pictures that reek of money spent and money to come, pictures that look safe—like those Biblical epics that came rumbling off the assembly lines in the fifties. Twentieth Century-Fox and Warner Brothers are jointly producing a burning-skyscraper picture, *The Towering Inferno*, with Steve McQueen, Paul Newman, William Holden, Jennifer Jones, Robert Wagner, Fred Astaire, Richard Chamberlain, and other assorted big names. It's Grand Hotel in flames at last. Universal, for starters, has signed up Anne Bancroft and George C. Scott for *The Hindenburg*, described as "a multilayered drama with a gallery of international characters." In other words, Grand Hotel in flames in the sky. Every couple of years, the American movie public is said to crave something. Now it's calamity, and already the wave of apocalyptic movies— which aren't even here yet—is being analyzed in terms of our necrophilia. The studio heads are setting up disaster epics like kids reaching hand over hand up a baseball bat—all because of the success of *The Poseidon Adventure*. I doubt whether there's a single one of the directors mounting these disaster specials—becoming commanders-in-chief in an idiot war—who wouldn't infinitely rather be working on something else. By the time the public is gorged with disasters and the epics begin to flop, the studio heads will have fastened on another get-rich-quick gimmick and the people who work for them will lose a few more years of what might have been their creative lives. The producers gamble on the public's wanting more of whatever is a hit, and since they *all* gamble on that, the public is always quickly surfeited, but the failures of the flaccid would-be hits never anger the producers the way the failures of the films that someone really fought for do. The producers want those films to fail; they often make them fail. A Sam Peckinpah film, an Altman film, a Kershner film—the executives get pleasure out of seeing those films fail. It's a *punishment* of the artist.

Since all the businessmen's energy goes into strategy and manipulation, they can outfox the artists damn near every time; that's really the business they're in. Their right of "final cut"—one of the great symbolic terms in moviemaking—gives them the chance to chop up the film of a director who has angered them by doing it his own way; they'll mutilate the picture trying to remove the complexities he battled to put in. They love to play God with other people's creations. Movie after movie is mangled, usually by executives' last-minute guesses about what the public wants. When they've finished, they frequently can't do anything with the pictures but throw them away. That's their final godlike act—an act easy for them to live with, because they always have the director to blame. To them, the artist is the outsider; he's not a member of the family, to be protected. A few years ago, when word was out in the industry that Brando didn't mean anything at the box office, the producer David Merrick fired him from a picture; I asked an executive connected with the production what Brando had done. "Nothing," he said. "Brando was working hard, and he was cooperative with everyone. But he suggested some ways to improve the script; they were good suggestions—the script was a mess. But legally that was interference, and Merrick could fire Brando and collect on the insurance." "But why?" I persisted. He shrugged at my ignorance. "What could make David Merrick bigger than firing Marlon Brando?" he said.

■　　■　　■

The star can be defined by what the producer says of him: "If he wants to burn down the studio, I'll hand him the match." That was said, I think, of Jerry Lewis, but it applies to such Hollywood figures as Frank Sinatra and, of course, Clint Eastwood and Robert Redford and Steve McQueen. What it means is very simple: the producers will hand them a match because the producers are banking the money. The producer is saying, "He can degrade me as long as I get mine out of it." And underneath that he's saying, "But wait until he has to come to me for something." The producers hate Brando for refusing to settle down and go for the money; they love-hate McQueen and Redford and Eastwood. They need them; they court them. And yes, they can make a deal with them, but only on the star's terms, and the producers are never allowed to forget it. If the chance ever comes, they'll make the star pay for that.

The country has never been as star crazy as it is right now; there aren't very many movie stars, but the phenomenon of stardom operates in television, in radio, in literature, in the academic world, in politics, in the women's movement. (The black movement hasn't been getting much publicity recently, because it lacks stars.) Yet can one watch a few TV "roasts"—those ugly-jolly orgies of mock insults and real insults and odious sentimental disclaimers in which celebrities are fêted—without becoming aware of the sense of betrayal that is just under the surface? The best performer at the roast is obviously the one who dares to be the most malicious, and the person honored is forced to be a good sport while others "kid" him, letting out their aggression while he tries to laugh. And then they embrace him and say they didn't mean it. The roast is the show-business form of Shirley Jackson's lottery. It's a public display of the anger and self-hatred of those caught in the system, a ritual gathering of sellouts hitting each other with bladders and pretending it doesn't hurt. And that's how they feel when they're *at the top*. Their contempt for the audience, like the stripper's, is probably what makes it possible for them to keep going. They begin to believe that Las Vegas is all there is. The roast is a metaphor for the truth of the business; that's why it has become impossible for the Academy Awards presentation to have any style or dignity. The members of the Hollywood community can't control their self-destructive impulses any longer; they can't resist humiliating themselves before the whole world. "If that's what people want," the performers say, "I'll give it to them." Essentially, they're all playing to Duddy Kravitz. He's the man backing the international motion-picture roast.

■　■　■

A reviewer who pans a producer's picture is just one more person telling him he has no taste. When the reviewers praise movies that are allowed to die, the moneyman's brute instincts are confirmed, and the reviewers' impotence gives him joy. "Why must we sit back and allow the critics to determine if a film is acceptable as a consumer product?" Frank Yablans, the president of Paramount, asked this June. He was speaking to some two hundred people who work in television, explaining to them that word of mouth, which can defeat downbeat reviews, will be Paramount's target. A reviewer speaks out once, or maybe twice. The advertisers are an invisible force pounding at the public day after day. Unfavorable reviews are almost never powerful enough to undo the saturation publicity. Besides, curiosity about an event like *The Exorcist* is a big factor; as the woman quoted in *Variety* said, "I want to see what everybody is throwing up about."

When other values are rickety, the fact that something is selling gives it a primacy, and its detractors seem like spoilsports. The person who holds out against an event looks a loser: the minority is a fool. People are cynical about advertising, of course, but their cynicism is so all-inclusive now that they're indifferent, and so they're more susceptible to advertising than ever. If nothing matters anyway, why not just go where the crowd goes? That's a high in itself.

People often make analogies between the world of live theater and the world of movies, and raise the question "Don't movie critics have too much power?" But in movies it's the businessmen who have the power. A reviewer's words can't be heard above the din unless they're amplified in the ads—which usually means reduced to a short, exclamatory quote and repeated incessantly. But that's only if the reviewer provided a quote for a picture that the company "has high hopes for"; if it's a picture that the company has lost interest in, there will be a few halfhearted ads, with apathetically selected quotes. Raves from even the dozen most influential papers and magazines can't make a success of *Mean Streets* if the company doesn't construct a campaign around those raves. The public indifference is a result of something that starts at the top of the movie company and filters down.

The younger audience—high-school and college students—grew up with the rating system. As kids, they couldn't escape to the movies, the way their parents did, and so movies weren't an important part of their lives (though television was). When *they* say they love movies, they mean the old movies that they're just discovering, and the new hits. Even the sub-teens want the events; they were born into sixties cynicism and saturation advertising.

The students now who discover movies in college and want to get into film production have a different outlook from the young counter-culture filmmakers of the sixties. They're not interested in getting into movie work in order to change movies; they just want to get into movie work. A young film student expressed anger to me about Elia Kazan, who had given a lecture at his university. Kazan had said that the studios wouldn't finance the subjects he was interested in, and offered him projects he couldn't face doing. The student, without a shade of sympathy for those caught in this basic Hollywood trap, said, "How can we listen to him? We would do anything to break in, and he says he's turning down projects!" Students have little interest in why a person refuses to direct the forty-sixth dope-heist picture or a romp about sprightly, beguiling swindlers; they don't care to hear some director say that he turned down *The Exorcist*. A hit makes a director a hero. A critic who speaks at a college now is almost certain to be asked such questions as "How many times do you see a movie before writing your critique?" and "Do you take notes?" The students are really asking, "How do you do it? How did you get to be a film critic?" They sometimes used to ask, "What do you think of Academy Awards?"—a question that was a sure laugh-getter from an audience that anticipated a tart rejoinder. Now they ask, "What [or who] do you think will win the Oscars this year?"

Stardom is success made manifest, success in human form, and, naturally, the yes-sayers are, in general, the biggest stars. College students are impressed and contemptuous at the same time. Can one imagine any picture so reactionary or vile that it would diminish Clint Eastwood's standing at a university? Even a reputation for corruption—for being willing to do anything for money—increases a star's stature, and the money gained gives him power and standing that are admired in a way that no-sayer's intransigence isn't, especially if his intransigence puts him out of the scene. There is nothing a star can do now that would really disgrace him. "Celebrity" has destroyed the concept of disgrace: scandal creates celebrity, and public misbehavior enhances it. Maybe *The Sting* is such a whopping hit because it's really a celebration of celebrity and stardom; it's not about anything but the golden yes-yes images of Redford and Newman. It doesn't need sex; it's got the true modern sex appeal—success.

In Los Angeles this spring, busloads of high-school students were brought in to listen to a Best-Sellers Panel composed of Helen Gurley Brown, Garson Kanin, Jacqueline Susann, and William Friedkin on the subject of how it feels to sell fifteen million books or to gross a hundred and twenty-five million dollars on a movie. From all accounts, there were no impolite questions, and no one made a rude noise when Kanin *(Tracy and Hepburn)* said, "We have to recognize that the public is smarter than we are. As individuals, one by one, perhaps no. But when that thousand-headed monster sits out there in the auditorium or sits reading your book of fiction, suddenly that mass audience is what the late Moss Hart called 'an idiot genius.'" This conceit of the successful—their absolute conviction that the crap that is sold is magically superior to the work that didn't sell—is the basis for the entrepreneurs' self-righteousness. The public has nothing to gain from believing this (and everything to lose), and yet the public swallows it.

■　■　■

The hits are not uniformly terrible, and in themselves they don't pose any great threat. But if this is all that people want from movies—if even educated people and people of taste and some sensibility settle for the nihilistic brassiness of the hits—there's no audience for new work. In the past ten years, filmmaking has attracted some of the most inspired college students—the aces and prodigies who in previous eras would have headed into poetry or architecture or painting or playwriting. There they are, poised and ready to take off, and there is no place for them to take off to except the same old Hollywood vise—tighter now, perfected. And there are the high-fliers who have been locked out all along—the dozens of artist-filmmakers who work in film not as a collaborative storytelling medium but as a highly individual art form, more closely related to the graphic arts than to Hollywood. Some of them, such as Ed Emshwiller, with his great trip film *Relativity,* and Jordan Belson, who has made flawless abstract visionary shorts, have already reached new peaks of film art; others, such as John Schofill, who works at scarily intense psychosexual imagery, may. Right now, there is no way for their work to reach movie theaters and no way for them to heat up and fertilize feature filmmaking, which needs renewal. Everything is ready for an age of great movies, except the entrepreneurs and the public.

Movies could easily go the way of the theater—and faster, since the moneymen have no aesthetic commitment whatever. And probably there'd be less lamentation for movies than for live theater. Because, of course, there's television. But it's not the same medium. And though if you don't read a book when it comes out you can read it a year later, if you don't see a movie when it comes out, and wait to see it a year later on television, you're not seeing what you could have seen in the theatre. (Nor do you see that movie if you wait to see it in a college, or at a film society in a cheap, grain 16-mm. reduction.) What's lost on television is the visual beauty, the spatial sense, the fusion of image and sound—everything that makes movies an art form. And movies made directly for television almost never have these qualities; one talks of TV movies in terms of pace and impact and tension, and occasionally—with the prestige ones—subject and performances, but who talks of television movies in terms of beauty? Movies made for TV, or movies made for a big screen and shown on TV, are reduced to just what the businessmen believe in—the bare bones of entertainment. There is something spurious about the very term "a movie made for TV," because what you make for TV is a TV program.

For perhaps most Americans, TV is an appliance, not to be used selectively but to be turned on—there's always something to watch. If a hundred million people see a movie in two showings on TV, that doesn't mean what it would if a hundred million people saw it in theaters. Sure, forty-two million people saw *The Autobiography of Miss Jane Pittman,* but they saw it sandwiched between two other shows. TV stars with audiences larger than the world has ever before known are eager to appear in a real movie—which, even if a hit, will be seen by only a handful, relatively speaking (until it, too, winds up on TV)—because they know that on TV they're part of the furniture. On TV they're mundane, they're reduced to the routinely, boringly tolerable. There's an aesthetic element in the phrase "larger than life," and the artists working in the movie medium instinctively take that into consideration. What is on the big screen has an aesthetic clarity denied to the box; when you're watching a movie in a theater, you don't need a voice telling you what you have just seen.

There have been some few subjects filmed for TV which nobody would finance for theaters, because it's generally understood that people won't pay to see a film on a subject like that of *I Heard the Owl Call My Name* or *Jane Pittman* or *The Execution of Private Slovik.* But a few TV shows with social themes shouldn't become the occasion for big headlines in the press about how television "has been growing bolder." Bold is just what these shows aren't; even when they're made as well as possible, they're mincingly careful. And they're not a key to new opportunities on TV so much as a key to the constriction of opportunities for moviemakers: moviemakers can't get backing for pictures with social themes—or with any real themes at all. Probably it's true that people wouldn't pay to see the films on social themes which they'll watch on television, but that's because those subjects are treated in the sober, limited TV manner. We have no way of knowing how the public might respond if a hugely talented filmmaker with adequate resources and a campaign to back him took on a large social theme. Nobody has had the chance in decades.

Television represents what happens to a medium when the artists have no power and the businessmen are in full, unquestioned control. People's TV expectations are so low and so routinized that *Brian's Song* can pass for an event, and a pitifully predictable problem play like *Tell Me Where It Hurts,* in which Maureen Stapleton plays a middle-aged housewife who joins a women's-lib group and has her consciousness raised, is received by the press as if it marked a significant advance. And what sort of opportunities does *normal* television offer for the development of talent? Here are the words of Brandon Stoddard, A.B.C.'s vice-president in charge of motion pictures for television:

> I am interested in emotional jeopardy, not physical jeopardy. I want the viewer to really care about the people and to feel something when it is over. . . . I have nothing against exploitative material if it is done right, and the way to do it right is to translate it into human drama rather than gimmicks. I don't want to know about the two Vampires in the casino in Las Vegas. I want to know about the man they are attacking and how it will affect his life. . . . We are looking everywhere for story ideas and even calling colleges to get some new blood into this.

Movies as an art form won't die and go to the heaven of television. If they die, they'll be truly dead. Even if the shift in the audience toward the crude and insensitive is only a temporary derangement, it could be sufficient to destroy movies. The good recent films—all together—can't possibly lose as much money as a single clinker like *Star!* or *Camelot,* but even if each one of them should manage to break even, and some of them to show a small or moderate profit, the businessmen will still see them as failures. The businessmen don't collect medals for moderate profits; they get their medals for box-office killers, and they don't want pictures by people who reject their values. When they tell a director, "Listen, what you call crap is what the public wants," it's not just an objective comment; they want the public to want this crap, and they've made stark sure it will. Since they've cold-decked public opinion, since they promote and sell only what they like, when they say, "That's what the public wants," it's the truth.

■ ■ ■

Nathanael West got it upside down. The locusts aren't those poor bastards from Oklahoma who want to touch a movie star and die in the sun; the locusts run the studios, and it's they who, in West's metaphor, will burn Los Angeles—they'll hand *everybody* a match. It's the smart empty people—not the dull-eyed but the beady-eyed—who are whipping up the orgiastic possibilities in irrational violence. It's the carnivore locusts at the top who tear the artists apart, but the writers and directors have often (unwittingly) aided them. Writers, who assume an ideal reader when they "do their own writing," accept the moguls' view of the public when they work for the movies. Not that they necessarily write down—probably most scenarists write as well as they can, considering the limitations imposed on them—but that they begin to subscribe to the moguls' attitudes, which are endemic in Hollywood, and so they come to believe in the necessity for those limitations. They don't assume an ideal viewer—they assume a hollowed-eyed, empty-souled, know-nothing hick.

And, in some crazy, vindictive way—as if the masses were their enemy—certain writers and directors enjoy satirizing the rootless, uncultured Americans. John Schlesinger in *Midnight Cowboy,* Tony Richardson in *The Loved One,* Antonioni in *Zabriskie Point*—liberals all, but aesthetes first—spin a new baroque out of the grotesqueness of American bad taste. They lose their socially conscious moorings when they treat American culture, just as American liberals and leftists from the East lose them in the West. Nathanael West—and what a misnomer he chose for himself—must have recognized that he was caught in an ideological bind in *The Day of the Locust.* In the middle of his apocalyptic climax, when the hollow-eyed people are gathering, he carefully exempts himself from political criticism by having his hero, Tod, observe, "He could see very few people who looked tough, nor could he see any working men. The crowd was made up of the lower middle classes." That handy, safe target of the left—"the lower middle classes." But, a few lines farther on, Tod describes the people and contradicts himself: "All their lives they had slaved at some kind of dull, heavy labor, behind desks and counters, in the fields and at tedious machines of all sorts, saving their pennies and dreaming of the leisure that would be theirs when they had enough." It's nonsense to think that working people don't get debased, and only the "lower middle classes" are susceptible to the deadening effects of mass culture, but if one makes this false split between the workers and the riffraff it's one hell of a lot easier to take movie money. Generations of screenwriters played the same game that West did, trying to convince themselves that they weren't doing any damage to anyone who really counted. The movie audience became a huge subhuman abstraction to them; it was a faceless joke, and they weren't accountable to it. In modern Hollywood, where most of the writing and directing are for TV, that is now the attitude toward the television audience.

Perhaps no work of art is possible without belief in the audience—the kind of belief that has nothing to do with facts and figures about what people actually buy or enjoy but comes out of the individual artist's absolute conviction that only the best he can do is fit to be offered to others. It's what makes a director insist on a retake even when he knows he's going to be penalized for it; it's what makes young dancers drop from exhaustion; it's what made Caruso burst his throat. You have to believe in the audience, and believe that your peak effort just barely makes you worthy of it. That's implicit when an artist says he does it "because he has to," and even when he says he does it "just for himself." An artist's sense of honor is founded on the honor due others. Honor in the arts—and in show business, too—is giving of one's utmost, even if the audience does not appear to know the difference, even if the audience shows every sign of preferring something easy, cheap, and synthetic. The audience one must believe in is the great audience: the audience one was part of as a child, when one first began to respond to great work—the audience one is still part of. As soon as an artist ceases to see himself as part of the audience—when he begins to believe that what matters is to satisfy the jerk audience out there—he stops being an artist. He becomes a businessman, marketing a commodity—his talent, himself.

■   ■   ■

There's no way for movies to be saved from premature senility unless the artists finally abandon the whole crooked system of Hollywood bookkeeping, with its kited budgets and trick percentages. Most directors are signed up for only one picture now, but after the deal is made the director gets the full de-luxe ritual: fancy hotels, first-class travel, expense money to maintain cool, silky blond groupies for traveling companions. The directors are like calves being fattened—all on the budget of the picture. The thieving, high-salaried executives and their entourage of whores and underlings are also traveling and living it up on that same budget; that's how a picture that cost $1,200,000 comes in on the books at $3,000,000, and why the director who has a percentage of the profits doesn't get any.

It isn't impossible to raise money outside the industry to make a movie—the studios themselves finance some of their biggest pictures with tax-shelter money (*Gatsby*, in part)—but even those who raise independent financing and make a picture cheaply (*Mean Streets* was brought in for $380,000, plus $200,000 in deferred costs, *Payday* for $767,000) are stuck for a way to distribute it and fall victim to the dream of a big Hollywood win. So they sell their pictures to "the majors" to exhibit, and watch helplessly as the films die or the swindled profits disappear. And they are beggars again. Brian De Palma's *Greetings* was made for $20,000, plus $23,000 in deferred costs in 1968; back in the fifties, Irvin Kershner made *Stakeout on Dope Street* for $30,000, plus $8,000 in deferred costs. If there had been an artists' co-op to distribute the films, the directors might have been able to use the profits to continue working, instead of pouring energy into planning films that they could never finance, and seeing the films they did make get sliced to ribbons.

If the directors started one distribution company, or even several (they could certainly get backing), they might have to spend time on business problems, but, with any luck, much less time on dealmaking sessions: those traumatic meetings at which the businessmen air their grievances while the artists anxiously vulgarize the projects they're submitting, hoping to make them sound commercial enough. If they have a book they want to film or if they try to get development money for a story idea, the lack of enthusiasm is deadly. One director says, "You look at them and you give up. And if, after a year or two years, they finally give you the go-ahead, then they cut you down to a twenty-five-day shooting schedule and *dare* you to make a picture." Right now, all but a handful of Hollywood directors spend most of their time preparing projects that they never get to shoot. They work on scripts with writers, piling up successions of drafts, and if they still can't please the producers and get a deal, the properties are finally abandoned or turned over to other directors, who start the process all over again, with new writers. The directors spend their lives not in learning their craft and not in doing anything useful to them as human beings but in fighting a battle they keep losing. The business problems of controlling their own distribution should be minor compared to what they go through now—the abuse from the self-pitying bosses, the indignity, the paralysis. And if the directors had to think out how their movies should be presented to the public—what the basis for the advertising campaign should be—this mightn't be so bad for them. If they had to worry about what a movie was going to mean to people and why anybody should come to see it, they might be saved from too much folly. A fatal difference between the "high" arts and the popular, or mass-culture, arts has been that in one the artist's mistakes are his own, while in the other the mistakes are largely the businessmen's. The artist can grow making his own mistakes; he decays carrying out the businessmen's decisions—working on large, custom-made versions of the soulless entertainment on TV.

There's no way of knowing whether a new audience can be found; it's a matter of picking up the pieces, and it may be too late. But if the directors started talking to each other, they'd realize that they're all in the same rapidly sinking boat, and there'd be a chance for them to reach out and try to connect with a new audience. If they don't, they'll never test themselves as artists and they'll never know whether an audience could have been found for the work they want to do.

The artists have to break out of their own fearful, star-struck heads; the system that's destroying them is able to destroy them only as long as they believe in it and want to win within it—only as long as they're psychologically dependent on it. But the one kind of winning that is still possible in those terms is to be a winner like William Friedkin or George Roy Hill. The system works for those who don't have needs or aspirations that are in conflict with it; but for the others—and they're the ones who are making *movies*—the system doesn't work anymore, and it's not going to.

The New Yorker, August 5, 1974

LACOMBE, LUCIEN

Introducing himself to a delicate, fine-boned Parisienne, the farm-boy hero of Louis Malle's new movie does not give his name as Lucien Lacombe; he gives the bureaucratic designation—Lacombe, Lucien. He presents himself, name inverted, because he is trying to be formal and proper, as he's been trained to be at school and at work, sweeping floors at his local, small-town hospital in southwest France. When he meets the girl, France Horn—and falls in love with her—his new job is hunting down and torturing people for the Gestapo. He likes it a whole lot better than the hospital. The title *Lacombe, Lucien* refers to the case of a boy of seventeen who doesn't achieve a fully human identity, a boy who has an empty space where feelings beyond the purely instinctive are expected to be.

The time is 1944, after the Normandy landings, and the Nazis and their collaborators won't be in power long. Lucien doesn't know that. He had tried to join the Resistance, but the local Resistance leader was his old schoolmaster, who thought him stupid, and Lucien stumbled into a job with the Nazis. Actually, he isn't stupid; he has the kinds of talents that don't show at school—he has a country boy's skills, and he knows how to survive in the wild. The schoolmaster is right, though, in perceiving that Lucien is apolitical and unprincipled—that he just wants some action. Lucien is good to his mother, and in normal circumstances he would work on a farm, taking care of his own and not bothering anybody, and he'd probably be a respected, unconscionably practical member of the community. But in wartime he's a perfect candidate for Nazi bullyboy. Malle's film is a long, close look at the banality of evil; it is—not incidentally—one of the least banal movies ever made. The actions are handled plainly, with restraint—with no attempt to shock anyone, or impress anyone; the actions are what we knew already. There's no special magic involved in the moviemaking technique—it's simple, head-on, unforced. The movie is the boy's face. The magic is in the intense curiosity and intelligence behind the film—in Malle's perception that the answers to our questions about how people with no interest in politics become active participants in brutal torture are to be found in Lucien's plump-cheeked, narrow-eyed face, and that showing us what this boy *doesn't* react to can be the most telling of all.

In *The Sorrow and the Pity* we watched former Nazis and collaborators give their accounts of their behavior, and with some of them we were left staring at big empty spaces. That's the space Malle attempts to define. It can't be done by setting up a character for us to identify with; the whole point of the film is that we have always been unable to identify with these people, and yet we don't know what makes us different from them—if we are. Malle can't think himself into Lucien's shoes; he could think himself into the very soul of the burnt-out, self-pitying hero of *The Fire Within*, but Lucien is outside the normal range of a dramatist's imagination. The screenplay Malle devised (together with the twenty-seven-year-old Patrick Modiano, author of three novels on the Occupation) tries not to dramatize and not to comment. The director sets up his wartime situation and puts in as Lucien a teenage country boy (Pierre Blaise) who has seen few films and has never acted before—a boy, that is, who can respond to events with his own innocence, apathy, animal shrewdness. Malle stages the action, but he uses the camera as an investigative instrument. His technique is to let the story seem to tell itself while he searches and observes. His gamble is that the camera will discover what the artist's imagination can't, and, steadily, startlingly, the gamble pays off.

We look at Pierre Blaise's face in a different way from the way we watch a trained actor. We look *into* it rather than react to an actor's performance. The enigma of a Lucien, whether he is a bullyboy of the right or the left, is the enigma of an open face and a dark, closed mind. Professional actors have the wrong kind of face for this sort of unborn consciousness, and they tend to project thoughts and feelings from the blank area. Pierre Blaise doesn't, and we trust our readings of his silent face almost as if we were watching a documentary. We *examine* it in that way, and we're more engaged than at most fictional films. There's nothing about Lucien that one can take for granted. Even those close to him don't feel close; his own mother (Gilberte Rivet, in a fine performance) isn't sure how to talk to him. His incomprehensibility is a mystery we're caught in, and Malle astutely surrounds Lucien and the girl with unfamiliar faces (actors from the theater, with little exposure in films), so that we won't have past associations to distract us. By the end, the case of Lacombe, Lucien has been presented to us. We know the evidence on which he will be judged a traitor, and we've also seen how remote that term is from anything he's ever thought about.

When things are going his way, Lucien is nothing more than a big puppy dog, eager for admiration, and his Gestapo mentor, a seedy, thieving French aristocrat, treats him as a pet, but the wrong tone, the wrong words, or a smile that suggests condescension, and he can be violent. The Parisian girl, France Horn, and her family—Jews who are trying to stay out of sight— have no weapons for dealing with him. They're helpless when Lucien moves out of the Gestapo headquarters at the local hotel and into their attic apartment, sharing France's bed. Mr. Horn (Holger Löwenadler), formerly a tailor to fashionable Paris, is so meticulously cultivated that he seems precious; to Americans it may come almost as a shock that he *has* a daughter—we associate his pursed-lips concern for social proprieties with put-down portraits of homosexuals. But Horn's punctiliousness is a serious—tragic—expression of the dignity he believes in. He cares deeply about the smallest nuances of a class society, yet he finds himself paying extortion money to Lucien's buddy, the son of a count who was part of his own clientele, and he is forced to accept Lucien—an uncouth *child*—at his table and in his daughter's bed. And, worse, he knows that his daughter is not unwilling.

Aurore Clément, who plays France Horn, had not acted before; Malle must have selected her for her fair coloring and tall, slim fragility and her ultra-civilized, poignant little face. She lacks an actress's tension, and so at times she seems a passive camera subject, but she gives us the double nature of France's response to Lucien: her amused derision of his ignorant attempts to play the courtier, and the sensual bond that draws them together. We see, even, that underneath France's fastidiousness and her sharp sensitivity there's a practical animal streak. Aurore Clément's beauty is almost prehensile, like the young Nicole Stéphane's in *Les Enfants Terribles,* and maybe it was this extra quality that attracted Malle. Her old-young face is incapable of surprise yet permanently marked by fear, like a doe's. The French heritage, in all its vaunted refinement, has made her hard in a way that connects with Lucien's pre-civilized obtuseness. She doesn't suffer, as her father does, from the humiliation of their position, and it may be Horn's recognition of this that makes him flail about and bicker with her— berating her as a whore and in the next breath begging her pardon. Lucien, we feel, is the last straw for Horn. After the long period of hiding, behaving prudently, and playing by whatever signals the scummy aristocrat sent out, Horn suddenly can't tolerate the pain of polite self-effacement any longer, and he begins to break. He dresses in his showiest boulevardier's finery and takes a promenade; he decides he must talk things out with Lucien "man-to-man," and when Lucien is too busy to talk at home he strolls over to Gestapo headquarters to wait for him.

Throughout the film, this Gestapo hotel-headquarters recalls the hotel gathering places in thirties French films, yet it has an unaccustomed theatricality about it. The collaborators who work there, live there, torture their victims there, and party there, too, have a wide range of motives. Nothing links them but their willingness to serve the Nazi cause, and that willingness is highly variable, since—not much more political than Lucien—they're primarily serving themselves. There's a former policeman who was discharged from his post; now, a high official, he gets shaved in his office while an adoring spinsterish secretary reads him the latest letters of denunciation from informers. The group also includes a onetime bicycle-racing champion (a nod, perhaps, to the bicycle champ in *The Sorrow and the Pity,* who said he "didn't see any Germans in Clermont-Ferrand") and a movie starlet, the aristocrat's girl friend, waiting for him to gather enough loot so they can take off for Spain. They're much like the ordinary characters in a French film classic, but they're running things now. The hotel is almost like a stage, and, wielding power, they're putting on an act for each other—playing the big time. Nazism itself (and Italian Fascism, too) always had a theatrical flourish, and those drawn into Gestapo work may well have felt that their newfound authority gave them style. The Nazi hotel here represents this troupe's idea of government. Lucien, the country bumpkin, going into the maid's room, at her invitation, or peeking through a doorway to see his old schoolmaster, whom he has drunkenly betrayed, being tortured, may recall the quite different figure in *The Blood of a Poet* wandering in the corridors of l'Hôtel des Folies-Dramatiques. Like Cocteau's poet, Lucien has fallen into a dreamworld. And he and the other collaborators have landed on their feet: they have become criminally powerful and can act out their impulses.

There is nothing admirable in Lucien, yet we find we can't hate him. We begin to understand how his callousness works for him in his new job. He didn't intend to blab about the schoolmaster; he was just surprised and pleased that he knew something the Nazis didn't. But he's indifferent when he witnesses the torture, and he shows no more reaction to killing people himself than to shooting a rabbit for dinner or a bird for fun. After the Maquis have raided the hotel, reprisals are ordered, and Lucien is sent, with an S.S. man, to arrest France and her grandmother (Thérèse Giehse). Lucien has no feelings one way or the other about hauling them in—so little sentiment that he reclaims a gold watch he looted earlier and gave to Mr. Horn in a buttering-up gesture. The German takes it away from him, however, and Lucien, piqued, shoots him. It is perfectly apparent that if the German had not pocketed the watch, which Lucien felt was properly his own, Lucien would have stood by as France was taken away. (He wanted his watch back because he didn't see why it should be wasted.) Yet with the S.S. man dead Lucien needs to get away, and he escapes, with France and her grandmother, to the countryside. When we see him in his natural environment, setting traps, killing game, making love to France, and once even lying flat on the ground and laughing like an innocent, confident boy, we know, with absolute conviction, that he has no sense of guilt whatever. His face is as clear as Lieutenant Calley's.

Malle's hero could have been placed almost anywhere at any time, but it is right for a French artist to place him where Malle did. The director Jean-Pierre Melville, who was himself a member of the Resistance, said in an interview that when he came out of the theater after seeing *The Sorrow and the Pity* he saw Roland Petit and Zizi Jeanmaire in the queue waiting for the next performance, and his first reflex was to pretend that he hadn't seen them—he felt as though he'd been caught coming out from a pornographic film. The pornography of *The Sorrow and the Pity* is in the shameful ordinariness of the people who betray their fellows. The movies, with their roots in stage melodrama, have conditioned us to look for evil in social deviants and the physically aberrant. The pornography that Malle delves into makes us think back to the protests of innocence by torturers and mass murderers— all those normal-looking people leading normal lives who said they were just doing their job. Without ever mentioning the subject of innocence and guilt, *Lacombe, Lucien,* in its calm, leisurely, dispassionate way, addresses it on a deeper level than any other movie I know.

■　■　■

Louis Malle has always been an alert and daring director who didn't repeat himself, but in recent years, since he broke with the smooth professionalism and surface sophistication of his early work and made the series of documentaries that form *Phantom India,* he appears to have begun anew. The picture he made after that experience, the high comedy *Murmur of the Heart,* set in 1954, suggested an artist's autobiographical first work, except that it showed a master's command of the medium. Now he has gone back farther, to the period of his childhood (he was born in 1932), to events he couldn't make sense of. *Lacombe, Lucien* is more of a test even than India: Malle could approach India in terms of his own sensibility, but in *Lacombe, Lucien* he is trying to seek out and create a sensibility utterly different from his own.

In all the most important ways, he succeeds, triumphantly. But in a million small ways he falls flat. Malle's earlier films were very precise, the work of an orderly, classical mind; they were films by a Frenchman who believed in reason, and although the Indian series brought out the humanist in him, he remained the *raisonneur*. This time, he's working on a subject that can't be thought out, and he's going on instinct. His greatest involvement is in the looser material, and when he stays with the gambler-improviser's intuitive method, he wins. In this film, Malle is best at what he's never done before—the almost wordless scenes, especially; he gets perhaps even more than he'd hoped for from Pierre Blaise's Lucien. In these scenes, it's not just that one can't separate Lucien's innocence and his corruption but that they really seem to be the same thing. However, Malle can't give a sense of life to all the situations he puts Lucien in. He seems to have lost interest in the scripted scenes, and there's a fatal hint of the obligatory in some of them. In setting up the atmosphere in the hotel, Malle probably knew that it was tricky to suggest that these Nazi collaborators, aping authority, are like bad actors. However, we have to extrapolate his subtle intentions, because the situations are often inert. The two scenes involving Lucien's affair with the hotel maid are glaringly unconvincing, and contradictory besides. In the first, before going to bed with him she gives him a little Resistance talk, telling him that the Americans are winning, and warning him against having any more to do with the Nazis; in the second, after he is involved with France Horn, the maid suddenly comes on like a woman scorned, a provincial Mrs. Robinson full of anti-Semitic fury. We can guess that her outburst is meant to indicate how an angry person can blame the Jews for his frustrations, but this sort of worked-out reason (spite, jealousy) is what we're used to—it's specious, without resonance, like the perfunctory reasons that are given for why the various people in the hotel have become collaborators. No doubt Malle means to tell us that their reasons *are* banal, but his handling of the people is so enervated that we just feel we've seen all these types with their quirks before.

Some artists have a natural feeling for the riches of chaos; when they don't pin things down for us to know exactly what's going on, we understand that they're not giving us that kind of meaning—they're giving us more than that. And Malle achieves that with Lucien, but he isn't skilled yet at merging scripted scenes with found material, and at times we feel that something has been left out. (What is France doing with those piled-up stones? Has her grandmother died?) In the scene of a Resistance doctor's arrest, when the doctor's phlegmatic teen-age son shows Lucien his model ship, it looks as if

Malle couldn't control the elements, and chose to retain the scene because of the overtones in the boy's physical resemblance to Lucien, and despite the boy's unconvincing lack of interest in his father's fate. Working with nonprofessionals in the leads and adapting the script to Lucien's emerging character, Malle probably had to cut scenes he needed that didn't pan out, but there are ellipses that aren't easy to account for—principally in Horn's sudden, suicidal carelessness. Some stages in Horn's breakdown seem to be missing, and his later scenes are lamely directed. Holger Löwenadler, a distinguished figure in the Swedish theater for over half a century (he appeared in Bergman's 1947 film *A Ship to India*, and in recent years he has toured Europe in Bergman stage productions, playing leads in Ibsen and Strindberg), prepares Horn's character so carefully in his early scenes that it's puzzling when the later ones are truncated. We miss Horn's shift to recklessness, and not enough is made of the moment when he appears all dressed up, his hat tilted rakishly over one eye. Is he deliberately calling attention to himself? There are brilliant ideas, like that "man-to-man" talk Horn wants with Lucien. (How can a Jew talk man-to-man at Gestapo headquarters, and what could Horn and that thug Lucien possibly talk about?) But Horn's breakdown is too fast, and we can't perceive why he is doing what he's doing; this is the wrong place for Malle to stand back and let the story just seem to happen—he has failed to provide the necessary information.

The picture is a knockout, and the flaws don't diminish its stature, so it may appear silly to discuss imperfections—which could be passed over as ambiguities. But it's because the picture is a major work that it seems necessary to distinguish between the great ambiguities of its theme and the piddling, diversionary gaffes and gaps in its execution. There's another reason for bringing up the crudenesses: they are the price that Malle the aesthete is willing to pay for discovery. Here is a director who achieved sleek technical perfection in his early, limited films and who is now saying that perfection is cheap and easy (which seems to be true for him). He's looking for something that he doesn't have the tools or the temperament to grab hold of, and he's catching it anyway.

Malle's renunciation of conventional drama—or his new indifference to it—cripples him in places where he still needs it. He hasn't fully cast off the hard shell of the brilliant young pro who made *The Lovers* and *Viva Maria!* and *Zazie*, but he's lost his slick. He's in the process of turning himself inside out and reaching into the common experience. Malle isn't used to playing by ear; he keeps looking at the notes and seeing they're wrong, revising them and hoping they're better. Yet somehow, with all the wrong notes he hits, and parts of the bass left out, he gets sounds that nobody's ever heard before.

The New Yorker, September 30, 1974

RICHARD LESTER'S JUGGERNAUT

Juggernaut is fast, crackerjack entertainment, with the cool, bitchy wit and the outrageously handsome action sequences of some of the best of the Bond pictures. It's surprisingly crisp fun, considering that it was directed by that most misanthropic of talented directors, Richard Lester. Though he eliminates practically every trace of human warmth, he manages to supply the characters with enough blackhearted existential bravado to keep the film sociable. Anybody who makes a picture like this one has to be a bit of a bastard, but Lester demonstrates what a sophisticated director with flair can do on a routine big-action project. Juggernaut is the name assumed by a bomb wizard who has planted seven whoppers on the luxury liner Britannic, carrying twelve hundred passengers on a transatlantic crossing.

Lester lets you know right from the start that if the genre is basically the same as that of *The Poseidon Adventure* the tone certainly won't be. Even before the ship (it's the Maxim Gorky doubling as the Britannic, and the ship's band looks suspiciously Slavic) leaves port, one sees Lesterisms. People who are handed rolls of festive paper streamers to throw drop them limply in disdain. The characters have none of the inviting smiles typical of the genre. Anthony Hopkins, a melancholy-faced police detective, says goodbye to his two children and his wife, dour Caroline Mortimer, who are sailing; she stays in an unexplained funk for the entire trip, from time to time staring abstractedly at her children. Clifton James, the mayor of an American city, has an aging wife, who, when it appears that they'll die, wants assurances that he has always been faithful; Lester undercuts the corn by having the wife, Doris Nolan, done up in a blond wig, like Bette Davis in her hag horror roles. Juggernaut himself, Freddie Jones, might be Anthony Burgess on a reasonably straightforward day. A ship's steward dies while saving a child's life, and absolutely nothing is made of it; it's typical of Lester that he refuses to make the child endearing and refuses to give the rescue an emotional glow. Considering how this child-in-danger situation is generally milked, Lester's cold-bloodedness is nifty. He doesn't go in for scenes of panic or screaming hysteria; instead, he has the ship's social director (Roy Kinnear) constantly rebuffed in his attempts to cheer people up. Where the usual disaster film gives us pathos, Lester gives us slapstick. The movie is a commentary on other directors' groveling for audience response.

Those not used to Richard Lester's neo-Noël Coward mixture of cynicism, angst, and anti-establishment sentimentality (is there anybody more British than an American convert?) may at first be thrown. He's a compulsive gagster, but the jokes are throwaway-fast and tinged with contempt. He uses famous actors, but he uses them like bit players—like props, almost. Omar Sharif, as the ship's captain, can't play in the same quick tempo as the rest of the cast (when he speaks, his words just don't seem to have originated in that head), but he isn't used as Omar Sharif, either. (Lester pulled the same stunt with Charlton Heston in *The Three Musketeers*, scaling him down from his heroic heights.) No doubt Sharif is on board to give the film his romantic box-office attributes, but he's not allowed to smile the famous smile, or even to look soulfully lovesick. He's kept rather grim, as if he were really an actor playing a role. For a sex interest (it isn't love), Sharif is given Shirley Knight as a sharp-witted international playgirl. Shirley Knight, who worked at top form with Lester in *Petulia* (her cookie scene with George C. Scott was the best part of that picture), hits it again here whenever she has tart, brainy lines, though she's burdened with some overly classy remarks about life and death.

The actors who get by with the worst of the lines—and still triumph—are Richard Harris, as the commander of the bomb-dismantling team, and David Hemmings, as his second-in-command. Harris, who delivers a long, drunken oration, might almost be playing Lester's glamorous alter ego; the team commander takes pride in being the best in his profession, though he says he doesn't believe in anything. It's the flossiest bit of rebel-hero nonsense since Humphrey Bogart. Lester likes to turn heroism into a joke, but in *Juggernaut* the derring-do isn't cancelled out, as it was in *The Three Musketeers*—quite the reverse. The cynical, dangling gags that counterpoint the gallantry make it more gallant. The picture has a structural flaw: it reaches its visual climax early, with the arrival of the dismantling team, who parachute down into giant storm waves and then fight their way up rope ladders to board the ship. The subsequent action sequences can't compete with the violent beauty of that arrival, and the actual dismantling of the bombs is too much like the prolonged safecracking scenes of heist pictures, though Lester and his cinematographer, Gerry Fisher, work microscopically close and achieve some almost abstract aesthetic effects. We don't get to see the damage caused by the bombs that explode, but the jaunty superciliousness is more entertaining than the bombs anyway. Lester has discovered a commercial use for his poisonous, flip wit: it provides just what Noël Coward's archness did—a smart, dissonant style to cover the traditional pieties.

The New Yorker, October 7, 1974

ABOUT BURT REYNOLDS, FROM REVIEW OF

THE LONGEST YARD

Not very long ago, Don Rickles, in his night-club dates, was considered the comics' comic, because he displayed his hostility to the audience; however, television makes "in" attitudes accessible to a wide audience, and now hostility is bursting out all over. Burt Reynolds has become popular by letting the public see his insider's jokey contempt for the whole entertainment business. He had been acting in the theater and on television since the late fifties and had appeared in a dozen movies without creating much of a stir, and when, in 1971, he began to appear on talk shows, other guests laughed nervously at hearing behind-the-scenes smart talk in public. But the TV audience enjoyed the dropping of barriers, and Reynolds was on his way. He showed an amazingly fast put-down wit, but he also showed something else, which the TV public was probably ready for: he made a joke of his profession. He came on as a man who had no higher values than the buck and the pleasures of the flesh—exactly what many people in the audience had always really believed stardom was about. His message was that stars were just bums, and that he himself was an honest, funny bum—too smart and gamy to give much of a damn about anything except having a good time, and too cocky to lie about it. His message was that he was having a ball being a stud celebrity. The belief is now widespread that the price of success is the loss of privacy, and that the successful person who fights this isn't playing fair. And there's a concurrent belief, almost as widely held, probably, that those rich, lucky people who have become stars—whether of sports, politics, entertainment, or anything else—are out for themselves. Reynolds not only accepted those terms but carried them further. His fun-loving "frankness" seemed the show-business truth, and when he was around, any earnestness looked a solemn fraud. His charm is that of a cheap crook who ingratiates himself by saying, "Look, we're all cheap crooks—why lie about it?"

The New Yorker, October 14, 1974

FROM SPIELER, REVIEW OF
PHANTOM OF THE PARADISE

B rian De Palma, the writer-director of *Phantom of the Paradise*, thrives on frowzy visual hyperbole. When he tries to set up a simple scene establishing that boy composer loves girl singer, he is a helpless amateur, but when he sets up a highly stylized paranoid fantasy with gyrating figures on a stage and an audience that is having its limbs hacked off, you can practically hear him cackling with happiness, and the scene carries a jolt. De Palma, who can't tell a plain story, does something that a couple of generations of student and underground filmmakers have been trying to do and nobody else has ever brought off. He creates a new Guignol, in a modern idiom, out of the movie Guignol of the past. *Phantom of the Paradise* is a rock horror show about a composer, Winslow (William Finley), who is robbed of his music, busted for drugs, and sent to Sing Sing—all at the instigation of Swan (Paul Williams), the entrepreneur of Death Records, who has made a

584

pact with the Devil for eternal youth. Winslow escapes from prison, is maimed by a record-pressing machine, and haunts Swan's new rock palace, the Paradise, where Phoenix (Jessica Harper), the girl he loves, becomes a star. This mixture of *The Phantom of the Opera* and *Faust* (via *The Devil and Daniel Webster*) isn't enough for De Palma. He heaps on layers of rock satire, and parodies of *The Cabinet of Dr. Caligari*, *The Hunchback of Notre Dame*, *Psycho*, and *The Picture of Dorian Gray*—and the impacted plots actually function for him. De Palma is drawn to rabid visual exaggeration and sophisticated, satirical low comedy. This slapstick expressionism is idiosyncratic in the extreme. It's De Palma's flukiness that makes *Phantom* so entertaining.

Though you may anticipate a plot turn, it's impossible to guess what the next scene will *look* like or what its rhythm will be. De Palma's timing is sometimes wantonly unpredictable and dampening, but mostly it has a lift to it. You practically get a kinetic charge from the breakneck wit he put into *Phantom;* it isn't just that the picture has vitality but that one can feel the tremendous kick the director got out of making it. And one can feel the love that went into the visual details of this production—the bird motifs, the shifting patterns of the interiors. De Palma's method is very theatrical, with each scene sharply divided from the next. He may play with crazy-house effects like a hyperactive kid, or he may set up a tricky scene with shrill, hot lighting—a magnesium flare—and have the camera circle some spangly, high-flier performers, providing almost a floating view. You get the feeling he's staring at them, as entranced as we are. His technique is inspired amateurishness; his work resembles what hundreds of student filmmakers have done, but there's a level of personal obsession which makes the material his own. Most student moviemakers are gullible: they harbor a naïve belief in the clichés they parrot. De Palma loves the clichés for their shameless, rotten phoniness. The movies of the past haven't made him their innocent victim; rather, they have wised him up. He doesn't just reproduce grotesque old effects; his driving, redeeming sense of humor cuts through the crap in movies at the same time that it cuts through the crap in the rock world. Few directors work in such a screwily personal way, but that sense of humor of his is like a disinfectant.

From the way his scenes plunge into vacuity whenever he tries to show ordinary human relations it's clear that his energy runs high only when he lets his carny spirit and his movie-fed imagination take over. Back in 1931—a decade before De Palma was born—a character in a movie listened to a preacher's daughter (Barbara Stanwyck) and said to her, "You've got the hot spiel in your blood." What the evangelical rhetoric had done to her, movies have done to Brian De Palma.

The New Yorker, November 11, 1974

LENNY

WHEN THE SAINTS COME MARCHING IN

L*enny,* the Bob Fosse film starring Dustin Hoffman, is for audiences who
want to believe that Lenny Bruce was a saintly gadfly who was martyred
for having lived before their time. Julian Barry, who wrote the Tom
O'Horgan 1971 stage show, starring Cliff Gorman, has written the screenplay, and the material is conceived for well-meaning innocents who never
saw Lenny Bruce and who can listen to Dustin Hoffman delivering bits of
Bruce routines and think, People just didn't understand him then—he isn't
shocking at all. There was every reason to believe that O'Horgan knew the
difference between Lenny Bruce the performer he'd been on the same bill
with back in the late fifties and the Lenny Bruce turn-on myth he helped
whip up. His *Lenny,* which came between his *Hair* and his *Jesus Christ Superstar,* was part of an effort to create a youth theater; the show dealt with
Bruce not as a man but as a sacrificial symbol surrounded by tribal symbols
on stilts and decked out in papier-mâché heads and grass skirts. It was James
Dean updated—Lenny Bruce as a misunderstood kid, the way *Jesus Christ Superstar* was to be Jesus as a misunderstood kid. Taking over the O'Horgan-
Barry material, Bob Fosse has eliminated the totemic haberdashery. His
staging goes all the way in the opposite direction: the film is in black and
white, in a semi-documentary style. But Julian Barry hasn't rethought
Bruce's life or fleshed out the characters, and the closer Fosse gets to them,
the more abstract they become. Lenny's wife, the stripper Honey Harlow
(Valerie Perrine); his mother, Sally Marr (Jan Miner); a fictitious manager
(Stanley Beck); and Lenny himself are still no more than symbolic figures,
and they inhabit an abstract, stage-bound world that doesn't seem to relate
to a specific period or to the cities where the key events of Bruce's life actually took place.

Fosse has learned a phenomenal amount about film technique in a
short time; *Lenny* is only his third movie (after *Sweet Charity* and *Cabaret*),
and it's a handsome piece of work. I don't know of any other director who
entered moviemaking so late in life and developed such technical profi-
ciency; Fosse is a true prodigy. *Lenny* is far removed in style from *Cabaret,* yet
it's controlled and intelligent. But the script is simply too thin for the
method Fosse uses. A searching, close-in documentary technique can sometimes provide glimpses of the riches of people's interior lives, but it is rarely
effective with actors: their controls are exposed, and we become more conscious of their acting than in a conventionally dramatized work. The idea
here seems to be that what the writer has failed to provide, the camera will
somehow probe. But since the characters have nothing to yield up, it probes
superficiality. Essentially, the method is to cut from episodes recalled by
Lenny's family and associates to Lenny performing a sliver of a routine that
seems to have developed out of each episode. However, the film never quite

586

achieves a "present": we might almost be watching him perform after the survivors were interviewed. The crosscutting between present and past is smoothly engineered, but it doesn't really do anything for us. I get the impression that, unlike O'Horgan, Fosse thought he was really getting at truth, and that he got so caught up in the complicated structure he didn't see that it surrounded a void. Despite the fluent editing and sophisticated graphics, the picture is the latest version of the one-to-one correlation of an artist's life and his art which we used to get in movies about painters and songwriters. Lenny's life becomes footnotes to his night-club acts—as if the acts needed footnotes!—and often the biographical account has the odd effect of making his stage acts seem like simple rationalizations of what was going on in his life. In the traditional movie, life is transmuted into art; here the hero's routines are so unfunny that no transmutation seems to have taken place.

Fosse may have tried so hard to stretch himself that he lost perspective (and his sense of humor) on this project. Within its serious conception, *Lenny* is very well made. But why does it take itself so insufferably seriously? Why the sociological black-and-white investigatory style for a subject like Lenny Bruce? The style says, Listen, kids, this is going to be about a very important man; be quiet, now—remember you're in church. The movie turns out to be the earnest story of a Jewish prophet who shouldn't have got involved with a shiksa junkie.

There really is no script. There was no play inside O'Horgan's production, either, but there were so many dervishes whirling that most of the audience didn't seem to mind. Gorman delivered large chunks of Bruce's material, and though he lacked the spiv comic's jabbing hostility, he was able to build up a rhythm with the audience. His actor's exertion and the sweetness he brought to the material fitted O'Horgan's sacrificial-lamb concept: the audience could appreciate the humor without feeling the danger that made Bruce's audiences prickle with nervous pleasure. Gorman seemed like such a nice boy up there, harried, and working hard. So does Dustin Hoffman, but he can't even work up a performing rhythm, because in the movie the shticks have been reduced to snippets and high points.

Hoffman makes a serious, honorable try, but he's the wrong kind of actor to play Bruce. Hoffman ingratiates himself with an audience by his shy smile, his gentleness, and his insecurity. He wins people over by his lack of physical confidence; you pull for him because he's so non-threatening—you hope that he isn't actually weak and that he'll prove himself. But that clenched, nasal voice of his is the voice of someone trying to get along in the nervous straight world Bruce fled; his putziness is just what Bruce despised. Hoffman is touchingly childlike (he was at his best on the TV show *Free to Be . . . You and Me,* when he read Herb Gardner's monologue about a child's first crossing a street by himself); there was nothing childlike about Lenny Bruce. He vamped the audience with a debauched, deliberately faggy come-hither that no one quite knew how to interpret; he was uncompromisingly not nice.

Who would be right to play him? Is there an actor with the hooded eyes and sensual come-on of a Persian hipster prince? Lenny Bruce had a treacherous glint under those heavy lids, and his cool pimp's mask of indifference was almost reptilian. He took off on the whole straight world, and that certainly meant the Dustin Hoffmans and it could mean you, because he was more of a hipster than anybody, and it was his vision and his rules (no rules at all) he played by. Hoffman's Lenny Bruce, like Gorman's, is on your side. Lenny Bruce was on nobody's side. The farthest-out hipster, like the farthest-out revolutionary, has an enormous aesthetic advantage over everybody else: he knows how to play his hand to make us all feel chicken. Bruce's hostility and obscenity were shortcuts to audience response; he could get and hold audiences' attention because they didn't know what or whom he was going to attack and degrade next, and they could sense that he wasn't sure himself. He was always open to darts of inspiration, so suspense was built in. He dropped the barrier between the vagrant obscene jokes that club comics, jazz musicians, and assorted con artists might exchange offstage and what was said publicly onstage. Educated left-wingers were probably his natural audience, because his gutter shpritz was often a more extreme and nihilistic form of what they were thinking, and the maggoty vitality of his language was a heady revelation to them. Words whizzed by that you'd never heard before and that may not have existed in any argot but his own, yet their sound was so expressive that the meaning got across. He flew recklessly low, and the audience, awed and delighted, howled at feeling so ridiculously dirty-minded, howled at the joke of how good it felt to be shameless. We hadn't known how many taboos we were living with, and how many humiliations and embarrassments we were hiding, until we heard him pop them one after another, like a string of firecrackers. That's what a Bruce routine did, and why it felt liberating. Bruce's gleeful, surreal, show-biz Yiddish-jive dirtiness was a mind-opener. He was always testing the audience and himself, and for religious people his blasphemy could only be a whack in the face. He wanted to reach audiences and hold them, yet the only way he knew how was to assault them with obscene jokes about everything that could conceivably be sacred to them. For the people sitting there, complacency was impossible. No matter how hip they thought they were, he would find ways to shock them. The prudish were almost forced to walk out.

Bruce's material is practically indelible for many of us who heard him, and his records stay in the mind for a decade, yet some of Bruce's best stuff is in the movie and we don't remember it ten minutes later, because the man who delivers the bits doesn't know why Bruce said them. The scriptwriter of *Lenny* must think that Bruce's material is so good that an actor can say it and that this will be enough. But those routines don't work without Bruce's teasing, seductive aggression and his delirious amorality. If they are presented as the social criticism of a man who's out to cleanse society of hypocrisy, the material goes flat. When Hoffman's Lenny tells the people in a club that he feels like urinating on them, Hoffman's tone is uncertain and his blank face says that he doesn't understand why Bruce felt that way. The screen never ignites: you're listening to Lenny Bruce's shticks and you don't even feel like laughing.

This Lenny, with his flower child's moral precepts, is a drag. When he does the famous Bruce bit about Jacqueline Kennedy trying to climb out of the assassination car, he attaches the moral that it's important to tell the truth about it in order to help other girls who might be in similar situations. When he assaults his night-club audience, singling out individuals as niggers, kikes, and greaseballs, he expounds on how much better the world would be if those words were freely shouted. Apart from the idiocy of the picture's endorsing this dubious theory and trying to wring applause for it, there's the gross misunderstanding of Bruce's methods. If Bruce did in fact stoop that low upon occasion, gathering sanctity around himself, the movie-makers should have had the brains to know that those explanations were false. I certainly don't recall Bruce's smiling at black patrons (as Hoffman does) to take the sting out of having called them niggers, but if he ever did, that wasn't Bruce the comic, it was Bruce the phony. His cruel jokes may have been a release for the audience (I think they were), but that's not why he did them. He didn't ridicule Jackie Kennedy's actions in order to help women, and he didn't use racial slurs in order to cleanse the national air. He did heartlessly cynical bits because there were only two possible audience reactions—to be outraged or to laugh. And either way he was the winner. But when he drove people out, he was the loser, too. He didn't want them to be outraged only: he was a comic, and he wanted them to laugh at what outraged them. Yet some people couldn't laugh at Bruce, because laughter was an admission that the ideas he was shocking you with weren't altogether new to you—or that, if you hadn't entertained them, you knew that you could. There was a good reason for him to become a counterculture hero: his scabrous realism never seemed a matter of choice. However, he went to the farthest lengths he could dream up, not out of missionary motives but out of a performer's zeal.

■ ■ ■

There are two views of Bruce competing for public acceptance now, and though a major-studio movie like *Lenny* is bound to set the pattern in which most people will think of Bruce for years to come, this movie suffers in just about every imaginable way by comparison with the Albert Goldman book *Ladies and Gentlemen Lenny Bruce!!* Goldman's greatest value is probably in supplying the show-business milieu that Bruce's humor came from. He provides a sense of how Bruce's act developed, and of who the audiences were, what the clubs were like, and what the other comics were doing. Goldman argues against the saintly view of Bruce, yet in his own way he falls into it—glorifying Bruce the junkie and putting down those who stayed clear of drugs. The book is brilliant, but it made me uneasy, as if Goldman were working off something on Bruce—maybe his own *not* being a junkie. Lenny Bruce got to him—Goldman admires him so much that he feels chicken for his own traces of cautious sanity.

The book has the involvement that is missing from the movie. I felt cold and remote while watching *Lenny,* with its plaster saint; the Goldman book, with its saint junkie, has overheated perils. The book is show business. Goldman gets the hype going and then doesn't go underneath it; the book stays hyped up, and the reader tires. You may begin to feel that Goldman wants the highs of a junkie without really getting hooked, and that he creates the hysterical hero to which his own prose is appropriate. He's so addictively involved that he assumes he's inside Bruce's head, and the interior view he gives is suspect. Goldman doesn't really see Bruce's suffering, because he thinks Lenny Bruce should know he's the great Lenny Bruce. He denies Bruce his pain. In his own way, Goldman competes with Bruce. He isn't just writing a biography; he does what Bruce did—he works the room.

The movie isn't show-biz enough; it's so busy with travail that it never gets any hype going—though Bruce was a hype artist. His view of the world came from the cruddiness and corruption of show business. Bruce spent his youth on the bottom rungs of the sordid club world, guided by his tough, lively mother, Sally Marr, also known as Boots Malloy, who worked as a comic in burlesque joints, managed comedians, and trained strippers. (In *Harry & Tonto,* Sally Marr plays the friendly old broad at the end who suggests to Art Carney that they get together.) And Bruce's seeing the world in show-biz terms was the key to his wit. In his "Religions, Inc." number, the Oral Roberts-type preacher greets Pope John on the phone with "Hey, Johnny, what's shakin', baby?" (This amiable near-obscenity isn't in the movie; if it were, Hoffman's Bruce might explain that it's not good for people to believe in the superstition that the Pope is holier than other men.) Many other comics have lifted Bruce's put-down style of treating the leaders of church and state as cheap hustlers, but when Bruce used show biz as the metaphor for everything squalid and hateful—and lively—in the world, it had a special impact. He was obsessed with bringing everything down to his own terms. Maybe most people who grow up in show business begin to see the world as an extension of it ("Life is a cabaret"), but the traditional performer glosses over the sleaziness with show-biz sentimentality. Even an insult comedian like Don Rickles lays on the sentimental shock absorbers; he titillates the audience by his naughtiness and then asks acceptance as a good boy. Bruce wouldn't play that show-biz game; he despised theatrical sentimentality as the worst form of sleaze (as in his great "Palladium" number). Sentimentality was a rotten, wet show; it disgusted him. Flattering the audience, squeezing for approval, offended his performer's instinct, which was far deeper in him than any social morality and was the base of his satirical outlook. It wasn't until late in his life that he got told that it was a moral base—and after that his instinct began to play him false.

Bob Fosse could have made a sensational movie if he had shown the backstage life that shaped Bruce's awareness, if he had given us a Lenny Bruce who enlarged his satirical perceptions of show biz to include the world—going from imitations of other performers and parodies of movies to parodies of religious show biz and, ultimately, to those labyrinthine, bebop satires of the law in which he was entangled. Maybe for Fosse that approach seems too close to home and too easy. He may devalue the show-biz sensationalism that he's practically a genius at, but the best bit in the movie is Gary Morton's performance as Sherman Hart, a comic based on Milton Berle (who pitched in for Bruce's funeral expenses), and Valerie Perrine's early striptease number has high theatrical dazzle. It's out of character for Honey, because Honey wasn't a top headliner, but if Fosse couldn't resist shooting the works and outblazing Blaze Starr, who will complain? Nothing in Honey's personality ties in with that high-powered strip, but Valerie Perrine gives an affecting, if limited, performance, and her Honey comes closer than Hoffman's Lenny to being a character. Hoffman has his moments; he looks better (and acts less gawky) when he's bearded, and he gets a jazzy performing style going on one piece of tape we hear, but he's respectable, like Paul Muni when he impersonated historical characters. No matter what he does, Hoffman never manages to suggest a hipster.

Lenny Bruce's story is a show-biz story. That's what the Julian Barry script, with its already dated leching-after-youth liberalism, fails to get at. Before his death, in 1966, Bruce himself began the moist process of canonization; it was his amorality that had shocked people, but now he began to claim that it was his morality. This movie swallows the lie that his motivating force was to make the audience well, and, having swallowed that, it can only defuse his humor. The moviemakers are working something off on Bruce, too: they're staking higher claims for themselves, trying to go beyond show business. The black-and-white earnestness of this movie and the youth-culture saintliness laid on Lenny Bruce are the ultimate in modern show-biz sentimentality.

The New Yorker, November 18, 1974

EARTHQUAKE

The people who reduced Los Angeles to rubble in *Earthquake* must have worked off a lot of self-hatred: you can practically feel their pleasure as the freeways shake, the skyscrapers crumble, and the Hollywood dam cracks. Nothing in L.A. looks as if it were meant to last anyway; it isn't a city you expect will sustain the ravages of time. When you peer up at glass houses perched on the edge of sandy cliffs, you feel that the people who put them there must have been stoned blind and giggling. Los Angeles, a mock paradise, is so perversely beautiful and so fundamentally unsatisfying that maybe just about everybody there secretly longs to see it come rattling down. In an earlier movie era, when a hurricane struck or a volcano erupted the scriptwriters always made it clear that the natural disaster was God's retribution for the sins of the trapped people. But who needs a reason to destroy L.A.? The city stands convicted in everyone's eyes. You go to *Earthquake* to see L.A. get it, and it really does. The picture is swill, but it isn't a cheat, like *Airport 1975,* which was cut-rate swill. *Earthquake* is a marathon of destruction effects, with stock characters spinning through. It isn't fun, exactly; it's ejaculatory, shoot-the-works filmmaking carried to the borderline of satire and stopping just short. Universal Pictures, which produced both, is a microcosm of the old Hollywood picture factories, streamlined for TV-age profits and totally cynical. These pieces of contemptuous entertainment might be the symbolic end point of the studio factory system, and there is something peculiarly gratifying about seeing the smoking ruins of the city that movies like this come from.

Earthquake is Universal's death wish for film art: these destruction orgies are the only way it knows to make money. The people who work on a picture like this are employees, and you can practically hear the executive producer, Jennings Lang, addressing them: There's no room for talent around here; this is belly-busting hard work, and if you want to make movies, this is what you'll do. And maybe the veteran director Mark Robson got into the spirit. He doesn't seem to want to leave any possible calamity effects for other epics to come, and as the bodies keep jumping, falling, or being shot, buried under walls and girders, or drowned, you begin to feel that he'd really like to kill off the whole cast, along with the thousands of extras. Stars like Richard Roundtree (playing a black, second-string Evel Knievel) disappear in the confusion without so much as a sendoff to eternity. Walter Matthau, serenely swacked throughout, may survive, but the picture doesn't care enough to make a point of it. A lot of well-known people are casually left in the debris.

The treatment of the film's two principal stars, Charlton Heston and Ava Gardner, could almost be the in joke of an industry that enjoys the idea of self-destructing. Gardner was one of the last of the women stars to make it on beauty alone. She never looked really happy in her movies; she wasn't quite there, but she never suggested that she was anywhere else, either. She had a dreamy, hurt quality, a generously modeled mouth, and faraway eyes. Maybe what turned people on was that her sensuality was developed but her personality wasn't. She was a rootless, beautiful stray, somehow incomplete but never ordinary, and just about impossible to dislike, since she was utterly without affectation. But to Universal she is just one more old star to beef up a picture's star power, and so she's cast as a tiresome bitch whose husband (Heston) is fed up with her. She looks blowzy and beat-out, and that could be fun if she were allowed to be blowzily good-natured, like the heroine of

Mogambo twenty years later, but the script here harks back to those old movies in which a husband was justified in leaving his wife only if she was a jealous schemer who made his life hell. Ava Gardner might make a man's life hell out of indolence and spiritual absenteeism, but out of shrill stupidity? *Earthquake,* though, isn't the sort of project in which the moviemakers care whether the role fits the performer. They get what they want. Ava Gardner's name lifts *Earthquake* out of the Universal-action-picture category.

Charlton Heston is the all-time king of prestige epics. However, the repressed acting, granitic physique, and godlike-insurance-salesman manner that made him so inhumanly perfect for fifties spectacles have also destroyed his credibility. He's not a bad actor, but he's humorlessly unresilient. He can't open up: his muscles have his personality in an iron grip. When Universal uses him in its action-disaster pictures, which are all really the same movie, sold by the yard, he underacts grimly and he turns into a stereotype of himself. In *Earthquake* Heston plays a big-time engineer who married the daughter (Ava Gardner) of the boss (Lorne Greene) and has fallen in love with a young screen-starlet widow (Geneviève Bujold), and when the city is all shook up he dashes from one heroic deed to the next, rescuing, rescuing, rescuing. He's a dependably heroic joke. No one is expected to believe in the acts he performs: he's a wind-up hero-machine, and ingenious special effects and trick photography can go on around him. At the end, the movie has the embarrassing problem of what to do with him to avoid the catcalls of a jaded audience, so it cynically trashes him along with Gardner and most of Los Angeles.

Heston's fatigued heroism serves a function: it enables us to retain an amused, disbelieving view. So do the shopworn incidents (the chief seismologist being out of town and his young assistant's warnings not being heeded; the workers on the dam lacking the authority to act in emergencies) and a poorly directed mad-rapist subplot involving Marjoe Gortner as a supermarket manager who lusts after Victoria Principal. The B-picture rituals keep everything unreal, so that, despite the "Sensurround" (rumbling noises on the track which make you feel that the vibrations will bring down the theater plaster), nobody's likely to become involved enough to be upset. And you don't go to this picture for involvement; even those who claim to be scared by it can't mean that in any more than an ooh-scare-me-some-more way. You feel no pang when the various characters get hit: the whole point of a pop disaster epic is for the audience to relish the ingenious ways in which they're brought down. When a drowned man pours out of a flooded elevator, you're meant to gasp at the shock, not lament his passing. I was glad that Gabriel Dell (Roundtree's manager and sidekick) was spared, because his acting had a little snap, but there was really only one person I didn't want picked off—Geneviève Bujold, dressed whimsically, always in pinks—and that was because she had a funny scene at the beginning and I hoped (vainly) that she'd have another. She's a witty comedienne, with a sense of style, and she's able to use her French accent teasingly here (instead of fighting it, as she was forced to do in *Anne of the Thousand Days*). She brings a touch of class to *Earthquake* and lightens the load.

What we really know when we watch this movie is that the destruction orgy on the screen is only a jokey form of the destruction orgy behind the screen, and we begin to take a campy pleasure in seeing the big-name actors and the old plot situations—and the motion-picture capital itself—totaled. L.A. isn't just the city that movies like this come from, it's also the city that movies that mean something to us come from, but Universal's callousness brings out a Roman-circus mentality in the audience, because actually that's the only way to have a good time at this picture. People who wanted to enjoy the degradation of their old favorites used to have to go to the gossip rags, but why should the movie executives let parasites rob them of revenue? Now the movies build that function in. Though you may rather enjoy *Earthquake*, you're not likely to applaud it, because you know that it's decadence you're responding to. Nero was considered crazy, but if he'd sold tickets and made money out of his pyromaniac spectacle, would he be considered smart, like Jennings Lang and the other executives who make profits out of financing bowdlerizations of old movies while refusing to finance new ideas?

They're not unaware; they know what they're doing out there. That's why they're rushing to open these disaster epics before the end of the year, fearing the public's interest won't stretch beyond that. Lew R. Wasserman, the board chairman of M.C.A., Inc., Universal's parent company, who has just completed eight years as the chairman of the Association of Motion Picture and Television Producers, was honored earlier this month by his colleagues. Three hundred and fifty top people in the industry gathered to pay him homage, and Gordon Stulberg, the president of Twentieth Century-Fox, who presented Wasserman with a gift from the association—an 1861 Italian "megalatoscopio," to add to his collection of motion-picture antiques—ventured a high-level sick joke: "We've come a long way to *Earthquake* and *Towering Inferno*." It is reported that the assembled guests laughed like mad.

The New Yorker, December 2, 1974

THE GODFATHER, PART II
FATHERS AND SONS

At the close of *The Godfather*, Michael Corleone has consolidated his power by a series of murders and has earned the crown his dead father, Don Vito, handed him. In the last shot, Michael—his eyes clouded—assures his wife, Kay, that he is not responsible for the murder of his sister's husband. The door closes Kay out while he receives the homage of subordinates, and if she doesn't know that he lied, it can only be because she doesn't want to. *The Godfather, Part II* begins where the first film ended: before the titles there is a view behind that door. The new king stands in the dark, his face lusterless and dispassionate as his hand is being kissed. The familiar *Godfather* waltz theme is heard in an ambiguous, melancholy tone. Is it our imagination, or is Michael's face starting to rot? The dramatic charge of that moment is Shakespearean. The waltz is faintly, chillingly ominous.

By a single image, Francis Ford Coppola has plunged us back into the sensuality and terror of the first film. And, with the relentlessness of a master, he goes farther and farther. The daring of Part II is that it enlarges the scope and deepens the meaning of the first film; *The Godfather* was the greatest gangster picture ever made, and had metaphorical overtones that took it far beyond the gangster genre. In Part II, the wider themes are no longer merely implied. The second film shows the consequences of the actions in the first; it's all one movie, in two great big pieces, and it comes together in your head while you watch. Coppola might almost have a pact with the audience; we're already so engrossed in the Corleones that now he can go on to give us a more interior view of the characters at the same time that he shows their spreading social influence. The completed work is an epic about the seeds of destruction that the immigrants brought to the new land, with Sicilians, Wasps, and Jews separate socially but joined together in crime and political bribery. This is a bicentennial picture that doesn't insult the intelligence. It's an epic vision of the corruption of America.

After the titles, the action begins in Sicily in 1901, with the funeral procession of Michael's murdered grandfather, and we realize that the plaintive tone that was so unsettling in the opening music is linked to funeral drums and to a line of mourning women. The rot in Michael's face starts here, in his legacy from his father. The silent nine-year-old boy walking behind the coffin with his strong, grief-hardened mother is Vito, who will become the Don, the Godfather (the role played in the first film by Marlon Brando). Shots are heard, the procession breaks up—Vito's older brother has just been killed. And in a few minutes Vito, his mother dead, too, is running for his life. The waltz is heard again, still poignant but with a note of exaltation, as a ship with the wide-eyed child among the hordes in steerage passes the Statue of Liberty. The sallow, skinny boy has an almost frightening look of guarded intelligence; not understanding a word of English, he makes no sound until he's all alone, quarantined with smallpox on Ellis Island. Then, in his hospital cell, he looks out the barred window and, in a thin, childish soprano, sings a Sicilian song. As he sings, we see the superimposed face of another dark-eyed little boy, a shining princeling in white with a pretty flower-face—Michael's son, the little boy who had been playing in the garden with the old Don Vito when he died. It is the rich princeling's First Communion, and there is a lavish celebration at the Corleone estate on the shore of Lake Tahoe. The year is 1958, and the surviving members of the

Corleone family, whose base of operations is now in Nevada, are gathered for the occasion.

The first film covered the period from 1945 to the mid-fifties. Part II, contrasting the early manhood of Vito (played by Robert De Niro) with the life of Michael, his inheritor (Al Pacino), spans almost seventy years. We saw only the middle of the story in the first film; now we have the beginning and the end. Structurally, the completed work is nothing less than the rise and decay of an American dynasty of unofficial rulers. Vito rises and becomes a respected man while his son Michael, the young king, rots before our eyes, and there is something about actually seeing the generations of a family in counterpoint that is emotionally overpowering. It's as if the movie satisfied an impossible yet basic human desire to see what our parents were like before we were born and to see what they did that affected what we became— not to hear about it, or to read about it, as we can in novels, but actually to see it. It really is like the past recaptured. We see the characters at different points in their lives, with every scene sharpening our perception of them; at one moment Michael embraces his young son, at another Vito cradles young Michael in his arms. The whole picture is informed with such a complex sense of the intermingling of good and evil—and of the inability to foresee the effects of our love upon our children—that it may be the most passionately felt epic ever made in this country.

Throughout the three hours and twenty minutes of Part II, there are so many moments of epiphany—mysterious, reverberant images, such as the small Vito singing in his cell—that one scarcely has the emotional resources to deal with the experience of this film. Twice, I almost cried out at acts of violence that De Niro's Vito committed. I didn't look away from the images, as I sometimes do at routine action pictures. I wanted to see the worst; there is a powerful need to see it. You need these moments as you need the terrible climaxes in a Tolstoy novel. A great novelist does not spare our feelings (as the historical romancer does); he intensifies them, and so does Coppola. On the screen, the speed of the climaxes and their vividness make them almost unbearably wounding.

Much of the material about Don Vito's early life which appears in Part II was in the Mario Puzo book and was left out of the first movie, but the real fecundity of Puzo's mind shows in the way this new film can take his characters further along and can expand (and, in a few cases, alter) the implications of the book. Puzo didn't write the novel he probably could have written, but there was a Promethean spark in his trash, and Coppola has written the novel it might have been. However, this second film (the script is again by Coppola and Puzo) doesn't appear to derive from the book as much as from what Coppola learned while he was making the first. In Part II, he has had the opportunity to do what he was prevented from doing before, and he's been able to develop what he didn't know about his characters and themes until after he'd made the first picture. He has also been able to balance the material. Many people who saw *The Godfather* developed a romantic identification with the Corleones; they longed for the feeling of protection that Don Vito conferred on his loving family. Now that the full story has been told, you'd have to have an insensitivity bordering on moral idiocy to think that the Corleones live a wonderful life, which you'd like to be part of.

The violence in this film never doesn't bother us—it's never just a kick. For a movie director, Coppola has an unusual interest in ideas and in the texture of feeling and thought. This wasn't always apparent in the first film, because the melodramatic suspense was so strong that one's motor responses demanded the resolution of tension (as in the restaurant scene, when one's heart almost stopped in the few seconds before Michael pulled out the gun and fired). But this time Coppola controls our emotional responses so that the horror seeps through everything and no action provides a melodramatic release. Within a scene Coppola is controlled and unhurried, yet he has a gift for igniting narrative, and the exploding effects keep accumulating. About midway, I began to feel that the film was expanding in my head like a soft bullet.

The casting is so close to flawless that we can feel the family connections, and there are times when one could swear that Michael's brother Fredo (John Cazale), as he ages, is beginning to look like a weak version of his father, because we see Marlon Brando in the wide forehead and receding hair. Brando is not on the screen this time, but he persists in his sons, Fredo and Michael, and Brando's character is extended by our seeing how it was formed. As Vito, Robert De Niro amply convinces one that he has it in him to become the old man that Brando was. It's not that he looks exactly like Brando but that he has Brando's wary soul, and so we can easily imagine the body changing with the years. It is much like seeing a photograph of one's own dead father when he was a strapping young man; the burning spirit we see in his face spooks us, because of our knowledge of what he was at the end. In De Niro's case, the young man's face is fired by a secret pride. His gesture as he refuses the gift of a box of groceries is beautifully expressive and has the added wonder of suggesting Brando, and not from the outside but from the inside. Even the soft, cracked Brando-like voice seems to come from the inside. When De Niro closes his eyes to blot out something insupportable, the reflex is like a presentiment of the old man's reflexes. There is such a continuity of soul between the child on the ship, De Niro's slight, ironic smile as a cowardly landlord tries to appease him, and Brando, the old man who died happy in the sun, that although Vito is a subsidiary character in terms of actual time on the screen, this second film, like the first, is imbued with his presence.

De Niro is right to be playing the young Brando because he has the physical audacity, the grace, and the instinct to become a great actor—perhaps as great as Brando. In *Mean Streets,* he was a wild, reckless kid who flaunted his being out of control; here he's a man who holds himself in—and he's just as transfixing. Vito came to America to survive. He brought nothing with him but a background of violence, and when he believes the only choice is between knuckling under to the gangsters who terrorize the poor in Little Italy—just as gangsters terrorized his family in Sicily—and using a gun, he chooses the gun. In his terms, it's a simple matter of self-preservation, and he achieves his manhood when he becomes a killer. Vito has a feudal code of honor. To the Italians who treat him with respect he's a folk hero—a Robin Hood you can come to in times of trouble. No matter what he does, he believes he's a man of principle, and he's wrapped in dignity. The child's silence is carried forward in the adult. De Niro's performance is so subtle that when he speaks in the Sicilian dialect he learned for the role he speaks easily, but he is cautious in English and speaks very clearly and precisely. For a man of Vito's character who doesn't know the language well, precision is important—sloppy talk would be unthinkable. Like Brando's Vito, De Niro's has a reserve that can never be breached. Vito is so secure in the knowledge of how dangerous he is that his courtliness is no more or less than noblesse oblige.

The physical contrasts between De Niro's characterization and Pacino's give an almost tactile dimension to the theme. Driving through the streets of Batista's Havana, which he's buying into—buying a piece of the government—Michael sees the children begging, and he knows what he is: he's a predator on human weakness. And that's exactly what he looks like. He wears silvery-gray nubby-silk suits over a soft, amorphous body; he's hidden under the price tag. The burden of power sits on him like a sickness; his expression is sullen and withdrawn. He didn't have to be what he is: he knew there were other possibilities, and he chose to become a killer out of family loyalty. Here in Part II he is a disconsolate man, whose only attachment is to his children; he can never go back to the time before that moment in the restaurant when he shot his father's enemies. In the first film, we saw Don Vito weep when he learned that it was Michael who had done the killing; Michael's act, which preserved the family's power, destroyed his own life. Don Vito had recoiled from the sordid drug traffic, but since crime is the most competitive business of all (the quality of what you're peddling not being a conspicuous factor), Michael, the modernist, recoils from nothing; the empire that he runs from Nevada has few links with his young father's Robin Hood days. It's only inside himself that Michael recoils. His tense, flaccid face hovers over the movie; he's the man in power, trying to control the lives around him and feeling empty and betrayed. He's like a depressed Brando.

There are times when Pacino's moodiness isn't particularly eloquent, and when Michael asks his mother (Morgana King) how his father felt deep down in his heart the question doesn't have enough urgency. However, Pacino does something very difficult: he gives an almost immobile performance. Michael's attempt to be the man his father was has aged him, and he can't conceal the ugliness of the calculations that his father's ceremonial manner masked. His father had a domestic life that was a sanctuary, but Michael has no sanctuary. He cannot maintain the traditional division of home and business, and so the light and dark contrasts are not as sharp as in the first picture. His wife knows he lied to her, just as he lies to a Senate investigating committee, and the darkness of his business dealings has invaded his home. Part II has the same mythic and operatic visual scheme as the first; once again the cinematographer is Gordon Willis. Visually the film is, however, far more complexly beautiful than the first, just as it's thematically richer, more shadowed, more full. Willis's workmanship has developed, like Coppola's; even the sequences in the sunlight have deep tones—elegiac yet lyrical, as in *The Conformist,* and always serving the narrative, as the Nino Rota score also does.

Talia Shire had a very sure touch in her wedding scenes in the first film; her Connie was like a Pier Angeli with a less fragile, bolder nature—a spoiled princess. Now, tight with anger, dependent on her brother Michael, who killed her husband, Connie behaves self-destructively. She once had a dream wedding; now she hooks up with gigolo playboys. (Troy Donahue is her newest husband.) Talia Shire has such beauty and strength that she commands attention. It's possible that she didn't impose herself more strongly in the first film because Coppola, through a kind of reverse nepotism (Miss Shire is his sister), deëmphasized her role and didn't give her many closeups, but this time—pinched, strident, whory—she comes through as a stunningly controlled actress. Kay (Diane Keaton), Michael's New England-born wife, balks at becoming the acquiescent woman he requires, so he shows her what his protection means. It's dependent on absolute fealty. Any challenge or betrayal and you're dead—for men, that is. Women are so subservient they're not considered dangerous enough to kill—that's about the extent of Mafioso chivalry. The male-female relationships are worked out with a Jacobean splendor that goes far beyond one's expectations.

There must be more brilliant strokes of casting here (including the use of a batch of Hollywood notables—Phil Feldman, Roger Corman, and William Bowers—as United States senators), and more first-rate acting in small parts, than in any other American movie. An important new character, Hyman Roth, a Meyer Lansky-like businessman-gangster, as full of cant and fake wisdom as a fund-raising rabbi, is played with smooth conviction by the near-legendary Lee Strasberg. Even his breath control is impeccable: when Roth talks too much and gets more excited than he should, his talk ends with a sound of exertion from his chest. As another new major character, Frankie Pentangeli, an old-timer in the rackets who wants things to be as they were when Don Vito was in his heyday, Michael V. Gazzo (the playwright actor) gives an intensely likable performance that adds flavor to the picture. His Pentangeli has the capacity for enjoying life, unlike Michael and the anonymous-looking high-echelon hoods who surround him. As the bland, despicably loyal Tom Hagen, more square-faced and sturdy now, Robert Duvall, a powerful recessive actor, is practically a genius at keeping himself in the background; and Richard Bright as Al Neri, one of Michael's henchmen, runs him a close second.

Coppola's approach is openhanded: he doesn't force the situations. He puts the material up there, and we read the screen for ourselves. But in a few places, such as in the double-crossing maneuvers of Michael Corleone and Hyman Roth, his partner in the Cuban venture, it hasn't been made readable enough. There's a slight confusion for the audience in the sequences dealing with Roth's bogus attempt on the life of Pentangeli, and the staging is a little flatfooted in the scenes in which the Corleone assassin first eliminates Roth's bodyguard and then goes to kill Roth. Also, it's a disadvantage that the frame-up of Senator Geary (which is very poorly staged, with more gory views of a murdered girl than are necessary) comes so long after the provocation for it. Everywhere else, the contrapuntal cutting is beautifully right, but the pieces of the Senator Geary story seem too slackly spaced apart. (The casting of G. D. Spradlin in the role is a juicy bit of satire; he looks and acts like a synthesis of several of our worst senators.) These small flaws are not failures of intelligence; they're faults in the storytelling, and there are a few abrupt transitions, indicating unplanned last-minute cuts. There may be too many scenes of plotting heads, and at times one wishes the sequences to be more fully developed. One never wants less of the characters; one always wants more—particularly of Vito in the 1917 period, which is recreated in a way that makes movies once again seem a miraculous medium.

This film wouldn't have been made if the first hadn't been a hit—and the first was made because the Paramount executives expected it to be an ordinary gangster shoot-'em-up. When you see this new picture, you wonder how Coppola won the fights. Maybe the answer is that they knew they couldn't make it without him. After you see it, you feel they can't make *any* picture without him. He directs with supreme confidence. Coppola is the inheritor of the traditions of the novel, the theater, and—especially—opera and movies. The sensibility at work in this film is that of a major artist. We're not used to it: how many screen artists get the chance to work in the epic form, and who has been able to seize the power to compose a modern American epic? And who else, when he got the chance and the power, would have proceeded with the absolute conviction that he'd make the film the way it should be made? In movies, that's the inner voice of the authentic hero.

The New Yorker, December 23, 1974

YOUNG FRANKENSTEIN

Gene Wilder stares at the world with nearsighted, pale-blue-eyed wonder; he was born with a comic's flyblown wig and the look of a reddish creature from outer space. His features aren't distinct; his personality lacks definition. His whole appearance is so fuzzy and weak he's like mist on the lens. Yet since his first screen appearance, as the mortician in *Bonnie and Clyde,* he's made his presence felt each time. He's a magnetic blur. It's easy to imagine him as a frizzy-haired fiddler-clown in a college production of *A Midsummer Night's Dream,* until he slides over into that hysteria which is his dazzling specialty. As a hysteric, he's funnier even than Peter Sellers. For Sellers, hysteria is just one more weapon in his comic arsenal—his hysteria mocks hysteria—but Wilder's hysteria seems perfectly natural. You never question what's driving him to it; his fits are lucid and total. They take him into a different dimension—he delivers what Harpo promised.

Wilder is clearly an actor who can play serious roles as well as comic ones, and he's a superb technician. Yet he also seems an inspired original, as peculiarly, elusively demented in his own way as the greatest original of them all, Jonathan Winters. You can't tell what makes clowns like this funny. The sources of their humor are split off from the technical effects they produce. (With Chaplin, there's a unity between source and technique—which isn't necessarily preferable.) Like Winters, Wilder taps a private madness. In *Start the Revolution Without Me,* he played a French nobleman who was offering a tidbit to the falcon on his wrist when his wife pointed out that the falcon was dead. With the calm of the utterly insane, he said to her, "Repeat that." Reality is what Wilder's weak stare doesn't take in.

Wilder plays the title role in Mel Brooks's *Young Frankenstein,* and in the first fifteen minutes or so—especially in a medical experiment on skinny, excruciatingly vulnerable Liam Dunn—he hits a new kind of controlled maniacal peak. The movie doesn't take Wilder beyond that early high, but it doesn't need to. It's a silly, zizzy picture—a farce-parody of Hollywood's mad-scientist-trying-to-be-God pictures, with Wilder as the old Baron Frankenstein's grandson, an American professor of neurology, who takes a trip to the family castle in Transylvania. Peter Boyle is the Frankenstein monster, and Madeline Kahn is the professor's plastic-woman fiancée, who becomes the monster's bride. It isn't a dialogue comedy; it's visceral and lower. It's what used to be called a crazy comedy, and there hasn't been this kind of craziness on the screen in years. It's a film to go to when your rhythm is slowed down and you're too tired to think. You can't bring anything to it (Brooks's timing is too obvious for that); you have to let it do everything for you, because that's the only way it works. It has some of the obviousness of *Abbott & Costello Meet Frankenstein,* and if you go expecting too much it could seem like kids' stuff—which, of course, it is, but it's very funny kids' stuff, the kind that made pictures like *Kentucky Moonshine* and *Murder, He Says* into nutbrain classics. You can go to see it when you can barely keep your eyes open, and come out feeling relaxed and recharged.

Wilder wrote the screenplay with Brooks, and he has a healthy respect for his own star abilities. Confidence seems to be making him better-looking with each picture; this time he wears a romantic, droopy mustache, and in full-face, with his eyes outlined and his long chin prominent, he gives a vain, John Barrymore-ish dash to the role. I could have done with less of his pixie hunchback assistant Igor—the English comic, Marty Feldman, who's done up like Barrymore as Richard III. The camera picks up the glints of Wilder's madness; Feldman projects to the gallery. He's too consciously zany; he's funny at times (and he uses a Groucho turn of phrase like a shiv), but he's heavy-spirited and cunning, in the Anthony Newley manner. He emphasizes the picture's worst defect: the director tends to repeat—and exhaust— effects. In the opening sequences, Wilder does a startling spinoff of Sellers's performance as Dr. Strangelove, but then, later on, Kenneth Mars, the Nazi playwright in *The Producers* and the Transylvania police inspector here— equipped with an artificial arm, like Lionel Atwill in the role in the old days—does a full-dress variation on Strangelove. Like Feldman, Mars seems meant to be funnier than he is; his impenetrable accent is one of those Brooks ideas that don't pan out. Sometimes Brooks appears to think he can force something to be a scream if he pounds away at it. Cloris Leachman makes a magnificent entrance as the castle housekeeper, but then, having a one-and-a-half-gag role, she has nothing left to do but make faces. However, Peter Boyle underplays smoothly; he suggests a puckish cutup's spirit inside his monster's bulk, and he comes through with a great sick-joke strangled voice in a musical number that shows what Brooks can do when his instinct is really working. He can make you laugh helplessly.

The picture was made in black-and-white, which holds it visually close to the pictures it takes off from, and Brooks keeps the setups simple. The details are reassuring: there's a little more Transylvanian ground fog than you've ever seen before, the laboratory machines give off enough sparks to let us know that's their only function, and the ingénue (Teri Garr, as Frankenstein's laboratory assistant) is the essence of washed-out B-movie starlet. The style of the picture is controlled excess, and the whole thing is remarkably consistent in tone, considering that it ranges from unfunny hamming (the medical student at the beginning) to a masterly bit contributed by Gene Hackman as a bearded blind man. (Hackman's inflections are so spectacularly assured I thought there was a famous comic hidden under the beard until I recognized his voice.) The movie works because it has the Mary Shelley story to lean on: we know that the monster will be created and will get loose. And Brooks makes a leap up as a director because, although the comedy doesn't build, he carries the story through. Some directors don't need a unifying story, but Brooks has always got lost without one. (He had a story in *The Twelve Chairs*, but he didn't have the jokes.) Staying with the story, Brooks even has a satisfying windup, which makes this just about the only comedy of recent years that doesn't collapse. Best of all, *Young Frankenstein* doesn't try to be boffola, like Brooks's last picture, *Blazing Saddles,* yet it has that picture's prime attractions: Wilder and Madeline Kahn. When she parodied Marlene Dietrich in *Blazing Saddles,* it wasn't the usual Dietrich imitation, because she was also parodying herself. Madeline Kahn has an extra dimension of sexiness; it's almost like what Mae West had— she's flirtatious in a self-knowing way. And everything that's wrong about her is sexy. You look at her and think, What a beautiful translucent skin on such a big jaw; what a statuesque hourglass figure, especially where the sand has slipped. She's so self-knowingly lascivious that she convinces you she really digs the monster. Madeline Kahn is funny and enticing because she's soaked in passion; when you look at her, you see a water bed at just the right temperature.

The New Yorker, December 30, 1974

SHAMPOO
BEVERLY HILLS AS A BIG BED

When George (Warren Beatty), the hairdresser hero of *Shampoo,* asks Jackie (Julie Christie), "Want me to do your hair?", it's his love lyric. George massages a neck and wields a blower as if he would rather be doing that than anything else in the world. When he gets his hands in a woman's hair, it's practically sex, and sensuous, tender sex—not what his Beverly Hills customers are used to. Their husbands and lovers don't have professionally caressing hands like the dedicated George's. Some ideas for films are promising, some are cocksure audacious, but a film about the movie colony featuring the lives of the rich, beautiful women who have a yen for their handsome hairdresser is such a yummy idea that it almost sounds like something a smart porno filmmaker would come up with. Exploited for gags, it might have been no more than a saucy romp, a modernized *Fanfan the Tulip,* and that may be what audiences expect—maybe even what some audiences want. But the way it has been done, the joke expands the more you think about it. *Shampoo* is light and impudent, yet, like the comedies that live on, it's a bigger picture in retrospect.

The attention George gives women is so exciting to him and to them that he's always on the go. He works in a fashionable salon, commutes to his assignations on a motorbike, and tells himself and his girl, Jill (Goldie Hawn), that they'll settle down as soon as he gets his own shop. The movie deals with his frantic bed-hopping during the forty-odd hours in which he tries to borrow the stake he needs from Lester (Jack Warden), the shyster tycoon who is married to Felicia (Lee Grant), a rapacious customer. Lester is also keeping Jackie, George's old girl friend, who is Jill's closest friend. *Shampoo* opens on Election Eve, November 4, 1968, when the hero's life has begun to boil over. The characters whirl in and out of bed with each other through Election Day and Night, watching the returns at a party at The Bistro, acknowledging Nixon and Agnew's victory by seeing in the dawn at another party, and preparing for the new era by shifting partners. The picture is a sex roundelay set in a period as clearly defined as the Jazz Age. (It's gone, all right, and we know that best when we catch echoes from it.) Maybe we've all been caught in a time warp, because the Beatles sixties of miniskirts and strobe lights, when people had not yet come down from their euphoria about the harmlessness of drugs, is already a period with its own bubbly potency. The time of *Shampoo* is so close to us that at moments we forget its pastness, and then we're stung by the consciousness of how much has changed.

Shampoo is set in the past for containment, for a formalized situation, just as Ingmar Bergman set his boudoir farce, *Smiles of a Summer Night,* in the operetta past of the *Merry Widow* period. What the turn-of-the-century metaphor did for Bergman the 1968 election, as the sum of an era, does for *Shampoo.* The balletic, patterned confusion of *Shampoo* is theatrical, and Los Angeles—more particularly, Beverly Hills, the swankest part of it, a city within a city—is, indisputably, a stylized, theatrical setting. But a bedroom-chase construction isn't stagey in Beverly Hills: *Shampoo* has a mathematically structured plot in an open society. Los Angeles itself, the sprawl-city, opens the movie up, and the L.A. sense of freedom makes its own comment on the scrambling characters. Besides, when you play musical chairs in the bedrooms of Beverly Hills, the distances you have to cover impose their own comic frenzy. As in a Feydeau play or some of the René Clair and Lubitsch films, the more complicated the interaction is, the more we look forward to the climactic muddle and the final sorting out of couples. The whirring pleasures of carnal farce require our awareness of the mechanics, and the director, Hal Ashby, has the deftness to keep us conscious of the structure and yet to give it free play. The plot isn't arbitrary; it's what George, who can never really get himself together, is caught in. The mixed pairs of lovers don't get snarled at the same parties by coincidence; they go knowing who else is going to be there, wanting the danger of collisions.

Shampoo expresses the emotional climate of the time and place. Los Angeles has become what it is because of the bright heat, which turns people into narcissists and sensuous provocateurs. The atmosphere seems to infantilize sex: sexual desire is despiritualized; it becomes a demand for immediate gratification. George's women have their status styles—money and sun produce tough babies—but George, the sexual courier, servicing a garden apartment as ardently as a terraced estate, is a true democrat. The characters are all linked by sex—and dissatisfaction. They're passionate people from minute to minute. They want to have something going for them all the time, and since they get it only part of the time, and it doesn't last long, they feel upset and frustrated. They're so foolish, self-absorbed, and driven that the film can easily seem a trifle—and at one level it is—but it's daringly faithful to the body-conscious style of life that is its subject, and it never falls into low farce by treating the characters as dumdums. They're attractively, humanly, greedily foolish, and some of their foolishness is shared by people much more complex. The movie gets at the kink and willfulness of the Beverly Hills way of life (which magnetizes the whole world), but it doesn't point any comic fingers. It's too balanced and Mozartean for that.

The scenarist, Robert Towne (Beatty, who shares the screenplay credit, contributed ideas and worked on the structuring with him), has brought something new to bedroom farce. The characters have more than one sex object in mind, and they're constantly regrouping in their heads. No one is romantically in love or devoted in the sense in which Bergman's characters are in *Smiles of a Summer Night. Shampoo* isn't about the bondage of romantic pursuit, it's about the bondage of the universal itch among a group primed to scratch. Ready and waiting, the characters keep all possibilities open. This variation on the usual love comedy is the trickiest, funniest, truest-to-its-freeway-love-environment ingredient of the movie. Except for George, who doesn't plan ahead, everyone is always considering alternatives. It's a small, rich, loose society, and its members know each other carnally in a casual way; it's in the nature of things that they take turns in the one big bed that is their world. Since the characters hold multiple goals, when they look depressed you're never sure who exactly is the object of their misery. The actors are much more free than in the confines of classic farce. They're free, too, of the stilted witticisms of classic farce: Towne writes such easy, unforced dialogue that they might be talking in their own voices.

Julie Christie's locked-in, libidinous face has never been harder, more petulant, or more magical than in her role as Lester's kept woman, who hates her position because she never gets to go anywhere with him. Jackie is coarse and high-strung (a true L.A. combo); she's a self-destructive winner, and Julie Christie plays her boldly, with a moody ruthlessness that I find uncanny. This is the first time Christie and Beatty have acted together since *McCabe & Mrs. Miller,* and each of them gains. Julie Christie is one of those screen actresses whose every half-buried thought smashes through; she's so delicate an actress that when she plays a coarse girl like Jackie there's friction in each nuance. On the stage last year in *Uncle Vanya* she was a vacuum; in *Shampoo* she's not only an actress, she is—in the high-class-hooker terms of her role—the sexiest woman in movies right now. She has the knack of turning off her spirituality totally; in this role she's a gorgeous, whory-lipped little beast, a dirty sprite.

Goldie Hawn, who began to come into her own as a screen actress in last year's *The Sugarland Express,* is probably going to be everything her admirers have hoped for. As the hysterical young Jill, she isn't allowed to be too hysterical; Hal Ashby doesn't let her go all frilly and wistful, either. She used to be her own best audience; now that she has stopped breaking up infectiously, we're free to judge her for ourselves. She has calm moments here—we see Jill's mind working without Goldie Hawn's goldfish eyes batting—and I think it's the first time I've noticed that she has a speaking voice. (She's always been a screamer.) She looks great in her baby dolls and minis, and it's a relief that her Jill doesn't have a mini baby-doll head. Lee Grant, who worked with Ashby in *The Landlord*, the film of his that *Shampoo* most resembles (though he was a beginner then, with nothing like the assurance he shows now), is such a cool-style comedienne that she's in danger of having people say that she's good, as usual. But she carries off the film's most sexually brutal scene: Felicia comes home late for an assignation with George and discovers that while he was waiting for her he has been occupied with her teenage daughter (Carrie Fisher), and she *still* wants to go to bed with him. She wants it more than ever. As her husband, Jack Warden is the biggest surprise in the cast. He's both a broad cartoon and an appealing character. Lester is triply cuckolded—George commutes between Lester's mistress and wife and daughter—and he's a heavy contributor to the Nixon-Agnew campaign, for business purposes. And yet he has more depth than anyone else in the movie. He's ready to investigate anything: invited to join a nymphs-and-satyrs bathing orgy, he considers getting into the water as he would a new investment, and thinks, Why not? Warden shows us Lester's pragmatic ruminations; we see that he's a business success because he's learned to make compromises in his own favor. While Nixon is on TV making his victory speech, Lester and George have it all out, in a final confrontation scene, and the astute Lester realizes that, despite the wear and tear on George's zipper, the hairdresser is no threat to him.

The central performance that makes it all work is Beatty's. George, who wears his hair blower like a Colt .45, isn't an easy role; I don't know anyone else who could have played it. Because of Beatty's offscreen reputation as a heterosexual dynamo, audiences may laugh extra hard at the scenes in which Lester assumes that a male hairdresser can't be straight, but that joke is integral to the conception anyway. Beatty makes George's impulsive warmth toward his customers believable. An uncomplicated Don Juan, George gets pleasure from giving pleasure. He doesn't smoke tobacco or dope; he doesn't pop pills; outside of soft drinks, the only beverage he takes in the whole film is a little white wine. George doesn't need to be raised high or brought down, and he has nothing to obliterate. Maybe when he's older, if he's still working in someone else's shop, he'll be embittered, and he'll be one of the garden-variety narcissists who must have attention from women (and secretly hate them). But at this point in his life, jumping happily to oblige any woman who wants him, he has the pagan purity of an adolescent. At the start of the film, George is in the middle of the whirligig, but by the end the game has moved on, and he's left behind, dreaming of a simpler life and longing for a sexual playmate from the past. "You're the only one I trust," he tells Jackie. The others are upward-mobile and moving fast, and they live as if upward mobility were a permanent condition. George wants something to hang on to, and he can't get it, because he's too generous. He lives in constant excitation, and so he's the closest to exhaustion. George is the only one of the characters who isn't completely selfish; he's the only one who doesn't function successfully in the society. The others know how to use people, but George, the compleat lover, does everything for fun. Making love to a beautiful woman is an aesthetic thing with him, and making her look beautiful is an act of love for him. He's almost a sexual saint.

Shampoo doesn't seem inspired the way Renoir's roundelay *Rules of the Game* does. It doesn't have the feeling that one gets from the Renoir film—that the whole beautiful, macabre chaos is bubbling up right this minute. And *Shampoo* is not as lyrical—or as elegantly moldy to the taste—as parts of Bergman's *Smiles*. It doesn't give the lunatic delight of *Bringing Up Baby*, which in its homegrown, screwball style also suggested an equivalent of Restoration comedy. But it's the most virtuoso example of sophisticated, kaleidoscopic farce that American moviemakers have ever come up with. And, as in *Rules of the Game*, the farce movement itself carries a sense of heedless activity, of a craze of dissatisfaction. In this game, George, who loves love too much to profit from it, has to be the loser. He's a fool (that's why Lester doesn't have him beaten up), but he's a pure fool (and Lester can appreciate that). George isn't a negligible dramatic creation. For the moviemakers, he's the foolish romanticism of youth incarnate, but some people may see him as a jerk and resent him. To them, possibly, the new romantic hero would be a cynical stud who gets it all and wins out. In its own way, *Shampoo* is a very uncompromising film, and it's going to cause dissension. People who are living the newer forms of the *Blow-Up* style, or want to, won't like this view of it. *Shampoo* may be put down as frivolous just because it really isn't; to lift a line from *The Earrings of Madame de . . .* , it's "only superficially superficial." Was it Osbert Sitwell who said that life might be considered a comedy only if it were never to end? *Shampoo* tosses the fact of death into the midst of the beauty shop; we suddenly learn that Norman (Jay Robinson), the languid, pettish proprietor, whom we'd assumed to be strictly homosexual, has just lost his teenage son in a car crash. It's an artifice—reality intruding upon the clowns at their revels, death as an interruption to the babble and trivial bickering of the beauty-salon world. But it's needed, and it's the right death—the accidental death of someone young, the only event, maybe, that can't be converted into gossip.

There are minds at work in this film: three principal ones—Ashby, Beatty, who produced it (it is his second production; the first was *Bonnie and Clyde*), and Towne. Hal Ashby says that he had fifty or sixty jobs (starting when he was ten years old) before he landed as a Multilith operator at the old Republic Studios in L.A., and decided he wanted to become a director. As the first step, he went to work in the cutting room, where he spent the standard eight years as an apprentice before he was allowed (by feudal union regulation) to edit a film. Afterward, he edited Norman Jewison's *The*

Cincinnati Kid, The Russians Are Coming, The Russians Are Coming, In the Heat of the Night, and *The Thomas Crown Affair,* and then, in 1968, Jewison, who was supposed to direct *The Landlord,* arranged with the moneymen to turn it over to Ashby. (*Shampoo* should cause *The Landlord* to get the attention it deserves.) His new film is only his fourth (*Harold and Maude* and *The Last Detail* came between), but he's developed quickly. Ashby's control keeps *Shampoo* from teetering over into burlesque. His work doesn't have the flash of an innovative, intuitive film artist, but for the script Towne has prepared, Ashby, the craftsman who serves the material, is probably the only kind of director.

Robert Towne didn't write a screenplay a director can take off from. *Shampoo* is conceived for the movies, and it's porous, yet the development of the themes is completely conceived. It isn't the basis for a director to work out his own conception; it *is* a conception. (Tall, his long face dark-bearded, Towne appears in one party shot in *Shampoo,* looking a little like Albrecht Dürer). It's more apparent now why Towne collided with Polanski over his script (also an original) for *Chinatown.* He provided a script that culminated—logically—with the heroine's killing her lover-father in order to save her daughter. A Gothic-minded absurdist, Polanski didn't see why he shouldn't end it with the death of the heroine and the triumph of the father, who had raped the land, raped his daughter, and would now proceed to corrupt the child he'd had by her. Towne doesn't pull everything down like that. It has taken a while to get a fix on his talent, because he's not a published writer, and because he didn't receive credit for some of the films he worked on, and didn't take blame for others *(The New Centurions).* His earliest screen credits are for *Villa Rides* and *The Tomb of Ligeia,* but even before those, in 1964, he wrote an episode for TV's *Breaking Point,* called "So Many Pretty Girls, So Little Time," about a Don Juan. Beatty brought him in to do the rewriting on *Bonnie and Clyde* (he was listed as "Special Consultant"), and when Coppola accepted his Academy Award for the screenplay of *The Godfather* he acknowledged Towne's contribution (he wrote one scene and tinkered with a few others). Towne also did a major rewrite on *Cisco Pike* (the film has certain similarities to *Shampoo*) and on *The Yakuza,* which hasn't opened yet, and he wrote the script (an adaptation) of *The Last Detail.*

Towne's heroes, if we can take Gittes, of *Chinatown,* and George, here, as fair examples, are hip to conventional society, and they assume that they reject its dreams. But in some corner of their heads they think that maybe the old romantic dream can be made to work. Gittes is basically a very simple man. He wants the woman he loves to tell him the truth about herself; the truth is very important to him. And George is even simpler. Towne's heroes are like the heroes of hardboiled fiction: they don't ask much of life, but they are also romantic damn fools who ask just what they can't get. His characters are so effective on the screen because they have sides you don't expect and—a Towne idiosyncrasy—they tell anecdotes, mostly inane, back-slapping ones (Jack Nicholson has several in *The Last Detail* and *Chinatown,* and Jack Warden gets off a real puzzler). With his ear for unaffected dialogue, and with a gift for never forcing a point, Towne may be a great new screenwriter in a structured tradition—a flaky classicist.

The New Yorker, February 17, 1975

COMING: **NASHVILLE**

Is there such a thing as an orgy for movie-lovers—but an orgy without excess? At Robert Altman's new, almost-three-hour film, *Nashville,* you don't get drunk on images, you're not overpowered—you get elated. I've never before seen a movie I loved in quite this way: I sat there smiling at the screen, in complete happiness. It's a pure emotional high, and you don't come down when the picture is over; you take it with you. In most cases, the studio heads can conjecture what a director's next picture will be like, and they feel safe that way—it's like an insurance policy. They can't with Altman, and after United Artists withdrew its backing from *Nashville,* the picture had to be produced independently, because none of the other major companies would take it on. U.A.'s decision will probably rack up as a classic boner, because this picture is going to take off into the stratosphere*—though it has first got to open. (Paramount has picked up the distribution rights but hasn't yet announced an opening date.) *Nashville* is a radical, evolutionary leap.

Altman has prepared us for it. If this film had been made earlier, it might have been too strange and new, but in the five years since he broke through with *M*A*S*H* he's experimented in so many directions that now, when it all comes together for him, it's not really a shock. From the first, packed frames of a recording studio, with Haven Hamilton (Henry Gibson), in bespangled, embroidered white cowboy clothes, like a short, horseless Roy Rogers, singing, "We must be doing somethin' right to last two hundred years," the picture is unmistakably Altman—as identifiable as a paragraph by Mailer when he's really racing. *Nashville* is simply "the ultimate Altman movie" we've been waiting for. Fused, the different styles of prankishness of *M*A*S*H* and *Brewster McCloud* and *California Split* become Jovian adolescent humor. Altman has already accustomed us to actors who don't look as if they're acting; he's attuned us to the comic subtleties of a multiple-track sound system that makes the sound more live than it ever was before; and he's evolved an organic style of moviemaking that tells a story

*I was wrong. It caused a stir, all right, but not at box offices.

without the clanking of plot. Now he dissolves the frame, so that we feel the continuity between what's on the screen and life off-camera.

•   *Nashville* isn't organized according to patterns that you're familiar with, yet you don't question the logic. You get it from the rhythms of the scenes. The picture is at once a *Grand Hotel*-style narrative, with twenty-four linked characters; a country-and-Western musical; a documentary essay on Nashville and American life; a meditation on the love affair between performers and audiences; and an Altman party. In the opening sequences, when Altman's people—the performers we associate with him because he has used them in ways no one else would think of, and they've been filtered through his sensibility—start arriving, and pile up in a traffic jam on the way from the airport to the city, the movie suggests the circus procession at the non-ending of *8½*. But Altman's clowns are far more autonomous; they move and intermingle freely, and the whole movie is their procession. *Nashville* is, above all, a celebration of its own performers. Like Bertolucci, Altman (he includes a homage to *Last Tango in Paris*) gives the actors a chance to come out—to use more of themselves in their characters. The script is by Joan Tewkesbury, but the actors have been encouraged to work up material for their roles, and not only do they do their own singing but most of them wrote their own songs—and wrote them in character. The songs distill the singers' lives, as the mimes and theatrical performances did for the actors in *Children of Paradise*. The impulse behind all Altman's innovations has been to work on more levels than the conventional film does, and now—despite the temporary sound mix and the not-quite-final edit of the print he ran recently, informally, for a few dozen people in New York, before even the Paramount executives had seen the picture—it's apparent that he needed the technical innovations in order to achieve this union of ideas and feelings. *Nashville* coalesces lightly and easily, as if it had just been tossed off. We float while watching, because Altman never lets us see the sweat. Altman's art, like Fred Astaire's, is the great American art of making the impossible look easy.

Altman does for Nashville what he was trying to do for Houston in *Brewster McCloud,* but he wasn't ready to fly then, and the script didn't have enough layers—he needs ideas that mutate, and characters who turn corners. Joan Tewkesbury has provided him with a great subject. Could there be a city with wilder metaphoric overtones than Nashville, the Hollywood of the C. & W. recording industry, the center of fundamentalist music and pop success? The country sound is a twang with longing in it; the ballads are about poor people with no hope. It's the simplistic music of the conquered South; the songs tell you that although you've failed and you've lived a terrible, degrading life, there's a place to come home to, and that's where you belong. Even the saddest song is meant to be reassuring to its audience: the insights never go beyond common poverty, job troubles, and heartaches, and the music never rises to a level that would require the audience to re-interpret its experience. Country stars are symbolic ordinary figures. In this, they're more like political demagogues than artists. The singer bears the burden of what he has become, and he keeps saying, "I may be driving an expensive car, but that doesn't mean I'm happier than you are." Neither he nor the politician dares to come right out and confess to the audience that what he's got is what he set out for from the beginning. Instead, he says, "It's only an accident that puts me here and you there—don't we talk the same language?" Listening to him, people can easily feel that he owes them, and everybody who can sing a little or who has written a tune tries to move in close to the performers as a way of getting up there into the fame business.

Nashville is about the insanity of a fundamentalist culture in which practically the whole population has been turned into groupies. The story spans the five days during which a political manager, played by Michael Murphy, lines up the talent for a Nashville rally to be used as a TV show promoting the Presidential candidacy of Hal Phillip Walker. Walker's slogan is "New Roots for the Nation"—a great slogan for the South, since country music is about a longing for roots that don't exist. Because country singing isn't complex, either musically or lyrically, Altman has been able to create a whole constellation of country stars out of actors. Some of them had actually cut records, but they're not primarily country singers, and their songs are never just numbers. The songs are the story being told, and even the way the singers stand—fluffing out a prom-queen dress, like Karen Black, or coolly staring down the audience, like the almond-eyed, slightly withdrawn Cristina Raines—is part of it. During this movie, we begin to realize that all that the people are is what we see. Nothing is held back from us, nothing is hidden.

When Altman—who is the most atmospheric of directors—discusses what his movies are about, he makes them sound stupid, and he's immediately attacked in the press by people who take his statements literally. (If pinned to the wall by publicity men, how would Joyce have explained the "Nighttown" sequence of *Ulysses?*) The complex outline of *Nashville* gives him the space he needs to work in, and he tells the story by suggestions, echoes, recurrences. It may be he's making a joke about how literally his explanations have been taken when in this picture the phony sentiments that turn up in the lyrics recur in other forms, where they ring true. Haven Hamilton, the bantam king of Nashville, with a red toupee for a crown, sings a maudlin piece of doggerel, with a heavy, churchy beat, about a married man's breaking up with his girl friend ("For the sake of the children, we must say goodbye"). Later, it's almost a reprise when we see Lily Tomlin, as the gospel-singing wife of Haven's lawyer, Ned Beatty, leave Keith Carradine (the hot young singer in a trio) for exactly that reason. Throughout, there are valid observations made to seem fake by a slimy inflection. Geraldine Chaplin, as Opal, who says she's from the BBC, is doing a documentary on Nashville; she talks in flights of poetic gush, but nothing she says is as fatuous as she makes it sound. What's funny about Opal is that her affectations are all wasted, since the hillbillies she's trying to impress don't know what she's talking about. Opal is always on the fringe of the action; her opposite is the figure that the plot threads converge on—Barbara Jean (Ronee Blakley), whose ballads are her only means of expressing her yearnings. Barbara Jean is the one tragic character: her art comes from her belief in imaginary roots.

The movies often try to do portraits of artists, but their artistry must be asserted for them. When we see an actor playing a painter and then see the paintings, we don't feel the relation. And even when the portrait is of a performing artist, the story is almost always of how the artist achieves recognition rather than of what it is that has made him an artist. Here, with Ronee Blakley's Barbara Jean, we perceive what goes into the art, and we experience what the unbalance of life and art can do to a person. When she was a child, Barbara Jean memorized the words on a record and earned fifty cents as a prize, and she's been singing ever since; the artist has developed, but the woman hasn't. She has driven herself to the point of having no identity except as a performer. She's in and out of hospitals, and her manager husband (Allen Garfield) treats her as a child, yet she's a true folk artist; the Nashville audience knows she's the real thing and responds to the purity of her gift. She expresses the loneliness that is the central emotion in country music. But she isn't *using* the emotion, as the other singers do: it pours right out of her—softly. Arriving at the airport, coming home after a stretch of treatment—for burns, we're told—she's radiant, yet so breakable that it's hard to believe she has the strength to perform. A few days later, when she stands on the stage of the Opry Belle and sings "Dues," with the words "It hurts so bad, it gets me down," her fragility is so touching and her swaying movements are so seductively musical that, perhaps for the first time on the screen, one gets the sense of an artist's being consumed by her gift. This is Ronee Blakley's first movie, and she puts most movie hysteria to shame; she achieves her effects so simply that I wasn't surprised when someone near me started to cry during one of her songs. She has a long sequence on the stage of the Opry Belle when Barbara Jean's mind starts to wander and, instead of singing, she tells out-of-place, goofy stories about her childhood. They're the same sort of stories that have gone into her songs, but without the transformation they're just tatters that she clings to—and they're all she's got. Ronee Blakley, who wrote this scene, as well as the music and lyrics of all her songs, is a peachy, dimpled brunette, in the manner of the movie stars of an earlier era; as Barbara Jean, she's like the prettiest girl in high school, the one the people in town say is just perfect-looking, like Linda Darnell. But she's more delicate; she's willowy and regal, tipping to one side like the Japanese ladies carved in ivory. At one point, she sings with the mike in one hand, the other hand tracing the movements of the music in the air, and it's an absolutely ecstatic moment.

Nashville isn't in its final shape yet, and all I can hope to do is suggest something of its achievement. Altman could make a film of this magnitude for under two million dollars* because he works with actors whose range he understands. He sets them free to give their own pulse to their characters; inspired themselves, they inspire him. And so we get motifs that bounce off each other—tough-broad Barbara Baxley's drunken fix on the murdered Kennedys, Shelley Duvall's total absorption in celebrity, a high-school band of majorettes twirling rifles, and Robert Doqui's anger at a black singer for not being black enough. All the allusions tell the story of the great American popularity contest. Godard was trying to achieve a synthesis of documentary and fiction and personal essay in the early sixties, but Godard's Calvinist temperament was too cerebral. Altman, from a Catholic background, has what Joyce had: a love of the supreme juices of everyday life. He can put unhappy characters on the screen (Keenan Wynn plays a man who loses the wife he's devoted to) and you don't wish you didn't have to watch them; you accept their unhappiness as a piece of the day, as you do in *Ulysses.* You don't recoil from the moody narcissism of Keith Carradine's character: there he is in his bedroom, listening to his own tapes, with one bed partner after another—with Geraldine Chaplin, whom he'll barely remember the next day, and with Lily Tomlin, whom he'll remember forever. You don't recoil, as you do in movies like *Blow-Up* or *Petulia,* because Altman wants you to be part of the life he shows you and to feel the exhilaration of being alive. When you get caught up in his way of seeing, you no longer anticipate what's coming, because Altman doesn't deliver what years of moviegoing have led you to expect. You get something else. Even when you feel in your bones what has to happen—as you do toward the climax of *Nashville,* when the characters assemble for the rally at the Parthenon and Barbara Jean, on the stage, smiles ravishingly at her public—he delivers it in a way you didn't expect. Who watching the pious Haven Hamilton sing the evangelical "Keep A'Goin'," his eyes flashing with a paranoid gleam as he keeps the audience under surveillance, would guess that the song represented his true spirit, and that when injured he would think of the audience before himself? Who would expect that Barbara Harris, playing a runaway wife—a bombed-out groupie hovering around the action—would finally get her chance onstage, and that her sexy, sweetly shell-shocked look would, at last, fit in perfectly? For the viewer, *Nashville* is a constant discovery of overlapping connections. The picture says, This is what America is, and I'm part of it. *Nashville* arrives at a time when America is congratulating itself for having got rid of the bad guys who were pulling the wool over people's eyes. The movie says that it isn't only the politicians who live the big lie—the big lie is something we're all capable of trying for. The candidate, Hal Phillip Walker, never appears on the screen; he doesn't need to—the screen is full of candidates. The name of Walker's party doesn't have to stand for anything: that's why it's the Replacement Party.

Nashville isn't full of resolutions, because Altman doesn't set up con-

_____

*The final cost, after the prints were made was about two million, two hundred thousand.

flics; the conflicts, as in Lily Tomlin's character, are barely visible. Her deepest tensions play out in the quietest scenes in the movie; she's a counterbalance to the people squabbling about whatever comes into their heads. There's no single reason why anybody does anything in this movie, and most of the characters' concerns are mundane. Altman uses a *Grand Hotel* mingling of characters without giving false importance to their unions and collisions, and the rally itself is barely pivotal. A lot happens in the five days, but a lot happens in any five days. There are no real dénouements, but there are no loose ends, either: Altman doesn't need to wrap it all up, because the people here are too busy being alive to be locked in place. Frauds who are halfway honest, they're true to their own characters. Even the stupidest among them, the luscious bimbo Sueleen (Gwen Welles), a tone-deaf waitress in the airport coffee shop, who wiggles and teases as she sings to the customers, and even the most ridiculous—Geraldine Chaplin's Opal—are so completely what they are that they're irresistible. At an outdoor party at Haven Hamilton's log-cabin retreat, the chattering Opal remarks, "Pure, unadulterated Bergman," but then, looking around, she adds, "Of course, the people are all wrong for Bergman, aren't they?" *Nashville* is the funniest epic vision of America ever to reach the screen.

The New Yorker, March 3, 1975

<hr>

EXCERPTS FROM THE DARNED
THE DAY OF THE LOCUST

One can go back to most writers one admired and re-experience what one admired them for, but with Nathanael West you're shocked by the élitist snobbery you once felt flattered to share. Cynical adolescents may accept *The Day of the Locust* as a brilliant Hollywood satire, on the order of *The Loved One*. What could be more attractive to them than West's view of the middle-aged and old as enraged grotesques, incapable of pleasure? He doesn't ask you to identify with his suffering grotesques—not even in *Miss Lonelyhearts*. He expects you to identify with his comic horror over their plight, and when you're young you're very vulnerable to West's highbrow-Christ attitude. But why is *The Day of the Locust* locked into so many people's minds as the definitive Los Angeles book? Maybe, in part, because of its thoroughgoing contempt for everything in Los Angeles. As a genre, Hollywood novels represent the screenwriters' revenge on the movies. In Hollywood, the writer is an underling whose work is trashed, or, at best, he's a respected collaborator without final control over how his work is used. Writing a Hollywood novel, he gets his own back: typically, he himself is the disillusioned hero, and the studio bosses, the producers, the flunkies are his boob targets—all those people who he feels have no right to make decisions about his work.

The writers romanticize the processes of corruption, seeing themselves as intellectual golden boys who go "out there"—as Edmund Wilson called it—and then turn their backs on that cheap glory, returning to write the fourth-rate book we've just plowed through. *The Day of the Locust* is far from fourth-rate, but it satisfies the loftiest expectations, since it deals with the victims of the movies—the poor in spirit who bought the commercial dreams. Edmund Wilson, one of the first to recognize West's literary worth, appreciated the book in the terms that generations of book reviewers have been using for Hollywood novels: "Mr. West has caught the emptiness of Hollywood; and he is, as far as I know, the first writer to make this emptiness horrible."

There's some truth in what Wilson said. The novel is about something, but it's not about as much as West wanted it to be—it's not about everything. West blew up his observations into a sweeping vision, and John Schlesinger takes the book seriously in all the wrong ways and compounds its overblown thesis—Faye becomes the bitch goddess, Homer is crucified, and masked figures, God help us, march toward the camera. Schlesinger's vice as a director has always been to score against his characters, crashing bricks on our skulls so we'll recognize how hideous they are.

There wouldn't be much to remember if it weren't for a few of the performers—especially Burgess Meredith. As Faye's father, Harry Greener, the washed-up old vaudevillian who sells "Miracle Solvent" door-to-door, Meredith does what is very likely his best acting in his forty-five years as a professional. Maybe you need forty-five years of experience to give this kind of performance. Meredith's Harry is a compulsive entertainer, a little, piggy-eyed, round-faced clown who failed on the stage but turns every place he's in—even his deathbed—into a theater. Harry Greener, boozy, his mind lost in a theater warp, doesn't know how *not* to put on an act. Life and show business are the same thing to him, and performing, wheedling, and conning have become indistinguishable. It's not a starring role, and it doesn't stand out and announce itself, yet Harry, the small-timer who has no world but the theater that never even knew he existed, is as fully lived-in a portrait as Olivier's Archie Rice. The conception is West's, but Meredith—strutting with a child's idea of raffishness, his face a frowzy high pink—makes you believe it. Meredith endows Harry with something of the frazzled indomitability of a Mickey Rooney, that giving-out even when one is faking giving-out. Like Rooney, Harry is manic by nature, and he never loses his awareness of the audience.

Billy Barty, who used to be Mickey Rooney's younger brother in the "Mickey McGuire" shorts, plays the dwarf gambler-tipster, Abe Kusich, and although his role is limited to a few scenes, he gives a major performance. In the novel, Abe, a macho dwarf, is an obscenely angry little man, but in realizing the character Billy Barty goes way beyond this. This Abe is dapper, with a hawk-eyed alertness to his rights and opportunities, and in the cock-fight, when he tries to breathe life into his dying rooster, his whole soul is engaged in his side's putting up a fight, and there's tenderness in his handling of the wretched, mutilated bird. Many years ago, in *Gold Diggers of 1933*, when Barty popped up in the "Pettin' in the Park" sequence, winked at Dick Powell, and handed him a can opener to use on Ruby Keeler's shiny tin costume, he seemed to embody Busby Berkeley's most wayward flights of fancy; now, like Burgess Meredith, he moves right into the character he's playing, and lives there. He gives Abe Kusich a rambunctious fullness that exposes West's sadness-of-the-monstrous for the self-pitying, self-aggrandizing bull it is. These two—Harry and Abe—escape West's patronizing categories; they have an independent existence that Tod, who represents West's own consciousness, doesn't.

The New Yorker, May 12, 1975

PART SEVEN

WHEN THE LIGHTS GO DOWN

1980

THE MAN FROM DREAM CITY—CARY GRANT

"You can be had," Mae West said to Cary Grant in *She Done Him Wrong*, which opened in January, 1933, and that was what the women stars of most of his greatest hits were saying to him for thirty years, as he backed away—but not too far. One after another, the great ladies courted him—Irene Dunne in *The Awful Truth* and *My Favorite Wife*, Katharine Hepburn in *Bringing Up Baby* and *Holiday*, Jean Arthur and Rita Hayworth in *Only Angels Have Wings*, Ingrid Bergman in *Notorious*, Grace Kelly in *To Catch a Thief*, Eva Marie Saint in *North by Northwest*, Audrey Hepburn in *Charade*. Willing but not forward, Cary Grant must be the most publicly seduced male the world has known, yet he has never become a public joke—not even when Tony Curtis parodied him in *Some Like It Hot*, encouraging Marilyn Monroe to rape. The little bit of shyness and reserve in Grant is pure box-office gold, and being the pursued doesn't make him seem weak or passively soft. It makes him glamorous—and, since he is not as available as other men, far more desirable.

Cary Grant is the male love object. Men want to be as lucky and enviable as he is—they want to be like him. And women imagine landing him. Like Robert Redford, he's sexiest in pictures in which the woman is the aggressor and all the film's erotic energy is concentrated on him, as it was in *Notorious*: Ingrid Bergman practically ravished him while he was trying to conduct a phone conversation. Redford has never been so radiantly glamorous as in *The Way We Were*, when we saw him through Barbra Streisand's infatuated eyes. But in *The Great Gatsby,* when Redford needed to do for Mia Farrow what Streisand had done for him, he couldn't transcend his immaculate self-absorption. If he had looked at her with desire, everything else about the movie might have been forgiven. Cary Grant would not have failed; yearning for an idealized love was not beyond his resources. It may even be part of his essence: in the sleekly confected *The Philadelphia Story,* he brought conviction to the dim role of the blue blood standing by Katharine Hepburn and waiting on the sidelines. He expressed the very sort of desperate constancy that Redford failed to express. Grant's marital farces with Irene Dunne probably wouldn't have been as effective as they were if he hadn't suggested a bedevilled constancy in the midst of the confusion. The heroine who chases him knows that deep down he wants to be caught only by her. He draws women to him by making them feel he needs them, yet the last thing he'd do would be to come right out and say it. In *Only Angels Have Wings,* Jean Arthur half falls apart waiting for him to make a move; in *His Girl Friday,* he's unabashed about everything in the world except why he doesn't want Rosalind Russell to go off with Ralph Bellamy. He isn't weak, yet something in him makes him hold back—and that something (a slight uncertainty? the fear of a commitment? a mixture of ardor and idealism?) makes him more exciting.

The romantic male stars aren't necessarily sexually aggressive. Henry Fonda wasn't; neither was James Stewart, or, later, Marcello Mastroianni. The foursquare Clark Gable, with his bold, open challenge to women, was more the exception than the rule, and Gable wasn't romantic, like Grant. Gable got down to brass tacks; his advances were basic, his unspoken question was "Well, sister, what do you say?" If she said no, she was failing what might almost be nature's test. She'd become overcivilized, afraid of her instincts—afraid of being a woman. There was a violent, primal appeal in Gable's sex scenes: it was all out front—in the way he looked at her, man to woman. Cary Grant doesn't challenge a woman that way. (When he tried, as the frontiersman in *The Howards of Virginia,* he looked thick and stupid.) With Gable, sex is inevitable: What is there but sex? Basically, he thinks women are good for only one thing. Grant is interested in the qualities of a particular woman—her sappy expression, her non sequiturs, the way her voice bobbles. She isn't going to be pushed to the wall as soon as she's alone with him. With Grant, the social, urban man, there are infinite possibilities for mutual entertainment. They might dance the night away or stroll or go to a carnival—and nothing sexual would happen unless she wanted it to. Grant doesn't assert his male supremacy; in the climax of a picture he doesn't triumph by his fists and brawn—or even by outwitting anybody. He isn't a conqueror, like Gable. But he's a winner. The game, however, is an artful dodge. He gets the blithe, funny girl by maneuvering her into going after him. He's a fairy-tale hero, but she has to pass through the trials: She has to trim her cold or pompous adversaries; she has to dispel his fog. In picture after picture, he seems to give up his resistance at the end, as if to say, What's the use of fighting?

Many men must have wanted to be Clark Gable and look straight at a woman with a faint smirk and lifted, questioning eyebrows. What man doesn't—at some level—want to feel supremely confident and earthy and irresistible? But a few steps up the dreamy social ladder there's the more subtle fantasy of worldly grace—of being so gallant and gentlemanly and charming that every woman longs to be your date. And at that deluxe level men want to be Cary Grant. Men as far apart as John F. Kennedy and Lucky Luciano thought that he should star in their life story. Who but Cary Grant could be a fantasy self-image for a President and a gangster chief? Who else could demonstrate that sophistication didn't have to be a sign of weakness— that it could be the polished, fun-loving style of those who were basically tough? Cary Grant has said that even he wanted to be Cary Grant.

And for women, if the roof leaks, or the car stalls, or you don't know how to get the super to keep his paws off you, you may long for a Clark Gable to take charge, but when you think of going out, Cary Grant is your dream date—not sexless but sex with civilized grace, sex with mystery. He's the man of the big city, triumphantly suntanned. Sitting out there in Los Angeles, the expatriate New York writers projected onto him their fantasies of Eastern connoisseurship and suavity. How could the heroine ever consider marrying a rich rube from Oklahoma and leaving Cary Grant and the night spots? Los Angeles itself has never recovered from the inferiority complex that its movies nourished, and every moviegoing kid in America felt that the people in New York were smarter, livelier, and better-looking than anyone in his home town. The audience didn't become hostile; it took the contempt as earned. There were no Cary Grants in the sticks. He and his counterparts were to be found only in the imaginary cities of the movies. When you look at him, you take for granted expensive tailors, international travel, and the best that life has to offer. Women see a man they could have fun with. Clark Gable is an intensely realistic sexual presence; you don't fool around with Gable. But with Grant there are no pressures, no demands; he's the sky that women aspire to. When he and a woman are together, they can laugh at each other and at themselves. He's a slapstick Prince Charming.

Mae West's raucous invitation to him—"Why don't you come up sometime and see me?"—was echoed thirty years later by Audrey Hepburn in *Charade:* "Won't you come in for a minute? I don't bite, you know, unless it's called for." And then, purringly, "Do you know what's wrong with you? Nothing." That might be a summary of Cary Grant, the finest romantic comedian of his era: there's nothing the matter with him. Many of the male actors who entered movies when sound came in showed remarkable powers of endurance—James Cagney, Bing Crosby, Charles Boyer, Fred Astaire—but they didn't remain heroes. Spencer Tracy didn't, either; he became paternal and judicious. Henry Fonda and James Stewart turned into folksy elder statesmen, sagacious but desexed. Cary Grant has had the longest romantic reign in the short history of movies. He might be cast as an arrogant rich boy, an unscrupulous cynic, or a selfish diplomat, but there was nothing sullen or self-centered in his acting. Grant never got star-stuck on himself; he never seemed to be saying, Look at me. The most obvious characteristic of his acting is the absence of narcissism—the outgoingness to the audience.

■ ■ ■

Cary Grant was a knockout in his dapper young days as a Paramount leading man to such suffering sinners as Sylvia Sidney, Carole Lombard, Tallulah Bankhead, Marlene Dietrich, Nancy Carroll. He appeared with this batch in 1932; Paramount threw him into seven pictures in his first year. In some two dozen roles in four years, he was a passable imitation of Noël Coward or Jack Buchanan, though not as brittle as Coward or as ingratiatingly silly as Buchanan. He played a celebrated javelin thrower in *This Is the Night,* a rotten rich roué in *Sinners in the Sun,* the husband of a diva in *Enter Madam* and of another diva in *When You're in Love.* He was a flier who went blind in *Wings in the Dark;* he wore a dinky mustache and was captured by the Kurds in *The Last Outpost;* he used a black bullwhip on the villainous Jack La Rue in *The Woman Accused.* But that's all a blur. He didn't have a strong enough personality to impose himself on viewers, and most people don't remember Cary Grant for those roles, or even much for his tall-dark-and-handsome stints with Mae West. He might never have become a star if it had not been for the sudden onset of screwball comedy in 1934—the year when *The Thin Man* and *Twentieth Century* and *It Happened One Night* changed American movies. His performances in screwball comedies—particularly *The Awful Truth,* in 1937, his twenty-ninth picture—turned him into the comedian-hero that people think of as Cary Grant. He was resplendent before but characterless, even a trace languid—a slightly wilted sheik. He was Mae West's classiest and best leading man, but he did more for her in *She Done Him Wrong* and *I'm No Angel* than she did for him. She brought out his passivity, and a quality of refinement in him which made her physical aggression seem a playful gambit. (With tough men opposite her, she was less charming, more crude.) Sizing him up with her satyr's eyes and deciding he was a prize catch, she raised our estimate of him. Yet Grant still had that pretty-boy killer look; he was too good-looking to be on the level. And although he was outrageously attractive with Mae West, he was vaguely ill at ease; his face muscles betrayed him, and he looked a little fleshy. He didn't yet know how the camera should see him; he didn't focus his eyes on her the way he learned to use his eyes later. No doubt he felt absurd in his soulful, cow-eyed leading-man roles, and tried to conceal it; when he had nothing to do in a scene, he stood lunged forward as if hoping to catch a ball. He became Cary Grant when he learned to project his feelings of absurdity through his characters and to make a style out of their feeling silly. Once he realized that each movement could be stylized for humor, the eyepopping, the cocked head, the forward lunge, and the slightly ungainly stride became as certain as the pen strokes of a master cartoonist. The new element of romantic slapstick in the mid-thirties comedies—the teasing role reversals and shifts of mood—loosened him up and brought him to life. At last, he could do on the screen what he had been trained to do, and a rambunctious, springy side of his nature came out. Less "Continental" and more physical, he became funny and at the same time sexy. He was no longer effete; the booming voice had vitality.

It was in 1935, when the director George Cukor cast him as a loud-mouthed product of the British slums—a con man and strolling player—in the Katharine Hepburn picture *Sylvia Scarlett*, that Grant's boisterous energy first broke through. He was so brashly likable that viewers felt vaguely discomfited at the end when Brian Aherne (who had given an insufferably egotistic performance) wound up with Hepburn. Grant, on loan from Paramount to RKO, doesn't play the leading-man role, yet his con man is so loose and virile that he has more life than anything else in the picture. Grant seemed to be enjoying himself on the screen in a way he never had before. Cukor said that Grant suddenly "felt the ground under his feet." Instead of hiding in his role, as usual, he expanded and gave his scenes momentum. *Sylvia Scarlett* was a box-office failure, but Grant knew now what he could play, and a year later, free to pick his own projects, he appeared in *Topper* and his fan mail jumped from two hundred letters a week to fourteen hundred. A few months after that, he got into his full stride with *The Awful Truth*.

What makes Grant such an uncannily romantic comedian is that with the heroine he's different from the way he is with everybody else; you sense an affinity between them. In *The Awful Truth*, he's a hearty, sociable businessman when he's with other people, but when he's with Irene Dunne you feel the tenderness that he conceals from others. The conventional bedroom-farce plot (filmed twice before) is about a couple who still love each other but have a tiff and file for divorce; during the period of the interlocutory decree, the husband has visiting rights to see their dog, and this cunning device enables Grant to hang around, romping affectionately with the dog while showing his (unstated) longing for his wife. Grant is a comic master at throwaway lines, and he turns them into a dialogue, as if he were talking to himself. The husband can't quite straighten out his marriage, yet every muttered, throwaway word expresses how badly he wants to. Grant's work with Irene Dunne in *The Awful Truth* is the most gifted stooging imaginable. She was betrayed by the costume designer: she's shrilly dressed. And though she is often funny, she overdoes the coy gurgles, and that bright, toothy smile of hers—she shows both rows of teeth, prettily held together—can make one want to slug her. The ancestor of Julie Andrews, Irene Dunne has a bad habit of condescending to anything oddball her character does—signalling the audience that she's really a lady playacting. But Grant stabilizes her and provides the believability. He's forceful and extroverted, yet he underplays so gently that his restraint enables her to get by with her affectations. Grant uses his intense physical awareness to make the scenes play, and never to make himself look good at the expense of someone else—not even when he could waltz away with the show. He performs the gags with great gusto, but he never lets us forget that the character is behaving like an oaf because he doesn't want to lose his wife, and that he's trying to protect his raw places.

Henry Fonda played roles similar to Grant's, and it isn't hard to imagine Fonda as the husband in *The Awful Truth* or as the paleontologist hero of *Bringing Up Baby*, but Fonda would have been more of a hayseed, and lighter-weight. And if Grant had played Fonda's role in *The Lady Eve* Grant wouldn't have been the perfect, pratfalling innocent that Fonda was: Fonda, with his saintly bumpkin's apologetic smile and his double-jointed gait, could play bashful stupes more convincingly than any other romantic star. However, it's part of the audience's pleasure in Grant that he isn't a green kid—he's a mus-cular, full-bodied man making a fool of himself. There were other gifted ur-bane *farceurs*. The best of them, William Powell, with his skeptical, tolerant equanimity, was supremely likable; he got the most out of each blink and each twitch of his lips, and he had amazing dimples, which he could invoke with-out even smiling. But Powell and the others didn't have romantic ardor hid-den inside their jokes. And although there were other fine romantic actors, such as Charles Boyer, their love scenes often turned mooshy, while Grant's had the redeeming zest of farce.

Perfection in drawing-room comedy was almost certainly Grant's dream of glory (it appears to have remained so), but he had, as a young vaudeville comedian, acquired the skills that were to turn him into an idol for all social classes. Drawing-room-comedy stars—no matter how artful—don't become that kind of idol. When we in the audience began to sense the pleasure he took in low comedy, we accepted him as one of us. Ray Milland, Melvyn Douglas, and Robert Young acted the screwball-comedy heroes proficiently, but the roles didn't release anything in their own natures—didn't liberate and complete them, the way farce completed Grant. Afterward, even when he played straight romantic parts the freedom and strength stayed with him. And never left him: he gave some embarrassed, awful performances when he was miscast, but he was never less than a star. He might still parade in the tuxedos and tails of his dashing-young-idiot days, but he was a buoyant, lusty performer. The assurance he gained in slapstick turned him into the smoothie he had aspired to be. He brought elegance to low comedy, and low comedy gave him the corky common-man touch that made him a great star. Grant was English, so Hollywood thought he sounded educated and was just right for rich playboys, but he didn't speak in the gentlemanly tones that American moviegoers think of as British; he was a Cockney. In the early sixties, when he was offered the role of Henry Higgins in the big movie ver-sion of *My Fair Lady*, he laughed at the idea. "The way I talk *now*," he said, "is the way Eliza talked at the beginning." Cary Grant's romantic elegance is wrapped around the resilient, tough core of a mutt, and Americans dream of thoroughbreds while identifying with mutts. So do moviegoers the world over. The greatest movie stars have not been highborn; they have been strong-willed (often deprived) kids who came to embody their own dreams, and the public's.

■ ■ ■

Archibald Alexander Leach, born in Bristol on January 18, 1904, was the only child of Elias James Leach and Elsie Kingdom Leach, their firstborn son having died in infancy. Elias Leach was tall, and in photographs he seems almost reprehensibly handsome, with a cavalier's mustache, soft, flashing dark eyes, and a faintly melancholy look of resignation. He is said to have been convivial and fond of singing—a temperament his wife definitely did not share. There wasn't much they did share. He came, probably, from a Jewish background, but went along with his wife's Anglicanism. He couldn't live up to her middle-class expectations, however. Elias Leach pressed men's suits in a garment factory, and although he worked hard in the first years of the marriage, he never rose far or made much of a living. Mrs. Leach pampered their protesting child, keeping him in baby dresses, and then in short pants and long curls. A domineering woman with an early history of mental instability, she was married to a pants-presser but she wanted her son to be a cultured, piano-playing little gentleman. The parents were miserable together, and the boy was caught in the middle. When Archie was nine, he returned home from school one day to find that his mother was missing; he was led to think she had gone to a local seaside resort, and it was a long time before he learned that she had broken down and been taken to an institution. In a series of autobiographical articles published in the *Ladies' Home Journal* in 1963, he wrote, "I was not to see my mother again for more than twenty years, by which time my name was changed and I was a full-grown man living in America, thousands of miles away in California. I was known to most people of the world by sight and by name, yet not to my mother."

After Mrs. Leach's removal, Leach and his son took up quarters in the same building as Leach's mother, but the boy was left pretty much on his own, fixing meals for himself most of the week, and trying to live up to his absent mother's hopes for him. He went to Boy Scout meetings, studied hard, and won a school scholarship; he planned to try for a further scholarship, which would take him to college, but found out that even with a scholarship college would be too expensive. From early childhood, he had been going to the children's Saturday movie matinées, and he later said that the sessions with Chaplin, Ford Sterling and the Keystone Cops, Fatty Arbuckle, Mack Swain, John Bunny and Flora Finch, and Broncho Billy Anderson were the high point of his week. When his mother was still at home, he had a party (the only children's party he remembers attending) that featured a candle-powered magic lantern with comic slides, to which he added his own joking commentary. His first contact with music hall came quite by chance. At school, he liked chemistry, and he sometimes hung around the lab on rainy days; the assistant science teacher was an electrician, who had installed the lighting system at the Bristol Hippodrome, and one Saturday matinée he took Archie, just turned thirteen, backstage.

It was probably the only free atmosphere the boy had ever experienced. He wrote later that backstage, in a "dazzling land of smiling, jostling people," he *knew*. "What other life could there *be* but that of an actor? . . . They were classless, cheerful, and carefree." He was lonely enough and had enough hustle to start going to the Hippodrome, and another theatre, the Empire, in the early evenings, making himself useful; he helped with the lights, ran errands, and began to pick up the show-business vernacular. When he learned that Bob Pender, a former Drury Lane clown, had a troupe of young knockabout comedians that suffered attrition each time a boy came of military age, he wrote, in the guise of his father, asking that Archibald be taken for training. Pender replied offering an interview and enclosing the railway fare to Norwich, and Archie ran away from home to become an apprentice. He was so tall that Pender accepted him, not realizing that he wasn't yet fourteen—the legal age for leaving school. It took a few days before Leach noticed that his son was gone. Earlier that year, Archie had taken a spill on an icy playground and broken an upper front tooth. Rather than tell his father, he had gone to a dental school and had the remainder of the tooth pulled out. His other teeth had closed together over the gap (giving him his characteristic upper-lip-pulled-down, tough-urchin grin) without his father's ever noticing. But, whatever Leach's failings, he appears to have meant well, and when it registered with him that the boy had run off, he tracked him down and brought him back. He might as well have saved himself the effort. Having given up his dream of college, Archie no longer cared about school, and he concentrated on acrobatics, so he'd be in shape to rejoin Pender as soon as he could. It was soon. Just after he turned fourteen, he and another boy attempted to explore the girls' lavatories, and he was expelled from school. Three days later, with his father's consent, he was a member of Pender's troupe. Only three months passed before he returned to Bristol in triumph—on the stage at the Empire, his old schoolmates in the audience.

■   ■   ■

Archie Leach found his vocation early and stuck to it. He studied dancing, tumbling, stilt-walking, and pantomime, and performed constantly in provincial towns and cities and in the London vaudeville houses. In the Christmas season, the troupe appeared in the traditional entertainments for children—slapstick musical-comedy versions of such stories as "Cinderella" and "Puss in Boots." Living dormitory-style, exercising and rehearsing, Archie had left his parents' class-ridden world behind. Once he'd joined up with Pender, he never lived with his father again, and he lost track of him over the years. The music-hall theatre became his world; he has said that at each theatre, when he wasn't onstage, he was watching and studying the other acts from the wings. In July, 1920, when Pender selected a group of eight boys for an engagement in New York City, the sixteen-year-old Archie was among them. They sailed on the S.S. *Olympic,* which was also carrying the celebrated honeymooners Douglas Fairbanks, Sr., and Mary Pickford. More than forty years later, Cary Grant described his reaction to Fairbanks: "Once even I found myself being photographed with Mr. Fairbanks during a game of shuffleboard. As I stood beside him, I tried with shy, inadequate words to tell him of my adulation. He was a splendidly trained athlete and acrobat, affable and warmed by success and well-being. A gentleman in the true sense of the word. . . . It suddenly dawns on me as this is being written that I've doggedly striven to keep tanned ever since, only because of a desire to emulate his healthful appearance." He and Fairbanks had much in common: shattered, messy childhoods, and fathers who drifted away and turned to drink. It appears that they were both part Jewish but were raised as Christians; and they both used acrobatics in their careers—though Fairbanks, a narrowly limited actor but a fine acrobat, was a passionate devotee, while Grant used acrobatics only as a means of getting into theatrical life. And, though they represented different eras, they were loved by the public in similar ways—for their strapping health and high spirits, for being *on* and giving out whenever they were in front of an audience, for grinning with pleasure at their own good luck. Grant's later marriage to Barbara Hutton—Babs, the golden girl, "the richest girl in the world"—had a fairy-tale resemblance to the Fairbanks-Pickford nuptials.

In New York City, the Bob Pender boys were a great success at the Hippodrome, which was considered the world's largest theatre. After the engagement was over, they got booked in the major Eastern cities and wound up back in New York at the top—the Palace. When the American tour ended, in 1922, and it was time to go home, Archie Leach and several of the other boys decided to stay. He had four solid years of performing behind him, but he had never actually been in a play, and though he'd been singing on the stage, he'd never spoken dialogue. The Pender troupe had been big time, but on his own he wasn't even small time—he had no act. In the first summer of job-hunting in New York, his savings went and he ate into the return fare Pender had given him for an emergency retreat. He must, however, have been an incredible charmer (it isn't hard to imagine), because, although he was only eighteen, he was invited to fill in at dinner parties, where he sat among the wealthy and famous—on one occasion, he was delegated to be the escort of the great soprano Lucrezia Bori. By day, after he finally landed work, he was a stilt-walker on the boardwalk at Coney Island, advertising Steeplechase Park. (It was many years before his status in life was commensurate with the regard people had for him.) In the fall, he shared quarters with a young Australian, who later became known as the costume designer Orry-Kelly; in those days, Kelly made and tried to sell hand-painted neckties, and Archie Leach peddled them along Sixth Avenue and in Greenwich Village. Around the same time, Leach and other ex-members of the Pender troupe got together in the new Hippodrome show, and joined up with some Americans and organized a vaudeville act. After trying it out in small towns in the East, they played the lesser vaudeville circuits through Canada and back across the country from California to New York. In 1924, having saved enough money to go their separate ways, the boys disbanded, some of them returning to England, Archie Leach to job-hunting in New York again.

He worked in juggling acts, and with unicycle riders, and with dancers; he was the audience plant with a mind-reading act. As a straight man for comics, he got one-night stands at churches and lodges, and brief engagements in the stage shows that movie theatres used to put on before the film. As his timing improved and he became more experienced, he got more bookings; he says that eventually he played "practically every small town in America." Then, when he was working in New York, a friend who was a musical-comedy juvenile suggested that instead of going on with his vaudeville career he should try to get into Broadway musical comedy, and introduced him to Reggie Hammerstein, who took him to his uncle, the producer Arthur Hammerstein. At the end of 1927, Archie Leach appeared in the role of an Australian—the second male lead—in the Otto Harbach–Oscar Hammerstein II show *Golden Dawn,* which opened the new Hammerstein's Theatre and ran there until the late spring. He'd got onto Broadway, all right—and Broadway was then in its frivolous heyday—but he hadn't got into musical comedy. It was operetta he was caught in, and, having signed a contract with the Hammersteins, that's where he stayed. Marilyn Miller wanted him as a replacement for Jack Donahue, her leading man in the Ziegfeld hit *Rosalie,* but Arthur Hammerstein and Ziegfeld were enemies, and instead (despite his pleas) his contract was turned over to the Shuberts—for three full years of operetta.

Archie Leach's first Shubert show was *Boom Boom,* a 1929 hit, starring Jeanette MacDonald. (*The New Yorker*'s reviewer, Charles Brackett, wrote that "*Boom Boom* can teach one more about despair than the most expert philosopher.") During its run, he and Jeanette MacDonald were both tested at Paramount's Astoria studio. She was immediately signed up to be the bubbly Maurice Chevalier's petulant, coy co-star in Ernst Lubitsch's *The Love Parade;* he was rejected, because he had a thick neck and bowlegs. Had he been signed as a singing star, he might have been stuck in a Mountie's hat, like Nelson Eddy. He did become a singing star on the stage. He played a leading role in a lavish and, apparently, admirable version of *Die Fledermaus* called *A Wonderful Night,* but it opened on October 31, 1929, two days after the stock-market crash, and it crashed too; for months it was performed to near-empty houses. In the summer of 1931, the Shuberts sent him to St. Louis for the open-air Municipal Opera season, where he was a great success in such shows as *Irene, Rio Rita, Countess Maritza, The Three Musketeers,* and the Broadway casualty *A Wonderful Night.* After that, he got a temporary release from the Shuberts and appeared on Broadway in the role of Cary Lockwood, supporting Fay Wray (who was already a popular movie actress) in *Nikki,* a musical play by her husband, John Monk Saunders, which flopped.

In 1931, Leach also appeared in *Singapore Sue,* a ten-minute movie short, starring Anna Chang, that Casey Robinson made for Paramount in Astoria; Leach, Millard Mitchell, and two other actors played American sailors in an Oriental café. Leach is striking; he grabs the screen—but not pleasantly, and he does have a huge neck. He's rather gross in general—heavy-featured, and with a wide, false smile. His curly-lipped sailor is excessively handsome—overripe, like the voluptuous young Victor Mature. Some of the early-thirties Hollywood publicity photographs of Grant are like that, too; the images have the pop overeagerness one often sees in graduation and wedding poses in photographers' shop windows. Self-consciousness and bad makeup must have overcome him on that first bout with the movie camera, because photographs of him in his stage performances show a far more refined handsomeness, and the Leach of *Singapore Sue* doesn't fit the image of him in accounts by his contemporaries.

Although Leach didn't appear in the smart shows, he was something of a figure in the New York smart set, and he was known to the Algonquin group in that period when the theatrical and literary worlds were one. Some people considered him an intellectual and a powerhouse talent of the future. Moss Hart later described him as disconsolate in those years; Hart and Leach were among a group of dreamers talking of changing the theatre (the circle also included Edward Chodorov and Preston Sturges) who met daily in Rudley's Restaurant at Forty-first Street and Broadway. It was a hangout where one got leads about possible jobs, and many performers frequented the place—Jeanette MacDonald, George Murphy, Humphrey Bogart. But Archie Leach was the only actor who was a regular at the Rudley rebels' table. The Anzac role he'd played in *Golden Dawn* must have clung to him, or perhaps, since he never talked much about his background, some of the others mistook his Cockney for an Australian accent, because they called him Kangaroo, and sometimes Boomerang. "He was never a very open fellow," Chodorov says, "but he was earnest and we liked him." "Intellectual" was probably the wrong word for Leach. They talked; he listened. He doesn't appear to have been much of a reader (except later on, during his marriage to Betsy Drake, when he became immersed in the literature of hypnotism and the occult), but there's no indication that anyone ever doubted his native intelligence. It's a wide-awake intelligence, though this may not be apparent from his public remarks of the sixties, which had a wholesome Rotarian tone he adopted during LSD treatments with a medical guru. In his youth, Leach liked to hang around people who were gifted and highly educated; always looking for ways to improve himself, he probably hoped that their knowledge would rub off on him. But there must have been more to it than that; he must have looked up to the brilliant young Rudley's group because the theatre he worked in didn't fully satisfy his mind. Uneducated outside the theatre, he was eager for spiritual leadership—for wisdom. In Hollywood, he was to sit at the feet of Clifford Odets, the leading wisdom merchant of the theatrical left (the sagacity was what marred Odets's plays). And during his many years of LSD sessions he was euphoric about how the drug had enabled him to relax his conscious controls and reach his subconscious, thus making him a better man—less selfish, fit at last for marriage, and so on. Obviously, he felt that he'd found a scientific route to wisdom.

When *Nikki* closed, on October 31, 1931, Leach decided to take a "vacation," and set out with a composer friend to drive to Los Angeles. He knew what he was after; many of the people he'd been working with were already in the movies. He had the situation cooled: he'd been earning from three hundred dollars to four hundred and fifty dollars a week for several years, and the Shuberts were eager to employ him if he returned. He had barely arrived in Hollywood when he was taken to a small dinner party at the home of B. P. Schulberg, the head of Paramount, who invited him to make a test (*Singapore Sue* had not yet been released), and after seeing it Schulberg offered him a contract. The studio executives wanted his name changed, and his friends Fay Wray and John Monk Saunders suggested that he use "Cary Lockwood." He proposed it when he went back to discuss the contract, but he was told that "Lockwood" was a little long. Someone went down a list of names and stopped at "Grant." He nodded, they nodded, and the contract went into effect on December 7th. He wasn't ever "discovered." Movies were simply the next step.

■   ■   ■

If Archie Leach's upward progress seems a familiar saga, it is familiar in the rags-to-riches mode of a tycoon or a statesman. What is missing from his steady climb to fame is tension. He became a performer in an era in which learning to entertain the public was a trade; he worked at his trade, progressed, and rose to the top. He has probably never had the sort of doubts about acting which have plagued so many later performers, and he didn't agonize over choices, as actors of his stature do now. A young actor now generally feels that he is an artist only when he uses his technique for personal expression and for something he believes in. And so he has a problem that Archie Leach never faced: When actors became artists in the modern sense, they also became sellouts. They began to feel emasculated when they played formula roles that depended on technique only, and they had to fight themselves to retain their belief in the audience, which often preferred what they did when they sold out. They were up against all the temptations, corruptions, and conflicts that writers and composers and painters had long been wrestling with. Commerce is a bind for actors now in a way it never was for Archie Leach; art for him was always a trade.

He was unusually long-sighted about his career, and prodigiously disciplined, and so he got into a position in which he didn't have to take any guff from anybody. The Hammersteins had sold him to the Shuberts when he wanted to go to Ziegfeld; and to get movie roles he had to commit himself to a five-year contract with Paramount. But that was the last time he let others have the power to tell him what to do. He was twenty-seven when he signed the contract—at a starting salary of four hundred and fifty dollars a week. Paramount didn't know what it had. It used him as a second-string Gary Cooper, putting him in the pictures Cooper was too busy for—or, even worse, in imitations of roles that Cooper had just scored in. In between, Paramount lent him out to other studios and collected the fees. He was no more than a pawn in these deals. M-G-M requested him for one of the top roles in *Mutiny on the Bounty,* a role he desperately wanted, but Paramount refused, and Franchot Tone won the part. A little later, Paramount lent him to M-G-M to support Jean Harlow in the piddling *Suzy.*

When the contract ended, in February, 1937, Cary Grant, just turned thirty-three, was raring to go. He never signed another exclusive contract with a studio; he selected his scripts and his directors, and this is probably what saved him from turning into a depressingly sentimental figure, like the later, tired Gary Cooper, or a drudge, like the big M-G-M stars. It was in his first year on his own, free of studio orders, that he became a true star. In comedy, Cary Grant just might be the greatest straight man in the business, and his specialty is to apply his aplomb as a straight man to romance.

The "lunatic" thirties comedies that made him a star are still enjoyed, but their rationale has dropped from sight. In essence, they turned love and marriage into vaudeville acts and changed the movie heroine from sweet clinging vine into vaudeville partner. Starting in 1934, when things were still bad but Roosevelt and the New Deal had created an upswing spirit, the happy screwball comedies were entertainment for a country that had weathered the worst of the Depression and was beginning to feel hopeful. Yet people had been shaken up. The new comedies suggested an element of lunacy and confusion in the world; the heroes and heroines rolled with the punches and laughed at disasters. Love became slightly surreal; it became stylized—lovers talked back to each other, and fast. Comedy became the new romance, and trading wisecracks was the new courtship rite. The cheerful, wacked-out heroes and heroines had abandoned sanity; they were a little crazy, and that's what they liked in each other. They were like the wise-cracking soldiers in service comedies: if you were swapping quips, you were alive—you hadn't gone under. The jokes were a national form of gallantry—humor for survival. Actual lunatics in these movies became enjoyable eccentrics, endearing nuts who often made better sense than anybody else (or at least as much sense), while the butts of screwball humor were the prigs and phonies, the conventional go-getters, the stick-in-the-mud conformists. Ralph Bellamy, the classic loser and opposite number to Cary Grant in *The Awful Truth* and again in *His Girl Friday,* still thought in the strict, stuffed-shirt terms of the Babbitty past. The word "square" wasn't yet in slang use, but that's the part Bellamy played—the man who didn't get the joke. Obliging and available, always around when you didn't want him (there was really no time when you did), he was the man to be jilted.

The comedies celebrated a change in values. In the movies of the twenties and the early thirties, girls who chased after riches and luxury learned the error of their ways, but after 1934 sin wasn't the big movie theme it had been. Adultery was no longer tragic; the unashamed, wisecracking gold diggers saw to that. Glenda Farrell, one of the toughest and most honestly predatory of the millionaire-hunters, put it this way in *Gold Diggers of 1937:* "It's so hard to be good under the capitalistic system." Impudence became a virtue. Earlier, the sweet, archly virginal heroine had often had a breezy, good-hearted confidante; now the roles were reversed, and the lively, resilient heroine might have an innocent kid sister or a naïve little friend from her home town who needed looking after. What man in the Depression years would welcome a darling, dependent girl? Maybe the hero's shy buddy, but not the hero. He looked for the girl with verve; often she was so high and buoyant she could bounce right over trouble without noticing it. It was Carole Lombard's good-hearted giddiness that made her lovable, Jean Arthur's flightiness, Myrna Loy's blithe imperviousness—and in *Bringing Up Baby* Katharine Hepburn was so light-headed, so out of it, that she was unbeatable. The mistreated, masochistic women who had been moping through the confessional movies, pining for the men who had ruined them and looking tenderly at their fatherless offspring, either faded (like Ann Harding, Ruth Chatterton, and Helen Hayes) or changed their styles (like Constance Bennett in *Topper,* Lombard in *Twentieth Century,* and, of course, Claudette Colbert in *It Happened One Night* and Irene Dunne in *Theodora Goes Wild* and *The Awful Truth*). The stars came down to earth in the middle and late thirties—and became even bigger stars. Marlene Dietrich, who had turned into a lolling mannequin, reëmerged as the battling floozy of *Destry Rides Again.* Just as in the late sixties some of the performers loosened up and became hip, thirties performers such as Joel McCrea and Fredric March became lighter-toned, gabby, and flip. An actor who changes from serious to comic roles doesn't have problems with the audience (the audience loves seeing actors shed their dignity, which has generally become a threadbare pose long before it's shed); it's the change from comic to serious that may confound the audience's expectations.

The speed and stylization of screwball humor were like a stunt, and some of the biggest directors of the thirties had come out of two-reel comedy and had the right training. Leo McCarey, who directed *The Awful Truth,* had directed the Marx Brothers in *Duck Soup* and, before that, Laurel & Hardy comedies for Hal Roach. George Stevens, who directed Grant in *Gunga Din,* was also a Hal Roach alumnus—cameraman on Laurel & Hardy and Harry Langdon shorts, and then a Roach director. *Topper,* with its sunny hocus-pocus and Grant as a debonair ghost, was actually a Hal Roach production; it was considered Roach's most ambitious project. Movies in the thirties were still close to their beginnings. Wesley Ruggles, who directed Grant in *I'm No Angel,* had been one of Mack Sennett's Keystone Cops; Howard Hawks, who directed Grant in several of his best thirties films, had started as a director by writing and directing two comedy shorts. The directors had graduated from slapstick when sound came in and Hollywood took over Broadway's plays, but after a few years all that talk without much action was becoming wearying.

The screwball movies brought back the slapstick tradition of vaudeville and the two-reelers, and blended it into those brittle Broadway comedies. When it was joined to a marital farce or a slightly daring society romance, slapstick no longer seemed like kid stuff: it was no longer innocent and was no longer regarded as "low" comedy. The screwball movies pleased people of all ages. (The faithful adaptations of stage plays had often been a little tepid for children.) And the directors, who had come out of a Hollywood in which improvising and building gags were part of the fun of moviemaking, went back—partly, at least—to that way of working. No longer so script-bound, movies regained some of the creative energy and exuberance—and the joy in horseplay, too—that had been lost in the early years of talkies. The new freedom can be seen even in small ways, in trivia. Grant's screwball comedies are full of cross-references, and gags from one are repeated or continued in another. In *The Awful Truth,* Irene Dunne, trying to do in her (almost) ex-husband—Grant—refers to him as Jerry the Nipper; in *Bringing Up Baby,* Hepburn, pretending to be a gun moll, tells the town constable that Grant is the notorious Jerry the Nipper. And the same dog trots through the pictures, as Mr. Smith in *The Awful Truth,* as George in *Bringing Up Baby* (and as Mr. Atlas in *Topper Takes a Trip* and Asta in the *Thin Man* movies). That dog was a great actor: he appeared to adore each master in turn.

Once Grant's Paramount contract ended, there seemed no stopping him. As long as the screwball-comedy period lasted, he was king. After *The Awful Truth,* in 1937, he did two pictures with Katharine Hepburn in 1938—*Bringing Up Baby* and *Holiday.* It was a true mating—they had the same high-energy level, the same physical absorption in acting. In 1939 he did *Gunga Din* and *Only Angels Have Wings,* and in 1940 *His Girl Friday, My Favorite Wife,* and *The Philadelphia Story.*

During those peak years—1937 to 1940—he proved himself in romantic melodrama, high comedy, and low farce. He does uproarious mugging in the knockabout jamboree *Gunga Din*—a moviemakers' prank, like *Beat the Devil.* Ben Hecht and Charles MacArthur stole the adolescent boys' fantasy atmosphere from *Lives of a Bengal Lancer,* then took the plot from their own *The Front Page,* mixed it with a slapstick *The Three Musketeers,* and set it in a Hollywood Kipling India. Douglas Fairbanks, Jr., plays the Hildy Johnson role—he plans to leave the British Army to get married and go into the tea business—and Victor McLaglen, in the Walter Burns role, and Grant, as the Cockney bruiser Archibald Cutter, scheme to get him to reënlist. When the three comrades fight off their enemies, they're like three Fairbankses flying through the air. Grant looks so great in his helmet in the bright sunshine and seems to be having such a marvellous time that he becomes the picture's romantic center, and his affection for the worshipful Gunga Din (Sam Jaffe) becomes the love story. The picture is both a stirring, beautifully photographed satiric colonial-adventure story and a walloping vaudeville show. Grant's grimaces and cries when Annie the elephant tries to follow him and Sam Jaffe onto a rope bridge over a chasm are his broadest clowning. (The scene is right out of Laurel & Hardy.) And he's never been more of a burlesque comic than when he arrives at the gold temple of the religious cult of thugs and whinnies with greedy delight at the very moment he's being shot at. The thug guru is shaven-headed Eduardo Ciannelli (the original Diamond Louis of *The Front Page*), who wears a loincloth and chants "Kill! Kill! Kill for the love of Kali!" Perhaps because the picture winds up with a bit of pop magic—an eye-moistening, Kiplingesque tribute to Gunga Din, shown in Heaven in the British Army uniform he longed to wear—the press treated it rather severely, and George Stevens, the director, was a little apologetic about it. He may have got in over his head. He had replaced Howard Hawks as director, and when he added his Stan Laurel specialties to the heroic flourishes Hawks had prepared, and after the various rewrite men (William Faulkner and Joel Sayre were among them) built on to the gags, the result was a great, bounding piece of camp. Grant has always claimed that he doesn't like to exert himself, and that his ideal role would be a silent man in a wheelchair, but his performance here tells a different story. (All his performances tell a different story.) The following year, when Grant played Walter Burns in *His Girl Friday* (this time an acknowledged remake of *The Front Page,* and, with Charles Lederer's additions, a spastic explosion of dialogue), he raised mugging to a joyful art. Grant obviously loves the comedy of monomaniac egotism: Walter Burns's callousness and unscrupulousness are expressed in some of the best farce lines ever written in this country, and Grant hits those lines with a smack. He uses the same stiff-neck, cocked-head stance that he did in *Gunga Din:* it's his position for all-out, unsubtle farce. He snorts and whoops. His Walter Burns is a strong-arm performance, defiantly self-centered and funny.

When Grant was reunited with Irene Dunne in *My Favorite Wife,* they had another box-office smash, but his playing wasn't as fresh as in *The Awful Truth.* This marital farce was really moldy (it was based on Tennyson's *Enoch Arden,* filmed at least a dozen times, starting in 1908), and Grant's performance as the rattled husband is a matter of comic bewilderment and skittish double takes. The presence in the cast of his close friend Randolph Scott (they shared a house for several years) as the rival for Irene Dunne's affections may have interfered with his concentration; he doesn't provide an underlayer of conviction. He's expert but lightweight, and the role and the bustling plot don't bring anything new out of him.

The Hollywood comedy era was just about over by then. The screwball comedies, in particular, had become strained and witless; the spoiled, headstrong runaway heiresses and the top-hatted playboy cutups had begun to pall on the public, and third-rate directors who had no feeling for slapstick thought it was enough to have players giggling and falling over the furniture. Right from the start, screwball comedy was infected by the germ of commercial hypocrisy. The fun-loving rich, with their glistening clothes, whitewall tires, mansions in the country, and sleek Art Deco apartments, exalted a carefree contempt for material values. The heroes and heroines rarely had any visible means of support, but they lived high, and in movie after movie their indifference to such mundane matters as food and rent became a self-admiring attitude—the attitude that is still touted in *Travels with My Aunt* and *Mame*. Like Mame, the unconventional heroines of the thirties were beloved by their servants. Irene Dunne in white fox and a trailing evening gown would kick her satin train impatiently to tell us that it was not money but love and laughter that mattered. The costume designers often went in for sprightly effects: Irene Dunne and Katharine Hepburn would be put into pixie hats that clung on the side of the head, dipping over one eye, while on top there were pagodas that shot up six or seven inches to a peak. All too often, the villains were stuffy society people or social climbers (as in *Mame*), and the heroes and heroines just too incorrigibly happy-go-lucky. Love seemed to mean making a fool of yourself. The froth hung heavy on many a screwball comedy, and as the pictures got worse and the Cary Grant parts began to be played by Lee Bowman and David Niven the public got fed up. The movement had already run down before the war started. In the forties, there were still some screwball comedies, but they were antic and shrill, except for a few strays: some of the Tracy-Hepburn pictures, and the comedies in which Preston Sturges reinvented slapstick in a more organic form—creating an image of Americans as a people who never stopped explaining themselves while balling up whatever they were trying to do.

■   ■   ■

Though he remained a top box-office star, Cary Grant fell on evil days. After 1940, he didn't seem to have any place to go—there were no longer Cary Grant pictures. Instead, he acted in pictures that nobody could have been right for—abominations like the 1942 anti-Nazi romantic comedy *Once Upon a Honeymoon,* in which he was an American newsman in Warsaw trying to rescue the American stripper Ginger Rogers from her Nazi husband (Walter Slezak). From the first frame, it was as clammily contrived as anything that Paramount had shoved him into, and in one pathetically insensitive sequence Grant and Rogers are mistaken for Jews and held in a concentration camp. His performance is frequently atrocious: he twinkles with condescending affection when the nitwit stripper develops a political consciousness and helps a Jewish hotel maid escape from danger. Mostly, he acted in stock situation comedies—comedies with no comic roots, like *The Bachelor and the Bobby-Soxer* (1947), in which Myrna Loy is a judge who works out a deal. Grant, a philandering artist, will go to jail unless he dates her schoolgirl sister (Shirley Temple) until the teen-ager's crush on him wears off. Escorting Shirley Temple—wearing his shirt open and acting like an adolescent—Cary Grant is degradingly unfunny. There's no core of plausibility in his role. Grant doesn't have the eyes of a Don Juan, or the temperament. When Grant is accused of being a skirt-chaser, it seems like some kind of mistake.

In the thirties, Grant would sometimes appear in a role, such as the despondent husband of a mercenary, coldhearted woman (Kay Francis) in the 1939 *In Name Only,* that suggested that he had unexplored dimensions. They remained unexplored. In 1941, when he departed from comedy, it was in just the sort of sincere tearjerker that Hollywood was always proudest of— *Penny Serenade,* with Irene Dunne again. The unrealistic casting of this inert, horribly pristine film is the trick: the appeal to the audience is that these two glamorous stars play an ordinary couple and suffer the calamities that do in fact happen to ordinary people. When tragedy strikes Cary Grant and Irene Dunne, it hurts the audience in a special way—*Penny Serenade* is a sweet-and-sour pacifier. Grant, who got an Academy Award nomination, could hardly have been better. Using his dark eyes and his sensuous, clouded handsomeness as a romantic mask, he gave his role a defensive, not quite forthright quality, and he brought out everything that it was possible to bring out of his warmed-over lines, weighting them perfectly, so that they almost seemed felt.

Nearly all Grant's seventy-two films have a certain amount of class and are well above the Hollywood average, but most of them, when you come right down to it, are not really very good. Grant could glide through a picture in a way that leaves one indifferent, as in the role of a quaint guardian angel named Dudley in the bland, musty Goldwyn production *The Bishop's Wife* (1947), and he could be the standard put-upon male of burbling comedy, as in *Every Girl Should Be Married* (1948) and the pitifully punk *Room for One More* (1952)—the nice-nice pictures he made with Betsy Drake, who in 1949 became his third wife. He could be fairly persuasive in astute, reflective parts, as in the Richard Brooks thriller *Crisis* (1950), in which he plays a brain surgeon forced to operate on a Latin-American dictator (José Ferrer). He's a seasoned performer here, though his energy level isn't as high as in the true Grant roles and he's a little cold, staring absently when he means to indicate serious thought. What's missing is probably that his own sense of humor isn't allowed to come through; generally when he isn't playing a man who laughs easily he isn't all there.

He was able to keep his independence because he had a good head for business. Within a short time of leaving Paramount, he could command a hundred and fifty thousand dollars a picture, and that was only the beginning. Later, he formed partnerships and produced his pictures through his own corporations—Grandon, Granart, Granley, and Granox. He didn't do what stars like Kirk Douglas did when they gained control over their productions: he didn't appear in Westerns, for the virtually guaranteed market. He was too self-aware for that; he was a lonely holdout in the period when even Frank Sinatra turned cowpoke. From the thirties on, Grant looked for comedies that would be mass-oriented versions of the Noël Coward and Philip

636

Barry and Frederick Lonsdale drawing-room and boudoir farces that Broadway theatregoers admired in the twenties. And so he settled for Sidney Sheldon (*The Bachelor and the Bobby-Soxer, Dream Wife*), or Stanley Shapiro (*Operation Petticoat, That Touch of Mink*), for Norman Panama and Melvin Frank (*Mr. Blandings Builds His Dream House*), or for Melville Shavelson and Jack Rose (*Room for One More, Houseboat*). He sought the best material and got the second-rate and synthetic, because good writers wouldn't (and couldn't) write that way anymore. His taste didn't change, but he didn't do the real thing—not even the real Lonsdale. His friends say he believes that the world doesn't understand fine language. With *People Will Talk* and *The Talk of the Town,* he was probably reaching toward Shaw. He got the loquacity without the wit.

Considering that he selected his roles, these choices indicate one of the traps of stardom. When actors are young, they're eager for great roles, but when they become stars they generally become fearful that the public won't accept them in something different. They look for roles that seem a little more worthwhile than the general run. With one exception—*None but the Lonely Heart*—Cary Grant appeared to be content throughout his career to bring savoir-faire to pratfalls, romantic misunderstandings, and narrow escapes. It seems reasonable to assume that he attained something so close to the highest aspirations of his youth that, as far as acting was concerned, he had no other goals—and no conflicts. Moss Hart said that Archie Leach's gloom vanished when he became Cary Grant.

■   ■   ■

The only trace of gloom in Grant's movies is in *None but the Lonely Heart,* which he made in association with Clifford Odets (as writer and director) in 1944. The film was an ironic interlude in Grant's career, coming, as it did, between the cloying whimsey of *Once Upon a Time,* in which he was a Broadway sharpie exploiting a boy who had a pet dancing caterpillar, and *Night and Day,* the ten-ton Cole Porter musical bio, in which he skittered about as a youthful Yalie before facing life with stoic courage and inscrutable psychic hangups. In *None but the Lonely Heart,* set in the East End of London, he plays Ernie Mott, a young Cockney—a restless drifter who lacks the will to leave the ghetto for good. Ernie grew up in oppressive poverty, but he wants to make life better for his mother, who runs a grubby antiques and secondhand-furniture shop. Made at Grant's instigation (he acquired the rights to the book), the film was a gesture toward the ideas he shared with the other dissidents at Rudley's, and, even more, a gesture toward his own roots—toward the grimness of his life before he apprenticed himself to the theatre. His mother was released from confinement in 1933 (that same year, his father died of "extreme toxicity"), and he established a surprisingly close relationship with her. Eccentric but hardy and self-sufficient, she had a whole new life after that twenty-year incarceration. She lived into her mid-nineties, and until she was in her late eighties she did all her own shopping and housework, and occupied her days with antiquing—driving fierce bargains when she spotted something she wanted. Grant has described her as "extremely good company." He wrote that "sometimes we laugh together until tears come into our eyes." In the thirties, he went to England several times a year to see her, and he took the socialite beauty Virginia Cherrill (Chaplin's leading lady in *City Lights*) to meet his mother before they were married, in London, in 1934—his first marriage, which was dissolved the following year. The outbreak of the Second World War must have brought his English past even closer to him; he was still a British subject, and in 1939 he became involved in activities to aid the British. Later, when the United States was in the war, he went on trips to entertain the troops and on bond-selling tours. (In one routine, he played straight man to Bert Lahr.) In June, 1942, less than two weeks before his marriage to Barbara Hutton, he legally changed his name and became an American citizen.

Grant's old name had long been a joke—to the public and to him. He had named his pet Sealyham Archibald, and when the dog ran away from his Los Angeles home (it is said that the dog ran out the door while Grant was carrying Virginia Cherrill over the threshold), he took large ads in the papers giving the dog's name. In *Gunga Din,* when Grant, as the soldier Cutter, receives an invitation to a regimental ball, he reads the salutation aloud—"Arch-i-bald Cutter"—chewing the syllables and savoring their preposterousness. As the editor in *His Girl Friday,* when Grant is threatened with prison by the mayor and the sheriff, he yammers out, "The last man to say that to me was Archie Leach, just a week before he cut his throat."

Yet when he played Ernie Mott in *None but the Lonely Heart* he became Archie Leach again; even the names are similar. *None but the Lonely Heart* was the first movie Clifford Odets had ever directed, and although the original material was not his but a best-selling novel by Richard Llewellyn, Odets gave it the rich melancholy of his best plays. Too much of it, however: the dirgelike, mournful, fogged-up atmosphere seemed fake and stagy. Odets worked up each scene (almost as one develops scenes in the theatre) and didn't get them to flow thematically, but he went all out. He brought off some hard-earned effects with an élan that recalled Orson Welles's first films, and there were unexpected crosscurrents. (Ernie's girl, played by June Duprez, was plaintive and distressed, and turned out not to be Ernie's girl at all.) It was an extraordinary début film, and it is an indication of the movie industry's attitude toward talent that Odets got only one other chance to direct—fifteen years later (*The Story on Page One,* in 1959). The complicated texture of *None but the Lonely Heart* made a pervasive, long-lasting impression. What can one remember of such Grant films as *Room for One More* or *Dream Wife* or *Kiss Them for Me* or *Houseboat?* But from *None but the Lonely Heart* one retains June Duprez's puzzlingly perverse face and voice; a scene of Grant and a buddy (Barry Fitzgerald) drunk in a tunnel, letting out their voices and teasing their echoes; and—especially—Grant and Ethel Barrymore together. She played his mother, and her great, heavy eyes matched up with his. In her screen roles, this statuesque, handsome woman usually substituted presence and charm and hokum for performance; she wasn't tedious, like her brother Lionel, but she was a hollow technician. Not this time, though. In a few scenes, she and Grant touched off emotions in each other which neither of them ever showed on the screen again. When Ernie, who has become a petty racketeer, is told that his mother has been arrested for trafficking in stolen goods, he has an instant's disbelief: "They got her inside, you mean—pinched?" Grant says that line with more fervor than any other line he ever delivered. And there are viewers who still—after three decades—recall the timbre of Ethel Barrymore's voice in the prison hospital when she cries, "Disgraced you, Son."

Grant is not as vivid in the memory as Ethel Barrymore is. Of the profusion of themes in the film, the deeply troubled bond of love between the mother and the son must have been a strong factor in his original decision to buy the book. Yet he didn't fully express what had attracted him to the material. His performance was finer than one might have expected, considering that in all his years on the stage he'd never actually done a play without music, and that he couldn't use the confident technique that made him such a dynamo in screen comedy, or the straightforward, subdued acting he depended on in the war film *Destination Tokyo.* Grant was always desperately uncomfortable when he played anyone who wasn't close to his own age, and though he may have felt like the Ernie of the novel (a dreamy nineteen-year-old, an unformed artist-intellectual), as an actor he was too set in his ways. The slight stylization of his comic technique—the deadpan primed to react, the fencer's awareness of the camera, all the self-protective skills he'd acquired—worked against him when he needed to be expressive. Cary Grant acts from the outside; he's the wrong kind of actor to play a disharmonious character, a precursor of the fifties rebel-hero. Grant isn't totally on the surface: there's a mystery in him—he has an almost stricken look, a memory of suffering—but he's not the modern kind of actor who taps his unconscious in his acting. Part of his charm is that his angers are all externally provoked; there are no internal pressures in him that need worry us, no rage or rebelliousness to churn us up. If he reacts with exasperation or a glowering look, we know everything there is to know about his reaction. When we watch Brando, the dramatic stage is *in* him, and the external aggressions against him are the occasions for us to see the conflicts within; the traditional actor's distance and his perfect clarity are gone. Life seemed simpler with Cary Grant's pre-Freudian, pre-psychological acting-as-entertaining. But he couldn't split Ernie Mott apart effectively, and he couldn't hold him together, either. And—it was nobody's fault—one reason Ernie wasn't as vivid a character as he needed to be was that it was Cary Grant trying to be grubby Ernie Mott. A movie star like Cary Grant carries his movie past with him. He becomes the sum of his most successful roles, and he has only to appear for our good will to be extended to him. We smile when we see him, we laugh before he does anything; it makes us happy just to look at him. And so in *None but the Lonely Heart,* in the role that was closest to Grant's own buried feelings—the only character he ever played that he is known to have consciously identified with—he seemed somewhat miscast.

It's impossible to estimate how much this failure meant to him, but more than a year passed before he plunged into the inanities of *Night and Day*—the only year since he had entered movies in which he made no pictures, and a bad year in other ways, too, since his marriage to Barbara Hutton broke up. However, Cary Grant appears to be a profoundly practical man; after the disappointing box-office returns from *None but the Lonely Heart* (he did get an Academy Award nomination for it, but the award was given to Bing Crosby for *Going My Way*), he never tried anything except Cary Grant roles. As far as one can judge, he never looked back. He remained a lifelong friend of Clifford Odets; he was proud to be accepted by Odets, and Odets was proud that the handsome, tanned idol was there at his feet. But Odets's passion no longer fired Cary Grant to make business decisions. When Odets was trying to set up picture deals and needed him as a star, he didn't return the calls. This didn't spoil their friendship—they had both been living in Los Angeles a long time.

■　■　■

No doubt Grant was big enough at the box office to have kept going indefinitely, surviving fables about caterpillars, and even such mournful mistakes as hauling a cannon through the Napoleonic period of *The Pride and the Passion.* But if Alfred Hitchcock, who had worked with him earlier on *Suspicion,* hadn't rescued him with *Notorious,* in 1946, and again, in 1955, with *To Catch a Thief* (a flimsy script but with a show-off role for him) and in 1959 with *North by Northwest,* and if Grant hadn't appeared in the Stanley Donen film *Charade* in 1963, his development as an actor would have essentially been over in 1940, when he was only thirty-six. In all four of those romantic suspense comedies, Grant played the glamorous, worldly figure that "Cary Grant" had come to mean: he was cast as Cary Grant, and he gave a performance as Cary Grant. It was his one creation, and it had become the only role for him to play—the only role, finally, he *could* play.

Had he made different choices, had he taken more risks like *None but the Lonely Heart,* he might eventually have won acceptance as an actor with a wide range. He might have become a great actor; he had the intensity, and the command of an audience's attention. But how can one tell? One thinks of Cary Grant in such a set way it's difficult even to speculate about his capacities. Yet, considering his wealth and his unusually independent situation, it's apparent that if he was constricted, it wasn't just Hollywood's doing but his own. Working within the framework of commercial movies, James Mason, who at one time also seemed a highly specialized star, moved on from romantic starring roles to a series of deeper character portraits. However, Mason had to move away from the sexual center of his movies to do it, and it's doubtful if Grant would have sacrificed—or even endangered—the type of stardom he had won. His bargaining power was probably more important to him than his development as an actor; he *was* a tycoon. Whatever his reasons were, they're concealed now by his brisk businessman's manner. He doesn't seem to know or to care whether his pictures were good or bad; he says that if they did well at the box office, that's all that matters to him, and this doesn't appear to be an affectation. He made a gigantic profit on the gagged-up *Operation Petticoat*, which he produced in 1959; his friends say that he makes no distinction between that and *Notorious*.

Cary Grant always looks as if he'd just come from a workout in a miracle gym. And it's easy for audiences to forget about his stinkers (they're not held against him), because he himself isn't very different in them from the way he is when he has a strong director and a script with some drive. It's his sameness that general audiences respond to; they may weary of him, but still he's a guaranteed product. (It's the pictures that aren't.) And if he didn't grow as an actor, he certainly perfected "Cary Grant." One does not necessarily admire an icon, as one admires, say, Laurence Olivier, but it can be a wonderful object of contemplation. (If Olivier had patented the brand of adorable spoiled-boy charm he exhibited on the stage in *No Time for Comedy,* he might have had a career much like Grant's—and, indeed, in *Sleuth* Olivier played the sort of role which would then have been all that could be expected of him.)

As a movie star, Grant is so much a man of the city that he couldn't play a rural hero or a noble, rugged man of action, and so much a modern man that he couldn't appear in a costume or period picture without looking obstreperous—as if he felt he was being made a fool of. In *The Howards of Virginia,* it wasn't just the hot-blooded fighter-lover role that threw him, it was also wearing a Revolutionary uniform and a tricornered hat, with his hair in a chignon; he waddled through the picture like a bowlegged duck. The thought of him in Biblical sackcloth or in a Roman toga or some Egyptian getup is grisly-funny. And he's inconceivable in most of the modern urban films: how could Cary Grant play a silent stud or a two-fisted supercop? Grant never quite created another character—not even in the limited sense that screen stars sometimes do, using their own bodies and personalities as the base for imaginative creations. There are no Fred C. Dobbses or Sam Spades in his career. It's doubtful if he could even play a biographical character without being robbed of his essence. As Cole Porter, he wanders around in *Night and Day* looking politely oblivious; he's afraid to cut loose and be himself, yet he's too constrained to suggest anything resembling Cole Porter, so the hero seems to have a sickly, joyless nature. Composing song after song, his Cole Porter appears to have less music in his soul than any other living creature. Grant relaxes a little just once, while singing "You're the Top" with Ginny Simms.

He sings quite often in movies—as in *The Awful Truth,* when he parodies Ralph Bellamy's version of "Home on the Range," or in *Suzy,* in which he does the number that is included in *That's Entertainment,* and he replaced Bing Crosby as the Mock Turtle in the 1933 *Alice in Wonderland,* and sang

"Beautiful Soup"—but he played an actual singing role in only one movie, early in his career: the disarmingly frilly 1934 *Kiss and Make Up,* one of Paramount's many imitations of the Lubitsch musical-comedy style. A sense of fun breaks through when he shows off his vaudeville skills—a confident, full-hearted exhibitionism. He frequently plays the piano in movies—happily and enthusiastically—and he does off the screen, too. For the past decade, since the breakup of his fourth marriage—to Dyan Cannon—following the birth of a daughter (his first child), he's been in retirement from the screen, but he's been active as an executive with Fabergé, whose president, George Barrie, used to play the saxophone for a living (Barrie composed the title song for *A Touch of Class,* produced by Brut, a subsidiary of Fabergé); they sometimes have jam sessions after board meetings, with Grant playing piano or organ. It's a corporate business right out of a thirties Cary Grant movie: in *Kiss and Make Up,* he actually ran a swank beauty salon. Grant belongs to the tradition of the success-worshipping immigrant boy who works his way to the top, but with a difference: the success he believes in is in the international high style of the worldly, fun-loving men he played—he's got Rolls-Royces stashed away in key cities. He has lived up to his screen image, and then some; welcome everywhere, more sought after than the Duke of Windsor was, in his seventies he's glitteringly—almost foolishly—hale.

Grant has had an apparently wide range of roles, but only apparently. Even in the era when he became a star, his sexual attraction worked only with a certain type of co-star—usually playing a high-strung, scatterbrained heroine, dizzy but not dumb. He would have been a disaster opposite Joan Crawford. With her gash smile, thick-syrup voice, and enormous tension, she required a roughneck titan like Gable to smite her; she would have turned Cary Grant into Woody Allen. A typical fan-magazine quote from Joan Crawford in her big-box-office youth was "Whatever we feel toward the man of the moment, it is he who is our very life and soul." It hardly matters whether Crawford herself was the author of those sentiments; that was the kind of woman she represented on the screen. It's easy to visualize Cary Grant's panic at the thought of being somebody's "very life and soul." He wanted to have a good time with a girl. It was always implicit that she had something going on her own; she was a free lance. She wasn't going to weigh him down—not like Crawford, who was all character armor and exorbitant needs. Crawford actually intended to take over the man of the moment's life and soul; that was what love meant in her pictures, and why she was so effective with skinny, refined, rich-hero types, like Robert Montgomery and Franchot Tone, whom she could scoop up. She gave the same intensity to everything she did; she inspired awe. But Grant didn't want to be carried away—nobody scoops up Cary Grant—and he didn't want an electrical powerhouse. (He's unthinkable with Bette Davis.) Once Grant became a star, there was a civilized equality in his sex partnerships, though his co-star had to be not only a pal but an ardent pal. When he appeared with Myrna

Loy, they were pleasant together, but they didn't really strike sparks. Loy isn't particularly vulnerable, and she isn't dominant, either; she's so cool and airy she doesn't take the initiative, and since he doesn't either (except perfunctorily), nothing happens. They're too much alike—both lightly self-deprecating, both faintly reserved and aloof.

In dramatic roles, the women stars of the thirties and forties could sometimes triumph over mediocre material. This has been one of the saving aspects of the movie medium: Garbo could project so much more than a role required that we responded to her own emotional nature. Her uniquely spiritual eroticism turned men into willing slaves, and she was often at her best with rather passive men—frequently asexual or unisexual or homosexual (though not meant to be in the course of the films). Garbo's love transcended sex; her sensuality transcended sex. She played opposite Clark Gable once, and the collision, though heated, didn't quite work; his macho directness—and opacity—reduced her from passionate goddess to passionate woman. And Garbo seemed to lose her soul when she played mere women—that's why she was finished when the audience had had enough of goddesses. But for a time in the late twenties and early thirties, when she leaned back on a couch and exposed her throat, the whole audience could dream away—heterosexual men as much as the homosexuals (whom she was, indeed, generally seducing in her movies). Something similar operated, to a lesser extent, with Katharine Hepburn. In the thirties, she was frequently most effective with the kind of juveniles who were called boys: they were male versions of sensitive waifs, all cheekbone. She was effective, but there wasn't much sexual tension in those movies. And, despite the camaraderie and marvellous byplay of her later series with Spencer Tracy, she lost some of her charge when she acted with him. She was humanized but maybe also a little subjugated, and when we saw her through his eyes there seemed to be something the matter with her—she was too high-strung, had too much temperament. Tracy was stodgily heterosexual. She was more exciting with Cary Grant, who had a faint ambiguity and didn't want her to be more like ordinary women: Katharine Hepburn was a one-of-a-kind entertainment, and he could enjoy the show. The element of Broadway conventionality that mars *The Philadelphia Story* is in the way she's set up for a fall—as a snow maiden and a phony. Grant is cast as an élitist variation of the later Spencer Tracy characters.

Cary Grant could bring out the sexuality of his co-stars in comedies. Ingrid Bergman, a powerful presence on the screen, and with a deep, emotional voice (her voice is a big part of her romantic appeal in *Casablanca*), is a trifle heavy-spirited for comedy. She was never again as sexy as in that famous scene in *Notorious* when she just keeps advancing on Grant; you feel that she's so far gone on him that she can't wait any longer—and it's funny. Although Grant is a perfectionist on the set, some of his directors say that he wrecks certain scenes because he won't do fully articulated passages of dialogue. He wants always to be searching for how he feels; he wants to waffle charmingly. This may be a pain to a scenarist or a director, but in his own terms Grant knows what he's doing. He's the greatest sexual stooge the screen has ever known: his side steps and delighted stares turn his co-stars into comic goddesses. Nobody else has ever been able to do that.

When the sexual psychology of a comedy was right for Grant, he could be sensational, but if it was wrong and his energy still came pouring out, he could be terrible. In Frank Capra's *Arsenic and Old Lace* (made in 1941 but not released until 1944, because, by contract, it couldn't open until the Broadway production closed) he's more painful to watch than a normally bad actor—like, say, Robert Cummings—would be, because our affection for Grant enters into our discomfort. As it was originally written, the Mortimer Brewster role—an acerbic theatre critic being pursued by his aggressive, no-nonsense fiancée—wouldn't have been bad for Grant, but the Capra film sweetened the critic and turned the fiancée into a cuddly, innocuous little dear (Priscilla Lane). Capra called Grant Hollywood's greatest *farceur,* but the role was shaped as if for Fred MacMurray, and Grant was pushed into frenzied overreacting—prolonging his stupefied double takes, stretching out his whinny. Sometime after the whopping success of *It Happened One Night,* Frank Capra had lost his instinct for sex scenes, and his comedies became almost obscenely neuter, with clean, friendly old grandpas presiding over blandly retarded families. Capra's hick jollity was not the atmosphere for Cary Grant, and he was turned into a manic enunch in *Arsenic and Old Lace.*

In drag scenes—even in his best movies—Grant also loses his grace. He is never so butch—so beefy and clumsy a he-man—as in his female impersonations or in scenes involving a clothes switch. In *Bringing Up Baby,* Katharine Hepburn takes his suit away, and he has nothing to wear but a flouncy fur-trimmed negligee. When Hepburn's aunt (May Robson) arrives and demands crossly, querulously, "Why are you wearing a robe?" Grant, exasperated, answers "Because I just went gay all of a sudden." It doesn't work: he goes completely out of character. Burt Lancaster was deliriously, unselfconsciously funny in a long drag sequence in *The Crimson Pirate* (a parody adventure picture roughly comparable to *Gunga Din*); he turned himself into a scrambled cartoon of a woman, as Harry Ritz had done in *On the Avenue.* That's what Tony Curtis and Jack Lemmon did in *Some Like It Hot—* only they did it by yielding to their feminine disguises and becoming their own versions of gorgeous, desirable girls. Bert Remsen does it that way in *California Split,* anxiously seeing himself as a gracious lady of quality. But Grant doesn't yield to cartooning femininity or to enjoying it; he doesn't play a woman, he threatens to—flirting with the idea and giggling over it. His sequence in a skirt and a horsehair wig in the stupid, humiliating *I Was a Male War Bride* was a fizzle. He made himself brusque and clumsy to call attention to how inappropriate the women's clothes were on him—as if he needed to prove he was a big, burly guy.

The beautifully tailored clothes that seem now to be almost an intrinsic part of the Cary Grant persona came very late in his career. Decked out in the pinstripes, wide lapels, and bulky shoulders of the early forties, Grant, with his thick, shiny black hair, often suggested a race-track tout or a hood. He was a snappy dresser, and when he was playing Ivy League gentlemen, his clothes were often kingpin flashy, in the George Raft manner. Happy and hearty, he looked terrific in those noisy clothes; he wore baggy pants in *Only Angels Have Wings* and was still a sexual magnet. But sometimes his slouch hats and floppy, loose-draped jackets seemed to dominate the actor inside. His strutting appearance was distracting, like a gaudy stage set. As he got older, however, he and his slim-line clothes developed such an ideal one-to-one love affair that people could grin appreciatively in the sheer pleasure of observing the union. In *North by Northwest,* the lean-fitting suit he wore through so many perils seemed the skin of his character; and in *Charade,* when for the sake of a dim joke about drip-dry he got under the shower with his suit on, he lost the skin of his character—even though that character was "Cary Grant."

■　　■　　■

It's a peerless creation, the "Cary Grant" of the later triumphs—*Notorious, To Catch a Thief, North by Northwest,* and *Charade.* Without a trace of narcissism, he appears as a man women are drawn to—a worldly, sophisticated man who has become more attractive with the years. And Grant really had got better-looking. The sensual lusciousness was burned off: age purified him (as it has purified Paul Newman). His acting was purified, too; it became more economical. When he was young, he had been able to do lovely fluff like *Topper* without being too elfin, or getting smirky, like Ray Milland, or becoming a brittle, too bright gentleman, like Franchot Tone. But he'd done more than his share of arch mugging—lowering his eyebrows and pulling his head back as if something funny were going on in front of him when nothing was. Now the excess energy was pared away; his performances were simple and understated and seamlessly smooth. In *Charade,* he gives an amazingly calm performance; he knows how much his presence does for him and how little he needs to do. His romantic glamour, which had reached a high peak in 1939 in *Only Angels Have Wings,* wasn't lost; his glamour was now a matter of his resonances from the past, and he wore it like a mantle.

Some stars (Kirk Douglas, for one) don't realize that as they get older, if they continue to play the same sort of parts, they no longer need to use big, bold strokes; they risk self-caricature when they show their old flash, and they're a bit of a joke when they try to demonstrate that they're as good as they ever were. But if they pare down their styles and let our memories and imaginations fill in from the past, they can seem masters. Sitting in an airport V.I.P. lounge a few years ago, Anthony Quinn looked up from the TV set on which he was watching *To Catch a Thief* and said, "That's the actor I always wanted to be"—which is fairly funny, not only because Quinn and Grant are such contrasting types but because Quinn has never learned the first thing from Cary Grant. He's never understood that he needs to dry out a little. Some actors are almost insultingly robust. If you should ask Anthony

Quinn "Do you know how to dance?" he would cry "Do I know how to dance?" and he'd answer the question with his whole body—and you'd probably wind up sorry that you'd asked. Cary Grant might twirl a couple of fingers, or perhaps he'd execute an intricate, quick step and make us long for more. Unlike the macho actors who as they got older became more strident about their virility, puffing their big, flabby chests in an effort to make themselves look even larger, Grant, with his sexual diffidence, quietly became less physical—and more assured. He doesn't wear out his welcome: when he has a good role, we never get enough of him. Not only is his reserve his greatest romantic resource—it is the resource that enables him to age gracefully.

What the directors and writers of those four suspense films understood was that Cary Grant could no longer play an ordinary man—he had to be what he had become to the audience. In box-office terms, he might get by with playing opposite Doris Day in *That Touch of Mink*, but he was interchangeable with Rock Hudson in this sort of picture, and the role was a little demeaning—it didn't take cognizance of his grace or of the authority that enduring stardom confers. The special charm of *Notorious*, of the piffle *To Catch a Thief*, and of *North by Northwest* and *Charade* is that they give him his due. He is, after all, an immortal—an ideal of sophistication forever. He spins high in the sky, like Fred Astaire and Ginger Rogers. He may not be able to do much, but what he can do no one else has ever done so well, and because of his civilized nonaggressiveness and his witty acceptance of his own foolishness we see ourselves idealized in him. He's self-aware in a charming, non-egotistic way that appeals to the very people we'd want to appeal to. Even when he plays Cockneys, he isn't English or foreign to us—or American, either, exactly. Some stars lose their nationality, especially if their voices are distinctive. Ronald Colman, with his familiar cultivated, rhythmic singsong, seemed no more British, really, than the American Douglas Fairbanks, Jr.; they were both "dashing" men of the world. Ingrid Bergman doesn't sound Swedish to us but sounds simply like Ingrid Bergman. Cary Grant became stateless early: he was always Cary Grant. Making love to him, the heroines of the later movies are all aware that he's a legendary presence, that they're trying to seduce a legend. "How do you shave in there?" Audrey Hepburn asks bemusedly in *Charade*, putting her finger up to the cleft in his chin. Her character in the movie is to be smitten by him and to dote on him. Actually, he had begun to show his age by that time (1963); it was obvious that he was being lighted very carefully and kept in three-quarter shots, and that his face was rounder and a little puffy. And although lampblack may have shielded the neck, one could tell that it was being shielded. But we saw him on Audrey Hepburn's terms: Cary Grant at his most elegant. He didn't need the show-stopping handsomeness of his youth; his style, though it was based on his handsomeness, had transcended it.

Everyone likes the idea of Cary Grant. Everyone thinks of him affectionately, because he embodies what seems a happier time—a time when we had a simpler relationship to a performer. We could admire him for his timing and nonchalance; we didn't expect emotional revelations from Cary Grant. We were used to his keeping his distance—which, if we cared to, we could close in idle fantasy. He appeared before us in his radiantly shallow perfection, and that was all we wanted of him. He was the Dufy of acting—shallow but in a good way, shallow without trying to be deep. We didn't want depth from him; we asked only that he be handsome and silky and make us laugh.

Cary Grant's bravado—his wonderful sense of pleasure in performance, which we respond to and share in—is a pride in craft. His confident timing is linked to a sense of movies as popular entertainment: he wants to please the public. He became a "polished," "finished" performer in a tradition that has long since atrophied. The suave, accomplished actors were usually poor boys who went into a trade and trained themselves to become perfect gentlemen. They're the ones who seem to have "class." Cary Grant achieved Mrs. Leach's ideal, and it turned out to be the whole world's ideal.

The New Yorker, July 14, 1975

SMILE

S*mile,* a comedy set in Santa Rosa during the Jaycee-sponsored California final of the national "Young American Miss" pageant, is about the American smile that certifies likability. It's about the booster spirit, and optimism as a way of life. There hasn't been a small-town comedy in so long that this fresh, mussy film seems to be rediscovering America. Though we laugh at the gaffes of the rawboned teen-age girls, the laughter isn't cruel. When the girls are interviewed, or when they have to perform in public, they look dumb, but they're not. They stumble and blurt out idiocies because what they're saying isn't what they feel at all. They're cued to talk cant about "helping others" by the chief judge of the contest—Big Bob Freelander (Bruce Dern), a mobile-home salesman and the biggest booster in town. He's a civic-minded man who lives by the beaming banalities that Bert Parks celebrates. Dern has a furtively hip style of comedy, and he's built for this part. He isn't tall and lanky in the heroic Western tradition—you don't think of that body in open spaces. His Big Bob is tall in a graceless, sexless way—he's one of those American men who haul their height around. Big Bob speaks in homilies that express exactly how he feels. He's a donkey, but he doesn't have a mean bone in his body. When Big Bob is attacked by his closest friend and forced into a moment of self-recognition, he's so shaken his face gets squinched up, like a pouting infant's. The film—a cousin to *Lord Love a Duck*—is an affectionate satirical salute to the square. (*Smile* has already opened around the country, though it's getting its first New York showing at the Film Festival.)

Are beauty contests too easy a target, as some of the film's negative reviews have charged? I don't think so. As a student at Berkeley, I was initiated into a women's honor society in a ceremonial that required each girl to wear a white formal and a gardenia corsage, and to carry a lighted candle. Who doesn't get stuck in false positions? Who hasn't been through stupid rituals? If many of us can't resist turning on the TV to watch at least one or two beauty contests each year, perhaps it's because these competitions seem like pockets of the past—pure fifties—and link in with our memories, the way seeing Fred Wiseman's *High School* brings back the indoctrination we went through and makes us realize it's still called education. There's not much heft to *Smile*, but Michael Ritchie, who directed, isn't the right director for big subjects anyway; he's not a director for depth, he's the man to turn loose on marginalia and surfaces. *Smile* supplies wonderful details of frazzled behavior, though Jerry Belson's script is often too blunt. Ritchie's direction is highly variable in quality; the picture doesn't hold together, and it lacks narrative flow—the jokes and the "talent" skits seem to be cut in rather haphazardly. But nobody is better at found (and pseudo-found) moments than Ritchie is. He's a whiz at setting up situations and then catching an embarrassed splutter or a woolly stare or a performer whose eyes wander desperately, and this film has his funniest off-guard bits yet. Maybe the hit-and-run continuity was the only way to convey the unresolved mixture of affection, disbelief, comic horror, camp, and imbecile suspense which is part of why some of us watch beauty contests.

In the past, Ritchie has had trouble with his women characters. In *Downhill Racer* and *The Candidate,* the women were lacquered figurines, and Ritchie gave the impression that he didn't have any idea what went on in their heads. And at the beginning of *Smile* we feel like connoisseurs when we look at the thirty-three contestants. (Young professional actresses—some of them former beauty contestants—are salted among non-professional Santa Rosa girls.) The camera itself seems to buttress the whole rationale of beauty contests: we appraise the skinny legs and the perfect little Aryan-goddess features, and people in the audience laugh automatically at ungainly conformations and chubby bodies. But when the girls are sorted out and we see what they are going through, there's no more of this appraisal or derision. Ritchie's attitudes don't seem ready-made this time; he seems to be willing to pick up new impressions. And willing to concede that the green, gawky girls aren't necessarily going to turn into packaged commodities (like the Candidate).

Miss Antelope Valley (Joan Prather), a straight-A brunette, realizes she's been had, and she can grin, shamefaced about what a fool she's been. Miss Anaheim (Annette O'Toole), a creamy redhead, is wised-up from the start. In the talent competition, she comes on overdressed, delivers a paean to "inner beauty," and uses it as the excuse to do a zingy striptease down to her tights, clutching a small lily to each breast. Not recognizing that Big Bob is looking for sincerity, she outsmarts herself and finishes as the fourth runner-up. But she's snappy and resourceful, like the girls Joan Blondell used to play. Only one contestant is really obnoxious—Miss Salinas, a self-made witch, programmed to smile and to wring the last ounce of advantage out of her Mexican-American background. Maria O'Brien (daughter of Edmond O'Brien and Olga San Juan) makes her a rollicky ethnic caricature, completely self-absorbed. Sucking up to the judges with presents of bowls of guacamole, she's the kind of gushing phony who can stare down a saint. She can even stare down a master phony like Brenda, the girls' thirty-ish den mother (Barbara Feldon), who always looks on the bright side, her chipper smile just sitting there. When Brenda's soggy-faced husband (Nicholas Pryor) gets fed up with her indefatigable cheer and complains to her, she comments "Another evening of sarcasm and self-pity!" and her inflections detonate. It was a mistake, though, to make her frigid and to use that as the reason for her husband's blubbering drunkenness. There's no wit in it. Barbara Feldon keeps trying, but Brenda lacks what Big Bob has—an essential innocence and good will. She isn't human enough to be a funny character or buggy enough to work as a cartoon. Feldon has the bad luck to be in several of the longer, broad-comedy scenes, and Ritchie doesn't pace them well. The only way he gets pace in a sequence is by editing; his longer scenes (like the Jaycees' nighttime get-together) are too schematic, and they don't develop the black-comedy hysteria that seems needed.

Smile might have been a classic American comedy if he'd been able to use the darting techniques on the Jaycees and the older townspeople which he used on the contest itself. However, I didn't mind the film's wobbling ineptness; it seems preferable to *The Candidate*'s stunningly cool, glib style, which went with its counterculture platitudes. In his earlier films Ritchie was misogynistic yet sentimental. In *Smile* he really appears to like most of the people on the screen. The film acknowledges the possibility that people can be cynical without being corrupt. Michael Kidd, the choreographer (who appeared on the screen once before, in *It's Always Fair Weather*), plays the once big-time, now fading choreographer brought in to stage the pageant. This jaded outsider is a hardboiled pro, observing the local shenanigans without surprise. He talks straight to the contestants, and when there's a petty crisis he resolves it by taking a lower fee. It's not a big thing, but he does it for the girls' sake, and it's the only clear-cut generous action I can recall in a Michael Ritchie film. Ritchie is no longer dividing the world between the manipulators and the manipulated. He has responded to the confusion and eagerness in the girls' smiles, and he's smiling back.

The New Yorker, October 6, 1975

THE STORY OF ADÈLE H.
ALL FOR LOVE

After a two-year break to read and to write, François Truffaut has come back to moviemaking with new assurance, new elation. *The Story of Adèle H.* (the closing-night selection of the New York Film Festival) is a musical, lilting film with a tidal pull to it. It's about a woman who is destroyed by her passion for a man who is indifferent to her—a woman who realizes herself in self-destruction. The only surviving daughter of the writer Victor Hugo, Adèle was sharing his exile in the Channel Islands during the reign of Louis Napoleon when she met the English Lieutenant Pinson, with whom she had a brief affair. When Pinson was transferred to Nova Scotia, she followed him. The film, based on her journals, begins with her arrival in Halifax in 1863—at the high point in her life, when she has had the courage to defy her family and cross the ocean.

A composer as well as a writer, Adèle (Isabelle Adjani) is educated, perceptive, wily; she's not taken in by Lieutenant Pinson (Bruce Robinson). She knows that he's essentially worthless—selfish, mercenary, fickle—and that he doesn't want her. But she constructs an altar to his photograph in the rented room where she waits out months, years. "Love is my religion," she writes in her journal. It may be necessary to this neurotic conception that the love object be himself negligible, even contemptible. How else can she—the gifted daughter of the most famous man in the world—know the full grandeur of self-abasement but with a tinhorn in a flashy uniform? How better punish her father for being a man of great accomplishments than to declare that she cares for nothing but love? By throwing herself in the dirt at the feet of a good-for-nothing, she proves her moral superiority to her father and all his worldly honors. You can see the pride she takes in being the lowliest of the low. With nothing to lose (she has already lost Pinson, before the start of the picture), there's nothing she won't stoop to. He's a gambler, so she bribes him with money. He's a womanizer, so she sends him a whore. All her waking moments are given to planning the blackmailing pressures that the unloved exert on those they claim to love. "Do with me whatever you will!" she cries, but the only thing he wants to do with her is to get rid of her. Spying on him, claiming to be his wife, breaking up an advantageous match he has arranged, turning up to make a scene when he's on maneuvers with his unit, she has him surrounded.

She's an appallingly devious woman, and as it becomes clear that she doesn't care anything about him, that all that matters to her is the purity of *her* feeling toward him, you begin to relate to the hounded Pinson, not because you're concerned for his career but because you can't help recognizing that it's only an accident—a joke, really—that he is the recipient of all this unwanted passionate attention. Weakly ladylike in appearance, Adèle looks a mere maiden—the sort of frail gentlewoman that men would help across the street in bad weather. But out of nowhere some hidden spring will snap, and she'll be rude and peremptory. Truffaut has one gasping at this dainty woman's fearless outrageousness. Adèle isn't a charmer, like Jeanne Moreau's Catherine in *Jules and Jim;* she's a limp, strung-out madwoman, so obsessed with love that she isn't even very sexy. The film doesn't have the raw, playful, sensual lyricism of *Jules and Jim;* it doesn't shift moods in that young, iridescent way. *Adèle H.* is damnably intelligent—almost frighteningly so, like some passages in Russian novels which strip the characters bare. And it's deeply, disharmoniously funny—which Truffaut has never been before. This picture is so totally concentrated on one character that it's a phenomenon: we become as much absorbed in Adèle as she is in Lieutenant Pinson. And our absorption extends from the character to a larger view of the nature of neurotically willed romanticism. The subject of the movie is the self-destructive love that everyone has experienced in one form or another. Adèle is a riveting, great character because she goes all the way with it.

One never for an instant condemns her or pities her. The triumph of *Adèle H.* is that she is a heroine. And, because of that, an archetypal creation. Her unshakable conviction that this one man—Lieutenant Pinson—is the only man for her may be woman's inverse equivalent of the Don Juan, forever chasing. Woman's mania transcends sex; the male mania centers on physical conquest. The woman values the dream of what she's almost had, or what she's had and lost; the Don Juan values only what he's never had. You could draw the connections geometrically: Adèle does what a woman can do to carry her social and biological position to maniacal extremes, and that's what—in male terms—a Don Juan does. Perhaps the one obsessive could intuitively understand the other. (Victor Hugo was an insatiable sexual prodigy right up to the end—a white-bearded satyr, tumbling new women each day.) Don Juanism has often been dealt with on the screen, but no one before Truffaut has ever treated a woman's crippling romantic fixation with such understanding, black humor, and fullness. Truffaut has found an exact visual metaphor for her neurosis. Toward the end of the film, Adèle, still dogging Pinson's footsteps, has followed him to Barbados. Living in the native quarter under the name Mrs. Pinson, she's a wintry wraith, out of place, belonging nowhere. The Lieutenant, now a captain, married, and fearful that her use of his name will cause more trouble for him, confronts her on the street. And she sails by him, as if she were from another world; she seems at peace, insensible to pain, with the calm of exhaustion. She has given herself over to love so completely that the actual man doesn't exist for her anymore. She doesn't even know him. It's inevitable, perfect. She has arrived at her goal.

Only nineteen when the film was shot, Isabelle Adjani is much younger than the woman she's playing. (Adèle Hugo was in her early thirties when she took off after Pinson.) She hardly seems to be doing anything, yet you can't take your eyes off her. You can perceive why Truffaut, who had worked on the Adèle Hugo material off and on for six years, has said that he wouldn't have made this "musical composition for one instrument" without Isabelle Adjani. She has a quality similar to Jean-Pierre Léaud's in *The 400 Blows*—not a physical resemblance but a similar psychological quality. The awareness and intelligence are there, but nothing else is definite yet; the inner life has not yet taken outer form, and so in the movie you see the downy opacity of a face in process, a character taking shape. We keep staring at Adèle to see what that face *means*. She's right for the role, in the way that the young Jennifer Jones was for Bernadette: you believe her capable of anything, because you can't see yet what she is. If the planes of Isabelle Adjani's face were already set in the masklike definition of a famous movie star's face (even child stars can get it), we couldn't have this participatory excitement—the suspense of seeing what Adèle is turning into. Isabelle Adjani has been a professional actress since she was fourteen without tightening; one French director says that she's James Dean come back as a girl. Considering how young she is, her performance here is scarily smart. She knows how to alert us to what Adèle conceals; she's unnaturally quiet and passive, her blue eyes shining too bright in a pale flower face. Truffaut had the instinct not to age her with makeup in the course of the film; we can see that years are passing, but the tokens of time are no more than reddened eyes, a pair of glasses, tangled hair, a torn, bedraggled gown. Aging her would have wrecked the poetry of her final, distraught image, and it's the poetry of the whole conception—the undecorated, pared-to-the-bone poetry—that gives the movie its force. The film is concrete, simple, literal, yet it all works on a metaphorical level. It's an intense, daring vision of the passions that women have kept hidden under a meek exterior. And Isabelle Adjani's soft, plangent quality (along with her trained, outsize talent) makes it possible for Adèle's heroic insanity to seem to explode on the screen.

It's a great film, I think—the only great film from Europe I've seen since *Last Tango*. Thematic ideas that have been plaguing Truffaut have fallen into place—especially the two-sisters theme of his *Two English Girls*. In that film, the girl could not be happy with the man she loved, because he had slept with her older sister, who had died. But Truffaut couldn't seem to express what engaged him in the material, which may have been an unworked-out allusion to the deceased Françoise Dorléac, who had appeared in a Truffaut film, and her younger sister Catherine Deneuve, who subsequently starred for him. It's possible that he was attracted to the story of Adèle Hugo by the fact that Adèle also had an older sister who died. Léopoldine Hugo was drowned at nineteen, along with her young husband, who was trying to save her, and she was temporarily immortalized in commemorative poems by her father; Adèle broke off her own engagement to her sister's husband's brother when she took up with Lieutenant Pinson. This time, however, Truffaut doesn't shy away from the competitive love-hate possibilities of the subject. Adèle is so wan because her energies are spent by violent nightmares: she tosses at sea, crying out as if she were drowning, while Maurice Jaubert's slightly jangling music intensifies the turbulence. (The score is from Jaubert's unpublished compositions—he died before the Second World War.) The water imagery is very powerful throughout. Adèle wrote letters to a brother, which were then transmitted to her father, for whom they were intended, and who replied. Midway in the film, we follow the oceanic trail of these letters; there's no apparent rational motive for this break in the action, yet it's highly effective. Adèle's biggest act of independence was to cross the waters all alone—a journey in bondage to a delusion. *Adèle H.* is her trip, and her divided spirit makes the whole movie vibrate.

Truffaut quoted the Brontës in *Two English Girls,* but this is his Brontë movie—finally brought off because he has given it his own thin-skinned, analytic spirit. His Gothic heroine brought up to date might have been conceived by Edna O'Brien Brontë. Truffaut is romantic *and* ironic: he understands that maybe the only way we can take great romantic love now is as craziness, and that the craziness doesn't cancel out the romanticism—it completes it. Adèle's love isn't corrupted by sanity; she's a great crazy. She carries her love to the point where it consumes everything else in her life, and when she goes mad, it doesn't represent the disintegration of her personality; it is, rather, the final integration. *Adèle H.* is a feat of sustained acuteness, a grand-scale comedy about unrequited love, and it's Truffaut's most passionate work. There's none of the puppyish reticence of several of his recent films. You get a sense of surging happiness from the way the picture moves; the ongoingness—the feeling of being borne on a current—recalls Vigo's *L'Atalante* and the sequence in Renoir's *A Day in the Country* when the flooding river represents the passage of the years. For some time, I've thought that Sven Nykvist was a peerless cinematographer, but on the basis of this film I'd say that Nestor Almendros, who shot it, is right up there with him. Almendros's unusual consistency was memorable in Eric Rohmer's summery *Claire's Knee,* and in *The Wild Child* the radiant orderliness of the interiors was part of the theme. *Adèle H.* is in desaturated, deepened color, with the faces always clear and the bodies swathed in clothing, dark, yet distinctly outlined against the darker backgrounds. It seems to me that I wasn't aware of the sky at any time during the movie. The images are dark on dark, like a Géricault, with the characters' emotional lives brought luminously close.

Adèle gets so close that when you hear the voice of her father answering her letters (she writes home only to ask for money, and to reproach him), you may begin to fantasize about his tone. He is always considerate, obliging, loving, yet somehow the paternal solicitude begins to weigh on one. Isn't he too humane, and impersonally so, as if he were demonstrating what a blameless father he is, and writing letters for the ages? His even-tempered voice from the other side of the ocean sounds very aloof when we're watching Adèle turn into a pile of rags: it cannot be easy to be the daughter (or son, either) of a great man. The godlike constancy of his tone recalls Cocteau's famous remark "Victor Hugo was a madman who believed himself to be Victor Hugo." Adèle Hugo used false names, her sister's name, any name but her own. Maybe she wasn't sure she had a right to it: it was rumored that her godfather, Sainte-Beuve, was actually her father. All the more reason for her to prove that, unlike her mother, and unlike her father, she was pure in her love. When Victor Hugo died, at eighty-three, he was buried like a divinity. His body was exhibited at the Arc de Triomphe, which was draped in black, and the route from the Étoile to the Panthéon, where his coffin was enshrined, was hung with crêpe and with shields bearing the titles of his works. Truffaut shows us photographs of the magnificent turn-out: a procession of two million mourners followed the coffin. Adèle was not among them; she spent her last forty years in an asylum, writing in her journal, in code. Victor Hugo is said to have had no equal as a poseur and a mythmaker, but, on Truffaut's evidence, his daughter, who lived to eighty-five, burning with faith to the end, may have surpassed him.

The New Yorker, October 27, 1975

MAHOGANY

Diana Ross doesn't act the starring role in *Mahogany*, she shoots up on it. As Tracy, a secretary from the South Side of Chicago, who becomes the first black model to crack the color bar and goes on to be a whirling international celebrity as well as a terrific haute-couture designer, and then gives it all up to help her black lover, Billy Dee Williams, fight to improve conditions at home, she has an overachiever debauch. (Even her lover's fight is high-level stuff—he's running for Congress.) At the bottom of the white world, Tracy sees vicious hardhats and has to deal with her nastily prejudiced boss, Nina Foch. When she rises to the top of the white world, she finds nothing there but decadence: pawing white lesbians leching for her honest black flesh; scrawny, stiff, stupid white models; Jean-Pierre Aumont as a rich aristocrat who tries to buy her. In between, she's discovered, packaged, and renamed Mahogany by Tony Perkins, a flitting homosexual photographer so impotent with women that he's supine even with Diana Ross. (That's carrying black revenge a bit far.) From Perkins's druggie-male-hustler mannerisms we can tell that he's trying to do something complexly ghastly with the role, but really the picture would be better off if he didn't. He's all too embarrassingly convincing when he's nuzzling Diana Ross's chest, and in the agony-in-the-bedroom scene, and what for? Even in its own recycled-tinsel terms, *Mahogany* is a series of missed opportunities. When the aristocrat wants Diana Ross's ravishingly emaciated body, she goes cold, like the white high priestesses of the Hollywood past; why didn't she do what we had earlier seen her do to a black man tailing her in Chicago—give him a line of brazen filth to turn him off? Diana Ross is almost irresistible when she makes a ribald, jittery style out of high-pitched mock-pickaninny teasing; that high, shrill voice is a soul scream. But this movie thinks it's giving her class when it gives her suffering-great-lady airs. At that, it does better by her than by anybody else; Beah Richards, who plays Tracy's indispensable seamstress, seems to get mislaid—she just evaporates.

Diana Ross's actual packager, Berry Gordy, chairman of the board of Motown Records, put *Mahogany* together after firing the director Tony Richardson, some of whose work remains. Since there is not one well-directed sequence in the entire film, Gordy seems to have had some reason to object to Richardson's work, but what a pity nobody had the power to fire Gordy. The formula is to pour black experience into discarded old-Hollywood molds, hoping for a lurid, jabbing new vitality. Gordy can't get that working from a do-it-yourself kit. Diana Ross could be what many of the black women in the audience clearly want her to be: their Streisand, their Liza Minnelli, their Lana Turner and Stanwyck and Crawford. And she could hold down the movie-queen color bar that she hurtled across in *Lady Sings the Blues*. But *Mahogany* is a brutal setback to her talent. She's a cyclone blowing through this movie: her performance isn't controlled, it isn't shaped, and she has nothing to do but dress up, pose for still shots that look like album covers, and be adorable. She's got her quick, funny, spontaneous style, and that hypnotic looseness—the wriggling, flowing jive movements that no trained screen actress has ever had—but there isn't any attempt at characterization, and she has no depth. Still, Ross doesn't make you want to avert your eyes until she gets the Crawford grimaces in the scenes just before she renounces the rotten life of the white swells. The scenarist (I assume it's John Byrum, who's credited, since the earlier screenplay, by Bob Merrill, isn't credited) tries to doll things up with kicky displays of decadence, and he has her doing a masochistic, writhing strip while holding up a lighted candle and dripping hot wax on herself. Somebody should have taken the lighted wick to Byrum's ideas. The folly of *Mahogany* runs deeper than the script, though. In a movie in which Perkins does his car-wrecking number out of *Phaedra* while Ross is synthesizing shards of Katharine Hepburn in *Woman of the Year*, Audrey Hepburn in *Funny Face*, and Lana Turner in *The Bad and the Beautiful*, it was decided that Ross should be a pure actress and not sing. Instead, she designed the clothes, which seem to be inspired by Chinese-restaurant décor.

In the Broadway movie house where I saw the picture, the black women laughed, shouted, and cheered Diana Ross on, though they didn't seem so happy about her learning her lesson and going home to be a politician's submissive wife. Black women appear to want the forties glamour dazzle that they haven't had before in their image, and they may want it so badly they don't mind the garish, sleazo *Mahogany*. Some of the black men in the audience were groaning, but some of them may accept it, too. However, this regression to outmoded white kitsch is a new ghettoization in the arts. Diana Ross has a mouth with a pout built in, like Lana Turner at her prettiest, and she's got a face-splitting grin like no white star who ever lived. The funkiest beauty the screen has known deserves better than white hand-me-downs.

The New Yorker, October 27, 1975

DISTANT THUNDER
A DREAM OF WOMEN

The color imagery of Satyajit Ray's *Distant Thunder* is so expressive that I regretted the need to look down to the subtitles; it took precious time away from the faces and bodies, with their hint of something passive, self-absorbed—a narcissism of the flesh. The setting is a torpid Bengali village in the early 1940s. Gangacharan (Soumitra Chatterji), a newly arrived Brahmin, is the only educated man for miles around; he's the schoolteacher, the priest, the doctor. The ignorant villagers treat him with reverence. "You are the jewel in our crown," they tell him, and he agrees. His condescension is all of a piece with his umbrella, his mustache and specs, and his preoccupied manner. He strokes himself in the moist, wilting heat; he sucks on a water pipe, inhaling wherever he goes—Gangacharan wants every kind of gratification he can get.

Soumitra Chatterji, Ray's one-man stock company, moves so differently in the different roles he plays that he's almost unrecognizable. He was the passionately romantic Apu in the last film of the trilogy, the husband in *Devi,* the suitor in tartan socks and English boots in *Two Daughters,* the guest in *Charulata,* the handsome, arrogant leader of the four young men in *Days and Nights in the Forest.* At first, his Gangacharan is almost physically dislikable—thin yet flabby, contemptuously pedantic; in the course of the film, as the feudal system that sustains this contempt is eroded, his body seems to change. The Second World War, which is so remote from the villagers that they don't know who is fighting, destroys the traditions that bind the community. The area is idyllically lush, but it isn't self-sufficient. When faraway supply ports for grain fall to the Japanese, and large shipments of food are needed for the Army, the price of rice soars. Speculators send it higher, and starvation and cholera will shortly follow. Famine approaches with the force of a natural disaster; the villagers are helpless.

During the early stages, the light is so soft, and the lily pads, the flying insects, the bathing women are so tranquil, that even when the women are hungry and picking snails out of the mud or digging for wild potatoes, the images are still harmonious. The film is delicately, ambiguously beautiful; the shadowing comes from our knowledge—and Gangacharan's knowledge—that the people we're looking at are endangered. It is a lyric chronicle of a way of life just before its extinction, and Ray gives the action the distilled, meditative expressiveness that he alone of all directors seems able to give. We're looking at something that we feel is already gone, and so the images throb. Or is it that *we* do? It comes to the same thing.

Whether intentionally or not, Ray has put something of himself into Gangacharan—of his own sense of guilt, of weakness, and of commitment. And something even more personal—his seeing the beauty in the Indian past almost completely in the women. The men in this village are ignorant and obsequious, and physically very unprepossessing; the rich ones hoard and profiteer, the poor panic, become violent, riot. But the women are conceived of as in a dream of the past—they might be iridescent figures on a vase. These women are uneducated and superstitious, they know nothing of the world outside; yet they're tender and infinitely graceful. Moving in their thin, clinging saris, they create sensuous waves of color in the steamy air. Gangacharan's bride, Ananga, is innocently childlike, undulant, luscious, with a pouty ripe-pink underlip; the brilliant orange-red spot in the middle of her forehead is like a cosmic beauty mark. Played by the actress Babita (that should mean Baby Doll), Ananga is the Indian version of a Hollywood darling. She seems to have been created for the pleasure of men; she has been bred to think of nothing but her husband, and she finds her pride and her fulfillment in pleasing him. She wants to be a tempting morsel so that her husband can take a juicy bite.

Ananga is just the ornament to his existence that this preening Brahmin would have found; everything in the society appears to be designed to assuage his ego. Yet he's intelligent, and he's not a bad fellow—merely infantile. When he realizes that he can't fulfill his end of the bargain, and his wife must do demeaning work to get food for them, the whole basis of their relationship changes. Gangacharan begins to care about someone besides himself. He loves her now not because she takes care of him but because of how she feels about taking care of him. There are other actresses in the film with a fine-grained quality that goes beyond Babita's almost pornographic charm—the one who plays Moti, the Untouchable, and another who plays a woman who gives Gangacharan food to take home to his wife. They, too, are gentle and undemanding—ideal traditional women.

Ray is one of the most conscious artists who ever lived, and in this film he means to show us the subservient status of women; the children Gangacharan teaches (by rote, drumming information into them) are, of course, all boys. The women remain illiterate, and locked into the vestiges of the caste system—Ananga and Moti are friends, but if they touch each other Ananga bathes. However, I wonder if Ray realizes the degree to which he shows a deep-seated distrust of Indian men and an equally deep trust in the selflessness of women. (Even Ananga's friend Chhutki, who trades her favors for food—giving herself to a hideously scarred kiln worker—wants to share the rice she gets.) Ray is not a vulgar chauvinist, exalting subservient women; quite the contrary. While the men in his films are weak and easily flattered—dupes, self-deceived by vanity and ambition—the women have conflicts that are larger, more dignified, involving a need for love, for independence, for self-expression. They are morally stronger than the men. This may, in part, reflect a belief that the women, having always been in a subservient position, were not corrupted by English rule in the way that the men were.

Still, in *Distant Thunder,* in a village far removed from that emasculating Anglicization, Ray perceives the women with such love that they become figures in a vision, and since he sees the men without that etherealizing intensity, there's an imbalance—poetry and prose. In the Apu trilogy, the hero was the embodiment of poetry, but here it is only at the end, when Gangacharan accepts a group of famine victims as his family, that he becomes as compassionate (and as fully human) as the women were all along. For Ray, the source of their strength is humility. And although one wouldn't propose any other course of action for Gangacharan, the way Ray sees him—made whole by his passive, chivalrous acceptance of what's coming—suggests a rather attenuated attempt at universalizing his situation. Satyajit Ray has rarely before dabbled in having his characters do what he so obviously believes is symbolically right; you expect a faint white light to begin whirring around Gangacharan's head. And when, with famine victims approaching their home, Ananga, with a shy, flirtatious smile of pride, speaks of the child she is carrying, this, too, seems to be symbolic of endurance in the midst of extreme adversity.

The music, which Ray composed, is also used portentously, signalling "distant thunder." And Ray has developed an alarming affection for melodramatic angles and zoom-fast closeups; when there's a violent action—the scarred man's overtures to Chhutki, or a rapist's assault on Ananga—he wants us to feel the dislocation. But it's intrusive, pushy; his style can't accommodate this visual abrasion. When a movie director suddenly loses his tact, he can shock viewers right out of the movie: cameras are cruel to the disfigured, and when Ray forces us to look close at the enlarged burned face of the kiln worker, we don't understand why. He's introduced like a Quasimodo, and though the more we see him, the easier it is to look at him, his becoming more sympathetic—so that we notice how attractive the good side of his face is—is too pedagogic, too symbolic. The rapist appears even more abruptly; we don't see his face—all we know about him is that he smokes cigarettes, like a Westerner. He remains a plot device, an illustration of the horrors these women experience, and hide, guiltily. Ray's use of emphatic techniques to heighten the impact of his material actually lowers it. When Ananga first mistakes planes flying overhead for insects, that's naïve and halfway acceptable, but when, later, the noise of the planes drowns out her screams as she's being raped, that's ladling it on. The ironies are too charged, as in the situations that American television writers come up with; this cleverness is the dramatist's form of yellow journalism. In Ray's work, what remains inarticulate is what we remember; what is articulated seems reduced, ordinary.

Distant Thunder is not one of his greatest films, yet it's still a Satyajit Ray film, and in how many directors' films does one anticipate greatness? With Ray, you puzzle if a picture is a little less than a masterpiece. If this one lacks the undertones of a *Days and Nights in the Forest,* it's probably because he's trying to do something that sounds straightforward but isn't quite clearly thought out. Ray wants to show us how war changes people (Bergman brought it off in *Shame*), but he also wants to make an indictment. And somehow he fails on both counts. Probably he fails on the first because he doesn't endow the villagers with enough complexity. And maybe he didn't think of them in complex enough terms because he had that second, social purpose in mind. When Gangacharan learns political lessons—when he discovers that what's wrong is that "the peasants do all the work and we live off them"—it's just plain fake. Gangacharan's sponging off the peasants—in the sense that he served them with bad grace, contemptuously, demanding a little more than was fair—is hardly a factor in the starvation. When we get the closing title, telling us that five million Bengalis died in the man-made famine of 1943, Ray uses the term "man-made" because it implies that the famine was a crime. But it looks more like a horrible pileup of accidents, plus some criminal greed, and thousands of years of no planning. His statement seems forced; his whole structure is forced, and yet the film is astonishingly beautiful. The character of Gangacharan—a mixture of slothful peacefulness and a sense of dissatisfaction which he takes out on the peasants and an inquisitive, modern mind—is a fine creation, except for terminal loftiness. And there's also a character Ray can't quite get a grip on: a beggar Brahmin with a gap-toothed rabbity smile that Gangacharan calls sly. It's that, and worse. Throughout the movie, whenever he appears, he seems to suck life away. He creates the most disturbing images, maybe because Ray sees him as both the life force and as dirty Death itself. At the end, it's he who arrives with his tribe of dependents—eight in all—to join Gangacharan's household. With his rags hanging on him and his staff in his hand, he's all four horsemen rolled into one. In the final image, the silhouetted figures of this old man leading his family are extended into a procession of the starving advancing on us. It's a poster design, and yet we're also prey to unresolved feelings about that sly beggar. The film is more puzzling than it seems at first; Ray is such an imagist that even his poster art slips into ambiguities.

I don't know when I've been so moved by a picture that I knew was riddled with flaws. It must be that Ray's vision comes out of so much hurt and guilt and love that the feeling pours over all the cracks in *Distant Thunder* and seals them up.

The New Yorker, November 10, 1975

THE MAGIC FLUTE
WALKING INTO YOUR CHILDHOOD

Since the only thing about reviewing movies that makes me unhappy is that I can't get to the opera often enough, Ingmar Bergman's film version of *The Magic Flute* is a blissful present. Filmed operas generally "open out" the action or else place us as if we were spectators at a performance, looking at the entire stage. Bergman has done neither—he has moved into the stage. He emphasizes the theatricality of the piece, using space as stage space, but with the camera coming in close. We get the pixillated feeling that we're near enough to touch the person who is singing; we might be dreamers sailing invisibly among the guests at a cloud-borne party. Bergman has often delighted in including little plays (plummy satires of stage acting) within his movies, and even movies (silent slapstick comedies) within his movies. He's used them not only to comment on his characters and themes but also for the joy of re-creating different performing styles. This time, the play inside the movie has become the movie, and he's sustained his ironic juggling all the way through. He can use what he knows (and loves) about the theatre.

Although the film was actually made in a studio, it is set within the Drottningholm Court Theatre, and at the beginning we see details of the baroque décor. Bergman retains the sense of the magical theatrical machinery of Mozart's time. When the three cherubim ascend in the basket of a balloon, the ropes don't move smoothly, and all through the film he calls our attention to toy moons and suns, to trick entrances, to what's going on backstage. We get the story of the performance as well as the story of the opera. The dragon who threatens Prince Tamino prances for applause; the three flirty temptresses who compete for Tamino also compete for the audience's approval. For Bergman, who says that he usually doesn't begin to write a part until he knows who's going to play it, it must have been like a game to find the singers he did, who look the roles to perfection. He must have used everything he's learned about how to get actors to trust him, because they act as if working in front of the camera were a natural thing. They don't have the wild-eyed dislocation of so many singers—that crazed stare that seems to be their amazed response to the sounds coming out of them. Those cherubim are the most winning cast members; they're three rosy-cheeked Pucks yet three child hams, and Bergman wants us to see the conscious pleasure they take in performing. They sing as if each note marked the happiest moment in their lives; you absolutely can't not grin at them.

Unlike *Don Giovanni* or *Così Fan Tutte*, *The Magic Flute*, Mozart's last opera, makes a special claim on one's affections, because its libretto is high camp. It's a peerlessly silly masterpiece: sublimely lucid music arising out of a parodistic fairy tale that celebrates in all seriousness the exalted brotherhood of the Freemasons. In most of the first act, the story seems to be a conventional romantic quest—a fairy Queen of the Night sends Prince Tamino to rescue her daughter, Pamina, from the evil sorcerer, Sarastro, who is holding her by force. But by the time the second act was written, Mozart and Schikaneder, his librettist, had shifted directions, and now Sarastro is the lord of enlightenment, High Priest of the Temple of Wisdom, and he's protecting Pamina from her demonic mother. This confusion arising from the belated decision to convert a fairy tale into a story about the mystic brotherhood (Mozart was a Mason) seems to add to rather than take away from the opera; the confusion serves as an ironic comment on the tangled stories of most librettos. In Bergman's version, Sarastro is Pamina's father—which does give the conflict between him and the Queen more substance, and even a bit of logic.

One could, if one wished, see all Bergman's themes in this opera, because it is a dream play, with many of the same motifs as *Smiles of a Summer Night, The Seventh Seal, Wild Strawberries,* and *Cries and Whispers.* In *Wild Strawberries,* the doctor, Isak Borg (I.B., like Ingmar Bergman), walked into his childhood, and that's what Bergman is doing here. But he isn't doing it realistically this time. In *The Magic Flute,* the need for love, the suicidal despair of loneliness, ambivalent feelings about one's parents, the fear of death are already ritualized, so Bergman can play with them, in mythological fantasy form. *The Magic Flute* takes place in a philosophical bubble in which you recognize your love—your other half—at once, because the names are in pairs. It's heavenly simplicity, in parody: Tamino is sent to rescue Pamina, and he's accompanied by the bird-catcher Papageno, who finds his Papagena. We know that we should identify with Prince Tamino—he's the pure-at-heart hero of legend, and Bergman has found a tenor (Josef Köstlinger) who looks like the handsome knights in the storybooks of one's childhood—but in *The Magic Flute* nothing works quite the way it's meant to, and it comes out better. Tamino goes through the trials and performs all the proper deeds, but he's a storybook stiff compared to Papageno, who flubs his tests. There's a lesson implicit in Tamino's steadfastness: he accepts his responsibilities and earns his manhood. But Papageno doesn't want responsibility—he just wants pleasure. He'll never be a "man"—he's an impetuous kid, a gamin, a folk hero. I think the reason Papageno isn't tiresome, like other buffoonish-everyman squires (and I include Sancho Panza), must be that he hasn't been burdened with practical, "earthy" wisdom; he's too goosy for that. He has his own purity—he's pure, impulsive id. Although Papageno isn't initiated into the priestly brotherhood with Tamino, and so will presumably never experience the divine wisdom of the consecrated, he is forgiven for his flimsy virtue. Papageno doesn't earn his prize, but he gets it anyway: his Papagena is easy as pie, a pushover, as carnally eager as he.

The brotherhood is clearly strictly male; like Papageno, women are considered too talkative. But Bergman tries to integrate the order by including women, from nowhere, among the men at the final ceremonial, when Sarastro retires as the leader, putting his spiritual kingdom in the hands of Tamino and Pamina. Bergman's gesture is understandable but a bit specious. The opera is based on strict polarities, turning on male-female. The Queen of the Night (Birgit Nordin) is a glittering coloratura harpy, served by witches-in-training, while Sarastro, the deep, friendly bass (Ulrik Cold, whose face belies his name), and his priests stand for sunlight, justice, and reason. Not surprisingly, the Queen and her vamps are a delight, while Bergman has to use all his ingenuity to keep the solemn priests from grinding the show to a halt. This is where his cinematographer, Sven Nykvist, turns wizard; since a film of *The Magic Flute* wasn't expected to create pandemonium at box offices around the world, it had to be shot in 16-mm., yet Nykvist got such extraordinary quality that even in the 35-mm. blowup for theatres there's a tactile dimension to the contrasting forces. This saves the dignified temple scenes, which are dull stretches in most live performances. Sarastro's dark-eyed, sympathetic face looks as if it would be warm to the touch, and Bergman's emblematic composition of two overlapping faces— used here for father and daughter—adds psychological shading to Sarastro's stepping down from his office. Though Sarastro defeats the nightmare-canary Queen (whose high trilling is a wickedly funny vocal metaphor for neurosis), the ending represents a new harmony of male and female, with joint rule by Tamino and Pamina. The melodic line of this opera, with its arias of men and women yearning for each other, is one of the rare perfect expressions of man-woman love.

The Magic Flute is a fairy tale that is also a parody of fairy tales; the libretto says that when you have your counterpart you'll never be lonely again. The working out of the story is so playful that you never forget you're in an enchanted landscape, yet the music—airily poignant—expresses the passionate desire for all this seraphic happiness to be true. The music is the distillation of our giddy longing for ideal romantic consummation; when we listen, we believe that there are partners ordained for us. *The Magic Flute* is a love poem that teases love; the women's costumes, cut low, show off the plushiest soft bosoms—it's all a teasing dream. The emotional quality of the music—delirium expressed in perfectly controlled, harmonious phrasing— may perhaps be compared to the flights of language in *A Midsummer Night's Dream,* but this music bypasses the mind altogether and goes right to the melancholy, rhapsodic core. *The Magic Flute* is about love as the conquest of death—and about love of the theatre as the conquest of death.

Eric Ericson conducts the Swedish State Broadcasting Network Symphony; the voices may not have the depth of feeling—that special rounded sweetness—that Dietrich Fischer-Dieskau, as Papageno, and Fritz Wunderlich, as Tamino, bring to the Deutsche Grammophon recording, with Karl Böhm conducting the Berlin Philharmonic, but they're wonderful enough, and Håkan Hagegård, who has a bright-eyed, crooked-toothed smile, is just what one wants Papageno to look like and to act like. Bergman was able to spare us the usual views of tongues and tonsils by having Ericson record the score first (in Swedish, which sounds remarkably pleasing), then playing it bit by bit while photographing the singers, who move their mouths in a more genteel manner than is feasible in actual performance. The synchronization is as close to impeccable as seems humanly possible.

The Magic Flute uses to the fullest that side of Bergman which I missed in *Scenes from a Marriage* (and I saw the complete, six-episode TV version). The telegraphic naturalism of that film seemed condescending, as if it represented Bergman's vision of how ordinary, uncreative people live; I responded most to the few minutes when Bibi Andersson was onscreen, because she appears to be closer in spirit to Bergman—she expresses the tensions of intelligence. Bergman seems more complexly involved in *The Magic Flute,* with only one exception: in the framing device, when he goes outside ironic theatricality to documentary-style shots of the "audience." During the overture and at the break between the acts, and a few times during the opera itself, he gives us family-of-man portraits of this audience, with special emphasis on a celestial-eyed little girl. The faces tell us that people of all ages, colors, and creeds enjoy Mozart; it's fiercely banal, like his sticking those modern youths in *Wild Strawberries* so we'd have something to identify with. This production, which is apparently the consummation of a dream Bergman has had for more than two decades, was financed to commemorate fifty years of Swedish broadcasting, and was presented on both Swedish and Danish television last New Year's Day. His cutting to the reactions of that princessy little girl, whom one wants to strangle, suggests that the production is designed to introduce opera to children. Some years back, I found *The Magic Flute* a wonderful first opera to take a child to, but for Bergman to institutionalize this approach—treating *The Magic Flute* as if it were *Peter and the Wolf*—devalues the opera and what he has done with it. He's undersold himself, for, apart from this visual platitudinizing, the picture is a model of how opera can be filmed. The English translation of Bergman's adaptation (he clarifies the text) is graceful, and the titles are unusually well placed on the frame. Having the titles there in front of you, you follow the libretto without losing anything; the story comes across even more directly than when you hear the opera sung in English. Bergman must have reached a new, serene assurance to have tackled this sensuous, luxuriant opera that has bewildered so many stage directors, and to have brought it off so unaffectedly. It's a wholly unfussy production, with the bloom still on it. He recently said, "Making the film was the best time of my life. You can't imagine what it is like to have Mozart's music in the studio every day." Actually, watching the movie, we can.

The New Yorker, November 17, 1975

THE MAN WHO WOULD BE KING

John Huston's *The Man Who Would Be King,* based on the Rudyard Kipling short story, is an exhilaratingly farfetched adventure fantasy about two roughneck con men, Danny and Peachy (Sean Connery and Michael Caine), in Victoria's India, who decide to conquer a barbarous land for themselves, and set out for Kafiristan, a region which was once ruled by Alexander the Great, to make themselves kings. With twenty rifles, their British Army training, unprincipled rashness, cunning, and a few wild strokes of luck, they succeed, for a time. As a movie, this Empire gothic has elements of *Gunga Din* and of a cynical *Lost Horizon,* along with something that hasn't been a heroic attribute in other Empire-gothic movies: the desire to become the highest-ranking person that one can envision. The heroes are able to achieve their goal only because of the primitiveness of the people they conquer, and this is very likely the stumbling block that kept the movie from being financed for the twenty-odd years that Huston wanted to do it. Maybe he was able to, finally, on the assumption that enough time has passed for the heroes' attitude toward the native populations of India and Kafiristan—the benighted heathen—to seem quaint rather than racist. Huston's narrative is both an ironic parable about the motives and methods of imperialism and a series of gags about civilization and barbarism. When savages in war masks are hit by bullets, the image is a sick-joke history of colonialism, and when the vulgarian heroes try to civilize the tribes they conquer, they obviously have not much more than their own military conditioning to draw upon. Danny and Peachy are British primitives who seek to turn the savages into Englishmen by drilling them in discipline and respect for authority. Danny becomes as sanctimonious about that mission as Victoria herself, and is baffled when the natives show ingratitude.

The script, by Huston and Gladys Hill, is a fine piece of craftsmanship, with every detail in place, and with some of Kipling's devices carried further, so that the whole mad, jinxed adventure is tied together. But *The Man Who Would Be King* isn't rousing, and it isn't a comedy, either. It's a genre movie made with full awareness of the campy pit into which it will sink if the laconic distancing ever lapses. Huston has to hold down the very emotions that most spectacles aim for; if he treated the material stirringly, it would take the audience back to the era when we were supposed to feel pride in the imperial British gallantry, as we did at some level, despite our more knowledgeable, disgusted selves, at movies like the 1935 *Lives of a Bengal Lancer.* This film doesn't dare give us the empathic identification with what's going on inside the heroes which we had with Gary Cooper and Franchot Tone in *Bengal Lancer.* And Huston, who has never been interested in spectacle for its own luxurious sake, doesn't make a big event of the adventure, the way Capra did with the arrival at Shangri-la—when he practically unveiled the city. Shot in Morocco, with Oswald Morris as cinematographer and Alexander Trauner as production designer, *The Man Who Would Be King* is in subdued reds and browns, and the persistent dusty earth tones underscore the transiency of the heroes' victory. There are no soaring emotions. Huston tells his whopper in a matter-of-fact tone, and he doesn't play up the cast of thousands or the possibilities of portentous spectacle in the bizarre stone "sacred city" of Alexander the Great, built on a mountain.

The director's love of the material is palpable; it makes one smile. Yet the most audacious parts of the film don't reach for that special clarity which makes action memorably poetic. There are lovely, foolish poetic bits—a panoramic view of warring armies pausing to genuflect when holy men walk through the battlefield, and the brave last flourish of Billy Fish (Saeed Jaffrey), the interpreter for the heroes, who dies charging their enemies, pointlessly, in the name of British military ideals—but these episodes are offhand and brief. Huston's is a perverse form of noblesse oblige—he doesn't want to push anything. He won't punch up the moments that are right there waiting, even though we might have enjoyed basking in them, and getting a lift from them. He sets up the most elaborate, berserk fairy-tale scenes and then just sits back; he seems to be watching the events happen instead of shaping them. Huston has said that Danny and Peachy are destroyed because of *folie de grandeur,* and that's what he risks, too. I admire his pride; he treats the audience with a sophisticated respect that's rare in genre films, and this movie is the best sustained work he's done in years. Even Edith Head's costume designs and Maurice Jarre's musical score rise to the occasion, and the animal noises (they sound like cows lowing through giant megaphones) that accompany the primitive rites are terrifyingly creepy. But Huston's courtliness has its weakness. No doubt he believes in telling the story as simply as possible, but what that means in practice is that he shoots the script. It's exemplary, and he's a good storyteller. But he's not such a great *movie* storyteller here. I don't think Huston any longer plans scenes for the startling sprung rhythms of his early work. The camera now seems to be passively recording—intelligently, beautifully, but without the sudden, detonating effects of participation. Huston has become more of an illustrator. And so the ironies in *The Man Who Would Be King* go by fast—when we want them to vibrate a little.

Huston's even-tempered narrative approach doesn't quite release all that we suspect he feels about the material. It may be that he's so far into the kind of thinking that this story represents that he doesn't take us in far enough. If he had regressed to an earlier stage of movie history and presented Kipling's jingoism with emotional force, the film might have been a controversial, inflammatory epic. If he had rekindled the magical appeal of that jingoism and made us understand our tragic vulnerability to it, it might have been a true modern epic. The way he's done it, the story works only on the level of a yarn. But it's a wonderful yarn. Huston shares with Kipling a revelling in the unexpected twists of behavior of other cultures, and he doesn't convert the story into something humanistic. The ignorant natives are cruel and barbaric; if they're given a chance, they don't choose fair play. And Huston leaves it at that—he doesn't pussyfoot around, trying to make them lovable. Huston has a fondness for the idiosyncrasies of the natives, and he doesn't hate the heroes who go out to exploit them. Huston is cynical without a shade of contempt—that's why the film is likable. Yet when you play fascinated anthropologist, equally amused by the British and the natives, you may have licked the problem of how to do Kipling now without an outcry, but you're being false to why you wanted to film the story in the first place. Despite the film's ironic view of them, Danny and Peachy, who can sing in the face of death, represent courage and gallantry. Huston may spoof this when he has Peachy bawl out Danny for rushing in to attack an enemy army, and Danny, who has won the battle single-handed, apologize that his "blood was up," but the love of this crazed courage is built into the genre, and even if you leave out the surging emotion of the arrival of the British relief column, it's the Britishers here—and their devoted Billy Fishes—who represent civilization. Their ways of killing are cleaner—they don't kill for pleasure. Huston's irony can't remove all this—it merely keeps it from being offensive.

The theme of *The Man Who Would Be King* gets at the essence of the attitudes underlying John Huston's work. Huston might be the man without illusions on a quest. Here, as in *The Maltese Falcon, The Asphalt Jungle, The Treasure of the Sierra Madre,* his characters are after money. But when Danny and Peachy are battling mountain snowstorms, risking blindness and death to get to the backward country they mean to pillage, one knows that it isn't just for gold—it's because conquering and looting a country are the highest score they can imagine. And when they view Alexander the Great's treasure, the jewels and gold pieces seem a little ridiculous; the treasure will be scattered, like the gold dust in *The Treasure of the Sierra Madre.* What matters in Huston films is the existential quest: man testing himself. It's a great pity that Huston didn't get to film Mailer's *An American Dream,* which is also about a man who would be king. (All Mailer's writing is.) Mailer's book, being in contemporary terms, might have challenged Huston right to the bone. The Kipling story, with its links to old adventure-genre movies, and its links to the childhood tastes we have disowned, doesn't quite.

Huston finds a grisly humor in the self-deceptions of ruthless people chasing rainbows; that might almost be his comic notion of man's life on earth. He earns esteem by not sentimentalizing that quest. (Yet his inability to show affection for characters who live on different terms shows how much the rogues mean to him.) Huston isn't too comfortable about any direct show of emotion; he's in his element (and peerlessly) with men who are boyishly brusque, putting down their own tender feelings shamefacedly. When he first prepared this script, Gable was to be in the Connery role and Bogart in the Caine role. Connery is, I think, a far better Danny than Gable would ever have been. Gable never had this warmth, and never gave himself over to a role the way Connery does. With the glorious exceptions of Brando and Olivier, there's no screen actor I'd rather watch than Sean Connery. His vitality may make him the most richly masculine of all English-speaking actors; that thick, rumbling Scotsman's voice of his actually transforms English—muffles the clipped edges and humanizes the language. Connery's Danny has a beatific, innocent joy in his crazy goal even when he's half frozen en route; few actors are as unself-consciously silly as Connery is willing to be—as he *enjoys* being. Danny's fatuity is sumptuous as he throws himself into his first, half-embarrassed lofty gestures. Connery plays this role without his usual hairpieces, and, undisguised—baredomed—he seems larger, more free; if baldness ever needed redeeming, he's done it for all time. Caine has the Bogart role, which means he's Huston's protagonist; Peachy is the smarter of the two, the wise-guy realist, loyal to Danny even when he's depressed by Danny's childishness. We see through Peachy's sane, saddened eyes the danger in Danny's believing himself a man of destiny, and Caine manages this with the modesty of a first-rate actor. He stays in character so convincingly that he's able to bring off the difficult last scene, rounding out the story conception, when it becomes apparent that Peachy has "gone native."

The central human relationship is between these two uneducated working-class blokes, who at first share a fantasy, and who remain friends—brothers, really, since they're Masons—even when their fantasies diverge. The entire plot hinges on Freemasonry—not however, used philosophically, as it was in *The Magic Flute,* though Kipling himself was deeply involved in the brotherhood, and Christopher Plummer, who plays him here, wears a Masonic watch fob. Plummer, hidden by a thick brush mustache, gives a blessedly restrained performance as the straitlaced young editor in India. In terms of historical accuracy, however, he's not young enough for the part. Brother Kipling—an "infant monster," Henry James called him—was only twenty-two when he published the story. In the movie, it seems appropriate that the watch fob should set the whole adventure in motion; the brotherhood that links the two rowdy crooks, the nearsighted journalist, and the shaven-headed monks in the temple of Kafiristan is like a schoolboys' secret society that has swept the world. In the story, Kipling was able to satirize his own gnomic vision of fraternity, and at times Huston and Gladys Hill, ringing changes on the mystic-fraternity theme—"rejuvenating" it—might almost be borrowing from Edgar Rice Burroughs. Huston seems to be enjoying himself in this film in the way he hasn't for a long time. It communicates the feeling of a consummated dream.

■   ■   ■

One of the incidental benefits of movies based on classics is that filmgoers are often eager to read the book; Allied Artists, which produced this film, and Bantam Books have just struck a low note by putting out a gold-covered paperback *novelization* of Kipling's story. This makeshift Kipling, written by Michael Hardwick, combines the story and the screenplay, unnecessary descriptions, and bits from Kipling's life to fill a hundred and thirty-seven pages. The whole new practice of film novelizations is a disgrace. It sickens the screenwriters who have written original screenplays to see their dialogue debased into a prose stew, but at least they are alive and in a position to fight against it. If they're suckered, it's partly their own damned greedy fault. But here is a movie inspired by love of Kipling—apparently, Huston first read the story when he was twelve or thirteen, and it meant enough to him to nag at him many years later—and this love has had the effect of temporarily displacing the story and putting drivel in its stead.

Hunger cannot be the excuse: Allied Artists and Bantam Books are not poor and desperate, and the profit to be made from this venture is not likely to be vast. What is the rationale for this garbagizing of literature? I don't think "The Man Who Would Be King" is a great story, but it's a good one—good enough to have turned people into Kipling readers, maybe, if it had been made readily available in an edition with one or two other Kipling stories, and with the movie-photo tie-ins that will attract readers to this gold beauty. Since Kipling's work isn't in screenplay form but in a highly readable form, the motive for this mass-marketed paperback seems almost like giggly mischief—a *folie* of debasement. That could be another term for business as usual. Allied Artists and Bantam Books, why are you doing this?

The New Yorker, January 5, 1976

NOTES ON THE NIHILIST POETRY OF SAM PECKINPAH—
THE KILLER ELITE

Sam Peckinpah is a great "personal" filmmaker; he's an artist who can work as an artist only on his own terms. When he does a job for hire, he must transform the script and make it his own or it turns into convictionless self-parody (like *The Getaway*). Peckinpah likes to say that he's a good whore who goes where he's kicked. The truth is he's a very bad whore: he can't turn out a routine piece of craftsmanship—he can't use his skills to improve somebody else's conception. That's why he has always had trouble. And trouble, plus that most difficult to define of all gifts—a film sense—is the basis of his legend.

■　■　■

Most movie directors have short wings; few of them are driven to realize their own vision. But Peckinpah's vision has become so scabrous, theatrical, and obsessive that it is now controlling him. His new film, *The Killer Elite*, is set so far inside his fantasy-morality world that it goes beyond personal filmmaking into private filmmaking. The story, which is about killers employed by a company with C.I.A. connections, is used as a mere framework for a compressed, almost abstract fantasy on the subject of selling yourself yet trying to hang on to a piece of yourself. Peckinpah turned fifty while he was preparing this picture, and, what with booze, illness, and a mean, self-destructive streak, in recent years he has looked as if his body were giving out. This picture is about survival.

■ ■ ■

There are so many elisions in *The Killer Elite* that it hardly exists on a narrative level, but its poetic vision is all of a piece. Unlike Peckinpah's earlier, spacious movies, with Lucien Ballard's light-blue, open-air vistas, this film is intensely, claustrophobically exciting, with combat scenes of martial-arts teams photographed in slow motion and then edited in such brief cuts that the fighting is nightmarishly concentrated—almost subliminal. Shot by Phil Lathrop in cold, five-o'clock-shadow green-blue tones, the film is airless—an involuted, corkscrew vision of a tight, modern world. In its obsessiveness, with the links between sequences a matter of irrational, poetic connections, *The Killer Elite* is closer to *The Blood of a Poet* than it is to a conventional thriller made on the C.I.A.-assassins subject, such as *Three Days of the Condor.* And, despite the script by Marc Norman and Stirling Silliphant that United Artists paid for, the film isn't about C.I.A.-sponsored assassinations—it's about the blood of a poet.

■ ■ ■

With his long history of butchered films and films released without publicity, of being fired and blacklisted for insubordination, of getting ornerier and ornerier, Peckinpah has lost a lot of blood. Even *The Wild Bunch,* a great imagist epic in which Peckinpah, by a supreme burst of filmmaking energy, was able to convert chaotic romanticism into exaltation—a film comparable in scale and sheer poetic force to Kurosawa's *The Seven Samurai*—was cut in its American release, and has not yet been restored. And Peckinpah was forced to trim *The Killer Elite* to change its R rating to a PG. Why would anybody want a PG-rated Peckinpah film? The answer is that United Artists, having no confidence in the picture, grabbed the chance to place it in four hundred and thirty-five theatres for the Christmas trade; many of those theatres wouldn't have taken it if it had an R and the kids couldn't go by themselves. The film was flung into those neighborhood houses for a quick profit, without benefit of advance press screenings or the ad campaign that goes with a first-run showing. Peckinpah's career is becoming a dirty, bitter game of I-dump-on-you-because-you-dump-on-me. Increasingly, his films have reflected his war with the producers and distributors, and in *The Killer Elite* this war takes its most single-minded form.

■ ■ ■

Peckinpah's roots are in the theatre as much as they're in the West; he loves the theatricality of Tennessee Williams (early on, he directed three different stage productions of *The Glass Menagerie*), and, personally, he has the soft-spoken grandness of a Southerner in a string-tie—when he talks of the way California used to be, it is in the reverent tone that Southerners use for the

Old South. The hokum runs thick in him, and his years of television work—writing dozens of "Gunsmoke" episodes, "creating" the two series "The Rifleman" and "The Westerner"—pushed his thinking into good-guys-versus-bad-guys formats. The tenderness he felt for Tennessee Williams's emotional poetry he could also feel for a line of dialogue that defined a Westerner's plain principles. He loves actors, and he enjoyed the TV-Western make-believe, but that moment when the routine Western script gave way to a memorably "honest" emotion became for him what it was all about. When Peckinpah reminisces about "a great Western," it sometimes comes down to one flourish that for him "said everything." And Peckinpah lives by and for heroic flourishes; they're his idea of the real thing, and in his movies he has invested them with such nostalgic passion that a viewer can be torn between emotional assent and utter confusion as to what, exactly, he's assenting to.

■   ■   ■

As the losing battles with the moneymen have gone on, year after year, Peckinpah has—only partly sardonically, I think—begun to see the world in terms of the bad guys (the studio executives who have betrayed him or chickened out on him) and the people he likes (generally actors), who are the ones smart enough to see what the process is all about, the ones who haven't betrayed him yet. Hatred of the bad guys—the total mercenaries—has become practically the only sustaining emotion in his work, and his movies have become fables about striking back.

■   ■   ■

Many of the things that Peckinpah says in conversation began to seep into his last film, *Bring Me the Head of Alfredo Garcia* (1974), turning it into a time-machine foul-up, with modern, airborne killers functioning in the romanticized Mexico of an earlier movie era. Essentially the same assassins dominate the stylized, darkened San Francisco of *The Killer Elite*. In a *Playboy* interview with William Murray in 1972, Peckinpah was referring to movie producers when he said, "The woods are full of killers, all sizes, all colors. . . . A director has to deal with a whole world absolutely teeming with mediocrities, jackals, hangers-on, and just plain killers. The attrition is terrific. It can kill you. The saying is that they can kill you but not eat you. That's nonsense. I've had them eating on me while I was still walking around." Sam Peckinpah looks and behaves as if he were never free of their gnawing. He carries it with him, fantasizes it, provokes it, makes it true again and again. He romanticizes himself as one of the walking wounded, which is no doubt among the reasons he wanted to direct *Play It As It Lays*. (He was rejected by the businessmen as being strictly an action director.) In that Murray interview, he was referring to the making of movies when he said, "When you're dealing in millions, you're dealing with people at their meanest. Christ, a showdown in the old West is nothing compared with the infighting that goes on over money."

■   ■   ■

Peckinpah swallowed Robert Ardrey whole; it suited his emotional needs—he *wants* to believe that all men are whores and killers. He was talking to Murray about what the bosses had done to him and to his films when he said, "There are people all over the place, dozens of them, I'd like to kill, quite literally kill." He's dramatizing, but I've known Sam Peckinpah for over ten years (and, for all his ceremonial exhibitionism, his power plays, and his baloney, or maybe because of them, there is a total, physical elation in his work and in his own relation to it that makes me feel closer to him than I do to any other director except Jean Renoir) and I'm convinced that he actually feels that demonic hatred. I think Sam Peckinpah feels everything that he dramatizes—he allows himself to. He's a ham: he doesn't feel what he doesn't dramatize.

■ ■ ■

Peckinpah has been simplifying and falsifying his own terrors as an artist by putting them into melodramatic formulas. He's a major artist who has worked so long in penny-dreadful forms that when he is finally in a position where he's famous enough to fight for his freedom—and maybe win—he can't free himself from the fear of working outside those forms, or from the festering desire for revenge. He is the killer-élite hero played by James Caan in this hallucinatory thriller, in which the hirelings turn against their employers. James Caan's Mike, a No. 1 professional, is mutilated by his closest friend, George Hansen (Robert Duvall), at the order of Cap Collis (Arthur Hill), a defector within the company—Communications Integrity Associates—that they all work for. Mike rehabilitates himself, however, by a long, painful struggle, regaining the use of his body so that he can revenge himself. He comes back more determined than ever, and his enemies—Hansen and Cap Collis—are both shot. But when the wearily cynical top man in the company (Gig Young) offers Mike a regional directorship—Cap Collis's newly vacated position—he rejects it. Instead, he sails—literally—into unknown seas with his loyal friend the gunman-mechanic Mac (Burt Young).

■ ■ ■

There's no way to make sense of what has been going on in Peckinpah's recent films if one looks only at their surface stories. Whether consciously or, as I think, part unconsciously, he's been destroying the surface content. In this new film, there aren't any of the ordinary kinds of introductions to the characters, and the events aren't prepared for. The political purposes of the double-crosses are shrouded in a dark fog, and the company itself makes no economic sense. There are remnants of a plot involving a political leader from Taiwan (he sounds off about democratic principles in the manner of Paul Henreid's Victor Laszlo in *Casablanca*), but that fog covers all the specific plot points. Peckinpah can explain this disintegration to himself in terms of how contemptible the material actually is—the fragmented story indicates how he feels about what the bosses buy and what they degrade him with. He agrees to do these properties, to be "a good whore," and then he can't help turning them into revenge fantasies. His whole way of making movies has become a revenge fantasy: he screws the bosses, he screws the picture, he screws himself.

■　　■　　■

The physical rehabilitation of the hero in *The Killer Elite* (his refusal to accept the company's decision that he's finished) is an almost childishly transparent disguise for Peckinpah's own determination to show Hollywood that he's not dead yet—that, despite the tabloid views of him, frail and falling-down drunk, he's got the will to make great movies. He's trying to pick up the pieces of his career. Amazingly, Peckinpah does rehabilitate himself; his technique here is dazzling. In the moments just before violence explodes, Peckinpah's work is at its most subtly theatrical: he savors the feeling of power as he ticks off the seconds before the suppressed rage will take form. When it does, it's often voluptuously horrifying (and that is what has given Peckinpah a dubious reputation—what has made him Bloody Sam), but this time it isn't gory and yet it's more daring than ever. He has never before made the violence itself so surreally, fluidly abstract; several sequences are edited with a magical speed—a new refinement. In *Alfredo Garcia,* the director seemed to have run out of energy after a virtuoso opening, and there was a scene, when the two leads (Warren Oates and Isela Vega) were sitting by the side of a road, that was so scrappily patched together, with closeups that didn't match, that Peckinpah appeared to have run out of zest for filmmaking. Maybe it was just that in *Alfredo Garcia* his old obsessions had lost their urgency and his new one—his metaphoric view of modern corporate business, represented by the dapper, errand-boy killers (Gig Young and Robert Webber as mirror-image lovers)—had thrown him off balance. He didn't seem to know why he was making the movie, and Warren Oates, who has fine shadings in character roles, was colorless in the central role (as he was also in the title role of John Milius's *Dillinger*). Oates is a man who's used to not being noticed, and his body shows it. When he tried to be a star by taking over Peckinpah's glasses and mustache and manner, he was imitating the outside of a dangerous person—the inside was still meek. And, of course, Peckinpah, with his feelers (he's a man who gives the impression of never missing anything going on in a room), knew the truth: that the actor in *Alfredo Garcia* who was like him, without trying at all, was Gig Young, with his weary pale eyes. In *The Killer Elite,* James Caan is the hero who acts out Peckinpah's dream of salvation, but it's Gig Young's face that haunts the film. Gig Young represents Peckinpah's idea of what he will become if he doesn't screw them all and sail away.

■　　■　　■

Peckinpah is surely one of the most histrionic men who have ever lived: his movies (and his life, by now) are all gesture. He thinks like an actor, in terms of the effect, and the special bits he responds to in Westerns are actors' gestures—corniness transcended by the hint of nobility in the actors themselves. Like Gig Young, he has the face of a ravaged juvenile, a face that magnetizes because of the suggestion that the person understands more than he wants to. It's a fake, this look, but Peckinpah cultivates the whore-of-whores pose. He plays with the idea of being the best of men and, when inevitably betrayed, the worst of men. (He's got to be both the best and the worst.) Gig Young has the same air of gentleness that Peckinpah has, and the dissolute quality of an actor whose talents have been wasted. Gig Young's face seems large for his body now, in a way that suggests that it has carried a lot of makeup in its time; he looks rubbery-faced, like an old song-and-dance man. Joel McCrea, with his humane strength, may have been Peckinpah's idealized hero in *Ride the High Country,* and William Holden may have represented a real man to him in *The Wild Bunch,* but Gig Young, who represents what taking orders from the bosses—being used—does to *a man of feeling,* is the one Peckinpah shows the most affection for now. Gig Young can play the top whore in *The Killer Elite* because his sad eyes suggest that he has no expectations and no illusions left about anything. And Peckinpah can identify with this character because of the element of pain in Gig Young, who seems to be the most naked of actors—an actor with no-where to hide. (Peckinpah's own eyes are saintly-sly, and he's actually the most devious of men.) Peckinpah could never for an instant identify with the faceless corporate killer played by Arthur Hill. When you see Arthur Hill as Cap Collis, the sellout, you know that it didn't cost Collis anything to sell out. He's a gutless wonder, something that crawled out of the woodwork. Arthur Hill's unremarkable, company-man face and lean, tall body are already abstractions; he's a corporate entity in himself. In Peckinpah's iconography, he's a walking cipher, a man who wasn't born of woman but was cast in a mold—a man whose existence is a defeat for men of feeling.

■ ■ ■

James Caan goes through the athletic motions of heroism and acts intelli-gently, but he doesn't bring the right presence to the role. His stoicism lacks homicidal undercurrents, and he doesn't have the raw-nerved awareness that seems needed. The face that suggests some of what Peckinpah is trying to express—the residual humanity in killers—is that of Burt Young, as the de-voted Mac. The swarthy, solid, yet sensitive face of Burt Young (he played the man looking at pictures of his faithless wife at the beginning of *Chinatown*) shows the weight of feelings. Mac's warm, gravelly croak and his almost gro-tesque simpleness link him to the members of the Wild Bunch. His is a face with substance, capable of dread on a friend's account. In *The Killer Elite,* his is the face that shows the feelings that have been burnt out of Gig Young's.

■ ■ ■

Peckinpah has become wryly sentimental about his own cynicism. When the Taiwanese leader's young daughter pompously tells the hero that she's a vir-gin, and he does a variation on Rhett Butler, saying, "To tell you the truth, I really don't give a shit," the director's contempt for innocence is too self-conscious, and it sticks out. Peckinpah wants to be honored for the punish-ment he's taken, as if it were battle scars. The doctor who patches up the hero says, "The scar looks beautiful"—which, in context, is a sleek joke. But when the hero's braced leg fails him and he falls helplessly on his face on a restaurant floor, Sam Peckinpah may be pushing for sympathy for his own travail. From the outside, it's clear that even his battle scars aren't all honorable—that a lot of the time he wasn't fighting to protect his vision, he was fighting for tortuous reasons. He doesn't start a picture with a vision; he starts a picture as a job and then perversely—in spite of his deal to sell out—he turns into an artist.

■   ■   ■

Much of what Peckinpah is trying to express in *The Killer Elite* is probably inaccessible to audiences, his moral judgments being based less on what his characters do than on what they wouldn't stoop to do. (In Hollywood, people take more pride in what they've said no to than in what they've done.) Yet by going so far into his own hostile, edgily funny myth—in being the maimed victim who rises to smite his enemies—he found a ferocious unity, an Old Testament righteousness that connects with the audience in ways his last few pictures didn't. At the beginning of *The Killer Elite,* the lack of sunlight is repellent; the lividness looks cheap and pulpy—were those four hundred and thirty-five prints processed in a sewer? But by the end a viewer stares fixedly, not quite believing he's seeing what he's seeing: a nightmare ballet. In the free-form murderous finale, with guns, Samurai swords, and lethal skills one has never heard of before, there are troops of Oriental assassins scurrying over the phantom fleet of Second World War ships maintained in Suisun Bay, north of San Francisco. Wrapped up in their cult garb so we can't tell one from another, the darting killers, seen in those slow-motion fast cuts, are exactly like Peckinpah's descriptions of the teeming mediocrities, jackals, hangers-on, and just plain killers that Hollywood is full of.

■   ■   ■

The film is so cleanly made that Peckinpah may have wrapped up this obsession. When James Caan and Burt Young sail away at the end, it's Sam Peckinpah turning his back on Hollywood. He has gone to Europe, with commitments that will keep him there for at least two years. It would be too simple to say that he has been driven out of the American movie industry, but it's more than half true. No one is Peckinpah's master as a director of individual sequences; no one else gets such beauty out of movement and hard grain and silence. He doesn't do the expected, and so, scene by scene, he creates his own actor-director's suspense. The images in *The Killer Elite* are charged, and you have the feeling that not one is wasted. What they all add up to is something else—but one could say the same of *The Pisan Cantos.* Peckinpah has become so nihilistic that filmmaking itself seems to be the only thing he believes in. He's crowing in *The Killer Elite,* saying, "No matter what you do to me, look at the way I can make a movie." The bedevilled bastard's got a right to crow.

The New Yorker, January 12, 1976

THE HINDENBURG
KAPUTT

Universal has gone back to one of the most primitive forms of movie advertising for *The Hindenburg*—TWO YEARS IN THE MAKING . . . PRESENTED AT A COST OF $15,000,000. And that's what it's selling: a hefty enterprise. Everything's been done to produce the illusion of a giant zeppelin sailing along, but the film doesn't have the flotation it needs—we don't experience the beatific sensations of lighter-than-air travel. In the late twenties and early thirties, before transatlantic plane service, people with enough money could make the crossing by dirigible; smoothly and noiselessly, they were wafted across the ocean in two and a half days. This form of vibrationless travel, perfected by the Germans, got a black eye when the Hindenburg—filled with explosive hydrogen, because the United States wouldn't sell Nazi Germany nonexplosive helium—blew up while coming down for a landing at Lakehurst, New Jersey, on May 6, 1937, with ninety-seven people on board. Thirteen passengers and twenty-two members of the crew were killed. Since there were newsreel cameramen waiting there to photograph the arrival, they recorded the disaster, and millions of people saw it in theatres. In thirty-four seconds, this great luxury airship, longer than two football fields, became a mass of flames, and its aluminum-alloy skeleton was exposed as it crashed. The movie is a fictional version of what happened on its last flight.

Zeppelins have an inflated-toy, sci-fi humor. Compared to the structure of planes, the fat-cigar shape seems amorphous, loony—a blob. Yet travel in them, with windows open to the fresh air, must have been intoxicating. There are so many easy ways that *The Hindenburg* could have suggested the giddiness—couldn't one of the passengers have at least picked up the hundred-and-twelve-pound aluminum grand piano in the lounge? But Robert Wise directed with tame, impersonal good taste; there's none of the blissful trippiness of being carried in the belly of a zeppelin, and none of the carnival vulgarity of the recent disaster thrillers. How can you agree to do one of these disaster epics and then con yourself into thinking that you can do it like a gent? There's a time-honored Hollywood device that enables those who compromise on all the important things to convince themselves that they're engaged in something of real importance: they give it social content. Robert Wise turned his disaster picture into an anti-Nazi disaster picture. The plot is an elaboration of the speculative thesis that the Hindenburg was destroyed by a saboteur's bomb, as an act of resistance to Hitler. But the elaboration of this plausible idea is so pompous that one might think Hollywood was taking credit for the explosion. The film builds up every kind of sympathy for the saboteur, who, being anti-Nazi, didn't intend for anyone to get hurt; he's infinitely courageous, and he even loves dogs. Wise brings all his flatulent seriousness to this endeavor. One gasbag meets another.

The introduction of the cast of characters is the most routinized part of the movies of this genre; it's like the animals going up the ramp to the Ark, and moviegoers have become connoisseurs of this assembling process. Robert Wise's convocation doesn't measure up. He was the director of such Academy Award-winning hits as *West Side Story* and *The Sound of Music,* and even a few pretty good pictures, but he'd never make it as Noah. He dawdles over the gathering of the clan, and the transatlantic swingers in *The Hindenburg* must be the frowziest bunch ever put together outside an ABC "Movie of the Week." Anne Bancroft plays the blasé doper Ursula, a sneering German countess whose hair has been coiffed to be so authentically thirties that it looks like black potato chips stuck to her head. (If Bancroft takes this *Ship of Fools*–Signoret spinoff role, what can the roles she rejects be like?) As soon as she speaks with that familiar New York intonation, her hauteur crumbles, though her eyebrows remain elevated. She's such a likable actress you want her to come off the great-lady pose. When she uses her classy allure on George C. Scott—a disillusioned Luftwaffe colonel—those eyebrows waggle like Groucho's. This cast really ought to get the troupers' award; perfectly good actors like William Atherton, Burgess Meredith, and Charles Durning all hang in there while Wise and his scenarist, Nelson Gidding, shuffle the subplots in order to create the impression of action. Wise tries to force conviction into the hollow characters; and dialogue that might pass if it were casually overlapped is delivered with such stick-to-itiveness that the actors could be bulldogs playing charades.

It's obvious that the logistics of this production were a real killer, and Albert Whitlock's matte effects are very fine trompe-l'oeil. Authenticity has been the keynote of this production—right down to the copying of the pattern of the Hindenburg's crockery and silverware. When moviemakers don't have strong feelings about what they're doing, solid research is the only kind of integrity left. This is a technically complicated primitive film that has been made in such a spirit of self-deception that it fails to work on the primitive level. It's so dry you begin to feel dehydrated and your mind goes on the fritz. Still, with the promotion it's got going for it (which may be included in that suspiciously high fifteen-million-dollar figure), chances are that it will do all right at box offices anyway—it can be *The Great Gatsby* of disaster movies.

The Hindenburg has, however, been the cause of a new complaint: some viewers (and members of the press, too) say that they've been gypped—that the disaster footage is *real* rather than *faked.* They don't like the ten-minute climax, which is the famous newsreel footage extended and intercut with newly shot scenes showing the actors—some perishing, some fleeing the wreckage. If the movie had begun with the newsreel material, followed by a large-scale detective story trying to account for the crash, probably no one would feel let down, but it's likely that Universal wanted to retain the formula of the recent fantasy-disaster money-makers, which have big, showcase climaxes. What Wise may not be able to accept is that, despite his efforts at authenticity, the movie is essentially every bit as fakey as *Earthquake* or *The Towering Inferno,* and the audience sits waiting for the final thrills. So when people complain, they're not necessarily being stupes: they could be expressing the feeling that the movie hasn't earned the right to ring in actual suffering; they may want the gaudy finish that would be more appropriate to the twerpy story. If it's possible to violate the disaster genre, *The Hindenburg* has done it. Blending documentary-catastrophe footage with simulated-catastrophe footage is fundamentally insensitive: how can a viewer look at true horrors and be a jaded connoisseur of movie thrills in practically the same instant? The mixture is like a visual *Ragtime* without satire. The original newsreel material is blown up, padded, interrupted, frozen, though when flames are shown in still shots you don't see more—all you get is the feeling that people are playing around and turning a newsreel into graphics. I had a very strong desire to see the newsreel as it was before all these graphics wizards got to work on it: I wanted the integrity of that famous thirty-four-second catastrophe respected. After the climax, the moviemakers appear to be clowning around when they give a report on which of the fictional characters have survived; when they provide the upbeat news that the pet Dalmatian on board, released from its cage by the saboteur, came through, they seem to be playing the audience for ninnies. At the close, Wise has tacked on to the sound track the words delivered to the 1937 radio listeners by a reporter at the scene: "Oh my, this is terrible. . . . This is one of the worst catastrophes in the world. . . . It's a terrific crash, ladies and gentlemen. . . . It's smoke and it's flames. . . . I don't believe it. . . . I'm going to have to stop for a minute. . . . This is the worst thing I have ever witnessed." Is Robert Wise, recent president of the Directors Guild of America, nostalgic for the relatively innocent days of radio reporting? Probably he is. But this ending may be less naïve than it seems. In the film, Scott, who is endowed with wry hindsight, calls the Hindenburg a flying dinosaur. Since the passengers who died in the actual explosion were the only passenger fatalities in nearly three decades of commercial dirigible service, what purpose does the film's contempt serve but to reinforce the impression given to the world by the newsreel and radio accounts? In order to make the disaster seem retribution for the Nazis and large enough to rival the fantasy horrors of recent hit films, this movie omits the most remarkable aspect of the Hindenburg story—that the media coverage of the crash resulted in the end of a mode of air travel which was superior to the airplane, and far safer. The crockery may be authentic all right, but the picture is a crock.

The New Yorker, January 12, 1976

NEXT STOP, GREENWICH VILLAGE
THE ARTIST AS A YOUNG COMEDIAN

In the fifties, when improvisational acts were booked into night clubs and coffeehouses, and the entertainers satirized middle-class interpersonal relations, young actors had a hip edge to their conversation. Freud had got into everything, and acting was now thought of in terms of awareness. Acting coaches who had been political activists turned into psychiatric philosophers. This is the atmosphere of Paul Mazursky's new, autobiographical comedy, *Next Stop, Greenwich Village.* The hero, a twenty-two-year-old Brooklyn College graduate, Larry Lapinsky (Lenny Baker), who has never wanted to be anything but an actor, moves out of the Brownsville apartment of his parents (Shelley Winters and Mike Kellin) into an apartment of his own in the Village. The film is about Larry's acting classes and his relations with his girl, Sarah (Ellen Greene), and his friends. Mazursky knows this scene so well that every word, every hangup, every awkward, flip hesitation rings a bell. *Next Stop, Greenwich Village* gives the best portrait of Village life ever put on the screen; the casualness, the camaraderie, and the sexual freedom are balanced by glimpses of the lives of those who are in the Village because they don't fit in anywhere else. Yet there's more to the movie than that. Like Alexander Portnoy, Larry is the son in the Jewish joke, but, unlike Portnoy, he isn't crippled by it. In both *Portnoy's Complaint* and *Next Stop, Greenwich Village,* guilt is funny; but the Philip Roth book is satire from within a fixation, and Portnoy is screaming with rage. Larry Lapinsky is rather like what the young Alex Portnoy might have been if he had recovered from his complaint. He learns to live with his guilt; that's the comedy of growing up which is celebrated in *Next Stop, Greenwich Village.*

As Larry's Mom, Shelley Winters is a hysteric on the loose, barging into his apartment in the middle of a party, embarrassing him so much he wants to crawl under the furniture. It is high-mania acting, like Winters's everhopeful Charlotte Haze in *Lolita.* Mrs. Lapinsky pours so much brute emotion into every small detail of her life that she has lost all sense of proportion; everything to do with her becomes of world-shaking importance. Her unused brains have turned her into a howling freak, but you can recognize in her the sources of her son's talent and wit. And, even seeing her through her son's agonized-with-shame eyes, you don't get too much of her—or, rather, you can't get enough of Shelley Winters's performance. With her twinkly goo-goo eyes and flirty grin, Shelley Winters is a mother hippo charging—not at her son's enemies but at him. Fat, morose, irrepressible, she's a force that would strike terror to anyone's heart, yet in some abominable way she's likable. She's Mrs. Portnoy seen without hatred. When Larry visits his parents, she hands him a bag of apple strudel to eat on the plane taking him, first class, to a job in Hollywood. Her husband says to her, "I told you he'd get angry," but Larry says, "I'm not angry. I'm crazy, but

I'm not angry." When he has said goodbye and is on his way to the subway, he stands on the Brownsville street listening to a fiddler and he eats the strudel.

Larry is crazy in a sane way: as a comedian, he puts his craziness to work for him. And that's Paul Mazursky's own greatest gift. What made his earlier films *(Bob & Carol & Ted & Alice, Alex in Wonderland, Blume in Love,* and *Harry & Tonto)* so distinctive was the acceptance of bugginess as part of the normal—maybe even the best part of it. In his films, craziness gives life its savor. When Mazursky makes fun of characters, it's not to put them down; quite the reverse—the scattier they are, the more happily he embraces them. (His quarrel is with the too controlled.) The star of *Next Stop, Greenwich Village,* the relatively unknown Lenny Baker, looks like a gangly young boy but has had almost a decade of professional experience, and he gives the central character the manic generosity that holds the film together. Starting as a runny-nosed, funny-looking kid, Larry becomes stronger and handsomer. Having survived his mother's aggression, he's got the craziness and the strength to make it as an artist.

On his own road from Brownsville through the Village and on to becoming a writer-director, Mazursky performed in improvisational cabaret theatre, wrote skits for "The Danny Kaye Show," and taught acting. Like Larry, who gets his break when he's cast as a tough punk, Mazursky got a role as one of the delinquents in *Blackboard Jungle* (1955), though he had gone West earlier, in 1951, to play a leading role as a psychopath who assaults a captive girl, in Stanley Kubrick's first feature, *Fear and Desire.* Mazursky has appeared in several of his own pictures (he was funniest as the itchy, voracious producer in *Alex in Wonderland*), and his directing style is based on the actors' intuitively taking off from each other, as they did in the coffeehouses. He does something that no other American movie director does: he writes, shapes, and edits the sequences to express the performing rhythm—to keep the actors' pulse. As a result, the audience feels unusually close to the characters—feels protective toward them. Mazursky brings you into a love relationship with his people, and it's all aboveboard.

This picture suggests that for Paul Mazursky (as for many theatre people) acting is at the basis of all judgment. Not all of Larry's friends are studying to be actors, yet one can interpret almost everything that happens to them in terms of acting. Ellen Greene's Sarah is intelligent and quick-witted, but she's already a little hard in the places where Larry is still sensitive—where you feel he'll always stay sensitive. (That's what will keep him an artist.) Sarah violates the rule that Larry's patriarchal acting teacher, Herbert (Michael Egan), says may be important "for the rest of your life": "The worst kind of joking you can do is to keep life out." According to Herbert, you shouldn't use your brain "to keep the stuff out," but "to take it in." Mazursky satirizes Herbert's litany, but very gently. (The famous acting teacher Herbert Berghof appeared in *Harry & Tonto* as Harry's New York friend the aged radical.) And Larry lives by Herbert's rule. He humors his parents, but he's really on his own; he has made the plunge—he's taking life in. Sarah, however, is still at home, and playing the lying-to-your-folks game along with the Greenwich Village game. She's a compromiser, and so elastic she doesn't know where she'll snap. Ellen Greene gives a beautiful, prickly, sensual performance; she has a big, avid mouth, which she uses for comic tics, taking us by surprise each time. The proof of her talent is that it's Sarah's hardness that makes her seem poignant. Being independent-minded has got mixed with something sharp and self-destructive; Sarah cuts herself off from people by acting sure just when she's least sure. This role is written with a respect for the ways in which savvy people with everything going for them can screw up. Mazursky keeps it all light and blowsy, yet the characters have depth, and a lot of damaging things are happening to them while they're frisking along. Sarah is attracted to Robert (Christopher Walken), a narcissistic, affectlessly calm poet-playwright. He's the sort of person who destroys a party—the one who says "Let's play the truth game." Robert is a passive sadist, who draws women to him and shrugs off any responsibility for what happens. And it's true that they've hurt themselves, but it's his passivity that has invited them to do it. Walken uses his light, high voice for an ambiguous effect, and he gives Robert an air of physical isolation that makes him seem always withdrawn from the rest of the group. When Larry, who has suffered because of him, accuses him of having nothing under his pose but more pose, it's as if Larry were using the old slang term and saying "You're a bad actor," meaning that he's untrustworthy, a crook—someone not in touch with himself. Robert might almost be the Nazi villain—he's every son of a bitch whose only interest in sex is for power. He's the only character without spontaneity, and the only one that Mazursky can't resolve his feelings about.

As a homosexual who is sick of role-playing but too frightened to stop, Antonio Fargas keeps just enough reserve to be affecting without pushing it; Lois Smith finds the archetypal Lois Smith role as the sodden Anita, a depressive who plays at suicide; Dori Brenner's Connie plays at being everybody's favorite good sport. And on the fringes of this group there's Barney (John Ford Noonan), a bearded, soft giant with a striking resemblance to Mazursky's old writing partner Larry Tucker. (Larry Lapinsky's first name may also be a nod to Tucker.) Most of these actors have been in movies before, but they didn't have Mazursky's lines to speak, or the hip timing he gets. The subsidiary characters help to form just the sort of human zoo that many of us live in. Jeff Goldblum plays a big, handsome young actor named Clyde Baxter—a goofed-up Victor Mature type. Lou Jacobi is the proprietor of a health-food lunch counter, whooping as if his whole life were vindicated when a customer comes in feeling rotten from having eaten a corned beef on rye. And Rochelle Oliver as Dr. Marsha and John C. Becher as Sid Weinberg, a casting director, contribute to making this picture Off Broadway's finest hour.

In refining his comic style, Mazursky has suffered a few losses. I miss the messy romanticism of *Blume;* there Mazursky was "too close" to the subject—he was gummed up in it, and the chaos felt good. This movie is set in his past, and the blood has cooled. But Mazursky's earlier scripts were splotchy; *Next Stop, Greenwich Village* has the intertwining of a classic American play. And if the mechanics seem a little too theatrical when Larry's Mom waddles into his apartment without knocking and pounces on him, still, in 1953 Village doors weren't always bolted. (Bolted doors wouldn't stop Shelley Winters anyway.) As in some other film shot by Arthur Ornitz, there doesn't appear to be a light source, and the color is muddy. You can't tell the blacks and browns and blues apart; Ornitz seems to get the shots to match by making them all dark. Luckily, this movie has so much else going for it that it can get along without visual beauty. Mazursky was so smitten by Fellini that his early films sometimes seemed to be commuting between cultures. But *Next Stop, Greenwich Village* isn't an imitation of *Amarcord,* it's Mazursky's own Amarcord. And I like it better than Fellini's. It isn't showy—Mazursky works on a small scale. Yet this satirist without bitterness and without extravagance looks to be a comic poet. His subject is the comedy of wisdom—how to become a good actor.

The New Yorker, February 2, 1976

TAXI DRIVER
UNDERGROUND MAN

Taxi Driver is the fevered story of an outsider in New York—a man who can't find any point of entry into human society. Travis Bickle (Robert De Niro), the protagonist of Martin Scorsese's new film, from a script by Paul Schrader, can't find a life. He's an ex-Marine from the Midwest who takes a job driving a cab nights, because he can't sleep anyway, and he is surrounded by the night world of the uprooted—whores, pimps, transients. Schrader, who grew up in Michigan, in the Christian Reformed Church, a zealous Calvinist splinter (he didn't see a movie until he was seventeen), has created a protagonist who is an ascetic not by choice but out of fear. And Scorsese with his sultry moodiness and his appetite for the pulp sensationalism of forties movies, is just the director to define an American underground man's resentment. Travis wants to conform, but he can't find a group pattern to conform to. So he sits and drives in the stupefied languor of anomie. He hates New York with a Biblical fury; it gives off the stench of Hell, and its filth and smut obsess him. He manages to get a date with Betsy (Cybill Shepherd), a political campaigner whose blondness and white clothes represent purity to him, but he is so out of touch that he inadvertently offends her and she won't have anything more to do with him. When he fumblingly asks advice from Wizard (Peter Boyle), an older cabdriver, and indicates the pressure building up in him, Wizard doesn't know what he's talking about. Travis becomes sick with loneliness and frustration; and then, like a commando preparing for a raid, he purifies his body and goes into training to kill. *Taxi Driver* is a movie in heat, a raw, tabloid version of *Notes from Underground,* and we stay with the protagonist's hatreds all the way.

This picture is more ferocious than Scorsese's volatile, allusive *Mean Streets. Taxi Driver* has a relentless movement: Travis has got to find relief. It's a two-character study—Travis versus New York. As Scorsese has designed the film, the city never lets you off the hook. There's no grace, no compassion in the artificially lighted atmosphere. The neon reds, the vapors that shoot up from the streets, the dilapidation all get to you the way they get to Travis. He is desperately sick, but he's the only one who tries to save a twelve-and-a-half-year-old hooker, Iris (Jodie Foster); the argument he invokes is that she belongs with her family and in school—the secure values from his own past that are of no help to him now. Some mechanism of adaptation is missing in Travis; the details aren't filled in—just the indications of a strict religious background, and a scar on his back, suggesting a combat wound. The city world presses in on him, yet it's also remote, because Travis is so disaffected that he isn't always quite there. We perceive the city as he does, and it's so scummy and malign we get the feel of his alienation.

Scorsese may just naturally be an Expressionist; his asthmatic bedridden childhood in a Sicilian-American home in Little Italy propelled him toward a fix on the violently exciting movies he saw. Physically and intellectually, he's a speed demon, a dervish. Even in *Alice Doesn't Live Here Anymore* he found a rationale for restless, whirlwind movement. But Scorsese is also the most carnal of directors—movement is ecstatic for him—and that side of him didn't come out in *Alice.* This new movie gives him a chance for the full Expressionist use of the city which he was denied in *Mean Streets,* because it was set in New York but was made on a minuscule budget in Southern California, with only seven shooting days in New York itself. Scorsese's Expressionism isn't anything like the exaggerated sets of the German directors; he uses documentary locations, but he pushes discordant elements to their limits, and the cinematographer, Michael Chapman, gives the street life a seamy, rich pulpiness. When Travis is taunted by a pimp, Sport (Harvey Keitel), the pimp is so eager for action that he can't stand still; the hipster, with his rhythmic jiggling, makes an eerily hostile contrast to the paralyzed, dumbfounded Travis. Scorsese gets the quality of trance in a scene like this; the whole movie has a sense of vertigo. Scorsese's New York is the big city of the thrillers he feasted his imagination on—but at a later stage of decay. This New York is a voluptuous enemy. The street vapors become ghostly; Sport the pimp romancing his baby whore leads her in a hypnotic dance; the porno theatres are like mortuaries; the congested traffic is macabre. And this Hell is always in movement.

No other film has ever dramatized urban indifference so powerfully; at first, here, it's horrifyingly funny, and then just horrifying. When Travis attempts to date Betsy, he's very seductive; we can see why she's tantalized. They're talking across a huge gap, and still they're connecting (though the wires are all crossed). It's a zinger of a scene: an educated, socially conscious woman dating a lumpen lost soul who uses one of the oldest pitches in the book—he tells her that he knows she is a lonely person. Travis means it; the gruesome comedy in the scene is how intensely he means it—because his own life is utterly empty. Throughout the movie, Travis talks to people on a different level from the level they take him on. He's so closed off he's otherworldly; he engages in so few conversations that slang words like "moonlighting" pass right over him—the spoken language is foreign to him. His responses are sometimes so blocked that he seems wiped out; at other times he's animal fast. This man is burning in misery, and his inflamed, brimming eyes are the focal point of the compositions. Robert De Niro is in almost every frame: thin-faced, as handsome as Robert Taylor one moment and cagey, ferrety, like Cagney, the next—and not just looking at the people he's talking to but spying on them. As Travis, De Niro has none of the peasant courtliness of his Vito Corleone in *The Godfather, Part II.* Vito held himself in proudly, in control of his violence; he was a leader. Travis is dangerous in a different, cumulative way. His tense face folds in a yokel's grin and he looks almost an idiot. Or he sits in his room vacantly watching the bright-eyed young faces on the TV and with his foot he slowly rocks the set back and then over. The exacerbation of his desire for vengeance shows in his numbness, yet part of the horror implicit in this movie is how easily he passes. The anonymity of the city soaks up one more invisible man; he could be legion.

Scorsese handles the cast immaculately. Harvey Keitel's pimp is slimy, all right, yet his malicious, mischievous eyes and his jumpiness are oddly winning. Jodie Foster, who was exactly Iris's age when she played the part, is an unusually physical child actress and seems to have felt out her line readings—her words are convincingly hers. Cybill Shepherd has never been better: you don't see her trying to act. She may actually be doing her least acting here, yet she doesn't have that schoolgirl model's blankness; her face is expressive and womanly. There's a suggestion that Betsy's life hasn't gone according to her expectations—a faint air of defeat. The comedian Albert Brooks brings a note of quibbling, plump pomposity to the role of her political co-worker, and Leonard Harris, formerly the WCBS-TV arts critic, has a professionally earnest manner as Palatine, their candidate. Peter Boyle's role is small, but he was right to want to be in this film, and he does slobby wonders with his scenes as the gently thick Wizard, adjusted to the filth that Travis is coiled up to fight; Boyle gives the film a special New York–hack ambience, and, as the cabby Doughboy, Harry Northup has a bland face and Southern drawl that suggest another kind of rootlessness. Scorsese himself is sitting on the sidewalk when Travis first sees Betsy, and then he returns to play a glitteringly morbid role as one of Travis's fares—a man who wants Travis to share his rancid glee in what the Magnum he intends to shoot his faithless wife with will do to her. As an actor, he sizzles; he has such concentrated energy that this sequence burns a small hole in the screen.

As a director, Scorsese has the occasional arbitrariness and preening of a runaway talent; sometimes a shot calls attention to itself, because it serves no visible purpose. One can pass over a lingering closeup of a street musician, but when Travis is talking to Betsy on a pay phone in an office building and the camera moves away from him to the blank hallway, it's an Antonioni pirouette. The Bernard Herrmann score is a much bigger problem; the composer finished recording it on December 23rd, the day before he died, and so it's a double pity that it isn't better. It's clear why Scorsese wanted Herrmann: his specialty was expressing psychological disorder through dissonant, wrought-up music. But this movie, with its suppressed sex and suppressed violence, is already pitched so high that it doesn't need ominous percussion, snake rattles, and rippling scales. These musical nudges belong back with the rampaging thrillers that *Taxi Driver* transcends. Scorsese got something out of his asthma: he knows how to make us experience the terror of suffocation.

Some actors are said to be empty vessels who are filled by the roles they play, but that's not what appears to be happening here with De Niro. He's gone the other way. He's used his emptiness—he's reached down into his own anomie. Only Brando has done this kind of plunging, and De Niro's performance has something of the undistanced intensity that Brando's had in *Last Tango*. In its own way, this movie, too, has an erotic aura. There is practically no sex in it, but no sex can be as disturbing as sex. And that's what it's about: the absence of sex—bottled-up, impacted energy and emotion, with a blood-splattering release. The fact that we experience Travis's need for an explosion viscerally, and that the explosion itself has the quality of consummation, makes *Taxi Driver* one of the few truly modern horror films.

Anyone who goes to the movie houses that loners frequent knows that they identify with the perpetrators of crimes, even the most horrible crimes, and that they aren't satisfied unless there's a whopping climax. In his essay "The White Negro," Norman Mailer suggested that when a killer takes his revenge on the institutions that he feels are oppressing him his eruption of violence can have a positive effect on him. The most shocking aspect of *Taxi Driver* is that it takes this very element, which has generally been exploited for popular appeal, and puts it in the center of the viewer's consciousness. Violence is Travis's only means of expressing himself. He has not been able to hurdle the barriers to being seen and felt. When he blasts through, it's his only way of telling the city that he's there. And, given his ascetic loneliness, it's the only real orgasm he can have.

The violence in this movie is so threatening precisely because it's cathartic for Travis. I imagine that some people who are angered by the film will say that it advocates violence as a cure for frustration. But to acknowledge that when a psychopath's blood boils over he may cool down is not the same as justifying the eruption. This film doesn't operate on the level of moral judgment of what Travis does. Rather, by drawing us into its vortex it makes us understand the psychic discharge of the quiet boys who go berserk. And it's a real slap in the face for us when we see Travis at the end looking pacified. He's got the rage out of his system—for the moment, at least—and he's back at work, picking up passengers in front of the St. Regis. It's not that he's cured but that the city is crazier than he is.

The New Yorker, February 9, 1976

ABOUT CAROLE LOMBARD, FROM REVIEW OF
GABLE AND LOMBARD

Carole Lombard probably wasn't a more skillful comedienne than Jean Arthur or Claudette Colbert, but she had a special luminous, Art Deco look that really went with the décor in those black-and-silver-and-white movies. She wore clothes superbly, in high-fashion style, with her slim hips thrust out; yet, unlike high-fashion models, she seemed more alive than other women. Her vibrancy was linked to her extreme whiteness—the blond hair, the pale skin, and the slinky, skin-tight white satins. In visual terms, she was the sexiest of the comediennes, and her daring décolletage and her free, loose, wiggly body were part of her manic charm in such movies as *Twentieth Century* (1934), *My Man Godfrey* (1936), *Nothing Sacred* (1937), and *True Confession* (1937). She threw herself into her scenes in a much more physical sense than the other women did, and her all-outness seemed spontaneously giddy. It was easy to believe that a woman who moved like that and screamed and hollered with such abandon was a natural, uninhibited cutup—naturally high-spirited.

In the Depression comedy, *My Man Godfrey,* Lombard was a rich, gorgeous nit who went to the city dump to find a "forgotten man." The man she found was played by William Powell. When she told him she needed to take him back to her party in order to win the scavenger hunt, he asked what that was, and sighing, she said, "A scavenger hunt is just like a treasure hunt, except in a treasure hunt you find something you want and in a scavenger hunt you find things you don't want and the one who wins gets a prize, only there really isn't any prize, it's just the honor of winning, because all the money goes to charity if there's any money left over, but then there never is." There was a delirious, breathless plaintiveness in Lombard at a moment like this—recognition dawning in her.

The New Yorker, February 23, 1976

SPARKLE

parkle, the story of the three daughters of a domestic servant who become a singing group, in the style of the Supremes, opened in April and closed a few weeks later. Now, partly because of the success of the Aretha Franklin album of the Curtis Mayfield score, the picture is being reissued in some cities. This means that moviegoers have another chance to see Lonette McKee, a young singer-actress so sexy that she lays waste to the movie, which makes the mistake of killing her off in the first half. But in that first part she and Dorian Harewood show a sixth sense for being alive. The fact that nobody has picked up on these two and starred them together is just one more proof that the new studio heads don't go to the movies.

Sparkle is the first film to be directed by Sam O'Steen, the well-known editor *(The Graduate, Rosemary's Baby, Chinatown),* who also directed *Queen of the Stardust Ballroom* for TV. He must have got carried away with the black cast and the smoky theatrical milieu, because the images are sometimes irritatingly dark, but he keeps them full of atmospheric detail, and the tawdry black-vaudeville scenes have the teeming, bodies-spilling-out-the-edges quality of Toulouse-Lautrec. The crowded look of the film helps to compensate for the Joel Schumacher script, which appears to be no more than a skeleton.

The outline for *Sparkle* follows the moral scheme of the old Production Code days: the "bad" characters (Lonette McKee as Sister, the hell-bent lead singer of the trio; Harewood as the teen-age boy who nonchalantly steals a car to take her out; Tony King as the dope pusher who hooks her) die or are punished, and the "good" characters (Irene Cara as the meek Sparkle who goes on as a single, and dimply Philip Michael Thomas as her hardworking young manager) are rewarded. As often happened in the old movie days, the "bad" performers are terrific and the "good" are insufferable.

Sister is a hot number, talented, smart, impudent—an inflammatory, exhibitionistic singer who wants to turn the whole world on. And as Lonette McKee plays her, Sister has the visceral beauty, the voice, and the sexual energy to do it. Sister puts the dirty fun of sex into her songs, with the raw charge of a rebellious, nose-thumbing girl making her way. She has barely had a taste of singing in public when she falls for the sadistic pusher who beats her up and degrades her; she goes downhill unbelievably fast—and the picture with her—and then she ODs. What isn't explained is the why of this relationship; instead, we move on to the way the dewy-eyed Sparkle achieves the fame Sister might have had. And in order to keep the story going the action shifts to the almost canine devotion of Sparkle's young manager; his true-hearted courage defeats the attempts of gangsters to muscle in on her career.

The subject that's passed over—why the thug wants to possess and destroy Sister, who so obviously has everything it takes to become a star, and why she's drawn to him—is a true modern subject, and not just for the rock world. Lonette McKee is the actress to drive this theme into one's consciousness, because she has the sexual brazenness that screen stars such as Susan Hayward and Ava Gardner had in their youth. You look at the sheer taunting sexual avidity of these women and you think "What man would dare?" And the answer may be: only a man with the strength to meet the challenge or a man so threatened by it that he's got to wipe the floor with the girl, and there are more of the latter. If the women who are "too much" for men fall for sharpies and rough guys who brutalize them, it probably has a lot to do with the scarcity of the other men, and something to do, too, with the women's insecurity about being too much. The stronger a woman's need to use her energy, her brains, and her talent, the more confusedly she may feel that she has a beating coming. Besides, having had to make her own way, and having—at some levels—been coarsened doing it, she may feel some rapport with the tough operators who are used to knocking people around. Whatever else these men are, they're self-made, and they instinctively know what she's going through and how to handle her.

Movies now seem to be almost begging for this theme to come out. It's highly unlikely that a woman can become a major screen star at this time unless she has a strong personality, yet if she does—like Jane Fonda, or Barbra Streisand, or Liza Minnelli—she's likely to be experienced as threatening by some of the audience (and by women who play by the standard rules as well as by men). These stars raise the problem in their relation to the audience which is implicit in their screen roles: resentment of their dominating presence. Yet at the movies audiences are far more interested in the "bad girls" than in the ingenues, and not just because wickedness gives an actress more of a chance; these roles give an actress a better chance because there's something recognizably there in those bad girls, even when it's frustrated, soured, and self-destructive. The "bad girl" is the cheapest, easiest way for the movies to deal with the women with guts.

In *Sparkle,* we can believe in Sister but not in the rise to rock stardom of the docile, unassertive Sparkle, because, given the social and biological circumstances of women's lives, a woman who isn't called a hard-driving bitch along the way is not likely to reach any top. A movie can show us the good girls winning the fellas, mothering the kids, succoring those who have met with adversity, but a good-girl artist is a contradiction in terms.

The New Yorker, September 27, 1976

JONAH WHO WILL BE 25 IN THE YEAR 2000
A CUCKOO CLOCK THAT LAUGHS

Jonah Who Will Be 25 in the Year 2000 stays suspended in the air, spinning—a marvellous toy, weightless, yet precise and controlled. Who would have expected the Swiss director Alain Tanner and his co-writer, John Berger, to turn out a bubbleheaded political comedy? Their last collaboration, *The Middle of the World,* ended with the words "There is no hope for rebirth," yet *Jonah* leaps about like an Easter bunny. This film is drunk and lit up on the possibilities of rebirth. At the same time, it has a fully developed sense of irony—the laconic kind that informed Renoir's *Boudu Saved from Drowning* and Buñuel's *The Discreet Charm of the Bourgeoisie.*

Jonah is set in Geneva, and the statue of Jean Jacques Rousseau (he was born there in 1712, the son of a watchmaker) presides over the film. *Jonah*'s spirit—romantic, Socialist, mystical—suggests that people were changed by the political upheavals of 1968 and that the new ways of thinking go beyond Marx, back to utopians such as Rousseau. That poetic social thinker, with his love of nature and man, didn't believe in original sin; he believed that the roots of evil were in the very existence of society, and that education should save children from contamination. There are eight key characters in *Jonah,* all in their twenties or thirties, and all seeking solutions to the problems brought to general consciousness by the events of 1968. Not one of them is a comfortable bourgeois; they're the sort of fantasists and obsessives who were considered marginal before 1968. They were fewer in number in those days and were likely to be called crackpots. Now that bourgeois norms have begun to look disreputable, these eight buggy dreamers aren't social outsiders. They're insiders, though in a precarious, existential way. In the course of the film, the eight become friends and accept each other's oddities without so much as a lifted eyebrow; they band together communally as the metaphorical parents of Jonah, and then disperse.

They're not a band of disciples; there's no faith they share. But each, in a small, self-contained way, is a prophet, or, at least, a prophetic crazy. They're all in this world, but each is also somewhere else, listening to his own different drummer. Snub-nosed, rounded Mathilde (Myriam Boyer), the most physical and the most innocent of them, finds fulfillment in pregnancy and massages people's tiredness away. Her husband, long-jawed Matthieu (played by an actor known as Rufus), a typesetter and union leader laid off in a cutback, goes to work for a produce gardener and sets up a Rousseauist school in a greenhouse. Marcel, the gardener (Roger Jendly), a withdrawn primitive artist, is engrossed in the life of animals, where he finds his answers to human problems. Marguerite, the gardener's rough-spoken wife (Dominique Labourier), a no-frills woman in witches' black, is fastened on organic farming. Big, worldly Max (Jean-Luc Bideau) has given up an organized political activity and works as a proofreader; roulette has become his game. Yet, though he doesn't believe in the revolution, he doesn't not believe, either; he's an agnostic about revolution—he's waiting. Meanwhile, he learns that a bank land swindle is under way and goes to warn the potential victims (and thus meets the farm couple, Marcel and Marguerite). Red-haired Madeleine (Myriam Mezière), a secretary in the dirty-dealing bank, gets Max copies of the documents he needs, though she has her mind fixed on the Tantras. Warm, tubby, intelligent Marco (Jacques Denis), a neighbor of the farm couple, is a high-school history teacher; his unorthodox methods and cloud-built theories please the students but not the administrators, and after he's fired he finds a new vocation working in a home for the aged. He falls in love with Marie (Miou-Miou), a cashier in a supermarket, who doesn't charge him for his liquor and wine. Marie is a French citizen, who must go back across the border each night. She's a border person in other ways, too: she filches food for elderly people on pensions. There may be some simple reason for all these prophets to have names starting with "Ma," or maybe there's no reason at all. (I hope the latter.)

Each of the eight Ma characters is a utopian of some sort, except for the disillusioned former activist, Max. By conventional standards, they are people who will never "amount to anything," and that's the originality of the film—it sees hope and renewal in all their methods, and honors Max, the Marxist turned gambler, as their spiritual ancestor, the man whose activities culminated in the events of 1968, and thus changed their world. The film honors precisely that "lunatic fringe" that the Marxists have always derided. Each of these people is autonomous, looks for his own answers, and acts upon them, and together, the film suggests, they can give birth to a Jonah who will have the acumen to connect their visions.

Tanner juggles all these extraterrestrial travellers, each of them into his own thing—a lunar colony interacting. *Jonah* moves so fast that one's mind races to keep up with what the characters are saying and doing; regarded with Tanner's appreciative detachment, their activities become a form of vaudeville. In movies, nobody has attempted anything quite like this whirling play of ideas. It may draw a little from Renoir's *Rules of the Game* and *The Lower Depths* and some from *La Chinoise* and other Godard films, but it's essentially a poetic original, simple and unstressed from shot to shot, with a visual luster. The colors are softer than in Godard; Tanner is more interested in the erotic qualities that go with different attitudes toward society, and each of the people has very distinctive flesh tones, suggesting sensuous contrasts. The ideas they expound are often woozy, and the history teacher's lecture on time, which is a key to the mechanism of the film, is the wooziest of all—it's impenetrable. I assume that the history teacher as seer is being satirized, and that this is also Tanner's and Berger's self-satire. I can't swear to that; what I take for droll, dry Swiss humor may be intended straight. But this slight perplexity may also be intentional: the film is willing to entertain possibilities for rebirth even if they're cracked or pickled. It doesn't ask us to believe anything. But we do believe that the *idées fixes* belong to the characters we see—at least, I did, for all except the earth mother, Mathilde. The phoniness of her lines ("I hate empty spaces. . . . Give me a child") seemed the authors' mistake rather than the character's self-view. Apart from this lapse, there's not a word I felt was wasted; I had confidence that Tanner and Berger wanted it just so. The whole film seems to have been conceived in a greenhouse.

Jonah doesn't operate on identification with a hero or on suspense. Yet it provides the kind of pleasure that one can generally get only from movies that involve us by those primal means. I hesitate to invoke the word "Brechtian," because, except for a few sixties films by Godard, that has generally meant a didactic pain. But before this nobody has had a Miou-Miou to sing a Brechtian cabaret song. She's the most purely enjoyable person in the movie. This tumble-dried blonde, the Brigitte Bardot the cat dragged in, doesn't look as if she could be an actress, but she certainly is. When this placid creature, with her broad-mouthed fey smile, breaks into a song, she turns on the charm like a scroungy Cinderella, creating instant empathy; yet she distances her character and kids the empathy. That naughty, plummy smile of hers makes her the director's confederate. In *Going Places*, a mean, funny film with sequences that had a Henry Miller–like erotic-fantasy quality, Miou-Miou was the abused girl who was so overjoyed when she had her first orgasm that she ran out to tell the news to the men who had called her frigid. It doesn't occur to the women Miou-Miou plays to hide anything; they're spacey right on the surface. In *Jonah*, she brings the missing magic to the Brechtian method; her Marie, a bewildered, feathery Pierrette, is as defiantly, forlornly romantic as Cyrano's plume dipped in horse manure. Marie has a friend in France, Old Charles, a retired railroad worker, to whom she brings stolen groceries; he is played by the veteran French character actor Raymond Bussières, familiar from *Casque d'Or* and films by Clouzot and René Clair. Together, Miou-Miou and Bussières act out fantasies in brief set pieces that do what Brechtian numbers are supposed to do, and without didactic jostling.

The whole film is designed as a collection of little routines—the red-haired Tantrist bringing the Marxist gambler to her exotic lair and spinning theories about the loss of semen which might have come right out of *Dr. Strangelove*, the history teacher meeting Old Charles and talking of railroads, and so on. They all add up to a vision of changes much like the ones that have taken place in this country, with many of the students who became politicized in the late sixties not retreating to bourgeois values but dispersing into various mystical movements. *Jonah* is so ingeniously constructed that one can enjoy it the way one enjoyed Renoir's egalitarian films of the thirties, relating to each character in turn. Yet the people are cultists and are conceived in Brechtian terms: we see their wheels going round. Tanner's inspiration was in allowing these metaphorical creations to be silly. They're silly, yet they're no sillier than the people I know in Berkeley, who are probably the brightest people I know. In life, bright people can bore one sense-less with their talk of crafts and ecology and children who are free to grow, and so it's a giddy surprise to discover how charming they are here on the screen, greening Switzerland with the same lunar poetry they've been using on America. When this genuinely eccentric movie gets its group of eight linked up, the themes of time, history, capital and labor, and education tie together, and Jonah the savior is born out of the whale of the old society. This is an Easter fable, all right, but with a dialectical bunny.

The New Yorker, October 18, 1976

FROM NOTES ON EVOLVING HEROES, MORALS, AUDIENCES—
JAWS, DOG DAY AFTERNOON, THE MAN WHO FELL TO EARTH

In *Jaws*, which may be the most cheerfully perverse scare movie ever made, the disasters don't come on schedule the way they do in most disaster pictures, and your guts never settle down on a timetable. Even while you're convulsed with laughter, you're still apprehensive, because the editing rhythms are very tricky, and the shock images loom up huge, right on top of you. There are parts of *Jaws* that suggest what Eisenstein might have done if he hadn't intellectualized himself out of reach—if he'd given in to the bourgeois child in himself. While having a drink with an older Hollywood director, I said that I'd been amazed by the assurance with which Steven Spielberg, the young director of *Jaws*, had toyed with the film frame. The older director said, "He must never have seen a play; he's the first one of us who doesn't think in terms of the proscenium arch. With him, there's nothing but the camera lens."

It's not only the visual technique of *Jaws* that's different. The other big disaster movies are essentially the same as the pre-Vietnam films, but *Jaws* isn't. It belongs to the pulpiest sci-fi monster-movie tradition, yet it stands some of the old conventions on their head. Though *Jaws* has more zest than a Woody Allen picture, and a lot more electricity, it's funny in a Woody Allen way. When the three protagonists are in their tiny boat, you feel that Robert Shaw, the malevolent old shark hunter, is so manly that he wants to get them all killed; he's so manly he's homicidal. It's not sharks who are his enemies; it's other men. When he begins showing off his wounds, the bookish ichthyologist, Richard Dreyfuss, strings along with him at first, and matches him scar for scar. But when the ichthyologist is outclassed in the number of scars he can exhibit, he opens his shirt, looks down at his hairy chest, and with a put-on artist's grin says, "You see that? Right there? That was Mary Ellen Moffit—she broke my heart." When Shaw squeezes an empty beer can flat, Dreyfuss satirizes him by crumpling a Styrofoam cup. The director, identifying with the Dreyfuss character, sets up bare-chested heroism as a joke and scores off it all through the movie. The third protagonist, acted by Roy Scheider, is a former New York City policeman who has just escaped the city dangers and found a haven as chief of police in a resort community on an island. There, feeling totally inadequate in his new situation, he confronts primal terror. But the fool on board the little boat isn't the chief of police who doesn't know one end of a boat from the other, or the bookman, either. It's Shaw, the obsessively masculine fisherman, who thinks he's got to prove himself by fighting the shark practically single-handed. Shaw personalizes the shark, turns him into a fourth character—his enemy. This fisherman is such a macho pain that it's harrowingly funny when he's gobbled up; a flamboyant actor like Robert Shaw, who wears a proscenium arch around him, has to be kidded.

The high point of the film's humor is in our seeing Shaw get it; this nut Ahab, with his hyper-masculine basso-profundo speeches, stands in for all the men who have to show they're tougher than anybody. The shark's cavernous jaws demonstrate how little his toughness finally adds up to. If one imagines George C. Scott or Anthony Quinn in the Robert Shaw role, these anti-macho jokes expand into a satire of movie heroism.

■　■　■

The actor who has put our new, ambivalent feelings about the warrior male to account is Jack Nicholson. Despite his excessive dynamism (and maybe partly because of it), this satirical actor has probably gone further into the tragicomedy of hardhat macho than any other actor. He exposes cracks in barroom-character armor and makes those cracks funny, in a low-down, grungy way. With his horny leers and his little-boy cockiness and one-upmanship, he illuminates the sources of male bravado. His whole acting style is based on the little guy coming on strong, because being a tough guy is the only ideal he's ever aspired to. This little guy doesn't make it, of course; Nicholson is the macho loser-hero. (In an earlier era, Nicholson would probably have played big guys.)

When you see the celebration of adolescent male fantasies in the film *The Yakuza*, directed by Sydney Pollack, or in a John Milius picture—*Dillinger* or *The Wind and the Lion*—you may wonder of the filmmakers, "Are these boys being naughty just because they're old enough not to be scolded by their mothers?" That's the kind of naughtiness Jack Nicholson keeps us aware of; he includes it in his performances. He's the kind of actor who gives you a character and then lets you follow him around the corner and watch as he reacts to what he just pulled off back there.

■　■　■

In *Dog Day Afternoon*, we don't want any explanation of how it is that Sonny (Al Pacino) lives in both heterosexual and homosexual marriages. We accept the idea because we don't really believe in patterns of behavior anymore—only in behavior. Sonny, who is trapped in the middle of robbing a bank, with a crowd gathering in the street outside, is a working-class man who got into this mess by trying to raise money for Leon (Chris Sarandon) to have a sex-change operation, yet the audience doesn't laugh. The most touching element in the film is Sonny's inability to handle all the responsibilities he has assumed. Though he is half-crazed by his situation, he is trying to do the right thing by everybody—his wife and children, the suicidal Leon, the hostages in the bank. In the sequence in which Sonny dictates his will, we can see that inside this ludicrous bungling robber there's a complicatedly unhappy man, operating out of a sense of noblesse oblige.

The structure of *Dog Day Afternoon* loosens in the last three-quarters of an hour, but that was the part I particularly cared for. This picture is one of the most satisfying of all the movies starring New York City because the director, Sidney Lumet, and the screenwriter, Frank Pierson, having established that Sonny's grandstanding gets the street crowd on his side against the cops, and that even the tellers are on his side, let us move into the dark, confused areas of Sonny's frustrations and don't explain everything to us. They trust us to feel without our being told how to feel. They prepare us for a confrontation scene between Sonny and Leon, and it never comes, but even that is all right, because of the way that Pacino and Sarandon handle their contact by telephone; Sonny's anxiety and Leon's distress are so pure that there's no appeal for sympathy—no star kitsch to separate us from the nakedness of the feelings on the screen.

This kind of male acting is becoming much more common in movies. In the past, the corruption of stardom has often meant that the actor was afraid of carrying a role through and exposing the insides of a character; a star began to have so large a stake in his own image that he was afraid of what the audience might think of the revelation. But new stars such as Pacino and Nicholson and Gene Hackman and Robert De Niro go as far into their characters as they can psychologically allow themselves to go; that's how they work.

■   ■   ■

Nicolas Roeg's *The Man Who Fell to Earth*, which stars David Bowie, is *The Little Prince* for young adults; the hero, a stranger on earth, is purity made erotic. He doesn't have a human sex drive; he isn't even equipped for it—naked, he's as devoid of sex differentiation as a child in sleepers. (He seems to be the first movie hero to have had his crotch airbrushed.) Yet there's true insolence in Bowie's lesbian-Christ leering, and his forlorn, limp manner and chalky pallor are alluringly tainted. Lighted like the woman of mystery in thirties movies, he's the most romantic figure in recent pictures—the modern version of the James Dean lost-boy myth. Nicolas Roeg has a talent for eerily easy, soft, ambiguous sex—for the sexiness of passivity. In his *Don't Look Now*, Donald Sutherland practically oozed passivity—which was the only interesting quality he had. And at the beginning of *The Man Who Fell to Earth* (which was shot in this country with an

American cast except for Bowie), when the stranger splashes down in a lake in the Southwest and drinks water like a vampire gulping down his life-blood, one is drawn in, fascinated by the obliqueness and by the promise of an erotic sci-fi story. It is and it isn't. The stranger, though non-human, has visions of the wife and kiddies he has left—an old-fashioned nuclear family on the planet Anthea. He has come to earth to obtain the water that will save his people, who are dying from drought, but he is corrupted, is distracted from his mission, and then is so damaged that he cannot return. Although Roeg and his screenwriter, Paul Mayersberg, pack layers of tragic political allegory into *The Man Who Fell to Earth*, none of the layers is very strong, or even very clear. The plot, about big-business machinations, is so uninvolving that one watches Bowie traipsing around—looking like Katharine Hepburn in her transvestite role in *Sylvia Scarlett*—and either tunes out or allows the film, with its perverse pathos, to become a sci-fi framework for a sex-role-confusion fantasy. The wilted solitary stranger who is better than we are and yet falls prey to our corrupt human estate can be said to represent everyone who feels misunderstood, everyone who feels sexually immature or "different," everyone who has lost his way, everyone who has failed his holy family, and so the film is a gigantic launching pad for anything that viewers want to drift to.

A former cinematographer, Roeg has more visual strategies than almost any director one can think of. He can charge a desolate landscape so that it seems ominously alive, familiar yet only half recognizable, and he photographs skyscrapers with such lyric glitter that the United States seems to be showing off for him (the better to be despoiled). The people pass through, floating, using the country without seeing its beauty. Roeg's cutting can create a magical feeling of waste and evil, but at other times his Marienbadish jumpiness is just trickery he can't resist. In *The Man Who Fell to Earth*, the unease and sense of disconnectedness between characters also disconnect us. Roeg teases us with a malaise that he then moralizes about. His effects stay on the surface; they become off-puttingly abstract, and his lyricism goes sentimental—as most other Christ movies do. In *Blow-Up* and *The Passenger,* Antonioni showed a talent (and a propensity) for mystification; it would be a present to audiences if just once he would use his talent frivolously—if, instead of his usual opaque metaphysical mystery, he'd make a simple trashy mystery, preferably in those *Réalités* travel spots he's drawn to. And it would be a blessing if Nicolas Roeg—perhaps the most visually seductive of directors, a man who can make impotence sexy—turned himself loose on the romance of waste.

■   ■   ■

Bowie's self-mocking androgyny is not a quality that one associates with the heroes of imperial nations. Imperial movie heroes are just about gone, and even much of what comes out on the American screen as sexism isn't necessarily the result of conviction; it may be the sexist result of simple convenience. In the movies or on television, the two cops in the police car don't have to think about each other. When a cop-hero's partner is shot, it's supposed to be worse than anything, but the reason it's worse than anything is always explained *after* he's been shot. Then the survivor—let's call him Frank—explains that Jim took the bullet for him, that Jim was the one Frank spent more time with than anyone else. And Frank's wife can say, "Frank and Jim were more married than we are"—and she says it sympathetically. She understands. The theme of mateship is such a clean, visible bond. It doesn't have the hidden traps of the relationship between men and women, or between lovers of the same sex. In a number of movies, the actors playing the two cops seem palpably embarrassed by the notion that women are those creatures who come into the story for a minute and you jump them. Some are embarrassed that that's all you do with them; others are relieved that that's all you have to do—because if there's anything more it may involve the problem of what men are supposed to be in relation to women.

Two human beings who are sexually and emotionally involved cause pain to each other, and it takes more skill than most writers and directors have to deal with that pain.

■   ■   ■

The changes in movies, responding to the changes in the national psychology, have come about mostly unconsciously. The comedies now are almost all made by Jewish directors—directors who are themselves anarchic comics. Comedies are no longer about how to win or how to be a success, but about trying to function in the general craziness. Some of the veteran directors may face insoluble problems—a director's craft isn't enough to see him through when that craft is itself an expression of the old, fixed patterns. In a country where the Protestant ethic doesn't seem to have worked out too well, it makes sense that directors of Catholic background—Francis Ford Coppola and Brian De Palma, of Italian-Catholic parents; Martin Scorsese, of Sicilian origins; Robert Altman, from a German-Catholic family in Kansas City, Missouri—speak to the way Americans feel now. These men have grown up with a sense of sin and a deep-seated feeling that things aren't going to get much better in this life. They're not uplifters or reformers, like some of the Protestant directors of an earlier era, or muckraking idealists, like some of the earlier Jewish directors. Pictures such as *Mean Streets* and *Taxi Driver, California Split,* and *Nashville, The Godfather, Part II,* and the new *Carrie* combine elements of ritual and of poetry in their heightened realism. The Catholic directors examine American experience in emotional terms, without much illusion—in fact, with macabre humor. The Western heroes faced choices between right and wrong; these directors didn't grow up on right-and-wrong but on good-and-evil—and then they lost the good.

■   ■   ■

If *Jaws* represents a new affability about the tough American male, it also contains a token of a new ruthlessness. There's a lull in the action, a becalmed interlude, which is filled by a long monologue delivered by Robert Shaw. He tells the ultimate shark horror story—it's worse, even, than anything that we see in the movie. The story he tells concerns the men of the *Indianapolis,* a heavy cruiser that was torpedoed after delivering key elements of the atomic bombs to be dropped on Japan. As Shaw, in drunken, sepulchral tones, describes the events, the survivors were attacked by sharks, which returned day after day, using the ever-smaller group of survivors as a feeding ground. Actually, it is not known how many of the Indianapolis crew died because of sharks, or how many died from exposure, or from injuries sustained when the ship was hit. The monologue, conceived by Howard Sackler, embellished to a length of nine pages by John Milius, and then trimmed by Spielberg and Shaw to a feasible length, could easily have dealt with a fictitious ship, but using the correct name gave it an extra plausibility. In the rest of *Jaws,* we're worked over right in the open, but in this Indianapolis episode we're fooled by a hidden confusion of historical fact and sadistic fantasy. The writers probably didn't consider—or were simply indifferent to—the nightmarish pain that their gothic embroidery would give to the relatives of the men who died in those waters.

■   ■   ■

The only morality that many of the best young filmmakers appear to have is an aesthetic morality. They may show us geysers of blood that tear us apart, but they're true to what they think is good filmmaking. In their movies, the human logic is secondary to the aesthetic logic. A movie is like a musical composition to them: they'll put in a bloody climax because they need it at a certain point. They're not afraid of the manipulative possibilities of the medium; they revel in those possibilities and play with them. Catholic imagery has a kind of ruthlessness anyway—the bleeding Jesus, the pierced, suffering saints. But even without a Catholic background, Spielberg is as ruthlessly manipulative as Scorsese or De Palma (though he doesn't rely on instinct as much as they do—he plans, like Eisenstein). Film is their common religion. For some people in the audience, their films may be too shocking; they overwhelm us emotionally in a way that more crudely manipulative directors don't, and so people tend to become much more outraged by a *Taxi Driver* than by a *Towering Inferno.*

New action films often seem to be trying so hard to beat the tube that they reach right out to grab us—not with the technique of a Steven Spielberg but by crowding out any aesthetic distance. There has always been an element of dread in the pleasure of suspense movies, but it was tangled up with childish, fairy-tale excitement and the knowledge that the characters we cared about would come out safe; the dread was part of the fun. But in many current movies the suspense is nothing more than dread. The only thing that keeps us watching some films is the fear of what the moviemakers are going to throw at us next. We don't anticipate the climactic scenes pleasurably; we await them anxiously, and after the usual two hours of assault the punishment stops, and we go home relieved, yet helplessly angry.

On the basis that they can't say they were bored, large numbers of people seem willing to accept heavily advertised shock-and-dread pictures (such as *Marathon Man*) as entertainment. But in a neat cultural switch, a sizable number of educated people who used to complain of Hollywood's innocuous pampering, and who went to foreign films for adult entertainment, now escape to bland French romances, such as the Lelouch pictures or *Cousin, Cousine,* to find the same innocent reassurance that the mass audience used to obtain. They've become afraid of American movies, and not just of the junk but of *The Godfather, Part II, Nashville,* and the best this country has to offer. They're turning to Europe for cuddly sentiments—for make-out movies. The success of *Cousin, Cousine,* a rhythmless, mediocre piece of moviemaking, may be in part attributable to its winsome heroine (Marie-Christine Barrault), who is sexy in a fleshy smiling-nun way, and in part to its silliness. With its wholesome carnality, *Cousin, Cousine* is so pro-life that it treats sex like breakfast cereal. It features adultery without dirt—adultery as carefree nonconformity—and the way the chorus of understanding kids applauds the parents' displays of innocent happy sensuality this could be the first Disney True Life Adventure about people.

The New Yorker, November 8, 1976

CARRIE
THE CURSE

Carrie is a terrifyingly lyrical thriller. The director, Brian De Palma, has mastered a teasing style—a perverse mixture of comedy and horror and tension, like that of Hitchcock or Polanski, but with a lulling sensuousness. He builds our apprehensions languorously, softening us for the kill. You know you're being manipulated, but he works in such a literal way and with so much candor that you have the pleasure of observing how he affects your susceptibilities even while you're going into shock. Scary-and-funny must be the greatest combination for popular entertainment; anything-and-funny is, of course, great—even funny-and-funny. But we come out of a movie like *Carrie,* as we did out of *Jaws,* laughing at our own childishness. It's like watching our team win a ballgame—we're almost embarrassed at how bracing it is.

This little gothic in a high-school setting has a script by Lawrence D. Cohen taken from Stephen King's unassuming potboiler about a miserable, repressed high-school senior—the daughter of a fanatically religious woman—who has never been accepted by other kids. Carrie (Sissy Spacek) is so withdrawn that she's a slug; her energy is released only telekinetically, in small ways that people don't recognize. (Objects have a habit of crashing when she's around.) At the beginning of the movie, she has her first period—at sixteen—in the gym shower, and doesn't know what's happened.

She panics—she thinks she's bleeding to death. Her ignorance makes her a scapegoat for the other girls in the gym; their ugly feelings about their own periods erupt, and, like junior versions of Russ Meyer's Supervixens, they laugh hysterically and pelt her with tampons and sanitary napkins. The gym teacher penalizes them for their cruelty, and a few of them scheme to get even with Carrie. Their plan is to have her elected prom queen and then humiliate her publicly. What we see that they don't see is the depth of Carrie's desire to be accepted by them. Her joy at having Tommy, the most popular boy in the class, ask her to the prom and at becoming prom queen transforms her; her home life is so horrible that this is her first taste of feeling beautiful, and she's a radiant Cinderella. De Palma, a master sadist, prolongs her moments of happiness; he slows the action down to a trance while we wait for the trap to be sprung, knowing that it will unloose her bottled-up telekinetic anger. It's a beautiful plot—a teen-age Cinderella's revenge. *Carrie* becomes a new trash archetype, and De Palma, who has the wickedest baroque sensibility at large in American movies, points up its archetypal aspects by parodying the movies that have formed it—and outclassing them.

De Palma was born in 1940 and started moviemaking when he was a sophomore at Columbia, in 1959. *Carrie* is his tenth feature. His eighth, *Phantom of the Paradise,* a rock-horror satire, was, I thought, an underground-movie explosion—a slapstick Guignol mad ball—but it got a substantially bad press and is just now going into general release. His ninth, *Obsession,* though no more than an exercise in style, with the camera swirling around nothingness, was great on-the-job training for *Carrie.* Here, the layered gags that have always been his specialty are joined to his new sweeping, circling camera movements. In the Joyce Carol Oates story "Where Are You Going, Where Have You Been?" a teen-age girl's desire for romance also turns into a teen-age nightmare, but the story has the ineluctable *National Enquirer* horror that often makes one recoil from Oates, wanting to go on reading yet not sure if one can bear what's coming. De Palma's humor—his delight in trashiness—saves us from that kind of distress. *Carrie* is a menstrual joke—a *film noir* in red. This picture has some of the psychic grip of *Taxi Driver,* yet isn't frightening in the same way, because it's essentially a pretty piece of paste jewelry. *Carrie* looks like a piece of candy: when De Palma is most distinctive, his work calls up so many junky memories it's pure candied exploitation—a funny archetypal nightmare. De Palma uses tawdriness as a tuning fork. No one else has ever caught the thrill that teen-agers get from a dirty joke and sustained it for a whole picture.

There are no characters in *Carrie;* there are only schlock artifacts. The performers enlarge their roles with tinny mythic echoes; each is playing a whole cluster of remembered pop figures. Sissy Spacek's Carrie goes to Bates High—Norman Bates ran the motel in *Psycho*—and her gym-shower scene is a variation on the famous *Psycho* shower. At home, Carrie is the unloved Patty Duke in the early scenes of *The Goddess,* but when, having made herself a dress, she goes to the prom, she's also Katharine Hepburn in *Alice Adams,* and when she's with her yellow-haired escort, the sensitive jock Tommy (William Katt), they're a puppy-love version of Streisand and Redford in *The Way We Were.* ("Love Among the Stars" is the theme the students have selected for their prom.) After Carrie's fall from grace, she's a teen-ager gone bad, an avenging angel with a fiery sword. At her command, fire hoses stand up like hissing serpents and attack her schoolmates, and she moves through the pandemonium with psychedelic grace, as remote as the queen in *She.*

De Palma has a background in theatre as well as in film; he's very canny about young performers (in his first, shoestring feature, *The Wedding Party,* he used Jill Clayburgh and Robert De Niro), and he appears to have had a freedom in casting which wasn't evident in *Obsession.* William Katt doesn't just look like Redford but acts like a fantasy of Redford at seventeen. The dark girl with the frizzies who persuades Tommy to take Carrie to the prom is played by Amy Irving; this girl's involvement in trapping Carrie is left too ambiguous, but Amy Irving is affectingly troubled in every scene she has, right up to the film's last shocker, when De Palma does a triumphant reprise of a poorly staged bit in *Deliverance.* (The shocker here is as startling as Finlay Currie's appearance in the graveyard in *Great Expectations.)* The older "normal" characters don't have much life; there's no ricochet effect from the movies they're drawn from, and they're just puppets. But the high-school students—each with a whopper crop of hair—bounce off the beach-party movies and *Peyton Place* and *Splendor in the Grass* and *American Graffiti.* The villains, the exuberant, beer-guzzling Billy (John Travolta, who might be Warren Beatty's lowlife younger brother) and his bitchy girlfriend Chris (Nancy Allen), with her lewd dimples and puffed ringlets, have the best dialogue—their language is so stunted that every second word is profane. When these two make out in a car, Andy Hardy is brought up to date: besieged by a voracious female, he's the Neanderthal stud in a porno. Later, when Billy and Chris are enjoying their viciousness to Carrie, they have a bile-green tinge like Margaret Hamilton in *The Wizard of Oz.*

Though few actresses have distinguished themselves in gothics, Sissy Spacek, who is onscreen almost continuously, gives a classic chameleon performance. She shifts back and forth and sideways: a nasal, whining child pleading for her mother's love, each word scratching her throat as it comes out; a chaste young beauty at the prom; and then a second transformation when her destructive impulses burst out and age her. Sissy Spacek uses her freckled pallor and whitish eyelashes to suggest a squashed, froggy girl who could go in any direction; at times, she seems unborn—a fetus. I don't see how this performance could be any better; she's touching, like Elizabeth Hartman in one of her victim roles, but she's also unearthly—a changeling. Though her showiest scenes are the luminous moments with her fresh-faced, lion-maned young Redford, her acting range is demonstrated in the scenes with her loony mother—played by Piper Laurie, in a spectacular return to the screen. (Her last film was *The Hustler,* in 1961). They're marvel-lously matched, and they perform duets on themes heard earlier from Tues-day Weld and Lola Albright in *Lord Love a Duck.* The skinny, croaking Carrie, with her long, straight reddish-gold hair, and the ripe woman, with her mass of curly red hair and deep, pipe-organ voice (the chest tones of an evangelist or of a woman giving testimony in church), are beautiful in such different Pre-Raphaelite ways that their scenes go beyond the simple mother-daughter conflicts of the rather crude script. Piper Laurie's face is soft—she's like a rosy Elizabeth Taylor—and you feel that the daughter is bound to her by ties of love and pain. This fundamentalist mother is pow-erful and sexy, yet she sees herself as a virgin damaged by sex. When the wounded daughter retaliates against her mother's assault, and the kitchen utensils fly into Mama, pinning her like St. Sebastian, Piper Laurie's face is relaxed and at peace—she's a radiant martyr in a chromo. Like Buñuel, De Palma has a sacrilegious sense of humor; he plays with a sense of sin.

The director James Whale worked sophisticated parody into some of his horror films, such as *The Old Dark House,* in 1932, and *The Bride of Franken-stein,* in 1935, but I don't think that before *Carrie* anyone had ever done a satiric homage to exploitation films. Who but De Palma would think of us-ing old-movie trash, and even soft-core pornos, to provide "heart" for a thriller? The banal teen-age movie meanness that the kids show toward Carrie gets the audience rooting for her, and it becomes the basis for her supernatural vengeance. This is the first time a De Palma picture has had heart—which may explain why De Palma, despite his originality, has never made it into the big winners' circle before. I liked the surreal sophomoric humor of his 1968 X-rated *Greetings,* with its draft-dodger hero; the style was deliberately offhand. In those days, De Palma didn't move the camera much; he used a lot of single-camera setups that went on for several min-utes—he let the actors play out their scenes. When he did move the camera, sometimes the movement was itself a gag—a parody of film "magic." His early films were cheaply made and badly distributed, but even so they didn't score with young audiences as they should have scored. Maybe this was the audiences' fault as much as his. Like some others of us, he probably as-sumed that counterculture movie-lovers had much hipper tastes than they turned out to have; they didn't go for the old patriotic, pro-war sentimental-ity, but they wanted more emotion and romance than De Palma, with his sense of the ridiculous, provided. However, he was always primarily a creator of comedy, an entertainer, so if the audience wouldn't change, he had to.

By the time of *Obsession,* De Palma had dropped his theatrical play-out-the-scene style; rock had unified the wild *Phantom of the Paradise,* but the camera itself did it for *Obsession.* He made a romantic movie without, as far as I can judge, a single romantic impulse; he was proving that he could tell a fluid, rhythmed story—that he could master camera magic. It was all calculation—camera movements designed to make an audience swoon. If the De Palma spirit was barely in evidence in *Obsession,* that was because the romantic conception operated on only one level; it lacked humor—this is where Paul Schrader, its scenarist, is weak (a weakness compensated for by the director and actors in Schrader's *Taxi Driver*). And *Obsession* lacked good, cheap dirt. In *Greetings*, Allen Garfield had hawked stag films; De Niro was a voyeur making Peep Art films in both *Greetings* and De Palma's *Hi, Mom!* After the rarefied phoniness of *Obsession*, De Palma has come back to his own exploitation themes in *Carrie;* the voyeur has got into the girls' locker room this time, bringing that romanticizing, hypnotic camera with him. De Palma was always a sexual wit; now he's a voluptuary wit, with the camera coming very close to Sissy Spacek's body, and with closeups of her wraithlike, hair-veiled face. We know her skin better than we know our own.

The technique is so absorbing that I don't think I blinked during *Carrie.* I assume that a virtuoso combination of the spiky editing of Paul Hirsch and the special effects by Gregory M. Auer is what gives us images such as Carrie's eye exploding a car. Mario Tosi's slithering cinematography seemed especially effective in Carrie's California-gothic home, and I assume that the art directors, William Kenny and Jack Fisk, made that possible. The music for *Obsession* was so emotive that the picture drowned in its score; the Pino Donaggio music for *Carrie* is modest and inoffensive, though more derivative than one might like. There are only a few places where the film seems to crr in technique. The speeded-up sound when the high-school boys are trying on tuxedos is a dumb, toy effect. And at the prom, when Carrie sees red, the split-screen footage is really bad: the red tint darkens the image, and there's so much messy action going on in the split sections that the confusion cools us out. But the film is built like a little engine, and it gets to us.

For a sophisticated, absurdist intelligence like De Palma's, there's no way to use camera magic except as foolery. He's uncommitted to anything except successful manipulation; when his camera conveys the motion of dreams, it's a lovely trick. He can't treat a subject straight, but that's all right; neither could Hitchcock. If De Palma were an artist in another medium—say, fiction or poetry—he might be a satirist with a high reputation and a small following. Everything in his films is distanced by his persistent adolescent kinkiness; he's gleefully impersonal. Yet, working in movies, he's found his own route to a mass audience: his new trash heart is the ultimate De Palma joke.

The New Yorker, November 22, 1976

NETWORK
HOT AIR

In *Network*, Paddy Chayefsky blitzes you with one idea after another. The ideas don't go together, but who knows which of them he believes, anyway? He's like a Village crazy bellowing at you: blacks are taking over, revolutionaries are taking over, women are taking over. He's got the New York City hatreds, and ranting makes him feel alive. There *is* something funny in this kind of rant—it was funny in Fred Wiseman's *Welfare*, too; with the number of things that are going wrong in the city, it's a bottomless comedy to see people pinning their rage on some one object, person, or group, or a pet collection of them. Cabdrivers used to get it off on Mayor Lindsay, liberals on the moon landings, and now Chayefsky's getting it off on television. Television, he says, is turning us into morons and humanoids; people have lost the ability to love. Who—him? Oh, no, the blacks, the revolutionaries, and a power-hungry executive at the UBS network named Diana Christensen (Faye Dunaway). In Chayefsky's 1958 movie *The Goddess,* the Marilyn Monroe-type heroine (Kim Stanley) sought movie stardom, fame, and adulation in order to compensate for her inability to love. This empty girl was supposed to symbolize our dreams; moviegoers were his morons then. Chayefsky said in 1958 that his heroine "represents an entire generation that came through the Depression with nothing left but a hope for comfort and security. Their tragedy lies in that they never learned to love, either their fellow humans or whatever god they have." God and love came together in his 1959 play *The Tenth Man,* which ended with an old man saying of the hero, whose demon (of lovelessness) had been exorcised, "He still doesn't believe in God—he simply wants to love—and when you stop and think about it, gentlemen, is there any difference?" This mushy amalgam of God and love is Chayefsky's faith, and if you don't share it you're tragic. The new goddess, the unprincipled career girl Diana Christensen, is explained in *Network* in these terms: "She's television generation. She learned life from Bugs Bunny. The only reality she knows comes to her over the TV set." What Chayefsky is really complaining about is what barroom philosophers have always complained about: the soulless worshippers at false shrines—the younger generation.

In Chayefsky's last film, *The Hospital* (1971), the fiftyish Jewish chief of medicine (George C. Scott) has lost his potency, fails at suicide, and is disappointed in his children; he blows off steam about what's wrong with the society but ridicules the Puerto Rican community-action groups who march on the hospital. After an affair with a young Wasp (Diana Rigg), who urges him to leave with her, he decides that *somebody* has to be decent and responsible, and so, with his potency restored, he stays to make his stand for sanity. Youth-baiting played a strong part in *The Hospital,* but Chayefsky's slapstick exaggeration of the chaos in a big-city institution has so much silly, likable crackpot verve that the diatribes against the disrespectful younger generation could be shrugged aside. *Network,* however, is all baiting—youth, TV, the culture, the universe. The UBS network has been taken over by a conglomerate, and Howard Beale (Peter Finch), a veteran anchorman whose ratings have slipped, is given two weeks' notice by executives who want to jazz up the news to make it more entertaining. Angry at being dumped, Beale goes out of control, and his blasts on the air about "this demented slaughterhouse of a world we live in"—blasts sprinkled with cusswords—accomplish what his restrained behavior didn't: his ratings go up. His best friend, the head of the news division—the fiftyish hero, Max Schumacher (William Holden), who is Paddy Chayefsky in the guise of the unimpeachable Ed Murrow—loses his fight to keep the news independent. The chief of operations (Robert Duvall) fires him and turns the news division over to Diana Christensen, the vice-president in charge of programming. So when Beale begins to have visions (either he's having a breakdown or he's in a state of religious exaltation) and is advertised as "the Mad Prophet of the airwaves," Schumacher is on the sidelines, and has nothing to do but hang around Diana Christensen, with whom he has an affair, and denounce her, television, and us soulless masses. The Mad Prophet and the sane prophet both deliver broadsides—enough to break a viewer's back. The screen seems to be plastered with bumper stickers.

The central gag in *Network*—Howard Beale becomes the first man killed because of lousy ratings—sounds like a good premise for a farce about TV, which has certainly earned farce status. (And, even if it hadn't, satire doesn't have to be fair to be funny.) But in the *Network* script Chayefsky isn't writing a farce: he's telling us a thing or two. And he writes directly to the audience—he soapboxes. He hardly bothers with the characters; the movie is a ventriloquial harangue. He thrashes around in messianic God-love booziness, driving each scene to an emotional peak. When Schumacher tells his wife (Beatrice Straight) that he's in love with Diana, his wife launches into a high-powered speech about "all the senseless pain that we've inflicted on each other," referring to his affair as "your last roar of passion before you settle into your menopausal years." It's a short, self-contained soap opera; she hits her peak—then she's invisible again. The director, Sidney Lumet, keeps the soliloquies going at a machine-gun pace. The movie might have been modelled on that earlier talk binge, Billy Wilder's *One, Two, Three;* Lumet is right—it's best not to let the words sink in. With Schumacher experiencing a "winter passion" and discussing his "primal doubts," you have to hurtle through to the next crisis. Lumet does Chayefsky straight, just as Chayefsky no doubt wanted. The film looks negligently made; the lighting bleaches the actors' faces, like color TV that needs tuning, and the New York views outside the office and apartment windows feel like blown-up photographs. The timing in most of the scenes is so careless that you may be aware of the laugh lines you're not responding to, and there's a confusing cut from Diana and Schumacher planning to go to bed together to Howard

Beale in bed by himself. *Network* even fails to show the executives at meetings getting carried away by the infectiousness of Diana Christensen's ideas—getting high on power. But Lumet keeps it all moving.

Chayefsky is such a manic bard that I'm not sure if he ever decided whether Howard Beale's epiphanies were the result of a nervous breakdown or were actually inspired by God. Yet Beale's story has a fanciful, Frank Capra nuttiness that could be appealing. Peter Finch's sleepy-lion head suggests the bland, prosperous decay of an anchorman whose boredom is swathed in punditry. His gray aureole is perfect: the curly, thick hair, cropped short, is the only vigorous thing about him. (Does Finch, who is British-Australian, seem American? Not really, but then does Eric Sevareid, who comes from North Dakota?) If Chayefsky meant Beale to represent his idealized vision of the crusading mandarin journalists of an earlier day who are now being replaced by show-biz anchorpersons, Finch is miscast, but his fuzzy mildness is likable, and in a picture in which everybody seems to take turns at screaming (Robert Duvall screams the loudest) Finch's ability to seem reserved even when he's raving has its own satirical charm. Unfortunately, when Beale's wild-eyed ramblings are supposed to make his ratings zoom up, you can't believe it; he doesn't give off enough heat.

Beale the Prophet's big moment comes when he tells TV viewers to open their windows, stick out their heads, and yell, "I'm mad as hell and I'm not going to take this anymore!" But is the viewers' obedience proof of their sheeplike response to TV or is it evidence that the Prophet has struck a nerve—that the public is as fed up as he is? Considering that the entire picture is Chayefsky sticking his head out the window and yelling (in Chayefsky's world, that's how you prove that you're capable of love), it must be that Beale's message is supposed to be salutary. Yet there's no follow-through on this scene, and that's where the movie goes completely on the fritz. Chayefsky whirrs off in other directions—Max's winter passion for Diana, and the Saudi Arabians taking over the conglomerate.

Early on, Howard Beale is awakened at night by the voice of the Lord or some Heavenly Messenger, who affectionately calls him "Dummy" and tells him what he must do on the air. The voice may be simply Beale's delusion, but how are we to interpret the turn of events when Beale is summoned to a meeting with the piggy-eyed master salesman Arthur Jensen (Ned Beatty), the head of the conglomerate, and Jensen addresses him as "Dummy"? Jensen, a corn-pone Grand Inquisitor, tells Beale that the multinational corporate state is the natural order of things now, and that he should embrace this one-business world, in which all men will be taken care of as humanoids. Converted, Beale asks the TV audience, "Is dehumanization such a bad word?" He preaches his new corporate faith—"The world is a business . . . one vast, ecumenical holding company." But people don't want to hear that their individual lives are valueless; he loses his ratings and is killed for it. Chayefsky, it seems, can be indignant about people becoming humanoids, and then turn a somersault and say it's inevitable and only a fool wouldn't recognize that. And he's wrong on both counts. There are a lot of changes in the society which can be laid at television's door, but soullessness isn't one of them. TV may have altered family life and social intercourse; it may have turned children at school into entertainment seekers. But it hasn't taken our souls, any more than movies did, or the theatre and novels before them. I don't know what's worse—Beale's denunciations of the illiterate public (Chayefsky apparently thinks that not reading is proof of soullessness) or Schumacher's pitying tone. When Schumacher tells Diana Christensen that she can feel nothing, while he's O.K. because he can feel pleasure and pain and love, you want to kick him. Doesn't Chayefsky realize that everybody can feel—even a kittycat?

The screw-up inside Chayefsky's message of kindness shows in the delight he takes in snide reactionary thrusts. Diana Christensen has no difficulty coöpting an Angela Davis-like activist (Marlene Warfield), the Communist central committee, and an extremist group that's a parody of the Symbionese Liberation Army and the Black Panthers. (Chayefsky can't even resist a sideswipe at Patty Hearst.) Christensen propositions them to perform terrorist crimes—kidnappings, robberies, hijackings—on a weekly basis, in front of a camera crew, and their only quarrel is over money. Whatever one's disagreements with Angela Davis, she's hardly a sellout. Yet Chayefsky's venom is such an exuberant part of him that the best scene in the movie is the slapstick negotiating session in which the black revolutionaries, their agents, and the network attorneys haggle over residuals and syndication rights, and a revolutionary who wants to be heard fires his pistol to get some order. This is in the paranoid-comic-strip style of Norman Wexler, the scriptwriter for *Joe*, *Serpico*, and *Mandingo*. Chayefsky's speeches may be about humanism, but baiting gets the old adrenalin going.

And what of Diana Christensen, the hopped-up *Cosmopolitan* doll with power on the brain? Look at her name: the goddess of the hunt, and some sort of essence of Christianity? In bed, on top of Schumacher, she talks ratings until orgasm. Chayefsky, in interviews, actually claims that he has created one of the few movie roles in which a woman is treated as an equal; this can be interpreted to mean that he thinks women who want equality are ditsey little twitches—ruthless, no-souled monsters who take men's jobs away from them. Diana Christensen is, Schumacher says "television incarnate"— that is, she is symptomatic of what's spoiling our society. And, in case we don't get Chayefsky's drift, he presents us with that contrasting image of a loving woman who has the capacity for suffering—Max's wife, to whom he returns after he leaves rotten Diana.

As Schumacher, Holden is in good form, and now that he has stopped trying to conceal the aging process his sunken-cheeked, lined, craggy face takes the camera marvellously—he has a real face, like Gabin or Montand. He does a lot for the movie—he's an actor with authority and the gift of never being boring—but he can't energize the phoniness of a man who claims to be superior to his society. This hero is trampling out the vintage where the sour grapes of wrath are stored. Dunaway chatters as Kim Stanley did in *The Goddess* (Chayefsky must believe that women talk because of their tinny empty-headedness), and even when she's supposed to be reduced to a pitiful shell by Holden's exposing her "shrieking nothingness" she's ticky and amusingly greedy. She snarls at underlings and walks with a bounce and a wiggle. In the past, Dunaway hasn't had much humor or variety; her performances have usually been proficient yet uneventful—there's a certain heaviness, almost of depression, about them. It's that heaviness, probably, that has made some people think her Garboesque. A beautiful woman who's as self-conscious as Faye Dunaway has a special neurotic magnetism. (The far less proficient Kim Novak had it also.) In this stunt role, her usual self-consciousness is turned into comic rapport with the audience; she's not the remote, neurotic beauty—she's more of a clown. And though her Diana isn't remotely convincing—she's not a woman with a drive to power, she's just a dirty Mary Tyler Moore—it's a relief to see Dunaway being light. She puts us on the side of the humanoids.

The watered-down Freudianism that Chayefsky goes in for—i.e., people want fame or power because they're sick—seems to get by almost everywhere these days. It became popular with those analysts who, taking Hitler's crimes as evidence, deduced that he was sexually crippled; they really seemed to think they were explaining something. And it spread in TV drama and in movies as a form of vindictive, moralizing condescension. The trick in *Network*, as in *The Goddess,* is to use a woman's drive toward fame or success as the embodiment of the sickness in the society. What's implicit is that if she could love she wouldn't need anything more. You couldn't get by with this bulling if a man were television incarnate. *Network* starts in high gear and is so confidently brash that maybe people can really take it for muckraking. But it's no more than the kind of inside story that a lot of TV executives probably would secretly like to write. Chayefsky comes on like a patriarchal Jackie Susann, and he likes to frolic with the folksy occult. What happened to his once much-vaunted gift for the vernacular? Nothing exposes his claims to be defending the older values as much as the way he uses four-letter words for chortles. It's so cheap you may never want to say ****
again. Chayefsky doesn't come right out and tell us why he thinks TV is *goyish*, but it must have something to do with his notion that all feeling is Jewish.

The New Yorker, December 6, 1976

LUMIÈRE

Every time Jeanne Moreau opens her mouth in *Lumière,* a *pensée* drops out. As the international screen star Sarah Dedieu, she is so solicitous of everyone's welfare that when she isn't reciting bits of Gallic wisdom of the heart or quoting weighty lines from Ingmar Bergman she picks up a book that's handily close by and reads us an enriching passage. It's no wonder, then, that lovers swarm all over Sarah and that her friends adore her—she gives fully of herself to each, and the lowliest worker on the set of the movie she's starring in may expect her loving consideration.

This appears to be how Moreau sees herself, and how she wants us to see her—as an impulsive, Colette-like woman eagerly sniffing a visiting friend's new perfume, or putting nasturtiums into a salad and serving it charmingly with her fingertips. The film, which marks her début as a director and also as a scenarist, is made up of treasured scraps; the script suggests a process of accretion rather than writing. Even the name Sarah Dedieu has the highest associations: not only Bernhardt but "Rachel when from the Lord," the actress about whom Proust speculated on "the power of the human imagination, the illusion on which were based the pains of love"; and, like Rachel, Sarah has had a lover named Saint-Loup. For a first film, the title *Lumière* is superbly confident, a dazzling pun, calling up not only the Creation, and Louis Lumière, the pioneer filmmaker who photographed actual events, but also the bright lights that theatrical people live in, the glow that stars give off, and the cry that is traditionally heard on movie sets—"Lights, camera, action!" The meaning is essentially the same as Chaplin's *Limelight,* and *Lumière* is perhaps the most elevated daydream of an actor's life since Chaplin's Calvero performed at a gala benefit, demonstrating to those who thought him a has-been that he was still the greatest performer of them all, and then died in the wings as the applause faded.

Watching the movie is rather like attending a queen's levee. Sarah awakes, sits up in her pomegranate-red nightie, her hair freshly done, as her servant brings in her fan mail. Admitted into her world of friends, we can see that she has no fears about her work, no pangs of anxiety about aging, no paranoia about the new actresses coming up. In the course of a week, she discards one lover firmly, honestly and takes on another—predestined for her, she feels. She visits the laboratory of Grégoire (François Simon), a cadaverous biologist, an ascetic so devoted to her that he is a husband in all but sex, and she listens to his scientific discourse with an absorption that makes us feel like bums: she does not merely understand science, she understands it with her whole soul. They walk together in white corridors that are like the inside of a machine; truly they are in a different world. At the end of the week, she wins something like the Academy Award, except it's at a ceremony where she is the only one being honored, and her girl friends and boy friends are all there, gathered round, to be happy for her. This bliss-out is the movie every actress must at some point have dreamed of making. Inadvertently, *Lumière* becomes a film about an actress's narcissism.

When word is brought to Sarah that her platonic husband was dying of a disease contracted because of his dedication to his work, and has killed himself, the camera moves in for a closeup. But she cannot react. We are invited to admire the virtuosity of her shocked impassivity. "That light," she complains. *"Le soleil m'enmerde."* Ah, yes, her star's ambience has blinded her to his suffering. Her grief must be terrible to be so bottled up. Then she goes to her movie set, takes off her flaming pomegranate cape, and, dressed appropriately in a Hamlet black tuxedo, breaks down. You feel you should applaud.

Jeanne Moreau has always made love to the camera—in effect, to the director. She has had her own way of changing her emotional coloring—surprising the director, entrancing him. The most dismaying aspect of *Lumière* is that she's making love to herself. In the sixties, Moreau used to say that she liked directors to decide for her what they wanted her to do, because "the ideas you can have about yourself are not very interesting." She said, "I think it is much better to see yourself through somebody's eyes." She was right. It's one thing to be seen as a goddess; it's quite another to see yourself as a goddess. And she was right when she discussed her "mystery" as "the director's mystery, for him to unravel." Of all the performers one can think of, she is probably the one who would naturally suffer the most from directing herself. The great thing about those sulky women she played in the early sixties was how little they said and how much they implied. Now that she's laying on the aphorisms, she isn't implying a thing. The flip-overs from mood to mood are visible, and there's nothing underneath to hold the tricks together.

Lumière suggests a refined, thin-blooded *All About Eve*. That American film is so telegraphic in style that the characters seem to be talking in headlines, but here the conversation is so gracefully marginal that you long for a headline or two. Sarah is offered to us as a chic, theatrical version of an earth mother, and as she drifts from appointment to appointment everything basic is left out. Moreau once said, "When I see something I want, I go *right* for it. I really won't let *anything* stand in my way. Shame, self-respect—nothing can stop me. I *always* get what I want." A decade later, she presents us with considerate, thoughtful Sarah Dedieu. But we never cared about whether Jeanne Moreau was nice; the point was, we couldn't take our eyes off her. We can, now that she's gone soft on herself; there is no strength of any kind in *Lumière*.

Rarely has there been so much camera movement to such static effect. The film is full of "artful touches": the camera plays peekaboo, or swirls whimsically, without dramatic impetus; a pair of women are photographed back to back, in a reversal of Bergman's face-to-face encounters; Sarah's shade of red turns up on her lovers—everybody in the movie is color-coördinated with her. In a prelude, shot in Moreau's house near Saint-Tropez, a quartet of holidaying actresses exchange confidences, and we are alerted that this is going to be a gentle, woman's view of women. The relaxed intimacy among the four is unlike the views of women's friendships which men directors have given, but it's a little too sun-sweetened; we seem to be in an idealized girls' dormitory, or an overage budding grove. The most animated moments in the movie involve Julienne (Francine Racette) and Caroline (Caroline Cartier), who probably represent Sarah at earlier stages in her life, just as Laura (Lucia Bosè), who has married rich, retired from the theatre, and become a little dull, probably represents what might have happened to Sarah if she had quit. As a director, Moreau brings out the possibilities in the young actresses. Francine Racette, a tall brunette, indecently pretty and with a monkey grin, is like a showgirl Katharine Hepburn; she has the popping-out-of-her-skin sexiness of the glittering Parisiennes of thirties movies—Jacqueline Delubac in the Guitry films, or Mireille Balin in *Pépé le Moko*. While Moreau sees the comedy in the seduction scene that Racette plays with a visiting American (Keith Carradine), Sarah's passions are treated with the utmost earnestness, even though she appears to have excruciating taste in men. The lover she sends packing is a mewling infant, and her new predestined soul mate (Bruno Ganz), a German writer whose books she says have "invaded my mind," is clammy and passive. But no one in the film expresses any awareness of her predilection for weak, asexual men, and her romantic scenes with the somber Ganz, which are a killing mixture of *La Notte* and *Now, Voyager,* are played absolutely straight, even when she rests her head, pictorially, on his manly shoulder. When Sarah is with her women friends, the scenes are arranged so that she can embrace them and be infinitely supportive and generous. The picture is a valentine to a wonderful woman's life of art and love. It shares a weakness of many other high-flown junk movies: it is less interested in pace than in culture.

Lumière is delicately dissociated; it nibbles around the edges of its subject, and this can be taken as feminine sensibility. But this is also what has given feminine sensibility a bad name. The affectation of *Lumière* is that its heroine is closer to the earth than men are, and yet has higher, more spiritual feelings than men. Which is where many men, too, have wanted to place women—leaving them out of the middle range, where the action is. There is no middle range in Moreau's picture—nothing between innocent girlish sensuality and poetic conceits. Jeanne Moreau keeps herself in too good a light. The film never rings true: it's a wrong-note sonata.

The New Yorker, December 20, 1976

KING KONG

The greatest misfit in movie history makes a comeback in the new *King Kong*. Monster, pet, misunderstood kid, unrequited lover, all in one grotesquely oversized body, the innocent ape is martyred once again. I wanted a good time from this movie, and that's what I got. It's a romantic adventure fantasy—colossal, silly, touching, a marvellous Classics-comics movie.

Kong has become a pop deity in the years since the 1933 version came out, and the tone of the new film, directed by John Guillermin, from a script by Lorenzo Semple, Jr., is different from that of the first. It had to be, since we know what's coming. Semple turns our knowledge to advantage by giving the characters lines that are jokes on them. Yet, with this *Beat the Devil* edge to the dialogue, the romantic appeal of the material is, if anything, even stronger this time around. The film doesn't have the magical primeval imagery of the first version; it doesn't have the Gustave Doré fable atmosphere. It's big in a much simpler, clunkier way, but it's also a happier, livelier entertainment. The first *Kong* was a stunt film that was trying to awe you, and its lewd underlay had a carnival hucksterism that made you feel a little queasy. This new *King Kong* isn't a horror movie—it's an absurdist love story. Taking into account the feelings that have developed about Kong, the moviemakers have pared the theme down to that of the instinctive animal-man of the collegiate graffiti: "King Kong died for our sins." (The hair on the college kids is noble-savage hair, and Kong has more of it than anybody.) The film moves unhurriedly, in a clean, straightforward progression to the ritual love-death. When the forty-foot Kong stands bleeding and besieged at the top of the World Trade Center, and his blonde (Jessica Lange) pleads with him to pick her up, so that the helicopters won't shoot at him, even Wagner's dreams seem paltry. This is opera at its campiest, yet that doesn't mean our feelings don't soar. We might snicker at a human movie hero who felt such passion for a woman that he'd rather die than risk harming her, but who can jeer a martyr-ape?

The plot is a tale of two islands—Skull Island, where Kong is god, and Manhattan, where he is a rampaging menace. In the first version, Robert Armstrong played an explorer-showman who made jungle pictures. Just before setting sail on a highly mysterious moviemaking expedition, he went looking for an actress to provide love interest for the film; he needed somebody desperate enough to sign on, no questions asked. After casing the women in the breadlines, he spotted a blonde (Fay Wray) stealing an apple in the Bowery; an orphan who had been working as an extra at the Astoria studios, she was unemployed, starving, and ready for anything. They sailed immediately, and on board, en route to the island, the tough showman tested her for her chores by photographing her screaming for her life. The hero was Jack (Bruce Cabot), the first mate, who rescued the girl after the savages on Skull Island abducted her to be the bride of Kong.

For the updating, this trio had to be reassembled in plausibly modern terms. Semple went a step beyond that, treating the updating as a comedy, and inviting us to peg the differences between old and new. The expedition to the island is now financed by Petrox, an oil company, and it's headed by Fred (Charles Grodin), who has convinced the Petrox executives that he'll make an oil strike. An "environmental rapist" with a flat haircut, trimmed long sideburns, and a dark mustache for twirling, Fred is a snarling villain out of an animated cartoon. Grodin roots around in the comedy of measliness: Fred is so money-hungry he's funny. And he's so fatuous he's the butt of all his own remarks—like the square-riggers Ralph Bellamy used to play. Jack (still called Jack) is now a Princeton paleontologist (Jeff Bridges) who specializes in primates; having heard where the ship is going, and having a suspicion of what's to be found on the island (he's the only one who does), he sneaks on board as a stowaway. Jack is more a hitchhiking hippie than an obsessed scientist, and there's a satiric point in casting the rough-hewn Bridges in this role: As the long-haired, shaggy-bearded friend of animals, Bridges is like man in his natural state in a Time-Life book on evolution; you can see him in one of those plates with a rock in his hand, except he's got a shirt on. His Jack is the human equivalent of Kong, and, like Kong, he falls for the blonde.

Semple has hold of an idea, all right: the big corporations *are* the show-business entrepreneurs now. But in using Petrox as an ecological target he gets awfully glib and topical, and remnants of the earlier conception still turn up, because the mythic structure requires them. Grodin's pomposity is ludicrously endearing when he's the company toady in the early sections. Coming ashore and putting his foot down on Skull Island, he attempts a historical pose, like General MacArthur returning to the Philippines, and can't make it; he doesn't have the conviction of a true fraud—he's a weasel, a cluck. However, the plot requires him to shift into the Robert Armstrong–showman role, and he loses his character in the process—his later scenes have no humor. Both the men's roles are pieced together out of scraps of old and new, but they're passable.

The movie is sparked mainly, I think, by the impudent new conception of the screaming-in-fear blonde, and Jessica Lange's fast yet dreamy comic style. Her Dwan has the high, wide forehead and clear-eyed transparency of Carole Lombard in *My Man Godfrey*. Dwan, an aspiring starlet, doesn't join the expedition; she's picked up along the way, unconscious, from a rubber raft in the ocean, the sole survivor of a yachting party. The yacht belonged to a movie mogul, and she'd been on board hoping to get a part that he'd promised her. Dwan (she changed it from Dawn) is one of the cloud-borne movie groupies who lead charmed lives. The way she's photographed, she seems to have stepped out of an expensive shampoo commercial; languorous and polymorphous, like a taller Tuesday Weld or a more slightly built

Margaux Hemingway, she has the sensuousness of a kitten. Dwan is so innocently corrupt she's as childlike as Kong himself, and her infantilism gives the picture a sexual chemistry that the movie-makers couldn't have completely planned—some of it just has to be luck. She has one-liners so dumb that the audience laughs and moans at the same time, yet they're in character, and when Jessica Lange says them she holds the eye, and you like her, the way people liked Lombard.

The story is no longer an ape going for a blonde but the loneliest creature in the world—the only one of his species—finding the right playmate. Dwan is the smart nit American *femme fatale*—a daisy, impulsive, well-meaning, yet so giddy, unstable, and self-centered that you know exactly why Kong is driven to despair. The elusive Dwan is the kind of crackbrain who can delight and exasperate the most controlled of men; this poor big ape never knows what hit him. Lolita accepted Humbert Humbert's devotion with barely a flicker of interest in how desperate he was; that's how Dwan is with the Great Ape. She concentrates on what she's interested in: if you told her World War III had just started, she'd say, "Save it and tell me later, would you? I'm off to the hairdresser." Kong, brought to New York, is caged and exhibited to the public at Shea Stadium. (It was a theatre in the earlier version.) He thinks that the photographers are hurting Dwan with their flashbulbs, so he breaks his bonds, tears up the place, and chases after her. Sniffing her out, trailing her to Manhattan, the obsessed, faithful ape is like Blume in Love. When he carries her off and reaches his final destination at the top of the World Trade Center, his eyes keep saying, "Do you love me?" And Dwan can't give him a truthful answer, any more than she can give Jack a truthful answer. Neither of them holds it against her. She's forgotten the question.

The central enjoyment in the film is Dwan's relationship with Kong; she humanizes him, as Streisand humanized Redford in *The Way We Were*—she makes you love him. On the island, she talks to him the same way she might have talked to her movie mogul in a Beverly Hills bedroom. When he's got her in his paw and she screams "Put me down!" many of us women know we've played that scene, and many men will know they've played the ape. This verbal gag becomes a visual gag when Kong breaks down the gates of a high wall to get to her: it's as if a man and a woman had been having a fight and the woman had done about the most infuriating thing she could do—locked herself away from him. Dwan may seem out of contact with reality, but there's a craftiness in her—an instinct for the main chance. Even with the ape, she half believes he can do something for her, and he does—he makes her a star.

The eroticism of the earlier *Kong* was rather nightmarish, especially for women—though black women may have experienced it differently, as a slap. Whites have sometimes spoken of the movie as a racial slur, but the black men that I've known have always loved it. It was their own special urban gorilla-guerrilla fantasy: to be a king in your own country, to be brought here in chains, to be so strong that you could roar your defiance at the top of the big city and go down in a burst of glory. This time, Kong is less threatening, and the sexual references are out on top. After the Skull Island savages abduct Dwan and put her on the altar as a full-moon sacrifice to Kong, they scurry back to safety on their side of the high wall and slide a prodigiously long, slick black bolt across the gate. However, it's almost an invasion of the viewer's privacy when one of the men on the expedition (Ed Lauter) quizzes Jack about what the ape wants with Dwan. Since the conception of the movie is a phallic joke carried to the level of myth, why raise this lame, prosaic question of what Kong wants? Obviously he wants to consummate his passion, and just as obviously he can't. He's the misfit extraordinaire. Like the earlier Kong, this one has no visible genitals; he doesn't need them—Kong is a walking forty-foot genital. What makes him such a pop mythic hero is that he's also pre-phallic—the Teddy Bear Christ of the sixties flower children, Christ as a mistreated pet.

Modernizing a forty-three-year-old pop fantasy is a tricky business. One might assume that the very first thing the moviemakers would do would be to work out a more authentic view of the culture on Skull Island and get away from the African "savages" from Central Casting of the thirties version, but there isn't much way to do that without disrupting the basic story. The original *King Kong* wasn't made innocently: it was an ingeniously made exploitation picture, and camp elements are integral to it. This version accepts what the material is and treats it playfully. (Contrary to rumors, the original has not been legally withdrawn; it is still available in 16 mm. and for television, and it will be available again in 35 mm. for theatres after a discretionary period—probably a year.) Some of the new details fizzle because they haven't been changed enough, others because the changes involve dated, sophomoric counterculture attitudes. The big presentation of Kong to the public at Shea Stadium is clumsily staged, and when this Kong emulates the first and tears down an elevated train, he might be playing with an antique toy; the sequence lacks excitement—it feels half-hearted, as if Guillermin did it because it was expected of him. The direction isn't as assured in the New York footage as it is on Kong's island or on the ship, but this may be because the script is weakest here. The special effects are generally enjoyable, though the full-moon scenes on the island are dark and don't give the impression of moonlight, Kong's fight with a serpent is lackluster, and, at the end, Kong's actual fall from the World Trade Center—which cries out for a slight slowing down, for a Peckinpah poetic image—is skimped and is over before we've seen it.

There are earlier scenes that stay with one: Kong dipping Dwan in a waterfall and blowing her dry, his cheeks puffed out like a fairy-tale illustration of Zephyrus, the billowing wind god; Kong when he's trapped, his head and arm lifting out of the miasmal fumes and dropping back, then his hand rising again and falling in defeat. The original version skipped over Kong's trip to New York, but this time we see him imprisoned in the hold of a supertanker, and Kong, morose, enslaved, with the ship's crew throwing food down into his cell, is a spectacular image of a degraded king. When he roars and beats against his prison, it's like the sound of a gorilla battering the bars of his cage at the zoo, but magnified so that the whole ship is pounding. The reverberations prevent Dwan from going to bed with Jack; they're ominous—Kong is shaking the universe. There's a lovely, campy sequence with Dwan's scarf, caught in a gust of wind, drifting down to Kong in the hold, and also a visit, when Dwan falls into his prison and he catches her. This is his finest scene: knowing the pain of being a prisoner, he frees her, and is grief-stricken as she leaves.

Guillermin is rather too Spartan; he rations the use of imagination. But he has an uncluttered style; he knows what point a scene should make and why. He sets a visual tone by the clean bigness of his images and by his long takes; if the original *Kong* was nightmarish, this one has a monumental comic dreaminess. The ape is always slow; his movements as he climbs the World Trade Center have the Bruckner feeling of heavy orchestration. When Guillermin needed a little more poetry, he may have been locked into his overall style. Still, the unity of the film is impressive: it doesn't fall into the choppiness that often results from extensive use of special effects. Guillermin, who is British, directed his first feature in 1949, when he was twenty-four, and worked steadily in a variety of genres—including two Tarzan pictures (the rousing *Tarzan's Greatest Adventure,* in 1959, might have been a warmup for this *Kong)* and two with Peter Sellers (the demonic-gangster melodrama *Never Let Go* and the Anglicized, hacked-up-by-the-producer *Waltz of the Toreadors)*—before settling into big international co-productions and action films (*Guns at Batasi,* 1964; *The Blue Max,* 1966; *The Bridge at Remagen,* 1969; *Skyjacked,* 1972; and *The Towering Inferno,* 1974). This picture must have been a backbreaking series of problems, yet, with his action director's experience, he has streamlined the myth. The original *Kong* had long passages without dialogue—just Max Steiner's music heaving, shrieking, and portending doom, and Kong grunting and beating his chest in triumph. (Oscar Levant once said that the film "should have been advertised as a concert of Steiner's music with accompanying pictures on the screen.") The new score, by John Barry, doesn't heighten the imagery with quite so many premonitory rumblings; it's more of a love poem—a great big swatch of mood music sweeping you along. It gives the picture an amplitude that goes well with Guillermin's big, bright-colored storybook imagery.

In a movie of this scale, Fred's lickspittle villainy comes across as trivializing, and the virtuous scientist Jack, with his gibes about the oil company and the environment, might also seem undersized if Jeff Bridges didn't have such heroic reserves of good humor. Without his amiable slouchiness, his hand pushing his dirty-blond hair off his face, his quick, natural-sounding delivery, Jack might have been a stick. (Instead, the role may help to give Bridges the popularity that he's earned in the past few years.) There is an awkward lapse toward the end—an insert of Jack cheering as Kong rips off pieces of the World Trade Center and hurls them at his attackers. This cue to the audience to be on Kong's side cheapens everything—Kong, the picture, us. Yet the story is paced majestically, and no mistake or excess seems to matter much, since Kong himself is an emotionally consistent protagonist, whose flickering expressions—lechery, bewilderment, tenderness—amuse us at the same time that we're in thrall. The picture works because, despite what you know, you believe in Kong as a living creature. You feel bad that the ape is killed—but you also feel tickled that you feel bad.

Guillermin, his boss (the producer Dino De Laurentiis), and his associates started with a powerful, silly idea that gets to people in a special way, and some of these people may regard the remake as desecration. Others may be put off by the scale of the advertising campaign and the very concept of a twenty-four-million-dollar movie. There is an element of obscenity in this kind of moviemaking—a remake that costs more than thirty-five times what the original did, and is so plugged into merchandising idiot items that the script's ecological claims acquire an extra layer of embarrassment. Nevertheless, the moviemaking team has come up with a pop classic that can stand in our affections right next to the original version. The most meritoriously intentioned movies are often stinkers, and this epitome of commercialism turns out to be wonderful entertainment. I don't think I've ever before seen a movie that was a comic-strip great romance in the way this one is—it's a joke that can make you cry.

The New Yorker, January 3, 1977

SILVER STREAK

When Richard Pryor appears on a TV talk show and he's asked questions, sometimes you can see that his squirming isn't simple contempt for the host, it's more like boredom and frustration—creative impatience. He knows he is trapped and isn't using the best part of himself: he's being forced to speak in his own voice, and he needs to take off into a character in order to be funny. We're not after the real Richard Pryor (whoever that might be), any more than we were ever eager for the real Peter Sellers to stand up. Pryor's demons are what make people laugh. If he had played the sheriff in *Blazing Saddles,* he'd have made him *crazy*—threatening and funny, both. Pryor shouldn't be cast at all—he should be realized. He has desperate, mad characters coming out his pores, and we want to see how far he can go with them.

Pryor's comedy isn't based on suspiciousness about whites, or on anger, either; he's gone way past that. Whites are *unbelievable* to him. Playing a thief in the new mystery comedy *Silver Streak,* he's stupefied at the ignorance of the hero (Gene Wilder), and he can't believe the way this white man moves. For about fifteen minutes, Pryor gives the picture some of his craziness. Not much of it, but some—enough to make you realize how lethargic it was without him. This movie not only casts him, though—it casts him as a friend to good-guy whites. We're supposed to be touched when he returns Wilder's wallet to him and affectionately advises him to "stay loose." But when he's soft-hearted about his buddy Gene Wilder, he's a bad actor. These moments come at the tag ends of scenes and could easily have been cut. Are they the moviemakers' unconscious revenge on Pryor's craziness? He saves their picture for a few minutes—he gives it some potency and turns it into the comedy they hoped for—and they emasculate him, turn him into a lovable black man whose craziness is only a put-on. Interracial brotherly love is probably the one thing that Richard Pryor should never be required to express. It violates his demonic, frazzled blackness. The suspense built into watching him is that we don't know what's coming out of him next, or where it's coming from. Those deep-set, somewhere-else eyes and that private giggle don't tell us much, but they do tell us this: his comedy doesn't come from love-thy-white-neighbor.

Most of *Silver Streak* is set on board a train from Los Angeles to Chicago, and the picture is so apologetic that it starts with a mess of exposition, explaining why each of the principal characters didn't take a plane. Wilder plays a Los Angeles publisher of how-to-do-it books, with a specialty in gardening, and the heroine, Jill Clayburgh, is the secretary of an art historian. After much badinage about the publisher's how-to-do-it expertise in the tending of flowers (i.e., sex), they go to bed, he lies back with his arms under his head, and she proceeds to do everything. This discrepancy isn't meant to be funny. The scriptwriter, Colin Higgins, and the director, Arthur Hiller, are merely showing us how liberated she is—liberation here meaning eagerness to perform oral sex. Besides, they need to have the man lying back and the secretary bent down over him, so that he can get a clear view of what happens outside the window: a murdered man falls from the top of the train and is caught on a hook, hanging upside down for a few seconds before dropping from sight. The next morning, the hero sees the new book the secretary's boss has written, and from the jacket photograph recognizes that the art historian is the dead man. *Silver Streak* is so helplessly unslick that it doesn't even have the wit to show Wilder looking at the book upside down.

The New Yorker, January 17, 1977

THE ENFORCER

D*irty Harry,* starring Clint Eastwood as Harry Callahan, the San Francisco police inspector who embodies a higher law, was a wizardly piece of vicious, brutal filmmaking; its sequel, *Magnum Force,* was poorly made but did have some cheap nastiness; the third in the series, the new *The Enforcer,* doesn't have the savvy to be sadistic. It's just limp. Yet each film has done bigger business than its predecessor. Have people become so accustomed to the series idea from television viewing that they go to another Dirty Harry movie because it's a known quantity? It may be that moviegoing is so expensive and people have been stung so often that they want to know what they're going to get. And maybe after a couple of Dirty Harry movies they're conditioned: they no longer need Eastwood plus violence plus fantasy—all they need is to see a picture of him.

In the first of the series, if Eastwood had thought out Dirty Harry we'd have had to hate that brutally self-righteous cop. But Eastwood played Harry as a comic-book saint. By now, he appears to be taking Harry's saintliness so seriously that he's tense with indignation; Harry can't relax, because of his sense of higher duty. Eastwood has lost the ominous sensuality he had in the spaghetti Westerns. The machinery has tightened up. He looks stricken—he hisses his lines angrily, his mouth pulled thin by righteousness. Is it time for Eastwood to turn villain? This drawn, creased face could have a George Macready sinister charm. Or has he gone past that already? At the climax of *The Enforcer,* when he yells "You ******* fruit!" as he kills his enemy, he looks ready to drool and climb the walls.

The Enforcer, produced by Eastwood's own company, with a hand-picked director, James Fargo, who was the assistant director on several Eastwood pictures, uses the same basic plot strategy as the Western *The Outlaw Josey Wales,* Eastwood's previous film. It sets up a collection of villains so disgustingly cruel and inhuman that Eastwood can spend the rest of the movie killing them with a perfect conscience. The Dirty Harry movies adapt to the latest in exploitative topicality; this time Harry is up against a terrorist group, the Revolutionary Strike Force. The members of this group are not really revolutionaries, though. They're just what Archie Bunker could have told Harry they'd be: pimps and hookers, who are in it for the money. And they've been directed to sneer and leer, like a gay landlord foreclosing the mortgage on the old homestead. There's also a black militant group with a panicky guru who serves as a police informer, and, of course, the usual contingent of liberal twits running the city government. When Harry, single-handed, goes in and rescues a batch of hostages from some robbers—an act that would make him the hero of every cop in town—he's reprimanded, and suspended from duty. They wouldn't try to get by with that on "Kojak."

Though the script, by Stirling Silliphant and Dean Ricsner, is just scaffolding, and there isn't one well-written line, a fast, lurid action film could have been made out of this garbage (as was done in *Dirty Harry)* if Eastwood and Fargo had got some velocity into their chases, and if they had created the atmosphere of corruption and lurking fear that would make us accept the idea of a city imperilled by thrill-seeking mercenaries. People get killed in this movie, but the violence has no rot or meanness in it. The staging is lackadaisical; the jowly revolutionaries shoot with one eye on the time clock. Does Eastwood's production company purposely choose bad actors to surround him with—to make him look better? Probably not—probably it's the director's fault that the actors look sedated. The movie comes to an amateurish full stop while the mayor's representative on the police board—a woman—shows her lack of comprehension of police problems; the acting is so archaic you expect her to pull out a lorgnette. The one smart move the filmmakers made was to cast Tyne Daly (she played Jack Lemmon's daughter in *The Entertainer*) as the heroine—a policewoman who is assigned to work with Callahan. Deliberately unglamorous in a clumsy work suit, Tyne Daly manages to show some believably human expressions of confusion and discomfort; she has worried eyes, and she isn't afraid to let her mouth go slack. It's such a warm performance that Eastwood's holy cool seems more aberrant than ever.

Harry is the source of the only venom we see; he's the one who's rancorous and strung out. And what is he snarling about? It's not that the villains are kidnappers and murderers—their real crime is that they're homosexual. In *The Eiger Sanction,* Eastwood sneered at the decadent killer (Jack Cassidy), whose dog was named Faggot; in *Magnum Force,* he mowed down a homosexual Nazi group inside the police department; in *The Enforcer,* he's got his "fruit." Is this the last outpost for the Western hero—killing homosexuals to purify the cities?

The New Yorker, January 24, 1977

ABOUT JOHN GIELGUD IN
PROVIDENCE

Gielgud has a longer death scene than Camille's; it's the whole movie. Every line in his fat role is an overwrought blooper, and he can't create a character out of what he's been given, yet he whoops it up with a marvellous zest. His polished effrontery makes him a sight to behold, just as it did a few weeks ago on Broadway, in *No Man's Land.* These days, he seems to delight in impersonations. He did a takeoff of W. H. Auden in the Pinter play, and here, in the garden scenes, in his rattan chair, wearing an off-white suit, a pale-pink shirt, and a broad straw hat, he does a neat Cecil Beaton. God, how this old knight loves to act, loves the sound of his great singsong. There's lip-smacking joy in his dirty-old-man rant. He's lean and wiry, turkey-faced, a tough old bird—so alive to the kinetic pleasures of play-acting that he bounces through the role, savoring its pipsqueak grandeur.

The New Yorker, January 31, 1977

IN **ARTHUR**

When John Gielgud was young, he looked like a tortured aesthete; he was lean and gaunt-faced and literally a highbrow—you couldn't imagine him playing a part like Hobson, the valet in *Arthur,* who is close kin to P. G. Wodehouse's Jeeves. Though Gielgud entered movies in 1924, he has rarely appeared in screen comedies, so his skill here has an element of surprise—he may be the most poised and confident funnyman you'll ever see. Gielgud can steal a scene by simply wearing a hat; it's so crisply angled that you can't take your eyes off him—you want to applaud that perfect hat. Gielgud has become more robust with the years, and he uses his hypercultivated tones—his speech is a form of trilling—as a supreme joke. As Hobson, he appears to be amused by his own astringency, his jowls, and the pursed mouth with which he can administer rebukes. Even when Gielgud gives the driest of dry inflections to his lines, his voice mellows them out. (For true dryness, you'd have to sit through *The Legend of the Lone Ranger* to hear another great comedian, Jason Robards, as President Ulysses S. Grant, rasp out at the end, "Who is that masked man?")

The New Yorker, July 27, 1981

THE LATE SHOW

In repose, Lily Tomlin looks like a wistful pony; when she grins, her equine gums and long, drawn face suggest a friendly, goofy horse. Either way, she takes the camera and holds it for as long as she wants to, with the assurance of a star. On TV, when she does one of her characters—such as the squinchy-eyed five-and-a-half-year-old Edith Ann, sitting sly and lonely in a big chair—you feel that she is creating this character out of the possibilities in herself. She can make you respond the same way in a movie role conceived by others. In *Nashville,* she played a sane woman who knew what mattered to her, and each time that she had a scene she brought calm into the movie. As Margo in the new detective film *The Late Show,* written and directed by Robert Benton, everything she does is a little off center. Margo is a nervous talker; her perceptions are faster than her ability to process them, and her conversation is a humming sound that she barely hears.

Margo came to L.A. to be an actress, and she still has ties to show business—she's trying to manage some performers. She's also trying to start a dress-designing business, while hanging on by dealing a little grass and transporting stolen goods. That's how she gets into the trouble that the movie is about: she keeps five hundred dollars that doesn't belong to her, and the hoods she's working for take her cat, threatening to strangle it unless she pays up. At first, Margo doesn't seem very smart, or particularly likable. But then she's so exhilarated by her prowess at driving a van away from a pursuing car that she cackles in triumph and begins to fantasize a whole new life for herself, and we see the gleam as she realizes that Ira Wells (Art Carney), the old private investigator who has been trying to find her cat, may be overweight and out of condition but he's different from the other men she knows. An instant later, she suggests that they could become a team like Nick and Nora Charles. Without any encouragement from the embarrassed yet pleased senior citizen, she dreams on, higher and higher, and her euphoria is openhearted. Lily Tomlin has the magical timing to do this dizzy, difficult scene in character and make it seem totally unrehearsed. If anyone else were playing Margo, she might be a mere kook; Tomlin makes her a genuine eccentric—she isn't just the heroine, she's the picture's comic muse.

In *The Late Show,* Robert Benton has followed the rules of the detective-movie genre, but he's also added something. The movie starts with Harry (Howard Duff), another detective trying to locate Margo's cat, showing up at Ira Wells's rooming house with a bullet hole in his stomach. Ira talks to Harry, watching, in a rage of helplessness, as his old friend dies. The film prepares us for Ira's determination to find out who murdered Harry. Ira doesn't unravel the mystery for us. We discover what's going on as he does; we react with him to the frightening things that happen when you break into a motel room at night and follow a trail of blood. Ira isn't cool, or fast on the draw, or able to outwit the scummy new-style operators; he's the hero because he is none of these things and is still determined to do the job. The something that's been added to the genre is that Ira Wells is scared. He's old and he's sick, with a perforated ulcer. He's humiliated by his physical weakness, and he can't take being roughed up anymore. Yet finding Harry's killers is his only way to prove to himself that he's not over the hill. In the standard detective movie, you have to accept the detective's integrity as a given; here you really believe in Ira's integrity, because that's all that old age has left him.

Spiritually, Ira Wells might be wearing a string tie, like the old Westerner Joel McCrea played in Peckinpah's *Ride the High Country.* There's an air of Sunday-suit formality about him. He's a dignified, big man, using a hearing aid and shifting his weight painfully from one foot to the other; you think his shoes must be pinching until you discover he's been carrying lead in one leg for over twenty years. He is what a private eye of the forties movies might have come to—living alone in a furnished room, without a car, retired because any two-bit chiseller can shove him around. Unprotected, Ira lumbers into a gangster's mansion, hoping to bluff his way through, only to have his bluff called. You feel his desperation—Art Carney seems to be working inside a nightmare that he's known for a long time. He gives Ira a human gravity, which contrasts with the inconsequentiality of the sharpie killers; they're comic heavies, lightly satirized, and this makes them even more of an insult to the old man. Eugene Roche plays Birdwell, a jolly fat-man fence, who treats Ira as harmless—calls him Pop, and gives him a hand-out. As the cheating Mrs. Birdwell, who lies as unconsciously as she draws breath, Joanna Cassidy has some of the luscious sluttiness that Rita Hayworth had in the late thirties. Mrs. Birdwell might be wearing sweaty satin; she's all curves, and she has a jive come-on, like James M. Cain's dirty charmers who can persuade a man to do anything.

This is only Robert Benton's second film, but he has become a much stronger director than he was on his first, *Bad Company,* in 1972. *(The Late Show* is the first script that he has written alone; he did *Bonnie and Clyde* in collaboration with his usual writing partner, David Newman.) Benton has learned the smartest thing anybody could learn from Robert Altman, who produced this picture—to pick actors with the ability to bring the characters up out of themselves, and then to encourage them to trust themselves and each other. Each character is an original. Lily Tomlin's Margo, who wanders off in her head and loses track of what's going on around her, needs a keeper, and she finds one in Art Carney's steady, close-lipped Ira. Eugene Roche makes the despicable Birdwell one of the loosest villains ever seen. Birdwell doesn't plan his swinishness—it comes so naturally to him he just plays it by ear. Birdwell the fence is a living ode to materialism; he loves his stolen goodies—his cajoling speeches about the joys of freeloading are de-livered like comic arias. And Bill Macy, who plays Margo's scrounging bar-tender friend Charlie, is practically reborn. Macy drops the middle-class intonations and gestures familiar from his dutiful Walter Findlay in the "Maude" series; with his hair combed back and a pencil-thin mustache, Charlie is a dude lizard. He's a failed talent agent, a cruddy, marginal man—not guilty and not innocent. The jokes involving Ruth Nelson as Ira's straitlaced landlady are a little coy; the director seems to want laughs with-out having enough conviction to go after them. And though as Birdwell's natty bodyguard John Considine has one plum scene—he's forced to jump into a swimming pool and tries to protect his cashmere jacket—his role isn't much more than a comic variant of the darkly handsome lowlife sheiks that Jack La Rue used to play. Considine had the springiness of a perfect fool in the role of Annie Oakley's philandering husband in *Buffalo Bill and the In-dians,* but here we're primed to find him funny, and the movie is too subtly toned for this kind of comic relief. The performers are so good that we want more of the characters than we get—it's slightly frustrating that the script holds them in check.

The Late Show never lets up; the editing is by Lou Lombardo (who has often worked with Altman) and Peter Appleton, and I can't think of a thriller from the forties that is as tight as this, or has such sustained tension. Chuck Rosher's cinematography does what's needed without making you feel you should applaud each shot, and the music, by Ken Wannberg, with saxophone themes that shift to strings for the sultry Mrs. Birdwell's con jobs, doesn't overdo the "haunting" bit. There may be a shortcoming. We expect the clichés of the genre to crack open and they don't. Benton knew he had the writing to fall back on, and he stuck to it too closely; his balanced approach to writing and directing evens things out so that the point of the picture is muted. If Benton hadn't written the script, he might have pushed some of the situations further, so that the cutthroat nastiness would give us shivers, as in *Double Indemnity*. Perhaps if Ira were the kind of man who had to fight his own susceptibility to Mrs. Birdwell, we might be drawn in deeper. From the bullet in his leg and the framed photo of Martha Vickers (the sweet psychopath of *The Big Sleep)* in his room, we get the idea that he's been played for a fool in the past. This is his "late show," and the whole conception requires that he be beyond temptation, but the cooling of his blood distances the crime plot. The events he uncovers don't mean enough to prickle in our imaginations, especially since, except for Howard Duff's Harry, we never see any of the murder victims alive. And the solution doesn't provide enough coherence—it's a paperwork solution. *The Late Show* doesn't quite pay off in the way a thriller is expected to—in thrills. It pays off in atmosphere, spooking us by the flip, greedy ordinariness of the evil. Benton's nostalgia for the genre works imaginatively in every detail of the film. What he lacks is low cunning. Working in the thriller genre, he's a sensitive craftsman infatuated with a painted whore. *The Late Show* is fast and exciting, but it isn't a thriller, exactly. It's a one-of-a-kind movie—a love-hate poem to sleaziness.

The New Yorker, February 7, 1977

ABOUT PAUL NEWMAN, FROM REVIEW OF
SLAP SHOT

What holds the picture together is the warmth supplied by Paul Newman. As Reggie, the player-coach of the Chiefs, a minor-league ice-hockey team, he gives the performance of his life—to date.

Newman is an actor-star in the way that Bogart was. His range isn't enormous; he can't do classics, any more than Bogart could. But when a role is right for him, he's peerless. Newman imparts a simplicity and boyish eagerness to his characters. We like them but we don't look up to them. When he's rebellious, it's animal energy and high spirits, or stubbornness.

Newman is most comfortable in a role when it isn't scaled heroically; even when he plays a bastard, he's not a big bastard—only a callow, selfish one, like Hud. He can play what he's not—a dumb lout. But you don't believe it when he plays someone perverse or vicious, and the older he gets and the better you know him, the less you believe it. His likableness is infectious; nobody should ever be asked not to like Paul Newman.

He's one of the few stars we've got in a normal emotional range. The Actors Studio may have contributed to the situation of many of our leading actors (such as Al Pacino): they can do desperately troubled psychological states—gloom, defeat, manic joy—but they're so inward you can't see them getting through a competently managed average day. Newman's range has become more normal with the years; in this he's rather like Mastroianni—he has grown by going deeper into the emotions of ordinary men. He's too modest and too straight inside for the strutting blowhard Buffalo Bill of *Buffalo Bill and the Indians;* Warren Beatty, who's not nearly as skilled an actor, could have done the role better. Newman is one of the least vain of stars; he used to smirk sometimes, but it wasn't vanity—it was nervous self-mockery, a shamefaced recognition of the effect that his handsomeness was having on other people. Now he has no need to be self-conscious; he's earned the right to be proud of how he looks. No other star in screen history has gone into middle age the way Newman has. At fifty-two, he doesn't have an ounce of flab on him; he shows no sign of deterioration—even his gray hair is curly and thick.

What Newman does here is casual American star-acting at its peak; he's as perfectly assured a comedian as Bogart in *The African Queen,* even though the role isn't particularly well written and the picture itself isn't in the same class. In *The Sting,* he was smooth and charming, but there was no hardness in him; he wasn't a con man for a minute. He's gone beyond that sweetie-pie succulence here. What he does as Reggie isn't very different from what he's done before: it's that the control, the awareness, the power all seem to have become clarified. He has the confidence now to value his own gifts as an entertainer. In a picture such as *Winning,* he was impressive but a little somber; there was nothing to crack open—he couldn't use his resourcefulness. Here his technique seems to have become instinct. You can feel his love of acting; he's not fighting it or trying to hide it.

The essence of his performance as Reggie is that Reggie has never grown up; he's beautiful because he is still a child. Reggie is scarred and bruised, and there are gold rims on his chipped teeth; you don't see much of his eyes. But with Newman leaner, and his bone structure more prominent, the childlike quality is inner, and the warmth comes from deeper down. He makes boyishness seem magically attractive. Whizzing around on the ice, Reggie is a raucous American innocent. He's thin-skinned but a little thick-headed—a good-natured macho clown who can't conceal his vulnerability. Newman gives Reggie a desperate, forlorn quality. He suggests an over-age jock's pain from accumulated injuries—and the despair under

Reggie's manic behavior. It's Newman's being a star who makes himself smaller that contributes to the funniest scene in the movie—which is also the only lusty, sensual scene. He's in bed with Melinda Dillon, who plays the runaway wife of an opposition-team player; she talks in a good-humored twang about her recent discovery of lesbian fun while he nuzzles her and looks up at her big breasts. There's a luscious infantile carnality about the scene—they're like kids playing doctor in a tree house.

How and why Newman broke through in *this* picture, I don't know; maybe his attempted stretch—and failure—as Buffalo Bill shook him up. But this is the kind of breakthrough that doesn't often happen with movie stars. And when a star grows as an actor, there's an extra pleasure in it for us. We know Newman so well in his star roles—he is so much a part of us— that we experience his development as if it were our triumph. Newman proves that stardom isn't necessarily corrupting, and we need that proof as often as possible.

The New Yorker, March 7, 1977

MARGUERITE DURAS—
THE TRUCK

Most of the well-known writers who have tried to direct movies have gone at it briefly and given up in frustration. Cocteau was an exception; Marguerite Duras is another. She has been writing scripts since 1959 (*Hiroshima, Mon Amour*) and directing her own scripts since 1966, and the control in her new film, *Le Camion—The Truck*—suggests that she has become a master. But there's a joker in her mastery: though her moods and cadences, her rhythmic phrasing, with its emotional undertow, might seem ideally suited to the medium, they don't fulfill moviegoers' expectations. Conditioned from childhood, people go to the movies wanting the basic gratification of a story acted out. Many directors have tried to alter this conditioning, breaking away from the simplest narrative traditions, and they've failed to take the largest audience with them. Duras doesn't even get near the mass of moviegoers, though somehow—God knows how—she manages to make her own pictures, her own way. Hers is possibly the most sadomasochistic of all director relationships with the audience: she drives people out of the theatre, while, no doubt, scorning them for their childish obtuseness. At the same time, she must be suffering from her lack of popularity. Her battle with the audience reaches a new stage in *The Truck*, in which the split between her artistry and what the public wants is pointed up and turned against the audience. She brings it off, but she's doing herself in, too. And so it isn't a simple prank.

724

There are only two people in *The Truck:* Marguerite Duras and Gérard Depardieu. They sit at a round table in a room in her home, and never leave it. Small and bundled up, her throat covered, her unlined moon face serene, half-smiling, Duras reads aloud the script of a film in which Depardieu would act the role of a truck driver who picks up a woman hitchhiker. He would drive and ask a question or two; the woman would talk. Depardieu doesn't actually play the truck driver: this actor, whose physical and emotional weight can fill up the screen, is used as a nonprofessional. He merely listens trustingly, a friend, a student, as Duras reads. Hers is the only performance, and there has never been anything like it: controlling the whole movie visibly, from her position on the screen as creator-star, she is so assured that there is no skittish need for makeup, no nerves, quick gestures, tics. The self-image she presents is that of a woman past deception; she has the grandly simple manner of a sage. Unhurriedly, with the trained patience of authority, she tells the story of her movie-to-be about the woman hitchhiker—a woman of shifting identities, who drops clues about her life which are fragments and echoes of Duras's earlier works. This woman, a composite Duras heroine, strews a trail of opaque references to Duras's youth in Indo-China (the daughter of two French teachers, Marguerite Duras spent her first seventeen years there), and when the hitchhiker talks to the truck driver about her disillusion with the politics of revolution, and says that she has lost faith in the proletariat, that she believes in nothing anymore—"Let the world go to rack and ruin"—she speaks, unmistakably, for Duras herself. *The Truck* is a spiritual autobiography, a life's-journey, end-of-the-world road movie; it's a summing up, an endgame. The hitchhiker travels in a winter desert; she's from anywhere and going nowhere, in motion to stay alive. Reading the script, Duras speaks in the perfect conditional tense, beginning "It would have been a film—therefore, it is a film." And this tense carries a note of regret: it suggests that the script is to be realized only by our listening and imagining.

Her seductive voice prepares us for the unfolding of the action, and when there is a cut from the two figures at the table to a big blue truck moving silently through cold and drizzle in the working-class flatlands west of Paris, we're eager to see the man and woman inside. But we don't get close enough to see anyone. The truck crawls along in the exurbanite slum, where housing developments and supermarkets loom up in the void, Pop ruins. Its movement is noiseless, ominously so; the only sound is that of Beethoven's "Diabelli" Variations, and the images and music never quite come together rhythmically. With nothing synchronized, the effect is of doomsday loneliness. Quiet is Duras's weapon. The Beethoven is played softly, so that we reach toward it. The stillness provides resonance for her lingering words—those drifting thoughts that sound elegant, fated—and for the music, and for the cinematographer Bruno Nuytten's love-hate vistas of bareness and waste, like the New Jersey Turnpike in pastels. The foreboding melancholy soaks so deep into our consciousness that when the director yanks us back to the room, you may hear yourself gasp at the effrontery of this stoic, contained little woman with her mild, Chairman Mao deadpan. When we were with the truck, even without seeing anyone in it we felt that "the movie"—our primitive sense of a movie—was about to begin. And it's an emotional wrench, a classic rude awakening, to be sent back to Square One, the room. The film alternates between sequences in the room and sequences of the rolling truck, always at a distance. Each time she cuts to the outdoors, you're drawn into the hypnotic flow of the road imagery, and though you know perfectly well there will be nothing but the truck in the landscape, you half dream your way into a "real" movie. And each time you find yourself back with Duras, you're aware of being treated like a chump, your childishness exposed.

Buñuel played a similar narrative game in parts of *The Discreet Charm of the Bourgeoisie,* parodying the audience's gullibility by involving us in scary ghost stories and then casually interrupting them. But that was only one of his games and he wasn't onscreen himself pulling the rug out from under us, the way Duras is, returning to her narration, all dulcet modulations, as if she thought we'd be delighted to listen. The audience reacts at first with highly vocal disbelief and then with outbursts of anger, and walkouts. Even those of us who are charmed by her harmonious, lulling use of the film medium and in awe of her composure as a performer are conscious that we have, buried under a few layers, the rebellious instincts that others are giving loud voice to. They're furious in a way they never are at a merely bad, boring movie, and this anger is perfectly understandable. But it's high comedy, too: their feelings have been violated by purely aesthetic means—an affront to their conditioning.

When *The Truck* opens at the New York Film Festival this week, there's likely to be a repetition of the scene in May at Cannes. After the showing, Marguerite Duras stood at the head of the stairs in the Palais des Festivals facing the crowd in evening clothes, which was yelling insults up at her. People who had walked out were milling around; they'd waited to bait her. It might have been a horrifying exhibition, except that the jeering was an inverted tribute—conceivably, a fulfillment. She was shaken: one could see it in the muscles of her face. But Robespierre himself couldn't have looked them straighter in the eye. There can't be much doubt that she enjoys antagonizing the audience, and there is a chicness in earning the public's hatred. *The Truck* is a class-act monkeyshine made with absolutely confident artistry. She knows how easy it would be to give people the simple pleasures that they want. Her pride in not making concessions is heroic; it shows in that gleam of placid perversity which makes her such a commanding camera presence.

She can take the insults without flinching because she's completely serious in the story of the despairing hitchhiker. In her method in *The Truck,* she's a minimalist, like Beckett, stripping her drama down to the bones of monodrama, and her subject is the same as his: going through the last meaningless rites. ("I can't go on. I'll go on.") What *The Truck* doesn't have is Beckett's bleak, funny commonness. Beckett sticks to lowlifers, and his plays are the smelly vaudeville of the living dead, the grindingly familiar slow music of moronic humanity. Duras is bleakly fancy, with a glaze of culture. She's all music, too, the music of diffuseness, absence, loss, but her spoken text is attitudinizing—desultory self-preoccupation, mystification. Not pinning anything down, she leaves everything floating allusively in mid-air. This is, God help us, a vice women artists have been particularly prone to. Who is this hitchhiker on the road of life? Ah, we are not to know. Indefiniteness is offered as superiority to the mundane, as a form of sensuousness. It's a very old feminine lure—presenting oneself as many women, as a creature of mystery, and, of course, as passive and empty, disillusioned and weary. Dietrich used to do it in sequins, feathers, and chiffon. Duras clothes it in Marxist ideology, and puts forth her disaffection as a terminal, apocalyptic vision: Nothingness ahead. Some of her remarks ("Karl Marx is dead," and so on) have a tinny, oracular ring. (You wouldn't catch out Beckett making personal announcements.) The hitchhiker's declaration that she no longer believes in the possibility of political salvation is meant to have shock value; the world—i.e., Paris—is being told what Marguerite Duras's latest stand is.

There are some people who are too French for their own good. True film artist though she is, Marguerite Duras has a sensibility that's infected with the literary culture of a *précieuse,* and partly because of the development of movies out of the common forms of entertainment, this sensibility exposes itself on the screen much more than it does on paper. Faced with the audience's impatience, Duras fights back by going further, defiant, single-minded. There's something of the punitive disciplinarian in her conception of film art; *The Truck* is a position paper made into a movie. It's accessible, but it's accessible to a piece of yourself that you never think to take to the movies. Let's put it this way: if you were studying for a college exam and knocked off to go see *The Truck,* you wouldn't feel you were playing hooky. Duras makes us aware of our own mechanisms of response, and it's tonic and funny to feel the tensions she provokes. Her picture has been thought out with such supple discrimination between the values of sound and image that one could almost say it's *perfectly* made: an ornery, glimmering achievement.

The New Yorker, September 26, 1977

PADRE PADRONE
THE SACRED OAK

The Taviani brothers have learned to fuse political commitment and artistic commitment into stylized passion. Their film *Padre Padrone* has the beauty of anger that is channelled and disciplined without losing intensity. When it appeared in competition at Cannes this year, there was no question among members of the jury but that it had to win the grand prize, the Golden Palm. It also won the independently awarded International Critics' Prize. No movie has ever won both before, and *Padre Padrone* wasn't even made as a theatrical feature—it was shot in 16 mm. for Italian television. Yet there has been very little talk about the film, which opened at the New York Film Festival on September 25th. Its subject—and, even more, the sudden flare-up of its scenes—may intimidate people. Paolo and Vittorio Taviani, who wrote and directed this adaptation of Gavino Ledda's 1974 autobiography, are not new filmmakers; Paolo was born in 1931, Vittorio in 1929, and they've been working in movies—starting with documentaries—since 1954. They've developed a dissonant technique that is remote from the terms of most moviemaking. *Padre Padrone* is a high-strung, intransigent work—deliberately primitive and barbaric. It's constructed as a series of epiphanies; each sequence has its own painterly design and is set off from the one before, as if a new slide were held up. The images are simplified down to their dynamic components, like the diagrams of great artists' compositions in painting texts, and this, plus the faintly psychedelic Romanesque color, creates a pungent, viselike atmosphere.

Gavino Ledda himself appears on the screen to introduce the story; a man in his mid-thirties, he stands in the village of Siligo, in northern Sardinia, at the school he attended for only a few days, and hands the actor (Omero Antonutti) who plays his father an indispensable prop—a large stick. Then Ledda disappears, and is replaced by the six-year-old Gavino (Fabrizio Forte) on the fateful day when his father comes to the school to take him away. Terrified, the boy urinates in the aisle. When the father and child are out of the room, the boys laugh at the puddle, and the father storms back in and shouts at them, "Your turn will come!" From their stricken faces it's clear that there is a terror they all live with.

Gavino says goodbye to his mother (Marcella Michelangeli), is taken to a sheepfold several miles from his family's home, and is left to live there alone. This is not the sylvan myth of the shepherd with his pipes; families here enslave their first children, so that the younger ones won't die of hunger. Gavino's father lashes him if he shows fear or tries to run away or talks with other boys in neighboring fields. Imprisoned in their sheepfolds and beaten into submission, Gavino and the other sink into apathy, with no outlet for their rancor except their unlucky animals. The oppression is systematized—a Gulag Archipelago that's been built into the mores of society for thousands of years. Forced to be a "wild child," Gavino lives in silence and illiteracy until he's twenty. The movie deals with his rebellion: his struggle for words.

The spirit of *Padre Padrone* isn't naturalistic; rather, it's animistic. This sets it apart from de Seta's classically structured, neo-realist *Bandits of Orgosolo* (1961), also a primal Sardinian story. Except for Disney-style films, *Padre Padrone* may be the only fully consciously animistic movie ever made. Without people to talk with, trained to listen for bandits, Gavino lives by sounds, and as he learns to listen to the rustling sacred oak tree we hear it, too, and we hear the dawn, the animals' thoughts, the cries of far-off people, the heavy breathing of a shepherd as he prepares for a sexual assault on his burro: breathing that gathers force as younger shepherds mount their sheep, still smaller boys attack their chickens, Gavino's father rushes home to his wife, and then men and women—the whole village—are heard panting. It's a gale, a squall that sweeps over the countryside. Sound is the Expressionist element in this movie. The heightened whispers of nature, the percussive clangings of Gavino's rage—these are uncontrollable sounds that come up out of the silence. But when Gavino, sullen-faced, spaced out in the stupor of loneliness, hears a distant accordion playing the waltz from *Fledermaus*, it's fiercely pleasurable. It's more than an accordion, it's a whole band. It's the world outside his field coming to him. Gavino slaughters two lambs and trades them for the accordion, and it's his first, furtive defiance of his father-master—an attempt to gain a piece of the human inheritance.

When the family fortunes improve, with the acquisition of an olive grove, the now fully grown Gavino (Saverio Marconi) is put to work there, and his father keeps him obedient by humiliating him, taunting him for his ignorance. And others humiliate him when he's called away for his military service: it's not just that he can't read but that he can't speak Italian—only his local dialect, which is forbidden. He begins to study—incessantly, voraciously—stays on as a volunteer so he can continue studying, and, finally, has a breakthrough. It's in radio class: the soldiers have had to build their own sets, and on test day an officer tries them out. If Gavino's radio works, he tells himself, he'll try for a scholarship, he'll study Latin and Greek, he'll go to college. The officer turns on the set and there is a second of silence and then, soaring up, the *Fledermaus* waltz of the accordion and band. The music has never sounded more joyous. This movie is not, however, naïvely triumphant in tone. There is a memorable sequence of Gavino in a tank during maneuvers calling out Latin words over his walkie-talkie to a soldier friend in another tank, and reciting lines from the Aeneid like a student prince, and he goes on to take a degree in linguistics. But Ledda himself, replacing the actor, comes on at the end to indicate that he can never be like those who haven't experienced a childhood of solitary confinement. The adult Gavino is left rocking his body back and forth, as we had seen the child Gavino rock in the sheepfold—a motion like the rocking of the blind or of caged primates. (Ledda's thesis at the University of Sassari was on Sardinian dialects—the language of the shepherds.)

The film has the air of a performance, each set piece bare yet carnal. Trying to find out what actually happened to the two missing lambs, the father eavesdrops on Gavino's night thoughts as if the boy were speaking aloud. When the members of Gavino's family lay out a well-to-do neighbor's corpse, each of them thinks of what he wants from among the dead man's possessions, and their voices fill the room. The shepherds bearing a statue aloft in a religious procession chatter about whores' not being satisfactory, because they don't have tails. And all through the film the oak tree, seen against the blackness of night, is a malevolent presence. The Tavianis' vision is on the nightmare side of primitivism, where the elements themselves are your enemies, and mindless cruelty seems grotesquely natural. The peasants' ignorance and greed are Boschian, mythological. As in Kosinski's *The Painted Bird*—the boy there loses his voice, loses the will to speak—the cruelty is almost rhapsodic. (This is the sensibility that Roman Polanski tries for.)

Though the acting is conceived to be slightly stolid—taciturn, distanced—the performances in the minor parts, such as Gavino's sisters and brothers, are often merely wooden; that, however, isn't distracting, like the carryings-on of Gavino's mother, a road-company Anna Magnani in an Italian version of *Sons and Lovers*. A small budget ($300,000) may explain the absence of sheep in the field where Gavino's father trains him but doesn't account for some imperfections: The sounds of the violent thrashings Gavino receives are a fraction of a second off synch—possibly for an intentional stylized effect; however, the viewer is uncertain whether this is deliberate or just sloppy. When the father opens his mouth as if to cry out and a chant comes from far away, from ancient time, the viewer is aware of the ambitiousness of the effect; it's like watching a dress rehearsal. Yet none of these blemishes is disturbing for long. What's disturbing is the tone: the Tavianis are barbaric in a very assured way.

When Ledda himself is on the screen, his plainness is emotionally overwhelming. A man not molded by society to be lettered who yet becomes so uses language differently from those who take their education for granted; he may make out of language something that no one thought of before. There is a mystery in Ledda's plainness: he is a "wild child" trying to tell us what life without us was about. He had to fight his father—a man built like an oak—and physically defeat him before winning the right to study, and when your slavemaster is your father and he wants to kill you for your defiance, that defiance must destroy all you've ever known. Ledda's isolation now that he has won that fight may be deeper than before. There is a moment in the film when the olive crop has been ruined by frost, and the father, suddenly puny, sits on his bed in his underwear, eating a dish of frozen milk—a child finding solace. And the grown-up Gavino, looking on, knows that his own hatred is pitiful. His progenitor, the tyrant, is smaller than the hatred, which will always be within him.

One's tenuous reservations about the picture come down to this: Ledda experienced the terror of being alone; the Tavianis didn't—they're interpreting it. They've learned from Brecht, they've learned from Godard. And their style is possibly—well, too stylish for Gavino Ledda's suffering and his struggle. They've put all their layers of modernism to work, and their method may be just a shade too intelligently dramatic; their perception insulates them. This could be the danger in being two—in talking everything out. A little plainness can be redeeming: Renoir knows that; De Sica did, too. Eisenstein didn't. The Tavianis know all about the uses of visual and aural austerity, but there's never a moment in this near-great movie when you hear the beat of a simple heart.

The New Yorker, October 3, 1977

JULIA
A WOMAN FOR ALL SEASONS?

To say that *Julia* is well lighted doesn't do Douglas Slocombe's cinematography exact justice. It's *perfectly* lighted, which is to say, the color is lustrous, the images so completely composed they're almost static—picture postcards of its heroine Lillian Hellman (Jane Fonda) as a national monument. This is conservative—classical humanist—moviemaking, where every detail of meaning is worked out, right down to each flicker of light in the bit players' eyes. The director, Fred Zinnemann, does all the work for you, the way George Stevens did in *A Place in the Sun.* He does it beautifully—and there are very few directors left who know how to do it at all; the younger directors who aspire to this style, such as Alan Pakula or Dick Richards, don't achieve anything like the smoothness of Zinnemann's control, the glide of one sequence to the next. The man who made *From Here to Eternity* and *The Nun's Story* and *The Sundowners* hasn't forgotten his trade. Yet there's a cautiousness and reserve in his control now. Though Zinnemann takes a very romantic view of his two heroines—Lillian and Julia (Vanessa Redgrave)—the film is impersonal, its manner objective. Zinnemann's imagery isn't as inflated as David Lean's; he doesn't hold the frames too long; *Julia* is never ponderous. But this is important-motion-picture land, where every shot is the most beautiful still of the month. *Julia* is romantic in such a studied way that it turns romanticism into a moral lesson.

"Julia," one of the stories in *Pentimento, A Book of Portraits* (1973), Lillian Hellman's second volume of memoirs, is an account of how her childhood friend Julia involved her in smuggling fifty thousand dollars into Nazi Germany ("to bribe out many in prison and many who soon will be"). Of the stories in the book, it comes closest to Hellman's plays and scenarios; it's the one most like a movie—specifically, the anti-Nazi adventure movies made in Hollywood in the forties. The author uses the smuggling operation as a suspense mechanism, and as a framework for her recollections about Julia. Zinnemann lets this suspense element slip between his fingers, indifferently, as if it would be vulgar to grip the audience's emotions. The Georges Delerue score is lovely, in Delerue's special, under-orchestrated way, and gives the imagery a reminiscent edge, but *it* doesn't provide suspense, either. Trying to be faithful to Lillian Hellman's recollections, Zinnemann and Alvin Sargent, the screenwriter, construct an ornate superstructure of narration, dissolves, flashbacks spanning decades, and telepathic visions. Yet without suspense this superstructure has no engine inside. The film is all mildly anticipatory; it never reaches a point where you feel "This is it." Sargent has demonstrated his craftsmanship in the past (the most gifted writers sometimes regress to the poetic follies of adolescence, and that probably explains his other Lillian, in *Bobby Deerfield*), and he's really trying this time. There's some shrewd, taut writing, but you can see that he's harnessed. The script fails to draw you in, and the invented scenes of the heroines as young girls are flaccid—a literary form of calendar art, and photographed like *September Morn*. The constraint and inertness must go back to the decision to treat the story as literary history, as a drama of conscience, a parallel to Zinnemann's *A Man for All Seasons,* with Lillian Hellman herself as a legendary figure, and the relationships she has written about—with Dashiell Hammett (Jason Robards), Dorothy Parker (Rosemary Murphy), Alan Campbell (Hal Holbrook), and others—assumed to be common knowledge. Pity the screenwriter impaled on the life of a living person. And Sargent is bound by that person's short account, to which a high degree of art has already been applied. He might have been liberated if he could have changed the names and fictionalized the story; that way, he could have plugged the holes in the material and supplied what's missing in the characters, and some skepticism. But then the film would have lost its air of importance, history, lesson. And, of course, its selling point. What other movie has had its trailer built into an Academy Awards presentation, the way *Julia* did last March, when Jane Fonda made a speech introducing Lillian Hellman, who, head erect, acknowledged a standing ovation?

The film opens with Jane Fonda's recitation of the epigraph to *Pentimento,* a passage about old paint on canvas aging and revealing what was underneath, what was obscured "because the painter 'repented,' changed his mind." Speaking as the elderly Lillian Hellman, she says, "I wanted to see what was there for me once, what is there for me now." The flashback structure, too, suggests that there will be shifting perspectives, and throughout the movie we wait for the revelation of something lost from sight, displaced, hidden. Yet the narrator also tells us, "I think I have always known about my memory: I know when it is to be trusted . . . I trust absolutely what

I remember about Julia." And actually there are no shadings that change, nothing brought up that was painted over, no hint of "repentance." Except for some needed exposition and some filler scenes, the movie limits itself to what the author provides, and her terse style locks her view of the past in place; there's no space for us to enter into it—not even any junk rattling around for us to free-associate with. What, then, is the point of the first quotation? This sort of fidelity—presumably for the sake of a polished, literate tone—fuzzes up whatever chances the film has for clarity in its first, complicated half hour. Lillian's memories of the years shared with Hammett and her efforts to write are interspersed with her memories of Julia, the opening night of *The Children's Hour,* the play that made her famous, and scenes on the train when she's carrying the bribe money across Germany to Berlin. You need to stare at the wigs to locate yourself in time. After a while, it becomes apparent that the filmmakers are trafficking in quotations and too many flashbacks because they can't find the core of the material.

They trust the author's memory, but can *we?* Who can believe in the Julia she describes—the ideal friend of her early youth, the beautiful, unimaginably rich Julia who never fails to represent the highest moonstruck ideals? If ever there was a character preserved in the amber of a girlhood crush, she's it. The gallant, adventurous Julia opens the worlds of art and conscience to the worshipful Lillian. She recites poetry and is incensed at the ugliness of the social injustices perpetrated by her own family; she goes off to study at Oxford, then to medical school in Vienna, intending to work with Freud; she plunges into the dangerous opposition to Hitler, writes letters to Lillian explaining the holocaust to come, and in the middle of it all has a baby. This saintly Freudian Marxist queen, on easy terms with Darwin, Engels, Hegel, and Einstein, might have been a joke with almost anyone but Vanessa Redgrave in the role. Redgrave's height and full figure have an ethereal, storybook wonder, and she uses some of the physical spaciousness that she had on the stage in *The Lady from the Sea;* she can be majestic more fluidly than anyone else (and there's more of her to uncoil). She has a scene all bandaged up in a hospital bed; unable to speak, she points with maybe the most expressive huge hand the screen has ever known. She handles the American accent unnoticeably—it's not that awful flat twang she used for Isadora. In closeups, Vanessa Redgrave has the look of glory, like the young Garbo in Arnold Genthe's portraits; her vibrancy justifies Lillian's saying that she had "the most beautiful face I'd ever seen." Redgrave is so well endowed by nature to play queens that she can act simply in the role (which doesn't occupy much screen time) and casually, yet lyrically, embody Lillian Hellman's dream friend. Zinnemann has very astutely cast as the teen-age Julia a young girl (Lisa Pelikan) who's like a distorted Vanessa Redgrave—a fascinating, dislikable, rather creepy look-alike, who suggests that the intellectual goddess didn't appear out of a white cloud.

It's the dark cloud—Jane Fonda's stubborn strength, in glimpses of her sitting at the typewriter, belting down straight whiskey and puffing out

733

smoke while whacking away at the keys, hard-faced, dissatisfied—that saves the film from being completely pictorial. It's a cloud-of-smoke performance; Bette Davis in all her movies put together couldn't have smoked this much—and Fonda gets away with it. It's in character. She creates a driven, embattled woman—a woman overprepared to fight back. This woman doesn't have much flexibility. You can see that in the stiff-necked carriage, the unyielding waist, even in the tense, muscular wrists, and in her nervous starts when anything unexpected happens. Her clothes are part of her characterization: Anthea Sylbert, who designed them, must have taken her cue from photographs of the author. These are the clothes of a woman who didn't choose them to be flattering—she chose them with a sense of her position in the world. They're expensive, selected with an eye to drama and to fashion—also not to get in her way. Outfitted in a style that combines elegance and impatience, Jane Fonda catches the essence of the Irving Penn portrait of Lillian Hellman reproduced in her first book of memoirs, *An Unfinished Woman* (1969). When she's alone on the screen, Fonda gives the movie an atmosphere of dissension, and she sustains this discordant aloneness in her scenes with everyone, except Julia, with whom she's soft, eager, pliant. Her deliberately humorless Lillian is a formidable, uningratiating woman—her hair sculpted out of the same stone as her face. If you like her, you have to like her on her own implacable terms. How does a viewer separate Jane Fonda's Lillian Hellman from the actual Lillian Hellman? It's impossible to make clear distinctions between the live woman that Jane Fonda draws from (the performance could be called an inspired impersonation), the self-portrait in the story, and the semi-fictionalized activities on the screen. Almost anything one thinks or feels about this character seems an intrusion on a life, yet an intrusion that has been contracted for by Lillian Hellman herself—perhaps somewhat unwittingly.

The story itself has a *submerged* core: all of Hellman's attitudes, everything that goes into her woman's variant of Hemingway-Hammett strippeddown, hardboiled writing. Her prose is strong and clear, and also guarded, reluctant, pried out of a clenched hand. In the kind of situation-centered play Hellman writes, she doesn't give much of herself away. Her memoirs are dramatized, too, yet they're more exciting as drama than her plays are, since you can feel the tension between what she's giving you and what she's withholding. One expects a writer to trust his unconscious, to let go sometimes—not always to be so selective. Lillian Hellman carries thrift and plain American speech to a form of self-denial. The clue to some of the tension in the story "Julia" comes elsewhere in *Pentimento*—in "Turtle," the most compact Hemingway-Hammett story in the book, yet the one that reveals the cost of being hardboiled. In "Turtle," there are only two important characters—Hellman and Hammett, with whom she lived off and on for almost thirty years—and it's evident that for him strong and clear and definite meant masculine, while doubts and unresolved feelings were weak nonsense: feminine. Lillian Hellman tried to write (and to live) in a way that

Hammett would approve of; he rejected much of what she actually felt, and she accepted his standards. (The question of why a woman of such strength and, in many ways, of such ruthless honesty should have deferred to the judgment of a man of lesser gifts than her own—that's the sexual mystery that would make a drama.)

The movie is about Hellman's career and doesn't really exist independently of one's knowledge of that career. The friendship between Julia and Lillian is obviously the emotional basis—the original material—for *The Children's Hour.* In that play, scandalmongers spread a sexual rumor about the relationship of two young women teachers, destroying their friendship and their hopes. Here, in *Julia,* Lillian is out drinking in a restaurant with Sammy (John Glover, who shows a nasty vitality, like an American Edward Fox), the brother of a former schoolmate. He says that "the whole world knows about you and Julia," and she slugs him, knocking him back in his chair and then slamming the table over on top of him as she leaves. (People in the theatre applauded.) In the melodramatic Victorian code that is integral to hardboiled writing, the suggestion of homosexuality is a slur—it sullies the purity of the two women's relationship. Only contemptible people—curs like Sammy—think like that. They don't know how to behave; they lack standards. (This was the theme that came out all too nakedly in Hellman's third book of memoirs, the 1976 *Scoundrel Time.*) The failure to look beyond "right" and "wrong" has limited Hellman as a dramatist, and in "Julia" (though not in other stories in *Pentimento)* she thinks in the same terms—judgmentally. "Julia" is an expression of outraged idealism—sexual, political, and in all areas of personal conduct. It is in this story that she shows the beginnings of her own political conscience, started and nurtured, according to her account, by Julia. And it is Julia's dedication to fighting Fascism and her subsequent mutilation and murder that serve as the concrete justification—the personal experience—behind Lillian Hellman's embittered attitude toward those she regards as cowardly or dishonorable. The motive force of the story is that those who have not lived up to her conception of honor stand morally condemned for eternity.

In the film, at the last meeting of Lillian and Julia, in a café near the railroad station in Berlin, Lillian turns over the money she has smuggled in, and Julia says to her, "Are you still as angry as you used to be? I like your anger. . . . Don't you let anyone talk you out of it." There's no way for viewers to understand what Julia is referring to: in their scenes together, Lillian has never demonstrated any anger. Julia has been the daring leader, railing at injustice, going off and doing something about it. Lillian has been the docile follower, the naïf. In the movie version of *A Man for All Seasons,* a respectable job of monument-making, Zinnemann enshrined the martyred Sir Thomas More as a man of conscience; audiences weren't forcibly reminded that what More got himself beheaded for was the belief that the Pope represented divine law. What people could take away from the film was that More stood by his principles and died for them. In *Julia,* it isn't nearly as clear why Lillian is a monumental figure. In the episode of carrying the money to Berlin, she's more of a hazard than anything else; the operation is so efficiently organized and she is supported by such resourceful anti-Nazi underground aides that she hardly seems to be needed at all.

And so it has to be from Lillian's mentors that we get her measure. As Hammett, Robards, who is gruff and funny at the beginning, has nothing to do once the film gets under way—he's just the all-wise, all-knowing Dash standing by, with love. But Dash is there for a reason: he's a judge of writing of such supreme authority—a Sainte-Beuve at the very least—that when he tells Lillian that *The Children's Hour,* which she has just finished, is "the best play anyone's written in a long time," there can be no question about it. Julia is the saintly political activist who certifies Lillian's anger as instinctive morality, and Dash is the stamp of approval that certifies her greatness.

The most difficult thing for an actor to suggest is what goes into making a person an artist—the tensions, the richness. And this is particularly difficult in the case of Lillian Hellman, who doesn't have that richness, and who in her own account makes herself so innocent of intellectual drives that anger seems to be her creative fount. If Julia's last advice to Lillian actually was to hang on to her anger, it was bad advice. Anger blinds Lillian Hellman as a writer. But anger is what holds the story "Julia" together, and the movie doesn't have it. At moments, Jane Fonda supplies something better, because she understands how to embody the explosive Hellman resentment. She gets at what anger does to you. It won't let you relax. It boxes you in: you're on your own. When—as Lillian—she walks into Sardi's on the opening night of her hit, twitching slightly from drunken nervousness, revelling in the attention she's getting while stiffly living up to her own image of herself as the distinguished playwright, you want more of her. You feel that Fonda has the power and invention to go on in this character—that she could crack this smooth, contemplative surface and take us places we've never been to. The film's constraint—its not seizing the moments when she's ready to *go*—is frustrating.

The New Yorker, October 10, 1977

THE AMERICAN FRIEND

Angst-dark primary colors—reds and blues so intense they're near-psychedelic, yet grimy, rotting in the thick, muggy atmosphere. Cities that blur into each other. Characters as figures in cityscapes or as exiles in rooms that are insistently not home. And, under it all, morbid, premonitory music. This is the festering mood of the young German writer-director

Wim Wenders's *The American Friend,* adapted from Patricia Highsmith's crime thriller *Ripley's Game.*

An American demi-crook, Tom Ripley (Dennis Hopper), operating out of Hamburg, suffers a small discourtesy: a Swiss picture restorer and framer, Jonathan (Bruno Ganz), who suspects Ripley of being involved in art forgery, declines to shake his hand. Minot (Gérard Blain), a gangster associate of Ripley's, needs the services of an assassin, and out of pique—it's no more than a perverse whim—Ripley suggests that Jonathan might be his man. Minot tricks Jonathan, who has a blood disease, into believing that his death is imminent, and proposes that he kill for hire—the target is someone he's never met—so that he'll have money to leave to his wife and child. Jonathan's moral values collapse once he thinks he's dying; suddenly something in him gives way—as (we fear) it might in any of us. He yields to the momentary temptation, and the trap closes; he's a criminal. There's a true thriller moment when this honorable, decent craftsman-shopkeeper carries out his mission. Feverishly, only half consciously, he shoots the victim on an escalator in the Paris Métro and then comes up into the daylight, and it's like waking from a nightmare—except that we know that now his whole life will be a nightmare.

Highsmith's thrillers—the sources of Hitchcock's *Strangers on a Train* and René Clément's *Purple Noon*—aren't concerned with bringing criminals to justice, and there's no moral principle or any other standard to separate the normal and the criminal. The symmetrical twist in the plot here is that Ripley develops an affection for Jonathan and tries to extricate him from Minot's clutches. (Does the title mean that an American friend is one who tries to help you after he's destroyed you?) Jonathan, who wanted to protect his family's future, is so changed that he leads a new, dislocated life in which he feels himself a stranger—a tourist who hasn't got his bearings. His wife barely knows him anymore; Ripley, who understands what is happening to him, replaces his wife as his mate.

Bruno Ganz's performance as Jonathan is one of the rare ordinary-decent-fellow portrayals that actually succeed (for a while, at least) in involving the viewer. Quiet, a man of inner strength, with watchful, anxious eyes and swansdown diction, Jonathan gives the film its only depth (except for the poignancy of the settings). Ganz doesn't talk, he croons—and you almost catch yourself leaning toward the screen. You feel you're reading Jonathan's soul each time you look at him; you soak into his face the way you soak into the rooms, the streets. If Wenders had written the role so that this patsy had some aggressive impulses that came out in the killing, or if he lost his inner dignity—if he were unpredictable—you could go on soaking into him. But there's not a lot of variety in Jonathan's soul. Ganz's character modulations are in too narrow a range; he's so inward that you begin to feel he's looking soulfully out of his deep brown eyes right down at his saintly tradesman's limp mustache. Jonathan is such a humble, anxious man that the picture needs a counter-force. A stronger Ripley might provide it. But as

Dennis Hopper plays him Ripley is nothing but a cowboy hat and a fatigued face and aberrant buoyant flings into the air: Hopper bounds up, arms raised high—the arms that are generally held close in to his slightly rigid body, as if he were chilled.

The psychological union that develops between Ripley and Jonathan—which should be the heart of the movie—is indicated by nothing more than Ripley's picking up a little kinetic novelty item in Jonathan's picture-framing shop and Jonathan's telling him to keep it (a gesture that could signify contempt as easily as generosity). Ripley gives Jonathan a kinetic gadget in return and fastens glassy, sweet-Jesus stares on him, which, by extrapolation, can be interpreted to mean that Ripley is moved by Jonathan's dedication to his craft. These scenes are particularly awkward because the film's sound is hollow. The performers speak German or English or French, whichever is appropriate to their characters and the moment, but the sound is poorly recorded and some scenes are inexpertly looped. This technical defect underlines the eccentricity of Hopper's decaying-juvenile blandness. It takes him an eternity of concentration to perform a minor action, such as pouring coffee into a thermos, and you could drive a truck between the syllables each time he speaks a line of dialogue. Ganz's accented English is far more fluent than his American friend's: it's as if Hopper had just mastered the beginnings of human speech and expected us to share his joy that words come out of his mouth, slowly, but . . . yes . . . they . . . do . . . come . . . out. Even an existential epigram comes out: "I know . . . less and less . . . about who . . . I . . . am . . . and . . . about . . . who . . . anybody . . . else . . . is." He mutters that into a tape recorder. For posterity. You can't risk losing thoughts like that. Has the tape been stored in a safe place?

Though Wenders overdoses on mood, he creates the right apprehensiveness for a Highsmith story. But he's trying to do eighteen other things, too; he "enriches" the plot with incidental speculative themes relating to the oppressiveness of modern society—losing more in clarity than he gains in depth. (It could be argued that he loses more in depth, too.) Jonathan is rootless—an expatriate from Zurich—and the American Ripley, the infant philosopher who talks like the computer in *Alphaville*, doesn't really live anywhere; he hops continents (via jump cuts) and camps out in his big house in Hamburg. It features a jukebox and looks like an American Colonial museum of Pop Art, so at first you don't even realize he lives on the same continent as Jonathan. The internationalization of modern cities is another theme: Wenders moves the action from New York to Hamburg, Paris, and Munich, and in each city he shoots the high-rise anonymity that could be anywhere. He finds new New Yorks all over Europe, and this certainly makes a point, but in order to make it he deliberately confuses the viewer about where the action is taking place.

All we know about most of the characters in the movie is that they are played by directors. Ripley and Minot are represented by actor-directors (Hopper and Blain), and Nicholas Ray, who directed the young Hopper in

Rebel Without a Cause, is cast as a famous painter who has pretended to be dead. He and Hopper have scenes together which, when they become penetrable, seem to relate to the painter's "forging" new paintings in his old style so they can be sold—a plot embellishment that has nothing whatever to do with Minot and the gangsters Jonathan has got involved with, who belong to porno-filmmaking rings. Other directors who turn up are Samuel Fuller as a Mafia chieftain, Jean Eustache, in a restaurant scene, Daniel Schmid as the man on the escalator, Peter Lilienthal as a hood, and Wenders himself, in an ambulance. This slyboots casting of directors as crooks has a deadening effect; except for Fuller, their acting is perfunctory (and, in the case of Ray, worse, since he tries for a mythic effect). In addition, Jonathan's shop and flat contain a magic lantern showing a speeding train, a zoetrope, a stereopticon, a praxinoscope; Jonathan's dedicated craftsmanship is thus linked to moviemaking. Yet none of this film-toy paraphernalia helps to create suspense or to move the action forward; rather, it suggests that though Wenders is attracted to the idea of telling a story he can't quite keep his mind on it. What about his own pride in craft? The simplest plot points are bobbled, and when there's mayhem, it isn't clear who the participants are or what the outcome is. We're never informed about Ripley's connection with Minot, which got the whole thing started. There's a gaping difference between moral ambiguity and this obscurity—which actually impedes the perception of moral ambiguities.

It's possible for a director to combine suspense narrative and essay, as Godard demonstrated in 1959 in *Breathless* and in several films in the sixties, doing it quickly, dartingly, in a visual style that could be read at a glance. But Wenders uses densely detailed imagery, his pacing is weighted, and there are no insights that relate to the characters—the film drags along on secondhand alienation. *The American Friend* doesn't have the nasty, pleasurable cleverness of a good thriller. Wenders has a moviemaker's visual imagination, and his unsettling compositions are neurotically beautiful visions of a disordered yet functioning world. Dramatically, though, the entire film is stagnant—inverted Wagnerianism. The unease of the generalized moral degradation overpowers Jonathan's individual story. Wenders has the style of someone who's aware of what he's doing, but that's not enough—look at Joseph Losey. Wenders is like a more garish, grainier Losey—Losey under mud. Is that why the film is being called a masterpiece? A great many new German films are being called masterpieces. After Vietnam and Watergate, it's understandable that Americans should begin to wonder if morally we are any different from the Germans, and experience a psychological rapprochement—a new closeness to directors who dredge around in guilt. With nihilism in the air here, the extreme moralism of the Germans may be appealingly exotic. (Moralism could be part of the new attraction of science fiction, too.) American directors may have lost the primitive-visionary qualities that make the new German films so mysterious, but they have an understanding of narrative that the young Germans don't have. *The American Friend* is a masterpiece for people who think a movie can't be worthwhile unless it makes you suffer. Emotionally, the drip drip of Wenders's poetic urban masochism—which is intended to be anti-bourgeois filmmaking—is indistinguishable from the heavy-going German films of the Emil Jannings period. Actually, Jannings was a more robust masochist than Bruno Ganz. And Wenders isn't satisfied by Ganz's anguish; he also gives Hopper a crackup and a lonely finish. Wenders is not only turgid, he's exhibitionistically turgid. There's too much imprecise, darkly lighted desperation in *The American Friend*. By the time it grinds to a halt, you feel your mind is clouded.

The New Yorker, October 17, 1977 ●

CITIZENS BAND (HANDLE WITH CARE)

andle with Care is exactly the kind of high-spirited light comedy that would have become a hit a few years ago. Today a picture is penalized if it isn't big enough, if it has no stars and no obvious selling point; hardly anybody hears about it. *Handle with Care* had, at least, some identity when it was called *Citizens Band*—its title when it was given regional playdates. Citizens Band is what it's about, literally and metaphorically. Now that it has lost that bit of identity, and is being advertised as if it were soft-core porno, it will probably have to wait, as *Smile* did, to be discovered by the public on Home Box Office and then—broken up and bowdlerized—on regular commercial channels. To expedite the bowdlerizing process, Paramount opened the picture in New York with its entire last sequence lopped off. This movie has one of the few fully rounded comic scripts of recent years, and in that sequence all the elements came together in a final fling; the amputation is the executives' way of punishing the film for their own ineptitude.

Paul Brickman, who wrote the screenplay, had an idea worthy of Preston Sturges: that the psychology of those who operate CB radio units might be like the psychology of crank phone callers, and breathers and obscene phone callers, too—that as disembodied voices, with identities borrowed from pop fantasies, and signal names to confirm their new self-image, people could live another life on the public airwaves. In the film, the CB users are secret celebrities, eloquent on the air, or, more often, aimlessly loquacious. Their voices have a tale-spinning seductiveness. But they dry up when they actually meet. Companionship comes easier to them across the airwaves; they feel safe then. CB functions as an authorized madness; it allows the characters to release their inhibitions while keeping one foot on the ground. The setting is a small Southwestern town where the people think they know each other; the story is about the collision of their free-floating ids.

The breathy carnal enticements of a young woman who calls herself

Electra overheat a bespectacled young man, Warlock (Will Seltzer); a listening trucker, Chrome Angel (Charles Napier), gets carried away and piles up his rig. A bratty little kid calls himself The Hustler and boasts of his sexual conquests; lonely old Grandma Breaker pours out reminiscences of her childhood. The hero, Spider (Paul Le Mat), lives in a shack with his father and runs a CB repair shop and, at his own expense, an emergency-rescue station. He's a Samaritan, dashing to the aid of truckers in trouble, and he becomes so incensed when the channels are tied up by chatterers who violate F.C.C. regulations that he turns vigilante and goes out to bust up their equipment. And so he invades the obsessions of a collection of harmless nuts, among them The Red Baron (Harry Northup), The Priest (Ed Begley, Jr.), and a gym teacher (Candy Clark) who used to be his girl but now dates his virulently competitive brother (Bruce McGill), the high-school gym coach. No heroism has ever been more transparent than Spider's. Paul Le Mat has some of the James Dean-Beau Bridges timid-dangerous-animal sensitivity; it's naïve, easily wounded, unconnected to thought, and that's why it's so attractive. Le Mat uses this disarming quality comically, so that it's tinged with American idiosyncrasy. The loose screws rattle around in Spider's head rather gently. His father, an alcoholic retired truck driver (Roberts Blossom), is morose and ornery with his son; on his CB he comes to life—his voice leaps to a youthful register, he's convivial, hopeful, practically a raconteur. When he won't answer his son, who's standing next to him, Spider has to get on the CB in order to get a response. Spider's vocal rhythms are totally unactorish; they're easygoing. But when he pleads with his father, there's a tightness in his throat and a faint childish whine. Spider is the small-town Boy Scout who has never grown up—he's still collecting medals from local civic organizations, beaming with embarrassment at the honor. He's a technology nut—a half-cocked hero—and he's been given as a sidekick a hugely fat adolescent friend (Michael Rothman), who helps him operate his emergency service and trudges after him.

Directed by the young Jonathan Demme, who has graduated from cheaply made exploitation films (Caged Heat, Crazy Mama, Fighting Mad), Handle with Care is a palmy, elegantly deadpan comedy; the jokes aren't pushed, so it takes viewers a few minutes to settle into the comic style, which has the mellow, light touch of thirties Renoir—who would have thought that there could be such a thing as redneck grace? The format is almost as complicated as that of Nashville: about fifteen characters (plus their alter egos) interact. The lunacies aren't frenzied; they just function as part of a normally wigged-out mode of existence. And the director's unstressed lyricism—the subdued colors, the unhurried flow, the dissolves—ties everyone together visually. There's nothing harsh in this comedy, not even its funniest, most hard-bitten character, Marcia Rodd as Portland Angel. Her timing—with a gulp or a hesitancy functioning as a gigantic double-take—is comparable to Lily Tomlin's work in The Late Show. Portland Angel is obdurate and smart; she stares incredulously when she listens to Ann Wedgeworth, who plays the bedraggled passionflower Dallas Angel. They are the two wives of the bigamous Chrome Angel, who happen to meet on a bus, and they're the best comedy team in years. The soft-headed Wedgeworth can convince herself of anything. Rodd, tough as they come, chews on Wedgeworth's gaga ideas as if they were jaw-breakers; she can't swallow them, and she's too polite. to spit them out. Charles Napier's Chrome Angel is a huge man with a great, jutting jaw; he looks like a Brian Keith made of granite, a thick-witted Steve Canyon. He's also lucky enough to have one of the friendliest mistresses in all movies—Alix Elias as Hot Coffee, a plump, motherly hooker. The impulsive, generous Chrome Angel helps her buy a motor home, so she can bring her service to her trucker-customers. Hot Coffee has a soothing, giggly disposition, and her nasal baby talk is blessed with a tiny speech impediment that's like a vocal dimple. When Chrome Angel's wives make their terrible discovery of each other and two happy homes are about to be torn asunder, Hot Coffee per-suades the two tearstained women to settle down with their husband in a ménage à trois; it's a triumph of giddy sweet reason. These three women give the film its eccentric peaks. Candy Clark, as the heroine, doesn't blend into the atmosphere the way they do. Her line readings are too deliberate, she slows things—almost imperceptibly, but there's a down. But hers are the only scenes that go on an instant too long.

There are perhaps twenty-five million CB sets in the United States, and at least one person in every twenty holds a CB license. If the film's satiric explanation of what this phenomenon is about isn't all-inclusive, it still must be an element in the CB appeal. In a sprawling country with people con-stantly on the move—literally spaced out—CB must be a new form of con-necting. And the film has caught the language of this subculture, in which technology and Yankee know-how are all mixed up with dreams of the past. This isn't a corn-pone special; it doesn't have a climactic car chase or a big fight. That's probably why Paramount failed to sell it in the small towns, where the Burt Reynolds comedy-melodramas succeed. It could be that *Han-dle with Care* is almost too likable a movie. Maybe it's too evenly directed; maybe it needed to be brought up to a higher pitch at certain points. It might not seem so small a picture if it had been. But its antic charm is in its even, unsurprised tone—in the absence of anger, the reasonableness to-ward creeps and crazies. There are a few times when you're afraid that the tone is becoming threatening and the action is about to descend into melo-drama. But the film sideswipes your fears and stays on course. There is no obsession—even the crackpot Red Baron's Nazi-racist harangues—that it does not de-fang. *Handle with Care* has the consistent vision of a classic com-edy; it undercuts all the characters' illusions without a breath of ill will.

The New Yorker, October 24, 1977

1900
HAIL, FOLLY!

At a certain point in their careers—generally right after an enormous popular success—most great movie directors go mad on the potentialities of movies. They leap over their previous work into a dimension beyond the well-crafted dramatic narrative; they make a huge, visionary epic in which they attempt to alter the perceptions of people around the world. Generally, they shoot this epic in what they believe is a state of superenlightenment. They believe that with this film they're literally going to bring mankind the word, and this euphoria conceals even their own artistic exhaustion. Afterward, in the editing rooms, when they look at the thousands upon thousands of feet of film they've shot, searching for ways to put it together, while the interest on the borrowed money rises and swells, and the businessmen or government representatives try to wrest control from them, their energy may flag and their confidence falter. Their euphoria had glossed over the initial compromises that now plague them—an unresolved, unfinished script, perhaps, or an international cast with no common language—and there is always the problem of excessive length. Griffith with *Intolerance,* von Stroheim with his ten-hour *Greed,* Abel Gance with his three-screen *Napoléon,* Eisenstein with his unfinished *Ivan the Terrible* trilogy, Bertolucci with *1900,* perhaps Coppola with his *Apocalypse Now* still to come—no one has ever brought off one of these visionary epics so that it was a hit like the director's preceding films that made it possible. Yet these legendary follies that break the artists' backs are also among the great works of film history, transforming the medium, discarding dead forms, and carrying on an inspired, lunatic tradition that is quite probably integral to the nature of movies.

Artists of an expansionist temperament are drawn to work in this medium, because movies are capable of being the closest thing there is to a total art. If success and personal acclaim win these artists their freedom, their love of the unexplored possibilities can't be contained; it spills over into dream epics. In movies, sanity is too neat, too limiting. Huston, Riefenstahl, Pudovkin, Welles, Dreyer, Fritz Lang, Visconti, Dovzhenko, Pabst, Max Ophuls, Francesco Rosi, Fellini, Peckinpah, Bondarchuk, John Ford, Altman, Scorsese, Kurosawa, Pontecorvo—does anyone doubt the self-destructive fulfillments that these artists would have reached out to if they'd had the chance? And isn't it a tragedy for us all—and for those who come after us—that they haven't? The calamity of movie history is not the follies that get made but the follies that don't get made.

Everybody knows that it is essential for there to be low-budget movies; how else can new young artists get their chance? And directors who work big carry the burden of guilt for the many smaller films that could have been made on the money they're spending. Not that they would have been

743

anyway—though generous-minded directors sometimes manage to use the power derived from their own success to help other filmmakers along. But even for the directors who profess belief in economy production, the contradictory aesthetic drive toward the big plunge is like a fever that passes from one great talent to the next. It may be that anyone with a large enough imagination who works in movies will catch it, unless, like an Ingmar Bergman, he reaches inward, downward, or, like Lubitsch, toward elegant condensation. The impulse is essentially the same as the one that led Tolstoy to write *War and Peace;* but in movies, no matter how great the director's talent and imagination are, he becomes swamped in the physical details of the production. He has to give so much of himself just to hold the production together that he can't sustain his creative energy. Writing a nineteenth-century novel on film—which is what this epic usually comes to be—means that you have to be a great con man, a great general, and a great artist, and if you weaken in any of those functions your golden bowl is cracked, perhaps shattered.

This form of gigantism is not to be confused with the producer-initiated or studio-initiated big-budget pictures (*Cleopatra, Doctor Dolittle, The Towering Inferno,* the forthcoming *The Swarm,* and so on). The artist-initiated epic is an obsessive testing of possibilities, and often it comes out of an overwhelming desire to express what the artist thinks are the unconscious needs of the public. It comes, too, from a conviction, or a hope, that if you give popular audiences the greatest you have in you they will respond. The moviemaker has an idealistic belief that no matter how corrupted mass taste is, people still retain the capacity to receive a vision. These epics try to vault over the film industry and go directly to the public.

The crazed utopian romanticism of Bernardo Bertolucci's *1900* reaches a new high pitch in movie idealism. A director *dies* on a picture of this magnitude with this degree of personal commitment; he has to be brought back to life so that he can move on. In the history of movies, *1900* represents a triumph, because after losing control of his movie the director regained it. After years of dissension and litigation (and that's par for the course), *1900* was finally shown at the New York Film Festival, and will open in a theatre on November 4th. The producer, Alberto Grimaldi, acknowledges that the film has been doing reasonably well overseas and will not lose money, and Bertolucci, treating the over-five-hour European version as a rough cut, has been able to refine it and release it here in his own four-hour-and-five-minute cut—so we don't have to try to piece out his intentions from a mangled version. This film is his; it represents almost five years of elation and anguish in the life of one of the three or four greatest young talents working in the movies.

1900 is about two boys born in the North Italian region of Emilia-Romagna on the same day in 1901. Alfredo (Robert De Niro) is the heir to the vast landholdings of his grandfather (Burt Lancaster), and Olmo (Gérard Depardieu) is the bastard grandson of the patriarch (Sterling

Hayden) of the peasant clan that lives on those holdings and labors for a share of the crop. *1900* opens on Liberation Day, April 25, 1945, then goes back to the birth of the boys and follows the course of their ambivalent friendship. Accepting the romantic convention that there is a lifelong bond between people who swam naked in a stream together as children, the film uses that bond as a dialectical opposition.

Alfredo inherits the estate after the death of his father (Romolo Valli) and marries a French girl, the neurasthenic sylph Ada (Dominique Sanda). But she is aesthetically repelled by his passive acquiescence in the Fascist takeover and leaves him. Olmo, "the elm tree," becomes a Socialist and lives with a comrade—a teacher, Anita (Stefania Sandrelli)—who is a militant peasant leader; she dies in childbirth, leaving him a daughter. The film includes the upheavals of a peasant uprising in 1908, the end of the First World War and the rise of the Fascists, who came to power in 1922, and the Fascist era. Then it returns to that pivotal day in 1945 when in fact the conquering Allies were "liberating" Italy from Fascism but when in Bertolucci's utopian fancy an agrarian revolution takes place. The peasants seem to be under the delusion that the liberation from Fascism means that they now own the land—they might be playacting a revolutionary spring festival (of the future). They stage a mock trial of Alfredo, the padrone, pronouncing him dead. Then, at the end of the day, the soldiers of the provisional government come and take away the peasants' guns, and Alfredo goes on as before. In an epilogue, he and Olmo are doddering old cronies, wrestling, quarreling, hugging each other in love and in anger—in bafflement at the emotions and the social forces that have thrown them together and thrown them apart.

Bertolucci is trying to transcend the audience appeal of his lyrical, psychological films. He is trying to make a people's film by drawing on the mythology of movies, as if it were a collective memory. *1900* is a romantic moviegoer's vision of the class struggle—a love poem for the movies as well as for the life of those who live communally on the land. (It may be that Bertolucci believes that he loves movies so much *because* they are the people's art.) Though in form *1900* is an opera-novel, and its homage is to Verdi, the great Emilian who died on the day (January 27, 1901) of the two boys' birth, the characters of the two grandfathers (Lancaster and Hayden)—giants of an earlier era—are drawn from American Westerns and adventure films. *1900* represents an attempt to fuse the American movies that fed Bertolucci's imagination and the visionary agrarian paean *Earth*, made by Dovzhenko, the most lyrical of all Russian directors. Bertolucci attempts to do this while taking another look at the Fascist material that he dealt with in his 1970 films, *The Conformist* and *The Spider's Stratagem*. The latter was also shot in Emilia, in a town near Parma, and was about the need for myth. It dealt with a man, born in 1900, who was killed during a performance of Verdi's *Rigoletto* and became an anti-Fascist martyr-hero. In that film, set in a town that Bertolucci called Tara, he used the town itself as an opera stage, and in a memorable sequence *Rigoletto* was heard pouring forth from loudspeakers in the ghostly, floodlit streets. The staging of *1900* is often similarly theatrical: This movie never goes farther from the estate than a city in Emilia, and the courtyard of the landowner's manor house is used, like Tara, as a giant set. Opera is in Bertolucci's blood and bones. When he stages scenes of peasants eating, the hearty bacchanalian imagery is out of Brueghel, but you wait for them to swallow their fake food and start singing. Bertolucci uses his peasants—actual Emilian peasants—as if they were a chorus, and as the film progresses they upstage the stars. (There is even a hunchback among them dressed as a jester and called Rigoletto.) He apparently believes that he can make the peasants larger than life by using the romantic conventions of opera, movies, and painting. He's trying for a "naïveté" like that of Verdi, who stayed within a tradition, adapting conventional forms, and he adapts the characters and devices of such movies as *Anthony Adverse* and *Gone with the Wind*. He knowingly risks grandiloquence, believing that this is the path to a people's art—that moviegoers want romance, myth, and their own struggles turned into poetry and fantasy.

There are sequences in *1900* as great as any ever filmed. The childhood scenes are steeped in memory—honeyed. Once again Vittorio Storaro is Bertolucci's cinematographer, and the lighting suggests that moment in art history when the Barbizon school gave way to the summer sun of Impressionism—when color burst open and became diffused, as if nature, like a film director, could no longer control its own exuberance. The little hellion Olmo, skinny-faced and barefoot, collecting frogs to sell to the manor house and wearing them tied together, still alive and wriggling, around his hat, is like Huck Finn in a surreal pastoral calendar. His freedom is balanced against the image of the plump-faced, spoiled, rich Alfredo, forced to eat those frogs' legs at dinner, and throwing up. The camera moves constantly, even in the interiors, which suggest a 1930s idea of *fin de siècle;* they have the tawny light of the Italian Impressionist Fattori—or a tilted, fuzzy Maxfield Parrish. In the most prodigious sequence, which appears to be one continuous shot, Bertolucci presents the peasant uprising of 1908 as a panoramic mural: poplars in the mist; the landowning hunters shooting ducks, which fall in the river; peasants who have been evicted from their land leaving on loaded wagons while, of those remaining, the men prepare to resist and the women stretch out on the road to block the oncoming cavalry, who ride up to their bodies, turn around, and leave. The camera executes almost a figure eight in this lyrical panning, tracking crane shot; it sweeps over the Po Valley, showing you the different, conflicting elements in the landscape. You're given the components of a novel at a glance, and every one of them is shown in relation to the others. Bertolucci has perhaps the greatest spatial-temporal sense of all film directors. The simultaneous actions that other directors have achieved only by cutting he puts in the same shot. The effect of this hunters-peasants-cavalry sequence is of a passage of visual music. Bertolucci is satisfied by its visual completeness, and he moves on to the next thing that interests him.

But for us in the audience his great sequences don't achieve their full power, because there's no follow-through. Years pass between sequences, when we want what happens next. Did the cavalry return? (Has there ever been a film that dealt successfully with so long a span of time? Maybe the *Godfather* films, jointly.) It's true that one remembers the great scenes from the nineteenth-century Russian novels, not the passages in between; but the greatness of those scenes derives from their meaning in the narrative, from the way they reverberate through what we have already read and what follows. There's a consistency of vision in Turgenev or Dostoevski or Tolstoy; we're told what we want to know. Bertolucci's great sequences don't make us think back or anticipate. He's attempting to achieve that Verdian naïveté, but, like many other directors now, he reproduces only the poetic form of the great moments from old movies (the cavalry sequence is an expansion on John Ford). There is a scene of a peasant celebration along the riverbanks which has a nostalgic yearning for simplicity; Bertolucci wants to make us feel the *goodness* of simplicity, the way John Ford did when he shot the frontier dance on the foundation for the church in *My Darling Clementine,* with Wyatt Earp (Henry Fonda), his hair pressed flat for propriety's sake, innocently hopping up and down with his lady. But there are too many divided emotions in *1900* for the riverbank scene to have its effect; Bertolucci does not have the gift of simplicity. After the Liberation Day opening, the childhood section—the first hour—flows seamlessly, until the sequence in which the boys go into town to a workers' Punch-and-Judy show that is broken up by mounted police. At this point, the continuity weakens. Yet even when the movie is flowing along there's an unease inside the virtuosity.

There is something off in the tone of *1900* right from the start. Partly it's the sound. In order to get the film financed (it cost eight million dollars), it had to be made with an international cast; there is no "original-language" version. The Italian version was all dubbed, but so many Italian directors employ visual effects they can achieve only by shooting silent and adding the sound later that Italians (and many other Europeans) ignore dead sound. We don't. In the English version that Bertolucci has prepared, Lancaster's performance has particular force, and that may be because his dialogue seems live. The track is a mixture of synch sound, post-synch sound, and dubbing, so within a scene there will be a shift in ambience—different hollows and bouncebacks, which weaken the emotion. Depardieu and Stefania Sandrelli are the only major performers whose voices are dubbed; De Niro, Dominique Sanda, Hayden, Donald Sutherland (who plays the Fascist Attila), and Laura Betti (who plays his paramour, Regina) all speak their own lines, but the post-synching has a slightly removed sound—and, of course, the minor players and the peasants who fill out the cast are dubbed. Visually and thematically, the film is conceived with so many contrasts, clashes, allusions, and symmetrical variations that one can see where the years of preparation went. The actual dialogue seems almost an after-thought, and the actors speak their lines without much confidence that they're worth saying. And so we're aware of the actors as actors, and of their different cultures. They're not all sure what they're meant to be conveying. And we're not, either.

The principal actors are characters but they're also puppets in this gigantic class-struggle puppet show, and so if we ask why it is that Alfredo, a decent, friendly fellow with an amused, wry glint in his intelligent eyes, is so weak that he allows his overseer Attila to tyrannize the peasant workers, the explanation can only be that at this point in history the landowning class had lost its strength, and had become passive collaborators in evil. Bertolucci doesn't show that Alfredo *needs* Attila—psychologically or economically. Alfredo's decision to keep the Fascist monsters Attila and Regina under his roof seems some sort of historical fatalism—as if he had the director's game plan in mind and behaved accordingly. And De Niro, acting the historical role assigned him—the withered seed of a once proud line—looks small, shrunken. As a child, Alfredo even has trouble with his penis: his foreskin is tight, while that of the peasant Olmo is loose and flexible. Alfredo is ineffectual—it's the Ashley Wilkes role—and De Niro, who might have tried to summon up some hamminess to see him through, didn't. He gives an ineffectual performance. There's an interior continuity in it, but there isn't any excitement—how could there be?

As a spokesman for the Socialist dream, Depardieu has the advantage of heroic physical presence; he has his wary jugface—he stares out at us like the rough-sensitive Botticelli in his self-portrait in *The Adoration of the Magi.* But he seems emblematic—without any clear personality—and his role is fragmented over the years. Some of his screen time is wasted in dangling scenes involving the theft of a gun—scenes we expect will connect with a later event. A larger disappointment is that the child Olmo, the fearless, unmanageable gamin who is the despair of his mother, doesn't grow up to be the firebrand one expects. When he returns from the First World War, he's a clear-eyed solid-peasant citizen, firm in the ways of courage and virtue. Bertolucci has set up the childhood sequences so that the boys seem destined to become the heroes of his epic—the carriers of history. We wait to see their lives become focussed, but then he pulls a dialectical switch. He deëmphasizes them, to indicate that they are not vital to the historical events of their time—they are merely figures borne along by the flood of history. Olmo may be a peasant leader, but it is those he leads who are the heroes. How many different games can a director play in a movie? Using two young stars known for their volatile, "dangerous" presence and turning them into supporting players—denying us individual heroes—Bertolucci betrays the romantic epic form.

Because of the switch from the two men to the peasants, the only characters who register fully are those who are allowed their movie-derived mythological roles—the grandfathers, Lancaster and Hayden, and, surprisingly, at moments Dominique Sanda. There is, mercifully, no capitalist class in this movie—only the remnants of feudalism. And as the feudal lord who still likes to sink his toes in earth and cow dung Lancaster expresses declining physical vigor with all the command of his thirty-odd years of movie heroics. He isn't the polished lord he played in *The Leopard;* he's a peasant at heart, a crude, honest man who despises Alfredo's father—his greedy hypocrite son who cheats the peasants and squeezes them dry. There's love in Bertolucci's portrait of the profane, raging old bull; even though he hangs himself in the stables, in disgust at his own impotence and the collapse of his world, there's no contempt for his act. And, though this isn't intentional, his death has more conviction than that of the man he respects and would like to consider a friend—the leader of the peasant clan, Hayden. This old peasant sits down to rest under an oak tree and slips away. Visually this is fine, but it's priggishly programmatic. Still, they're both old oaks, and if Hayden's performance isn't as strong as Lancaster's, he has his noble, weather-beaten presence. His hair is worn short, cut way up high on his head, and his neck is long and straight, with cords like organ pipes; he resembles the famous photograph of Dovzhenko that is reproduced in *Agee on Film.*

Except for her work with Bertolucci, and in De Sica's *The Garden of the Finzi-Continis*, Dominique Sanda's performances have been stilted, amateurish. With Bertolucci, she is all visual: the image, the essence, of movie glamour, Garbo without depth—a trifling Garbo. As Ada, she has a weird, boneless seductiveness, like the young Lauren Bacall become a wraith. She's all curves, her body a crescent and her crushed upper lip conveying ironic secret promises. It may be that Bertolucci doesn't know what to do with his "thinking woman"—the militant Anita, whose exhortations to the peasants have no conviction. But when this gauzy vamp Ada slithers across the screen, with her gowns floating half off, or with a soft big-brimmed hat framing her come-hither smiles, she's the past recalled, all right, and you don't want to let it go. Ada, a virgin Futurist bohemian who smokes furiously and drives a Bugatti, is all affectation—self-dramatizing spoofery. She composes free verse, but if she has an art it's the art of the moue, and she has been given the funniest lines in the picture. She and Alfredo's homosexual uncle Ottavio (Werner Bruhns) represent charming, frivolous decadence, and the film doesn't try to turn them into villains.

Fascism here is demonological—so lewdly melodramatic that it makes Visconti's excesses in *The Damned* seem courtly. In the second half of *1900*, when Attila and Regina—the Fascist Macbeth and Lady Macbeth—come to power, the imagery changes to the dark mists of autumn and winter. Their posturings are like a hurdy-gurdy variation on the strident, Expressionist horror of Eisenstein's mad Ivan the Terrible. It's Fascism as a strain of diseased, perverted sexuality, and it explodes in a couple of scenes of shocking, Kabuki-wild violence. Attila and Regina are everything dirty, and we can almost hear the hiss of electric sparks shooting out of their heads. (Is it relevant that Bertolucci's father's name was Attilio?) These two are meant to embody the aggressive forces of the bourgeoisie; Alfredo and Ada's white wedding is followed by Attila and Regina's vile rites—they sodomize and murder a child. (The sequence would mean more to an audience if Bertolucci had indicated that the wedding aroused in Attila and Regina a need to defile it. When they go off to their debauchery, it's as if they did this every afternoon before tea.) Dressed all in black, at six feet four and with pale-blue eyes, Sutherland is already somewhat hyperbolic, and with a grotesque false high forehead he's a black-shirted vampire. All this curling of lips, baring of jagged teeth, and flashing of demented eyes must be what the director wanted, but only a very dedicated liberal would play a Fascist in this manner. Bertolucci wove a Hammer-Films gothic thread into his tapestry. What Attila and his guttural, leering accomplice Regina represent is what Fascism and Nazism became for those who made lampshades out of human skin, but it doesn't account for the attraction of Fascism and Nazism as political movements. The nightmare sadism gives *1900* a spaghetti-Western view of class struggle. This, too, must be partly intended: Bertolucci, who worked on the story of Sergio Leone's *Once Upon a Time in the West,* has used Leone's composer, Ennio Morricone; his creamy elegiac score heightens the emotion in the first half but suddenly, in the second, takes a dive into Peyton Place schlock–Chopin piano music.

The framing device—that pivotal Liberation Day—is the allegorical aspect of *1900,* and its worst stumbling block. Alfredo, held prisoner, is detached in his attitude; shuffling along in a cardigan, with a slack, dumb grin and a mustache two inches wide, he's no more than a nose-picking clerk. His trial, with the complaints of his accusers, who hold him to account for their rotting teeth and missing fingers, is coyly didactic, telling you that you should live right—under a playful veneer that makes you squirm. There are echoes of Chairman Mao's Little Red Book. It's a Maoist-Brechtian Judgment Day. Bertolucci's utopian future, with Olmo's daughter skipping among the haystacks, doesn't improve on the shots of little girls playing in the sun which were used by Griffith to demonstrate how beautiful life would be once people stopped being intolerant.

A solemn protest march ends the first half of the film: a funeral march displaying the charred bodies of four old men, who were in a *casa del popolo*—a workers' meeting hall—that the Fascists set on fire. The march signifies the unity of the workers, and it is magnificently staged, with a uniformed brass band playing the "Internationale"; it is set off from ordinary events by being photographed in a simplified palette—but it's Communist-color-coördinated! The caskets are lined in red, and every mourning marcher, every horse wears a patch of exactly the same shade. Ribbons, bows, scarves, furbelows—they're all one ravishing, sumptuous red. This is visual Verdi; it's splendid—a Communist fantasy march. But a viewer doesn't know whether to exult in the beauty or to laugh. Is Bertolucci a Communist for the sake of color? Are we rooting for a team? Red banners fly from the train that bears the young Olmo and the other striking workers' children off to where they can be fed; a huge patchwork canopy—a rainbow of reds—is unfurled on Liberation Day. Isn't this aesthetic Communism as flighty as Ada's aesthetic anti-Fascism?

Bertolucci has somehow resolved his own political contradictions in a dream of a happy agrarian future that hasn't budged beyond the turn of the century. The belief that permeates this movie is that Communism will preserve the folk culture of the peasants. Still nostalgic for life "before the revolution," Bertolucci now thinks that that life can be preserved only after the revolution. His is an anthropologist's Communism: he doesn't want the peasants corrupted into selling native artifacts to tourists; he doesn't want them exposed to credit cards and 100% virgin acrylic. It may be that in Emilia (the birthplace of Italian Socialism as well as of Verdi and Bertolucci), a prosperous region that has been partly administered by Communists since the end of the Second World War, the peasant culture has in fact flourished. But this film is addressed to the world outside Emilia, where the sumptuous innocence of Bertolucci's vision suggests Marie Antoinette playing shepherdess. *1900* represents the thinking of someone who grew up at the movies and accepted the myth that all problems can be brought to a happy resolution. Communism is going to usher in a folk utopia, and an artist who loves style above all else can make a people's film by drawing upon the standard metaphors of American and Soviet movies.

Bertolucci has said that all his films are "desperately autobiographical," and in this one the desperation shows. He has cast De Niro, an actor whose responsiveness to the camera derives from his reserves of passion and, having cast this man as himself, has not allowed him *any* passion. Bertolucci, locking himself away, locked out De Niro as an actor—gutted him. His Alfredo is an unfinished man: a man who hasn't tested himself. He's too emasculated even to suffer. Alfredo is the pampered, bourgeois liberal that Bertolucci guiltily fears himself to be, while Olmo is his proletarian dream self, and at the end it's as if the class struggle were just two boys trying to out-macho each other, still checking to see who has the bigger penis. Under the class struggle, that's the theme all the way through. Most directors are at their best when they deal with what's closest to them. In this film, Bertolucci is at his feeblest every time he gets near the adult Alfredo. He stays as far away as possible. This director has gone so much further than most movie directors that he's run up against what novelists and dramatists run up against: the desire to escape oneself. He has fled to the lives of the peasants and put an optimist's bland smile on top of the despair of his *Last Tango in Paris*. His utopia rests on the belief that peasants live in a pre-Freudian state; they have no conflict except with their oppressors. They're not plagued with the problems of bourgeois artists—they have loose foreskins. There is a connection between the film's blissed-out politics and the way Bertolucci treats the Fascist plunderers. He's not afraid to show violence, but he doesn't allow himself to identify with the person doing the violence. It is Dostoevski's identifying more with the characters who go out of control than with the others that makes reading him deeply terrifying. Bertolucci rejects the vile, violent possibilities in himself. That's why he lets Donald Sutherland go so far in his performance that human iniquity is turned into a cartoon. Bertolucci wants to believe in his peasants—who are so firm in their goodness, so split off from the Fascist criminality that they're less than human.

This film is about Bernardo Bertolucci's need for myth, and his self-denial. For those who are infatuated with what they loathe, the battle with themselves never stops. *1900* has all of Bertolucci's themes and motifs; one could call it the Portable Bertolucci, though it isn't portable. It's like a course to be enrolled in, with a guaranteed horror every hour. *1900* is a gigantic system of defenses—human fallibility immortalized. The film is appalling, yet is has the grandeur of a classic visionary folly. Next to it, all the other new movies are like something you hold up at the end of a toothpick.

The New Yorker, October 31, 1977

ABOUT RUDOLF NUREYEV IN
VALENTINO

Ken Russell uses Rudolf Nureyev in *Valentino* the way he used Twiggy in *The Boy Friend;* he gets the publicity value out of Nureyev's screen-acting début and doesn't worry about providing plausible material for him, giving him partners who will set him off, or protecting him. Twiggy was cast as a Cinderella, but with Russell as her godmother she remained a waif. Nureyev, however, despite his inexperience in speaking lines, is not a novice performer—and he knows how to laugh at himself. This is a movie about a legendary silent-screen idol whose voice isn't known (Rudolph Valentino died in 1926), played by a legendary dancer whose voice isn't known, either. Hearing Nureyev is something of an unveiling, and his effort to adapt his facial movements (the movements of someone who grew up speaking Russian) to an Italian accent gives his performance an extra, *cinéma vérité* hazardousness. Nureyev doesn't have the bloom of Valentino, who was only thirty-one when he died. However, the disparity in age hardly matters; in a Ken Russell picture, the yowling characters aren't even recognizable as members of the human race. *Valentino* was shot in England and Spain, and there has been little attempt to match the sleekness of the remembered Valentino—the beautifully dressed, almond-eyed Latin in his California Spanish, Art Nouveau streamlined décor. Nureyev's high cheekbones, his imperious sniff, and the set of his full mouth are more reminiscent of Yul

Brynner when he first played in *The King and I*. Nureyev doesn't evoke Valentino, but from time to time he has a captivating, very funny temperament of his own.

Seen up close, Nureyev has a camp devil loose in him; he has the seductive, moody insolence of an older, more cosmopolitan James Dean, without the self-consciousness. His eagerness to please would be just right for frivolous, lyrical comedy, and he could play cruel charmers—he has the kinky-angel grin. With the right director—Bob Fosse to release his athleticism, or someone like Michael Ritchie, perhaps, to catch the fickle, contradictory shades of feeling and register his easiest movements—he could be a supremely entertaining screen performer. He's a showman through and through. He has the deep-set eyes of a Zen archer: the public is the target. At the ballet, one may be too aware of him as a personality, yet what can be faintly distasteful there—his being a star before he's a dancer—is what makes him a full presence on the screen. He has to be photographed carefully: his nose (ski run, pointed, with flaring nostrils) is problematic, and when he's tense or the lighting is bad, he gets that jaded gigolo look of Alain Delon. But he doesn't have the mime's masklike expressions that wreck most dancers as screen actors, and his justly celebrated "Blakean torso" is never rigid. He moves with the élan that dancers are supposed to have but usually don't, and when his face is relaxed, he suggests what Sabu should have grown up to be—a smiling, primitive-sophisticated rajah. His narcissistic menace is more complexly amusing than Valentino's famous smoldering menace. It's this narcissism that makes him (like James Dean) seem untamable—a "natural" rebel.

The surprise of Nureyev onscreen (although one should have guessed it from his work on the ballet stage) is how generous this narcissism is. He wants to give out; that has to be why he sets himself such a sweatshop schedule of performances with one dance company after another. Now thirty-nine, he must have considered that the movies could provide him with a new outlet. There's choreography, or directing a dance company, of course; but could a man who loves to perform as much as Nureyev does function successfully behind the scenes? He's old for a *premier danseur* but not for a movie actor. (Burt Lancaster, for example, made his first movie when he was about thirty-four; Pacino was thirty-one when he caught public attention in *The Panic in Needle Park;* Bogart didn't hit his full stride until he was in his forties.) Nureyev's generosity extends even toward the dancing required of him here, which, despite Russell's own dance background, is staged insultingly. The initial number—a tango, with Valentino, as a dance instructor, teaching Nijinsky (Anthony Dowell)—is photographed from much too far away, and others are so cheaply conceived that Nureyev is featured tapping or whizzing around to show off his speed, as if he were the José Iturbi of dance.

The New Yorker, November 7, 1977

CLOSE ENCOUNTERS OF THE THIRD KIND
THE GREENING OF THE SOLAR SYSTEM

C *lose Encounters of the Third Kind* is the most innocent of all technological-marvel movies, and one of the most satisfying. This film has retained some of the wonder and bafflement we feel when we first go into a planetarium: we ooh and aah at the vastness, and at the beauty of the mystery. The film doesn't overawe us, though, because it has a child's playfulness and love of surprises. There is a moment that is startlingly funny in its obviousness when a whole landscape of people in India who are ecstatically chanting a five-note theme are asked where these sounds came from, and a mass of arms are raised straight up, forefingers pointing. In routine science-fiction films, any bodies from space are alien invaders; they come from *out there,* and we start running or shooting. But in *Close Encounters* they come from *up there*—they're sunburst Gods arriving through Blakean Old Testament clouds. This isn't nuts-and-bolts, *Popular Mechanics* sci-fi; it's beatific technology—machines from outer space deified. And to cap it all, the intelligent creatures in these machines are benevolent. They want to get to know us. This vision would be *too* warm and soul-satisfying if it weren't for the writer-director Steven Spielberg's skeptical, let's-try-it-on spirit. He's an entertainer—a magician in the age of movies. Is Spielberg an artist? Not exactly—or not yet. He's a prodigy—a flimflam wizard-technician. The immense charm of *Close Encounters* comes from the fact that, for all its scale and expense (nineteen million dollars), this is a young man's movie—Spielberg is still under thirty—and there's not a sour thought in it. (The title is from a book by the astronomer Dr. J. Allen Hynek—close encounters of the first kind are sightings, the second kind are physical evidence, and the third involve actual contact. Sightings aren't necessarily close and they're not encounters, and physical evidence isn't an encounter, either, but the title sounds good, anyway.)

The basic story is scanty: this unidentified-flying-objects movie is about those who are "looking for answers." In Muncie, Indiana, an electrical-power-company lineman named Roy (Richard Dreyfuss), a three-year-old boy named Barry (Cary Guffey), the boy's mother (Melinda Dillon), and a collection of innocuous misfits, retired folks, and artists all catch sight of the flaring lights of spacecraft; some of them are sunburned, and a vision is implanted in them. They become obsessed with a shape they don't understand—a lumpy, sawed-off pyramid or mountain. At the same time, an international team of scientists, headed by a clearheaded Frenchman, Lacombe (François Truffaut), is dashing about the globe picking up word of other signals, which direct the team to a mountain in Wyoming. It is the spot the aliens have chosen for a rendezvous with us earthlings, and the dreamers—the invited guests—converge upon it. But military personnel who are working with the scientific team cut most of them off. It's a going-to-Bethlehem story. Only those with enough faith and luck make it.

Close Encounters is a vindication of village crazies. Those people always give you the feeling they know something you don't, and in this scientific fairy tale it turns out they do. God is up there in a crystal-chandelier space-ship, and He likes us. The stoned, the gullible, the half-mad, and just plain folks are His chosen people. To be more exact: *It* likes us. (The extra-terrestrials appear to have evolved beyond sex.) The largest craft, the mother ship, is a great celestial body—a symmetrical, rounded Christmas-tree orna-ment as big as a city. When it descends from on high, looming over the mountain and hovering there, no storybook illustration can compete with it. This is something only movies can do: dazzle you by sheer scale—and in this case by lights and music as well. Spielberg is the son of an electrical-engineer, sci-fi-addict father and a classical-pianist mother, and in the climax of the film he does justice to both. Under the French scientist's direction, the earthlings are ready with a console, and they greet the great craft with an oboe solo—variations on the five-note theme; the craft answers in deep, tuba tones. The dialogue becomes blissfully garrulous. And with light flooding out from the windows of this omniscient airship—it's like New York's skyscrapers all lighted up on a summer night—there is a conversational duet: the music of the spheres. This is one of the peerless moments in movie history—spiritually re-assuring, magical, and funny at the same time. Very few movies have ever hit upon this combination of fantasy and amusement—*The Wizard of Oz*, perhaps, in a plainer, down-home way.

Close Encounters, too, is a kids' movie in the best sense. You can feel the pleasure the young director took in making it. With his gift for investing ma-chines with personality, Spielberg is the right director for science fantasy. He made a malevolent character of a truck in *Duel,* his famous made-for-TV movie. In his first theatrical feature, *The Sugarland Express,* he had cars danc-ing, feuding, bonding. In his second film, *Jaws,* he turned a computer-operated shark into a personal enemy. And now he's got his biggest mechanical toys: the mother ship and the flying-saucer herald angels—whirring through the skies, flashing their lights. Some are intergalactic Pucks teasing earthlings and leading them on fools' chases; some are stately geometric forms spinning languorously. Each is like a musical divertimento, a delight unto itself. *Jaws* was a nightmare movie; this is a dream. In *Jaws,* the harrowing terror kept building; here the mystical good humor builds—the story envelops you. With Truffaut as Lacombe, the sympathies of the sci-entist don't have to be explained; he is essentially the educated man of good will that Truffaut played in his own *The Wild Child.* Truffaut suggests effi-ciency plus innate refinement; his forehead is noble, his features are mod-elled in a seraphic smile, and he's small. His Lacombe is a calm, wise child who responds to the vision of the dreamer-misfits—shares their instinctive trust of what is in space. (And when, at last, he communicates with a visitor

755

from above, there is a fleeting suggestion of Jean Renoir's lopsided grin in the extraterrestrial's young-old face.)

There are, of course, limitations to science-fiction movies. People used to love to be frightened by ghost stories—those evil portents of a world beyond death, with their intimations of haunted, macabre sex. Those stories belonged to an age when people lived in fear of their own impulses, and in dread of punishment. And movies were able to bring out the stories' primitive-sophisticated power—their suggestiveness. Science fiction, the modern successor to tales of the supernatural, lacks those psychological dimensions, it doesn't have the whole nighttime apparatus of guilt and superstition clinging to it. The attraction of science fiction is that it's an escape into an almost abstract unknown. Those who are frightened of, despairing about, or bored with this world like to turn their hopes to other worlds in space, but they're not much interested in people. Imagination and idealism are expressed in simplified, allegorical terms. Generally speaking, when a speculative fantasy deals with human conflicts in any depth, it ceases to be called science fiction. The persistent fault of sci-fi movies has been the split between the splendor of their special effects and the stilted mediocrity of their characters, situations, and dialogue. There has probably never been a first-rate characterization in an American science-fiction movie—how could there be, since the stories don't depend on character? (That's why science fiction used to be considered a pulp genre.) It's difficult to think of even one well-written role. Kubrick's *2001* was no exception: its only character who made any impression was Hal, the voice of the computer. In *Star Wars*, audiences fell in love with R2D2 and C3P0; people had the same reaction to Robby, the robot in *Forbidden Planet*, and to the drones in *Silent Running* (which was directed by Douglas Trumbull, who supervised the special photographic effects in *Close Encounters*). In sci-fi movies, the robots have personalities; the actors usually don't. *2001* wasn't a pop escapist fantasy, like *Star Wars;* it was an attempt at a more serious view of the future, which was seen as an extension of now, a super-ordinary world. In Kubrick's conception, there was no richness, no texture—it was all blandness. He might as well have been saying, "I have seen the future and it put me to sleep." Spielberg's movie is set right now, and it has none of that ponderous seriousness—but it's the same bland now that sci-fi enthusiasts seem to think we live in. The banality is really in *their* view of human life.

With a vast, clear sky full of stars, and a sense of imminence—much of the movie feels like being inside the dome of an enchanted cathedral waiting for the Arrival—terse, swift, heightened dialogue is called for. Instead, we hear casual, ordinary-man language, and, although it has an original, colloquial snap, Spielberg just doesn't have the feeling for words which he has for images. And he doesn't create the central characters (Barry's mother and Roy), or develop them, in a *writer's* way; he's thinking about how to get them into the positions he wants them in for his visual plan. Roy is supposed to be the Hitchcockian ordinary man in extraordinary circumstances; for

Hitchcock that could be Cary Grant, but for Spielberg it means a sincere attempt to show how a lumpy average man living in pop-culture emptiness could get caught up in a quest. Richard Dreyfuss's Roy waddles in rear view, and becomes moist-eyed when he longs for knowledge. We seem to be asked to respond to Roy for being out of condition and, at times, out of control. There's a fine dinner scene in which Roy's children, who love him, are upset by the compulsiveness of his behavior; they can feel him growing away from them. But Spielberg doesn't follow through on the change in Roy; he jumps to a low-comedy marriage-breakup scene. And after we've had a few closeups of Roy's hectic fervor, as he attempts to share his U.F.O. experience with his pragmatic wife (Teri Garr), her dry philistinism has a hard-edged, comic-strip appeal. With her one-track mind, she's a frozen pizza in Roy's yearning-mystic eye. As one of the crackpots—a man who has seen Bigfoot as well as flying saucers—Roberts Blossom has the look of a true believer. That's what Dreyfuss lacks. Spielberg is far more successful with Barry, the three-year-old, whose pure lust for otherworldly entertainment is delicately funny. Barry, the toddling light-worshipper who sees the sky as a giant toy shop, is closer to the heart of Spielberg's vision than Roy, whose "looking for answers" Dreyfuss strains to represent.

Steven Spielberg is probably the most gifted American director who's dedicated to sheer entertainment. He may have different aims from the aims of people we call artists, but he has integrity: it centers on his means. His expressive drive is to tell a story in shots that are live and hopping, and his grasp of graphic dynamics may be as strong as that of anyone working in movies now. The spatial relationships inside the frame here owe little to the stage, or even to painting; Spielberg succeeds in making the compositions so startlingly immediate that they give off an electric charge. He puts us right in the middle of the action, yet there's enough aesthetic distance—he doesn't assault us. Though the perspectives don't appear forced or unnatural, they're often slightly tilted, with people moving rapidly in or out of the frame, rarely intersecting the center and never occupying it. By designing the images in advance, Spielberg is able to cut without any confusion. Nobody cuts faster on shots full of activity than he does, yet it's never just for the sake of variety: it's what the movie is about that generates the images and the cutting pattern, and there's a constant pickup in excitement from shot to shot—a ziggety forward motion. Even the weakly motivated sequences (which are needed for a later, visual payoff)—such as Roy's going batty, and tearing up his garden and throwing mud and plants in through his kitchen window, or the mountain scaling out of *North by Northwest*, which comes across as a delaying tactic—are partly saved by Spielberg's visual energy. *Close Encounters* is big and complex (in addition to Vilmos Zsigmond, who was the director of photography, other famous cinematographers—William A. Fraker, Douglas Slocombe, John Alonzo, and Laszlo Kovacs—worked on it), and there are sequences, such as the one in India, that are fine in themselves yet don't have Spielberg's distinctive graphics. But he never loses the emotional drive of his subject, and he gives audiences full opportunity to luxuriate in the sensuousness of the spectacle. It's too bad that John Williams, who did the score, thinks he's still working on *Jaws.* Movie music in general has reached the point where if it isn't meant to cheer you or to scare you, the composer doesn't know what to do. Except for the great duet here, Williams provides emotional noise, rising and shrilling in the Bernard Herrmann manner. The score fails to match the witty use of rapturousness in such images as that of Barry trotting out of his house at night—just a speck on the prairie under a blanket of stars and a huge roiling cloud.

Close Encounters shows an excess of kindness—an inability (or, perhaps, unwillingness) to perceive the streak of cowardice and ignorance and confusion in the actions of the authorities who balk the efforts of the visionaries to reach their goal. Having devised a plot in which the government systematically covers up information about U.F.O. sightings, Spielberg is much too casual about how this is done and imprecise about why. He has a paranoid plot, but he hasn't dramatized the enemy. The obstacles here are just Air Force and Army men doing their duty, and these authorities are shrugged off by the cranks, or humbly accepted. Roy and the others don't have the incapacitating hatred of smooth-talking authority which would make us respond to their frustrations—would make us feel what was unhinging them. Impersonality doesn't enrage Spielberg, because he hasn't got at the personality hidden in it. Stock villainy isn't what's needed—something deeper is. He had similar trouble with the corrupt local merchants and politicians in *Jaws;* their corruption was tired, ritualized—it was necessary for the plot, that was all. In *Close Encounters,* there is nothing behind what the military men do except bureaucratic indifference. But that means they don't know what they're doing—and to be so totally blind is tragic, crazy emptiness. Spielberg has a genuine affection for harmless aberrants, but he doesn't fathom the dangerous aberrance of authority—particularly an authority that in its own eyes is being completely reasonable. In terms of his plot, Spielberg needs some Terry Southern in his soul, or maybe even some Norman Wexler. He needs to show us how scared bureaucrats are of something they can't understand and don't know how to handle.

Steven Spielberg is commercial without really being commercial: that is, he's a popular entertainer who doesn't have a feeling for the profane, sneaky pleasures of tawdriness. *Close Encounters* is so generous in its feelings that it makes one feel maternal and protective; there's also another side of one, which says, "I could use a little dirty friction." Most directors who make sweet movies are unskilled, and you're supposed to forgive them their incompetence because of their niceness. Spielberg may be the only director with technical virtuosity ever to make a transcendently sweet movie. *Close Encounters* is almost the opposite of *Star Wars,* in which a whole planet was blown up and nobody batted an eye. It seems almost inconceivable, but nobody gets hurt in this movie, except the occupants of one police car, who are so delirious in their pursuit of a flying object that they hurtle off the highway into the air, and then bounce down to earth in a ditch—and they may be too surprised to be hurt. The film is like *Oklahoma!* in space, with jokes; it's spiritual cotton candy and it goes down easy. The summer-skies atmosphere is achieved by certain exclusions: the film is virtually sexless, and the aliens don't deliver any invitations to the Soviet bloc, so there's no political scrambling in the race to the rendezvous. Mercifully, there's no cosmological philosophizing, either: nobody stands around arguing about what the manifestations prove. As was the case with *2001,* though, the publicity is full of the usual announcements about the data in it not having been disproved. And statistics about how many millions of people claim to have seen flying saucers are used to give the film an almost official status, as if it were a daring inquiry into facts that the government is hiding from us. These publicity claims of credibility and usefulness only take away from what should be the film's enduring appeal as fantasy.

Close Encounters is a beautiful, big, enjoyable film that sends you out happy. It might be even better if there weren't so many people at the end looking upward with transfigured faces. *Star Wars* had its guru, Alec Guinness, in his neo-*Lost Horizon* trappings, and this film, too, has its gaseous naïveté. But it has the visionary magic to go with it. If Roy and Lacombe and the other dreamers do a lot of blinking and staring up with wet eyes, it's not like *The Miracle of Our Lady of Fatima*—here we at least get to see what they're staring at. And we watch Roy ascend the stairway to Heaven. Spielberg is busy, like that fine humbug Wizard of Oz, pressing buttons on his light panel. He puts on a great show.

The New Yorker, November 28, 1977

THAT OBSCURE OBJECT OF DESIRE
CUTTING LIGHT

The great thing about Luis Buñuel's *That Obscure Object of Desire* is that it gives you the feeling that it was made by a happy man. The film was shot in Seville and Paris, and Buñuel's happiness shines especially in the luxuriance of Seville. This city is like an older, more southern, Mediterranean San Francisco; the surfaces shimmer, and the film is almost pink with happiness. The feeling that permeates *That Obscure Object of Desire* is that for Buñuel now life is more important than art. It is for everybody, maybe, but when artists are raging—straining to express themselves—they don't feel that way. Buñuel no longer has any trouble expressing himself: art has become simple for him, as it did for Matisse in his later years, with his cut-and-pasted papers. What Buñuel is expressing is his own pleasure in his command of the medium: he's at peace with himself, and art has become pure play for him. This has never happened in movies before: no one Buñuel's age (seventy-seven) has gone on making personal films, on material of his own choice.

"Cutting to the quick in color reminds me of the sculptor's direct carving," Matisse said. He had found a freedom he'd always wanted, and some of his late cutouts may be as good as anything he ever did: shallow great art. Though lighter, less palpable than the paintings, these cutouts have an energetic physical roughness, because of the scissors. They're airy—never static. Buñuel broke through with his buoyant late style in *The Discreet Charm of the Bourgeoisie* (1972). All the gloom, the cruelty, the outraged idealist's harshness seemed to have been transcended, and it was his humor that remained—that, and his moviemaking technique, which magically became almost weightless, yet with a storyteller's energy, uncomplicated, without fuss or pressure. Some men grow embittered as they age, but Buñuel got his bitterness out early on, and in old age he began to have a marvellous time, using what he'd learned. His films began to be set in his own period—a floating timelessness.

The Discreet Charm of the Bourgeoisie (made when he was seventy-two) had the surprise of relaxed virtuosity, as if he'd just discovered, at last, how to make movies, by a new, ironically matter-of-fact, thin-textured method—the visual equivalent of simple declarative sentences. His Surrealist vaudevillian's sense of parody had become more delicately precise, and his indifference to dramatic logic was total; the "sentences" might contradict and destroy each other. He showed this detached utter sureness of style again in 1974, in *Le Fantôme de la Liberté*, and he shows it now in *That Obscure Object*. But if age can give you a serenity that isn't available to youth, it also takes something away. There's a price you pay for serenity. *That Obscure Object* is far more pleasing than *Le Fantôme* was, but it's a little monotonous, and if the anti-bourgeois, anti-institutional jokes aren't exactly predictable, still one laughs not because they're funny but because one recognizes that they're distinctively Buñuelian—they have the cadence of Buñuel's wit.

The style of the film is peerlessly urbane; it moves along at a raconteur's pace as Mathieu (Fernando Rey), a rich, worldly French widower of perhaps fifty, boards the Seville-to-Paris train and makes the acquaintance of the other passengers in his first-class compartment. He seems a cultivated man, perfectly self-controlled, but before the train leaves Seville he dumps a bucket of water on a battered young woman who attempts to come on board, and seems rather pleased with himself. Observing that his travelling companions are nonplussed, he explains that she is "the worst of all women," and during the journey he entertains them with the story of why he drenched the terrible Conchita, whom he first met when she was hired as a maid in his home in Paris, and whom, over the years, he has supported, and even lived with, but never won. In *The Discreet Charm of the Bourgeoisie*, a group of people were never able to eat a meal; the film proceeded by interruptions. In *That Obscure Object,* Mathieu is never able to consummate sex with Conchita. She alternates between promises and postponements: she teases him, fleeces him, enrages him. She offers herself to him and then comes to bed armored in intricately laced heavy-canvas drawers; Conchita frustrates Mathieu to tears of exhaustion—and he loves her. The ambiguous element is that she also claims to love him, but says, "If I gave in, you wouldn't love me anymore." Is she really denying him because she loves him? This could be her gambit; it could be the truth.

That Obscure Object is the fifth movie version of Pierre Louÿs's short novel about a femme fatale, *La Femme et le Pantin,* published in 1898. It was filmed in 1920, starring Geraldine Farrar, again in 1929, with Conchita Montenegro, and again in 1935, when Josef von Sternberg made the most famous version, *The Devil Is a Woman,* starring Marlene Dietrich. Buñuel wanted to do the story in the late fifties, but the producer and he disagreed about both the treatment and the star; the producer wanted Brigitte Bardot, who ultimately did the film—*A Woman Like Satan* (1958)—with Julien Duvivier directing. Buñuel got back to it when his style—and his outlook—had grown beyond it. The movie that Buñuel might have made in the late fifties would surely have been more provocatively irrational, more *animal* than the film he has made now. In the sixties, when he made *Belle de Jour,* he still had a dirty, sadistic, funny streak; if he had filmed the Louÿs story then, we might have felt a mean glee when Conchita taunts this rich, refined old goat who has everything in life he wants except her. But the runaround that Conchita gives Mathieu in *That Obscure Object* doesn't have much libidinal impact; repressed material doesn't poke up to startle us. The special quality of Buñuel's late, storyteller's style is that there are no layers, nothing hidden; that's what makes it so serene.

Buñuel has modernized the story; he has set it in a world askew where the old forms and courtesies persist—appearances still count—and terrorist explosions are casual happenings. When Mathieu is out in his limousine, his discreet, correct valet (André Weber) sits up front next to the chauffeur; the class relationships are intact, though no one is surprised when a car in front of them is booby-trapped—revolutionary acts are just one of the inconveniences of city life. The film is randomly punctuated with muggings, bombings, hijackings, murders. The initials of the illegal organizations are sexual acronyms, and the blasts that these groups set off are the only orgasms poor Mathieu ever gets near. Yet these Surreal touches don't detonate the emotions in the Mathieu-Conchita tangle; they seem part of another game. Buñuel's deftness at amusing himself was just right for the social satire of *The Discreet Charm*—no passions were involved. Here the tone is satirical, though the subject is passion. The tone suggests that Conchita is simply taking this lordly boulevardier for a grand ride—that her putting him in bondage is the revenge of the poor on the rich, and of women on men. But the idea of the mysterious unknowability of women (it was hot stuff in silent pictures) still clings to the story.

The psychological weakness of the script (and this was a problem in the von Sternberg version, too) is that Conchita is seen totally from the man's point of view—there's no clue to what her actual feelings are. Since Conchita is a literary conceit—a deliberately unresolved character—the part requires an actress who can capture our imaginations and tease us, as she teases Mathieu. Buñuel had cast Maria Schneider in the role, but they severed relations after a few days of shooting and he decided to fill the part with two actresses—Carole Bouquet, a tall French girl, and Angela Molina, a Spanish girl, who's shorter, more rounded—plus a third woman to speak the French dialogue for both of them. (Fernando Rey is dubbed by Michel Piccoli.) The script, by Buñuel and his collaborator, Jean-Claude Carrière, shows no sign of having been rewritten to take advantage of the stunt of using the two women as one; perhaps there wasn't time. There's no interplay of qualities or gestures; they simply shift interchangeably, with their natural characteristics providing some contrast. Bouquet, who's like an angular, sly Ali MacGraw, is poker-faced, except for a squint of amusement and a foxy, crooked smear of a smile. She's the more tantalizing, modern Conchita, while Molina is physically impulsive, and sensual in a traditional heaving and weeping, heavy-eyed way. Using the two actresses doesn't add any meaning; perhaps there's less than if there were only one. We have to believe that Mathieu sees something extraordinarily erotic in Conchita (even if we don't); we have to believe in his passion, or else the basic love tragedy isn't funny. And with these two women ducking in and out as if they were playing charades, Mathieu's relationship to Conchita seems to depend on which actress will turn up in the next shot.

Fernando Rey is probably the most believable man of the world in contemporary movies; even the tilt of his hat here is a rotting signal of wealth and breeding. And so when Mathieu, in his finely tailored leisure clothes, is seen to pick up a burlap sack and carry it on his back like a hump, the audience laughs. But it's not because this sack has any resonance in the film— the resonance is in our memories of other enigmatic tricks, in other Buñuel films. Buñuel's Surreal tomfoolery—sprinkling his films with disconnected jokes—has become a trademark, and one could almost take this aspect of *That Obscure Object* as self-homage; it suggests a variant form of what turns up more heavily and blatantly in Hitchcock's late films. It isn't self-homage: it's simply that Buñuel has the same turn of mind he has always had, though without the violence underneath to make the connections for us. The gags seem reprises rather than originals because they're not shocking. He sets up the Louÿs story, then treats it glancingly—as a joke to hang other jokes on. All his films are cosmic comedies now; it's not expression that he seeks but play—the entertainment of the senses.

Here is a master, for whom every shot is a demonstration of joyous ease—like Matisse picking up his scissors and cutting light. Working without waste or calculation, Buñuel makes films more directly—from inside himself to up there on the screen—than perhaps anyone else ever has. His technique has become so direct that he seems freed from technique, and the effect is of supreme clarity. But now that he has sprung past all the technological hurdles, what themes can he find that will be at one with his new freedom? The projects that were once wickedly alluring are no longer worthy of him. The wholeness of spirit that informs *That Obscure Object of Desire* outshines the story; the artist delights us even as the film disappoints us.

There is a special affection that moviegoers have for Luis Buñuel—not just because of our familiarity with his films (that can work against him, as it does in places in *That Obscure Object*) but because in an industry that rewards sentimentality he's kept his no-slobbering, disenchanted attitude. And so when enchantment floods in on him it has a clean radiance. The light of Seville is very soft here.

The New Yorker, December 19, 1977

SATURDAY NIGHT FEVER
NIRVANA

There is a thick, raw sensuality that some adolescents have which seems almost preconscious. In *Saturday Night Fever,* John Travolta has this rawness to such a degree that he seems naturally exaggerated: an Expressionist painter's view of a young prole. As Tony, a nineteen-year-old Italian Catholic who works selling paint in a hardware store in Brooklyn's Bay Ridge, he wears his heavy black hair brushed up in a blower-dried pompadour. His large, wide mouth stretches across his narrow face, and his eyes—small slits, close together—are, unexpectedly, glintingly blue and panicky. Walking down the street in his blood-red shirt, skintight pants, and platform soles, Tony moves to the rhythm of the disco music in his head. It's his pent-up physicality—his needing to dance, his becoming himself only when he dances—that draws us into the pop rapture of this film. In his room in his parents' cramped house, he begins the ritual of Saturday night: shaving, deodorizing, putting on gold chains with a cross and amulets and charms, selecting immaculate flashy tight clothes. The rhythm is never lost—he's away in his dream until he's caught in a bickering scene at the family dinner table. He leaves his home; his friends pick him up on the street, and then they're off to the dream palace—2001 Odyssey—where Tony, who is recognized as the champion dancer, is king.

Inside the giant disco hall, the young working-class boys and girls, recent high-school graduates who plod through their jobs all week, saving up for this night, give themselves over to the music. Sharing an erotic and aesthetic fantasy, they dance the L.A. Hustle ceremonially, in patterned ranks—a mass of dancers unified by the beat, stepping together in

763

trancelike discipline. Suggested by Nik Cohn's June 7, 1976, *New York* cover story, "Tribal Rites of the New Saturday Night," this movie has a new subject matter: how the financially pinched seventies generation that grew up on TV attempts to find its own forms of beauty and release. The Odyssey itself (the picture was shot in the actual Bay Ridge hall) has a plastic floor and suggests a TV-commercial version of Art Deco; the scenes there are vividly romantic, with the dancers in their brightest, showiest clothes, and the lights blinking in burning neon-rainbow colors, and the percolating music of the Bee Gees. The way *Saturday Night Fever* has been directed and shot, we feel the languorous pull of the discothèque, and the gaudiness is transformed. These are among the most hypnotically beautiful pop dance scenes ever filmed.

The director, John Badham, who is in his thirties, has made only one previous film, *The Bingo Long Traveling All-Stars and Motor Kings*, but he's well known for his work in television (*The Law* is probably his most impressive credit). The son of an English actress, Mary Hewitt, Badham grew up in Alabama, where his mother had her own TV talk show; his younger sister Mary played Gregory Peck's daughter in *To Kill a Mockingbird*. He went on to Yale, where he, the lyricist Richard Maltby, Jr., and the composer David Shire (who worked on the score of this picture) are reported to have been fervently devoted to putting on musicals, and he has staged *Saturday Night Fever* with a flowing movement that makes it far more of a sustained dance film than *The Turning Point*. When the patrons of the Odyssey clear the floor for Tony and he does a solo, he's a happy young rooster crowing in dance. And Badham, working with the choreographer Lester Wilson, the editor David Rawlins, and the cinematographer Ralf D. Bode, has designed this number so that it's as smoothly seductive to us as to the onlookers. There's no dead break between the rhythmed sequences at the Odyssey and the scenes when Tony is in hamburger joints with his friends or at a dance studio with Stephanie (Karen Lynn Gorney), the girl who's "different" from the other dancers, or on trips to the Verrazano-Narrows Bridge or, later, to Manhattan. These, too, have their musical beat—and are scored to songs by the Bee Gees and other groups, or to Walter Murphy's variations on Beethoven's Fifth, or to Shire's "Salsation" or his Gershwin-like "Manhattan Skyline." The film's sustained disco beat keeps the audience in an empathic rhythm with the characters: we're physically attuned to their fear of being trapped—of losing the beat.

It's a straight heterosexual film, but with a feeling for the sexiness of young boys who are bursting their britches with energy and desire—who want to *go*—which recalls Kenneth Anger's short film *Scorpio Rising* (1963). Anger celebrated the youth and sexuality and love of speed of motorcycle gangs while mocking their fetishistic trappings—the swastikas and black leather and chains that they used to simulate fearlessness. Those boys lived in a homoerotic fantasy of toughness, and their idols were James Dean and

Brando, as the motorcyclist in *The Wild One*. The boys in *Saturday Night Fever* have more traditional desires, though in a new, pop form. Their saint is Al Pacino—the boy like them who became somebody without denying who he was. When Tony looks in the mirror, it's Pacino he wants to see, and he keeps Pacino's picture on his wall. (He also has posters of Bruce Lee, of Farrah Fawcett-Majors, and of Sylvester Stallone and Talia Shire in *Rocky*.) It's not just that Pacino is for the Bay Ridge boys what Brando was for their parents; Brando represented the rebellious antithesis of the conventional heroes of his time, while Pacino stands alone. These boys are part of the post-Watergate working-class generation with no heroes *except* in TV-show-biz land; they have a historical span of twenty-three weeks, with repeats at Christmas.

The script was written by Norman Wexler (*Joe, Serpico, Mandingo, Drum*), and it has his urban-crazy-common-man wit—the jokes that double back on the people who make them. And Badham's kinetic style, which shows the characters' wavering feelings and gives a lilt to their conversations (especially those between Tony and Stephanie), removes the ugliness from Wexler's cruder scenes; the comedy is often syncopated. But Norman Wexler can't seem to keep his mind on anything for long; you never wait more than four scenes for any issue to be resolved, and then he hops off to something else. The picture is like flash cards: it keeps announcing its themes and then replacing them. Trying for conventional family conflicts, it wanders into a deadening subplot about Tony's older brother—a priest who has lost his vocation—which is only a cut above "All in the Family." Trying for "action," it brings in a gang rumble, with unwelcome echoes of *West Side Story*, and when one of Tony's friends dies (for no more substantial reason than to strengthen Tony's moral fiber), the episode throws the whole last part of the picture off course. Yet the mood, the beat, and the trance rhythm are so purely entertaining and Travolta is such an original presence that a viewer spins past these weaknesses.

John Travolta doesn't appear to be a "natural" dancer: his dances look like worked-up Broadway routines, but he gives himself to them with a fullness and zest that make his being the teen-agers' king utterly convincing. He commands the dance space at the Odyssey, and when the other dancers fall back to watch him it's because he's joyous to watch. He *acts* like someone who loves to dance. And, more than that, he acts like someone who loves to act. It's getting to be a joke—another Italian-American star. *Saturday Night Fever* is only Travolta's second movie (he was the Neanderthal beer-guzzling Billy in *Carrie*); he has become a teen and pre-teen favorite as Vinnie Barbarino in the "Welcome Back, Kotter" TV series, though, and in his one previous starring appearance, in the TV movie *The Boy in the Plastic Bubble*, he gave the character an abject, humiliated sensitivity that made the boy seem emotionally naked. One can read Travolta's face and body; he has the gift of transparency. When he wants us to feel how lost and confused Tony is, we feel it. He expresses shades of emotion that aren't set down in scripts, and he knows how to show us the decency and intelligence under Tony's un-couthness. Tony's mouth may look uneducated—pulpy, swollen-lipped, slack—but this isn't stupidity, it's bewilderment. Travolta gets so far inside the role he seems incapable of a false note; even the Brooklyn accent sounds unerring. At twenty-three, he's done enough to make it apparent that there's a broad distance between him and Tony, and that it's an actor's imagination that closes the gap. There's dedication in his approach to Tony's character; he isn't just a good actor, he's a generous-hearted actor.

Playing opposite him, Karen Lynn Gorney, whose facial style is as tense and hard as his is fluid and open, has a rough time at first. The story, un-fortunately, introduces Stephanie in *West Side Story* lyrical terms as the won-derful dancer Tony wants to meet, and Gorney isn't much of a dancer. She's proficient—she can go through the motions—but the body is holding back. So the film overworks soft-lighting effects. It takes a while before it's clear that Stephanie is a little climber and show-off—a Brooklyn girl who gives herself airs and talks about the important people she comes into contact with in her office job in Manhattan. Her pretensions to refinement are des-perately nippy and high-pitched. (She's reminiscent of the girl Margaret Sullavan played in *The Shop Around the Corner.*) She's a phony (Tony spots that), but with a drive inside her that isn't phony (he spots that, too). As the role is written, this girl is split into so many pieces she doesn't come across as one person; you like her and you don't, and back and forth. You can't quite figure out whether it's the character or the actress that you're not sure about until Gorney wins you over by her small, harried, tight face and her line readings, which are sometimes miraculously edgy and ardent. The de-termined, troubled Stephanie, who's taking college courses to improve her-self, is an updated version of those working girls that Ginger Rogers used to play (as in *Having Wonderful Time*). The surprising thing is that Stephanie's climbing isn't put down; in a sense, the picture is a celebration of individual climbing, as a way out of a futureless squalor.

You feel great watching this picture, even if it doesn't hold in the mind afterward, the way it would if the story had been defined. The script at-tempts to be faithful to the new, scrimping, dutiful teen-agers, who never knew the sixties affluence or what the counterculture was all about; for them maturity means what it traditionally meant—leaving home and trying to move ahead in the world. Once again in movies, Manhattan beckons as the magic isle of opportunity—not ironically but with the old Gershwin spirit. The awkwardness is in treating Tony as a character in passage from boyhood to maturity. The script drops the dancing, as if it were part of what Tony has to grow out of. But the dancing has functioned as a metaphor for what is driving him on to Manhattan, not what he's leaving behind. There is a happy going-to-the-promised-land, boy-gets-girl ending yet it misplaces Tony's soul, so it doesn't feel as up as it should. At its best, though, *Saturday*

Night Fever gets at something deeply romantic: the need to move, to dance, and the need to be who you'd like to be. Nirvana is the dance; when the music stops, you return to being ordinary.

The New Yorker, December 26, 1977

COMING HOME
MYTHOLOGIZING THE SIXTIES

Jane Fonda isn't playing a character in *Coming Home*, she's playing an abstraction—a woman being radicalized. The time is 1968, the place is Los Angeles, and she's Sally Hyde, the proper, repressed wife of a hawkish Marine captain (Bruce Dern). Sally has been married for several years but has no children and nothing to do after her husband leaves for Vietnam, so she volunteers for work in the veterans hospital. On the day she signs up, she crashes into Luke (Jon Voight), who was an athlete when she knew him in high school and is now a paraplegic in a rage of helplessness. She discovers that the men injured in Vietnam are embittered by neglect, and that the other officers' wives, frozen-faced, sitting in their club all groomed and primped, don't want to know about it. As she works among the men, her identification shifts away from the idle-class women. She trades her sexless, crisply laundered clothes for T-shirts and jeans; she stops straightening her hair and lets it frizz up and tangle. Dramatists have always had a terrible time showing their characters "growing," and have usually had to resort to speeches announcing the interior changes; movies can spread the transformation, more novelistically, over a period of months or years. Sally Hyde gradually (and entertainingly) loses her inhibitions, but she develops only to the level of doctrinaire awareness which has been reached by the people who put *Coming Home* together, and this means that the character has a hollow tone—the same inauthenticity that the home-front heroines had in Second World War movies. Fonda develops that sorrowing-woman smile. The other characters are playing abstractions, too. Voight, round-faced and blond-bearded, is like a Kris Kristofferson who studied acting. He handles the transition from rage to boyish romantic hopes with star magnetism, and he gives his scenes a sexual undercurrent that may help put the movie over at the box office. But his role (with scenes that appear to have been suggested by actions of the paraplegic anti-war activist Ron Kovic) could be a parody of the new sanctimoniousness. Luke is a feeling human being, gentle and firm—stuffed with grand compassion. He embraces the distressed and comforts them with thoughts such as "You have enough ghosts to carry around." The measure of Voight's stature as an actor is that he very nearly gets by with his pontifical lines. Sally's friend Vi (Penelope

Milford) is a miniskirted version of the smart, knowing, heart-of-gold working girl of thirties movies. She wises us up with her social perceptions; she explains that she went back where her home used to be but "they tore down my past and built a shopping center." Her salty, pithy, neo-Odetsian dialogue carries the label "gallant proletarian." We may not have had other movies with so much remorse about the Vietnam War, but we've been here before.

Coming Home started out to be about how the Vietnam War changed Americans, and turned into a movie about a woman married to a hawk who has her first orgasm when she goes to bed with a paraplegic. Sally Hyde's hospital collision with Luke is actually the only strong dramatic sequence, and the porny romanticism of their affair has a morbid kick to it. The musical prelude to the sex is reverential—moviemakers haven't found a slicker way of combining purity and eroticism since Marlene Dietrich unknowingly married a runaway monk (Charles Boyer). Viewers could go on fantasizing about this bedroom scene, except that Sally announces the obvious: "That's never happened to me before."

The politics of the film are extremely naïve, and possibly disingenuous. *Coming Home* doesn't oppose the Vietnam War on political grounds. The film embodies a pure-pacifist attitude toward Vietnam: the war is condemned on the basis that our soldiers are maimed and killed in it. Except for a sex scene or two, *Coming Home* is the sort of film a Protestant church group might put out—blandly humanitarian. Though it was shot by Haskell Wexler, a wizard of fast-moving strong graphics, it has a Waspy glaze to it—a soft, pastel innocuousness, as if all those involved were so concerned to get the message across without offending anyone that they fogged themselves in. Jane Fonda's face seems a little vague and pasty, as if she didn't want to stand out too much; her features seem to have disappeared. She's trying to act without her usual snap, and the result is so unsure she comes flutteringly close to a Norma Shearer performance.

The picture has a peculiar, anticipatory tension: you wait so long for something to happen you're ready to jump out of your skin. At first, it seems that the director, Hal Ashby, just has a drifting, dawdling approach to getting under way. Then you realize that this amorphous, inappropriately dreamy movie reflects Ashby's approach to the subject—maybe to any subject now. A former editor, Ashby is generally referred to as a meticulous craftsman; he took more than four months to shoot *Coming Home* and then eight months to supervise the cutting. Can it be that it's so sloppily made because he took so long over it? He plans in the sense of wanting to have enough to edit, and then he has too much. He must get overwhelmed by choices, and so far inside whatever he's shot that he loses the spine of the story. Ashby's two best-known films, *The Last Detail* and *Shampoo,* had tightly structured scripts by Robert Towne, and Ashby, working within trim shooting schedules, stayed with those scripts. But he had greater control of his next picture, *Bound for Glory,* and he and his editor, Robert C. Jones, added explicit, messagey scenes and extended the film until it meandered into shapelessness. The *Coming Home* project, initiated by Jane Fonda, began with a script by Nancy Dowd. Then Waldo Salt was brought in for a rewrite, and the Dowd script was mostly discarded. And then when John Schlesinger, who was expected to direct, left the project, and Ashby was hired, he brought in his former editor, Robert C. Jones, who gets his first credit as a writer. The script that emerged from all this labor and God knows how many conferences is a mixture of undeveloped themes, and is so thinly textured that Ashby has filled in the dead spaces by throwing a blanket of rock songs over everything. (It's disconcerting to hear words like "strawberry fields forever" when you're trying to listen to what people are saying to each other.) The music isn't used for a strong beat or for excitement; it's more like a deliberate distraction, as if Ashby had got bored with the movie and wanted to hear what was going on in the next room.

Ashby's mood scenes can be very personal and touching; a sequence with Luke on the hospital basketball court telling Sally that he's being discharged from the place and Sally on the other side of the fence telling him that she's going to Hong Kong to see her husband does everything it needs to do and more—the feelings spill over, and stay with us. The whole picture is evocative of that messy time; it's permeated with free-floating anxiety, and Luke's stricken eyes serve as an emblem of the country's guilty confusion. *Coming Home* idles, it goes from scene to scene intuitively, romantically, until Sally's visit to Hong Kong; after that the cutting is often like a door slamming in our faces, and, without any dramatic preparation, there's bam-pow crosscutting between simultaneous events. In one sequence, Vi's despondent younger brother Bill (Robert Carradine) is having a fit of depression at the hospital, and Luke, having been on the phone with him, realizes the condition the boy is in and rushes to his aid. We see Luke wheeling himself to his car, folding up his wheelchair and driving off, and then arriving at the hospital and racing through the ward. But in between we see the paraplegics at the hospital staring at Bill and halfheartedly calling out to him, instead of spinning down the corridor to get help. One's time sense is violated; movie crosscutting was more highly developed than this in D. W. Griffith's day. The plot device of having Luke and Sally under F.B.I. surveillance is introduced at such an unstrategic moment that we half expect the F.B.I. men to burst in on their big love scene and beat Luke up. The captain returns from the war limping from a leg wound—ignobly received—and overnight his limp is gone. And what is Sally doing in the scene in which she stands holding out her arms to her husband? Every time there's a cut to her, obediently playing statue, we can practically hear the director thinking, Time stands still; this moment is an eternity. Bad moments are the real eternity.

What the film shows us goes against the grain of what it asks us to accept. The captain is such a charmless, reactionary stiff that when he comes home and Sally says she loves him, we don't believe her. With Bruce Dern in the role, Captain Hyde—who is supposed to be driven mad by the war—looks buggy-eyed and crazily distracted even before he goes to Vietnam;

when the war deranges him, who can tell the difference? It's a fatally wrong
piece of casting. Everything to do with Hyde is false, creepy, awful—he's like
a psychotic Andy Gump. We feel no regret over anything that happens to
him; the director has so little imaginative sympathy for a war supporter like
Hyde that we don't feel Hyde's bewilderment at the ugliness of what his
men have been doing. *He* doesn't seem a casualty of war.

At the beginning, we see Sally's open eyes while she's enduring intercourse with her husband. Later, we watch her face during her orgasm with
Luke; this scene is the dramatic center of the movie. The question in the
viewer's mind is, What will she feel when her husband comes home and they
go to bed? Will she respond, and, if she does, how will he react? The psychological structure of the situation practically demands that he discover
her infidelity by the sexual change in her. His attitude would then help determine whether the marriage will become a real one or will end. Instead,
he finds out by means of the F.B.I. eavesdroppers; we never learn how he
would react to the new, responsive Sally, and Ashby has no ending—just a
lot of cutting back and forth.

Allowing for the differences in the wars, *Coming Home* may be the post-
Vietnam equivalent of the post–Second World War movie *The Best Years of
Our Lives,* which also dealt with returning veterans in smooth, popular
terms. Maybe, considering the squalor and disruptiveness of the Vietnam
War, we can't expect much more than this depoliticized, melodramatic elegy
with shame spreading in the sunshine. There's a pettiness of spirit here.
People are judged too easily, and by class. Why are the other officers' wives
shown as so coolly indifferent to the conditions in the veterans hospital?
Mightn't some of them have been so insulated by their own lack of experience or so lonely and fearful of what could happen to their husbands that
they dreaded the thought of the hospital? (And were there no officers
among the seriously wounded?) There's a strong element of self-admiration
in the film's anti-Vietnam attitudes. It's not enough that Hyde is wrong
about the war; he's got to be a lousy lover, too, while the good war protester
Luke—paraplegic though he may be—is so life-affirming that he brings Sally
Hyde to life. Are liberals really such great lovers?

The New Yorker, February 20, 1978

THE FURY
SHIVERS

There's an ecstatic element in Brian De Palma's new thriller *The Fury:* he
seems to extend the effects he's playing with about as far as he can without losing control. This inferno comedy is perched right on the edge. It

may be to De Palma what *The Wild Bunch* was to Peckinpah. You feel he never has to make another horror movie. To go on would mean trying to kill people in ever more photogenically horrific ways, and he's already got two killings in *The Fury* which go so far beyond anything in his last film, *Carrie,* that that now seems like child's play. There's a potency about the murders here—as if De Palma were competing with himself, saying "You thought *Carrie* was frightening? Look at this!" He's not a great storyteller; he's careless about giving the audience its bearings. But De Palma is one of the few directors in the sound era to make a horror film that is so visually compelling that a viewer seems to have entered a mythic night world. Inside the world, transfixed, we can hear the faint, distant sound of De Palma cackling with pleasure.

Most other directors save the lives of the kind, sympathetic characters; De Palma shatters any Pollyanna thoughts—any expectations that a person's goodness will protect him. He goes past Hitchcock's perversity into something gleefully kinky. In *Carrie,* he built a two-way tension between our hope that the friendless, withdrawn, telekinetic heroine would be able to sustain her Cinderella happiness at the school prom and our dread of what we feared was coming. De Palma builds up our identification with the very characters who will be destroyed, or become destroyers, and some people identified so strongly with Carrie that they couldn't laugh—they felt hurt and betrayed. *The Fury* doesn't have the beautiful simplicity of the Cinderella's-revenge plot of *Carrie*, and it doesn't involve us emotionally in such a basic way; it's a far more hallucinatory film.

The script, which John Farris adapted from his novel, is about two teenagers, spiritual twins who have met only telepathically. They are superior beings; in a primitive tribe, we are told, they would have become the prophets, the magicians, the healers. In modern civilization, they become the prisoners of a corrupt government (ours), which seeks to use them for espionage, and treats them impersonally, as secret weapons. In the opening scenes, set on a beach in Israel, the psychic boy, Robin (Andrew Stevens), is captured by an agent, Childress (John Cassavetes). The picture deals with the efforts of Robin's father, Peter Sandza (Kirk Douglas), to find him. The search centers in Chicago, where Sandza enlists the help of the psychic girl, Gillian (Amy Irving). Douglas gives a creditable professional-powerhouse performance; his quest has a routine action-film quality, though, and doesn't affect us emotionally. Once again, the suffering center of a De Palma film is a young girl. Amy Irving (she was the chestnut-haired, troubled Sue Snell, the survivor of the prom, in *Carrie*) brings a tremulous quality to *The Fury;* she's lyrical in the most natural way. The script is cheap gothic espionage occultism; she humanizes it. Both Gillian and Robin have the power to zap people with their minds. Gillian is trying to cling to her sanity—she doesn't want to hurt anyone. And, knowing that her power is out of her conscious control, she's terrified of her own secret rages. There's a little of the young Sylvia Sidney in Amy Irving's apprehensive, caught-in-the-glare-of-headlights beauty. Her sense of alarm makes us feel that real lives are at stake. With her blue, heavy-lidded almond eyes, she can look like an Asiatic princess in a fairy tale or a mask of tragedy. Farris's complicated, rickety plot doesn't give Robin an opportunity to demonstrate his prodigious gifts before Childress corrupts them. And it doesn't develop the core relationship of Robin and Gillian, so that we'd feel her need to get to him (and to avenge him). This film's dark, symphonic terror might seem almost abstract if Amy Irving weren't there all the way through, to hold it together. De Palma's virtuosity and her unaffected performance play off against each other, to the great advantage of both.

There's a third major collaborator: Richard H. Kline, whose deep-toned, velvety cinematography keeps the whole movie vibrating. Kline, who shot the 1976 *King Kong,* knows how to light to create hyperbolic imagery; scenes such as a telepathic vision on a staircase and gunfire on the streets at night have the luster of a binful of garnets, amethysts, cat's-eyes. The compositions have so much depth and heavy shadow that objects stand out as if they were in 3-D; one can touch the metallic sheen of the cars, respond to Robin as a sculptural presence (he's shot to resemble Donatello's *David*). There's also a fourth major collaborator: John Williams, who has composed what may be as apt and delicately varied a score as any horror movie has ever had. He scares us without banshee melodramatics. He sets the mood under the opening titles: otherworldly, seductively frightening. The music cues us in. This isn't going to be a gross horror film; it's visionary, science-fiction horror. De Palma is the reverse side of the coin from Spielberg. *Close Encounters* gives us the comedy of hope, *The Fury* the comedy of cruelly dashed hope. With Spielberg, what happens is so much better than you dared hope that you have to laugh; with De Palma, it's so much worse than you feared that you have to laugh.

Obviously, De Palma was offered this project because Robin and Gillian have telekinetic powers, like Carrie's, and, just as obviously, although he uses some effects similar to those in *Carrie,* he's too original not to have embroidered them and turned them into something different. The violence is presented in such a stylized, aestheticized way that it transcends violence. When Peter Sandza is in a commandeered Cadillac at night in a pea-soup fog and the cars chasing him go up in balls of flame, the scene is so spectacularly beautiful that it hardly matters if one doesn't know why he sends his car flying into Lake Michigan; maybe he's just blowing off steam—having a destruction orgy because De Palma felt that this flourish was *visually* necessary to complete the sequence. There is a joke involving an amusement-park ride which is surely one of the great perverse visual gags of all time; one knows exactly what's going on, yet here, too, one is struck by the languorous richness of the scene. The joke itself has been aestheticized. Most directors are so afraid of losing our attention that if two people are sitting together talking we're not allowed to see what's happening around them. De Palma pans around the rooms and landscapes slowly—a Godardian ploy—to give us more and more to look at, and to key up our expectations. He doesn't quite make good on his promises: he doesn't provide the crucial actions—the payoffs—within the circling, enlarging movements. But the expansiveness is essential, because of the stodgy dialogue; he anticipates the boredom of the ear by providing excitement for the eye.

No other director shows such clear-cut development in technique from film to film. In camera terms, De Palma was learning fluid, romantic steps in *Obsession;* he started to move his own way in *Carrie*—swirling and figure skating, sensuously. You could still see the calculation. Now he has stopped worrying about the steps. He's caught up with his instructors—with Welles in *Touch of Evil,* with Scorsese in *Mean Streets.* What distinguishes De Palma's visual style is smoothness combined with a jazzy willingness to appear crazy or campy; it could be that he's developing one of the great film styles—a style in which he stretches out suspense while grinning his notorious alligator grin. He has such a grip on technique in *The Fury* that you get the sense of a director who cares about little else; there's a frightening total purity in his fixation on the humor of horror. It makes the film seem very peaceful, even as one's knees are shaking.

The Fury isn't tightly structured; there are rising and falling waves of suspense, and De Palma's visual rhythms outpace the story. (Sometimes the characters talk as if they hadn't noticed that the movie has gone past what they're saying.) Randall Jarrell once quoted some lines from Whitman and commented, "There are faults in this passage and they *do not matter.*" The visual poetry of *The Fury* is so strong that its narrative and verbal inadequacies *do not matter.* No Hitchcock thriller was ever so intense, went so far, or had so many "classic" sequences.

Carrie Snodgress returns to the screen in the role of Hester, Peter Sandza's lover and confederate; she's so pale and thin-faced that she's unrecognizable until one registers her eyes and hears that purring, husky voice of hers which seems to come out of furrowed vocal cords. Her plaintive, low-pitched normality helps *The Fury* to touch the ground now and then; fortunately, she goes out of the picture in a tense, slow-motion death-knell sequence that does her full honor. Fiona Lewis, who plays the woman Childress assigns to watch over Robin and satisfy his sexual needs, is not so lucky; she goes out of the picture in perhaps the most gothic way that any beloved has ever been dispatched by her lover. Her exit is topped only by that of Childress, and this is where De Palma shows his evil grin, because we are implicated in this murderousness: we want it, just as we wanted to see the bitchy Chris get hers in *Carrie.* Cassavetes is an ideal villain (as he was in *Rosemary's Baby*)—sullenly indifferent to anything but his own interests. He's so right for Childress that one regrets that there wasn't a real writer around to provide dialogue that would match his gloomy, viscous nastiness. He's been endowed with a Dr. Strangelove dead arm in a black sling (and there's a nice touch: his dead arm hurts), but only his end is worthy of him. This finale—a parody of Antonioni's apocalyptic vision at the close of *Zabriskie Point*—is the greatest finish for any villain ever. One can imagine Welles, Peckinpah, Scorsese, and Spielberg still stunned, bowing to the ground, choking with laughter.

The New Yorker, March 20, 1978

FEAR OF MOVIES—

NATIONAL LAMPOON'S ANIMAL HOUSE, EXORCIST II: THE HERETIC, HEAVEN CAN WAIT, HOOPER, CONVOY, THE LAST WALTZ, EYES OF LAURA MARS, INTERIORS

Are people becoming *afraid* of American movies? When acquaintances ask me what they should see and I say *The Last Waltz* or *Convoy* or *Eyes of Laura Mars,* I can see the recoil. It's the same look of distrust I encountered when I suggested *Carrie* or *The Fury* or *Jaws* or *Taxi Driver* or the two *Godfather* pictures before that. They immediately start talking about how they "don't like" violence. But as they talk you can see that it's more than violence they fear. They indicate that they've been assaulted by too many schlocky films—some of them highly touted like *The Missouri Breaks.* They're tired of movies that reduce people to nothingness, they say—movies that are all car crashes and killings and perversity. They don't see why they should subject themselves to experiences that will tie up their guts or give them nightmares. And if that means that they lose out on a *Taxi Driver* or a *Carrie,* well, that's not important to them. The solid core of young moviegoers may experience a sense of danger as part of the attraction of movies; they may hope for new sensations and want to be swept up, overpowered. But these other, "more discriminating" moviegoers don't want that sense of danger. They want to remain in control of their feelings, so they've been going to the movies that allow them a distance—European films such as *Cat and Mouse,* novelties like *Doña Flor and Her Two Husbands,* prefab American films, such as *Heaven Can Wait,* or American films with an overlay of European refinement, like the hollowly objective *Pretty Baby,* which was made acceptable by reviewers' assurances that the forbidden subject is handled with good taste, or the entombed *Interiors.*

If educated Americans are rocking on their heels—if they're so punchy that they feel the need to protect themselves—one can't exactly blame them for it. But one can try to scrape off the cultural patina that, with the aid of the press and TV, is forming over this timidity. Reviewers and commentators don't have to be crooked or duplicitous to praise dull, stumpy movies and disapprove of exciting ones. What's more natural than that they would share the fears of their readers and viewers, take it as a central duty to warn them off intense movies, and equate intense with dirty, cheap, adolescent? Discriminating moviegoers want the placidity of *nice* art—of movies tamed so that they are no more arousing than what used to be called polite theatre. So we've been getting a new cultural puritanism—people go to the innocuous hoping for the charming, or they settle for imported sobriety, and the press is full of snide references to Coppola's huge film in progress, and a new film by Peckinpah is greeted with derision, as if it went without saying that Bloody Sam couldn't do anything but blow up bodies in slow motion, and with the most squalid commercial intentions.

This is, of course, a rejection of the particular greatness of movies: their power to affect us on so many sensory levels that we become emotionally accessible, in spite of our thinking selves. Movies get around our cleverness and our wariness; that's what used to draw us to the picture show. Movies—and they don't even have to be first-rate, much less great—can invade our sensibilities in the way that Dickens did when we were children, and later, perhaps, George Eliot and Dostoevski, and later still, perhaps, Dickens again. They can go down even deeper—to the primitive levels on which we experience fairy tales. And if people resist this invasion by going only to movies that they've been assured have nothing upsetting in them, they're not showing higher, more refined taste; they're just acting out of fear, masked as taste. If you're afraid of movies that excite your senses, you're afraid of movies.

■　■　■

In his new book *The Films in My Life,* François Truffaut writes, "I demand that a film express either the *joy of making cinema* or the *agony of making cinema.* I am not at all interested in anything in between; I am not interested in all those films that do not pulse." Truffaut's dictum may exclude films that some of us enjoy. You couldn't claim that *National Lampoon's Animal House* expresses either the joy or the agony of making cinema. It's like the deliberately dumb college-football comedies of the thirties—the ones with Joan Davis or Martha Raye—only more so; it's a growly, rambunctious cartoon, and its id anarchy triumphs over the wet-fuse pacing, the blotchy lighting, and the many other ineptitudes. In its own half-flubbed way, it has a style. And you don't go to a film like *Animal House* for *cinema,* you go for roughhousing disreputability; it makes you laugh by restoring you to the slobby infant in yourself. (If it were more artistic, it couldn't do that.)

But that sort of movie is a special case. Essentially, I agree with Truffaut. I can enjoy movies that don't have that moviemaking fever in them, but it's enjoyment on a different level, without the special aphrodisia of movies—the kinetic responsiveness, the all-out submission to pleasure. That "pulse" leaves you with all your senses quickened. When you see a movie such as *Convoy,* which has this vibrancy and yet doesn't hold together, you still feel clearheaded. But when you've seen a series of movies without it, whether proficient soft-core porn like *The Deep* or klutzburgers like *Grease,* you feel poleaxed by apathy. If a movie doesn't "pulse"—if the director isn't talented, and if he doesn't become fervently obsessed with the possibilities that the subject offers him to explore moviemaking itself—it's dead and it deadens you. Your heart goes cold. The world is a dishrag. (Isn't the same thing true for a novel, a piece of music, a painting?)

This pressing against the bounds of the medium doesn't necessarily result in a good movie (John Boorman's debauch *Exorcist II: The Heretic* is proof of that), but it generally results in a live one—a movie there's some reason to see—and it's the only way great movies get made. Even the madness of *Exorcist II* is of a special sort: the picture has a visionary crazy grandeur (like that of Fritz Lang's loony *Metropolis)*. Some of the telepathic sequences are golden-toned and lyrical, and the film has a swirling, hallucinogenic, apocalyptic quality; it might have been a horror classic if it had had a simpler, less ritzy story. But, along with flying demons and theology inspired by Teilhard de Chardin, it had Richard Burton, with his precise diction, helplessly and inevitably turning his lines into camp, just as the cultivated, stage-trained actors in early-thirties horror films did. Like them, Burton had no conviction in what he was doing, so he couldn't get beyond staginess and artificial phrasing. The film is too cadenced and exotic and too deliriously complicated to succeed with most audiences. But it's winged camp—a horror fairy tale gone wild, another in the long history of moviemakers' king-size follies. There's enough visual magic in it for a dozen good movies; what the picture lacks is judgment—the first casualty of the moviemaking obsession.

What Boorman has in surfeit is what's missing from *Heaven Can Wait:* there isn't a whisper of personal obsession in the moviemaking. The film has no desire but to please, and that's its only compulsiveness; it's so timed and pleated and smoothed that it's sliding right off the screen. This little smudge of a movie makes one laugh a few times, but it doesn't represent moviemaking—it's pifflemaking. Warren Beatty moves through it looking fleecy and dazed, murmuring his lines in a dissociated, muffled manner. The film has to be soft-focussed and elided—a series of light double takes—because if Beatty raised his voice or expressed anything more than a pacific nature, the genteel, wafer-thin whimsy would crumble.

There's no way I could make the case that *Animal House* is a better picture than *Heaven Can Wait,* yet on some sort of emotional-aesthetic level I prefer it. One returns you to the slobbiness of infancy, the other to the security of childhood, and I'd rather stand with the slobs. I didn't much mind *Heaven Can Wait* when I saw it. Some of the lines have Elaine May's timorous, unaccountable weirdness. (Those jokes of hers come at you like wobbly cannonballs; you're never sure which ones will hit.) And in their marginal roles Dyan Cannon (a frenzied, lascivious bunny) and Charles Grodin (a discreet lizard) play off each other like cartoon confederates. It wasn't bad. Why, then, does it offend me when I think about it? Because it's image-conscious celebrity moviemaking; Beatty the star (who is also the producer and the co-director and even takes a co-writing credit) wants to be a nice guy, the same way Burt Reynolds does in *Hooper*. They go soft on themselves and act on one cylinder. They become so *dear*—Beatty the elfin sweet Jesus, and Reynolds the macho prince who hides his saintly heart—that they're not functioning as artists; they've turned into baby-kissing politicians.

As Hooper, Reynolds risks his life and injures himself in order to protect a little mutt, and afterward, while in pain, he's bawled out by a huffy official from an animal-protection society who doesn't recognize his devotion to dogdom. But *we're* sure not kept in the dark. In this slapstick celebration of the "real people" in Hollywood—the stunt men—the director, Hal Needham, lays out the gags for us as if we were backwoodsmen, and when it's time for him to show his stuff by staging the breathtaking stunts that the movie keeps telling us about, he fumbles every damn one of them. The camera is always in the wrong place; it's as if Needham had a tic that made him turn his head at the crucial moment. And it's almost a sickness—the repetition mania, the falling back on exhausted conventions. The hero has a live-in girlfriend (Sally Field) who is an irrelevant drag on the action, just like the worrying wives of old. As Hooper goes off to perform the most dangerous stunt of his life, she delivers the line that emerged from the compressed lips of generations of movie wives: "I won't be here when you get back." Was there ever one of them who carried out the threat? (The alternative was the John Ford woman, who said, "Matt, be careful.")

Reynolds has a faithful audience for pictures in which he doesn't attempt anything he hasn't done before. A half-cocked piece of movie-making like *Hooper*, with its neo–John Wayneism (we red-blooded men who aren't afraid of risking our bodies are the true chivalrous knights of America, the only ones you can trust), is accepted as "a kick." The public has genuine affection for Reynolds's West Coast wise-guy swagger, and it doesn't seem to matter to people that in *Hooper* his merriment often seems a tired reflex. (That moon face crinkles on call.) Even if the press treated *Hooper* or a Clint Eastwood picture as contemptuously as it did *Convoy*, those pictures might not be hurt at box offices.

It's no accident that the directors who have an appetite for the pleasure and complexity of moviemaking are so often abused in the press. Their films are likely to grip people, and in impolite ways. These directors can't resist subverting the old forms that give comfort to audiences. And, given the hell of dealmaking and the infinite number of things that can go wrong during a production, a director who cares about the rhythm and texture of his imagery is likely to turn into a mixture of pompous bore, master strategist, used-car salesman, maniac, and messiah—in short, a major artist. And yes, he'll try for too big an effect, or he'll upset the balance of a neatly structured pipsqueak script. The pressures of dealmaking squeeze the juice out of him, but still, in his sheer burning desperation to make movies, he'll try to turn a dud into *something*. And maybe he'll sustain that drive for only a part of the picture and he'll let the rest of it go to hell. How can moviemakers sustain their energy? How can they believe they should give the public of their best when the kids want to get Greased over and over and the literate adults go off to their cozy French detective comedy? Whom can they make movies *for*? They have every reason to be bitter and confused. (And they are, they are.)

■　■　■

Audiences hiss the sight of blood now, as if they didn't have it in their own bodies. They hiss those bloody scenes that have the power to shock them, even when the blood isn't excessive. Bergman gets away with shocking effects; in *Cries and Whispers,* he even shows vaginal blood, and no one dares hiss. But in *Eyes of Laura Mars,* where the first flash of bloodletting comes right at the beginning, and in *The Fury,* where the bloodshed is stylized, hyperbolic, insane, audiences who seem hypnotized by the urgency in the moviemaking still hiss the blood. They seem to be saying, "I don't need this!" They hiss the blood as if to belittle it, to make it less menacing. And these movies are treated with condescension.

Movies have upset repressive people right from the start, but the old Hollywood studio heads learned to appease pressure groups by keeping a lid on sacrilege and eroticism, and by making sharp moral distinctions between the violent acts committed by good guys and those committed by bad guys. Probably the movie that did the most to overturn all this was *Bonnie and Clyde,* in 1967. Lingering sensuously on violent imagery, the director, Arthur Penn, brought our hidden, horrified fascination into the open. Eisenstein had plunged us into violence, and so had Buñuel and Kurosawa and many others, but this was an American movie made by an American director—in color—and it was saying, "Don't turn your head away, there's something horrible and rapturous going on." Louis B. Mayer and the old Hollywood simplicities were finally undermined. In 1969, Peckinpah's *The Wild Bunch* came out—a traumatic poem of violence with imagery as ambivalent as Goya's. And as the Vietnam War dragged on and Americans became more and more demoralized and guilt-ridden, our films splattered blood at us—so much blood that going to the movies was often a painful, masochistic experience. The lurid didacticism was generally hypocritical: every crummy action-adventure picture that didn't know how to keep the audience's attention except by piling on massacres pointed to the war as a justification. And people became particularly incensed over the balletic, slow-motion scenes; although there's a psychological rationale, as well as an aesthetic one, for this "eternity in an instant" treatment of falls and accidents and horrors, it began to seem a mere device to force us to stare at gruesomeness.

People had probably had it with movie violence long before the war was over, but they didn't feel free to admit that they really wanted relaxed, escapist entertainment. Now that the war has ended, they talk about violence in movies as if it would plunge us back into that guilty mess. There's a righteousness in their tone when they say they don't like violence; I get the feeling that I'm being told that my urging them to see *The Fury* means that I'll be responsible if there's another Vietnam. During a brutal fight in *Who'll Stop the Rain,* there were cries in the audience—on the order of "O.K., enough!"—and applause for the cries. These weren't the good-natured cat-calls that are heard at stupid movies; it was an escape from the power of the fight. It's a way of closing off what you feel. I think I first became conscious of this audience mechanism back in the mid-forties, when I saw *Dead of Night* on its opening day in a crowded theatre and the audience laughed rau-cously during Michael Redgrave's greatest—most terrified—moments. The tension had got too much for them, and they turned philistine, rejecting their own emotional immersion in his performance. That's what people are doing now, on a larger scale. Maybe it's partly because they want to put the war behind them, but there's more to it: they're running away from flesh and blood on the screen. They have lost the background of security that used to make it easy for them to respond to suspense stories. Now, when they're always conscious of the violence in the society and are afraid that it's going to be coming at them when they leave the theatre, they don't want to see anything frightening on the screen. They've lost the hope that things are going to be better—that order will return. So they go to the movies to be lulled—to be gently rocked to sleep. (*Heaven Can Wait*—the acclaimed movie of the summer—is a lullaby.) What may be behind all this is the re-pression of the race issue. People feel that there's violence out there, and they want to shut it out. Movies, more than any other form of expression, are capable of bringing us to an acceptance of our terrors; that must be why people are afraid of movies.

■ ■ ■

Was *Convoy* punished because of the blood Peckinpah has made us look at in the past? It got the bum's rush, though it's a happy-go-lucky ode to the truckers on the roads, a sunny, enjoyable picture, with only ketchup being splattered (in a mock fight in a diner). The lighting suggests J.M.W. Turner in the American Southwest, his eyes popping with surprise. Seeing this pic-ture, you recover the feelings you had as a child about the power and size and noise of trucks, and their bright, distinctive colors and alarming individ-uality. Peckinpah uses the big rigs anthropomorphically. Each brawny giant in the procession has its own stride; some are lumbering, others are smooth as adagio dancers, while one bounces along and its trailer shimmies. At night, when a frightened driver pulls out of the line to go off alone in the darkness, the truck itself seems to quaver, childishly. The trucks give the per-formances in this movie, and they go through changes: when the dust rises around them on rough backcountry roads, they're like sea beasts splashing spume; when two of them squeeze a little police car between their tanklike armored bodies, they're insect titans. The whole movie is a prankish road dance, and the convoy itself is a protest without a cause: the drivers are just griped in general and blowing off steam. They want the recreation of a protest.

Sam Peckinpah talks in code, and his movies have become a form of code, too. *Convoy* is full of Peckinpah touches, but you can't tell the put-on from the romantic myth; his cynicism and his sentimentality are so intertwined by now that he's putting himself on. He has a mocking theme here that's visual: the spaciousness of the land and the pettiness of men's quarrels. But the script doesn't play off this disparity, and so, when the spaciousness overwhelms the lawman's spite that set the convoy in motion, it's the plot (rather than mankind) that seems silly. The film barely introduces the characters, and one of the funniest, J.D. Kane's Big Nasty, who talks in a voice so deep it might be his mammoth truck talking, is lost sight of. And here, as in *Cross of Iron*, Peckinpah can't shoot dialogue; he doesn't seem to know anymore how people talk. (Also, the post-synchronization is so poor that the voices seem disembodied.) The visual music of the moving trucks is enough to carry the film for the first hour, but when the truckers stop for the night at an encampment, the movie stops; there's no narrative energy to keep it going.

The actor at the front of the convoy, Kris Kristofferson, isn't convincing as a horny trucker grabbing a sad-eyed waitress (Cassie Yates) and hopping into the truck for a quickie; Kristofferson lacks the common touch that might have given the movie some centrifugal force. But, with his steely blue eyes, and his hair and beard blowing in the wind, he's as majestic as the big trucks, and his reserve is appealingly heroic. Kristofferson doesn't overact, and his charm is so low-key and easy that even the disembodied sound doesn't damage him—it goes with his faintly detached personality. The sound is rough on the other performers, though; they seem not quite there. Kristofferson is partnered by Ali MacGraw, who has never seemed anywhere, and some of the resentment directed against the film may be because of her. She is a truly terrible actress, of the nostril school. (Did she study under Natalie Wood?) As the camera comes closer, the nostrils start flexing—not just for anger, for *any* emotion. Her role makes her seem soft and spoiled and rich, and she doesn't react to a situation, she comments on it, in a hideously superior way. When she's really working hard, she adds a trembling lip (reminiscent of Jackie Cooper as a child) to her tiny repertory of expressions. She isn't around a lot, though, and Kristofferson doesn't pay much attention to her (which saves him).

It isn't clear whether Peckinpah walked away from *Convoy* after presenting his first cut, or was barred from the final editing, or how much Graeme Clifford, who finally put it together (he was the editor on Nicolas Roeg's *Don't Look Now*), is responsible for. But there are lovely editing transitions and fast, hypnotic rhythms and graceful shifts of stationary compositions. Sequences with the trucks low in the frame and most of the image given over to skies with brilliant white clouds are poetic gestures, like passages in Dovzhenko. The film has a springiness of spirit, and a lust for drifting white desert sand; it's so beautiful (yet funny) that often you don't want the camera to move—you want to hold on to what you see. Probably Peckinpah intended to make a simple action movie, but something in him must have balked at that. He saw the trucks and the skies and he kept shooting, like Eisenstein when he saw the faces of the Indians in Mexico.

■   ■   ■

No American movie this year has been as full of the "joy of making cinema" as Martin Scorsese's *The Last Waltz,* his film of The Band's Thanksgiving, 1976, concert in San Francisco. He shot it while he was still involved in *New York, New York*—which was full of the "agony of making cinema." In *The Last Waltz,* Scorsese seems in complete control of his talent and of the material, and you can feel everything going right, just as in *New York, New York,* you could feel everything going wrong. It's an even-tempered, intensely satisfying movie. Visually, it's dark-toned and rich and classically simple. The sound (if one has the good luck to catch it in a theatre equipped with a Dolby system) is so clear that the instruments have the distinctness that one hears on the most craftsmanlike recordings, and the casual interviews have a musical, rhythmic ease. Why was it so hard to persuade people to go see it? Were they leery of another rock-concert film? Were they tired of hearing about Scorsese? All of that, maybe, and possibly something more. They swooned and giggled over *A Star Is Born,* but *The Last Waltz* is a real movie, and it must have given off some vibration that made them nervous. They couldn't trust the man who'd made *Mean Streets* and *Taxi Driver* to give them a safe evening.

■   ■   ■

The fun of a movie thriller is in the way it plays on our paranoid fantasies; we know that we're being manipulated and yet—if the manipulation is clever enough—we give over to it. But can people respond to this as entertainment if they're on such edgy terms with themselves that they're afraid of being upset? In the press coverage of *Eyes of Laura Mars,* the reviewers seem to be complaining that it's a thriller—or, rather, an effective thriller. Their being frightened seemed to make them resent the film as immoral. *Eyes of Laura Mars,* Irvin Kershner's seductive whodunit, is up against attitudes that a comparable fantasy, such as Polanski's *Rosemary's Baby*—also about justifiable female paranoia—didn't have to face. *Laura Mars* operates on mood and atmosphere, and moves so fast, with such delicate changes of rhythm, that its excitement has a subterranean sexiness. It's a really stylish thriller, and Faye Dunaway, with long, thick dark-red hair, brings it emotion and presence, as well as a new erotic warmth. (Her legs, especially the thighs, are far more important to her performance than her eyes; her flesh gives off heat.) More womanly and more neurotically vulnerable—even tragic—than before, she looks as if she'd lived a little and gone through plenty of stress. She's glamorously beat out—just right to be telepathic about killings. Caped and swathed in clothing, with her glossy pale face taut against the lustrous hair (so thick it's almost evil), she's both Death and the Maiden. No Hollywood sex goddess has ever presented so alluring an image of kinky Death herself.

The scabrous is part of the elegant in this film; Laura Mars is a celebrity fashion photographer who specializes in the chic and pungency of sadism. The pictures she shoots have a furtive charge; we can see why they sell. Her photographic sessions, with burning cars and half-naked models strutting around their prey, are set up so that we get a sense of friction between the models, who are acting as killers and victims, and the buzzing, over-intense city, where everyone seems to be on a stage. Laura's pictures are, in fact, single-image versions of high-style blood thrillers, such as *Laura Mars*. The humor in the movie is in the mixture of people who drift through the celebrity-circus milieu. Models who in their poses look wickedly decadent may be just fun-loving dingalings; unself-conscious when they're nude, they put on their gaunt insouciance with their clothes. In this high-fashion world, decadence is a game. But the creepiness of the environment isn't. The frames are packed with abrasive movement, and we see the dreck right next to the glamour, the dirty fingers that handle the expensive photographs. In the rush and bickering confusion of Laura's work life, she's dependent on her scruffy, wild-eyed driver (Brad Dourif), who's into God knows what, and her agent-manager (René Auberjonois), who probably hates her, because he has to take care of all the technicalities of time and place and money while she's being "creative." She has no one to trust. And so the harassed, frightened Laura falls in love with a police lieutenant (Tommy Lee Jones), who comes from a different, working-class world and represents simple values, old-fashioned morality. In many ways, it's a subtle, funny movie. Laura's voice is heavy with emotion, the policeman's is light and high and boyish; they're as unlikely a pair of lovers as you would ever hope to see. With the help of Michael Kahn, who was the editor, Kershner glides over the gaps in the script and almost manages to trick viewers past the mediocre lighting. He gets us to experience the jangled, onstage atmosphere viscerally. Brad Dourif's excitable driver makes us laugh, because he epitomizes New York's crazed messengers and hostile flunkies; he's so wound up he seems to have the tensions of the whole city in his gut. The film has an acid-rock texture, while Tommy Lee Jones, with his cat burglar's grace, his sunken eyes, rough skin, and jagged lower teeth that suggest a serpent about to snap, takes us into the world of punk.

In *Laura Mars*, you barely see any violence; it comes across by suggestion and a few quick images. But it's violence of a particular kind (and this may explain the angry, moralistic reactions to the film): the danger is to the eyes. If the killer had gone for the throat, probably the movie wouldn't be so frightening and wouldn't be considered immoral. (Of course, it wouldn't have any point, either.) *Laura Mars* violates our guardedness about our eyes. The most dreaded thing that can happen to what many regard as their most sensitive organs happens in this picture; like *Un Chien Andalou*, it attacks what we're watching the movie with. *Eyes of Laura Mars* hasn't the depth of intention (or the art) to upset us profoundly; it doesn't go at the eyes like *King Lear* or *Oedipus Rex* or the *Odyssey*, it just touches lightly on our dread.

But this movie has enough "pulse" to make us register how horribly vulnerable our bodies are. And people in the audience who are used to TV, with its car crashes and knifings and shootings that have no pain or terror in them, and no gore, feel violated: how dare a movie scare them, and how dare it attack their taboo about the eyes? Has their world become so close to a paranoid fantasy that they no longer experience any of the primal fun in being frightened?

One film has shocked me in a way that made me feel that it was a borderline case of immorality—Hitchcock's *Psycho,* which, because of the director's cheerful complicity with the killer, had a sadistic glee that I couldn't quite deal with. It was hard to laugh at the joke after having been put in the position of being stabbed to death in the motel shower. The shock stayed with me to the degree that I remember it whenever I'm in a motel shower. Doesn't everybody? It was a good dirty joke, though, even if we in the audience were its butt. I wouldn't have wanted to see *Psycho* that first time alone in a theatre (and I sometimes feel a slight queasiness if I'm by myself late at night somewhere watching a horror film on TV). But that's what a theatrical experience is about: sharing this terror, feeling the safety of others around you, being able to laugh and talk together about how frightened you were as you leave.

Those people who are trying to protect themselves from their own violence and their own distress by not going to see anything that could rock the boat are keeping a very tense cool. There's something crazily repressive in the atmosphere. They're rejecting the rare films that could stir them, frighten them, elate them. And they're accepting the movies in which everything happens affectlessly and even bloody violence can be shrugged off. Within a few years, everything has turned around. Violence that makes you feel afraid has replaced sex as what's offensive, exploitative, dirty; since the end of the war, particularly, this kind of violence has become pornographic—it's as if we thought we could shove muggers and urban guerrillas under the counter. Movie sex, meanwhile, has become trivialized—made casual. It's posh call-girl sex, *Playboy* sex; there's no hatred or possessiveness or even passion in it. (Imagine the sour rage and depth of desire a director like Peckinpah might show us if he made a movie about sex.) What does it mean when someone says to you in a prissy, accusing tone that he "doesn't like" violence? Obviously, he's implying that your ability to look at it means that you *like* it. And you're being told that you're made of coarser stuff than he is. He's found a cheap way to present his cultural credentials. There's something snobby in all this; sex is chic but violence is for the animals. The less worldly still ask, "Why can't they make movies about *nice* people?" It's the comfort of order that's wanted—everything in its place. It used to be that well-brought-up ladies were not expected to be able to stand the sight of blood; they were expected to be so protected from sex and blood and flesh and death that they would faint if exposed to what the common people had to learn to look at. It was considered an offense to them to bring up certain subjects in their presence. Now the same sort of delicacy is once again becoming a mark of culture and breeding. Squeamishness—surely with terror and prurient churnings under it?—is the basis of this good taste.

■   ■   ■

The people in Woody Allen's *Interiors* are destroyed by the repressiveness of good taste, and so is the picture. *Interiors* is a puzzle movie, constructed like a well-made play from the American past (such as *Craig's Wife*), and given the beautiful, solemn visual clarity of a Bergman film, without, however, the eroticism of Bergman. *Interiors* looks so much like a masterpiece and has such a super-banal metaphysical theme (death versus life) that it's easy to see why many regard it as a masterpiece: it's deep on the surface. *Interiors* has moviemaking fever, all right, but in a screwed-up form—which is possibly what the movie is all about. The problem for the family in the film is the towering figure of the disciplined, manipulative, inner-directed mother (Geraldine Page). She is such a perfectionist that she cannot enjoy anything, and the standards of taste and achievement that she imposes on her three daughters tie them in such knots that they all consider themselves failures. Alvy Singer, the role Woody Allen played in *Annie Hall,* was just such a compulsive, judgmental spoilsport, and Allen's original title for that film was *Anhedonia*—the lack of the capacity for experiencing pleasure.

Among the many puzzling aspects of *Interiors:* How can Woody Allen present in a measured, lugubriously straight manner the same sorts of tinny anxiety discourse that he generally parodies? And how intentional is most of what goes on under the friezes and poses? Are we expected to ask ourselves who in the movie is Jewish and who is Gentile? The characters are so sterilized of background germs that the question is inevitably raised, and one of the film's few overt jokes is an overheard bit from a television show in which an interviewer asks a boy, "What nationality were you at the time of your birth?" and the boy answers, "Hebrew." Surely at root the family problem is Jewish: it's not the culture in general that imposes these humanly impossible standards of achievement—they're a result of the Jewish fear of poverty and persecution and the Jewish reverence for learning. It's not the joy of making cinema that spurs Woody Allen on (as he made clear in *Annie Hall,* he can't have that kind of joy), it's the discipline of making cinema. The movie, with its spotless beaches, is as clean and bare as Geraldine Page's perfect house: you could eat off any image. The prints of *Interiors* were processed on a new film stock, and during the showings for the press and people in the industry in Los Angeles, Allen had the print returned to the lab after every screening to be washed. Which makes this the ultimate Jewish movie. Woody Allen does not show you any blood.

The father (E. G. Marshall) asks his wife for a divorce and then marries a plump, healthy, life-force woman (Maureen Stapleton), and so there are two mothers. The tall, regal first mother, an interior decorator (who places a few objects in a bare room), wears icy grays and lives among beiges and sand tones; the plebeian stepmother bursts into this hushed atmosphere wearing mink and reds and floral prints. This is the sort of carefully constructed movie in which as soon as you see the first woman caress a vase and hover over its perfection you know that the second woman will have to break a vase. The symbolism—the introduction of red into the color scheme, the broken vase, and so on—belongs to the kind of theatre where everything was spelled out. But under this obviousness there are the layers of puzzle. The two mothers appear to be the two sides of the mythic dominating Jewish matriarch—the one dedicated to spiritual perfection, the other to sensual appetites, security, getting along in the world, cracking a few jokes. It's part of the solemn unease of the film that no one would want either of them for a mother: they're both bigger than life, and the first is a nightmare of asexual austerity, the second an embarrassment of yielding flesh and middle-class worldliness. If the two are warring for control of Woody Allen, the first (the *real* mother) clearly has him in the stronger grip. She represents the death of the instincts, but she also represents art, or at least cultivation and pseudo-art. (As a decorator, her specialty, like Woody Allen's here, seems to be the achievement of a suffocating emptiness.) Maureen Stapleton, the comic life force, lacks *class*. The film might be a representation of the traditional schizophrenia of Jewish comics, who have had the respect for serious achievement planted in them so early that even after they've made the world laugh they still feel they're failures, because they haven't played Hamlet. Groucho Marx talked morosely about not having had the education to be a writer, and said that his early pieces for *The New Yorker* were his proudest achievement. For Woody Allen, the equivalent is to be the American Ingmar Bergman.

The three daughters represent different aspects of the perfectionist neurosis. The oldest (Diane Keaton) is a well-known poet, determined, discontented, struggling with words while unconscious of her drives; the middle one (Kristin Griffith) is a TV actress, dissatisfied with her success, and snorting cocaine; the youngest (Mary Beth Hurt), who looks like a perennial student, rejects sham and flails around, unable to find herself. In plays, the youngest is generally the one who represents the author, and whenever you see a character who's stubbornly honest you know that you're seeing the author's idealized vision of some part of himself. With Mary Beth Hurt, if you have any doubts all you have to do is look at how she's dressed. (You'll also notice that she gets the worst—the most gnomic—lines, such as "At the center of a sick psyche there is a sick spirit." Huh?) She's unsmiling—almost expressionless—closed in, with specs, hair like shiny armor (it says hands off), and schoolgirl blouses and skirts. She's like a glumly serious postulant, and so honest she won't dress up; determined not to be false to her feelings, she actually dresses down for her father's wedding to the "vulgarian," as she calls her. (She's there under duress, and her clothes are an implicit protest.)

She's the Cordelia, the father's favorite who refuses to lie, even to the mother, whom she alone in the family truly loves (she guiltily hates her, too).

The men's roles are relatively minor; Sam Waterston's part, though, is the only one that's unformed in the writing and doesn't quite fit into the formal plan. Geraldine Page is playing neurosis incarnate, and the camera is too close to her, especially when her muscles collapse; this failure of discretion makes her performance seem abhorrent. But Maureen Stapleton livens things up with her rather crudely written role. Hers is the only role that isn't strictly thematic, and you can feel the audience awake from its torpor when she arrives on the scene and talks like a conventional stage character. Diane Keaton does something very courageous for a rising star. She appears here with the dead-looking hair of someone who's too distracted to do anything with it but get a permanent, and her skin looks dry and pasty. There's discontent right in the flesh, while Kristin Griffith, the TV sexpot, appears with fluffy hair, blooming skin, and bright white teeth—the radiance that we normally see in Keaton. This physical transformation is the key to Keaton's thoughtful performance: she plays an unlikable woman—a woman who dodges issues whenever she can, who may become almost as remote as her mother.

For Allen, who is a very conscious craftsman, it is surely no accident that the mother's impoverished conception of good taste is sustained in the style of the film. But what this correlation means to him isn't apparent. *Interiors* is a handbook of art-film mannerisms; it's so austere and studied that it might have been directed by that icy mother herself—from the grave. The psychological hangups that come through are fascinating, but the actors' largo movements and stilted lines don't release this messy material, they repress it. After the life-affirming stepmother has come into the three daughters' lives and their mother is gone, they still, at the end, close ranks in a frieze-like formation. Their life-negating mother has got them forever. And her soul is in Woody Allen. He's still having his love affair with death, and his idea of artistic achievement (for himself, at least) may always be something death-ridden, spare, perfectly structured—something that talks of the higher things. (If this, his serious film, looks Gentile to people, that may be because for Woody Allen being Jewish, like being a comic, is fundamentally undignified. This film couldn't have had a Jewish-family atmosphere—his humor would have bubbled up.) The form of this movie is false, yet it's the form that he believes in, and the form of *Interiors* is what leads people to acclaim it as a masterpiece.

People like Woody Allen for a lot of good reasons, and for one that may be a bummer: he conforms to their idea of what a Jew should be. He's a younger version of the wise, philosophic candy-store-keeper in *West Side Story*. His good will is built partly on his being non-threatening. He's safe— the schlump who wins, without ever imposing himself. People feel comfortable with him; the comedy audience may even go to *Interiors*—to pay its respects to the serious Woody. Woody Allen's repressive kind of control—the source of their comfort—is just what may keep him from making great movies. *Interiors* isn't Gentile, but it *is* genteel. He's turned the fear of movies—which is the fear of being moved—into a form of intellectuality.

The New Yorker, September 25, 1978

BERTRAND BLIER—
GET OUT YOUR HANDKERCHIEFS, CALMOS (FEMMES FATALES), GOING PLACES

The French writer-director Bertrand Blier has an authentic, lyrical impudence in *Get Our Your Handkerchiefs,* which was shown at the New York Film Festival on September 29th and 30th. This is the third in his series of male erotic fantasies. Blier, who is a novelist and the son of the well-known plump character comedian Bernard Blier, started to direct movies in the sixties, and then in 1974 made *Going Places* (the original title is *Les Valseuses,* French slang for testicles), and in 1976 *Calmos* (it turned up, without publicity, in New York last year under the title *Femmes Fatales* and disappeared almost immediately). Perhaps *Handkerchiefs,* a more subdued, deeper variation on the themes of those two films, will make it easier for audiences to respond to what he's about and to look at his earlier work without becoming incensed. When *Going Places* was released here, in 1974, it was variously described as "sordid," "loathsome," and "disgusting," and just this past March it was taken off the Home Box Office schedule because of complaints from affiliate stations. What is the picture's crime? Probably that viewers find themselves laughing at things that shock them. At one point, the two young roughneck protagonists (Gérard Depardieu and Patrick Dewaere) board a train and observe a beautiful, pure-looking young mother (Brigitte Fossey) nursing her baby in an otherwise empty car. They offer this madonna money to give them a sip and, apparently terrified of refusing, she accedes. When she gets off the train, her husband, a scrawny, pasty-faced soldier on furlough, is waiting, and as she walks to join him she has a silly, happy grin on her flushed face. Audiences have come to accept the dirty joking in Buñuel films; the years, the honors, the press have given it a pedigree. But Blier's joking is so unself-conscious that it makes Buñuel's seem preconceived, almost pedantically outrageous. Blier gives us the kind of joke that can't be done by implication or symbolically—that has to be absolutely literal. This kind of joke has found only verbal form before, yet Blier visualizes it—as if that were the most natural thing in the world to do. The two roughnecks act out their sex reveries—in which, no matter what a woman says, she's really begging for it, so they're doing her a favor if they force themselves on her. And people watching this may be so fussed about the disreputability of what excites them that they can't accept the humor of their own situation. *Going Places* is an explosively funny erotic farce—both a celebration and a satire of men's daydreams—and some people find its gusto revolting in much the same way that the bursting comic force of the sexual hyperbole in Henry Miller's *Tropic of Cancer* was thought revolting.

Going Places shakes you up and doesn't seem to leave you with anything to hang on to. It's easy to find it upsetting and degrading. But that's part of what makes it funny. The two men's crude energy is overwhelming, grungy, joyous. Life to them is like a big meal: they go at it like hungry workmen tearing at a carcass of beef, with greasy fingers. They aren't hippies rejecting middle-class materialism; they have none of the sanctimonious counterculture glamour of the pals in *Easy Rider*. They're closer to the joyriding lowlifers in *The Wild One*. These two pals talk in rough lower-class accents and don't fit into modern urban France, with its homogeneous middle-class culture. They're outsiders without jobs or money who want to live the life of the rich and satisfy their appetites. So they help themselves to things: they snatch purses, steal cars, pilfer shops, and make passes at almost every woman they get near. They're not professional criminals; they just rip people off. They harass shopkeepers and work them up into a rage, but, in terms of the film, this is the only excitement the smug, bored shopkeepers get, and it's way in excess of any damage that the boys actually do. The atmosphere is that of classic farce, as in Ben Jonson: these two are no worse than the respected members of the bourgeoisie, they're just less skillful in their methods. It takes a half hour or so before a viewer grasps that the two pals (one is twenty-five, the other twenty-three) are guileless raw innocents and that almost everything they do backfires on them.

The tone of *Going Places* is startling, both brutal and lyrical. The men are barnyard characters with the kind of natural magic that the kids have in Vigo's *Zero for Conduct* and that Jean Renoir's Boudu has; there's a poetic logic in what they do. They pick up a compliant scraggly-blond waif, a beautician (Miou-Miou), who is so used to being treated as something inanimate—as garbage—that she thinks she is garbage. The two guys beat her up and abuse her. Yet they also like her, and they take turns trying to bring her to orgasm—one of them even encouraging and coaching the other. But she remains sad and frigid, and they become furious with her. In between their heterosexual episodes, Depardieu jumps Dewaere (he yelps); he has also suffered the indignity of being shot in the groin, sustaining what the doctor calls "an abrasion of the left testicle." After the failure with Miou-Miou, the two go off to find an experienced older woman who will feel something; they wait outside a women's prison, confident that discharged prisoners will be sex-starved, and a middle-aged woman (Jeanne Moreau) who has spent ten years inside emerges. They treat her royally, with food and attention, and she gives them a great night of sexual maternal passion.

But in the morning she kisses them both as they sleep and commits suicide by putting a gun to her vagina. Shocked by this first encounter with real madness and pain, they go back to their frigid little beautician; they weep and she comforts them, and then, out of a sense of responsibility to the dead woman, the three of them travel to another jail to await the release of her son. He turns out to be physically unappealing and not quite right in the head, but when the four of them are off in the country at a hideaway and the two pals are fishing they hear their frigid girlfriend, who is in bed with the crazy jailbird, making cries of sexual arousal, and in a minute she rushes out, radiant, to tell them the happy news of her first orgasm. (They pick her up and dunk her in the river.) Once aroused, she is always eager, and the two pals keep swapping places in the back seats of stolen cars.

The social comedy in Blier's work is essentially sexual comedy: sex screws us up, we get nicked in the groin or jumped from behind, idiots make out better than we do, and some people are so twisted that no matter what we try to do for them they wreck everything. And sex between men and women is insanely mixed up with men's infantile longings and women's maternal passions. Sexually, life is a Keystone comedy, and completely amoral—we have no control over who or what excites us.

Going Places was perhaps the first film from Europe since *Breathless* and *Weekend* and *Last Tango in Paris* to speak to us in a new, firsthand way about sex and sex fantasies; it did it in a terse, cool, assured style influenced by Godard, yet with a dreamy sort of displacement. (Godard achieved something similar in the postcards sequence of *Les Carabiniers*—also a two-pals movie.) When Blier's two pals are not in movement, they're disconsolate; they can't think of what to do with themselves from day to day. The landscapes without other people, the deserted places they go to, suggest a sex-obsessed dream world. These are cavemen who give women what in their exuberant male fantasies women want. The dialogue is slangy, the mood buoyant—flagrantly funny in a special, unpredictable way. You have no idea what may be coming. The distinctive aspect of Blier's method of work is that although his scripts are completely written in advance of the shooting—and he doesn't improvise—he writes in an improvisational manner. Most scenarists, like dramatists, think out their structure in terms of the development of a situation—with conflict and resolution. They instinctively plan it out and know where they're going. Blier writes psychological picaresques: he begins with a group of characters and a certain tone, and then he may veer off and go wherever his subconscious takes him. Where he ends up probably surprises and partly mystifies him, as it does us. But generally he's right to trust his impulses, because they take him somewhere we might not have got to in any other way. Crazy connections get made—things unexpectedly tie together. And there is, finally, an underlying set of themes which emerges, and it's much richer than if he'd stuck to a conscious plan. The limitation—if one chooses to regard it as that—of Blier's go-with-your-subconscious method is that, naturally, his films all have the same themes. But he has the wit to treat his own subconscious as a slapstick fantasy land.

■   ■   ■

Blier's method worked in *Going Places,* and it works in *Handkerchiefs,* but something went wrong in his sexual extravaganza *Calmos* (and the picture failed, even in France). The first half hour or so of *Calmos* is a hilariously scandalous dirty-boy romp. Blier has such economy that he goes right into the comedy; there are no preliminaries, no waste—you're laughing before you've settled into your seat. There are two pals again, but now they're forty-year-old boulevardiers who look like wax grooms on a stale wedding cake. One is a gynecologist (Jean-Pierre Marielle), and the other a baby-blue-eyed pimp (Jean Rochefort). The doctor can't bear to look at women's genitals anymore; the pimp is exhausted by women's sexual demands—he feels women are chasing him even in his sleep. When the doctor's wife (Brigitte Fossey), hoping to tantalize him, offers herself for bondage—tells him she's ready for *anything*—he asks for foie gras. It's a dumb joke, but her nudity and his uncontrollable disgust make it lewdly, visually funny. The comedy is derived partly from a banal premise, a reversal of women's saying that they have a headache. But the men's satiation—their demonstration of revulsion against sex—has real comic conviction. The two men run away together into the countryside, to a village where they eat and drink and wear old clothes and begin to stink. Calm, that's what they want. Eating is the only thing they can get excited about. They sit at a Rabelaisian feast, along with the local curé (Bernard Blier) and his helper, in an old house, and the cinematographer, Claude Renoir, makes the house, the food, the landscape sinfully beautiful. This opening is an inspired exploitation porno fantasy, with Renoir's images (and the music, by Georges Delerue) providing a feeling of grandeur and folly. But then the story enlarges and takes a science-fiction turn. It shifts from the lunacy and regressions of these two men to the sexual revulsion of men en masse. Blier and his co-scriptwriter, Philippe Dumarcay (who also worked on *Going Places*), lose the flavor and the characters, and the picture falls back on the stored-up debris of mass culture. The two men are joined by other escaping men; women demanding gratification come after them with guns, and it's a full-scale tedious war of the sexes until, finally, the two pals, old men now and shrivelled in size, are dropped out of a cloud onto an island, where they walk through the pubic hair of a giant black woman and slip into her vagina just as her giant black lover arrives to deflower her, and crush them. *Calmos* is an overscaled back-to-the-womb satiric fantasy—a male daydream about the impossibility of escape from the sexual wars.

How much distance does Blier have from his characters' foolishness? Well, at least enough to make us laugh at them. In a sense, *Calmos* is about sex rather than about women. A couple of guys coming out of a bar late at night might talk like this—about wanting to go home just to sleep but knowing that there's a woman waiting up for them, and not being able to face it.

It's about the demands of sex on men who spent their youth chasing women and now—jaded—want a break from it. There's no macho in the male bonding of the Marielle and Rochefort characters; they just want to be left alone for a while—they want to go off and live like pigs. It's a funny idea, and though *Calmos* abandons it, there are still things to look at all through the picture. It was a stroke of genius to use Renoir and Panavision: the images have clarity, depth, richness, sweep, and the color is deeper even than Decae's. Early on, there's a streetcar full of avid women—a not too bright idea that is given a redemptive comic intensity by Renoir's lighting. Throughout, the women are made repellently beautiful—they have a neon voraciousness. Brigitte Fossey, a blond cat with a perfect tiny mouth, is like sensual porcelain. The light on her is so metallic and cold that her makeup seems to be dry ice. Any man would fear to come to her: who could live up to the glittering desire in her cat eyes? And even the idea of the giantess (shot on a beach in Guadeloupe) is almost redeemed by Renoir's use of Eastman color and Panavision. No one but Blier has matched such raunchiness and such visual beauty; you have to have a true respect for raunchiness to do that.

■　　■　　■

The title *Get Our Your Handkerchiefs* suggests a mockery of such movies as *Love Story,* but it also carries another suggestion—that we *should* be prepared to weep at the perplexities of love. It's a gentler, more refined comedy than either of the others; our laughter is never raucous. The wildness of *Going Places* hasn't disappeared, though—now it's underneath. The impression that the film gives is of freshness and originality, and of an unusual serenity. Feelings are expressed that haven't come out in movies before, and in a personal voice of a kind we think of as novelistic, yet nothing is wasted in the shots. Everything is to the point, and so we sit trustingly as things drift along and work themselves out. Here, as in the two other pictures, we never know where the story is going, and there's a considerable shift of direction midway, but this time it's all reassuringly quiet. The music is by Mozart, by Delerue (writing in the spirit of Mozart), and by Schubert, and this has an additional modulating, controlling effect. The style is almost chaste.

The two protagonists are played by the stars of *Going Places,* Depardieu and Dewaere (it was written with them in mind), but they're not the boors they were before—there's no violence in them. They're polite, harmless workingmen—Depardieu a driving-school instructor, Dewaere a playground supervisor. The picture opens at Sunday lunch in a Paris café. Jug-faced and serious, the powerfully built Depardieu is eating robustly while his lovely dark wife (Carole Laure) pecks at her food. Suddenly, he begins expostulating; he explains to her that she doesn't eat because she's sick of his face. He says that he loves her and wants to make her happy, so he'll bring her the man sitting opposite her whom she's been staring at and wants to go to bed with. There's something Neanderthal about his clumsiness; he's telling her of his consideration for her while making a public spectacle of her misery and their sexual failure. He goes over, introduces himself to the bearded stranger (Dewaere), propositions him, and says, "If you get her to smile, you'll be my pal." From this first scene—which is as deft and quick and funny as scenes in Sacha Guitry's comedies, such as *Lovers and Thieves*—Blier is playing with his characters and with us. The wife certainly looks bored and depressed, but we don't see her eyeing Dewaere—who wears glasses, and looks rather vague and self-absorbed. He accepts the invitation, though, and becomes the wife's lover, and the men then take turns trying to impregnate her—it being their theory that she is silent and morose because a woman needs a child. What we do see once the two men become pals (without Dewaere's getting her to smile) is that neither one makes any emotional contact with her. Dewaere has the complacency of a literate simpleton. He owns five thousand of the Livre de Poche paperback classics; reading them and listening to Mozart are his life. And he proselytizes, and converts Depardieu to his interests, while the wife scrubs and knits. When a neighbor (Michel Serrault, the star of *Lovers and Thieves*) bangs on their door at night to complain of the sound of a Mozart record, Depardieu sits him down and converts *him.*

So far, it's an enchanting quirky sex comedy. The situation of the sterile wife and the rattled husband has its classic-farce overtones; the cuckolded husband is generally rich and decrepit, of course, but this is a classic farce in modern slang, with a barrel-chested, virile young husband who cuckolds himself with complete casualness, on the spur of the moment. Yet the film's texture is soft and sensual; there's a velvety underlayer to the scenes. Jean Penzer's cinematography suggests another world—like something shot from a diving bell. Because of Blier's method, nothing is ever explained. It's clear the two men are chumps. But if they don't have any idea what's going on in the wife's mind, neither do we. And the secret of the film—its essence—is that Blier doesn't, either. Carole Laure, with her neat little choirboy head and her slender, sinuous body, is treated as an object throughout. But never with contempt. And Carole Laure is a wonderful reactor. Her elusive, doleful shades of feeling delight us, even though we can't be sure what they mean; we can't tell if her knitting is a way of escaping the men's idiocy or if her mind is blank, or both, but we enjoy entertaining the possibilities. Are the men right to think she will be happy only if she has a child? Maybe so, but they go about trying to give her one without ever getting through to her. Their obtuseness—their clumsiness—may be the reason they can't reach her, but then perhaps it's her unreachability that makes them so clumsy. She has the natural, yielding grace of a sapling.

In the second half, the classical elements vanish, and the picture becomes more mysterious, leisurely, and meditative. In all three of these films, the movement is from the city to the country—to the primeval wilderness—and it's always the men's propulsion. This time, the two men decide that the wife they've been sharing needs country air, and the three of them go off to be counsellors at a summer camp for the underprivileged. The camp has one wealthy child, a thirteen-year-old boy (the child who plays the part is billed only by his nickname, Riton, to protect him from notoriety); he has been sent there by his parents to obtain experience of the underprivileged, whom he will be dealing with when he takes over the family's industrial enterprises. He's a smart brat, with a genius I.Q., though he looks unformed; there is no suggestion of horniness about him, and the first time we see him, when the other children are picking on him, we might easily take him for a girl. But he's far more clever than the two pals, and he hasn't had any reason to feel that he's clumsy; he has his child's guile and seductiveness. He says and does the shrewd things that thirteen-year-olds must want to say and do but don't have the courage for, or the knowledge, except in their dreams. He uses entreaties drawn from Cherubino in *The Marriage of Figaro*. And he gets through to the wife. The men were right: she wanted a child.

The woman takes this little boy to her bed, and can't live without him, even if that means he must be kidnapped. When he has been sent away from her to boarding school, and is in the dorm at night telling his awed fellow-students the story of his conquest, and the woman herself tiptoes in and, in full view of all those boys, kisses him, we're watching a mythological romance. There are all the obstacles, such as the boy's parents, to be taken care of, but the two men (who turn into her clown attendants) help her, though it lands them in jail. How can they not help? The boy prodigy is like their Mozart. The film goes off in this weird direction, yet it all seems uncannily logical and prepared for. At the end, the woman has her child lover and is pregnant as well.

It's bewildering yet mysteriously right, satisfying, down to the pensive sounds of Schubert at the end. There's a gravity to this film—to Blier's generous, amused giving in to a sense of defeat. At some level, he has the feeling that what women want men for is to perpetuate the species—that they really want a child. And he has compounded this fantasy by having a child father the child, thus eliminating the need for men altogether. *Handkerchiefs* is a farce that turns into a fable. Now we recognize why everything about the young wife is so ambiguous—that melting look in her eyes, her shimmering beauty. Now we can understand Dewaere's double take when he was spending a night with her and said he wondered what her husband was doing, and she said "Who?" This is a sleeping-beauty fable, but told from the point of view of a man's erotic fears. This woman is to be awakened not by a prince but by a princeling. At the moment that her child lover is seducing her, in the sleeping quarters at the summer camp, the two chumps come down the hallway, pause outside her door, and discuss whether to go in. They decide that there's no reason to worry—the boy is too young. It's a funny moment, yet there's poetic tension in it, and the hallway has a palpable sensual beauty. They're losing out forever.

All three of these films are about two pals who don't really understand women—and their not understanding women is part of their bond. The teamwork of the actors is the true marriage. Depardieu, with his beautiful long jaw and his loping walk, and Dewaere, with his nearsighted vagueness (he's like a more delicate Timothy Bottoms), move together rhythmically. Marielle and Rochefort twitch and grimace and drop their eyelids in perfect counterpoint; their show of revulsion at women is the flirtation dance of impotent roués. The pal teams in these movies have intuitive rapport. They hang loose when they're together.

In *Handkerchiefs*, Blier's fantasy themes seem to turn against the male fantasist. There's pain along with the humor. The thirteen-year-old who arouses the wife is a variation of the jailbird who aroused the beautician, but, once aroused, the lovely wife does not want the men—she wants only the child. The two men who were so happy with the mother figure played by Moreau, and who wanted to be suckled on the train, are now rejected by the mother. Marielle and Rochefort at least found their way back to the womb, but Depardieu and Dewaere seem to be locked out. All they've got is each other, and at the end they're going off together, maybe to live happily like pigs. But that's not how it looks. Discharged from jail and carrying their belongings, Depardieu and Dewaere peer through an iron gate into the window of the solid, rich home where the wife they have lost sits contentedly knitting baby clothes, and then disappear down the road.

Blier's poetic logic is so coolly, lyrically sustained in *Get Out Your Handkerchiefs* that nothing that happens seems shocking. You feel you understand everything that's going on. But only while it's happening—not afterward. Afterward, you're exhilarated by the wit, and by your own amusement at how little you understand. What does the woman respond to in the child? His need? His foxiness? His strength? His childishness? It's a mystery. Sex is emotional anarchy.

Blier doesn't attempt to present a woman's point of view; he stays with the man's view of women, and that gives his films a special ambience. For a woman viewer, seeing *Handkerchiefs* is like a vacation in a country you've always wanted to visit. Reading a book such as *From Here to Eternity*, a woman enters an area of experience from which she has been excluded; seeing a Blier film, a woman enters a man's fantasy universe stripped of hypocrisy. Blier's films have no meanness about women; the wife in *Handkerchiefs* isn't neurotic—just elusive. Women are simply seen as different. A man friend of mine used to say, "If the first Martian who lands on earth is a male, I'll have more in common with him than I do with all the women on earth." Blier's is an art of exaggeration: he takes emotions and blows them up so big that we can see the things people don't speak about—and laugh at them. *Get Out Your Handkerchiefs* makes you feel unreasonably happy.

The New Yorker, October 16, 1978

THE WIZ

When I read the Oz books as a child, I loved their plainness. The fairy tales that we inherited from Europe were usually translated and adapted in fancied-up styles that didn't resemble how Americans talked. But there were no poetic embellishments in L. Frank Baum—it was magical prosiness. A child could feel he was being talked to straight. And in the Oz series the magic itself had an ordinary, everyday quality; the things that were endowed with personality were ridiculous domestic objects—a saw-horse or a lumpy old sofa. There was a basic topsy-turvy egalitarianism: animals, children, inanimate objects, witches, and fairies all talked the same simple Yankee language. Baum had spent his youth in the theatre (he joined a touring company when he was nineteen), but it wasn't until I began reading the books aloud to my own child that I realized how much showmanship there was in them: the characters were vaudeville comics, the jokes were stage patter, and there was an acceptance of the corny enjoyment in puns and parodies. Even the outsize toys that came to life were like the "transformations" in stage shows for children. (In the new film, there's a suggestion of this in a robot camera and especially in a walking mike that looks like a Grandville lithograph.) Probably all these common stage devices were part of what I had experienced as blessed plainness. With the illustrations as a guide, a child reads along and projects himself into this funny, amiable vaudeville show; that may be part of why those of us who loved the books (and we were legion) had a special identification with them. We, too, joined a touring company. When I'd read ten or eleven of the books aloud and my daughter was ready to read the rest of the series by herself, I felt as if I'd been dropped along the road.

Baum's material is so essentially theatrical and unserious that it's adaptable to the song-and-dance gifts of almost any culture, and, in fact, white viewers can easily accept Michael Jackson as the Scarecrow, Nipsey Russell as the Tinman, and Ted Ross as the Lion. They give their roles black show-biz equivalents of the musical-comedy and burlesque styles that Ray Bolger and Bert Lahr, in particular, brought to the 1939 film. As far as the performers are concerned, the only problem is the insufferable Dorothy, who's some sort of superstar neuter, smiling through tears, with her arms always raised to the heavens. And she doesn't have the face of a dreamer. Judy Garland, with her fleshy vulnerability, provided a contrast to her three companions, but Diana Ross is as much an artifact as they are.

The New Yorker, October 30, 1978

MIDNIGHT EXPRESS
MOVIE YELLOW JOURNALISM

Midnight Express puts the squeeze on us right from the start. First, there are titles explaining that the movie is "based on a true story" that began in 1970 in Istanbul. Before we see anything more, we hear ominous percussion music: the thump thump of Billy Hayes's heart. We're inside this college boy's chest, pulsating with his panic as he straps two kilos (about four pounds) of hashish around his torso and goes out to the airport to catch the flight that will take him home to New York. By the time he gets to customs, he's sweating in terror and his chest is about to burst, and then, at the very moment of boarding the plane, he is apprehended.

For the next two hours, this innocent American is subjected to the most photogenic brutalization that the director, Alan Parker, and the screenwriter, Oliver Stone, can dream up. The "true story" of Billy Hayes—that is, the relatively simple account given in the book by Hayes and William Hoffer, which was probably already somewhat heightened—is used merely as a taking-off place for the moviemakers' sadomasochistic and homoerotic imaginations. Parker and Stone pile on the horrors, and, together with the composer, Giorgio Moroder, and his synthesizer, jack them up to a frenzy. The film is like a porno fantasy about the sacrifice of a virgin. When he's arrested, Billy (Brad Davis)—the beautiful male ingenue, with his well-fed, muscular American body—is stripped, in a smoky room, for the delectation of the cruel Turks. He's cast as Lawrence of Arabia, for the roughest of rough trade. Surrounded by these garlicky, oily men with hairy nostrils who talk in their incomprehensible language, like members of another species, he's isolated with his fear, and the pounding in his chest is joined by electronic buzzing and heavy bell sounds. He's thrown in jail and, on his first night, he's hung up by the ankles and clubbed—and there's the strong suggestion that he's also sodomized—by the head guard, Hamidou (Paul Smith), a huge, sadistic bullock of a man with great clumps of hair growing from the rims of his ears, like outcroppings of lust. When Billy meets another American inmate, Jimmy (Randy Quaid), a hothead whose thoughts pop like firecrackers, he says, "I'm Billy Hayes—at least, I used to be."

We watch him deteriorate as the film rushes from torment to torment, treating his ordeals hypnotically in soft colors—muted squalor—with a disco beat in the background. The prison itself is more like a brothel than a prison; the film was shot mostly in a nineteenth-century British barracks in Malta, which was turned into a setting worthy of this de Sade entertainment. (It even has a flooded catacomb.) When you see Max (John Hurt), a drugged-out, emaciated English prisoner, caress a kitty, you wait for something terrible to happen to it; it does, and you get to see that, plus Max's stricken face. When you observe that there are child prisoners, you brace yourself, and, sure enough, they're cold-bloodedly tortured. Yet this picture, which represents itself as an unsparingly realistic, hard-hitting view of the brutalities of prison, has an interlude to tease us. Suddenly, a steaming sauna appears in a patch of sunlight in the middle of this foul dungeon, and an amiable Swede is giving Billy a lyrical scrubdown. The Swede kisses Billy solemnly and the music rises for a triumphal wedding celebration, but the marriage isn't consummated: with a Madonna smile, Billy gently—one might say with polite regrets—declines the offer. That's the only overt sexual advance in the movie; you'd think sex among prisoners meant whimsical, tender friendships—among Westerners, that is. (The dirty Turkish prisoners are sodomites, who also keep knifing each other.) This Billy-the-pure scene is part of the director's preparation for his big number. Billy is so lacerated by deprivation and torture that his mind snaps and he goes wild and attacks a Turkish informer, chasing him back and forth, beating him, and then grabbing him for what at first appears to be a horrifying, harsh kiss. Billy bites the Turk's tongue off and, in sensuous slow motion, triumphantly spits it out. By that time, the electronic hype has been so effective—the audience has been coiled so tight—that there are people in the theatre cheering this insane revenge. Billy's gleeful bloody madness—his face drips gore—marks a new, stepped-up phase. He's dragged off to the section for the criminally insane, where the misery is so decorative it's almost Felliniesque. When his girlfriend, Susan (Irene Miracle), comes to see him in this Turkish snake pit, he is a gibbering, whimpering animal, masturbating with desire for her. It's five years, all told, before he escapes.

Midnight Express is single-minded in its brutal manipulation of the audience: this is a clear-cut case of the use of film technique split off from any artistic impulse. Parker seems almost vindictive in the way he prods the viewers—fast, efficiently, from one shock to the next. You get the feeling that what he and his team set out to do was to take this darling American boy Billy and subject him to the most garish tortures they could without running into an X rating. The moviemakers are British, but with virtually no film industry in Britain now, they're working with American financing and with Peter Guber (of *The Deep*) as executive producer; they're demonstrating that they can be vivid and ferocious enough for the international "action" market. There's a mean-spiritedness in this fake-visceral movie which has got mixed together with the cause of imprisoned young pothead smugglers like Billy Hayes.

It's symptomatic that the director's control is least effective with the actors. Brad Davis's Billy is a standard young actor's imitation-James Dean performance, without much assurance. There's a heroism of physical force in most of the powerfully built American men stars; Davis—unlike the actual resourceful Billy Hayes—exudes weakness. This may be what attracted the moviemakers to him; their Billy is conceived as a victim—they deify weakness. But Davis isn't a strong enough actor to hold the screen when he plays scenes with Quaid or Hurt. And the director damages both of them by zeroing in on them as soon as they're introduced; he seems to be saying, "Perform." Quaid grabs attention simply by his usual overacting, which he tries to pass off as Jimmy's nuttiness; it isn't until late in the movie that we respond to the way Jimmy's one-cylinder high-combustion mind works and feel the comedy in the doggedness of his attempts to escape. Hurt, however, as he demonstrated on television—as Quentin Crisp in *The Naked Civil Servant,* and as Caligula in *I, Claudius*—is a truly great interpreter of eccentrics; he has such inner force that he can play the most passive of roles, as he does here (he barely moves a muscle), and still transfix the audience. Hurt has some good lines as Max, and he delivers them in a dry deadpan, like a wasted English Buck Henry. Max is so spiritually exhausted that he doesn't have the emotional energy required for facial expressiveness: he's an almost burned-out light bulb with just a few dim flashes of the filament left. Yet he's the most moving character in the film.

The director works in xenophobic, melodramatic terms: the Americans, the Englishman, and the Swede are civilized and sensitive, and the Turks are bestial, sadistic, filthy. There are no ambiguities, there is no depth. Alan Parker doesn't waste his sympathy on Turkish prisoners, and his idea of irony is to have the hairy-eared Hamidou (the actor is actually an American with degrees from Brandeis and Harvard) whipping Jimmy with a leather belt while the Turks are at their prayers to Allah—Jimmy's yells of pain provide the melody to the praying chorus. The film is a crude rabble-rouser: like a wartime atrocity movie, it keeps turning the screws to dehumanize Billy's jailers, and even his lawyer, who's a fat nose-picker. At the same time, it's sanctimonious about Billy's victimization: he writes florid, high-toned letters to Susan which we hear him read, and, worse, at a hearing he makes a messagey speech to the court, lecturing it on the meaning of crime and punishment and mercy, and denouncing the Turks as "a nation of pigs." The facts of Billy Hayes's case as presented in the book (which is by no means as anti-Turkish as the movie) make a solid, strong claim on our feelings: sentenced to four years and two months for possession of hashish, he had almost completed his term and was awaiting release when he was sentenced to an additional term of thirty years for smuggling—all for the same two kilos. But the film's cheap grandstanding—indicting a whole people on the presumption that the brutality of prison guards represents the national way of life—destroys those feelings. (It is not made clear that it was the American government which put pressure on the Turks to keep dope from being smuggled into the United States: we gave them an assistance program in criminology and trained their customs officials. The Turks have been trying to oblige us.)

Why are people lining up at theatres to see this picture? I assume that there are others besides me who felt squeezed so much that they grew to hate the picture more and more. (I didn't hope for Billy and his friends to escape—just for the movie to be over.) But *Midnight Express* may be something close to an all-purpose fantasy. For those who are part of the drug culture (which is by now almost the national culture), it can serve as a confirmation and extension of their fears. This movie is being sold as a journalistic exposé—the ads say, "Walk into the incredible true experience of Billy Hayes. And bring all the courage you can." And even if people who have read the book know that most of the juiciest episodes in the movie were invented, they can still respond to it emotionally, because it's what they want to see—the worst that could happen, and the depths to which they could be driven. What could be more satisfying to students and young dopers than this intoxicating view of the horrible pitfalls of smuggling dope—an ultimate romantic horror show. (The Billy of the movie doesn't just go biting-tongue-off mad; he also becomes a murderer.) Confinement in foreign prisons constitutes the martyrdom of the drug culture, and it's about the only part of that culture which the movies had missed until now. This story could have happened in almost any country, but if Billy Hayes had planned to be arrested to get the maximum commercial benefit from it, where else could he have got the advantages of a Turkish jail? Who wants to defend the Turks? (They don't even constitute enough of a movie market for Columbia Pictures to be concerned about how they're represented.)

And this picture is not only a full-scale fantasy for the drug culture but the cautionary tale that parents have been waiting for. Here, at last, is the movie that puts Vietnam behind us. It has been a long time since middle-aged people could say to their kids, "You don't know how lucky you are to be Americans, safe and protected." Billy's shame when he writes to his parents for help rehabilitates the shame that disobedient children used to feel in movies of the twenties and thirties. In prison, Billy feels totally abandoned, forsaken, left to rot. The love that fills his being when his father (Mike Kellin) comes to try to help him is so traditionally boyish that it recalls Lon McCallister in his doughboy uniforms, and Van Johnson waving to Mom as he went off to war. Billy is never more James Dean–like than when he weeps and his father weeps. There hasn't been this kind of reconciliation-between-the-generations scene in many years. (It recalls *East of Eden*.) When Billy's father says that his bowels are running because of the Turkish food he ate, and that for the rest of his stay "I'm not takin' any more chances—I'm gonna eat at the Hilton every night: steak and French fries and lotsa ketchup," he's making the fundamental point of the movie (as older people will see it). Stay out of Turkish jails, don't do anything you shouldn't, eat right, this is what can happen to you if you're not a good boy. *Midnight Express*, with its sadistic sexual current, is a there's-no-place-like-home story, of a very peculiar variety. Hysterically sensual on the surface but with basic honor-thy-parents-and-listen-to-them glop at the center, it manipulates cross-generationally.

This fantasy even has a special appeal to liberals: the package is presented as social protest, as a modern *J'Accuse*. There's a final crawl title: "On May 18th, 1978 the motion picture you have just seen was shown to an audience of world press at the Cannes Film Festival . . . 43 days later the United States and Turkey entered into formal negotiations for the exchange of prisoners." And ringing upbeat music—exaltation music, like slow disco Muzak—accompanies this remarkable piece of journalistic self-congratulation. The producers sell this prison rhapsody as an example of bold muckraking that had immediate results—so, in a sense, the film claims that it has already proved its worth. Actually, the United States and Turkey have been talking about a prisoner-exchange agreement for several years, and last January the United States sent a draft proposal to Turkey, which is still under negotiation; no prisoners have yet been transferred. (What happened in forty-three days? Nothing.) The music that says "Rise and salute our accomplishment" is really telling us to salute bunko artists.

The actual Billy Hayes, who has been out flacking for the film on the talk shows, was quizzed about that accomplishment in a recent interview in the *Los Angeles Herald Examiner.* Here are his answers:

HAYES: I believe, and certainly hope that to some degree, how great or how small is very hard to say, that [the film] *Midnight Express* has been instrumental in making this prisoner-exchange treaty happen.
QUESTIONER: Did you have anything to do with that?
HAYES: No, I don't think I had anything to do with it, directly. But I think anybody who's spoken about it, who's tried to spread an awareness of the fact that there are people who are being beaten, tortured, and thrown into prison for years for what is not even a crime in some places, had something to do with it. If *Midnight Express* does nothing else, it's making people aware that this kind of thing happens.

It's wonderful—isn't it—that there are young dopers coming along who have already mastered the politician's art of squirming off a hook and floating in a sea of generalizations.

The New Yorker, November 27, 1978

THE DEER HUNTER
THE GOD-BLESS-AMERICA SYMPHONY

A "magnificent hermaphrodite born between the savage and the civilized": that's how Balzac described Hawkeye, the Deerslayer—the idealized frontier hero of James Fenimore Cooper's Leatherstocking Tales. The steelworker hero of Michael Cimino's *The Deer Hunter* is the newest version of this American "gentleman" of the wilderness, and the film—a three-hour epic that is scaled to the spaciousness of America itself—is the fullest screen treatment so far of the mystic bond of male comradeship. It is steeped in boys' adventure classics, with their emphasis on self-reliance and will power, and their exaltation of purity of thought—of a physical-spiritual love between men which is higher than the love between man and woman, because (presumably) it is never defiled by carnal desire. The American wilderness of our literature is (as D. H. Lawrence wickedly put it) the boys' Utopia. *The Deer Hunter* is a romantic adolescent boy's view of friendship, with the Vietnam War perceived in the Victorian terms of movies such as *Lives of a Bengal Lancer*—as a test of men's courage. Yet you can feel an awareness of sex just under the diffused sensuality of the surface. The whole movie, with its monumental romanticism and its striving for a symphonic shape, is sexually impacted. It takes the celibacy of football players before the big game and attaches it to Vietnam. The hero, Michael (Robert De Niro), and his friends—Nick (Christopher Walken) and Steve (John Savage)—are as chaste as Normal Rockwell Boy Scouts; they're the American cousins of hobbits.

Cimino, who is thirty-nine, has directed only one previous film—*Thunderbolt and Lightfoot,* with Clint Eastwood and Jeff Bridges, in 1974, which he also wrote. He's a New Yorker who studied graphic design, went into the Army, and was a medic attached to a Green Beret unit training in Texas. When his interest turned to movies, he worked in documentary film and in commercials before he was able to use writing as a way to break into directing. His first credit was on *Silent Running,* in 1971; then he (and also John Milius) worked on the script of *Magnum Force* for Clint Eastwood, who had already arranged to give Cimino his chance on *Thunderbolt and Lightfoot.* His new film is enraging, because, despite its ambitiousness and scale, it has no more moral intelligence than the Eastwood action pictures. Yet it's an astonishing piece of work, an uneasy mixture of violent pulp and grandiosity, with an enraptured view of common life—poetry of the commonplace.

When we first see the three men, it's 1968 and they are in a steel mill, on the floor of the blast furnace; at the end of the shift, they go from the blazing heat to the showers. It's their last day on the job before they report for active duty, and the other workers say goodbye to them. Then they move through the casual sprawl of their hilly mill town, Clairton, Pennsylvania, to their nearby hangout—Welsh's bar—to guzzle a few beers and loosen up. Each step of their day is perceived in ritual terms. The big ritual is to come that night: Steven's wedding at the Russian Orthodox Church and then the celebration at the Clairton chapter of the American Legion, which is also the farewell party for all three. We spend about three-quarters of an hour in the church and the hall; the moving camera seems to be recording what's going on in this microcosmic environment—to be giving us an opportunity to observe people as they live their lives. The long takes and sweeping, panning movements are like visual equivalents of Bruckner and Mahler: majestic, yet muffled. Because of the length of this introductory section, and because it isn't dramatically focussed, we feel an anticipatory ominousness. Derivative as this opening section is (it's easy to see the influence of Coppola and Visconti, and probably Minnelli, too), it conveys a very distinctive love of rootedness and of the values of people whose town is their world. (It's the sort of world we used to see in French films of the thirties, with Raimu.) Cimino brings an architectural sense into his collaboration with the cinematographer, Vilmos Zsigmond, whose style here recalls his smooth long takes in *Deliverance* but has a crisp vitality, like his more recent work in *Close Encounters*. There may be a touch of *National Geographic* in the first views of the beautiful, gaudy interior of the Byzantine-primitive church, yet Cimino and Zsigmond take the curse off the usual limitations of Panavision and the heightless wide screen by panning down, down, slowly. They provide such an illusion of height that it's hard to believe the screen is the same shape that George Stevens once said was good only for high-school-commencement pictures. In the church, we see the faces of people we have already met; our eye is caught by John Welsh (George Dzundza), the cherub-cheeked bar owner, singing in the chorus. Here and in the Legion hall, there are uninterrupted panning movements in which we see people singing and dancing, flirting and fighting, and moving from one group to another. And it has a detailed clarity: we feel that we're storing up memories. There's something nostalgic about this ceremonial view of ordinary American community life even as it's going on. This town of Clairton is actually a composite of a number of locations, most of them in Ohio, but it becomes a clear geographical entity for us, and even the double mobile home that Michael and Nick share feels so accurate that it, too, seems rooted. Nothing was shot in a studio.

Cimino's virtuoso staging has a limitation: the brilliance of his panoramic ensembles sometimes gives us the idea that in seeing so many things so quickly we have come to know these people. They don't actually reveal much more than the convivial crowds in a beer commercial do, yet, we're made to feel that what we see is all they are. (A great director would plant doubts in us.) And even with the dozen or so principal characters, the casting and the actors' physiognomies and intuitive byplay do most of the work of characterization; the dialogue is usually just behavioral chatter. When Cimino wants to make a point, it's usually an outsize point—a portent or an omen that reeks of old-movie infantilism. Someone draws Michael's attention to a nimbus around the sun, and he explains what the Indians used to say this formation meant. (Is Cimino invoking the mythology of Hawkeye and the great chief Chingachgook?) Steven and his bride, who is pregnant but not by him, are served wine in a double-cupped goblet, by the priest, who tells them that if they drink it down without spilling a drop they will have luck all their lives, and we see the small stains forming on the bride's white lace bodice. (Here it's *Smilin' Through* that's invoked.) Nick, the best man, makes Michael promise that, whatever happens to him, he will be brought back to this place, these trees. A grim-faced Green Beret just returned from Nam comes into the Legion bar during the party; the men ask him "What's it like over there?" and he replies with an obscenity. And so on. Cimino's talent is for breadth and movement and detail, and the superlative mix of the Dolby sound gives a sense of scale to the crowd noises and the voices and the music; we feel we're hearing a whole world. But Cimino doesn't know how to reveal character, develop it, or indicate what's going on in a human relationship. When Linda (Meryl Streep), one of the brides-maids, catches the tossed bridal bouquet, and Nick asks her to marry him and she says yes, we don't know if she's in love with him or with Michael, with whom she's exchanged glances earlier, or what Michael feels. Probably, Cimino doesn't know; he may think it doesn't matter. Michael keeps his dis-tance from people, and he seems too pure to have anything particular in mind when he looks at Linda; he's saving his vital juices for chivalry.

After the party is over and the bride and groom have left for their week-end honeymoon, Michael and Nick and their pals—John Welsh and skinny, dark Stan, played by John Cazale, and huge, bearded Axel, played by Chuck Aspegren—climb into Michael's white '59 Cadillac with tail fins and drive to the mountains, for a last, ritual hunt before Vietnam. A couple of the men are still wearing their rumpled tuxedos, but Michael, who is the leader of the group yet also a man apart, emotionally hidden, and with a compulsive orderliness that makes the others uncomfortable, has stripped down and dressed for his date with the deer. Unlike such makers of epics as Coppola and Bertolucci, Cimino doesn't seem to want his themes to rise to our full consciousness (or perhaps even to his own), but he can't resist eroticizing the hunt—it's a sexual surrogate, a man's-man wedding. Michael climbs to the top of a virgin mountain and, with a snowcapped peak behind him and a male choir in the sky singing a Russian Orthodox liturgical chant and rain clouds swirling about him, stalks a buck and fells it with one clean shot. That's his consummation.

The five hunters drive back down to Welsh's bar, and there follows a scene that is possibly too clever: fat, baby-faced Welsh plays a Chopin noc-turne, and the others listen attentively. It's a moment of communion before the parting of the ways. The music is lovely, and if one of the men—the ami-able nonentity Axel, perhaps—had only fallen asleep this scene might have been as great as it wants to be. But with all of them demonstrating their in-nate sensitivity, showing us that beer sloshers' savage breasts are soothed by music and that their inarticulate feelings go far beyond what they talk about, it's too much like those scenes in which roomfuls of Hitler's lieutenants all swooned to Wagner. And it's just a shade too effective, too theatrical, when Cimino cuts from this solemn grace to the noise and hell of Vietnam.

It's in the contrast, though, between the Clairton sequences, with all those people joined together in slowly rhythmed takes, and the war in Viet-nam, where everything is spasmodic, fast, in short takes, with cuts from one anguished face to another, that Cimino shows his filmmaking instinct and craft. But also his xenophobic yellow-peril imagination. It's part of the nar-rowness of the film's vision that there is no suggestion that there ever was a sense of community among the Vietnamese which was disrupted. We are introduced to Asians by seeing a soldier (North Vietnamese, or, perhaps,

Vietcong—we can't be sure) open the door of a shelter, find women and children cowering inside, and then thoughtfully lob in a grenade. Michael, a Green Beret Ranger in an advance reconnaissance unit, spots the soldier machine-gunning a fleeing woman and her child, yells "No!," and hits him with a flame thrower. The impression a viewer gets is that if we did some bad things over there we did them ruthlessly but impersonally; the Vietcong were cruel and sadistic. The film seems to be saying that the Americans had no choice, but the V.C. enjoyed it. Michael meets up with Nick and Steven again, and the three are taken prisoner and are tortured strictly for their captors' pleasure. The prisoners are forced to play Russian roulette in teams while the Vietcong gamble on which one will blow his head off.

The Vietnam War—and, more particularly, Russian roulette—serves Cimino metaphorically as the Heart of Darkness; Michael, the disciplined Deer Hunter, doesn't succumb. He has the will and courage to save the three of them. These prison-camp torture sequences are among the finest-edited action scenes that I know of; they are so fast and powerful—and so violent—that some people will no doubt be forced to walk out. They are the very center of the film—the test it was preparing for. Although Michael, the superman who forces his friends to develop the will to survive, belongs to the boys'-book world of grit and sacrifice, the sheer force of these pulp atrocity scenes takes over one's consciousness. I say "pulp" because the Vietcong are treated in the standard inscrutable-evil-Oriental style of the Japanese in Second World War movies and because Russian roulette takes over as the ruling metaphor for all the action scenes in the rest of the movie, even in the later episodes in Saigon and back home. Why is Russian roulette used this way? Possibly because it goes so completely against the American grain—it's like a metaphor for the General Westmoreland theory that Asians don't value human life the way we do. But also because it has a boyish vain-glory about it: does one have the guts to pull the trigger? It's a boy's kicky idea of courage.

If *The Deer Hunter* had been a serious consideration of boys'-book values, it might have demonstrated that they did not apply in the mechanized destructiveness of modern warfare—that Michael was basically as vulnerable as everybody else. But the fact is that Cimino believes they do apply, and so Michael is put up against curs and sadists; he's in a Victorian test of manhood. And no doubt many people will go along with the film and accept Michael, the superior being, as a realistic hero, because of the general understanding that comradeship and depending on your buddies and helping them is finally all that you can believe in when you're in the midst of war. Cimino, who believes in those Hemingwayesque one-clean-shot values that Michael (whom he has obviously named for himself) represents, has framed the whole war in terms of that kind of courage. Everything that happens appears to be the result of the atrocities of the Vietcong. Yet the film's point of view isn't clear. The American helicopters are like Walpurgisnacht locusts coming down on your head, and no one who believed that the Americans behaved honorably in Vietnam would have staged the evacuation of Saigon as Cimino has done, with thousands of Vietnamese abandoned and despairing. And, although Michael proves himself by performing extraordinary feats of valor, he is not ennobled by them, as movie heroes used to be. *The Deer Hunter* is Beau Geste-goes-to-Vietnam, all right, but with a difference: when Michael returns to his home and goes up to the mountain peaks again, and the male choir chants, he has the deer in front of him but he doesn't kill it. Cimino has made a film that vindicates the boys'-book values (without them, Michael and his friends would not have survived the prison camp) and then rejects them.

This movie may offend conventional liberal thinking more by its commitment to parochial, "local" values than by any defense of the Vietnam War—for it makes none. Neither does it take any political position against the war. But the film's very substance—the Clairton community in contrast with the Asian chaos—is the traditional isolationist message: Asia should be left to the Asians, and we should stay where we belong, but if we have to go over there we'll show how tough we are. This parochialism may be the key to why some people will reject the film in toto—even find it despicable in toto. Although cosmopolitan values were actually the ones that got us into Vietnam (the government planners weren't small-town American Legionnaires; they were Harvard men), it has become the custom to pin the guilt on the military "hawks." Michael is not a liberal hero, like the Jon Voight character of *Coming Home;* we can feel (without being told) that he's grounded in the rigid values of people who are suspicious of science and world affairs and anything foreign. Cimino is as careful to leave controversy out of his idealized town as Louis B. Mayer used to be. Clairton is abstracted from even those issues that people in beer joints quarrel about; no one ever asks what the Americans are doing in Vietnam, there are no racial jokes, and there isn't as much as a passing reference to strikes or welfare, or anything else that might show dissension, anger, or narrowness. And, of course, there are no homosexuals in the town (or even in the war); if there were, the film's underpinnings would collapse, and its eerie romanticism would become funny. In this film, evil itself is totally unsexual; Russian roulette is the perfect solution—Nick, who has had his soul burned out by it, goes AWOL and disappears into the dives of Saigon, where civilians play that game. Without sharing the implicit God-and-country, flag-on-the-door political assumptions of *The Deer Hunter,* one can see, I think, that, even with its pulp components and the racism of the Saigon dens-of-vice scenes and its superman hero, it is not merely trying to move people by pandering to their prejudices—it is also caught in its own obsessions. And, because it plays them out on such a vast canvas, it has an inchoate, stirring quality. Audiences can project into *The Deer Hunter* in a way they couldn't with such male-comradeship films as *Butch Cassidy and the Sundance Kid,* because it gives us the feeling that it's got a grand design lurking somewhere in those sensual rhythms and inconsistent themes.

In traditional American literature—in Mark Twain, say—the boys with pluck run away from proprieties, restrictions, manners, chores. Women represent the civilization that must be escaped. But in *The Deer Hunter* women are not even that much: they exist only on the margins of the men's lives. Steven's mother (Shirley Stoler, in a poor, mostly one-note performance) is a virago, his bride is a sallow weakling, and the bridesmaids are overly made-up and have too many curls; they're plump—stuffed with giggles. The only woman we see in Clairton who could attract a man of substance for more than a quick fling is Meryl Streep's Linda, who works in the supermarket; Streep has the clear-eyed blond handsomeness of a Valkyrie—the slight extra length of her nose gives her face a distinction that takes her out of the pretty class into real beauty. She doesn't do anything standard; everything seems fresh. But her role is to be the supportive woman, who suffers and endures, and it's a testament to Meryl Streep's heroic resources as a mime that she makes herself felt—she has practically no lines. There were three writers on this project in addition to Cimino (Deric Washburn, Louis Garfinkle, and Quinn K. Redeker worked on the story with him, and Washburn did the screenplay), but Linda is a presence rather than a character. She's a possibility glimpsed, rather than a woman, or even a sex object—least of all, a sex object. Michael and Nick, the two central characters, both have some sort of commitment to her, without our knowing what either of them feels for her—it's a very limp triangle. She is the film's token of romance, and Cimino's unwillingness to go beyond Victorian tokenism muddies the film when Michael returns from Vietnam and his relations with Linda consist mostly of the exchange of unhappy, solicitous looks. Does he love her but feel that she's pledged to Nick, who he thinks is dead? (There's no clue to why he would think Nick was dead.) Michael shows no physical desire for Linda. They lie on a bed together, he fully clothed—should we know what they're thinking? We don't. And when, for one night, they're under the covers together, without their clothes, and he rolls over on top of her, the scene is deliberately vague, passionless. He never even kisses her—would that be too personal? He was hotter for the deer.

Finally (and improbably), Michael learns that Nick may still be alive, and goes back to Vietnam to find him and pull him out from the Heart of Darkness. The scenes in Vietnam, with all those people clamoring to survive, and with him going back in there to rescue a man who doesn't care to live, are so sweeping yet so slick that they're like Coppola without brains or sensibility. Exotic steaminess is pushed to the melodramatic limit, as Michael, looking for his friend, passes through the inferno of war and enters Saigon's sin city, operating in the midst of flames and human misery. The film's last hour, in which it loses its sure progression and its confident editing, would have been far less wobbly if Michael had not come home until after he had made this rescue attempt. As it is, he returns from Vietnam twice, and during the period when he's home for the first time the story weaves back and forth, with fumbling scenes of Michael trying to make up his mind whether he should go see Steven, who's in a hospital. This period is unformed; it lacks resonance and gives us the impression that we're missing something—that pieces of the plot have been cut out.

It's possible that Cimino grew as an artist during the years of making this film (the production costs doubled, to thirteen million) but was locked into certain fantasy conceptions, and was never able to clarify the characters without violating the whole deer-hunting mystique he'd started with. And even after he'd shot the sequences that re-created the obscenity of the evacuation of Saigon, he was still committed to the gimmickry of the roulette game of life and death. *The Deer Hunter* is a small-minded film with greatness in it—Cimino's technique has pushed him further than he has been able to think out. His major characters don't articulate their feelings; they're floating in a wordless, almost plotless atmosphere, and their relations aren't sharp enough for us to feel the full range of the film's themes. Too many of the motifs are merely symbolic—are dropped in rather than dramatized. At times, we feel that we're there to be awed rather than to understand. We come out knowing the secondary characters—John Cazale's weak Stan (who hits women and kills deer sloppily) and George Dzundza's music-loving Welsh and John Savage's simple-hearted, ingenuous Steven—far better than we know Michael or Nick.

This isn't because De Niro and Walken don't do their jobs. Walken seems completely authentic one minute and totally false the next, because he has so little that's definite to project that he's straining. Yet he has never been so forceful on the screen, and when he's feverish and wet in the Vietnamese jungle and his hair is plastered down on his head, his large eyes, sharp chin, and jutting cheekbones suggest Falconetti in *The Passion of Joan of Arc;* he has a feminine delicacy without effeminacy. He's right for his part, but his rightness for it is all that the part is. And this is true of De Niro. He's lean, wiry, strong. Physically, he's everything that one wants the hero to be. (The only thing that's unheroic about him is that he's still using the cretinous grin he developed for *Bang the Drum Slowly.*) He fails conspicuously in only one sequence—when he's required to grab Nick's bloody head and shake it. You don't shake someone who's bleeding, and De Niro can't rise above the stupidity of this conception; even his weeping doesn't move us. We have come to expect a lot from De Niro: miracles. And he delivers them—he brings a bronze statue almost to life. He takes the Pathfinder-Deerslayer role and gives it every flourish he can dream up. He does improvisations on nothing, and his sea-to-shining-sea muscularity is impulsive. But Michael, the transcendent hero, is a hollow figure. There is never a moment when we feel, Oh my God, I know that man, I am that man.

The New Yorker, December 18, 1978

INVASION OF THE BODY SNATCHERS
PODS

Invasion of the Body Snatchers is more sheer fun than any movie I've seen since *Carrie* and *Jaws* and maybe parts of *The Spy Who Loved Me*. The scriptwriter, W.D. (Rick) Richter, supplies some of the funniest lines ever heard from the screen, and the director, Phil Kaufman, provides such confident professionalism that you sit back in the assurance that every spooky nuance you're catching is just what was intended. It's a wonderful relief to see a movie made by people who know what they're doing. They're also working with a deliciously paranoid theme: trying to hang on to your human individuality while those around you are contentedly turning into vegetables and insisting that you join them. The film takes off from the 1956 *The Invasion of the Body Snatchers*, directed by Don Siegel—a low-budget Allied Artists movie (about $350,000) that has an honored place in film history, because of its realistic atmosphere (it's set in a drab, isolated small town that seems to close in on the characters) and the solid, frightening theme, which is essentially the idea that Ionesco developed in *Rhinoceros*. (Americans seem to have better luck when they treat surreal paranoid ideas in low-down science-fiction form.) Siegel's version was subjected to executive bowdlerizing: most of the humor was excised, and a prologue and an epilogue were tacked on to provide a hopeful resolution. Even so, it's a tight little economy-package classic. The new version is wilder and more fantastic, with perhaps the best use of Dolby stereo yet—the sound effects have you scared and laughing even before the titles come on. This Phil Kaufman version is so sumptuously made that it looks very expensive, even though it was done on what is now considered a small budget (under three and a half million, with a sizable chunk of that going into the post-production work on the sound.) The pre-title rumbling roar suggests how God might have started the Creation if only He'd had Dolby. The first images, which are of diaphanous gelatinous spores wafting upward, have a spectral comic beauty; it's like being in a planetarium while something awesomely, creepily sexy is taking place. This is a full-scale science-fiction horror fable, a realization of the potentialities of the material. For undiluted pleasure and excitement, it is, I think, the American movie of the year—a new classic.

The story is set in San Francisco, which is the ideally right setting, because of the city's traditional hospitality to artists and eccentrics. Probably nowhere else have people considered so many systems of thought and been through so many interpersonal wars; San Franciscans often look shell-shocked. The various outcroppings of the human-potential movement have had an unexpected result: instead of becoming more individual, people in therapeutic groups get so self-absorbed in their various quests that they appear dulled out. And so when the gooey seeds from space come down in the rain over San Francisco and cling to leaves and establish root systems and blossom, and each flower pod develops into a fetus that grows large enough to replace an individual as he sleeps, while the old body crumbles into a small pile of garbage, it is not surprising to hear the reborn flower people proselytizing for their soulless condition as a higher form of life. "Don't be trapped by old concepts," one of them says. The story simply wouldn't be as funny in New York City, where people are not so relaxed, or so receptive to new visions. There are no a-priori rejections in San Francisco.

The hip-idyllic city, with its gingerbread houses and its jagged geometric profile of hills covered with little triangles and rectangles, is such a pretty plaything that it's the central character. The movie itself is like a toy; it's all filigree, in the way that *The Manchurian Candidate* is. As the malignant growth sprouts brilliant-red blossoms, we hear the film's first words: in the blank, bored tone of someone who's trying to fill up the time, a teacher who's out with her class says, "There's some more flowers, kids. Go pick them." That has got to be a famous first line. For the opening third of the picture, almost every scene has a verbal or visual gag built into it, and throughout there's a laciness to the images—to the way the interiors include exterior views of the whimsical, Victorian-dollhouse architecture, and the bright-colored sanitation trucks gobbling up waste matter.

Elizabeth (Brooke Adams), who works at the Department of Health, picks one of the carnal red flowers on her way home. When she gets there, Geoffrey (Art Hindle), her laid-back lover, is sprawled out watching basketball on TV; he kisses Elizabeth without taking off his earphones and gets excited only when he hears a terrific play—he pushes her aside so he can see it. Geoffrey, who's a dentist, is so quintessentially laid back you don't know what keeps him vertical, or in such good shape. He just seems to have been manufactured with muscles: that's the model. The flower is left near his side of the bed, and in the morning he no longer goes with the flow; he gets up with a stolid sense of mission, dresses up as if he were a Rotarian huckster, and takes a bundle out under his arm and tosses it into a waiting garbage truck. And as he goes about the city he makes eye contact with other people, who all know what's on each other's minds—it's as if they were governed by Muzak. (Watching the clear-faced, neatly dressed, upstanding Geoffrey, you suspect that Werner Erhard was the original spore.) Scared by the change in him, Elizabeth tells her boss, Matthew (Donald Sutherland), that Geoffrey isn't Geoffrey, that "something is missing." But then she goes to a cocktail party celebrating the publication of a new how-to-be-happy book by Dr. Kibner (Leonard Nimoy), the city's leading chic psychiatrist, who suavely explains that she thinks Geoffrey has changed—has become less human—because she's looking for a chance to get out of their relationship. (Kibner is as smug as the psychoanalyst in *Cat People* explaining to Simone Simon that she only fantasizes turning into a leopard.) And Elizabeth, who knows she's beginning to have romantic urges toward her boss, half accepts Kibner's explanation.

In most science-fiction movies, the stalwart characters would have nothing to lose to the pod people; they have already been vegetablized by the lack of imagination of the filmmakers. But Kaufman and Richter have managed to give substance to the fear of losing one's individuality, by creating believable, likable characters. Brooke Adams doesn't have the sullen-washerwoman look she had in *Days of Heaven;* her turned-down mouth has an odd attractiveness, and her Elizabeth is smart and resilient, with a streak of loony humor. (She spins her eyeballs, like the great Harry Ritz.) Even her flat voice is funny here: she uses vocal affectlessness as a deadpan, and rings trick low notes on it. (The women in this movie are every bit as strong and sharp—and foolish—as the men, without any big point being made of it.) As heroes go, Sutherland may not be a world-beater, but at least he's plausible and stays in character. And the other leads play genuine San Francisco weirdos. Jeff Goldblum, who knows enough to disregard his handsomeness, and to stick with a huffy, distracted timing that is purely his own, is Jack Bellicec, a furiously angry poet who is proud of taking six months to decide on a word, and Veronica Cartwright is his wife, Nancy, who works in their Turkish-bath establishment—Bellicec Baths—as desk clerk and masseuse. Veronica Cartwright has such an instinct for the camera that even when she isn't doing anything special, what she's feeling registers. She doesn't steal scenes—she gives them an extra comic intensity. When Nancy Bellicec greets someone by scrunching up her face, her whole goofy soul is in her expression. What the film catches with this devoted pair is their domestication of nuttiness—they wouldn't love each other so much if they weren't both a little cracked. San Francisco is a city full of people who are sure they could write better than the successful writers in their midst, and probably could, but they're too busy living and griping to try. Jack's contempt for the best-selling Dr. Kibner is the contempt of a writer who doesn't put anything on paper for the fraud who does. Phil Kaufman (who makes his home there) and Rick Richter (who was on the locations throughout the shooting) have got the conversational tone of the culture down pat. The Bellicecs must protect their eccentricity: it's the San Francisco brand of humanity. This film is almost like a surreal variant of Simone Weil's thesis that the people who resisted the Nazis weren't the good, upright citizens—they were the dreamers and outcasts and cranks. There's something at stake in this movie: the right of freaks to be freaks—which is much more appealing than the right of "normal" people to be normal.

There are some amazing special effects: the plant tendrils that sneak over sleeping people, and the fetal pods that bleed when they're crushed, and a dog joke that is perhaps a nod to *The Fly* and *The Mephisto Waltz* and the famous dog in *Yojimbo* but is also pure Dadaism. *Invasion of the Body Snatchers* gives the impression of a supernatural and fantastic visual style, though the cinematography, by Michael Chapman, is very straightforward. This may be because of the unusual delicacy of his work. The daylight scenes, with sharp primary colors that aren't posterish in the Godardian way, because of a softening use of secondary colors, emphasize the orderly movements of the pod people, which are so at odds with the iridescent bauble of a city. At night, of course, the city is theirs. Much of the photogenic power of the material (it's based on Jack Finney's early-fifties *Collier's* serial *The Body Snatchers*) comes from the fear of night and sleep: if a character closes his eyes, he may not be himself when he wakes up. When the first version was made, the filmmakers thought of calling it *Sleep No More.* Chapman has a special feel for night subjects, as he demonstrated in *Taxi Driver* and *The Last Waltz,* though his work on Kaufman's *The White Dawn* was also eerie and mysterious. He shows a gift here for bringing out the personality of the city locations; there's a finely drawn, cluttered grace in his San Francisco, and it intensifies the horror, in the same way that the characters' idiosyncratic styles of humor do. When the four principals run down Telegraph Hill, with a phalanx of pod people in pursuit, and dash to the Embarcadero, they cast long shadows, like figures in one of de Chirico's almost deserted piazzas. Parts of this film have a hellish beauty, like Cocteau's *Orpheus* and, more recently, *The Fury.*

There are small disappointments. Elizabeth tells Matthew of the conspiratorial meetings of the pod people before we actually see them meet. And Matthew has a sequence of racing from one telephone booth to another which is charged with meaningless tension and has no particular payoff. Perhaps the scenes in which pods are being dispatched to other cities are not as elegantly staged as they might be. And there may be a few times when the generally dazzling score, by Denny Zeitlin, the jazz pianist turned San Francisco psychiatrist, overpowers the action, but the music is a large contributor to the jokes and terrors. There is also a truly inspired electronic effect, devised by the sound expert Ben Burtt: the pod people make a shrieking, warning cry that suggests an inhuman variant of the rhythmic trilling-screaming sounds of the women in *The Battle of Algiers.* In that film, it was a cry for freedom; here it's a cry for conformity.

There's a great entertainment-movie tradition of combining high jinks and artistry, and this film belongs to it. Michael Chapman, the cinematographer, can be spotted in a corridor, leaning against a mop and Robert Duvall, who played Jesse James in Kaufman's first major studio film, *The Great Northfield Minnesota Raid,* is visible as a priest on a playground swing. (As a benediction for the movie?) Don Siegel turns up, playing a cabdriver. And there's a reënactment of what is generally remembered as the end of the 1956 version (it's how the movie would have ended if the studio hadn't slapped on the "Get me the F.B.I." epilogue), with Kevin McCarthy, the star of that version, once more banging on car windshields. He yells, "They're here! Help! They're here!" But this time he isn't saved—he's finished off. There are also fog-enshrouded shots of the Transamerica pyramid. (Transamerica is the parent company of United Artists, which financed this picture.) *Invasion of the Body Snatchers* doesn't take itself too seriously, yet it plunges into emotional scenes with a fast, offhand mastery. At night, Matthew stands on the terrace of his apartment, where he and his three friends have holed up, and looks down at the four adult-size fetuses that are almost

ready to replace them. He wants to smash those bodies, but he can't destroy
the ones of his friends, because they're so close to human that it would be
like killing people he loves. He can smash only his own reproduction. This
set of variations on the 1956 film has its own macabre originality; it may be
the best movie of its kind ever made.

The New Yorker, December 25, 1978

FROM REVIEW OF PETER WEIR'S
THE LAST WAVE

The maudlin hysteria in the film links it to some of the Hollywood movies
of the late-sixties-early-seventies period. (This may help to account for
the respectful tenderness with which it has been treated in much of the
press.) It's the kill-us-because-we-deserve-to-die syndrome. Instead of seeing
the victims of expansionist drives and colonial policies—the aborigines or
blacks or Indians—as people whose rights were violated and must be restored as quickly as possible, these movies romanticize the victims. They are
seen in terms of what whites are supposed to have repressed. A few generations ago, whites saw the victims of white civilization (as racist bigots still
do) in terms of sexuality and savagery; now the victims are seen in terms of
magic, dreamspeak, nobility, intuition, harmony with nature. The white bigots saw them as mentally inferior; the modern, guilt-ridden whites see them
as spiritually superior. . . .

It's implicit in *The Last Wave* that the crime against the aborigines is
what alienated the whites from their dreams, and that because of this crime
a Biblical flood is coming—punishment and purification. It doesn't seem to
matter that the flood will flush away the aborigines as well. This film is so
infatuated with white guilt that the aborigines are created in our lost self-
image. The lithe, graceful Chris (Gulpilil, the star of Roeg's *Walkabout*),
who's on trial, and the dignified, wily shaman, Charlie (Nandjiwarra
Amagula), are what self-hating whites emotionally need them to be: our betters. Aborigines who cling to their tribal rites are seen as uncorrupted, and
the shaman, like an old Indian chief, is revered because he's such a photogenic custodian of our consciences. (We all know that, in order to survive,
many people of oppressed races have developed inner strength, but this
strength also shines forth in many white faces—in the inhabitants of
Appalachia, for example—or in almost any group at a time of crisis.)

The decadent white race is represented by the sickly paleface lawyer,
and surely there isn't an actor with less natural rhythm than Richard Chamberlain. But if the filmmaking team hired Chamberlain with malice afore-
thought why didn't anybody explain to him that he needn't wear himself

out acting? Chamberlain has got by in a few roles—as Aramis in Richard Lester's *The Three Musketeers,* because he could be in motion, and in the TV *Count of Monte Cristo,* when he was bearded and dashing. But throughout this film we listen to vaguely alarming distant sounds on the track while the lawyer muses about his intimations that things aren't . . . quite right. And Richard Chamberlain is not an actor you want to spend quiet moments with. He can't stop quivering his lips to connote sensitivity and contracting his nostrils for apprehensiveness and pulling in his cheek muscles for ineffable sorrow. He keeps us conscious that he's acting all the time. His toes act in his shoes.

The New Yorker, January 22, 1979

PART EIGHT

TAKING IT ALL IN

1984

The movies have been so rank the last couple of years that when I see people lining up to buy tickets I sometimes think that the movies aren't drawing an audience—they're inheriting an audience. People just want to go to a movie. They're stung repeatedly, yet their desire for a good movie—for *any* movie—is so strong that all over the country they keep lining up. "There's one God for all creation, but there must be a separate God for the movies," a producer said. "How else can you explain their survival?" An atmosphere of hope develops before a big picture's release, and even after your friends tell you how bad it is, you can't quite believe it until you see for yourself. The lines (and the grosses) tell us only that people are going to the movies—not that they're having a good time. Financially, the industry is healthy, so among the people at the top there seems to be little recognition of what miserable shape movies are in. They think the grosses are proof that people are happy with what they're getting, just as TV executives think that the programs with the highest ratings are what TV viewers want, rather than what they settle for. (A number of the new movie executives come from TV.) These new executives don't necessarily see many movies themselves, and they rarely go to a theatre. If for the last couple of years Hollywood couldn't seem to do anything right, it isn't that it was just a stretch of bad luck—it's the result of recent developments within the industry. And in all probability it will get worse, not better. There have been few recent American movies worth lining up for—last year there was chiefly *The Black*

Stallion, and this year there is *The Empire Strikes Back.* The first was made under the aegis of Francis Ford Coppola; the second was financed by George Lucas, using his profits from *Star Wars* as a guarantee to obtain bank loans. One can say with fair confidence that neither *The Black Stallion* nor *The Empire Strikes Back* could have been made with such care for visual richness and imagination if it had been done under studio control. Even small films on traditional subjects are difficult to get financed at a studio if there are no parts for stars in them; Peter Yates, the director of *Breaking Away*—a graceful, unpredictable comedy that pleases and satisfies audiences—took the project to one studio after another for almost six years before he could get the backing for it.

There are direct results when conglomerates take over movie companies. At first, the heads of the conglomerates may be drawn into the movie business for the status implications—the opportunity to associate with world-famous celebrities. Some other conglomerate heads may be drawn in for the girls, but for them, too, a new social life beckons, and as they become socially involved, people with great names approach them as equals, and it gets them crazy. Famous stars and producers and writers and directors tell them about offers they've had from other studios and about ideas that they have for pictures, and the conglomerate heads become indignant that the studios they control aren't in on these wonderful projects. The next day, they're on the phone raising hell with their studio bosses. Very soon, they're likely to be summoning directors and suggesting material to them, talking to actors, and telling the company executives what projects should be developed. How bad are the taste and judgment of the conglomerate heads? Very bad. They haven't grown up in a show-business milieu—they don't have the background, the instincts, the information of those who have lived and sweated movies for many years. (Neither do most of the current studio bosses.) The conglomerate heads may be business geniuses, but as far as movies are concerned they have virgin instincts; ideas that are new to them and take them by storm may have failed grotesquely dozens of times. But they feel that they are creative people—how else could they have made so much money and be in a position to advise artists what to do? Who is to tell them no? Within a very short time, they are in fact, though not in title, running the studio. They turn up compliant executives who will settle for the title and not fight for the authority or for their own tastes—if, in fact, they have any. The conglomerate heads find these compliant executives among lawyers and agents, among lawyer-agents, among television executives, and in the lower echelons of the companies they've taken over. Generally, these executives reserve all their enthusiasm for movies that have made money; those are the only movies they like. When a director or a writer talks to them and tries to suggest the kind of picture he has in mind by using a comparison, they may stare at him blankly. They are usually law-school or business-school graduates; they have no frame of reference. Worse, they have no shame about not knowing anything about movies. From their point

of view, such knowledge is not essential to their work. Their talent is be
able to anticipate their superiors' opinions; in meetings, they show a six
sense for guessing what the most powerful person in the room wants to
hear. And if they ever guess wrong, they know how to shift gears without a
tremor. So the movie companies wind up with top production executives
whose interest in movies rarely extends beyond the immediate selling possibilities; they could be selling neckties just as well as movies, except that they
are drawn to glamour and power.

This does not prevent these executives from being universally treated as
creative giants. If a studio considers eighty projects, and eventually twenty of
them (the least risky) go into production, and two of them become runaway
hits (or even one of them), the studio's top executive will be a hero to his
company and the media, and will soon be quoted in the *Los Angeles Times*
and *The New York Times* talking about his secret for picking winners—his intuitive understanding, developed from his childhood experiences, that people want a strong, upbeat narrative, that they want to cheer the hero and
hiss the villain. When *Alien* opened "big," Alan Ladd, Jr., president of the
pictures division of Twentieth Century-Fox, was regarded as a demigod; it's
the same way that Fred Silverman was a demigod. It has nothing to do with
quality, only with the numbers. (Ladd and his team weren't admired for the
small pictures they took chances on and the artists they stuck by.) The media now echo the kind of thinking that goes on in Hollywood, and spread
it wide. Movie critics on TV discuss the relative grosses of the new releases;
the grosses at this point relative to previous hits; which pictures will pass the
others in a few weeks. It's like the Olympics—which will be the winners?

■   ■   ■

There are a lot of reasons that movies have been so bad during the last couple of years and probably won't be any better for the next couple of years.
One big reason is that rotten pictures are making money—not necessarily
wild amounts (though a few are), but sizable amounts. So if studio heads
want nothing more than to make money and grab power, there is no reason
for them to make better ones. Turning out better pictures might actually
jeopardize their position. Originally, the studios were controlled by theatre
chains—the chains opened the studios in order to have a source of supply.
But the studios and the theatre chains were separated by a Supreme Court
order in 1948 and subsequent lower-court rulings; after that, the studios, operating without the protection of theatres committed in advance to play
their product, resorted to "blind bidding" and other maneuvers in order to
reduce the risk on their films. It's only in the last few years that the studios
have found a new kind of protection. They have discovered that they can get
much more from the sale of movies to television than they had been getting,
and that they can negotiate presale agreements with the networks for guaranteed amounts before they commit themselves to a production. Licensing
fees to the networks now run between $3,000,000 and $4,000,000 for an average picture, and the studios negotiate in advance not only for network

TV syndication (about $1,500,000 for an average pic-
~~~~~~levision (between $1,000,000 and $1,500,000), but for
~~~~s, cassettes, and overseas television. And, of course, they
~~~~ign distributors and to exhibitors here, and much of that
~~~~so committed in advance—sometimes even paid in advance. So
~~~n is budgeted at $8,500,000, the studio may have $14,000,000 guaran-
~ed and—theoretically, at least—show a profit before shooting starts, even
if $4,000,000 is allowed for marketing and advertising. And the studio still
has the possibility of a big box-office hit and *really* big money. If a picture
is a large-scale adventure story or has superstars, the licensing fee to the networks alone may be between $15,000,000 and $25,000,000, and the total advance guarantees may come to almost double the budget. Financially, the
only danger in an arrangement like this is that if the film goes seriously over
budget the studio can still lose money. That's why directors who have the
reputation of always coming in on schedule are in steady demand even if
they've had a long line of box-office failures and their work is consistently
mediocre, and why directors who are perfectionists are shunned as if they
were lepers—unless, like Hal Ashby, they've had some recent hits.

The studios no longer make movies primarily to attract and please
moviegoers; they make movies in such a way as to get as much as possible
from the prearranged and anticipated deals. Every picture (allowing for a
few exceptions) is cast and planned in terms of those deals. Though the studio is very happy when it has a box-office hit, it isn't terribly concerned
about the people who buy tickets and come out grumbling. They don't
grumble very loudly anyway, because even the lumpiest pictures are generally an improvement over television; at least, they're always bigger. TV accus-
toms people to not expecting much, and because of the new prearranged
deals they're not getting very much. There is a quid pro quo for a big advance sale to television and theatres: the project must be from a fat, dumb
best-seller about an international jewel heist or a skyjacking that involves a
planeload of the rich and famous, or be a thinly disguised show-business biography of someone who came to an appallingly wretched end, or have an
easily paraphrasable theme—preferably something that can be done justice
to in a sentence and brings to mind the hits of the past. How else could you
entice buyers? Certainly not with something unfamiliar, original. They feel
safe with big-star packages, with chase thrillers, with known ingredients. For
a big overseas sale, you must have "international" stars—performers who are
known all over, such as Sophia Loren, Richard Burton, Candice Bergen,
Roger Moore, Clint Eastwood, Burt Reynolds, Alain Delon, Charles
Bronson, Steve McQueen. And you should probably avoid complexities:
much of the new overseas audience is subliterate. For a big advance sale to
worldwide television, a movie should also be innocuous: it shouldn't raise
any hackles, either by strong language or by a controversial theme. And
there must be stars, though not necessarily movie stars. It has recently been
discovered that even many Americans are actually more interested in TV

personalities than in movie ones, and may be roused from their TV-viewing to go see a film with John Denver or John Ritter. In countries where American TV series have become popular, our TV stars may be better known than our movie stars (especially the ones who appear infrequently). A 1979 Canadian film, *Running,* starring Michael Douglas, who has appeared in a TV series and was featured in *The China Syndrome,* cost $4,200,000; by the time it was completed, the various rights to it had been sold for over $6,000,000. The lawyer-financier who set up the production of *Foolin' Around,* which stars Gary Busey, said he would not have made the picture without the television insurance of a supporting cast that included Tony Randall, Cloris Leachman, and Eddie Albert. Nobody needs to have heard of these independently packaged pictures for them to be profitable, and, in some cases, if it were not contractually necessary to open the film in theatres in order to give it legitimacy as a movie, it would be cheaper not to, because the marketing and advertising costs may outstrip the box-office revenue (unless that, too, was guaranteed). On productions like these, the backers don't suffer the gamblers' anxieties that were part of film business in the fifties and sixties, and even in the early seventies. Of course, these backers don't experience the gamblers' highs, either. Movie executives now study the television Q ratings, which measure the public's familiarity with performers, and a performer with a high rating (which he attains if he's been in a long-running series or on a daytime quiz show) is offered plum movie roles—even if this means that the script will have to be completely rewritten for his narrow range or bland personality.

■   ■   ■

There is an even grimmer side to all this: because the studios have discovered how to take the risk out of moviemaking, they don't want to make any movies that they can't protect themselves on. Production and advertising costs have gone so high that there is genuine nervous panic about risky projects. If an executive finances what looks like a perfectly safe, stale piece of material and packs it with stars, and the production costs skyrocket way beyond the guarantees and the picture loses many millions, *he* won't be blamed for it—he was playing the game by the same rules as everybody else. If, however, he takes a gamble on a small project that can't be sold in advance—something that a gifted director really wants to do, with a subtle, not easily summarized theme and no big names in the cast—and it loses just a little money, his neck is on the block. So to the executives a good script is a script that attracts a star, and they will make their deals and set the full machinery of a big production in motion and schedule the picture's release dates, even though the script problems have never been worked out and everyone (even the director) secretly knows that the film will be a confused mess, an embarrassment.

Another new factor makes a risky project still riskier; if a movie doesn't have an easily paraphrasable theme or big stars it's hard to sell via a thirty-second TV commercial. (The networks pay a lot for movies, but they get much of it back directly from the movie industry, which increasingly relies on TV commercials to sell a film.) It's even hard for the studio advertising departments to figure out a campaign for newspapers and magazines. And so, faced with something unusual or original, the studio head generally says, "I don't know how to market it, and if I don't know how to market it, it will lose money." The new breed of studio head is not likely to say, "It's something I feel we should take a chance on. Let's see if there's somebody who might be able to figure out how to market it." Just about the only picture the studios made last year that the executives took a financial risk on was *Breaking Away*. And despite the fact that it cost what is now a pittance ($2,400,000) and received an Academy Award Best Picture nomination, Twentieth Century-Fox didn't give it a big theatrical re-release (the standard procedure for a nominated film) but sold it to NBC for immediate showing, for $5,000,000. So a couple of weeks after the Awards ceremony, just when many people had finally heard of *Breaking Away* and might have gone to a theatre to see it, it appeared, trashed in the usual manner, on television. The studio couldn't be sure how much more money might come in from box offices and grabbed a sure thing. In order to accept the NBC offer, the studio even bypassed pay TV, where the picture could have been seen uncut. It was almost as if *Breaking Away* were being punished for not having stars and not having got a big advance TV sale. And the price was almost insulting: last year, Fox licensed *The Sound of Music* to NBC for $21,500,000, and licensed *Alien* to ABC for $12,000,000, with escalator clauses that could take the figure up to $15,000,000; Columbia licensed *Kramer vs. Kramer* to ABC for nearly $20,000,000, and United Artists got $20,000,000 for *Rocky II* from CBS. But then how do you summarize in a sentence the appeal of a calm, evenhanded film about fathers and sons, town boys and college boys, and growing up—a modest classic that never states its themes, that stirs the emotions by indirection, by the smallest of actions and the smallest exchanges of dialogue?

■　■　■

If a writer-director conceives a script for a fiery young actor—K., a young man with star potential who has not yet had a role that brought him to the consciousness of the public—and shapes the central character to bring out K.'s volatility and ardor, he is likely to be told by the studio head, "K. doesn't do anything to me." That rules out K., even if the studio head has never seen K. act (and chances are he wouldn't remember him if he had). The studio head doesn't care if K. could become a star in this part; he wants R., because he can get a $4,000,000 network sale with the impassive, logy R., a Robert Wagner type who was featured in a mini-series. And if the point is pressed, the studio head may cut off discussion with some variation of "I must know what I'm doing, or I wouldn't be in this job." If he is feeling expansive, he may go on with "I won't say that you can't make a good film with K., and some people— some critics and your friends—will like it. But a good picture to me is a successful picture—one that will make money." If the writer-director still persists, it's taken as a sign of stupidity. A finer-grained executive—one of the rare ones who loves movies—may put it to him this way: "I like K., I like you, I like the script. But I can't recommend it. It's an expensive picture, and the subject matter makes it a long shot. And if I back too many long shots that don't come in, I'm out on my ass." That's the distillation of executive timidity, and maybe it's better to get it from the coarser man: you can have the pleasure of hating him—you aren't made to sympathize with his plight. Since all the major studios basically play by the same rules, the writer-director will wind up with a picture that is crucially miscast and has a vacuum at its center. By the time it is released and falls by the wayside, and he is publicly humiliated, K., disgusted at not having got the part, may have accepted a dumb role in a TV series and become a hot new TV personality, whom all the movie studios are propositioning.

Chances are that even if the writer-director had been allowed to use K., he would have been completely enraged and demoralized by the time he started shooting, because the negotiating process can stretch on for years, and anyone who wants to make a movie is treated as a hustler and an adversary. "Studios!" said Billy Wilder, paraphrasing an old complaint about women. "You can't make pictures with 'em, and you can't make pictures without 'em." Everybody in the movie business has the power to say no, and the least secure executives protect themselves by saying no to just about anything that comes their way. Only those at the very top can say yes, and they protect themselves, too. They postpone decisions because they're fearful, and also because they don't mind keeping someone dangling while his creative excitement dries up and all the motor drive goes out of his proposal. They don't mind keeping people waiting, because it makes them feel more powerful. I'm describing trends; of course, there are exceptions—those who are known (and sometimes revered) for quick decisions, like David Picker in his United Artists days, and Daniel Melnick in his brief stints at M-G-M and Columbia, and David Begelman at Columbia and now at M-G-M. But most of the ones who could say yes don't; they consider it and string you along. (Hollywood is the only place where you can die of encouragement.) For the supplicant, it's a matter of weeks, months, years, waiting for meetings at which he can beg permission to do what he was, at the start, eager to do. And even when he's got a meeting, he has to catch the executive's attention and try to keep it; in general the higher the executive, the more cruelly short his attention span. (They're television babies. Thirty seconds is a long time to them.) In this atmosphere of bureaucratic indifference or contempt, things aren't really decided—they just happen, along bureaucratic lines. (Generally, it's only if a picture is a hit that executives talk about having given it the go-ahead. They all angle for credit in the media.) During the long wait, the director has lost the cinematographer he wanted and half the performers; in order to get the necessary approvals, he has agreed to actors he knows are wrong, and he has pared down the script to cut costs, chopping out the scenes that once meant the most to him but that he knows he can't get in the tight, ten-week shooting schedule he has been forced to accept. And then, at the last minute, a few days before shooting is to start, the studio is likely to slice the budget further—and he's down to a nine-week schedule, which means trimming the camera moves that were half the reason he'd been eager to work on the idea in the first place. Is it any wonder if the picture that comes out has a sour spirit?

It may just barely come out anyway. If there's an executive shakeup during production or after the film is completed (and shakeups take place every few months), the new studio head has nothing to gain if the film succeeds (he can't take credit for initiating it); he may find it to his strategic advantage for the film to fail. The executives—bed-hoppers, who go from one berth to another—have no particular loyalty to the studio, and there isn't the lower-echelon executive stability to launch a film initiated during the old regime with the same care as one initiated during the new regime. It all depends on the signals that come from the top.

■   ■   ■

If a big star and a big director show interest in a project, the executives will go along for a $14,000,000 or $15,000,000 budget even if, by the nature of the material, the picture should be small. And so what might have been a charming light entertainment that millions of people all over the world would enjoy is inflated, rewritten to enlarge the star's part, and overscaled. It makes money in advance and sends people out of theatres complaining and depressed. Often, when people leave theatres now they're bewildered by the anxious nervous construction of the film—by the feeling it gives them of having been pieced together out of parts that don't fit. Movies have gone to hell and amateurism. A third of the pictures being made by Hollywood this year are in the hands of first-time directors, who will receive almost no guidance or help. They're thrown right into a pressure-cooker situation, where any delay is costly. They may have come out of sitcoms, and their dialogue will sound forced, as if it were all recorded in a large, empty cave; they may have come out of nowhere and have never worked with actors before. Even if a director is highly experienced, he probably has certain characteristic weaknesses, such as a tendency to lose track of the story, or an ineptness with women characters; he's going to need watching. But who knows that, or cares enough to try to protect the picture? The executives may have hired the director after "looking at his work"—that is, running off every other reel of one of his films. They are busy people. Network executives who are offered a completed movie commonly save time by looking at a fifteen-minute selection from it—a précis of its highlights—which has been specially prepared for them. God forbid that they should have to sit through the whole thing.

What isn't generally understood is how much talent and hard work are wasted—enough, maybe, to supply the world with true entertainment. A writer who is commissioned to adapt a book and turns in a crackerjack script, acclaimed by the studio executives, who call him a genius, then stands helplessly by as the studio submits it to the ritual lists of the stars and the directors whom they can get the biggest guarantees on. And as, one by one, the stars and directors who aren't right for the project anyway take months to read it and turn it down, the executives' confidence in the script drains away. If a star expresses tentative interest, contingent on a complete rewrite they will throw out the snappy script and authorize a new script by a sodden writer who has just had a fluke hit, and when the star decides to do something else anyway, they will have a new script written for a different star, and another and another, until no one can remember why there was ever any interest in the project. It may be shelved then, but so much money has already gone into it that in a couple of years some canny producer will think it should be brought back to life and reworked to fit a hot new teen-ager from television—who eventually will decide not to do it, and so on. To put it simply: A good script is a script to which Robert Redford will commit himself. A bad script is a script which Redford has turned down. A script that "needs work" is a script about which Redford has yet to make up his mind. It is possible to run a studio with this formula; it is even possible to run a studio *profitably* with this formula. But this world of realpolitik that has replaced moviemaking has nothing to do with moviemaking. It's not just that the decisions made by the executives might have been made by anyone off the street—it's that the pictures themselves seem to have been made by anyone off the street.

The executives are a managerial class with no real stake in the studio; they didn't build it, it's not part of them, and they're moving on—into a big-ger job at another studio, or into independent production (where there's more money), or to form their own companies. The executives just try to hold things together for the short period that they're going to be around; there isn't even an elementary regard for the conservation of talent. And, as in any chaotic bureaucracy, the personalities and goals of those at the top set the tone for all the day-to-day decisions; the top executives' apathy about the quality of movies infects the studio right down the line. The younger ex-ecutives who are pushing their way up don't want to waste their time con-sidering scripts that may not attract a star. For them, too, a good picture is a picture that makes money, and so after *The China Syndrome* clicked at box offices, they could be heard talking about what a wonderful craftsman its di-rector, James Bridges, was, and after *The Amityville Horror*, with its unbeliev-ably clunky script, by Sandor Stern, showed big grosses, they wanted to sign up Stern as a writer-director. At the bottom as at the top, the executives want to score; they want a hit, not just for the money but for the personal plea-sure of the kill.

■   ■   ■

Part of what has deranged American life in this past decade is the change in book publishing and in magazines and newspapers and in the movies as they have passed out of the control of those whose lives were bound up in them and into the control of conglomerates, financiers, and managers who treat them as ordinary commodities. This isn't a reversible process; even if there were Supreme Court rulings that split some of these holdings from the conglomerates, the traditions that developed inside many of those businesses have been ruptured. And the continuity is gone. In earlier eras, when a writer made a book agreement with a publisher, he expected to be working with the people he signed up with; now those people may be replaced the next day, or the whole firm may be bought up and turned into a subdivision of a textbook-publishing house or a leisure-activities company. The new people in the job aren't going to worry about guiding a writer slowly; they're not going to think about the book after this one. They want bestsellers. Their job is to find them or manufacture them. And just as the studios have been hiring writers to work on screenplays, they are now beginning to hire writers to work on novels, which the publishers, with the help of studio money, will then attempt to promote to best-sellerdom at the same time that they are being made into movies. The writer Avery Corman has suggested "the horrifying prospect of a novelist being fired from his own book." It won't horrify the people who are commissioning these new books—pre-novelizations.

There are certain kinds of business in which the public interest is more of a factor than it is in the manufacture of neckties. Book publishing, magazines and newspapers, movies and television and live theatre—these are businesses, of course, but traditionally the people who work in them have felt privileged (by birth or ability or talent or luck, or by a combination of those factors). That has been true not only of the actors and journalists but of the entrepreneurs and the managers. There have always been a few businessmen in these fields who had the sensibility of artists (without the talent or the drive); if they had a good critical sense and a generous nature, they were appreciators of artists and didn't resent them. And so they became great producers in the theatre and movies, or great book and magazine editors. Contemporary variants of these people insist on being celebrity-artists themselves, and right now they all seem to be writing and directing movies.

In movies, the balance between art and business has always been precarious, with business outweighing art, but the business was, at least, in the hands of businessmen who loved movies. As popular entertainment, movies need something of what the vulgarian moguls had—zest, a belief in their own instincts, a sentimental dedication to producing pictures that would make their country proud of their contribution, a respect for quality, and the biggest thing: a willingness to take chances. The cool managerial sharks don't have that; neither do the academics. But the vulgarians also did more than their share of damage, and they're gone forever anyway. They were part of a different America. They were, more often than not, men who paid only lip service to high ideals, while gouging everyone for profits. The big change in the country is reflected in the fact that people in the movie business no longer feel it necessary to talk about principles at all. They operate on the same assumptions as the newspapers that make heroes of the executives who have a hit and don't raise questions about its quality.

■ ■ ■

When the numbers game takes over a country, artists who work in a popular medium, such as the movies, lose their bearings fast. There's a pecking order in filmmaking, and the director is at the top—he's the authority figure. A man who was never particularly attractive to women now finds that he's the padrone: everyone is waiting on his word, and women are his for the nod. The constant, unlimited opportunities for sex can be insidious; so is the limitless flattery of college students who turn directors into gurus. Directors are easily seduced. They mainline admiration. Recently, a screenwriter now directing his first picture was talking about his inability to find a producer who would take some of the burden off him; he said he needed a clone—someone who would know what was in his mind and be able to handle a million details for him. But anyone observing this writer-director would know that he needs a real producer, and for a much more important reason: to provide the sense of judgment he has already lost. Nobody really controls a production now; the director is on his own, even if he's insecure, careless, or nuts. There has always been a megalomaniac potential in moviemaking, and in this period of stupor, when values have been so thoroughly undermined that even the finest directors and the ones with the most freedom aren't sure what they want to do, they often become obsessive and grandiloquent—like mad royalty. Perpetually dissatisfied with the footage they're compulsively piling up, they keep shooting—adding rooms to the palace. Megalomania and art become the same thing to them. But the disorder isn't just in their heads, and a lot of people around them are deeply impressed by megalomania. What our directors need most of all, probably, is a sense of purpose and a subject that they can think their way through. Filmmakers want big themes, and where are the kinds of themes that they would fight the studios to express? It's no accident that the two best recent American movies are both fantasy fairy tales—childish in the fullest, deepest sense. Working inside a magical structure, Carroll Ballard in *The Black Stallion* and Irvin Kershner in *The Empire Strikes Back* didn't have to deal with the modern world; they were free to use the medium luxuriantly, without guilt. You can feel the love of moviemaking—almost a revelry in moviemaking—in their films, as you can also in Walter Hill's *The Long Riders*, despite its narrative weaknesses and a slight remoteness. But we don't go to the movies just for great fairy tales and myths of the old West; we also hope for something that connects directly with where we are. Part of the widespread anticipation of *Apocalypse Now* was, I think, our readiness for a visionary, climactic, summing-up movie. We felt that the terrible rehash of pop culture couldn't go on, mustn't go on—that something new was needed. Coppola must have felt that, too, but he couldn't supply it. His film was posited on great thoughts arriving at the end—a confrontation and a revelation. And when they weren't there, people slunk out of the theatres, or tried to comfort themselves with chatter about the psychedelic imagery. Trying to say something big, Coppola got tied up in a big knot of American self-hatred and guilt, and what the picture boiled down to was: White man—he devil. Since then, I think, people have expected less of movies and have been willing to settle for less. Some have even been willing to settle for *Kramer vs. Kramer* and other pictures that seem to be made for an audience of over-age flower children. These pictures express the belief that if a man cares about anything besides being at home with the kids, he's corrupt. Parenting ennobles Dustin Hoffman and makes him a better person in every way, while in *The Seduction of Joe Tynan* we can see that Alan Alda is a weak, corruptible fellow because he wants to be President of the United States more than he wants to stay at home communing with his daughter about her adolescent miseries. Pictures like these should all end with the fathers and the children sitting at home watching TV together.

The major studios have found the temporary final solution for movies: in technique and in destiny, their films *are* television. And there's no possibility of a big breakthrough in movies—a new release of energy, like the French New Wave, which moved from country to country and resulted in an international cross-fertilization—when movies are financed only if they fall into stale categories of past successes. But once the groups that are now subsidizing studio-made films begin to weary of getting TV shows when they thought they were buying movies, there should be a chance for some real moviemaking. And when the writers and directors have confidence in what they want to express, if they can't find backing from the studios they ought to be able to find backers outside the industry who will gamble on the money to be made from a good picture, once it is complete. It's easier to make money on movies now: there are more markets, and we know now that the films themselves have a much longer commercial life than early moviemakers could have guessed. The studios may find that they need great moviemakers more than the moviemakers need them. Billy Wilder may be right that you can't make pictures with 'em, but of course he's wrong that you can't make pictures without 'em. There are problems both ways, but there may be fewer problems without them, and less rage.

It would be very convincing to say that there's no hope for movies—that audiences have been so corrupted by television and have become so jaded that all they want are noisy thrills and dumb jokes and images that move along in an undemanding way, so they can sit and react at the simplest motor level. And there's plenty of evidence, such as the success of *Alien*. This was a haunted-house-with-gorilla picture set in outer space. It reached out, grabbed you, and squeezed your stomach; it was more gripping than entertaining, but a lot of people didn't mind. They thought it was terrific, because at least they'd felt something: they'd been brutalized. It was like an entertainment contrived in Aldous Huxley's *Brave New World* by the Professor of Feelies in the College of Emotional Engineering. Yet there was also a backlash against *Alien*—many people were angry at how mechanically they'd been worked over. And when I saw *The Black Stallion* on a Saturday afternoon, there was proof that even children who have grown up with television and may never have been exposed to a good movie can respond to the real thing when they see it. It was a hushed, attentive audience, with no running up and down the aisles and no traffic to the popcorn counter, and even when the closing credits came on, the children sat quietly looking at the images behind the names. There may be a separate God for the movies, at that.

The New Yorker, June 23, 1980

DRESSED TO KILL
MASTER SPY, MASTER SEDUCER

In *Dressed to Kill,* a suspense comedy about sex and fear, set in Manhattan, everybody is spying on everybody else, or trying to. And the director, Brian De Palma, who also wrote the script, is the master spy. In two early De Palma pictures, Robert De Niro played an underground filmmaker who made Peep Art movies, and in the second one he also tried to get into the action. At the start of *Sisters* (1973), a blind girl is taking off her clothes; a well-dressed black man catches sight of her—will he go on watching? It turns out that they are both part of a TV game show called "Peeping Toms." The beginning of *Carrie* (1976) is like an adolescent boy's dream of sneaking into the girls' locker room at high school and hiding there, unseen, as the girls strip and soap themselves and brush their hair in the misty, steamed atmosphere. Now, at the opening of *Dressed to Kill,* Kate Miller (Angie Dickinson), a beautiful, aging golden blonde, married yet frustrated, and longing to be made love to, is in her shower, at her most defenseless, smiling ever so slightly in pleasure, and as the camera moves around her she seems to have an aureole—an autoerotic glow. We in the audience are put in the position of voyeurs inside Kate's languorous masturbation fantasy, sharing her secrets. (In some shots, she has been given the dream body an aging woman might have in her fantasies.)

Over the years, De Palma has developed as an artist by moving further into his material, getting to deeper levels of erotic comedy and funnier levels of violation. If he has learned a great deal from Hitchcock (and Welles and Godard and Polanski and Scorsese and many others), he has altered its nature with a funky sensuousness that is all his own. The gliding, glazed-fruit cinematography is intoxicating but there's an underlay of dread, and there's something excessive in the music that's swooshing up your emotions. You know you're being toyed with. The apprehensive moods are stretched out voluptuously, satirically—De Palma primes you for what's going to happen and for a lot that doesn't happen. He sustains moods for so long that you feel emotionally encircled. He pulls you in and draws the wires taut or relaxes them; he practically controls your breathing. His thriller technique, constantly refined, has become insidious, jewelled. It's hardly possible to find a point at which you could tear yourself away from this picture.

A few minutes in, De Palma stages an almost perfect love comedy, in miniature: Kate Miller, whose day began with a bout of miserable thumping intercourse with her husband, Mike (Fred Weber), to the accompaniment of the weather report on the radio, followed by a session with her analyst, Dr. Elliott (Michael Caine), who rejected her sexual invitation, sits on a bench in a room at the Metropolitan Museum. This woman, who looks—as they used to say—"made for love," is visibly aching for it. Distracted, dreaming away the time, she watches a little Oriental girl skip off from her mother and her mother's male companion, who a moment later run after her. She glances up at a portrait of a woman (by Alex Katz) that seems to look back at her, contemplatively, as if to say, "So what are you going to do now?" A handsome stud of perhaps thirty-eight, in dark glasses, a casual gray pullover, and a well-tailored dark jacket, sits down next to her. Unable to meet his eyes, Kate looks down at her hand, in two-toned gloves with strips of leather running up the fingers, and then she look farther down, to his expensive two-toned leather shoes. It's commodity fetishism. Kate takes off a glove, exposing the diamond on her third finger, left hand, and the man disappears. Perceiving with dismay that she has driven him off, she gets up, dropping her glove, and looks for him. The camera (the Panavision version of the Steadicam) darts from gallery to gallery as she searches anxiously. But when the man, having backtracked, picked up her glove, and put it on, touches her shoulder with his gloved hand, she is so startled she bolts away. Then, realizing that he meant to return the glove and that her frayed nerves had made her look a panicky fool, Kate follows him. The man teases her, leading her in a chase through the rooms, with contemporary paintings as witnesses to the cat-and-mouse courtship game. The music here is subdued (the friend next to me whispered, "It sounds like Bernard Herrmann on Quaaludes"), and though it becomes more frantic the chase still has an eerie sheen of culture. With almost no words, this loveplay edged by the man's contemptuous assurance goes through so many permutations that it suggests a speeded-up seduction out of *Les Liaisons Dangereuses*—a hundred pages turned into a visual scherzo. The quick sequence is extraordinarily revealing: when Kate, hopelessly outmaneuvered, stands indecisively in galleries that have two or three entrances, you can see that she's vulnerable to attack from any direction. The desperation in Kate's sexual loneliness makes it possible for Angie Dickinson to show a much warmer expressive range than might be expected—you can read every nuance of desire, embarrassment, and trepidation on her face.

There's very little dialogue altogether in *Dressed to Kill;* what talk there is is casual, funny, and often good-naturedly off-color. Most of the film's humor, though, is visual, and it's not innocent at all. Visual humor is generally slap-stick; this isn't. You could try to single out the gags that make *Dressed to Kill* visually funny, but describing the gags wouldn't convey its humor. What makes it funny is that it's permeated with the distilled essence of impure thoughts. De Palma has perfected a near-surreal poetic voyeurism—the styl-ized expression of a blissfully dirty mind. He doesn't use art for voyeuristic purposes; he uses voyeurism as a strategy and a theme—to fuel his satiric art. He underlines the fact that voyeurism is integral to the nature of movies. In the Metropolitan sequence (the interiors are actually the Philadelphia Mu-seum of Art), we catch glimpses of figures slipping in and out at the edges of the frame, and there are other almost subliminal images; we're playing hide-and-seek along with Kate, and her pickup. Later, there's a visually lay-ered police-station sequence: the principal characters—Mike; Dr. Elliott; Kate's whiz-kid son, Peter (Keith Gordon); a loud, brash investigator, Detec-tive Marino (Dennis Franz); and a pretty, investment-minded hooker, Liz Blake (Nancy Allen)—are in different rooms or in the hallway, but they can see each other through the glass partitions, and the interplay among these people, most of whom have never met before, seems to be happening on about eighteen different levels of deception, eavesdropping, and all-around peeping. And there's a subway chase, in which the reddish-blond Liz, who has witnessed a murder and is being pursued by the killer, stands, for protection, near a couple of young black men playing a tape recorder, but then they're joined by their pals, and the gang of hoods turns on her; everybody has de-signs on poor Liz. In this paranoid urban nightmare of a sequence, it's once again now-you-see-it-now-you-don't, as hidden figures scurry by. Throughout the film, De Palma plays with the visual theme of outside and inside voyeur-ism (the person peeking through windows is always much safer than the per-son who sneaks inside), and he also keeps dividing things in two—often the screen itself. This film has some of the most graceful use of the split screen (and screen-within-the-screen devices) in recent years, especially when the im-age is divided between Dr. Elliott at his place and Liz at hers; she gets a tip from her stockbroker on one phone and raises the necessary money by ar-ranging a "date" with her escort service on another—for her, Phil Donahue on the TV is just a background noise, while the doctor, watching the same show, is giving it close attention.

De Palma's sense of humor makes him the least respectable of the front-rank American directors. He presents extreme fantasies and pulls the audience into them with such apparent ease that the pleasure of the sus-pense becomes aphrodisiacal. And he does what Hitchcock always said he wanted to do—such as have Cary Grant really be a murderer at the end of *Suspicion.* (Hitchcock came closest to actually doing it when he bumped off Janet Leigh in *Psycho.*) De Palma goes ahead and takes the risk all the time. Yet though he draws the audience in by the ironic use of sentimental con-ventions, when he explodes the tension (the shocks are delivered with sur-gical precision), those people in the audience who are most susceptible to romantic trickery sometimes feel hurt—betrayed—and can't understand why the rest of us are gasping and laughing. Life plays obscene jokes on soft, creamy-pink Kate Miller, who wants nothing more than to give and receive pleasure; just when she's happy and sated and feels grateful, she discovers something so humiliating that she gets the cold shakes. Life also played obscene jokes on the teenage Carrie (Sissy Spacek), who wanted only to be accepted by the other kids at school. Life played a brutally dirty trick on the father (Kirk Douglas) in *The Fury* (1978), who wanted only to be reunited with his son. Like Hitchcock, like Polanski, like Buñuel, De Palma has a prankish sense of horror. Most parodists of gothic tricks flatten them out (as in *High Anxiety*); De Palma's humor heightens them—he's probably the only American director who knows how to use jokiness to make horror more intense. Through visual storytelling, he can get at the currents of sexiness and fear and guilt that were the hidden strength of the great silent horror films, but he taps those currents for a different purpose. De Palma replays film history as farce. He has kept the dirty fun of a bad boy at the center of his art. It gives his work a lurid, explosive vitality.

Dressed to Kill isn't as imaginatively dark as *The Fury:* the evil was luxuriant in that one—nightshade in bloom. There's nothing here to match the floating, poetic horror of the slowed-down sequence in which Amy Irving and Carrie Snodgrass are running to freedom: it's as if each of them and each of the other people on the street were in a different time frame, and Carrie Snodgress's face is full of happiness just as she's flung over the hood of a car. And the story told in *Dressed to Kill* doesn't have the richness of the pop fairy-tale theme of *Carrie*. It's a thinner-textured movie, but—perhaps because De Palma did the writing by himself—it's all of a piece in a way that those films weren't. His dialogue is much more sly than that of the scenarists he has generally worked with—there are no flat, laughable lines like the ones that marred *The Fury*.

There are no weak performances, either. In the pivotal role of Dr. Elliott, Michael Caine demonstrates once again what an unself-centered actor he is: he's willing to be reserved and a little creepy—he does no reaching for sympathy, and he never turns on the charm. Clearly, he's considering the total effect rather than just his own part, and he's willing to strengthen the picture by providing authority and letting the women shine. The element that gives the movie its balance may be the director's liking for the characters played by Nancy Allen (she was the blond viper, Chris, in *Carrie*) and Keith Gordon. He first paired the two in *Home Movies*, the primal-family slapstick comedy that he filmed at Sarah Lawrence, using students and professionals, during the break he took after making the excitingly hellish *The Fury* (which must have been like working in a danger zone). In this anomalous, often very funny comedy, Keith Gordon played an adolescent filmmaker, who was given Star Therapy by the Maestro (Kirk Douglas) who told him that he behaved like an extra, and that he had to learn to put his name above the title, because "Everyone is the star in the movie of his own life." (Keith Gordon had a plaintive moment when he said, "I didn't get a script.") Working on a family theme in light, knockabout terms seems to have loosened De Palma and brought him a simpler, streamlined touch. In *Home Movies*, Keith Gordon won the sexy girl played by Nancy Allen—a night-club ventriloquist with a lewd rabbit—but he seemed almost presexual. In carrying these two performers over as the hero and heroine of *Dressed to Kill*, De Palma has made this innocence work for him. As Nancy Allen plays her, Liz Blake must be the most practical, out-in-the-open girl since the young, gum-chewing Ginger Rogers. In the Paris setting of *Roberta*, Ginger was said to have the best figure in Europe, and no one in a theatre was ever heard to deny it; if Nancy Allen were to play that role, there wouldn't be any rebuttals this time, either. Liz Blake is everybody's target, and four-eyed Peter, who's obsessed with computers, is the teen-age prodigy who rescues her. (As a boy, De Palma, who started out at Columbia in physics and then switched to fine arts, used to design computers for science fairs; he was married to Nancy Allen last year.) Peter has the preoccupied seriousness of an adolescent eccentric, but he becomes a person to reckon with right before our eyes, and it's easy to see why Liz grows fond of him. Even when she says things like "I'll miss having you on my tail," they're spoken in an oddly straightforward way; if she knows more about sex, he knows more about everything else. Nancy Allen is a breezy comedienne, and Keith Gordon is a great young straight man. *Dressed to Kill* seems to have merged De Palma's two sides: he has created a vehicle in which he can unify his ominous neo-Hitchcock lyricism with the shaggy comedy of his late-sixties *Greetings* days, when he used to let background jokes dominate the foreground. Without the misfit romance and the many casual bits, such as the rapid changes of expression on a young cabdriver's face and the changes of clothing on Detective Marino (winner, hands down, of the worst-dressed-cop award), *Dressed to Kill* would be too chic, too stylish. It needs every bit of its shag. This picture is such a unified, confident piece of work that De Palma can even make the image hazy and provide a stylized chorus of observers out of Bedlam—giving it away that something isn't really happening—and still you're terrified.

De Palma has been able to retain control of most of his films by working in the suspense genre, on a small budget. His development has been mostly outside the industry, or on its margins, and, with only a few exceptions, such as *The Fury*, which cost six million dollars, he has worked on minuscule budgets or small ones; *Dressed to Kill*, which is being released by Filmways (the new name for A.I.P.), came in at six and a half million. (The average cost of a major studio movie this year is nine million.) De Palma knows how to get style on the cheap. Though he didn't have his usual editor, Paul Hirsch (who was busy on *The Empire Strikes Back*) and worked with Jerry Greenberg, the timing of the cuts in the Metropolitan sequence and in the subway sequence is daringly precise. And the way that cinematographer Ralf Bode's images connect with the slightly debauched music—it's like a rhapsody on forties movies—by Pino Donaggio seems exactly right. (Donaggio also did the scores for *Carrie* and *Home Movies*.) The whole film gives you the feeling of evenly controlled energy. De Palma shows the kind of restless intelligence which suggests that he will want to work in many different forms, and certainly he needs more chances to work on a larger scale, as he did in *The Fury*. But he doesn't have to move away from thrillers to prove he's an artist. In his hands, the thriller form is capable of expressing almost everything—comedy, satire, sex fantasies, primal emotions.

There is a peculiarity about *Dressed to Kill:* when the explanation comes, it's weightless. You've probably already figured out most of it anyway, and since everything else plays on several levels, this scene, which has only one, seems prosy and obligatory. You recognize how carefully the murder motive was prepared and how everything fits together, but the explanation has no tingle: you don't feel its connections with what makes the picture frightening. The explanation scene in *Psycho* was even prosier, and there is a slight suggestion of parody here, but more likely the resemblance is an homage; the kicker is that it's an homage to—arguably—Hitchcock's worst scene. The parody comes right after it, in the restaurant scene, when Liz plays teacher to Peter, and a woman at a nearby table (a pantomime role, by Mary Davenport, who was Keith Gordon's mother in *Home Movies*) overhears such bewildering clinical information being delivered in a matter-of-fact tone that her face crumples. Here De Palma sabotages the rational explanation, which goes rattling on. Then, at the end, he uses a ploy—a pause and then a starting up again—that resembles the endings of *Carrie* and *The Fury*, but to get a different psychological effect. In those pictures he jolted the audience out of the gothic atmosphere, and most of us left the theatre laughing. This time, the spell isn't broken and he doesn't fully resolve our fear. He's saying that even after horror has been explained, it stays with you—the nightmare never ends.

The New Yorker, August 4, 1980

THE CHANT OF JIMMIE BLACKSMITH

The great Australian film *The Chant of Jimmie Blacksmith*, which was made in 1978 and has finally opened here, has almost nothing in common with the other Australian films of recent years. All of them partake of some of the fascination of movies set in unfamiliar terrain, but this one is large-scale and serenely shocking, with the principal characters shot against vast, rolling landscapes that are like wide, wide versions of the flat, layered backgrounds in Chinese wash drawings. *The Chant of Jimmie Blacksmith* was adapted from Thomas Keneally's novel, which is based on the case of Jimmy

Governor, a half aborigine who went on a rampage and killed seven whites in 1900, the very year of Federation. (His hanging was delayed until after the ceremonies, so as not to embarrass the proud young nation by reminding it of what had been done to the natives.) The movie is about the cultural chasm that divides the natives and the European-spawned whites, and it's horribly funny, because the whites are inadequate to their own cruelties. The emotional effects of what these displaced Irish and Scottish and English do are much larger than the people themselves. The director, Fred Schepisi (pronounced Skepsee), has a gift for individualizing every one of the people on the screen; it takes him only a few licks to let us perceive how they justify themselves to themselves. Men who were at the bottom in Europe now command thousands of acres. Scrabbling tightwads, these white landowners got where they are by self-denial. Penny-pinching is a moral tenet to them, and they don't regard cheating the helpless aborigines as cheating, because the aborigines don't know how to save their money anyway. The aborigines live in the remnants of a tribal society with an elaborate structure of claims: men are obliged to give a share of their earnings to their kin, even if their kin are drunken and diseased and want the money only to go on a binge. And men offer their wives to visiting kin as a form of hospitality. To the whites, giving money away is unfathomable laxity, and since the black women are so easily available the white men treat the aboriginal settlements as brothels. The black women don't even have to be paid for their services, except with a bottle of cheap sherry for their husbands. The settlements are conveniently situated on the outskirts of the towns, far from the eyes of white women and children.

Jimmie Blacksmith (Tommy Lewis) is a product of one of these visits to a tin shanty, and because he learns quickly and is half white, the Reverend Mr. Neville (Jack Thompson), who runs the Methodist mission school, and Mrs. Neville (Julie Dawson) take him into their home when he's of an age to be useful. They train him to be polite and docile and teach him how important it is to gain a good reputation for work. Jimmie goes through his tribal initiation rites, but he grows up determined to escape the debased existence of aborigines in their hovels by working hard, buying land, and, as Mrs. Neville has advised him, marrying a nice white girl off a farm, so his children will be only a quarter black and the next generation scarcely black at all.

Sent out into the world, with the blessing of the Nevilles, he's a half-caste Horatio Alger figure, determined to show that his word is his bond and that he will stick to a job until it's done. Proper and well-mannered, he looks for work among clerks and prospective employers who call him Jacko and refer to him as a boong, a darkie, and a nigger. He doesn't take offense: these whites don't understand yet that he's different from the uneducated blacks. He smiles, so that they will see how willing he is, and eventually he gets his first job—making a post-and-rail fence to mark the boundaries of a huge farm. As he digs holes in the hard, dry earth, the vistas are lonely and bare; far in the distance, delicately etched trees look pale blue. After months of back-breaking work, Jimmie finishes the job, is underpaid, and is ordered off the property; denied a letter of recommendation as well, he flares up and tells the man that he knows why—it's because the man can't write. Jimmie is knocked flat. He goes from one fence-building job to the next, and we see how his employers react to his eagerness to prove himself a good worker. No matter how long and hard he works or how servile his behavior is, he never wins the civility or praise he longs for. These isolated farmers are terse, close-mouthed, as if even a little companionable chat would be profligacy, a waste. They can't resist finding fault with Jimmie's work and shorting him on his pay; thrift and mistrust have become second nature to them. Besides, they need to see him fail: it confirms the necessity of keeping the savages in their place. Since the aborigines have no legal rights, the farmers can feel generous-hearted for paying any part of what was agreed to. When Jimmie complains, he looks slightly wall-eyed from terror. The farmers show their fears in their tight faces whenever there's more than one black on their land. Jimmie has a half brother, laughing Mort (Freddy Reynolds), a teen-age aborigine who giggles with contentment. He walks enormous distances to come be with Jimmie and give him a hand on his jobs, but this additional presence upsets the bosses, who accuse Jimmie of turning their land into "a blacks' camp."

When Jimmie visits his tribal shantytown with Mort, a claim is made on them for money; Mort gives his little bit happily, but Jimmie flings a roll of bills down on the ground in disgust because his inability to save money eats away at his hopes. He gets a job as a tracker and general underling with the New South Wales Mounted Police; barefoot in a thick, outsize uniform, he's a caricature of a policeman. He thinks of the uniform very righteously, though, and when the police raid a settlement, trying to find out which of the aborigines stabbed a debauching white man, Jimmie does just what his boss, Constable Farrell (Roy Barrett), tells him to do: he rides in smashing his club down on the head and shoulders of anyone within range. Then he proves his diligence by turning in the culprit—an old friend. It isn't until the brutish Constable Farrell gets boozed up and tortures and kills the prisoner that Jimmie wakes from his illusion that he is part of the master race. Barrett is so strong an actor that when the constable's full sadism comes into play you want to cower in your seat; Jimmie is forced to understand that he is as powerless as the mutilated corpse.

He runs off and finds work as a sweeper and cook's helper at a shearing contractor's, where a dim-witted, rutting servant girl (Angela Punch), a blond waif who has been coupling with the goatish cook (played by Thomas Keneally), presents herself to him, half naked. She becomes pregnant, and so he gets himself a white wife. His next employer, Newby (Don Crosby), allows him to put up a one-room shack, where he and his bride can live while he builds a fence around the Newby domain. Beyond him, there are always the pastel hills—so remote they're almost part of the sky—and the faint blue trees. The immensity of the plains mocks Jimmie's hope of gaining a good reputation; trying to improve himself, he's like a hair-raisingly foolish cross between Jude the Obscure and Gunga Din. Jimmie's pathetic wife brings him his only chance of realizing his ambition to have a home, like a white man. Yet when he hears the first cries of his wife's baby, his bare feet grip the earth in dance steps that suggest an atavistic rite. Unconsciously, he seems to be expressing his continuity with nature and his tribe. Mort arrives in a spirit of celebration, accompanied by a cousin and by Jimmie's uncle Tabidgi (Steve Dodds), a tribal elder, who is worried about Jimmie's marriage to a white woman and has brought him a talisman to keep him safe. They stay on and on, with the uncle sousing while Mort helps with the work, until Newby raises the familiar cry that the place is being turned into "a blacks' camp." Mrs. Newby (Ruth Cracknell) and Miss Graf (Elizabeth Alexander), a young schoolteacher who lives with the Newbys, want to save Jimmie's wife from the fate of living among blacks anyway, and so Newby tries to get rid of Jimmie and his black kin by starving the whole group out. Jimmie is baffled by the whites' hatred, baffled that these people—the only ones on his travels who have ever shown him any kindness—are humiliating him by denying him money for groceries and are trying to persuade his wife to leave him and become a servant to Miss Graf, who is getting married. They represent what he wanted a white wife for—he wants to be them. And so, of course, they enrage him the most.

When Jimmie explodes, you may feel a sudden chill that is quite unlike what you have felt at other films, because his actions don't come out of conscious militancy or a demand for political justice. They come out of helplessness and frustration. The speed of Jimmie's first, irrevocable action makes the image seem like something happening in a delirium; his motion is so fast you replay it in your head and it stays with you—an insane ritual. It's as if he had let his unconscious take over. Jimmie acts on the level on which he has been experiencing the insults and the condescension. After the first explosion, he says he has declared war. But even then he doesn't wage war directly against the men: he attacks the men's most prized possessions—their robust, well-fed women, their pink-and-white children. His prime target—though only semiconsciously—is the supercilious schoolie, Miss Graf. She is everything plump and prissy that Jimmie has aspired to. Her immaculate, high-toned respectability represents sexuality to him, just as the "gins"—the unpaid black prostitutes lying on the dirt floors of their hovels—represent it to the ranchers. His war is race war, sex war—a freakish parody of textbook war which is probably an accurate reflection of the forces let loose in colonial uprisings. It's a conflict between two debased, threatened cultures—one individualistic, one tribal—and it's Jimmie, rather than a full-blooded aborigine, who explodes because he has tried the individualistic white way and has been rejected. He and Mort go back over the hundreds of miles he has covered; he retraces his steps to take revenge for each humiliation he has suffered.

If the film has a hero, it's Mort, who loses his happy laugh when he is drawn into Jimmie's war, and never fully regains it. We feel for Jimmie, but we don't love him as we love Mort, who is instinctively kind and selfless. Mort is something like the noble Indians and Negroes of American literature, but he's not a warrior or a mighty hunter. There's nothing overtly heroic about him; he's essentially passive and relaxed—a loyal, easy-going bum in ragged tweeds. This bum makes us see what the Europeans have destroyed; he's the simplest yet the most civilized person in the movie. The tribalism he accepts means that he doesn't have to prove himself, like the tormented Jimmie: he is part of everything. Jimmie suffers from the perils of Christian individualism; he wants respect, property, whiteness, and his failure rots him and twists him. Mort has nothing yet feels rich. We understand Jimmie and his divided soul only too well, but we don't *understand* Mort—he's both transparent to us and totally mysterious. People in ethnographic documentaries sometimes combine these qualities, but this is just about the only time I have ever seen primitive mystery made flesh in an acted movie. It couldn't have simply happened this way through a lucky accident of casting, because, of course, the past eighty years have taken their toll of tribalism. (Now it is having a *conscious* resurgence, and it's no more simple or instinctive than reawakened tribal consciousness among American Indians or the neo-African movements among American blacks.) Mort became a Methodist, but it rolled right off him. Jimmie was so flagrantly naïve that he believed what the white missionaries taught the blacks; he's their patsy. The Reverened Mr. Neville comes to understand this, in horror and confusion: he has been giving his life to destroying the blacks. Yet how could Jimmie have improved his lot except by being the good native grateful to work for the whites? The alternative was drunkenness, and death at an early age from consumption or pneumonia.

The Chant of Jimmie Blacksmith is a triumph of casting and of coaching. With a shooting schedule of only fifteen weeks, and locations requiring that the crew travel five thousand miles, Schepisi had the job of blending a large company of the finest (white) stage and screen performers with aborigines— most of them nonprofessionals who were trained while the film was being made. (The star, Tommy Lewis, was a nineteen-year-old half-caste college student.) The professionals had to be really skillful, so as not to dominate their scenes with the amateurs; there are fine shadings in the work of actors such as Brian Anderson, who plays the objective-minded butcher and hangman, and Peter Carroll, who plays the wheezing red-haired McCreadie, an intelligent, neurasthenic schoolteacher who is taken hostage by Jimmie and is then carried piggyback to safety by Mort. The aboriginal performers—the men, particularly—come through vividly. They have the advantage of their unusual (to us) physiognomies. At times, Freddy Reynolds (Mort) and some of the others—whose features are not African, yet whose skins are dark—look like the actors in blackface who played Negroes in *The Birth of a Nation* and other early American films; they seem so different from American blacks that it sometimes throws you off when they're referred to by the same epithets. Two professionals among them are wonderful as sots: Jack Charles as the murdered prisoner, and Steve Dodds as the dazed Tabidgi, who is tried for murder and simply says, "You'd think it would take a good while to make up your mind to kill someone and then to kill them, but take my word for it, it only takes a second." (Of all the turn-of-the-century locations, only one arouses suspicion: the graffiti in a deserted sacred place are disconcertingly bright and much too legible—the four-letter desecrations spell irony.)

Schepisi, who was born in Melbourne on December 26, 1939 (his grandfather was an immigrant from a small island north of Sicily), began working in advertising at fifteen and went on to TV commercials and government documentaries. In 1970, he made a half-hour short called *The Priest,* which was part of the omnibus film *Libido,* and five years later he completed an autobiographical feature, *The Devil's Playground,* about his early-teen years in a seminary. (Keneally, a friend of his, played a priest.) An epic is not easily made, especially one that deals with the queasy emotions that attend the creation of a society built on racial oppression, yet *Jimmie Blacksmith* is only Schepisi's second feature; it's a highly sophisticated production, made in Panavision (the cinematographer was Ian Baker), and one of the rare movies in which a wide screen is integral to the conception. Schepisi has trimmed fourteen minutes since the film was shown at Cannes in 1978, and though wide-screen imagery is difficult to edit for speed, he has achieved a glancing, leaping emotional progression that's very calm, very even. The score, by Bruce Smeaton, never crowds the viewer's emotions but is right there when it's needed. Schepisi picked great material, and in mapping out the screenplay he took much of the dialogue right from the book. This is generally a mistake, but not with Keneally, who is a dramatist as well as a novelist. He writes dialogue that jumps up from the page, bites you on the nose, and makes you laugh.

Published here in 1972, Thomas Keneally's novel is no longer in print; the library copy that I read hadn't been checked out since January, 1973. How did this book slip into neglect? Was it because the literary-publicity machine was in its modernist phase, when the most highly honored novels were intricate literary puzzles? Or did the thought "arid," so closely associated with Patrick White, smudge the wrong Australian? I began the novel around one in the morning, intending to read only a few chapters before going to bed. Although it's a short book (just a hundred and seventy-eight pages), I stayed up until five, reading it slowly, because I didn't want to diminish the pleasure by going too fast. The book is like Nat Turner's story as a great lusty ironist—an Irish Nabokov, perhaps—might have written it. I didn't want to lose the full shape of the story by interrupting it until the next day; anyway, I had to read it in one sitting, because the rhythms propel you forward. They're oral rhythms—not just in the dialogue but in the prose cadences. The book itself is the chant, and it's inexorable. The novel and the movie add to each other. Keneally's passion comes out in barbaric, pixillated humor; Schepisi's vision is less comic, but his work is visually impassioned, and it, too, seems inexorable. The smooth, high-strung tone is set right at the start, and I don't think there's an inexpressive frame of film in the entire movie. Schepisi's chant has a different rhythm: Keneally writes spiccato, Schepisi's moviemaking is legato. Keneally writes with the comic virulence of an Irish-Australian observing the stingy Scots, who can't open their fists even when they're the lords of a great land; Schepisi sees the meanness set against the expanses, sees the patterns of dark to light, with the people at the dark bottom of the image and the birds flying from the pastels to the whiteness at the top. Each, in his way, makes you feel that he has captured a nation's rhythm.

In recent years, the movies with the clearest social vision appear to be those rooted in a particular time and place: in the Sardinia of the Taviani brothers' *Padre Padrone,* with its patriarchal system; in Francesco Rosi's *Christ Stopped at Eboli* (which gave you the feeling that the camera arrived in the remote, mountainous peasant village with Carlo Levi in the thirties and left with him, and that the land and the people returned to darkness). Maybe it's because movies spouted so much humanitarian ideology in the past, and Hollywood showed us so many faceless throngs, that these exact, personal visions bringing us up close to their subjects have special, ecstatic force. *The Chant of Jimmie Blacksmith* is a dreamlike Requiem Mass for a nation's lost honor; that Schepisi should have financed it partly by his work on TV commercials is a joke that all moviemakers can appreciate. Keneally's book is full of jokes. A sample: "Press cartoonists sketched the nascent motherland. . . . In one hand she held perhaps a tome with a title such as 'British Civilization,' in the other a blank parchment entitled 'The Fresh New Page of Democracy.' She rather resembed Miss Graf."

The New Yorker, September 15, 1980

THE STUNT MAN
AS SWIFT AS BUZZARD FLIES

The *Stunt Man* catches you up with its rowdy, satirical opening sequence: between the snaps of clapper boards with the credits, we see a series of paranoid reactions to chance happenings, with one reaction sparking the next. All nature is a powder keg of grievances. On a sunny, bright day, a police car honks at a dog sleeping in the middle of the road, the dog snarls viciously, and the movie is off and spinning. A telephone lineman throws a rock at a big buzzard; darting away, the buzzard hits a helicopter carrying a cameraman and a movie director, and somebody in the plane (the pilot or the cameraman) rasps out, "That God damn crazy bird . . . he was trying to kill us!" The voice of the not yet visible director, Eli Cross (Peter O'Toole), is heard: "That's your point of view. Should we stop and ask the bird what his was?" Then Cross takes a bite from an apple and tosses it away; the apple lands on the roof of a café and rolls down onto the top of the police car, which is just being parked, giving the two policemen a start. Inside the café, a trucker reaches out to make a pass at a waitress, and the pet Chihuahua that she carries close to her breast snaps at him ferociously. A scroungy-looking young man with stubble on his chin, Cameron (Steve Railsback), sees the policemen coming in, and terrified, he goes to the pinball machine, where he finds a free ball; the policemen come over and put handcuffs on him, but he bolts out the door and keeps going, while they shoot at him. A short distance away, he knocks down the telephone lineman, grabs the man's tool belt, and heads for the woods, where he uses the tools to split the handcuffs apart. Running past the sawhorse barricades closing a road, he starts across a river bridge and tries to hitch a ride in the only car in sight—a shiny, glamorous old Duesenberg. The young, yellow-haired driver, who is alone, stops, and Cameron thinks he's being picked up, but when he gets in, the driver shoves him out with his foot and speeds away, leaving him sprawling and bruised; then the Duesenberg turns around and heads right toward him. Thinking that the driver means to kill him, Cameron grabs a construction bolt and throws it at the car, hitting the windshield. But the car doesn't come near him. By the time he picks himself up—a few seconds only—it has disappeared and the bridge is deserted. Looking down, he sees bubbles where the water has closed over the Duesenberg, and, hearing an engine above, he looks up and sees the helicopter, which comes down close. Cameron runs across the bridge and through fields until he comes to an oceanside resort area. He cuts off the legs of his jeans, so that he'll look like a vacationer in shorts, and joins the crowd that is watching a movie crew prepare to shoot a war scene on the beach. There's a non-stop quality about this chain-reaction prologue. The music—cheery, jangling, circusy music, by Dominic Frontiere—might almost be driving Cameron on. It seems to pick him up and keep him whirling; he gets only a short breather before he's in movement again. The music doesn't reach any kind of completion: it's a repeated vamp that starts up— loud and boisterous—each time the mood of the film is frazzled and everything is in motion.

Eli Cross's first, disembodied words state the theme of *The Stunt Man:* it's about the paranoia of snap judgments. All through the movie, people grasp only a fragment of a situation and misinterpret what is going on because they perceive that fragment in terms of their fears that everything—a buzzard, an apple, a yellow-haired man in a Duesenberg—is against them. The film itself is designed to demonstrate how difficult it is for Cameron—or you—to know what's really happening. You joyride through this picture, sorting out what you're seeing as it races ahead. At first, the thought may cross your mind that the cameraman in the helicopter is photographing Cameron, and that he's part of a movie being made; this thought gets discarded fast, as you realize that Cameron intruded on the making of a movie, and that Burt, the man in the Duesenberg who shoved him out and spun the car around, was a stunt man, doubling for the blond hero. Burt didn't have time for more civil behavior because his drive had to be coördinated with the helicopter—and he had intended to go over the side of the bridge. (He had also intended to survive, of course, but Cameron's cracking his windshield was a factor he hadn't taken into account.) When Cameron shows up at the beach, Eli Cross, who recognizes him from the bridge, pretends to the police that he was the driver of the Duesenberg, and that nobody got killed. Cross, who has a permit to shoot for three more days at the resort, doesn't want the police to close him down, so he protects Cameron. The actors and crew know perfectly well that Cameron is a stranger, but Cross decrees that because of Burt's return from the bottom of the river he is henceforth to be known as Lucky Burt, and everyone complies, shortening it to Lucky. When Cameron is afraid that he won't be able to fool the police, Cross reassures him: "You will be disguised as a stunt man who doubles for an actor who plays an American flier who poses as a German soldier who, like yourself, is a fugitive." Clean-shaven, wearing makeup, and with yellow hair, Cameron becomes the stunt man.

Working with material that could, with a few false steps, have turned into a tony reality-and-illusion puzzle, the director, Richard Rush, has kept it all light-headed and funny—it's slapstick metaphysics. *The Stunt Man* is a virtuoso piece of moviemaking: a sustained feat of giddiness that is at the same time intense. Rush isn't afraid to hook you and to keep hooking you. Despite the elaborateness of what he and his scenarist, Lawrence B. Marcus (best known for *Petulia),* were aiming at, he didn't forget what he'd learned in exploitation pictures, when his subjects were hippies, drugs, and motorcycles. Rush uses the pacing and exhilarating, so-bright-it's-luminous visual style he developed on A.I.P. releases in the late sixties, when he was working with the cinematographer Laszlo Kovacs on such pictures as *Psych-Out* and *Hell's Angels on Wheels* and *The Savage Seven*. Those movies were crude with a special, hopped-up American trashiness; that was true, too, of such later Rush films as the more ambitious (and more disreputable) *Getting Straight* and *Freebie and the Bean*. Rush is a kinetic-action director to the bone; visually, he has the boldness of a comic-strip artist, and maybe because *The Stunt Man* is about subjects close to him—paranoia and moviemaking, which may be the subjects closest to almost all dedicated moviemakers—there's a furious aliveness in this picture. The cinematographer, Mario Tosi, has brought back the airiness and energy of that early Kovacs lighting (which even Kovacs has lost). There's nothing delicate or subtle in this movie, but there's nothing fussy or dim in it, either. The music is the film's motor; it starts up with the varoom of Rush's motorcycle gangs.

The Stunt Man suggests what Truffaut's *Day for Night* might have been if its director-hero had been a flamboyant fire-eater instead of a modest, self-effacing clerk, or what Fellini's *8½* might have been if its director-hero had been John Huston or David Lean rather than "Guido," and if he had been seen from the slapstick, satirical outside rather than from the soft, warm inside. There is, of course, a reason for Eli Cross's being heard before he is seen: in the beginning was the word. And when Peter O'Toole lets out his strong, raucous voice, you know that there's only one cock-a-doodle-doo man on this movie set, and he's it. He doesn't need a megaphone. O'Toole's Eli Cross may be as definitive a caricature of a visionary movie director as John Barrymore's Oscar Jaffe in *Twentieth Century* (1934) was of theatrical genius. Cross is a shameless manipulator, who tricks people to get what he wants, but probably he long ago lost track of the difference between what he wants and what his legend requires of him. He plays to his own legend, and he does it with the crazed strength of the totally self-centered. The only thing that matters to him is the movie he's at work on, and, like Oscar Jaffe, this God is on his uppers: He needs a hit. But there's something that means much more to Cross than box-office success: his most basic need is to do something mad—and to be acclaimed and vilified for it, of course.

Remarkable as O'Toole has often been in gentle roles (as in the 1969 *Goodbye, Mr. Chips*), it's great to see him playing a hellion. Using his words like a cat's playthings, pouncing on them, teasing, and then showing his claws, he gives a peerless comic performance. It's apparent that Eli Cross has been conceived by Rush and Marcus and O'Toole as a protean figure—a man who has in him all the basic human attributes. He's fierce-tempered and tough; like Sam Peckinpah, he carries teeth-gnashing orneriness to an art form. Yet he's also an Audrey Hepburn gamine—ethereal and fey. The chief of police (Alex Rocco), who is enraged by his high-handedness, yells at him that he's a "fruit with a camera." Yes, of course he is. Eli Cross could be called almost anything and it wouldn't be wrong and it wouldn't insult him. He's a capering showoff with a tricky glint in his eyes. He opens them wide, like someone sincere and insincere; he mesmerizes whomever he's talking to. Eli Cross acts all the time, and he's completely aware of his craggy magnificence—he holds his gaunt, high-boned face to the light the way the other Hepburn does. (O'Toole has acted with both.) Wearing a black turtleneck and black pants, and with his arms hanging at his sides holding his chest together, he's a spiffy Hamlet. He never wears an ordinary shirt; in his knits and the high-necked blouses that emphasize his thinness and height, he's a slinky dowager. Perhaps it's not that no human possibilities are closed to him but that no glamorous poses are closed to him. (Directors and stars often fight because they're competing for the same pose.) Yet Cross *does* live in another world. O'Toole revels in the histrionics of this thick-skinned, thin-skinned, dreamlit optimist who chews a hunk of bubble gum as if it were a plug of tobacco. Seated in the basket chair of his crane, Cross drops down into the film frame to say something to Lucky or he swings in from the side and floats off again. He's always hovering overhead, dangling from his helicopter or his crane; he uses his basket chair like a divinity's kiddie car, popping into the frame to make a grand entrance. Cross is on top of everything, dominating everyone's life; he knows what everyone is doing, whom they're sleeping with, and what they're thinking—and which ones are out spreading vicious gossip, and why. To the cast and the crew he is God the Father as a son of a bitch.

Cross turns his visage into a heroic, world-weary mask, but Cameron has only a stricken, naked face. Cross has a use for Cameron beyond hiding the fact of Burt's death from the police: with his director's hyper-intuitiveness—the one attribute that all fanatic movie directors seem to share or, at least, to pride themselves on—Cross detects in Cameron's animal desperation something of the madness he needs for his film. As Steve Railsback plays Cameron-Lucky, the role suggests James Dean's crushed loners, with a trace of Tommy Lee Jones in this fugitive's inability to trust anyone. Rush and Marcus tease the audience and build suspense by withholding information: for most of the movie, all we know about Cameron is that he spent two years in 'Nam. (Vietnam today is used as a catchphrase—a plot convenience—the way the Foreign Legion used to be.) And his quick physical responses—which convinced Cross that he could replace the stunt man—tell us of his will to live. But, just as Cameron doesn't know how to interpret the situations in which he finds himself, we don't know if he's a perverse, brutal murderer or merely a kid who got into trouble. Railsback (he played Manson on TV in *Helter Skelter*) manages to suggest a pure, lacerated sensibility that would fit either of these explanations, and many others as well. It's far from easy to make a scared, self-pitying man with terrible judgment appealing but Railsback does it. He's helped by the physicality of his role (though much of it is, no doubt, an illusion provided by stunt men doubling for him). Rush takes a sizable liberty with the way movies are actually made—shot by shot, with considerable time spent in moving the camera and arranging the lights and setting up all the elements. Instead, he presents the scenes of Lucky's stunts as if they were shot together in continuous long takes, so we see a chase (reminiscent of a chase in *Gravity's Rainbow*) in which he is pursued by German soldiers and shot at by planes while he runs across rooftops, slides down turrets, leaps from tower to balcony, crashes through a skylight to fall on a brothel bed between two naked bodies, and is caught by carousing Huns in the beer hall downstairs, who sadistically toss him around over their heads—and all the time that insistent, vamping music is driving the action forward. The shifting camera angles in what is presented as if it were accomplished as fast as we're seeing it give the moviemaking sections of the film a hurtling, exhilarating speed. Rush is well-named. (Actually, superlative editing was needed to achieve the effect of these long takes, which parallel the chain reactions of the opening; it was done by Jack Hofstra and Caroline Ferriol.)

Lucky gets tipsy on his own prowess and on the thought of the big money that the stunt master (Chuck Bail) tells him he has coming for it. He falls in love with stardom, in the person of Nina (Barbara Hershey), the actress who is the heroine of the movie being made, and when they're together he gets up from her bed, puts on her wig, and holds her costume in front of him—he entertains the fantasy of doubling for her as well as for the hero. Maybe it's the location that has got to him: most of the picture was shot around the Hotel Del Coronado, near San Diego—the same gabled and turreted romantic folly that figured in *Some Like It Hot.* If there were such a thing as a masterpiece of a location, the Hotel Del Coronado as it is used in *The Stunt Man* would be it. The cameras are positioned so skillfully that this location satisfies the needs of the film we see being shot as well as the more complex needs of the film we're seeing. When the crew is photographing soldiers being blown up on the beach, with ancient little planes flying over the water and strafing them, we also see the hotel that will not be visible in the shots, and during Lucky's stunts we take in how the illusion of the First World War period can be created from a few bits of roof, with the parking lots and the palm trees kept out of the compositions.

Starting with the misunderstood bird, and the apple falling on the top of the café, this movie is in love with sky and roofs, planes and cranes; it touches earth as little as possible, except in the character of Sam, the dumpling screenwriter, who is designed to be the Sancho Panza to Cross's Don Quixote. Sam—the practical worrywart whose dialogue Cross throws out as he improvises his way toward madness—may be the best role Allen Goorwitz has had, and the best performance he has given since he (when he used the name Allen Garfield) and Robert De Niro did a comedy routine together in De Palma's *Hi, Mom!* back in 1970. The conversations between squat Sam and lean, tall Cross are a comedy routine, too, with Sam claiming that his "magical madhouse" scene is better than *Marat/Sade,* and Cross throwing it out anyway. Goorwitz's byplay and timing are impeccably deceptive: at first you think Sam is a quintessential jerk; a little later he doesn't seem quite so dumb; and by the time he's offering Lucky advice he has actually become lovable and wise.

There are also scenes that might touch earth if the music didn't drive the picture forward. (We move on so fast we don't hear the thud.) I have men friends who like Barbara Hershey's flower-child persona; one of them said, "I always wanted to get to know her—I felt if I met her she'd be mine." "What about her acting?" I asked. "What acting?" he said. If Barbara Hershey isn't perceived as an actress (and very likely she isn't by most people), it's probably a mistake to cast her as one. Nina, I assume, is meant to keep us guessing about when she's playacting and when she isn't, but Hershey, whose technique consists primarily of an affected naturalness, playacts all the time. She certainly doesn't have the style to deliver a line such as "I *am* the movies." Her performance gets off to a bad start: Nina is first seen made up as an elderly woman, but the camera is too close for us to be fooled, she moves all wrong, and whoever did her rubbery, wrinkled makeup might as well have signed his name across her forehead. And when the ruthless Cross plays a rotten trick on Nina in order to get her to express shame on camera, Hershey's expression of shame is so small and drippy that the sequence misses its punch. We can see that Cameron is attracted to stardom (or what he thinks is stardom—he has seen Nina in a dog-food commercial), but what attracts Nina to him? Is she flattered by his fixation on her? Or does his being hunted by the police constitute stardom in her eyes—the attraction of danger? Or is she excited by the physical risks he takes, or touched by the sense of terror he communicates? I have a feeling that these possibilities are supposed to keep us off balance, constantly revising our interpretation, but all that really comes across is that Nina "falls in love" with Lucky, and there's no tension in their tender scenes together. The tension in the movie is between O'Toole and Railsback; the romantic scenes are dead spaces in which even the camerawork goes flooey. There are other failures. The whole conception of Cross's finding in Cameron the madness he needs disintegrates when Cross shoots the sequence that is supposed to show this madness: the action, involving Lucky dancing on the wing of a plane, takes too long to get started, and it doesn't seem mad—only awkward and silly.

Even if a line such as "I *am* the movies" were made to sparkle, it would still, like many of the lines and situations that do sparkle, cast too familiar a glow. The clever bits are often drawn from the stockpile of movie gags and anecdotes. And there are scenes—such as the crowd on the beach applauding the bombing and strafing, then seeing the bloodshed and becoming hysterical, thinking that live ammunition has been used, then laughing as the mutilated corpses get up, and applauding again—that have a secondhand surreal irony, even though they work, (The crowd's hysteria is extraordinarily effective, because the audience in the theatre is also momentarily confused by the illusion of real blood.) The rowdiness saves this film from its stale ideas, which are often on a par with Sam's "magical madhouse." There's also a more central flaw. When Rush and Marcus prepared the script, which is based on the 1970 novel by Paul Brodeur, they created different characters while retaining some of the situations and paraphrasing bits of the dialogue. Marcus did an amazing job of turning serious reality-and-illusion convolutions into a game we could all play. The book provided the controlling metaphor, however, and the subjects of paranoia and moviemaking are not linked in the way they would have been if the story had originated with a moviemaker and a screenwriter rather than in the imagination of a New York novelist. Cameron brings his suffering into the world of moviemaking. The suspense in the picture comes from his fear that he is trapped—that if the police don't get him the crazy Eli Cross will. He feels sure that Cross means to kill him at the end of the three days, when he is to recapitulate the stunt of the Duesenberg going off the bridge. Cameron has it all wrong, of course. Cross is the one who said, "That's your point of view. Should we stop and ask the bird what his was?" And it's Cross who frees him from his paranoid delusion. But a movie set is not where you go to get your paranoia cured—it's where you get it inflated. Ask Richard Rush—a big, commanding figure—who had a heart attack last October, following the decision of Melvin Simon Productions (which financed this project after he had spent six years being turned down by the major studios) not to include the film in its distribution arrangements with Twentieth Century-Fox, leaving Rush to spend almost a year trying to get the best picture he has ever made into theatres. (After it ran to enthusiastic audiences in Seattle and became a hit in Los Angeles, Fox took it on, a few weeks ago, and it is now going to open in New York. Finally shot in 1978, and completed in 1979, *The Stunt Man* was first announced as a 1971 release.) Moviemaking is a seedbed of paranoia. On the set, directors—with their feelers out, intuiting what everyone is thinking—are the paranoid kings of backbiting kingdoms. They have to be paranoid to survive, and it makes them look twenty years older than they are. Once when I was at a large party in Los Angeles, a famous director suddenly screamed from across an adjoining room at me and another guest, "I know you're talking about me!" He was right. Working from observation, Peter O'Toole has put the paranoia in Eli Cross, and there's truth in this great caricature, up until the moment when Cross turns benign, like your friendly neighborhood shrink. What's left out of the story line is the suspiciousness and terror and calculation that gnaw away at directors and turn them into bedevilled stunt men.

The New Yorker, September 29, 1980

MELVIN AND HOWARD
THE MAN WHO MADE HOWARD HUGHES SING

Jean Renoir instinctively understood what he had in common with characters very different from himself, and when his people are at their most ludicrous—when they are self-pitying or infuriatingly contentious—he puts us inside their skins, so we're laughing at ourselves. Asked to explain how it was that he didn't separate his characters into the good ones and the bad ones, Renoir's answer was always "Because everyone has his reasons," and in his best films we don't need those reasons explained—we intuit them. The young American director Jonathan Demme has some of this same gift, and his lyrical comedy *Melvin and Howard,* which opened the New York Film Festival on September 26th, is an almost flawless act of sympathetic imagination. Demme and the writer Bo Goldman have entered into the soul of American blue-collar suckerdom and brought us close enough to see that the people on the screen are us. Demme and Goldman have taken for their hero a chucklehead who is hooked on TV game shows and for their heroine his wife, who when she's off on her own and needs to work turns go-go dancer. And they have made us understand how it was that when something big—something legendary—touched these lives, nobody could believe it.

The lawyers and judges and jurors who were involved in the 1976–78 legal proceedings over the Howard Hughes will known as the Mormon will looked at Melvin Dummar, raked over his life, and couldn't believe that Hughes (who died in April, 1976) would have included Dummar among his beneficiaries. If you've seen Melvin Dummar on television, you may have observed that he's very touching—he looks like a more fair-haired Andy Kaufman as Latka Gravas in the TV series "Taxi," and he has that square, engaging naïveté that is so thoroughgoing it seems like a put-on. Dummar does, in fact, have links to TV: he is the representative debt-ridden American for whom game shows were created. He won a prize on "Truth or Consequences" but was unsuccessful on "The Dating Game"; he once appeared on "Let's Make a Deal" wearing a string of oranges around his neck and a hat shaped like an orange, and another time in the same hat but with a duck on top with a sign that said "Quacking up for a deal." Actually, Dummar was on "Let's Make a Deal" four times within a period of five years (which is probably a record); in the hearings on the will, an attorney said that this was a violation of federal law, and it was used against him to indicate that since "theatrics and lying" were a way of life for him, he could have faked the will and invented the story that he gave to account for the bequest—the story of how one night around Christmas of 1967 or early January of 1968 he had found Hughes in the desert and given him a ride. Even Dummar's dreams were turned against him: an attorney grilling his second wife in order to discredit him asked, "Mrs. Dummar, didn't your husband once write a song which he entitled 'A Dream Becomes Reality,' with this as one of the lines—'A beggar becomes a king'?" And, of course, the attorney had a point: the Hughes bequest did seem just like another one of Dummar's dreams, though it probably wasn't. The new nonfiction detective story *High Stakes,* by Harold Rhoden, makes a very spiky and convincing argument for the authenticity of the Mormon will, which the whole country laughed at because of the inclusion of Melvin Dummar, who seemed like a pudgy hick. (Johnny Carson got a lot of mileage out of Melvin Dummar jokes; for a while he was the national chump.) Even the many eminent institutions that were also named as beneficiaries didn't put up much of a fight for the will. Maybe their officers couldn't believe Melvin Dummar belonged among the hallowed names. More likely, these officers, knowing that the scary, powerful Summa Corporation, which controlled Hughes's wealth, would not relinquish this fortune without a costly battle in the courts which Summa, with the Hughes resources, could prolong into infinity, decided that it was wiser simply to string along with the general attitude in the media that a will in which Melvin Dummar was a beneficiary had to be a forgery. (The will, dated March, 1968, which would have effectively dissolved the Summa Corporation, left one-quarter of Hughes's estate to medical research, one-eighth to four universities, and the remainder to be divided into sixteen parcels, among beneficiaries such as the Mormon Church, the Boy Scouts, orphans, Hughes's ex-wife, relatives, business associates, and

Dummar, whose one-sixteenth would have amounted to over a hundred and fifty million dollars.)

But what if the meeting between Melvin Dummar and Howard Hughes took place just as Dummar said it did? What might have caused Hughes to remember Melvin a few months later and put him in his will? That's what *Melvin and Howard* tells us. By their own imaginative leap, Demme and Goldman make us understand what Howard Hughes might have seen in Melvin Dummar that the lawyers and reporters didn't see. Paul Le Mat (he was the disarming, spacy young hero in Demme's *Citizens Band*) is such an easy-going, non-egocentric actor that he disappears inside the role of big, beefy Melvin—a sometime milkman, sometime worker at a magnesium plant, sometime gas-station operator, and hopeful song-writer. Driving along the California-Nevada interstate at night in his pickup truck, Melvin has a bovine boyishness about him. He keeps himself in good cheer in the desert by singing "Santa's Souped-Up Sleigh"; the lyrics are his own, set to a tune he bought by mail order for seventy dollars, and when he sings— ostentatiously keeping time—you feel there's not a thing in that noggin but the words of the song. Jason Robards plays Howard Hughes, who hits a snag while racing his motorcycle in the desert and is flung into the air. He is lying in the freezing darkness when Melvin spots him—a bony old man in beat-out clothes, with a dirty beard and straggly long gray hair. When Melvin helps him into the front seat of the truck, next to him, he's doubled over in pain, and even as Melvin is wrapping him up to warm him there's a malevolent, paranoid gleam in his eyes. Melvin, who takes him for an old wino—a desert rat—is bothered by his mean expression, and in order to cheer him up (and give himself some company) he insists that the old geezer sing his song with him, or get out and walk.

Jason Robards certainly wasn't a beacon to his profession in last year's *Hurricane* or in the recent classic of nincompoopery *Raise the Titanic,* and it may be true that, as he says, he works in movies "to make it possible to work on the stage." But I doubt if he has ever been greater than he is here. This Hughes is so sure that people are only after his money that he distrusts everyone; he has bribed and corrupted so many high officers in business and government that he believes in nothing but the power of bribery. His thinking processes are gnarled, twisted; he begrudges the world the smallest civility and lives incommunicado from everyone. And here he is singing "Santa's Souped-Up Sleigh" while sneering at its cornball idiocy and looking over disgustedly, in disbelief, at the pleasure that this dumb bunny next to him takes in hearing his song. In recent years, Robards's Yankee suavity has occasionally been reminiscent of Walter Huston: his Ben Bradlee in *All the President's Men* recalled Huston in *Dodsworth,* and here, when his Howard Hughes responds to Melvin's amiable prodding and begins to enjoy himself on a simple level and sings "Bye, Bye, Blackbird," he's as memorable as the famous record of Huston singing "September Song." His eyes are an old man's eyes—faded into the past, shiny and glazed by recollections—yet intense.

You feel that his grungy anger has melted away, that he has been healed. He and Melvin talk about how the desert, after rain, smells of greasewood and sage, and at dawn, just as they approach the lights of Las Vegas, where Hughes gets out, they smile at each other with a fraternal understanding that's a cockeyed, spooky miracle.

In an interview in the *Times* last year, Jason Robards pointed out that Robards was Hughes's middle name and that both of them had Loomises among their relatives. "They couldn't have cast anyone else as Howard Hughes," he said. "I figured I didn't have to do any preparation for the part. It's all built in genetically." What's built in genetically may be the way Jason Robards responds to an acting challenge: the son of an actor father and an actor all his life, he goes for broke in a way that never suggests recklessness. He just casually transports himself to new dimensions (that maybe nobody else has ever been in), as if he had been breathing that air all his life. Robards isn't on the screen for long, but Hughes suffuses the movie. You know he's there without your even thinking about him; he might almost be looking down on Melvin, watching what's happening to him. And this is what the picture is about. The moviemakers have understood the position that Howard Hughes has arrived at in American mythology, and they have used the encounter in the desert to confer a moment of glory on Melvin Dummar. Eight years later, when Melvin finds himself named in the will and realizes that the old coot who said he was Howard Hughes *was* Howard Hughes, he is awed—it's like being touched by God. When reporters, neighbors, and the curious and the crazy gather at his gas station, he hides in a tree and peers out at the crowd in terror.

Most of the movie is about Melvin's life during those eight years—the life that will look so makeshift and shoddy when it's examined in a courtroom. Later in the morning after the encounter in the desert, Melvin's truck is repossessed, and his wife, Lynda (Mary Steenburgen), packs her things and takes their little daughter and goes off to live with another man, pausing only to murmur a regretful goodbye to the sleeping Melvin. They get a divorce, then remarry when she's hugely pregnant, but this marriage doesn't last long. Lynda can't stand Melvin's buying things that they never get to keep, and he can't stop kidding himself that his expensive, installment-plan purchases are somehow practical—that they're investments. So they never have anything—finally not even each other.

Mary Steenburgen was oddly tremulous in *Goin' South,* and though in *Time After Time* she was very sweet in an out-of-it way—a stoned cupcake— she didn't have the quickness or the pearly aura that she has here. Her Lynda Dummar has a soft mouth and a tantalizing slender wiggliness, and she talks directly to whomever she's talking to—she addresses them with her eyes and her mouth, and when they speak she listens, watching their faces. When she listens, she's the kind of woman a man wants to tell more to. Mary Steenburgen makes Lynda the go-go dancer so appealing that you realize she's the dream Melvin attained and then couldn't hang on to. Melvin is a hard worker, though, and he believes in family life. When Lynda leaves him, he's appalled by her exhibiting herself in strip joints; he keeps charging in and making scenes. Lynda is hurt by his attitude; she loves to dance, and she doesn't think there's anything lewd about what she's doing. In a way, she's right: Lynda could shimmy and shake forever and she still wouldn't be a hardened pro. Her movements are sexy but with a tipsy charm and purity. When her boss bawls her out because of a commotion that Melvin has just caused, she quits on the spot, whips off the flimsy costume that belongs to the boss, throws it in his face, and walks through the place naked, and she does it without making an event of it—it's her body. Melvin's second wife, Bonnie (Pamela Reed, who was Belle Starr in *The Long Riders*), isn't a romantic dream, like Lynda. She's a down-to-earth woman with a couple of kids who propositions him with a solid offer—marriage and her cousin's gas station in Utah, in a package deal. She makes the offer almost hungrily. Promising him a good marriage and a good business, she's like a sexual entrepreneur who feels she can use his untapped abilities and turn him into a success.

This is a comedy without a speck of sitcom aggression: the characters are slightly loony the way we all are sometimes (and it seldom involves coming up with cappers or with straight lines that somebody else can cap). When the people on the screen do unexpected things, they're not weirdos; their eccentricity is just an offshoot of the normal, and Demme suggests that maybe these people who grew up in motor homes and trailers in Nevada and California and Utah seem eccentric because they didn't learn the "normal," accepted ways of doing things. When Lynda is broke and takes her daughter, Darcy (the lovely, serious-faced Elizabeth Cheshire), to the bus station in Reno to send her to Melvin, she's frantic. Her misery about sending the child away is all mixed up with her anxiety about the child's having something to eat on the trip, and she's in a rush to put a sandwich together. She has bought French bread and bologna, and she takes over a table and borrows a knife from the man at the lunch counter so she can cut the bread; she salvages lettuce and tomatoes from the leftovers on someone's plate, and sends Darcy back to the counter to get some mustard and then back again to get some ketchup. The unperturbed counterman (played by the real Melvin Dummar) finds nothing unusual in this, and asks, "Is everything all right?" There's no sarcasm in his tone; he seems to understand what she's going through, and he wants to be helpful. She says, "Everything's just fine, thank you very much." She has dominated everyone's attention—she has practically taken over the station—yet the goofiness isn't forced; it's almost like found humor. It's a little like a throwaway moment in a Michael Ritchie film or a slapstick fracas out of Preston Sturges, but there are more unspoken crosscurrents—and richer ones—in Demme's scenes. While you're responding to the dithering confusion Lynda is causing in the bus depot, you're absorbing the emotions between mother and child. Darcy is often very grownup around her mother, as if she knew that Lynda is a bit of a moonbeam and needs looking after. But at the depot Darcy herself is so excited she becomes part of the confusion. Later, during Melvin and Lynda's remarriage ceremony in a Las Vegas "wedding chapel," Darcy is so impressed and elated that her whole face sparkles; she's like an imp Madonna. Throughout the movie, the children—Lynda's or Bonnie's, and sometimes all of them together—are part of an ongoing subtext: they're never commented on, and they never do anything cute or make a move that doesn't seem "true."

When Jonathan Demme does a thriller like *Last Embrace*, he seems an empty-headed director with a little hand-me-down craft, but in *Melvin and Howard* he shows perhaps a finer understanding of lower-middle-class life than any other American director. This picture suggests what it might have been like if Jean Renoir had directed a Preston Sturges comedy. Demme's style is so expressive that he draws you into the lives of the characters, and you're hardly aware of the technical means by which he accomplishes this— the prodigious crane and tracking shots that he has worked out with his cinematographer, Tak Fujimoto, and the fluid, mellow colors that probably owe a lot to Toby Rafelson's production design. The comedy doesn't stick out; it's part of the fluidity. And if you respond to this movie as I did, you'll hardly be aware (until you think it over afterward) that it has no plot, in the ordinary sense. (This could handicap it, though, in movie markets; the pitfall that a picture like this presents is that there's not a hard-sell scene in it. It's a soft shimmer of a movie, and the very people whom it's about and who might love it if they gave it a chance may not be tempted to see it.) There are a couple of flaws: the sequence of Melvin taking the will to the Mormon Church in Salt Lake City is so fast and cryptic it seems almost like shorthand, and if you've forgotten the stories that filled the papers a few years ago you may not understand what's going on; and the following sequence, of Melvin hiding from the crowd, doesn't have quite the clarity or the dramatic fullness that it needs. And there is a small lapse of taste: a shot too many of the blond Mrs. Worth (Charlene Holt), one of Melvin's milk-route customers—she lifts her head heavenward and mugs silly ecstasy at the prospect of his returning the next day, for another carnal visit. The dialogue is as near perfection as script dialogue gets—it's always funny, without any cackling. Bo Goldman, who is in his late forties, shared writing credits on *One Flew Over the Cuckoo's Nest* and *The Rose*, but this is his only unshared credit. (After spending a day with the real Melvin Dummar, Goldman decided he wanted to write the script; then he stayed with Dummar for a month and "got to love him," and came to know the two wives and Dummar's friends and relatives and neighbors.) The people in the movie— the large cast includes Charles Napier, John Glover, Gloria Grahame, Dabney Coleman, Michael J. Pollard, Martine Beswick, Susan Peretz, Naida Reynolds, Herbie Faye, and Robert Wentz—all seem scrubby and rumpled and believable; you feel that if you hung around Anaheim or L.A. or Reno you'd run into them. Maybe if you had been at the Sex Kat Klub at the right time, you'd have seen the dancer next to Lynda who was strutting her stuff with a broken arm in a big plaster cast.

Melvin and Howard has the same beautiful, dippy warmth as its characters. Paul Le Mat's Melvin, who barely opens his mouth when he talks, opens it wide when he sings. His proudest moment is probably the hit he makes at the dairy's Christmas party when he grins confidently as he sings a ballad about the gripes of a milkman. (The words, like the words of "Santa's Souped-Up Sleigh," are by the real Melvin Dummar.) Le Mat's Melvin often has a childlike look of bewilderment that he seems to be covering up by his beaming optimism. He's very gentle; he threatens physical violence only once—when he thinks that the assistant manager of the dairy (Jack Kehoe) is trying to rook him out of the big color TV set he has won as Milkman of the Month. Watching a game show, "Easy Street," on that set, he's like an armchair quarterback, telling the contestants which doors to choose to win the prizes. When Darcy is bored by it, he tries to justify his obsession by explaining how educational these shows are, but she isn't conned—she goes out to play.

Demme stages a segment of "Easy Street" (modelled on "Let's Make a Deal") which opens up the theme of the movie by giving us a view of game shows that transcends satire. Lynda, who has been selected as a contestant, appears in an aquamarine dress with tassels and an old-fashioned bellhop's hat, and when she does a tap dance that's as slow as a clog dance the audience starts to laugh. But she keeps going, and though she has more movement in her waving arms than in her tapping feet, she's irresistible. It's the triumph of adorable pluckiness (and the uninhibited use of her beautiful figure) over technique. The host of "Easy Street" (Robert Ridgely) combines malicious charity with provocative encouragement, and the enthusiastic applause confirms the notion that every TV audience loves someone who tries sincerely. In Ritchie's *Smile,* it was plain that the teen-age beauty contestants were not nearly as vacuous as they were made to appear (and made themselves appear), and here it's evident that Lynda the winner, jumping up and down like a darling frisky puppy, is putting on the excitement that is wanted of her. She's just like the pretty women you've seen on TV making fools of themselves, except that you know her; you know the desperation that went into choosing that tawdry dress and that's behind the eagerness to play the game—to squeal and act gaga and kiss everybody. The host personifies the game show, as if he were personally giving all the prizes. He's a pygmy metaphor for Howard Hughes. The game show is the illusion that sustains Melvin: that if you pick the right door, what's behind it is happiness.

Shortly after the probate trial on the Mormon will, the judge who had presided died of cancer; at his funeral service one of the speakers said that on his deathbed the judge told him that he hoped to meet Howard Hughes in the next world—that he had a question he wanted to ask him. The movie shows us a triumphant Melvin Dummar: he knows the answer. He also knows he'll never see the money. (Maybe Howard Hughes was the naïve one, if he thought that he could smash the monster corporation he had created.) Melvin Dummar was touched by a legend. Howard Hughes came to respect him, and so do we.

The New Yorker, October 13, 1980

ORDINARY PEOPLE
THE IRON-BUTTERFLY MOM

You know you're in for it when you see the solemn white titles against a black background—and in silence. Is it going to be Robert Bresson cauterizing your funny bone? When the discreet classical music starts—a piano, first just one hand and then the other, on Pachelbel's Canon in D—you know it's going to reek of quality, and that it's going to be an attempt at the austere manner of *Kramer vs. Kramer* and *Scenes from a Marriage.* Movie stars who become directors sometimes seem to choose their material as a penance for the frivolous good times they've given us. Paul Newman made *Rachel, Rachel,* and now Robert Redford has made *Ordinary People,* which is full of autumn leaves and wintry emotions. It's an academic exercise in catharsis; it's earnest, it means to improve people, and it lasts a lifetime. The story is about the Jarretts, a Protestant family living in an imposing brick house in Lake Forest, a wealthy suburb of Chicago. Conrad (Timothy Hutton), a high-school student, has the shakes, and dark circles around his eyes, because he can't sleep, and we soon learn that he has only recently emerged from a psychiatric hospital, where he spent four months and had electric-shock treatment, following a suicide attempt. His mild, ineffectual father, Calvin (Donald Sutherland), who is a successful tax lawyer, is worried about him but can make only inane, formal attempts to reach him, and his control-freak mother, Beth (Mary Tyler Moore), whose chief interest is golf, expresses little feeling for him beyond polite aversion. It boils down to Strother Martin's sick joke in *Cool Hand Luke:* "What we've got here is a failure to communicate." There is so little communication in this family that the three Jarretts sit in virtual silence at the perfectly set dinner table in the perfectly boring big dining room; it's a suburban variant of American Gothic. From time to time, Calvin, with a nervous tic of a dimpling smile—it seems to get stuck somewhere in his cheek muscles—tries to make contact with his son, and urges him to see the psychiatrist recommended by the hospital.

Conrad begins to have sessions with this psychiatrist, Dr. Berger (Judd Hirsch), whose office is pleasantly grubby, cluttered, and warmly inviting. Dr. Berger is not a monosyllabic Freudian who waits for the patient to bring up what's bugging him (or the movie would last *many* lifetimes). He's a free-method activist who grapples with the problems; he talks to Conrad, he prods and yells and emotes. And he's the model of what this uptight Protestant kid would be if he were cured: Jewish. (But then why do so many Jews go to shrinks? Ah, that's a different story.) With Dr. Berger shouting "Feel!" at him, Conrad soon begins to have breakthroughs: he learns what you knew as soon as you heard that he had an older brother who was accidentally drowned when they were out sailing together on Lake Michigan—his mother, who loved the brother, blames Conrad, and he feels guilty because he survived. (You knew because it's the standard TV-style explanation; you're consistently ahead of the storytelling, the way you almost always are when you watch a prestigious TV movie—which this really is.) Moving along on the road to recovery, Conrad starts speaking up and expressing his feelings at home, becomes more outgoing, and begins to date a pretty girl (Elizabeth McGovern) who has a deep, purring voice and a funny, understanding manner. But the loosening of his emotional tensions opens up a can of worms in the family. His seeing a psychiatrist makes Beth rigid with disapproval, and when Calvin, talking to a friend at a party, mentions that the boy is going to a doctor, Beth's face twists with anger. (This is the kind of movie in which the mother keeps the dead boy's room intact—a shrine that probably has its own cleaning lady.) Calvin, who realizes the cruelty of his wife's rejection of their son, goes to see Dr. Berger in order to explain what Conrad is up against at home, and after hedging and fumbling he finally comes out with it and says that he guesses he came to talk about himself. At this point, the movie cuts away. And it's at this point, if you had any doubts before, that you know the movie is going to be a cheat.

The way *Ordinary People* is structured, if Conrad's brother hadn't been accidentally drowned everything in the family would have been hunky-dory, neat and happy, and there wouldn't be a picture. Obviously, the film means to get at something much deeper and more widespread: it means to get at the harm that repression causes, and to suggest that orderly patterns of polite living can make it almost impossible for people to express their feelings except by an explosion, like Conrad's attempted suicide. But every time *Ordinary People* comes close to anything messy or dirty or sexual it pulls back or cuts away. What is Calvin's relationship with Beth based on, anyway? (It's not likely that she turns into a hot pixie at night: there are military-looking stripes on her bathrobe.) How did Beth's love for the son who was drowned—a love that, in the one flashback glimpse we get of it, appears to have been flirtatious—affect her and her husband? Did it make Conrad hate his brother? There's a nasty, almost conscious incestuousness lurking in Beth and never brought to the surface, and even at his most neurotic Conrad is still a "nice boy." (There are no drugs in this picture, and no teen sex; he meets his girl at choir practice.) The movie is just as sanitized as the fantasy of upper-middle-class life it sets out to expose. And it's just as empty and orderly: Calvin has the possibility of becoming a decent, whole person, because he is willing to open himself to Dr. Berger, but Beth, who rejects

Calvin's plea that she also go, is too proud to admit to any weakness or need; shaking uncontrollably at the thought of her life collapsing, she still rejects help, and she is doomed to freeze-dry.

As this Wasp witch, whose face is so tense you expect it to crack, Mary Tyler Moore also seems to be doing penance for having given audiences a good time. Her idea of serious acting seems to be playing a woman who has a mastectomy (*First You Cry*, on TV), a suicidal, bedridden quadriplegic (*Whose Life Is It, Anyway?*, on Broadway), and this self-deceiving woman who cares more for appearances than for her husband and son. Are fine comediennes still to be called courageous for giving performances as locked in dreariness as Carol Burnett's were when she went through her overage-bachelor-woman pregnancy in *The Tenth Month* and lost her son in *Friendly Fire*? As Beth, Mary Tyler Moore holds her pinched seriousness aloft like a torch. The fault isn't just in her acting; it's also in the writing and in the directing. She has been made into a voodoo doll stuck full of pins. This movie is *Craig's Wife* all over again: Beth is the compulsively neat, dedicated-to-appearances, unloving Harriet Craig, the perfect wife. But this time as a mother. She is so completely Harriet Craig that I didn't believe it for an instant when she left the house at the end. Even within its own terms, the film goes wrong here. The impersonal, ice-palace house is what Beth is married to—the house *is* Beth. It's not for living, it's for show, and it's her proof that everything is just as it should be. Beth would have stayed in her house, like Harriet Craig, and the men would have left. What are they going to do with it, anyway? Invite Dr. Berger in to mess it up and make it homey?

Ordinary People delivers on the promise of that silent opening—a certificate of solemnity. The pace is unhurried, and as a director Redford doesn't like to raise his voice any more than Beth does. Like many other actor-directors, he doesn't reach for anything but acting effects. The cinematographer, John Bailey, lights the images well enough (though the only lighting that's at all arresting is in the high-school swimming-pool scenes), but *Ordinary People* has that respectable, pictorial, dated look that movies get when the director has a proficient team of craftsmen but doesn't really think in visual terms. Redford shows taste and tact with most of the actors, and there are well-observed moments. Yet every nuance seems carefully put in place, and the conversations are stagy, because there's nothing in the shots except exactly what we're supposed to react to, just as there is nothing in Beth's character or in Calvin's except what's needed to fit a diagram of suburban suffocation. Redford's work is best in the light, funny scenes, when Conrad gets a chance at byplay with kids his own age. Alvin Sargent, who wrote the script, which is based on the popular 1976 novel by Judith Guest, wrote some bits of sharp repartee for Conrad. Mostly, though, the dialogue is intelligent in an over-modulated, point-making way, and often it's psychobabble in full bloom. (Calvin to Beth: "I don't know who you are. . . . I don't know if I love you anymore, and I don't know what I'm going to do without that." Beth's only response is to look stricken. Who wouldn't be stricken listening to this crap?) The movie is not above shamelessness: surely we could have been spared the symbolic broken dish and the information that this monstrous woman wouldn't even let her sons have a pet? And when Conrad tries to hug his mother, she sits as straight as a plank of wood, with her eyes wide open in the timeworn manner of actresses demonstrating frigidity. In general, the more emotional the scenes are, the worse they play.

Casting Timothy Hutton, the nineteen-year-old son of the late Jim Hutton, as Mary Tyler Moore's son was astute; he matches her physically, in a very convincing way. (And casting the beautiful Meg Mundy as Beth's mother was also a shrewd decision.) Hutton appears to be phenomenally talented whenever he has a chance at a light or ironic bit, and he has strangely effective moments, as in a scene when a girl (played by Dinah Manoff) whom he wants to talk to leaves him and his eyes look miserable and haze over. But he loses conviction at times, and he has an awkwardly staged scene when he has to accept his father's love and put his head on his father's shoulder. (Sutherland doesn't seem to know what to do with that head resting on him; he isn't allowed to grab the boy and hold him, the way Dr. Berger does when the promiscuous kid hugs *him*.) Sutherland, who slides into stillness and passivity almost too easily, gives a rather graceful performance, considering that Calvin isn't a character—he's just a blob created to be tyrannized by Beth. Sutherland has only one scene that's really all his: in Dr. Berger's office, when Calvin doesn't quite know what he wants to say, Sutherland uses his wonderful long hands to express more than words could. Judd Hirsch's role has the juiciness of burlesque, and Hirsch uses his terrific comedy timing; he gets laughs and manages to pick up the pace, but he's just doing wise, warm Jewish shtick. According to this movie, if Wasps can just learn to express their emotions they'll be all right. The point of view seems predicated on the post–Second World War Hollywood idea that Wasps don't know how to suffer. If you want suffering, get Jews or Italians, because when Wasps suffer, it doesn't show on the screen. (Hollywood Jews and Italians know how to act at dinner tables, too: they scream and quarrel.)

Why is this tragic view of the death of the Protestant family ethic drawing crowds? Maybe because the movie is essentially a simpleminded, old-fashioned tearjerker, in a conventional style. People weep for Beth, who can't change—who can't let herself change. We are given to understand that she would like to come out of her shell but she can't. She's trapped in the pride and discipline and privacy that she was trained to believe in. She was *bred* not to say what's on her mind. And the movie, which treats her, finally, with sympathy yet holds out no hope for her, makes her seem rather gallant. She seems the last standard-bearer for the Wasp culture that the film indicts. With its do-gooders' religion, *Ordinary People* says that the willingness to accept psychiatry divides people into the savable and the doomed. Yet maybe because the film's banal style speaks to the audience in aesthetically conservative terms, this movie about the hell that uptight people live in somehow turns into a nosegay for Wasp repression. Beth will go down with the ship: she will never "communicate."

The New Yorker, October 13, 1980

THE ELEPHANT MAN
THE FROG WHO TURNED INTO A PRINCE

T*he Elephant Man* is a very pleasurable surprise. Though I had seen *Eraserhead,* which is the only other feature directed by David Lynch, and had thought him a true original, I wasn't prepared for the strength he would bring out of understatement. It might be expected that the material—the life of John Merrick, the grievously eminent Victorian who is sometimes said to have been the ugliest man who ever lived—would push Lynch into the kind of morbid masochism that was displayed in the various versions of *The Hunchback of Notre Dame* and *The Phantom of the Opera.* But this young director (he's thirty-four) has extraordinary taste; it's not the kind of taste that enervates artists—it's closer to grace. The movie shows us what the monster feels about himself and what his view of the world is and what he sees when he looks out of the single rectangular slit in his hood (which suggests an elephant's eye). He must see everything framed, as on a screen, and the movie gives us this sense of framed imagery—of action marked off, with curtains drawn over the surrounding material. (The stitching around the slit gives it depth, and at one point, when the hood is hanging on the wall, the camera moves right into the dark opening.) You may find yourself so absorbed that your time sense changes and you begin to examine the images with something of the same wonder that John Merrick (John Hurt) shows when he looks at the spire of St. Philip, Stepney, from his window at the London Hospital, where he finds refuge.

The Elephant Man has the power and some of the dream logic of a silent film, yet there are also wrenching, pulsating sounds—the hissing steam and the pounding of the start of the industrial age. It's Dickensian London, with perhaps a glimpse of the processes that gave rise to Cubism. Coming from an art-school background, Lynch has rediscovered what the European avant-garde film artists of the twenties and early thirties, many of whom also came from a painting and design background, were up to, and he has combined this with an experimental approach to sound. In Merrick's fantasy life, his beautiful young mother is trampled by elephants when she is carrying him in her womb, and the sounds of those great beasts as they attack her in his dreams are the hellish sounds of industrial London, whose machines will produce their own monstrous growths. *The Elephant Man* isn't as daringly irrational as *Eraserhead,* which pulls you inside grubby, wormy states of anxiety, but it pulls you into a serene, contemplative amazement. Lynch holds you in scenes with almost no action: Merrick may be alone on the screen preening, or fondling the brushes and buffers in his gentleman's dressing case, or just laying them out in an orderly pattern and waltzing around them, like a swell, and you feel fixated, in a trance.

When Frederick Treves (Anthony Hopkins), the doctor who is to become Merrick's friend, first tracks him down in the illegal, hidden sideshow where he's being exhibited as the Elephant Man, Treves goes through what seem to be endless slum passageways and alleys into an abyss—the darkness where the monster huddles. Finally, he sees the pathetic deformed creature, but *we* don't. We see only Treves's reaction, and his tears falling. The grace in Lynch's work comes from care and thought: this is a film about the exhibition and exploitation of a freak, and he must have been determined not to be an exploiter himself. The monster is covered or shadowed from us in the early sequences and we see only parts of him, a little at a time. Lynch builds up our interest in seeing more in a way that seems very natural. When we're ready to see him clearly, we do. By then, we have become so sympathetic that there's no disgust about seeing his full deformity. John Hurt has had the screen long enough to make us respond to his wheezing, groaning sounds and his terrified movements, so we don't see merely the deformations, we see the helpless person locked in the repulsive flesh. Even before Merrick begins to speak to Treves and to recite poetry and to reveal his romantic sensibility, we have become his protectors. He's a large lumplike mass at first, but as we get to know him, and respond to his helplessness, he begins to seem very slight—almost doll-like. There's nothing frightening about him, and he's not repellent, either. His misshapen body and the knobby protuberances on his forehead suggest a work of art—an Archipenko or one of Picasso's bulging distortions.

The only horror is in what we experience on his behalf. When a young nurse sees him and screams, it's *his* recoil we respond to. There is a remarkable sequence after Merrick has been kidnapped from the hospital by his London exploiter and taken to be exhibited again, this time on the Continent. Too sick to stand and in despair, Merrick doesn't gratify the ticket buyers, and he is beaten so brutally that the other fairground freaks decide to free him. The giant strong man breaks the lock of the cage next to the baboons where Merrick has been put and lifts him out in his arms, and there is a dreamlike procession of the freaks in the woods along a riverbank as they help him to escape. They buy him his passage back to England, and a small group of them take him to the ship. (We're apprehensive then, because he's going to be alone.) He arrives in London by train, and as he makes his way slowly and painfully through the station his cloaked, hooded figure attracts the attention of a puzzled boy, who demands to know why he's wrapped up as he is and pelts him with a peashooter. Other kids follow him and taunt him; with only the eye slit on one side, when he clumsily tries to move faster to get away he inadvertently knocks down a little girl. People begin to chase him, and he rushes down a flight of stairs; on the landing, someone tears off his hood and he runs down more stairs and staggers into a urinal. A mob comes in after him, backing him against a wall; he moans that he is not an animal and collapses. This whole sequence is saved from being a cheap ecstasy of masochism by the fairy-tale design of the shots and the lighting. Using black-and-white Panavision, the veteran cinematographer Freddie Francis does lighting here that recalls his expressive work in *Sons and Lovers* and *Room at the Top* and *Saturday Night and Sunday Morning.* The smoke that softens everything is like J. M. W. Turner clouds, but carrying poison. With the help of the production designer, Stuart Craig, Lynch and Francis use the grays to set a tone of emotional reserve yet make the whites and the sooty blacks, which bleed out of their contour lines, seem very passionate (the way they are in the Londoner Bill Brandt's photographs). The imagery is never naturalistic, and Lynch never pulls out all the stops.

Every time the director does something risky and new or reinterprets something very old, you know you're watching real moviemaking. Though the sound isn't nearly as inventive as it was in *Eraserhead,* whenever it's hyperbolic, like the noise of the big gongs that wake Merrick on his first night at the hospital, it has a disturbing excitement. And Samuel Barber's "Adagio for Strings" on the track has an elegiac lyricism—stately, but mellow, too. Lynch is least successful with the conventional melodramatic scenes. When the night porter at the hospital invades Merrick's room with gawkers, and two whores are shoved onto his bed, we want to climb the wall along with Merrick, and not just out of empathy: the staging is crude. And almost all the scenes of the drunken villain, Bytes (Freddie Jones), the exploiter and kidnapper, seem long, probably because you can read his standard evil piggy expressions a mile away. The scenes of Anne Bancroft as Mrs. Kendal, the actress whose visits to Merrick turn him into a celebrity (which leads to his being taken up by London society), feel obligatory. The first time she's close to Merrick, Mrs. Kendal shows a flicker of disgust that she covers with her actressy poise—that part is good. But after that we need to read her feelings in her eyes, and all we register is her smiley, warm mouth; she's gracious in a great-lady way that doesn't provide any clue to why she becomes involved. The dialogue in the script, by Christopher DeVore and Eric Bergren, with the later collaboration of Lynch, is no more than serviceable, and it's less than that in Bancroft's role; she's used like a guest star, and though she's more toned down than in other recent appearances, she seems to have dropped in from another era. Hannah Gordon, who plays Mrs. Treves, has the clearer, better part: when Treves brings Merrick to tea and presents him to his wife, Merrick is so overwhelmed at meeting a beautiful woman that he snuffles and weeps. And she, of course, weeps, too. (There's no sun in this tale of a terrible enchantment, and a tear shed for Merrick is a jewel.)

John Gielgud is in strapping form as the head of the hospital, and Wendy Hiller, as the chief nurse, matches him in vinegary elegance, syllable for syllable, pause for pause. John Hurt and Anthony Hopkins—both specialists in masochism—might have leaked so much emotion that the film would slip its sprockets. But Hopkins comes through with an unexpectedly crisp, highly varied performance—the kind you respect an actor for. He lets Hurt (was ever actor better named?) have a monopoly on our sympathy, and Hurt, using his twisted lips and his eyes, but mostly his voice and his posture and movements, makes of Merrick an astonishingly sweet-souled gentleman of his era. If he were not encased in loathsome flesh, we could never believe in such delicate, saintly humility. But the film makes us understand that in a time when ugliness was thought to come from within, Merrick had to become a dandy of the soul in order to feel human. Once he's out of his cloak and into a suit, he has a soft, sidling walk, askew but airy. He's only in his twenties (he died at twenty-seven), and his wish to be good is childlike and a little cracked, but his kindness seems to come from a mystic simplicity. There's no irony in the film when he becomes a society figure—an oddity and a pet to be pampered. We see his sheer delight in being accepted among people with nice manners; his fawning gratitude is from the heart. He isn't concerned with Treves's problems of conscience about whether he, too, is exploiting Merrick's condition. Merrick knows that Treves has brought him from agony to peace. The director doesn't stray from the Victorian framework he constructs; nothing is interpreted (not even the recurrent mother-being-raped-by-elephants dream), and so nothing is sentimentalized in a modern manner.

This is not the usual movie—in which the story supports the images and holds everything together. Lynch's visual scheme is so imaginative that it transcends the by now well-known story, and scene by scene you don't know what to expect. You're seeing something new—subconscious material stirring within the format of a conventional narrative. There is perhaps nothing as eerily, baldly erotic as that moment in *Eraserhead* when two lovers deliquesce into their bed—disappearing in the fluid, with only the woman's hair left floating on top. But there is something indefinably erotic going on here; it's submerged in the film's rhythm and in the director's whole way of seeing. And wherever you look there are inexplicably satisfying images: a little barrel-chested mutt bulldog waddles across a London street with its tail stretched straight out, like a swagger stick; at the medical college, when Treves, assuming a matter-of-fact tone, presents Merrick in all his glorious deformity to the assembled doctors, a man with a big furry beard turns on the light at the start of the presentation and turns it off at the close—a silly detail to remember, but it's part of the texture, like the carriage horse that suggests a phantom, and the illumination on the cobblestones that makes them look like fish scales, and the night scene on the Continent that might be a painting, except that dawn comes up. In Merrick's dream of the trampling elephant feet, the camera swerves and swoops across the bodies of the great beasts in strange panning movements that suggest the way Merrick, who must sleep sitting up with his head on his raised knees (because of its weight), would dream, with his head wobbling and jerking. And in perhaps the most elusive series of effects, when Merrick realizes his lifelong ambition

of going to the theatre and sees a Drury Lane performance of the pantomime "Puss in Boots," it becomes a fantasy of magical transformations, with
ducks and a lion and fairies flying on wires and people who seem to be on
horseback, except that the horses' legs are their own, and an ogre behind
bars, and swans—deliriously snooty cardboard swans. You can't be sure what
you're seeing: it's like disconnected memories of the earliest stories you
were told. The creatures—animal, human, birds, spirits—are all mixed up
together, and the bits of glitter that fall on them have the dreamlike quality
of the overturned world in the glass ball that fell from Kane's hand. In this
sequence, too, there is a suggestion of the wobbling movement of the heavy
head. Late that night, when Merrick, in his fresh nightshirt, smooths his
clean white bedsheets—it's like another form of preening—his body seems
weightless. He is ready to leave it.

The New Yorker, October 27, 1980

STARDUST MEMORIES
THE PRINCE WHO TURNED INTO A FROG

At the beginning of Woody Allen's *Stardust Memories*, there is a Bergman-
esque nightmare sequence, silent except for the sound of ticking.
Woody Allen is on a stalled train, and as he looks around he sees big-
nosed misery on the other faces; his fellow-passengers are self-conscious grotesques who might have been photographed by Diane Arbus. Peering out
the window, he can see that on the next track there's another stalled train
that is headed in the same direction, and it's full of swinging, beautiful people living it up and having a ball.

He motions to the conductor that he's on the wrong train and tries to
get out, but he's sealed in. This visual metaphor has almost the same meaning as the Groucho epigram that was quoted twice in *Annie Hall:* "I wouldn't
want to belong to any club that would have me for a member." The clubs
from which Groucho was excluded were, of course, the gentiles' clubs, and
he was expressing his chagrin at being lumped with the other Jews. (Excluded from a California beach club, Groucho wrote the organization,
"Since my daughter is only half Jewish, could she go in the water up to her
waist?") *Stardust Memories* might be described as an obsessional pastiche. It is
modelled on Fellini's *8½*, and the bleached-out black-and-white cinematography suggests a dupe of a dupe of *8½*, with some allusions to the clown's
pasty despair at the start of Bergman's *The Naked Night*. The theme recalls
Preston Sturges's *Sullivan's Travels*, which is about an acclaimed director
who doesn't want to go on making popular comedies—he wants to be stark,
tragic, and realistic.

Woody Allen calls himself Sandy Bates this time, but there's only the merest wisp of a pretext that he is playing a character; this is the most undisguised of his dodgy mock-autobiographical fantasies. The setting is the Hotel Stardust, a resort on the New Jersey seashore, where a woman film critic (played by Helen Hanft) conducts weekend seminars; for a fee, the guests spend a weekend looking at the work of a filmmaker and discussing it with him—and they also get to press his flesh. This weekend, Sandy Bates is the celebrity-in-residence; he runs his new picture as well as clips from his comedies, and the discussions are intercut with flashbacks, hallucinations, and fragmentary encounters. The actors slip in and out of the films and his life. Feeling besieged, he goes through a vague sort of crisis, possibly brought on by the seminar guests. Each of them wants something from him—he is asked to appear at a benefit for cancer, to give some personal article to an auction, to sign a petition, to read a script, to answer an imbecilic question. And these pushy fans who treat him in such an overfamiliar way are gross or big-nosed and have funny Jewish names. They're turned into their noses; they leer into the lens, shoving their snouts at Sandy Bates. They chide him (indulgently) for his recent seriousness, and he complains, "I don't want to make funny movies anymore. They can't force me to. I look around the world and all I see is human suffering."

In *Stardust Memories,* Woody Allen degrades the people who respond to his work and presents himself as their victim. He seems to feel that they want him to heal them; the film suggests a *Miss Lonelyhearts* written without irony. (Maybe Sandy Bates means he sees human suffering when he looks around his apartment: his walls are decorated with blowups of news photographs, such as the famous one of the execution in a Saigon street during the Tet offensive, and they change like mood music. Is this evidence of Sandy Bates's morbidity, or is it how he proves that he's politically and socially with it? Is there any way it can't be a joke? *What* is going on in this movie?) Woody Allen has often been cruel to himself in physical terms—making himself look smaller, scrawnier, ugly. Now he's doing it to his fans. People who, viewed differently, might look striking or mysterious have their features distorted by the camera lens and by Felliniesque makeup; they become fat-lipped freaks wearing outsize thick goggles. (They could serve as illustrations for the old saw that Jews are like other people, only more so.) People whose attitudes, viewed differently, might seem friendly or, at worst, overenthusiastic and excited are turned into morons. Throughout *Stardust Memories,* Sandy is superior to all those who talk about his work; if they like his comedies, it's for freakish reasons, and he shows them up as poseurs and phonies, and if they don't like his serious work, it's because they're too stupid to understand it. He anticipates almost anything that you might say about *Stardust Memories* and ridicules you for it. Finally, you may feel you're being told that you have no right to *any* reaction to Woody Allen's movies. He is not just the victim here, he's the torturer. (A friend of mine called the picture *Sullivan's Travels Meets the P.L.O.*)

The hostility of the standup comic toward his night-club audience is often considered self-evident, but the hostility of a movie director toward the public that idolizes him doesn't have the same logic behind it, and it's almost unheard of. Woody Allen has somehow combined the two, and his hostility takes a special form. He's trying to stake out his claim to be an artist like Fellini or Bergman—to be accepted in the serious, gentile artists' club. And he sees his public as Jews trying to shove him back down in the Jewish clowns' club. Great artists' admirers are supposed to keep their distance. *His* admirers feel they know him and can approach him; they feel he belongs to them—and he sees them as his murderers.

Conceivably, a comedy could be made about an artist who thinks that those who like his work are grotesque and those who don't are stupid. This misanthrope would have to be the butt of the comedy, though; his pain would have to be funny—like the pain that Portnoy felt about his life's being a Jewish joke. But Woody Allen doesn't show the ability to step back from himself (as he did when he was making comedies); even the notion of doing this particular film in black-and-white is tied up with his not being able to step back. He sees himself only from the inside, and he asks us to *suffer* for the pain he feels about his success. At times, he sets up scenes as if he recognized that this pain is absurd, but he can't achieve—or doesn't want to achieve—the objective tone that would make us laugh. He brings in characters who seem designed for a payoff—an old school chum who complains that he isn't rich and famous like Sandy, an actress who once played Sandy's mother in a film and has now undergone cosmetic surgery and thinks she has become a beauty—but he stages their scenes in what appears to be a deliberately off-key, quavering tone, so that everything turns uncomfortable, morose, icky. And whether it's because of Woody Allen's desire to show us his loss of faith in these gags, or because of the cinematographer Gordon Willis's penchant for dark abstractions, they are shot at such a distance that the purpose of the scenes becomes opaque. (The actress-mother is seen in distant, cruel silhouette.)

The film has a single moment of comic rapport: Sandy visits his tough, lively married sister (played by Anne DeSalvo), and they take relish in a shared bitchy laugh about their mother. Yet even this visit begins with an aggressively rancid scene making fun of the sister's loud, uncouth friends—particularly a fat woman who was raped the night before; inexplicably, she wears a T-shirt with the word "Sexy" across her huge bosom. And the purpose of the visit seems to be to burlesque Sandy's relatives. The furnishings of the sister's apartment and the corpulent idiocy of her husband, stuffing his face while pumping on an Exercycle, shriek of bad taste. (The writhing wallpaper in her bedroom suggests something dreamed up for a decorator's Halloween party.) The only concession to vitality in the movie (besides the sister) is in the great jazz recordings used as the score, though in this atmosphere the music sounds like Fellini Dixieland.

Starting with the two trains, there are a number of potentially funny situations, but they don't come out funny. You're not sure how to react: the gags are strained—they seem poisoned by the director's self-pity. You can't laugh at the nightmarish melancholy of those dark, pimply train passengers, or at the ugliness of the seminar guests and the sister's pals. And though Woody Allen's attitudes may have a lot in common with those of Diane Arbus, you can't respond as you would to her photographs. The deep malignity in her work gives those photographs an undeniable punch. Woody Allen assembles people and makes them grotesque, but he uses them in such a casual way that he trivializes the ugliness he puts in front of us. There's no power in the images; he trivializes even his own malignity by his half-joking manner. And he doesn't appear to see any comedy in the fact that the only undemanding, unpushy characters in the movie—the three women in Sandy's life—are all gentile. These women are also indifferent to his work; at least, they don't offer opinions of it. They don't have enough independent existence for us to be sure what they're supposed to represent, and what attracts them to him—if not his films and his fame—isn't made apparent. But we can see what attracts him to them: they're the only women on the landscape in "quiet good taste," the only ones with hair that doesn't look like plaster of Paris or frizzed wire. Charlotte Rampling, who is posed in closeup after closeup—a ship's figurehead, like Anouk Aimée in *8½*—suggests a decaying goddess. She seems to be used just for her physiognomy—for her bony chest and wide mouth (its corners run right into her cheekbones). Marie-Christine Barrault is used for her matronly-milkmaid-goddess look and the beautiful big teeth that can turn threatening. Jessica Harper is used for her wide brow and perverse, waifish grin. The first two are like toys that Sandy Bates has lost interest in; Harper is a possibility glimpsed which he doesn't care enough about to pursue.

The Jewish self-hatred that spills out in this movie could be a great subject, but all it does is spill out. The ostensible subject is the beleaguered artist and what the public demands of him. In a *Newsweek* cover story in 1978, Woody Allen was quoted: "When you do comedy you're not sitting at the grown-ups' table, you're sitting at the children's table." From the tone of this film, you would think that vulgarians were putting guns to Woody Allen's head and forcing him to make comedies. Considering the many respectful, indeed laudatory reviews he got for *Interiors,* which, he says, even "turned a little profit," and considering the astonishing success of *Manhattan,* in which he tried to be both Ingmar Bergman and Charlie Chaplin—a wet mixture if ever there was one—his contempt for the public seems somewhat precipitate.

Woody Allen, who used to play a walking inferiority complex, made the whole country more aware of the feelings of those who knew they could never match the images of Wasp perfection that saturated their lives. He played the brainy, insecure little guy, the urban misfit who quaked at the thought of a fight, because physically he could never measure up to the big strong silent men of the myths—the gentile beefcake. Big strong men know that they can't live up to the myths, either. Allen, by bringing his neurotic terror of just about everything out front, seemed to speak for them, too. In the forties and fifties, when Bob Hope played coward heroes the cowardice didn't have any political or sexual resonance, but in the late sixties and the seventies, when Woody Allen displayed his panic he seemed to incarnate the whole anti-macho mood of the time. In the sloppy, hairy counterculture era, Americans no longer tried to conform to a look that only a minority of them could ever hope to approximate. Woody Allen helped to make people feel more relaxed about how they looked and how they really felt about using their fists, and about their sexual terrors and everything else that made them anxious. He became a new national hero. College kids looked up to him and wanted to be like him.

That's why it seems such a horrible betrayal when he demonstrates that despite his fame he still hates the way he looks, and that he wanted to be one of *them*—the stuffy macho Wasps—all along. There were moments of betrayal in his other films, such as the peculiar jokiness of his using actors smaller than he as his romantic rivals (the Hollywood doper played by Paul Simon in *Annie Hall*, and Jeremiah, played by Wallace Shawn, in *Manhattan*). But people in the audience could blot out the puzzling scenes of *Annie Hall* and *Manhattan*. In *Stardust Memories*—awful title!—he throws so much at you that you can't blink it away. If Woody Allen were angry with himself for still harboring childish macho dreams, that would be understandable, but he's angry with the public, with us—as if *we* were forcing him to embody the Jewish joke, the loser, the deprived outsider forever. Comedy doesn't belong at the children's table, but whining does.

One of the distinctions that is generally made between a "commercial" artist and a "pure" one is that the former is obsessed with how the audience will react, while the latter doesn't worry about the audience but tries to work things out to satisfy his inner voice. That Woody Allen should try to become a "pure" artist by commenting on his audience seems a sign that he's playing genius. In *Manhattan*, he reworked too much of *Annie Hall*; it was clear that he needed an infusion of new material. In *Stardust Memories*, we get more of the same thoughts over and over—it's like watching a loop. The material is fractured and the scenes are very short, but there was not a single one that I was sorry to see end. *Stardust Memories* doesn't seem like a movie, or even like a filmed essay; it's nothing. You see right through it to the man who has lost the desire to play a character: he has become the man on the couch. He thinks he has penetrated to the core of what life is, and it's all rotten. No doubt he feels that this is the lousy truth; actually, it's just the lousy truth of how he feels. But we've all felt like that at times; he hasn't discovered anything that needs to be shared with the world.

In *Manhattan*, Woody Allen began to use his own face more naturally than he had before on the screen; he didn't turn into a caricature anymore—it was a naked face, sometimes too naked. He is even more relaxed in *Stardust Memories*, and in the absence of other characters you may get fed up with his nakedness and, as his depression enters into you, begin to think about what's in his head. I referred to Woody Allen's recent films as dodgy because I don't think anybody knows how we're supposed to react to the protagonist's metaphysical head cold—his carrying on about death and the shallowness of his friends. He keeps shifting: at one point in a movie he seems to be its moral center, at another point he's a sniper who turns petty grievances into moral issues, and at other times he's the frailest, weakest person around, trying to manipulate people in terms of his needs. In *Annie Hall,* in *Manhattan,* and now in *Stardust Memories,* the protagonist's high moral tone is often out of scale with what he's indignant about and he just sounds like a crank, but we can't tell when Woody Allen means him to sound like one and when Woody Allen really is one.

No movie star (not even Mel Brooks) can ever have been more explicit on the screen about his Jewishness than Woody Allen, and he was especially so in his Academy Award–winning romantic comedy, *Annie Hall*—the neurotic's version of *Abie's Irish Rose* and the TV series "Bridget Loves Bernie." The hero, Alvy Singer, announced that he was paranoid about being Jewish, and at dinner with Annie's Midwestern Wasp family he had a flash and saw himself through their eyes as a Hassidic rabbi—not just the outsider but the weirdly funny outsider, too ridiculous to be threatening. What's apparent in all his movies is that for him Jewishness means his own kind of schlumpiness, awkwardness, hesitancy. For Woody Allen, being Jewish is like being a fish on a hook; in *Annie Hull* he twists and squirms. And when Alvy sits at that dull Wasp dinner and the screen divides and he sees his own family at dinner, quarrelling and shouting hysterically, the Jews are too heavily overdone for comedy. Here, as almost everywhere else in Woody Allen's films, Jews have no dignity. That's just about how he defines them and why he's humiliated by them.

There was self-love as well as self-hatred involved in *Annie Hall,* however: Alvy was very quick to decide that almost everyone connected with show business (except for him) was a sellout. Though the story, which turned into a conflict between East Coast and West Coast, faded before it worked itself out, that fading became part of the meaning: relationships fail, and we're not quite sure why. Diane Keaton's Annie was full of thoughts that wilted as she tried to express them, and her lyrical, apologetic kookiness gave the film softness, elusiveness. She was fluttery and unsure about everything, yet she went her own way, leaving Alvy to continue his love affair with death—an affair that he seemed to think represented integrity and high seriousness. What made the movie run down and dribble away was that while Woody Allen showed us what a guilt-ridden, self-absorbed killjoy Alvy Singer was, always judging everyone, he (and not just Alvy) seemed bewildered that Annie wearied of Alvy's obsessions and preferred to move on and maybe even have some fun. By the end, Alvy and the story had disappeared; there was nothing left but Woody Allen's sadness.

At the opening of *Manhattan,* Woody Allen's Isaac Davis spoke about the corruption of the city's inhabitants in what came across as a satirical commentary; the audience howled. Then that commentary turned out to be the point of view of the picture. But the audience was right to howl: Allen based his case for general moral decay on the weaknesses (not even cruelties) of two or three selfish, confused people. You could indict Paradise on charges like that. In *Annie Hall*, he gave us an L.A. full of decadent pleasure lovers, and his *Manhattan* was also full of naughty, self-centered types: he contrasted their lack of faith with the trusting, understanding heart of a loyal child— played by Mariel Hemingway. (What man in his forties but Woody Allen could pass off a predilection for teen-agers as a quest for true values?) It was clear that he thought we all ran around being rotten and chic, and had to come to terms with our shallowness in order to be saved. (At least he gave us a *big* child to lead us.) Woody Allen the moralist has restated his imponderable questions about man's destiny so often that in *Stardust Memories* even he sounds tired of them; he tosses them out unemotionally—it's his ascetic reflex. He may be ready to become a Catholic convert. If Woody Allen finds success very upsetting and wishes the public would go away, this picture should help him stop worrying.

The New Yorker, October 27, 1980

USED CARS

U sed Cars has a wonderful, energetic heartlessness. It's an American tall-tale movie in a Pop Art form, with a theme similar to that of *Volpone*. Remember the convict's advice that Nelson Algren quoted? "Never play cards with a man called Doc. Never eat at a place called Mom's. Never sleep with a woman whose troubles are worse than your own." This movie adds "Never buy a used car from a dealer whose slogan is 'Trust us.'" Its premise is that honesty doesn't exist. If you develop a liking for some of the characters, it's not because they're free of avarice but because of their style of avarice. Jack Warden plays twin brothers—the amiable codger Luke Fuchs and the vicious cutthroat Roy L. Fuchs—who run rival used-car lots across the street from each other in the booming Southwest. Luke has a bad heart, and every time he thinks of his skunky brother it gets worse; the only thing that keeps his business going is Rudy Russo. This fast-talking supersalesman, played by Kurt Russell, is so rambunctiously, ingeniously crooked that he's a standout—a star in the world of the mendacious. He's slick and sleazy—a vulgarian through and through. Kurt Russell was sensationally effective when he starred in the TV film *Elvis* early in 1979; here he goes further. His leap into satire blots away the ten Disney pictures he appeared in, between the ages of fourteen and twenty-four. His Rudy has an authentic loudmouth uncouthness; when he's momentarily stumped, his tongue seems to thicken

helplessly. He's a son of a bitch, but not a bad guy. The film pits this crass, ferociously ambitious hero against the sneaky Roy L. They're feuding cartoon animals, both using dirty tricks. And when they land in court, the judge (Al Lewis) looks as if long, long ago he smelled something very rotten; it confirmed what he had suspected and he never let himself forget it.

The movie has a flow of visual-slapstick details and off-color verbal nuances that aren't ever punched up or commented on; they just keep flashing by. You see from the corner of an eye that the Mexican, Manuel (Alfonso Arau), who sells Rudy two hundred and fifty used cars (some of them taxis), conducts his illicit business out of his home in an old airplane that sits in the desert surrounded by cactus. The story line is built of small, wild frauds and jack-in-the-box jokes; they're all interconnected, and, amazingly, every one of them pays off. The film's super-hip use of corn is a home-grown surrealism that the director, Robert Zemeckis, and his co-writer and producer, Bob Gale (they were both born in 1951), have developed out of earlier American slapstick routines. The intricacy of the gag patterns is all theirs, and so is the way in which the clusters of gags come together—the momentum creates the illusion of being out of control. Zemeckis and Gale are compulsive jugglers, adding more and more balls. But this isn't simple gag comedy with kickers; the comedy is also in the characters, who keep kicking all the time. *Everybody* in the movie is funny—even Toby, Luke's dog. (Actually, you laugh more when the jokes involve Toby than you do the rest of the time, because whenever Toby is part of the chicanery on the lot, there's a cut to his trick and there isn't much else going on in the frame.) The whizzing plot mechanism may make some people feel that they've never been invited aboard—that the picture is speeding ahead without them. And it's vulgarly funny—which may repel some from boarding. Others have said they find it too cruel: there is a sequence in which Roy L. hires a demolition-derby driver to go across the street, pose as a customer, and take Luke for a ride so scary he'll have a heart attack, and Roy L.—he thinks—will inherit Luke's lot. When Luke staggers back into his office in his death throes, the scene might appear unconscionably prolonged if you weren't reacting to the jokes ricocheting off his stagger. Maybe it's just the timing in that sequence that throws some people off; the audience has no problem laughing when Rudy and his pals conceal Luke's death by burying him on the lot, sitting up in a 1959 Edsel.

The action is so fast that at times it's like an adolescent stunt, carried out convulsively—a fit. Everything is staged for motion; there isn't a static thought in this movie. The jokes aren't scattershot: *Used Cars* has the crazy consistency of a picture like *Bringing Up Baby* or *Shampoo*. The bluffs and the scams all play on the theme of trust (just as everything does in Melville's *The Confidence Man*). It's easy to see why Steven Spielberg, who sponsored Zemeckis and Gale, was drawn to their manic bravura: their moviemaking is a giant version of the toys he set in motion in *Close Encounters*. Spielberg was executive producer of their first feature, the 1978 *I Wanna Hold Your Hand*,

and his picture *1941* was made from their screenplay, with John Milius as executive producer; both Spielberg and Milius were executive producers on *Used Cars*. All three of these Zemeckis-Gale projects have been commercial disappointments, and a friend of mine who couldn't stand *1941* said it was like having your head inside a pinball machine for two hours. I know what he meant: *1941* shows you talent without sensibility. And that's also why *Used Cars* seems adolescent, and maybe even pre-human. Like *1941,* it has a carnival atmosphere, and yes, there is something of a pinball machine about it. In both cases, the moviemakers start with a comic premise and take it as far as they can, expanding it with a soaring madness that seems to bring a metallic sheen to the images. What this way of working doesn't allow for is humanistic considerations; such considerations have rarely figured in farce, but Americans may have become touchy. When you see any version of *Volpone* on the stage or the screen, you're not likely to be offended by what it says about human greed, deception, mean-spiritedness. You think of the greed *Volpone* delights in as satiric distortion. But it can rub you wrong to see a used-car lot where everyone swindles everyone else; you may think you're seeing a metaphor of American life rather than a slapstick exaggeration.

Cold-bloodedness shouldn't need to be defended; you can't have pratfalls without it, and the sense of fun in Zemeckis and Gale's hyperbolic slapstick does more for us than pitting virtuous characters against the swindlers would. (It would be demeaning if every movie had to be "balanced," like a political discussion on TV, or like the Marx Brothers pictures made at M-G-M, which, at Irving Thalberg's insistence, were given a supposedly sane crooner and ingénue to balance the insane comedy.) In the context of *Used Cars,* anyone trying to be sane or virtuous would come across as a goosey dimwit, like poor Gloria Jean in *Never Give a Sucker an Even Break.* Zemeckis and Gale's movie is really a more restless and visually high-spirited version of the W. C. Fields comedies.

This picture is entirely made up of comic turns, and at its best there isn't a sincere emotion in it. Rudy's burly sidekick, Jeff, played by Gerrit Graham (he was Beef in *Phantom of the Paradise*), believes in omens, and not just in a small way—he believes totally in omens, and so he lives in spaced-out terror. Most of the time, he looks like a dodo bird in shock, and the gorgeous bimbos he generally has at his side are like feathered trophies. Luke's shell-shocked mechanic, Jim, whose standards of honesty are set by how things are done at Luke's lot, is played by Frank McRae. Given the workaday world in which Jim functions as an honest man, he can't help being funny. David L. Lander and Michael McKean (who's like an American Dudley Moore) play Freddie and Eddie, a pair of electronic wizards who help Rudy and Jeff cut into a Presidential address with their used-car commercials; Freddie and Eddie are like twin brothers, too, and they speak in a doubletalk jargon that suggests the language of robots. The film slides a bit when Rudy falls in love with Luke's long-estranged blond daughter, Barbara Fuchs, because Barbara seems too dainty and too easily duped. Though

Deborah Harmon, who plays the part, has a good, eccentric voice and gives her lines little twists, her role doesn't have the hot-ziggety verve to match up with Kurt Russell's. The movie needed to go all the way; it shouldn't have pulled back into this pallid conventionality. (When Rudy says "Trust me" to Barbara, he actually means it.) The film recovers a bit, though. By the end, Barbara, who has appeared in time to take over her father's lot, is wising up, and she becomes a gyp artist, snookering a little old lady with a painted-over taxi. In the big finale, when, in order to keep Roy L. from grabbing the business away from Barbara, two hundred and fifty teen-age student drivers race Manuel's two hundred and fifty jalopies across the prairie, and Rudy jumps from car to car, like the hero of a Western jumping from horse to horse to stop the heroine's runaway coach, the picture adds up the way whoppers told by magnificent liars do.

Surprisingly, the cast works together more smoothly than the group that Spielberg assembled for *1941* did. And the gags interlock even more symmetrically. *1941* had a choppy beginning; it seemed to start with the story already under way, and Spielberg overdid some of the broad, cartoon aspects—several of the performers seemed to be carrying placards telling you what was wacko about them. But the U.S.O. jitterbug number is one of the greatest pieces of film choreography I've ever seen, and the film overall is an amazing, orgiastic comedy, with the pop culture of an era compacted into a day and a night. Its commercial failure in this country didn't make much sense to me. It was accused of gigantism, and it did seem huge, though part of what was so disarmingly fresh about it was the miniature re-creation of Hollywood Boulevard at night in 1941, with little floodlights illuminating the toy cars tootling around the corners and toy planes flying so low they were buzzing through the streets.

Spielberg and Zemeckis & Gale share a mania for comic invention, and there's the feeling of a playroom about their work. That has been true of the acknowledged masters of slapstick, though. Why hasn't *Used Cars* (which received some enthusiastic reviews) done better? The only big reason I can come up with is that maybe you have to be hooked on filmmaking to respond to it, because the jokes run all through and there aren't slowdowns or pauses for laughs. I loved the film, but I didn't laugh out loud a lot, because I was too busy looking at it. I've never seen another movie with the same kind of ravishing, bright Pop lighting, and the cinematographer, Donald M. Morgan, turns the used-car lot at night into a cityscape on the far side of the moon. The movie could be used for a film-school demonstration of dynamic composition and production design (even the clothes are photogenic and funny—Rudy and Jeff dress like natty astro-cowboys, in jeans and iridescent satin shirts). And the editing is by one of the modern masters, Michael Kahn. Maybe the failure is that of the moviemakers, who are so absorbed with their playthings that they fail to draw the audience in. But it could also be that *Used Cars* is so elegantly made and so continuously funny that audiences don't respond the way they would if the jokes were clumsily signalled. You have to bring something to this party. Rudy isn't just a creative sleazo. Why does he work for Luke, whose business is failing, rather than for the get-up-and-go Roy L.? For the challenge, of course. He's selling cars now, but he's still young: he's selling cars only until he can come up with the rest of the sixty thousand dollars it will take to buy the nomination for state senator. He's an American dreamer; he wants to go where the big bucks are. *Used Cars* is a classic screwball fantasy—a shaggy celebration of American ingenuity. Trust me.

The New Yorker, November 10, 1980

DIVINE MADNESS

Watching Bette Midler in *Divine Madness,* which was filmed on three successive nights at specially arranged performances at the Pasadena Civic Auditorium, you don't know where her energy and spirit come from. She goes from one mood to another in triple time (like a Betty Hutton with brains)—as if she's so alive that all these emotions just spurt out. In *The Rose,* she was probably able to give her passionate, skilled performance by drawing from the same source that Streisand drew from in *Funny Girl:* these "untrained" artists had invented their own training—they had been treating each song they sang as an encapsulated, highly emotional story. Midler—a comedienne who sings—and Streisand are very different, though. When Streisand sings, her command of the audience is in her regal stillness; she distills her own emotions. You feel that she doesn't need the audience—that she could close her eyes and sing with the same magnetic power. Streisand's voice is her instrument; Midler's audience is her instrument. She plays on us and we bring her to life, or at least she makes us feel that we do.

Midler holds you by her changes. She moves like a flighty, mincing Mick Jagger, with a high-heeled, tippy-toed prance and a furious jiggle, and even when her feet don't move, her features do. Everything about her soft and curvy short-waisted body is contradictory: she has narrow hips, slim legs, full breasts, plump upper arms, and slender, expressive hands. When she talks to the audience, telling jokes about a trip to Europe, she shakes like a rowdy burlesque queen, and her toothy smiles are radiantly lewd. When she sings, she's an emotional whirligig, spinning from a cackle to a torchy moan so fast that we're floored by the convictions she brings to each—she can turn gleaming-eyed parody to pure emotion. Midler gives a song a workout, going at it again and again, and topping one big finish with another. Along the way, she may swing it, wail it, shout it, rock it, and throw in some scat, gospel, funk, and punk. She's a bosomy clown who flirts, then weeks, and then clowns again while keeping the passionate, tragic tone. Singing "Stay with Me," which is the climax of her first set of songs, she's suddenly startlingly beautiful; the camera angles on her suggest posters Lautrec didn't get to do. The film critic Michael Sragow wrote that "her face resembles the masks of comedy and tragedy melted into one"—there is an exciting Expressionist bleariness about her.

Except for a prologue skit, in which the house manager gives numb-skull instructions to the ushers, *Divine Madness* is essentially a one-woman show: Bette Midler is alone on the stage with her backup trio, the Harlettes. Probably the greatest of all recorded-performance films is the 1979 *Richard Pryor Live in Concert*—when we watch that film we can't account for Pryor's gift, and everything he does seems to be for the first time. Bette Midler mystifies us, too. A crazed, sunny effervescence takes over her face—her demon is a dirty imp. Like Craig Russell, she seems to have a whole troupe of people inside; there's a spooky echo-chamber effect. But *Divine Madness* doesn't have the unity of the Pryor film, and it doesn't get a performance rhythm going, as that did. The separate numbers, with their costume changes, break it up, and Midler's entrances, such as her arrival in a sequined mermaid's tail and a power-driven wheelchair as Delores DeLago, the Toast of Chicago, seem better calculated for the stage than for the camera.

Bette Midler's pneumatic body is very important to her effects. (She's such a tiny Big Mama.) She looks great when she wears a revealing short, spangly dress with thin shoulder straps, and she has a puffed-up physical alertness in the forties swimsuit she wears for "Boogie Woogie Bugle Boy." (It would be even better if she weren't wearing a ribbon that says "Miss Community Chest"; she has gone way past this tired camp.) She has a triumphant moment in a witty enveloping costume that makes her a bride from the front and a groom from the back, for "Chapel of Love," and she's also lighted resplendently during this number. The director, Michael Ritchie, and the cinematographer, William A. Fraker, do discreet, handsome work; they don't try to hide her performance sweat—they let us see that she can be fleetingly beautiful in many different ways, and that her willingness to be grotesque is part of what makes that possible. She has the ability to change glitz to shimmer. *Divine Madness* shows us a great entertainer, though it's not stirring, like *The Rose*, where we could see the dramatic reasons for the incontinent changes of feeling. Here Midler seems to be dipping into a cornucopia—Santa's bag of presents—and she brings the contrasting emotions out so fast that they're somewhat devalued; the meanings crowd each other.

But the only major weakness is that after the first set the song numbers go downhill, and the film gets to be too much. It would have been better with the last quarter lopped off, starting with Midler's mime—a boozing bag lady wearing rainbow-colored rags and carrying an umbrella, who falls asleep on a bench. Some numbers begin poorly and then get better, but once she comes on with that soulful umbrella the jig is up. The bag lady, who is trying to capture the bird of happiness, shows us her longings and her need for fantasy. We've been taking these longings for granted from the start; now Bette Midler lays them out, and all this vulnerability is pretty grim. (It's blobby, like Red Skelton's mime.) The show takes a nose dive with "Rain" and a Kurt Weillish "Ready to Begin Again"—it's inspirational, in the worst sense—and a badly staged "Do You Want to Dance?" Though she almost picks things up at the very end with the gospel sound of "I Shall Be Released," the sodden banality of that damn bag lady lingers in the air. Bette Midler, who is maybe better at bawdiness than any other woman entertainer alive, doesn't need to push her range into show-biz sincerity (which she destroys in Delores DeLago's rendition of "My Way"). And something else goes wrong in this last quarter of the show: she's swathed in tattered clothing and she loses her physicality. We need to see Bette Midler's body in movement. When she tries to be still and make it just on her singing, her act dies. It's not that she's a bad singer but that her voice alone isn't very distinctive—it lacks personality. The joy she communicates is in the feeling she gives you that she needs to move and bounce and take those quick trotting steps—just as she needs to sing and grin and tell dirty jokes.

The New Yorker, November 10, 1980

RAGING BULL
RELIGIOUS PULP, OR THE INCREDIBLE HULK

As Jake La Motta, the former middleweight boxing champ, in *Raging Bull,* Robert De Niro wears scar tissue and a big, bent nose that deform his face. It's a miracle that he didn't grow them—he grew everything else. He developed a thick-muscled neck and a fighter's body, and for the scenes of the broken, drunken La Motta he put on so much weight that he seems to have sunk in the fat with hardly a trace of himself left. What De Niro does in this picture isn't acting, exactly. I'm not sure what it is. Though it may at some level be awesome, it definitely isn't pleasurable. De Niro seems to have emptied himself out to become the part he's playing and then not got enough material to refill himself with: his La Motta is a swollen puppet with only bits and pieces of a character inside, and some semi-religious, semi-abstract concepts of guilt. He has so little expressive spark that what I found myself thinking about wasn't La Motta or the movie but the metamorphosis of De Niro. His appearance—with his head flattened out and widened by fat—is far more shocking than if he were artificially padded. De Niro went from his usual hundred and forty-five pounds to a hundred and sixty for the young fighter, and then up to two hundred and fifteen for La Motta's later days. (No man has ever made a more dramatic demonstration of the aesthetic reasons that people shouldn't get bloated.) And the director, Martin Scorsese, doesn't show us the trim, fast fighter and then let us adjust to his deterioration; he deliberately confronts us with the gross older La Motta right at the start, in a flash-forward.

At first, we may think that we're going to find out what makes Jake La Motta's life special and why a movie is being made about him. But as the picture dives in and out of La Motta's life, with a few minutes of each of his big fights (he won the title in 1949), it becomes clear that Scorsese isn't concerned with how La Motta got where he did, or what, specifically, happened to him. Scorsese gives us exact details of the Bronx Italian neighborhoods of the forties—everything is sharp, realistic, lived-in. But he doesn't give us specific insights into La Motta. Scorsese and De Niro, who together re-worked the script (by Paul Schrader and Mardik Martin, based on the book *Raging Bull*, by La Motta with Joseph Carter and Peter Savage), are trying to go deeper into the inarticulate types they have done before; this time they seem to go down to pre-human levels. Their brutish Jake is elemental: he has one thing he can do—fight.

Raging Bull isn't a biographical film about a fighter's rise and fall; it's a biography of the genre of prizefight films. Scorsese loves the visual effects and the powerful melodramatic moments of movies such as *Body and Soul, The Set-Up,* and *Golden Boy.* He makes this movie out of remembered high points, leaping from one to another. When Jake is courting the fifteen-year-old platinum-blond Vickie (Cathy Moriarty), he takes her to a miniature-golf course, and their little golf ball rolls into a little wooden church and never comes out. The scene is like one of a series in an old-movie montage showing the path to marriage. But Scorsese just puts in this one step; probably for him it stands for the series. And his neutral attitude toward La Motta is very different from that of forties movies. An idle remark by Vickie—that Jake's opponent in his next match is good-looking—makes Jake so jealous that he goes in and viciously, systematically destroys the kid's face. The movie doesn't throw up its hands in horror; it just looks on. Jake, who enforces long periods of sexual abstinence before his fights, becomes obsessed with the idea that Vickie is cheating on him; you feel that he *wants* to catch her at something. His suspicions lead him to smack her around and to beat up his brother Joey (Joe Pesci), who is his manager, sparring partner, and closest friend. The questions that come to mind (such as why Vickie stays with Jake, or why she leaves when she does, or even whether in fact she *is* unfaithful) clearly aren't germane to Scorsese's interest. Vickie doesn't react much; she accepts Jake's mounting jealousy passively.

Scorsese appears to be trying to purify the characters of forties movies to universalize them. Vickie is an icon—a big, lacquered virgin-doll of the forties. Tall and strong-looking, Cathy Moriarty has a beautiful glassy presence, like Kim Novak in her *Man with the Golden Arm* days, and the same mute sexuality. She recalls other iconographic presences—Jean Harlow, Lana Turner, and the knowing young Gloria Grahame—but she's tougher and more composed. Sitting at the edge of a swimming pool, her Vickie is a *Life* cover girl of the war years. She has sultry eyes and speaks in flat, nasal Bronx tones. It's lucky that Moriarty is big, because when Jake comes at her angrily, like a slob Othello, she looks as if she could take care of herself; there's no pathos. Joe Pesci's Joey is stylized in a different way: he may bring to mind the brother in a movie about a show-biz family. His speech sounds like patter, as if he were doing a routine with Abbott and Costello or the Three Stooges; he has the vocal rhythms of a baggypants comic from burlesque, and though his lines aren't especially funny, his manner is, and the audience responds to him gratefully, because he's so much saner and less monotonous than the Neanderthal Jake. It's Pesci's picture, if it's anybody's, because we can understand why Joey does what he does. Even when he goes out of control and smashes a taxi door repeatedly against a mobster who is caught half in, half out, we know that he's doing what Jake charged him to do. (As the big, gentle mobster, played by Frank Vincent, who's quietly effective, is having his bones broken, voluptuous, forlorn Mascagni music rises. Here, as in much of the movie, Scorsese's excesses verge on self-parody.)

Scorsese is also trying to purify forties style by using the conventions in new ways. If you look at forties movies now, the clichés (which bored people at the time) may seem like fun, and it's easy to see why Scorsese is drawn to them. But when he reproduces them, he reproduces the mechanical quality they once had, and the fun goes out of them. The cardinal rule of forties-studio style was that the scenes had to be shaped to pay off. Scorsese isn't interested in payoffs; it's something else—a modernist effect that's like a gray-out. Early on, when Jake's first wife is frying a steak for him and he complains that she's overcooking it, she hollers and picks up the steak as if she were going to throw it at him, but instead she puts it on his plate. The violence in the scene is right on the surface (she doesn't hold anything back), yet nothing comes of it, and shortly after that she disappears from the movie. We don't get the explosion we expect, but we feel the violence. Scorsese shows us Jake—snorting to himself, and with his belly hanging out—going to see Vickie to get his World Middleweight Championship belt so he can hock the jewels from it, and the scene withers away. Yet we remember his banging on the belt to pry the jewels loose. Scorsese's continuity with forties movies is in the texture—the studio artificiality that he makes sensuous, thick, viscous; there are layers of rage and animosity in almost every sequence.

Raging Bull isn't just a biography of a genre; it's also about movies and about violence, it's about gritty visual rhythm, it's about Brando, it's about the two *Godfather* pictures—it's about Scorsese and De Niro's trying to top what they've done and what everybody else has done. When De Niro and Liza Minnelli began to argue in Scorsese's *New York, New York,* you knew they were going to go from yelling to hitting, because they had no other way to escalate the tension. Here we get more of these actors' battles; they're between Jake and Joey, and between Jake and Vickie. Listening to Jake and Joey go at each other, like the macho clowns in Cassavetes movies, I know I'm supposed to be responding to a powerful, ironic realism, but I just feel trapped. Jake says, "You dumb f—k," and Joey says, "You dumb f—k," and they repeat it and repeat it. And I think, What am I doing here watching these two dumb f—ks? When Scorsese did *Mean Streets, Alice Doesn't Live Here Anymore,* and *Taxi Driver,* the scenes built through language and incident, and other characters turned up. But when he works with two actors and pushes for raw intensity, the actors repeat their vapid profanities, goading each other to dredge up some hostility and some variations and twists. And we keep looking at the same faces—Jake and Joey, or Jake and Vickie. (They're the only people around for most of this movie.) You can feel the director sweating for greatness, but there's nothing *under* the scenes—no subtext, only this actor's version of tension. Basically, the movie is these dialogue bouts and Jake's fights in the ring.

The fights are fast and gory and are shot very close in. We're not put in the position of spectators; we're put in the ring, with our heads right up against the heads of the two fighters who are hammering away at each other, with slow-motion eruptions of blood and sweat splashing us. We're meant to see the fists coming as they see them, and feel the blows as they do; the action is speeded up and slowed down to give us these sensations, and the sound of the punches is amplified, while other noises are blotted out. These aren't fights, really; they're cropped, staccato ordeals. The punches are a steady series of explosions—a drummer doing death rolls. The pounding immediacy is grandiloquent—almost abstract.

The picture seems to be saying that in order to become champ, Jake La Motta had to be mean, obsessive, crazy. But you can't be sure, and the way the story is told Jake's life pattern doesn't make much sense. When he loses the title and gives up fighting, he opens a night club, where he's the m.c. and the comic, clowning around with the customers. I had no idea where this cheesy jokester came from: there was certainly no earlier suggestion that Jake had a gift of gab. And there is nothing to prepare us for the poster announcing that he's giving readings from Paddy Chayefsky, Shakespeare, Rod Serling, Budd Schulberg, and Tennessee Williams; we're in a different movie. At the end, before going onstage for his public reading, Jake recites Brando's back-of-the-taxi speech from *On the Waterfront* while looking in his dressing-room mirror. Scorsese is trying to outdo everything great, even the scene of De Niro talking to himself in the mirror in *Taxi Driver.* What does it mean to have La Motta deliver this lament that he could have been a contender instead of a bum when it's perfectly clear that La Motta is both a champ *and* a bum? (Is it a deliberate mockery of the simplicity of Schulberg's conception?) The whole picture has been made looking in a mirror, self-consciously. It takes a while to grasp that La Motta is being used as *the* fighter, a representative tormented man in a killer's body. He's a repulsive, threatening figure who seems intended to be all that and yet to have an element of greatness. He's a doomed strong man—doomed by his love for his wife and by his ability to fight. It's all metaphors: the animal man attempting to escape his destiny. When Jake, in jail on a morals charge, bangs his head and his fists against the stone walls of his cell and, sobbing in frustration, cries out, "Why? Why? Why? It's so f—king stupid! I'm not an animal," it's the ultimate metaphor for the whole film.

The tragedy in Scorsese's struggles with the material in both *New York, New York,* and *Raging Bull* is that he *is* a great director when he doesn't press so hard at it, when he doesn't suffer so much. He's got moviemaking and the Church mixed up together; he's trying to be the saint of cinema. And he turns Jake's life into a ritual of suffering. In the middle of a fight, Jake is sponged by the men in his corner, and he has been injured so much that the water is dark: they're washing him in his own blood. Scorsese is out to demonstrate that he can have for his hero a brutish hardhead, a man with no redeeming social graces, and make you respect him. He must have been drawn to La Motta's story by its sheer plug-ugliness: here was a fighter who didn't even look graceful in the ring—he crouched and slugged. And Scorsese goes to cartoon lengths to establish that Jake is a bad guy: Jake actually threatens to kill and eat a neighbor's dog. Scorsese doesn't want us to *like* Jake, because he wants us to respond on a higher level—to Jake's energy and his pain. He wants us to respect Jake despite everything we see him do. We're supposed to believe in his *integrity*. The Mafia bosses force Jake to throw a fight before they'll let him have a chance at the title. He throws the fight by just standing still and taking the blows; afterward, he weeps. It's a fall from grace: he has given up the only thing that counts. We're supposed to think, Jake may be a pig, but he *fights*. Scorsese appears to see Jake as having some kind of loony glory. But if you respond, possibly it's not to La Motta's integrity but to De Niro's; he buries the clichés that lesser actors might revel in, and is left with nothing to anchor his performance. He does some amazing things, though. In the ring taking punches, Jake seems to be crying, "Crucify me! Crucify me!" With anyone but De Niro in the role, the picture would probably be a joke. But De Niro gives you a sense of terrible pain that is *relieved* when he's in the ring. The film's brutality doesn't seem exploitative; it's mystical.

The magazine *Film Comment* has a feature, "Guilty Pleasures," which it runs intermittently: movie people list the works they wouldn't try to defend on aesthetic grounds but have enjoyed inordinately. When Scorsese offered some of his favorites in 1978, a thread ran through many of his selections. He says, "*Play Dirty* isn't a sadistic film, but it's mean. The characters have no redeeming social value, which I love." Of *Always Leave Them Laughing,* he says, "I admire the guts it took for Berle to make this autobiographical film about a completely dislikable guy." Of the hero of *I Walk Alone,* he says, "He has only one way to deal with his problems: brute force." Of *Dark of the Sun,* he says, "The sense of the film is overwhelmingly violent; there's no consideration for anything else. The answer to everything is 'kill.' " Scorsese likes movies that aren't covered in sentimental frosting—that put the surliness and killing and meanness right up front. But *Raging Bull* has the air of saying something important, which is just what he loved those cheapo pictures for not having. By making a movie that is *all* guilty pleasures, he has forged a new sentimentality. *Raging Bull* is about a character he loves too much; it's about everything he loves too much. It's the kind of movie that many men must fantasize about: their macho worst-dream movie.

Scorsese is saying that he accepts totally, that he makes no moral judgment. I think that by the last fight we're not supposed to care whether Jake wins or loses—we're supposed to want to be in there, slugging. Even the black-and-white is macho: it has something of the flashy, tabloid look of the original *Naked City* movie. But it's so hyper that you're aware of the art, which kills the tabloid effect. We don't get to see the different styles of La Motta's opponents: Scorsese doesn't care about the rhythm and balance of fighters' bodies. There's no dancing for these fighters, and very little boxing. What Scorsese concentrates on is punishment given and received. He turns the lowdown effects he likes into highbrow flash reeking of religious symbolism. You're aware of the camera positions and of the images held for admiration; you're conscious of the pop and hiss of the newsmen's cameras and the amplified sound of the blows—the sound of pain. Scorsese wants his B-movie seaminess and spiritual meaning, too. He wants a disreputable, lowlife protagonist; then he suggests that this man is close to God, because he is God's animal.

By removing the specifics or blurring them, Scorsese doesn't produce universals—he produces banality. What we get is full of capitals: A Man Fights, A Man Loses Everything, A Man Bangs His Head Against the Wall. Scorsese is putting his unmediated obsessions on the screen, trying to turn raw, pulp power into art by removing it from the particulars of observation and narrative. He loses the lowlife entertainment values of prizefight films; he aestheticizes pulp and kills it. *Raging Bull* is tabloid grand opera. Jake is the Brute Life Force, and the picture ends as he experiences A Surge of Energy. It's a Felliniesque ending: Life Goes On. The picture is overripe, ready for canonization. An end title supplies a handy biblical quote.

The New Yorker, December 8, 1980

ABEL GANCE'S **NAPOLÉON**

Abel Gance's art is the art of frenzy, tumult, climax. He dashes toward melodramatic peaks and goes over the top. The result is overwhelmingly literary, highfalutin, romantic, and foolish. His corn is purple—and it makes you gasp with pleasure because he achieves his effects by the most innovative means. He's like an avant-garde De Mille. Gance has a nineteenth-century theatrical sensibility, but he's also obsessed with the most avant-garde film techniques, and he uses these advanced methods to overpower you emotionally. When he succeeds, you're conscious of the humor of your situation—you applaud, you cheer, because the exhilaration of his technique freshens the stale, trashy ideas, gives them a grand lunacy.

In Gance's greatest film, *Napoléon,* which had its première at the Paris Opéra in 1927, and was presented at Radio City Music Hall in a reconstructed version at the end of January and the beginning of February, Napoleon (Albert Dieudonné) is a Man of Destiny. Before that, when he's still a boy (Vladimir Roudenko), he's a Boy of Destiny. In the opening section, a fortress-like military school is in the distance, while in the foreground the courageous twelve-year-old Napoleon commands his outnumbered troops in a snowball fight. The camera seems to encompass miles of landscape, yet there's so much activity within the shots, and the movement of the boys is so quick and darting and funny, that the effect is of your eyes clearing—of everything becoming bright. Gance cuts from the long shots to closeups, and adds superimpositions, and then the cutting becomes fast and rhythmic, with Napoleon's face flashing by in one frame of every four, and you realize that the principal purpose of this jazzy blinking is to give you a feeling for speed and movement—and for the possibilities of the medium. Gance doesn't dawdle; he starts off with pinwheels, sparks, madness.

Back in 1927, a lot of people must have got off the carousel right there, saying, "It spins too fast, it makes me dizzy—and it's stupid." And maybe when Francis Ford Coppola, who served as impresario for the New York showings, opens the film more widely, some new people will. Years ago, when I was managing theatres, each time I ran an Abel Gance picture there were intelligent, highly educated people who would patiently explain to me how freakishly moldy the ideas were. I would impatiently respond that they weren't allowing themselves the goofy rapture they might feel if they could just give over for a little while. I said that Gance's technique transcended his ideas—that there was a fever in his work which came out of love of the medium itself, and that this love was the real subject of his movies. (I didn't convince anybody.) The problem for these people wasn't that Gance was avant-garde—it was that he was avant-garde and old-fashioned. This is a mixture that some moviegoers just can't swallow.

■   ■   ■

Napoléon was originally made as a six-hour silent film, in color (the prints were tinted and toned by a dye process), and with sections designed to be run on a triple-width screen, by a process called Polyvision. Gance intended this work—thought to have been twenty-six or twenty-eight reels—to be shown in two-hour chunks on three successive nights. But even at the 1927 Paris opening (under the title *Napoléon vu par Abel Gance*) it was, instead, abridged and run in one night. The six-hour original played briefly, on a three-night basis, in eight European cities; then the film was chopped down into so many different versions (some of them reëdited by Gance himself) that it took the English filmmaker and film historian Kevin Brownlow years to assemble this new, relatively complete version. He estimates that twenty to forty minutes of footage are still missing; and a subplot of about fifteen minutes has been cut for the new American opening. At Radio City, where the film was run at twenty-four frames per second (it was originally run at approximately twenty frames per second), it lasted about four hours. (There's a simulation of the original color for an instant at the very end.) Gance actually intended his six-hour movie, which ends with the young Napoleon leading his army in Italy, to be just the first *(Première Époque: Bonaparte)* in a cycle of six Napoleonic films.

■ ■ ■

The opening "Youth of Napoleon" section includes the revenge of Napoleon's enemies—the boys who have lost the fight in the snow. The subtitles tell us that both the masters and the pupils feel an antipathy to this proud, fierce child, and that his only consolation is his pet eagle; after the fight his enemies let the eagle out of its cage, and the bird flies into the night. Not knowing which boys are responsible, Napoleon goes from bed to bed, systematically challenging every one of them; he takes on the whole dormitory. The brawl turns into a pillow fight (the ancestor of the celebrated lyric, feathery sequence in Vigo's *Zero for Conduct*), and as he fights them all and the feathers start to fly the screen divides into four separate shots, then into six, then into nine. And with all nine images in motion the screen becomes a fantasia of boys, pillows, feathers. There's so much movement that the separate images dissolve in the whirling mass. The fight is broken up by the masters, who punish only Napoleon, sending him to spend the night outdoors; he has fought with honor, though, and as he huddles alone in the cold his eagle returns to him. The audience applauds the gaudy, romantic inevitability of the bird's return. (The eagle will be Napoleon's totem throughout the picture.) This early section has a charm that is reminiscent of Mack Sennett and Chaplin, and even the small touches are likable. During the snow fight, a scullion who admires Napoleon's courage warns him that his enemies are putting rocks in their snowballs. After the pillow fight, a stinky little boy (one of the two who let the eagle out) lies snug in his bed; he snores, and a bit of down puffs out of his mouth.

■ ■ ■

Gance works directly on our senses. When images that are no more than a few frames long are intercut repeatedly in a fixed pattern, there's a flickering, blinding effect, like a strobe. And when he divides the screen into multiple images, so that we see seething forms, he's obviously trying to affect us at a subconscious level. I think Gance always meant to be a prophet showing mankind the Way, but he's a prophet only in terms of movie techniques. As a thinker, he is essentially a fantasist, a mythmaker enslaved by his own schoolboy gush.

It's amusing to see the boy Napoleon treated as a Genius, but in the next sections—Napoleon and the French Revolution, and then the Italian Campaign—when the young man Napoleon is treated as the embodiment of the French Revolution, you know you're in the grip of a crazy. There are certain subjects that pose special hazards for great moviemakers, and they are just the ones that attract them the most: the Promethean conquerors, the mad kings, the Men of Destiny, the visionaries. The imaginative moviemaker knows that there are no limits to what is possible in the movie medium, and belief in his own omnipotence rises in him like sap. Imperial moviemakers can't settle for less than the imperial subjects that have no clearly defined limits. (It's no accident that Welles wanted to do *Heart of Darkness* or that Kubrick wanted to do a *Napoleon*.) The trap of these subjects is not merely that they grow to excessive length, that they become misshapen, or are unfinished because funds run out, or that they get mutilated, but that the moviemaker, who begins with a sense of holy mission, winds up not knowing what he meant to say, and the scale of his epic makes the utopian humanistic message he settles for look puny. There's an incoherence that seems almost integral to visionary epics: the bravura techniques have everything to do with exploring the medium, but they have nothing to do with the filmmaker's "statement" about pacifism or revolution or tolerance or a world nation. There's a kind of Pyrrhic poetry about Coppola's having put up more than a quarter of a million dollars to reopen this film in Radio City Music Hall, and with his father, Carmine Coppola, in the pit, conducting the sixty-piece American Symphony Orchestra. Back around 1920, it was D. W. Griffith who arranged for the American opening of Gance's 1919 film *J'Accuse*.

■   ■   ■

Gance's life has been a tragedy of waste. When *Napoléon* opened, he was only in his mid-thirties, and he has spent the rest of his life (he is ninety-one now) mainly on commercial subjects and unfulfilled grand projects. This cannot be completely blamed on tight-fisted, shortsighted businessmen. The fact is that most of Gance's epic ideas reek of nineteenth-century grandiloquence. He isn't rounded (as, say, Renoir was). His films are superb in glimpses or in sequences, but they're not unified by simple emotion, as Griffith's epics were. They're held together by obsession, by fervor. When Gance tries for simple, ordinary feelings, he's usually at his worst. It isn't that he treats the simple moments as filler and pays little attention to them but that he makes something kitschy and embarrassing of them. He layers them with obvious ironies, whole-hog patriotism, facetiousness. For him, common experience is comic relief. In *Napoléon*, during the Terror two government clerks try to save people they like from the guillotine by chewing and swallowing their dossiers, but one of them keeps gagging. Josephine's son (about twelve) sits in a room where Napoleon is courting his mother, and the kid enjoys every minute of it. (That'll be the day!) When Napoleon marries Josephine, the wedding ceremony is comically brief. (Napoleon is a man in a hurry.)

What Gance offers us is not merely a Napoleon without politics; his is a divine Napoleon. Gance's Man of Destiny has a mesmeric gaze. When Napoleon meets with any opposition, Dieudonné's eyes light up like the eyes of the kids in *Village of the Damned*. The power of Napoleon's gaze was famous, but this is a horror-film comedy routine. When he turns his piercing stare on them, rioting crowds back away, and even unruly generals do his bidding. Others don't need to be glared at: characters such as Fleuri (Nicolas Koline), the admiring scullion who later becomes an innkeeper, and his daughter, Violine (the lovely, teen-age Annabella), turn up from time to time, so they can symbolize the good common people and worship Napoleon from afar.

There is no doubt that Gance takes a mystical view of his hero. When Napoleon attacks the British, and the messy battle goes on for seventy-two hours and ends in hand-to-hand combat in rain and mud, a subtitle announces: "He is in the thick of fire. He is in his element." (Some of the night fighting scenes were originally in blue, others in red.) Everything is explained by "fate." Before Napoleon and Josephine have met, he is a young officer in the street outside a fortune-teller's shop, while she is inside being told that she will be a queen. Gance is shameless: everything is foretold, ordained, or revealed in a hideous presentiment. It's clear that Gance conceived of his huge cycle of films as a glorification of Genius. His hyperbolic romanticism knows no bounds: in one scene Napoleon stands alone on a peak overlooking the ocean, and a subtitle tells us that Ocean is his friend and they meet as equals. When Gance tries to "humanize" this hero, he shows him embarrassed and fumbling in his courtship of Josephine. We come away from a Griffith epic, such as *Intolerance,* or even *Orphans of the Storm* (which is also set in the French Revolution), with a feeling for the characters, and a sense of pleasure in the whole story, and memories of small, surprising moments. We come away from *Napoléon* exulting in Gance's extraordinary inventiveness and spirit. In the same sense that his Napoleon is the Revolution, Gance is the film we have been watching.

■   ■   ■

He can be a great show. When Napoleon is in Corsica, with a price on his head, he takes down the French flag, which he believes the Corsicans are unworthy of; he jumps from a building onto a horse and, clutching the flag, rides away to escape a large group of horsemen pursuing him. Suddenly we're in a Western chase, but in this Western the camera is more interested in the movement of the horses' legs than in the possibility that the posse might catch up to the hero. (For some of the inserts, Gance strapped the camera to the back of a horse.) Pursued all the way to the sea, Napoleon hops into a dinghy and unfurls the tricolor for a sail. It's a piece of flamboyance that makes one laugh and applaud. What follows is even higher on the hog: A sirocco comes up, and the little boat is flung about in the splashing waves—and we're flung about, too. Gance built an underwater camera, which, he said, he placed at the level of the waves, so the image would not be "that seen by a person looking at the waves, but rather that of one wave seen by another." This storm at sea is intercut with the political storm at the National Convention in Paris, with Danton orating and Robespierre crushing the Girondists. In order to produce a parallel sense of vertigo from the waves of the surging crowd, Gance mounted the camera on a pendulum, which swung over the extras' heads. It's a freak sequence: a forced metaphorical connection between two phenomena, and an essentially verbal metaphor besides. It's obvious and hokey, yet the effect is smashingly modern, with the swaying camera whipping us right into the movement of the crowd, and back and forth, in ever quicker shots. And then the two storms are superimposed. What we admire is, of course, Gance's zingy virtuosity.

In the first Gance picture I ever saw, his 1936 sound film *Un Grand Amour de Beethoven,* released here as *The Life and Loves of Beethoven,* the sequence of Beethoven going deaf was invested with so much passion that it was almost painful. Beethoven (the magnificent, plug-ugly Harry Baur) couldn't understand what was happening to him. Charging outside, with his big blunt face stricken, he could see the bells ringing, see the blacksmith at work, see the noisy washerwomen. But he couldn't hear anything—and we shared the silence with him. Then we heard a sudden pealing of bells, and all the other sounds that he was henceforth denied. The sequence was so emotionally devastating that when he swung a clenched fist at the camera as he died, his anger seemed completely just. Gance's 1922 *La Roue* has a comparable passage about the onset of its railwayman-protagonist's blindness. (The Russian giants of the twenties studied a print of Gance's original thirty-two-reel version, and this film's lightning-fast montages of engines and pistons, rails and wheels, were probably a chief influence on Russian montage.) Gance's 1937 sound remake of his anti-war film *J'Accuse* ends with a sequence so overpowering that it obliterates the rest of the film. In this finale, the war dead rise to confront the living; the mutilated, the crippled get up and march toward us. In George Romero's 1968 *Night of the Living Dead,* the onslaught of the dead is used for a gruesome horror effect; in Gance it's a nightmare miracle, and awesome. The soldiers just keep marching toward us—a vast army of the dead filling the screen.

Gance is a master of a certain kind of theatrical rhetoric; he must think in tropes. In *Napoléon,* at the climactic moments the eagle appears. It lights on the topmost part of a ship carrying Napoleon, it settles on a pole in the camp where he's sleeping after his victory over the English at Toulon, and, at the end, the eagle spreads its wings across the three screens.

■　■　■

All through *Napoléon,* you can see why Gance had to invent the Polyvision wide-screen process (which was the predecessor of Cinerama and Cinema-Scope). Whenever there's a mob onscreen, the action seems to be pushing against the sides of the frame. That square frame is like a straitjacket to Gance; you feel that he can't accept it and work within it—that he *has* to push it wider. I never got this sense of confinement from Griffith (who often used a flexible frame—blacking out the top and bottom for a proportionately wider image, or blacking out the sides for a narrow vertical image) or from Eisenstein or the other Russians. Gance needs a wider canvas because he just naturally tries to encompass more than the square can hold. Though he has a dazzling compositional sense, the halls with crowds seated or jumping to their feet look compressed and static. When, at the climax, Napoleon addresses his army in Italy and the screen opens up to triptych width, the squeezed look disappears and Gance's compositional style seems, at last, fulfilled. (At Radio City, three synchronized projectors were used, though something like this effect can—and probably will—be accomplished by putting the triple-width section on 70-mm film.) Napoleon reviews his troops, and we see the whole damned army stretched out over the landscape. It's like a photographic map—the country is laid out in front of us. We see the encampments, tents, the troops, and Napoleon himself, high on a peak, addressing them. And there is an effect that suggests 3-D (which Gance also experimented with while making this picture): several horses and riders cross in front of the vista and seem to ride right into the theatre. This concluding section is a triumph: the three images are sometimes one continuous panoramic view; at other times the center panel is complemented by the wings in a contrapuntal effect, or all three are different. And the extravagance is compounded by two, sometimes three, sets of superimpositions. (There were also three earlier, brief uses of the triptych width in *Napoléon,* but apparently Gance, despairing because it didn't seem that anyone would ever be interested in the footage, destroyed it.) Gance, the visionary who reached out to bring more and more into his frames (some scenes have as many as six thousand extras), must have felt a strong temperamental affinity with Napoleon, the visionary conqueror. Gance—he appears here, with gold loops in his ears, in full-screen closeups, as the handsome, lordly Saint-Just—has often been described as looking like an eagle.

■ ■ ■

One of the reasons that *Napoléon* failed with the public may be that Gance works on such a large scale that he uses his performers for their physiognomies—their look—rather than for any contribution they might make to the film as actors. We see them in luminous, expressive closeups—faces abstracted from the action—and we see them in long shots. But there is little of the middle distance, where we might get to know the characters they're playing. We don't find out what the Revolution is about or what Danton and Robespierre stand for. The kind of mind that thinks in tropes doesn't dramatize particulars. The crowds at the National Convention don't represent anything to us—they're just people milling around. They're illustrations of history. When Antonin Artaud, who plays Marat, appears, the Radio City audience applauds him for who he is; his acting wouldn't call up any cheers. Artaud gives a hyperactive, bulging-eyed performance (though he was gentle and superbly modulated in Dreyer's 1928 *The Passion of Joan of Arc*.) The thin, elegant Pierre Batcheff (he was the cyclist in the Buñuel-Dali 1928 *Un Chien Andalou*) plays Josephine's lover, General Hoche; he has almost nothing to do, but he does make you wonder why Josephine tosses him over for Nappy, who is still just an intense, glowering little nerd. Dieudonné (he looks like Rod Stewart on a stormy day) has presence, but he seems much older than Napoleon was at this time (all of twenty-six), and, with his pale eyes and thin, dark-lipsticked mouth, he's rather off-putting. This Napoleon may be fire and eagle and all, but we never get a sense of the man, or of the tactician, either. All we know is that his will is steely, his military plans are brilliant, he loves his mother, and he's on a divine mission—he's going to spread the French Revolution to other countries by conquering them. Gance doesn't seem to notice anything odd about the idea of bringing self-respect to people by defeating them in war.

There is a truly disingenuous sequence: Gance attempts to purify Napoleon's plans by a supernatural device. After the rush-rush wedding and a hurried night with his bride, Napoleon, at dawn, heads for Italy. (He allows himself only three months for its conquest.) But on the way, just after taking leave of Josephine, he stops at the empty Convention hall. It is inhabited by the phantoms of the guillotined Revolutionary leaders—Danton and the others. These dead speak to him: They tell him that the Revolution cannot prosper without a strong leader, and they ask him to be that leader. They tell him that the Revolution will die if it doesn't expand beyond France, and that he must spread it. And he solemnly promises these apparitions that he will liberate oppressed peoples and create a united Fatherland. (He was racing off to "liberate" Italy anyway, so it's rather funny that he reacts as if the dead had just laid this burden on him.)

■ ■ ■

Josephine (Gina Manès), who carries a lapdog, is a tough, worldly tart. Her brutal nature may perhaps show too clearly on the outside—she has a hard jaw, as if she'd been chewing on things too long. When Napoleon's face is in the center panel, with a globe of the world on a side panel, and then Josephine's face, in all its leering glitter, is superimposed on that globe, we are supposed to see that his pure dream of a universal state is being corrupted. She is the temptress who comes between him and his Destiny. The film ends with Napoleon still triumphant, though there are mystic forebodings of defeats to come. The strange thing about the structure is that, as everything has been set up, Napoleon should win out over his enemies. There is so little sense of political or military reality in this film that the only way Napoleon's defeats can be prefigured is by mystic hints and Josephine's enigmatic, dirty smile. It's as if Christ were done in by Eve.

■ ■ ■

At Radio City, *Napoléon* had the right setting and a great audience. I had seen the triptych section set up with three projectors and three little screens in the auditorium of the San Francisco Museum of Art in the forties, and the group of us there were wild-eyed with excitement about what we saw. We were only the lunatic fringe, though. At Radio City, there were as many people in the audience as there were on the screen, and for a spectacle film designed to work on mass emotions a big screen and a crowd make an enormous difference. During the two-storms sequence, you could feel a third storm—waves of audience response. It's inspiriting to be in a large audience so knowledgeable about movies that it reacts with surprise and excitement to each unusual technical device, and with enjoyment to the romantic flourishes. In the twenties and thirties, people were rebelling against the nineteenth-century sentiments expressed here (and talkies had brought in a new realism), and in the forties if the film had played to a large crowd it might have appeared obscene. But the picture's flowery pannationalism just seems a curiosity and a camp now. This could be the time for Gance, because there are so many more people now who recognize what he was doing technically. It could even be the right time for Gance the size freak, because after the years of TV and tiny art houses you begin to feel how much size matters. The score that Carmine Coppola conducted—and composed, with some acknowledged borrowings from Berlioz and others—helped the film enormously; over the years, I have seen *Napoléon* in several versions, and it never moved as fluently as it did with this music. I've never heard the score that Honegger wrote for the 1927 opening, or the new score that Carl Davis prepared for the London showings last year, but this one has pulse and spirit. (It's an incredible workout for the orchestra, and for the conductor, who must be close to seventy—four hours of almost continuous playing.) There was only one spot where I thought the synchronization of the score and the images failed: the organ interlude during the Battle of Toulon episode. An organ doesn't have the right sound for battle, or for councils of war, either. And even after Napoleon called for "Order, calm, silence" the organist was rushing on excitedly.

■　　■　　■

If a huge, hip audience can do wonders for a film, it can also expose blunders: when Charlotte Corday comes to murder Marat, she is ushered into the room where he is soaking in his bathtub; a curtain is drawn (as if we were at a theatrical performance), and then it's pulled back after he has been stabbed. Stage and screen conventions have got confused here, and the audience broke into laughter. (Marat's death is staged as a "living picture"—an exact re-creation of the famous painting.)

After the Terror, the subtitles inform us, there is a reaction of joy, and people celebrate at balls. The one that Napoleon goes to is the Victims' Ball, attended by those who have narrowly escaped the guillotine or lost relatives to it. Gance has shown a fine eye for beautiful women throughout, but suddenly he seems to have shifted centuries, because the sparkling-eyed beauties at this party carry on like flappers at a twenties artists' ball. The men are properly costumed, but the women are in the kind of dresses that go with cloches. Two of them sit in a swing high above the crowd, wearing only little wisps of clothing; others dance, bare-legged and bare-bottomed, with, here and there, a breast exposed. (This jazzy revel is reminiscent of the cubistic Charleston montage in Lubitsch's 1926 *So This Is Paris*, except there are no black musicians.) Watching this twenties orgy during the French Revolution, I thought it might have been Gance's gesture toward his backers—an obligatory scene, like the car chases that have been forced on Hollywood directors in recent years. But then I remembered (and found) a still of a shindig from Gance's 1935 *Lucrezia Borgia*, starring Edwige Feuillère, which I'd saved because the garlanded maidens dancing semi-nude had such a howling thirties look. Maybe Gance goes into little time warps.

Napoléon is full of aesthetic contradictions, and seeing it with an audience that enjoys them adds to the picture's freshness. When you watch a Gance film, you're seeing a film made by a man who was born in the nineteenth century (in 1889) and who mastered a twentieth-century art while remaining a romantic dandy of the past. Gance is still ahead of most film artists, yet he has always been behind movie audiences. He's a double anachronism, a living time warp. This man, who sold his first scripts in 1909, once wrote a play for Sarah Bernhardt, and his thinking (if his later movies, such as the 1964 *Cyrano et D'Artagnan,* accurately express it) hasn't changed. But he's such a passionate wizard that in his hands the old declamatory conventions sometimes become iconographic right before your eyes. There are masters whose technique is invisible (Renoir, De Sica, Satyajit Ray), so that what you respond to is the stories and the people. And there are masters of bravura, such as Gance and Welles, who often seem wildly "cinematic" because they are essentially theatrical. This isn't a negative observation: it may be that they love movies so much because they loved the theatre.

The New Yorker, February 16, 1981

ABOUT CHRISTOPHER WALKEN IN
THE DOGS OF WAR

The casting of Walken in the lead gives this picture the fuse it needs; without him—with some stalwart, tough-looking actor—it might seem just a crisp example of an action film. But Walken, with his pale, flat-faced mask of pain and his lithe movements, suggests a restless anger. His eyes look spooked, like a cat's, and you feel he'd be cold to the touch.

The New Yorker, March 23, 1981

ATLANTIC CITY

Burt Lancaster started out, back in the 1946 *The Killers,* as a great specimen of hunkus Americanus. In Louis Malle's new comedy, *Atlantic City,* from a script by John Guare, Lancaster uses his big, strong body so expressively that if this were a stage performance the audience would probably give him a standing ovation. I don't see how he could be any better. He plays Lou, an old-timer who tries to keep up appearances; he irons his one good silk tie before going outside. Still dreaming of the good old days, when he was a flunky and bodyguard for big-time racketeers, Lou scrounges for a living as a numbers runner, making his rounds of Atlantic City's black slums and picking up bets of fifty cents or a dollar. He also takes handouts—and abuse—from Grace (Kate Reid), the widow of a mobster he used to work for. She has an apartment in the same building where he has a small, seedy room; she stays in bed, pampering herself, while he shops and cooks for her and walks her dog—a tiny poodle, which he hates. Grace is a hypochondriac and complainer, and she razzes him mercilessly; he accepts her reproaches, though he snarls to himself in weary resentment. You sense that he barely hears her anymore; Lou's thoughts are elsewhere. When he's in his room and looks out the window, across the airshaft, he can see into the apartment where Sally (Susan Sarandon) lives; hiding to the side, he watches her nightly ablutions when she comes home from her waitress work at the Oyster Bar in the Resorts International casino. She puts a tape of *Norma* on her cassette-player, cuts lemons in half, and rubs the juice onto her upper body. Excited, Lou hurries down to Grace's apartment, puts a record on, and crawls into bed with her.

Lancaster's acting in *The Killers* wasn't at all bad, but his physical presence was so powerful in the busy years that followed that he became a caricature of an action star. Sometimes he was a satiric caricature (as in the 1952 *The Crimson Pirate*), and sometimes he was an impressive, highly sexual man of action (as in the 1953 *From Here to Eternity*), but in his many attempts to extend his range beyond action roles—in *Come Back, Little Sheba* (1952), *The Rose Tattoo* (1955), *The Rainmaker* (1956), *Separate Tables* (1958), *The Devil's Disciple* (1959), *The Young Savages* (1961), *Judgment at Nuremberg* (1961), *Birdman of Alcatraz* (1962), *A Child Is Waiting* (1963), and, most notably, in *Sweet Smell of Success* (1956)—you could often see him straining for seriousness, and it shrivelled him. (When Lancaster put on a pair of specs, he looked as if he'd been bled by leeches.) Probably no other major star took so many chances, and a couple of times—as the prince in Visconti's *The Leopard* (1963), and as the patriarch in Bertolucci's *1900* (1976)—he came through with a new weight of emotion. In those pictures, he seemed able to use his bull-like physicality with a new dignity and awareness. He was more physical than ever, but physical in the way that Anna Magnani (with whom he was teamed in *The Rose Tattoo*) was—battered, larger than life, vain, naked. In shallow action roles, he played bloody but unbowed; when he was working with Visconti or Bertolucci, he wasn't afraid to be bloody and bowed. And that's how he is here, but more so, because this time he isn't playing a strong man brought down by age and social changes: he's a man who was never anything much—he was always a little too soft inside—and Grace won't let him forget it.

Though I have a better time in the theatre at John Guare's plays than I do at the plays of any other contemporary American, I would not have guessed that his charmed, warped world and his dialogue, which is full of imagery, could be so successfully brought to the screen. In a Guare play, the structure isn't articulated. There's nothing to hold the bright pieces together but his nerve and his instincts; when they're in high gear, the play has the excitement of discovery—which you don't get in "well-crafted" plays. You're not stuck with the usual dramatic apparatus—the expository dialogue and the wire-pulling to get the characters into the planned situations. Instead, you get gags, which prove to be the explanations. *Anything* may turn up in a Guare play. In Joseph Papp's Public Theatre production of Guare's *Marco Polo Sings a Solo,* set on an Arctic island in 1999, Anne Jackson, who played Joel Grey's mother, revealed that her son was the first person in history to have only one parent: she was a transsexual, she explained, and had conceived him with semen saved from before her sex-change operation. In the same play, another character talked about Chekhov's *The Three Sisters:* "Those poor girls, all the time trying to get to Moscow. The town they lived in was only forty-eight miles from Moscow. In 1999 that town is probably part of greater downtown Moscow. They were in Moscow all the time." Guare's vaudeville jokes subvert traditional conceptions of drama. Anyone who has ever been embarrassed for the actors who had to fling a prop dead bird around the stage in *The Sea Gull* would have appreciated Anne Jackson's aside to the audience apropos of some similar props: "I don't know much about symbols, but I'd say that when frozen flamingos fall out of the sky, good times are not in store." In a foreword to the published version of his play *The House of Blue Leaves,* Guare wrote that what had got him out of a creative cul-de-sac was watching Olivier perform on successive nights in Strindberg's *The Dance of Death* and Feydeau's *A Flea in Her Ear.* In his imagination, they blended, he said, and became one play, and he asked himself why Strindberg and Feydeau shouldn't get married, or at least live together.

I have resorted to quoting from *Marco Polo* because I would like to suggest Guare's comic style without uncorking *Atlantic City.* Let me just indicate how the jokes function: Lou reminisces about the glories of this resort town in the days when there were real songs, like "Flat Foot Floogie with the Floy Floy," and he adds, "The Atlantic Ocean was something then." You laugh in recognition that for him life has lost its savor. Guare's one-liners are more deeply zany than we're accustomed to. His characters sound as if they had all invented themselves and their life histories right on the spot. And Guare has a way of shaping a funny line of dialogue so it goes loop-the-loop into pathos. Sometimes I think that his is the only kind of theatrical pathos that's really enjoyable; it erupts suddenly when a character's invention can't go any further and he's left with truth. But it's still part of a gag. Kate Reid's Grace, lying amid boxes of chocolate and rose satin quilted covers, may remind the lucky few who saw Guare's most intense and macabre play, *Bosoms and Neglect*, of her performance as the bedridden, blind, and cancerous old Irish mother, Henny. (When Henny is in the hospital for surgery, her son visits a woman he picked up in Rizzoli's—a blond bibliophile who tries to seduce him with her first editions. He describes his mother's torments, and she cries, "I suddenly have this image of being blind. Oh God. Never to be able to browse.") Guare was one of the three writers who worked with Miloš Forman on the 1971 *Taking Off*, but the film's sensibility was Forman's. *Atlantic City* is a collaboration much like that of Elia Kazan and Tennessee Williams on, say, *Baby Doll*. Louis Malle has entered into Guare's way of seeing—a mixture of observation, flights of invention, satire, perversity, anecdote, fable. And depth of feeling—what Lancaster, in the finest performance he has ever given (with the possible exception of his work in *1900*), brings to the film. And he brings it to the jokes.

Near the beginning of the film, one of the vast, curvy old Baghdad-by-the-sea buildings that date from Atlantic City's days as a resort community is dynamited; this rock-candy relic is making way for the new hotel-casinos, which have been shooting up since New Jersey legalized gambling there, in 1976. (It was chosen partly because it's on an island and can be closed off from the mainland.) Malle's Atlantic City is very different from the seedy, decrepit one in which Bob Rafelson shot *The King of Marvin Gardens*, in 1972. The destruction and construction that go on in all cities are accelerated in the new Atlantic City; it suggests a giant movie lot, where sets are built and struck. This spa that became a racketeers' paradise during Prohibition and is now on its chaotic way to becoming Vegas with a beach is an improbable place; it gives a hallucinatory texture to the characters' lives. And it's the ideal place for a Guare comedy—everything arriving and departing in one fell swoop. Atlantic City is the film's controlling metaphor. Malle and Guare must have let the city itself set the motifs: demolition and construction; decay and renewal; water, baths, ablutions; luck. The city says so much on its own that the moviemakers don't have to press down for meanings; if anything, they need to hold back (and they do).

When the rambling pleasure palace crumbles, the film takes up the story of another relic—Lou. The movie is a lyric farce, in which Lou and Sally, and Grace also, realize their dreams, through a series of accidents and several varieties of chicanery. Sally has been training to become a croupier, under the tutelage of the Frenchman (Michel Piccoli) who gave her the Elizabeth Harwood tape of *Norma*. Her plans are disrupted when her wormy husband (Robert Joy) hitchhikes into town with her pale, sweetly zonked younger sister Chrissie (Hollis McLaren), who is hugely pregnant by him. They turn up, scuzzy from the road and with their packs on their backs, at the sleek casino where Sally works. Sally's husband expects her to let them crash at her place until he can dispose of a bundle of cocaine that he stole in Philadelphia. Once he arrives, nobody in the movie seems to have any principles or to have heard of honesty. (Chrissie doesn't even believe in gravity.) Lou—through a fluke—gets hold of the money from the cocaine, and starts behaving like the sport he has always wanted to be. He spreads the wealth around and squires Sally to an expensive restaurant; she's eager to learn more about the world, and, little as he knows, he's a fount of knowledge compared with her.

The role of the ignorant Sally, a back-country girl from Saskatchewan who hopes to work her way to Monte Carlo, is essentially that of Gabrielle in *The Petrified Forest,* and, for once, Susan Sarandon's googly-eyed, slightly stupefied look seems perfect. She doesn't rattle off her lines in her usual manner; she seems to respond to the freshness and lilt of the dialogue. In Malle's last film, *Pretty Baby,* she was mysteriously beautiful when she was posing nude for photographs, but she gave an inexplicably petulant and vapid performance; she did so much ruminating she was cowlike. Susan Sarandon has sometimes come through in strange circumstances, though; the permutations of her rattle provided the sprightliest moments of *The Other Side of Midnight.* Maybe she seems so skillful here because this is the best part she's ever had on the screen. Her double takes are very delicate; she keeps you tuned in to her feelings all the time. Sally's expression is frazzled yet affectionate when she looks at her Hare Krishna–ite little sister. Hollis McLaren (she was the half-mad girl in *Outrageous!*) brings a winsome dippiness to the role of gullible Chrissie, a flower child born into the wrong era. Simplicity like Chrissie's seems almost soothing, but not if you're her sister and don't know what to do with her. What can you do with a pregnant angel?

When I see a Guare play, I almost always feel astonished; I never know where he's going until he gets there. Then everything ties together. He seems to have an intuitive game plan. That's how this film works, too. It takes Malle a little while to set up the crisscrossing of the ten or twelve major characters, but once he does you can begin to respond to the interior, poetic logic that holds this movie together. By the second half, *Atlantic City* is operating by its own laws in its own world, and it has a lovely fizziness. Everything goes wrong and comes out right. It's no accident that Guare said Feydeau had helped him out of a cul-de-sac. We get the pleasure of seeing everything sorted out, as it is in a classic farce, except that the perfect pairings, the slippers that fit, the kindnesses rewarded have the dadaist quality of having been plucked out of the air.

The casting is superb, and each time a performer reappears you look forward to what he's going to do this time. There are just a few minor disappointments. Acting in English, Piccoli doesn't have his usual nuanced control (he overemphasizes his lines), but he certainly knows how to play a practiced European lecher; in one scene he circles around Sally, like a weary dancer. A murder sequence in a hydraulic parking structure is perhaps too tricky; it looks as if it was a bitch to shoot and edit. But there are almost constant small pleasures, such as Lou's meeting an old pal, Buddy (Sean Sullivan), who has become a washroom attendant, and swapping stories, and a hospital sequence, in which Robert Goulet, on behalf of Resorts International, presents the casino's check for a quarter of a million dollars to the Atlantic City Medical Center, the Frank Sinatra Wing, and sings to an audience of patients brought down to the lobby to make the presentation a media event. (It's like an epic-size Bill Murray routine.) One sequence appears to drift, but then has a great conclusion: Sally and Lou go to the house that she plans to share with nine other croupiers-in-training. (Each of the ten is studying to deal a different game—baccarat, blackjack, and so on.) Sally takes Lou to the room she needs to paint, and when they're alone he tells her that he watches her at night. She is moved and he can see that she is going to let him make love to her. He pushes her blouse down from her shoulders and looks at her ripe young flesh, and his watery eyes are full of reverence and regret.

This picture has just about everything that *Pretty Baby*, which was also made in this country, and in English, lacked. Every line of dialogue in *Pretty Baby* was stiff. It was clear that the person who made the film was a director, but it was hard to believe that he'd ever worked with actors before. In *Atlantic City*, Louis Malle is in full control and at his ease, and his collaboration with John Guare produces a rich, original comic tone. Sometimes the most pleasurable movies seem very slight, because they don't wham you on the noggin. Malle's skill shows in the way he keeps this picture in its frame of reference, and gives it its own look. Visually, it's extraordinary, though in a way that doesn't hit you on the noggin, either. The lighting is vivid but muted and indirect. A whole room may be in focus, yet with very little light—no more than the modulated light you see on cloudy days. The cinematographer, Richard Ciupka, is a young Québécois (the film was financed partly by Canadian funds); his work here suggests Storaro—it's like studio lighting but softer. The whole city seems to be in deep focus; you're sharply aware of old and new, age and youth. The ocean breezes are chilling to Lou; he's bundled up as he makes his rounds. But by the end he enjoys looking at the ocean again. The movie is a prankish wish-fulfillment fantasy about prosperity: what it does to cities, what it can do for people. There's a closing image of a massive building—the wrecking ball keeps pounding it, and it keeps refusing to yield. When you leave the theatre, you may feel light-headed, as if there were no problems in the world that couldn't be solved.

The New Yorker, April 6, 1981

EXCALIBUR
BOORMAN'S PLUNGE

John Boorman is an intoxicated moviemaker, with a wonderful kind of zeal—a greed to encompass more and more and more in his pictures. His action scenes are rarely comprehensible. He can't get any suspense going. He doesn't seem to understand the first thing about melodrama. He has no particular affection for humor. And his skills are eccentric and his ideas ponderously woozy. But I don't know of any other director who puts such a burnish on his obsessions. Moviemaking is clearly the first of them, with mythology a close second. I would never have imagined that I could enjoy a retelling of the Arthurian legends which was soaked in Jung and scored to themes from Carl Orff's "Carmina Burana" and Wagner, but Boorman's *Excalibur* has its own kind of crazy integrity. At first, I couldn't quite believe what I was seeing: a serious, R-rated fairy tale. Boorman had been trying to get this project financed for the past decade, and he'd been mulling it over for much longer than that. No doubt he got the go-ahead because of the success of *Star Wars,* which is essentially the Arthurian story set in "a galaxy far, far away," but he has done the legends straight. Children may be enthusiastic about *Excalibur,* but it hasn't been made as a family movie, and though Excalibur is clearly The Force, symbolized in the magic sword, which is effective only when used for good purposes, Boorman doesn't linger on that. He doesn't bring a comic-strip sensibility to the material, and he doesn't make the narrative easy to understand, in the manner of the Hollywood *Knights of the Round Table* (1953), with Robert Taylor as Lancelot and Ava Gardner as the Queen. What Boorman has in mind is probably closer to *The Seventh Seal.*

He just plunges into the Dark Ages, smiting us with raging battles, balls of flame, mists of dragon's breath, knights with horns and tusks jutting out of their armored heads, and battle-axes that hack off limbs, which seem to ricochet off the armor. He sails through the Arthurian stories, from Arthur's conception and birth to his death, without pausing even for the awesome, triumphant moment when the boy Arthur pulls the sword from the stone where his dying father had placed it. This scene is staged with townspeople gathered, some saying that his pulling out the sword means he's the King, some saying that it doesn't and he isn't, and with all this clutter and dissension there's no tingle at seeing the visualization of one of the high points of fairy lore. Something in Boorman must rebel at the thought of a dramatic climax. The film is almost all action, with very little at stake for us, because we hardly have a chance to meet the characters before they're off and running. The hackings aren't any more upsetting than the hackings in *Monty Python and the Holy Grail;* in fact, the ones in *Monty Python* may have been more disturbing, because they were funny and gruesome at the same time. In *Excalibur,* they're neither. You don't see the limbs or heads that are lopped off; you see the red-stained armor. The hackings are part of the visual texture, along with the spiked elbows and the jutting metal earmuffs that look as if they could kill a stag at bay.

The imagery is impassioned, and it has a hypnotic quality. You feel there's something going on under the narrative; you're very much aware of shine and glitter, of hair and skin—the imagery has a tactile life of its own. Boorman doesn't bother with episodes that don't stir him; there's no dull connective tissue. The film is like Flaubert's more exotic fantasies—one lush, enraptured scene after another. The images are crystal-clear, gold-tinted, jewelled; it's a stained-glass movie. But, of course, the Flaubert exotica—such as *Salammbô,* which, as Francis Steegmuller writes, covers a great literary canvas with "the colors of violence and physical suffering, and above all with the color of blood"—are the ones that many readers find too rich.

The dialogue in *Excalibur* is near-atrocious; written by Rospo Pallenberg and Boorman, it reveals what Boorman thinks he's doing. He thinks he's showing us the primal harmony of man and the magic forces of earth and air, and then man's loss of magic, which passes into the unconscious. Jung believed that his investigations carried on the work of Merlin and the alchemists, and Merlin (Nicol Williamson) is the presiding spirit of this movie—its resident pundit and ironic relief. He's presented as the peacemaker: he counsels first Uther Pendragon (Gabriel Byrne) and then Uther's son, Arthur (Nigel Terry), against violence, and makes deals with them, granting them magical favors in exchange for their behaving peaceably. Wearing a silver skullcap with an encrusted jewel—a third eye—in the middle of his forehead (the cap could be a leftover from Max von Sydow's Ming the Merciless headgear in *Flash Gordon*), Merlin is both seer and jester. He's always threatening to disappear for an aeon or two, or for eternity, but he keeps showing up to tell us how despondent he is about men's brutality and his own ineffectuality. He's a soft touch—he does favors that he knows he shouldn't, and they have fatal consequences. He's also a real talker, Mercutio-style, and he informs us of the meaning of what we're seeing. "The one God comes to drive out the many gods," he announces, thus presaging the ascendancy of Christianity, and soon King Arthur dispatches his knights on the quest for the Holy Grail. Merlin's speeches are wisdom droppings. Nicol Williamson toys with them; he uses a lilt and his deepest basso growl, but he's better off when he gets to do Gaelic incantations and we can just enjoy his vocal purring. It's as sensual as a love aria sung in a language that we don't know a word of.

Boorman's last two movies—*Zardoz* and *Exorcist II: The Heretic*—were also attempts at mythmaking, and we might have considered them classics if we hadn't known English. If we'd been able to imagine that the words were as lyrical and hallucinogenic as the images, we might have acclaimed Boorman instead of falling on the floor laughing (as a friend assures me he did when he saw *Zardoz*) or throwing things at the screen (which happened at some theatres showing *The Heretic).* Boorman is telling the Arthurian legends straight, all right—as straight as he can ever do anything. One of the great things about modern movies which distinguish them from the pictures that used to be made by the studio factories is that the artists' nuttiness comes out now. If they're mediocrities, their nutty movies can be much worse than the movies that used to be patched and smoothed. But if they're giants, their work may have a virtuoso looniness all its own. Boorman is a giant. But he's a sensualist with images and a pedant with words. It isn't enough for him just to present an immensely complicated series of legends; he also tries to build in a Jungian interpretation, so that the movie, adapted from Sir Thomas Malory's *Le Morte d'Arthur,* will demonstrate what man lost when he gained modern consciousness—how he has never been "whole" since, and all that jazz. Boorman's self-seriousness gets in the way of his artistry. In *The Heretic,* the dialogue and how it was directed were ruinous; Richard Burton's recitatives were theological gibberish. Merlin's fanciful remarks are far more entertaining, though the central role that Boorman gives him takes time and emphasis away from Arthur and his knights.

Boorman appears to have got so caught up in his theory of the lost magical Oneness that he leaves a gaping hole in the middle of the Arthurian stories. When Arthur has become a man of peace and his kingdom (roughly Europe) is flourishing and his court at Camelot is the center of culture, where's the chivalry? We get only a few glimpses of Camelot in long shot, and when we're inside, the knights look bored. (There was more even to the Kennedy Administration—they gave a few good parties.) We don't experience the realization of the paradisiacal dream, and so we're not horrified by its collapse. But the Arthurian stories support Boorman's visual style much more gracefully than his last two films did. I loved watching *The Heretic,* but I couldn't recommend it to anyone without starting to grin shamefacedly. *Excalibur* is much simpler: it spans three generations—first Uther and his feuding with the other Celtic lords, then Arthur's reign, and, finally, the challenge to Arthur's power by his demonic son, Mordred. The movie might have been clearer still if the knights had had their names embroidered on their chain mail or painted on their foreheads. (Who is to say that this wasn't sixth-century practice?) Since the actors are almost all new to movies, it takes a while to sort the knights out.

The actors become more attractive and much more impressive as they age and we get to know them better. This is particularly true of Nigel Terry's Arthur and of Perceval (played by Paul Geoffrey)—undistinguished youths who grow shaggy beards and develop presence and depth. (When Paul Geoffrey, who gives perhaps the most affecting performance, is bearded, he resembles Francis Ford Coppola.) Boorman seems to be caught in a bind, though. He can visualize what the men were doing in the sixth century— jousting, riding, and, no doubt, polishing their armor. (Lancelot's has such a silvery-white gleam that he can't have had time for much else). But what were the women up to? Nothing but mischief, apparently, and Boorman can't seem to get them matched to the same century as the men. How do you get pretty women to look like barbarians? Boorman's Guenevere (Cherie Lunghi) is a hot chick with a mop of gorgeously dishevelled curly dark hair; she's like the young Susan Hayward wearing a Pre-Raphaelite gown to a disco joint. The Lady of the Lake floating in the water might be Bo Derek. And as the treacherous Morgana (who in Hollywood versions used to be called Morgan le Fay) Helen Mirren is such a slinky witch that she looks as if she were practicing to play opposite Snow White in gay-bar theatricals. (Nobody in the movie seems to have any fun except Merlin and Morgana when they're huddled together talking about potions and spells. There's a conspiratorial intimacy between them; he's like a master cook imparting the secrets of the kitchen to a guileful apprentice.)

Somehow—maybe by sheer force of will—Boorman keeps the women's scenes from collapsing into camp. He needs the women; they're essential to the stories, because they're the source of evil. The Arthurian legends, like the stories of Helen of Troy and of Adam and Eve, are repositories of a peculiarly male mythology: woman the temptress causes man to fall from grace, to fight and kill. Yet though Boorman is in love with images and the whole movie has an erotic sheen, the adultery that shakes the kingdom is almost chaste. When hot little Guenevere follows Lancelot (Nicholas Clay) into the forest and chums up with him, they look so innocent, curled up together naked, like babes in the wood, that you can't accept the idea that this trivial frolic destroys the Golden Age of Camelot and brings starvation and pestilence on the land. The effect is altogether disproportionate to the cause, and you feel that something is off, that something is missing. No matter how this adultery was presented, it might be difficult for modern audiences to accept it as earthshaking, but Boorman makes it just about impossible. What's off, I think, is the scale of the characters.

The film's Germanic-Byzantine-Celtic style often suggests Fritz Lang's *Siegfried* and *Kriemhild's Revenge,* which were also serious dream-world epics. There's no problem of disproportion between action and consequences in Lang's movies, though, because the characters are scaled heroically. Boorman is telling magical, heroic tales about men and women as large as gods, but he has populated the screen with the kids next door: they're not big enough in spirit, in aspirations, in dreams, or in passions for the myths built on their adventures. The stories are of characters who are sorcerers or part phantom, part man, or who assume different guises. Arthur is himself born of magic: Uther persuades Merlin to transform him into the likeness of the husband of the dancer Igrayne (Katrine Boorman), so that he can sleep with her. Arthur's son, Mordred (Robert Addie), is conceived through a similar magical deception, concocted by Morgana, who is Arthur's half sister as well as the mother of his son. When Mordred is fully grown, he wears golden spiked armor and, on his head, a gold gargoyle mask that his own sneering mouth completes. This apparition of evil comes closer to mythological scale than Arthur or Lancelot or Guenevere or any of the others do.

Love and lust are so human that they're easy to forgive; the picture doesn't seem to have a real issue. You think, Is that what the Arthurian legends come down to—not gods, just these little people with their warts? Boorman denies us the elation that we expect to experience at the end of a heroic story. He has made the characters so small that the myths themselves shrink in his telling. The picture gives us a different kind of elation, though. The Dark Ages section, with its armored brutes—they're like crustaceans tearing each other apart—is a thrilling piece of moviemaking. The second and third sections don't have the same concentration, but they do have shots—such as the one of the aged Arthur and his aged knights riding through a Klimt-like grove of flowering trees—with the mystic ambience of silent-movie fairy tales. If *Excalibur* is a lamebrainstorm of a movie, it's at least a genuine storm. There's a stubborn, freakish discipline in the way Boorman refuses to hold the iridescent images for the extra beat that would make an audience exclaim at their beauty. Even when there's an effect that might make the audience's flesh tingle—like the scene on a hill when the knights stand in the ring that will soon become the emblem of their fellowship—Boorman barely waits for you to take it in. Where Fritz Lang would let you bask in the imagery, Boorman has so much he wants to do that he hurries you past. Was there really an iron snout protruding from someone's face armor? Those slimy creatures that crowded around Merlin as he rested in the shadowy foliage—were they his familiars? And when his eyes turned that dark, evil red, what tricks was he up to? Which were the knights hanging on the tree, where Morgana had trapped them? The picture moves along so inexorably, with lances going through chests in barbaric, orange-amber landscapes, that there isn't time to absorb all the components of the shots. When Merlin leads Morgana down into some dank rotten place—a grotto in the netherworld—the set could almost be an homage to Fritz Lang and his great designers. Boorman's cinematographer, Alex Thompson, his production designer, Anthony Pratt, and Trevor Jones, who prepared the score and conducted it, must have given him their fealty as well as their talent, because amazingly, he does this kind of spectacle on the (relative) cheap. Using the Irish landscape and the Ardmore Studios, near Dublin, he is able to do for ten million dollars what would probably cost at least twice that if it was attempted here. At times, I was aware that there weren't quite as many extras as we're used to seeing, and there's a little joke near the end: the dragon's breath comes out of the old hag Morgana, and Arthur, who is leading his handful of surviving knights in a battle with Mordred's men, says, "In this fog, they won't know how few of us there are." It sounds like a reproach to the production manager.

Boorman's medieval battles don't have the same kind of impact as the great battle in the mud in Welles's *Falstaff;* every shot in the *Falstaff* battle scenes registers in your mind and helps to build the sequence. Boorman doesn't build. *Excalibur* is all images flashing by—ravishing images—and though we can't retain them, we drink them in. Each, in some weird way, seems to be on its own. This may help to explain the film's hypnotic effect: the events keep gliding into each other. We miss the dramatic intensity that we expect the stories to have, but there's always something to look at. The images keep coming, and the cadences are bizarrely even. Every now and then, there's an inchoate swelling—as in the royal-wedding sequence, where the sensuousness of metal and flesh makes you feel that something might be about to explode. Boorman sets an aestheticized mood, and by quivering, wiredrawn control he sustains it. At times, he's doing something close to free-associating visually. It's as if he were guiding us down a magic corridor and kept parting the curtains in front of us.

The New Yorker, April 20, 1981

FROM WHIPPED

The marketing executives are the new high priests of the movie business. It's natural. They're handling important sums of money. And they dispense the money dramatically, in big campaigns that flood out over the country. It's not unusual for more to be spent on marketing a picture than on making it, and this could become commonplace. (Everybody takes it for granted that more is spent selling soap than manufacturing it.) Right now, the easier a project looks to market, the easier it is to finance. And the scope of what these priests think they can sell becomes narrower all the time. Except for the occasional prestige picture that offers middle-class group therapy (*Ordinary People, The Four Seasons*), it's all fantasy. There isn't a human being on the screen. Having lost the habitual moviegoers, the studio heads have no confidence that if they approve projects they like, an audience will be attracted; they're trapped by empirical evidence to the contrary. And so they listen to the marketing men, with their priestly jargon—"normatives," "skewed," "bimodal audience." The mysterious phrases are soothing to the worried studio heads. And when the new geniuses are given what they want—comic-strip pulp or slobby horror—they swing into action heroically. Daggers menace us in TV commercials, magazines, and newspapers, and *sometimes* the slob movies do become hits. But if you boil out the feathers what it comes down to is: When there's a flop, the marketing men cluck their tongues and say, "Well, boys, the picture just didn't have it." When there's a big hit, the marketing men pound their chests like King Kong and say, "Boy, did we know how to sell it!"

These marketing divisions are a relatively new development. (In earlier years, there were two much smaller departments—advertising and sales.) Their growing power isn't in any special effectiveness in selling pictures; it's in their ability to keep pictures that don't lend themselves to an eye-popping thirty-second commercial from being made or, if they're made, from being heard of. In the new Hollywood wisdom, anything to do with people's lives belongs on TV. (As a result, television now makes contact with us in ways that movies no longer do.)

Like poor relations, the print media are the residual legatees of the huge marketing campaigns for pictures. The thinking is that anything associated with a big new hit will become a hot ticket. So magazine editors, ever eager to increase their newsstand sales, prepare their cover stories. Alan Alda, publicizing *The Four Seasons,* is the perfect cover boy for the women's magazines; if his film makes money, the writers and editors will feel they guessed right. I can't think of a single occasion when a small movie that really needed help got a slick-magazine cover, no matter how much the in-house critic liked it. The magazines try to ride on a hit picture's tail wind.

The New Yorker, June 15, 1981

BLOW OUT
PORTRAIT OF THE ARTIST AS A YOUNG GADGETEER

At forty, Brian De Palma has more than twenty years of moviemaking behind him, and he has been growing better and better. Each time a new film of his opens, everything he has done before seems to have been preparation for it. With *Blow Out,* starring John Travolta and Nancy Allen, which he wrote and directed, he has made his biggest leap yet. If you know De Palma's movies, you have seen earlier sketches of many of the characters and scenes here, but they served more limited—often satirical—purposes. *Blow Out* isn't a comedy or a film of the macabre; it involves the assassination of the most popular candidate for the Presidency, so it might be called a political thriller, but it isn't really a genre film. For the first time, De Palma goes inside his central character—Travolta as Jack, a sound-effects specialist. And he stays inside. He has become so proficient in the techniques of suspense that he can use what he knows more expressively. You don't see set pieces in *Blow Out*—it flows, and everything that happens seems to go right to your head. It's hallucinatory, and it has a dreamlike clarity and inevitability, but you'll never make the mistake of thinking that it's only a dream. Compared with *Blow Out,* even the good pictures that have opened this year look dowdy. I think De Palma has sprung to the place that Altman achieved with films such as *McCabe & Mrs. Miller* and *Nashville* and that Coppola reached with the two *Godfather* movies—that is, to the place where genre is transcended and what we're moved by is an artist's vision. And Travolta, who appeared to have lost his way after *Saturday Night Fever,* makes his own leap—right back to the top, where he belongs. Playing an adult (his first), and an intelligent one, he has a vibrating physical sensitivity like that of the very young Brando.

Jack, the sound-effects man, who works for an exploitation moviemaker in Philadelphia, is outside the city one night recording the natural rustling sounds. He picks up the talk of a pair of lovers and the hooting of an owl, and then the quiet is broken by the noise of a car speeding across a bridge, a shot, a blowout, and the crash of the car to the water below. He jumps into the river and swims to the car; the driver—a man—is clearly dead, but a girl (Nancy Allen) trapped inside is crying for help. Jack dives down for a rock, smashes a window, pulls her out, and takes her to a hospital. By the time she has been treated, and the body of the driver—the governor, who was planning to run for President—has been brought in, the hospital has filled with police and government officials. Jack's account of the shot before the blowout is brushed aside, and he is given a high-pressure lecture by the dead man's aide (John McMartin). He's told to forget that the girl was in the car; it's better to have the governor die alone—it protects his family from embarrassment. Jack instinctively objects to this coverup but goes along with it. The girl, Sally, who is sedated and can barely stand, is determined to get away from the hospital; the aide smuggles both her and Jack out, and Jack takes her to a motel. Later, when he matches his tape to the pictures taken by Manny Karp (Dennis Franz), a photographer who also witnessed the crash, he has strong evidence that the governor's death wasn't an accident. The pictures, though, make it appear that the governor was alone in the car; there's no trace of Sally.

Blow Out is a variation on Antonioni's *Blow-Up* (1966), and the core idea probably comes from the compound joke in De Palma's 1968 film *Greetings:* A young man tries to show his girlfriend enlarged photographs that he claims reveal figures on the "grassy knoll," and he announces, "This will break the Kennedy case wide open." Bored, she says, "I saw *Blow-Up*—I know how this comes out. It's all blurry—you can't tell a thing." But there's nothing blurry in this new film. It's also a variation on Coppola's *The Conversation* (1974), and it connects almost subliminally with recent political events—with Chappaquiddick and with Nelson Rockefeller's death. And as the film proceeds, and the murderous zealot Burke (John Lithgow) appears, it also ties in with the "clandestine operations" and "dirty tricks" of the Nixon years. It's a Watergate movie and on paper it might seem to be just a political melodrama, but it has an intensity that makes it unlike any other political film. If you're in a vehicle that's skidding into a snowbank or a guardrail, your senses are awakened, and in the second before you hit you're acutely, almost languorously aware of everything going on around you—it's the trancelike effect sometimes achieved on the screen by slow motion. De Palma keeps our senses heightened that way all through *Blow Out;* the entire movie has the rapt intensity that he got in the slow-motion sequences in *The Fury* (1978). Only now De Palma can do it at normal speed.

This is where all that preparation comes in. There are rooms seen from above—an overhead shot of Jack surrounded by equipment, another of Manny Karp sprawled on his bed—that recall De Palma's use of overhead shots in *Get to Know Your Rabbit* (1972). He goes even further with the split-screen techniques he used in *Dressed to Kill* (1980); now he even uses dissolves into the split screen—it's like a twinkle in your thought processes. And the circling camera that he practiced with in *Obsession* (1976) is joined by circling sound, and Jack—who takes refuge in circuitry—is in the middle. De Palma has been learning how to make every move of the camera signify just what he wants it to, and now he has that knowledge at his fingertips. The pyrotechnics and the whirlybird camera are no longer saying "Look at me"; they give the film authority. When that hooting owl fills the side of the screen and his head spins around, you're already in such a keyed-up, exalted state that he might be in the seat next to you. The cinematographer, Vilmos Zsigmond, working with his own team of assistants, does night scenes that look like paintings on black velvet so lush you could walk into them, and surreally clear daylight vistas of the city—you see buildings a mile away as if they were in a crystal ball in your hand. The colors are deep, and not tropical, exactly, but fired up, torrid. *Blow Out* looks a lot like *The Fury;* it has that heat, but with greater depth and definition. It's sleek and it glows orange, like the coils of a heater or molten glass—as if the light were coming from behind the screen or as if the screen itself were plugged in. And because the story centers on sounds there is great care for silence. It's a movie made by perfectionists (the editor is De Palma's longtime associate Paul Hirsch, and the production design is by Paul Sylbert), yet it isn't at all fussy. De Palma's good, loose writing gives him just what he needs (it doesn't hobble him, like some of the writing in *The Fury),* and having Zsigmond at his side must have helped free him to get right in there with the characters.

De Palma has been accused of being a puppeteer, and doing the actors' work for them. (Sometimes he may have had to.) But that certainly isn't the case here. Travolta and Nancy Allen are radiant performers, and he lets their radiance have its full effect; he lets them do the work of acting, too. Travolta played opposite Nancy Allen in De Palma's *Carrie* (1976), and they seemed right as a team; when they act together, they give out the same amount of energy—they're equally vivid. In *Blow Out,* as soon as Jack and Sally speak to each other you feel a bond between them, even though he's bright and soft-spoken and she looks like a dumb-bunny piece of fluff. In the early scenes, in the hospital and the motel, when the blond, curly-headed Sally entreats Jack to help her, she's a stoned doll with a hoarse, sleepy-little-girl voice, like Bette Midler in *The Rose*—part helpless, part enjoying playing helpless. When Sally is fully conscious, we can see that she uses the cuddly-blond act for the people she deals with, and we can sense the thinking behind it. But then her eyes cloud over with misery when she knows she has done wrong. Nancy Allen takes what used to be a good-bad-girl stereotype and gives it a flirty iridescence that makes Jack smile the same way we in the audience are smiling. She balances depth and shallowness, caution and heedlessness, so that Sally is always teetering—conning or being conned, and sometimes both. Nancy Allen gives the film its soul; Travolta gives it gravity and weight and passion.

Jack is a man whose talents backfire. He thinks he can do more with technology than he can; he doesn't allow for the human weirdnesses that snarl things up. A few years earlier, he had worked for the Police Department, but that ended after a horrible accident. He had wired an undercover police officer who was trying to break a crime ring, but the officer sweated, the battery burned him, and, when he tried to rip it off, the gangster he hoped to trap hanged him by the wire. Yet the only way Jack thinks that he can get the information about the governor's death to the public involves wiring Sally. (You can almost hear him saying, "Please, God, let it work this time.") Sally, who accepts corruption without a second thought, is charmed by Jack because he gives it a second thought. (She probably doesn't guess how much thought he does give it.) And he's drawn to Sally because she lives so easily in the corrupt world. He's encased in technology, and he thinks his machines can expose a murder. He thinks he can use them to get to the heart of the matter, but he uses them as a shield. And not only is his paranoia justified but things are much worse than he imagines—his paranoia is inadequate.

Travolta—twenty-seven now—finally has a role that allows him to discard his teen-age strutting and his slobby accents. Now it seems clear that he was so slack-jawed and weak in last year's *Urban Cowboy* because he couldn't draw upon his own emotional experience—the ignorant-kid role was conceived so callowly that it emasculated him as an actor. As Jack, he seems taller and lankier. He has a moment in the flashback about his police work when he sees the officer hanging by the wire. He cries out, takes a few steps away, and then turns and looks again. He barely does anything—yet it's the kind of screen acting that made generations of filmgoers revere Brando in *On the Waterfront:* it's the willingness to go emotionally naked and the control to do it in character. (And, along with that, the understanding of desolation.) Travolta's body is always in character in this movie; when Jack is alone and intent on what he's doing, we feel his commitment to the orderly world of neatly labelled tapes—his hands are precise and graceful. Recording the wind in the trees just before the crash of the governor's car, Jack points his long, thin mike as if he were a conductor with a baton calling forth the sounds of the night; when he first listens to the tape, he waves a pencil in the direction from which each sound came. You can believe that Jack is dedicated to his craft, because Travolta is a listener. His face lights up when he hears Sally's little-girl cooing; his face closes when he hears the complaints of his boss, Sam (Peter Boyden), who makes sleazo "blood" films—he rejects the sound.

At the end, Jack's feelings of grief and loss suggest that he has learned the limits of technology; it's like coming out of the cocoon of adolescence. *Blow Out* is the first movie in which De Palma has stripped away the cackle and the glee; this time he's not inviting you to laugh along with him. He's playing it straight, and asking you—trusting you—to respond. In *The Fury,* he tried to draw you into the characters' emotions by a fantasy framework; in *Blow Out,* he locates the fantasy material inside the characters' heads. There was true vitality in the hyperbolic, teasing perversity of his previous movies, but this one is emotionally richer and more rounded. And his rhythms are more hypnotic than ever. It's easy to imagine De Palma standing very still and wielding a baton, because the images and sounds are orchestrated.

Seeing this film is like experiencing the body of De Palma's work and seeing it in a new way. Genre techniques are circuitry; in going beyond genre, De Palma is taking some terrifying first steps. He is investing his work with a different kind of meaning. His relation to the terror in *Carrie* or *Dressed to Kill* could be gleeful because it was Pop and he could ride it out; now he's in it. When we see Jack surrounded by all the machinery that he tries to control things with, De Palma seems to be giving it a last, long, wistful look. It's as if he'd finally understood what technique is for. This is the first film he has made about the things that really matter to him. *Blow Out* begins with a joke; by the end, the joke has been turned inside out. In a way, the movie is about accomplishing the one task set for the sound-effects man at the start: he has found a better scream. It's a great movie.

The New Yorker, July 27, 1981

MOMMIE DEAREST
DUNAWAY ASSOLUTA

Faye Dunaway gives a startling, ferocious performance in *Mommie Dearest.* It's deeper than an impersonation; she turns herself into Joan Crawford, all right, but she's more Faye Dunaway than ever. She digs into herself and gets inside "Joan Crawford" in a way that only another torn, driven actress could. (She may have created a new form of *folie à deux.*) With her icy features, her nervous affectations, her honeyed emotionalism, Dunaway has been a vividly neurotic star; she has always seemed to be racing—breathless and flustered—right on the edge of collapse. In *Mommie Dearest,* she slows herself down in order to incarnate the bulldozer styles in neurosis of an earlier movie era; her Joan Crawford is more deliberate and calculating—and much stronger—than other Dunaway characters. As Joan the martinet, a fanatical believer in discipline, cleanliness, order, Dunaway lets loose with a fury that she may not have known was in her. She goes over the top, discovers higher peaks waiting, and shoots over them, too. Has any movie queen ever gone this far before? Alone and self-mesmerized, she plays the entire film on emotion. Her performance is extravagant—it's operatic and full of primal anger; she's grabbing the world by the short hairs. Maybe Dunaway had to get into this hard-nosed Crawford drag—the mannish shoulders, the popping eyes and angry mouth—before she could yell this loud. Her back is stiff, her voice is thick with barely suppressed rage, and her diction has become ridiculously cultured. This congealed-syrup voice is the only voice Joan has got. She's a very scary, sinewy woman; wearing a silver lamé gown fitted at the waist, she looks like a high priestess with breastplates. In a scene in the sterile Crawford mansion, Joan is on her hands and knees vigorously scrubbing her own shrine. She's proving her right to be a star the only way she knows—by compulsive, punishing work. She has to scrub the floor because the maids don't get it clean enough; if they did, they wouldn't be maids.

The film includes the nocturnal rampages that were the most talked-about episodes in the book by her adopted daughter, Christina Crawford, on which the movie is based. In one, Joan, prowling through her children's closets, finds a flaw—an expensive little frock on a wire hanger—and goes out of her head. In another, Joan responds to the news that she's finished at M-G-M by systematically cutting down her rose garden; she's wearing a sequin-top evening gown as she chops away at a tree. Dunaway brings off these camp horror scenes—howling "No wire hangers!" and weeping while inflecting "Tina, bring me the axe" with the beyond-the-crypt chest tones of a basso profundo—but she also invests the part with so much power and suffering that these scenes transcend camp. The destruction orgy that follows her discovery of the wire hanger may recall the gothic flamboyance of *What Ever Happened to Baby Jane?*, and her smeary cold cream gives her the white face of a Kabuki demon. Yet she's so wrecked, so piteous—and so driven—that she isn't funny. You can't help laughing at the movie, but you can't laugh at her. When she beats Tina with the offending wire hanger, or whomps her with a can of Old Dutch Cleanser, the horror isn't ridiculous, because you feel her tension and madness; you feel the strength of her need to smash this child, who isn't the malleable doll she fantasized when she bought her. (Movie stars were pioneer customers in the blond-blue-eyed-baby traffic.) Dunaway doesn't hold back: when Joan abuses Christina, you know that the child represents all the disappointments and disorder in Joan's life.

Dunaway gets at the mania for precision and order which often comes with age—it's almost always part of the running battle between parents and children, and sometimes goes as far as weird geometrical obsessions about where things should be. And for an aging star trying to deal with the pressures of the business world—someone who has labored to develop competence and needs order so that she can function—precise arrangements can be the only peace that's attainable. (It's too bad that the film doesn't provide any specific allusions to her early life, so that we could visualize the squalor she has climbed out of.) There's an aesthetic involved in Joan's rejection of wire hangers: when everything is symmetrical and expensive, she

905

knows where she is—she can feel that she lives in harmony, unthreatened. There's no *mess*. Order is beauty to her, and the satisfaction she takes in it keeps her going. She's providing her kids with the perfection she yearned for, and they don't appreciate it. So she blows sky-high and shows them real disorder—the mess they deserve.

Dunaway has only one sequence that's merely camp (and it's an entertaining lowdown number): after the death of Joan's last husband—Alfred Steele, of Pepsi-Cola—when she lets the company board of directors know that she's not going to be pushed around, she belts out, "Don't f—k with me, fellas. This ain't my first time at the rodeo." She's like a rowdy female impersonator, savoring the jolt she gives the fellas—and the audience. It's a release the audience needs.

The Joan Crawford of this movie has the insecurities of an aging beauty and the strident aggressiveness of a two-fisted butch lesbian. It's an overheated, horrifying combination. And she's both mother and father to her adopted kids; actually, she is so authoritarian that she's neither mother nor father—she's a demented androgyne. There is nothing appealingly soft in this boss-lady bawling out instructions, so it's flabbergasting to see the rapport that the normally smooth Dunaway feels with this tough, crazy grotesque. It's one star speaking for another, saying that the business devours your sanity and your femininity. The picture sets up Crawford as Lady Macbeth of Hollywood. In a pre-title sequence, she is awakened by an alarm clock; it's 4 A.M. She unstraps her facial mask while getting out of bed, scrubs her face and arms briskly (she could be sandpapering herself), and plunges her face into ice to tighten the skin. There's anger mixed with a sense of duty in the determination of her movements as, wordlessly, she puts on garments from her perfect closets and walks through the chaste halls and into a waiting limousine, where she studies her script—*The Ice Follies of 1939*—and autographs photos on a special tray-desk. Not a second is wasted: everything she does is purposeful. She appears to be overzealous, inhuman. But Dunaway takes this star-machine Joan Crawford and shows you that she isn't evil or inhuman—she's frighteningly human.

Dunaway goes at the role with such magnificent loony empathy that her posture and movements and the way she runs recall Crawford's self-consciousness, and sometimes when her movements are most like Crawford's they're also quite crazy. Beyond your horror for the child whom Joan tries to subjugate, you're involved in Joan's need to enforce her perverted idea of discipline. The little girl (Mara Hobel) who plays the child Christina has a prematurely wise face; she's like a pixie dwarf. And in the scene with this creepy, narcissistic child sitting at the mirror pretending to be her creepy, narcissistic mother, only to have her mother pounce on her and, as punishment, hack off her golden curls, the mother and the daughter are both so hysterically upset and the mother is so unrelenting, cropping more and more of the hair, as if to root it out, that the nightmarish collision of temperaments begins to suggest a great subject: the horrible misunderstandings between all parents and children—their need to "correct" us, our need to spite them, our raw nerves that they can pinch, theirs that we can press down. Diana Scarwid, who takes over from Mara Hobel when Tina is about thirteen, holds you by letting you watch Tina's secret thoughts. The adolescent Tina is a fresh-faced yet hidden person—she has to be hidden to survive. She's not docile—she's careful and cagey. But every once in a while she forgets herself and speaks her mind, and she's in real trouble. Scarwid has good low tones in her voice which suggest the ordeals Tina has been through, and she brings the role a twinkle, a gleam of rude humor, that seems to sustain Tina through her mother's most fiendish persecutions. On the occasion when it deserts her, and she raises her voice and talks back to her mother, Joan tries to choke her; Tina is rescued by a writer from *Redbook* (played in a believable, I've-seen-everything way by Jocelyn Brando) who's in the house doing a puff piece on the star's home life. Nobody is really in a position to help the children: Joan wouldn't put up with anybody strong enough to fight her. Her secretary-companion, Carol Ann (Rutanya Alda), who sees Tina's misery, is a wan, pinched acolyte. When she prays for Joan to win the Academy Award (for *Mildred Pierce*), there's a good possibility that she's really saying, "O God, save us from what we'll have to go through if they don't give it to her."

The best that can be said about the movie itself is that it doesn't seem to get in the way of its star. Mostly, it's bare and uninhabited. Produced by Frank Yablans and directed by Frank Perry, from a script they patched together (which was also worked on at various times by Tracy Hotchner and by Robert Getchell), it takes place in limbo. There's no illusion of any life going on around the action, which is staged right up front; you can practically hear the camera motor crank up for each shot, and when a crowd gathers, it seems to number eleven at the most. The film is a jumbled scrapbook of Crawford's life from her middle years to the end, with continuity that's slightly berserk. After the pre-title morning ritual, which goes on until Joan comes out of the makeup room at the studio and is ready to present herself to be photographed (this is the only sequence that's ingenious in visual terms), the film cuts back to her at home. Right after she wins the Academy Award, the film cuts to her wire-hanger fit, as if it were later that night. (Does the picture mean to suggest that she's so far gone that nothing can appease her? Or is there no relationship between the two sequences?) Some of the most promising episodes aren't shaped. The one in which the grown-up Tina, who has become an actress and is appearing in a soap opera, becomes ill and is hospitalized and the elderly, drunken Joan fills in for her is just a limp, squashy mess. There's an unexplained, tatty little scene with Tina accepting an award on Joan's behalf while Joan lies in bed weepy-eyed, watching the ceremony on TV. And Alfred Steele is presented as if he were a butter-and-egg salesman from Topeka rather than the head of an international corporation; Joan seems to lead him by a nose ring. And did the movie go through a budgetary crisis? Joan forces Al to spend excessive amounts of company money on a huge apartment that is to be their show-place, and then we never get to see the finished thing. There's too much of a beginning to some of Scarwid's scenes—we're almost watching her pre-pare for them. And Perry violates her performance with shots of the adoles-cent Tina necking which feature flashes of her white panties. But he doesn't intrude on Dunaway—he gives her long takes so she can go into her arias, and she sustains them. She becomes as grim and harsh as the actual Joan Crawford was—in her films of the forties and fifties, especially, when her falseness was so regal and heavy that you couldn't cut through it. You didn't feel the presence of anything else underneath. In the obit that George Cukor wrote, he said, "Whatever she did, she did whole-heartedly." Strenu-ously, rather; she was incapable of lightness, of delicacy. In a scene in which Joan is rehearsing for *Mildred Pierce*, Dunaway looks like her, but you're aware of an enormous difference: this is *Mildred Pierce* with a real actress in the part.

The emotional violence in this film is potent; you can't get it out of your mind. There are probably people in the audience saying to themselves, "If Joan Crawford had adopted me, I would have known how to handle her"—and forgetting how they fought with their own parents. And there are prob-ably others to echo the sentiments of Larry Rivers, who got up after a screening of *Mommy Dearest* and said, "You know what I just realized—I *am* Joan Crawford." Somehow, the movie is balanced: you see both sides. There's no question that Joan is guilty of battering her child, but Tina isn't exactly innocent—she has to test Joan in order to get her bearings in the world. The surprise of the movie is that you can watch Joan's killer instinct at work and still not hate her. When the little Tina deliberately interrupts her mother's session with a handsome stud, you know what the session means to Joan, be-cause you've seen her preparing for him, preening herself and anxiously checking out the leg she then casually displays to him. You've seen her jog-ging, working out: she has constructed herself almost mechanically—a post-industrial Venus. She wants to be perfect, like her spotless mansion. Her assumption of a charitable social role and her generosity to her fans are not just self-serving. She works to provide them with an ideal, and feels generous to those who can never accomplish what she has and yet believe in the ideal. Dunaway sees a grandeur in Joan Crawford, and by the size and severity of the torments she acts out she makes Crawford seem tragic. After Michael Redgrave played the insane ventriloquist in *Dead of Night,* bits of the charac-ter's paranoia kept turning up in his other performances; it could be hair-raising if Faye Dunaway were to have trouble shaking off the gorgon Joan.

The New Yorker, October 12, 1981

PIXOTE
CHILDHOOD OF THE DEAD

There are three million abandoned children in Brazil—swarms of scavenging, thieving street kids. Unwanted—many of them children of prostitutes or unmarried mothers—they're born into vagrancy; turned loose by parents who can't feed them or send them to school, they learn to pick pockets and grab purses and hustle. It's their only way of surviving. In the Brazilian movie *Pixote* (pronounced roughly "pee-*shoat*"), a judge has been murdered on a street in São Paulo, and the police have to take some action, so they routinely round up dozens of these kids, including the ten-year-old Pixote (Portuguese slang for Peewee), and throw them in a reformatory. There, behind rotting walls, Pixote (Fernando Ramos da Silva) watches as several of the larger boys gang-rape a kid not much older than he is. He sees boys beaten and killed, and he learns to say nothing when the guards and officials come around and ask questions. A bully spits in his milk and he drinks it down, because if he doesn't he'll be in trouble with one group or another. He stares as if he weren't there—his round eyes go dead, and his truculent baby face is indifferent. But he's a little camera taking it all in, and he's quick—he learns how to maneuver.

A group of boys, including Pixote, break out, and he and three others stick together like a family; they snatch enough purses and wallets to make their way to Rio de Janeiro and begin dealing cocaine. Outsmarted by the adult criminals, the kids buy an aging, drunken prostitute from a pimp and go into business with her: she brings men home and they rob them, at gunpoint. When you see children who are treated as an urban infestation—who *are* an urban infestation—you recognize the enormous difference between countries where kids get an education and countries where large numbers of them don't. (The slum children who were recruited to act in this movie can't read or write.) As the director, Hector Babenco, sees it, there's something essential missing in Pixote: no one has ever made him feel that his life had any value. He's a snub-nosed infant asserting his wants, and when they're denied his mouth turns down and he changes into a baby gangster—a runt Scarface. He kills innocently, in the sense that he doesn't understand the enormity of the crime.

When the boys are on the grayish beach in Rio, Babenco isn't doing travel-poster shots of Sugar Loaf. *Pixote* has its own look—a very distinctive pinkish glow, as if the film stock were infused with the colors of dawn—and there are lovely pale salmon tones and grays and browns. The incidents don't appear to be set up for the camera—things just seem to be happening and every image is expressive. (Well, maybe not every one: when the whore brings an American back to her fleabag, he's such a crude, swag-bellied gringo that the picture seems, fleetingly, to be pandering to audience hostility.) What goes on in this movie is different from what goes on in Amer-

909

ican movies. The imagination at work is both romantic and anti-romantic, and the mixture has the intensity that reaches back at least as far as *Don Quixote*. (Babenco, who wrote the script with Jorge Duran, from the novel *Infância dos Mortos*, by José Louzeiro, may have chosen the film title for its ironic echo of Quixote.) Brazil is steeped in poverty and paganism and Christianity and Pop; starving teen-age transvestites—Indian and Negro—put on wigs and call themselves Marilyn. Babenco's imagery is realistic, but his point of view is shockingly lyrical. South American writers, such as Gabriel García Márquez, seem to be in perfect, poetic control of madness, and Babenco has some of this gift, too. South American artists have to have it, in order to express the texture of everyday insanity. In Colombia a few years ago, I saw soldiers stationed on street corners who wore gold spiked helmets and carried machine guns; they didn't look down as a shrivelled little girl of perhaps eight, bent over parallel to the pavement from the weight of a huge bundle of wood on her back, passed by at their feet. The little girl, who will undoubtedly be deformed, walked past buildings with enormous billboards advertising American action movies; Yul Brynner, Burt Lancaster, and other stars are giant deities looming over the cities.

When Pixote and his pals mug somebody, the camera pulls back so that we have a view of the whole area: we get the social picture, and we see them dart in, score, and run off. It's fast teamwork, like a football scrimmage; each mugging has its own choreographic plan. But most of the incidents in the film aren't so distinctly shaped. They're loose and sometimes a little blobby. (When the kids and the whore, Sueli, lock one of her customers in the trunk of his car and drive off to celebrate—they park, turn up the car radio, and dance—we're distracted by wondering what's happening to the poor guy in the trunk. In other scenes, we wonder what happens to the fresh corpses.) Throughout the film, though, even when the acting is minimal there are no wrong notes in it. (Babenco says that the children themselves "guided" him, and came up with ideas that changed perhaps forty per cent of the script.) And the lighting is extraordinary: in the second half, and particularly after Sueli appears, the tones shift from the pastels to bright pinks and reds, and at night a boy's Afro acquires an orange aureole from the light reflected from neon signs. But Babenco doesn't build the film rhythmically, and you don't feel the dramatic intensification that you do when a structure is beautifully worked out. (There's a particularly confusing episode in which the guards pack some of the boys into a van and send them to a prison.) *Pixote* doesn't have the purity of *Shoeshine* or the surgical precision of *Los Olvidados*. It's effective cumulatively, and, because of the strength of feeling that Babenco has put into it, it becomes more and more devastating. Babenco is only a first-generation South American (his parents—Russian and Polish Jews—left Europe in the mid-thirties and went to Argentina), but he's not afraid to be florid, and his excesses are some of his finest moments.

At its best, *Pixote* isn't a political film, except in the larger sense in which films such as Vigo's *Zero for Conduct* and Jean Genet's *Un Chant d'A-mour* are political films. I think *Pixote* has some relation to those two pictures—certainly it shares their feeling for the ecstatic—and it may also relate to several Fellini movies. It has a fairly obvious thesis: when you see the handsome Babenco in the prologue and then meet Pixote, the child resembles the director so startlingly that it's almost as if Babenco were saying, "This could have happened to me or to you or to anybody who was deprived of minimal care and affection." The film is too pat and predictable when the kids start being destroyed by their contact with adults. And it's too clever when Pixote sits on Sueli's bed staring at the TV, then at Sueli and one of his pals going at it, and back at the TV; you register that the kids are making another attempt—a grotesque attempt—to construct the family they never had. Babenco is wildly ambitious, in the manner of gifted young artists: he's attempting to be a poet while making points for us to process. But the richer characters—Lilica (Jorge Julião), a seventeen-year-old transvestite homosexual, and the whore Sueli (Marília Pera)—transcend the demonstration. Jorge Julião, who hasn't acted before, and Marília Pera, who is a leading Brazilian stage actress, give such full performances that they take the picture to the ecstatic levels that Babenco hoped for.

The swanlike Lilica, who has a classic transvestite look, is in terror of his next birthday. (In Brazil, children under eighteen can't be prosecuted for criminal acts; they're merely sent to reform schools, like the one we've seen.) Lilica is a soft creature, flamingly nelly—an imitation of a young girl without parody. Emotionally, he's the most courageous kid of the bunch. The brutality he has seen inflicted on others hasn't made him callous; it has deepened his understanding and made him more loving. Pixote's soul hasn't been awakened; Lilica seems all soul. He's like a male version of the Giulietta Masina character in *Nights of Cabiria,* except that he's smarter and funnier, and much younger. He suffers romantic tragedies, but he doesn't go long without falling in love again.

Sueli is the whoriest whore imaginable. When we first see her, she has just given herself an abortion; she's feverish and full of hate. Pixote is frightened by the sight of the bloody fetus, and she cruelly, vindictively forces him to understand what it is. In the scenes with her, as she begins to have a swell time with the kids, dancing and drinking and coupling, the movie achieves a raw, garish splendor. Sueli is alive in the most brutal sense. When Pixote, who has accidentally killed one of the other kids while trying to help him, vomits, she takes him in her arms and consoles him. He puts his mouth to her breast and hangs on, suckling. He won't let go. What he's doing is perhaps too overtly Oedipal and symbolic, but it's an amazing scene, because of Sueli's violent response. She's repelled by his attempt to become her child; she pulls him off her and throws him out. This sick, broken-down streetwalker may have cradled him in her arms for a minute, but she doesn't want the burden of this child any more than she wanted the fetus she threw in the waste can.

After I saw *Pixote,* I had an opportunity to speak with Babenco, and since the street kids in the movie are all boys, I asked, "What of the girls?" His answer was "Their lives are ten thousand times as bad." I was left wondering whether his two women characters—a treacherous drug dealer, Debora, also aging, who kills one of the four boys, and Sueli, who takes Lilica's young lover away from him and destroys the remnants of the family—are supposed to be an indication of how poisoned the girls' lives are, or are part of a melodramatic myth. The film is apparently nonjudgmental, but at a deeper level it's judgmental as hell.

No matter what act of horror Sueli has participated in, she's elated—ready for a high time. She takes a savage's delight in the spoils. She may suddenly weep, even as she's dancing, but the tears are strictly for herself. Sueli needs Pixote and the other kids to make a party out of the horror of her life; horror *is* her party, and after some gullible john has been robbed she dances as if at a tribal celebration. She's a mother who thrusts children away or takes them as lovers. Babenco must have intended her to be the opposite of what he intended the children to be. (The kids do horrible things, but they don't rejoice in them.) Lilica's is the most sexual presence in the movie; he represents tenderness, love. Sueli represents annihilation—and the uglier her deeds are, the more hauntingly beautiful she becomes. (That's where Babenco shows class, and a genuine feeling for the mythic.) Marília Pera, who appeared in the first of Babenco's two earlier features, is best known as a comedienne. Playing Sueli must have been a deliverance for her; dusky and aquiline-faced, she has an Anna Magnani–like presence—horrifying and great. Babenco is too didactic about Pixote's blank slate; the sociological component of this film doesn't get at much that we don't know, and what the camera is going to find in most of the boys' faces has been predetermined. But Marília Pera's face registers the immediacy of the moment. Her Sueli is like a raging sun; when the inexpressive kids revolve around her and feel they own her, it's almost as if she were their only chance to learn what can be in a face.

It's not the boys' innocence that the movie seems to be about but their innocence in relation to the camera. Pixote sits still and the camera gets nothing from his impassive face; we may halfway accept Babenco's notion that he's so young that there's nothing written on it yet, and that his impassivity is his survival technique. But isn't it really that he's a blank because he's not an actor? Sueli darts around and the camera picks up everything she feels. The picture comes to life with Sueli, because she's the whore spawned out of men's darkest imagining, in the way that Medea and Clytemnestra and Lady Macbeth and Jocasta and Euripides's fierce Helen of Troy were spawned, and because the actress is so sharply and completely there.

The picture isn't quite great, maybe because you can see it struggling to be, and the end (a lyric, ironic switch on the *Vitelloni* ending) is awfully portentous, with the rejected Pixote, gun in pocket, kicking a can as he walks down the railroad tracks—a baby bandit on his way. You know it's supposed to make you think. But what I thought about was a male fantasy of barbaric, rejecting females, and an actress whose display of passion wiped the little non-actor kids off the screen. *Pixote* is good enough to touch greatness; it restores your excitement about the confusing pleasures that movies can give.

The New Yorker, November 9, 1981

THE DEVIL'S PLAYGROUND

The people in Fred Schepisi's *The Devil's Playground* are like sculptured figures that glow with their own light. You're not aware of surfaces, of skin. You're aware of the substance of the flesh. The Marist Brothers at the seminary around which most of the film is set seem to be looking into themselves, puzzled and deeply disappointed by their own physicality. And the pubescent boys gaze with thunderstruck eyes at the eruptions of their bodies. The movie is always on the borderline of comedy, because they have all—monks and seminarians alike—been taught that "an undisciplined mind is the Devil's playground," yet they can't get their minds off their bodies. They can't control the urges that the Church's teachings say they must control. They're in a losing battle with their flesh.

Schepisi is odd man out—the artist in the Australian film renaissance, which is otherwise a celebration of the work of intelligent, slightly impersonal craftsmen. That may be why it took him five years to complete this semi-autobiographical first feature (it's set in the fifties) and why it has taken another five years for the film to get a New York opening. (*The Devil's Playground* was finished in 1976; Schepisi's second picture, the 1978 *The Chant of Jimmie Blacksmith*—a masterwork—opened here in 1980.) *The Devil's Playground* treads a delicate tightrope; there has probably never been a film that treats priestly shame—amounting to agony in some cases—with such understanding. Most of the monks have genuine affection for the boys they teach, and sympathy for the plight of little kids bewildered by their erections. And the monks are acutely aware of each other's concealed torments. They're tolerant of the drinking of Brother Victor (Nick Tate), who goes into the city wearing civvies, picks up two women and flirts and teases right up to the verge of actual sex, and then just barely makes his escape, gasping to the younger monk waiting for him, "They nearly had me." And when Brother Francine (Arthur Dignam), the most agonized of all, and the most repressive with the students, instructing them that "Your body is your worst enemy," has been drinking wine with the other brothers, he suddenly lets out a torrent of rage and self-disgust and shouts, "The body won't be denied." The men in the room with him look away, look inward; they are aware of each other's miseries, but each is thinking, Why has this horrible thing—sexuality—been inflicted on me? They remain very still, yet they're pulsing, like the figures in Rodin's *The Burghers of Calais*.

Schepisi's passion is expressed visually—in his thematic use of water imagery, in the voluptuous shifting of dark and light, in the matte green of the monks' billiard table, and in the deep green of the huge, overhanging trees on the seminary grounds and the paradisal trees in the countryside, with twisted, mossy limbs. His use of color eroticizes the environment. Outside the seminary, the greens and the aquas are tense, acid, and at a family picnic there are bright pinks and reds that look electrified next to the greens and the blues. Trees and grass have a special vibrancy—they, too, seem to glow with their own light.

Schepisi is a rarity—an artist whose sense of justice and proportion is as highly developed as his sensual aesthetic. He's sane and balanced in his treatment of the characters. At the center of the story is the cheerful thirteen-year-old Tom (Simon Burke), whose pigeon-toed front teeth give him the grin of a friendly child-satyr. Tom thinks he has a calling to the religious life (as Schepisi did at thirteen), but he's the joke of the seminary, because, as the monks observe, he has a constant erection. (A very old monk gently tries to dissuade him from his vocation.) For Tom, sexuality is a source of pleasures he can't resist. For the sallow, fanatic Brother Francine, it's an agonizing burden that threatens him. On a trip to the city, he sneaks off to a public swimming pool and gapes at exposed flesh—at men's hairy underbellies, at women's breasts slightly askew in their wet bathing suits—and his huge dark eyes bulge with shame for his voyeurism and his lust. The most intense eroticism in the film is in a dream that tortures Brother Francine: underwater, naked, his face in shock, expressionless, and his eyes wide open, staring, he is surrounded by beautiful naked nymphs— all of them for his pleasure, except that he's incapable of feeling pleasure even in a dream. Arthur Dignam brings a self-dramatizing fervor to the role: Brother Francine, isolated with his fantasies, is contemptuous of the lesser suffering of the other monks. This mortified zealot, whose emotions are a tangle, has the richest (and most sepulchral) voice in the film.

The sound of *The Devil's Playground* is a comic cantata: the boys' voices are in various stages of changing, and the kids are as surprised as we are by the spooky, quavering tones that come out of them. The monks' voices are educated, modulated—avuncular. But in some cases (such as Brother Victor), the rough, slangy Australian vulgate comes through. And in the case of Father Marshall—played by the Australian novelist Thomas Keneally, from whose book Schepisi adapted *Jimmie Blacksmith*—an Irish lilt can be heard. The bald and bewhiskered Father Marshall, a missionary who officiates at the boys' three-day retreat, is a heightened version of the other monks. A friendly leprechaun, he goes out of his way to ease the boys' fears. (He gives Tom a vial of holy water from Lourdes so that he can put a drop of it on his tongue—to help him with his bed-wetting.) But when Father Marshall delivers a sermon it's pure fundamentalist hellfire and damnation, holding up to the boys images such as a fiery worm consuming their entrails for eternity, and real terror hovers in the air. The combination of dogmatic teachings and the onset of puberty drives some of the boys more than a little crazy: three of them become involved in secret purification rites, and their leader, thinking he's ready to walk on water, is drowned.

Schepisi wrote himself a beautiful script: it's all theme and variations, yet nothing seems forced. Instructed that they must not talk during their retreat, the boys awkwardly dispose themselves on the shore of a lake. The silence is oppressive to them—it feels false and silly—and Tom tosses a pebble into the water. Others toss pebbles—a whole volley of pebbles—and then a fat boy slips in, with a big, thudding splash, and the tension is broken and they all laugh together. Almost every incident in the film gives us, like this one, an intuitive perception of how the boys' impulses are thwarted and how the kids consciously or unconsciously fight back. The monks are simply the boys at a more advanced stage of repression and guilt; locked in by their feelings of unworthiness, they're on permanent retreat.

Perhaps Tom's encounter with a young girl is a shade too idyllic. And when he was visiting with her and with his family I was a little confused about where they all were. And perhaps the old monk who counsels Tom against striving for priestly celibacy and perfection is too kindly; it might be better if he didn't mutter "It's unnatural"—Schepisi needn't tell us what he's showing us. But there are few flaws, and they're piddling ones. I don't really see how this movie could be much better. Schepisi is a great filmmaker, with his own softly rhythmed style. The full, widescreen images glide by; the cadences are elusive—like Scott Fitzgerald's prose rhythms. Schepisi's two features, this one and *Jimmie Blacksmith,* are not like the work of any other director. In this first film, even the way that the music comes in on scenes and rises up during the underwater dream is very personal. I had the feeling that everything in the film was breathing. When a director so clearly knows what he's doing, you can sit back and smile with pleasure. The details are satisfying: the way the boys ignore the crabbing of the seminary cook; the suave righteousness with which the head of the school refuses to give Tom the address of a friend he wants to write to who has been expelled; the crew-neck sweater that Brother Victor wears on his flirtatious foray into town—just clerical enough for him to feel a little safe. The film gives you the impression that Schepisi has got the whole thing right. He must have freed himself very thoroughly: this isn't an anti-clerical movie. Far from it. Schepisi loves these tormented comedians. But he looks at them with humorous pagan eyes.

The New Yorker, December 7, 1981

ON GOLDEN POND

O
n *Golden Pond* is an unbelievably literal-minded movie. It opens with images of sunset on a lake, and we hear the cry of a loon; there are views
of two loons in the water and closeups of flowers. Katharine Hepburn
and Henry Fonda, arriving at their summer house in Maine, get out of a car,
and it's a stage entrance, with both of them so busily in character that I felt
a slight throb in the temple—a foreboding. When Hepburn, fluttering girlishly and listening with poetically cocked head, announced, "The loons, the
loons. They're welcoming us back," and Fonda, crotchety as could be, let us
know that he was too deaf to hear what she was carrying on about, I knew
what I was in for. *On Golden Pond* is the kind of uplifting experience that
traffics heavily in rather basic symbols: the gold light on the pond stands for
the sunset of life; the loons, whom Hepburn refers to as a husband and wife,
represent Ethel and Norman Thayer (Hepburn and Fonda). Do you dig it?
Do you have the stomach for it? Directed by Mark Rydell, from Ernest
Thompson's adaptation of his own 1978 play, the movie is a doddering valentine in which popsy Norman, who's having his eightieth birthday, and
mopsy Ethel, who's nearing her seventieth, crack jokes, weather domestic
crises, and show us the strength of solid Yankee values. Or is it "good American stock," or Hepburn's pedigreed cheekbones? Fonda is seventy-seven,
and Hepburn is seventy-five, and the media have been turning them into
monuments. This film is a rather indecently premature memorial service.

Surely the only way to show respect for elderly performers is to hold
them to the same standards that they were held to when they were younger,
and it's almost impossible for Hepburn and Fonda to do anything resembling a creditable job of acting in a vehicle like *On Golden Pond*. It comes out
of the Theatre of Safety. It's shaped so that it seems to be getting at the
problems of old age (Norman's eyes and ears are failing, his memory is
spotty, and his body is becoming more and more unreliable), but then Norman's crankiness is made to seem sly—a form of one-upmanship. He's
meant to be a lovable curmudgeon. And he and Ethel are such an adoring,
lovey-dovey old pair that there are no recriminations and just one regret—
and that is taken care of in the course of the film. It concerns their child—
their daughter, Chelsea (Jane Fonda), now forty-two, and still bitter and
resentful because she has never felt that she could please her father or that
he cared about her.

Ernest Thompson takes a roundabout route to the rapprochement of
father and daughter. Chelsea, whose first marriage failed, arrives for her father's birthday, bringing her new lover, Bill (Dabney Coleman, bearded), a
Los Angeles dentist, and his thirteen-year-old son, Billy (Doug McKeon), an
unhappy little tough, whom she and Bill park with the Thayers for a month
while they vacation in Europe. Wouldn't Billy be happier in a summer camp,
with kids his own age? Oh, but then we couldn't be faced with the gruesome
prospect of watching canny old Norman reclaim the boy—get his mind off

chasing girls and onto fishing and diving and other outdoor sports—and change him into an ideal, tenderhearted kid. Somehow, the affection that springs up between the old man and Billy makes it possible for Chelsea, on her return, to gain self-respect by doing the backflip dive that she was afraid to do as a young girl, and to talk—talk "meaningfully," that is—to her father for the first time. Naturally, the picture ends with Norman and Ethel saying their annual goodbye to the lake; there are more shots of the sunset on the water, and Mr. and Mrs. Loon, whose baby has learned to fly and has gone off on its own, come round to say goodbye to Norman and Ethel.

This isn't material for actors, no matter what their age. It's material for milking tears from an audience. Hepburn and Fonda are playing America's aged sweethearts—A Married Couple for All Seasons. Norman and Ethel are more in love than on the day they were married; he is a retired professor (apparently without any anxieties about inflation or other money worries), and they have always lived graciously. It's no accident that the publicity sketch showing Henry Fonda, in a fishing hat, and the smiling faces of Hepburn, Jane Fonda, and Doug McKeon looks like a knockoff of a Norman Rockwell *Saturday Evening Post* cover. That's the world that the film tries to evoke. But the sketch has a sickly, creepy quality, and so does the movie. Henry Fonda appears to give an honest performance, but his clean-old-man role is conceived so grotesquely that I found it impossible to like Norman—and our liking him is the linchpin of the whole enterprise. Hepburn is a special case: she's heady, as if exhilarated by her own acting. She overdoes Ethel's being entranced with nature, and she horribly overdoes Ethel's devotion to Norman, so that it calls attention to Ethel's own wonderfulness. Ethel is meant to be a capable, down-to-earth woman, but Hepburn leaps about weightlessly—she never comes close to touching the ground. She has become a Kate Hepburn windup doll—chipper and lyrical, floating in the stratosphere, and, God knows, spunky. Her star turn is a parody of the great Hepburn performances—it's all pirouettes.

The director has not done himself proud. Listening to the dialogue is like being at a bad play: you can count out the beats in the pauses. And some of the shots go on a few frames too long, so that you see the actors' false emotions freezing and the people look the way they do in the sketch. Doug McKeon is stiff, as if he had played Billy a thousand times already and were bored past showing any emotion. And Rydell has the actors hitting some very strange notes. In the only scene that Billy has alone with his father, Bill threatens to send him back to his mother if he doesn't behave, and there is such ugly menace in his tone that I had the vagrant thought that Chelsea was making another big mistake in her life—that Bill, the bearded dentist who talks L.A. psychodrivel, was some sort of weirdo con man. There certainly seems to be something suspicious about him when he has a conversation with Norman and his face switches expressions crazy-fast—he's like a speed freak trying on attitudes. It turns out that Bill is meant to be a charming fellow and the right husband for Chelsea—it's only Mark Rydell who has taken leave of his senses. In extenuation of Dabney Coleman's performance, it should be pointed out that Norman mocks Bill so cruelly and so sneakily that it might be difficult for any actor to know how to read Bill's lines.

As the playwright has set things up, Norman, who has the bulk of the one-liners, gets laughs by jokes about his own enfeeblement and then gets more laughs by being on top of the situations and zapping people who think he's feeble. We're meant to enjoy the way he picks on people and makes them feel foolish, and we're also asked to weep (and people around me certainly *were* weeping) for his frailty, for his courage, for the beauty of his love affair with his wife of forty-eight years. The author is both ruthless and shameless—a real winning combination. He even gives Norman a bit of an angina attack onstage (sorry about that—on camera). The fakery at the core of the material is that Norman is a mean old son of a bitch to his daughter and to just about everyone else except his wife and Billy. Yet we're asked to dote on him, and Chelsea is made out to be a neurotic mess for not having responded to his true loving nature. Chelsea is a terrible role, and Jane Fonda plays it so tensely that she's like an actress in a soap opera telegraphing her psychiatric miseries. (In a lakeside scene, in a bikini, she looks spectacular, yet she keeps her body held in so tight that you can't believe she's breathing.) Ethel, who is so understanding with her husband, is starchy and impatient with her daughter, telling her, "All you can do is be disagreeable about the past. What's the point? . . . Life marches by, Chelsea. I suggest you get on with it." That's not a mother talking—it's a headmistress. Yet we're supposed to applaud Ethel's no-nonsense stoicism. Ernest Thompson works the audience for any approval he can wring out of it.

Some sections of the press are doing backflips of their own. What is going on when *Time*, in a reverential cover story on this movie and Hepburn and Fonda, uses terms such as "breeding" and gets right down to lineage: "Both their families were established in the colonies by the 18th century, and the pedigree shows in the two who took up acting"? Hepburn and Fonda have not, then, merely "ascended to proud new peaks"; they are Our Betters. I don't think this snobbery should be blamed on the Reagans. I think it's a worshipfulness (and maybe envy) that overcomes some people when they look at Hepburn's imperious bones. They feel she must belong to a superior race. (Henry Fonda is let in on a pass, because he has played so many great liberals.)

There's a moment, after Norman and Billy have become buddies and are out fishing together, when the movie gives us a quick-flash reminder that the subject is mortality: Billy hauls in a dead loon and then, in his new, reformed manner, asks Norman, man to man, if he's afraid of dying. The movie is like a striptease without nudity. It's a death tease; nobody dies—the only corpse is that loon, and it isn't even one of Norman and Ethel's beloved loons. All the talk about death and dying is really very cozy, because Norman is demonstrated to be such a tough old bird that he can still outwit everybody around. And there can be few people in the world as snugly protected in their old age as he is, with a selfless wife dedicated to his care. Even the symbols—the golden-sunset years, the pair of loons—are soothing. This twaddle is a pacifier—it's a regression to the movies with cute and wise old codgers.

The New Yorker, December 7, 1981

PENNIES FROM HEAVEN
DREAMERS

ennies from Heaven is the most emotional movie musical I've ever seen. It's a stylized mythology of the Depression which uses the popular songs of the period as expressions of people's deepest longings—for sex, for romance, for money, for a high good time. When the characters can't say how they feel, they evoke the songs: they open their mouths, and the voices on hit records of the thirties come out of them. And as they lip-sync the lyrics their obsessed eyes are burning bright. Their souls are in those voices, and they see themselves dancing just like the stars in movie musicals.

Visually, the film is a tarnished romance. The sets are stylized—not just the sets for the dance numbers but also the Chicago streets and stores, the movie houses, the diners and dives, which are designed in bold, formal compositions, for a heightened melancholy. This is our communal vision of the Depression, based on images handed down to us: motionless streets and buildings, with lonely figures in clear, cold light. The film actually re-creates paintings and photographs that are essences of America. There's a breathtaking re-creation of Edward Hopper's *Nighthawks* coffee shop, and it's held for just the right length of time. There's Hopper's interior of a movie house with a woman usher leaning against the wall, and there are bleary faces and purplish red-light-district scenes by Reginald Marsh, and thirties photographs of desolation, such as a dark flivver parked in front of a plain white clapboard house. These images blend in and breathe with the other shots. The whole movie seems a distillation of that forlorn, heavily shadowed period, while the songs express people's most fervent shallow hopes. When the hero, Arthur, a sheet-music salesman, a big talker just smart enough to get himself into trouble, goes on his selling trips, from Chicago to Galena, in 1934, the land is flat and deserted, with almost nothing moving but his little car chugging along the road.

As Arthur, Steve Martin has light-brown hair cut short, and when he calls up a song he has an expression of eagerness and awe that transforms him. You forget Steve Martin the TV entertainer, with his zany catch phrases and his disconnected nonchalance. Steve Martin seems to have forgotten him, too. He has a wild-eyed intensity here that draws you right into Arthur's desperation and his lies. Arthur believes the words of the songs, and he tries to get to the dream world they describe. At home in Chicago, he pleads with his wife for a little sex: he mimes a love song—"I'll Never Have to Dream Again"—and Connee Boswell's voice comes out of him. It's our first exposure to the film's device, and though we're meant to laugh or grin, Connee Boswell is saying something for Arthur that his petite and pie-faced wife, Joan (Jessica Harper), refuses to hear, and the mixture of comedy and poignancy is affecting in a somewhat delirious way. Joan cringes at Arthur's touch; she thinks his attempts to make love to her are evidence of a horrible, sullying perversion. Then, in the little town of Galena, when he's in a music store trying to get an order, a shy schoolteacher, Eileen (Bernadette Peters), walks in; Arthur mimes Bing Crosby singing "Did You Ever See a Dream Walking?" and Eileen dances to the music, and the two of them form romantic, thirties-movie-star silhouettes in his mind. Eileen is pale and gentle, a brown-eyed blonde with soft curls—tendrils, really. She looks malleable, like the young Janet Gaynor. Eileen lives in a song world, too, and she's eager to believe Arthur's lie that he isn't married. She also has a spicy, wanton side; she turns into a Kewpie doll when she mimes Helen Kane's boop-boop-a-doops in "I Want to Be Bad." She has everything that Arthur wants, except money. As the story develops, it's so familiar it's archetypal; it's a manic-depressive libretto. Alfred Kazin has written about the passion of "a period—the thirties—that has had no rival since for widespread pain and sudden hope." That's what this black-humor musical, which Dennis Potter adapted from his six-segment BBC mini-series, is about.

The lip-syncing idea works wonderfully; it's in the dialogue interludes that the movie gets off on the wrong foot. Most of these scenes need to be played faster—to be snappier and more hyperbolic, with little curlicues of irony in the performances to point things up. For example, we see a gigantic billboard showing Carole Lombard with a huge black eye in Faith Baldwin's *Love Before Breakfast*. (It's the same billboard poster that appears in a famous photograph by Walker Evans, taken in Atlanta in 1936.) A little while later, with the Lombard poster looking on, a love-starved man grabs a blind girl, and when we next see her, dead, she has a black eye. The director, Herbert Ross, plays it straight, and so instead of being bizarrely, horribly funny it's peculiar. Black humor played too slow *is* peculiar; it may seem that the misery level is rising awfully high. Ross's deliberate pace makes the film's tone uncertain. Sometimes he doesn't go all the way with a shocking joke, or he muffles it, so the audience doesn't get the release of laughter. There's so little movement during the dialogue that the characters seem numbed out, and the audience's confidence in the film is strained—the discomfort of some of the viewers is palpable. I think our emotions get jammed up. Yet the scenes in themselves—even those that are awkwardly paced and almost static—still have a rapt, gripping quality. And even when a scene cries out for a spin, a further twist of artifice, the actors carry the day. Bernadette Peters has ironic curlicues built in, and her exaggerated

Queens diction (which is certainly eccentric for an Illinois girl) gives her her own cheeping-chicky sound.

Besides Arthur and Joan and that heavenly angel cake Eileen, there are two other major characters. Vernel Bagneris (the director and star of the long-running show *One Mo' Time*) plays a homeless, stuttering street musician and beggar, the Accordion Man, whom Arthur picks up on the road, and it's Bagneris who mimes the title song. The version he lip-syncs isn't the happy-go-lucky Crosby version from the totally unrelated 1936 film that was also called *Pennies from Heaven;* it's that of Arthur Tracy, which is much darker and much more potent. The sorrow of the Depression and the hoping beyond hope are concentrated in this song and in the Accordion Man himself. Arthur Tracy's wrenching voice—it has tears and anguish in it—comes pouring out of the stuttering simpleton, and, as if the song had freed him, the Accordion Man dances, sensually, easily. With a photo-collage of the Depression behind him, and a shower of shimmering gold raining down on him he stretches and struts. I never thought I'd go around with the song "Pennies from Heaven" pulsating in my skull, but the combination of Arthur Tracy and Vernel Bagneris is voluptuously masochistic. Popular singers in the thirties brought out the meaning of a lyric as fully as possible, and the original recordings, which are used here, have the true sound of the period. (The bridges between these old arrangements and the dances—and the dance sequences themselves—are said to have been orchestrated "using antique recording equipment" to preserve the thirties sound; however it was accomplished, the result is worth the effort.) Where the movie misses is in the timing of the contrapuntal gags: after the Accordion Man has had his shimmering-gold epiphany, Arthur, feeling like a real sport, hands him a quarter. Ross somehow buries the connection, the shock. Everything in the material is double-edged; it's conceived in terms of extremes—the melodrama and the pathos on one side and the dream world on the other. Normal life is excluded. But the director keeps trying to sneak it back in; he treats the piled-on sentimental gloom tenderly, as if it were meant to be real life. (Would he be this afraid of the cruel jokes in *The Threepenny Opera?*)

The other major character—almost as much transformed as Steve Martin—is Christopher Walken, with dark, slicked-down hair. As Tom the pimp, who puts Eileen on the street, he has the patent-leather lounge-lizard look of a silent-movie wolf, and his scenes play like greasy magic. In his first movie musical, Walken, who used to dance on Broadway, has more heat and athletic energy than he has shown in his straight acting roles. He has never been quite all there on the screen; he has looked drained or packed in ice. (That's what made him so effective as the chief mercenary in *The Dogs of War*—that, and the tense way he walked in New York, like an animal pacing a cage.) Here, there's sensuality in his cartooned apathy, and when he first spots Eileen his eyeballs seem to pop out on springs. In a mock striptease in a saloon, he shows how powerfully built he is, and he's a real hoofer. He takes the screen in a way he never has before—by force, and with lewd amusement, particularly when he bares a grotesque valentine tattoo on his chest.

There hasn't been this much tap dancing in a movie musical in many years. Arthur does a derby-and-plaid-suit vaudeville routine with two other salesmen, who are played by Tommy Rall (best known to moviegoers as Ann Miller's partner in the 1953 *Kiss Me, Kate)* and spaghetti-legged Robert Fitch (best known to theatregoers as the original Rooster in *Annie).* It's a fast, showy number—to the Dorsey Brothers Orchestra's playing and the Boswell Sisters' singing "It's the Girl"—and the three men have wonderful frilly gestures as they curve and sway to imitate femininity, and use their hands to model their dream girls' shapes in the air. Steve Martin doesn't slow his celebrated partners down; he's spectacular—he really is Steve (Happy Feet) Martin. In the film's most startling sequence, set inside the Hopper movie theatre with the weary blond usher, Arthur and Eileen sit watching *Follow the Fleet.* Arthur is transfixed, and as Astaire sings "Let's Face the Music and Dance" Arthur begins singing, too. He goes up on the stage, and Eileen joins him—two tiny, sharply edged figures in deep, rich color against the huge black-and-white screen images of Astaire and Rogers dancing, and they really seem to be there. They dance along with the stars on the screen, and then the two minuscule figures shift into black-and-white, and take over. Arthur is in tails, Eileen in a copy of Ginger's glittering gown with its loose fur cowl. And a chorus line of men in tails appears, tapping, like the men in *Top Hat.* It makes you gasp. Do Steve Martin and Bernadette Peters really dare to put themselves in Astaire and Rogers's place? Yet they carry it off. You may still be gasping when Arthur and Eileen leave the theatre (the exterior is a Reginald Marsh) and hear newsboys shouting the headlines. The police are looking for Arthur.

Herbert Ross has never shown much audacity in his other screen work, and when a director has been as successful as Ross has been with bland muck *(The Sunshine Boys, The Turning Point, The Goodbye Girl),* and has even been honored for it, it certainly takes something special to make him plunge in. Ross didn't go in far enough, but this is still quite a plunge. Dennis Potter's idea—obvious, yet strange, and with a pungency—provided the chance of a lifetime; Ross's collaborators must have felt it, too, and possibly they came up with ideas he couldn't resist. He had a superlative team. The production designer was Ken Adam, who designed the eight most imaginative James Bond pictures and also *Dr. Strangelove, Barry Lyndon,* and *The Seven-Per-Cent Solution.* The film's greatest splendors are those re-created visions—particularly the coffee shop with Arthur and Eileen as nighthawks, and Jimmy's Diner, which has a sliding glass wall, so that the Accordion Man can slip out into the rain to dance. Among its more obvious splendors is an Art Deco Chicago bank in which Arthur, who has tried to get a loan to open his own music shop and been turned down, dreams that he's deluged with money: to the music of "Yes, Yes!," performed by Sam Browne and the Carlyle Cousins, he and the banker (the matchless Jay Garner) and a batch of chorines perform in a dance montage that suggests the harebrained variations of Busby Berkeley montages.

The choreographer, Danny Daniels, does each number in a different theatrical style, and he palpably loves the styles that he reworks, especially the lowdown, off-color ones, like Walken's "dirty" sandwich dance—he's wedged between two blowzy whores. With the exception of a few routines with chorus girls as Rockette-style automatons, Daniels's choreography isn't simply dance—it's gag comedy, in which each dancer has his own comic personality. The dances are funny, amazing, and beautiful all at once. There are no problems of pacing here (except that a few numbers are too short and feel truncated). Several of them are just about perfection. And with teasers—comedy bits that prick the imagination. Bernadette Peters has a big production number ("Love Is Good For Anything That Ails You") that's like a dance of deliverance. Her classroom is transformed into something palatial and white, with children tapping on the tops of miniature grand pianos, and with her in silver and white, shimmying down the center aisle. (All the costumes are by Bob Mackie.) And when Arthur dreams of himself as a happy man, settled down with both Joan and Eileen, the three of them mouth "Life Is Just a Bowl of Cherries," like a radio trio. It's an indication of the depth of Jessica Harper's performance as the little witch Joan, shrivelled by repression and hatred, that it takes a second to recognize her as the pretty brunette in the trio.

The cinematographer, Gordon Willis, provides the lighting to carry out Ken Adam's visual ideas, and it's different from anything that I can remember Willis's ever doing before. The movie is about ordinary experience in a blazing, heightened form, and Willis keeps the level of visual intensity phenomenally high. At times, the color recalls the vivid, saturated tones in the 1954 *A Star Is Born*: the images are lustrous, and are often focussed on the pinpoint of light in the dreamer-characters' eyes when they envisage the pleasures celebrated in the songs. Eileen's eyes switch on and off, and so do the Accordion Man's; Arthur is possessed by the dream—his eyes are always on. My eyes were always on, too: even when I wanted to close up the pauses between the actors' lines, there was never a second when I wasn't fascinated by what was happening on the screen.

Despite its use of Brechtian devices, *Pennies from Heaven* doesn't allow you to distance yourself. You're thrust into the characters' emotional extremes; you're right in front of the light that's shining from their eyes. And you see the hell they go through for sex and money. Arthur, the common man with an itch, will do just about anything. When he blurts out something about his wife to Eileen, he covers his traces blubbering about how horribly she died in an accident, and then uses the invented tragedy to soften up Eileen so he can hop on top of her. He's a bastard, but you're not alienated from him; the songs lead him by the nose. As it turns out, the one character whose dream comes true is the pinched and proper Joan, who has dreamed of taking revenge on Arthur for his sexual demands on her.

There are cruel, rude awakenings; maybe they should be more heartlessly tonic, more bracing. But they do give you a pang. When Eileen is happily dreaming away in her classroom, seeing it as a tap dancers' paradise, with the children tapping and playing musical instruments, the principal comes in, enraged by the noise that the kids are making, and he takes a ruler and smacks the hands of a fat boy—a boy who has been proudly blowing on a tuba in her dream. The injustice to the boy—the humiliation—is one of those wrongs that some people are singled out for. The boy is fat, Arthur is horny, Eileen is gullible, the Accordion Man is inarticulate. This double-edged movie supplies a simple, basic rationale for popular entertainment. It says that though dreamers may be punished for having been carried away, they've had some glorious dreams. But it also says that the emotions of the songs can't be realized in life.

There's something new going on—something thrilling—when the characters in a musical are archetypes yet are intensely alive. This is the first big musical that M-G-M has produced on its lot in over a decade. The star, Steve Martin, doesn't flatter the audience for being hip; he gives an almost incredibly controlled performance, and Bernadette Peters is mysteriously right in every nuance. Herbert Ross and Ken Adam and Danny Daniels and Gordon Willis and Bob Mackie and the whole cast worked at their highest capacities—perhaps were even inspired to exceed them. They all took chances. Do you remember what Wagner said to the audience after the première of *Götterdämmerung*? "Now you have seen what we can do. Now want it! And if you do, we will achieve an art." I am not comparing *Pennies from Heaven* with *Götterdämmerung*. But this picture shows that the talent to make great movie musicals is out there, waiting.

The New Yorker, December 21, 1981

SHOOT THE MOON

There wasn't a single scene in the English director Alan Parker's first three feature films (*Bugsy Malone, Midnight Express, Fame*) that I thought rang true; there isn't a scene in his new picture *Shoot the Moon* that I think rings false. I'm a little afraid to say how good I think *Shoot the Moon* is—I don't want to set up the kind of bad magic that might cause people to say they were led to expect so much that they were disappointed. But I'm even more afraid that I can't come near doing this picture justice. The characters in *Shoot the Moon*, which was written by Bo Goldman, aren't taken from the movies, or from books, either. They're torn—bleeding—from inside Bo Goldman and Alan Parker and the two stars, Diane Keaton and Albert Finney, and others in the cast.

Diane Keaton is Faith Dunlap, and Finney is her husband, George. The Dunlaps have been married about fifteen years and have four school-age daughters. George is a nonfiction writer who's had a rough time, whipping up free-lance articles to meet the bills. But now he has become reputable, and they are doing better financially and are comfortable in their big old house in Marin County, across the bay from San Francisco. Their relationship has been poisoned, though. Faith knows all George's weaknesses and failures, and her knowledge eats away at his confidence. "You always remember the wrong things," he tells her. So he's having an affair, and feeling so rotten about it that he sobs when he's alone. And though he tries to keep the affair secret from Faith, she learns about it and is devastated. She can't look at him; her anxious eyes turn away. When he says, "You look really pretty," she can't stop herself from saying, "You seem surprised." Her angry misery is almost like a debauch; it makes her appear sodden. When she's with him, her face sinks—it's the dead weight of her sense of loss. At a book-awards ceremony in San Francisco, she overhears photographers who have taken pictures of the two of them decide on the caption "George Dunlap and friend." She blurts out, "I'm not his friend. I'm his wife." The movie begins on the eve of the day when she drives him out of the house, and it covers the next months of separation.

Their oldest daughter, the thirteen-year-old Sherry (Dana Hill), who has known about her father's adultery, feels that it's treachery to her and to the whole family. She can't forgive him, and after he has moved out she refuses to talk with him or to go along when he drives the younger girls to school or takes them away for the weekend. She shuts him out of her life, and the bond he feels with her is so strong that this is even more intolerable to him than being shut out of his own home. The other girls are sunshiny, but Sherry's face goes slack, and she looks burned out, like her mother. Faith, though, can look young and animated when she isn't with George; the years just fall away when she smiles her ravishing, clown's smile. Sherry's mood doesn't lift. She has had the most love and the most pain. She's the embodiment of what went wrong between her parents, and she's always there.

The movie isn't labored, like Ingmar Bergman's *Scenes from a Marriage*. It's essentially the story of the husband and father as supplicant for re-admission into the family, but it touches on things without seeming to address them directly. It's like a person with many sides. There are gags that pay off and keep on paying off—they turn into motifs. And sometimes the lines of dialogue that seem funny or ironic go through a variation or two and become lyrical. Parker has caught the essence of Bo Goldman's melancholic tone in the theme music—"Don't Blame Me," picked out on the piano with one finger. That, too, is turned into a joke and then has its original tone restored. There's an amazingly risky sequence, set in the restaurant of a Northern California inn, where George and Faith meet by chance and have a rowdy spat that's played off against screwball-comedy circumstances, with an elderly, quavering-voiced woman singer using the theme song in a hopeless attempt to drown out their shouting, and a man at the next table taking exception to their loud use of vulgar language. Many of the scenes have details that touch off very personal feelings: George pulling down the note pad that hangs on a string in his car to write excuses for his children's being late to school; one of the girls leaning toward *The Wizard of Oz* on the TV and chanting the Wicked Witch's threats slightly ahead of Margaret Hamilton. In this movie, the people have resources; they try things out. They take a step forward, and then maybe they move back. The tension that George feels with Faith is gone when he's with his perfectly shallow new lover (Karen Allen). She tells him, "You're my friend, George. I like you. I love you. And if you don't come through I'll find somebody else." She means it; she's adaptable.

The kids had a real presence in Bo Goldman's script for *Melvin and Howard* (his other screen credits include co-writing *One Flew Over the Cuckoo's Nest* and *The Rose*), and they have an even stronger one here. The family has been close in the loose, Northern California manner; the kids talk as freely as the parents do, and they're at ease, the way the house is. The girls have moments of imitating their high-and-mighty and short-tempered parents and then dissolving in giggles; they bitch each other heartlessly and then do something in perfect unison. When they squeal and carry on as they watch their parents on TV at the book awards, you know that this movie was written from observation and directed that way, too. The interaction of the four girls with each other and with their parents and the interaction of the girls with each parent's new lover are part of the substance of the movie. Alan Parker has four children, and Bo Goldman is the father of six; that may be the bond that made *Shoot the Moon* possible. This movie isn't just about marriage; it's about the family that is created, and how that whole family reacts to the knotted, disintegrating relationship of the parents. The children's world—a world of fragmented, displaced understanding—overlaps that of the adults and comments on it. And the texture of domestic scenes with bright, sensitive kids squabbling and testing keeps the film in balance. Bo Goldman has too much theatrical richness in his writing to make an audience suffer. He lets people be the entertainers that they are in life.

The four girls are inventive—they slip in and out of roles. Instinctive vaudevillians, they're always onstage. And whenever they're around, the movie is a variety show. Faith is sensitive to the comedy and drama of her family—she's constantly soothing and adjusting, and helping the seven-year-old get equal billing. When the morose, separated George takes the three younger kids out, he works so conscientiously to keep them happy that he sounds completely false; they feel his strain and try to humor him. When they're with him and his new lady, they try to play their parts, to keep tension to a minimum. (The comedy here is in how transparently they assume these roles.) And the sign of Sherry's confusion is her insistence on bringing up just the things nobody wants to have brought up, on forcing her parents into bad scenes. Yet she is never a pain. She keeps the atmosphere raw, and rawness is what makes this movie get to you.

Albert Finney, who has been sleepwalking in his recent movie appearances, is awake and trying out his reflexes. There's a profound difference in Finney; this is not a performance one might have expected from him. He uses all the impacted sloth and rage that show in the sag and weight of his big, handsome face. Locked out, George looks stunned, as if he'd been hit over the head—you can see the emotions fermenting in him that he himself isn't conscious of. He doesn't know that he's going to explode when he does. In a sequence in which he goes to the house doggedly determined to give Sherry her birthday present, Faith tells him that Sherry won't see him, and bolts the door. All he knows is that he has to get to Sherry. He kicks at the door and then he suddenly smashes a glass panel, sticks his arm in and pushes the bolt, rushes upstairs, grabs the child and spanks her, brutally. Sherry reaches for a scissors and holds him off with it. And then they huddle together, sobbing, and he, unforgiven, caresses her, pleading for a chance. It's one of the saddest, greatest love scenes ever put on film; you feel you've lived it, or lived something so close to its emotional core that you know everything each of them is going through. When George leaves, in disgrace, he trudges out carrying the present; then, a few paces away from the lighted house, he suddenly breaks into a run. Both as a character and as an actor, Finney seems startled and appalled by what has been let loose in him. His scenes seem to be happening right in front of us—you watch him with the apprehensiveness that you might feel at a live telecast. Keaton is Faith, but Finney seems both George and Finney. He's an actor possessed by a great role—pulled into it kicking and screaming, by his own guts.

Diane Keaton may be a star without vanity: she's so completely challenged by the role of Faith that all she cares about is getting the character right. Faith's eyes are squinched and you can see the crow's-feet; at times her face is bloated from depression, and she has the crumbling-plaster look of an old woman. Keaton is tall but not big, yet she gives you a feeling of size—of being planted and rooted, while George is buffeted about. He doesn't know how he was cast loose or what he's doing at sea. He has done it to himself and he can't figure out why. Throughout the movie, he's looking for a dock—he's reaching out to his wife. But Faith is unyielding; she doesn't want more pain. Very few young American movie actresses have the strength and the instinct for the toughest dramatic roles—intelligent, sophisticated heroines. Jane Fonda did, around the time that she appeared in *Klute* and *They Shoot Horses, Don't They?*, but that was more than ten years ago. There hasn't been anybody else until now. Diane Keaton acts on a different plane from that of her previous film roles; she brings the character a full measure of dread and awareness, and does it in a special, intuitive way that's right for screen acting. Nothing looks rehearsed, yet it's all fully created. She has a scene alone in the house in the early days of the separation—soaking in a tub, smoking a joint and singing faintly (a Beatles song—"If I Fell"), getting out to answer the phone, and then just standing listlessly, wiping off her smudged eyeliner. It's worthy of a Jean Rhys heroine; her eyes are infinitely sad—she's cracking, and you can sense the cold, windy remnants of passion that are cracking her. But this scene is a lull between wars. Faith is rarely alone: she still has her life around her—she has the kids and the house. (And that house, with its serene view, is itself a presence; it's upsetting when George smashes the door.) Faith can ignore George and start having a good time with a rather simple new fellow (Peter Weller)—a workman-contractor who puts up a tennis court for her in the grove next to the house. But George can't ignore her, because she's still holding so much of his life—the kids, the house, all the instinctive adaptations they had made to each other. George can't take anything for granted anymore.

Alan Parker and Bo Goldman circle around the characters, observing their moves and gestures toward each other; the movie is about the processes of adaptation. That's why that sequence at the inn is so funny and satisfying. In *Melvin and Howard,* it was a great moment when Howard Hughes got past his contempt for Melvin and they spoke together about the smell of the desert after the rain, and finally were friends and so close that they didn't need to talk. In *Shoot the Moon,* the only time that George and Faith reconnect is in their drunken dinner at the inn when they start eating out of the same plate and yell at each other, and then they wind up in bed together. What a relief it is for George—for a few hours he can live on instinct again.

This film may recall Irvin Kershner's 1970 *Loving*—a story of separating that had a high level of manic pain. But the wife in that (played with great delicacy by Eva Marie Saint) wasn't the powerhouse that Faith is. Faith doesn't back down when she and George fight, and her angry silence is much stronger than George's desperate chatter—Faith has no guilt. *Shoot the Moon* may also call up memories of *Long Day's Journey Into Night,* in the theatre or on the screen. But in that, too, the husband held the power. George is powerless. He has an extraordinary reconciliation scene with Sherry: she runs away from her mother on the night of a party celebrating the completion of the tennis court, and comes to find him, and they talk together on a pier, sitting quietly, with George's brown cardigan pulled around them both to keep out the chill. But when he takes Sherry back home and sees Faith and her lover and their guests and the strings of festive lights on the tennis court, he's filled with a balky, despairing rage—you can almost see his blood vessels engorging. He has been stripped of too much of his life; throughout the film he has been losing emotional control, breaking down—he can't adapt.

Alan Parker doesn't try to rush things or to prove himself. His energy doesn't come all the way through to the surface, as an American director's might; it stays under, and it's evenly distributed. George becomes resentful of any sign of change in Faith's or the children's lives, but the film doesn't over-emote—it looks at him and the others very steadily. It's a measure of the quality of Parker's direction that no one in the picture asks for the audience's sympathy. When George is self-pitying, as he is in a sequence of visiting the ruins of Jack London's house and telling his kids what a great author London was and how someone set fire to the house the night before the great author was supposed to move in, his maudlin tone is played off against the girls' questions and remarks about London's marriages and children; they all project their own feelings onto the Londons—it becomes a comedy routine. This is an unapologetically grown-up movie. Though Alan Parker doesn't do anything innovative in technique, it's a modern movie in terms of its consciousness, and in its assumption that the members of the movie audience, like the readers of modern fiction, share in that consciousness.

Probably Parker couldn't have brought it all off with such subtlety and discretion if he hadn't had the collaborators who were with him on his other features—the producer Alan Marshall, the cinematographer Michael Seresin, the production designer Geoffrey Kirkland, and the editor Gerry Hambling. They must have helped free him to devote his full attention to the cast. He directs the actors superbly. Diane Keaton and Albert Finney give the kind of performances that in the theatre become legendary, and, in its smaller dimensions, Dana Hill's Sherry is perhaps equally fine. And the three child actresses—Viveka Davis as Jill, Tracey Gold as Marianne, and Tina Yothers as Molly—are a convincing group of sisters and the very best kind of running gag. Even George Murdock, who has a single appearance as Faith's dying father, is remarkable—the old man has a clear head. Parker has created a completely believable family and environment (the picture was all shot on location), and he has done it in the wet days and foggy light of a country and a culture that aren't his own. And he has given us a movie about separating that is perhaps the most revealing American movie of the era. *Shoot the Moon* assumes the intelligence of the audience, as *Bonnie and Clyde* did; it assumes that people don't need to have basic emotions labelled or explained to them. When you see *Shoot the Moon,* you recognize yourself in it. If there's a key to the movie, it's in one simple dialogue exchange. It comes at the inn when George and Faith are in bed, lying next to each other after making love. She talks about how much she used to love him and then:

FAITH: Just now for an instant there—I don't know—you made me laugh, George—you were kind.
GEORGE: You're right, I'm not kind anymore.
FAITH: Me neither.
GEORGE: You're kind to strangers.
FAITH: Strangers are easy.

The New Yorker, January 18, 1982

DINER

Diner, written and directed by Barry Levinson, is a wonderful movie. Set in Baltimore, around Christmas of 1959, it's like a comic American version of I Vitelloni. A fluctuating group of five or six young men in their early twenties hang out together. They've known each other since high school, and though they're moving in different directions, they still cling to their late-night bull sessions at the Fells Point Diner. Shrevie (Daniel Stern), who has nothing to say to his young wife, ducks out on her, and the others take their dates home, and then they all make a quick dash back to the diner—where, magically, they always seem to have plenty to talk about. They're so relaxed together that they can sound worldly and sharp; they may never sound this quick-witted again. Levinson, who is making his début as a director, has a great ear; he's as sure on the nuances of dialogue and as funny as Paul Mazursky was in Bob & Carol & Ted & Alice and Next Stop, Greenwich Village. And when Levinson hits the contrasting notes—such as Shrevie's outburst at his affable young wife, Beth (Ellen Barkin), that leaves her emotionally annihilated—there are times when the lyrical intensity of the lines lifts you right out of the situation, transcends it. Conversations may roll on all night at the diner—it's kidding, reassuring patter—but when these boys are out with girls they're nervous, constricted, fraudulent, half crazy. They can't be the same people with women that they are with each other.

Diner is a great period piece—a look at middle-class relations between the sexes just before the sexual revolution. If any men (or women) think they regret the changes, this is the movie they ought to see. Although the trappings have changed, the dynamics are still much the same—except among people who make a real effort not to fall back on them. Set when it is, this film can show those painful dynamics at the last period in our history when people could laugh (albeit uneasily) at the gulf between men and women. It takes place just before this gulf became an issue of sexual politics—before it began to be discussed as a problem. (Perhaps that's the real change: the earnest psychiatric language took over.) The most innocent of the group is smiling, coddled Eddie (Steve Guttenberg, in a performance with such perfectly inflected Paul Newman–like grins that it atones for a lot, even his appearances in The Boys from Brazil and Can't Stop the Music). Eddie lives for football, and the Baltimore Colts, who are about to play the New York Giants, are his passion. He's scheduled to get married on New Year's Eve, but only if his bride-to-be passes a "monster" football-trivia test that he has scheduled for her; she's cramming for it. His rationale is that he wants to be sure they'll be able to communicate after they're married. There's a beautiful, bone-chilling moment when this simple, warm kid asks Shrevie what marriage is really like, and Shrevie, who has just said that he can't hold a five-minute conversation with his wife, thinks it over for a few seconds before telling him, "It's O.K."

The sleaziest and most charismatic figure of the group is Boogie, played by Mickey Rourke, who was the young professional arsonist in *Body Heat*. With luck, Rourke could become a major actor: he has an edge and magnetism, and a sweet, pure smile that surprises you. He seems to be acting to you, and to no one else. There's nothing standard about Rourke—he has an off-kilter look, like Louis Hayward, but with depth. Here, with his hair swept back, he's Boogie the flashy, experienced chaser, the gambler who's in bad trouble with his bookie, the guy who thinks of crooked ploys but can't really carry them out. Boogie works in a beauty parlor in the daytime, sits up till all hours at the diner, and still finds time to chase girls. Though completely unsettled and sweaty from exhaustion, he's ready for anything. He's also the most tender in his dealings with women, and the most gallant. Boogie courts women; he likes them. And you can see what makes him appealing to women; he's charming. But he has no real connection with them except sex.

Fenwick (Kevin Bacon), a smart, self-destructive dropout, is half drunk, half flipped out all through the film. He plays reckless practical jokes that get him and three of the others arrested; he's withdrawn, in a bitter funk. It's not until you see him alone, watching the "College Bowl" TV quiz show and gleefully beating the contestants to the answers, that you realize how consciously he's throwing himself away, and when you see him with his mealy-mouthed brother and discover that his father is the only parent who won't bail his kid out, you get a sense of why he's so screwed up. Fenwick is so infantile that the only girl he goes with is a highly developed eleventh grader. Kevin Bacon, with his pointed chin, and the look of a mad Mick, keeps Fenwick morose and yet demonic. You can see why the others try to take care of him and shield him. Fenwick will do more for his friends than he'll do for himself; he'll do anything he can think of to help Boogie with his debt—which means trying, failing, getting more drunk.

These are amazing performances—all four of them. You don't need to follow these characters' lives for years to get a sense of what will happen to them. And as Shrevie's young wife, Beth, Ellen Barkin, with her tough wistfulness, does things I've never seen before. Beth is crass and almost lewdly ordinary, yet her bruised, beat-out expressions stay with you. Barkin has a broad face, and at moments her Beth suggests the punchy Brando of *On the Waterfront*, with his slow reaction time. When Shrevie, who works in a store selling TV sets and refrigerators, tells her not to play any of the records in his collection, because she gets them mixed up, you feel that he enjoys putting her down. He's a fetishist about his records. They have been his own private world—what he cared about most—and it's slipping away from him; singing along with the music in his car, he looks utterly lost. (When the gang disintegrates, he'll be the worst off.) Sports, chasing girls, conversation, the early rock music are all linked together for the group at the diner. The movie isn't about sex but the quest for sex, the obsession with making out, which, for Shrevie, at least, has ended in the nothingness of marriage.

Levinson is less successful with the more proper Waspy characters. Timothy Daly, as a graduate student in another city, who has returned to be the best man at Eddie's wedding, is saddled with a beautiful, bland television-producer girlfriend (Kathryn Dowling). Their scenes aren't as well written as the others; they don't have the back-and-forth movement. But there are fully rounded marginal characters—Modell (Paul Reiser), a moocher who's often part of the group, is so funny when he tries to coax Eddie out of half his roast-beef sandwich or tries to bum a ride from him that the two of them seem to have had this bickering relationship since childhood.

Levinson never allows us to think that we know everything there is to know about these characters. They have sides—all of them—that are hidden from us and from each other. Levinson doesn't violate his characters by summing them up—he understands that we never fully understand anybody. Near the beginning, when several members of the group have gone to the Christmas dance at their old high school Boogie discovers that Fenwick has sold his date (whom he really likes) for five dollars; Boogie goes looking for him and finds him in the basement of the building smashing windows. Boogie asks him why he's doing it, and Fenwick says, "Just for a smile." Yes, he's a crazy masochist, but he is also really looking for a smile; he's trying to amuse himself. And Modell the reticent moocher, a dark, persistently self-righteous fellow, with small, suspicious eyes, turns out, at the wedding, to be a hilarious speechmaker. Nobody is merely what he seems. This movie is so beautifully detailed that the parents are as many-sided as their kids. The bride's football exam, with her father there judging the fairness of the scoring, is a perfect piece of loony Americana. So is the wedding, with the Baltimore Colts marching song and the bridesmaids' dresses in the Colts' colors (blue and white), and Beth trying to teach her record-aficionado husband to dance, and just about all the characters we have met gathered together listening to Modell making his toast.

Some twenty-six records are heard during the movie—the singers include Lil Green, Elvis Presley, Bobby Darin, Fats Domino, Sinatra, Jerry Lee Lewis, and Chuck Berry—but I was so caught up in the characters that I barely registered what was playing when. That may be an indication of the kind of talent Levinson has. He isn't thrillingly visual, and there are a few sequences (such as the intermingling of a TV soap opera with a messy real-life situation) in which his idea is a few jumps ahead of his ability to carry it out. But he's a storyteller with fresh stories to tell, and they're all bound together. You have the impression that he lets things take their own shape. His background is as a writer and performer; he wrote for "The Carol Burnett Show" and for Mel Brooks on a couple of movies, and he and a partner, Valerie Curtin, wrote . . . And Justice for All. Diner is that rare autobiographical movie that is made by someone who knows how to get the texture right. Levinson likes actors, the way Mazursky does. Boogie, being roughed up and trying to push his assailant away, the kid who wanders around quoting from Sweet Smell of Success—these are scenes that are just about perfectly rendered.

Levinson has a great feel for *promise*. At the diner, the boys are all storytellers, and they take off from each other; their conversations are almost all overlapping jokes that are funny without punch lines. The diner is like a comedy club where the performers and the customers feed each other lines—they're all stars and all part of the audience. The diner is where they go to give their nightly performances, and the actors all get a chance to be comedians.

The New Yorker, April 5, 1982

RICHARD PRYOR LIVE ON THE SUNSET STRIP

When Chaplin began to talk onscreen, he used a cultivated voice and high-flown words, and became a deeply unfunny man; if he had found the street language to match his lowlife, tramp movements, he might have been something like Richard Pryor, who's all of a piece—a master of lyrical obscenity. Pryor is the only great poet satirist among our comics. His lyricism seems to come out of his thin-skinned nature; he's so emphatic he's all wired up. His 1979 film *Richard Pryor Live in Concert* was a consummation of his years as an entertainer, and then some. He had a lifetime of material at his fingertips, and he seemed to go beyond himself. He personified objects, animals, people, the warring parts of his own body, even thoughts in the heads of men and women—black, white, Oriental—and he seemed to be possessed by the spirits he pulled out of himself. To those of us who thought it was one of the greatest performances we'd ever seen or ever would see, his new one-man show *Richard Pryor Live on the Sunset Strip* may be disappointing yet emotionally stirring. His new routines aren't as fully worked out; Pryor hasn't been doing the stage appearances that he used to do—hasn't, in fact, given any one-man shows since the 1979 film was shot—so these routines haven't been polished and sharpened, and they're not as varied. The material—specially prepared for this film, which was shot at two performances at the Hollywood Palladium—is rather skimpy, and a lot of it is patterned on routines from the first. Pryor doesn't seem as prickly now—he doesn't have the hunted look, or the old sneaky, guilty gleam in his eyes. He says he isn't angry anymore, and he seems to have been strengthened—he's more open. This probably has something to do with the vast public outpouring of affection for him after his near-fatal accident in June, 1980, when (as he acknowledges here) the dope he was freebasing exploded and set him on fire.

Pryor must have realized that millions and millions of people really wished him well, felt grateful for the pleasure he'd given them, and wanted him to live. How does an ornery, suspicious man who brought the language and grievances of the black underclass onto the stage deal with acceptance? (This is not a problem that Lenny Bruce, who brought the backstage language of the tawdriest levels of show business onto the stage, ever had to face.) Pryor doesn't appear sweetened, exactly. Even in the films in which he has played Mr. Nice Guy to children or whites, the stickiness hasn't clung to him; he's shed it. And he's always come clean with the audience. Pryor's best jokes aren't jokes in the usual sense—they're observations that are funny because of how he acts them out and because of his inflections. He constantly surprises us and makes us laugh in recognition. He tells us what we *almost* knew but shoved down, so when we laugh at him we feel a special, giddy freedom. That hasn't changed—he isn't soft in *Sunset Strip*. He tries on some benign racial attitudes and then drops them very fast—that's how you know he's still alive and kicking. He's different, though. You may sense that there has been a deepening of feeling, that there's something richer inside him, something more secure.

At the same time, he's adrift as a performer, because he isn't sure that he's got his act together. And he hasn't. The pressure of a one-man show before a huge crowd and on camera must be just about heart-stopping if you haven't been working in front of big live audiences. And that first film made him a legend; he has the pressure here of an audience expecting history to be made. This film doesn't build the performance rhythm that the 1979 film did; it's very smoothly put together, but in a meaningless way—you don't feel that you're experiencing *Pryor's* rhythms. Is the editing bad, or were the editors trying to stretch the material to this eighty-eight minute length? (Why are there so many cutaways—at just the wrong time—to laughing, dressed-up people in the front rows? You half expect to see a star or two among them. It makes the movie feel canned.) Haskell Wexler headed the camera crew, and the color looks true and clear, and Pryor, in his scarlet suit, black bow tie and shirt, gold shoes, and a snazzy designer belt with a piece hanging straight down, is vividly close to us. But he has trouble getting going. He has hunches—he touches on things and you wait to see what he'll do with them. And most of the time he doesn't do anything with them; they don't develop into routines—he just drops them. Midway, he starts getting into his swing, in a section about his experiences during the filming of parts of *Stir Crazy* in the Arizona State Prison. He goes on to talk about a trip he took to Africa, and it's a scene—he can live it. He turns himself into a rabbit, a bear, a lion, a couple of cheetahs, and a fearful gazelle. You feel his relief when he does the animals; a lot of the time he has been looking for his place on the stage, and now he has something physical to do. But then there's a sudden break. Voices, ostensibly from the audience, can be heard. One of them calls, "Do the Mudbone routine," and, rather wearily, saying that it will be for the last time, Pryor sits on a stool and does the ancient storyteller Mudbone, who in the seventies was considered one of his great creations. And the movie goes thud. This section feels like an interpolation—it doesn't have the crackle of a performer interacting with an audience. It's almost as dead as what happens when Johnny Carson asks an aging celebrity to tell the joke he used to tell that always broke Johnny up. Pryor looks defeated, shot down. The sudden dullness is compounded by his sitting: we're used to seeing him prowling—accompanied, when the spots hit the curtain behind him, by wriggling shadows.

When he picks up his act again, he talks about freebasing, and the feelings he had about his pipe—it talks to him, and he becomes the pipe. We feel as if we were actually listening to his habit talking to him. And he builds up a routine about his wife and his friend Jim Brown telling him what cocaine was doing to him. But "the pipe say, 'Don't listen.' " And then he tells about the hospital and about Jim Brown's visiting him every day. He's a great actor and a great combination of mimic and mime; he's perhaps never more inspired than when he assumes the personality of a rebellious organ of his body or of an inanimate object, such as that pipe—or Jim Brown. This is the high point of the film. When he becomes something or someone, it isn't an imitation; he incarnates the object's soul and guts. But he doesn't have enough material to work up the rhythmic charge he reached before Mudbone. What he has in *Sunset Strip* is the material for a forty-minute classic.

The picture is full of wonderful bits, such as his demonstration of how he loses his voice when he's angry at his wife, and to those unfamiliar with Pryor's infectiousness and truthfulness and his unfettered use of obscenity, and to all those who missed his 1979 film, it may be a revelation. But the greatness of *Richard Pryor Live in Concert* was in the impetus of his performance rhythm—the way he kept going, with all those characters and voices bursting out of him. When he told us about his heart attack, he was, in almost the same instant, the helpless body being double-crossed by its heart, the heart itself, a telephone operator, and Pryor the aloof, dissociated observer. We registered what a mysteriously original physical comedian he is, and we saw the performance sweat soaking his collarless red silk shirt. (There's no visible sweat this time.)

If he fulfilled his comic genius in *Live in Concert*, here he's sampling the good will the public feels toward him. Audiences want him, they love him, even in bum movies, and he appears to be experiencing a personal fulfillment. But he hasn't yet renewed himself as an artist: it may seem cruel to say so, but even the routine on his self-immolation is a pale copy of his heart attack. In the first film, there was a sense of danger; when he used the word "nigger," it was alive and raw. When he uses it here, it just seems strange. He's up against something very powerful: the audience may have come expecting to see history made, but history now is also just seeing Richard Pryor. He knows that he doesn't have to do anything. All he has to do is stand there and be adored. And he knows there's something the matter with this new situation, but he doesn't know how to deal with it.

The New Yorker, April 5, 1982

DIVA
RHAPSODY IN BLUE

The French romantic thriller *Diva* dashes along with a pell-mell gracefulness, and it doesn't take long to see that the images and visual gags and homages all fit together and reverberate back and forth. It's a glittering toy of a movie, like *Touch of Evil* or *The Stunt Man* or *Zazie dans le Métro*. This one is by a new director, Jean-Jacques Beineix (pronounced simply Ben-ex, with the stress on the second syllable), who understands the pleasures to be had from a picture that doesn't take itself very seriously. Every shot seems designed to delight the audience. Now thirty-five, Beineix has been working as an assistant to other directors for ten years; he begins his own directing career as a Euro-disco entertainer with a fabulous camera technique. The movie doesn't have the purity of conception of those other toys. It isn't quite in their class, and though you may come out of it with some of the same exhilaration, it isn't really memorable. But the images are so smooth yet tricky and hip that Beineix might be Carol Reed reborn with a Mohawk haircut.

The diva of the title is an awesomely beautiful black American soprano called Cynthia Hawkins (and played by the American Wilhelmenia Fernandez), who inspires a fanatic following, like that of Maria Callas. But the glorious Cynthia has a major eccentricity: she refuses to make recordings, because she wants the public to have the full experience of a singer's presence. Jules, the eighteen-year-old hero (Frédéric Andrei), a skinny young postal messenger in Paris, with an official cap that's too big for his face, is, perhaps, Cynthia's most dedicated fan. He rides his motorbike all the way to Munich and other cities she performs in, and when she gives a concert in Paris he sneaks his Nagra tape machine in and makes a recording—he wants to be able to listen to her at home. Her voice is thrilling in the hushed, expectant atmosphere; her off-the-shoulder satin gown reveals a creamy brown arm, and her lips push out toward us as she articulates the words. Jules' face is full of adoration; a tear collects in one eye and falls, while his hands skillfully regulate the dials. It's at this point that the picture opens, and from there on we follow the chaos that envelops Jules because of this tape and a second tape that he knows nothing about. A barefoot prostitute, running away from two assassins and trying to reach a policewoman to turn over a casette revealing names and details of a narcotics-and-vice ring, sees the killers coming at her, and, just before being murdered, she drops the tape in the saddlebag of Jules' bike. The wide-eyed music lover Jules is the subject of two intertwined chases. The police and the killers are after him for the prostitute's exposé, and a pair of Chinese record pirates from Taiwan are trying to get his concert tape, so that they can use it to blackmail Cynthia Hawkins into signing with them—they threaten that if she doesn't they'll release the illicit recording.

For a while, Jules innocently goes on about his life. In a music store, he watches a young Vietnamese girl, Alba (played by the fourteen-year-old Thuy An Luu), as she calmly snitches a record and brazens it out with the suspicious clerk. The unfazable Alba is the post-Godardian tootsie—in her short-short skirts and transparent plastic coat, she's a lollipop wrapped in cellophane. Alba appears to have no inner life at all, to be totally—and enchantingly—a creature of surface attitudes, all pose. In the street, outside the store, she tells Jules that the record is a present for a guy who's in his cool phase, and takes him to meet the guy—Gorodish (Richard Bohringer), the most dream-born of the characters (and ultimately, perhaps, the least successful element). When you see this movie, which opened in Paris in March, 1981, and is still running (it has just won some of the top French prizes—Best First Film, and Best Photography, Sound, and Music), you get a clearer sense of what went wrong for Coppola in his *One From the Heart.* Much of what Coppola seemed to be aiming for—the dreamy-disco fun in the detritus of tech commercialism (bashed-in old cars, broken signs, painted skies on billboards)—Beineix had already got onto the screen. And Beineix made it work, because his picture has the baroque characters to go with it—a dozen or so of them—and an amusing enough suspense plot to support it (though the plot is so smart it outsmarts itself in places, and the introduction of a fairy godfather does seem a bit of a cheat). Jules lives in a warehouselike garage and auto graveyard that's reached by a huge car-lift elevator, and Gorodish (he could be thirty-five or forty) lives in a vast bluish space so large Alba skates around in it. Kinetic sculptures slosh water back and forth, and Gorodish works on the waves of a giant jigsaw puzzle of the sea, while piling up Gitanes cigarette boxes, with their wavy blue and white lines. When all hell breaks loose around Jules, Gorodish in his white suit helps him hide out by packing him into his white Citroën and taking him to a lighthouse-castle that's magical in the blue dawn light. Gorodish seems to be a punkers' deus ex machina, wise in the ways of criminals. He knows how to deal with the forces in society, and, effortlessly, he has the wherewithal to do it. The hero of a novel by Delacorta—which, adapted by Beineix and Jean Van Hamme, was the basis of the film—Gorodish is the bemused Mr. Cool. The conception may be all too airily French. Gorodish is a tease of a character—a Zen master of gadgetry—and he's enjoyable. But toward the end, when he takes over, something gets dampened. Gorodish isn't either believably human or high-wire enough to be a creature of fantasy. He's in between.

Jules' garage, with its crippled Rolls-Royce and its posters for events long past, looks much like Frederic Forrest's dream refuge in *One From the Heart,* but there's a sizable difference. Forrest's company was Reality Wrecking, and he wandered through the painted Las Vegas set morosely. Beineix accepts the faddish, constantly changing reality; he didn't build this vision—it isn't a set, it's Paris as he sees it, and he shows the crazy, dissociated pleasures in it. He isn't even saying that this is a condemned playground; he doesn't make any moral judgment—he's having too much fun looking at the players. *Diva* is the human side of *Alphaville*. Even gags, such as Alba in Jules' garage hopscotching on a nude woman painted on the floor, or Gorodish wearing a diver's mask and snorkle as he chops onions, seem to come out of their characters. And conceits, such as Alba sitting on top of Gorodish's refrigerator as if she were Helen Morgan on the piano, or affectations, such as Jules strolling in the Tuileries with Cynthia Hawkins and holding a white umbrella above her head to frame her beauty, seem exactly what these characters would do. Beineix presents people who charm us because they arrange their reality to suit their whims. They're unselfconscious about being self-conscious. Godard showed us people who were turning into cartoons; the people here don't mind being cartoons—they amuse themselves at it. They make their lives scintillate.

When Cynthia listens to Jules' tape of her singing, she realizes she was wrong to be against recording. But in a way she wasn't. If you put on the record of Wilhelmenia Fernandez singing her big number in the movie—the aria from the first act of Catalani's *La Wally*—you may decide that Cynthia Hawkins was right, because without her beauty and the drama of her presence and the charged setting that the movie gives her performance, her voice isn't quite as overwhelmingly glorious. A movie can do for a performer most of what a live stage appearance can do, and then some. (What singer in a solo recital could afford a whole orchestra behind her?) Actually, the entire movie demonstrates the richness that you can get only from movies. If it's about anything, it's about the joy of making them. (At the lighthouse, Alba serves Jules coffee out of a coffeepot that could be a miniature version of the lighthouse itself.)

Diva is a later stage of what Godard was getting at in *Masculine Feminine* and in his other movies about "the children of Marx and Coca-Cola"—except that now Marx is gone and New Wave music and video games have settled in. What Marxists and other puritans have never wanted to allow for is the fun to be had with the material goodies that capitalism produces (such as entertaining movies). Godard knew it, recognized that alienation wasn't all torment, and then somehow blotted it from his mind. (When he became more political, he *wanted* us all to be tormented.) Alba, the wise-child playmate, may be shell-shocked, but she's having a good time. The young actress Thuy An Luu is completely at ease in front of the camera; if that's the result of fundamental indifference (and it may very well be), it works to her great advantage here. Jules is the Jean-Pierre Léaud of Godard's films with a love of music and a sweeter nature; he wears an invisible aureole, but he's still a fan. Cynthia treats him like a lovely pet, and that seems just about right—he's birdlike. (Wilhelmenia Fernandez' American-accented French and her amateurishness as an actress are ingratiating. It's her bad luck, though, to be caught in the only real lapse of judgment in the movie: Cynthia invites Jules to stay with her while she practices, and then proceeds to sing "Ave Maria"—the banality of the choice momentarily strips her of glamour.)

Beineix may not be interested in what's underneath, but he has a great feeling for surfaces. A chase through the Métro and an escape to a pinball-machine and video-game arcade are so ravishing that they're funny, intentionally. The whole high-tech incandescence of the film is played for humor. Beineix takes it for granted that we'll make all sorts of connections between his images and other movies we've seen—Cynthia Hawkins at the start is like Arletty's Garance in *Children of Paradise;* a police informer who works on a boardwalk operating a Wheel of Chance has layer upon layer of movie associations; there's a little salute to Marilyn Monroe in *The Seven Year Itch;* and Welles is in the huge deserted bluish factory where the all-knowing Gorodish arranges a meeting with the villain—it recalls *The Trial.* Welles is everywhere. But Beineix doesn't force the connections on us. Everything is deft, flamboyant yet light—Jules takes Cynthia Hawkins' pearly satin gown and flings it around his neck, like a First World War aviator's scarf, as he rides off on a borrowed motorbike. In the factory, Gorodish's tape-recorded voice directs the villain. Every shot seems to have a shaft of wit. It's Welles romanticized, gift-wrapped. It's a mixture of style and chic hanky-panky, but it's also genuinely sparkling. The camera skids ahead, and you see things you don't expect. Beineix thinks with his eyes.

The New Yorker, April 19, 1982

E.T. THE EXTRA-TERRESTRIAL

Steven Spielberg's *E.T. The Extra-Terrestrial* envelops you in the way that his *Close Encounters of the Third Kind* did. It's a dream of a movie—a bliss-out. This sci-fi fantasy has a healthy share of slapstick comedy, yet it's as pure as Carroll Ballard's *The Black Stallion.* Like Ballard, Spielberg respects the conventions of children's stories, and because he does he's able to create the atmosphere for a mythic experience. Essentially, *E.T.* is the story of a ten-year-old boy, Elliott, who feels fatherless and lost because his parents have separated, and who finds a miraculous friend—an alien, inadvertently left on Earth by a visiting spaceship.

If the film seems a continuation of *Close Encounters,* that's partly because it has the sensibility we came to know in that picture, and partly because E.T. himself is like a more corporeal version of the celestial visitors at the end of it. Like *Close Encounters, E.T.* is bathed in warmth, and it seems to clear all the bad thoughts out of your head. It reminds you of the goofiest dreams you had as a kid, and rehabilitates them. Spielberg is right there in his films; you can feel his presence and his love of surprises. This phenomenal master craftsman plays high-tech games, but his presence is youthful—it has a just-emerged quality. The Spielberg of *Close Encounters* was a singer with a supple, sweet voice. It couldn't be heard in his last film, the impersonal *Raiders of the Lost Ark,* and we may have been afraid that he'd lost it, but now he has it back, and he's singing more melodiously than we could have hoped for. He's like a boy soprano lilting with joy all through *E.T.,* and we're borne along by his voice.

In Spielberg's movies, parents love their children, and children love their siblings. And suburban living, with its comfortable, uniform houses, is seen as a child's paradise—an environment in which children are protected and their imaginations can flourish. There's a luminous, magical view of Elliott's hilly neighborhood in the early-evening light on Halloween, with the kids in their costumes fanning out over the neatly groomed winding streets as each little group moves from one house to another for trick-or-treat, and E.T., swathed in a sheet and wearing red slippers over his webbed feet, waddles along between Elliott and his teen-age brother, Michael—each of them keeping a firm, protective grip on a gray-green four-digit hand. E.T. isn't just Elliott's friend; he's also Elliott's pet—the film catches the essence of the bond between lonely children and their pets. The sequence may call up memories of the trick-or-treat night in Vincente Minnelli's *Meet Me in St. Louis,* but it's more central here. All the imagery in the film is linked to Halloween, with the spaceship itself as a jack-o'-lantern in the sky, and the child-size space visitors, who have come to gather specimens of Earth's flora, wrapped in cloaks with hoods and looking much like the trick-or-treaters. (The pumpkin spaceship is silent, though when you see it you may hear in your head the five-note theme of the mother ship in *Close Encounters,* and the music that John Williams has written for *E.T.* is dulcet and hushed—it allows for the full score that the movie gets going in your imagination.)

E.T. probably has the best-worked-out script that Spielberg has yet shot, and since it seems an emanation of his childlike, playful side and his love of toys, it would be natural to assume that he wrote it. But maybe it seems such a clear expression of his spirit because its actual writer, Melissa Mathison, could see what he needed more deeply than he could himself, and could devise a complete structure that would hold his feelings in balance. Mathison was one of the scenarists for *The Black Stallion* and is a co-writer of *The Escape Artist;* it probably isn't a coincidence that all three of these films have young-boy heroes who miss their fathers. Writers may be typecast, like actors; having written one movie about a boy, Mathison may have been thought of for another, and yet another. In *E.T.,* she has made Elliott dreamy and a little withdrawn but practical and intelligent. And very probably she intuited the necessity for Elliott, too, to be bereft—especially since Spielberg himself had experienced the separation of his parents. Mathison has a feeling for the emotional sources of fantasy, and although her dialogue isn't always inspired, sometimes it is, and she has an ear for how kids talk. Henry Thomas, who plays Elliott, and Kelly Reno in *The Black*

Stallion and Griffin O'Neal as the boy magician in *The Escape Artist* are not Hollywood-movie kids; they all have an unusual—a magical—reserve. They're all in thrall to their fantasies, and the movies take us inside those fantasies while showing us how they help the boys grow up. Elliott (his name begins with an "E" and ends with a "T") is a dutiful, too sober boy who never takes off his invisible thinking cap; the telepathic communication he develops with E.T. eases his cautious, locked-up worries, and he begins to act on his impulses. When E.T. has his first beer and loses his inhibitions, Elliott, at school, gets tipsy, and in biology class when each student is required to chloroform a frog and then dissect it he perceives his frog's resemblance to E.T. and sets it free. (His classmates follow suit.) The means by which Elliott manages to kiss a pretty girl who towers over him by at least a head is a perfectly executed piece of slapstick.

It's no small feat to fuse science fiction and mythology. *E.T.* holds together the way some of George MacDonald's fairy tales (*At the Back of the North Wind, The Princess and the Goblin, The Princess and Curdie*) do. It's emotionally rounded and complete. The neighborhood kids whose help Elliott needs all come through for him. Even his little sister, Gertie (Drew Barrymore), is determined to keep the secret that E.T. is hidden in Elliott's room. And when Elliott's harried mother (Dee Wallace) rushes around in her kitchen and fails to see E.T.—fails to see him even when she knocks him over—the slapstick helps to dominate the feeling of enchantment and, at the same time, strengthens it. Adults—as we all know from the children's stories of our own childhoods, or from the books we've read to our children—are too busy and too preoccupied to see the magic that's right there in front of them. Spielberg's mellow, silly jokes reinforce the fantasy structure. One of them—Elliott on his bicycle dropping what look like M&M's to make a trail—seems to come right out of a child's mind. (Viewers with keen eyes may perceive that the candies are actually Reese's Pieces.) Among the costumed children radiating out on Halloween is a tiny Yoda, and the audience laughs in recognition that, yes, this film is part of the fantasy world to which Yoda (the wise gnome of *The Empire Strikes Back*) belongs. And when E.T.—a goblin costumed as a ghost—sees the child dressed as Yoda and turns as if to join him it's funny because it's so unaccountably right.

Henry Thomas (who was the older of Sissy Spacek's two small sons in *Raggedy Man*) has a beautiful brainy head with a thick crop of hair; his touching serio-comic solemnity draws us into the mood of the picture. When one of the neighborhood kids makes a fanciful remark about E.T., Elliott reprimands him, rapping out, "This is reality." Dee Wallace as the mother, Peter Coyote as a scientist who from childhood has dreamed the dream that Elliott has realized, and the other adult actors are the supporting cast. Henry Thomas and E.T. (who was designed by one of the authentic wizards of Hollywood, Carlo Rambaldi) are the stars, and Drew Barrymore and Robert Macnaughton, as the teen-ager Michael, are the featured players. Elliott and his brother and sister are all low-key humorists. When Michael first sees E.T., he does a double take that's like a momentary paralysis. Elliott has an honestly puzzled tone when he asks Michael, "How do you explain school to a higher intelligence?" Little Gertie adapts to E.T. very quickly—he may have the skin of a dried fig and a potbelly that just misses the floor, but she talks to him as if he were one of her dolls.

Spielberg changed his usual way of working when he made *E.T.*, and you can feel the difference. The visual energy and graphic strength in his work have always been based on his storyboarding the material—that is, sketching the camera angles in advance, so that the graphic plan was laid out. That way, he knew basically what he was after in each shot and how the shots would fit together; his characteristic brilliantly jagged cutting was largely thought out from the start. On *E.T.*—perhaps because the story is more delicate and he'd be working with child actors for much of the time—he decided to trust his intuition, and the film has a few fuzzy spots but a gentler, more fluid texture. It's less emphatic than his other films; he doesn't use his usual wide-screen format—he isn't out to overpower you. The more reticent shape makes the story seem simpler—plausible. The light always has an apparent source, even when it gives the scenes an other-worldly glow. And from the opening in the dense, vernal woodland that adjoins Elliott's suburb (it's where we first hear E.T.'s frightened sounds), the film has the soft, mysterious inexorability of a classic tale of enchantment. The little shed in back of the house where Elliott tosses in a ball and E.T. sends it back is part of a dreamscape.

The only discordant note is the periodic switch to overdynamic camera angles to show the NASA men and other members of the search party whose arrival frightened off the space visitors and who keep looking for the extra-terrestrial left behind. These men are lined up in military-looking groups, and the camera shows us only their stalking or marching bodies—they're faceless, silent, and extremely threatening. Their flashlights in the dark woods could be lethal ray guns, and one of them has a bunch of keys hanging from his belt that keep jangling ominously. The rationale is probably that we're meant to view the men as little E.T. would, or as Elliott would, but most of the time neither E.T. nor Elliott is around when they are. Later in the movie, in the sequences in a room that is used as a hospital, it's clear that when adults are being benevolent in adult terms they may still be experienced by children as enemies. But the frequent intrusive cuts to the uniformed men—in some shots they wear moon-travel gear and head masks—are meant to give us terror vibes. They're abstract figures of evil; even the American-flag insignia on their uniforms is sinister—in modern movie iconology that flag means "bad guys." And this movie doesn't need faceless men; it has its own terror. Maybe Spielberg didn't have enough faith in the fear that is integral to any magical idyll: that it can't last.

When the children get to know E.T., his sounds are almost the best part of the picture. His voice is ancient and otherworldly but friendly, humorous.

And this scaly, wrinkled little man with huge, wide-apart, soulful eyes and a jack-in-the-box neck has been so fully created that he's a friend to us, too; when he speaks of his longing to go home the audience becomes as mournful as Elliott. Spielberg has earned the tears that some people in the audience—and not just children—shed. The tears are tokens of gratitude for the spell the picture has put on the audience. Genuinely entrancing movies are almost as rare as extraterrestrial visitors.

The New Yorker, June 14, 1982

ABOUT RICARDO MONTALBAN IN
STAR TREK II: THE WRATH OF KHAN

The director, Nicholas Meyer, has made the dialogue scenes jazzy without violating the characters, and, using the contrast between Ricardo Montalban's fiery Khan and William Shatner's pasty Captain Kirk as the psychological center, he keeps the movie whipping from one incident to another.

Montalban, who was born in Mexico in 1920, is one of those potentially major actors who never got the roles that might have made them movie stars. He appeared to have everything else—a marvellous camera face, the physique of a trained dancer, talent, a fine voice (he could even sing), warmth, and great charm. Maybe the charm was a drawback—it may have made him seem too likable, a lightweight (though it didn't stop Charles Boyer). In Montalban's first English-language picture, M-G-M's *Fiesta,* in 1947, which featured Esther Williams as a matador, he danced with Cyd Charisse. M-G-M next had him dancing with Charisse and Ann Miller in a Kathryn Grayson–Frank Sinatra film called *The Kissing Bandit;* it was said that the dancing was added after the executives saw the movie—they wanted to give the customers *something.* He kept working—in pictures such as *On an Island with You,* with Charisse and Esther Williams, and *Neptune's Daughter,* and *Sombrero,* starring Vittorio Gassman, and the low-budget *My Man and I,* in which he played a sexy handyman and displayed his pectorals, and *Latin Lovers,* in which he carted Lana Turner around in a tango. He had secondary parts in *Sayonara* and *Hemingway's Adventures of a Young Man,* and in *Cheyenne Autumn,* and he brought conviction to every role that anyone could bring conviction to, but, after almost twenty years in Hollywood, there he was in 1966 in *The Singing Nun,* with Debbie Reynolds, and, with Lana again, in *Madame X.* He seems to have lived a (lucrative) horror story, especially when you think of the TV commercials and his ever-ready smile on "Fantasy Island." It may be that Khan in the 1967 TV episode "Space Seed" was the best big role he had ever got, and that the continuation of the role in *The*

Wrath of Khan is the only validation he has ever had of his power to command the big screen.

Montalban is unquestionably a star in *The Wrath of Khan* (and his grand manner seems to send a little electric charge through Shatner). As a graying superman who, when foiled, cries out to Kirk, "From Hell's heart I stab at thee!," Montalban may be the most romantic smoothie of all sci-fi villains. Khan's penchant for quoting Melville, and Milton (which goes back to "Space Seed"), doesn't hurt. And that great chest of Montalban's is reassuring—he looks like an Inca priest—and he's still champing at the bit, eager to act: he plays his villainy to the hilt, smiling grimly as he does the dirty. (He and his blond-barbarian followers are dressed like pirates or a sixties motorcycle gang.) Montalban's performance doesn't show a trace of "Fantasy Island." It's all panache; if he isn't wearing feathers in his hair you see them there anyway. You know how you always want to laugh at the flourishes that punctuate the end of a flamenco dance and the dancers don't let you? Montalban does. His bravado is grandly comic. Khan feels he was born a prince, and in all the years that he was denied his due (because of Kirk, in his thinking) his feelings of rage have grown enormous. They're manias now; nothing can stop him from giving in to them. His words and gestures are one long sigh of relief—he's letting out his hatred. This man, who believes that his search for vengeance is like Ahab's, makes poor pompous Kirk even more self-conscious. Kirk is Khan's white whale, and he knows he can't live up to it—he's not worthy of Khan's wrath.

The New Yorker, June 28, 1982

BLADE RUNNER
BABY, THE RAIN MUST FALL

Ridley Scott, the director of the futuristic thriller *Blade Runner,* sets up the action with a crawl announcing that the time is early in the twenty-first century, and that a blade runner is a police officer who "retires"—i.e., kills—"replicants," the powerful humanoids manufactured by genetic engineers, if they rebel against their drudgery in the space colonies and show up on Earth. A title informs us that we're in Los Angeles in the year 2019, and then Scott plunges us into a hellish, claustrophobic city that has become a cross between Newark and old Singapore. The skies are polluted, and there's a continual drenching rainfall. The air is so rotten that it's dark outside, yet when we're inside, the brightest lights are on the outside, from the giant searchlights scanning the city and shining in. A huge, squat pyramidal skyscraper (the new architecture appears to be Mayan and Egyptian in inspiration) houses the offices of the Tyrell Corporation, which produces those marvels of energy the replicants, who are faster and stronger than human beings, and even at the top, in the penthouse of Tyrell himself, there's dust hanging in the smoky air. (You may find yourself idly wondering why this bigwig inventor can't produce a humble little replicant to do some dusting.)

The congested-megalopolis sets are extraordinary, and they're lovingly, perhaps obsessively, detailed; this is the future as a black market, made up of scrambled sordid aspects of the past—Chinatown, the Casbah, and Times Square, with an enormous, mesmerizing ad for Coca-Cola, and Art Deco neon signs everywhere, in a blur of languages. *Blade Runner,* which cost thirty million dollars, has its own look, and a visionary sci-fi movie that has its own look can't be ignored—it has its place in film history. But we're always aware of the sets as sets, partly because although the impasto of decay is fascinating, what we see doesn't mean anything to us. (It's 2019 back lot.) Ridley Scott isn't great on mise en scène—we're never sure exactly what part of the city we're in, or where it is in relation to the scene before and the scene after. (Scott seems to be trapped in his own alleyways, without a map.) And we're not caught up in the pulpy suspense plot, which involves the hero, Deckard (Harrison Ford), a former blade runner forced to come back to hunt down four murderous replicants who have blended into the swarming street life. It's a very strange tenderloin that Ridley Scott and his associates have concocted; except for Deckard and stray Hari Krishna–ites and porcupine-headed punks, there are few Caucasians (and not many blacks, either). The population seems to be almost entirely ethnic—poor, hustling Asians and assorted foreigners, who are made to seem not quite degenerate, perhaps, but oddly subhuman. They're all selling, dealing, struggling to get along; they never look up—they're intent on what they're involved in, like slot-machine zealots in Vegas. You know that Deckard is a breed apart, because he's the only one you see who reads a newspaper. Nothing much is explained (except in that opening crawl), but we get the vague impression that the more prosperous, clean-cut types have gone off-world to some Scarsdale in space.

Here we are—only forty years from now—in a horrible electronic slum, and *Blade Runner* never asks, "How did this happen?" The picture treats this grimy, retrograde future as a given—a foregone conclusion, which we're not meant to question. The presumption is that man is now fully realized as a spoiler of the earth. The sci-fi movies of the past were often utopian or cautionary; this film seems indifferent, blasé, and maybe, like some of the people in the audience, a little pleased by this view of a medieval future—satisfied in a slightly vengeful way. There's a subject, though, lurking around the comic-strip edges: What does it mean to be human? Tracking down the replicants, who are assumed not to have any feelings, Deckard finds not only that they suffer and passionately want to live but that they are capable of acts of generosity. They have become far more human than the scavenging people left on Earth. Maybe Scott and the scriptwriters (Hampton Fancher and David Peoples), who adapted the 1968 novel *Do Androids Dream of Electric Sheep?*, by the late Philip K. Dick, shied away from this subject because it has sticky, neo-Fascist aspects. But this underlying idea is the only promising one in the movie, and it has a strong visual base: when a manufactured person looks just like a person born of woman—when even the eyes don't tell you which is which—how do you define the difference?

Scott's creepy, oppressive vision requires some sort of overriding idea—something besides spoofy gimmicks, such as having Deckard narrate the movie in the loner-in-the-big-city manner of a Hammett or Chandler private eye. This voice-over, which is said to have been a late addition, sounds ludicrous, and it breaks the visual hold of the material. The dialogue isn't well handled, either. Scott doesn't seem to have a grasp of how to use words as part of the way a movie moves. *Blade Runner* is a suspenseless thriller; it appears to be a victim of its own imaginative use of hardware and miniatures and mattes. At some point, Scott and the others must have decided that the story was unimportant; maybe the booming, lewd and sultry score by Chariots-for-Hire Vangelis that seems to come out of the smoke convinced them that the audience would be moved even if vital parts of the story were trimmed. Vangelis gives the picture so much *film noir* overload that he fights Scott's imagery; he chomps on it, stomps on it, and drowns it.

Blade Runner doesn't engage you directly; it forces passivity on you. It sets you down in this lopsided maze of a city, with its post-human feeling, and keeps you persuaded that something bad is about to happen. Some of the scenes seem to have six subtexts but no text, and no context either. There are suggestions of Nicolas Roeg in the odd, premonitory atmosphere, but Roeg gives promise of something perversely sexual. With Scott, it's just something unpleasant or ugly. The dizzying architectural angles (we always seem to be looking down from perilous heights) and the buglike police cars that lift off in the street and rise straight up in the canyons between the tall buildings and drop down again give us a teasing kind of vertigo. Scott goes much further, though. He uses way-off-kilter angles that produce not nausea, exactly, but a queasiness that prepares us for the feelings of nausea that Deckard is then seen to have. And, perhaps because of the what-is-a-human-being remnant in the story, the picture keeps Deckard—and us—fixated on eyes. (The characters' perambulations include a visit to the eyemaker who supplies the Tyrell genetic engineers with human eyes, and he turns out to be a wizened old Chinese gent—as if eyemaking were an ancient art. Maybe Tyrell picks up some used elbows in Saigon. His methods of operation for creating replicant slaves out of living cell tissue seem as haphazard as bodywork on wrecked cars.) In Nicolas Roeg's films, the characters are drained, and they're left soft and androgynous in an inviting way; Scott squashes his characters, and the dread that he sets up leads you to expect some release, and you know it's not the release you want.

All we've got to hang on to is Deckard, and the moviemakers seem to have decided that his characterization was complete when they signed Harrison Ford for the role. Deckard's bachelor pad is part of a 1924 Frank

Lloyd Wright house with a Mayan motif. Apart from that, the only things we learn about him are that he has inexplicably latched on to private-eye lingo, that he was married, and that he's tired of killing replicants—it has begun to sicken him. (The piano in his apartment has dozens of family pictures on it, but they're curiously old-fashioned photos—they seem to go back to the nineteenth century—and we have no idea what happened to all those people.) The film's visual scale makes the sloppy bit of plot about Deckard going from one oddball place to another as he tracks down the four replicants—two men, two women—seem sort of pitiable. But his encounters with the replicant women are sensationally, violently effective. As Zhora, who has found employment as an artificial-snake charmer, Joanna Cassidy has some of the fine torrid sluttiness she had in *The Late Show*. (Nobody is less like a humanoid than Joanna Cassidy; her Zhora wasn't manufactured as an adult—she was formed by bitter experience, and that's what gives her a screen presence.) And, in the one really shocking and magical sequence, Daryl Hannah, as the straw-haired, acrobatic Pris, does a punk variation on Olympia, the doll automaton of *The Tales of Hoffmann*.

The two male replicants give the movie problems. Leon (Brion James, who brings a sweaty wariness and suggestions of depth to the role) has found a factory job at the Tyrell Corporation itself, and his new employers, suspecting that he may be a renegade replicant, give him a highly sophisticated test. It checks his emotional responses by detecting the contractions of the pupils of his eyes as he attempts to deal with questions about his early life. But this replicant-detector test comes at the beginning of the picture, before we have registered that replicants *have* no early life. And it seems utterly pointless, since surely the Tyrell Corporation has photographic records of the models it has produced—and, in fact, when the police order Deckard to find and retire the four he is shown perfectly clear pictures of them. It might have been much cannier to save any testing until later in the movie, when Deckard has doubts about a very beautiful dark-eyed woman—Tyrell's assistant, Rachael, played by Sean Young. Rachael, who has the eyes of an old Murine ad, seems more of a zombie than anyone else in the movie, because the director tries to pose her the way von Sternberg posed Dietrich, but she saves Deckard's life, and even plays his piano. (She smokes, too, but then the whole atmosphere is smoking.) Rachael wears vamped-up versions of the mannish padded-shoulder suits and the sleek, stiff hairdos and ultraglossy lipstick of career girls in forties movies; her shoulder comes into a room a long time before she does. And if Deckard had felt compelled to test her responses it could have been the occasion for some nifty repartee; she might have been spirited and touching. Her role is limply written, though; she's cool at first, but she spends most of her screen time looking mysteriously afflicted—wet-eyed with yearning—and she never gets to deliver a zinger. I don't think she even has a chance to laugh. The moviemakers haven't learned that wonderful, simple trick of bringing a character close to the audience by giving him a joke or having him overreact to one. The people we're watching are so remote from us they might be shadows of people who aren't there.

The only character who gets to display a large range of emotions is the fourth of the killer replicants, and their leader—Roy Batty (the Crazed King?), played by the tall, blue-eyed blond Dutch actor Rutger Hauer, whose hair is lemon-white here. Hauer (who was Albert Speer in *Inside the Third Reich* on television last May) stares all the time; he also smiles ominously, hoo-hoos like a mad owl and howls like a wolf, and, at moments, appears to see himself as the god Pan, and as Christ crucified. He seems a shoo-in for this year's Klaus Kinski Scenery-Chewing Award. As a humanoid in a homicidal rage because replicants are built to last only four years, he stalks through the movie like an evil Aryan superman; he brings the wrong kind of intensity to the role—an effete, self-aware irony so overscaled it's Wagnerian. His gaga performance is an unconscious burlesque that apparently passes for great acting with the director, especially when Hauer turns noble sufferer and poses like a big hunk of sculpture. (It's a wonder he doesn't rust out in all that rain.) This sequence is particularly funny because there's poor Harrison Ford, with the fingers of one hand broken, reduced to hanging on to bits of the cornice of a tall building by his one good hand—by then you've probably forgotten that he *is* Harrison Ford, the fellow who charms audiences by his boundless good humor—while the saucer-eyed Hauer rants and carries on. Ford is like Harold Lloyd stuck by mistake in the climax of *Duel in the Sun*.

Ridley Scott may not notice that when Hauer is onscreen the camera seems stalled and time breaks down, because the whole movie gives you a feeling of not getting anywhere. Deckard's mission seems of no particular consequence. Whom is he trying to save? Those sewer-rat people in the city? They're presented as so dehumanized that their life or death hardly matters. Deckard feels no more connection with them than Ridley Scott does. They're just part of the film's bluish-gray, heavy-metal chic—inertia made glamorous. Lead zeppelins could float in this smoggy air. And maybe in the moviemakers' heads, too. Why is Deckard engaged in this urgent hunt? The replicants are due to expire anyway. All the moviemakers' thinking must have gone into the sets. Apparently, the replicants have a motive for returning to Earth: they're trying to reach Tyrell—they hope he can extend their life span. So if the police want to catch them, all they need to do is wait for them to show up at Tyrell's place. And why hasn't Deckard, the ace blade runner, figured out that if the replicants can't have their lives extended they may want revenge for their slave existence, and that all he's doing is protecting Tyrell? You can dope out how the story might have been presented, with Deckard as the patsy who does Tyrell's dirty work; as it is, you can't clear up why Tyrell isn't better guarded—and why the movie doesn't pull the plot strands together.

Blade Runner is musty even while you're looking at it (and noting its relationship to Fritz Lang's *Metropolis* and to von Sternberg's lighting techniques, and maybe to Polanski's *Chinatown* and *Fellini's Roma,* and so on). There are some remarkable images—for example, when the camera plays over the iron grillwork of the famous Bradbury Building in Los Angeles the iron looks tortured into shape. These images are part of the sequences about a lonely, sickly young toymaker, Sebastian (William Sanderson), who lives in the deserted building. Sebastian has used the same techniques employed in producing replicants to make living toy companions for himself, and since the first appearance of these toys has some charm, we wait to see them in action again. When the innocent, friendly Sebastian is in danger, we expect the toys to come to his aid or be upset or, later, try to take reprisals for what happens to their creator, or at least grieve. We assume that moviemakers wouldn't go to all the trouble of devising a whole batch of toy figures only to forget about them. But this movie loses track of the few expectations it sets up, and the formlessness adds to a viewer's demoralization—the film itself seems part of the atmosphere of decay. *Blade Runner* has nothing to give the audience—not even a second of sorrow for Sebastian. It hasn't been thought out in human terms. If anybody comes around with a test to detect humanoids, maybe Ridley Scott and his associates should hide. With all the smoke in this movie, you feel as if everyone connected with it needs to have his flue cleaned.

The New Yorker, July 12, 1982

THE ROAD WARRIOR
ACTION

T *he Road Warrior* is intense, and it's all of a piece. The Australian director George Miller grabs you by the throat—or lower—and doesn't let go until it's over. The picture probably won't leave you feeling crummy the way junk-food movies usually do, because in visual terms, at least, *The Road Warrior* is terrific junk food. Miller must have the jittery nervous system of an exploitation filmmaker linked to the eyes of an artist. The picture has its own distinctive tautness (there's nothing left to trim) and its own special dark, almost violet light that doesn't suggest either night or day—it's as if the outdoors were lit by torches. The film might be taking place in the lustrous, paranoid dreams of a man who had gorged, happily, on action movies—on *Death Wish* and *Death Race 2000* and *Walking Tall,* on A.I.P. wheelers and samurai epics, on images of Vikings, Apaches, sadomasochists, and hotrodders, on Bronson and Eastwood, on demolition derbies and medieval jousts. Set in a post-apocalyptic Wasteland, *The Road Warrior* is a mutant, sprung from virtually all action genres. It's an amazing piece of work; it's like "Starsky and Hutch" at switch blade speed. The jangly, fast editing suggests wit; so does the broad blacktop highway that cuts across the desert nothingness. Australia is certainly the right place for this fantasy—the parched horizons tell you why men would turn into motor maniacs. *The Road Warrior*, which is in Panavision and Dolby, could be the prototype of future road movies—perhaps of all action movies. But I didn't find it great fun to watch. The crashes, the flames, and the persistent instant-myth music (you barely need to add water) are rather wearing. (If there were such a thing as Jungian music, this would be it—unless Carl Orff staked an earlier claim.) The picture doesn't mean anything to me—not, at least, what it does for a lot of men I know, especially the ones who haven't had a real fix since the last Sergio Leone picture, a decade ago. (At times, *The Road Warrior* could be a spaghetti Western directed by George A. Romero.)

That *was* Wasteland with a capital W. *The Road Warrior*, which in other countries is known as *Mad Max 2*, is a sequel to Miller's first film, the 1979 *Mad Max*—an openly sophomoric bash. *Mad Max* was a revenge fantasy turned into a futuristic cartoon; the constant car-wrecking had a two-fisted deliriousness. It was of the exploitation genre that the critic David Chute, with no pejorative intention, calls "crash-and-burn," and it was Australia's biggest international box-office success ever (though not in this country: a jarringly dubbed version played here, on the theory that Americans wouldn't be able to understand the Australian vulgate). But Miller—who, as he makes clear in an interview with Chute in the July-August *Film Comment*, looked for the reasons for the film's success and believed he had found them when he was introduced to Jung, via Joseph Campbell's *The Hero with a Thousand Faces*—became convinced that he had unconsciously struck something very deep. And so this new film comes equipped with a prologue describing its hero's past in prose poetry. Sample: "In the roar of an engine, he lost everything . . . And became a shell of a man . . . a burnt out, desolate man, a man haunted by the demons of his past . . . A man who wandered out . . . into the Wasteland . . . And it was here, in this blighted place, that he learned to live again." You can hear those dots, and the words are spoken in fruity, cultivated tones.

Maybe Miller's belief that he has tapped into the universal concept of the hero is what makes *The Road Warrior* so joyless. It isn't simply stupid—it's trying-to-be-smart stupid. It's abstract in an adolescent way. And though Max, the road warrior (Mel Gibson), is mythologized in that prologue, he doesn't have anything particularly heroic to do. *The Road Warrior* is much hipper than a Western such as George Stevens' 1953 *Shane* (which was already in the mythmaking business: Alan Ladd's drifter was meant to suggest Galahad on the range), but it follows the same basic pattern. The boy whose piteous cry "Shane!" clung to people's ears when the picture ended has become the Feral Kid (Emil Minty), a wolf-boy orphan with a deadly metal boomerang for a toy, who attaches himself to the loner Max. And the apathetic Max encounters a new version of the homesteaders: some few decent men and women have survived the Third World War (two big powers fighting over oil) and have banded together in a small, walled encampment around a dinky refinery, where they have been refining the last remaining oil into gasoline and hoarding it, so that they can get in their battered vehicles and make a run to the seashore, two thousand miles away. These homesteaders are under siege by punkish post-nuclear-war bikers—savages on motorcycles, slightly updated from their Roger Corman days. Rampaging vandals who tear people apart for pleasure, they're led by a masked body builder, the Humungus. He wears leather-and-metal straps crossing his muscles, and his men are comic-strip terrors, each accoutred in his own rough-trade style—fashion plates of the newest in nightmare adornment. The huge, garishly strong Wez (Vernon Wells), whose yellow-haired punk boyfriend sits behind him on his bike, sports a fire-red Mohawk strip of hair on his shaved head, plumes and football pads at the shoulders, a studded codpiece, and a hideously businesslike metal crossbow on his gauntlet. His buttocks are bare. These nouveau barbarians, who look ready to storm an s-m bar, are determined to get the homesteaders' gas, and have set up camp just a few miles away from the enclosure.

Miller doesn't show any interest in characterization, except for what can be obtained by astute casting. His performers aren't required to act—only to present their faces and bodies to the camera. Yet he has a gift for placing them in the very wide frame so that even if they are almost silent we respond to them as individuals. The people at the refinery are decked out in what looks like homespun burlap (and, when the weather changes, what looks like homespun fur)—they're clothed in virtue, like early Christians in a De Mille epic—but each face makes an impression, no matter how brief its screen time. And there's a real film instinct at work in Miller's treatment of Bruce Spence, who plays a stork-legged, rotten-toothed aviator who uses snakes to guard his autogyro. The first time we see him, he appears out of the sand, like a trapdoor spider. This fellow looks like an assemblage of hopeless parts, and in most movies he'd bite the dust, yet with his gummy, horsey grin, his overexcited jumping up and down (is there a punk record playing in his head?), and his talking to himself—muttering about the things he remembers from the era when there were arts and traditions—he somehow survives. He's like his ragtag plane and the other pieced-together, souped-up vehicles that can still go. By the end, he has even managed to get himself a pretty girl, with a loyal spirit. Bruce Spence's aviator is more hopeful and tenderhearted and adaptable than Mel Gibson's glum Max, whose parts match up quite handsomely.

Bruised and puffy, Max has no edges, he stands about blandly, uncertainly, on the sidelines—Brutus in leather armor—while others make decisions. His finest moment—and perhaps Miller's most lyric, fairy-tale image—is totally passive: the wounded Max, carried on the tiny autogyro, floats high above the blasted desert landscape and the human debris. This vaguely Wagnerian shot is beautiful on its own; it doesn't have any dramatic meaning, because we don't know what has been going on in Max's mind.

And when he is partly healed and has decided to join the homesteaders, who have nursed him, he still seems split—it isn't clear whether he has become fond of the good folk or just wants revenge on the bikers. It's because Mel Gibson is carrying all of George Miller's mixed ambitions on his shoulders that he has no stature as a hero. And it's because of this underlayer of indecisiveness that the action doesn't have a real kick. We're told in the prologue that Max has lost his reason for living; this film is supposed to be about his spiritual rebirth and the first stirrings of a new civilization, but he remains sullen and withdrawn. And civilization may be a long time coming: Miller, following the moldiest Hollywood tradition, cues us to exult along with the good guys whenever one of them kills a baddie. The picture gets whatever charge it has from the spectacle of devolution.

Miller is barely in his mid-thirties (he studied medicine and worked as a doctor while he was making short films that prepared the way for *Mad Max*), yet if you think of him as one of the kinetic moviemakers, such as John Carpenter and Romero, he's a giant. And his chase sequence with Max driving an oil truck makes the comparable truck chase in Spielberg's *Raiders of the Lost Ark* look lame—as Spielberg, who has expressed admiration for Miller, might be the first to acknowledge. But Miller apparently doesn't see the limitations of the kind of material he's working with, and he has given it an art-film aspect. I don't mean the visionary shots, such as the bikers circling in the dust (as if they had all the gas in the world), riding round and round the enclosure, like old movie Indians on horses terrorizing the fort. Since this is basically a mindless film, I don't fault Miller for sacrificing credibility to beauty. And it's amusingly sloppy that in order to stage the climactic chase and battle, which is a variant of the settlers in their wagon train heading out through Indian territory, Miller asks us to accept a piece of visual idiocy: the refinery is surrounded by flat, dry desolation as far as the eye can see, yet when Max believes he's leading the homesteaders on their run he heads straight for the bikers' campfires, as if that were the only route he could take. What I regret is George Miller's thinking there's mythic depth in sickly-stale elements—the lonely Feral Kid who worships Max, and the aviator's devotion to Max (like Walter Brennan's fealty to Bogart), and Wez's love for his blondie, and Max's not allowing himself to have any fellow-feeling except for his pooch (a great-looking bandy-legged Australian Cattle dog, with a black monocle around one eye, a white around the other), and all the other familiar bits.

Miller gets effects, all right, but they're not the perverse, erotic effects that seem promised; the picture is weirdly not kinky—maybe because he's trying to be seriously kinky. *The Road Warrior* is sappy-sentimental, and, for all its huffing and puffing, it doesn't blow any houses down; it has no resonance of any kind. Something rather solemn comes across in the prologue and the afterword, and in the use of actual documentary shots of warfare to substantiate the film's apocalyptic claims (a terrible mistake in judgment for a comic-strip movie, no matter how elegant), and in the important-person,

Charlton Heston–like poses that Max assumes—especially the cantilevered-hip position, with all the weight on one leg. Miller consciously uses Mel Gibson as an icon; that's enough to squeeze the juice out of any actor.

At a point near the end of the picture, after the tanker chase, the limitations of action-genre moviemaking stare right out at Miller: this is when we discover that while we've been watching Max driving, and fighting off the big brute Wez, the important things have been happening elsewhere. The decent folk in burlap have used their heads and planned their strategy; what we were watching was the kid stuff—"action." For once, Miller seems at a loss; he doesn't appear to know whether or not this revelation should be treated as a joke on Max, and so he muffles the scene. The script (by Terry Hayes and Miller, with Brian Hannant) has provided this ironic episode—a twist on *The Treasure of the Sierra Madre*—that undercuts Miller's serious approach to the crash-and-burn genre, but as a director he's no longer willing to laugh at himself, and he retreats to the safety of muzzy mythologizing. And so the wolf boy (who is our narrator) grows up and, like many of his kind, learns to talk like a BBC announcer, but with an Australian accent. And Max, who has to remain a loner so he'll fit the Jungian hero pattern, is left behind, brooding. He's like Steve McQueen at the end of each episode of his old bounty-hunter TV series, with nothing to look forward to next week but more killing.

George Miller is enormously gifted as a moviemaker, and he has fused his crazily derivative material; this cultural compost heap has yielded a vision. But when you get caught up in his way of thinking, you can convince yourself that the more indebted to old movies your material is, the richer it is, and the more archetypal—and that junk food is the only true nourishment. There's nothing under the film's clichés—nothing to support the visceral stress that Miller's single, continuous spurt of energy puts on us. And there's no humor, finally, under that incessant music. If Max had it in him to laugh at how he was used—to laugh the way Walter Huston did at the end of *Sierra Madre*—there might be some point to the picture. The introspective Max never gets past his own joylessness. We're supposed to regard him as a hero because he's a fearless driver. Is he fearless because, not caring if he lives or dies, he has less to lose than his enemies? Or is it that he's a survivor because he's alone? Either way, he never acknowledges that he has anything at stake, and he's no hero to me. This is a phony genre picture. Genre pictures are meant to be entertaining; this one wants to be much more. It's an abstract presentation of male paranoid fantasizing, with an air of intelligence. The male audience can think it's prophetic (Max was used); maybe the male audience can even think it's deep. (It's definitely not a picture for heterosexual couples on dates.)

We may not feel crummy after the movie, but we feel hollow. I would think that even those who are elated while they're watching it feel hollow. *The Road Warrior* is for boys who want to go around slugging each other on the shoulder and for men who wish that John Wayne were alive and fifty again.

The film has been greeted by superlatives from reviewers, because of what I think may be a tragic misunderstanding of the appeal of movies in earlier periods: the widely expressed idea that what people used to go to the movies for was simply action and fireworks, a basic, easy-to-follow story, and the good winning out over the bad—that all they wanted was genre films. It might be closer to the facts to say that people accepted the routinized genre pictures when they couldn't get something wonderful, because they understood that great movies didn't come along every day. It's scary to read critics praising action pictures that are no more than embodiments of male dynamism and suggesting that these are the only real movies—what the people want—even after TV has done action to death. I know that I didn't go to the movies to see car crashes or galloping horses or gangsters shooting each other, though I often went to films in which these things happened; I went because I wanted to "see the picture"—to become involved in the characters' intertwined lives and to experience the worlds that all the hacks and craftsmen and artists who worked in the movies could bring into being. We're often told now that moviegoers never sought anything more than they get from *Star Wars* or *Raiders,* and I want to testify that this is a falsehood. It's one that movie and TV executives have been known to embrace. When critics in the press and on TV embrace it, they're engaged in another form of shoulder punching.

The New Yorker, September 6, 1982

MY FAVORITE YEAR
ACTORS AS HEROES

My *Favorite Year* is about hero worship, and—surprise!—it's for it. The picture is set in New York in 1954—the year that the live Saturday-night TV series "Your Show of Shows" was at its peak popularity. That was the year NBC divided it into two shows by separating its stars, Sid Caesar and Imogene Coca, and created a third asset by signing their producer, Max Liebman, to put on specials. "Your Show of Shows" was followed by "Caesar's Hour," in which big Sid was teamed with Nanette Fabray, and these two series have merged in people's memories, where Sid Caesar has the hallowed status of genius, because of his own gifts and because of the writers who worked on his shows—Neil and Danny Simon, Carl Reiner, Larry Gelbart, Lucille Kallen, Joe Stein, Mel Brooks, and Woody Allen, among others. *My Favorite Year* is a fictional treatment of life backstage during the days when those soon-to-be-famous writers were brainstorming together, shouting ideas into the air or, as in the cases of the shy Neil Simon and Woody Allen, whispering their jokes to a fearless, brass-lunged confederate. It helps to know the legends, because some of the scenes aren't fully shaped, but if you didn't know anything about Sid Caesar or his writing team you could still laugh at *My Favorite Year*—the characters and situations are alive on their own. This show-business farce is the first film directed by Richard Benjamin, and the lighting is gummy, the views of Broadway are a blur, and the staging sometimes creaks—it even klonks. But the film has a bubbling spirit, and I was carried along by the acting and by Benjamin's near-libidinous reverence for his smartass characters. This man is crazy about actors—not a bad start for a director.

As Stan (King) Kaiser, the brawny star of the TV show "Comedy Caval-cade," Joe Bologna suggests an introverted ox. Absent-minded, slugged—like a heavyweight who has just gone ten rounds—he stares down at the small people who work for him as if he couldn't remember what they were there for. He stares down even at people who are taller than he is. What makes Bologna so authentic is that he has a manic force field, and it was precisely the comics with this kind of aggressive aura (Sid Caesar, Milton Berle, Jackie Gleason, the young Steve Allen) who came across the strongest on early, live TV. Somehow, TV filtered out their threat, and viewers didn't register it. (What viewers experienced was simply their energy.) But back-stage how could anybody miss it? Bologna's King Kaiser is a looming pres-ence, and there doesn't have to be trouble for him to smell it; violent and depressive, he holds his ground, and if his punches knock someone out he has a self-congratulatory reflex—with a gigantic paw, he shifts the weight in his crotch. An inarticulate comic who has surrounded himself with talker-writer prodigies, King has no awe of them: he knows that he—not the writers—makes people laugh.

One layer of the script, which is by Norman Steinberg and Dennis Palumbo, is about the truculent, half-mad King in relation to the writers in their rumpus-room office. They, of course, think they're the reason he gets laughs. Sy, the senior gagman (Bill Macy), rants about everything they have to do; even his personal grievances are all-encompassing. Bill Macy has a true comic artist's understanding of sleaze, as he proved in *The Late Show* (he was the failed talent agent turned bartender), and he has a gift for bringing unexpected depth and detail to a role, as he demonstrated in the otherwise tinny *Serial* (he was the suicide). When Sy holds forth to the other writers about what he's going to say to King, he sounds as if his life is on the line; when King confronts him, he retreats instantly. He's so smooth it's a transformation—it's on the order of a recantation. This rancorous old warhorse of a gagwriter has all the mechanisms to survive in the business; when he goes home, he probably sleeps like a baby. (He's no saner than King—just more verbal.) As the only woman in the bunch, the nifty Anne DeSalvo makes you understand at once why the attractive but self-deprecating Alice would be accepted, and how much she enjoys being part of this competitive craziness where anyone's best lines may be stepped on.

The youngest of the writers—and the film's protagonist—is a small chipmunk called Benjy, whose actions are probably based partly on the exploits of the young Mel Brooks (his company co-produced the film), with maybe some borrowing from the early life of Woody Allen. The role is played by Mark Linn-Baker, who is dark-haired and has a round face with pointy features—even a pointy chin. His Benjy is button-eyed and shiny—a snookums. He looks as if when he opened his mouth a cheep or a chirp would come out. This Brooklyn worrywart with cultural yearnings and conflicts about becoming a gagwriter is like a Jewish-intellectual version of Eddie Bracken. It's a tricky role; at times Linn-Baker is borderline ghastly, and at other times he seems just what was needed, and quite inventive. Then you may be dubious again—especially in the scenes between Benjy and the producer's assistant, played by Jessica Harper, whom he considers his girl. (Her boss, the teeth-gnashing producer, is played by Adolph Green, who certainly has a lot of teeth to gnash.) You'd never guess what a remarkable performer Jessica Harper can be from what she does here; she has no role to play, and the only time she doesn't seem like a bad actress is when she's telling Benjy why she isn't interested in him—she's saying things you agree with. What finally saves Linn-Baker is that Benjy is given the task of keeping an eye on the week's guest star—a screen star he idolizes—and making sure that this notorious womanizing boozer stays sober. In his first big movie role, Linn-Baker has the good luck to play most of his scenes with Peter O'Toole.

As the guest from Hollywood—the peacock Alan Swann, who is part John Barrymore and part Errol Flynn (maybe the best parts of each)—O'Toole is simply astounding. In recent years, he hasn't had the press he deserves—particularly in England. Maybe, having had the nobility of a certain kind of stardom conferred upon him, he is thought not to have kept his side up. His recent performances seem to be an answer to that; he's saying, "See, I'm not gone—you're just looking in the wrong place." And he has been getting better as an actor. When you watch him work in *The Stunt Man* or on TV in *Masada* or here, it's clear that he doesn't impress himself with what he's doing. And he doesn't hold back a thing—not even what stars usually hold back to make you know they're stars. While others turn into immobile figureheads, he has become a master of physical comedy—a whirlwind on the order of Barrymore in *Twentieth Century*. O'Toole's Alan Swann arrives at the TV production facilities and collapses—apparently dead drunk, but not quite unconscious. He hears King's decision to bump him from the show and hears Benjy make an impassioned plea that they keep him. And when he's on his feet he acknowledges his debt to Benjy. At that moment, we're his, and, as a result, we know why Benjy is his. Drunk, Alan Swann isn't merely swozzled—he's liquefied. But in his woozy eyes you can still see his imagination at play, and you recognize that he exults in his diction and the fine, trained voice that echoes back. Even when Swann is drunk, he's acting a great actor drunk. Self-destructive as Swann is, he still has some control. When we first see this wasted dude, he isn't wearing a watch, but he arrives for rehearsals on the dot. He honors his commitments, as he honors his debt to Benjy. Swann is a pro, and wants to work, just as King Kaiser does. King is a star because he's funny, and so he has got to be funny. Alan Swann knows that as a romantic-daredevil hero it's his job to make people fall in love with him. Each in his own area is a cock of the walk, and in the film's climax they stand together as heroic equals and fight off their common enemy.

The picture is a triumph of casting—not least in giving us Lainie Kazan as the chipmunk's mother. I never thought that I'd be capable of saying anything complimentary about Lainie Kazan; watching her sing and bulge on television, I have sometimes cowered—I've wanted to throw a blanket over the set. But her fleshiness is perfect here; it goes with her fossilized hairdo and her leering smile. Padded (I assume) and stuffed into her dress, this new Lainie Kazan goes beyond shtick; when she talks about what's real, she seems to become a real mother. And, powerhouse comic mama though she is, she's—well, sexy. When Alan Swann, who has accompanied Benjy to Brooklyn for dinner, looks at her, there's tribute in his eyes; his expression says, "This woman is not just this kid's mother." The whole Brooklyn sequence is generous-hearted; everybody is ridiculous but no one is put down for it. And running through the film there are jokes that spin off each other. As a crooked union leader in a pin-striped suit who is trying to kill King Kaiser for repeatedly satirizing him on the show, Cameron Mitchell has great animal noises rumbling out of him. When the live "Comedy Cavalcade" is to start, King Kaiser is dressed in his own version of the pin-striped suit—it has shoulder pads sticking out so far you could fly with them. Then he becomes confused and begins to think it's the Musketeers routine that's coming up. Talking out loud to herself, the wardrobe mistress (Selma Diamond) honks, "He thinks he's in the wrong costume every week." But it turns out that King is right to be confused, because inadvertently the union-crook routine and the swashbuckling skit merge.

The jokes are good, but it's Peter O'Toole's Swann—the film's wild card—who makes it memorable. I can't think of another major star, with the possible exception of Ralph Richardson, who would have the effrontery (about what great actors should allow themselves to do) to bring this sly performance off—and Richardson didn't develop this kind of funky daring until he was too advanced in years for it to be romantically effective. O'Toole and Linn-Baker almost bring off a close-to-impossible-to-play sequence in which Swann takes Benjy to the Stork Club. Swann is asked to speak to an elderly adoring fan (Gloria Stuart, as deep-bosomed as ever, and, except for what looks like a gray, elderly-lady wig, nearly as beautiful). He understands what his romantic persona is, and he plays it immaculately, sweeping the woman into his arms and waltzing with her. Though the Club scenes end in a sloppy bit (the usual tray of pastries gets spilled), O'Toole's tone is so sure that the waltzing episode doesn't become maudlin or self-congratulatory.

Swann is always aware of the impression he's making; when he enters a room, his feelers are out. He enjoys living up to the public's dream of him—

his courtliness is part of his sense of the fitness of things. But this same man drinks out of cowardice and is in absolute terror when he realizes that the TV show must be done live, in front of a studio audience and twenty million people at home. Benjy persuades him to go on by telling him that he couldn't have played all those movie heroes if he didn't have some of that courage in him; by the end, Swann has justified Benjy's idolatry. Maybe this movie is so satisfying because it believes in what it's saying: that stars have the heroism to do things most people couldn't do—that there's a reason these heroes are heroes. You can almost see Richard Benjamin (part Benjy himself) grinning, his sheep's eyes wet with admiration for Peter O'Toole, who does the equivalent of pratfalls on his face—smacking himself against walls and floors—and then may do something so foxy-subtle that some of the moments between Swann and Benjy transcend comedy and become fable.

The plot appears to be casual—even a bit scatty—yet when you think the movie over, the layers of reference in the script come together. They chime the way they do in the best-constructed farces, and it's a very pretty sound, especially when they chime ironically. Sy and the other gagwriters who think they're the reason for King's success—how do they feel when at the climax of the TV show everything crashes and the script is discarded, and the studio audience goes berserk with laughter? King gets an ovation. Imagine what it will be like on Monday when he walks into the writers' office and says "Top it."

The New Yorker, October 4, 1982

COME BACK TO THE 5 & DIME JIMMY DEAN, JIMMY DEAN
THE MAGICIAN

Robert Altman's *Come Back to the 5 & Dime Jimmy Dean, Jimmy Dean* shouldn't work, but it does. Every idea and line of dialogue in Ed Graczyk's play, which centers on the reunion of a James Dean fan club on the twentieth anniversary of his death, is derivative in a fake-poetic, fake-magical way; it reeks of the worst of William Inge, of Tennessee Williams misunderstood. In structure, it's a Texas-small-town, women's version of O'Neill's *The Iceman Cometh,* with each woman forced to reveal her hideous truth—what her whole pitiful system of pretensions has been covering up. And it has its Iceman: a member of the group who left town and now returns to blast the lid off these cowardly lives. I doubt if a major film director has ever before voluntarily taken on as thoroughgoing a piece of drivel as this one. Yet when Altman gives a project everything he's got, his skills are such that he can make poetry out of fake poetry and magic out of fake magic. When he'd finished this film, he went off to the University of Michigan to stage Stravinsky's *The Rake's Progress,* which features a machine for converting stones into bread.

Altman had a humiliating defeat when he directed *Come Back to the 5 & Dime Jimmy Dean, Jimmy Dean* on Broadway early this year; afterward, he restaged the one-set play in a New York studio with basically the same cast and shot it in Super 16-mm. in nineteen days, at a cost of nine hundred thousand dollars—put up by Mark Goodson Productions and Viacom (which acquired the right to show the film on its cable division, Showtime). When *Come Back* was blown up to 35-mm., there may have been a small loss of vibrancy (the peach-pink tones seem to have grayed out a bit), but it still has a glow. Discussing his plans to film plays for cable TV, Altman told *Newsweek,* "There has to be a new style—not a play, not a movie," and *Come Back* is somewhere in between. The material develops like a well-made theatre piece: the playwright withholds crucial information about the characters' past experiences, then gradually strips away their lies. And although Altman has trimmed the text of the Broadway version, the dialogue retains the over-explanatory quality that is typical of the stage. There's a lot of talk. But he uses an unusually fluid camera style. The movement inside the 5 & Dime setting is delicately purposeful—he keeps us aware of the women's faces and shoulders, of how they stand or touch or hover over one another. While Graczyk's dialogue is coming out of them, the camera peruses the ones who are speaking and the ones who are listening. We're physically close to them, as we're physically close to the actors in Bergman's films. But Altman doesn't burrow into a character the way Bergman does, starting in closeup and pushing farther and farther in. Altman's camera doesn't have that relentlessness; the characters don't look pinned down—they appear to be caught in passing, on the wing, and that's part of what makes this film seem so magical. Moving in apparent freedom, the principal actresses go at their roles so creatively that, I think, they've found some kind of acting truth in what they're doing. They bring conviction to their looneytunes characters.

When you come out, you may be saying to yourself, "If Robert Altman can do that with a piece of sausage, think what he could do with a good script." But it's possible that Sandy Dennis, Cher, Karen Black, and, in a lesser role, Marta Heflin are able to do so much with their parts because of the cheesy mythmaking undertones of the material. If the roles made better sense, the actresses might not be able to plunge so far down into themselves or pull up so much emotion. It's *because* this glib, religioso play is so derivative that the actors have found so much depth in it. When actors peel away layers of inhibition, they feel they're uncovering "truth" and it's traditional for directors and acting teachers to call it that. But this truth may be derived from their stored-up pop mythology—atrocity stories from sources as diverse as comic books, TV, and Joan Didion, and tales of sacrificial heroes and heroines that go back beyond the birth of movies to the first storytellers.

"Truthful" acting may be affecting to us because it represents the sum total of everything the actors have been affected by. It comes from areas far below conscious technique; it's true to their psyches. To use the theatre term, the performers here have made the roles "their own." They may think they're finding meanings in the material, but actually they're adding them. If they didn't—if they stayed with the surface of this play—they'd be dead.

As the more than slightly mad Mona, Sandy Dennis is the linchpin of the production, and if you're not fascinated by the way Mona tries to distance herself from the life about her and from her own sensuality you might find the film intolerable. Sometimes it may seem that not much separates a superb Sandy Dennis performance from an irritating one, since she uses some of the same mannerisms in both. But when her tics are right for a role she can zoom off and come up with things no one else would have dreamt of. I found her impossible in her starring vehicles (the 1967 *Up the Down Staircase* and the 1968 *Sweet November*) but a droopy joy in the 1970 *The Out-of-Towners* and unfailingly funny in the 1977 *Nasty Habits*. And she brought something weirdly human to last year's *The Four Seasons*. (She was the only person in it I could have any feeling for.) Mona is her most extravagant creation: nervous and nostrilly and ladylike, a woman who hides in dowdy clothes yet can't resist wearing her thick, curly red hair soft and loose—floating about her, aureole style. Even Mona's affectations—which center on how fine-grained and sensitive and asthmatic she is—are of the flesh. She's compellingly strange and repressed, yet carnal, and, I think, very beautiful (she's a little like Piper Laurie in *Carrie*), and when she's angry she's frighteningly bossy. She gets "burned up," and you can see why the people around her don't challenge her stories: Mona's grip on her fantasies is the strongest thing about her. I admired the performance that Sandy Dennis gave in Altman's 1969 *That Cold Day in the Park*, but it was a much more held-in character; Mona—a delusionary romantic—is far more stirring. And Sandy Dennis takes more chances as an actress now. The way the role is written, Mona is a hand-me-down from Tennessee Williams; complaining of the small-minded small-town people, she's a cow-country Blanche DuBois. She has some of Blanche's frailty; that's why it's so shocking when she yells—you don't expect her to be able to sustain that much emotion.

The town that the 5 & Dime is in is close to the site where parts of *Giant* were filmed in 1955, and it's Graczyk's conceit that working as extras in the crowd scenes was the biggest event in the lives of the local people, and that for the hyper-impressionable Mona, the boyish young star of the movie, James Dean, was a Christ figure. When she gave in to her desires and had sex with a boy one hot summer night, she convinced herself that it was James Dean the Saviour who came into her body, that she was "chosen," and that the son she bore—Jimmy Dean—was his.

The action flashes back and forth between 1955 and the reunion year, 1975, without any attempt to make the actors appear younger or older: it's as if Altman had said, "There's so much illusion hopping around in this material, let's not play games with makeup—let's treat the audience as adults who can accept the convention that the actors are meant to be both young and old." And so the actors are liberated, and the décor takes on the job of telling us which period we're in, and does it easily, painlessly. Actually, the camera's frequent scanning of the 5 & Dime—a variety store with a soda fountain—is oddly pleasurable. The set has a mirrored wall, and Altman uses mirrors for the illusion of space (and for time changes, too, and tricks of memory). The action even passes through them. In Louis Malle's *My Dinner with André,* which also uses a large mirror, there are times while André is talking when the movie seems to transport you, and this happens in the Altman film, too. Its modulations are transporting, and Pierre Mignot's cinematography is airy and lyrical without any show-biz glitter. Although the action is all in the store, there seems to be plenty of room, and the movie breathes as if it were shot outdoors. Altman keeps looking at the world, and it's never the same; what we're responding to is his consciousness at work (and play). The sunlight coming through the shop's glass front and the dusty pastel colors are part of the film's texture, along with the women's hair and heads and hands, which are always touching, moving. Present and past interpenetrate, and Altman keeps everything in motion. (The closeups are pauses, not full stops.) His feeling for the place is almost as tactile as his feeling for the performers. When the characters' passions well up, the camera is right there, recording the changes in their neck muscles, their arms, their cheeks. But it never crowds them.

As Sissy, the waitress at the 5 & Dime—a strutting good-time girl, who's the opposite of Mona—Cher is direct and simple in her effects, as if it were the easiest thing in the world to slip into the character of an aging small-town belle with a Texas accent. When Sissy and Mona fight, you feel the emotional violence in these two women who can't help being contemptuous of each other. And though Sandy Dennis is amazing in these scenes, Cher holds her own. Cher could play Arletty roles—at least, she could if Altman were directing her—and not just because her fine cheekbones and long, slender arms suggest Artletty's particular type of dark patrician beauty (the look of an archaic figure on a vase) but because she has the funny tough-broad quality to go with it. There was a richness in Arletty's whory elegance—she made you feel she'd learned even from the things she wished she could forget. Cher doesn't seem rich in experience that way, but without any of the kook fiddling about that she did on TV—staying completely in character, without tricks or reminders of who she is—she's stunningly unself-conscious.

Karen Black, who makes a late, carefully prepared-for entrance (like the Iceman), has the showiest role, and she plays it with spectacular tawdry world-weariness; her Joanne is like a gay-bar version of Angie Dickinson, tailored white suit and all. Joanne, with her low voice and the stiff hairdo of a TV anchorwoman, is heartsick and past hope, yet still loving. She's the most sinned-against—a living hard-luck story. And her masochism is presented as glorious gallantry. Slinking around—prowling the 5 & Dime—she embodies all the ironies that Ed Graczyk could pile onto her, and damned if Karen Black doesn't bring them all off. (The material develops an edge when she appears.) Joanne is the third—and the most "hurting"—of the film's three mutilated goddesses. And Karen Black keeps the mawkishness from splashing all over the set. I think this isn't just the best performance she has given onscreen—it's a different kind of acting from what she usually does. It's subdued, controlled, quiet—but not parched. When she and Cher get a little drunk and laugh uproariously, there's a healthy raucous feeling in it.

Two of the former members of the club have driven from Dallas for the anniversary. Marta Heflin's Edna Louise, a mousey blond mother of six (and pregnant again), submits to the bullying of her hefty, richer friend, Kathy Bates's Stella Mae, who has a brassy voice and wears a cowgirl hat. It's a Laurel & Hardy relationship, with the puny and timorous Edna Louise becoming rather endearing. Perhaps because Edna Louise allows Stella Mae to walk all over her, she's the only character who's exempted from exposure; Edna Louise is a dishrag, and so she's meant to be the happy one of the bunch—touched by grace. Graczyk's schema is offensive (and so obvious you may find yourself moaning), but Marta Heflin's performance is sweetly, appealingly meek. Kathy Bates has a good prurient bit toward the end (before it becomes labored), but her loud belligerence seems too practiced. Altman doesn't appear to have shaken the stage rhythm out of her delivery. This fault is even more pronounced in Sudie Bond's performance as the crabby fundamentalist Juanita, the widow who runs the 5 & Dime. Juanita isn't well integrated into the camera rhythms, either; her expressions and her words seem frozen—as if she had worked up the character long before and had nothing more to bring to it. But Altman handles the only male actor—Mark Patton, as Joe (who looks a little like James Dean)—with fine discretion, using him as a partly hallucinatory figure; he materializes as Mona thinks of him.

Altman's overall directing is a model of tenderness and tact. His touch seems as sure here as it was wobbly in most of the pictures he has made since *Nashville,* in 1975. He's a great director. But there is still the puzzler: it's not just the actors who have swallowed Graczyk's big, windy ironies—Altman bit on them, too. A banner welcoming the club members who have returned for the 1975 anniversary tells us the name of the group: the Disciples of James Dean. The 5 & Dime has two enshrined portraits—one of Christ, one of Dean. Altman lightens these ironies; his humor doesn't fail him. There are a few clinkers, though. One of the women makes the flat-out statement that the group knew all along that Mona wasn't telling the truth; surely "suspected" would have been more felicitous? And there's a symbolic notion that's too ripe even for parody: the 1975 scenes take place during a drought, and the storm that's expected passes over—there's no rain. Graczyk's play is actually much worse than the material of Altman's most forgettable films. Its only advantage is that it has given him a cast-iron structure. Though the opening scenes that set up the characters and the time shifts seem very free and flimsy (and are initially off-putting), every detail is pinned in place. I think Altman may have been attracted by the trashy play because it's a remote variant of his 1977 film *Three Women,* which he himself wrote (and which disintegrated in solemnities). He's drawn to archetypal American figures, and to characters who represent our well-known warped and impoverished values. Mona, to whom a movie star is God; Sissy, who thinks her chest is her passport to glory; Stella Mae, the boastful materialist; Juanita, the tight-faced hypocrite—they're all designed to muckrake themselves, and Altman may have felt that the play was "saying something." But he has made it effective by going way beyond its prosaic intentions. Yes, the characters are warped by their illusions, but Altman has a poetic intuition of the way illusions wrap around people's lives, and his technique—all the artifice he brings to the staging—becomes one with the themes of illusion and deception. And the pop mythology that the actresses bring to the film can be startling in its intensity, because where the lines are written for pathos, he tops it with a satirical twist. His comedy and artifice save the day.

Commercial failure can affect an artist's judgment as badly as overconfidence can; his tastes may regress. When Altman came to New York last year to work in the theatre, he told the *Times,* "I think I've been too isolated." His wanting to stage *Come Back* is proof of that. But whatever has gone flooey in Robert Altman's choice of material, he's in his prime as a director. Actually, he's in too good form for this play: he outclasses it. People who are caught up in the performances and the style may be appalled by the text, and those who are keen on Gracyzk's writing will probably wish the film were done in the head-on-collision, blurting-out manner of, say, *On Golden Pond.* The movie is a genuine oddity—like *The Night of the Iguana* performed by a company of seraphim. The rake's machine for converting stones into bread is, of course, a devil's trick—a fraud. Altman's magic is the real thing.

The New Yorker, November 15, 1982

TOOTSIE, GANDHI, AND SOPHIE

*T*ootsie began with Don McGuire, who wrote what is said to have been a wild screenplay. After it was sold and Dick Richards was set to be the director, Robert Kaufman was hired to do a new draft. When Dustin Hoffman read Kaufman's version, he agreed to play in the picture, and brought in his playwright pal Murray Schisgal (with whom he had once tried to concoct a movie about a man impersonating a woman) to rework the material. Then the director, Dick Richards, was replaced by Hal Ashby, and Larry

Gelbart was hired for yet another version. After that, Hal Ashby was replaced by Sydney Pollack, and Elaine May (who chose to be anonymous) was signed to do a rewrite; after her came the team of Barry Levinson and Valerie Curtin, and after them, Robert Garland. And with some of these people doing more than one draft, when the screenplay had to be submitted to the Writers Guild for arbitration over the issue of who should get the screen credit, three large cardboard boxes were needed to transport the more than twenty scripts. Pollack must have saved whatever he could of the best in each of them—*Tootsie* sounds as if one superb comedy writer had done it all. There is talk in Hollywood now of forming the I Also Wrote/I Almost Directed *Tootsie* Club. (The writing credit went to Larry Gelbart and Murray Schisgal.)

One of the things that Hollywood used to be good at was producing enjoyable, seemingly effortless entertainments, such as the Hepburn-Tracy *Pat and Mike,* Jean Harlow in *Bombshell,* Claudette Colbert in *Midnight,* Jean Arthur and Ray Milland in *Easy Living,* the Hepburn and Grant *Bringing Up Baby,* and later on, *Some Like It Hot*—films that were factory products and commercial as all hell but took off into a sphere of their own. Those movies continue to give so much pleasure that they have a special glamour. *Tootsie*—a modern addition to this company—has what the best screwball comedies had: a Can-you-top-this? quality. (And they often got it from relays of top writers—who were on the payroll, anyway, in those days.) Paying off this project's earlier writers and directors added heavily to its cost, and it took a rather scandalous one hundred shooting days—some of them, according to press and TV accounts, given over to squabbles between Hoffman and Sydney Pollack. But when the result is a *Tootsie* the expenses seem justified. And when Hoffman delivers the kind of performance he gives here, the talk in the media about his being overpaid seems beside the point. This movie is inconceivable without him. Once Hoffman was committed to the project, the scriptwriters began to shape the central character to fit him, and then they went further. In its final form, *Tootsie* is based on Dustin Hoffman, the perfectionist; he's both the hero and the target of this satirical farce about actors.

The central character, Michael Dorsey, is a brilliant, "uncompromising" New York actor whom no one wants to hire, because he makes things hell for everybody. A stickler for the "truth" in an actor's performance, he overcomplicates things. He's a nut—acting is his mania. So, despite his gifts and his reputation among the young actors whom he coaches, at thirty-nine he's still frustrated—scrounging for a living and finding jobs as a waiter. At the start of the movie, he hasn't had any acting work in two years, and when his girlfriend (Teri Garr) goes up for an audition for a role in a soap and is rejected as the wrong type, he decides to try for the part himself. Made up as a woman, he presents himself as Dorothy Michaels, and lands the job.

Michael is dressed in skirts for about half the movie. This isn't a simple female impersonation, on the order of *Charley's Aunt.* Michael finds himself when he's Dorothy—not because he has any secret desire to be a woman but because when he's Dorothy he's acting. He's such a dedicated, fanatical actor that he comes fully alive only when he's playing a role, and you can see it in his intense, glittering eyes. There are always several things going on in Hoffman's face. He lets us see that Michael's mind is working all the time, and that he's making an actor's choices. Michael is thinking out Dorothy while he's playing her—he's thinking out what a woman would do. When he's giving a performance as Dorothy, he feels a freedom that he doesn't have when he's just Michael. Dorothy, in her fussy, high-necked dresses, has a definite personality—we in the audience become fond of her. She's a flirt, a joker: *she* doesn't have to take herself as seriously as Michael, the artist (who's all nerves), takes himself. She has a much less knotted personality than he has—he allows her to have the charm he denies himself. She also has a Southern accent, and a rather troubling voice; it slips around in a hoarse, neuter sort of way. But Michael is a meticulous actor: Dorothy's vocal patterns and her phrasing are very different from his. And when she's at the TV studio, playing the role of Emily Kimberly, the hospital administrator in "Southwest General," she takes on a brisk huffiness. Hoffman's performance works at so many different levels in this movie that when Michael is in women's clothes you keep watching his crooked, lipsticky smile and his mascaraed eyes, to see what's going on in his head. And when Michael is only Michael, you miss Dorothy, and Emily, too. You can believe that Michael would be a hit playing Emily Kimberly, because this scrappy woman, with thick wrists and oddly sharp, crooked teeth and a bouffant red hairdo, is more eccentrically, believably alive than anyone you're likely to see on the soaps. The performers I've caught (in my limited exposure as I flick from one channel to the next) have been a glazed, strangely slowed-down race of people, plagued by uncertainty; they move as if they were under water and seem to spend their lives on the telephone. Emily, who's fast-talking, overexcited, and absolutely sure of everything she says, would be bound to stir things up.

It's the film's notion that when Michael plays Emily he is driven to depart from his scripts and improvise whenever he feels that the lines she has been given aren't true to her character, and that his improvisations—his peppery rejoinders when the male head doctor is being condescending to Emily—endear him to women viewers. It would be easy to say that the movie was itself being condescending to women—that it was suggesting that it took a man to be tough and forthright enough to speak up for women's rights. Dorothy does seem to be bringing enlightenment into her co-workers' lives, and there's an element of self-congratulation (and self-aggrandizement, too) in the way Michael delivers his spontaneous feminist speeches. But it's also perfectly in character for Michael, experiencing male condescension for the first time, to feel it as an insult to Emily, his creation, and have her erupt in anger. Michael loves his characters more than he loves himself—Emily has to be fearless, a standard-bearer. Michael compulsively embroiders on the role of Emily and enlarges it; even in a hospital soap he's on a quest for the truth of his character. Michael isn't adaptable; he's a total, egocentric idealist. That's what has made him too cantankerous to be a working actor.

When Dustin Hoffman smiles—as Dorothy—he may be more sheerly likable as a movie star than he has ever been before. He gives a master actor's performance: he's playing three characters, and they're shaped so that Dorothy fits inside Michael, and Emily fits inside Dorothy. Even Hoffman's self-consciousness as an actor works in this performance; so does his sometimes grating, rankling quality (which is probably his idea of sincerity). The climactic scene that ends Michael's imposture isn't as well thought out as the rest of the picture, and the cutaway is abrupt; the scene needs reverberations or an aftermath—it's just shucked off. And there's an undercurrent that I could do without: the suggestion that Michael, through playing a woman, becomes a better man—more in touch with himself and all that. This doesn't come through strongly enough to do the movie much harm. It's the kind of increment of virtue that actors and directors speak of proudly, though, when they're giving interviews to papers or on television; they can make it sound as if this were why they made the picture—to improve our characters and their own, too.

What's good about Michael's playing Dorothy is that it enables Hoffman to show a purely farcical side of himself, and he has some inspired moments. After Michael has fallen in love with Julie (Jessica Lange), the star of "Southwest General," who has become very much attached to Dorothy, he has a scene in which he eagerly agrees to babysit with her infant, without having the faintest idea of what he may be letting himself in for. We can see Michael's harried mind clicking along inside Dorothy even during the babysitting. He tries everything he can think of to amuse the child, and after he has been sitting on the floor trying to quiet the kid by stuffing food into her, he falls back in exhaustion. With his legs spread out under his skirt and his big, fluffy head of hair sunk on his small body, he looks like a broken doll. And there's a brief gag scene with Michael, whose career has just been shattered, walking by a mime in Central Park who's in a precarious pose and knocking him over with a malicious touch—no more than a finger. This is the only time Michael ever shows any doubt about his vocation, and it's a passing, aberrant impulse—as if his head didn't quite know what his hand was up to.

Sydney Pollack, who was an actor in his earlier years, originally went to Hollywood (in 1961) as a dialogue coach for John Frankenheimer, essentially he's still a dialogue coach, and this works better for him here than it ever has before. Having dealt with stars most of his life, he knows how impossible they can be, and he has been able to make *Tootsie* something practically unheard of: a believable farce. The picture has more energy than anything else he has done; it's almost alarmingly well cast, and the lines of dialogue collide with a click and go spinning off. Pollack himself gives some jabbing, fast readings; he plays a major role—that of Michael's agent—with zest. Teri Garr has developed a shorthand style of comedy that's all her own, and the audience has such strong empathy with her that she can get her flighty, pent-up character across to us in a few terse movements and phrases. The actress she plays dramatizes her reaction to everything; she's always shrieking or on the verge of shrieking—in disbelief at what is happening to her. Yet Teri Garr always takes us by surprise; she has become the funniest neurotic dizzy dame on the screen. As Michael's roommate, an avant-garde dramatist, Bill Murray keeps dropping into the movie and making an observation or a comment, and his inflections break up the audience every time. (He is said to have ad-libbed his role.) As a lecherous, foolish old ham who plays the head doctor in the soap, the veteran performer George Gaynes has a small comic triumph; once you've laughed at him, even the sight of him triggers more laughs. Dabney Coleman, as the director of the soap, doesn't seem to have come up with anything fresh, but Charles Durning, who plays Julie's farmer father, does some shrewd underplaying, especially in a scene in which you can feel how badly he wants to wallop Michael.

When Jessica Lange appears, the movie changes from the crackling, rapid-fire presentation of the hopes versus the realities of out-of-work actors' lives to something calmer, and perhaps richer. She has a facial structure that the camera yearns for, and she has talent, too. Her face is softer here than in *Frances;* her Julie is a dream girl, and she's like a shock absorber to Michael. When he, dressed as Dorothy, sees her, some of his irascibility melts away. Julie has honey-colored hair, and a friendly smile; she looks freshly created—just hatched, and pleasantly, warmly spacy (enough to be deeply impressed by Dorothy's high-principled talk about the theatre). Jessica Lange helps to keep the movie from being too frenetic. There is none of the usual actress's phoniness in her work; as Julie, she says her lines in such a mild, natural way that it makes perfect sense for Michael to stop in his tracks and stare at her in wonder. The picture is marvellous fun.

■ ■ ■

Leaving the theatre where I saw *Gandhi,* I felt the way the British must have when they left India: exhausted and relieved. Directed by Richard Attenborough, the film (which runs three hours and eight minutes) has no dramatic center; perhaps in compensation, the action all seems to take place in the dead middle of the screen. In his interviews, Attenborough appears to have an instinct for the telling detail, the anecdote that reveals character, but that's part of what he lacks as a moviemaker. *Gandhi* is reverential and holy, like the pictures that used to be made about Jesus. Gandhi, too, goes by in a cloud of serenity, and everyone who sees him knuckles under (with the exception of a few misguided fellows, of course). Ben Kingsley, the English actor of half-Indian extraction who plays the Mahatma, looks the part, has a fine, quiet presence, and conveys Gandhi's shrewdness. He has also mastered a smile that's part compassion, part wince of pain. Kingsley is impressive, the picture isn't. It isn't a disgrace—it just isn't much of anything. The first half builds up considerable interest in Gandhi; the second half is scattered—as if it had been added to or subtracted from at random. And

Kingsley can't give his role a core, because it has been written completely from the outside. During the picture, we never feel that we know Gandhi, and when it's over we still have no insight into what went on in his head. All we get to take home is the shine in Kingsley's eyes.

Members of the press have been congratulating Attenborough for making an old-fashioned movie, but that was hardly a matter of choice for him. Attenborough works in the tradition of orderly, neat imagery: in his India even poverty is clean and barbered. His sensibility is conventional, like that of the studio heads of three or four decades ago. The picture is respectable. It skitters over some of the principal events in Gandhi's public life and tidies up his rather kinky domestic relations. Spanning fifty-five years, it's a schoolbook Life of Gandhi, and can be regarded worshipfully.

There are many famous performers in the cast: the British brigade includes John Gielgud, Trevor Howard, John Mills, Michael Hordern, John Clements, Ian Bannen, Ian Charleson, and villainous Edward (twisty-face) Fox; Athol Fugard plays General Smuts, Candice Bergen is supposed to be Margaret Bourke-White, and Martin Sheen is a reporter, though he can't have much to report, because when historic encounters are going on in front of him he's looking down at his feet. Several of the Indian actors are look-alikes for the figures they're playing, but the Nehru look-alike (Roshan Seth) doesn't have Nehru's elegant presence, and Gandhi's enemy Jinnah (Alyque Padamsee), who wants India to be divided into two countries (as indeed it was), is too obviously a decadent bad guy. There are some amiable people on the screen such as the round-faced Saeed Jaffrey as Patel, but except for Gandhi there are no characters of any consequence, and the material is unshaped—you can't tell what goes on in *anybody's* head. The film's Gandhi is a one-man independence movement; he doesn't discuss nonviolence with other Indian leaders or with his own aides—he lays it down as a decree. And the only drama is in his courage and the courage of his nameless followers, as they carry out acts of civil disobedience and allow themselves to be beaten, maimed, killed. Nonviolent resistance can be very appealing to movie audiences—nonviolent rebels pose no threat to us. And, of course, audiences here can make the association and recall that this policy worked for Martin Luther King, Jr. It worked for King as it had for Gandhi—because he, too, was able to publicize the confrontations, and thus to shame white Americans, as Gandhi shamed the British. But in countries where movements for freedom don't have access to television and the press, nonviolent resistance isn't a political maneuver—it's just a morally superior way of getting yourself mangled. (The soldiers who attacked the refugees in the Lebanese camps were probably delighted that their victims were unarmed, and the Nazis who ran the death camps took pains to insure that theirs wouldn't put up a fight.)

There's a great subject here—a man without any public office, or even a clerical title, who becomes the leader of a nation by sheer force of spiritual authority. But can Gandhi's story be told without a trace of irony? Gandhi didn't use his fasts and his emanciated body just to embarrass the British; he used them against his own people, too. And here is his replica on the screen using his own martyrdom as a tactic—pushing guilt on everybody and getting his way. Basically, he's using the same diabolic tricks as the Jewish mothers that TV comics complain about. And Gandhi had a manipulative genius for timing and publicity. He made a virtue of what was practical. He was also often rigidly impractical—a side of him that, understandably, is omitted from the film. Many scenes break off as if they'd been cut before they were played out. Possibly, the script, by John Briley (there was an earlier version, by Gerald Hanley, and another, by Robert Bolt, and some rewrite work by Donald Ogden Stewart), suggested more of what formed Gandhi and set him apart. Still, it must have been written basically as the life of a saint. When the film's Gandhi says things like "All through history, the way of truth and love has always won," we must be meant to take them straight, be uplifted, and burn incense.

Attenborough himself is no slouch when it comes to publicity—the *Times* alone has had at least eight articles and news stories about the movie—and the accounts of his twenty-year struggle to get it made sit heavy on reviewers' heads. I don't think these accounts are necessarily false, or exaggerated; he has probably gone through some gruelling bad times to make this movie, and the subject may very well have become an obsession with him. But that doesn't mean that he's an obsessive artist. He steered a middle course so that the picture wouldn't offend people. What this amounts to is an empty, schoolboy's (or actor's) form of hero worship. Attenborough seems, more than anything else, infatuated with Gandhi. (Attenborough to a *Newsweek* correspondent: "I adore courage.") The movie is, as he hoped, generally inofffensive, but, apart from those scenes in which the unarmed Indians wait to be attacked by their armed adversaries, it's also, I think, unaffecting. This has to do with the kind of moviemaker Attenborough is. He has scenes with crowds of perhaps hundreds of thousands, but his images are less expressive than the footage we could see on television every night when masses of Iranians gathered in the streets to do obeisance to Ayatollah Khomeini. You have to read about Attenborough's deep commitment to the subject, because you couldn't guess it from what's on the screen. There is no trace of a point of view; the film feels as if it were directed by a committee. The movies that Satyajit Ray has made and the ones that Louis Malle shot in India in the late sixties—the feature-length documentary *Calcutta* and the seven-part series *Phantom India*—have the spirituality that this officially approved, laundered *Gandhi* doesn't have. When I've seen the Satyajit Ray films or those by Malle, I've felt that I was beginning to perceive something of the torpor and beauty of India; *Gandhi* makes me feel that I've been on a state visit.

■   ■   ■

Sophie's Choice, an unusually faithful adaptation of William Styron's Holocaust Gothic, is, I think, an infuriatingly bad movie. It comes to us stuffed with literary references and encrusted with the weighty culture of big themes: evil, tortured souls, guilt. The director, Alan J. Pakula, did the screenplay himself. He didn't write it, he penned it, and the film tells us that (1) survivors of the death camps carry deathly guilt within them and (2) William Styron is right up there on Parnassus with Thomas Wolfe, Walt Whitman, Emily Dickinson, and Hart Crane.

As Sophie, Meryl Streep is colorful in the first, campy, late-forties scenes, in a Brooklyn house divided into apartments and known as the Pink Palace, when, red-lipped and with bright-golden curls, she dimples flirtatiously and rattles on in Polish-accented, broken English, making her foreignness seem zany. This giddy, triste Sophie charms Stingo (Peter MacNicol), a young Southern writer—the stand-in for Styron—who has moved into the room right under hers. And there's an oddly affecting (though stagey) comic scene when Sophie and her lover, Nathan (Kevin Kline), babble to Stingo at the same time, seemingly unaware that each is drowning out the other. But once the flashbacks to Sophie's tormented past start up and the delayed revelations are sprung on us, and we know we're supposed to feel the lurid thrill of everything she did to survive, I felt more sympathy for Meryl Streep, the actress trying to put over these ultimate-horror scenes, than I could for Sophie herself. Streep is very beautiful at times, and she does amusing, nervous bits of business, like fidgeting with a furry boa—her fingers twiddling with our heartstrings. She has, as usual, put thought and effort into her work. But something about her puzzles me: after I've seen her in a movie, I can't visualize her from the neck down. Is it possible that as an actress she makes herself into a blank and then focusses all her attention on only one thing—the toss of her head, for example, in *Manhattan,* her accent here? Maybe, by bringing an unwarranted intensity to one facet of a performance, she in effect decorporealizes herself. This could explain why her movie heroines don't seem to be full characters, and why there are no incidental joys to be had from watching her. It could be that in her zeal to be an honest actress she allows nothing to escape her conception of a performance. Instead of trying to achieve freedom in front of the camera, she's predetermining what it records.

Meryl Streep's work doesn't hold together here, but how could it? Sophie isn't a character, she's a pawn in this guilt-and-evil game played out by Sophie the Catholic, Nathan the Jew, and Stingo the Protestant. Styron got his three characters so gummed up with his idea of history that it's hard for us to find them even imaginable. And, with Sophie as the careworn flirt and Stingo as the heir to Southern chivalry, Nathan *has* to be unpredictable, or nothing would happen. (Maybe that's the reason for psychotics in fiction.)

MacNicol, in the usually lifeless part of the onlooker who's going to write the story we're seeing, gives the best and the only sustained performance: his auburn hair is cut very short, and he looks the twenty-two-year-old he's meant to be; he keeps an intensity going—he's right there, completely involved in the lovers' sadomasochistic trials. In the ads for the movie, Meryl Streep and Kevin Kline are posed like Garbo and John Gilbert—older Endless Lovers. But Kline is saddled with the kind of flamboyant role that never works—the brilliant, suffering genius. What is a poor actor supposed to do when he's given florid, tortured speeches to deliver? I kept waiting for him to cry "O Bright Ironic Gods!" It's an unplayable part—there's not a single believable moment in it.

What Pakula never figured out was how to get all this crazed romanticism in motion. There's nothing to move the picture forward during the scenes in which Nathan discovers that Sophie has *Look Homeward, Angel* in Polish, or Stingo receives *Leaves of Grass* as a present from Sophie and Nathan, or Stingo recites Emily Dickinson to Sophie, or the three of them are having an epiphany on Hart Crane's Brooklyn Bridge. The movie is a novel being talked to us. And Styron's novel is all come-on. The book has the kind of plotting that points relentlessly at a character's secret and then has to have the character lying constantly, so that the lies can be stripped away. Styron does a dance of a thousand veils with what he regards as the Mystery of Our Time. The movie, following the book, is a striptease. Styron builds the novel toward momentousness, but it's a structure of titillation. And maybe he's afraid we might be tired of the Nazis, so he works to nab us: he sweetens things along the way, throwing in Gothic goodies like the Pink Palace. (Was it inspired by the 1963 movie *What a Way to Go!*, with Shirley MacLaine trying to cheer up her husband, Pinky, by having the rooms in their mansion all painted pink?) The whole plot is based on a connection that isn't there—the connection between Sophie and Nathan's relationship and what the Nazis did to the Jews. Eventually, we get to the Mystery—to Sophie's Choice—and discover that the incident is garish rather than illuminating, and too particular to demonstrate anything general. When you read the book, you can see that there are no unmarked cards in Styron's deck, and you feel you're being played for a sucker. The inert movie takes the book so seriously that you may feel it's Pakula who's the sucker.

The New Yorker, December 27, 1982

THE NIGHT OF THE SHOOTING STARS
MEMORY

T*he Night of the Shooting Stars* (the original Italian title is *La Notte di San Lorenzo*) is so good it's thrilling. This new film by Vittorio and Paolo Taviani (who made the 1977 *Padre Padrone*) encompasses a vision of the world. Comedy, tragedy, vaudeville, melodrama—they're all here, and inseparable. Except for the framing-device scenes that take place in a blue-lighted, fairy-tale present, *Shooting Stars* is set in a Tuscan village and its environs during a summer week in 1944, when the American troops were rumored to be only days away, and the Germans who had held the area under occupation were preparing to clear out. But this setting is magical, like a Shakespearean forest; it exists in the memory of Cecilia, who is telling the story of what happened that August, when she was a sultry six-year-old hellion (played by Micol Guidelli), and her family was part of a group of a dozen villagers who had decided to disobey official orders. Convinced that the Germans, who had mined their houses, meant to destroy the whole town—San Martino—that night, they stole out after dark and went to find the Americans. The directors (who also wrote the script, with Giuliani G. De Negri) are great gagmen—they aren't afraid to let Cecilia exaggerate. She remembers herself as a tiny six-year-old who is independent of adults and smarter than life. It doesn't take much stretch of our imaginations to grasp that accidents that befell the child—such as tumbling onto a basket of eggs—have become enlarged. The basket itself has assumed heroic proportions, and, having been blamed for what she couldn't help, the little girl takes a demonic joy in smashing the two eggs that are still intact. The Cecilia we see never complains and always finds ways to amuse herself; when she has witnessed an on-the-run wedding (the groom is AWOL, the bride's pregnancy is close to term) even the hops she takes, out of sheer pixilated excitement, are a bit higher than life. At this rushed wedding, an old man drinks a ceremonial glass of wine and gives a recitation about what happened to Achilles and Hector as if the Trojan War had taken place in his own lifetime. I think you could say that *Shooting Stars* is about how an individual's memories go to form communal folklore, and vice versa, so that we "recall" what we've heard from others as readily as what we've actually seen or heard. And the myth becomes our memory—the story we tell.

The Tavianis' style here is intellectualized, but their effects are unaccountable and gutty. Right at the start, in the chaos of a war that's lost but not yet over, and with Army deserters making their way home and hiding out from the Germans and the local Black Shirts, and with families split between Resistance fighters and Fascists, and nobody sure what the Germans will do before they pull out, San Martino is victimized by a practical joker who plays "Glory, Glory Hallelujah" on his phonograph. It's a marching version, with drums and woodwinds, of the old camp-meeting hymn that became "John Brown's Body" and later the "Battle Hymn of the Republic," and it begins softly, as if John Brown's brigades were at a distance and coming closer, and the townspeople, who have been cowering in their cellars, think that the Americans, their liberators, have arrived, and rush out to greet them. One boy is so sure of it, he sees them.

Galvano (played by Omero Antonutti, the powerful father of *Padre Padrone*) is the leader of the group that sneaks away in the night; at times he's like a theatre director. He tells his people to wear dark clothes for camouflage, and the whole troupe scrambles into black coats and coverings at the same time—it's like backstage at the opera, with everyone getting ready for the masquerade scene. And then there's another, quicker routine: the dogs who must be left behind, because their barking would betray the group, bark because they're being left behind. At last, Galvano's villagers are out in the country. They have been told that the Germans will blow up the town at 3 A.M., and when it's close to three they stand still and listen. We hear their thoughts, and then, exactly at three, distant shelling can be heard, and we see closeups of ears, like enlarged details of paintings by Uccello. The villagers listen to the destruction of San Martino—the only world they know—and we see their hands clenching their house keys, and see their expressions. Galvano doffs his hat and weeps for San Martino; a man throws his key away. It's an unostentatiously beautiful passage. The people mourn, but they're too excited to feel crushed: they're out on the road looking for Americans. In the morning, they take off their black clothes. The August landscapes are golden, and Cecilia is proud of her pleated red print pinafore. It's made of the same material as her mother's sundress; they're wearing matching mother-daughter outfits.

Shooting Stars keeps opening up and compressing as it cuts back and forth between what happens to the group in the hills and what happens to the others, back in San Martino, who believed the authorities when they told them that they'd be safe if they took refuge in the cathedral. The elderly bishop, who has collaborated—has done what he was told—offers bland assurances to everyone while praying to God that he will really be able to protect his flock. (His prayer has a note of apprehensiveness; life is making a skeptic of him.) So many townspeople gather inside that the bishop runs out of wafers, but the people have brought loaves of bread with them and they break these into bits. He consecrates the bread, and everyone is given the Host—the ritual has never seemed more full of meaning. When the crowded cathedral explodes, the door blasts open and smoke pours forth; two priests bring the bishop out, and, dazed, he slumps in the square. The pregnant bride had become too ill to go on with the trekkers in the country, and her mother had hauled her back on a litter and taken her into the cathedral; now the mother tries to carry the mortally wounded, unconscious girl out, and the bishop, pulling himself to his feet, helps her. For a minute, they're both slightly bent over, facing each other and tugging at the helpless girl; they're forehead to forehead, and their eyes lock. It's an insane, cartoon effect—"This is what trusting in God and the Fascists gets you!"—and it makes the pain of the situation more acute. *Shooting Stars* is so robust that even its most tragic moments can be dizzyingly comic. When Richard Lester attempted black humor on the horrors of war (in the 1967 *How I Won the War*), the scenes were jokey and flat, and the people were no more than puppets. In *Shooting Stars,* black humor is just one tonality among many, and the exhausted mother and the double-crossed bishop aren't diminished by being revealed as dupes; having shared their rock-bottom moment, we feel close to them. Many voices are joined in these memories, and though the people who have headed out for freedom may look more courageous, the film doesn't degrade the ones who stayed behind. They had their reasons—children, old age, fears. In one way or another, they're all like that woman with the pregnant daughter.

Out on the roads, a Sicilian girl who has been shot by German soldiers—who is already dead—flirts and makes small talk with some stray G.I.s, Sicilian-Americans from Brooklyn, before she accepts her death. The only other movie director I know of who could bring off an epiphany like this is the Ukrainian Dovzhenko, the lyrical fantasist of the silent era. The Tavianis present their wildest moments of fantasy in a heightened realistic form; you believe in what you're seeing—but you can't explain why you believe in it. I think that we're eager to swallow it, in the same way that, as children, we put faith in the stories we heard at bedtime, our minds rising to the occasion, because what happened in them was far more real to us than the blurred events of our day. And for the grown woman Cecilia the adventures that she took part in have acquired the brilliance and vitality of legend.

San Martino is probably much like the town of San Miniato, between Pisa and Florence, where the brothers were born (Vittorio in 1929, Paolo in 1931), and which was the site of a massacre carried out by the Germans. (Their first short film—*San Miniato, July 1944,* made in 1954—was about this massacre.) The full fresco treatment they give the events of that summer in *Shooting Stars* is based partly on wartime incidents that they themselves witnessed when they were adolescents; they have said that everything they show actually happened—that the events they didn't witness they picked up "one by one . . . from all kinds of sources, official and otherwise." It's this teeming, fecund mixture, fermenting in their heads for almost forty years, that produces this film's giddy, hallucinated realism.

The movie is not like anything else—the Taviani brothers' pleasure in the great collection of stories they're telling makes it euphoric. It's as if they had invented a new form. In its feeling and completeness, *Shooting Stars* may be close to the rank of Jean Renoir's bafflingly beautiful *Grand Illusion,* and maybe because it's about the Second World War and Renoir's film was about the First, at times it's like a more deracinated *Grand Illusion.* Trying to pick the name by which he'll be known in the Resistance, a man who sings in church decides that he wants to be called Requiem. A married couple who belong to Galvano's group are out in the middle of nowhere, listening to the sounds of a warplane overhead, and the man holds his wife's compact up so she can see to put on her lipstick. Galvano's hungry people come across a watermelon patch, and the film becomes a bucolic festival; one girl can't wait for a melon to be cut open—she smashes it with her bottom. At night, all of them sleep piled on top of each other in a crater—a shell hole—as if their bodies had been flung there in a game of pick-up-sticks. And the image is so vivid that somehow you don't question it. Was this crater with its groundlings conceived as a secular joke on the seraphic figures floating in the painted domes of churches? You don't boggle at anything in this movie. The Tavianis have the kind of intuition that passeth understanding. An era is ending, the society is disintegrating, but they take a few seconds to show us Galvano, who has gone to a stream to bathe, standing still in the water, completely at peace—his mind a blank. It's a transcendent image. He could be anywhere and the water would renew him; he has a sense of balance. Galvano gets to consummate his lifelong dream, but before he goes to bed with the woman he has loved for forty-years—the woman who hasn't been accessible until now, because she became part of the landed gentry—they kiss, and he tells her apologetically that his kiss would be better if he hadn't lost three teeth. What he's saying is "Do you know what you've made us miss?"

The film's greatest sequence is hair-raisingly casual—a series of skirmishes in a wheat field. Still looking for the American troops and spotting nothing but Germans, the villagers come to a wheat field and meet up with a group of Resistance fighters who need help with the harvest (or the Fascists will get it), and the villagers lend a hand. And suddenly all the ideological factions that have been fighting in the country are crawling around in the tall wheat. There's a civil war taking place in the fields, with men who all know each other, who in some cases are brothers or cousins, going at each other with clubs and guns and pitchforks. These are not noble peasants. Two old friends wrestle murderously, each demanding that the other surrender; the gentle bridegroom kills a fifteen-year-old Fascist, who is grovelling in terror, and the kid's father falls to the earth and scoots in a circle like an animal in agony. Scenes from this battlefield could turn into Anselm Kiefer's huge straw landscapes, which are like windswept, overgrown memorials that have come up out of the past—out of war and mud and destruction. At one chaotic moment, a couple of people who are tending a wounded old woman reach out at arm's length for the flask of water that a couple of other people have just given to a wounded man, and then, realizing that they're enemies, both pairs start shooting at each other—from a distance of about three feet. It's a pure sick joke, like something Godard would have tried in *Les Carabiniers* if he'd thought of it. In *Shooting Stars,* you're never reminded of a filmmaker who isn't a master.

The Taviani brothers say that if there is a theme running through their movies it's "From silence to communication," but they try to spoof their own theme, too. When Cecilia and another little girl meet up with two G.I.s, Cecilia's friend picks the one she likes, and he gives her a chocolate bar, but Cecilia's G.I. indicates that he has nothing to offer her. Silently, she makes funny ugly faces at him, and he replies in kind, and then, wanting to give her some token, he improvises—he blows up a condom as if it were a balloon, and she dances off with her prize. This, like several other scenes in the movie, is reminiscent of Rossellini's 1946 film *Paisan;* the Tavianis, who saw that film when they were university students in Pisa, say that it was *Paisan* that made them decide to become moviemakers. And so maybe this G.I.-

condom scene can be passed over—it's effective in the thin, overcooked manner of *Life* journalism in the forties. It's an amusing parody of a whole batch of romantic encounters in wartime movies, but it's also a dismayingly pat little number.

In a sense, everything in *Shooting Stars* is a theatrical routine (but not on that level). The Tavianis' style keeps you conscious of what they're doing, and, yes, the technique is Brechtian, but with a fever that Brecht never had. The Tavianis make stylized unreality work for them in a way that nobody else ever has; in *Shooting Stars* unreality doesn't seem divorced from experience (as it does with Fellini)—it's experience made more intense. They love style, but it hasn't cost them their bite—their willingness to be harsh and basic. During the brief period when a movie is actually being shot, a director often wishes that he had someone to help him—someone who knew what was inside his head. These two do, and that may account for the calm assurance of the film and its steady supply of energy. Every sequence is a flourish, but there's heft in the Tavianis' flourishes, and no two have the same texture or tone. The shaping of the material is much more conscious than we're used to. The movie builds, and it never lets up—it just keeps channelling its energy in different directions. Even when *Shooting Stars* is at its most emotionally expansive, you're aware of the control the directors have. What they're controlling is exaltation. That's the emotional medium they're working in.

They use sound in a deliberately primitive way: the sound here— whether it's from nature or Verdi or the score by Nicola Piovani—makes memories flood back just as odors sometimes bring things back. It's sound of great clarity, set against silence. (A superb fanfare is heard during the film's main title—a fanfare followed by cannon fire and then, for a moment, nothing.) The memories the sound brings back come up out of the muck and are heavily filtered; they're distorted, and polished until they gleam. And the directors' visual techniques—their use of dissolves, especially—keep you conscious of the processes of memory etching in and eroding. The film's impassioned style is steeped in nostalgia. Cecilia's mythicized memories are her legacy to her own child, to whom she is telling this story at bedtime. For the Tavianis, as for Cecilia, the search for the American liberators is the time of their lives. For an American audience, the film stirs warm but tormenting memories of a time when we were beloved and were a hopeful people.

The New Yorker, February 7, 1983

THE YEAR OF LIVING DANGEROUSLY

A new-style old-time "dangerous" steaminess builds up as Mel Gibson and Sigourney Weaver eye each other. When he watches her dancing to a record of Jerry Lee Lewis's "Whole Lotta Shakin' Goin' On" and one of her spaghetti straps keeps slipping off her shoulder, or when they're running together in the rain and she's giggling like crazy, the movie has "hot stuff" written all over it. The director, Peter Weir, knows what's spectacular about Sigourney Weaver: her brainy female-hunk physicality—her wide-awake dark eyes, the protruding lower lip, the strong, rounded, outthrust jaw, and her hands, so large that when she embraces Gibson her five fingers encompass his back. Weaver has practically no character to play but she suggests a privileged woman who feels perfectly free to enjoy her prerogatives, and that's a turn-on for the audience, because what a set of prerogatives!

Mel Gibson is a highly accomplished screen actor; that was apparent in *Gallipoli*, too. But he's very young (twenty-seven), and something bland and ordinary seems to be poking through the sullen, burned-out fellow he plays in *The Road Warrior*. Here Gibson's being too young for his foreign correspondent role isn't a disadvantage. When he sees Weaver across the room, he's agog—he has a puppyish look. He's like Henry Fonda staring at Barbara Stanwyck in *The Lady Eve*: he's moony, a bumbler. And his open-mouthed gawking at Weaver amuses her; she's so wild about him she's charmed by his callowness—she laughs at him the way Stanwyck laughed at the mesmerized Fonda (and made him fall all over himself). Gibson still doesn't have a very distinctive personality as an actor, but his character's jangled nerves are good for him; he uses his eyes more here—he has more tension and dash—and he brings a spunky, romantic-comedy quality to his role. When the two stars are together, the movie has the hectic, under-the-surface energy that is Weir's brand of magic. Gibson and Weaver cause a scandal by leaving a party at the Embassy; they get in a car and he drives, hellbent, as if nothing could stop them, and he plows right through an army roadblock. The guards shoot at them, and the gun bursts are like applause for their sexiness.

The New Yorker, February 21, 1983

ABOUT ROBERT DE NIRO IN
THE KING OF COMEDY

Robert De Niro's Rupert Pupkin is Jake La Motta without his fists. In *Raging Bull*, De Niro and Scorsese had things boiled down, so that Jake's entire character was the chip on his shoulder. This time there's no chip. If De Niro, disfigured again here, has removed himself from comparison with other handsome young actors, it's not because what he does now is more than acting. It's less; it's anti-acting. Performers such as John Barrymore and Orson Welles and Laurence Olivier have delighted in putting on beards and false noses, yet, no matter how heavy the disguise, they didn't disappear; they still had spirit, and we could feel the pleasure that they took in playing foul, crookback monsters and misers—drawing us inside and revealing the terrors of the misshapen, the deluded. A great actor merges his soul with that of his characters—or, at least, gives us the illusion that he does. De Niro in disguise denies his characters a soul. It's not merely that he hollows himself out and becomes Jake La Motta, or Des the priest in *True Confessions,* or Rupert Pupkin—he makes them hollow, too, and merges with the character's emptiness.

In most of De Niro's early performances—in *Hi, Mom!,* even in *The Gang That Couldn't Shoot Straight,* and in *Mean Streets, The Godfather, Part II, Taxi Driver,* and *New York, New York*—there was bravura in his acting. You could feel the actor's excitement shining through the character, and it made him exciting to watch. But, for all his virtuosity, his Monroe Stahr in *The Last Tycoon* was lifeless, and his Michael in *The Deer Hunter* heroic yet never quite human. And then he started turning himself into repugnant, flesh effigies of soulless characters. Rupert is chunky and thick-nosed, and he has a foul, greasy mustache; is it so De Niro can remove himself further from the character and condescend to him even physically? Rupert waves his arms when he talks; they work in pairs, as if he didn't have the brains to move them independently of each other. De Niro cunningly puts in all the stupid little things that actors customarily leave out. It's a studied performance; De Niro has learned to be a total fool. Big accomplishment! What De Niro is doing might be based on the Warholian idea that the best parody of a thing is the thing itself.

Rupert doesn't really talk to or listen to anyone else in the movie; whatever he's doing, he's always in rehearsal, trying out his new moves. Scorsese and De Niro close him in, just as Hal Ashby and Jerzy Kosinksi closed in the Peter Sellers character in that dim, prolonged one-joke satire *Being There,* and for the same purpose: to tell us that TV is making such fools of us that we'll accept a moron—as a statesman in *Being There,* and as an entertainer in *The King of Comedy.* Sellers' stillness, his unhappy expression, his stately misery in those itchy old clothes, and the Oriental-sage formality of his speech didn't make much sense—how could these be the effects of a simpleton's watching TV? But Sellers did create a solemnly dull character: a baffled, easily hurt, wanting-to-please moron. Pupkin is a nothing.

The New Yorker, March 7, 1983

TALES OF ORDINARY MADNESS

E very once in a while, the highly accomplished Ben Gazzara gets a film role that he's itching to play and a director who's in love with that marvellous oily, enigmatic face of his. Gazzara is handsome yet guarded, like an armadillo. He could be a survivor of an ancient (and untrustworthy) race. As Charles Serking, the drunken, permanently hung-over, semi-famous poet in the Italian director Marco Ferreri's *Tales of Ordinary Madness,* he gets to cut loose and do things on screen that he has never done before—that probably nobody has done onscreen before. Ferreri is known for carrying ideas to extremes (*The Ape Woman,* of 1964, *La Grande Bouffe,* of 1973, *The Last Woman,* of 1976), and his script is based on the stories and the spirit of the American poet and novelist Charles Bukowski, a master of rut who writes about the gutbucket pain and elation of being human. The specific story drawn on for this movie (made in English) is "The Most Beautiful Woman in Town," from the City Lights book *Erections, Ejaculations, Exhibitions and General Tales of Ordinary Madness.* The story is written in the first person, and that's who Gazzara is playing—his Serking is an interpretation of Bukowski.

Tales of Ordinary Madness isn't for people who are disturbed by four-letter words or sexual acts performed with lewd gusto. That should still leave quite a few of us. It's a startling movie, partly because it's so simply presented. Though it's about many of the same themes as an Ingmar Bergman picture, it isn't stark—it has the matter-of-fact, one-thing-after-another plainness of an Abbott and Costello movie. Serking, a skid-row scrounger with a gray beard and with seat-sprung pants hanging down from his shrunken body, swigs from a bottle in a brown paper bag and sniffs like a stray dog at a succession of fat, mean, and sleazy women. The sleazier they are, the more he likes them. He sees the brutish comedy in what he's doing, and that's part of why he does it. (At times, he's a lot like Mailer the grizzled challenger.) Between sexual bouts, he reads his poetry at a college, raises hell at a foundation that tries to treat him as an artist-genius, drinks until he pukes, and then drinks some more. The movie, with its artist-bum as hero, has a slight resemblance to the 1970 *Tropic of Cancer,* in which Rip Torn played Henry Miller, but this bum Serking is also a sufferer, and the picture is far more sexually explicit. It goes beyond raunchiness—it's naked. And the bare, functional filmmaking intensifies our awareness of what the coupling human beings on the screen are doing to each other—there's nothing else to look at. Visually, the film seems washed out at the start, and then it becomes brighter; sunlight seems to become one of Ferreri's themes. It isn't likely that anyone imagined that Joseph Strick, who directed *Tropic of Cancer,* shared Miller's excitement about women of any age or shape. Here you feel that Ferreri, who has his own wild man's understanding of comedy, has also got right down inside Bukowski's self-mocking lust and self-dramatizing temperament. Certainly Gazzara has felt his way in—his reptilian eyes shine with the mischief his role makes possible. They almost pop out in his scenes with Susan Tyrrell, as a loco who's perhaps the gamiest and funniest of the women he has bouts with. (She yells so violently during sex he has to cover her mouth.)

Except for side excursions to the college, to the foundation in New York, and to the ocean, the movie is set in Bukowski's old habitat, Los Angeles, where he has spent most of his life. (His books sell moderately well there and spectacularly well in Europe, especially in Germany, and he now lives a more stable and prosperous existence in San Pedro, California.) Serking's L.A. is mostly Hollywood at its crummiest—flophouses, rooming houses, cheaply built garden apartments, and bars where broken-down hookers hang out. It's in one of these bars that Serking meets Cass, "the most beautiful woman in town." Ornella Muti, who plays the role, fully lives up to the description; she's as lithe as a cat, and has the soft radiance of the young Hedy Lamarr in the coital scenes of *Ecstasy.* And Ferreri, who has worked with her before (in *The Last Woman*), lights her to perfection. (He appears to take more care with her scenes than with the rest of the film.) Ornella Muti's Cass is sloe-eyed, and high-waisted, with the long legs of a Balanchine dancer. Convent-bred, she's mysteriously, uncannily beautiful—a carnal Madonna who punishes herself by working as a prostitute. Cass, whose beauty would open any doors, picks up men in the cheapest sour-smelling dives. This degradation isn't enough: she mutilates her flesh. She's intelligent but crazy, and she has nothing binding her to life.

This beautiful woman, with her inverted narcissism—she costumes herself in dramatic, mood-fitting ensembles, with special attention to the neck she has sawed away at—is like a mad nun. Cass is a trite, preposterously over-dramatic creation—a fallen angel with crosses dangling from her ears and a faraway look in her eyes—and yet something about her rings true. She has elements of every self-destructive Catholic girl I've ever known or heard of; her self-love and her self-hatred aren't just a made-up subject. And her ringing true helps to validate Serking's attitudinizing and his despair. Cass is a sex goddess, she's walking poetry—and Serking, who loves her, can't hang on to her. He gets her out in the sun, but he can't infuse his own love of life into her.

The early parts of this movie have a shocking comic power (and sometimes the comedy drains away and leaves a deliberately sad tawdriness), but the sequences don't have much impetus. After Cass's story takes shape, though, the picture develops its own kind of rhythm. And by the end Serking, whose pants are always about to fall down to his knees, begins to seem—well, valiant. He's resigned to failure, but he keeps trying—he wants to believe in the dream he had of a life with Cass. Meanwhile, there are all those Hollywood locos, and even a fresh young thing who asks him "Where does poetry come from?" That heartfelt question may call for a half grapefruit in the face, but the vain Serking, touched, responds very tenderly. After all, for him women hold the mystery of creation.

At the beginning of the movie, when Serking is speaking in a deep voice in an ornate, sparsely filled college auditorium, he says, "To do a dangerous thing with style is what I call art." It's a dangerous thing for Ferreri (who wrote the script with Sergio Amidei and Anthony Foutz) to use that line. Inevitably, it leads to thoughts of: Is *Tales of Ordinary Madness* art? A lot of skepticism wells up in me when poets go into their living-on-the-edge, deep-in-the-lower-depths boogie. From time to time, Serking does a voice-over narration, and it could be a parody of the tough-guy narration in the Raymond Chandler detective movies, with Serking on a quest for truth and beauty. He says things like, "the defeated, the demented, and the damned—they're the real people of the world, and I was proud to be in their company." Since the director doesn't appear to have the best grasp of how Americans talk, it's sometimes hard to tell whether this kind of flatulence is meant to be taken straight. Chances are it is, but it also fits the character Gazzara is playing. Ferreri uses his deadpan simplicity to bring out the infantilism of middle-aged macho clowns who know they're being infantile and getting high on excess but don't know how to grow up, and don't want to, anyway. There's genuine audacity and risk-taking in this movie. It may not have the energy of great art, but its nakedness has an aesthetic force. When you come out of the theatre, you know you've seen something; it wasn't just another picture.

The great thing about Marco Ferreri is that he gets to the point. In one image—Serking rams an enormously fat woman's crotch with his head—the film sums up what a number of Rabelaisian writers have struggled to say about their desire to go back to the womb. That image cuts through the fake profundities that the film falls for. And even when Gazzara is lamenting bourgeois stultification and crying out "Can't we awaken? Must we forever, dear friends, die in our sleep?" He knows that these are the words of a poseur. He makes Serking a big enough poseur to be a macho-clown artist.

The New Yorker, March 21, 1983

TENDER MERCIES

In *Tender Mercies*, Robert Duvall, as Mac Sledge, a legendary country-and-Western singer and song-writer who has become an alcoholic wreck, begins to recover through the kindness of Rosa Lee (Tess Harper), the young widow of a soldier killed in Vietnam. She lets him stay at her motel and gas station on the desolate Texas prairie, and he does handyman jobs to pay for his keep, but they haven't actually exchanged much more than a few yups and nopes when, about half an hour into the picture, he says, "I guess it's no secret how I feel about you. A blind man could see that." Which is quite a surprise, because nobody could see it. There hasn't been the slightest interplay between them—not so much as a soft expression or a good hot look. And I'm afraid that I was further confused because Rosa Lee has been so blank-faced and terse that I'd thought she was meant to be—well, simple, dim-witted. So it took me a while to get into the film's conception and realize that in this scheme of things simple meant deep, and that this woman of few words is supposed to represent frontier-woman steadfastness and true, enduring values. She's patience, normality, perfection. (What she isn't is a character.) Once I got it straight, I knew how I was supposed to react to her faint smile of gratification as she watches Mac—now her husband—getting himself dunked, along with her nine-year-old son, in the baptismal tank at her church. Mac is born again. Being with Rosa Lee and the boy has healed him. And he ends her loneliness, and provides the boy with the father he never had. (Mac's conversion, like his falling in love, takes place off camera; that could be one of the mercies referred to in the title.)

It used to happen that you paid to see a movie and you got back your weight in homilies. A lot of people must miss this; tired of the new junk, they want the old junk—like the stuff they used to get from the alleged Golden Age of Television. Audiences appear to be deeply moved by this barebones picture, which is said to be honest and about real people. Duvall's Mac is pure, wrinkled granite; he's such a recessive personality that the few seconds of emotion he lets come through seem to convince some viewers that they're seeing great acting. But it may be that Duvall puts too much emphasis on the integrity (i.e., the shell) of the character: his integrity as a performer means that we lose out. For example, I think he needed to give more to the scene in which Sue Anne, his eighteen-year-old daughter by his first marriage (to a high-powered country-music star), comes to see him, hoping for the understanding she doesn't get from her mother. Sue Anne is played by Ellen Barkin, whose few scenes are the high points of the movie. She has something rare in a young actress: power. And she has a great face for acting—her eyes are about a mile apart. Her lines aren't any more expressive than the rest of what the scriptwriter, Horton Foote, master of arid realism, provides, but she makes you feel Sue Anne's messy hopes so acutely that when this girl asks her father if he remembers a song he used to sing to her and he stands there, impassive, it's bewildering. After she leaves, he recites the lyrics of the song so we'll know he remembers everything, and that he is—in the language of this movie—hurting. I don't understand why he couldn't have given her a sign of acknowledgment that he remembered—he can see that she needs it. Duvall appears to operate on the premise that the less Mac Sledge shows the more he feels. (I've never seen a star performance so dependent on a squint; Mac's T-shirts should read "Life Makes Me Wince.")

I kept waiting for *Tender Mercies* to get started—to get into something. I was still waiting when it was over and I was back out on the street. The Australian director Bruce Beresford, who makes his American début with this inspirational film, has shot it in bright sunshine out in the middle of nowhere; the motel-gas station is as isolated as the mansion in *Giant.* (It's a mystery how Rosa Lee ever expected to make a living from it.) I was grateful when a van pulled up and several local young men—musicians—piled out; they've come to pay their respects to Mac, and though they seem like the kind of guys who can spit watermelon seeds real far, they serve to populate the screen and provide a few minutes of affability. And it helps to see Betty Buckley, who stirs things up a bit in her role as Dixie—Mac's first wife, the red-haired singer whom he had brutalized in the days when he was a mean drunk. Onstage, Betty Buckley's Dixie is a brassy trouper—a hardworking second-rater; too bad that offstage she has lines like the complaint about her daughter: "I gave her everything in the world she ever wanted." (I didn't make that up, but then neither did Horton Foote.) Mostly the picture consists of silences; long shots of the bleak, flat land, showing the horizon line (that, too, gives a film integrity); and Duvall's determination to make you see that he's keeping his emotions to himself, and Tess Harper staring out of her cornflower-blue headlights. These two have matching deep-sunk eyes; the theme song—which Duvall sings in a dry, unmusical voice—is called "It Hurts to Face Reality." *Tender Mercies* is proof that a movie doesn't have to be long to be ponderous.

The New Yorker, May 16, 1983

RETURN OF THE JEDI

Some of the trick effects might seem miraculous if the imagery had any lustre, but *Return of the Jedi* is an impersonal and rather junky piece of moviemaking. There doesn't seem to be enough light, and the editing isn't crisp (particularly in the first third). *Jedi* features a tribe of potbellied woodland creatures, the furry, cuddly Ewoks, who suggest a cross between koala bears and puli dogs; the Ewoks help their friend Princess Leia (Carrie

Fisher) by toddling about the forest bashing her enemies—one fiercely de-termined Ewok scrambles into an aircraft that looks like a kiddie car, and he becomes a daredevil ace. The sequence should be magical, because God only knows how all this was done, but the images are muddy and the slap-stick is repetitive. The forest is unenchanted and, like the other settings, in the desert, all too earthly. And though we want to be able to remember this glade full of raffish little Teddy bears, the effects are gruelling; they tend to cancel each other out. This is partly because of what has become recogniz-able as the George Lucas approach to fantasy: it's bam bam pow—he's like a slugger in the ring who has no variety and never lets up. This third film of the *Star Wars* trilogy (which, we are told, constitutes the middle section of a nine-film cycle) is, except for a slow beginning, paced like its predeces-sors and like *Raiders of the Lost Ark,* which Lucas also produced. But I think that the groaning exhaustion that had me sighing with relief when *Jedi* was finished can also be blamed on its British director, Richard Marquand (*Eye of the Needle,* the TV series "The Search for the Nile"). Every time there's a possibility of a dramatic climax, a chance to engage the audience emotion-ally with something awesome, Marquand trashes it—and not deliberately, as Richard Lester might, to show us that he's too hip for that, but out of what appears to be indifference yet may just be a weak visual imagination. Even the scene that should be the emotional peak of the whole mythic trilogy—the moment when the young protagonist, Luke Skywalker (Mark Hamill), removes the black visor and the helmet that have concealed Darth Vader's face—has no thrill. There isn't a gasp to be heard in the entire theatre. Luke looks into the eyes of his nightmare father, and he might be ordering a veggieburger.

In *The Empire Strikes Back,* when Han Solo (Harrison Ford) was frozen into sculpture—his face protruding from a bas-relief, the mouth open as if calling out in pain—the scene had a terrifying grandeur. Though *Empire,* re-leased in 1980, didn't have the leaping, comic-book hedonism of the 1977 *Star Wars* and, as the middle, bridging film of the trilogy, was chained to an unresolved, cliffhanger plot, it was a vibrant, fairy-tale cliffhanger. The direc-tor, Irvin Kershner, brought the material a pop-Wagnerian amplitude; the characters showed more depth of feeling than they had in the first film, and the music—John Williams' variations on the *Star Wars* theme—seemed to saturate and enrich the intensely clear images. Scenes from that movie lin-ger in the mind: the light playing on Darth Vader's gleaming surfaces as this metal man, who's like a giant armored insect, fills the screen; Han Solo sav-ing Luke's life on the ice planet Hoth by slashing open a snow camel and warming him inside; Luke's hand being lopped off, and his seemingly end-less fall through space; Chewbacca, the Wookie, yowling in grief or in comic fear, his sounds so hyper-human you couldn't help laughing at them; the big-eared green elf Yoda, with shining ancient eyes, who pontifically in-structs Luke in how to grow up wise—Yoda looks like a wonton and talks like a fortune cookie. The effects in *Empire* appeared to be integral to the story and the characters; in *Jedi* the effects take over. Everything has lost its tone: when Leia finally frees Han Solo from his living death as sculpture, the scene has almost no emotional weight. It's as if Han Solo had locked himself in the garage, tapped on the door, and been let out.

Probably the most difficult thing facing the director of a fantasy that is dependent on mechanical effects is how to make the images flow. George Lucas couldn't do it when he directed *Star Wars,* but he kept the movie hopping, by cutting it into short, choppy scenes. Kershner is a master of visual flow, and, joining his own kinks and obsessions to Lucas's, he gave *Empire* a splendiferousness that may even have transcended what Lucas had in mind. Maybe because of the cascading imagery of *Empire* (which was almost as impassioned as John Boorman's *Excalibur,* and was also funny), Marquand's work looks especially klunky and drab. The characters seem to be robbed of their essences. Chewbacca's personality has drained away. The spark is gone from Yoda's eyes; the little green sage looks swollen and baggy—he has been given horrible fuzz all over, as if he were a peach—and the way he's lighted he isn't even green. Billy Dee Williams' Lando, the gambling man, has been made a general in the rebel forces; perhaps the high rank is meant to compensate for his being on the margins of the movie. (He checks in now and then to remind us of a war that's supposed to be going on somewhere.) Worse, the bravado is gone from Han Solo; this sad palooka is so callow he seems to have regressed. Leia, older and sleeker now, looks at him affectionately, like an indulgent mother who has learned to live with her son's dopeyness. The director doesn't appear to have any use for him: when Han Solo is freed from the block of stone, he's blind, and the picture doesn't even bother to emphasize the moment when he regains his sight. This must be the only movie ever made in which the romantic lead has his sight restored to him in an aside.

Leia herself has acquired more importance in the scheme of things, but in a rather unsatisfying way. We've been assuming that men become knights because of their valor, and Luke, striving to become a Jedi, has been tested over and over. Yet Leia becomes strong and wise—a fighter—because of her lineage. The scriptwriters (Lawrence Kasdan and Lucas) remove the trilogy's moral underpinnings when they tell us that you can become a Jedi knight, with the Force to do good, by heredity. (It's a very un-American notion.) Throughout *Jedi,* we can see that Luke is meant to be maturing and gaining wisdom, but, like Han Solo and Leia, he's colorless. In *Empire,* these three seemed capable of real exhilaration and real suffering. In *Jedi,* they're back to being comic-strip characters wandering through a jokey pastiche of the Arthurian legends.

The movie is openly silly, with obvious parody references to *The Wizard of Oz, The Adventures of Robin Hood, King Kong, Tarzan, the Ape Man,* and everything else, including itself. Some of the silliness is in the ingenious manner of L. Frank Baum, and it's wonderful: the Ewoks fighting off the Empire's soldiers by the strategies that Robin's men used in Sherwood Forest; the Ewoks taking the chatterbox C-3PO, in his gold-colored casing, for a god and putting him on a throne, whereupon he proceeds to draw upon his memory bank and tell them the story of everything that has happened in the three movies—he turns it all into bedtime stories for drowsy Teddy bears. (That's the most endearing idea in the trilogy; it's like something Mark Twain couldn't quite work into *A Connecticut Yankee in King Arthur's Court.*) A batch of new creatures turn up, and one of them, an ogre, Jabba the Hutt, might have come out of a woodcut by Tenniel: he has a walruslike body, a pyramidal head that merges with it, and—superb touch—the wrinkled eyelids of a dowager. And he has a tiny companion perched on him—a parrotlike monkey, or is it a winged Chihuahua? But most of the new critters—monsters that the epicene Jabba has gathered around him at his underground castle—haven't been given much semblance of life. Some, such as the minotaurs, are drooling, cartoon heavies in masks; many have opaque, shoe-button eyes or seem Muppety; others haven't waited to be adapted by toy manufacturers—they're stuffed animals to start with.

Although the dialogue of the first two films also alternated gee whizzes with flat exposition, I don't remember the construction being so bald a series of "Meanwhile, back at" episodes, and I don't recall broken promises, such as solemn pronouncements about Luke's "destiny" which turn out to be all wet. In this kind of movie, in which practically everything is foretold, shouldn't we be able to trust the prophecies that are intoned? Why else include them? And when Luke, dressed in a Hamlet getup, tells Darth Vader's master, the Emperor of the dark side—who's shrouded like Death in *The Seventh Seal*—"Soon we'll both be dead," it's gibberish, an embarrassment. This Emperor, who commands legions of Storm Troopers is an embarrassment anyway. He's photographed too close in, so our time with him is spent staring at the variations in his makeup and the black liquid that the actor is sloshing around his teeth, trying for a ghastly look. There's also an oddly callous development. In one scene, Luke, bargaining with Jabba for Han Solo's life, casually offers the ogre a present: C-3PO and R2-D2. It's as if Dorothy offered the wicked witch a swap—the Cowardly Lion, the Scarecrow, and the Tin Woodman in exchange for Toto. Luke's apparent willingness to betray his loyal friends comes across as mean, even if he intends it only as a tactic.

Chances are that none of this will make any highly visible difference to the children who are clamoring to see the picture. *Empire* left kids dangling; this one has the payoffs. And Lucas may be on to something: that for children (and some adults) a movie that's actively, insistently exhausting can pass for entertainment. Lucas produces the busiest movies of all time; they're made on the assumption that the audience must be distracted every minute. *Return of the Jedi* is packed with torture scenes, and it bangs away at you; it makes you feel that you've seen it all before. I don't mean to suggest that Lucas intends to shortchange audiences; quite the reverse. He gives them a load of movie—so much that their expectations are rammed down their throats. But by now it's clear that his conception of a good show for kids is junky at heart. *Return of the Jedi* is a fun-machine movie. It's the new form of pulp, and when it's made on the scale of *Jedi* slovenliness is an inevitable part of it. A picture with as many special effects as *Jedi* costs a major fortune, and to make it so that the tricks are not just approximations of what was hoped for could double that cost. One answer might be to plan films with fewer tricks, better scripts, and directors who love to see the sparks that actor can give off. Lucas's answer is to pile on the effects—and, with the rumbling noises of things blowing up in Dolby, you're physically under bombardment. There's no blood in the killings in *Jedi,* but is killing without blood really preferable? The picture is indecently affectless: it ends with the triumph of the good guys and the grand celebration of a (bloodless) nuclear explosion—with no worry, no aftermath, no fallout.

The performers aren't encouraged to bring anything to their roles, and they become dispirited: their faces go slack. Denis Lawson, the jack-of-all-trades innkeeper of *Local Hero,* is one of the featured performers in *Jedi,* and you'd never know he was anything special; if the young Alec Guinness or Peter Sellers were in the role, you'd never know he was bursting with talent, either. (Returning to the role of Obi-Wan-Kenobi, even the elderly Guinness, with all his sly skill, barely makes an imprint on this picture.) The cast may be full of comic marvels who were never allowed to do anything but put on masks or sit behind a mockup of the controls of a bomber so that sound-effects wizards could fit the racket in. I can believe that kids will be excited by *Jedi.* They have lived their imaginative lives with the Star Wars characters for six years; each three-year wait has had to be filled with imagination, and so the characters have acquired depth. (Children may not have had such prolonged experiences with any other characters unless they've got into, say, the Oz books.) But I can't believe that *Jedi* will give kids any deep pleasure, because there's no quality of personal obsession in it, or even of devotion to craft. What a director like Richard Marquand does is take the fantasy out of fantasy.

It's one of the least amusing ironies of movie history that in the seventies, when the "personal" filmmakers seemed to be gaining acceptance, the thoughtful, quiet George Lucas made the quirkily mechanical *Star Wars*—a film so successful that it turned the whole industry around and put it on a retrograde course, where it's now joining forces with video-games manufacturers. If a filmmaker wants backing for a new project, there'd better be a video game in it. Producers are putting so much action and so little character or point into their movies that there's nothing for a viewer to latch on to. The battle between good and evil, which is the theme of just about every big fantasy adventure film, has become a flabby excuse for a lot of dumb tricks and noise. It has got to the point where some of us might be happy to see good and evil quit fighting and become friends.

The New Yorker, May 30, 1983

PART NINE

STATE OF
THE ART

1985

ABOUT STEVE MARTIN, FROM REVIEW OF
THE MAN WITH TWO BRAINS

A comic's naked desire to make us laugh can be an embarrassment, especially if we feel that he's hanging on that laugh—that he's experiencing our reaction as a life-or-death matter. Steve Martin is naked, but he isn't desperate. (He's too anomic to be desperate.) Some performers can't work up a physical charge if the audience doesn't respond to them, but Steve Martin doesn't come out on a TV stage cold, hoping to get a rhythm going with the people in the studio. He's wired up and tingling, like a junk-food addict; he's like a man who's being electrocuted and getting a dirty thrill out of it. Steve Martin doesn't feed off the audience's energy—he instills energy in the audience. And he does it by drawing us into a conspiratorial relationship with him.

Pop culture is a relatively recent phenomenon. It's only in the last two decades that moviemakers have come along whose attitudes were shaped by the movies they grew up on, and whose subjects were often drawn from those old movies. And it's only in the past decade that a new generation of comics has been shaping its material as a satirical spinoff of the Catskill traditions they grew up on. The Steve Martin we see is a marionette, like the Devo punks; what holds the strings is the pop culture that he has processed. But he's not protesting the overload of his nervous system. His core is burned out, and he's a happy idiot, all spasms and twitches, and videotape for nerve endings.

When Martin comes onstage, he may do, say, just what Red Skelton used to do, but he gets us laughing at the fact that we're laughing at such dumb jokes. Martin simulates being a comedian, and so, in a way, we simulate being the comedian's audience. Martin makes old routines work by letting us know that they're old and then doing them immaculately. For him, comedy is *all* timing. He's almost a comedy robot. Onstage, he puts across the idea that he's going to do some cornball routine, and then when he does it it has quotation marks around it, and that's what makes it hilarious. He does the routine straight, yet he's totally facetious. He lets us know that we're seeing silliness in quotes. There he is, spruced up and dapper in a three-piece white suit; even his handsomeness is made facetious. Steve Martin is all persona. That's what's dizzying about him—and a little ghoulish. He and some of the other comics of his generation make the *idea* that they're doing comedy funny.

It's as if Steve Martin's showmanship had two stages—as if first he came on and said, "Imagine a clod like me dancing like Fred Astaire." An old-style comedian would then fall on his face, or if he were Jack Benny fancying himself as Heifetz he'd produce one sour note after another. But Martin's steadfast concentration allows him, in the second stage, to do just what he said he'd do—he dances like Fred Astaire.

The New Yorker, June 27, 1983

TWILIGHT ZONE—THE MOVIE

Richard Matheson lives up to his formula for an ideal "Twilight Zone" in the fourth episode, which is a reworking of his script for the 1963 "Nightmare at 20,000 Feet," and, with the Australian George Miller (the director of *The Road Warrior*) in charge and John Lithgow as star, the result is a classic shocker of the short form—something that ranks with the Alberto Cavalcanti segment of *Dead of Night,* the one with Michael Redgrave as the ventriloquist. Miller can't get any distance from his subject: almost all the action takes place in the confines of a plane during a storm, and most of it in the tight space where Lithgow, as Valentine, is seated squirming and wriggling, sick with fear. The whole episode is about this one passenger's freaking out. (Redgrave's ventriloquist was coming apart, too, and Matheson and Miller may be paying their respects to *Dead of Night* by including among the passengers a little girl with a ventriloquist's dummy.) Working within strict spacial limits, and with Lithgow almost always on camera, Miller builds the kind of immediacy and intensity that Spielberg built at the high points of *Jaws.* Miller's images rush at you; they're fast and energizing. And it's in no sense a putdown to say that the short format is perfect for him. The mechanical virtuosity he sustains here would be too overwhelming in a full-length movie—it would seem inhuman. Here, Lithgow makes everything credible. You're never aware of his pumping himself up; hysteria seems to come naturally to him. He does something that's tough for an actor to do: he shows fear without parodying it and yet makes it horrifyingly funny to us. And when you see an actor with this kind of finesse working inside such bizarre material, the finesse itself is outlandish and makes us laugh.

John Lithgow is six foot four, and he's built large, and cuddly, like a Teddy bear. Onscreen (and on the stage, too), he has a special gift for far-out characters, such as the transsexual Roberta Muldoon in *Garp*. Lithgow domesticates flakes; he lets us observe which screws are loose and which are fixed firmly in place. Valentine, the respectable author of a book on computer microchips, is about as far out as a role can get. Valetine has been shaking too much to shave; he has soft stubble on his chin. Those who are subject to anxiety attacks may have a double anxiety attack when they recognize that an attack is starting. Valentine is soaked in cold sweat. He isn't fat, but he's fleshy, and when the sweat pours he's like an animal in terror—a baby-faced ox. And he's writhing with shame because he can't control himself. He knows that the other passengers and the stewardesses (who had to help him back to his seat after he'd panicked in the john) think he's distraught, and maybe they think he's crazy. What else would account for the squalling sounds he has been making, or the way he has been twisting himself on the tiny seat, like a human pretzel? And now, looking out his window, he thinks he sees a form outside, skittering about on the wing of the plane. Peering through the wind and the heavy, sleeting rain, he can't be sure if it's an animal or a person. The other people on the plane look where he points and see nothing. Can it be just an illusion—a projection of his fear? Abject and humiliated as he is, sedated by the head stewardess and trying to act rational, he nevertheless has a compulsion to see what's out there. He lifts his drawn window shade. The shadowy gremlin is attacking the plane, clawing at the wing and tearing out an engine.

Lithgow's performance is like a seizure; the art is in the way he orchestrates it emotionally. With his white face all scrunched up, and anxiety burning out his brain, he takes us with him every step of the way, from simple fear to dementia to stupor, and every step is funny. Valentine never stops embarrassing himself. It's a comic orgy of terror.

The New Yorker, July 25, 1983

ZELIG

Zelig, the new picture by Woody Allen, is a lovely small comedy, but it can't bear the weight of the praise being shovelled on it. If it's a masterpiece, it's a masterpiece only of its own kind; it's like an example of a nonexistent genre, or a genre from another country—something mildly eerie that feels Eastern European, about a man who's on the verge of disappearing and finally he does. Allen had a vertiginous, original idea for a casual piece, like his Madame Bovary story, and he worked it out to perfection. The film has a real shine, but it's like a teeny carnival that you may have missed—it was in the yard behind the Methodist church last week. Insignificance is even its subject.

The son of an Orthodox Jewish actor, Leonard Zelig (played by Allen) wants to be safe, accepted, liked; being a nothing himself, he takes on the characteristics of whatever strong personalities he comes in contact with. In the faddist twenties, his freakish transformations (which are beyond his conscious control) make him a celebrity—he becomes the rage. The movie, which is in the form of a documentary about Zelig, the Human Chameleon, is worked out meticulously, using trick effects that put Allen into old newsreels and stock footage, as well as into expertly faked footage that looks old. Mia Farrow, who, like Woody Allen, is seen only in simulated found bits of film, plays a young psychiatrist, Dr. Eudora Fletcher, who tries to cure Zelig, and, falling in love with him, is loyal even when the press and the public turn against him. And this mock documentary, which is an intricately layered parody, includes interviews "today" with people who knew him, including the elderly Eudora (played by Ellen Garrison), who reminisces about him, in her levelheaded way. And it has its guest-star savants. In a takeoff of *Reds,* Allen uses modern cultural figures—such as Susan Sontag, Irving Howe, Saul Bellow, Bruno Bettelheim—as "witnesses" to Zelig's career, and they each interpret that career in terms of their specialty. (A few of them are perhaps too self-aware—too smiley about satirizing their own ideas. But Woody Allen has got one thing exactly right: as soon as they talk in abstractions we tune out on what they're saying.)

The picture is thoroughly charming. It's quick and deft and it races along. I admired the delicate care with which it was made, I kept smiling happily, and I laughed out loud once, at something so silly I wasn't sure why it got to me. But when I see comparisons with *Citizen Kane* in the papers, I don't know what the writers are talking about. When you went to the movies in the pre-television days the picture would come on right after the newsreel. And at the end of the newsreel in *Citizen Kane* the picture does start up. At the end of the newsreel in *Zelig,* the picture is over. I felt good, but I was still a little hungry for a movie. There's a reason *Zelig* seems small: there aren't any characters in it, not even Zelig. It's a fantasy about being famous for being nobody. Zelig is played humbly and gracefully; Woody Allen never disrupts the movie's smooth, neutral surfaces—at times he's as meek and abashed as Stan Laurel. Even when Zelig has taken on the black skin of a jazz trumpeter, or the blubber of a fatty, or the profile of a Mohawk Indian, he isn't really strong or sure of himself. There's something frail and shy—and still—about him in any guise. He's emotionally mute.

Zelig is an end-of-the-alphabet man, the one who comes last, and he's so anonymous that he can be everywhere. He melts into any situation. Yet whether he's on the field at spring training in Florida waiting his turn at bat after Lou Gehrig and Babe Ruth, or innocently causing a fracas by showing up next to Pope Pius XI on the balcony at St. Peter's, or peeking from behind Hitler on the stage at a giant National Socialist Party rally, he's always looking into a camera, looking for himself. The movie is so densely about a man's obsession with himself—with his misfortune, his nothingness—that it's suffocatingly sad to think about. (Maybe that's why it suggests an Eastern European sensibility.) One of the newsreel announcers tells us that Zelig continues to "astound scientists" who observe his transformations, and for a while eminent doctors use him like a guinea pig; his half sister takes him away, and she and her husband put him in sideshows, exhibiting him as a freak, like the Elephant Man. We see him at one zero point when the doctors are conducting experiments on him: He's sitting by himself in a hallway, "a human cipher," eating a hard, unbuttered roll that has been handed to him. People walk past on their errands without registering his existence; he barely registers it. Woody Allen is poignant here in the way that Chaplin was often poignant, and it's creepy, because you feel that these rich, gifted, accomplished writer-director-comedians who have won their artistic freedom, who have many friends and are attractive to lovers, who are admired the world over, are showing you the truth of how at some level they still feel utterly alone and lost, like wormy nothings. And you don't know how to react to it. *Zelig* is fastidiously controlled and dry, but at the core—that lonely figure chewing dutifully, without pleasure—it's bathed in tears. Yet that, too, is presented fastidiously.

This film is an unusually gentle, modulated comedy. It could be rambunctious, what with Zelig having not just one but two ticker-tape welcomes to New York, and inspiring Jazz Age songs and dance crazes, and all of this coming to us as part of the stylized, hyperbolic past that we see in old newsreels. But Allen plays everything off against Zelig's sad nothingness. It's an ingenious stunt. Like the unbuttered-roll scene, which is totally visual (its strength comes from the placement of the walkers-by in relations to the camera), the whole movie has been thought out in terms of the film image, turning American history into slapstick by inserting this little lost sheep in a corner of the frame. (The effect is something like what you get when you read *Ragtime.*) Allen couldn't have told the story of Leonard Zelig any other way—the pathos would have been crushing. It's the fakery that dries it out and keeps it light. Zelig is always just glimpsed, and the movie darts on. It's incredibly artful; it's all touches—like the enlightened-modern-woman expression on Eudora's face as she publicly smokes a cigarette. The clothes, the paraphernalia seem exactly right yet funny—the care that has gone into the trivia is itself absurd. The movie is said to be about modern man's anxiety and his quest for identity, about conformism, the emptiness of celebrity, the fickleness of the public, etc. And it *is* about all these themes, but it's very "real"; you don't have to have read Kafka or worried about existential predicaments to get it.

Zelig has a literary precursor—Melville's Confidence Man, whose appearance also kept changing, but Zelig is the Confidence Man without a game (and without the author's passion). Zelig has relatives, too, such as Chekhov's Olga, in "The Darling," who changes to suit her husbands, and Toto, in the Zavattini–De Sica film *Miracle in Milan,* who tries to make physically afflicted people feel better by imitating their afflictions. Woody Allen's originality is in shafting the almost universally accepted idea that everyone is someone. His movie is a chiding demonstration that everyone is not someone. That's real subversion. (At least a third of all Tin Pan Alley lyrics may be shot to hell.) Allen doesn't build up any rage about it, or much hilarity, either. Even the hysteria that might be expected to accompany such drastic role confusion as Zelig's is missing; Zelig's nothingness is simply a given—an idea that Woody Allen gets to play with. And he puts it through its permutations.

At one level, the picture is a skewed fairy tale about a patient winning his shrink: she's the best person in the world, she cares for you, she's faithful to you and follows you all over the globe to help you. And the movie is at its most inventive and its wittiest, I think, when Mia Farrow's Eudora is having difficulty treating Zelig because he, with his adaptation mechanism, thinks that he, too, is a psychiatrist. She devises a strategy to get through to him. Since she cannot convince him that he isn't one, she does it indirectly—she tells him that she is a sham, an impostor, that she has been deceiving him and isn't really a psychiatrist. Zelig is visibly upset, and we see his distress as he begins to feel that he's an impostor, too. But her cleverness backfires: his only way of dealing with his agitation is to disappear.

Throughout the movie, Zelig keeps disappearing, and Woody Allen's conception of him is of a very withdrawn, recessive person. Though Eudora pursues Zelig and there's an apparently happy resolution of his troubles—he learns to use his disorder and, presumably, gains an identity—that doesn't quite jibe with what we see. Mia Farrow, perhaps the most thin-skinned of actresses—luminously so—is unearthly, weightless, a Peter Pan. She has refinement in her bones. And hand in hand she and Woody Allen play together with tactful ease. She has never seemed more finely chiselled or more beautiful, but she wears huge specs and her slender face seems to disappear behind them. She's the invisible shrink. I got the feeling that Woody Allen as director was changing her, making her more like himself—that he was making her recede. And that she, like a chameleon, was becoming as faded and indistinct as he is. But she also changes him. She doesn't challenge him (as Diane Keaton did in her pictures with him); she frees him from stress, and he comes up with fresh, delicate scenes, like the one in which, under hypnosis, he murmurs, "I love you," and then, in a whimper, "You're the worst cook . . . those pancakes. I love you . . . I want to take care of you. No more pancakes." When he's with her, they're both childlike, withdrawn, far away. The whole picture goes by so fast and the people are at such a remote distance that it seems evanescent, and though the aged Eudora is still around to be interviewed, Zelig seems to have vanished—evaporated. He should be back, though. The term "Zelig" will probably enter the language to describe all the nonpersons we meet.

The New Yorker, August 8, 1983

THE LEOPARD

It's deeply satisfying to see, finally, Luchino Visconti's magnificent 1963 film *The Leopard* in Italian, with subtitles, and at its full length—three hours and five minutes. It had been cut to two hours and forty-one minutes when it opened in this country, in a dubbed-into-English version that didn't always seem in sync, and with the color brightened in highly variable and disorienting ways. Now the movie has its full shape, and it couldn't have arrived at a better time. The new movies—especially the new American movies—have reached a low, low point. And here is a work of a type we rarely see anymore—a sweeping popular epic, with obvious similarities to *Gone With the Wind*. Set in Sicily, beginning in 1860, it's *Gone With the Wind* with sensibility—an almost Chekhovian sensibility. It doesn't have the active central characters that the American epic has; there's no Scarlett or Rhett. But it has a hero on a grand scale—Don Fabrizio, Prince of Salina, played superlatively well by Burt Lancaster. And it's so much better at doing the kind of things that *Gone with the Wind* did—showing you how historical events affect the lives of the privileged classes—that it can make you feel a little embarrassed for Hollywood. *Gone with the Wind* is, of course, a terrific piece of entertainment; *The Leopard* is so beautifully felt that it calls up a whole culture. It casts an intelligent spell—intelligent and rapturous.

The Visconti epic is based on the posthumously published, best-selling novel by Giuseppe Tomasi di Lampedusa—an impoverished Sicilian prince, like his hero. (The Lampedusa coat of arms bore a leopard.) The movie isn't what we normally call "novelistic," though; everything comes to us physically. Visconti suggests Don Fabrizio's thoughts and feelings by the sweep and texture of his life. The fabrics, the medal-laden military uniforms, the dark, heavy furniture, the huge palaces, with their terraces and broad marble staircases, and the arid, harsh landscapes they're set in are all sensualized—made tactile. Burt Lancaster has always been a distinctively physical actor, and this is a supremely physical role. We know the Prince by his noble bearing and the assurance of his gestures—they're never wasteful. He's at ease with authority; you can believe that he's the result of centuries of aristocratic breeding. There's grandeur in the performance, which Lancaster has acknowledged he modelled on Visconti himself (who, though not a Sicilian, was a count whose family titles were among the oldest and most noble in Europe). It is not merely that the Prince is in tune with his surroundings. They have formed each other: he and the Salina country palazzo basking in the yellow light outside Palermo are one.

The Prince's estates have dwindled, money is running low, but he keeps up the family traditions. He's not a romantic—he's a realist. He'll protect aristocratic values for as long as he can, and he'll do his best to protect the future of the Salina family—his wife and seven children, his nephew—and the household priest and all the other attendants. He bends to the times only as much as he needs to. In 1860, Italy was in the middle of a revolution. Garibaldi and his followers—the Redshirts—were trying to unify Italy and free the south and Sicily from Bourbon rule. The Prince's favorite nephew, the spirited, gallant Tancredi (Alain Delon), goes off to join Garibaldi; he goes with the Prince's blessing and a small bag of his gold—the Prince understands that the Bourbons will fall. He's a man with few illusions, a man of sense who suffers fools all the time and tries to cushion his impatience. When Garibaldi lands on Sicily with an army of about a thousand men, and there are skirmishes in the streets of Palermo, the Prince's neurasthenic wife (Rina Morelli) becomes hysterically frightened—she's a whimperer—and he, recognizing that they may be in danger, takes her and their brood to safety at the family holdings across the island in Donnafugata. Along the way, the servants lay out a picnic—they spread a vast white linen cloth, and dish after dish, while the grooms take care of the horses. (Corot should have been invited.) At Donnafugata, the Prince leads the procession of his people, weary, and covered with dust from the road, into the cathedral. Seated in the Salina family pews, they're like corpses—petrified, deadwood figures.

The movie is about the betrayal of Garibaldi's democratic revolution, and about the wiliness of opportunists like Tancredi. ("Black and slim as an adder" was how Lampedusa described him.) Tancredi makes his reputation as a heroic fighter while he's an officer with Garibaldi's Redshirts, but as soon as power shifts to the Mafia-dominated, middle-class landgrabbers, he changes into the uniform of the new king—*their* king, Victor Emmanuel II, from the House of Savoy. He doesn't so much as blink when he hears the gunshots that mark the execution of the last of Garibaldi's loyal troops. The young Delon is perhaps too airy for the role. With his even features, small teeth, and smooth cheeks, he's a very pretty art object, perfectly carved. He'd make a fine, spry figure in an operetta, but he doesn't have the excitement or force to give Tancredi's actions the weight they might have had. (This Tancredi is as shallow as that other opportunist—Scarlett.) But the film is essentially about the Prince himself—the aging Leopard—and how he reacts to the social changes.

Lancaster provides the film's center of consciousness. We see everything that happens through Visconti's eyes, of course, but we feel we're seeing it through the Prince's eyes. We couldn't be any closer to him if we were inside his skin—in a way, we are. We see what he sees, feel what he feels; we know what's in his mind. He's fond of—and a little envious of—Tancredi, with his youth and verve. The Prince—he's only forty-five, but forty-five was a ripe age in the mid-nineteenth century—has perceived what the result of the revolution will be: the most ruthless grabbers will come out on top. There's a despicable specimen of the breed close at hand—the rich and powerful mayor of Donnafugata, Don Calogero (Paolo Stoppa), who is eager to climb into society. The Prince has a daughter who is in love with Tancredi, but the Prince understands that this daughter—prim and repressed, like his wife—is too overprotected and overbred to be the wife Tancredi needs for the important public career he's going after. And Tancredi, who has nothing but his princely title and his rakish charm, requires a wife who will bring him a fortune. And so when Tancredi is smitten by Don Calogero's poised and strikingly sensual daughter, Angelica (the lush young Claudia Cardinale, doing a bit too much lip-licking), the Prince arranges the match. (All this is presented very convincingly, and it's probably silly to quibble with a masterpiece, yet I doubt if a warmhearted father—and especially one sensually deprived in his relationship with his wife—would be so free of illusions about his daughter. And it seemed to me that he was more cut off from his children—one of the striplings is played by the very young Pierre Clementi, who has the face of a passionflower—than a man of his temperament would be, whatever his rank.)

Lighted by the justly celebrated cinematographer Giuseppe Rotunno, the movie is full of marvellous, fluid set-piece sequences: the dashing Tancredi's goodbyes to the Salina family when he goes off to join Garibaldi; the picnic; the church sequence. The original Italian prints may have had deeper brown tones and more lustrous golds—some of the scenes have a drained-out look—but there's always detail to exult in. Each time the Salina family assembles for Mass or for dinner, it's a big gathering. Some of the smaller, less opulent sequences are ongoing political arguments, like the ironic dialogue between the Prince and the timid worrywart family priest (Romolo Valli), or between the Prince and a family retainer who is his hunting companion (Serge Reggiani, overacting). This poverty-stricken snob, who's loyal to the Bourbons, is shocked that the Prince would approve of his nephew's marrying a girl whose mother is "an illiterate animal." The political issues that the film deals with are, of course, simplified, but they're presented with considerable cogency, and they're very enjoyable. Of the smaller sequences, perhaps the most dazzling is the conversation between the Prince and a petite, intelligent professorial gentleman (Leslie French) who has come with the official request that he stand for election to the Senate.

(Victor Emmanuel II is a constitutional monarch.) Here, the Leopard—refusing the offer—shows his full pride. It's the most literary passage in the movie; it's the rationale of the script: the Prince explains the Sicilian arrogance and torpor, and how he and the land are intertwined. I doubt if any other director has got by even halfway with a fancy dialogue of this kind, yet it's stunningly successful here. Lancaster has held his energy in check through most of the performance; now he comes out blazing, and he's completely controlled. He has a wild, tragicomic scene, too, when the weasel-eyed Don Calogero comes to discuss Tancredi's proposal to his daughter. The sickened Prince listens to him, and then, in a startling move, picks up the little weasel, plants a quick, ceremonial kiss on each cheek to welcome him into the family, and plunks him down. It happens so fast we barely have time to laugh. Don Calogero's greed shines forth then in the satisfaction with which he enumerates each item of the dowry he will bestow upon Tancredi; it's as if he expected the Prince to cry "Hosanna!" for each acre, each piece of gold.

Probably the movie seems as intense as it does because the action isn't dispersed among several groups of characters, the way it usually is in an epic. We stay with the Prince almost all the time. Except for the fighting in the streets, there's only one major sequence that he isn't in—an episode in which Tancredi and Angelica wander about in unused parts of the rambling Salina palace in Donnafugata. The Prince's absence may not be the reason, but this episode doesn't seem to have any purpose or focal point, and it's also the only time the film's tempo seems off. Whenever the Prince is onscreen—whether in his study, where the telescopes indicate his interest in astronomy, or in the town hall, controlling his distaste while drinking a glass of cheap wine that Don Calogero has handed him—we're held, because we're always learning new things about him. And in the concluding hour, at the Ponteleone Ball—certainly the finest hour of film that Visconti ever shot (and the most influential, as *The Godfather* and *The Deer Hunter* testify)—it all comes together. At this ball, the Salinas introduce Angelica to society—to all the many Sicilian princes and aristocrats. Visconti's triumph here is that the ball serves the same function as the Prince's interior monologue in the novel: throughout this sequence, in which the Prince relives his life, experiences regret, and accepts the dying of his class and his own death, we feel we're inside the mind of the Leopard saying farewell to life.

Everything we've seen earlier, we now realize, was leading to this splendid ball, which marks the aristocrats' acceptance of the parvenus who are taking over their wealth and power. (The poor will stay at the bottom, and—in the Prince's view, at least—will be worse off than before; the new ruling class will not be bound by the tradition of noblesse oblige.) The Prince, strolling away from these overheated rooms, sees a bevy of adolescent girls in their ruffles jumping up and down on a bed while chattering and screaming in delight—overbred, chalky-faced girls, like his daughters, all excited. In a room where people are seated at tables feasting, he glances in revulsion at a colonel covered with medals who is boasting of his actions against Garibaldi's men. He begins to feel fatigued—flushed and ill. He goes into the library, pours himself a glass of water, and stares at a big oil—a copy of a Greuze deathbed scene.

It's there, in front of the painting, that Tancredi and Angelica find him. She wants the Prince to dance with her, and as she pleads with him their bodies are very close, and for a few seconds the emotions he has been feeling change into something close to lust. He envies Tancredi for marrying for different reasons from his own; he envies Tancredi for Angelica's full-blown beauty, her heartiness, her coarseness. He escorts her to the big ballroom, and they waltz together. It's Angelica's moment of triumph: he is publicly welcoming her into his family. He is straight-backed and formal while they dance, but his thoughts are chaotic. He experiences acute regret for the sensual partnership he never had with his wife, and a nostalgia for the animal vitality of his youth. His intimations of his own mortality are fierce. After returning the shrewd, happy Angelica to Tancredi, he goes to a special small room to freshen up. Coming out, he sees into an anteroom—the floor is covered with chamber pots that need emptying. Eventually, the ball draws to a close, and people begin to leave, but a batch of young die-hard dancers are still going strong: they're hopping and whirling about to livelier music now that the older people have left the floor. The Prince arranges for his family to be taken home, explaining that he will walk. When he passes down the narrow streets, he's an old man. The compromises he has had to make have more than sickened him—they've aged him. His vision of the jackals and sheep who are replacing the leopards and lions ages him even more. He is emotionally isolated from his wife and children; he no longer feels any affection for the sly-faced Tancredi. He's alone.

The Leopard is the only film I can think of that's about the aristocracy from the inside. Visconti, the Marxist count, is both pitiless and loving. His view from the inside is not very different from that of Max Ophuls in *The Earrings of Madame de . . .*—which was made from the outside (though it was based on the short novel by the aristocratic Louise de Vilmorin). Ophuls' imagination took him where Visconti's lineage (and imagination) had brought him, and he gave us a portrait of a French aristocrat by Charles Boyer which had similarities to Lancaster's performance. But we weren't taken inside that French aristocrat's value system with anything like the robust fullness of our involvement with Lancaster's Leopard. If it weren't for the Prince's wiry, strong, dark-red hair and his magisterial physique—his vigor—I doubt if we'd feel the same melancholy at the death of his class. The film makes us feel that his grace is part of his position. We're brought to respect values that are almost totally foreign to our society. That's not a small thing for a movie to accomplish.

The New Yorker, September 19, 1983

ABOUT RIP TORN IN
CROSS CREEK

In the past, Rip Torn's emotions have generally been twisted, and he has often had a mean, hipster's glint. His meanness was fun; it was tonic. But his being *on* was sometimes the essence of his acting and of his characters. They fed off being on—that's what made them seem sadistic, sharklike. Self-hate was Rip Torn's specialty. Here, he's essentially decent; he's untwisted, and you see more sides to him than in his usual roles. There's a warm free-flowing stream of emotion in his performance; both the character and Torn himself seem capable of sorrow (and of generosity). As Marsh Turner, he wears a feather in his hat. He's a gallant, responsible husband and father who's also a grandstanding rowdy. Then, within a few minutes of screen time, he turns into a weeping, broken man; drunk and in despair, he throws an empty liquor keg through a shop window in town; returning home, he bangs things in misery, breaking up furniture. Marsh Turner's emotions rear up very large, and he simply discharges them—when he's bashing chairs or tables, it's like brushing a tear away. It's a rampaging role, but Torn doesn't seem to be afraid of anything, and he gives his character a pleasure in performance—something that American actors rarely do. He endows this backwoods man with his own love of whooping it up in front of people, and with an awareness of the impressions he makes. It's a demonstration of a wild-man actor's art—he lets us see how rage and tears verge on each other. It's crazy, great acting, and the picture would be stone cold without it.

The New Yorker, October 3, 1983

THE RIGHT STUFF

The Right Stuff gives off a pleasurable hum: it's the writer-director Philip Kaufman's enjoyment of the subject, the actors, and moviemaking itself. He's working on a broad canvas, and it excites him—it tickles him. Based on Tom Wolfe's 1979 book, the movie is an epic ramble—a reënactment of the early years of the space program, from breaking the sound barrier up to the end of the solo flights. It covers the years 1947 to 1963, especially the period after 1957, when government leaders, who felt they'd been put to shame by the Soviet Union's sorties into space, rushed to catch up; they initiated Project Mercury, assembled a team of official heroes—all white, married males—and began to exploit them in the mass media. Henry Luce, the founder of *Life,* which had perfected the iconography of a clean-living

America during the Second World War, bought exclusive rights to all NASA coverage of the space program and put the newly selected astronauts under contract; *Life* then presented them and their wives as super-bland versions of the boys and girls next door. The movie contrasts the test pilots who risk their lives in secrecy with these seven publicly acclaimed figures who replace the chimps that were sent up in the first American space capsules. They're synthetic heroes, men revved up to act like boys. Walking in formation in their shiny silver uniforms, the astronauts, whose crewcuts give them a bullet-headed look, are like a football team in a sci-fi fantasy. But they're not quite the square-jawed manikins they pretend to be; creatures of publicity, they learn how to manipulate the forces that are manipulating them. They have to, in order to preserve their dignity. They're phony only on the outside. Their heroism, it turns out, is the real thing (which rather confuses the issue).

As the lanky Sam Shepard embodies him, Chuck Yeager, the "ace of aces" who broke the sound barrier in 1947, evokes the younger, breathtakingly handsome Gary Cooper. And Yeager and the other test pilots have a hangout near the home base of the U.S. flight-test program: a cantina in the Mojave Desert, with a wall of photographs behind the bar—snapshots of the flyers' fallen comrades. Presided over by a woman known as Pancho (Kim Stanley), the place recalls the flyers' hangout in the Howard Hawks picture *Only Angels Have Wings* and the saloons in Westerns. Shepard's Yeager is the strong, silent hero of old movies—especially John Ford movies. On horseback in the desert, he looks at the flame-spewing rocket plane that he's going to fly the next morning, and it's like a bronco that he's got to bust. Kaufman uses Sam Shepard's cowboy Yeager as the gallant, gum-chewing individualist. He has some broken ribs and a useless injured arm when he goes up in that fiery rocket, and he doesn't let on to his superiors; he just goes up and breaks the sound barrier and then celebrates with his wife (Barbara Hershey) over a steak and drinks at Pancho's. He expresses his elation by howling like a wolf.

Even if the actual, sixtyish Chuck Yeager, now a retired Air Force brigadier general, weren't familiar to us from his recent appearances in TV commercials, where he radiates energy and affable good-fellowship, we can see him in the movie (he plays the bit part of the bartender at the cantina), and he isn't a lean, angular, solitary type—he's chunky and convivial. Sam Shepard is playing a legend that appeals to the director. He's Honest Abe Lincoln and Lucky Lindy, a passionate lover, and a man who speaks only the truth, if that. This legendary Yeager has too much symbolism piled on him, and he's posed too artfully; he looms in the desert, watching over what happens to the astronauts in the following years as if he were the Spirit of the American Past. Sam Shepard's Yeager appears in scenes that have no reason to be in the movie except, maybe, that Phil Kaufman has wanted for a long time to shoot them. (The worst idea is the black-clad death figure, played by Royal Dano, who, when he isn't bringing the flyers' widows the bad news or singing at the burial sites, sits at a table in Pancho's, waiting.) Kaufman must assume that the images of Yeager will provide a contrasting resonance throughout the astronauts' sequences. But Sam Shepard isn't merely willing to be used as an icon—he uses himself as an icon, as if he saw no need to act. And he can't resonate—he isn't alive. The movie is more than a little skewed: it's Kaufman's—and Tom Wolfe's—dreamy view of the nonchalant Yeager set against their satirical view of Henry Luce's walking apple pies. This epic has no coherence, no theme to hold it together, except the tacky idea that Americans can't be true, modest heroes anymore—that they're plasticized by the media.

Like Tom Wolfe, Phil Kaufman wants you to find everything he puts in beguilingly wonderful and ironic. That's the Tom Wolfe tone, and to a surprising degree Kaufman catches it and blends it with his own. The film's structural peculiarities and its wise-guy adolescent's caricature of space research all seem to go together to form a zany texture. It's a stirring, enjoyable mess of a movie. Kaufman plays *Mad*-magazine games, in which the woman nurse (Jane Dornaker) testing the astronauts is a comic ogre with a mustache and the space scientists are variants of Dr. Strangelove—clowns with thick German accents. (Scott Beach, who plays the Wernher von Braun figure, wears a wig that sits on his head like a furry creature that took sick and died there.) Counterculture gags are used for a sort of reverse jingoism. When the scientists get together to celebrate their victories, they sing in German. When Lyndon Johnson (Donald Moffat) can't understand what von Braun is saying, he's a Lyndon Johnson cartoon, and the dialogue has the rhythm of a routine by two old radio comics. Most of the low comedy doesn't make it up to that level; Kaufman has a healthy appetite for foolishness, but his comic touch is woozy—some scenes are very broad and very limp. (Even Jeff Goldblum, as a NASA recruiter, can't redeem all the ones he's in.) And there are coarse, obvious jokes: the astronauts come on to the press like a vaudeville act—playing dumb and giving the reporters just what they want—while the Hallelujah Chorus rises on the soundtrack. The action zigzags from old-movie romance to cockeyed buffoonery to the courage (and exaltation) of men alone in tiny capsules orbiting the earth at eighteen thousand miles an hour. Kaufman relies on the contrasts and rhythms of the incidents to produce a cumulative vision, and it doesn't happen. The picture is glued together only by Bill Conti's hodgepodge score. But a puppyish enthusiasm carries it forward, semitriumphantly. And the nuthouse-America games do something for it that perhaps nothing else could have done: they knock out any danger of its having a worthy, official quality, and they make it O.K. for the flights themselves to be voluptuously peaceful.

The flights—a mixture of NASA footage and fictional material, with marvellous sound effects—are inescapably romantic. Working with the cinematographer Caleb Deschanel (*The Black Stallion*) and with the San Francisco avant-garde filmmaker Jordan Belson, who does special visual effects, Kaufman provides unusually simple and lyrical heavenly scenes. As a scriptwriter, he may try to come in on a wing and a prayer, and as a director he may have too easygoing a style for the one-two-bang timing needed for low comedy, but he's a tremendous moviemaker, as he demonstrated in *The Great Northfield, Minnesota Raid* (1972), *The White Dawn* (1974), *Invasion of the Body Snatchers* (1978), and *The Wanderers* (1979). He has a puckish side; it comes out here in a rather unshaped deadpan joke using Australian aborigines to account for the mysterious "celestial fireflies" that Ed Harris's John Glenn reports seeing. Kaufman's re-creation of the middle and late fifties is realistic and affectionate without any great show of expense. (He was able to fake most of the locations in the San Francisco area, which doubles here for Florida, Texas, Washington, D.C., and New York, and Australia, too.) And he doesn't take the bloom off space by knocking us silly with the grandeur of it all. *The Right Stuff* has just enough of Jordan Belson's tantalizing patterns and rainbow fragments to suggest the bliss that Chuck Yeager felt high above the desert and that the astronauts experience while they're inside their spinning capsules. Strapped in and almost immobile, John Glenn is also the beneficiary of a magical effect that he himself can't see. The lights from the equipment that are reflected in the windows of all the astronauts' helmets hit him just right; we see two tiny lines of jewelled lights streaking down his face, one from each eye. "Astro tears" the movie crew called them. (They suggest Jesus in space.)

Phil Kaufman makes it possible for some of his characters to show so many sides that they keep taking us by surprise—especially Ed Harris's John Glenn, the strict Presbyterian, who probably comes the closest to fitting *Life*'s image of an American hero. This Glenn, who reprimands his teammates for their willingness to oblige astronaut groupies, and is grimly humming "The Battle Hymn of the Republic" to keep himself together as he sits trussed up in his capsule, hurtling back into the earth's atmosphere, is perfectly capable of using patriotism as a put-on: at the Mercury team's first big press conference, in Washington, he assumes the role of spokesman, flashes his quick, big smile, and is real pleased with himself. Blond and blue-eyed, and, at thirty-two, considerably younger than John Glenn was at the time, Ed Harris has some of the bleached pallor of Robert Duvall, and when he's sitting out in space, loving it, his pale-eyed, staring intensity may remind you of Keir Dullea's starchild face in *2001*. But Harris has a scary, unstable quality that's pretty much his own. He holds his head stiff on his neck, and he's the kind of very still actor who can give you the willies: he often has the look of someone who's about to cry, and a flicker of a smile can make you think the character he's playing is a total psycho.

Your feelings about Harris's Glenn are likely to be unresolved, except in Glenn's scenes with his wife, Annie (played with delicate, grinning charm and mischief by Mary Jo Deschanel, the actress wife of the cinematographer). In an early scene, Kaufman establishes that they have an understanding of each other that goes beyond words. It has to, because the enchanting Annie is a stutterer who can't get a sentence out. Her husband knows how to read every blocked syllable; the two of them are so close they communicate almost by osmosis, and even when she's making fun of his gung-ho wholesomeness he giggles happily, secure in the intimacy they share. Then, on the day of his scheduled flight, the NASA people ask him to talk to his wife on the phone and persuade her to "play ball" with the television newscasters who are outside the Glenns' house waiting to come in and interview her. Vice-President Johnson is also out there, in his limousine; he wants to come in to reassure her on TV. On the phone, she's distraught—she can barely speak her husband's name. But he intuits what she's trying to say; it's as if he could read her breathing. She faces terrible humiliation—she wants to know if she has to let them all in. Glenn has the single most winning speech of the whole three-hour-and-twelve-minute movie when he tells her he is, he manages to express that no, she doesn't have to let anybody in. And, good Presbyterian that his rage at the networks and the politicians without ever using a cussword (which is a feat comparable to her non-verbal communication—they're both handicapped). The scene is perhaps the wittiest and most deeply romantic confirmation of a marriage ever filmed. When Glenn is back on earth and the two of them are riding in a ticker-tape parade in his honor, they're a pair of secret, victorious rebels.

The movie probably has the best cast ever assembled for what is essentially a docudrama—although a twenty-seven-million-dollar docudrama, and one with an individual temperament, isn't like anything we've seen on TV. Scott Wilson appears as the test pilot Crossfield, and Levon Helm is Ridley, Yeager's mechanic. Pamela Reed brightens up the scenes she's in; she's all eyes as Trudy, the secretly estranged wife of the astronaut Gordon Cooper. And I felt my face twitching, as if I were about to laugh, whenever Dennis Quaid's Gordo was on the screen, because he has a devilish kid's smile, with his upper lip a straight line across his face. Quaid plays Gordo as a self-reliant, tough kid—a wised-up Disney boy, the savviest Huck Finn there ever was. When he gets his turn in the heavens—Cooper makes the last solo flight into space—his split-faced grin is perhaps the standout image of the film. He's cynical and cocky—a materialist in every thought and feeling—and so when his face tells us that he's awed by what he sees, we're awed by what we see in his face. It may seem ungrateful to point out the results of realism, but most of the actors playing astronauts are martyred by their haircuts; their features look naked, their noses as big as a bald eagle's beak. Scott Glenn, who plays Alan Shepard, has gone even further than the others. He looks a little like Hoagy Carmichael, but he seems to be deforming himself; if this is meant to be an aspect of the astronaut's character, it isn't delved into. Scott Glenn has got so wiry, gaunt, and muscular that his skin appears to be pulled taut against his bones, and when he laughs his whole face crinkles, like a hyena's.

If we're often preoccupied by the men as physical specimens, this has a good deal to do with the subject, but it may also be because we're not sure how to interpret their meaningful glances at each other. Are we intended to see comradeship there, and mutual respect, or do the expressions mean "They're buying it!" or "This is the life!" or "My head is numb"? We in the audience are put in the position of being hip to what's going on even when we don't really get it. What, for example, are the astronauts thinking as they watch old Sally Rand do her feather-fan dance in their honor in Houston in 1962? (The dancer who impersonates her is, blessedly, younger and more gifted.) The jazzy hipness in the film's tone comes down to us from Tom Wolfe—it's an unearned feeling that we're on to things. Probably Kaufman thinks that he's conveying a great deal more to us than he is. Certainly he's trying to "say something" when he cuts Sally's fan dance and the expressions of the astronauts watching her right into footage of Sam Shepard's Chuck Yeager being brave again (and still unsung). But he's making points on an epic scale rather than telling an epic story. He hasn't dramatized what he wants to get at; he has attitudinized instead—setting the modern, hype-bound world against a vision of the past that never was. Though it's a docu-drama and some incidents are included simply for the record, *The Right Stuff* is drawn not from life but from Tom Wolfe's book and Kaufman's nostalgia for old-movie values.

The mishap that the astronaut Gus Grissom (that terrific actor Fred Ward) is involved in gives us, briefly, something solid that makes us feel very uncomfortable. As the film presents it, the gloomy-souled Grissom panics during the splashdown of his capsule and is desperate to get out. The helicopter that is to pick up the capsule is hovering overhead, maneuvering into position. Though the film doesn't make it absolutely clear, when the hatch blows open and Grissom climbs out (and the capsule sinks) the implication is that he opened it. He claims that it simply malfunctioned and opened by itself, but clearly the NASA people don't accept his account, because he receives considerably less than a hero's welcome, and his wife, Betty (Veronica Cartwright), feels horribly let down by the second-rateness of the ceremonies in his honor. I wish that Kaufman had followed through on the disturbing, awkward quality of this incident, which grips us at a different emotional level from the other scenes. I realize I'm asking for a different kind of movie, but if he'd taken a different approach to the Gus and Betty Grissom episode he might have opened up some of the implications of the phrase "the right stuff" that have bothered me ever since Tom Wolfe's book came out.

Yeager is, of course, the movie's archetype of "the right stuff"—the model of courage, determination, and *style*. The astronauts don't have an acceptable style, but the movie half forgives them, because, as it indicates, this isn't their fault—the times are to blame. The men themselves have the guts and the drive, and they win Kaufman's admiration. But then there's Fred Ward's Gus Grissom, who may at a crucial moment have failed to demonstrate "the right stuff." Isn't this all painfully familiar? Doesn't it take us back to the Victorian values of *The Four Feathers* and all those other cultural artifacts which poisoned the lives of little boys (and some girls, too), filling them with terror that they might show a "yellow streak"?

Being far more of an anti-establishmentarian than Tom Wolfe, Kaufman probably felt that he had transformed the material, but he is still stuck with its reactionary cornerstone: the notion that a man's value is determined by his physical courage. You'd think that Kaufman would have got past this romantic (and perhaps monomaniacal) conception of bravery. (With this standard, whatever you fear becomes what you compulsively measure yourself by.) I assume that people who are jellyfish about some things may be very brave about others. And certainly during the counterculture period there was a widespread rejection of the idea of bravery that this film represents. According to Wolfe, "the right stuff" is "the uncritical willingness to face danger." Yet the film's comedy scenes are conceived in counterculture terms.

The movie has the happy, excited spirit of a fanfare, and it's astonishingly entertaining, considering what a screw-up it is. It satirizes the astronauts as mock pilots, and it never indicates that there's any reason for them to be rocketing into space besides the public-relations benefit to the government; then it celebrates them as heroes. As a viewer, you want the lift of watching them be heroic, but they're not in a heroic situation. More than anything else, they seem to be selected for their ability to take physical punishment and accept confinement in a tight cylinder. And about the only way they can show their mettle is by *not* panicking when they finally get into their passive, chimp positions. (If they discover that they're sick with terror, they can't do much more about it than the chimps could, anyway.) It's Yeager who pronounces the benediction on the astronauts, who tells us that yes, they *are* heroes, because they know (what the chimps didn't) that they're sitting on top of a rocket. (I imagine that the chimps had a pretty fair suspicion that they weren't frolicking high in a banana tree.) If having "the right stuff" is set up as the society's highest standard, and if a person proves that he has it by his eagerness to be locked in a can and shot into space, the only thing that distinguishes human heroes from chimps is that the heroes volunteer for the job. And if they volunteer, as they do in this film, out of personal ambition and for profit, are they different from the chimp who might jump into the can eagerly, too, if he saw a really big banana there?

The New Yorker, October 17, 1983

UNDER FIRE
IMAGE MAKERS

In the opening scenes of *Under Fire,* rebel soldiers in Chad are trying to move a caravan of elephants carrying crates of weapons across a patch of open field, and Nick Nolte, as Russell Price, a photojournalist, trots alongside, snapping pictures of the ponderous beasts and the drivers sitting way on top of them and their freight. Suddenly, a helicopter gunship appears, blasting, and the scene turns into a horrifying shambles of elephants running and men shot down as they scurry for the bush. Wherever he is, the big, blond Russell Price goes on taking pictures. He is covered with cameras; they're his only luggage, and they swing as he moves. He switches from one to the other, and with each small click of the shutter we see—in a freeze-frame that is held for just an instant—what he has shot. The director, Roger Spottiswoode, a Canadian-born Englishman who's thirty-eight now, began working in London studios at nineteen and already had several years of experience, including work as an editor on Sam Peckinpah's *Straw Dogs,* when he came to live in this country, in 1971. He edited two more Peckinpah films and Walter Hill's *Hard Times,* worked with Karel Reisz, first as editor, then as second-unit director and associate producer, and also wrote the first draft of *48 Hrs.* before he got a chance to direct (with *Terror Train* and *The Pursuit of D. B. Cooper*). He was ready—maybe more than ready—for *Under Fire.* It has been made with breathtaking skill. Price's photographs—those freeze-frames, most of them in black-and-white, some in color, and each with its small, staccato click—fix the faces, the actions, the calamities in our memories, and the film is so cleanly constructed that they have a percussive effect. They're what *Under Fire* is about.

When Price hitches a ride on a truck carrying rebel troops out of the area, he's not the only American (or the only blond) among the black men. Oates (Ed Harris), a mercenary with the grin of a happy psychopath, sits among the rebels thinking he's among the soldiers of the government that's paying him. Price sets him straight, and he chuckles; he doesn't care who he kills anyway—it's his sport. When Price gets back to his hotel, the foreign press corps—which includes Claire (Joanna Cassidy), a radio reporter who is just breaking up with her lover, Alex (Gene Hackman), and Alex himself, a celebrated war correspondent and Price's closest friend—is preparing to move on to the next big trouble spot, Nicaragua. And we realize that what we have seen is, essentially, the prologue. But we have already grasped the most important thing about Price, who risks his carcass as a matter of course: he's an image man. And, seeing through his eyes as he clicks the shutter, we intuitively recognize how good he is at what he does. There's a purity about his total absorption in images. Price doesn't even have to do the kind of interpretation that the reporters do; he doesn't have to try to make sense of things. Nolte's loping, athletic grace as he moves alongside fighting men adds to the feeling we get that Price is an artist and an autom-aton, too. His whole body is tuned up for those clicks. He couldn't explain why he shoots when he does; he simply *knows*. And Nolte has what is per-haps an accidental asset for the role: his eyes are narrowed, as if by a life-time of squinting through cameras, and his eyelids look callused.

It doesn't take long to grasp that Price and Claire and Alex regard their lack of involvement in what they cover as part of being professionals. They are observers, not participants, and they're proud of it. It's the essence of their personal dash and style—the international form of the swaggering cyn-icism of *The Front Page*. They all risk their lives with a becoming carelessness. But that's almost the only thing they have in common with the heroes and heroines of old Hollywood movies. One conspicuous difference is that they're grownup people in their forties; Alex may even be fifty.

The movie is set in 1979, during the last days of the rule of General Anastasio Somoza, the dictator-president whose family was put in power and kept there by the United States. And in a sense the Sandinist revolution— the imagery of it—is the star. This is trompe-l'oeil moviemaking, with Mex-ican locations in Oaxaca and Chiapas dressed up in the shantytown building material of Nicaragua (uncut beer-can sheets), and the political graffiti and the pulsing, hot colors—turquoise and flaming pink. The young Sandinistas who dart through the streets in striped T-shirts, with bright handkerchiefs masking their faces, have the street-theatre look that is so startling in the book *Nicaragua,* Susan Meiselas's 1981 collection of photographs of the in-surrection. Spottiswoode knows not to make realism drab; there's dust and anger everywhere, but the country is airy and alive with color. Produced at a cost of eight and a half million dollars (Nolte and Hackman worked for much less than their usual fees) and with only fifty-seven shooting days, the film is a beautiful piece of new-style classical moviemaking; everything is thought out and prepared, but it isn't explicit, it isn't labored, and it cer-tainly isn't overcomposed. No doubt the cinematographer John Alcott, whose speed is turning him into a legend—he's the man who doesn't bother with light meters, he just looks at the back of his hand—gave it its tingling visual quality. The dialogue is exciting, too. The script, by Ron Shelton, working from a first draft by Clayton Frohman, is often edgy and maliciously smart. Terry Southern at his peak did no better than the lines Shelton has written for Richard Masur as Somoza's American publicity expert—the man trying to improve Somoza's "image"—as he offers condo-lences to the lover of a correspondent murdered by Somoza's troops: "Jesus Christ, a human tragedy. What can I say?" (Shelton was a professional base-ball player for some time; he has been writing scripts for three or four years, but except for some rewrite work he did on *D. B. Cooper,* this is the first to be filmed.) What gives the movie its distinction is that the articulate, sophis-ticated characters don't altogether dominate the imagery. The Nicaraguans (some of them played by Mexicans, others by Nicaraguan refugees in Mex-ico) aren't there just to supply backgrounds for the stars.

With its concentration on the journalists—the outsiders—*Under Fire* is a little like Peter Weir's *The Year of Living Dangerously,* but visually and in its romantic revolutionary spirit it's more like the Cuban scenes in *The Godfather, Part II* and Gillo Pontecorvo's *The Battle of Algiers* and *Burn!* Spottiswoode isn't inflammatory in the way that Pontecorvo is, but in his more subdued impassioned manner he presents the case for the 1979 revolution—the one that the United States government has been trying to undo by backing the insurgents known as contras or anti-Sandinistas. (I assume that the title of the film comes from the words of Augusto César Sandino, the leader of a peasant army, who was murdered in 1934: "It is better to die as rebels under fire than to live as slaves.")

The revolutionaries, with their poetic peasant faces, are presented in a grand, naïve, idealized movie tradition. Anger doesn't make the Sandinistas mean or violent, and there's no dissension among them. (It's how we want to think revolutionaries are.) They don't have any visible connections to the Communist powers, either. Even so, this is one of the most intelligently constructed political movies I've ever seen. Its fictional inventions serve a clear purpose. Although the Sandinistas have always been led by a group, the story posits a single leader—Rafael—who gives the people hope. Rafael is featured in the graffiti—his face is the emblem of the revolution—but he has never been photographed, and the story involves the attempt of Price and Claire to find him, and the various forces that manipulate them before and after their search. One of these forces is a wily Frenchman, Jazy, who works for the C.I.A., and, as played by Jean-Louis Trintignant, he's a suave, lecherous imp. You know he's a dangerous little sleazo (he says he works for everybody, and he probably does), but he's also knowledgeable and witty. And when Somoza's men throw Price in the clink "for taking too many pictures" and kick him around, it's Jazy—a pal of Somoza's—who gets him released. Jazy is the kind of pal of Somoza's who amuses himself with Somoza's leggy young mistress, Miss Panama (Jenny Gago). The General himself is played by René Enriquez (of "Hill Street Blues"), who in fact is a Nicaraguan and was acquainted with Somoza. His performance is a finely nuanced caricature: this Teddy-bear Somoza deludes himself that he's an aristocrat with thousands of years of tradition behind him. He has perfected a form of infantilism—he sees only what he wants to see and hears only what he wants to hear. He's so locked in himself he's like a product of inbreeding—a genetic idiot who thinks he's a grandee.

The corrupt environment creates tensions in the gentle, affable Price: anger at the way Somoza's bullies treated him, and deeper anger at the way they brutalized the priest he shared a cell with. And something happens that upsets him so much that, photogenic as it is, he momentarily forgets to take a picture. When he and Claire are on one of their trips trying to find Rafael and are being escorted by Sandinistas, he sees the mercenary Oates hiding. Oates is out of his skull; he's an obscenity. (He stands in for all the mercenaries running loose in Third World countries.) But Price, being a journalist and regarding himself as "neutral," doesn't reveal Oates' presence. Then, as he and Claire are walking along and talking to their young Sandinista guide—who wears a Baltimore Orioles cap, because the Nicaraguan Dennis Martinez is on the team—Oates kills the kid. It's a spiteful, showoffy murder, and Price knows he could have prevented it. He's sickened; he's full of grief and disgust. It's Claire (whom he loves) who points out to him that he didn't take a picture; the artist-automaton broke down and behaved humanly, and that night is their first together.

When Price and Claire reach Rafael's hiding place and Price is asked to perform a crucial service for the rebels, he is emotionally prepared. He is asked to fake a photograph for them, and he does it, though this is a betrayal of his art and, if it becomes known, will almost inevitably wreck his reputation. Events then move very quickly. Shortly afterward, Price discovers that a whole series of photographs he took (just for himself) on the unmasked Sandinistas at Rafael's headquarters have been stolen and are being used by the demented mercenary Oates—a one-man hit squad—to identify the rebel leaders. Even Price's pure images are being polluted; they're being used every which way. They're marking his subjects for extinction.

Before Price came to Nicaragua, he was an overgrown small boy playing with what he loved to do: take pictures. (And this is why Nolte is a perfect choice for the role. He can be dumb, unthinking, oxlike, yet with a controlling intelligence and a central sweetness and decency.) In Nicaragua, where somebody's using you all the time, Price is in a new situation. Detachment can have hideous results, as he saw when the Orioles lover was killed. Whatever Price's misgivings as a professional photojournalist with a reputation for integrity, and whatever the effects of the action on his future, when he fakes the picture to help the Sandinistas he isn't destroyed by doing it—he's humanized. He is letting himself be governed by his own core of generosity. These are the terms of the movie, in which Price the photojournalist is a metaphor for movie director. Making movies, this picture says, isn't about purity. It's about trying to suggest the living texture in which people make choices that may—from an academic point of view—appear unethical, crazy, wrong.

The movie fills our heads with images of people under fire. There are terrified peasants and Somoza's equally terrified national guardsmen—probably peasant boys who signed up because they were hungry. At one point, Price and Claire are in a car in a provincial town, and the driver panics when guardsmen direct him to stop; he backs up, and, with guardsmen firing at them, Price and Claire jump out into the street and try to hide. There's not much sense to anything that happens during the insurrection. Peasants in dirt streets stare at a shiny big automobile in flames. Refugees in the provincial city of León mill in the streets trying to escape the national guardsmen who are shooting at them, and they're simultaneously attacked by planes. In some neighborhoods of Managua, guardsmen fire into the flimsy beer-can shacks, and shoot everything in the streets that moves—even

squealing pigs. It's in this sequence that the movie reënacts the 1979 killing of Bill Stewart, the ABC correspondent, at a national-guard checkpoint in Managua. After kneeling and holding his hands out, to show that he had no weapons, Stewart was told to lie down, with his arms over his head, and was then—for no particular reason—shot, while his cameraman went on photographing the scene. I hadn't been aware of how that footage had stayed in the back of my head for four years, but at the movie, as soon as I saw the guardsmen standing there in the street, and saw one of the characters mosey up to them to ask directions, I knew what was coming; Stewart's death was still so vivid that this reënactment almost seemed to be in slow motion, and, with Price's shutter-click frozen frames, in a sense it was. The killing has an eerie inevitability about it. *Under Fire* isn't just reproducing a famous incident here, it's making us conscious of the images we've got stored up. It brings the Nicaragua of countless news stories right to the center of our consciousness. We knew more about the place than we thought we did. And Jerry Goldsmith's spare, melodic score (one of the best movie scores I've ever heard) features a bamboo flute from the Andes with a barely perceptible electronic shadow effect—a melancholy sound that takes you back. It tugs at your memories.

There's a good reason, I think, for the use of grownup people as the principal characters. These grownups aren't surprised or scandalized by what they see, and their lack of surprise is part of the unusual quality of *Under Fire*. There's no gee-whizz acting. After Hackman's Alex—who has been "hanging in there" with Claire, hoping she'll change her mind about wanting her freedom—decides to head back to the States and take the anchorman's job he has been offered, Claire says goodbye to him and watches as he goes off in the taxi that's taking him to the airport. Partway down the street, Alex sees Price walking up; he jumps out, and they hug each other. As he goes off again in the cab, Claire and Price both stand watching as it becomes smaller down the street and heads toward the hill in the distance. It's a beautiful shot, and expressive, too, because nobody (the audience least of all) wants Hackman to go. He's totally believable as a network's choice for anchorman—it's the quality in him that makes him so valuable to the movie (and picks up its energy level when he returns.) Hackman seems leaner here than in his last films, and he's faster—he's on the balls of his feet. As the famous Alex, he maintains a surface jauntiness—he's professionally likable. But Alex has ideas ricocheting in his head, and whether he's sitting down at the piano in a Managua night club and singing or just basking in his celebrity he's never unaware of what's going on around him. He's always sizing things up—taking mental notes. He has an expansiveness about him; he's full of life (the way Jack Warden was in *Shampoo*). The three major characters have to be people who have been around, because outrage is not the motivating emotion of *Under Fire*, as it was in, say, Costa-Gavras's *Missing*. Spottiswoode and Shelton may be appalled, but they're not shocked. And they're not interested in presenting characters going through the usual vir-

gin indignation. The United States has been setting up or knocking down Nicaraguan governments since 1909; the movie can hardly pretend to be showing us things we don't—at some level—already know. *Under Fire* is about how you live with what you know.

Joanna Cassidy, who has the pivotal role, is a stunning woman with a real face, and as Claire she has a direct look—the kind of look that Claire Bloom's characters have sometimes turned on people, and that Jane Fonda has had in her best roles. Joanna Cassidy is tall (Trintignant looks really petite when he's next to her), and as Claire she has the strength of a woman who's had to set her jaw and keep her smile for long stretches. Claire has had to be tough, and toughness deeply offends her. She has been struggling to keep some softness. The film catches her at a key time in her physical development. Running through the streets, she moves with extraordinary grace, and you certainly know why Price takes pictures of her sleeping nude. But her job has yielded her everything that it's going to. She has an almost grownup daughter, whom she talks to on the phone and on tapes—she would like to be with her. This is a time in her life when doubts have settled in. The foreign press corps, like the mercenaries, jump from one chaos to the next; they go where the armaments shipments are going. They keep the people at home "informed," but to the people they descend on they must seem like powerful celebrities who could change things if they would just tell "the truth." Claire is doing her job almost automatically now, and her mind has a roving eye. When Price's automatic-response system fails him—when he doesn't take a picture of the dead kid right next to him—it's a change in him she can respond to. None of this is spelled out for us; it's all there in Joanna Cassidy's performance and in Nolte's response to her physical presence. As Price, he doesn't use the low, growling voice that he had in *48 Hrs.,* and his beefiness is all sensitivity. Nolte never lets you see how he gets his effects. His big, rawboned body suggests an American workingman jock, but he uses his solid flesh the way Jean Gabin did: he inhabits his characters. He's such a damned good actor that he hides inside them. That's *his* sport.

I have been wondering why some members of the press show so little enthusiasm for this picture. (It certainly couldn't be more timely.) Possibly the movie ladles too much guilt on journalists. (The mercenary who has been poisoning Price's life bids him a cheery farewell—"See you in Thailand.") But I can think of only a few scenes that aren't brought off and only one that's clumsily staged: the last appearance of Trintignant's fascinatingly crisscrossed Jazy. Three frightened young Sandinistas who have come to his house to kill him wait around while he explains his political rationale to Price—his fear of the future Communist takeover. I think there's something in *Under Fire* that's bugging the press the way it was bugged a couple of years ago by *Absence of Malice.* Price's faking the photograph and accepting the penalties that will follow may be bewildering to the run of journalists who make decisions about what to report on the basis of their own convenience

and advantage all the time. Since they do it unconsciously, they can easily be aroused to indignation at Price's conscious act. Maybe they know that they wouldn't do what he does, and they think that that means he's morally inferior to them. And maybe, like other professional groups, they don't like movies about them that don't glorify them.

Spottiswoode could be a trace too sane; the actors go as far as they can with what they've got to work with, but possibly he doesn't go quite far enough (and neither, possibly, does the script). Spottiswoode doesn't have the wild, low cunning that the great scenes in Peckinpah's films have—he doesn't spook us. But he does everything short of that. In its sheer intelligence and craft this is a brilliant movie.

The New Yorker, October 31, 1983

YENTL

Barbra Streisand's *Yentl* is rhapsodic yet informal; it's like a gently surprising turn of phrase. Set in the thriving Polish-Jewish communities of an imaginary, glowing past, the movie has its own swift rhythms. Its simplicity and unity are somewhat reminiscent of Jacques Demy's *The Umbrellas of Cherbourg* (1964); perhaps that's because the composer Michel Legrand wrote the scores for both, and the songs carry both films' emotional currents (though in totally different ways). Adapted from the Isaac Bashevis Singer story "Yentl the Yeshiva Boy," the Streisand film tells of a young woman who grows up in a tradition-bound community in which bright boys—yeshiva boys—live to study Torah. Coddled and prized, they sit at their books all day long, memorizing and reciting, debating moral issues, and attempting to fathom the unfathomable. Women are excluded from scholarship, but Yentl has a passion for religious study—she thinks it's the only way of life that's worthwhile. And so when her widower father (who has secretly taught her) dies, she dresses as a boy, sneaks away at night and goes off to enroll in a yeshiva in a distant town.

The beginning of *Yentl* is shaky. Streisand wants to make sure we get the idea that women are kept in ignorance, and she's a trace insistent. And the end is, I think, a flat-out mistake. But most of *Yentl* is, of course, its middle, which is glorious; it's like that of the story, though with different shades of humor. Yentl, a woman crowding thirty, passes as an adolescent student and feels like one. She's carefree and goofy; she has found herself—as a boy. (Yentl in disguise is definitely a boy, not a man. That's how the masquerade was conceived by Singer, and it works for Streisand the way it did for Katharine Hepburn when she passed as a boy in *Sylvia Scarlett*.) You can believe that the people in the Jewish quarter accept this smart, smooth-faced student, who has taken the name of Anshel, as male, because she isn't so very different from a lot of precocious, little-shrimp kids who seem to grow only in the head. Anshel is a sprite: as the yeshiva student, Streisand doesn't have an image of Barbra Streisand to play, and she lets herself be this slender and defenseless kid showing off his knowledge. When Streisand is playing a character, it releases something in her—a self-doubt, a tentativeness, a delicacy. She seems physically lighter, her scale is human, and you can share something with her that you can't when she's planted there as Streisand (and seems domineering). The basic concept of this movie lets her release herself, and as the yeshiva boy she's giddy and winsome.

Her singing voice takes you farther into the character; the songs express Yentl's feelings—what she wants to say but has to hold back. Her singing is more than an interior monologue. When she starts a song, her hushed intensity makes you want to hear her every breath, and there's high drama in her transitions from verse to chorus. Her phrasing and inflections are so completely her own that the songs make the movie seem very personal. Her singing has an ardent, beseeching quality—an intimacy. And her vocal fervor lifts the movie to the level of fantasy.

Streisand sings with such passionate conviction that she partly compensates for the sameness of Legrand's tunes. A few of them are exciting in context, but "This Is One of Those Moments" and "Tomorrow Night" are so dull they seem to be all recitative, and Legrand's music simply doesn't have the variety, the amplitude, to do justice to Yentl's full emotional range. The Alan and Marilyn Bergman lyrics don't rise to the poetic richness of the occasion, either; songs such as "No Matter What Happens" and "A Piece of Sky" are tainted with feminist psychobabble and Broadway uplift. Streisand's eerily way-out-there-by-itself voice soars, striving to achieve new emotional heights, and the music is on a treadmill. But as the director Streisand does graceful tricks with the songs. She uses them to take the audience through time and space. Yentl begins a song, and it continues in voice-over as the action races ahead. The songs are montages and comedy routines, too, with images of what Yentl is singing about edited to the rhythm of the music. During the song "No Wonder," a dialogue scene takes place while Yentl/ Anshel sings a wry, funny commentary on it, and it's all brought off rather softly, without fuss. As a musical, *Yentl* conveys the illusion that the songs simply grow out of the situations—which isn't altogether an illusion.

The movie loses its sureness of touch now and then, but it's unassuming. It's a homey, brightly lighted fantasy. Yentl's teacher papa (Nehemiah Persoff) has the apple cheeks and jolly gray beard of a Yiddish Kris Kringle. And when he dies and she leaves home, a big bird who represents his spirit hovers overhead, accompanying her on her travels. The place Yentl grew up in, the inn where she breaks her journey, the town where she passes the examination and is accepted as a yeshiva student—they all have the familiarity and the pastness of places we know from folktales. Only the big, clanging gates of the Jewish quarter, which are closed at night, seem unusual, and it may take a second or two to register what they are, because the movie doesn't emphasize the specific nature of its folklore. It takes it for granted. (In a scene in which Yentl, dressed as a boy, pays for a ride on a farmer's wagon and then isn't allowed to climb on board, the point that the people on the wagon are gentiles who are pulling a trick on her isn't fully shaped for the audience, and some moviegoers may be mystified.) But *Yentl* isn't a sweet, tame musical. Coming out of that ornery, mischievous Singer story, it couldn't be. There's a running theme in Singer: human beings keep trying to flirt with God, hoping that someday a line of communication can be established, but sex always gets in the way. Their wonderful good intentions are thwarted by the tingle of the groin.

Dressed as a boy, Yentl is no longer resentful of male privileges, and for the first time she feels attracted to a man. At the inn, just after she has left home, she meets the virile, bearded Avigdor, played by Mandy Patinkin (who makes the impact here that he failed to make in *Ragtime* and *Daniel*). Avigdor is friendly and warm. He's also charged up sexually. After years of the repressed life of a yeshiva student, he can hardly wait to be married to the luscious ripe peach who is pledged to him. Yentl, who is aroused by his sensual fever, accepts his suggestion that she come to his yeshiva, and when, as Anshel, she is accepted there and is considered a prodigy, Avigdor's eyes sparkle with pride. He plays big brother to her, and she becomes his study partner.

Maybe the magic of this Singer story (and of many of his other tales) is that the folkloric characters have been imbued with a drop of D. H. Lawrence's blood, yet they live in a time when confusing sexual urges are explained as the work of demons. "Yentl the Yeshiva Boy" is a folktale told by a sly trickster: its elements don't stay within the conventions of folklore. (It's as if the story were a river, and fish were trying to jump out of it.) Things take a turn toward the disturbing in "Yentl the Yeshiva Boy"; they become quite turbulent. There's darkness on the one hand and ribald comedy—even sex farce and burlesque—on the other, but the storyteller remains imperturbable.

In the movie, when Avigdor's fiancée, Hadass (Amy Irving), a beauty out of the erotic pages of the Old Testament, enters the picture, it becomes a series of dilemmas and metaphors. The three principal characters look at each other with longing, and sometimes with fear and bewilderment. They can't sort their emotions out. Avigdor, not knowing that Anshel is a woman, feels a closer companionship with her than he has ever known with anybody else of either sex. When Hadass's father cancels the wedding and Avigdor is distraught, Anshel, his confidant, shares in his pain. And the brooding, pitiful Avigdor, having lost Hadass, and loving his friend Anshel, wants Anshel to marry her; that way, Avigdor won't feel he has totally lost her. He threatens to go away if Anshel doesn't agree to the plan. Meanwhile, Hadass, whose love for the burley, strong Avigdor is a mixture of attraction and terror, begins to love Anshel for his gentleness—Hadass has found a "man" she doesn't feel afraid of. The baffled Yentl, who sees in Hadass everything that she herself didn't want to be and couldn't have been—who sees that Hadass is like a slave girl when she's around men—is jealous of her and at the same time touched by her. Hadass's submissiveness is mysteriously sultry. And Yentl/Anshel—as if in a trance, thinking to hold on to Avigdor and also captivated by Hadass—asks for her hand in marriage.

One moment, Yentl is a yeshiva boy, taking pleasure in being the smartest kid in the class; the next moment, she's got herself in a fix. There's only one end to this story, and it's the one that Singer gave it: Yentl must go down the road in search of another yeshiva. She is condemned to the life of study that she has chosen (and a Chassidic scholar can never learn enough). It isn't difficult to figure out the thinking behind the film's ending, in which Yentl, restored to women's clothes, goes off to America, where, presumably, freed from the binding traditions of the Old World, she can live as a woman and still continue her studies. The thinking is that you have to give the movie audience hope. (And there's even an attempt to show that Hadass will be changed by her encounter with Yentl/Anshel—that, Lord help us, she has had her consciousness raised.) Streisand tries to turn a story about repressed, entangled characters into a sisterhood fable about learning to be a free woman. She tries to transform a quirky folktale into a fairy tale. And it feels almost like a marketing choice.

But this is by no means a playing-it-safe movie. It's a movie about restrictive social conventions and about internal conflicts—about emotions and how they snarl you up. There are no chases, no fistfights or fights of any other kind. The picture is closer to the sensibility of the Ernst Lubitsch musical comedies than it is to films such as *The Turning Point* and *Rich and Famous*. And even when the characters' sex roles are blurred—when they're lost in a multitude of roles—Streisand as director keeps them all clear. Her vision is sustained—until the end. The closing shipboard sequence seems a blatant lift from the "Don't Rain on My Parade" tugboat scene in *Funny Girl;* it feels like a production number, and it violates the whole musical scheme of the movie. It also has Streisand wearing immigrant chic and playing the Streisand image. This misstep must have come from an excess of virtue. Streisand wants to give the audience an educational and spiritual message. She wants Yentl to be—gulp—a role model. Where Streisand's instinct as an artist fails her is in her not recognizing that Yentl exists on a magical plane, and that the attempt to make her a relevant, contemporary heroine yanks her off it. The script, by the English playwright and television writer Jack Rosenthal and Streisand, prepares for this ending by placing the action in 1904, but the Chassidic life that the movie shows belongs to an earlier, make-believe past. At the start of the film, a book peddler calls out "Storybooks for women! Sacred books for men!" By 1904, the novels—*War and Peace,* perhaps, or *Anna Karenina* or *The Brothers Karamazov* or *Middlemarch* or volumes of Dickens or Balzac—might have had more to tell Yentl than she could get out of the sacred texts. (A girl who couldn't study Torah may not have known how lucky she was. When Yentl sings defiantly "Where is it written what it is I'm meant to be?" the answer is: In those sacred books that she's so high on.) This musical creates its own frame of reference; its spirit is violated by earnest intentions. Streisand wants to create a woman hero, but when you read Singer, Yentl isn't the hero—the story is. And at its best the movie is the hero, too.

Streisand's long obession with the material is well known; she began thinking about the story as a possible film in the late sixties, and bought the screen rights in 1974. Whatever the box-office results, her instinct was sound. It *is* the right material for her. And now that she has made her formal debut as a director, her work explains why she, notoriously, asks so many questions of writers and directors and everyone else: that's her method of learning. And it also explains why she has sometimes been unhappy with her directors: she really did know better. *Yentl* is never static or stagy; the images move lyrically. The same intuitions that have guided Streisand in producing her records and her TV specials have guided her here—and taken her into some of the same traps. But, even if you object (as I do) to the choice of songs on her records and the manner of those specials, they're highly professional. Within her own tastes, she aims for perfection. Shooting on Czech locations and in English studios, and with the cinematographer David Watkin, Streisand has made a technically admirable movie, with lovely diffuse, poetic lighting and silky-smooth editing. And she brings out the other performers' most appealing qualities. It's a movie full of likable people. Steven Hill, who plays Hadass's father, gives marvellous line readings, and he has something of the same gnomish charm as Nehemiah Persoff's Papa; they're the elders as a child sees them. And Amy Irving's Hadass has a comically human dimension. The half-closed eyes of this slave princess as she serves dinner make her look as if she were deep in an erotic dream, but they are actually the result of her having had to be up at dawn to buy the fish. Her sleepy, plaintive beauty is the perfect foil for Yentl's skinny, anxious face. When Amy Irving just stands there, with her mass of thick, curly dark-red hair and with ornaments dripping from her head and body, she seems to be overcome by her own heavy perfume. She's dopey and she's sumptuous—she's the image of what women have wanted to be freed from, yet can't help wanting to be.

Streisand and Amy Irving play off each other with a kind of rapport that you don't see in movies directed by men. They have a scene in which Hadass, now in love with Anshel, tries to help him conquer his physical timidity—tries to seduce him—and Yentl is in pain as she backs away. It's a deeply ambiguous scene; thought went into it, as well as care. And toward the end of the film Streisand and Patinkin play a bedroom scene in which Avigdor, who has been sexually attracted to Anshel in the vagrant moments when he wasn't sick with love for Hadass, shows the limits of his understanding of a woman's needs. The scene is simply different from scenes conceived and directed by men; it has a different flavor. Avigdor is revealed as essentially a big, sweet Jewish hunk who could never accept a woman as an equal, and when he and Yentl part, the tapering, feminine hand she holds up in farewell puts a seal on his blindness. The whole movie has a modulated emotionality that seems distinctively feminine. That's part of why the independent-woman-on-her-way-to-the-new-land ending is so silly. There is something genuinely heroic in the mixture of delicacy and strength that gives this movie its suppleness. Within the forty-one-year-old star-director are the perfectly preserved feelings of a shy, frightened girl of twelve. She's also shockingly potent. So was Colette—and there's a suggestion of her in the Yentl who runs her fingers over books as if they were magic objects.

The New Yorker, November 28, 1983

ABOUT JOHN CANDY IN

SPLASH

This gigantic, chubby Puck has been great in brief appearances (seventeen movies in the past five years), but the role of Freddie the playboy is the first role big enough for him to make the kind of impression he made in the SCTV shows and in his guest shots on "The New Show." John Candy is perfectly named; he's a mountainous lollipop of a man, and preposterously lovable. As Freddie, who carries a cooler with beer when he goes to play racquetball with his brother Allen (Tom Hanks) and appears on the court cradling a beer in one hand and smoking a king-size cigarette, he doesn't have a hypocritical bone in his body. When he encourages his brother to give in to temptation, he's not playing devil's advocate; Freddie the girl chaser gives in to his own giddiest impulses—he doesn't want Allen to be deprived. Candy has the same function here that Michael Keaton, the brainstorming hipster of *Night Shift,* had. He stirs things up and spars with Tom Hanks. As a bon vivant and man about town, Freddie takes an almost lewd pleasure in his own vanity; he fancies himself debonair and light on his feet, and he is. But he also makes you aware of his bulk by the tricks in his verbal timing: when Hanks has said something to him and you expect him to answer, his hesitation—it's like a few seconds of hippo torpor—is what makes his answer funny. There's a certain amount of aggression built into a frame as big as Candy's: he simply occupies more space than other people do. But Candy doesn't have anything like John Belushi's insane volatility or the gleam in his eyes that told you he was about to go haywire and smash things up; Candy is the soul of amiability—it's just an awfully large soul.

Freddie is the older brother you always wanted to have. He's Falstaff at fourteen, and the picture probably wouldn't work without him; he doesn't add weight, he adds bounce and imagination.

The New Yorker, March 19, 1984

THE BOSTONIANS
THE WOMAN QUESTION

When Henry James wrote *The Bostonians,* which was first serialized in *The Century Magazine* and then published in book form, in 1886, his sentences hadn't yet hit the grand stride of his later manner. His writing wasn't as imperturbably cadenced as it was to become in the maniacal, formal perfection of the novels he brought out after the turn of the century (*The Wings of the Dove* in 1902, *The Ambassadors* in 1903, *The Golden Bowl* in 1904). It's easier to recognize the greatness of those later novels: they are so circumspect and finespun they're almost abstract. You can get heady from the rarefied air. And even those of us who take an intense pleasure in their super-subtlety can recognize that there's a kind of battiness about them. It's James's battiness that we come to love, breathing to the roll of those arch, loony sentences—equilibristic feats that seem to constitute a world of their own. *The Bostonians* has a more earthly kind of greatness. Set in the period after the Civil War, among the abolitionists, who are now—it's 1875 —turning their energies to the emancipation of women, it's a wonderful, teeming novel, with darting perceptions. It's perhaps the most American of James's novels—not just because it is set here but because all the characters are Americans, and because Boston, with its quacks and mystics, its moral seriousness and its dowdiness, is contrasted with New York's frivolous "society" and the South's conservatism. James had immersed himself in Hawthorne's work (he published his biography of him in 1879), and he may have been influenced by Hawthorne's novel about the Brook Farm socialists and idealists, *The Blithedale Romance.* He sees Boston as the capital city of the high-minded—the freethinkers, whom he views satirically, yet admiringly, too. The book is packed with rude (and detailed) psychological observations, and with ironies that aren't quite focussed—he's still in the process of discovering them when the story ends. It's the liveliest of his novels, maybe because it has sex right there at the center, and so it's crazier—riskier, less controlled, less gentlemanly—than his other books. He himself seems to be pulled about, identifying with some of the characters and then rejecting them for others. I think it is by far the best novel in English about what at that time was called "the woman question," and it must certainly be the best novel in the language about the cold anger that the issue of equal rights for women can stir in a man. I first read the book when I was in my early twenties, and it was like reading advance descriptions of battles I knew at first hand; rereading it, some forty years later, I found it a marvellous, anticipatory look at issues that are more out in the open now but still unresolved.

The mind-lock of the central male character, the tall, distinguished-looking, and intelligent young Mississippian Basil Ransom, is chilling. Ransom thought women "essentially inferior to men, and infinitely tiresome when they declined to accept the lot which men had made for them." Their rights "consisted in a standing claim to the generosity and tenderness of the stronger race." James is so sensitive to nuance that every time Ransom puts on his mask of chivalry and addresses a woman chaffingly, jocularly—gallantly—you just about feel your teeth grate. Impoverished by the war in which he fought, Ransom, who belongs to the aristocratic, plantation-owning class, has come to New York to be a lawyer and to try to repair the family fortunes. On a visit to Boston, to make the acquaintance of a distant relative, the wealthy, ascetic blue-stocking Olive Chancellor, he accompanies her to a meeting at the home of a Miss Birdseye, an elderly leader of the suffragettes. The featured speaker is a lovely, flaming-red-haired young girl, Verena Tarrant, who is the daughter of a mesmerist faith healer and has a golden voice and a "gift" for inspirational oratory. Her father has to "start" her—he puts her in a semi-trance, but then she keeps going on her own. Verena has been brought up as a perfect hypnotist's subject: she has been trained to surrender her mind. Both Olive Chancellor and Ransom are drawn to her, and the novel becomes a tug-of-war between the repressed lesbian Olive, who takes Verena into her fine house on Charles Street and grooms her to be a spokeswoman for the emancipation movement, and Ransom, who likes women to be "private and passive." He thinks that the movement is a "modern pestilence," and he's only half joking when he blames the Civil War on women—the abolitionists, he says, were "principally females." He is offended by the idea of Verena's speaking in public—he wants her for himself alone.

The book has a whole gallery of women, with James's tone ranging from the affectionate (almost adoring) satire of the aged, selfless Miss Birdseye (based on Hawthorne's sister-in-law, the abolitionist Elizabeth Peabody), who is "in love . . . only with causes," to the caricature of Verena's mother, the inane, ever-hopeful-of-attaining-a-high-social-position Mrs. Tarrant. There is the diminutive Dr. Prance, a shorthaired, no-nonsense Boston physician with a friendly, dry manner of speech; she is absorbed in her work and has no inclination to listen to emotional feminist rhetoric. And there is Mrs. Burrage, the shrewd, rich New Yorker who arranges for Verena to speak at her home, because her son is in love with the girl and, besides, the movement is the latest fashion.

Virtually everyone in the novel loves Verena. She's a darling. She's one of James's incorruptible American innocents—the girls (Daisy Miller is the most obvious example) who are so often his trusting, ingenuous heroines.

Ransom speaks for the author when he tells Verena, "You are outside and above all vulgarizing influences." And like James's other generous-hearted innocents—his fatally impressionable girls who fall in love with the wrong men—she wants to please. James shows us the mechanisms of the Southerner's manly will and certitude which would make him attractive to a soft and trusting girl. Poor pale Verena, who's only nineteen, is a conventional, perky, flirty girl. She's an asset to the movement just because she's agreeable and pretty rather than forceful. And it's because of her submissiveness—she can't say no—that she becomes the battlefield for the battle of wills between Ransom and Olive Chancellor, who, on meeting Verena, feels that she has found "what she had been looking for so long—a friend of her own sex with whom she might have a union of soul." Alone with Verena for the first time, Olive immediately asks, "Will you be my friend, my friend of friends, beyond everyone, everything, forever and forever?" Verena, the mesmerist's daughter, is, of course, willing. She's like an actress eager for a role. She has an appealing manner but no content; she's an exaggerated version of many men's (and women's) feminine ideal—she's an empty vessel. Ransom and Olive are at war over a vacuum. (At times, this book comes close to modern magic realism; it's no wonder it was a terrible flop when it came out.)

Olive takes on the task of educating Verena, and they study together—they study the history of "feminine anguish." James writes, "Olive had pored over it so long, so earnestly, that she was now in complete possession of the subject; it was the one thing in her life which she felt she had really mastered." And she wants revenge: she feels that men must pay. James is at his most devastating with the humorless Olive Chancellor. He writes that "the most sacred hope of her nature was that . . . she might be a martyr and die for something." And he shows us how Olive unconsciously coerces Verena while talking the rhetoric of freedom. Yet he comes to stare in wonder at Olive's quivering sensibility and her capacity for suffering. She says, of not having the vote, "I feel it as deep, unforgettable wrong. I feel it as one feels a stain that is on one's honour." She develops such neurotic exaltation that even her creator is impressed. In her intertwined folly and nobility, Olive, who has taken on protégée after protégée, and had each one desert her and the cause to which she has consecrated herself—always for a man—is the most heroic figure in the novel.

There's every reason in the world to read the book, and to do it before you see the movie (so that you don't let the movie images saturate what you read). The only good reason to see the film version is Vanessa Redgrave's performance as Olive Chancellor. Her voice shaking with emotion, she gives this woman who is "unmarried by every implication of her being" mythological size. Physically, she's so much stronger and riper than the tremulous fanatic of the book that she stands as proof of the absurdity of women's position in the society. With her powerful neck and broad shoulders, she's like a mature swan; she's gloriously neurasthenic. (And an actress who can be glorious in a role in which she never gets to laugh is a miracle worker.) She brushes off Ransom's flowery condescension as a minor indignity.

Vanessa Redgrave gives the film the force of repressed passion, and I don't know how she does it with so little help. (My companion suggested that she pulled the performance out of her skin.) *The Bostonians* was produced by Ismail Merchant, and directed by James Ivory, from a script by Ruth Prawer Jhabvala, and although it's not as limp as some of their other collaborations, they don't dramatize the great material they selected, and Ivory doesn't shape the performances. Christopher Reeve's handsome, mustachioed Ransom has too likable a presence; he's wholesomely romantic, and when he delivers the rigid-minded, contemptuous-of-women lines that James wrote, his crinkly smile and boyish affability take the sting out of them. He's more Rhett Butler than Basil Ransom. That makes him pleasant, dumb fun to watch, but the tensions that are necessary to the theme don't build. His Ransom isn't bitter; he isn't replaying the Civil War, determined that this time the South will win. And you just don't feel the irony of the bird-in-a-cage life he offers Verena. With Reeve as Ransom, that life seems rather jolly. I don't know what to make of Madeleine Potter's film début as Verena. Her plaintive, Trilby-like Verena is certainly not the fresh, sparkling ingénue that the material calls for; she's more odd than anything else, and she's overcontrolled. Her pallor is rather depressive. (I've seen Potter on the stage and have found her problematic there, too: she works hard, but it isn't acting, exactly—not yet, anyway; it's more like thoughtful pretending.)

Some of the other performers seem so right for their roles that you may want to yelp in pain at the way they're wasted. Jessica Tandy could do so much more with the angelic Miss Birdseye, and Linda Hunt is just a shade away from bringing out the full ironic possibilities in Dr. Prance. Nancy Marchand is luckier: as the New York society woman Mrs. Burrage, she gets to play a long scene (right from the book) in which the drama is allowed to develop—a conversation between Mrs. Burrage and Olive Chancellor, with Mrs. Burrage trying to strike a bargain, suggesting that Olive should encourage Verena to marry her son, as the lesser evil, and as a way of keeping her in the suffrage movement, which the Burrages will back with money and influence. Marchand's face perfectly expresses the "detestable wisdom" that, according to James, Olive sees in her; it's as if you'd looked into Mrs. Burrage's soul and a ravaged old panderer returned your gaze. The only other performer who makes an impression is, surprisingly, Wesley Addy, as Verena's ineffectual father, Dr. Tarrant, the mesmerist who doesn't have enough conviction or energy to be a real charlatan. Addy (who from some angles looks like a fuddled version of Jean Cocteau) brings just enough grotesquerie to his facial contortions—Tarrant seems always to be on the verge of saying something that no one will listen to. Other performances—such as Barbara Bryne's Mrs. Tarrant, John Van Ness Philip's young Burrage, Nancy New's Adeline (Olive's sister), and Wallace Shawn's newspaper reporter, Mr. Pardon—don't come through at all, or, as in the case of Pardon, come through awkwardly, as if the lines were being read from the script without ever entering the actor's consciousness.

The movie follows the book faithfully, except for an attempt at an upbeat ending—a story-conference type of ending—to reassure us that the movement will go on. (Is there some danger that we'll think it stopped?) Until then, the film's worst mistake is that it's full of short scenes in which nothing develops—glimpses of Ransom walking in the woods with Verena or standing on the shore with her at what's meant to be Cape Cod. These glimpses are simply intended to carry the narrative further—they're like those vacuous montages of couples cavorting in photogenic surroundings which were so common in sixties movies, persisted into the seventies, and then finally seemed to be consigned to commercials and MTV. They're filler in *The Bostonians*, and an embarrassment, because what is crucial to Henry James is that every scene have its exact emotional weight. In *The Bostonians*, he hadn't yet got to the point he reached in the later novels, where a single line of dialogue would explode and reverberate back over everything we'd read; *The Bostonians* has many explosions of meaning, and at the end there's a climactic one, in which you'd have to be a fool (or a saint, like Miss Birdseye) not to register that Basil Ransom isn't just expressing his devotion to Verena, he's also skewering Olive Chancellor. That has been part of his motivation from the start. He's sticking it to her.

Ivory's *The Bostonians* is the Henry James novel without the revelations. And the movie's upbeat ending deprives Olive of her tragic stature. But, in its own insignificant, washed-out way, it goes along fairly inoffensively until the last sequence, when we're given the impatient sounds of a large Boston audience that has come to hear Verena speak and is being kept waiting. The shouts and stomping noises from the audience are so unconvincing that the movie falls to pieces. The whole last section is nightmarishly mangled; it's as if the director had said, "Let's really foul this thing up."

The New Yorker, August 6, 1984

UTU
MIRRORS

Geoff Murphy, the director of the New Zealand film *Utu*, has an instinct for popular entertainment. He also has a deracinated kind of hip lyricism. And they fuse quite miraculously in this epic about the relations between the Maori, the dark-skinned Polynesians who started migrating to the volcanic islands that form New Zealand around a thousand years ago, and the British, who began to migrate there in large numbers in the eighteen-thirties. By 1870, the year in which the movie is set, the British were the government (and within the next few decades confiscated millions of acres of Maori land—much of it as "punishment for rebellion"). Murphy uses the conventions of John Ford's cavalry-and-Indians Westerns, but he uses them as a form of international shorthand—to break the ice and get going, and for allusions and contrasts. His primary interest isn't in the narrative; it's in how the characters think and what they feel. By 1870, the Maori, trained and educated in mission schools, speak English and are imbued with Englishness. And they certainly know how to mock the English—playing off the Englishmen's expectations that they will behave like ignorant savages.

Te Wheke (Anzac Wallace), the troublemaker at the center of the story, is a literate, Europeanized Maori with a taste for Shakespeare. He's a uniformed scout with the British colonial forces who returns to his tribal settlement—a village friendly to the British—and finds that the huts are still smoking: the cavalry rode in and set them ablaze after casually slaughtering everyone there, leaving the bodies where they fell. In grief and rage at the death of his people, he feels the need to exact *utu*—the Maori word that means honor and includes ritualized revenge. Te Wheke's honor requires that he achieve balance through reciprocal acts—*utu* can be attained only by the shedding of blood.

By the thirteenth century, the Maori in New Zealand were having disputes over land, and warrior-cannibal tribes built fortified villages and ate or enslaved the enemies they defeated. Since the justification for the raids and killings was the need for *utu,* the members of the tribe that had been attacked would then have the same need, and the warfare was continuous—it was the normal way of life. Because of this tradition, the Maori weren't united even in resisting European encroachment on their land. Some were with the British troops, some tried to remain neutral, and by 1870 the hostile Maori were so demoralized by defeat and slaughter that they couldn't manage much more than occasional guerrilla raids. As more and more land-hungry British settlers arrived, the wars between the Maori and the British became wars of atrocities (on both sides).

Te Wheke prepares for his return to the barbaric, mystical heritage of the warrior tribes by having his face carved to symbolize his new purpose. In the Maori variant of tattooing, deep lines are cut, so that the skin in between stands out in ridges; Te Wheke, with curves and spirals covering his face, has a new aura. He's like a living version of the totemic figures exhibited in the Maori show at the Metropolitan Museum of Art. With his long, thick black hair and his mustache and elated eyes adding to the symmetrical pattern, he suggests the posters for the Broadway show *Cats*. He's a commanding presence—a Maori Che Guevara. He's also engaged in a form of make-believe—he's a travesty of an ancient warrior. When he's dressed for *utu* in his red British Army jacket, and with a military cap perched on his matted hair, it's as if all the contradictions in the society were popping out of his skin—as if he couldn't contain them anymore. He formally announces his *utu* in a rural Christian church after chopping the pastor's head off. He challenges the bewildered white and Maori parishioners by assuming the open-mouthed pose of the totems and jiggling his protruding tongue at them.

Joined by a band of guerrilla recruits, Te Wheke sets out on his rampage. The code that governs *utu* does not require that the specific perpetrators of the offense be killed; any members of their tribe will do—so all Europeans are fair game. When the guerrillas attack the idyllic farmhouse of the Williamsons—Bruno Lawrence (of *Smash Palace*) and the fine actress Ilona Rodgers—they assault the two and proceed to desecrate everything European; they shoot up Mrs. Williamson's china, loot the place, and dance to the pounding of her grand piano before shoving it out the window. Picking up a volume of Shakespeare, Te Wheke entertains himself by reading a passage from *Macbeth* before setting fire to the house. It's an insane vandalization, and he knows it, but he's committed to this mad course of action because the history of his country appears to have left him with no other recourse.

At times, when you're looking at Maori, with their beautiful broad, relaxed faces, you can't tell which side they're on; then you realize that this confusion is part of the subject. They're on both sides: almost everyone in the movie wavers in his allegiance from time to time—even the young Lieutenant Scott (played with a likable mixture of callowness and élan by Kelly Johnson), who has been posted here by the British War Office, because he has been with the Boers putting down the natives in skirmishes in South Africa and has learned new, experimental counter-insurgency tactics. He turns out to be a flop, because he was born in New Zealand and becomes attached to a lovely, fleshy Maori girl; he can't give his work the wholehearted, career enthusiasm he had in South Africa. And the girl (played by an eighteen-year-old Maori student, Tania Bristowe), who is tied in with Te Wheke's band, acts the part of dusky enticer to Scott but feels closer to him than she does to her Maori friends; she gets to the point where she's marked for execution by both sides. As for Te Wheke, he runs his army as a parody of the white man's army. He and his guerrillas deck themselves out in a ragtag assortment of parts of British military uniforms and scraps of Victorian clothing they've picked up in raids on farms, and have hatchets and knives and guns tucked into their belts and boots. They have turned themselves into the Europeans' images of them as butchers and buffoons. (They're like American blacks playing Jungle Bunny.) If that's what the Europeans think they are, that's what they'll be. That's all that's left for them to be. In murdering the British, they're murdering themselves anyway. In a trancelike sequence, Te Wheke's guerrillas take over a wagon full of supplies for the militia and use it to ride in for a surprise night attack; along the road, one of the men rips open a sack of flour, plunks his face down in it, and says, "I've only been one of them for a minute, and already I hate you Maori." As the wagon rolls on, his white face is almost phosphorescent in the moonlight—he's like a phantom.

Mimicry goes on at so many levels in this horror comedy of colonialism that the viewer may be laughing, exhilarated by constant discovery, yet be a little discombobulated and scared. Murphy throws you at the start—he may want to disorient you, as Te Wheke disorients people—and he keeps you in a state of suspension. A few scenes go by before it's clear that the movie is cutting back and forth between the trial of the captured pattern-faced Te Wheke and the events that led the smooth-faced man to transform himself. At the trial, when Wiremu (Wi Kuki Kaa), a smart, fair-minded Maori who's a mercenary with the British forces, explains what has been going on to the officer, Te Wheke yawns. Wiremu, who plays chess with the racist colonel and puts a crimp in his theory of Maori inferiority by winning, has noble twin arches in his upper lip (like V. S. Naipaul)—he's smiling even when he isn't smiling. (He has some of Naipaul's gravity, too.) I doubt if any other director has treated the conventions of this colonial-epic form with Murphy's offhand audacity. He turns the form into a mirror of racism.

Murphy uses an abrupt, lurch-ahead editing that works well (except at the beginning), and there are real streaks of madness in the pursuit story. This isn't an impassioned lament, like the great Australian film *The Chant of Jimmie Blacksmith;* the lamenting quality is implicit in the material. And *Utu* doesn't have a strong protagonist; there are a whole string of leading characters—Lieutenant Scott, the young Maori girl, and others—who take over for a sequence or two and then recede, but may return. Left for dead, Bruno Lawrence's bald, bearded Williamson gets on Te Wheke's trail with the obsessiveness of a man who has lost his wife and seen the destruction of everything he has worked for. He's in the same position as Te Wheke, and has only one desire: to kill him. Slogging through the countryside carrying a quadruple-barrelled shotgun that he has put together (it's the size of a baby cannon), going for days and nights without sleep, and speaking in a dry rasp of a voice that gets lower and lower, Williamson is the only other character with the intensity of Te Wheke, who keeps firing at him but can't seem to kill him. Williamson has the same trouble killing Te Wheke. One with too much hair, the other with hair in the wrong place, they're like the pairs of adversaries in Sergio Leone's *Once Upon a Time in the West,* and we expect them to meet in a final shootout. But Murphy and his co-writer, Keith Aberdein, skewer your expectations, and you think, Of course, it's richer this way. Murphy throws you curves all through the picture: Te Wheke will suddenly be singing "Old MacDonald Had a Farm," or the soundtrack will make a satirical comment on the action, using "Marching Through Georgia," or Lieutenant Scott will casually survive being shot a few times, or Te Wheke's grimaces will remind you of Toshiro Mifune's Macbeth in *Throne of Blood.* (Anzac Wallace's performance as Te Wheke—his first acting—may owe something to his own experiences as a wild, sociopathic thief; he spent fourteen years in prison before becoming reconciled to living with other people, leading an industrial strike, and becoming a union organizer.) There are other reminders of Kurosawa, and of *Macbeth,* too, when Te Wheke stages his own version of moving Birnam wood to Dunsinane.

Te Wheke's Shakespearean flourish in the Williamsons' vandalized home may be somewhat fancy and more than somewhat trite, but Geoff Murphy has the popular touch to bring it off. This fellow, who in the late sixties was a scat singer and trumpet player in Bruno Lawrence's rock group and travelling road show, and also its visual-effects man, seems to be directing with a grin on his face. (After years of working in film, Murphy had a big hit—relative to a country of only three million people—in 1980, with *Goodbye Pork Pie,* which played around the world; that's probably what enabled him to get hold of the three million dollars it took to make *Utu.*) The score, written by John Charles, who was also with the road show, and recorded by a traditional Maori flautist and the New Zealand Symphony Orchestra, takes risks, and most of the time the risks come off gloriously. The film has sweep, yet it's singularly unpretentious—irony is turned into slapstick.

As the militia ride out to go after Te Wheke, young Lieutenant Scott asks Wiremu, "Whose side are you on?" Wiremu answers, "Same side as you, sir. I was born here, too." The fatalistic, pragmatic Wiremu knows there's no side to be on; there's no justice. It's obvious that the British will win, and just as obvious that Te Wheke is a folk hero. He's a hero even when he has become so cruel that he is more like a bug than a man, and his own followers are disgusted by him. No doubt Murphy was conscious of taking a balanced, nonjudgmental position, but you feel that the material itself—and his own instincts—dictated it. He couldn't have made this movie any other way, because it's a comedy about the characters' racial expectations of each other, which come out of the tragedy of their history—a history too grotesque for tears. In one sequence, the soldiers are tracking the guerrillas, and Te Wheke, catching their scent, sniffs the air; his dogs, also sniffing, turn their heads this way and that. Murphy's absurdism is a matter of temperament—it's part of the texture of the movie, which appears to be a reasonably accurate version of a totally crazy birth of a nation.

Probably what Murphy does that makes a viewer respond so freely is that he distances us—very slightly—and makes comedy out of the distancing. (He's a joshing, razzing director.) And because we're not asked to respond in the banal ways that action-adventure movies usually impose on us—there's no one we could conceivably root for—we're free to respond to much more. We're turned loose inside this epic, and the freedom is strange and pleasurable. Some of it has to do with the Maori, who have the placid features of Gauguin's Polynesians but appear to be completely expressive, and have such a fluent, unaffected wit that they seem to be plugged into the cosmos in a different way from the British. (In a scene out in a remote woodland area, Lieutenant Scott, talking companionably to a Maori soldier, says that Maori laugh at things that aren't funny. He gives as an example a horrible prank that some Maori played on the British—adding human meat to a barrel of pickled pork. When he finishes the story, the Maori laughs.) And some of the pleasure has to do with the quality of the light and the uncanny splendor of the New Zealand landscapes. There's a vista of an army encampment—small white tents dotting the pale-green hills—that's like a child's dream of outdoor living. Much of the film was shot in high country in wet weather, and the cinematographer, Graeme Cowley, lets us see the mountains and forests and mist-covered farms as if we just happened to look up and there they were. In New Zealand, no one is ever more than seventy miles from the sea, and maybe that helps to account for the feeling of exaltation and spirituality that hovers over this film. We know this basic story of colonialism from books and movies about other countries, but the ferocity of these skirmishes and raids is played off against an Arcadian beauty that makes your head swim.

The New Yorker, October 15, 1984

STOP MAKING SENSE

Stop Making Sense makes wonderful sense. A concert film by the New York new-wave rock band Talking Heads, it was shot during three performances at the Hollywood Pantages Theatre in December, 1983, and the footage has been put together without interviews and with very few cutaways. The director, Jonathan Demme, offers us a continuous rock experience that keeps building, becoming ever more intense and euphoric. This has not been a year when American movies overflowed with happiness; there was some in *Splash,* and there's quite a lot in *All of Me*—especially in its last, dancing minutes. *Stop Making Sense* is the only current movie that's a dose of happiness from beginning to end. The lead singer, David Byrne, designed the stage lighting and the elegantly plain performance-art environments (three screens used for back-lit slide projections); there's no glitter, no sleaze. The musicians aren't trying to show us how hot they are; the women in the group aren't there to show us some skin. Seeing the movie is like going to an austere orgy—which turns out to be just what you wanted.

Clean-shaven, with short hair slicked back, and wearing white sneakers and a light-colored suit, with his shirt buttoned right up to his Adam's apple, the gaunt David Byrne, who founded the group, comes on alone (with his acoustic guitar and a tape player) for the first number, "Psycho Killer." He's so white he's almost mock-white, and so are his jerky, long-necked, mechanical-man movements. He seems fleshless, bloodless; he might almost be a black man's parody of how a clean-cut white man moves. But Byrne himself is the parodist, and he commands the stage by his hollow-eyed, frosty verve. Byrne's voice isn't a singer's voice—it doesn't have the resonance. It's more like a shouter's or chanter's voice, with an emotional carryover—a faintly metallic wail—and you might expect it to get strained or tired. But his voice never seems to crack or weaken, and he's always in motion—jiggling, aerobic walking, jumping, dancing. (They shade into each other.) Byrne has a withdrawn, disembodied, sci-fi quality, and though there's something unknowable and almost autistic about him, he makes autism fun. He gives the group its modernism—the undertone of repressed hysteria, which he somehow blends with freshness and adventurousness and a driving beat. When he comes on wearing a boxlike "big suit"—his body lost inside this form that sticks out around him like the costumes in Noh plays, or like Beuys' large suit of felt that hangs off a wall—it's a perfect psychological fit. He's a handsome, freaky golem. When he dances, it isn't as if he were moving the suit—the suit seems to move him. And this big box that encloses him is only an exaggeration of his regular nerd-dandy clothes. Byrne may not be human (he rejects ordinary, show-biz forms of ingratiation, such as smiling), but he's a stupefying performer—he even bobs his head like a chicken, in time to the music.

After Byrne's solo, the eight other members of the group come on gradually, by ones and twos, in the order in which they originally joined up with him, so you see the band take form. Tina Weymouth, the bass player, who also sings, comes on next; a sunny, radiant woman with long blond hair, she's smiling and relaxed. (She couldn't be more unlike Byrne—he's bones, she's flesh.) Watching her, you feel she's doing what she wants to do. And that's how it is with the drummer, Chris Frantz, and the keyboard man, Jerry Harrison, and the others in the sexually integrated, racially integrated group. The seven musicians and the two women who provide vocal backing interact without making a point of it; you feel that they like working together, and that if they're sweating they're sweating for themselves, for their pleasure in keeping the music going. They're not suffering for us; they're sharing their good times with us. This band is different from the rock groups that go in for charismatic lighting and sing of love and/or sex. David Byrne dances in the guise of a revved-up catatonic; he's an idea man, an aesthetician who works in the modernist mode of scary, catatonic irony. That's what he emanates. Yet when the other Talking Heads are up there with him for a song such as "Once in a Lifetime" the tension and interplay are warm—they're even beatific. The group encompasses Byrne's art-rock solitariness and the dissociation effects in the spare—somewhat Godardian—staging. The others don't come together with Byrne, but the music comes together. And there's more vitality and fervor and rhythmic dance on the stage than there is with the groups that whip themselves through the motions of sexual arousal and frenzy, and try to set the theatre ablaze.

It's slightly puzzling that this band's music absorbs many influences—notably African tribal music and gospel (the climactic number here is "Take Me to the River")—yet doesn't have much variety. The insistent beat (it stays much the same) works to the movie's advantage, though. The pulse of the music gives the film a thrilling kind of unity. And Demme, by barely indicating the visual presence of the audience until the end, intensifies the closed-off, hermetic feeling. His decision to keep the camerawork steady (the cinematographer, Jordan Cronenweth, used six mounted cameras, one hand-held, and one Panaglide) and to avoid hotsy-totsy, MTV-style editing concentrates our attention on the performers and the music. The only let-down in energy, I thought, was in Byrne's one bow to variety—when he left the stage for the Tom Tom Club number. It's a likable number on its own, but it breaks the musical flow. (It's also the only number with a cluttered background, and it has a few seconds of banal strobe visuals.) One image in the film also stuck in my craw: a shot of a little boy in the audience holding up his white stuffed unicorn. It's just too wholesome a comment on the mu-sic. But these are piddling flaws. The movie was made on money ($800,000) that was raised by the group itself, and its form was set by aesthetic consid-erations rather than a series of marketing decisions. (This is not merely a rock concert without show-biz glitz; it's also a rock-concert movie that doesn't try for visual glitz.) Many different choices could have been made in the shooting and the editing, and maybe some of them might have given the individual numbers (there are sixteen) more modulation, but in its own terms *Stop Making Sense* is close to perfection.

The sound engineering is superb. The sound seems better than live sound; it *is* better—it has been filtered and mixed and fussed over, so that it achieves ideal clarity. (The soundtrack-album versions of some of the songs that are also on the Heads' 1983 album *Speaking in Tongues* are more up, more joyous.) The nine Talking Heads give the best kind of controlled performance—the kind in which everyone is loose. At the end of the con-cert, they're still in control, but they're also carried away. And Jonathan Demme appears to have worked in exactly the same spirit.

The New Yorker, November 26, 1984

CHOOSE ME

The love roundelay *Choose Me*, written and directed by Alan Rudolph, on a budget of $835,000, is pleasantly bananas. The characters, who wander in and out of a bar called Eve's Lounge, are lighted as if Edward Hopper lived across the street and Reginald Marsh prowled the alley; they're all vaguely amnesiac, and their dialogue is overintellectualized in a hammy-hilarious way. The songs are performed by Teddy Pendergrass, and he's just right—he does what Tom Waits is supposed to do. The entire movie has a lilting, loose, cho-reographic flow to it. Rudolph and his cinematographer, Jan Kieser, have de-veloped a swoony camera style befitting the romanticism of a movie in which everyone is obsessively looking for love. A friend once wrote me that ten min-utes into Rudolph's first film, *Welcome to L.A.*, he had the urge to walk out and find somebody doing something: running a jackhammer, fixing a tire, cutting hair—anything routinely useful. This movie may give him the same urge, but it's fun in something like the way that Jacques Demy's 1961 *Lola* was fun. *Lola* was about a girl whose faith in her illusions was vindicated; *Choose Me* is about a group of lovers whose madnesses and illusions interlock. It's giddy in a magical, pseudo-sultry way—it seems to be set in a poet's dream of a red-light district. And though you can't always tell the intentional humor from the unintentional, this low-budget comedy-fantasy has some of the most entertaining (and best-sustained) performances I've seen all year.

Eve is played by Lesley Ann Warren, who has a rare kind of off-and-on beauty. She has acres of eyelids in a face that can seem young and fresh or agelessly old. At moments she's Garboesque, but in the next breath she may remind you of someone as contemporary as Susan Sarandon or Margot Kidder. Her acting isn't as steady as that of the other key performers, but she brings her pivotal role the mystery that is essential to the film. (In some odd way that I won't attempt to explain, her beauty authenticates Rudolph's vision.) Geneviève Bujold has the dippiest and funniest role: she dispenses sex-therapy advice on a radio show, and when she's feeling hot she gets listeners hot. Over the years, Bujold has developed a marvellously close rapport with moviegoers; she can make us feel we're reading her mind. And here she has us entering into every twist of her character's nuthead frigidity and nymphomania; after a while, we giggle happily at sight of her, anticipating that she'll do something naughty, and she doesn't let us down. Rae Dawn Chong is the film's biggest surprise. As the part-black wife of a European racketeer, she puts a sophisticated, comic spin on her line readings, and she's ripely sensual and dirty-minded. The movie has elements of interracial fantasy; the hookers in the street outside Eve's place pair up and triple up with their johns in racially mixed combos—they meet and go off together like dancers, in rhythm with the music. Rae Dawn Chong's amours are more intense, and much more fleshly. She's presented like the occasional exotic black woman in French movies—her husband calls her *"mon petit chocolat"*—but her wit is strictly American. The only big flaw in Rudolph's sex-farce construction is that she's left stranded about half an hour before the close of the picture, and the romanticism loses some of its lift when she isn't around.

The central male role—the starring role—is played by Keith Carradine, who may never have been this impressive before, even in his performances for Robert Altman. He's playing a perhaps crazy stud, who comes to Eve's bar straight from the mental ward. It's a literary conceit of a role—the kind that almost invariably makes an actor look like an idiot. He has to suggest that he's a lunatic who's saner than anyone else, and yet emanate danger and untrustworthiness. Carradine carries it off, while boyishly hopping into all three of the women's beds. He's not callow anymore. The years have given him a handsome, sculptural presence, and he manages to validate every bad idea Alan Rudolph throws at him. Other directors aren't this lucky.

The New Yorker, December 24, 1984

MRS. SOFFEL
FEVER DREAM

Mrs. *Soffel* gets into a great subject: repressed, often well-educated women who fall in love with prisoners—men in cages. In our day, we read news accounts of a woman lawyer helping her client escape from prison, or a woman professor abetting a jailbreak, or a business or professional woman reading about a prisoner, visiting him, marrying him. *Mrs. Soffel* is based on an actual case that goes back to 1902, when the wife of the warden of the Allegheny County Jail in Pittsburgh helped two prisoners—the Biddle brothers—escape from Murderers' Row, and ran off with them. As the movie tells it, Kate Soffel (Diane Keaton) isn't radicalized in any ideological sense, and Ed Biddle (Mel Gibson) and his brother Jack (Matthew Modine) aren't political, or even big-time. They're just holdup artists who have been condemned to be hanged because someone got killed when they robbed a grocery store. But they're young and handsome, the fiery-eyed Ed swears that they're innocent of murder, and they've developed a considerable following among the impressionable women of Pittsburgh. Teen-age girls bring flowers to the prison, and the next-to-oldest of Kate's four children—the naïve twelve-year-old Margaret (Jennie Dundas)—is staunch in her belief that though the Biddles have committed ninety robberies, they're laboring-class rebels who have never hurt anyone; she pastes newspaper clippings in a scrapbook so she'll have a record of all the injustices done to them. Their case becomes political.

Working from a script by Ron Nyswaner, the young Australian director Gillian Armstrong doesn't lay out the reasons for what happens; she evokes them partially, suggestively, inviting you to feel your way into Kate Soffel's disappointment with her marriage. We can see the torment and dissatisfaction in Kate's face, and the neurasthenia that has kept her in bed for three months, and keeps her from sharing a bedroom with the husband she married eighteen years ago, when she was seventeen. (At first, we see that she's sick and that she's married to Edward Herrmann; soon we suspect that she's sick because she's married to Edward Herrmann.) The family lives in the warden's quarters, which are built right into the jailhouse structure, and the ornately furnished rooms seem airless and confining. Surrounded by husband, children, and servants, the imprisoned Kate sits in her tightly bound clothes; under the curls on her forehead, her eyes are full of misery. As the warden's gracious, devout wife, she makes her own rounds, taking Bibles to the inmates and offering words of moral guidance. But there's something about her that makes you uneasy; she's telling the prisoners that faith will do something for them that it has obviously failed to do for her.

What's daring in the way Gillian Armstrong presents this love story is that we don't quite trust the emotions of either Kate Soffel or Ed Biddle. She's sickly, frustrated, unstable; he's an opportunist, with only one opportunity—to make her love him so madly that she'll bring him and Jack the saws they need to get out. From behind bars, he works on her, quoting the Bible in a ringing, romantic voice, challenging her by telling her he's not a believer. He asks her to read to him—that keeps her close. He writes her a poem; he touches her, grabs her, kisses her. (And Jack, in the cell next to Ed's, grins.) But Kate isn't a fool, and she's twelve years older than Ed; she's aware of how he's trying to use her. At the same time, she's sexually aroused by him—he's like a trapped animal reaching out to her, pulling her up against his cell.

Mel Gibson, who miscast can seem a lightweight, is superb here. Much wirier than in his earlier roles, he's convincingly passionate, shrewd, relentless. There's concentrated emotionality in this performance—an all-out romanticism that you don't expect from an actor who's only twenty-eight. As Ed, he's like the young Henry Fonda, but with a streak of something darker, more volatile, and more instinctively knowing. Ed comes on so strong that we don't know quite how to read him—especially since much of the time he's behind bars and we see only part of his face. He puts the squeeze on Mrs. Soffel, and it makes her feel alive; it takes a while before we realize that she does the same for him. Diane Keaton has trouble with the period role: her fast, distraught manner of speaking, the words she emphasizes, the ones she throws away—it's all very specifically modern. So is her conception of neurosis, and so, I think, is the tender, easy manner Kate has with her children. (Shouldn't she be more erratic, taking out some of her suffering on them, or, at least, be negligent and indifferent?) But she has a moment here that's freakishly inspired: Ed has been holding her against the bars and she has been speaking like a moral exemplar when suddenly, in mid-sentence, she lets out a dirty little giggle. We know then that Kate is living in a fever dream and doesn't want to wake up. And the post-hippie diction and the other surface flaws in Keaton's performance fade into relative insignificance, because the things that come from inside are so startlingly right. Kate has a broad, lewd smile when she holds out her Bible to Ed—with the saws in it; then she reads the Good Book out loud to the brothers, keeping watch for them as they saw away.

The movie is set in winter, in the grime and fumes of an industrial city at its worst, and then in snow-covered farmland as the three try to escape to Canada. There isn't a single image that looks ordinary or stale; Armstrong and her cinematographer, Russell Boyd, give us a completely fresh vision of the American past, and the whites glisten in Boyd's deep-toned shots. But Armstrong may have overdone the ominousness and gloom of the early scenes—the murk indoors and the sootiness outdoors may make the movie hard for viewers to get into. Even if you know that Pittsburgh used to need its street lights on in the middle of the day, the darkness may seem affected. If you give the movie a chance, though, it justifies the early dreamlike funereal underlay. Each of Armstrong's three features has been amazingly different from the others. As a piece of filmmaking, the first, the feminist princess fantasy *My Brilliant Career* (which she made in 1978, when she was only twenty-seven), was careful, pictorial, leisurely. The second, the pop musical *Starstruck,* set in modern Sydney and starring the blithe new-wave singer Jo Kennedy, was visually jangly and all over the place, but exuberant and likable. Clearly, Armstrong adapts herself to her subjects, and this time her style has an edginess: the scenes have unexpected tempos, the perspectives on the richly furnished Soffel household are always slightly unsettling, and we never know when we'll hear the clanging of the iron gates and doors. The prison is a major presence—it's the prison from which the actual Mrs. Soffel and the Biddles fled into the night. Designed by Henry Hobson Richardson to resemble a fortified church and built in the eighteen-eighties, it's oppressive yet in its way exalted—an architectural marvel that is still in use, housing five hundred inmates. With its majestic cell-block atrium, and the warden's quarters as part of the structure, it's a perfect setting for a Gothic romance.

This stone-and-iron monster is so solid that you may get the feeling that at first Kate Soffel could enjoy the titillating danger that Ed Biddle represented because she felt cloistered and secure—she could go anywhere in the prison, but he was safely behind bars. She could go to him, but he couldn't come to her. One thing that makes their love story different from the familiar ones is that they finally come clean with each other. She abandons her protected status; he abandons the public poses that turned her little daughter into a groupie. (And Gibson has a rare kind of delicacy when Ed offers Kate proof of his love.) There are some surprising elements in this movie—such as the confusion of the prison break, the shock of seeing Ed and Jack in the warden's quarters, the hostility that Ed and Jack's friends feel toward Kate, and the brotherly bond between the Biddles that we're aware of throughout. They match up well physically, but that's only a small part of it; Modine enables you to see how Jack takes his cues from Ed, and why Ed feels responsible for him.

Mrs. Soffel lacks humor, and its themes don't fully emerge. (The fault may be in the screenplay—that it just doesn't go far enough.) But the movie builds an excitement that has something to do with the fact that the flight of the Biddles with Kate in tow is deranged. They're killing each other by staying together, yet you can see that staying together is all that matters to them. When the three of them are out in the snow, rushing toward the border, the hurrying about makes Kate flush, and her eyes and teeth shine—she seems elated and glamorous. She's experiencing freedom, and the feelings that were buried in her are released. When a stranger says something grossly insensitive in her presence, and she slaps him, all her senses seem to be whirring. She's a Victorian madwoman heroine.

The New Yorker, January 7, 1985

THE COTTON CLUB
ECHO CHAMBER

I f a whiz-kid director from the three-minute-rock-video field tries his hand at a Jazz Age gangster musical, the result might be *The Cotton Club*. Francis Coppola, who co-wrote and directed it, seems to have skimmed the top off every twenties-thirties picture he has seen, added seltzer, stirred it up with a swizzlestick, and called it a movie. The shots don't look as if he were framing for the movie camera; they're framed for video excitement. His only goal seems to be to keep the imagery rushing by—for dazzle, for spectacle. The thinking (or the emotional state) behind his conception appears to be that it's all been done before, and that what remains is to feed your senses. He just wants to look at pretty girls, movement, color. He's watching his brain cells twinkle.

The action is centered on the famous Harlem late-night supper club that from 1923 to 1936 was situated upstairs over a theatre on the corner of 142nd Street and Lenox Avenue—a speakeasy with a great floor show, in which "colored" headliners and the "tall, tan, and terrific" Cotton Club Girls (who were required to be "high yaller," under twenty-one when hired, and at least five feet six) performed for a white clientele. The club was a showcase for the "primitive" joyousness and sensuality of the black singers and dancers, and the revues, which were produced by whites and ran for an hour and a half or two hours, with the last of the three nightly shows starting at 2 A.M., had motifs in keeping with the club's advertising itself as a "window on the jungle . . . a cabin in the cotton." (The jungle predominated, and the club itself was decorated jungle style.) Seven hundred socialites, celebrities, Broadway stars, bootleggers, and assorted mobsters could be seated at the tiny tables, arranged in a horseshoe around the dance floor; among them might be Mayor Jimmy Walker, Fred Astaire, Irving Berlin, Fanny Brice, Charlie Chaplin, and such underworld figures as Legs Diamond, Dutch Schultz, and Lucky Luciano. Starting in 1927, the house bandleader was Duke Ellington, and he soon began broadcasting a nightly radio show live from the stage; when the show went national, on a weekly basis, the whole country heard of the Cotton Club and listened to its music. And people went on listening after Ellington left for other commitments and Cab Calloway, who at first had just filled in, replaced him. The entertainers, who were the highest paid in Harlem, included Bessie Smith, Josephine Baker, Lena Horne, Ethel Waters, Bill Robinson, and, later, Buck and Bubbles, and the Nicholas Brothers. Financed by a syndicate of white mobsters, the club had a slightly flexible Jim Crow policy: twelve seats could be filled by Negro dignitaries, racketeers, and the families and friends of the performers, and a few more if the applicants were well groomed and very light-complexioned. (This exclusionary policy was somewhat further eased under pressure from Ellington, though people of color were likely to be seated at the back, near the kitchen.)

The movie has its own racial problems: white moviegoers will rarely attend pictures on black themes or with black stars, and so Richard Gere was signed up to play the leading role—on a contract in which he stipulated that he was to appear as a cornet player—before there was anything resembling a role or a script. After a few attempts at scripts failed, Coppola was brought in; he had trouble, too, and enlisted a collaborator, the novelist (and former film critic) William Kennedy. Together, they hatched some thirty to forty versions—an insane number. But how do you make a movie about the Cotton Club starring a white cornet player when there were no white musicians at the Cotton Club?

In diagrammatic terms, the intricate plot that Coppola and Kennedy devised isn't bad. They introduced another famous Harlem nightspot—the Bamville Club—where Gere could go to blow his horn in jam sessions, and then they worked out a gimmicky scene in which Gere, a smiling-eyed young Irishman, saves Dutch Schultz (James Remar) from a stick of dynamite planted by assassins. In gratitude, Dutch puts him on the payroll, and hires his loutish brother (Nicolas Cage), too. This still doesn't give Gere much connection to the Cotton Club, except that he sometimes goes there with Schultz, a married man, who uses Gere as escort to his teen-age mistress (Diane Lane). Having compounded the initial lunacy of the white-cornettist hero, Coppola and Kennedy created a parallel set of black brothers (Gregory and Maurice Hines)—tap dancers who get their big chance at the Cotton Club. These parallel plots don't converge; there's no more than an occasional "Hi" as Gere and Gregory Hines go past each other on the street or at the club until close to the end, when Dutch Schultz, enraged, wants to kill Gere, and Hines, with his dancer's speed and agility, kicks the gun out of Schultz's hand. But the two sets of brothers give the movie an illusion of symmetry: both sets have families and fights, and Gere's troubles with the tough, tarty Diane Lane are matched by Gregory Hines' troubles with a light-skinned showgirl and singer, played by Lonette McKee. By then the movie is packed with characters and complications and incidents that it doesn't have time for; it's so overloaded with plot that it might just as well have no plot at all. And I haven't even mentioned that the black crooks who control the Harlem numbers racket are being challenged by the Irish and Jewish mobsters, and then the Italians—led by Lucky Luciano (Joe Dallesandro)—move in. Maybe because of the need to work around that horn-player hero, Coppola and Kennedy kept adding elements until the plot became a composite of the old Warners musicals and gangster pictures. Coppola apparently believes this pastiche to be an authentic, epic view of the Jazz Age. Describing it to an interviewer from *Film Comment,* he said, "It's a story of the times: it tells the story of the blacks, of the white gangster, about entertainers, everything of those times, like Dos Passos, and the lives all thread through with 'Minnie the Moocher' and 'Mood Indigo.'"

Actually, it's an echo chamber of a movie. When Warners made those pictures that were snatched from the headlines, the crude, simplified characters had a tabloid immediacy. Reproduced here in composite form, they have no inner life and no emotional force. *The Cotton Club* is so dense about so little. It's a movie made by a director who has lost his sense of character. The joke of the long effort to concoct a script around the star Gere is that there are no stars in any of Coppola's recent movies *(One from the Heart, The Outsiders, Rumble Fish);* stars may be signed on, but when the movies come out there's just a bunch of bewildered performers wondering why they don't make a stronger impression.

If there's something more upsetting about this movie than there is about other failed epics, it's that a great time in the history of black people has been screwed over. Yes, the Cotton Club was a racist institution, but it was something more, too: it was part of a liberating social upheaval—not the most creative part but the most conspicuous part. And if some of those white swells were slumming when they went up to Harlem to watch "the coloreds" they put on their evening clothes to do it. There was joy in those black entertainers, and there was heat. That was what the white audience recognized; that was what the radio listeners responded to. It's what the Jazz Age was about: the emergence of black music—hot jazz—and the thrill that white artists and white audiences felt as black artists began to enter the cultural mainstream, moving from Harlem to Broadway and across the country. In the thirties, when I was a kid in San Francisco, I thought I would die from pure pleasure when I saw Buck and Bubbles perform in the stage show that came on before the movie at the Golden Gate Theatre; I'd sit through the picture over and over so I could watch John W. Bubbles glide through his tap numbers, smiling crookedly, his eyes hooded, as if he knew that kids like me had never seen anything so slinky sexy. I thought he was evil, but I loved it.

Coppola, with his staccato imagery fragmenting the songs and dances, knocks the life out of the performers. The tall, sinuous Lonette McKee, with her long, expressive arms upraised, actually gets to complete a number (the torchy "Ill Wind"), but she has none of the impudent energy she showed in the 1976 *Sparkle*. And the Hines brothers' dancing is fast and proficient yet uninspired. If you look at a clip of the Nicholas Brothers, say, in the 1942 *Orchestra Wives,* where they dance to "I've Got a Gal in Kalamazoo," you just about go crazy from the sheer aesthetic excitement of what they're doing—they're flying. The way Coppola shoots dance, nobody flies. In a sequence at the all-male Hoofers Club, Honi Coles and the other great tappers are just starting to limber up and go into their moves when they're chopped into dancing feet without bodies and wiggling bodies without feet. Coppola doesn't seem to know that it's criminal not to let these artists do their thing. The movie is all his thing—he keeps the images scrambling ahead. It's a self-defeating technique: he's so antsy that he doesn't stop to let us look at what we've come to see. The picture opens with the dancing bodies of the Cotton

Club Girls in smoky color. Their dancing—intercut with black-and-white titles and angled spotlights that establish the film's visual style—is routine and impersonal. It never becomes anything more, and during the whole movie we never get close enough to these girls to see their faces, their spirit. We never get to see what we might expect to be at the heart of the movie: how the black performers and the white customers (and bosses and floor-show staff) feel about each other.

The movie certainly has a visual style: Art Deco with *film noir* lighting, and montages that skitter through the years, signifying what's happening to the country and the principal characters. But this dark, lacquered style doesn't come out of the material; it's a fashionable style that's imposed, like the visual formats of videos. Coppola doesn't build a dance through editing, as Busby Berkeley did; the jazz singers and dancers are in the background to be broken into. They're used to give the movie contrasts and sheen—to give it more of a spin. When Diane Lane and Richard Gere have their big sex scene, burnished rainbows fill the room, and then the shadow of the curtains makes lace patterns on her bare body; these effects are what we get instead of the emotion that the moment might be expected to call up. Coppola gives us all this design and he doesn't seem aware of what's missing. He's not taking old techniques and applying them; he's just taking them.

Musicals of the past rarely had fully written characters, but they didn't need them, because the actors' personalities filled out the roles. Here most of the actors are hardly allowed to show they're alive. It's a toss-up whether Nicolas Cage or Diane Lane has the worst part. Cage easily passes as Gere's younger brother, but he is made such a crude dope that there isn't a single scene in which we're happy he's around. Diane Lane was eighteen when she played her role, and that's roughly the age of Dutch's moll, but she's encased in makeup and wigs. And though most of the dialogue in the movie is reasonably pungent, her lines express a callous, moronic cynicism. Statements such as "Money's the only thing that ever saves you" don't do a lot for an actress, and her performance is equally blunt. (In the kissing scenes, she and Gere chew each other's lips so hungrily that something besides passion seems implied, but what?) Gregory Hines doesn't come off as badly, but his role is miserably misconceived. When he's smitten at first sight of Lonette McKee, the audience can share his emotion, but you expect him to be hip and to court her with his talent. When, instead, he chases after her, calf-eyed and stupidly sincere, and gets into backstage squabbles, he becomes embarrassing—you don't want to look at him. As for Gere (whose role is based partly on George Raft), with his hair brushed back flat and brilliantined, and a natty little mustache, he flashes a pretty smile and is more agreeable than usual. But there's nothing to draw us into his simp-sheik character. (In his brief appearance as Luciano, Joe Dallesandro, who's reminiscent of De Niro in *The Godfather, Part II,* has a much more romantic presence.)

A few of the actors seem to be invincible. Lighted from below, Julian Beck, of the Living Theatre, who plays Sol, a corrupt-to-the-bone hit man, looks like an Old Testament vulture. He takes his time and delivers his world-weary remarks in amusingly ghostly, sinister tones—he could be the John Carradine of the avant-garde. And Bob Hoskins, as Owney Madden, the cunning gangster who operates the club, and Fred Gwynne, as his henchman, Big Frenchy DeMange, who welcomes the guests, are like a vaudeville comedy team. Big Frenchy, as gloomy as a basset hound and always formal, walks a step behind the little bulldog Owney and stands behind him when he's seated; he seems to be Owney's butler and bodyguard, and his partner, too. When they finally have a full scene together, after Big Frenchy has been kidnapped and Owney has ransomed him, they one-up each other belligerently, but in rhythm, and with undercurrents of so much affection that it's the most touching moment in the movie—even though it doesn't make a lot of sense.

This Hoskins-Gwynne scene stands out because it doesn't just refer to old-movie scenes about friendship; you actually experience the emotion. In most of the movie, you don't get the feelings that made old-movie scenes memorable—you just watch people referring to those old scenes. (An example: the break between the Hines brothers causes us no pain, and their reunion has no exhilaration.) That's why the movie's plot doesn't give you the pleasures of a plot. Coppola uses the plot pro forma—he doesn't invest it with meaning. The movie is Felliniesque (especially in its last section, which cuts between Grand Central Station and a Grand Central set on the Cotton Club stage), and Coppola, like Fellini, assumes the role of the master of ceremonies, the eye of the hurricane. But his expansiveness has become strictly formal. Emotionally, he seems to have shrunk. The way he directs the cast here, people exist to reflect light.

The New Yorker, January 7, 1985

A PASSAGE TO INDIA
UNLOOS'D DREAMS

The title of E. M. Forster's *A Passage to India* is an homage to one of the loveliest sections in Whitman's *Leaves of Grass,* and, unlike Forster's other, more neatly constructed novels, this one has an all-embracing, polymorphous quality, an openness. Forster had lived in India before and after the First World War, and in story terms the novel, published in 1924, is about the tragicomedy of British colonial rule. The liberal, agnostic author projects himself into the Indian characters—into the humiliation they feel at being governed by people who have no affection for them, who don't like them. In its larger intentions, the novel is about the Indians' spirituality, their kindness, their mysticism. The novel's flowing, accepting manner is related to Eastern philosophy. It embodies that philosophy, yet when Forster attempts to explain it—when he tries for mystery and depth—the writing seems thin, fuzzy, inflated. (When his exaltation goes flat, it's like flat Whitman; it's like hearing someone dither on about oneness with the universe.) I don't think the novel is great—it's near-great, or not-so-great, maybe because mysticism doesn't come naturally to an ironist, and in *A Passage to India* it seems more willed than felt. But the novel is suggestive and dazzlingly empathic. Forster never falls into mere sympathetic understanding of the Indians; he's right inside the central Indian character—the young Muslim Dr. Aziz. He embraces Aziz, all right; it's the British he pulls away from.

The movie version, adapted, directed, and edited by David Lean, is an admirable piece of work. Lean doesn't get in over his head by trying for the full range of the book's mysticism, but Forster got to him. In its first half, the film (it lasts two hours forty-three minutes) has a virtuoso steadiness as the story moves along and we see the process by which the British officials and their wives, who arrive in the fictitious provincial city of Chandrapore with idealistic hopes of friendship with the Indians, are gradually desensitized to the shame experienced by the natives, and become imperviously cruel. The movie shows us the virtual impossibility of communication between the subject people and the master-race British, and between the Muslims and the Hindus, at the same time that we observe the efforts of two Englishwomen to bridge the gulfs—to get to know the Indians socially.

Mrs. Moore (Peggy Ashcroft), an elderly woman, whose son Ronny (Nigel Havers) has been in India for a year as city magistrate in Chandrapore, comes to visit him, accompanied, at his suggestion, by Adela Quested (Judy Davis), whom he expects to marry. Mrs. Moore is displeased to see her son turning into a dull sahib, and the young, inexperienced Miss Quested, who has never been out of England before, is shocked by Ronny's new callousness and the smugness of the people he emulates. Mrs. Moore, who has little patience with her son and his warnings about the dangers of mingling with the natives, strikes up an immediate, instinctive rapport with Dr. Aziz (Victor Banerjee), a glistening-eyed, eager doctor-poet, whom she meets by chance in a mosque. And later the two women have tea with Fielding (James Fox), the principal of the local Government College, who, to help them socialize, invites two Indian guests—Aziz and a Hindu scholar, Professor Godbole (Alec Guinness). Dr. Aziz, a bit heady with the joys of this social intercourse with English women who treat him as an equal, and unable to invite the group to his squalid one-room cottage, proposes an excursion—a picnic at the distant Marabar Caves.

And that's where, despite Aziz's careful, elaborate planning, everything comes to grief. Hearing the echo in a cave, Mrs. Moore is overcome by heat and fatigue, premonitions of death, and the feeling of a void where God should be. While Mrs. Moore rests, Miss Quested goes on alone with Dr. Aziz and a guide, and soon comes rushing from a cave suffering, perhaps, from what Whitman called "unloos'd dreams"—she is hysterical, and is convinced that Dr. Aziz has attempted to rape her. He is arrested, and the British, with their surface unflappability and their underlying paranoia about the Indians, react as if they were under siege. The British colony closes ranks, except for Fielding, who asserts his belief in the doctor's innocence, and the now irritable and distressed Mrs. Moore, who, without waiting to testify on the doctor's behalf, starts the journey home. For the others, the supposed attack on Miss Quested is further proof of the racial inferiority of the Indians. Besides, as the Superintendent of the Police explains at the trial, it's a matter of scientific knowledge that the darker races are attracted to the fairer, but not vice versa.

Forster's plot is a very elaborate shell game: in the book, just when you think the nugget of truth about Miss Quested's accusation has been located Forster evades you again. He's very lordly, in his way; it's a cosmic comedy—each group of players has its own God. (The inscrutable Hindus, with their policy of self-removal, are wittier than the British Christians, with their disdain. The Muslims are anxious.) Lean isn't as playful, but he has his own form of lordliness. He knows how to do pomp and the moral hideousness of empire better than practically anybody else around. He enlarges the scale of Forster's irony, and the characters live in more sumptuous settings than we might have expected. But they do live. Lean knows how to give the smallest inflections an overpowering psychological weight. The actors don't sink under it.

Lean's control—a kind of benign precision—is very satisfying here, because of the performers (and the bright-colored, fairy-tale vividness of the surroundings). By the time he gets to the trial, everything has been prepared, and, in a departure from Forster's mode, he delivers suspense, drama, excitement. The courtroom scenes are far more climactic than in the novel, but Lean has necessarily shaped the material to his own strengths. This isn't the *Passage to India* that Satyajit Ray hoped to make—though he, too, wanted Victor Banerjee to play Dr. Aziz (and he had met with Peggy Ashcroft). And perhaps Ray might have been able to convey the spiritual grace that Forster was reaching for. But Lean's picture is intelligent and enjoyable, and if his technique is to simplify and to spell everything out in block letters, this kind of clarity has its own formal strength. It may not be the highest praise to say that a movie is orderly and dignified or that it's like a well-cared-for, beautifully oiled machine, but of its kind this *Passage to India* is awfully good, until the last half hour or so. Having built up to the courtroom drama, Lean isn't able to regain a narrative flow when it's over. The emotional focus is gone, the tension has snapped, and the picture disintegrates. The concluding scenes, in which he follows the general plan of the book, wobble all over the place. But by then we're pretty well satisfied anyway, and we don't mind staying a little longer with these actors, even though they seem lost.

The cast is just about irreproachable, with the exception of Guinness, who's simply in the wrong movie. The presence of Victor Banerjee makes you feel embarrassed for Guinness. It's dangerous for an actor to try that Peter Sellers–Indian routine when he's next to the real thing. (You keep expecting Guinness to break into a soft-shoe or do something silly with his turban.) As Dr. Aziz, the slim, compact Banerjee, with his handsome, delicately modelled face (the round eyes, the cupid's-bow mouth), belongs to this society—he's like a piece of erotic sculpture, a sensual cherub. When he gets ready to go out, he puts a black line under his eyes with a swift, practiced motion; he makes the most of his beauty. This soft-voiced Bengali actor is more fluid emotionally than anyone else in the cast; Dr. Aziz's feelings of generosity, servility, hurt, and rage slide into each other, and we get the impression that this is what trying to please the British has done to the man. He's too easily hurt; he's all exposed nerves and excitability. He's the most "human" of the characters, because he's so far from being like the English—and the more he tries to be like them, the farther away he is.

As Miss Quested, Judy Davis has none of the bloom that she had in *My Brilliant Career;* she's pale and a trace remote—repression has given her a slightly slugged quality about the eyes. But she's still very attractive in Western terms. Her broad-rimmed hats and virginal, straight-cut dresses are simple and uncoquettish. You like watching her—she has an unusual physical quiet, and her mouth is very expressive (despite the brick-colored lipstick she wears throughout). And it's clear that India represents her first chance to live. She longs for adventure, though she's frightened of it. And she's drawn to Dr. Aziz, though she doesn't know how to get closer to him. So it isn't until the trial that we register that to the Indians she looks tall, flat-chested, and sexually undesirable. To them the charge of attempted rape is something of an insult to Dr. Aziz's taste. All along, there's a lascivious fear that runs through the proper behavior of the British—a fear of India's voluptuous erotic traditions. And Lean has interpolated a sequence that makes this unmistakable: alone on a bicycle ride, Miss Quested chances upon an overgrown park with a temple covered with statuary—coupling bodies. She's fascinated, and as she walks about looking at what the statues are doing she seems transformed— awakened and beautiful. But the statues are suddenly swarming—a bunch of chattering, screeching monkeys come down to the bottom of the temple and onto the statues. They're like little demons blending with the lovers, and they charge at Miss Quested, terrifying her, and chase her as she dashes away on her bike. This dramatization of Miss Quested's fear of sex is very effective. (It's actually more affective than the major episode of Marabar.) But we can feel its function: it's to cue us for her hysteria at the caves, and that's not how Forster's material works. (Lean gives us a pointed reminder of the temple scene when Miss Quested is on her way to the courthouse and a man in a monkey suit jumps on the running board. This is a real blunder; for a second, it throws us out of the movie.) But Judy Davis's performance is close to perfection; her last scene (in England) is a little skewed, but that's no more than a flyspeck. Despite her moment of hysteria, this Miss Quested is a heroically honest figure who, in testifying as she does at the trial, escapes being raped of her soul by Ronny and the British colonial community.

As Mrs. Moore, Peggy Ashcroft comes through with a piece of transcendent acting. She has to, because Mrs. Moore is meant to be a saint, a sage, a woman in tune with the secrets of eternity. Forster never devised anything for her to do; in the novel, she simply is a sacred being—she's an enigma, like Professor Godbole. It may have been in an attempt to convey her wisdom that Lean gave her what is probably the worst line in the script: "India forces one to come face to face with oneself. It can be rather disturbing." (Substitute "Transylvania," and that's a line for Dracula to speak.) Except for Mrs. Moore's brief rapport with Aziz, who tells her she has the kindest face he has ever seen on an English lady, she's simply a weary, practical-minded woman who's very sure of things. She's not much of a mother—she's quite out of sympathy with her son Ronny—and she has no particular feeling for Miss Quested. She's a cantankerous old lady, yet Peggy Ashcroft breathes so much good sense into the role that Mrs. Moore acquires a radiance, a spiritual glow. It makes us like her. Fielding, the character who behaves most courageously, doesn't seem to have stirred Forster's imagination much; Forster was probably too much like Fielding for Fielding to interest him. The character is always on the verge of being too decent, but James Fox (he was the weakling master turned slavey in *The Servant*) gives the part a doggedness that saves it.

The novel wants to be about unresolvability; the movie doesn't, and isn't. What's remarkable about the film is how two such different temperaments as Forster's and Lean's could come together. There's a tie that binds them, though: Lean certainly hasn't softened Forster's condemnation of the British officials' poisonous thick-skinned detachment. Like the book, the movie is a lament for British sins; the big difference is in tone. The movie is informed by a spirit of magisterial self-hatred. That's its oddity: Lean's grand "objective" manner—he never touches anything without defining it and putting it in its place—seems to have developed out of the values he attacks. It's an imperial bookkeeper's style—no loose ends. It's also the style that impressed the Indians, and shamed them because they couldn't live up to it. It's the style of the conqueror—who is here the guilt-ridden conqueror but the conqueror nevertheless. Lean has an appetite for grandeur. That may explain why, at the start, he puts the Viceroy on the ship with the two women (and why, the caves in India not being imposing enough, he dynamited and made his own). But his appetite for grandeur also accounts for such memorable images as the red uniforms and headgear on the Indian band mangling Western music in the brilliant sunshine at the whites-only club, and the ancient painted elephant that lurches along from the train to the caves with Dr. Aziz, Mrs. Moore, and Miss Quested on its back.

The New Yorker, January 14, 1985

WITNESS

In the new Peter Weir movie, *Witness,* an eight-year-old Amish boy (Lukas Haas), on his first trip to a city, sees a murder taking place in the men's room of Philadelphia's Thirtieth Street train station. In order to protect the boy and his mother, Rachel, a widow (Kelly McGillis), from the killers, John Book (Harrison Ford), the police captain who's in charge of the investigation, tries to hide their identities, and, with a bullet wound in his side, drives them back to their farm in Lancaster County before he collapses. At that point, the film has already built up the contrast between the devout, gentle Amish and the greedy, brutal Philadelphians—seen through the eyes of the child, who takes in everything. In the days of silent pictures, the distinction between rural virtue and big-city vice was a standard theme. The girl on the farm was steadfast; she represented true, undying love. The city girl was fast and spoiled and selfish. This split between good farmers and bad urban dwellers takes an extreme form in *Witness.* Last year's rural trilogy *(Country, Places in the Heart,* and *The River)* prepared the way: moviegoers have been softened to accept the idea that people who work the land are uplifted by their labor. And *Witness* goes the trilogy one better by having its farming people part of a pacifist religious community that retains an eighteenth-century way of life and stresses "plainness." (The Amish reject *buttons* as decorative.) Also, in the past twenty years we have been battered by so much evidence of crime in the cities that moviegoers may be ready to believe that city people are, of necessity, depraved. *Witness* seems to take its view of the Amish from a quaint dreamland, a Brigadoon of tall golden wheat and shiny-clean faces, and to take its squalid, hyped-up view of life in Philadelphia from prolonged exposure to TV cop shows. Murder is treated as if it were a modern, sin-city invention.

Though you can feel in your bones that a solemn cross-cultural romance is coming, the first section of the story moves along at an even clip until John Book's collapse. There's even a bit of visual comedy in the train station, when the little boy, in his black suit and broad black hat, thinks he sees another member of the sect: he walks over to an elderly Orthodox Jew, and the two look at each other in wordless rejection. But the narrative is becalmed during Book's recuperation at Rachel's farm, because the screenwriters (Earl W. Wallace and William Kelley) haven't provided him with any plan of action. When he rushes Rachel and the boy back to safety among the Amish, it's because he has learned that the killers are his superiors in the police department, who are involved in a twenty-million-dollar narcotics deal. But once he knows that, his mind seems to go dead. During his stay among the Amish, he gets out to a nearby town and phones the only cop he can trust—his partner—who wonders if they should go to a reporter or to the F.B.I. The suggestions seems to fall into a void, and Book just waits for the killers to track him down and show up at the farm. Maybe the movie is trying to tell us that the whole American system is so rotten that Book has no recourse—that there's no agency that isn't contaminated. Whatever the moviemakers had in mind, the way the story is set up there's nothing for us to look forward to but the arrival of the bad guys and the final fit of violence.

While we wait, *Witness* is a compendium of scenes I had hoped never to see again. There's the city person stranded in the sticks and learning to milk a cow, and—oh, yes—having to get up at 4:30 A.M. to do it. There's the scene with this city person sheepishly wearing clothes that are too short and look funny on him, so that the countrywoman can't restrain herself from giggling. There's the barn-raising (out of *Seven Brides for Seven Brothers*) and all the hearty fellowship that goes with it. There's the natural woman who stands bare-breasted and proud; in earlier American movies, the film frame used to cut her off at the bare shoulders, but you got the idea. *Witness* also takes first prize in the saying-grace department: a whole community of people bow their heads over their vittles. It's like watching the Rockettes kick. We can't have prayers in the public schools, but movies are making up for it.

Weir, an Australian filming in this country for the first time (*Witness* was shot in Pennsylvania), has succumbed to blandness. Book's stay at the farm is like a vacation from the real world; the rural images have a seductive lyricism that's linked to the little boy's dark, serious eyes. He's a subdued child—boyish only in his quiet curiosity and low-key playfulness. Lukas Haas is a good little actor—his shyness is lovely—but the moviemakers' conception of the boy is so idealized it's as if they'd never been driven nuts by the antics of a real, live child. This kid never develops beyond our first view of him. He doesn't argue with his mother, he doesn't complain, he doesn't make any noise. He's a miracle of politeness and obedience—a walking ad for fundamentalist orthodoxy. But Lukas Haas at least stays in his perfect character. As his mother, Kelly McGillis is like a model in a TV commercial that reproduces a seventeenth-century painting of a woman with a pitcher of water or milk. She shifts uneasily between the heroic naturalness of Liv Ullmann and the dimpled simpering of the young Esther Williams. She's so dimply sweet that when she's happy she's like a wholesome, strapping version of a Disney Mouseketeer.

The moviemakers try to balance things by introducing the suggestion that the sect is narrow-minded; Rachel is warned that her interest in John Book is causing talk among the Amish and could result in her being "shunned." But the whole meaning of the movie is that her life and her child's life are far better than anything the two could experience in the outside world. And, of course, John Book comes to love Rachel and her bonnet too much to want to expose her to the ugliness outside. (The spoiled city woman is represented here by Patti LuPone, who plays Book's divorcée sister—a tense urban type to the ultimate degree.) It's suggested that the women in the community don't take part in the decision-making, but never that there's anything basically repressive or stultifying about living in this authoritarian society without music* or dance, without phones or electricity, without the possibility of making friends in the outside world. The picture isn't interested in what life in such a closed-in community might actually be like for a woman or a child. The farm country is used as a fantasyland for the audience to visit; it has its allure, but you're ready to leave when Book goes—you wouldn't want to live there and get up at 4:30 A.M. and work like a plow horse. *Witness* uses the Amish simply as a way to refurbish an old plot. And as soon as you see Rachel's galumphing Amish suitor (Alexander Godunov), with his dear, mischievous grin, you know that the film is going to avoid any real collision of cultures, and the risk of giving offense. The suitor is there so that John Book can make the right, noble decision. He makes the decision for both himself and Rachel. The implication is that, coming from the world of violence and being a man who uses a gun—i.e., a sinner—he knows that there's no possibility of true happiness out there.

The picture is like something dug up from the earliest days of movies: it starts off, during the titles, with the wind blowing through the wheat, and the actors often looked posed. Weir seems less interested in the story than in giving the images a spiritual glow. (It's easy to imagine this picture being a favorite at the White House.) It must be said that Harrison Ford gives a fine, workmanlike performance, tempered with humor. The role doesn't allow him any chances for the kind of eerie intensity he showed in his small part as a burned-out Vietnam veteran in the 1977 *Heroes,* and he doesn't have the aura that he has as Han Solo and as Indiana Jones, but he burrows into the role and gives it as much honesty as it can hold. He's not an actor with a lot of depth, but he has an unusual rapport with the audience—he brings us right inside John Book's thoughts and emotions. Granting him all that, I must also admit that the only time I really warmed to him here was when he suddenly broke out of character and, his face lighting up demonically, parodied a TV commercial as he cried out, "Honey, that's *great* coffee!" (It's a free-floating joke, like Jack Nicholson's "Here's Johnny" in *The Shining.*) It's a measure of how sedate the movie is that you feel a twinge (as if you were being naughty) when you laugh.

But my instincts tell me that this idyllic sedateness could be the film's ticket to success. In its romanticism and its obviousness, *Witness* has got just about everything to be a *Lost Horizon* for the mid-eighties. There's the charming, obedient child, and there's the widow whose eyes flash as she challenges John Book to look at her nakedness. (And—I swear I didn't make this up—a storm is raging on the night she flashes him. It's the same storm that used to rage for Garbo when her passions rose.) There's the implicit argument that a religious community produces a higher order of human being than a secular society. There's something for just about everyone in this movie—even the holistic-medicine people. John Book's bullet wound

*When I wrote this, I forgot that the sect permitted some vocal music—the men sing after the barn-raising.

is healed by folk remedies: Rachel gives him herbal teas and applies poultices to the affected area. (I'm disposed to have some trust in the efficacy of these methods, but I still wish that just once somebody in a movie who was treated with humble ancient remedies would kick off.) Scenes like the one in which some showoff kids try to provoke the Amish to fight can be discussed by editorial writers and in schools. All those dug-up scenes are probably just what is going to sell the movie. There's a little paradox here: *Witness* exalts people who aren't allowed to see movies—it says that they're morally superior to moviegoers. It's so virtuous it's condemning itself.

The New Yorker, February 25, 1985

THE MAKIOKA SISTERS
GOLDEN KIMONOS

A friend of mine says that when you go to a Kon Ichikawa film "you laugh at things, and you know that Ichikawa is sophisticated enough to make you laugh, but you don't know why you're laughing." I agree. I've just seen Ichikawa's 1983 *The Makioka Sisters,* which opened in New York for a week's run and will open nationally in April, and although I can't quite account for my response, I think it's the most pleasurable movie I've seen in several months—probably since *Stop Making Sense,* back in November. The last hour (the picture runs two hours and twenty minutes) is particularly elating—it gives you a vitalizing mix of emotions. It's like the work of a painter who has perfect control of what color he gives you. At almost seventy, Ichikawa—his more than seventy movies include *Kagi, Fires on the Plain, An Actor's Revenge, Tokyo Olympiad*—is a deadpan sophisticate, with a film technique so masterly that he pulls you into the worlds he creates. There doesn't seem to be a narrative in *The Makioka Sisters,* yet you don't feel as if anything is missing. At first, you're like an eavesdropper on a fascinating world that you're ignorant about. But then you find that you're not just watching this film—you're coasting on its rhythms, and gliding past the precipitous spots. Ichikawa celebrates the delicate beauty of the Makioka sisters, and at the same time makes you feel that there's something amusingly perverse in their poise and their politesse. And he plays near-subliminal tricks. You catch things out of the corner of your eye and you're not quite sure how to take them.

The Junichiro Tanizaki novel on which the film is based was written during the Second World War and published in 1948, under the title *A Light Snowfall* (and it has been filmed twice before under this title—in 1950, by Yutaka Abe, and in 1959, by Koji Shima), but it has become known here as *The Makioka Sisters.* The women are the four heiresses of an aristocratic

Osaka family. Their mother died long ago, and their father, who was one of the big three of Japan's shipbuilders, followed. Tsuruko (Keiko Kishi), the eldest of the sisters, lives in the family's large, ancestral home in Osaka and controls the shrinking fortunes of the two unmarried young girls. The film is set in 1938, and the traditions in which these women were raised are slipping away, along with their money. Tsuruko and the next oldest, Sachiko (Yoshiko Sakuma), have married men who took the Makioka name, but its prestige has been tarnished by the behavior of the youngest of the sisters, Taeko (Yuko Kotegawa), who caused a scandal five years earlier, when she ran off with a jeweller's son and tried to get married, though the Makioka family's strict code of behavior required that Yukiko (Sayuri Yoshinaga), the next to youngest, had to be married first. The scandal was augmented, because the newspaper got things wrong—wrote that Yukiko had eloped and then, when Tsuruko's husband complained about the error, mucked things up more in correcting the mistake. Taeko still lives in Sachiko's home, along with Yukiko, but she's trying to achieve independence through a career. She wants to start a business, but Tsuruko won't give her her inheritance until she's married, and she isn't allowed to marry. It's Catch-22. She's flailing around, and waiting for the demure Yukiko to say yes to one of her suitors.

Each suitor is brought to a formal ceremony—a *miai*—where the prospective bride sits across a table from the prospective groom, with members of their families and go-betweens seated around them. At thirty, Yukiko is a veteran of these gatherings, but she has still not found a man to her liking. During the year that the movie spans, there are several of these *miai*—each a small slapstick comedy of manners. The last, when Yukiko finally meets what she has been waiting for (and the camera travels up the suitor's full height), has a special tickle for the audience, because you can see exactly why Yukiko said no to the others and why she says yes to this one.

These *miai* are just about the only formal, structured events; in between them, Taeko gets into highly unstructured emotional entanglements—falling in love with a photographer who becomes ill and dies, taking up next with a bartender, becoming pregnant, sampling a few lower depths, and planning to go to work, which means another scandal. While Taeko wears Western clothes and goes off on her own, the exquisite, subdued Yukiko stays in her sister's house. (The two married women's houses are like theatres-in-the-round, with the four sisters and the servants as each other's audience.) Is Yukiko the priss that her Southern-belle curls and her old-fashioned-girl manner suggest? Not by what you catch in glimpses. Yukiko, who clings to the hierarchic family values of the past, with all the bowing and the arch turning away of the head and the eyes cast down, is inscrutable, like Carole Laure in Blier's *Get Out Your Handkerchiefs*. But we see the come-on in her modesty. That's what's enchanting in the older sisters, too. Taeko, the animated modern girl, the one asserting her sexual freedom, is the last teasing, the least suggestive, but when she's with the others and in a kimono she's lovely. They're beauties, all four of them, with peerless skin tones, and they move as if always conscious that they must be visual poetry. (And they are, they are.)

Yukiko appears to be the most submissive, but she's strong-willed, and she has a sly streak. Living in Sachiko's house, she dresses with the door open to the hall Sachiko's husband passes through. And when she sees him looking at her bare thigh, she covers herself slowly, seductively. Sachiko, who observes what's going on, gets so fussed she starts tripping on her kimono and bumping into things. When she sees her husband kissing Yukiko, she crushes a piece of fruit in her fist and shoves it into her mouth to keep from crying out. And she renews her efforts to find Yukiko a suitable husband.

Ichikawa has said, in an interview, that he took his cue from the book's original title, *A Light Snowfall*. He said that light snow, which melts away instantly, "expresses something both fleeting and beautiful," and that he looked at the sisters in these terms. And that may help to explain why it's so difficult to pin down the pleasure the film gives. It's like a succession of evanescent revelations—the images are stylized and formal, yet the quick cutting melts them away. It's not as if he were trying to catch a moment— rather, he's trying to catch traces of its passing. When the four stroll among the cherry blossoms in Kyoto, the whole image becomes cherry-toned and they disappear.

Ichikawa's temperament brings something more furtive and glinting to the material than Tanizaki gave it in the novel. (In its spirit, the movie actually seems more closely related to other Tanizaki novels, such as *Kagi*, than it does to this one.) The film builds to its last hour; what's distinctive about the buildup is that the darts of humor don't allow you a full release. Taeko's first bid for independence involves becoming an artist, and her sisters speak of her work in perfectly level, admiring tones. Sachiko even pays for a show at a gallery. Taeko's art is the creation of dolls—exact, lifelike small reproductions of girls in heavy makeup and elaborate gowns, and with eyes that open and close. They could be little Makioka sisters. This is sneak-attack humor, played absolutely straight—Ichikawa is satirizing the material from within. And when this kind of suppressed joke plays right next to sequences such as a display of shimmering golden kimonos that the Makioka girls' father had bought for Yukiko's wedding presents, with one after another placed center screen—a glorious celebration of textures and color—an unusual kind of tension and excitement builds in the viewer.

I don't know enough about the Osaka culture to interpret the film as social criticism or as an elegy to a vanishing form of feminine grace. (Ichikawa himself comes from the Osaka area.) But the actresses are perfectly believable as the works of art that women like the Makioka sisters were trained to be. And it's easy to be entranced with the world that the film creates. (The industrialization of Japan is kept on the periphery.) When the banking company that Tsuruko's husband works for transfers him to Tokyo, and Tsuruko doesn't want to leave the Makioka home—a cool palace of polished wood that seems built on an intimate scale—you don't want to leave it, either. The rich colors, the darkness, the low-key lighting—they're intoxicating. When Tsuruko decides to make the move, and her husband falls to his knees to thank her, it has the emotional effect of a great love scene. But the film's finest moment comes at the very end. It's a variation of Joel McCrea's death scene in Peckinpah's *Ride the High Country,* when the old marshal falls out of the film frame. Yukiko is going off to be married; she boards the train in soft vanishing snow, and we realize that she meant far more to Sachiko's husband than a casual flirtation. We see him alone, getting drunk, and he looks terrible—he's all broken up. Then images of the four sisters among the cherry blossoms are held on the screen in slow motion that's like a succession of stills. At last there's only Yukiko's head in the center of the screen, and the head of her disconsolate brother-in-law passes across the screen behind her and out of her life.

The horrible thing about Peckinpah's recent death was that he was the most unfulfilled of great directors. Like Peckinpah, Ichikawa has had more than his share of trouble with production executives, but he has weathered it, and there's a triumphant simplicity about his work here. This venerable director is doing what so many younger directors have claimed to be doing: he's making visual music. The themes are worked out in shades of pearl and ivory for the interiors and bursts of color outside—cherry and maple and red-veined burgundy. He's making a movie that we understand musically, and he's doing it without turning the actors into zombies, and without losing his sense of how corruption and beauty and humor are all rolled up together.

The New Yorker, March 11, 1985

HEARTBREAKERS

Eli (Nick Mancuso) and Blue (Peter Coyote), the two central characters in *Heartbreakers,* are inseparable friends, and it's easy to perceive their longtime affection for each other. It's in the half looks they exchange; it's in the way they move down the street together, and in the things they take for granted. The movie is about what's underneath their buddy relationship: their competitiveness, their jealousy of each other, their resentments—all the unresolved feelings that go into making them rivals. Women are their battlefield. The darkly handsome Eli takes over his father's business (a women's-apparel factory), and he lives in a swank little house, drives a neat car, and isn't short of funds, so maybe there's a natural balance in the fact that the women he likes are attracted to Blue, a driven, unsuccessful painter, always broke.

Bobby Roth wrote and directed this low-budget feature (his fourth), and it was photographed on locations in his home town, Los Angeles, by the Berlin-born cinematographer Michael Ballhaus, whose wide-ranging credits include seventeen Fassbinder films. When Eli and Blue are hanging out at places like Fatburger or the gym The Sports Connection, they fit right in. Both in their mid-thirties, they're like hip American versions of the men in Bertrand Blier's *Get Out Your Handkerchiefs;* they're attractive to women and they have no trouble making out, but women mystify them. At the beginning of the movie, Blue realizes that Cyd (Kathryn Harrold), who has been living with him for five years in a loft with few of the amenities—it doesn't even have a real bed—is "slipping away" from him. She wants something more substantial than his idea of an artist's life; she complains that when he's painting he forgets all about her. Blue is sick at the thought of losing her, and he expresses his anxieties to Eli. But all he says to Cyd is "If you're not happy, leave," and despite her feelings for him she takes up with the attentive, dependable Chuck King (Max Gail), an abstractionist who sells and isn't as passionately involved in his work as Blue. (The paintings in this movie seem exactly right: King's patterned canvases look like Blue's description of them as wallpaper. If Blue were more generous, he might call them agreeable, workmanlike wallpaper.) Cyd's leaving Blue precipitates the events of the movie. Desperate to win her back, he tries to pull his life together. He quits his crummy job at a printshop—he tells the boss he can't stand printing porno stuff anymore. And then he talks a gallery owner into giving him a show by capitalizing on his (somewhat embarrassed) attraction to fetishes: he produces a series of high-camp Pop paintings—porny pinups that feature a dominatrix, Candy (the late Carol Wayne), decked out in a wig, high heels, garter belts, merry widows, and leather.

Meanwhile, Eli, who is shorter and more muscular than Blue, and looks younger and healthier, loses his father, takes on heavier business responsibilities, and, after years of doing well with women but feeling empty because they don't mean more to him than casual sex, spots the girl he thinks is *the* girl. Liliane (played by Carole Laure, the willowy French-Canadian actress who was the pivotal figure in the Blier film) is an assistant at the gallery where Blue is to have his show, but her principal occupation appears to be doing calisthenics, aerobics, and dance movements. (The results seem worth every bit of the compulsive effort.) When Liliane isn't working out, she's wiggling like an exotic temptress, with her long dark hair sheathing her snaky body. Carole Laure suggests a haunted, feverish sensuality, and she gets by with all of Liliane's sultry squirminess, even when the editing doesn't protect her and she's seen rolling her eyes like a latter-day Tondelayo (the sexy savage of *White Cargo* who drove men wild with lust). The key difference between Liliane and Tondelayo is that Liliane fancies herself a feminist. Her idea of controlling her life is to have sex with Eli in his car but refuse to go to bed with him; she's like a soulful dominatrix, and she keeps him spinning.

Roth doesn't quite sustain the Eli-and-Blue parallel-lives construction;

he seems more involved with Blue—maybe because he dealt with a character in Eli's situation in his film *The Boss' Son*. And there could be another reason. In photographs, Roth looks like a cross between Coyote's Blue and Mancuso's Eli, and in an interview with the *Times* he said that the two characters "were actually two sides of myself—the political artist side and the businessman-Jewish-son side—and they were based on composites of all my male friends." But he must have identified much more strongly with the artist side; the film couldn't be so full of tension and temperament if he hadn't. Roth has an intuitive feeling for movement—movement that appears natural yet is heightened. The picture doesn't look as if it had been photographed in separate shots; the movement seems fluid, continuous. There's always something going on between Mancuso and Coyote; they're a good team, even though Mancuso on his own is a dark, polite blank—Heathcliff out to lunch. He suggests a generic businessman-son, with no specifics and little personality—just a faint disaffection. (Eli is smooth-faced and withdrawn even in the hospital scene where his dying father—played by George Morfogen, who's a fine physical matchup—expresses contempt for him.)

Sometimes the characters open their mouths and what comes out isn't dialogue—it doesn't deepen the scene or move it along. And sometimes the characters simply don't have enough to say, and the scenes feel muffled or hollow, as if the director wasn't quite sure what he was getting at—as if he was hoping for a revelation. (Roth may need to work with a writer.) *Heartbreakers* engages a viewer, but it doesn't hold together in the memory, because it's all moods and moments, and much of the emotion swirling about is inchoate—for example, Liliane's weeping after sex, and even in the wonderful scene where Eli asks Blue to dance with Liliane so he can watch and torment himself. It's a mood-poem movie. (At times, it's like a more realistic Alan Rudolph film; at other times it's a little like one of Cassavetes' drunken-buddy pictures.) And the mood is basically set by Peter Coyote. He's more open to the camera than anyone else; his face and body say more. Mancuso's handsomeness is like a mask, but Coyote, who often looks ravaged, meets the other actors more than halfway. The women's attraction to him is convincing; their subsequent anger, disappointment, and depression are convincing, too.

Blue wants women to be around when he takes a break from his work; he doesn't want to be bothered when he's working. He expects the women he likes to be far more independent than they are—he is surprised to discover that he can't deal with them on his terms without hurting them. (The saddest is Candy, the hooker-model with the whips, who's a sweet, maternal pussycat.) The movie catches the confusion in the relations of the sexes without sentimentalizing that confusion. (Blue's name is the film's most sentimental touch, and it can be partly explained by the fact that his paintings are actually the work of the artist Robert Blue.) What binds the two guys is their bewilderment about women. They seem to blame each other for a good measure of their emotional frustration (and their rage erupts when they play racquetball).

The women in this movie are all likable, yet they're screwed-up and, from the men's point of view, utterly impossible. The women don't want the guys to be overprotective or to treat them as helpless, yet they expect to be taken care of. The men don't know which signals to follow, and the women don't know which signals they're sending out, because their feelings are contradictory. They want to be respected as modern, independent women, and they want to be cuddled like little girls. Courting Liliane, Eli keeps trying to tune in to whatever frequency she's operating on, but he never finds it. Blue can't believe that Cyd, who acknowledges that she loves him, will stay on with Chuck King. There's nothing dirty or spiteful or anti-woman in Roth's approach; it simply recognizes how insane all this is.

Heartbreakers deals with sex in a matter-of-fact way and in an American idiom—in our body language, with our shorthand, and in our lofts and apartments. The characters are frazzled in ways we recognize. Coyote's Blue looks like the kind of guy who has tended his boyishness over the years; he has the not-quite-grownup American look—an anguished boyishness. And when his sold-out show and his unaccustomed solvency don't bring Cyd back, his face takes on new expressions of uncertainty and pain. Blue's capacity for unconcealed suffering is what makes him Roth's hero. At the opening of the movie, when Blue is afraid he's losing Cyd, he goes to Eli's place to talk to him, and Eli and his date (Jamie Rose), who are giddy and charged up and just about to have sex, forget about it and take him out to comfort him. He really cares about Cyd, and that's more emotionally involving for them than the flirty relationship they were engaged in.

It's Blue's depth of emotion—what Eli calls his "passion"—that Eli can never forgive him for. It's what, in the framework of this movie, distinguishes the artist from the businessman. There's an undeniable element of fanciness in the conception, and I wish the movie weren't awed by Blue. Are his glossy pinups an expression of his passion? Or of something lesser—a callow obsession, perhaps, or even a way of taking revenge on Cyd? There's an element of revenge in Blue's becoming successful—he's showing her what she passed up. (Generally, the kind of close relationship between men that *Heartbreakers* is about doesn't last after one of them marries, and this might suggest that Blue isn't as serious about Cyd as he wants to believe he is.) Roth doesn't go deep enough, but he succeeds in using the two men as a way into the American culture of sex, circa the mid-eighties, and he captures something of West Coast bohemianism. He characterizes everyone; people who nod at Eli or Blue in a breakfast spot turn up again, and you begin to get a sense of them as the regulars in the places Eli and Blue go to. Blue has no illusions about the kind of gallery he's showing at; it's the hot gallery of the moment, run by a dealer (James Laurenson) who takes sixty per cent. But this dealer knows what he's up to, and he's as happy as a baby boy when he puts over an unknown like Blue. He prances in triumph, and sings "For I Am a Pirate King." Roth uses time-lapse photography as a comic device to show us the gallery filling up for the opening of Blue's show. When things are in full swing, Blue's old boss from the printshop comes over to congratulate him and to twit him, too, about his having been fed up with porno stuff; it's a fine small exhange.

If the movie is a little unformed, that's because Roth is attempting to be truthful to his own experience and the lives of those around him. He's trying to express lives in flux. This is the sort of attempt that usually turns into an unreleasable picture, a straining-for-seriousness embarrassment. But Roth has his wits about him, and Peter Coyote rings true whether he's drunkenly razzing Chuck King or sobbing in a crowded diner. *Heartbreakers* becomes more involving as it goes on, and when it's over, you feel you've seen something (even if you're not quite sure what).

The New Yorker, April 22, 1985

ONCE UPON A TIME IN AMERICA
TIDAL

When Sergio Leone's epic *Once Upon a Time in America* opened here in June, 1984, in a studio-hacked-down version (cut from three hours and forty-seven minutes to two hours and fifteen minutes), it seemed so incoherently bad that I didn't see how the full-length film could be anything but longer. A few weeks later, though, the studio people let me look at it, and I was amazed at the difference. I don't believe I've ever seen a worse case of mutilation. In the full version, the plot, which spans almost a half century, was still somewhat shaky, but Robert De Niro's performance as the Jewish gangster, Noodles, took hold, and the picture had a dreamy obsessiveness. I was excited about it and expected to review it a few weeks later, when it was to be released. But the opening was postponed, the weeks stretched into months, and by the time the full (or reasonably complete) epic showed at the New York Film Festival and began slipping into a few theatres, other films were making a more urgent claim.

There's a special reason it lacked urgency: like the rest of Sergio Leone's work, *Once Upon a Time in America* has no immediacy, no present tense. And being in many ways a culmination of his career it's probably the least anchored of his films. Leone, who grew up in the Italian studio world (his father, Vincenzo Leone, was a pioneer director), isn't interested in observing the actual world—it probably seems too small and confining. He's involved in his childhood fixations about movies—stories enlarged, simplified, mythicized. (He only makes epics.) There's no irony in the title: he uproots American Westerns and gangster pictures and turns them into fairy tales and fantasies. In this movie, a Jewish deli on the Lower East Side in 1921 is on a street as broad as Park Avenue and has a storeroom the size of a football field. Leone doesn't care about the fact that it was the crowded, constricting buildings that drove the kids into the streets. He directs as if he had all the time in the world, and he has no interest in making his characters lifelike; he inflates their gestures and slows down their actions—every lick of the lips is important.

After we've seen conventional gangster pictures, the characters may become enlarged in our memories because of what they do and how the actors look as they're doing it. Leone doesn't bother to develop the characters—to him, they're mythic as soon as he puts them on the screen. And in this movie, though he gives almost an hour to the childhood years of his gang of six Jewish boys (and a couple of girls), the camera solemnizes and celebrates these kids of ten and twelve and fourteen from the start. It's like watching the flamboyant childhood of the gods. In a sense, what Leone gives us is predigested reveries; it's escapism at a further remove—a dream-begotten dream, but a feverish one, intensified by sadism, irrational passions, vengeance, and operatic savagery. (In the genre he created, the spaghetti Western, the protagonist didn't wait for his enemies to draw; he shot first.) Leone has found the right metaphor here: the movie begins and ends in an opium den, where Noodles puffs on a pipe while episodes of his life of killings and rapes and massacres drift by and a telephone rings somewhere in the past. The action is set in 1921, 1933, and 1968—but not in that order.

In its full length, the movie has a tidal pull back toward the earliest memories, and an elegiac tone. Partly, I think, this is the result of De Niro's measured performance. He makes you feel the weight of Noodles' early experiences and his disappointment in himself. He makes you feel that Noodles never forgets the past, and it's his all-encompassing guilt that holds the film's different sections together. De Niro was offered his choice of the two leading roles—Max, the go-getter, the tricky, hothead boss of the group, and the watchful, indecisive Noodles, the loser, who spends the years from 1921 to 1933 in prison. I respect De Niro's decision, because he may have thought that the passive Noodles, whose urges explode in bursts of aggression against women, would be a reach, would test him. But I think he made a mistake in terms of what was best for the movie, which, despite its hypnotic bravura, lacks the force at its center that a somewhere-between-twenty-one-and-forty-five-million-dollar epic (depending on who is asked) needs. James Woods, who plays Max, dominated the short version; he actually provided its brighter moments, and it's a sad thing when you go to a movie and look forward to seeing James Woods, whose specialty is acting feral. In the full version, De Niro gives the film its dimensions. He keeps a tiny flame alive in his eyes, and his performance builds, but Leone doesn't provide what seems essential: a collision between Noodles and Max—or, at least, some development of the psychosexual tensions that are hinted at. (When

Noodles and Max are young teen-agers and are murderously beaten by a rival gang, Noodles lies writhing and Max crawls toward him—it's like Jennifer Jones and Gregory Peck at the end of *Duel in the Sun*.) The film's theme is the betrayal of the immigrants' dream of America; Max—ever greedy for more money, more power—represents the betrayer. By leaving the two men's competition and love-hate as just an undercurrent, the film chokes off its dramatic core. And Noodles often seems to be contemplating his life instead of living it. He's at his most assured—he comes into his own—when Noodles is about sixty; there's something old about him from the start. (No one is less likely to be called Noodles.)

Leone wants the characters to be as big as the characters he saw on the screen when he was a child, and he tries to produce that effect with looming closeups and heroic gestures; the key thing for his actors is to have the right look. Yet, despite his having breathed and talked this movie for almost ten years before he started production, he made some flagrant mistakes when he got down to the casting. After you've seen his *Once Upon a Time in the West,* you can't get the iconographic faces (Henry Fonda, Charles Bronson, Jason Robards, Woody Strode, Claudia Cardinale, Jack Elam, and all the others) out of your mind. But it's almost impossible to visualize all of the five adult gang members in *America,* even right after you've seen the movie. Worse, they don't have the basic movie-gangster characteristic: they don't emanate danger. And although Deborah, the dancer-actress that Noodles loves all his life, is marvellously vivid in her young girlhood, when she's played by Jennifer Connelly (who's so clear-eyed she walks away with the twenties passages), the role of the adult Deborah is taken over by Elizabeth McGovern, who's classically miscast. McGovern's hairstyle is ferocious, she's unflatteringly photographed, and she moves like a woman who has never got used to being tall. She looks dispirited, and the flair she shows in her comedy roles isn't visible—she's so bad you feel sorry for her. (She's also the victim of a glitch in the film's time scheme: Deborah goes off to Hollywood in 1933, and then we learn in 1968 that she's now a big star.) McGovern's inability to live up to the idea that she's De Niro's great love weakens the film's showpiece romantic sequence, set in a vast Art Deco oceanfront restaurant on Long Island—a restaurant that is closed for the season but that Noodles has rented for the evening, with a full staff and a dance orchestra. The scene is meant to reveal Noodles' yearning nature; it's clear that Leone was thinking about Gatsby and lost dreams.

The other actresses fare much better. Tuesday Weld is in peak form as a nympho moll who becomes Max's girl. She isn't doing that anomic acting that made her tedious in films like *Play It As It Lays* and *Who'll Stop the Rain;* she looks great, and she has a gleam of perversity. She brings the film some snap and humor, and Woods has his best scene when he's elated at showing the other guys how little she means to him—it may be the best scene he has ever played. And, as a young woman that Noodles takes up with, Darlanne Fleugel is Art Deco incarnate; streamlined and blond, she wears her sleek thirties gowns with spectacular ease. Her performance is simple and in beautiful control, and De Niro has a relaxed elegance around her. The film could have used much more of her; she sets off its architectural motifs—its arches and scallop shapes.

Unlike Westerns, where everything is even literally out in the open, gangster movies have a special appeal: we want to know more about the concealed lives of these hidden outlaws, and how they work. (That was part of the excitement of the *Godfather* pictures—the fullness of the crime-family details.) Leone doesn't have enough interest in the real world to make the gang's dealings with bigger mobs and its union tie-ins even halfway intelligible. That's a real disappointment. You can't figure out the logistics of the crimes; you don't know what's going on. What's probably going on is that Leone, with his dislocated myths, is like Noodles amid the poppy fumes— he's runing old movies in his head. There's nothing in the movie to differentiate Jewish crime from Italian crime or any other kind. Leone's vision of Jewish gangsters is a joke. As a friend of mine put it, "it wasn't just that you never had the feeling that they were Jewish—you never had the feeling that they were anything."

The movie isn't really about America or about Jewish gangsters. But you can see why Leone was drawn to the subject: it was to create his widescreen dreamland view of the Lower East Side. That setting, filmed partly on a Brooklyn street near the waterfront, with the Williamsburg Bridge in the background, partly in Montreal, and partly on constructed sets in Rome, made it possible for him to transmute the Lower East Side settings of American gangster films—to give the genre a richer, more luxuriant visual texture. It's typical of Leone's grandiloquent style that the opium den, in the back room of a Chinese theatre, is sumptuous and large. And the Long Island restaurant that we see is impossibly lyrical and grand (the building is actually the Excelsior Hotel in Venice); it has to be archetypal for Leone, and it has to have an aura. Even though some of what he shows you defies common sense, visually he justifies his lust for the largest scale imaginable. He uses deep focus to draw details from the backgrounds into your awareness. The film is drenched in atmosphere, and you see more and more in the wide frames. You see howlers, too. One of my favorites is the gang's storing its booty of a million dollars in a locker in Grand Central in the twenties and Noodles' going to retrieve it in the thirties. But I imagine that if anybody had explained to Leone that those lockers were cleared every seventy-two hours he'd have brushed the fact aside as mere realism.

Just about all the incidents (including the palatial rented restaurant and the loot in the locker) echo scenes in Hollywood's gangster movies. There's the heart-tugger: the youngest and littlest member of the gang is the first to be killed. There's the black-humor gag: Max drives a hearse to pick up Noodles at the penitentiary gates, with a hooker who's ready and waiting stowed in a coffin. About all that's missing is that Noodles, being Jewish, doesn't have a boyhood friend who becomes a priest. Leone reworks the old scenes and embroiders on them. Our group of gangsters meet Tuesday Weld (and Noodles rapes her) in the course of an out-of-town robbery, when they're wearing hankies over their faces; when they encounter her again in New York, they reintroduce themselves by tying their hankies on their faces. (The fellows ask her to guess which one raped her, and they unzip.)

The movie might seem a compendium of kitsch—in a certain sense, it is. But it's kitsch aestheticized by someone who loves it and sees it as the poetry of the masses. It isn't just the echoing moments that keep you absorbed. It's those reverberant dreamland settings and Leone's majestic, billowing sense of film movement; the images seem to come at you in waves of feeling. Despite the film's miscasting and its craziness, Leone sustains the moods for an almost incredible three hours and forty-seven minutes—most of it unusually quiet. The movie has a pulse; it's alive. But not now. It's alive in some golden-brown past of the imagination.

The New Yorker, May 27, 1985

THE SHOOTING PARTY AND RAMBO: FIRST BLOOD PART II

The first thing that charmed me about *The Shooting Party*, which is set in the English countryside in the autumn of 1913, was the swiftness and wit with which we are introduced to the characters. A large number of landed gentry, aristocrats, servants, gamekeepers, beaters, and loaders have gathered at the Nettleby estate for a three-day shoot, and the camera, flitting like a butterfly, hovers over a couple of people talking about someone else, whirls over to that person in conversation, and from there to whoever is being talked about, and so on. This Alan Bridges film isn't merely based on Isabel Colegate's 1980 novel; it's a film of the novel, a transcription in the literal sense—"the arrangement of a composition for a medium other than that for which it was originally written." It's a novel acted out for us. But by devices such as those hovering, whirling introductions, and by the quality of the performances, and the economy and fleeting elegance of the whole production, Alan Bridges carries the "Masterpiece Theatre" approach to the level of art.

The novel is highly compressed: it's a set of variations on the end-of-an-era theme, with dozens of characters in less than two hundred pages. Colegate sets them up, one by one, in a few sentences—deft, sneaky details of their backgrounds—and then lets them speak for themselves. The dialogue is sly and pithy. At times, it's reminiscent of Oscar Wilde, and the adapter, Julian Bond, hasn't tried to improve on it. Whole scenes have the Colegate verbal rhythms intact, and a viewer can bask in the beautiful bounce and precision of the dialogue, which is spoken by the kind of cast you assemble when you fantasize about who should be in the movie of a novel you've just read. It's a dream of a cast.

James Mason is the aging baronet Nettleby, the host, whose wife (Dorothy Tutin), we are given to understand, used to be a gregarious creature, always on the go. Now she's content to bicker with the head gardener, keep an eye on her grandchildren, and play a killer game of bridge. Nettleby is the central figure—the embodiment of the values that are already frayed and will disintegrate in the war to come. And James Mason, in his final movie (he died last July, at seventy-five), goes out in glorious style. His Nettleby is a supremely civilized man; he sees other people for what they are, but he also sees the reasons for it. He speaks harsh words to only one person, the cold fish Lord Hartlip (Edward Fox), whom he reprimands for "not shooting like a gentleman," and he does so in a tone of pained regret. Mason uses a mild, aging man's voice in this role, and his querulous, cracked inflections make us smile. His face and, especially, that plangent voice are so deeply familiar that when we see him in a role that does him justice there's something like an outpouring of love from the audience to the man on the screen.

Mason validates our feelings: he uses his own physical deterioration for the role, yet he never turns into a grand old man or indulges in a quaver that isn't a funny, integral part of the country squire who's conscious that he's ineffectual—that he's losing his grip. In a scene midway, Nettleby, who breeds game birds on the estate so that he can provide his guests with these splendid shooting sprees, is confronted by a protester, played by John Gielgud, who marches into the middle of the shoot carrying a placard that says "Thou Shalt Not Kill," and the old squire and the old zealot—each, in his own way, disaffected—converse. The scene is right out of the novel, but Mason and Gielgud are like soft-shoe artists; they bring suavity to their teamwork, with Mason matching his melancholy warble to Gielgud's melodious whine. They're even more hilarious than Gielgud and Ralph Richardson were on the stage in *No Man's Land*, because that was just two great actors sparring; here the two can tease each other from inside the characters they're playing. They're so amused they're almost laughing—they're in actors' heaven. And when, toward the close of the film, Mason has a scene that's overladen with the possibilities of pathos and grandeur—it's a scene with Gordon Jackson as a poacher whose cussedness the squire has come to respect—he pulls back; he underplays, magically. No one could accuse James Mason of not acting like a gentleman.

Bridges, whose 1982 film *The Return of the Soldier* opened here in February, has a special gift for these evocations of a world seen in a bell jar, and now, with Geoffrey Reeve as producer and Fred Tammes as cinematographer, he has refined his techniques. A late bloomer (he was born in 1927), Bridges goes beyond being pictorial and literary. He sharpens the novel's wry observations on the Edwardian era and at the same time infuses a sensuous sweetness into the material. The film isn't Chekhovian, exactly (though Mason is); it's more like a distillation of what's alluring about the Masterpiece Theatre productions—wonderful actors, given the chance to speak a celebrated writer's lines. And it's brought off with a sovereign ease. On TV, a novel like *The Shooting Party* would be a six-part series, full of longueurs, and shorteurs, too. Here, after we've met the key members of the party, the movie puts us (as the novel does) among actions and conversations going on simultaneously. And as the events become more intense Bridges picks up the pace and tightens the film's emotional hold on us. Many of his performers are veterans of the prestigious series shows with which he has long been associated, but actresses such as Cheryl Campbell (who was Vera Brittain in "Testament of Youth") and Judi Bowker (who was in "The Glittering Prizes") make a stronger impression in their brief screen time than they do in their much longer stints on TV—maybe because the pictorial setups are held so long on TV that we tire of them, and the images don't stay with us. As Lady Aline, the flighty, adulterous wife of Edward Fox's Lord Hartlip, who disgraces himself in the shoot, Cheryl Campbell is at one moment a pert-faced, nosy gossip, and at the next a tantalizing sensualist being caressed by her own long, wavy blond hair. It's a quicksilver performance that recalls Joan Greenwood at her most seductive. And Judi Bowker as the guileless Lady Olivia, the wife of thickheaded Lord Lilburn (Robert Hardy), looks at the camera with a direct gaze that makes her seem infinitely beautiful. When the tall, slim young barrister Lionel Stephens (Rupert Frazer) declares his love for her, you think, Of course—how could he look into her clear eyes and not imagine depths of mystery?

The movie has a few misdirected elements. One is a small subplot involving a love letter that Stephens writes to Olivia and then tears up and tosses into a wastebasket, from which it's retrieved by a young footman, who copies it and gives it to the servant girl he's courting. (She's a prosaic soul and disapproves of it as tosh.) Somehow, this episode comes through confusingly. And there's also some fuzziness about the identity of several of the characters. Though it doesn't really matter which of the assembled people are related to the Nettlebys, we don't know that at first, and I kept wondering which of them were the Nettlebys' children. It turns out that they have only a son, who is a diplomat and is out of the country, and that his wife, Ida (Sarah Badel), is the mother of all four grandchildren, including the flirtatious nineteen-year-old Cicely (Rebecca Saire) and the ten-year-old Osbert (Nicholas Pietrek), who has a pet mallard named Elfrida Beetle. We—and several of the guests and servants—fear for Elfrida when she's loose on the grounds on the third day; that's the day the shooters, having dispatched hundreds of pheasants, rabbits, and woodcocks, go after ducks.

Does it seem arch or frivolous that the characters fuss over a little boy's possible loss of a pet duck in a movie that's ostensibly about the Twilight of the Empire? Actually, it's Elfrida and all the other singularities that form this vision of an aristocracy reduced to playing games of death. Yes, we can see that the advancing line of beaters and the line of shooters with their loaders behind them are like lines of soldiers, and we recognize that these expensively got-up people, who regard their class as the flowering of the social order, and the British Empire as the best there has ever been, are on the edge of oblivion. Once again, a shooting party is being used as a symbol for the greater violence to come. But Colegate's tone is lightly self-mocking. (The moviemakers didn't find a way to adapt one of the elements that link with the Gielgud character and round out Colegate's conception. She sees the pheasants as fed and protected from predators, then cast forth from their Eden and "forced to take to the air reluctantly—heavy birds, a flight of more than a few feet exhausts them—forced up and out to meet a burst of noise and a quick death in that bright air.")

What keeps the picture from abstractness and overfamiliarity is that it's full of the English affection for gentle lunacy. Gordon Jackson plays the poacher as Colegate described him: "His conversational manner had always tended towards the histrionic." Aline Hartlip, who sees herself as passion's plaything, also manages to cadge some money from her hostess. The wide-eyed Olivia, never having had a romantic thought about Lionel Stephens, responds to his avowal of love—and the news he brings that their souls knew each other before—with the sudden discovery that, yes, she loves him, too.

The movie is about the tight fit of the jacket worn by the Hungarian count (Joris Stuyck) and the way Nettleby refers—fondly—to the immensely rich Sir Reuben Hergesheimer (Aharon Ipalé) as "the Israelite." It's about the traditions, loyalties, and idiosyncrasies that bind a social order. It's about the ceremonies of dressing for dinner and becoming part of the procession to go into the dining room and being seated at the table, where conversation is a form of theatre. Most of all, it's about how, given the chance, actors can take us beyond what we read in a book. Edward Fox, a master of twisted psyches and gnarled vocal tones, can make us feel the loneliness inside the miserable, arrogant Hartlip, who has nothing to be proud of except his reputation as the best shot in England—a reputation that Lionel Stephens, without giving the matter much thought, challenges. And Dorothy Tutin wraps the role of Lady Minnie Nettleby around her like a dowdy old sweater. (I enjoyed even the unplanned things, like the way Robert Hardy's fatuous Lord Lilburn recalls Nigel Bruce as the stocky, expostulating Dr. Watson, and the way Gielgud from some angles is a ringer for I. B. Singer.)

The Shooting Party isn't likely to appeal to the teen-agers at the shopping mall. What would they make of the characters' allusions to Ruskin and to George Meredith's *The Egoist*, which have been retained from the novel, or of a remark (Julian Bond's addition) that Lady Minnie makes to Lady Aline—"I've always thought your men more Ibsenite than Chekhovian"? (I'm not sure I know what to make of that, either.) There's probably no more preciously literate scene in movies than the explanation of how Elfrida Beetle got her name, but the scene is consciously, whimsically silly. This is one of the rare movies that can be said to be for an educated audience without that being a putdown.

■ ■ ■

Rambo: First Blood Part II explodes your previous conception of "overwrought"—it's like a tank sitting on your lap firing at you. Jump-cutting from one would-be high point to another, *Rambo* is to the action film what *Flashdance* was to the musical, with one to-be-cherished difference: audiences are laughing at its star and progenitor, Sylvester Stallone, who comes across as a humanoid Christ figure with brown leather skin and symmetrical scars. Rambo has been programmed with (a) homoeroticism, (b) self-pity, (c) self-righteousness, (d) sweat, and (e) an insatiable need to be crucified over and over. He has a sour pout on his face, and he's given to deep, enigmatic utterances, such as "To survive a war you have to become war."

According to *Rambo*, we didn't lose the war in Vietnam—the United States soldiers weren't allowed to win it. And when it ended, our government made a deal to pay war reparations of four and a half billion dollars to North Vietnam for the return of our captured men, then reneged on the deal and tried to forget all about the prisoners of war.* Rambo goes in and brings a bunch of survivors out. Of course, he has his moments of pleasure: he has bits of his flesh sliced off by a sadistic, Nazi-like Russian (Steven Berkoff), he's spread-eagled on an electrified rack by torturers who think they can make him talk, he's branded in the face with a red-hot knife, he's immersed in pig glop while hanging crucifixion style. And, boy-oh-boy, what this killer Christ does to those Commies! He shoots them with his bow and arrows—arrows with explosive points that send them up in fireballs.

The jungle greenery is very lustrous; the cinematographer, Jack Cardiff, gets something of the effect in color that Josef von Sternberg got in black-and-white in a studio-made jungle in his 1953 *Anatahan*—it's as if each leaf had been oiled and buffed. And with the bare-chested Stallone slipping through these leaves the effect is mighty odd: you're supposed to be intoxicated by his lumpy muscles. The way he's photographed, he's huge—our national palooka—and the small Vietnamese in their ill-fitting uniforms don't look as if they had a muscle (or a brain) among them. They just stand around stupidly, waiting to be blown up; you may want to yell at them "Take cover!" But who could be heard above the soundtrack alerting you to watch for the next killing, and the audience's catcalls and the giggly cheers for Rambo's Zen marksmanship and his gorgeous fireballs? (The film reaches climax when two boats crash in flames.) The director, George P. Cosmatos, gives this near-psychotic material—a mixture of Catholic iconography and

*There is some factual basis for this: in 1973, President Nixon promised President Pham Van Dong $3.25 billion in U.S. economic aid, but Congress refused to grant the money.

Soldier of Fortune pulp—a veneer of professionalism, but the looniness is always there. Rambo's old Green Beret colonel calls him "a pure fighting machine," yet, like Rocky, Rambo always has to have bigger guys in his movies—real bruisers, like the Russian giant here—to beat him up. We mustn't forget that his namesake is Arthur *(A Season in Hell)* Rimbaud: trying to explain Rambo to a corrupt official, the colonel says, "What you choose to call hell, he calls home."

What Sylvester Stallone chooses to call a movie is a wired-up version of the narcissistic jingoism of the John Wayne–Second World War pictures. Its comic-strip patriotism exploits the pent-up rage of the Vietnam vets who feel that their country mistreated them after the war, and it preys on the suffering of the families who don't know what happened to their missing-in-action sons or brothers, fathers or husbands. A Sylvester Stallone hit movie has the same basic appeal as professional wrestling or demolition derbies: audiences hoot at it and get a little charged up at the same time.

David Morrell, whose novel *First Blood* was the basis of the first Rambo picture, has written the novelization of this sequel, from the screenplay by Stallone and James Cameron. It's a love letter to Rambo's weaponry—his nasty serrated knife and his bow and exploding arrows. In the author's note at the front of the book, Morrell tells us who "created" the weapons and where we should write to order them. I can hardly wait for my set to arrive.

The New Yorker, June 17, 1985

PRIZZI'S HONOR AND THE HOME AND THE WORLD
RIPENESS

If John Huston's name were not on *Prizzi's Honor,* I'd have thought a fresh new talent had burst on the scene, and he'd certainly be the hottest new director in Hollywood. The picture has a daring comic tone—it revels voluptuously in the murderous finagling of the members of a Brooklyn Mafia family, and rejoices in their scams. It's like *The Godfather* acted out by The Munsters, with passionate, lyrical arias from Italian operas pointing up their low-grade sentimentality. The 1982 novel, by Richard Condon, is a lively, painless read. His riffs about the corruption of American business and politics have a rote paranoia—they have no sting—but the characters are entertainingly skewed, and the story moves along and keeps you smiling. The movie does something more. When it's over, you may think of slight resemblances to *Beat the Devil* and *The Maltese Falcon,* but its tone is riper. The behavior on the screen is bizarrely immoral, but it has the juice of everyday family craziness in it. And the zest that goes into the Prizzis' greediest swindles is somehow invigorating. You'd think this movie was the work of a young director because of the elation you feel while it's on, and afterward, too. Even *The Man Who Would Be King* didn't have the springiness that this has. The only thing about *Prizzi's Honor* that suggests a veteran director, or even hints at Huston's age (he's seventy-eight), is the assurance of his control. He directed this movie (his fortieth) on pure instinct—on the sum of everything he knows. It's as if his satirical spirit had become irrepressible—the devil in him made him do it.

Huston has a cast of devil's helpers, who have been coached in the jerky rhythms and combative dialect of Sicilian Brooklynese by the actress-playwright Julie Bovasso. She played John Travolta's mother in *Saturday Night Fever* and its sequel, and that's who they talk like. They sound like truculent trolls. As Charley Partanna, the enforcer (i.e., hit man) for the brotherhood, Jack Nicholson has added a facial effect: his upper lip puffs out and curls under, which thickens Charley's speech. (When he's fully in character, he's frog-faced and fishy-eyed, like a blown-up Elisha Cook, Jr.) Charley is a loyal and dedicated company man, but he's not too sharp; he's like a hardhat who's only good at his trade—he needs to be cranked up to think. And Nicholson's performance is a virtuoso set of variation of your basic double take and traditional slow burns. At times, Charley is like Jackie Gleason's vain Ralph Kramden in "The Honeymooners": he seems to want to waddle and shake more rolls of flesh than he's got. (Like Kramden, he wants to occupy a bigger space in the world.) Then he'll go limp and lacklustre, like Art Carney's Ed Norton. Nicholson's Charley plugs the "Honeymooners" kind of ordinariness into this Mafia world. And when he falls for a West Coast girl—a Polish blonde, Irene (Kathleen Turner), whom he meets at the Prizzi wedding that opens the movie—he's like a man conked out by a truckload of stardust. He's gaga. But Nicholson doesn't overdo his blurred expressions or his uncomprehending stare; he's a witty actor who keeps you eager for what he'll do next. There are reasons for audiences' good will toward him: he'll do anything for the role he's playing, and he has a just about infallible instinct for how far he can take the audience with him.

Charley's essential average-guyness is the movie's touchstone: this is a baroque comedy about people who behave in ordinary ways in grotesque circumstances. The Condon book is a takeoff on *The Godfather,* and Huston follows it right down to putting a spin on the details (like the quick glimpse of the wedding couple, so you can see that the bridegroom is shorter than the bride), but the parody isn't too broad—not even with Nicholson's inflated upper lip complementing Brando's pushed-out lower lip. (In a scene in which Charley, the romantic clod, is told that he is to be the next head of the family, Nicholson produces a small, eye-rolling flourish: for an instant—a passing shade of thought—he sees himself as Brando, the don.)

The title is, of course, satiric. The movie is about what the Prizzis do in the name of honor. Old Don Corrado Prizzi (William Hickey) is a shrunken little man, ghouley and wormy, with tiny, shocking bright eyes. These slitted, almost closed eyes are so alive they jump out at you. (They're like the director's eyes—they're the soul of the movie.) At eighty-four, this slippery master chiseller snoozes most of the time, but he still runs the mob, and he's plotting his "monument"—a banking maneuver that should net the family some seventy million dollars. Hickey, an esteemed New York acting coach, actually in his fifties, has always had a special energy, and his mock seriousness here is just what the mummified old don needs. Don Corrado can barely walk anymore (he shuffles), but he lives to rook people, and Hickey makes you feel the mean joy he takes in it. When the don wants to say something, he doesn't speak, exactly—he is so much into his own rhythms that he sing-songs his remarks. But age hasn't softened him. And an old don has an advantage that other oldsters don't have: when this little geezer gives orders to the members of his family, they obey.

Don Corrado's two sons are big men. The firstborn, Dominic (Lee Richardson), who's in his sixties, runs the dirty side of the operations; the younger, better-educated, and slicker Eduardo (Robert Loggia), who's in his fifties, handles the "legitimate" investments and mingles with financial leaders and high-ranking men in government. Richardson and Loggia play their roles just tilted enough for you to register what it's like for men Dominic's and Eduardo's ages to be dominated—still—by their father: it keeps all their childhood tensions going.

The member of the family who is closest in spirit to the tricky old don is his granddaughter Maerose (Anjelica Huston), whose eyes are never at rest, either. Dominic, Maerose's rigid-minded father, has made her a family outcast, because some years earlier, when she and Charley were engaged and got into a scrap, she took off in a drunken rage and had an affair. She has been exiled to Manhattan, where she works as an interior decorator, but she's as busy plotting as the don himself. As Anjelica Huston plays her, the raven-haired Maerose is a Borgia princess, a high-fashion Vampira who moves like a swooping bird and talks in a honking Brooklynese that comes out of the corner of her twisted mouth. Anjelica Huston seems to have grown into her bold features: she's a flinty beauty here—she has the imperiousness of a Maria Callas or a Silvana Mangano. And, with that Brooklyn cabbie's diction, and Maerose's fixation on vengeance against her father, Anjelica Huston is an inspired comedienne, especially when she parodies penitence and sidles into a room dolorously, her head hanging on her shoulder. The stunning Maerose loves scandalizing the family, and comes to the wedding—the bride is her younger sister—in a scarlet-banded, one-shouldered black gown. Maerose has more in her face than anyone else has; she has irony and the strangeness of what's hidden. She's like a bomb ticking away in the background of the movie.

By contrast, Kathleen Turner's ravishingly pretty Irene seems pallid. Turner has built up a lot of audience good will, too, and she has her moments; Irene's intonations are hilariously ritualized when, after participating in a kidnap and a murder, she chirps "See you at dinner" to Charley and pecks him like a suburban housewife as he drives off with the kidnap victim.

But her role doesn't really develop, and it suffers from an omission: Irene needs a scene to show the shift in her from the woman who's playing Charley for a sap—the woman who smiles to herself when she's got him hooked—and the woman who warms to the adoration of such a big man in the Mafia. (Charley is the kind of romantic who, after they've declared their love for each other, in a swank Mexican restaurant in L.A., takes note of what the orchestra is playing and says, "This is gonna be our song.") And Turner is at a disadvantage: Irene isn't from Brooklyn and doesn't have the chance to talk in the clan's comic lingo.

The central group is completed by Charley's father, Angelo "Pop" Partanna (John Randolph), who is the Prizzis' *consigliere* and Don Corrado's closest friend. As Condon described Pop, his "sweetness and amiable good cheer about murder and corruption were legendary in the environment," and that's how Randolph plays him. He's always beaming, and when he looks at Charley, the hit man, the crinkles around his eyes radiate all over his face: there never was a father who took greater pleasure in his son. When the two are together, we see the father-son relationship in its ideal form. These two confide in each other the way fathers and sons do in storybooks for boys. I don't think Randolph has ever done anything this mellow before: Pop is overflowing with happiness, and when, toward the end, the kidnap and killing (which are tied in with the banking maneuver) cause unforeseen troubles, the childlike anxiety in his face suggests a perturbed saint.

It's impossible to say who's happier—Pop, who dotes on his son, or Don Corrado, who has always had his own way. Or the audience. I found myself laughing all the way through. Though some people don't respond to the movie at all, laughter seems to bubble up in most of us. Probably that's because characters like Pop and the don are only slightly warped versions of other doting parents, other tyrants. It's the context of Mafia connivery that makes their happiness, like Charley's romanticism, seem blissfully silly. (Being a mobster appears to produce the same result as a lobotomy: some vital connection in the brain is severed.)

Huston has made a character comedy out of Condon's prankish satire of American corruption. He has been so confident and free that he has included moviemaking jokes, like the use of obvious stock shots of planes whipping back and forth across the country to represent Charley and Irene carrying on their coast-to-coast romance. The characters come equipped with certain eccentricities of the "environment," such as the habit—apparently developed among people who make inordinate amounts of money—of saying "a dollar" when they mean a thousand dollars. When they refer to seven hundred and twenty dollars, they're actually talking about heavy cash. Except for the failure to round out Irene's character, the script, by Condon and, later, Janet Roach (who worked on the structuring of the scenes), is a beauty, and the Alex North score, with its lush, parodistic use of Puccini, and some Rossini, a little Verdi, and a dash of Donizetti, too, actively contributes to the whirling texture of the scenes. Even the musical jokes that you're not quite conscious of work on you, and the music seems to bring out the lustre of Andrzej Bartkowiak's cinematography. Everything in this picture works with everything else—which is to say that John Huston has it all in the palm of his big, bony hand.

You can feel a prickly excitement in the theatre. It's the kind of excitement that makes you say, "God, I love movies"—or, at least, "God, I love this movie."

■　　■　　■

It's a different kind of love that Satyajit Ray's *Ghare-Baire,* or *The Home and the World,* brings out, but it's love all right. Adapted from a novel that Rabindranath Tagore wrote in 1912 (Ray prepared a script for it in the forties, long before he made his first film, *Pather Panchali*), it deals with a great modern subject that has come up in Ray's work over and over: the emancipation of women, and what it does to them and to the men who love them. This is central to *Ghare-Baire,* which is the story of the emergence of a young wife from the seclusion and ignorance of purdah into the complexities of becoming more fully human—or, at least, adult—and having choices. The core situation is much like the one in James Joyce's play *Exiles*—the husband, in his pride, wanting the wife to be free to be faithful—but that's only the film's starting point.

Victor Banerjee (the Dr. Aziz of *A Passage to India*) is Nikhil, a maharajah in Bengal with a Western education and liberal views. His wife, Bimala (Swatilekha Chatterjee), is conventional in her beliefs, and is content to live in the women's quarters of his palace and be visible to no man except him. But he loves her and is proud of her, and wants her to be a modern woman, able to move in the world. She first saw him at their wedding: how will he ever know whether she really loves him if she doesn't have the opportunity to choose him—to prefer him to other men? For ten years, Bimala is taught by an English governess and encouraged to think for herself and develop her creativity. At last, in 1907, Nikhil persuades her to take the momentous walk with him down the corridor that leads from the women's apartment to the main rooms of the palace. There, in the drawing room, he introduces her to his friend the handsome, fiery radical Sandip (Soumitra Chatterjee, the Apu of *The World of Apu,* and a principal actor in eleven other Ray films). And then the refined, uncoercive Nikhil watches passively—helplessly—as she becomes enthralled by Sandip's cocksure masculinity and his revolutionary rhetoric.

The movie is about the destruction of the marriage, and the riots and bloodshed caused by Sandip's terrorist supporters. It's a large theme—a double tragedy, in the home and in the world—presented in a formal style that owes almost nothing to the conventions of American or Western European films. The screen frame is almost square, and the scenes—most of them inside the rooms of the palace—are in deep, glowing colors. The main characters talk, and the camera just stays on them and waits until they finish, yet these conversations develop a heart-swelling intensity. In a sense, the method is like that of amateur moviemakers who think that all they need to do is put actors in a room and photograph them reading their lines as if they were on a stage. The difference is that Satyajit Ray, who has been making movies for thirty years, didn't start with this simplicity—he achieved it. His approach—the intimacy of his focussing on the actors in their setting—may be influenced by Ozu or late Dreyer, but it isn't remotely austere or ascetic. India takes care of that.

When you're inside the palace, there's a lot of India outside the windows. The home and the world are interpenetrating metaphors. The interiors seem to be lighted through stained-glass windows, and the colors, the fabrics, the way the actors move—everything is erotic, ambiguous, in the process of being transformed. The richness of the performances—those of Victor Banerjee and Swatilekha Chatterjee in particular—and the colors and textures of the interiors are like an electric field. The conversations in golden light and shadows have their own kind of voltage. You watch these graceful people in draped garments in their lethargic, patterned décor, and everything in the country seems draped, hanging, defeated—and hectic, too.

The story takes place during the chaotic aftermath of Lord Curzon's partition of Bengal into Muslim and Hindu states, when the nationalist movement that Sandip is part of is trying to impose a boycott against all foreign goods (by claiming that imports are at the root of Indian poverty). Yet Bimala is becoming educated—becoming free—by imbibing English traditions. When this Indian woman sings, in English, the song that she has been taught by her governess—"Tell me the tales that to me were so dear, Long long ago, long long ago"—the confusion of cultures is insanely poignant.

Bimala is girlish and coquettish in the early scenes in the women's quarters, and part of the fascination of the movie is that Swatilekha Chatterjee grows with her role, and becomes more absorbing the longer you see her. She's not a mere ingénue; she's a full-bodied, rounded beauty, and her Bimala has an earthy, sensual presence. But Bimala and Nikhil obviously have no children, and we don't see them in passionate embraces, either. Nikhil's love for her seems more spiritual than physical.

For much of their ten-year-marriage, each time Nikhil suggests that Bimala leave purdah behind she looks down, smiling defensively. It isn't her compulsion; it's his. She doesn't want to come out of the women's quarters—all incense and silks, Arabian Nights cushions and English bric-a-brac. The rooms are stuffed—surfeited—with treasures; Bimala seems to emerge from inside a jewel. Maybe it's because the drive isn't hers that she's so overwhelmed by Sandip's fervor, and so easily taken in. Nikhil could guide her—could explain what the boycott is doing to the poor in the area. But he wants her to wise up by herself; he wants her to jump over the giant hurdle of growing up in ignorance, and see through the political line of a messiah like Sandip. He tells her to use her "woman's intuition"—surely the last thing she should trust in making a choice between his passive principles and Sandip's ruthless magnetism. This gracious, recessive maharajah (with zero carnality) is the innocent one.

Nikhil seems almost to will the destruction of his marriage. We never get inside his kindness, his virtue, his high-mindedness—or his weakness. Yet this doesn't seem a defect in the film but, rather, part of its richness and its mystery. Toward the end, Bimala, who was wheedled into independence by her husband, becomes desperate to express that independence—recklessly, heedlessly. When it comes to truthfulness about women's lives, this great Indian moviemaker Satyajit Ray shames the American and European directors of both sexes.

The New Yorker, July 1, 1985

PART TEN

HOOKED

1989

SONGWRITER
LIVING OUT A SONG

The least publicized of the American movies that have just opened in New York, *Songwriter* is the freest and funniest of the bunch—the most sophisticated, too. It's about the devious and sometimes felonious tricks that Doc Jenkins (Willie Nelson), a country-and-Western composer, uses to extricate himself from his legal entanglement with a Nashville gangster entrepreneur, who takes all the profits from his songs. Fed up with life on a tour bus—with the camaraderie, the partying, and the confusion—and unable to make any money from recordings of his music, Doc has turned to what his ex-wife, Honey (Melinda Dillon), calls "mogulling." He has been managing the career of his old singing partner Blackie Buck (Kris Kristofferson), the roué of the road, who loves the cash and the near-anonymous sex. And in the course of the movie Doc takes on another client, a woman singer—Gilda (Lesley Ann Warren), a sweet, insecure, boozing hysteric—who provides the leverage that Doc needs to outwit the gangster.

Songwriter is a satirical comedy about an artist trying to break free of the crooks who are binding him, but it never loses its sense of perspective on what a wily, frisky old pirate Doc himself is. With the stud in his ear, and his headband and long hair and graying reddish beard, Willie Nelson's Doc Jenkins is like a country-music version of Alec Guinness's scalawag painter Gulley Jimson in *The Horse's Mouth*. The theme, which comes through explicitly in the songs that Nelson and Kristofferson wrote for the movie, is that artists are driven to become con artists in order to survive. And since the material is loosely based on Willie Nelson's own life and legend and financial misadventures (it's said that the song "Night Life," which he sold in 1961 for a hundred and fifty dollars, went on to be recorded by over seventy performers and sold more than thirty million copies), Nelson plays his role with considerable bite. Doc is tough and determined—he's trying to save his life, and get back to Honey and sanity. He needs some solid ground under his feet, and he needs to make music on his own terms.

The script, by Bud Shrake, provides Nelson and Kristofferson with a steady flow of sharp lines, and though the picture starts off at full tilt and it's cut fast, leaving you to fill in for yourself, the director, Alan Rudolph, has a freewheeling responsiveness to the performers, and he allows room for the two stars' amiability and their ad libs. You can feel how much they enjoy singing together and drinking and hanging out together. Their mellowness is the essence of their "outlaw" country music, and it's right there on the screen; they harmonize even when they're not singing. Kristofferson, who's usually so detached that he seems camera shy, looks completely happy when he's just up on a stage performing in front of a crowd. Playing a vain, laid-back sensualist, the silver-bearded Kristofferson has a smiling glow; he has never been more at ease or a more chesty cavalier, or carried a larger sign that says, "I'm a good guy, but I don't want to be bothered."

Working with Shrake's material, which is much less high-toned and art-conscious than his own (his last picture was *Choose Me*), Rudolph is able to bring out the scrounginess and ribaldry of the down-home music scene. Whenever the mellowness threatens to get too warm and friendly, Rip Torn comes on and sideswipes the action. As a crumbum promoter who specializes in ripoffs—he draws audiences by advertising stars that he hasn't booked—Torn is the picture's insurance against gentility. Everything he says sounds mean and dirty, and even when you can't understand his snarled-out words he makes you laugh. (He's like W. C. Fields letting out his broadsides, but he's much speedier.) This grumbler feels he isn't getting his due—his whole being shouts it. And the moviemakers were smart enough to realize that Doc and Blackie would be as smitten by his cocky pride as we are. He becomes their pal, and soon three sets of beer-soaked whiskers are lined up at a honky-tonk bar.

The picture offers a wide range of rowdy slapstick, and some that's fairly highbrow and still rowdy. The performers seem up for everything that's handed to them. A girl who works for Doc at his headquarters in Austin, Texas, after he pulls up stakes in Nashville is played by a blond newcomer, Rhonda Dotson. She resembles the appealingly mysterious Marina Vlady of *Two or Three Things I Know About Her* and has something of Teri Garr's manic alertness and dippiness, too, but in a softer form. She's a romantic comedienne with awesome poise—she manages to be a lovely, still presence among the frantic people she shepherds. And, as the gangster whom Doc fears, Richard C. Sarafian (the director of *Vanishing Point*) is big,

and has a whomping comic menace; this gangster has the deadpan, self-righteous conviction that he's fully justified in screwing Doc—that that's business. The way Sarafian plays him, he's so totally, aberrantly self-centered that you get to like the slob. (His smile recalls the lopsided idiot's grin on Peter Sellers' face in *Being There*.) Melinda Dillon has a special gift: as Honey, she blends right in with the gags. She doesn't have nearly enough screen time, but she gives a gentle, very pleasing performance. And you develop respect for the director's craftsmanship when you see how gracefully he plays down the idyllic scene in which Doc comes to see Honey and the kids, and sits right down to play guitar with his little girl, who shows him what she has learned.

Lesley Ann Warren's Gilda is a showier part, and the performance is spectacular. When we first see Gilda, she's a singer with no belief in herself and no class; she's an incredibly beautiful girl in a red dress bumping and grinding like a dumb floozy's idea of a hot mama. She's touchingly gawky, as if not sure how to move her long-limbed body, but her red lips and the excitement in her eyes are dazzling. And the cinematographer, Matthew Leonetti, knows that you don't get a camera subject like Lesley Ann Warren very often. Gilda winds up her rendition of "Great Balls of Fire" with a couple of pelvic twitches, and you're conscious of the intersection where her abdomen disappears into her thighs, and conscious that the men around her must want to dive into it. You can't say much more about her singing at this point than that it's loud, but Doc sees the possibilities in the total package. When he grooms her to go out as the opening act for Blackie, she begins to learn something about taste and musicianship, and her voice flowers. Besides being one of the great beauties of the screen, Warren can sing.

Plainness, naturalness, that's Willie Nelson's style, and he's a master at it—not just in his singing but in his acting, too. About the only thing that was lacking in his performances in *Honeysuckle Rose* and *Barbarosa* was an actor's tension—what Rip Torn has with such pungency that the atmosphere around him seems to reek. Nelson keeps (and polishes) his plainness here—it's his glory. And as Doc he's intense and almost Zen-like in his moment-to-moment decisiveness. Maybe because he respects the hipness of Shrake's dialogue, the suggestion of a few grains of sand in his throat—the grittiness that keeps his singing voice from being too sweet—works in his line readings. His jazz-inspired musical phrasing carries over, too. Nelson delivers a line so fast that he seems to be brushing it off, but though his lines have the casualness of throwaways, they're like the exit lines of a matinée idol—they linger in the air. For the first time onscreen, he's consciously using himself as an icon, and Kristofferson is doing it, too. They're looking at themselves in the mirror and they're also seeing each other as mirror images. You can sense the canniness that it took both of them to become stars. That's what the interplay between them comes out of, and they both recognize it and are undercutting each other in the friendliest possible manner. They're living out a song.

In the movie, Doc finds a way to outwit the Nashville operators. But Nelson and Kristofferson haven't found a way to outwit Tri-Star. The newest of the major production companies, Tri-Star is flush with the success of *Rambo,* and in only the third year of its existence it is trashing movies as buoyant and entertaining as *Songwriter*—not giving this one even a token New York campaign or so much as a press screening. (The music was one of only three song scores nominated for an Academy Award earlier this year, but there's no space in the minuscule newspaper listing to say so.) *Songwriter* opened in New York at a tiny theatre—Film Forum 2, on Watts Street; if the movie has disappeared, there's some consolation in its being available on video cassette. But that doesn't make up for the fact that Lesley Ann Warren can give a performance as stunning as the one she gives here and not have it recognized. *Songwriter* is so good-natured it's like a fairy-tale satire. Is it possible that the gents at Tri-Star saw themselves in the caricatured Nashville thugs, and took revenge by deciding that there would be no audience for the picture?

The New Yorker, July 29, 1985

STEVEN BACH'S
FINAL CUT

When a new, inexperienced administration at United Artists gave the go-ahead to Michael Cimino's Western *Heaven's Gate,* the project, which had been turned down by executives at other studios (and by at least one of the previous administrations at United Artists), was clearly booby-trapped. The new management team, put in position by the officers of U.A.'s conglomerate parent, Transamerica, were aware of the risks, but their predecessors, who had left, en bloc, to form Orion Pictures, jeered at them in the press, and they were overeager to establish themselves by coming up with a slate of films that would confer prestige on them. Proposed at seven and a half million dollars, eventually budgeted at roughly eleven and a half million, and written off finally at forty-four million, *Heaven's Gate* brought nothing but torment to the executives of United Artists, which is now virtually defunct. (Transamerica, humiliated by the publicity, sold the company to Kirk Kerkorian's M-G-M, which wanted it because of its distribution apparatus, and dismantled the production side.) About the only good that has ever come from the movie is the new book *Final Cut: Dreams and Disaster in the Making of "Heaven's Gate"* (Morrow), by Steven Bach—perhaps the best account we have of American moviemaking in the age of conglomerate control of the studios, and (though this isn't made explicit) in the druggy age.

Steven Bach was part of the new U.A. team, and was head of production when *Heaven's Gate* was premièred, late in 1980—the book might be called *Apologia pro Fiasco Suo*. It's that, but it's considerably more than that. There are a lot of emotions bumping into each other under the surface of Bach's precise, thoughtful, sometimes hilarious and macabre story. He begins by describing the formation of United Artists, in 1919, by Charlie Chaplin, Douglas Fairbanks, Mary Pickford, and D. W. Griffith; outlines the steps that led the company to become a subsidiary of Transamerica in 1967; and then gets into the whole *Heaven's Gate* debacle. That picture is only a part of what is going on at the studio, though—it's one debacle among many. (There are also imagined future triumphs, but the regime and the company didn't last long enough.) Bach is particularly good in his observation of how the marketing and distribution people start taking over the decision-making process about what films should be given the go-ahead—a power grab that's also taking place at other studios and helps to explain why we've been getting so many teen pix in the last few years. And the choices that were made by the U.A. team are covered in an interlocking series of fine, juicy anecdotes indicating why U.A. turned down what it did and financed what it did, and why it lost projects it wanted and had to settle for others.

The book is a short course in the realpolitik of how projects come to be accepted; it's set in a cutthroat business, where betrayal is the rule, not the exception. It takes Bach a while to grasp that, and his loyalty and affection go to the man who doesn't fit the pattern. The hero of Bach's story isn't Bach. It's shy Andy Albeck, the new president of United Artists—not because he was the right man for the job (he wasn't) but because he treated his staff and the people he dealt with fairly and considerately. Bach's greatest contribution may be his recognition that even in the movie business there are decencies that transcend success or failure. (Neither he nor Albeck is still in the business.) That's what gives the book its distinction: it has the touching, melancholic quality of a story told by someone who knew he was on a sinking ship but felt honor-bound not to try to save himself.

As I see it, Bach—intelligent and knowing as he is—wasn't the right man for his job, either. From his own description of the day-to-day workings of United Artists, it appears that there was a vacuum of leadership even before the decision was taken to make *Heaven's Gate,* and that he was part of that vacuum. In all probability, Michael Cimino could read Steven Bach a lot better than Bach could read Cimino. And if Cimino could, others could, too. The new management team looking for projects that would redound to U.A.'s glory and keep Transamerica proud and happy were perfect patsies. The movie business attracts flimflam artists, megalomaniacs, and pathological liars from all over the world; the essential part of the head of production's job is having the instincts and the experience to know what and whom to say yes to. And in a period when—because of the widespread consumption of pills, cocaine, and God knows what—stars' and directors' track records may not be a valid guide to how they will perform next time, the executive needs genius instincts. And he has to exercise them before a picture begins rolling, because once it starts he has about as much control over the director as a hospital administrator has over a doctor during surgery.

When Cimino's picture is out of control and is costing the company a million dollars a week, Bach is in a terrible bind. His account of the steps he takes—talking to an eminent director about possibly replacing Cimino, asking advice from an eminent producer, and so on—makes for good reading. But what he's doing is remarkably tepid and ineffective. Obviously, if he fires Cimino, whose last picture, *The Deer Hunter,* has just won five Academy Awards, including Best Picture and Best Director, he and the other officers of U.A. will be vilified in the press and go down in history as hatchet men and philistines. But he doesn't seem to be doing anything but wasting time giving people in the Hollywood community the chance to sympathize with him. When you get down to it, Bach conveys an impression of connoisseurship, erudition, and understanding while misunderstanding the problem: he's the problem. He doesn't do much except wring his hands until the last weeks of filming, when it finally registers on him that he has to show some force. By then, Cimino, who's utterly dedicated to his amorphous vision, has shot over two hundred hours of film.

Bach looks back to a golden age in the fifties when the heads of United Artists "were able to draw upon a pool of thoroughly trained, knowledgeable professionals to whom independence was not synonymous with indulgence, self- or otherwise." He looks back to the time "before poetic license had become the intellectual justification for all manner of creative licentiousness." This hokey nostalgia isn't worthy of him. When he complains about "licentiousness" and lack of discipline, he's really saying that he couldn't handle Michael Cimino. Maybe nobody could have, but the members of the U.A. team were the ones who said yes to him, because they thought they could. I admire the sensitivity and taste that Steven Bach shows in this book, but these are not the qualities that make a studio head. Whether artists have self-discipline or not, executives are supposed to be disciplined people with the strength and the smarts to impose discipline on others when it's needed. That's what they draw astronomic salaries for.

The New Yorker, August 12, 1985

SWEET DREAMS

In *Sweet Dreams,* Jessica Lange plays the pop-and-country singer Patsy Cline with a raw physicality that's challenging and heroic. "Patsy didn't hold anything back," Lange has been quoted as saying. "Patsy had a way of hitting life head-on." That's exactly how Lange plays her. It took courage for

Lange to abandon her blond silkiness and appear as a raw, small-town Southern girl with bushy dark hair who dresses in outfits that her mother makes for her. (Patsy's mother seems to have cornered the market in shrill-blue fabrics.) And it took intelligence not to tone up the story with genteel movie-star conceits. Lange's interpretation of Patsy Cline's character is based on the best possible source—her singing—and she creates a hot, woman-of-the-people heroine with a great melodic gift. Almost insistently clumsy and completely unpretentious, her Patsy is like an American backcountry version of the young Anna Magnani. The singing voice that comes out of her is from the vocal tracks of recordings that Patsy Cline made between 1960 and 1963. (In some cases, new instrumental tracks with new background singers have been laid on.) It takes a few songs before you get used to Lange's body with Patsy Cline's voice, but as Lange's Patsy rises to stardom, bouncing and dancing as she sings, you feel the unity: Patsy's voice is generating Lange's performance.

Patsy Cline was one of the rare full-throated belters with the ability and stamina to belt musically, exultantly, and Jessica Lange's body lives up to the sound. So does her speaking voice, which she modulates so that it's in the same range as Patsy's singing. Growing as confident as the singing voice coming out of her, Lange even puts a raucous growl on a line of dialogue to match Patsy's growl. Lange and Patsy Cline's voice energize the picture, give it a vigor that women have rarely had a chance to show in starring roles. *Sweet Dreams,* which was directed by Karel Reisz *(Saturday Night and Sunday Morning, Morgan!, Isadora, The Gambler, Who'll Stop the Rain, The French Lieutenant's Woman),* is a woman's picture of a new kind—a feminist picture not because of any political attitudes but because its strong–willed heroine is a husky, physically happy woman who wants pleasure out of life. Lange's Patsy Cline doesn't have to talk about her art: we can see that she's happiest and rowdiest and most fully alive when she sings, and when she's rolling in the hay. What the movie makes you feel is her lust for living. And what makes the movie different from the women's pictures of the past is that there's no call for the heroine to be punished, and no suggestion that she shouldn't want *more. Sweet Dreams* doesn't step back from her; she's taken on her own terms.

The big weakness in this kind of bio-pic is that once it's on the rails (*Sweet Dreams* starts in 1956) you can see where it's heading: Patsy is going to marry Charlie Dick (Ed Harris) and be battered on the climb to stardom, and she's going to die in a plane crash in 1963, at the age of thirty. And you recognize the signposts: honky-tonks, the Grand Ole Opry, top of the charts. So in basic story terms it's almost inevitably going to seem banal. *Sweet Dreams* doesn't transcend this limitation, but the fighting and boozing are kept to a minimum, and, scene by scene, the script, by Robert Getchell (who wrote *Alice Doesn't Live Here Anymore*), has a funny, edgy spontaneity, a tang. Getchell cuts through the familiarity of the material by providing mean, lowdown banter for Patsy and Charlie, with innuendos right out on top. And he writes scenes between Patsy and her mother (the soft-faced Ann Wedgeworth, a marvellous comedienne) that have a lovely, tickling humor. Patsy's mother was married at sixteen and raised three children by herself—by her sewing. She has never had anything to her name. Yet she's imbued with middle-class moral niceties, and she giggles shyly, as if she were the fluttering essence of gentility. She's disturbed and titillated—in about equal parts—by Patsy's swinging hips and uncouth language. So, of course, Patsy delights in shocking her. These scenes have a real mother-daughter rapport; they stir so much recognition that they're small comedy classics. (Wedgeworth plays prudishness as a sly form of flirtation.) Almost every scene in the movie comes up with something that nips at you and makes you laugh or takes you by surprise. And you like the people more when you hear them taunting and kidding each other. Patsy gives a delayed party to celebrate her younger sister's graduation from high school; she explains the delay to the guests (she didn't have the money earlier), and then she explains why the event called for a major celebration: her sister is the first person in the family to graduate from high school. And with that wry, proud announcement a whole raft of details you've been noticing fall into place.

Patsy and Charlie are passionately in love but have never learned to control their tempers or their impatience. They flare up at each other, and Patsy the smartmouth gives as good as she gets; they keep destroying their own happiness. But they keep experiencing it, too. After Charlie has been drafted, Patsy goes to see him at Fort Bragg and they go to a motel; she makes a very simple postcoital speech—she tells him, "You can't go to your grave sayin' you weren't ever loved"—and it has a resonance that carries through the movie. Ed Harris brings out Charlie's tragic, pitiable sweetness. This husband, who's in awe of his wife's talent, wants a stable marriage more than he wants anything else in the world, yet he has never known how to live on an even keel. Charlie comes on at first bristling with sexual confidence, but the essence of Harris's acting style is the intensity he brings to quietness. Gradually, Charlie loses his bravado, and becomes quieter, more bewildered, and his big scene—a jailhouse monologue about the death of his father—is perhaps the most hushed, most introspective moment he has.

When Charlie and Patsy dance (to music such as Sam Cooke's "You Send Me," on a car radio), it's just about their only tranquil time together. They weave and sway rhythmically; they barely move their feet. The stillness is hypnotic, and it's the only time when Charlie seems at peace and in control of things. Harris has done this erotic swaying in other movies recently—with Amy Madigan in *Places in the Heart* and *Alamo Bay*—but it's effective here, too. When Patsy, dressed in a cowgirl outfit, appears on the Arthur Godfrey show, Charlie watches her at home on TV, and he dances alone to the rhythm of her singing. It's sexy, but it's also desolate. When he and Patsy dance together, it points up the marriage of opposites: the mysteriously quiet man who's suspended in the middle of nowhere, who never finds himself, and the woman who has it all, who knows her gift almost from childhood. It's Patsy's singing—the sureness of it—that attracts him. As Charlie is presented, he's sure he knows how to have a good time, and he's sure of his sexual prowess, but of not much else.

Sweet Dreams should look better than it does: the sets and costumes are fine, but the cinematography is very ordinary, especially in the interiors, and a few sequences are almost ostentatiously dark. There are also a couple of scenes that raise issues without any follow-up, leaving gaps in the continuity. Reisz's staging isn't inspired, either, though he comes through now and then. But Reisz, a Czech-born Englishman, brings the American humor out of the script, and he does beautiful work with Ann Wedgeworth and with Ed Harris. He doesn't interrupt Patsy Cline's songs, and he stays out of Jessica Lange's way. She doesn't have the opportunities for brilliant nuances that she had in the dud movie *Frances,* and her performance may not have the suggestion of worldly ripeness or the affecting qualities that Beverly D'Angelo brought to her few scenes as Patsy Cline in *Coal Miner's Daughter,* but when Lange's Patsy slings her strong young body around she gives off a charge. Lange has real authority here, and the performance holds you emotionally. This is one of the few times I've seen people cry at a movie that wasn't sentimental—it's an honest tearjerker. People can cry without feeling they've been had.

The New Yorker, October 21, 1985

DREAMCHILD

The English film *Dreamchild* is about a moment of epiphany. Just before her eightieth birthday, in 1932, Mrs. Alice Hargreaves (Coral Browne) sails to New York to speak at the Lewis Carroll centenary celebration at Columbia University. The voyage is disorienting, and her mind goes back to her childhood days, and to the lazy boating party of July 4, 1862, when the young Reverend Charles Dodgson, Lecturer in Mathematics at Christ Church, Oxford, where her father was the Dean, had attempted to entertain her and her sisters by spinning the nonsense tale that grew to be *Alice's Adventures in Wonderland.* Later, during the ceremonies at Columbia, when a men's choir sings the Mock Turtle's song, "Will you, wo'n't you, will you, wo'n't you, wo'n't you join the dance?," she remembers the Reverend Mr. Dodgson's shyness on another summer day. There were adolescent boys on the excursion, along with the grownups, and she was self-conscious in their presence. When Mr. Dodgson, feeling her rejection of him, tried to recite, he stuttered. She had giggled in embarrassment; her giggles had set off giggles from one of her sisters, and that had got *her* going again. The humiliated, pink-faced little Dodgson had stuttered so much he had to break off in the middle of the "Will you, wo'n't you." Apologetic when she saw how hurt he was, the young Alice had gone over to him, kissed him gently on the cheek, and embraced him. It's only now, at this commemoration and with her own death close at hand, that the elderly Alice, remembering how he shrank back from her touch, grasps how deeply tormented he was, and that he loved her. The full force of the revelation shakes her while she speaks at Columbia. She recognizes that she knew it then, yet didn't quite know it. And she almost loses control. It's a fine, affecting scene: Coral Browne suggests the shock to the wide-eyed little girl who is alive in her still, and it's clear that that girl—Dodgson's dreamchild—has learned enough in her eighty years to value his love now for what it was.

Nothing I've seen Coral Browne do onscreen had prepared me for this performance. In the past, this Australia-born actress (who's in her early seventies) seemed too bullying a presence; she was too stiffly theatrical for the camera, and her voice was a blaster. Here, as Mrs. Hargreaves, she has the capacity for wonder of the Alice of the stories, and when she's overtaken by frailty her voice is querulous and fading. Through most of the film, her decisive tones suggest the practical-mindedness and vanity that link her with the bright, poised, subtly flirty Alice at ten (played by Amelia Shankley), whose conversations with her sisters have an angelic precision. The sound of these imperious little-princess voices blended in idle chitchat is plangent, evocative. It makes you happy and makes you respond to the happiness of the Reverend Mr. Dodgson as he loiters outside the little girls' windows, eavesdropping.

Ian Holm, who plays Dodgson, has to achieve almost all his effects passively, by registering the man's acute and agonizing self-consciousness and his furtive reactions to what goes on around him. As Holm interprets Dodgson's stifled emotional life, pleasure and terror are just a hairbreadth apart. The freedom of imagination that Dodgson shows in the poems and stories he writes for little girls (there were many of them—generations of them—after Alice) disappears in his dealings with the adult Oxford world. Dodgson the Don is a priss—a scholarly celibate who is obsessive about purity of thought. The movie, which was directed by Gavin Millar, from a screenplay by Dennis Potter, doesn't have to formulate most of this; it's all there in Holm's performance. It's all there in the single shot of Dodgson feeling so gratified by Alice's pecking at his cheek that he must retreat from her, squirming in his oversize stiff collar. (His clothes make him look like a wizened naughty little schoolboy, a close relative of his dressed-up brainchildren in Tenniel's illustrations.) It's a wonderful performance— sneaky-dirty in its recessiveness, funny and painful at the same moments.

The picture is a curio; it's anomalous in the way the projects that Dennis Potter (*Pennies from Heaven, Brimstone and Treacle*) instigates often are, and its structure and techniques suggest a literate TV show rather than a movie. Despite the collaboration of Jim Henson's Creature Shop, *Dreamchild* is not a movie for a wide audience; it simply isn't conceived in the broad, narrative patterns that please most moviegoers. Yet it's very enjoyable; it has a twinkling subtext, and in some scenes it achieves levels of feeling that the new mainstream films don't get near. It's about how children can hurt us, and it's about how a man who forbids himself any transgressions against propriety—a man who looks to be dying inside—can split his life between writing "nonsense" and writing mathematical treatises and never, ever crack. I wish that we could have seen other areas of Dodgson's life. How did this prodigy comport himself when he was around the artists he knew, such as Ruskin, Millais, Ellen Terry, Tennyson, and the Rossettis? Did he allow something of the sweet, fey fellow who amuses Alice to come through? And was it creepy for Alice when she passed beyond his favored age range and saw him transfer his devotion to her successors—other bright little Victorian girls?

But Dennis Potter has his own obsessions, and American pop entertainment of the thirties is one of them. The movie is plotted around the impoverished Mrs. Hargreaves' trip to New York, in the company of an adolescent girl (Nicola Cowper) whom she has taken from an orphanage to serve as her nurse-companion. This girl also serves as the film's ingénue. Potter has devised a ramshackle romance between her and a young American (Peter Gallagher), a brash reporter who, having been fired from his job, becomes Mrs. Hargreaves' agent and sets her to delivering product endorsements on the radio and in the press. This aspect of the movie is like a parody tribute to Hollywood's newspaper comedy-romances (such as *Love Is News*), with Gallagher, who is all curly lips and dimples and black eyebrows, doing the Irish charm and blarney that the young Tyrone Power was a wizard at. The romance allows for some pleasant enough musical numbers. ("I Only Have Eyes for You" is sung at a tea dance at the Waldorf-Astoria, and Mrs. Hargreaves has a scene at a radio station that serves no great purpose except to allow us to hear a crooner's gloriously nasal rendition of "I'm Confessing That I Love You.") But Millar, the director, who has a lovely touch with Dodgson and the Dean's little daughters, doesn't seem to know what to make of Potter's quirky affection for Hollywood's exhausted conventions, and Mrs. Hargreaves' Potteresque adventures in the Art Deco New York wonderland have wobbly tonalities. (I began to visualize an old-fashioned Hollywood story conference, with Potter trying to explain his ideas to a studio head like Louis B. Mayer or Harry Cohn.)

The conception is pure fluke, but it almost works. The picture is magically smooth, and it's full of felicities, such as Nicola Cowper's unsentimental ingénue (this orphan is a fast learner) and Peter Gallagher's playing the high-pressure charmer in a loose, affable style. Billy Williams' cinematography has a glowing dreaminess; his lighting helps us over the transitions between 1932 and 1862, and into the glimpses of the world inhabited by the eerie Lewis Carroll–Tenniel–Jim Henson creatures. There are six of them here, complexly detailed creations, and rather malign—as they are in the book. (They're almost too fascinating for the brief appearances they make.)

The Gryphon and the sorrowful Mock Turtle live among ledges of rock on a darkling seashore with rippling plastic waves—a Fellini-like night world of the imagination that the aged Mrs. Hargreaves visits. The March Hare has broken, yellowish-gray teeth and soiled-looking whiskers, and he seems to be chewing even while he's speaking. He, the Mad Hatter, and the Dormouse, and the Caterpillar, too, converse in the same matter-of-fact, egalitarian manner that the visiting little Alice does. They—and little Alice herself—rattle around in Mrs. Hargreaves' mind as she experiences a second childhood in the cocky splendors of New York. She knows that her flashing back is a sign of senility, but her new experiences are jogging her out of her confining Victorian primness, and when she flashes back she sees the riches that she has cut herself off from for seventy years.

The New Yorker, October 21, 1985

RE-ANIMATOR

R*e-Animator* makes good on its title. At first, it just makes you smile or giggle, but pretty soon you laugh out loud, and as the ghoulish jokes escalate you feel revivified—light-headed and happy, the way people do after an evening at Charles Ludlam's Ridiculous Theatrical Company. The picture is close to being a silly ghoulie classic—the bloodier it gets, the funnier it is. This is the same blood that flows through the Hammer horror movies; it's theatre-of-the-absurd blood, slapstick blood. *Re-Animator* is the first film directed by Stuart Gordon, who was one of the founders of the Organic Theatre, in Chicago, in 1969; the screenplay, which Gordon wrote along with a couple of the Organic's playwrights—Dennis Paoli and William J. Norris—was adapted from a series of six stories that H. P. Lovecraft published in 1922. The movie features a bunch of relative newcomers who have had their training in regional theatres, and they perform with a straight-faced, hip aplomb. (They need it.)

Nothing fazes Herbert West, the medical student who comes to Misketonic University in (the apocryphal) Arkham, Massachusetts, from Zurich, bearing an unbreakable bottle full of a fluorescent greenish-yellow serum. He injects it in any corpse that's handy, restoring the dead to hideous, unpredictable activity. The pale, imperturbable Herbert, with his grave manner and his forced little smile, is played by Jeffrey Combs with pursed lips and a clammy-prissy set of the jaw. Herbert, the re-animator, is like a crawly little slug, and he has something of the obsessiveness of Dwight Frye as Dracula's spider-eating assistant. (He laughs only in hysteria.) Herbert's moment of greatest triumph is the resuscitation of the medical school's treacherous, hypocritical chief neurosurgeon (David Gale) after he has been decapitated. This fellow spends the rest of the movie literally holding his head in his hands, but being in two parts doesn't seem to slow him down much; he continues with his vile scheming. Resuscitation has done something to him, though: his libido appears to have been liberated. The severed head is soon busily engaged in making love to the Dean's beautiful blond daughter. David Gale has a long-jawed, sorrowful look—he suggests Boris Karloff—and his eyes roll in lascivious delight as he licks the soft flesh of the helpless, spread-eagled blonde (Barbara Crampton) who has been trussed to a table in the morgue.

These scenes are like pop Buñuel; they're explosively batty, yet the actors manage to keep their professional dignity. Barbara Crampton, who's creamy pink all over, is at her loveliest when she's being defiled; lying there in the morgue with the head moving around on her, she's like a nude by Fragonard or Boucher floating on a ceiling. Skinny-faced Bruce Abbott, who plays her adoring fiancé—he goes in and out of a state of shock—and Robert Sampson (a familiar face from TV), who plays the Dean, her adoring father, round out the key members of the cast. Sampson has what is perhaps my favorite scene. Tied in a straitjacket and locked inside a cubicle, the Dean can't see out, but his daughter and the surgeon (still in one piece at this point), who are in the next room, can see him through one-way glass. In torment, the Dean bangs against the glass, and the vicious surgeon, who is courting the daughter with expressions of concern for her father's mental health, slams back at him furtively with his elbow. The maddened Dean butts his head against the glass, banging at the surgeon. The hatred in this exchange—the pure aggressive meanness in it—is just about peerless, though no doubt some will prefer the wilder moment that comes late in the movie when Herbert decides to try yet another experiment with his greenish-yellow guck, and gives the surgeon's trunk a mighty overdose. The body parts spin off in a scene that recalls the Schwarzenegger robot being dismantled while the machine keeps going in *The Terminator* (which recalled the relentless Yul Brynner robot of *Westworld*), but that joke is topped here when the surgeon's intestines fly out and coil around Herbert like a boa constrictor. (This is an Organic Theatre movie).

It's monkeyshines like these that raise this horror-genre parody to the top of its class. *Re-Animator* doesn't give you a lot of time to think. The score, by Richard Band, has a whoopiness about it, like Bernard Herrmann with hiccups, and Gordon brings the movie in at an hour and twenty-five minutes. Early scenes featuring a re-animated cat named Rufus, who has the scream of a banshee, seem the climax of decades of cat jokes. These jokes hit you in a subterranean comic zone that the surrealists' pranks sometimes reached, but without the surrealists' self-consciousness (and art-consciousness). This is indigenous American junkiness, like the Mel Brooks–Gene Wilder *Young Frankenstein*, but looser and more lowdown. The dialogue isn't particularly polished—the comedy isn't so much in what the characters say as in what they do. There's a suggestion of *The Beast with Five*

Fingers, and there's a sequence that recalls Romero's *Night of the Living Dead,* but this is a much rowdier movie—it's not out to scare you, it's out to make you laugh at what other movies have scared you with, and at what they'd have scared you with if they hadn't pulled back. (*Re-Animator* wasn't submitted to the Ratings Board.)

Stuart Gordon's début film carries something intangible from live theatre. The mockery here is the kind that needs a crowd to complete it; ideally, you ought to see it with a gang of friends.

The New Yorker, November 18, 1985

ABOUT KATE NELLIGAN, FROM REVIEW OF
ELENI

I n the three-part TV presentation of *Thérèse Raquin,* in 1981, Kate Nelligan had a marvellous sexual vibrancy that kept getting harsher, more animal. The 1981 movie *Eye of the Needle* might be a standard genre piece if it weren't for Nelligan as the lonely wife. The way she plays the part, all the woman's accumulated spiritual and sexual longings come pouring out; when a big emotion goes through her, it's like the wind snapping a sheet. Nelligan doesn't editorialize on the emotions that her characters are gripped by; she cauterizes those emotions—burns away everything easy or too girlishly appealing. She can do that and still be lyrical, as she demonstrated on the stage in New York in 1984, in her performance as O'Neill's virginal Irish-American farm girl in *A Moon for the Misbegotten.* And in New York early this year she gave one of the least heralded great performances I've ever seen, in Edna O'Brien's *Virginia.* Speaking Virginia Woolf's own words, in a play that is constructed almost as a monologue, she did an ecstatic, transcendent piece of acting, bringing out the beauty of Woolf's language without ever losing the tough complexity of mind that went into it. At the end, when she released her concentration, I looked down at my clasped hands, and the knuckles were white. There is something immaculate about Nelligan's sustained intensity—you never feel she's protecting herself. But her clean acting style is all wrong for the mythmaking propensities of *Eleni.* She's a scrupulous actress trying to play a believable heroic woman when the Red-baiting script calls for a shameless humbug—a lusty, defiant young Katina Paxinou.

The New Yorker, December 2, 1985

THE COLOR PURPLE

During the making of *The Color Purple,* Steven Spielberg's version of the Alice Walker novel about black women's lives in the South in the first half of the century, the advance publicity suggested that he was attempting something "serious." But when you see the movie you realize that he was probably attracted by Walker's childlike heroine, Celie, and the book's lyrical presentation of the healing power of love. He may not have understood this, because he approaches the material with undue timidity. It's no wonder the novel was popular. On the first page, the fourteen-year-old black drudge Celie is raped by the man she believes to be her father. She gives birth to two children by this brute; he takes the babies away, and she has no idea what he has done with them. Tired of her, he forces her to marry another brute—a widowed farmer who needs her to take care of his children. This man uses her sexually and beats her. When her younger sister, Nettie—the only person who cares for her and doesn't think she's ugly—runs away from the raping father and comes to stay with her, her husband makes advances to Nettie and, when Nettie fights him, throws her off the property. Poor Celie toils on, with never a kind word coming her way, until her husband brings home Shug Avery, a honky-tonk singer—his true love and sometime mistress—who is sick and needs care. Celie falls in love with the raucous, gutsy Shug (short for "sugar"), and Shug, seeing Celie's true worth, makes love to her. It's the turning point of Celie's life: after experiencing sexual pleasure, she becomes confident of her self-worth, goes out into the world, and returns to make a success of herself running a small business.

But *The Color Purple* isn't just the story of Celie; it's an extended-family saga spanning generations and two continents. (The cast-out Nettie has gone to Africa, with a missionary couple.) The novel is about the bonding of the generous, artistically gifted, understanding black women (no matter how worn down they are, they never speak a harsh word to a child). It's also about the insensitivity, cowardice, and meanness of the black men (Nettie is able to brief us on how the men oppress the women in Africa, too). The glue that holds it all together is a pop-folk religiosity that also serves to keep the book's anti-male attitudes in check. Walker allows some of the lazy, lecherous oppressors to redeem themselves by accepting their inferiority to their wives and developing their aptitudes for cooking and sewing. So the many characters all come together for a series of reconciliation scenes.

Probably Alice Walker gets by with so much rampant female chauvinism because it's put in the mouth of her battered fourteen-year-old heroine. The book—or, rather, the best part of it, roughly the first third—is made up of Celie's letters to God, which are written in a raw, cadenced dialect, an artful version of a rural near-illiterate's black English. The book has a joyous emotional swing to it, and this swing can carry a reader right through inspirational passages such as the one where Shug teaches Celie that God is inside her and inside everybody else, that everything wants to be loved and "it pisses God off if you walk by the color purple in a field somewhere and don't notice it."

Spielberg has been quoted in *The New York Times* as being worried about "doing a movie about *people* for the first time in my career," and fearing that he'll be "accused of not having the sensibility to do character studies." But the Walker material has about as much to do with character studies as Disney's *Song of the South* did. Spielberg's *The Color Purple* is probably the least authentic in feeling of any of his full-length films; the people on the screen are like characters operated by Frank Oz. But they're not much phonier than the people in the book: Spielberg's problem is that he can't give the material the emotional push of that earthy folk style of Walker's. He just doesn't have the conviction that she has.

Spielberg's version comes from a man who filters everything through movies. He sees Georgia in 1909 the way a European director might; visually, the picture suggests *Song of the South* remade by Visconti. When Celie (played in the early scenes by Desreta Jackson and then by Whoopi Goldberg) and Nettie (Akosua Busia) do their jive talk—clapping their hands in fast, intricate rhythms as they chant—it seems to be going on in a faraway, magical kingdom, in a field of pink flowers from the florists who supplied the daffodils for David Lean's *Doctor Zhivago*. Spielberg has all this facile, pretty camera technique, but he can't find an appropriate tone, and so the incidents don't click into place. The movie is muffled, bombed out, and a gooey score by Quincy Jones calls attention to the emotional void— Jones seems to have been waiting all his life to metamorphose into Max Steiner.

Spielberg soft-pedals the lesbian side of the Celie and Shug romance, and the men may be more buffoonish than they are in the book and so less threatening, but he has tried to be faithful to Walker. This doesn't do the movie a lot of good. Working from a script (by Menno Meyjes) that hasn't reshaped the novel into a dramatic structure, Spielberg has trouble getting about two dozen characters in and out of the action, which spans some thirty years. (Performances, such as Rae Dawn Chong's as Squeak—Celie's stepson's mistress, who wants to be a singer—have obviously been truncated.) A scene of several women standing on Celie's porch is the worst piece of staging this director ever dreamed up. It tops even the crowd scene where the people singing outside a church converge with the people singing inside—a jubilee that reminds you of fire drills in junior high. And this is the only film that Spielberg has ever made where the editing looks to be from desperation. The crosscutting between Nettie's experiences in Africa and Celie's life back home is staggeringly ineffective. In one sequence, we hop back and forth between Celie, who has just learned of her husband's full treachery to her and picks up a straight razor to shave him, and Shug, who is at a distance and starts running to the house because she intuits that Celie is about to cut his throat, and Nettie in Africa dashing to a ritual of initiation where children are to have their faces incised. The passage rivals the famous parody of editing in *The Apprenticeship of Duddy Kravitz,* where Denholm Elliott played a drunken filmmaker who, having been hired by a father to record his son's bar mitzvah, got carried away with his art and intercut the gathering with bloody primitive rites. (Spielberg's African ritual may even be a first on film: a coed tribal initiation.)

Except for the dimpled Oprah Winfrey as the powerhouse Sofia, whose mighty punch at a white man lands her in jail for twelve years, the performers don't make a very strong impression. Whoopi Goldberg's Celie may be a little less "real" than the title character in *E.T.,* but, given the conception of Celie—who has to be meek and then discover her power—she does a respectable job. (If we feel a letdown when she takes over from Desreta Jackson's teen-age Celie, it's because Jackson is warmer and more open to the camera.) Willard Pugh is likable and peppy as Celie's stepson, who keeps falling through roofs, and Danny Glover, in the difficult role of the husband who slaps her around, probably does as well as anybody could with material such as the stupid comedy routine where he proves the ineptness of men by trying to prepare a meal for the bedridden Shug and burning everything. (It's the kind of humiliation that Katharine Hepburn went through long ago in *Woman of the Year*) it's no less offensive when the sexual tables are turned; As Shug, Margaret Avery is in a tough spot, because of all the press attention to Tina Turner's being offered the role and turning it down. (You can't help imagining how Turner might have played it.) Margaret Avery makes a terrific entrance, grinning, with a jagged front tooth sticking out, and she looks great singing in a glittering red dress in a juke joint. (She's dubbed by Tata Vega.) But then an awful thing happens, which has to be at least partly the director's fault: she plays the rest of her scenes in a refined, contemporary manner that dulls out all interest in Shug. If you're among the millions of people who have read the book, you probably expect the actors to be more important than they turn out to be. The movie is amorphous; it's a pastoral about the triumph of the human spirit, and it blurs on you.

The New Yorker, December 30, 1985

DOWN AND OUT IN BEVERLY HILLS

S et in a pastel consumers' paradise, Paul Mazursky's new comedy, *Down and Out in Beverly Hills,* is almost immorally luscious. The cinematographer, Don McAlpine, gives you a vision of the sensuousness of money wrapped in sunshine, and Mazursky introduces you to a race of anxious people who feel "unfulfilled." Driving downtown in his Rolls-Royce with the top down, a self-made millionaire—a manufacturer of wire hangers—listens to Dr. Toni Grant's psychological advice on the radio. You're often at a loss to know why you're laughing, but jokes you can't explain may be the best kind, and Mazursky is a master of them. When he gets rolling, you're not responding to single jokes—it's the whole gestalt of the movie that's funny.

Down and Out takes off from the play, by René Fauchois, that served as the basis for Renoir's 1931 film *Boudu Saved from Drowning* (which was first released in the United States in 1967). A bum (Michel Simon in the Renoir film) is rescued from drowning by a middle-class man, who tries to turn him into a responsible citizen like himself. In the new version, Nick Nolte is the shaggy, smelly drifter; left with nothing when his scroungy dog, Kerouac, deserts him, he stuffs his pockets with ornamental stones from the grounds of a Beverly Hills mansion and walks into the clear blue swimming pool. Though slightly built, Dave Whiteman (Richard Dreyfuss), the wire-hanger magnate who owns the house, struggles manfully to pull him out and then gives him artificial respiration while Mrs. Whiteman (Bette Midler) and the servants look on in horror. The bum's filthiness is a moral affront to them.

A creamy-skinned, pampered Beverly Hills matron, Barb Whiteman can't believe what's happening when her husband insists on taking the ungrateful, foul-tempered fellow—Jerry—to the guest cabaña. Like Boudu, Jerry isn't one of the "deserving poor"; he's a dropout who wants to be left alone, and his eyes don't communicate—they don't tell you a thing. But he settles in fast, and in the next few weeks he ingratiates himself with the lady Barb, with the Whitemans' hot live-in maid Carmen (Elizabeth Peña), with their cool daughter Jenny (Tracy Nelson), and everybody else he encounters. Matisse, the family dog, who growls and yaps at Dave, does tricks for big, lazy Jerry, decked out now in silk lounging robes.

Like Mazursky's last picture *Moscow on the Hudson, Down and Out in Beverly Hills* is what a friend of mine calls "cultural comment without a hair shirt." This movie is silky in every department—the clothes, the bedding, Dave's white Rolls, which is the twin of his record-producer neighbor's white Rolls. I don't think conspicuous consumption has ever been made so integral to a way of life; it *is* the way of life here. Trying to persuade Jerry to rejoin the world and go to work, Dave takes him to his hair salon for some grooming, buys him expensive clothes, and drives him down to the plant where the hangers are made; a paternalistic employer, he's proud of the health care he provides the workers, proud of the business he built up. But Jerry is way past wanting a job. He's lord of the sunshine manor. One day, he persuades Dave to take him to the beach and meet his bummy old pals, and at sundown graying Dave and big, muscular Jerry talk together silhouetted against the opalescent water and the pale distant mountains. The beauty of this Southern California world plays off our sense of reality, even though it's as real as can be. All through the picture, Mazursky uses the deluxe settings and the natural splendor as comic counterpoint to the dialogue. Beverly Hills is presented as a bastion of the new rich, where nobody feels fully accepted. The record-producer neighbor (Little Richard) shouts in protest that the police department comes out in greater force for Whiteman's (accidental) burglar alarms than it does for his own (accidental) alarms, because he's black; he claims that Whiteman rates a police helicopter and he doesn't. An unspeakably rich Iranian neighbor is offended because the Whitemans don't think to invite him to their New Year's party. Dave's father always worries that he won't have enough of the white meat of the turkey.

Mazursky and his co-scriptwriter, Leon Capetanos, aren't afraid to plant the beginnings of their gags and then have them pay off an hour later; the movie keeps erupting as gags reach maturity and crisscross each other. And it's full of the kind of social detail that makes Beverly Hills different from communities of the old rich. (Seeing Whiteman looking harried, the Japanese gardener suggests a vacation and offers him the use of the place he has bought in Hawaii.) As an actor, Little Richard uses the maniacal energy that went into his singing: the millionaire record producer's denunciation of the police department is a virtuoso piece of rant, with just a hint of a whine in its singsong, gospel rhythms. He stands outside in his silk dressing gown, singsonging furiously, and when he says the name "Whiteman" he gives it a twist. The whole movie spins off that name.

Bette Midler has never before been this seductive on the screen. This is only the fourth picture she has starred in, and you see a softer, less funky Midler; she's playing the role of a bored, dissatisfied housewife who has something extra—a warped charm rather like that of Teri Garr, but riper, juicier. Barb looks as if she might be listening to angels tinkling coins; money has beautified her, and so have a succession of gurus and yogis. Whether Barb Whiteman is reclining in the enormous peach-colored bedroom she shares with Dave (it's blissfully harmonious, like a motel in Nirvana) or sitting cross-legged before the statue of an Oriental idol or trotting through the halls jiggling in her frilly dresses and making tippy-taps with her high heels, her eyes are pixillated. She's ready for anything. (I think I'd be happy to watch an evening of Midler just doing her bobble-jiggle walks.)

Richard Dreyfuss's Dave Whiteman is devoted to his cool, slender, above-it-all daughter, irritated by his confused, semi-androgynous son (Evan Richards), and wild about Carmen, whose bed he pads off to as soon as Barb closes her eyes. Dave plays straight man to everybody in the movie; he even plays straight man to the little black-and-white Border collie Matisse, who gets laughs by chasing him around. Lean now, Dreyfuss is more precise and agile than he used to be, and he uses his slightness for comic effects vis-à-vis Nolte. When Dave is trying to hold the unconscious man's head above the water, he looks as if he were being overpowered by Jerry's bulk (and the stones). And when Jerry, shaven and groomed, walks down the street with Dave he towers over the blithe little guy. Dreyfuss isn't acting up a storm; he just slips into the character of Dave the patsy and stays with it. He hasn't been on the screen for a few years, so we get to rediscover what an enjoyable actor he can be. His Dave is the traditional henpecked husband brought up to date: Dave is henpecked upstairs by Barb and downstairs by the demanding Carmen. Elizabeth Peña plays Carmen as tantalizing and sulky; she has a bedroom mouth, and when it says no to Dave the rejection is brutal, because that mouth looks as if it were made to say nothing but yes.

Nick Nolte looks great as Jerry; his high cheekbones and strong physique and fair hair—the abundance of it—suggest a Nordic seafarer but one with the sneaky, foxy eyes of a con artist. He looks a bit like Kris Kristofferson here but much more powerful. And he has that deep rumble of a voice which seems to come from under the ocean floor. Jerry never tips his hand; he's as much of a mystery at the end as he was at the beginning, and that seems right, because explaining his background would diminish the movie—would suggest that it's about clearing up the mystery of who and what Jerry used to be. But the Beverly Hills we see is about the wonders of rootlessness; a shrewd bum *should* rule the roost. Taxpaying residents may panic when stray leaves fall on their plush greensward; it takes a bum like Jerry to be lordly enough to pee on the plants.

The film has some minor flaws. In the opening scenes, Jerry, looking for his mutt Kerouac, abandons the shopping cart with his pack rat's hoard of possessions, and he never goes to reclaim it. (Perhaps the cart-pushing fellow we see under the end titles is meant to have taken it.) And the advice that Jerry gives the Whitemans' son is no different from what a radio psychologist might give him. So when it backfires you expect Mazursky to come up with a snapper of some sort. (The boy is made too poignant anyway; Mazursky treats his sexual-identity problems in the constrained way he treated the heroine's rising consciousness in *An Unmarried Woman*.) And the film makes the mistake of leading you to expect a resolution that it can't provide. But these are nits. The picture is peppy and pleasurable in the way that *Moscow on the Hudson* is, and with a modulated visual texture that makes it one of the most sheerly beautiful comedies ever shot. Mazursky, who appears in a small part, as Dave's accountant, wears the wild curly wig of a bandit. He isn't afraid of uproarious silliness. I haven't laughed at cuts to a dog reacting since *Used Cars,* but Matisse provides the capper to some dizzying slapstick numbers. The dog's startled response to Barb's orgasmic vocalizing is stupendous. And there's a wonderful feeling of a warrior at his rest when Nolte relaxes sleepily in the peach bedroom with Matisse snuggling on his hip.

The New Yorker, February 10, 1986

HANNAH AND HER SISTERS

Woody Allen's *Hannah and Her Sisters* is an agreeably skillful movie, a new canto in his ongoing poem to love and New York City which includes *Annie Hall* and *Manhattan*. The principal characters are members of a show-business family, with the stable, dependable Hannah (Mia Farrow), a successful actress who manages a career and children with equal serenity, as the pivotal figure. At the start, the whole clan gathers at her sprawling Upper West Side apartment for Thanksgiving dinner. It includes her two flailing-about sisters: the wildly insecure cocaine-nut Holly (Dianne Wiest), whose acting career has never taken off, and the unsure-of-herself Lee (Barbara Hershey), who goes to A.A. and turns to men she can look up to. It includes the three sisters' bickering show-business-veteran parents: their boozy, habitually flirtatious mother (Maureen O'Sullivan) and their affable, but underconfident father (Lloyd Nolan). And it includes Hannah's financial-consultant husband (Michael Caine), who is swooning with passion for Lee, and an assortment of friends and relatives. Not in attendance is Lee's artist lover (Max von Sydow), who has no patience for social chatter. The movie ends at another Thanksgiving celebration, two years later; by then, Holly has pulled herself together, Hannah's husband has had his fling with Lee, and Hannah's ex-husband, Mickey Sachs (Woody Allen), a TV writer-producer, has rejoined the clan. And things are rosier. Like Ingmar Bergman's *Fanny and Alexander,* which was also about a theatrical family, the film is full of cultured people, and it has a comfortable, positive tone. Bergman's central character, Alexander, was clearly based on Bergman as a child; Allen's heroine is clearly based on Mia Farrow. And, like Bergman, whose cast included old friends, an ex-wife, an ex-lover, and a few of his children, Allen uses several actors he has worked with before, has Mia Farrow's mother playing Hannah's mother, and uses Farrow's actual apartment and seven of her eight children.

Hannah is meant to be the still center of the film, but mute would be more like it. Casting Mia Farrow as an ideal creative, nurturing woman in demure, plain-Jane dresses, Allen turns her into an earth-mother symbol and disembodies her. Most of the time, Hannah the Madonna seems barely animate. Allen has got her so subdued and idealized that she seems to be floating passively in another world. Barbara Hershey has a luscious presence here. She has a sexual vibrancy about her, and she fits her role—it's easy to believe that her brother-in-law would become obsessed with her. But Allen hasn't written enough sides for her—or for anyone else—to play. Dianne Wiest does all she can with her role—she makes a style out of neurosis. Her Holly is so fouled up that she's always angry at herself and everybody else, too. Her nerves aquiver, she seems to be holding back either screams or tears; she lives in a tizzy. (And she's so completely lacking in confidence that she's bound to match up with the Woody Allen character.) But Allen's script, for all its shrewdness about sisterly relations and its considerable finesse, doesn't cut very deep. There's a basic, bland unadventurousness about the picture: it never makes us wonder about anything. Hangups are there to be got through; the characters are like patients in the hands of a benevolent, godlike therapist.

Hannah and Her Sisters would be lifeless without Woody Allen's presence as Mickey Sachs, who is convinced he has a fatal disease. It needs his mopey personality, and it needs his jokes, even though they're throwbacks to earlier gags. It's a funny thing about Woody Allen: the characters he plays learn to accept life and get on with it, but then he starts a new picture and his character is back at square one. Mickey is a hypochondriac, terrified of dying and obsessed with the same old Woody Allen question: If there's no God and no afterlife, what's the point of living? Mickey takes a year off from his work in TV to ponder the meaninglessness of everything. He tries to find faith in Catholicism and then, for a moment, in Hare Krishna (because of the sect's belief in reincarnation); he attempts suicide. Then he sees the Marx Brothers in *Duck Soup,* and when they sing "Hail, Fredonia" he realizes that he wants to enjoy life for as long as he can. He'll settle for romantic love, for a "relationship." But we've been through all this with him before.

Still, the picture needs him desperately, because the other roles are so thin that there's nobody else to draw us into the story. Michael Caine flails around confusedly trying to bring something to a role that's out of bedroom farce but that he seems expected to give other dimensions to. At first, you attribute Caine's discomfort to the character's crush on Lee, but afterward he goes on being ill at ease. Maureen O'Sullivan (who was born in 1911) comes through with a ribald-old-trouper performance that's gutsier than anything she ever did in her M-G-M years. But it's a small role. So is that of Lloyd Nolan (born in 1902), who made his final appearance here; he brings to his part the dapper weariness of a vain man whose wife goads him unconscionably—he may suspect that tormenting him is what keeps her on her toes and beautiful. In a larger role, Max von Sydow has nothing to play but an aspect of the earlier Woody Allen characters: he's a rigid intellectual, a man so devoted to high culture that he's exasperated by other people's delight in pop. He's like the Woody Allen of *Stardust Memories,* and his determination to educate Lee recalls the Woody of *Annie Hall.*

This character's gloom and the way he cuts himself off from other people tell us that Woody Allen is saying here that the high arts are not everything—that we also need the ease and relaxation of pop culture, that superficiality isn't all bad. Allen's love for the romantic, "civilized" pop music of the past is expressed throughout the movie, which features Rodgers and Hart songs, a couple of Harry James recordings, and some Count Basie, as well as Gustav Leonhardt playing Bach. Allen draws the line at high-powered rock, though: part of Holly's coming to her senses is her graduating from the downtown life of CBGB to classical music. Woody Allen can't seem to get rid of a streak of draggy pedantry; he's still something of a cultural commissar. (I could have done without the quick tour of Manhattan's architectural marvels that's included in the movie)

Like Bergman, Allen shows his intellectuality by dramatizing his quest for meaning and then shows his profundity by exposing the aridity of that quest. This celebration of family is essentially a celebration of sanity and of belonging to a group—of satisfying the need for human connections. It's a tribute to human resilience, a look-we-have-come-through movie, and the people who were deeply moved by *Manhattan* are likely to be still more deeply moved by *Hannah*. The infertile Mickey even becomes fertile; the picture goes the traditional life-affirming route. Yet what he has come through to is so lacking in resonance that it feels like nowhere. *Hannah* is very fluid in the way it weaves the characters in and out; Allen's modulated storytelling has a grace to it. The picture is certainly better than three-fourths of the ones that open, and it's likable, but you wish there were more to like. It has some lovely scenes—I was particularly taken with the one in which Holly and a good friend (played by Carrie Fisher) are out in a car with a man (Sam Waterston) whom they're both interested in, and at their last stop before calling it a night they discuss the logistics of which one he should drop off first. Yet, over all, the movie is a little stale, and it suggests the perils of inbreeding It might be time for Woody Allen to make a film with a whole new set of friends, or, at least, to take a long break from his sentimentalization of New York City. Maybe he'd shed the element of cultural self-approval in the tone of this movie. There's almost a trace of smugness in its narrow concern for family and friends; it's as if the moviemaker has seen through the folly of any wider concern.

Woody Allen has joined a club that will have him, and that may help to explain the awesome advance praise for the film. Like the Robert Benton picture *Kramer vs. Kramer,* which also stirred up enormous enthusiasm in the press, *Hannah* evokes the "family/style" pages in the *New York Times* and all the books and editorials and "Hers" columns about people divorcing and remarrying and searching to find meaning in their lives. It's about people that members of the press can identify with; it's what they imagine themselves to be or would like to be. They're applauding their fantasy of themselves.

All the vital vulgarity of Woody Allen's early movies has been drained away here, as it was in *Interiors,* but this time he's made the picture halfway human. People can laugh and feel morally uplifted at the same time. The willed sterility of his style is terrifying to think about, though; the picture is all tasteful touches. He uses style to blot out the rest of New York City. It's a form of repression, and from the look of *Hannah and Her Sisters,* repression is what's romantic to him. That's what the press is applauding—the romance of gentrification.

The New Yorker, February 24, 1986

MY BEAUTIFUL LAUNDRETTE

My Beautiful Laundrette is the unprepossessing title of a startlingly fresh movie from England. The director, Stephen Frears, threads his way through life in South London among the surly white street gangs who live on the dole with no hope of anything better and the Pakistani immigrants who are trying to make their way upward. The movie begins in a small apartment with a Pakistani father phoning his brother to arrange a summer job for his son, whom he expects to start college in the fall, and it gradually expands until you get the sense of the Pakistanis moving in everywhere, and forming a community inside a larger slum community. As the assorted skinheads, punkers, and thugs see it, the "Pakis" were allowed into England to do the dirty work, to be *under* them, yet are getting ahead of them; and these thugs, with their remnants of colonial, master-race attitudes, take out their frustrations on the unlucky Pakistanis who cross their path. That's the milieu of the movie; it's intrinsically fascinating, and you wouldn't normally see it. You're taken into it by guides who know their way around, and you're caught up in the texture and decay of modern big-city life. Though it's South London, you have the feeling that this is what's around you, too—that your blinders have been taken off. The movie defines a world and the people in it, and keeps redefining them. In the foreground is a homosexual romance between a dark-eyed, softly handsome, almost flowerlike Pakistani teenager, Omar (Gordon Warnecke), who grew up in this neighborhood, and a young dyed-blond-on-brunet street lout, Johnny (Daniel Day-Lewis). They chummed together years before, as schoolkids, and they become partners when Omar, having taken the summer job washing cars in his uncle's parking garage, persuades the uncle to let him have a ratty-looking failed launderette.

Omar's mother couldn't take the cultural dislocation of the move to London and killed herself. Papa (Roshan Seth), a member of a distinguished family that was highly respected in Pakistan, was a left-wing intellectual journalist in Bombay, and he expects Omar to become an educated man and carry on the family traditions, though he himself is now a vodka-soaked dreamer, a near-invalid too sodden to get out of bed. There's not much left of Papa except bright eyes and a tongue that's still quick. Omar's uncle (Saeed Jaffrey) has been amassing money; it's the only way he sees for a Pakistani to win respect in London. A plump sensualist, he's a slumlord and low-level capitalist entrepreneur, with a handful of enterprises, some of them shady. Saeed Jaffrey—he was Billy Fish, the interpreter, in *The Man Who Would Be King*—plays the uncle as a man who's a slave to his appetites; he loves his white-Londoner mistress (Shirley Anne Field), he loves his wife and daughters, he loves the sweet, docile Omar. He wants Omar to marry his playful, smart, uncontrollable daughter, Tania. He wants everybody to be happy, and he wants to be sated with sex and oiled and massaged like a pasha.

Omar, who's eager to learn and not afraid of hard work, is soon making pickups of dope and porno videos, and, as amoral as a puppy, he steals from a racketeer relative. That's how he and Johnny get the money to transform the run-down launderette into a neon-decorated establishment that looks like the flashiest new disco in town. It's a slum dweller's dream of hot chic, and on the re-opening day Omar and Johnny are so exhausted and elated that they have to make love before letting the customers in. As Daniel Day-Lewis (son of the poet C. Day Lewis and grandson of Sir Michael Balcon, who was the head of Ealing Studios) plays Johnny, he's morally aware in ways that Omar isn't. He doesn't enjoy being a dull-eyed, semi-fascistic loafer; he hates the hanging around doing nothing that has been his life, and he has outgrown his old street gang—he's too intelligent to go on shouting insults at Pakis and threatening them. But he still feels a loyalty to his old pals—he knows how pathetic they are under their loudmouth jeering and Paki-bashing. When he's in a car with Omar, and the racketeer relative, who's driving, angrily runs down and cripples a gang member, an old friend of his, and then speeds off, Johnny is torn by conflicting loyalties. And Omar has his conflicts, too. He uses his come-hither eyes on Johnny, but he also plays boss to him—exacting revenge for all the times that Johnny and other street toughs insulted him. Race and sex, resentment and pride, and just plain ignorance are hopelessly (and comically) intertwined in this story.

The scriptwriter, Hanif Kureishi, who's not yet thirty, was born in South London, to a Pakistani father and a white English mother. His first play was staged at the Royal Court Theatre when he was eighteen; it was about the immigrant experience, which he has kept at in all his work since. *My Beautiful Laundrette* was written for television, and Frears made it in 16-mm., on a budget of under $850,000. After it was shown at several European festivals and opened in English theatres, Frears was asked why he hadn't got together a bigger budget and shot it in 35-mm. He answered, "You couldn't seriously have gone out and said to a financier, 'I'm going to make a film about a gay Pakistani launderette owner,' and confidently expected that there'd be an audience." As it turned out, the blowup to 35-mm. is near-miraculous; it's only in the first scene or two that a viewer is conscious that the definition is not as sharp as it might be. Frears has directed more than a dozen films for British TV since his first, in 1971 (the most famous is probably the 1979 *Bloody Kids*); he has also made a couple of theatrical films (*Gumshoe,* with Albert Finney, in 1971, and *The Hit,* with Terence Stamp and John Hurt, in 1984). What we see in *My Beautiful Laundrette*—the title grows on you—is a sensual, highly developed visual style. The 16-mm. may even contribute to the film's informal, dropped-in-on quality. Kureishi's script is filled to the rafters with characters and incidents, and the way Frears stages the various interactions it's almost as if they were simply going on in the environment and he and his cinematographer, Oliver Stapleton, just happened to pick up on them. This is particularly true for the women characters. With the exception of Shirley Anne Field's good-natured, aging bawd, the women's roles aren't as fully developed as the men's, but the women's visual presence is so strong that we get a sense of what their lives are—particularly that of the hit-and-run driver's wife (Souad Faress), who's always sticking her head out in hallways to see what's going on, and the unmanageable Tania (Rita Wolf), who becomes more attractive and impressive with each appearance. Even the loving relationship between Omar's Papa and uncle develops new meaning when we finally see the two together, and see how they accept each other's weaknesses.

Over the years, Frears has refined a magical instinct for just how long we want to see a face and just how long a scene needs to be. If he could bottle this instinct, it could be called "Essence of Moviemaking." His images here are quick and unexpected, and they feel exactly right. But Frears' editing rhythms that seem so right are actually very odd. *My Beautiful Laundrette* doesn't feel like any other movie; it's almost as if he's cutting to the rhythm of Pakistani-accented English—to what you can hear even in the quirky lilt of the title. The stew of interrelationships that Kureishi supplies seems appropriate to the Pakistanis' ornate ceremoniousness; it even suggests Islamic decorative art. The Pakistanis bring their tastes with them, but what comes through even more strongly is that Western capitalist culture appeals to their senses and blends with their traditions. Omar's eyes shine when he sees flashing lights; his relatives love their VCRs. Frears and Kureishi are unapologetic about showing Pakistanis as lowlifes or as possession-crazy, and they don't hem and haw about showing that Omar is a bit of a harem girl, slithering through various groups. He brings nothing into any environment; he just takes on protective coloration. You gradually get a sense of how he operates—he's a young man on the make. The people in this movie want something more than they have, and you feel the enticement of their goals: Omar wants flash. Tania wants independence. Johnny wants to get away from the street kids who feel that they're in a dead-end society, and so he joins up with the Pakistanis who know that this society is the best they can hope for, and try to wriggle through the cracks.

Frears is responsive to grubby desperation and to the uncouthness and energy in English life—he's responsive to what went into the punk-music scene and to what goes into teen-age-gang life. You could feel it in the way he released the energy of the young hood Myron, played by Tim Roth, in *The Hit.* That picture had something: a style, a tone, a streak of humor. But its flamboyant existentialism was spare and abstract; the picture was empty compared with this one—it was all craft and artifice. Here Johnny is more central to the action than Myron was, and Daniel Day-Lewis's performance gives the movie an imaginative, seductive spark. As the skinny-faced John Fryer in the 1984 *The Bounty,* Day-Lewis stuck out; he seemed like a bad actor. But if he can do only certain kinds of roles Johnny must be in his very best range. When Johnny refocusses his attention, it shows in his face, and when he looks at himself in the mirror to fluff his hair, his face is different from how it is when he looks at other people. This Johnny wants to make something of himself, and he'll go through more than his share of humiliation to do it. He also enjoys wooing the cuddly Omar. He can't resist touching Omar with his tongue when they're out on the street, right in front of the launderette, with white-racist rowdies all around them. He can't resist being frisky, because it's dangerous, and that makes it more erotic. The movie captures some of the wonderful, devil-may-care giddiness that's part of the joyride of teen-age sex. Johnny and Omar behave as if they had invented the thrills of perilous public display; for all they know, they did. And the messy tensions of the multiracial South London community feed into the tenderness of their love affair.

It's an enormous pleasure to see a movie that's really about something, and that doesn't lay on any syrupy coating to make the subject go down easily. (It's down before you notice it.) Frears and Kureishi take a pile of risks in this movie, and take them in stride.

The New Yorker, March 10, 1986

FROM REVIEW OF THE TAVIANI BROTHERS'
KAOS

In the epilogue, Omero Antonutti, who was the father in *Padre Padrone* and the peasant leader in *Shooting Stars,* plays the aging, world-famous Nobel Prize winner Pirandello, a dapper gentleman with a pointy little goatee, returning after many years to his family home. Getting off the train from Rome, he sees a couple of boys taking turns diving down a pile of sand, and the image stirs something in him. When he's in the house and has a vision of his dead mother, he asks her to tell him once again about an adventure she had as a child—a story he has never been able to put on paper—and we go back in time as she describes the day when her own mother took her brood of six children in a red-sailed fishing boat for the three-day trip to visit their father, a political exile, in Malta. On the way, the boat stopped at a volcanic island—a mountain of white pumice—and she and her brothers and sisters stripped to their underclothes, climbed up the slopes, and, flapping their arms, floated down the powdery white sand to bathe in the sea. As they slide into the turquoise water, the clouds of pumice drifting down with them merge with the skies and the foaming whitecaps of the Mediterranean. The children are flying through whiteness, and the music carries the sound of a bell, recalling the swooping, soaring crow (of the earlier scenes). The Tavianis themselves are flying high here: the images seem to comprise all memories of childhood pleasure and all nostalgia. The music, the sights, the longings that the children have evoked all come together, and for a moment we're not sure how many of our senses are being affected. And, of course, we can see why the Tavianis have their Pirandello figure say that he could never find a way to tell this story: you need to be a moviemaker to fuse sensory impressions as the Tavianis have done here. For sheer transcendence, these moments are peerless; we're with the children, cascading through eternity.

The New Yorker, March 10, 1986

8 MILLION WAYS TO DIE

Hal Ashby's *8 Million Ways to Die* is about cops and robbers, coke and hookers. (These are the pillars of new American action movies—the ones that aren't about showing the Commies how mighty is our moral wrath.) The Ashby film is based on Lawrence Block's mystery novels featuring the detective Matthew Scudder; the best known of these books is *Eight Million Ways to Die*—which, of course, refers to New York City, where the stories are set. So it's a bit dislocating when the movie opens with a fine aerial view of traffic on the L.A. freeways. Scudder (Jeff Bridges) is now a narcotics detective for the L.A. County Sheriff's Department, and that first dislocation is one of many. The movie has an overlush pictorial exoticism, as if being coked out comes with the territory. The locales, which include a cliff at Malibu with a tram that takes you up to a casino-bordello, and a cocaine importer's curvy, pseudo-Gaudí house, suggest an effort to find a dark, baroque beauty and sexiness in the corrupt city. (It's as if Ashby imagines himself shooting *The Third Man* in the bombed-out ruins of Vienna.) *8 Million* is both intensely visual and exhausted—"blown away." It's more enjoyable than the other pictures that Ashby has made in the last half-dozen years, yet it's permeated with druggy dissociation and you can't always distinguish between what's intentional and what's unintentional. Plot points don't connect, as though they don't matter, the actors often sound as if they're making up their lines, and on three separate occasions Scudder and another man engage in lengthy, belligerent confrontations, exchanging obscenities and telling each other off. As far as the narrative is concerned, these macho shouting matches might be intermissions. What they tell us is that Ashby is less interested in the thriller aspect of the film than in men in a semi-stupor challenging each other. And the crazy confusion of these challenges is halfway amusing—you don't know what's going on, or if the director does, either. Violence and dreaminess are blended.

At the outset, Scudder, driven to drink after he has had to shoot a man, has taken a leave of absence from the Sheriff's Department and joined A.A. He's been free of booze for six months when a bright-eyed, coke-snorting young hooker called Sunny (Alexandra Paul) hires him to protect her. Sunny is one of a string of a dozen or so whores who are available to the patrons of the swank casino, and the film's grandiosity klonks a viewer on the head fairly early, when this fresh-faced sweetie takes off her clothes in Scudder's apartment and rhapsodizes about the glow of her pubic hair in the street light. Not in the moonlight but in the street light. Her words may be the ultimate in eighties film-noir self-consciousness. (Is there something in druggy subjects that encourages directors to make imitation film noir? Film noir itself becomes an addiction.) At first, Scudder thinks that Sunny is frightened of Chance (Randy Brooks), the black ex-convict who operates the casino, but after she is murdered his suspicions settle on a sleek Colombian-American racketeer, Angel Maldonado (Andy Garcia), who frequents the place and is enamored of Sarah (Rosanna Arquette), the top hooker of the bunch. The script, credited to Oliver Stone and David Lee Henry (other hands were also involved), is crude stuff, but it suggests more hardboiled narrative drive than Ashby delivers. (That might be what prompted the production company to fire him after the wrap—the completion of principal photography.) The story isn't filled in, and the spaces in the narrative contribute to the coked-out feeling. At times, Ashby might be waiting around for something in his brain to crystallize. He doesn't give the scenes the emotional shading that would make them play, and the actors are left exposed to ridicule, as if this were a cheap exploitation film instead of an expensive one. Except for Andy Garcia, the Cuban-born actor who was the trim, attentive homicide detective in *The Mean Season,* and who cuts loose here—he does Latino sleaze and volatility to hammy perfection, flashing his eyes like semaphores—the performances are negligible. That includes Bridges, and Arquette, too. When she's trying to be hard-edged, she chops her lines short and makes funny faces. (And the hopes that people have had for her, on the basis of her work—and her look—in *The Executioner's Song,* keep withering away.) As for Bridges, he generally tries something different in each role, but he can't get hold of much this time; a passivity seems to engulf him, and the picture swings over to Garcia, who's simply more fun to watch.

8 Million Ways to Die is like a continuation of other drug-traffic movies that Oliver Stone has written *(Midnight Express, Scarface, Year of the Dragon).* It's pulpier and tawdrier than you might expect from Ashby, but it's also woozy, and it luxuriates in the glamour of being physically and emotionally spent, as if droopiness were sexy. Ashby seems to smear his materials on the screen; that includes such devices as blobs of color and breathy sounds on the track. He loves visionary, watery finales—he has Bridges and Arquette romping on the beach at the end, embracing and walking along, just two happy kids. And you feel as if you're seeing a mind shutting off in front of your eyes. He directs like a gonzo flower child.

The New Yorker, May 19, 1986

MONA LISA

The imperious black call girl Simone (Cathy Tyson) works on a strict schedule that requires a chauffeured car to take her to luxury hotels and private residences. One night, after she has finished her rounds, and her driver, George (Bob Hoskins), is heading for her apartment, she asks him to stop as they go past the rows of streetwalkers soliciting along a London bridge. Sitting half hidden in the back of the car, she stares at the battered, painted girls; her face looks pinched—haunted—as if she never slept, as if her memories were shadows that would never lift. In these shots in the new English film *Mona Lisa,* directed by Neil Jordan, an Irish novelist turned moviemaker, the streetwalkers are standing around the car. George sees Simone's face in the mirror swimming at the center of a sea of women's faces. It's an emotionally hypercharged image; it's hellish, yet it's also sensuous, dreamy, mythic. And in that moment we see him fall in love with her. When a pimp recognizes Simone and sticks his head in the car's open front window, shouting insults at her, George, in a fury, bashes the guy's head against the top and bottom of the open window and shoves the bloody mess out. As George drives on, the women's faces blur and disappear; they stay in your consciousness, though, throughout the movie, which is lurid in a beautiful way.

George is the central character. At one time an East End petty criminal, he has just come out of prison; he took a seven-year rap in place of the vice lord Mortwell (Michael Caine), and has been given the chauffeuring job as his recompense. Neil Jordan (and David Leland) wrote the script with Hoskins in mind; he's in every scene, and he's tremendous. This short, chunky actor is a powerhouse, yet he doesn't wear you out, the way some powerhouse performers do. As George, he's a decent, simple guy and a romantic at heart, but when he attacks a couple of big bruisers and knocks them down, he's completely convincing. Jordan intends the movie to be an adult version of the fairy tale of the Frog Prince, told from the frog's point of view. But that isn't the image that comes to mind. Hoskins' George is a little like a Cockney version of Edward G. Robinson's tough guys and a little like Bruno Lawrence at his most impassioned and explosive in *Smash Palace.* He's intensely sympathetic, yet brutish—especially when he's trying to assert that he's as good as anybody—and he charges his enemies like a chesty bull terrier. When he starts work as Simone's chauffeur, he doesn't know how to behave in the fancy lobbies where he is to pick her up; being ill at ease makes him belligerent, and he calls too much attention to himself. Simone is furious. She does nothing but curse and complain, and that makes him touchier and more obstreperous. The friend sitting next to me summed him up: "He's like a testicle on legs."

When George shows his devotion to the uncommunicative Simone—the Mona Lisa of the story—she sets him to searching the red-light districts of London for the girl that she was hoping to find when she asked him to stop the car. She and this little blonde—a fifteen-year-old heroin addict who was her friend when she was working the streets—were in the control of the same vicious pimp. George makes his way through the strip joints and erotic shows and whores' hangouts, and is sickened when he sees defenseless young girls covered with bruises. He finds Simone's friend and breaks into the mansion where she's being used in a blackmail scheme; she's so strung out and wrecked that he has to carry her piggyback to the car. (At first, George doesn't understand what's the matter with her. The script sometimes requires him to be more thickheaded than seems plausible, and the audience grasps things faster than he does. But we can accept this as a convention.) We see the drugs and kinkiness and cruelty as the good-hearted, appalled George sees them. He also sees that his old boss Mortwell is in the rotten thick of it. In this movie, vice is pitiful and powerfully ugly, and hallucinatory, too.

Most of the picture was shot on location in London and Brighton, but Jordan's London and Brighton never look merely realistic; the lighting (by the cinematographer Roger Pratt) heightens their emotional resonances. And Jordan—this is his third movie, after *Angel* (1982), set in Northern Ireland and released here as *Danny Boy,* and *The Company of Wolves* (1984)—shows a gift for making the emotional atmosphere visual, and vice versa. He works in a heated-up rhetorical style that's something like a visual equivalent of Norman Mailer's method in *An American Dream.* It's thought-out pop, and Jordan is perhaps too aware of the mythic layers in the material—an awareness that comes out in old-movie conceits and symbolic touches and contrasts and balances. You get the feeling that Jordan has hovered over this garden of references (with its dwarf and its white horse) very lovingly. He may be one of those people who become so involved in dreams and the unconscious that they go at everything consciously, like a diligent graduate student. Even his playfulness is pointed. You hear Nat King Cole's 1950 recording of the Jay Livingston and Ray Evans song "Mona Lisa" during the titles; you hear it again (as in a forties movie) on George's car radio. When George visits his burly old pal Thomas (Robbie Coltrane) and you see a reproduction of the Leonardo painting stuck on the side of the refrigerator in Thomas's private junk yard, it may be a bit fussy. And when George and Simone run for their lives, racing through the carnival stands on the pier at Brighton, it may not be such a great idea for them to jostle a display of red hearts and make them fall to the boardwalk. But the way Jordan uses clichés they become part of a fluid, enjoyable texture, a melodramatic impasto with an expressive power of its own. It's his romanticism that pulls you along. And if there's an element of intellectual vanity or preciousness in the film's system of references Hoskins and Tyson and Coltrane and Caine redeem it. They haven't thought things out too much; they draw on their intuitions—and, yes, their unconscious. They do it naturally and confidently, and Jordan has made this possible. He may be overaware of how he wants us to read the film's meaning, but he goes with the performers. He appears to let them set the rhythms in some of the key dialogue scenes; the result is oddly irregular and lifelike (in this stylized thriller), and very pleasing.

Cathy Tyson was raised in Liverpool and is, at twenty, a member of the Royal Shakespeare Company. She's a head taller than Hoskins, and has a slender-faced poignancy that makes Simone's foulmouthed anger seem like a self-violation. Simone's anger is inseparable from pain and loneliness, and when she drops her haughtiness and shows some fellow-feeling for George a viewer experiences the scene as if it were a spring bouquet, even though the ambiguousness and tension in the atmosphere aren't dispelled. This is Cathy Tyson's first movie, and I think it helps that we've never seen her before: her Simone is as mysteriously stirring to us as she is to George. Tyson also has remarkable control: there are few feminist tags on her performance, but her beauty incarnates everything that the sadistic pimps beat down in the process of turning girls into dependent dumb cows. It makes perfect sense that Simone has no love left in her for men. (And it makes perfect sense that Jordan, who was born in 1950 and is the father of two girls, has the empathy that he shows here, and makes George the father of a girl as a way of deepening *his* empathy.) The faintly out-of-it character—Coltrane's big, blubbery Thomas—has a calming influence on George and on the picture. Thomas's eccentric sanity is lightly amusing, and very easy to take, even though it's apparent that he's a function of the plot; he's in the movie to be a true friend to George, to understand his follies, and to warn him about Mortwell right at the start.

The name Mortwell is a bit much and is probably intended to be, and so is the white rabbit that George gives this crime boss. (It provides the final baroque touch that, so to speak, fulfills the name.) But Mortwell is not a character you can just dismiss, and I can't recall a screen star of Michael Caine's rank who has had the talent and the willingness to play a man so foul and repugnant. It's said that all Caine's scenes were shot in four days, and there aren't really many of them, but they add up to a portrait of an abomination. Mortwell panders to the vices of the rich and the poor, and he does it in a routine, matter-of-fact way. His pallor and his fish-faced smile reveal that he knows he's not peddling nuts and bolts, but he views the girls he deals in as if they were something less than hardware. Mortwell is everything that the little mug George will never understand; he's what Simone has had to come to understand. And it's a scary performance: after more than fifty pictures, Caine still comes up with shocking surprises. As Mortwell, Caine is believably evil, just as Hoskins, as George, is believably kind yet violent. It may be no more than an accident of casting that these two actors are also onscreen together in *Sweet Liberty,* and that they were together in the 1983 *Beyond the Limit* (the film of Graham Greene's *The Honorary Consul*). But in some way that perhaps Caine and Hoskins—who are both playing Cockneys here—understand, they operate on the same energy level. They take paper conceptions and turn them into characters who are more alive than anybody else in their pictures. Caine manages to do this even when he's playing a piece of ordure like Mortwell.

Mona Lisa reeks of noirishness. Worse, it reeks of intellectualized noirishnesss. But the whole movie has some of the potency of cheap music that's represented by the title song. I succumbed.

The New Yorker, June 16, 1986

TOP GUN

The strapping Kelly McGillis spends her time in *Top Gun* sidling into rooms and leaning against doorways, or slouching or bending, so she won't overpower her co-star, the relatively diminutive Tom Cruise. In some scenes, she stands slightly behind him, resting on his shoulder with her body contorted into an S so their heads will be on a level. And all the while she does her full-blown best to leer at him sexily. The best part of the movie comes when he's suffering: he speaks in a little-boy voice and looks such a Nautilized, dinky thing. Trying to instill courage in him, she says throatily, "When I first met you, you were larger than life."

In Nabokov's *Lolita,* Humbert Humbert tortures himself with images of his nymphet in the arms of "kissy-faced brutes"; that's what *Top Gun* is full of. When McGillis is offscreen, the movie is a shiny homoerotic commercial featuring the élite fighter pilots in training at San Diego's Miramar Naval Air Station. The pilots strut around the locker room, towels hanging precariously from their waists, and when they speak to each other they're head to head, as if to shout "Sez you!" It's as if masculinity had been redefined as how a young man looks with his clothes half off, and as if narcissism is what being a warrior is all about.

In between the bare-chested maneuvers, there's footage of ugly snub-nosed jets taking off, whooshing around in the sky, and landing while the soundtrack calls up Armageddon and the Second Coming—though what we're seeing is training exercises. Photographed up close in a heavy make-believe fog, the planes turn into mythic beasts, the men in the ground crews are adjuncts of these beasts, and the high-powered music simulates a prime-val storm. But once the planes are in the sky the jig is up. When aerial dog-fights are staged with jets, the pilots are barely visible—you can't tell them apart—and it's all so quick and depersonalized there's nothing to see but hunks of steel flashing by.

What is this commercial selling? It's just selling, because that's what the producers, Don Simpson and Jerry Bruckheimer, and the director, Tony (Make It Glow) Scott, know how to do. Selling is what they think moviemaking is about. The result is a new "art" form: the self-referential commercial. *Top Gun* is a recruiting poster that isn't concerned with recruiting but with being a poster.

The New Yorker, June 16, 1986

MIKE'S MURDER

A few days after seeing the newly manufactured, disposable *Legal Eagles,* I noticed that Debra Winger's last picture to be released, *Mike's Murder,* was listed for Showtime in *The New York Times* TV schedule, and that the *Times'* advice was "Skip it." Please, don't skip it next time it comes around—or, if you can, rent it. I wasn't able to see this film during its unheralded, minuscule New York run in 1984, but I caught up with it on HBO last year. It's not a movie that had much likelihood of being a hit, but its view of the cocaine subculture (or culture) of L.A. is probably the most original and daring effort by the writer-director James Bridges, and it has two superb performances—a full-scale starring one by Winger, and a brief intense one by Paul Winfield. She's a radiantly sane young bank teller who has an affair with a curly-haired, clear-faced young tennis instructor called Mike (Mark Keyloun). She likes him—you can see her eagerness, even though she knows how to be cool and bantering with him. And when they're together you can believe that there's something going on between them. But it's a wobbly affair: she hears from him randomly over the course of two years. Whenever the mood hits him, he calls her, and once he asks her to drive him to an estate where he plans to hole up—he tells her he has been dealing, and that he's being chased for encroaching on some other guys' territory. One night, he's supposed to come over late, but he doesn't show. She gets a call from a friend of his telling her he's dead, and that he talked about her all the time. His death is abrupt, bewildering. She can't let go of him so quickly—not without understanding more about him—and she tries to find out anything she can. What she learns is that he scrounged off homosexual lovers (that's where Winfield, a record producer, comes in), and she discovers how slimy-paranoid the drug world is, and how quick on the trigger it can be with kids like Mike if they get just a little greedy. She learns a bit, too, about the pleasure-besotted underpinnings of the L.A. entertainment world. (Warner Brothers had been unhappy about the *Mike's Murder* project from the start, and the cast and crew took a thirty-per-cent reduction in salary to keep costs down and insure the film's independence. Then the Warner executives refused to release it until Bridges made some cuts and changes, and they probably breathed a few sighs of relief as they buried it.)

Winger has thick, long, loose hair and a deep, sensual beauty in this movie. Bridges wrote the role for her after directing her in *Urban Cowboy,* and you feel the heroine's expanding awareness in Winger's scenes with Keyloun and her scenes with Winfield. It's a performance that suggests what Antonioni seemed to be trying to get from Jeanne Moreau in *La Notte*, only it really works with Winger—maybe because there's nothing sullen or closed about her. We feel the play of the girl's intelligence, and her openness and curiosity are part of her earthiness, her sanity. There's a marvellous sequence in which Mike calls her after an interval of three months and wants her to come to him right that minute. She says, "How about tomorrow night?" He says, "You know I can't plan that far in advance," and gets her to talk to him while he masturbates. He says he loves her voice, and though we don't see him, we hear a callow sweetness in his tone; he wants to give her satisfaction, too. He talks hot, and she's sort of amused, and goes along with it. I don't know of anyone besides Winger who could play a scene like this so simply. She's a major reason to go on seeing movies in the eighties— but not in *Legal Eagles*.

The New Yorker, June 30, 1986

BLUE VELVET
OUT THERE AND IN HERE

"Maybe I'm sick, but I want to see that again."
—OVERHEARD AFTER A SHOWING OF *BLUE VELVET*

When you come out of the theatre after seeing David Lynch's *Blue Velvet*, you certainly know that you've seen something. You wouldn't mistake frames from *Blue Velvet* for frames from any other movie. It's an anomaly—the work of a genius naïf. If you feel that there's very little art between you and the filmmaker's psyche, it may be because there's less than the usual amount of inhibition. Lynch doesn't censor his sexual fantasies, and the film's hypercharged erotic atmosphere makes it something of a trance-out, but his humor keeps breaking through, too. His fantasies may come from his unconscious, but he recognizes them for what they are, and he's tickled by them. The film is consciously purplish and consciously funny, and the two work together in an original, down-home way.

Shot in Wilmington, North Carolina, it's set in an archetypal small, sleepy city, Lumberton, where the radio station's call letters are WOOD, and the announcer says, "At the sound of the falling tree," and then, as the tree falls, "it's 9:30." Not more than three minutes into the film, you recognize that this peaceful, enchanted, white-picket-fence community, where the eighties look like the fifties, is the creepiest sleepy city you've ever seen. The subject of the movie is exactly that: the mystery and madness hidden in the "normal." At the beginning, the wide images (the film is shot in CinemaScope ratio: 2.35 to 1) are meticulously bright and sharp-edged; you feel that you're seeing every detail of the architecture, the layout of homes and apartments, the furnishings and potted plants, the women's dresses. It's so hyperfamiliar it's scary. The vivid red of the roses by the white fence makes them look like hothouse blooms, and the budding yellow tulips are poised, eager to open. Later, the light is low, but all through this movie the colors are insistent, objects may suddenly be enlarged to fill the frame, and a tiny imagined sound may be amplified to a thunderstorm. The style might be described as hallucinatory clinical realism.

When Mr. Beaumont, of Beaumont's hardware store, is watering his lawn and has a seizure of some sort—probably a cerebral hemorrhage—the water keeps shooting out. It drenches his fallen body, and a neighbor's dog jumps on top of him, frisking and trying to drink from the spray. The green grass, enlarged so that the blades are as tall as redwood trees, is teeming with big black insects, and their quarrelsome buzz and hiss displaces all other sounds. When Jeffrey Beaumont (Kyle MacLachlan), home from college to be near his stricken father and take care of the store, walks back from a visit to the hospital, he dawdles in a vacant lot and spots something unexpected in the grass and weeds: a human ear with an attached hank of hair, and ants crawling all over it. The ear looks like a seashell; in closeup, with the camera moving into the dark canal, it becomes the cosmos, and the sound is what you hear when you put a shell to your ear—the roar of the ocean.

Jeffrey's curiosity about the severed ear—whose head it came from and why it was cut off—leads him to Lumberton's tainted underside, a netherworld of sleazy interconnections. A viewer knows intuitively that this is a coming-of-age picture—that Jeffrey's discovery of this criminal, sadomasochistic network has everything to do with his father's becoming an invalid and his own new status as an adult. It's as if David Lynch were saying, "It's a frightening world out there, and"—tapping his head—"in here."

Wholesome as Jeffrey looks, he's somewhat drawn to violence and kinkiness. But he doesn't quite know that yet, and it's certainly not how he explains himself to Sandy (Laura Dern), a fair-haired high-school senior and the daughter of the police detective investigating the matter of the ear. She has become Jeffrey's confederate, and when she questions the nature of his interest in the case he speaks of being involved with "something that was always hidden," of being "in the middle of a mystery." Sandy tantalizes him with what she's overheard the police saying, and he tantalizes her with the strange, "hidden" things he learns about. During their scenes together, an eerie faraway organ is playing melodies that float in the air, and the sound italicizes the two kids' blarney. It's like the organ music in an old soap opera; it turns their confabs into parody, and tells us that they're in a dream world. Sometimes when Jeffrey tells Sandy what he thinks is going on it's as if he had dreamed it and then woke up and found out it had happened. Jeffrey himself is the mystery that Sandy is drawn to (perhaps the tiny gold earring he wears is part of his attraction), and you can't help giggling a little when she turns to him with a worried, earnest face and says, "I don't know if you're a detective or a pervert." She's still a kid; she thinks it's either/or. Jeffrey is soon withholding some of his adventures from her, because they're not just mysteriously erotic—they're downright carnal, and, yes, he's smack in the middle of it all. He has been pulled—with no kicking or screaming—into the inferno of corrupt adult sexuality.

Dorothy Vallens (Isabella Rossellini) is soft and brunette and faintly, lusciously foreign; she has had a child, and she's enough older than Jeffrey to have the allure of an "experienced woman." A torch singer in a night club outside the city limits, she wears a moth-eaten mop of curls and lives at the Deep River Apartments in musty rooms that look as if they'd sprouted their own furniture. The gloomy walls—mauve gone brown—suggest the chic of an earlier era, when perhaps the building was considered fashionable (and the elevator worked). Sandy has told Jeffrey that the police think Dorothy Vallens is involved in the mutilation case, and have her under surveillance. Jeffrey puts her under closer surveillance. The moviemaker doesn't do any interpreting for you: you simply watch and listen, and what ensues rings so many bells in your head that you may get a little woozy.

Hiding in Dorothy's closet at night, Jeffrey peeks at her through the slatted door while she undresses. She hears him and, grabbing a kitchen knife, orders him out of his hiding place and forces him to strip. When he has nothing on but his shorts, she pulls them down and begins fondling him, but sends him back into the closet when she has a caller—Frank the crime boss, Mr. Macho Sleazeball himself, played by Dennis Hopper. Frank is an infantile tough-guy sadist who calls her "Mommy," wallops her if she forgets to call him "Daddy," and wallops her harder if she happens to look at him. All this seems to be part of their regular ritual; he demands his bourbon (as if he's sick of telling her), has her dim the lights, and he takes out an inhaler mask (for some unspecified gas) to heighten his sensations during sex. (The gas is probably a booster to whatever drugs he's on.) He also uses a fetish—the sash of Dorothy's blue velvet bathrobe. Jeffrey, in his closet, doesn't make a sound this time; he's transfixed by what he can just barely see. It's like a sick-joke version of the primal scene, and this curious child watches his parents do some very weird things. After Frank leaves, Jeffrey attempts to help the weary, bruised woman, but all she wants is sex. She's photographed in a clinch, with her face upside down and her ruby lips parted in a sly smile that exposes her gleaming front teeth—especially the one that has a teasing chip, as if someone had taken a small bite out of it.

When Jeffrey comes to see her again, he knocks on the door. She greets him eagerly—almost reproachfully—with "I looked for you in my closet tonight." (That line is a giddy classic.) The third night, they're on her bed after a round or two of intercourse. Trying to overcome his reluctance to hit her, she asks, "Are you a bad boy . . . do you want to do bad things?" We know the answer before he does. He's having trouble breathing.

Isabella Rossellini doesn't show anything like the acting technique that her mother, Ingrid Bergman, had, but she's willing to try things, and she doesn't hold back. Dorothy is a dream of a freak. Walking around her depressing apartment in her black bra and scanties, with blue eyeshadow and red high heels, she's a woman in distress right out of the pulps; she has the plushy, tempestuous look of heroines who are described as "bewitching." (She even has the kind of nostrils that cover artists can represent accurately with two dots.) Rossellini's accent is useful: it's part of Dorothy's strangeness. And Rossellini's echoes of her mother's low voice help to place this kitschy seductress in an unreal world. She has a special physical quality, too. There's nothing of the modern American woman about her. When she's naked, she's not protected, like the stars who are pummelled into shape and lighted to show their muscular perfection. She's defenselessly, tactilely naked, like the nudes the Expressionists painted.

Jeffrey, commuting between Dorothy, the blue lady of the night, and Sandy, the sunshine girl, suggests a character left over from *Our Town.* (He lives in an indefinite mythic present that feels like the past—he's split between the older woman he has sex with but doesn't love and the girl he loves but doesn't have sex with.) Kyle MacLachlan is in just about every scene, and he gives a phenomenal performance. As the hero of *Dune,* he may have been swallowed up in the sand, but here he's ideally cast. His proper look is perfect for a well-brought-up young fellow who's scared of his dirty thoughts (but wants to have them anyway). And when Jeffrey and Laura Dern's Sandy first meet and they make each other laugh, you relax with them and laugh, too, because you know that the two performers are going to work together like magic. Laura Dern brings a growing-up-fast passion to Sandy's love for Jeffrey, and she has an emotional fire that she didn't get to demonstrate in *Mask* or *Smooth Talk.* Lynch takes a plunge when he stages the high-schoolers' party that Sandy takes Jeffrey to: the two of them begin to dance and begin to kiss, and can't stop kissing. "Mysteries of Love," the song that they're dancing to, is scored using an organ, but now the organ isn't mocking them—the music swells to do justice to their feelings. The sequence may recall Sissy Spacek's romantic whirl at the prom in De Palma's *Carrie,* but the tone is different: we're being told that these two are not going to let go of each other, that they're moving into the unknown together. And the song, with lyrics by Lynch and music by Angelo Badalamenti (who wrote the score), carries the emotion over to the later scenes when Sandy's belief in Jeffrey is tested. (The movie may frighten some adolescents, as *Carrie* did, though the violent images aren't obtrusive; you don't quite take them in at first—it's only as the camera is pulling back from them that you see them clearly.)

As the uncontrollable Frank, in his slick leather outfits, Dennis Hopper gives the movie a jolt of horrific energy. Frank is lewd and dangerous; you feel he does what he does just for the hell of it. (He uses his inhaler to heighten the sensation of murder, too.) And as Ben, one of Frank's business associates, Dean Stockwell is a smiling wonder; you stare at his kissy makeup, the pearly jewel that he wears halfway up his ear, his druggy contentment. Frank refers to Ben as "suave," but that's not the half of it. Miming to Roy Orbison's song "In Dreams," about "the candy-colored clown they call the sandman," he's so magnetic that you momentarily forget everything else that's supposed to be going on.

Actually, it's easy to forget about the plot, because that's where Lynch's naïve approach has its disadvantages: Lumberton's subterranean criminal life needs to be as organic as the scrambling insects, and it isn't. Lynch doesn't show us how the criminals operate or how they're bound to each other. So the story isn't grounded in anything and has to be explained in little driblets of dialogue. But *Blue Velvet* has so much aural-visual humor and poetry that it's sustained despite the wobbly plot and the bland functional dialogue (that's sometimes a deliberate spoof of small-town conventionality and sometimes maybe not). It's sustained despite the fact that Lynch's imagistic talent, which is for the dark and unaccountable, flattens out in the sunlight scenes, as in the ordinary, daily moments between parents and children. One key character is never clarified: We can't tell if Sandy's father (played by George Dickerson) is implicated in the corruption, or if we're meant to accept him as a straight arrow out of a fifties F.B.I. picture. Lynch skimps on these commercial-movie basics and fouls up on them, too, but it's as if he were reinventing movies. His work goes back to the avant-garde film-makers of the twenties and thirties, who were often painters—and he himself trained to be one. He takes off from the experimental traditions that Hollywood has usually ignored.

This is his first film from his own original material since *Eraserhead* (which was first shown in 1977), and in some ways it's linked to that film's stately spookiness. Lynch's longtime associate, the cinematographer Frederick Elmes, lighted both films, and he has given *Blue Velvet* a comparable tactility; real streets look like paintings you could touch—you feel as if you could moosh your fingers in the colors. There are also reminders of the musical numbers in *Eraserhead*, which were like a form of dementia. (Lynch used an organ there, too.) With Rossellini singing at the club, and vocalists like Bobby Vinton on the soundtrack and tunes layered in and out of the orchestral score, *Blue Velvet* suggests a musical on themes from our pop unconscious. There are noises in there, of course, and Alan Splet, who started working with Lynch when he was doing shorts and has been his sound man on all his features (*Eraserhead* was followed by *The Elephant Man,* in 1980, and *Dune,* in 1984), combines them so that, say, when Jeffrey walks up the seven flights to Dorothy's apartment the building has a pumping, groaning sound. It could be an ancient furnace or foghorns or a heavy old animal that's winded. The mix of natural sounds with mechanical-industrial noises gives the images an ambience that's hokey and gothic and yet totally unpretentious—maybe because Lynch's subject is normal American fantasy life. Even that fetishized blue velvet robe is tacky, like something you could pick up in the red brick department store on Main Street.

Blue Velvet is a comedy, yet it puts us—or, at least, some of us—in an erotic trance. The movie keeps ribbing the clean-cut Jeffrey, yet we're caught up in his imagination. It must be that Lynch's use of irrational material works the way it's supposed to: at some not fully conscious level we read his images. When Frank catches Jeffrey with "Mommy" and takes him for a ride—first to Ben's hangout and then to a deserted spot—the car is packed with Frank's thugs, Dorothy, in her robe, and a large-headed, big-bellied woman in a short, pink skirt who has been necking with one of the guys. When Frank parks and he and his thugs start punching out Jeffrey, the pink-skirted woman climbs up on the roof of the car and, to the sound of that sandman song, dances aimlessly, impassively, like a girl in a topless bar. (She's in her dream world, too.) In a later scene, a man who has been shot several times remains standing, but he's no longer looking at anything; he faces a one-eared dead man sitting up in a chair, with the blue velvet sash in his mouth, and the two are suspended in time, like figures posed together in a wax museum, or plaster figures by George Segal retouched by Francis Bacon. Almost every scene has something outlandishly off in it, something that jogs your memory or your thinking, like the collection of fat women at Ben's joint, who look as if they were objects in a still-life. Or there may be something that just tweaks your memory, like the worrywart old maid—Jeffrey's Aunt Barbara (Frances Bay). Or a bit of comedy that's underplayed, like the shot of Jeffrey's mother (Priscilla Pointer) and Sandy's mother (Hope Lange) getting to know each other and looking interchangeable. (The only scene that feels thin—that lacks surprise—is Dorothy's lushly romanticized reunion with her child; for a few seconds, the film goes splat.)

It's the slightly disjunctive quality of Lynch's scenes (and the fact that we don't question them, because they don't feel arbitrary to us) that makes the movie so hypnotic—that, and the slow, assured sensuousness of his editing rhythms. This is possibly the only coming-of-age movie in which sex has the danger and the heightened excitement of a horror picture. It's the fantasy (rather than the plot) that's organic, and there's no sticky-sweet lost innocence, because the darkness was always there, inside.

The film's kinkiness isn't alienating—its naïveté keeps it from that. And its vision isn't alienating: this is American darkness—darkness in color, darkness with a happy ending. Lynch might turn out to be the first populist surrealist—a Frank Capra of dream logic. *Blue Velvet* does have a homiletic side. It's about a young man's learning through flabbergasting and violent experience to appreciate a relatively safe and manageable sex life. And when Sandy's father, speaking of the whole nightmarish business of the ear, says to Jeffrey, "It's over now," the film cuts to daylight. But with Lynch as the writer and director the homily has a little zinger. Sandy, who may have watched too many daytime soaps, has dreamed that the morbid darkness will be dispelled when thousands of robins arrive bringing love—a dream that she tells Jeffrey (to the accompaniment of organ music twitting her vision). When a plump robin lands on the kitchen windowsill, it has an insect in its beak.

The New Yorker, September 22, 1986

DOUBLING UP
FROM REVIEW OF
SOMETHING WILD

The movie gives you the feeling you sometimes get when you're driving across the country listening to a terrific new tape, and out in nowhere you pull in to a truck stop and the jukebox is playing the same song. The director Jonathan Demme is in harmony with that America and its mixture of cultures.

Starting with David Byrne and Celia Cruz singing Byrne's "Loco De Amor" during the opening credits, and ending with a reprise of Chip Taylor's "Wild Thing" by the reggae singer Sister Carol East, who appears on half of the screen while the final credits roll on the other half, the movie has almost fifty songs (or parts of songs)—several of them performed onscreen by The Feelies. The score was put together by John Cale (who did the track of Demme's first picture, *Caged Heat,* in 1974, for Roger Corman); Laurie Anderson worked on this score, too, and it has a life of its own that gives the movie a buzzing vitality. Some years back, and long before Demme made *Stop Making Sense* or his videos, he said, in an interview in the now defunct *Soho News,* that "music was my first love; movies came second." He brings them together here in a lighthearted way. It's a little reminiscent of the use of music in *Easy Rider,* but it's more of a rap. The singing voices keep talking back to us in the way that they often do from car radios and tape decks, or at noisy parties. I like the doubling up of the energy sources; it turns the film into a satirical joyride. *Something Wild* is a road movie, and car music is primal American pop. How else could we live through the distances we travel? Shallow entertainment helps keep us sane. This kind of music is, in its way, the equivalent of the genre movies that are often just what we want and all we want.

Something Wild is rough-edged. It doesn't have the grace of Demme's *Citizens Band* and *Melvin and Howard* or the heightened simplicity of his *Stop Making Sense.* It has something else, though—a freedom that takes off from the genre framework. And Demme has used it to weave the stylization of rock videos into the fabric of *Something Wild.* Probably no other director could have performed this feat so spontaneously or unself-consciously; the doubling up works integrally for him—it fulfills impulses that were there in Demme right from the start of his career. And he's made something new: a party movie with both a dark and a light side.

The New Yorker, November 17, 1986

CRIMES OF THE HEART

Beth Henley's play *Crimes of the Heart* may suggest a quaint variation of early Tennessee Williams (*The Glass Menagerie* especially) or William Inge, or even Paul Zindel or Horton Foote, but it isn't bad. It has a goofy charm. Henley has a streak of campiness in her, and she curls the edges of the dialogue with Southernisms, or what we take to be Southernisms. ("How's my hair?" "Fine." "Not pooching out in the back, is it?" "No." That same non-pooched-out woman complains of a polka-dot dress she was given for her child: "The first time I put it in the washing machine, I mean the very first time, it fell all to pieces. Those little polka dots just dropped right off in the water.") The three actresses who star in the movie version—Diane Keaton, Jessica Lange, and Sissy Spacek—bring it such overflowing wit and radiance that they waft it up high. The play is thin, and the playwright's screen adaptation is just the usual "opening out," but the actresses put so much faith in their roles that they carry the movie, triumphantly. It's too bad that the director, Bruce Beresford, didn't know how to give it a push and make it spin. With these three actresses sparking off each other, he might have caught something like the whirling magic of Robert Altman's *Come Back to the 5 & Dime Jimmy Dean, Jimmy Dean*. But the movie has some élan anyway, because these women working together are something to see. They giggle over the stagy exposition, treating it like choice, well-loved gossip.

The sweet and dippy Babe (Sissy Spacek), the youngest of the MaGrath sisters of Hazlehurst, Mississippi, has shot her rich lawyer husband and faces trial. The oldest, Lenny (Diane Keaton), has been too shy to have boyfriends; at thirty, she takes care of Old Granddaddy, has a routine job, and keeps up the family home. The middle sister, Meg (Jessica Lange), may have had a few too many boyfriends; she started smoking and drinking at fourteen, and the town regards her as a tramp. Now Lenny sends word of the shooting to Meg, in Hollywood, where she has tried to make a career as a singer, and she returns. The three are united in the house they grew up in, and their childhood alliances and petty jealousies start up all over again, along with a fierce, us-against-the-world family loyalty. A friend of mine in Oregon went to see Diane Keaton in *Mrs. Soffel* at my urging, and then wrote me that "at its best *Mrs. Soffel* is about the mystery of where love and courage come from." I think it could be said that at its best *Crimes of the Heart* is about the comedy of where love and courage come from. It's goofiness is integral: it's a comedy about wacked-out normality. The characters say dumb things with such simple conviction that they seem to have a glimmer of truth. When Babe wonders "why Mama hung herself," Meg says, "I don't know. She had a bad day. A real bad day."

It's no surprise that Keaton and Lange are full-scale funnywomen; the news here is that Spacek, after all the tiresome studied acting she has been doing in recent years—she's dull as an achiever heroine or a suffering heroine, she's dull when she searches for depth—can still play on instinct and be terrific. (Yes, she was lovely and gave a fine performance in *Raggedy Man,* but it lacked the oddball zing of what she does here.) Spacek looks as if she'd rediscovered how much fun acting could be, and she isn't afraid to play a character as weird as her Carrie was. Babe verges on the bizarrely unbalanced, and the trick in playing her is to make her human—to make her motives accessible. Spacek empties the foxiness out of her face and plays this zany Babe with a propulsive sureness. Her twang gives a flourish to her lines, and when she has her star turns—a series of slapstick disasters that she has to bring off all by herself—she's *up* for them. She has real voltage here; she holds her own with big Jess and gurgly, wild-eyed Keaton—and with energy to spare.

Lange must have gained something from playing the forthright Patsy Cline in the 1985 *Sweet Dreams.* She seems liberated from the "image" fears that constrict the acting of so many stars, and any anxieties about the self-exposure in screen acting seem gone, too. It's a strong, unabashed performance. She's as confidently sexual as any American screen star past or present, and when this woman gets to shake her chassis it's some chassis. From our first view of Meg, on the bus heading back to Hazlehurst, we know she's had some rough times. What we're not prepared for is the gusto that Lange brings to Meg's schoolgirl meannesses. Meg can't resist showing Lenny that she knows her one poor little secret, and she has no compunction about doing the dirty to Babe, who told it to her. The way Lange plays this scene, Meg enjoys her sisterly one-upmanship so much that she's rather lovable when she spills the beans. Underneath, she conveys the feeling that keeping a secret is just a piddling convention anyway. And Lange goes beyond the individual character: she leaves us with the image of a smiling tough cookie in a blue denim jacket and a short skirt that sets off her long legs—a rowdy, down-to-earth American archetype, everybody's favorite waitress. (I came to like her faded denim better and better; she wears it like a badge of honor.) Lange seems an effortless comic virtuoso here—there's no fussiness in her acting. Her soft voice has a defiant edge, and she's economical even in her delivery of the film's best line. When Babe is worried because the husband she shot has threatened to send her to an insane asylum,

Meg reassures her by saying, "Why, you're just as perfectly sane as anyone walking the streets of Hazlehurst, Mississippi."

Keaton's Lenny is abashed about everything; she has so many timidities she's in a constant tizzy. Keaton is a master of high-strung unsureness; when she plays comedy, she has a miraculous gift for fumbling in character—for showing you the emotional processes that lead the character to say what she does. What makes Warren Beatty's performance in *McCabe & Mrs. Miller* stay in the mind in a way his other performances don't (not even his Clyde Barrow) is that he shows you McCabe fighting through his own clumsiness and confusion, trying to express what he doesn't fully understand. That's what Keaton's Lenny does. Her tangled feelings spill out in all directions, and what makes her a great comic presence is that she always reveals more than she means to. Babe and Meg talk about how she has been turning into Old Grandmama—Lenny wears her grandmama's sun hat and gardening gloves, and she huddles, and hides her body in shapeless pinafores. (In some ways, the play, which was first performed in 1979, is Beth Henley riding the 1977 *Annie Hall* down South.) Keaton's nervous old-maid Lenny is a much richer character than you could guess from reading the play. She's a wonderful mixture of raw shyness and unconscious, eye-batting flirtatiousness, and her "fumbling" lifts the character right off the page. Even her feeling her way into a Southern accent seems to become part of the character. And Keaton is great at playing a sense of injustice for laughs: Lenny's resentment of Meg for having been granted childhood privileges denied to the two others wells up in her uncontrollably, as if she were still thirteen. She's had so few experiences as a grownup that she keeps their childhood alive all through the movie. She's the responsible sister—a thirty-year-old hopelessly good little girl longing to be naughty.

As a cousin of the sisters—an officious bitch who's so much like Mae, the mother of the no-neck monsters in *Cat on a Hot Tin Roof,* that she comes across almost as an homage to Tennessee Williams—Tess Harper gets laughs with a minimum of waste motion. They're stagy, predictable laughs, though, and in these moments that the stars don't dominate, you can recognize how much they bring to the material. Without them, the fluidity is gone, and there's nothing but artifice; the movie stops. The director's work seems negligible (he doesn't show any flair for slapstick in the scene of Lenny flapping a broom and chasing her cousin out of the house), but it's inoffensive. David Carpenter is likable as Babe's impressionable yet hardheaded young lawyer. And Sam Shepard appears in the small part of horn-rimmed Doc—the fellow Meg ran out on when she went to Hollywood to satisfy her granddaddy's idea that she had a big career ahead, and the fellow Lenny has always had a crush on. Shepard plays his scenes with the drab seriousness of a weak man who was left in the lurch once and holds no hard feelings but doesn't intend to let it happen again. When Doc and Meg talk together, their voices are in quiet, lovers' tune; you can believe that she might have been happy with him, and that strengthens the importance of the mostly offscreen Old

Granddaddy (Hurd Hatfield), who raised the girls and screwed up their lives.

The movie has a bad opening: the first scene, in which Lenny picks up Babe's things at the mansion where she shot her husband and carts them back to the MaGrath house, does more to dislocate us than to give us our bearings. And when we get our first view of the MaGrath place it's perhaps more architecturally pixillated than seems appropriate to the emptiness of the sisters' lives there. But though the moviemakers' efforts to make the play "visual" fail, the actresses give it their vitality. And they avoid the danger in Beth Henley's material—the trap that *Nobody's Fool,* which is based on Henley's autobiographical script, falls into. At her worst, Henley turns the heartbreak and boringness of small-town life into cute tics. In *Nobody's Fool,* the young heroine (Rosanna Arquette) behaves as if she were brain-damaged, but we're supposed to take her sickly romantic carrying on as an indication that she's going to become an artist. The picture dotes on her; it swoons over her while we in the audience stare numbly. *Crimes of the Heart* has some of the same mixture of looniness and lyricism, but the actresses are smart and generous and inspired. So the three women's looniness really is lyric. Lenny's *hysteria* is lyric. It's as if the three actresses said to the director and the rest of the cast, "Just back off, and let us become sisters." And they became sisters.

The New Yorker, December 15, 1986

LITTLE SHOP OF HORRORS

Little Shop of Horrors is jivey, senseless fun. The stupidity is appealing, the way it is in great comic strips. These moviemakers aren't trying to edify us or make us see beauty in the skid-row settings—they're just out to make us feel brainlessly slaphappy gaga. The film is taken from the Off Broadway musical that was based on Roger Corman's 1960 quickie—he is said to have shot it in two days and a night, from a script that Charles Griffith threw together. (Corman's picture didn't originate in a flight of imagination; it came out of sheer expedience—he was offered the set.) It's impossible to guess what made Howard Ashman (words) and Alan Menken (music) think there was the basis for a stage show in this junky travesty of sci-fi genetic-mutation pictures, but they had a historic Pop insight: they understood that the show's appeal would be in its undisguised mental deficiency.

Nothing in the new movie, directed by Frank Oz, is realistic. This is still a stage musical on exaggerated sets with exaggerated people. It takes its period from the date of the Corman movie, and its setting is the downtown-

Manhattan skid row of reddish tenements and overstuffed garbage cans, with singing winos curled up in doorways, and vocalizing bag ladies, and a Greek chorus of three cheeky black girls—teen-agers who hang out on the streets, wiggling like chorines and commenting on the action in the Motown-Supremes sound of the period. Smooth and knowing, these lolli-pops like to view the street action from the corner in front of Mushnik's flower Shop, but Mushnik (Vincent Gardenia) chases them away, even though there are no customers for them to annoy. Business doesn't pick up until Mushnik's assistant, Seymour (Rick Moranis), puts in the window a strange little flowering cactus, potted in a coffee can, that he bought from an ancient Chinese after a total eclipse of the sun. The plant, which lures customers and changes the fortunes of Mushnik, Seymour, and the shop clerk Audrey (Ellen Greene), is a carnivore, but only Seymour, who takes care of it—and lets it suck blood from his fingertips—knows that. This sug-gests musical Grand Guignol, but the Guignol aspects are tame. The movie isn't out to horrify you; it uses humor to turn shock into bliss.

Ellen Greene's platinum-blond Audrey arrives for work with a shiner, and in her idea of proper attire for a salesgirl: stiletto heels and the black femme-fatale dress of forties thrillers, with neck scooped low. Her clothes look laminated to her body, which is so frail, narrow-shouldered, and tiny-waisted that you can't believe the fleshy boobs that puff out of her décolletage. She might be a mutation, like a ravenous plant, and Seymour, who adores Audrey, christens his prize specimen—which has a shark mouth, like hers—Audrey II.

Ellen Greene seems to have created the sexpot-waif Audrey out of some dreamy dementia—she's not like any other heroine you can think of. Audrey is so romantic she isn't quite all there. She "dates" a biker-dentist, played by a dark-haired Steve Martin—a sadist who leaves her battered after every encounter. But she pines for considerate Seymour—the gentleman nebbish. (When he's overexcited, she slaps him smartly and lisps, "You're hysterical.") Ellen Greene originated the role, and played it for eighteen months in New York and Los Angeles and six months in London; it has per-haps got overly stylized—it's a little rigid. Frank Oz might have helped to compensate for her familiarity with the part by suggesting the kind of sub-tlety and nuance that the camera can pick up (and he might have compen-sated for the general airlessness of the studio-set musical by more fluidity in the production). But this is niggling; in its own broad, blatant terms, the movie works. And Ellen Greene is a weird little wow. Ever since I saw her in Mazursky's 1976 *Next Stop, Greenwich Village*, I've been in thrall to her talent. "Thrall" may be the word for it, too, because she seems to wrap a hypnotic state around herself; watching her, you just about enter into it. When she shifts from her mousy little-Audrey manner of speech to her big Broadway singing voice (it's like pent-up passion being released), you're even more transfixed—you don't know where that sound can be coming from.

Greene in her trance-state cocoon gives the movie its peculiar aura.

She's an authentically peculiar diva, like Bernadette Peters. With a more conventional ingénue—one who didn't twist knots into the dumb-blonde stereotype—it might collapse. Audrey is oddly valiant, and she's matched up well with Moranis, who's very appealing here. It seems right that when these two look at each other they see their romantic ideals. And though the picture might have gained if the naïveté of their romance, which is fine at the start, had developed, the cartoon characters that don't change are O.K., too. These two are balanced against the much wilder cartoons played by Steve Martin and, in a brief but glorious turn, Bill Murray. Their sequence together is a classic encounter between sadistic dentist and pain-freak patient; when you see it, it's like stumbling on a piece of historic footage, like an encounter between legendary crazies such as Bert Lahr and Joe E. Brown. Martin's dentist is a confident brute until this scene. He plays his status-conscious professional man like a mad satire of Elvis Presley in his concert entrances, when he stalked onstage as if to assault the audience. But when this sadist comes up against Murray, who's even more bughouse than he is, he's undone. And when Murray, in the dentist's chair, climaxes and grabs Martin's shoulder Martin is enraged and disgusted. Furious that the patient enjoyed the pain, he throws him out. It's a piece of transcendent slapstick. Murray plays the masochist so tenderly that through sheer force of imaginative lunacy he's practically the star. (And Martin helps to redeem himself for *Three Amigos!*)

At first view, Audrey II is small and rather feminine: it has something creepy yet coquettish and alluring about it. And it seems to have its own light source—it suggests star quality. Seymour talks to plants, of course, and this one answers. It demands "Feed me! Feed me!" and Seymour, suckling it with his blood, shows a screw-loose humility. Audrey II grows quite a bit before it orders Seymour around in the deep, rumbling basso of Levi Stubbs, the lead singer of the Four Tops; it's a threatening big black bopper that sings, "I'm a mean, green mother from outer space." As the plant grows bigger, the joke doesn't, and Audrey II becomes more mechanical-looking. But Stubbs' growl is awesome. And there's at least one neat gag: Audrey II uses a tendril to dial the telephone. And there's a wonderful comic-strip image of Audrey II surrounded by its offshoots, all of them singing, "I'm a mean, green mother."

Oz, the Muppeteer, isn't an experienced or, from the evidence here, an especially talented film director, and you have to be willing to accept a movie that's all smack in front of your face; you might almost be glued to a puppet theatre. But it goes from one plot-advancing smash number to the next, and it has wonderful details. There's a skid-row parody of Busby Berkeley with the street people definitely not in symmetry—they're all askew. And a shot of the dentist seen from inside a patient's full-screen mouth—Steve Martin is like a little devil with his pitchfork tools. The three streetwise teenagers (Tichina Arnold, Tisha Campbell, Michelle Weeks) wear witty girl-group dresses and girl-group smiles; they prance right into the shop where something awful is happening and slink out again, carefree figures of doom. Comic actors drop in for bits: John Candy is almost terrific as a Wolfman Jack–style radio host; as the first customer to be attracted by little Audrey II in the window, Christopher Guest flashes a bright, sweet smile.

The movie has an elusive midnight-movie feeling to it. It's nothing but blown-up cartoon-style friskiness, and it keeps slugging you. But it makes you feel as inexplicably sappy and contented as a kid used to feel on Sunday morning lying on his stomach reading the funnies. Only, this is bigger, brasher, with its own kind of higgledy-piggledy ecstasy.

The New Yorker, January 12, 1987

PLATOON

Oliver Stone, who wrote and directed *Platoon,* based on his own experiences, dropped out of Yale at nineteen, taught Chinese students in Vietnam, did a stint in the merchant marine, and finished a novel (in Mexico), which he couldn't get published. Feeling, he says, that he needed to atone for his life of privilege and his individuality—that he had to be an anonymous common soldier—he enlisted in the Army, and on his twenty-first birthday, in September, 1967, he was on his way back to Vietnam, where he saw action with the 25th Infantry along the Cambodian border. In the next fifteen months, he was wounded twice and decorated twice. He came home, he acknowledges, a freaked-out pothead; at one point, his stockbroker father paid off some people to get him out of jail for marijuana possession. In 1969, he enrolled in the N.Y.U. film school, where he had Martin Scorsese as a teacher and pulled himself together. "Scorsese gave me film as a way to use my energies," he said to Peter Blauner in a recent interview in *New York.* We can surmise that Stone became a grunt in Vietnam to "become a man" and to become a writer. As *Platoon,* a coming-of-age film, demonstrates, he went through his rite of passage, but, as *Platoon* also demonstrates, he became a very bad writer—a hype artist. Actually, he had already proved this in his crude scripts for *Midnight Express* and *Scarface.* (He was also co-writer of *Conan the Barbarian, Year of the Dragon,* and *8 Million Ways to Die.*) Stone has an action writer's special, dubious flair: his scripts have drive—they ram their way forward, jacking up the melodrama to an insane pitch. Luckily, he's a better director than writer.

Salvador, the early-in-1986 film that Stone directed and co-wrote, had a sensationalistic propulsiveness, and a hero (James Woods) whose hipster hostility was integral to the film's whole jittery, bad-trip tone. I don't think *Platoon* is nearly as good a movie. Although Stone was born in 1946, this is like a young man's first, autobiographical—and inflated—work. Written in

1976, eight years after his war experiences, the script is swamped by his divided intentions: he's trying to give us an account of what it was like to be an infantryman in Vietnam in 1967–68, and to present this in all its immediacy and craziness, but he's also trying to compose a requiem for that war. The results are overwrought, with too much filtered light, too much poetic license, and too damn much romanticized insanity.

The picture begins with an epigraph from Ecclesiastes ("Rejoice, O young man, in thy youth!"), and then the music, Samuel Barber's "Adagio for Strings" (which was used so chastely in *The Elephant Man*), comes on in a soupy orchestration by Georges Delerue—and the movie is grandiloquent before it even gets rolling. The first images draw us in, though: Charlie Sheen's twenty-one-year-old Chris Taylor—the Oliver Stone character—arrives in the confusion of Vietnam, and the plane that brought him is loaded with body bags for the return trip. Just about everything to do with Chris's initial disorientation, his getting to know the men in the platoon, and the pre-dawn jungle ambush in which he sees the enemy advancing but is paralyzed with fear and can't warn the other men, and then is wounded, has dramatic life in it. So does the small talk. There's a good, if perhaps too eloquent, sequence with the men in a hooch, drinking and doping, listening to rock 'n' roll and dancing; in a psychedelic, homoerotic bit, an older soldier blows pot smoke through a rifle and Chris inhales it—it's like the seductive smoke-through-the-prison-wall in Jean Genet's *Un Chant d'Amour.* And there's a fine, scary scene in which the men are attacked in their foxholes and the bursts of fire are like a light show in the middle of a nightmare.

There are scenes unlike any I've seen before, in which we can see the soldiers' frustration, and how they're caught in a revenge fever. Then, when they take a small village suspected of aiding the Vietcong, their rage against the villagers builds in waves and finds release in violence against animals, a helpless grinning idiot, women, children. The film shows Chris taking part in the cruelty and then gaining control of himself, and grasping at first hand what many of us at home watching TV grasped—that whether the Vietnamese won or lost in the fight it was what we were doing to them that was destroying us. The film is about victimizing ourselves as well as others; it's about shame. That's the only way in which it's political; it doesn't deal with what the war was about—it's conceived strictly in terms of what these American infantrymen go through.

Platoon has many things to recommend it, but its major characters aren't among them. Chris is a pleasant-faced blank—not the actor, the character—and, regrettably, he narrates the movie by reading aloud the letters he writes home to his grandmother. You might think that Stone would be too hip to add the explanatory emotions this way—particularly after Sheen's father, Martin, recited the tormented, purploid prose that Michael Herr wrote for the narration of *Apocalypse Now.* The voiceovers here are perhaps even more stupefying, since they're easier to comprehend. They're populist sentiments reminiscent of the Joad family conversations in *The Grapes of Wrath.*

> Well here I am—anonymous alright, with guys nobody really cares about—they come from the end of the line, most of 'em small towns you never heard of—Pulaski, Tennessee, Brandon, Mississippi, Pork Bend, Utah, Wampum, Pennsylvania. Two years high school's about it, maybe if they're lucky, a job waiting for 'em back in a factory, but most of 'em got nothing, they're poor, they're the unwanted. . . . They're the best I've ever seen grandma, the heart and soul—maybe I've finally found it way down here in the mud—maybe from down here I can start up again and be something I can be proud of, without having to fake it, be a fake human being. Maybe I can see something I don't yet see, learn something I don't yet know.

It's like some terrible regression. Stone's gone back to being a literary preppy.

He's thinking like a preppy, too. Chris finds two authority figures in the platoon: the two sergeants, who were once friends, and are personifications of good and evil. Willem Dafoe's Sergeant Elias is a super-sensitive hippie pothead, who cares about the men—he's a veteran fighter who's kept his soul. Tom Berenger's Sergeant Barnes is a kickass boozer—a psycho, whose scarred, dead-eyed face suggests the spirit of war, or the figure of Death in a medieval morality play. The movie is about the miseries of Nam, but it's also about the tensions that develop between the factions in the platoon who line up with one or the other—Love or Hate, Life or Death, Christ or the Devil. And it's about Chris's learning—and, worse, telling us—that "we weren't fighting the enemy; we were fighting ourselves," and, yes, that he feels "like the child of Barnes and Elias."

This melodramatic shortcut—and Stone's reduction of all the issues of the war to make them fit the tags "good" and "evil"—may make you wonder if he is using filmmaking as a substitute for drugs. (The picture itself, in representing the heads as the good guys, makes a case for the socializing, humanizing qualities of dope; God Himself seems to be on the side of the dopers.) Stone is in such a hurry to get a reaction out of us that he can't bother to create characters with different sides. The two sergeants are posed and photographed to be larger than life, but the roles are underwritten. Dafoe's tough, courageous Elias is like a young Klaus Kinski playing innocent miss, and Berenger's glamorous, scarred-up Barnes, who has been shot seven times but can't be finished off until he wills it, looks as if he were a killing machine carved out of jagged rock, though he moves with a slithering grace. The two are mythic figures out of nowhere—Elias who's high only on drugs and goodness, Barnes who's high on war. The men in the platoon may suddenly be trashed by a line. Round-faced Forest Whitaker, who plays gentle Big Harold, is going along all right until after the atrocities against the villagers, when he has to say, "I'm hurtin' real bad inside." That's the end of his performance.

Stone tries for bigger effects than he earns. When he doesn't destroy things with the voice-over banalities or a square line of dialogue, he may do it with a florid gesture, such as having the Christus, Sergeant Elias, run away from the Vietcong who are firing at him, run toward a departing helicopter, which is his only chance for life, and lift his arms to Heaven. There are too many scenes where you think, It's a bit much. The movie crowds you; it doesn't give you room to have an honest emotion.

You knew you were getting pulp in *Salvador* because it was grungy; here the pulp is presented pedagogically, and it's made classy and meditative, but it's laid on thick—that idiot gets his head bashed in by Americans trying to wipe the grin off his face. Is it powerful? Sure it is. (This kind of routine played well in the twenties and thirties, too, when the bad guys in Westerns did it, and it wasn't as graphic then.) Stone has talent: he shot this epic in the Philippines on a tight budget—roughly six and a half million dollars. He's a filmmaker, all right, but he lacks judgment. Just about everything in *Platoon* is too explicit, and is so heightened that it can numb you and make you feel jaded. You may suspect that at some lowdown level Stone (he appears as the major blown up in his bunker at the end of the film) is against judgment. Elias is supposed to represent true manliness, but if Stone's other films tell us anything—if this film tells us anything—it's that he's temperamentally more on the side of crazy stud Barnes. The preppy narration extolling the nobility of the common man is worse than a "privileged" boy's guilt—it's a grown man's con.

Stone's moviemaking doesn't suggest that he was a young, idealistic Chris Taylor going to war to find himself in the comradeship of the anonymous but, rather, that he was a romantic loner who sought his manhood in the excitement of violent fantasy. Stone seems to want to get high on war, like Barnes. The key scene in the movie is directed so that it passes like a dream. In a remote area, Chris calmly, deliberately shoots a fellow-soldier. There is no suggestion that Chris is an innocent corrupted by having got used to violence. The murder is presented as an unambiguous justified execution. This oddly weightless pulp revenge fantasy is floating around in Stone's requiem, along with a lot of old-movie tricks.

I know that *Platoon* is being acclaimed for its realism, and I expect to be chastised for being a woman finding fault with a war film. But I've probably seen as much combat as most of the men saying, "This is how war is."

The New Yorker, January 12, 1987

THE STEPFATHER
KILLER-DILLER

Young kids often think that a lunatic is a horrible-looking bogeyman coming at them out of the darkness. But as you get older the psychopaths who plague your imagination are the smooth-faced Ted Bundys and the bland ones, like John List, the New Jersey accountant and Sunday-school teacher who arranged his 1971 disappearance so fastidiously that the five members of his family whom he left dead in his house weren't discovered for a month. He himself was described in "Wanted" posters as "6-1, 185 lbs Caucasian male, with no distinguishing features." The imagined scene of carnage at the List home provides the starting point for *The Stepfather,* which Joseph Ruben directed, from a dandy screenplay by the crime novelist Donald E. Westlake that devises a logic for the killer and follows him as he goes on his way to a new life. Jerry Blake, as he calls himself in the town he moves to, wants to be the head of an ideal family. He's an obsessive conformist, who's attracted to widows with children, in picture-postcard houses. As Terry O'Quinn plays the part, Blake has a waxen handsome ordinariness; a realtor now, he could be your trustworthy realtor in a TV commercial. But with any strain in the middle-class surface of his life—the troubles that his sixteen-year-old stepdaughter (Jill Schoelen) gets into at school, the unexpected willfulness of his wife (Shelley Hack)—his idealized vision is imperilled. And since he's a perfectionist who sees anything less than the ideal as total failure, if he can't restore an even tenor he's furiously, self-righteously angry. And he prepares to move on.

The Stepfather is a cunning, shapely thriller—a beautiful piece of construction. But it could easily be overlooked, because it has a placid surface that resembles B-picture banality. Ruben—his last film was the 1984 *Dreamscape,* with Dennis Quaid—is a craftsman, who uses this banality for a purpose. The movie is all implication: everything that's going on is held in check, and the restraint is menacing, with each scene moving quietly into the next. Jerry Blake's persona has a narrowly limited capacity for expressiveness. Ruben presents this subject by making what could be said to be a repressed movie; the excitement here is deep down—and the fun of the movie is deep down, too. Nothing is withheld from you, yet nothing happens quite as you expect. (The surprises all fit together, though.) The atmosphere suggests a Joyce Carol Oates twist on the American dream. Jerry the model citizen who's out in the open whistling "Camptown Races" becomes more frightening the more we see of him. The horror is there waiting all the time. It's in what's missing from the man we see, and the skill of the picture is that it keeps us creepily conscious of what's missing.

Ruben, whose first movies after he'd taken theatre and film courses at Michigan and got a degree at Brandeis included *The Pom-Pom Girls,* still has his affinity with teen-agers, and the sixteen-year-old girl who recoils from her stepfather's touch on her arm has healthy instincts that she can't explain. She knows right down to her toes that he's got some kind of fix on her and that he doesn't love her bamboozled mother. The scenes between the girl and smarmy Jerry have a special tension, because of her not covering up the revulsion she feels for him and because of his soft-soaping attempts to win her over. She stands between him and his dream of a perfect family life. It's a battle to the death.

They're the two main characters, and I didn't see a hitch in either performance. Jill Schoelen, a spirited, dark young beauty, has been acting since she was a child and has appeared in lots of TV and in several movies; O'Quinn has put in his time on and off Broadway as well as in TV and films. She comes through with the right raw freshness, and he with hypercontrol. We become so familiar with Jerry's steady gray-blue eyes and his eerie intuitiveness that if he momentarily flips out and loses track of which identity he's using it's like a crazy crack in a frozen lake. We're shocked: we know—just as he knows—that it can't be sealed up again. At one point, when a fissure appears he grins so foolishly it's like a giggle. At moments, he parodies his own unctuousness: strapping a corpse behind the wheel of a car, he says, "Buckle up for safety," as if he were a grammar-school traffic officer.

Jerry attempts to win his stepdaughter's affection by giving her a puppy; he's doing what the father figures on the old *SatEvePost* covers would do. His hobby is building birdhouses that are painted and divided like doll houses—he evidently intends them for birds who live respectable family lives. His carpentry tools are arranged methodically in his good-manly-dad shop in the basement. That's a *SatEvePost* cover, too, although not when he's incensed about the girl's suspiciousness and talks to himself about what a sweet little girl she is while he handles those lethal instruments. And when we get a look at a practically identical arrangement of tools in the basement of the house he lived in earlier, everything important about him seems to be buried. He seems to be alive only in these dark areas—in what's underneath "no distinguishing features."

Westlake's way of using the carnage at the start—to foreshadow what may happen—is a daring stunt. And he introduces the girl's therapist (Charles Lanyer) and Jerry's previous wife's brother (Stephen Shellen)—characters you expect will serve mechanical plot functions—and then throws you curves. (He has written a pip of a meeting between Jerry and the therapist in an empty house, and a quick collision between Jerry and the brother that's even better.) Working with this sharp script, Ruben sets up a scene between the mother and the daughter so that we see the solidity of their affection for each other and understand how muddled they both get when Jerry comes between them. Ruben uses the girl's boyfriend (Jeff Schultz) to demonstrate how sound of head the two kids are, in contrast with the fantasy-driven Jerry, who catches them in a chaste goodnight kiss and yells rape.

The Stepfather doesn't have the cocky zest of *Dreamscape;* the subject doesn't allow for it. This is closer to the genre of the Hitchcock–Thornton

Wilder *Shadow of a Doubt* (though the killer here isn't a charmer, like the Joseph Cotten character, and the mood is very different). With the Vancouver area doubling for Seattle in the opening section, and then for the fictitious towns nearby, Ruben uses everyday settings. They could be called plain, but they're well lighted (by John W. Lindley), and this young director turns plain into precise—the appurtenances of middle-class life become a bit crawly. And the picture's submerged sexual content goes way beyond the usual scare movie. *The Stepfather* is almost cruelly plausible; luckily, Ruben and Westlake are entertainers.

The New Yorker, February 9, 1987

THE HOUR OF THE STAR

Every so often, you're watching a movie about ordinary, deprived, unlucky people and something numinous happens and they're no longer ordinary. You may feel that transformation at De Sica's *Umberto D.* and *Miracle in Milan*, at early Fellini, and at the work of the Taviani brothers. You may feel it at Jacques Demy's *Lola* and Hector Babenco's *Pixote*. It's as if the characters' souls became magically visible, and when that happens the movie becomes piercingly close to you. You feel protective of it, and momentarily alienated from people who don't respond as you do.

So it's not a good idea to see *The Hour of the Star* with the wrong companions. A lot of the scenes don't quite work, but the transforming power of art is very strong in this movie, a first feature by the Brazilian Suzana Amaral, the mother of nine, who, at the age of fifty-two, shot it in four weeks, in 1985, for $150,000. Amaral didn't suddenly turn primitive moviemaker. She's from a family that is well known in the arts, and though she had quit college to marry she began to study film at the University of São Paulo when she was in her late thirties, and she worked in television and made more than forty documentaries and short films before coming to this country and enrolling in the graduate program at N.Y.U. film school, where she took a master's degree in 1978. She's a knowledgeable artist, and it's so rare for anyone to attempt what she's trying for here that I can feel myself wanting to overpraise the results. What I can say with honor is that at moments the picture comes very close to the effects achieved by De Sica and the others.

Working from a script that she and Alfredo Oroz adapted from the 1977 novella by Clarice Lispector, Amaral tells the story of Macabéa (Marcelia Cartaxo), a nineteen-year-old orphan from a depressed rural section in the northeast, a girl with no skills or education—without looks or personality, or even training in keeping herself clean—who comes south to

São Paulo, a city of fourteen million. It wouldn't occur to this girl that the world could be changed; she probably wouldn't notice if it were. She barely knows what people are saying to her: her dialect is different from theirs. She lives in a rented room in the slums with three other girls, all named Maria; she absorbs trivia from radio shows, goes to her job as a typist, and mimics the behavior of her co-worker Gloria (Tamara Taxman), a veteran of the dating wars, whose five abortions are her battle stripes. Macabéa apologizes politely to her boss for her hopelessly inept one-finger typing, for the smudges on the paper and the holes she makes; he can't bring himself to fire her. So she hangs on. The distance between her timid, passive existence and her fantasy life is so vast as to set off poetic reverberations. Wrapped in the isolation of ignorance, she doesn't think about things like improving her typing; she simply wants to be a movie star.

Amaral has been quoted as saying, "My film is not a feminist film; it's a feminine film." And that's what gives it its special qualities of heartbreak and revelation. It's as if *Umberto D.* had concentrated not on the old professor but on the young servant girl. It's like a fuller version of the story of the Sicilian girl killed by the German soldiers in *The Night of the Shooting Stars.* Amaral has taken a character who might be considered far more marginal than either of those girls, put her at the center of our attention, and made us feel what it's like for her when she looks at men with hopeful interest, trying to make eye contact with them. Later, we feel what it's like for her when she's dating Olimpico (José Dumont), a vain—and mean— metalworker, who's almost as ignorant as she is but puts her down because he's embarrassed that he can't get a snappier girlfriend. He's the sort of man who turns nasty when a woman asks questions he doesn't know the answers to. Macabéa has a little of Gelsomina (from *La Strada*) in her. When she sings an aria that she's heard on the radio, Olimpico hits her on the head because it annoys him and then lifts her high in the air, gyrating with her; he's playing the strongman, just like the brute Zampanò.

Macabéa is clumsier than Gelsomina, heavier-spirited; she seems more enduring. She's devastated, though, when she experiences a betrayal. Macabéa has hooded eyes, and when she suffers they become the eyes of a forest creature at bay: she loses all hope. Gloria, who has thoughtlessly betrayed her, tries to square things by paying for her to go to Madame Carlot (Fernanda Montenegro), a *macumbeira*—an illegal witch doctor– fortuneteller—whose flashy old-whore makeup and bangles seem to lend color to Macabéa. The *macumbeira,* who is fascinated by the girl's innocence, gives her ready-made dreams, and the film completes its trajectory from neorealism to magic realism. Like *Umberto D., The Hour of the Star* has moments of uncanny humor and painful intuition, but at the end it has a plunging happiness that is inseparable from horror. The hallucinatory effect seems somewhat alien to Amaral's temperament; she's better at the plain, level scenes—they have a truer magic. Still, this Latin-American mash of dreams and reality and American advertising art and images from the movies—a vision similar to what you get from Manuel Puig's novels—has an awkward, mystic sanctity. All the moldy colors seem to come together and to be struck by sunshine. It's contrived with too much trickery (flash-forwards and slow motion), yet it's affecting.

Visually, the movie has a trancelike quality right from the start, when Macabéa, looking in a mirror, moves her hands over her face, as if connecting the sense of touch with the image. As the unloved girl, the twenty-three-year-old Marcelia Cartaxo, who was performing with a regional theatre group when she was selected for the role, is grim and lumpish—she seems misshapen—and you can't believe she could look any other way. Then, in a scene where Macabéa has wangled a day off from work and is luxuriously alone in the rented room, she dances to the radio, watching herself in the mirror and swirling a sheet around her as if it were a bridal costume, and, yes, she seems to be what she longs to be—a pretty girl who could please a man. But when she's there with the Marias or is out in the city she's like a lost member of an ancient race. She's a misfit—her dinky white barrette a badge of her miserable virginity. Yet she accepts her life, accepts the slums, accepts her failure to please her boss, with a stolid meekness. She has inarticulate yearnings but no consciousness; she's all unconscious. She's simply *there*, looking to be a slave to a pathetic, twisted Olimpico. (Amaral doesn't extend much sympathetic imagination to Olimpico.)

Macabéa's story can be perceived many different ways; it's certainly a metaphor of male-female relationships and of the barely literate poor in the burgeoning big cities of the Third World, such as Mexico City, São Paulo, and Seoul. And to some degree Amaral is working inside the skin of her subject. The story connects at all sorts of points with the life of a woman who in her childhood wanted to be a movie star and, after raising nine children and divorcing her husband of twenty years, has become a star in the world of movies—the picture has been gathering major prizes at festivals. It's not a great movie, but it's good enough to get to you, and the image of Marcelia Cartaxo's Macabéa is what does it—the terrible aloneness of this mass woman, this nothing of a woman whom you wouldn't notice on the street. Umberto D. stood for all the proud, angry old people who couldn't live on their pensions, but he was himself, too—his own ornery old man. Macabéa is most herself in her moments of contentment: she smiles serenely as she celebrates her Sunday by taking a ride in the subway. It's Suzana Amaral's triumph that this girl gets away from her. Numbed as she is, she's as alive as Amaral or you or I, and more mysteriously so.

The New Yorker, February 23, 1987

LAW OF DESIRE
MANYPEEPLIA UPSIDOWNIA

Big-bosomed, short-waisted, and long-legged, Tina (Carmen Maura) has a hot, roiling temperament; after she has given her nightly performance in Cocteau's monologue-play *The Human Voice,* which her famous brother Pablo (Eusebio Poncela) directed, she walks toward a café with him and her daughter Ada, and, seeing a couple of street-cleaners who are busy with their spraying, she calls out to them to hose her down. Soaked, her short knit dress clinging to her wide hips, she's deliciously happy at the café, until the cool, chic Pablo tells her that she overacted. Overacting is what she's all about; it's what the Madrid writer-director Pedro Almodóvar's *Law of Desire* is all about. Tina has a slutty splendor: she swivels around on her clicking high heels, prays to the Virgin, and fills little Ada's head with her sentimental gabbing. She's overacting womanhood, which is the role of her life. She started out as Pablo's brother; as a teen-ager, she ran off with their father and had the operation to please him, but he finally left her, and she hasn't had anything to do with a man since. Little Ada is actually the daughter left behind by her lesbian lover. Almodóvar adds another layer of topsy-turvydom: Carmen Maura, the transsexual here (and the slum mother in his *What Have I Done to Deserve This!*), is a powerful actress in the manner of the early Anna Magnani, with the trippiness and self-mockery of Bette Midler; the strikingly beautiful lesbian is played by a low-voiced male transvestite.

If Tina lives in make-believe, so does the less flamboyant Pablo, who adores her. In story terms, Pablo, who imagines himself a discreet homosexual, is the protagonist. The sexual effrontery of his stage productions and his classy homoerotic films (which delight the public) have made him a glamorous celebrity, with a wide choice of lovers. (His sleek dark-blond hair, cleft chin, and steely-blue eyes help him along.) Pablo's liaisons don't make him happy, though, because he's in love with a curly-haired young working-man, Juan (Miguel Molina), who values his companionship—a rather steamy companionship—but isn't fully committed to homosexuality, or to Pablo's upper-bohemian style. One night, Pablo takes home Antonio (Antonio Banderas), a government minister's son, who has been stalking him; by morning, Antonio loves him and is determined to possess him completely. Determined also to possess anyone dear to Pablo, Antonio becomes the central horror of Pablo's life. And the film winds up in a demonstration that Antonio's desire, which is grotesque, uncontrollable—crazy—simply can't be denied. It gets so all-encompassing that Pablo has to respond to it. This will come as no surprise to people who have found themselves in bed with people they despise, or with ex-spouses or ex-lovers whom they have fought to get rid of—a sexual paradox that can have a passionate, oh-well-what-the-hell quality on the screen.

Almodóvar's tone is not like anyone else's; the film has the exaggerated plot of an absurdist Hollywood romance, and even when it loses its beat (after a murder) there's always something happening. This director manages to joke about the self-dramatizing that can go on at the movies, and at the same time reactivate it. The film is festive. It doesn't disguise its narcissism; it turns it into bright-colored tragicomedy. (Almodóvar is the director who might have brought off the sultry spirit of Manuel Puig's *Kiss of the Spider Woman*.) I've never been to Spain, but the temperament of Almodóvar's Madrid—*his* temperament—goes with the world I know. Partly, this may be because his sensibility is steeped in Hollywood movies and underground films, but it's more than that. In a recent interview in *The New York Times* he said, "My rebellion is to deny Franco. . . . I refuse even his memory. I start everything I write with the idea 'What if Franco had never existed?' " Well, that's America.

He opens with a metaphor of moviemaking—an autoerotic film is being shot in a studio—and he goes on side excursions that are also metaphorical. Some of these are the best jokes in the movie—such as Tina's taking Ada to the church where she used to sing as a choirboy, and introducing the child as her daughter to the courteously befuddled, somewhat pained choirmaster priest. And straight-faced gags keep popping up, such as Pablo's telling Tina she should get a guy and go straight. Even better: the ten-year-old Ada, worried about her developing body, asks Tina whether she'll soon grow breasts, and Tina says, "Sure. At your age, I was flat as a board." This gagster-artist Almodóvar loves Tina's religious view of herself as a woman; she has surrendered to the movies she saw as a boy. Her eyes shine when her sentimental fantasy of herself as a woman and a mother is intact; when some guy rudely disturbs it, she unconsciously throws a punch like a man. Carmen Maura, whose plumpish figure is baffling, succeeds in looking neither masculine nor feminine—her Tina is a great satirical flip-flopping creation.

Almodóvar seems to have skimped on the three men. They're wonderful romantic types, but they're involved in the more conventionally melodramatic side of the story, and in some fairly conventional homosexual romanticism. And they're almost too sensually handsome, too well built. Eusebio Poncela's Pablo lacks a goosey, comic side; he's stone-faced in scenes involving letters to Juan and Antonio—scenes that could have a flaky vivacity. (His porno movies can't be as much fun as we're led to think they are.) And Miguel Molina's Juan is boringly, honorably straight and decent. (Is Almodóvar, who comes from a rural, working-class background, taking this hardworking lad more seriously than he should?) Luckily, the well-heeled Antonio isn't held down by virtue, and the actor Antonio Banderas gets to suggest a little of the spoiled-rotten instability of Bellocchio's pug-dog hero (Lou Castel) in *Fists in the Pocket*. Banderas has a sly, funny side: when Antonio first goes home with Pablo, he explains that he's never been with a man before, and when Pablo mounts him he has a comedian's chagrined, quizzical look that says, "This isn't going to work." (Pablo makes it work, all right.)

Antonio has already interrupted their lovemaking to ask Pablo if he has any diseases. Pablo answers contemptuously, implying that if you care about sexual pleasure you can't worry about such matters. His manner says, "Go home, little boy, if you're worried about syphilis." It's the grand attitude of an earlier era. *Law of Desire* is a homosexual fantasy—AIDS doesn't exist. But Almodóvar is no dope: he's a conscious fantasist, and the movie is as aware of AIDS as the audience is. This wild man has a true talent. When Tina gives to the poor, her expression is exalted—she's Jesus and she's Eva Perón.

The New Yorker, April 20, 1987

STREET SMART

Is Morgan Freeman the greatest American actor? Back in 1980, in a late-night-over-drinks conversation, a friend and I wound up agreeing that maybe he was. That was after seeing him in plays and on television and, earlier that night, in *Brubaker.* As a death-row prisoner who broke out of his hole and started to strangle another convict, he gave the film a sudden charge that the moviemakers didn't seem to know what to do with. Freeman just shot out onto the screen, and then his character was dropped from the story. After seeing him in the new Jerry Schatzberg film, *Street Smart,* I don't think that my friend and I were too far off. This is probably the first major screen role he's ever had, and he turns a haphazardly written Times Square pimp into something so revealing that it's a classic performance. Tall and slim, and looking like a very handsome, elongated Richard Pryor, he gives the role of Fast Black a scary, sordid magnetism, and he gives the picture some bite. Fast Black is old for a pimp; he's heading toward fifty, and he has watchful eyes; they're weary and shifty—you wouldn't want to look into them. This man's coiled power is in his complete lack of scruple; it's in his willingness to resort to violence. So it's best not to make the mistake of thinking that you can put anything over on him. He's seductive—he has a veneer of affability—but he's all contradictions; you never know where you are with him except right this minute, and the minute can be cut short. Magically, Morgan Freeman sustains Fast Black's authenticity; it's like sustaining King Lear inside *Gidget Goes Hawaiian.*

Christopher Reeve plays Jonathan, a privileged young man trying to be a smooth hotshot; he has gone from Harvard to free-lance writing for a weekly "lifestyle" magazine like *New York.* Lately, his facility has been failing him, and when he pitches ideas the editor (André Gregory) barely listens to him, until he comes up with "twenty-four hours in the life of a pimp." The editor jumps at it and wants it fast; Jonathan assures him that he has the contacts, and then he goes out to try to find them. He can't, so he fabricates the story—that's what the screenwriter, David Freeman, did when he published "The Lifestyle of a Pimp" in *New York* for May 5, 1969. It created no big stir; there were no dire results, and no big-time benefits, either. In the movie, though, we get the screenwriter's fantasies of all the things that could or should have happened. Doggedly, he piles them on: Jonathan's fiction appears as a cover story and is such a wow that he becomes the editor's pet and a celebrity; he's hired to appear on the local TV news as a roving reporter specializing in street life; his apocryphal pimp is somehow thought to be based on Fast Black, who is facing a murder charge; Fast Black seeks Jonathan out and gets to know him, and when the editor wants to meet the pimp it's Fast Black that Jonathan introduces; both the assistant D.A. and Fast Black's lawyer are now on Jonathan's tail; a judge orders him to turn over his nonexistent notes, and he goes to jail when he refuses. Eventually, after Jonathan's girlfriend (Mimi Rogers) has been knifed and a prostitute called Punchy (Kathy Baker) has been killed, the new, wised-up, devious Jonathan gives in to Fast Black's pressure, fakes notes that clear the pimp of the murder charge, and then, in the screenwriter's final (most synthetic) twist, outwits Fast Black for all time.

Often underrated, Jerry Schatzberg can make viewers feel the beauty and excitement of everyday grit. (He even brings off the trick of using Montreal for most of the Manhattan locations.) Schatzberg knows how to tell a story visually: in a hotel-room scene between Jonathan and Punchy, the movements of the actors and the camera show us layers of sexual gamesmanship building up. He makes the script look and play better than it deserves to. But he can't give it conviction, rootedness. He can't conceal the author's thin, brassy attitudes: this screenwriter is out to show that everybody is corrupt, that everybody uses everybody, and so on. Most of the performers do their damnedest. Kathy Baker's Punchy looks as if she'd be called Punchy; at times she's as forlorn as an alcoholic who has been falling face down. Baker's face seems to go out of focus, as if her expressions had changed too fast for the camera—but in sexual situations her face takes on an all-out intelligent sexiness. As a hooker, she makes you feel she's a pro who delivers pleasure. (She even gets by with seducing Jonathan to Aretha Franklin singing "Natural Woman.") André Gregory is terrific as the heartless, dryly self-amused editor. Trim and dandified, he's more than pleased with himself: he's his own yes man. Gregory is some kind of eccentric genius: this editor inflects smugness, cackling at his own cleverness, leaving a trail of media slime.

Morgan Freeman wears long fingernails (proof that Fast Black is not a laboring man); he has the accompaniment of funky music and Miles Davis's trumpet; and he's terrifying in a battle of wills with Punchy, who has made the mistake of thinking they're friends. But Christopher Reeve has no peculiarities, no distinctive musical backup, and no threat. He's a big nothing.

Reeve is willing to play Jonathan as a suck-up who's trying to make his name. But as an actor he's physically too inexpressive to play inexpressiveness; it isn't the character who's a lug—it's Reeve. (When Jonathan's girlfriend marvels at his wonderful article and asks where the material came from, he crooks a finger to his skull. I blinked, expecting the finger to go right through.) Reeve has a personality when he's Superman; here, though, he doesn't seem to do anything but play what's on paper (diffidently), and it isn't enough. In the scenes where Jonathan thinks he can hold his own with Fast Black and discovers he's a helpless babe, Reeve isn't bad. His clumsiness works when he's up against Morgan Freeman's dancerlike swiftness; this taut actor can whip him with an eyelash. But when Jonathan gains the cunning to out-street-smart Fast Black it's a joke—an Ivy League white boy's dream of glory. We're supposed to take his victory as proof that he's learned his lesson and become a dirty realist. Actually, it's just a confirmation that the plot is a sham. Screenwriters who come on with the scoop that we're all pimps should just speak for themselves.

The New Yorker, April 20, 1987

TAMPOPO

The title *Tampopo*, which is Japanese for "dandelion," is the name of a fortyish widow (Nobuko Miyamoto) who is trying to make a go of the rundown noodle shop on the outskirts of Tokyo that her late husband operated. The name—it's the name that the restaurant acquires, too—fits her. She's a weedy sort of flower—a meek, frazzled woman raising a young son and doing her best to please the customers. She can't, though, because she's a terrible cook, and knows it. One day, a courtly truck driver, Goro (Tsutomu Yamazaki), and his helper eat at the shop, and Goro, who wears a dark-brown cowboy hat straight across his brow, like the righteous hero of a solemn Western, gets into a fight on her behalf. Seeing him take on five men, she is inspired by his courage. She tells him that meeting him has made her want to be a real noodle cook, and, in his formal, majestic way, he makes it his mission to teach her.

Juzo Itami, who wrote and directed this flapdoodle farce, is the son of a pioneer director. Born in 1933, he spent time as a commercial artist before becoming a well-known film actor (he played the bank-executive husband of the oldest sister in Kon Ichikawa's *The Makioka Sisters*), and he's also a popular essayist. He turned to directing in 1984 with *The Funeral*, a prizewinner in Japan, which also starred Nobuko Miyamoto (who is his wife). *Tampopo*, his second film, has its own brand of dippiness. The subtexts connect with viewers' funnybones at different times, and part of the fun of the movie is listening to the sudden eruptions of giggles—it's as if some kids were running around in the theatre tickling people.

The picture is made in a free form, crosscutting between two sets of food adventurers. The main story is that of Tampopo, the cowboy-samurai Goro, and their band of friends as they penetrate the secrets of other noodle shops, bribing and finagling to get hold of valuable recipes. The secondary story takes up the culinary-erotic obsessions of a pair of lovers: a gangster (Koji Yakusho), in a white hat and suit, and his ready-for-everything cutie (Fukumi Kuroda). These two demonstrate that eating and sex can be the same thing. The proof is in the orgasmic moment when they pass a raw egg yolk back and forth from his mouth to hers, over and over, until it bursts and dribbles down her chin. This is undoubtedly one of the funniest scenes of carnal intercourse ever filmed, and it's shot in hot, bright color that suggests a neon fusion of urban night life and movie madness.

Itami uses his background in commercial art: every now and then, the characters assume shiny Pop poses, and the images have the slightly crazed look of heightened reality. (It's a little like the heightening in *Blue Velvet*.) The whole movie—an understated burlesque of Westerns, samurai epics, and gangster films—is constructed like a comic essay, with random frivolous touches. (Goro wears his hat in the bathtub, like Dean Martin in *Some Came Running*, and it works on its own—it's entertaining.) The characters are agreeable monomaniacs: they often speak in the stiltedly civilized language of food critics. (A noodle may be profound or synergetic; it may have depth without substance.) Itami loves filmed anecdotes. He shows us a woman dying just as her kids have sat down at the table, and her husband telling them excitedly, "Keep on eating! It's the last meal Mom cooked! Eat, eat while it's hot!" The scene is a brief sacramental black comedy. On the rosier side, there's a disconsolate little boy whose parents have decreed that when he's out playing he must wear the sign "I only eat natural foods. Do not give me sweets or snacks." When a man gives him an ice-cream cone, you get the feeling that the man wants to spite the parents more than he wants to give pleasure to the child. And there are such diversions as a restaurant scene with a class of young ladies being instructed in how to eat spaghetti without slurping. Elsewhere in the restaurant—in a private room—the man in the white suit is supping on crawfish in cognac, from his cutie's navel.

The film dawdles at times, and it has its lapses: Goro gives Tampopo her cooking lessons to the accompaniment of too much triumphal music; later, the jocular use of ragtime is a bit of a pain. And when Goro is giving Tampopo her workouts, to toughen her up for cooking, the spoof of *Rocky* is cloddish. But the lapses don't last long, and the picture has a frisky texture. Reminiscences of *Shane* and *Pépé le Moko* and Kurosawa's *Yojimbo* and films by Godard, Sacha Guitry, John Ford, and Sergio Leone may slip in and out of your consciousness while Tampopo struggles to get the broth right and goes to visit the Old Master, a chef who is surrounded by shaggy-haired vagrants discussing French food and wine. The Old Master decides to rally to Tampopo's cause, and his gourmet bums (they're like Japanese Hell's Angels) sing him on his way. When the skinny-necked, fine-featured Master joins up with Tampopo's other noodle warriors, the image seems posed as if for a calendar.

The film's greatest charm is in Juzo Itami's delicate sense of fatuity. He may have developed it during his years of acting. (He was in the American films *55 Days at Peking* and *Lord Jim* as well as in Ichikawa films and, more recently, *The Family Game*, by Yoshimitsu Morita.) Tampopo, who seems to transform from within, like the American heroines of the thirties, weeps for joy when her band of friends and teachers pronounces her cooking perfection. Goro lives by his code, and he beams with satisfaction at a task accomplished. He's as proud of the refurbished restaurant, Tampopo Noodles, as he would be if he'd saved a medieval village. He looks at the throng of customers waiting to get in and knows he's no longer needed. Stately as ever, he heads out to his truck; the Old Master gets on his bicycle; and the whole group of mother's helpers disbands.

Itami's movie background is a satirist's treasure trove. There's a startling scene in which the white-suited sensualist buys a huge oyster from a woman diver; he tries to swallow it right out of the shell to which it's still attached and it bites him on the lip. Stirred by his appetite, the diver feeds the rambunctious oyster to him out of her palm, then licks the blood off his mouth. The gangster—the movie's dream hero—comes to the classic gangster finish. But even after he's shot down in the streets on a rainy night and his loyal moll pleads "Don't die!" he won't stop talking about what he wants to eat. He's got a recipe for wild boar stuffed with yam . . . And, with the whole history of movies reverberating in her voice, the moll says, "We'll eat wild boars in winter," as the gangster relinquishes his white fedora and puts it on her perfectly beautiful head.

The New Yorker, June 1, 1987

ROXANNE

Steve Martin is improbably light on his feet in the love comedy *Roxanne.* He's C.D., the fire chief, whose agility expresses the ticktock workings of his mind. C.D.'s body seems able to do anything his mind wants it to, and with the speed of thought. But he has an anomaly: a nose so long that birds can perch on it and he can sniff out distant fires. When he bangs this metanose into things and he shakes his head as if to clear it, he's suddenly W. C. Fields. As he saunters through the streets of the ski-resort town of Nelson, Washington (nestled against the mountains, it seems a dream-built town, but it's actually Nelson, British Columbia), he may do a precise little hop and a skip or waft himself in the air. The man and his timing are the same: he has a snap to him. And everything he does—like fighting two bullies—is a routine: assorted spins, kicks, whacks, and the bullies are knocked unconscious. Each routine is completed, and clicks into place. Early on, he puts a coin in a newspaper-vending machine, looks at the front page, screams, puts another coin in, and puts the paper back. And the gag tells us how lucky he feels to be high up in this town, far from the horror. His willingness to pay money to make the gesture tells us something else about him. He dances down the street because he craves movement, he loves gestures.

As C.D., Martin seems to crossbreed the skills of Fields and Buster Keaton, with some Fred Astaire mingled in. He's a wonder, which is what he should be, because C.D. stands for Cyrano de Bergerac. The script is Martin's updated version of the play that Rostand wrote in 1897, for Coquelin. Film footage of Coquelin in the role shows him tossing his sword about and juggling it in the duel-of-wits scene; he uses his physical dexterity much as Martin does. But Martin, who tells the story in a modern vernacular, isn't dashing—he's jaunty. His tart, low-key script solves the updating problems tactfully, buoyantly. (The scene that explains why C.D. can't have his nose bobbed also gives him a chance to see himself in the mirror while holding up cards with different noses.) And, as a comic, Martin is in a conspiracy with us to stay a beat or two ahead of us. That's what we pin our trust on, and he does it more than ever here. His timing has Buster Keaton's inspired airiness. Nothing Martin does in this movie seems familiar, yet he's always the man we've come to see. He's in character as Steve Martin, only more so.

His lightness is a form of purity. It cuts down on the mawkish appeal of *Cyrano*—that it's shaped as an actor's masochistic fantasy. (In the play, the star can wallow in the feeling of being unloved because of "fate.") Yet he keeps the romanticism. Daryl Hannah is the stargazer Roxanne, a graduate student in astronomy who has rented a house in Nelson for the summer so she can study the skies. This new Roxanne isn't chaste, but she's not sullied, either. The experience she's had makes her seem more desirable, more voluptuous. And Daryl Hannah's height, the confident swing of her walk, and the fullness of her mouth and chin make her a spectacular Roxanne—a convincing embodiment of a flawed man's ideal. Wearing white clothes, she gives off a womanly radiance—a combination of carnality and moonglow— and in one sequence she wears two little Christmas-tree angels as earrings. Somehow, these dangling angels become emblematic; they take over for the white plume in the play. They stand for the unabashed ingenuousness of the film.

C.D. is, of course (as just about everybody will remember from high school, or earlier), too nose-conscious to tell his new friend Roxanne of his love for her. It's a measure of the success of this adaptation that when Roxanne impetuously takes a fancy to young Chris (Rick Rossovich), the strapping new firefighter brought in by C.D. to raise the level of the volunteer squad, it isn't distressing. By then, we have enough confidence in Martin's script and the verve of the director, Fred Schepisi, to know that the movie won't go clammy on us. And when the dumb lug Chris inveigles C.D. into carrying on his courtship rites for him—reciting speeches to Roxanne, writing impassioned letters—and Roxanne falls in love with C.D.'s words, thinking they're Chris's, the deception never gets a chance to be sickly. For one thing, Martin has had the script inspiration to whip up a character, the barmaid Sandy (Shandra Beri), who doesn't awe Chris the way Roxanne does. Chris doesn't need to be poetic and intense for Sandy, and as soon as we hear the easy way they talk together we know they're a perfect match. His attraction to Roxanne has been a mistake, like hers to him. And Martin's adaptation, without wrecking the play, speeds up Roxanne's coming to her senses. The moviemakers know that Rostand's idea of beauty (in the Brian Hooker translation) is too limited for an age that encompasses punk, an age in which looking unusual may be taken for an achievement, or, at least, a "statement."

Schepisi is a fluid yet right-on-the-button director, starting with the first scene, in which the spruce, angular, gray-haired C.D. jumps out of his front door and greets the day with a twist of his hips. It's like the beginning of oddball classics such as *The Bank Dick,* which didn't fuss around with overtures—they just got on with it. It's like that, but it keeps going more gracefully, without the jerky starts and stops. Schepisi's control probably helps to account for the warmth and likableness of Daryl Hannah's performance and for the quality of surprise in the scenes between Chris and Sandy; these two have the conversational rhythm of good-natured dopes. (Shandra Beri gives her idle talk just the right weight, and she's got a barmaid's sociable smile down pat.) Schepisi does well by the encounters in the town café. (Its owner is played by Shelley Duvall.) His blitheness comes through at the firehouse: the squad of volunteer firefighters are this movie's Keystone Cops; they're fumblers, unromantic clowns. (C.D. is a clown *because* he's romantic; he makes every day different for himself.) Schepisi uses the town of Nelson as if it were the firefighters' playpen. It's also a safehold, a haven for lovers. As the director uses it and as Ian Baker shoots it, this otherworldly, lost-in-a-trance locale is a major contributor to the film's mellow, dotty charm. You want to go to the town; you want to go back to the movie.

A false nose in closeup is riveting, of course, and we in the audience can't help looking for signs of where this thingamabob is attached to a real nose (and in at least one scene—with the bird—the joining makeup is visible). But the moviemakers do something very smart: Steve Martin makes his appearance as C.D. and we laugh at his quick-thinking moves before he turns his profile and we see the extension of the nose that sticks straight out. It doesn't do what the bandage did to Jack Nicholson's nose in *Chinatown*—it doesn't uglify him. This is a funny nose, an absurd nose, and it never really seems to mar his face.

In Hawthorne's story "The Birthmark," a magnificent woman's tiny defect is the source of tragedy because her husband can't accept it. Here

C.D.'s aberration is comic because Roxanne isn't bothered by it. The movie is finally as simple as that: a love story about two sane people. It's like *Annie Hall* without anhedonia.

The New Yorker, June 15, 1987

THE WITCHES OF EASTWICK

Jack Nicholson entertains himself in *The Witches of Eastwick:* he snuffles and snorts like a hog, and he talks in a growl. And damned if he doesn't entertain us, too. As Darryl Van Horne, who describes himself as "your average horny little devil," he has half-closed piggish, insinuating eyes, and his big, shaggy head doesn't look as if it belonged on those small, fleshy shoulders. His wardrobe is an astonishment: it suggests a pasha or a samurai, and he changes garments in the middle of his conversations. He seems to have given more attention to assembling his flowing brocade robes than he ever gave to assembling his body. He's so repulsive he's funny.

The movie wavers between satirizing a hyper-sexed male's misogyny and revelling in it. Directed by George Miller (of the *Mad Max* movies), from a rickety script credited to Michael Cristofer, it's a farce that resembles its source, John Updike's 1984 novel, only in its high gloss, the general outlines of the leading characters, some purloined lines of dialogue, and Darryl's entertainingly uncouth turns of phrase. When Nicholson has a dirty word to deliver, he punts it right into your face. And he has invented some furiously demented slapstick; he's an inspired buffoon. (Nobody is likely to fall asleep at this movie.)

The three women in the fictional New England town of Eastwick—Cher as a sculptor, Susan Sarandon as a cellist and music teacher, Michelle Pfeiffer as a reporter on the *Word*—aren't the busy adulteresses that they are in the novel. They're three good-hearted beauties (a brunette, a redhead, a blonde) who have lost their husbands by death, divorce, and desertion. They're lonely, and they practice a little harmless magic just to keep from being bored. It turns out that their combined longing for a man is potent enough to lure Darryl the lech from New York City. Once ensconced in a comically vast mansion, he seduces each of them, and soon they're all frolicking together in his indoor swimming pool. But though the women are in sexual bliss with Darryl, they're so upset by his cruel tricks (he causes the death of a puritanical local woman, the owner of the *Word*, played by Veronica Cartwright) that they decide not to have anything more to do with him. When he starts punishing them, they turn to witchcraft, in self-defense, to get rid of him. Except for this mechanical structure, nothing is carried through; about half the scenes don't make much sense, and the final ones

At the beginning, Kubrick's photographic style is oppressively close in; he holds the camera so tight on the actors' faces that he doesn't give them room to act. When the recruits' heads are shaved, they're shot like Falconetti in *The Passion of Joan of Arc,* only no emotions are being expressed—that's a big "only"—and so there's no beauty in the imagery. The boys are under a microscope. When the sergeant tells them that they're "maggots" and all "equally worthless," there's nothing in Kubrick's approach to suggest anything different.

The lean, mechanical-man sergeant has a pet victim: a slow, overweight recruit whom he calls Gomer Pyle (Vincent D'Onofrio). The sergeant degrades him mercilessly, and pits the other men against him by penalizing the whole platoon for Pyle's failures. And Kubrick concentrates our attention on poor, doughy-faced Pyle; he's a fatty, like Dim the droog in *A Clockwork Orange.* (D'Onofrio had to put on sixty pounds to get the role.) But Kubrick isn't a psychological director; he doesn't seem to care anything about motivations. And so Pyle, whom Kubrick uses to demonstrate that the system for turning kids into killers can spin out of control, is no more than a comic horror, like a sad, fat crazy in an exploitation film.

In the novel, when Joker, who has tried to help the slow learner Pyle, joins the rest of the platoon in beating him while he yelps and moans, a scary-sick ambivalence gets its grip on the reader, and all the action in Nam that follows intensifies that ambivalence. The Joker of the book is like a living Catch-22: he's telling the story (it's a first-person narrative), and when he discovers that the war is turning him into a vicious racist killer we're right there inside him, as baffled by his emotions as he is, yet never doubting them. He has been brainwashed, like the others, and he becomes part of the fighting machine that the sergeant has built. In the movie, Joker joins in the beating but nothing in the second section seems to follow from it. And although the subsequent material is episodic—almost random—as it follows Joker, who eventually finds someone he knows from boot camp, we don't see through his eyes. Angular and sharp-featured, he's remote, spectral—he's supposed to be smart, but he, too, seems dim.

After the first part reaches climax, the movie becomes dispersed, as if it had no story. It never regains its forward drive; the second part is almost a different picture, and you can't get an emotional reading on it. Joker serves as a combat correspondent with the 1st Marine Division, and is assigned to write upbeat, "public relations" stories about the American soldiers' kindness to the natives, and to invent anecdotes that show we're winning the war. When he meets up with his buddy from Parris Island, he goes out on a patrol with him. They're part of a squad that sticks together during the Battle of Hue, the final round of the Tet offensive, in 1968. But when a sniper picks the men off, shooting them limb by limb, like a gourmand saving the tenderest bits for last, and we hear the men's cries, we can barely remember who they are. And we don't know why we're following Joker. His streak of humor seems ornamental—a curlicue, like the Peace might as well have a sign posted: "We're desperate for a finish." But even at its trashiest the movie keeps bumping along. It has its moments, such as the townspeople's initial inability to remember Darryl's name.

And those three beauties *are* beauties. Cher, though, mysteriously ravishing as she is, has too many closeups. The camera feasts on her heavy-lidded exoticism for so long that we can't help noticing that she isn't playing a character. And she doesn't relate to anyone else: she might be acting in front of a mirror. Sarandon is more luxuriantly physical, and she makes contact with the other performers—especially with Nicholson, in a scene where he accompanies her cello playing and she gets so hot her instrument starts smoking. Sarandon's huge eyes are made for batting, and she knows it. She has become a terrific comedienne. (A friend of mine says she wears her eyes on her sleeve.) Pfeiffer has less to do, but her kitty-cat comedy style is soft and fluid; she blends right in with the others. They're a supple trio—not a brittle bone among them. Nicholson has waited all his acting life for a harem like this.

The New Yorker, June 29, 1987

FULL METAL JACKET

Chances are that when Stanley Kubrick's Vietnam film *Full Metal Jacket* is at midpoint a lot of moviegoers will be asking themselves what it's going to be about, and when it's over they still won't know. The picture stays reasonably close to its source, Gustav Hasford's compressed, white-hot Vietnam novel *The Short-Timers,* which came out in 1979; much of the dialogue is taken directly from the book. Yet the short, spare novel has an accumulating force of horror and the movie doesn't, though it prepares for it in the long first section, set in the Marine Corps training camp at Parris Island, South Carolina. Private Joker (Matthew Modine) and the other recruits are methodically brutalized by the hateful gunnery sergeant (Lee Ermey), whose small-mindedness and impersonality are faintly funny. The man shouts abuse at us just about nonstop for three-quarters of an hour, and he punctuates his shouting with slaps on the trainees' faces, punches in the gut, and other assorted punishments. This section is basic training stripped down to a cartoonish horrorshow; it's military S&M. Kubrick seems to know exactly what he's doing here. He's so narrowly geared to the immediate purpose that he fails to establish the characters who will figure later in the film, but he achieves his effect: the process of turning young boys into robots has a sadistic, pounding compulsiveness. The moviemaking suggests a blunt instrument grinding into your skull. This can easily be taken for the work of a master director.

button he wears on his uniform (to contrast with "Born to Kill," which he has painted on his helmet).

A Vietnamese hooker flips up her miniskirt, the better to show off her bottom for a marine's camera. That's the only suggestion of spontaneity in the film. Kubrick has become a hermetic, deliberate director, who painstakingly records scenes over and over again until he achieves—what? It can't be performances he's after. He shows so little interest in the actors that they come across as the dullest cast he's ever worked with. Only the sergeant and Pyle leave any visual recall, and that's not because of their performances—it's their physiques, their faces. A sequence in which the men in the squad encounter a television crew and are asked to talk about what they're fighting for is flabby, because Kubrick doesn't discover anything in them to reveal. And it can't be the atmosphere—the feel of the place—that he's after. He began as a photographer shooting pictures for *Look,* but now he lives near London, and he didn't go to Southeast Asia or the Philippines—Asia was brought to him. (The movie was shot in England.) So our vision of the war is changed. We don't get the image of a handful of black and white intruders in a land of Asians; it's a handful of Asians who are the intruders. There they are in the rubble of Hue under gray, lowering English skies, with some imported palm trees in the distance. Even when the marines are being trained it's disorienting to hear someone refer to the Island, because we have no sense that the men we're watching are on an island, or anywhere in particular. Yet it isn't so much the English locations that are the problem—it's the spirit behind using them.

It must be ideas that Kubrick is trying to get at. The screenplay, by Kubrick, Michael Herr, and Hasford, has attitudinizing speeches—the kind that sound false no matter how true they are. When a marine talks about how "we're killing fine human beings," his language is inert. Generally, the men talk in a profane military slang that can't always be deciphered but makes its point: that clean English can't express how they feel. The themes are familiar. The sergeant's boast that before basic training is over, the men will be able to shoot as well as Charles Whitman and Lee Harvey Oswald, who learned their marksmanship in the Marines, is in the novel, but in the movie it becomes a *Dr. Strangelove* joke. And the whole theme of the reprogramming of human material recalls *Clockwork Orange*—except that there it was from sociopathic to social, and here it's the reverse. But somehow the book's overriding idea—how these brainwashed men were destroyed from within—gets lost. This war was more intensely confusing than earlier wars (in which marines were also trained to be a fighting machine). Second World War books and movies seem reasonable compared with the psychedelic, acid-rock horror that you find in accounts of Vietnam, where the emotions of combat are heightened by a druggy poetics of guilt. The Joker of Hasford's book hated the helplessness of an old Vietnamese farmer the way he hated the infantile, blubbering Pyle. He was shooting at his own helplessness. It was his fierce revulsion that made him do horrible things; some part of him protested against being turned into a killer.

In the movie, Kubrick doesn't allow his "hero" to do those horrible things. So we don't get a sense of his inner conflict. Joker just seems a detached sort of wise guy, with a superior manner; perhaps his mocking attitude is supposed to help the hip young audience identify with him. He doesn't really connect with anything. And the Peace symbol he wears isn't a sign of the protest he can't quite acknowledge; it's explained as a symbol of the Jungian duality of man. What is emotional in the book is made abstract. The movie has no center, because Kubrick has turned this hero into a replica of himself: his Joker is always at a distance—he doesn't express his feelings. So the movie comes across as not meaning anything. But it has a tone that's peculiar to Kubrick. His cold-sober approach—the absence of anything intuitive or instinctive or caught on the wing—can make you think there's deep, heavy anti-war stuff here. The gist of the movie, though, seems to be not that war makes men into killers but that the Marine Corps does. (In *2001,* we were told that it was enough to be a man to be a killer.) Here's a director who has been insulated from American life for more than two decades, and he proceeds to define the American crisis of the century. He does it by lingering for a near-pornographic eternity over a young Vietnamese woman who is in pain and pleads "Shoot me! Shoot me!" This is James M. Cain in Vietnam.

It's very likely that Kubrick has become so wrapped up in his "craft"— which is often called his "genius"—that he doesn't recognize he's cut off not only from America and the effects the war had on it but from any sort of connection to people. (The only memorable character in his films of the past twenty years is Hal the computer.) What happened to the Kubrick who used to slip in sly, subtle jokes and little editing tricks? This may be his worst movie. He probably believes he's numbing us by the power of his vision, but he's actually numbing us by its emptiness. Like a star child, Kubrick floats above the characters of *Full Metal Jacket,* the story, the audience. Moviemaking carried to a technical extreme—to the reach for supreme control of his material—seems to have turned Kubrick into a machine.

The New Yorker, July 13, 1987

JEAN DE FLORETTE

Jean de Florette is set in a wide-screen Provence in the early nineteen-twenties. Clearly, man is the viper in this harsh paradise—man in the form of the tough, greedy old peasant César Soubeyran (Yves Montand), called Le Papet, the grandpa, though he has never married and has no descendants. Le Papet wears a smile of self-satisfaction, even when he causes the death of a neighbor, whose land, with its spring of fresh mountain water, he covets for his dull-witted nephew, Ugolin (Daniel Auteuil). To make sure that those who inherit the property will sell out fast, Le Papet and Ugolin hide the spring under a load of cement. A poacher sees them doing it, and just about all the men in the area know that there has always been a source of water there, but they are a closemouthed, tight group, and when the new owner, the hunchback Jean de Florette (Gérard Depardieu), turns out to be an educated city fellow, who has learned about farming from books, nobody tells him about the mountain spring. This nature-loving dreamer has a devoted wife (Elisabeth Depardieu), who used to sing in opera, and a delicate little daughter named Manon. Depardieu wears "GOOD MAN" in capital letters across his wide brow; in smaller letters we can read "He has poetry in his soul." And for slightly over two hours we watch him trudge across his land hauling two barrels of water that are fastened across his hump. When there's no rain and his plants shrivel and his rabbits die, it's our doom. Our only relief comes when the director, Claude Berri, cuts to Le Papet and Ugolin, who monitor Jean's misery, plot against him, and gloat. Their dinnertime talk, in the darkness of an old stone house that is partly sunk in the earth, is the film's regularly scheduled den-of-thieves time.

Adapted from the first volume of Marcel Pagnol's two-part novel *The Water of the Hills,* published in 1963 (it was derived from a picture he made in 1952), *Jean de Florette* is to be followed, later this year, by *Manon of the Spring.* Both films have been much honored in France, and the New York opening of *Jean de Florette* has been preceded by respectful—even awed—publicity. It isn't hard to see why. The scheming Le Papet and Ugolin stand for the dark, elemental forces. Clear-eyed Jean is no match for their mingy-mindedness. We're seeing a big theme about "fate" being played out—the fate that used to be dramatized in silent-film epics and in sprawling realistic novels. But those works often had an unruly imaginative power. Berri, who did the adaptation with Gérard Brach, has conceived of his two films as a majestic, faithful version of the Pagnol books. He has said that it was his task to give the material "a cinematic rhythm," but "there was no need for imagination." That's what *he* thinks. *Jean de Florette* doesn't have the motor of a work conceived as a film. It's a copy, with no life of its own.

The movies that Pagnol himself made from his own material didn't have much life, either. As a scriptwriter, Pagnol drew upon many sources; Zola and Alphonse Daudet were among them, and several of his finest films, including *Harvest* (1937) and *The Baker's Wife* (1938), are from stories or novels by Jean Giono. The young Orson Welles cited *The Baker's Wife,* starring Raimu, as proof that "a story and an actor, both superb" can result in "a perfect movie" even if the directing and the editing are not "cinematic," and many of us would agree. But in the movies that Pagnol produced from his own plays the emotional texture is thinner and the talk is talkier (to American ears, anyway). The films in the famous Pagnol trilogy—*Marius*

(1931), *Fanny* (1932), *César* (1936)—are static and seem to last forever. Whether the director is Alexander Korda, who did the first, or Marc Allégret, who did the second, or Pagnol himself, who did the third, the director is the caretaker of the text, and that's all he is. These are writer-controlled movies; literal-mindedness and pedestrianism are built into them. (It was no accident that Pagnol was the first moviemaker to be elected to the Académie Française.) And Berri, in some sort of ultimate homage to Pagnol, has honored his shallow, academic side.

One of the French film traditions that the New Wave seemed to have washed away for good was the folklore of greed in which the ignorance and meanness of the peasants were supposed to be cosmi-comic. Ugolin (that name!), who actually rather likes Jean and his family and half wants to be their friend, is a figure right out of those rustic fables. He and Le Papet and their opposite number, the sainted hunchback, are characters without any subtext. Berri seems dedicated to these people who live by the seasons and have rich earth under their fingernails. But his sincerity doesn't live up to Verdi's "La Forza del Destino" on the soundtrack. The actors say the lines that Pagnol wrote decades ago, and then time passes and they say some more lines. (It's "Masterpiece Theatre" with subtitles.) Montand, in his wide-wale brown corduroy jacket, is a pillar of peasant chic. And though Berri may have felt courageous making a movie about a hunchback, this hunchback is Gérard Depardieu, who's a six footer. His hump was made in box-office heaven.

The New Yorker, July 13, 1987

HOPE AND GLORY

It's hard to believe that a great comedy could be made of the blitz, but John Boorman has done it. In his new, autobiographical film, *Hope and Glory,* he has had the inspiration to desentimentalize wartime England and show us the Second World War the way he saw it as an eight-year-old—as a party that kept going day after day, night after night. The war frees the Rohans (based on Boorman's family) from the dismal monotony of their pinched white-collar lives and of their street, with its row of semidetached suburban houses; now they have the excitement of the bomb blasts, the dash to the shelters, the searchlights combing the night skies, the stirring patriotic bilge on the wireless, and the equality that's ushered in with the ration books. Bill Rohan (Sebastian Rice Edwards) diligently collects shrapnel, and, along with the other eight- and nine-year-old boys, pokes through the ruins, smashing whatever's left to smash. Boorman lets his characters say the previously unsayable. Bored with crouching indoors during the nightly raids by the Luftwaffe and listening to the shelling and sirens, the fifteen-year-old Dawn (Sammi Davis), the eldest of the three Rohan children, runs outside for the exhilaration of movement, watches the firefighters at work on a blazing house, and dances in the Rohans' postage-stamp-size front garden. "It's lovely!" she calls to Bill as he hesitates on the porch. Seeing something by the curb, he runs out and picks it up—"Shrapnel! And it's still hot." He tosses it from hand to hand, cooling it. His mother, Grace (Sarah Miles), suddenly laughs at the sight of the burning house down the street, and is shocked at her own reaction. She calls out, "Come in at once, or I wash my hands of you!" And then, as Boorman writes (the script has been published by Faber & Faber): "A shell bursts right overhead and they duck into the open doorway. The four of them are framed there, looking up at the savage sky where the Battle of Britain rages. Bill watches, enraptured."

Boorman's approach makes perfect sense. He doesn't deny the war its terrors: there's an astonishing scene where Grace and the two younger children are heading out to the shelter but don't make it; bright white shellbursts knock them back and fling them about the living room as if they were slow-motion marionettes. Yet he gives everything a comic fillip. Bill and the other schoolkids have to wear gas masks when they go to the school shelter, and the headmaster makes them put their time to use by reciting multiplication tables; exquisitely repulsive sucking-air sounds come out. At one point, when Grace and her kids are at the movies, watching a newsreel of the Battle of Britain, a notice on the screen tells them that there's an air raid and they should take shelter. As Grace leads them up the aisle, Bill says, "Can't we just see the end?" Dawn tells him, "They've got the real thing outside." "It's not the same," he says. And that's true for the movie we're watching: it's the life that goes on outside the theatre, but selected, heightened, polished. And, in the case of *Hope and Glory,* life outside has been given an extra dose of good sense—a jolly luminousness.

The picture recalls what Ingmar Bergman tried to do in *Fanny and Alexander*—to create a whole vision of life out of a man's memories of what, as a child, he perceived about his family. But, rich as Bergman's film is, he got bogged down in Gothic fantasies and Victorian conventionality; he's never at peace with the child's amoral side. Boorman treats the memories more lightheartedly. So his mother didn't love his father and they weren't happy together, but he *survived.* The war came along and shook things up, and if his father (David Hayman), who was like a shrivelled patriotic schoolboy, tried to escape the sense of shame he felt about slipping down from the middle class to the rootless life of the semis, and enlisted, expecting adventures but finding himself put to work as a clerk-typist—well, at least he got to visit his family. And when that semidetached house—emblem of coal pollution and conformity—burned down (in a "normal" fire that couldn't be blamed on the Nazis) nobody missed it. Its destruction provided the excuse for Grace and the children to move into her parents' big, open, ramshackle bungalow on the Thames, where Bill and his six-year-old sister, Sue

(Geraldine Muir), could fish and play. And since this was at Shepperton, near the studios that Alexander Korda built, and movie crews frequently worked along the river, Bill could develop the interests that turned him into John Boorman.

The movie is wonderfully free of bellyaching. Grandfather (Ian Bannen) is a gruff, demanding old buzzard who gets drunk at Christmas and subjects the whole clan to his toasts to all the ladies he remembers with lewd satisfaction. But he also instructs Bill in the lore of the river. Now and then, Bill can tease him and get away with it, and when, just hours before the beginning of the fall term, Bill's grim, dreaded school is bombed and burned out, Grandfather laughs like a cartoon anarchist. It's as if his and Bill's dreams had exploded the place. And not theirs alone: arriving for the first day of servitude, the pupils see the bomb debris and riot in the school-yard. It's a whoop-de-do celebration, because their holidays will be extended; it's also an orgy of hatred for the headmaster, who likes to cane kids, raising welts on their palms. He has told them that discipline wins wars; now the bombs have put a stop to his tyranny. That's the joy of the movie: the war has its horrors, but it also destroys much of what the genteel poor like Grace Rohan have barely been able to acknowledge they wanted destroyed.

Boorman keeps his energy up in all the scenes. He doesn't get so personal he loses control, and he doesn't fall into any of his Jungian pits. The many things that could go wrong didn't; the picture moves along lightly, one incident after another, a collage of memories, dreams, newsreels, old movies, fake old movies. It's like a plainspoken, English variant of the Taviani brothers' *The Night of the Shooting Stars*, which was also the Second World War as seen through the eyes of a child. In that film, the child, grown up, mythicizes her war experiences, converting them into bedtime stories to tell her own child, and Boorman has written that his script began with the stories he told his kids at bedtime. Many of his characters and anecdotes are like archetypes, but they're grounded in definite, "real" characters and situations. They're never forced on us; they simply take hold—maybe because we're always in on the jokes. The picture has a beautiful pop clarity.

Sammi Davis's dimply, pleasure-loving Dawn is always changing her mind. She wants sex but not love and is furious when she falls for a Canadian jokester soldier with dimples of his own (Jean-Marc Barr). Sammi Davis (she was the blond teen-age prostitute in *Mona Lisa*, and she's the blind girl in *A Prayer for the Dying*) makes Dawn's bluntness wittily uncouth; she turns just about every line she has into a kicker. And, as Grace's friend Molly, Susan Wooldridge (she was Daphne Manners in *The Jewel in the Crown*) has moments when she's almost as no-nonsense "common" as Dawn. A few of the characters—such as Molly's husband, Mac (Derrick O'Connor)—don't have any comic turns and so they don't add up to much. And not all the performances are dazzling. (Sarah Miles is actressy without being much of an actress.) But you feel that you're seeing the people with refreshed eyes.

Sebastian Rice Edwards' Bill is everything he should be: funny, tough-minded, open-faced. And although the role of Sue takes less doing, Geraldine Muir is a hilarious little trouper. Her misconstruction of what she sees through the keyhole when she watches Dawn and the Canadian and what she sees when she watches Mummy and Daddy is a small classic.

The picture itself is big—a large-scale comic vision, with ninety-foot barrage balloons as part of the party atmosphere. In the opening scenes, kids in a movie theatre are throwing bits of paper at each other, creating a blizzard. Boorman's touch here is so sure it's as if he were handing us popcorn, and saying, "Throw it if you want; just have a good time."

The New Yorker, October 5, 1987

FATAL ATTRACTION
THE FEMININE MYSTIQUE

F*atal Attraction* is just about the worst dating movie imaginable—a movie almost guaranteed to start sour, unresolvable arguments—but long lines of people curl around the block waiting to see it. At a New York publishing party, a dull but presentable corporate lawyer (Michael Douglas), a settled married man, exchanges glances with a bold-eyed, flirtatious woman (Glenn Close), a book editor. She's wearing a Medusa hairdo—a mess of blond tendrils is brushed high off her forehead and floats around her face. She's made up to get attention, yet she resents it: the lawyer's plump pal (Stuart Pankin) tries a pleasantry on her, and she gives him a drop-dead stare. We see all the warning signals that the lawyer doesn't, and when he runs into her again, on a weekend when his wife and six-year-old daughter are out of town, we sense the hysteria behind her insinuating repartee and the hot looks she fastens on him. She makes all the overtures; he's not particularly eager, but she semi-transforms her frighteningness to sexiness, and he, being frightened, finds it sexy. She makes spending the night together seem casual and grownup—makes him feel he'd be a total wimp to say no—and he goes with her to her loft.

Like a femme fatale in a Cecil B. De Mille picture, she comes from hell: her loft is in the wholesale-meat district, where fires burn in the street. The director, Adrian *(Flashdance)* Lyne, puts on bravura demonstrations of frenetic passion. The two have sex, with her seated on the kitchen sink, and when she reaches for the faucet and splashes her hot face Lyne shoots it as if the water were wildly erotic. After more sex, they go to a Latin club for some (comically) supercharged dancing, then have sex in the elevator to the loft. By morning, the lawyer has had enough, but she pressures him, and he doesn't find it easy to get clear of her. When the weekend is over and he's determined to say goodbye and go back uptown she stops him, temporarily, by slashing her wrists. In the weeks that follow, she hounds him at his office and his home, insisting that he can't use her and then discard her. The picture is a skillfully made version of an old-fashioned cautionary movie: it's a primer on the bad things that can happen if a man cheats on his wife.

Once the woman begins behaving as if she had a right to a share in the lawyer's life, she becomes the dreaded lunatic of horror movies. But with a difference: she parrots the aggressively angry, self-righteous statements that have become commonplaces of feminist fiction, and they're so inappropriate to the circumstances that they're the proof she's loco. They're also Lyne's and the scriptwriter James Dearden's hostile version of feminism. (Dearden's script is an expansion of the forty-two-minute film *Diversion,* which he wrote and directed in England in 1979.) Glenn Close expresses the feelings of many despairing people; she plays the woman as pitiable and deprived and biologically driven. But in the movie's terms this doesn't make the character sympathetic—it makes her more effectively scary, because the story is told from a repelled man's point of view. Lyne and Dearden see her as mouthing a modern career woman's jargon about wanting sex without responsibilities, and then turning into a vengeful hellion, all in the name of love. They see the man as ordinary, sane, hardworking—a man who loves his beautiful homebody wife (Anne Archer) and bright little daughter (Ellen Hamilton Latzen). He's the opposite of a lech; he was a little tickled at being seduced. Yet the woman plays the *Madama Butterfly* music and doesn't regard it ironically; alone in her stark loft, she really sees herself as having been mistreated. When she seeks revenge, she might be taking revenge on all men.

The horror subtext is the lawyer's developing dread of the crazy feminist who attacks his masculine role as protector of his property and his family. It's about men seeing feminists as witches, and, the way the facts are presented here, the woman *is* a witch. She terrorizes the lawyer and explains his fear of her by calling him a faggot. This shrewd film also touches on something deeper than men's fear of feminism: their fear of women, their fear of women's emotions, of women's hanging on to them. *Fatal Attraction* doesn't treat the dreaded passionate woman as a theme; she's merely a monster in a monster flick. It's directed so that by the time she's wielding a knife (from that erotic kitchen) you're ready to shriek at the sight of her. But the undercurrents of sexual antagonism—of a woman's fury at a man who doesn't value her passion, doesn't honor it, and a man's rage at a woman who won't hold to the rules she has agreed to, a man's rage against "female" irrationality—give the movie a controversial, morbid power that it doesn't really earn.

It's made with swank and precision, yet it's gripping in an unpleasant, mechanical way. When we first hear that the little daughter wants a bunny rabbit, an alarm goes off in our heads. And after the lawyer buys the rabbit we wait to see what obscene thing the demon lady will do to it. Educated people may want to read more into *Fatal Attraction,* but basically it's a gross-out slasher movie in a glossy format. (It has special touches, such as a copy of Oliver Sacks' *The Man Who Mistook His Wife for a Hat* next to the bed in the loft.) The violence that breaks loose doesn't have anything to do with the characters who have been set up; it has to do with the formula they're shoved into.

The picture has De Mille's unbeatable box-office combination—an aura of sexiness and a moral message. We know that the lawyer isn't going to chase after the blonde, because Lyne softens Anne Archer's features and sexualizes every detail of the cozy marriage. And the movie is edited so that the audience is breathing right along with the husband as he watches his wife put on her extra-moist lipstick. There are also bits of contrast, like the pal's making fun of himself, or the husband's experiencing a surreal embarrassment, trying to carry the blonde from her sink to her bed and being hobbled by his pants and shorts, which are caught around his ankles. Lyne uses these moments to break into the dreamlike tension of the male erotic reveries of the soft nest at home and of the tempestuous, kinky sex in the loft. The husband loves his wife and prefers her in every way to the interloper, whose rapacity scares him even before she threatens his way of life, even before she sends him porno tapes full of hate. The movie has its sex in the dirty sink, but it's pushing the deeper erotic satisfaction of the warm, sweet life at home. The key to its point of view is that dull, scared everyman husband. The woman was ready to go nuts; if it hadn't been this ordinary guy she tried to destroy, it could have been another. She carries madness, disease, the unknown. This is a horror film based on the sanctity of the family—the dream family. It enforces conventional morality (in the era of AIDS) by piling on paranoiac fear. The family that kills together stays together, and the audience is hyped up to cheer the killing.

The New Yorker, October 19, 1987

THE LAST EMPEROR
THE MANCHURIAN CONFORMIST

In 1908, the not quite three-year-old Pu Yi was forcibly separated from his mother and set on the Dragon Throne in Peking's Forbidden City. Honored as a god—as the Lord of Ten Thousand Years—he was the titular ruler of a third of the people on earth. Deposed in 1912, by the republican revolution, he was a feudal has-been but didn't know it for several years, because he was allowed to remain in the Forbidden City with his courtiers, chamberlains, and aristocratic ladies, and several hundred eunuchs. He went on playing emperor and presiding over empty ceremonies until 1924, when Nationalist forces evicted him. He was nineteen; he packed up his No. 1 wife (the empress) and his No. 2 wife, his wealth and his entourage, and moved to the coastal city of Tientsin, where he lived the life of a Western-style playboy—he partied. Then, in the early thirties, he was wooed by the Japanese: accepting their offers, he became the puppet emperor of Japanese-occupied Manchuria, and stayed in office during the Second World War—until the arrival of Soviet paratroopers, in 1945. He spent five years in Soviet custody. When Mao's Communists took power in China and wanted him returned, Stalin sent him home, and for ten years he was "reëducated" in a war-criminals prison. Pardoned in 1959, he worked as an unskilled under-gardener in Peking's Botanical Gardens and then as an archivist until his death, of cancer, in 1967. All that he left behind was an autobiography, and that was written by Communist hacks. It deals with his repentance.

This desperately unlucky man—a cork bobbing on the tides of history—is the subject of Bernardo Bertolucci's *The Last Emperor*. Pu Yi's life story seems made for irony. It could be told so that we'd see his ups and down-down-downs as an extreme example of the crazy bad breaks we all are handed. His life has the pattern for Preston Sturges slapstick—Sturges might see him as a peppy fellow always fighting the storms and getting knocked into the water, the Emperor of China as a poor, sad schmuck. And if Bertolucci wanted to make *The Tragedy of a Ridiculous Man*—which was the title of his last picture—Pu Yi would be the perfect subject. But Bertolucci, and Mark Peploe, who wrote the script with his help, have a different approach. They use three child actors as Pu Yi at three, at ten, and through his wedding, at fifteen, and then John Lone takes over for him at eighteen and plays him to his end, at sixty-two. The movie doesn't have the juicy absurdity that seems to pour right out of the historical story. And it suppresses the drama. But it has a dull fascination.

Bertolucci doesn't intend us to see Pu Yi as the hero or the anti-hero, or even the comic victim, of his life. Rather, he's a man without will or backbone who lives his life as spectacle—who watches his life go by. And since he experiences his life as spectacle we're given only spectacle—a historical pageant without a protagonist. There's an idea here, but it's a dippy idea—it results in a passive movie. There's no toughness in Peploe's writing; the dialogue is waxy. And Bertolucci, given the opportunity to shoot the palaces and courtyards and labyrinthine walled paths of the two-hundred-and-fifty-acre Forbidden City, works so gracefully that the movie is all vistas, all squat façades and heavy silks, reds and brilliant yellows. The chinoiserie is pleasant enough, but Bertolucci's staging, Vittorio Storaro's cinematography, and Ferdinando Scarfiotti's sets aren't in the service of anything in particular, and they make no real mark on you. That's also true of Peter O'Toole's performance as the boy emperor's tutor, a Scotsman, who was reputedly skilled in intrigue but is presented here as no more than a stiff, kindly fellow.

There are tiny set pieces that can get to you. When Pu Yi's wet nurse is taken away, because he's too attached to her, he chases the palanquin carrying her but can't catch up; years later, in Manchuria, his porcelain-doll empress (the gifted Joan Chen) is taken away by the Japanese because they can't control her, and he chases the car and, of course, doesn't catch up. These rhyming incidents of helplessness—of loss—are disturbingly poignant: you feel them like slivers under your skin. And though Pu Yi is a prisoner in the Forbidden City, he's a pampered prisoner, so that when he must leave—when the Nationalist soldiers fall into ranks at the gates and he comes out leading the motorcade, sitting between his two wives—it's like the expulsion from Eden. Images such as that of hundreds of bannermen with coxcomb headgear, or the regiments of eunuchs—who are about to leave the City—standing in formation holding little terra-cotta jars, so that when they are buried they can be buried as whole men, have some staying power. The movie is full of felicities, but the central idea of a man who watches his life go by is only an intellectual conceit. It doesn't make contact with the audience.

Bertolucci's typical men have been passive—the rich or privileged ones especially (Fabrizio in *Before the Revolution,* the Trintignant character in *The Conformist,* the De Niro character in *1900*). Here the whole mood of the film is passive. In a sense, we're being told to watch history acting on people, and the filmmaking itself is not active enough to show us how the people respond. John Lone has the sensuous, modelled features of a matinée idol; he's mysteriously poised and formal—he suggests something between Eastern and Western acting—and there's a tension in his star presence. But the movie, which renounces psychology, gives no weight to Pu Yi's undefined sexuality or to his cruelty; he's written as a figurehead. Lone is gutted as an actor—the conception doesn't allow him to show anything like the fears that Trintignant communicated. All Lone can do with Pu Yi is make him a magnetic figurehead. The child actors who play Pu Yi get a chance to show some spontaneity, and we can smile at how straight they stand in their imperial getups. And we see how the courtiers and the ladies control the growing child by giving him sensual pleasure or withholding it. They're like unscrupulous parents. They're hiding behind columns listening when Pu Yi's tutor is with him. When Pu Yi wants to go off to Oxford, they pick an eligible seventeen-year-old Manchu princess for him, and when she covers the little fifteen-year-old boy's face with lipsticky kisses their hands loosen her clothes so he can get at her.

Lone has to carry the film's dubious message. Bertolucci and Peploe want us to believe that Pu Yi really was reëducated: that he became a model citizen through the ministrations of the governor of the prison, a kindly, shrewd first-generation Communist (Ying Ruocheng), and that in his later years, when he worked as an under-gardener, he experienced freedom for the first time. They want us to believe that his repentance was genuine, and that what some might disparage as Communist brainwashing actually cleaned away his decadence and healed him. They come up with a scene in which Pu Yi, near death, visits the Forbidden City, which is now a tourist attraction, talks to a child there, and, going to his old throne, digs down to find the cricket cage he left there years before, and hands the cage, with its still-living cricket, to the child. The scene would work better if the moviemakers had planted the detail of how long crickets can survive, but it would still have a fuddy-duddy humility about it.

If we're to believe that the reëducation was a success, we have to see it. And Bertolucci and Peploe are too passive to dramatize it. The movie gives us no way to judge whether Pu Yi is pleased merely to have survived, like the caged cricket—survived the revolutions, the prisons, and his own suicide attempts—or has found some deep inner contentment as a Communist citizen. His empress, who has the political instincts he lacks, speaks up freely before she's taken away from him. His No. 2 wife (Wu Jun Mimei) walks out on him in Tientsin, taking nothing—not even an umbrella to ward off the rain. She's soaked but free, like the romantic heroines in movies of long ago. The scene has no substance, yet you know that Bertolucci admires this adventurous woman, while Pu Yi, like the Trintignant and De Niro figures, seems to stand for the part of him that he feels should be expunged—the coddled little boy who grows up wanting to cling, as Pu Yi does, to his mother, his wet nurse, his golden throne, his paradise. The only way I can make sense of this movie is to see it as the reverie of a man who can't justify himself as an artist, who doesn't trust his instincts and keeps leaning on Marxism and other outside forms of discipline, who feels that he needs to be reëducated, changed—that his artistry should be put at the service of ordinary people. He's brainwashing himself in this movie, trying to tell himself that he shouldn't be the star of his life—that he'd be happier as an extra.

Bertolucci is not the kind of moviemaker who can make epics for a huge international audience: he doesn't have the gusto, the animal high spirits, or the low cunning. And, working with Mark Peploe, he can't show us what Pu Yi is missing. Pu Yi is just as passive near the end, when he's a lowly gardener, as he was when he was a weakling playboy—perhaps more so. But now that he's an extra we're supposed to see him as a happy, free man. This makes no sense: Is he never to assert himself? Is happiness supposed to be the acceptance of castration? Pu Yi might as well be given a little terra-cotta jar.

Bertolucci makes pretty pictorial music, but two hours and forty-six minutes is a long time for a movie to dance. Maybe it wouldn't be if his sense of rhythm hadn't become erratic. A scene in which the adolescent Pu Yi plays a game with the eunuchs—he stands on one side of a huge cloth banner, they on the other, and he feels them, trying to guess who is who—has its more explicitly erotic echo when Pu Yi is in bed, under a flesh-toned satin cover, with both his wives, and we watch the rippling movements of cloth. A fire outside darkens the flesh tones—a wonderful idea—but the satin ripples for much too long. The voluptuous lyricism has gone out of Bertolucci's sensual scenes; they've become obvious. And he has taken to redoing his own earlier effects. Parts of the movie suggest that he moved *The Conformist* to Manchuria, but when he stages a lesbian seduction it isn't lush and enticing—it's right out of the Ridiculous Theatrical Company. The seducer, who announces "I'm a spy, and I don't care who knows it," is also an opium addict, a concubine, and a would-be aviatrix who dresses all in leather; she wins the empress by sucking her toes, putting a ring on one of them, and declaring, "Now we're engaged." (The Manchurian scenes are disconcertingly cartoonish, with slimy Japanese on nefarious errands, and the empress stuffing her mouth with flower petals.) The film's most shocking moment comes when Pu Yi, still a boy, is not allowed to go out of the Forbidden City to see his mother, who has killed herself; he takes the pet mouse that he carries in his pocket and smashes it against the City gates. The scene is especially shocking to those who saw *1900* and retain a vivid memory of Donald Sutherland, as the Fascist Attila, smashing a cat. These scraps of Bertolucci's past hint at a problem: he can't get a new vision together, and he's in danger of self-parody.

To enjoy the picture, you have to settle for the set pieces and the many quick, unstressed details, such as a glimpse of women's bound feet, or images such as that of a single huge red star in a detention center, and a single fedora in a crowd of prisoners, on Pu Yi. The Forbidden City itself is visually pleasing but not exactly glorious. Peter O'Toole has said that it wasn't until the movie was actually being shot and he was riding in a golden palanquin, ten feet in the air, that he saw the Imperial Palace as "a sea of yellow triangular and rectangular loops" and realized that the whole Forbidden City was intended to be seen from the height of a palanquin—that it was a maze designed for the eyes of lordlings, not earthlings. I don't understand why the moviemakers didn't get the camera up there. What better way for Bertolucci to show us the true meaning of a life of privlege? Is it possible that Bertolucci (whose movies tell us that he can't tear himself away from that life) didn't want to make the Forbidden City too alluring? It isn't just himself he's trying to reëducate.

The New Yorker, November 30, 1987

THE DEAD
IRISH VOICES

The announcement that John Huston was making a movie of James Joyce's "The Dead" raised the question "Why?" What could images do that Joyce's words hadn't? And wasn't Huston pitting himself against a master who, though he was only twenty-five when he wrote the story, had given it full form? (Or nearly full—Joyce's language gains from being read aloud.) It turns out that those who love the story needn't have worried. Huston directed the movie, at eighty, from a wheelchair, jumping up to look through the camera, with oxygen tubes trailing from his nose to a portable generator; most of the time, he had to watch the actors on a video monitor outside the set and use a microphone to speak to the crew. Yet he went into dramatic areas that he'd never gone into before—funny, warm family scenes that might be thought completely out of his range. He seems to have brought the understanding of Joyce's ribald humor which he gained from his knowledge of *Ulysses* into this earlier work; the minor characters who are shadowy on the page now have a Joycean vividness. Huston has knocked the academicism out of them and developed the undeveloped parts of the story. He's given it a marvellous filigree that enriches the social life. And he's done it all in a mood of tranquil exuberance, as if moviemaking had become natural to him, easier than breathing.

The movie is set on the sixth of January, 1904, the Feast of the Epiphany. The Morkan sisters and their fortyish niece—three spinster musicians and music teachers—are giving their annual dance and supper, in their Dublin town house, and as their relatives and friends arrive the foibles and obsessions of the hostesses and the guests mesh and turn festive. The actors—Irish or of Irish heritage—become the members of a family and a social set who know who's going to get too loud, who's going to get upset about what. They know who's going to make a fool of himself: Freddy Malins (Donal Donnelly)—he drinks. Even before Freddy shows up, the two Misses Morkan—ancient, gray Julia (Cathleen Delany), whose fragile face seems to get skinnier as the night wears on, and hearty Kate (Helena Carroll)—are worried. They're relieved when their favorite nephew, Gabriel Conroy (Donal McCann), arrives, with his wife, Gretta (Anjelica Huston); they can count on Gabriel to keep an eye on Freddy for them. It's the reliable, slightly pompous Gabriel—a college professor and book reviewer—who has an epiphany this night, and we, too, experience it.

During the party, Gabriel tries to entertain Freddy's excruciating old bore of a mother (Marie Kean), a self-satisfied biddy who smiles a sweet social smile at Gabriel but treats her son with contempt. Mrs. Malins wears an evening hat perched on her white ringlets and sits with one hand on her fancy walking stick; she's so old she seems to have the bones of a little bird, yet Freddy looks to her for approval, like a child. When he sees her expression, he's left openmouthed, chagrined, and with a faint—almost imperceptible—stutter. He shrinks. She thinks she would like him to be like Gabriel, but she and Freddy match up beyond one's saddest dreams. She sneers at him for not being the manly son she can be proud of, and turns him into a silly ass. Ever hopeful, he's crushed over and over again, his mustachioed upper lip sinking toward his chin.

Gabriel looks more authoritative than he feels. A stabilizing presence, and the man whose task it is to represent all the guests in a speech thanking the hostesses, he's like an observer at the party, but he's also observing himself, and he's not too pleased with how he handles things—especially his response to a young woman who chides him for spending his summer vacations abroad and for not devoting himself to the study of the Irish language. He would like to be suave with her, but he's so full of doubts about himself that he gets hot under the collar. And Gabriel feels his middle-aged mediocrity when he's speechifying. He plays the man of literary eminence, toasting Aunt Julia and Aunt Kate and their niece, Mary Jane (Ingrid Craigie), after calling them the Three Graces of the Dublin musical world. But when the assembled guests drink to them he sees the ladies' gaiety go beyond gaiety. They can't contain their pleasure at being complimented; Julia's hectic, staring eyes fill with tears, and a high flush appears on her ancient girlish dimples. And he gets a whiff of mortality.

The movie itself is a toast to Irish hospitality and to the spinster sisterhood of music teachers, which has probably never before been saluted with such affection. Starting with the sound of an Irish harp under the opening titles, and with frequent reminders of the importance of the pianists who play for the dancing at the party, the picture is about the music that men and women make, and especially about the music of Irish voices. At supper, the characters go at their pet subjects: opera past and present, and famous tenors, dead and alive. They know each other's positions so well that they taunt each other.

One of the guests—a tenor, Mr. D'Arcy (Frank Patterson)—has declined to sing, but after most of the others have left he succumbs to the pleading of a young lady he has been flirting with, and sings "The Lass of Aughrim." Gretta Conroy, who has been making her farewells and is coming down the stairs to join Gabriel, stands hushed, leaning on the bannister listening. Mr. D'Arcy's voice, resonating in the stairwell, has the special trained purity of great Irish tenors; the whole world seems still while he sings, and for a few seconds after. And Gabriel, seeing his wife deeply affected, is fired with sexual longing for her. He hopes to awaken her passion. But in the carriage she's sad and silent, while he makes clumsy conversation. When they reach the hotel where they are to spend the night, she falls asleep in tears after telling him about her youth in Galway and about a consumptive young boy, Michael Furey, her first love, who sang that song, "The Lass of Aughrim." Michael Furey had left his sickbed to come see her on a rainy night in winter, and died a week later, when he was only seventeen.

In the course of the evening, Gabriel has been evaluating how he's doing, and feeling more and more like a solemn stuffed shirt. Now everything he thought he knew about Gretta and himself has been sent whirling. He feels that his own love for her is a dismal thing compared with the dead boy's, and he gets beyond his own ego—he's moved by the boy's action. He thinks about carnal desire and about "the vast hosts of the dead." He sees Aunt Julia as she had looked a few hours earlier when she danced with him, and imagines that she will be the next to go. And Huston, having intensified our vision of the family life that the final passages of the story come out of, implicitly acknowledges that he can't improve on their music. In the story, these passages are Gabriel's thoughts. Here Huston simply gives over to them, and we hear them spoken by Gabriel, as the snow outside blends the living and the dead. Joyce's language seems to melt into pure emotion, and something in Gabriel melts.

Huston moved to Galway in the early fifties, and it was his home base for roughly twenty years—it's where Anjelica Huston and his son Tony Huston, who wrote the script, grew up. But when he made this movie he shot the Dublin interiors in a warehouse in Valencia, California, and the snow was plastic. Huston wasn't strong enough to travel; he completed the film early in the summer, and died in August, after his eighty-first birthday. The picture he left us is a tribute to Joyce, whose words complete and transcend what we've been watching. But the humor is from the two of them, and from the actors.

The movie is a demonstration of what, in Huston's terms, movies can give you that print can't: primarily, the glory of performers—performers with faces that have been written on by time and skill, performers with voices. It's as if Huston were saying, "Making a movie of a classic isn't anything as simple as just depriving you of the work of your imagination. Your imagination couldn't create these people for you. Only these specific actors could do it." And, of course, they could do it only with Huston guiding their movements and Tony Huston providing their words. And, yes, your imagination is now tied to these actors, but they bring a spontaneity and joy into the movie which you don't experience from reading the story.

It isn't simply that they physically embody the characters; they embody what the movie is saying. When Aunt Julia, once a respected local soprano, is prevailed on to sing, and comes out with "Arrayed for the Bridal," the quaver in her thin voice is theme music. So is her vaguely rattled look. Poor, effusive Freddy tells her that he has never heard her sing so well, then goes even further and tells her he has never heard her sing half so well. That's right out of the story, but it's different when we can see and hear the woman he's praising so idiotically. Cathleen Delany is superb as Julia, whose memory is fading, and who sometimes forgets where she is. There's a moment at the beginning when she's in the receiving line and looks at someone blankly; asked if she doesn't remember the person from last year, she rallies with "Of course, of course." She's leaving this world, but she's still a firm social liar. Donal Donnelly isn't just a great drunk; he knows how to play a drunk sobering up. By the end of the party, Freddy is almost a man of the world. Marie Kean's Mrs. Malins is such a smiley little dragon she makes you laugh; the performance is high clowning. And Helena Carroll's Aunt Kate is wonderfully obstreperous when she berates the pope for turning women (like her sister) out of the choirs and putting in little boys. Ingrid Craigie's Mary Jane, the peacemaker, soothes Aunt Kate's sense of injury (you know it's an oft-indulged sense of injury) and steers people to safe ground; Mary Jane has a softness about her, a loving docility. Dan O'Herlihy is the Protestant Mr. Browne, a florid old gent who is delighted to hear Kate lashing out at the pope; he fancies himself a gallant and jovially drinks himself to sleep. Huston never before blended his actors so intuitively, so musically.

The change in his work is in our closeness to the people on the screen. Freddy is such a hopeful fellow, always trying to please, that we can see ourselves in his worst foolishness. We can see ourselves in Julia and Kate and in the stiff, self-tormenting Gabriel. And when Anjelica Huston's Gretta speaks of Michael Furey and says, "O, the day I heard that, that he was dead," we hear the echoes of the pain that she felt all those years ago. We hear them very clearly, because of the fine, unimpassioned way that the actress plays Gretta, leaving the tragic notes to Gabriel. Gretta's is only one of the stories of the dead, but Joyce wrote the work right after his Nora told him of her early great love, and it's the most romanticized, the most piercing. The stillness in the air during Frank Patterson's singing of the melancholy "Lass" is part of the emotional perfection of the moment. But the film finds its full meaning in the stillness of Donal McCann's meticulous tones at the end—in Gabriel's helpless self-awareness. He mourns because he is revealed to himself as less than he thought he was. He mourns because he sees that the whole world is in mourning. And he accepts our common end: the snow falls on everyone.

The New Yorker, December 14, 1987

THE LONELY PASSION OF JUDITH HEARNE

In the 1935 *Alice Adams,* the affectations of Katharine Hepburn's Alice would make her dislikable if you didn't feel the desperation behind them—if you didn't feel as if you were inside her skin. I was sixteen when the film was first shown, and during the slapstick dinner-party scene, when Alice was undergoing agonies of comic humiliation, I started up the aisle to leave the theatre, and was almost out the doors before I snapped to my senses, and rushed back and sat down. Something similar happened to me a few days ago when I was watching Maggie Smith's performance in *The Lonely Passion of Judith Hearne:* during Judy's most self-exposing moments, I caught myself trying to escape by glancing down, as if I had urgent business with my notepad. Judy, who lives in Dublin, is all pretension, like Alice. Everybody sees through her, and she knows it, but she can't get rid of her own mealymouthed phoniness: it's ingrained in her. Educated in an exclusive convent school for the daughters of the wealthy, she's a spinster in her late forties or fifties, with nothing but her airs, her polished turns of phrase, and a little jewelry left her by her aunt, along with a moldering gray mink stole. She's impoverished—she doesn't get enough to eat. She keeps up her prim, ladylike manner, though, and when she moves into new lodgings her land-lady's brother, James Madden (Bob Hoskins), who has just returned after thirty years in New York City, thinks she must have a bit of money. He asks her out, hoping she'll invest in a business venture he's dreaming up, and she believes herself to be in the midst of a romance.

The movie is about a great deal more than a near-comic misunderstand-ing. It's about the loneliness that Judy tries to conceal from the people at the rooming house—she pretends she has friends and social commitments. It's about her secret drinking. And it's about the deprivation that she feels every waking minute, and about the Catholicism that has always provided her with ready-made answers to everything. Mortified when she learns that Madden isn't interested in her as a woman, she turns to her priest—gruff, bearded Father Quigley (Alan Devlin)—whose fieriness in the pulpit has im-pressed her. She confesses her drinking; she explains that she gave her youth to tending her bedridden aunt, and when the aunt died it was too late for her to get an office job—meaning that it was also too late to get a man. She tells Father Quigley of her isolation, and he brushes her off with dogma: if she has faith in God, she can't be lonely. All her life, she has been kept in the position of a child taking the Church fathers' word for every-thing. Now she demands to be treated as a grownup and given straight an-swers. She doesn't understand that Father Quigley doesn't have them: he's a company man handing out the company line, and when she isn't content with it he gets testy.

Brian Moore's *The Lonely Passion of Judith Hearne* is perhaps the finest novel ever written about a woman who's a spinster in spite of her sensual na-ture. It's a beauty of a novel—a work of surpassing empathy—written when Moore was only twenty-seven and, having left Ireland (partly, he has said, be-cause of the religious stranglehold on the country), was living in Canada. The book was published in 1955 and began to be optioned for the stage and the screen almost immediately. José Quintero was among the theatre peo-ple; he hoped to do it with Geraldine Page. John Huston optioned it, in-tending to film it with Katharine Hepburn; Daniel Petrie had Rachel Roberts in mind; Irvin Kershner planned on Deborah Kerr. But nobody had the rights and the financing at the same time until this year. Then George Harrison, whose company, HandMade Films, backed *Mona Lisa* and *A Pri-vate Function,* gave the go-ahead to Jack Clayton and Maggie Smith, who worked from Peter Nelson's clear, intelligent adaptation. Clayton is a felici-tous choice to direct a character-study movie about a woman's rage against the Church for her wasted life. For one thing, he's Catholic. And Clayton—his first feature was *Room at the Top,* with Simone Signoret, and he made *The Innocents,* with Deborah Kerr, and *The Pumpkin Eater,* with Anne Bancroft—knows how to show women's temperatures and their mind-body interactions.

Maggie Smith lets you read every shade of feeling in Judith Hearne's face. Judy's blue-green eyes are full of misgivings; her thin lips have spokes—nervous pucker lines—and her pinched expression accentuates the long space between nose and mouth. She looks like a gigantic mouse—a mouse who's grown to the height of a giraffe. It's a staggering performance. Maggie Smith becomes the essence of spinster—she makes you feel the ghastliness of knowing you're a figure of fun. When Judith Hearne is at her most proper, she wears a hat flat across her head. (It looks like a poached egg.) Her ludicrous appearance is the image of old-maid torment, and you know you've laughed at women who looked like this—or, at least, you've wanted to. Now you get what it's like to be on the other side of that laugh. Smith makes us understand that when Judy's childish literal-mindedness about religion is shaken, her faith is gone. The Judy who's painfully self-conscious and polite is still a romantic little girl at heart. But when she has some gin in her and she runs down the church aisle and batters on the small gold doors of the tabernacle, demanding that God make his presence known to her—that he open up and take her in with him—her voice is deep and angry. She's suddenly a force of nature, gone crazy-sane.

Hoskins' Madden is a vulgarian who's impressed by Judy's refinement, until he discovers she gives piano lessons—that's the tipoff there's no money there. Madden, who's plump and has a limp, affects sportiness; he's like a little mechanical man when he and Judy go walking and he holds up his arm, crooked at the elbow, for her to hang on to. He has a beady-eyed, out-of-control intensity in the scenes where he lusts after the fresh young slavey Mary (Rudi Davies) who does the dirty work in the rooming house. But Hoskins' acting doesn't have the surprise of Ian McNeice's performance as Madden's nephew Bernard, the landlady's son. A grown man who has already been to university, he looks like a wax angel made of rotten tallow. He's a Dickensian horror, with lewd pink flesh and yellowish hair. (McNeice was Young Wackford Squeers in the 1981 New York *Nicholas Nickleby*.) His belly hangs out of his red silk pajama bottoms, but his mother (Marie Kean) dotes on him and keeps stuffing him; Bernard is writing an epic poem, which he expects will take five more years of being fed and fussed over. It's McNeice's feat that he plays Bernie as a sybaritic slime yet also makes us understand why the sixteen-year-old Mary waits each night for him to sneak up to her bed. Bernie is playful with her—he shows her a good time. (And he's certainly the only one who does.) The picture needs the baroque touch that McNeice provides: Bernie has enough elfish perversity to help offset the shallow, virtuous ending. (Madden is brought back so that Judy can reject him and go forth without illusions.)

The people in this movie are accustomed to the everyday perversity that passes for rectitude: adults tell on each other, like mean-spirited schoolkids. The book is set in Belfast, the movie in Dublin, but it's the same Church, the same infantilization. The devout landladies can't resist the chance to squeal to the mothers of Judy's piano pupils about her drinking. At one point, she goes to give a lesson, and the woman of the house won't let her in—closes the door in her protesting face. Judy goes on talking for a second: she says (to herself), "I used to play in musicales." And there's a cut to Judy at the piano performing for fashionable guests, with Wendy Hiller sitting there as the aunt, regal in her finery. It's a satisfying transition, because we can see that even in Judy's palmier days she was repressed and gawky and not much of a musician. Smith and Wendy Hiller are magnificent together. You feel an ugly, claustrophobic intimacy in the Judy-and-her-aunt relationship: all the love is from Judy's side, and it's self-deception. (She can't admit to herself that her aunt is a tyrant.) Part of what makes the two actresses match up as family is their bond of love and respect for their profession. They both have beautiful restraint. If Wendy Hiller went too far in the aunt's petulant, hysterical scenes, we wouldn't believe that Judy would stay all those years to look after her. And if Maggie Smith went too far in Judy's outbursts at God, we'd stop feeling that we were inside her skin. And the movie would let us off the hook.

The New Yorker, December 28, 1987

MOONSTRUCK
LOONY FUGUE

Cher is right at home in the screwball ethnic comedy *Moonstruck*. She doesn't stare at the camera and act the goddess. She moves around, she shouts, and when she lets her hair down a huge dark mass of crinkly tendrils floats about her tiny face. (What a prop!) Cher isn't afraid to be a little crazy here, and she's devastatingly funny and sinuous and beautiful. She plays Loretta, a widowed bookkeeper in her late thirties, who lives with her Italian-American family in a big old brownstone in Brooklyn. Doing the levelheaded thing, she accepts the marriage proposal of a timid dullard (Danny Aiello), a bachelor in his forties, and, when he has to fly to Palermo, she does what he asks: she invites his estranged younger brother (Nicolas Cage), a baker, to come to the wedding. Up to that point, you may not be sure how to take the flat-out, slightly zonked dialogue. But when Cher and Nicolas Cage—each with droopy eyelids—start lusting for one another, a fairy-tale full moon lights up the movie. Cage is a wonderful romantic clown: he's slack-jawed and Neanderthal and passionate. He may be the only young actor who can look stupefied while he smolders. And no one can yearn like Cage: his head empties out—there's nothing there but sheep-eyed yearning. *Moonstruck* is an opera buffa in which the arias are the lines the characters deliver, in their harshly musical Brooklyn rhythms. Looking as if he's in a sick trance, the baker tells Loretta he's in love with her; she has just been to bed with him, but when she hears this she slaps him two quick whacks and says, "Snap out of it!" In her dry way, she's more irrational than he is. And when you see that the whole cast of family members are involved in libidinal confusions the operatic structure can make you feel close to deliriously happy.

Working from a script by John Patrick Shanley, the director, Norman Jewison, doesn't go for charm; he goes for dizzy charm. And that's what wins you over. He sets a hyperemotional mood; even the performances of the bit players are heightened. And the musical score, arranged by Dick Hyman, keeps twitting you. It starts, under the titles, with Dean Martin singing "That's Amore," and it reaches a juicy peak with the voices of Renata Tebaldi and Carlo Bergonzi in *La Bohème*. Hyman mixes musical emotion and a teasing parody of musical emotion, and you can't separate them, even when the parody is very broad. That's essentially what Shanley and Jewison are up to: they've blended a slapstick temperament with the pleasures that the synthetic elements in American movies used to give us. And so you get such counterpoint as the baker, whose thought processes are primeval, telling Loretta about the accident that turned him against his brother, and Loretta calmly explaining what happened, in a parody of Freudian explanations that's pure bughouse. And, with David Watkin lighting the scenes and Lou Lombardo (who edited *The Wild Bunch* and *McCabe & Mrs. Miller*) giving them a spin, the picture has a warm, fluky dazzle. Its originality is that the mockery doesn't destroy the overblown romanticism—it intensifies it.

This is ethnic comedy, but it's not noisy or monotonous. Jewison scales down the bullying stage techniques of actors you've been backing away from for years; everything is modulated, so that each voice can be heard. Vincent Gardenia is Loretta's irascible father, whose prosperous plumbing business sustains life in the brownstone. Olympia Dukakis, heavy-lidded, like Cher, and with a similar deadpan matter-of-factness, but with the dry-husk voice of a mummy, is the plumber's worldly-wise wife; she knows he's straying but can't figure out the reason. This woman is of a philosophical bent: she doesn't worry about who—it's the why that plagues her. Louis Guss is her mild brother, who runs a deli with his companionable wife, played by the great, leering Julie Bovasso—she's like a female Bert Lahr. (She also trained the cast in its fugue of contentious Brooklyn accents.) Feodor Chaliapin (the son of the legendary singer-actor) is Loretta's grandfather, who lives in the brownstone with his five dogs—he coaches them (in Italian) to howl at the full moon. John Mahoney is a lonely, lecherous professor of communications at N.Y.U., who dates his impressionable students but has an eye for an older woman, too—he makes overtures to Loretta's mother. Anita Gillette is a fortyish tootsie who has been having a cuddly affair with Loretta's father, and Nada Despotovich is a wistful young girl who works in the bakery and pines for the dopey, tempestuous baker. Most of the characters are gathered at the breakfast table in the closing scenes, when the plot is tied together. And Shanley's theatrical artifice works, partly because he accepts the characters as comic stereotypes—he doesn't try to give them depth—and partly because the actors love their lines, and, as characters, they can flaunt the excessiveness of their emotions. These characters make comedy turns out of everything they do.

Moonstruck is slender, and at times it's a little too proud of its quaintness. When the characters raise their champagne glasses in a toast "To family!" you may dimly recognize that this picture could become a holiday perennial. But you're probably grinning anyway, because the toast has a flipped-out quality. *Moonstruck* isn't heartfelt; it's an honest contrivance—the mockery is a giddy homage to our desire for grand passion. With its own special lushness, it's a rose-tinted black comedy.

The New Yorker, January 25, 1988

THE UNBEARABLE LIGHTNESS OF BEING
TAKE OFF YOUR CLOTHES

Going to see Philip Kaufman's *The Unbearable Lightness of Being*, I didn't remember anything of the Milan Kundera novel. But as the movie started I knew just what was coming next and I loved seeing it happen—it was like a dream that you long to return to, and lo! there it is. I think I know why the novel, with all its flashing wit, evaporated: the characters were counters to demonstrate a theory that wasn't demonstrated—convincingly, that is—and so neither the characters nor the ideas sank in very deep. The charm (and limitation) of the novel was its Continental dandyism: Kundera was more cultivated—more elegantly European—than a great writer needs to be. He was too conscious of his themes, his motifs, his paradoxes. He was a rational spokesman for playfulness; there's something the matter with that—it's playfulness as a literary method. (He also sees it as a tradition.) But while watching the movie I began to feel more affection for the novel. Kaufman cuts down on the pastry pensées, and the movie has some of his adventurous spirit. It's a prankish sex comedy that treats modern political events with a delicate—yet almost sly—sense of tragedy. It's touching in sophisticated ways that you don't expect from an American director.

The movie begins in 1968, during the Prague Spring, the culmination of the period of freedom of expression and artistic flowering known as "socialism with a human face," which ended when Soviet tanks rumbled into the city on August 21st. The key word in the title is "lightness." It retains some of its happy, buoyant associations, but it also refers to being cut off from your history, your culture, your memory. To simplify: Unbearable lightness refers to our recognizing that we go through life only once—it's like going onstage unrehearsed. And, more specifically, it's the suspended state of a person in an occupied country—especially if the person, like Tomas (Daniel Day-Lewis), is part of an advanced society under the domination of a backward society. (It's also the floating state of an exile.)

Tomas, a hedonist, a womanizer, and an eminent young brain surgeon, is perhaps at his lightest when he's barred from the practice of medicine and works as a window washer; he enjoys it, and it gives him a chance to practice his speciality, if the woman whose windows he washes invites him in. Tomas, a tall, boyish satyr with thick, curly dark hair that stands up a full three inches, looks at women from under bushy eyebrows and smiles crookedly—seductively. Day-Lewis has acquired a faint Czech accent, and he hits funny, voluptuous low notes when he says abruptly, "Take off your clothes," adding, when persuasion is necessary, "Don't worry—I'm a doctor." (Tomas is an ironic lech.)

He stays clear of love and its entanglements, never spending a whole night with a woman—not even with his longtime sex partner Sabina (Lena Olin), a painter. She's as independent as he is; that's the basis of their friendship. But when Tereza (Juliette Binoche), a childlike barmaid whom he meets when he's sent to perform an operation at a spa in a small town, follows him to Prague and comes to his flat, he takes her in. Tereza knows nothing of his non-involvement policy; she holds tight to his hand while she sleeps, and in spite of himself he loves being bound to her. He admires the pictures she takes; he asks Sabina to help her get a job in photography, and with that help Tereza's work begins to appear in magazines. Tereza and Tomas are married, and he buys her a puppy—they name it Karenin. (She was carrying *Anna Karenina* when they first met.) But his philandering goes on, and she suffers horribly from jealousy—she dreams about having to watch him in bed with Sabina.

Tereza doesn't know real happiness until the arrival of the Soviet tanks. Rushing around taking pictures and pressing rolls of film into the hands of foreign journalists to publish out of the country, she experiences the euphoria of being part of the whole nation in actively hating the Russians. Tomas, meanwhile, dashes around pulling her back from danger, and they join in the anti-Soviet demonstrations. (Through masterly trompe-l'oeil techniques, shots of the actors have been inserted in documentary footage of the crowds defying the soldiers.) When the excitement dies down, Tereza persuades Tomas to accept an offer he has had from a hospital in Geneva, and they join the vast exodus from Czechoslovakia. (Sabina has left ahead of them.) In Geneva, Tereza shows some of her best photographs of the invasion to an illustrated magazine, but the Russian crackdown is already old news to the editors. A woman staff photographer, trying to be helpful, suggests that she try fashion photography, and also offers to introduce her to the editor in charge of the garden section, who might need some photographs of cactuses. When Tereza objects, saying "I'd rather be a waitress, or stay at home," the helpful pinhead says, "But will you be fulfilled sitting at home?"

In the film's centerpiece, Tereza, who has fantasies of accompanying

Tomas to his assignations, decides to try her hand at nudes and gets Sabina to pose for her. After Tereza completes the long session, Sabina picks up the camera, says, "Take off your clothes," and, when the half-undressed Tereza tries to hide, chases her with the camera, and another session begins. When it's over, these two women, who represent the poles of Tomas's life—Tereza (weight) lives for him, Sabina (lightness) has to be her own woman—stay stretched out by the fire, quiet, then laughing. The sequence has an erotic formality: it's ridiculously, beautifully resonant—you feel you're watching a classic pas de deux.

At intervals throughout the movie, a scene will have a mysterious seed of comedy. An example: Tomas pauses to watch a group of elderly men in the swimming pool at the spa; they surround a floating chessboard on which two of them are having a match. I can't explain exactly what gives this scene its lovely estrangement, but I know that if Miloš Forman, who was a student of Kundera's at the Prague film school, where Kundera taught literature, had made the movie the scene would be folk humor, and it wouldn't have the slight distancing it has here—the beatitude of the image of the old men at their games, their bodies in the pool seen as in an idyll. (The cinematography is by Sven Nykvist.) Other examples: the scene in bed when Tereza sniffs Tomas's hair and, smelling another woman, whimpers; and the scenes of Sabina in her black net bra and panties, with a black bowler hat on her head—the hat that is the emblem of her sex play. Almost all of Sabina's scenes are tantalizing. Lena Olin (she was the girl in Ingmar Bergman's *After the Rehearsal*) seems to incarnate the many meanings tucked away in the phrase "the unbearable lightness of being"—the freedom and elusive sadness. She's glorious.

And the movie has scenes that may not stir a reaction until a few hours or a few days after you've seen it, when you suddenly remember the deft use of an old movie device (the clinking of glasses on a tray as the first hint of the tanks in the street) or, perhaps, the pinkness of a pet piglet named Mephisto that a smiling, congenial farmer (Pavel Landovsky) carries around on his visit to Prague. (With its long snout and big ears, the pretty little creature suggests a toy elephant.) Or perhaps you think back on Franz (Derek de Lint), the professor whom Sabina takes for a lover in Geneva. His eyes shine with bright-blue virtue; he looks as if he had never known a hangover. He is so straightforward and good that she has to escape him. (His goodness is too heavy for her.) And, late in the film (it runs a short two hours and fifty-three minutes), there's a closeup of Karenin—showing just one blurry eye—that may remind some moviegoers of the image of the hare in Renoir's *The Rules of the Game*.

But it's the way the variations of jealousy and erotic attraction are played out by the three principal actors—an Englishman, a Swedish woman, and a Frenchwoman, all playing Czechs—that give the movie its wonderfully unresolved texture. The main difference between the movie and the novel is that Day-Lewis is about ten years younger than Kundera's forty-year-old hero, and so the whole spirit of the film has become younger, and less defeated. Phil Kaufman has an exuberant American temperament—he has never let go of the best of the late sixties and early seventies. The sex scenes are rambunctious, with a legs-flying youthfulness. And when Sabina tells Tomas that Franz is the best man she has ever met, only he doesn't like her hat, and she puts it on and she and Tomas whirl in an embrace, the moment has an Ernst Lubitsch giddiness. The material is all there in the book, but Kaufman has instinctively loosened it; if he hadn't, he'd have come out with only a literary adaptation instead of this movie, which is his as much as Kundera's—perhaps more his. (And so it may delight the onetime film-school professor.)

The script, by Jean-Claude Carrière and Kaufman, is possibly too faithful to the book in retaining some gimmickry about the number six. And after Tereza goes back to Prague, to the old flat, and Tomas follows her (and has his passport confiscated), there are a few late plot developments that aren't quite prepared for. (One of them involves Erland Josephson as a barroom janitor who was formerly the Czech ambassador in Vienna.) And I'm not sure that the conception of the gamine Tereza as photographic artist is much more than a literary conceit. But the young Binoche gives the role a sweet gaucheness and then a red-cheeked desperation—the push and pathos of a Clara Bow or a young Susan Hayward. She verges on peasant-madonna darlingness, but that's what the conception requires. Tereza is a waifish little mantrap; she has the appeal of teen-age sexy petiteness. That's what gets to Day-Lewis's Tomas: she has a built-in pornography.

In the novel, the authorial voice leads us along, and the main characters have little depth; only Lena Olin is fully able to compensate for this. But Day-Lewis endows Tomas with a sneaky wit; this lusty Tomas—who *looks* Central European—is a cutup who draws you into his flirtations. Day-Lewis is a vocal trickster, too: he manipulates his Czech accent to throw you curves. A muscular toothpick with a long, skinny face and that cushion of hair, he's playing something new in movie heroes: a harlequin intellectual. And when Tomas is a pleasure seeker without a passport, working on a farm, Tereza, who's backward, like the police state, has him where she wants him. (Janet Malcolm has pointed out that the name Tereza echoes the Czech concentration camp Terezin.) But there's also a strong element of conventionality in Kundera's structure, and you can interpret Tomas's commitment to Tereza as his redemption—his gaining the weight that saves him from the unbearable lightness of being. Kundera—the spokesman for playfulness—is himself divided, a puritan as well as a dandy. (He toys with the idea of life as a concentration camp.) The novel feels the pull of gravity, and this weakens the film's ending. Yet the film's spirit carries through.

Kundera has often spoken of Laurence Sterne, the author of *Tristram Shandy,* as one of his idols. I didn't catch that when I read *Unbearable Lightness,* but there are glimmers of it in Day-Lewis's performance, and in Phil Kaufman's confident waywardness. Kaufman has made movies that should have been hits—the 1978 *Invasion of the Body Snatchers* and, in 1983, *The Right Stuff*. This time, he has made a movie that probably doesn't stand much chance of reaching a wide audience. But it puts him in a different class as an artist. It also puts him and his backer, Saul Zaentz, at the top of the heap for courage.

The New Yorker, February 8, 1988

HIGH TIDE
THE LADY FROM THE SEA

Every now and then, I hear from young women who say that they want to write or direct movies but have no interest in car chases, coke busts, or shoot-outs. They want to make movies about personal relations and emotional states. Generally, I encourage them, while acknowledging my dread of the mess of vague, inchoate feelings that could be the result. I caution them that it takes more talent and more tough-mindedness to put a sensibility on the screen than it does to film a gunfight, and, lest they think that their desire is a specifically feminine one, I point out movies such as Kershner's *Loving,* Alan Parker's *Shoot the Moon,* Ichikawa's *The Makioka Sisters,* and Satyajit Ray's *Days and Nights in the Forest* and *The Home and the World*. But young women directors may be drawn to get at emotional states with less plot apparatus—almost nakedly.

Gillian Armstrong reports that when she began work on her new picture, *High Tide,* she pinned a note above her desk: "Blood ties. Water. Running away." That note tells us what the movie is about more truthfully than a plot summary would. Shot from a script by Laura Jones, *High Tide* is a woman's picture in the way that *Stella Dallas* was—it's about the mother-daughter bond. But it's also a woman's picture in a new way: Gillian Armstrong, the Australian who directed *My Brilliant Career* at twenty-seven and then made *Starstruck* and *Mrs. Soffel,* has the technique and the assurance to put a woman's fluid, not fully articulated emotions right onto the screen. And she has an actress—Judy Davis, the Sybylla of *My Brilliant Career* and the Adela Quested of David Lean's *A Passage to India*—who's a genius at moods.

As Lilli, one of three backup singers for a touring Elvis imitator, Judy Davis is contemptuous of the cruddy act, contemptuous of herself. Too smart for what she's doing, Lilli is a derisive tease—a spoiler. Feeling put down, the dumb-lug Elvis fires her, and she's left alone at the beginning of winter in a ramshackle beach town on the magnificent, wind-swept coast of New South Wales. There, stuck in the Mermaid Caravan Park while she tries to scrounge up the money to pay for repairs on her car, she encounters her teen-age daughter, Ally (Claudia Karvan).

When Lilli's young surfer husband died, she felt lost; she gave up the baby to her mother-in-law, Bet (Jan Adele), and has been drifting ever since, and getting stinko and passing out. Bet, a singer in talent shows at the local restaurant-night spot, who works at a fish-packing coop and runs a soft-ice-cream stand, is a rowdy, belligerent woman, and she's devoted to Ally: Bet has taken care of her for thirteen years, but has no idea how unhappy the girl is—the rules Bet lays down to protect the kid cut her off from other kids and make her miserable. Lilli has an immediate rapport with the lonely Ally, even before she knows that Ally is her daughter, and after she knows, she can't take her eyes off the kid. When they're at the public baths at the same time, Lilli stares at Ally's legs under the stall door; Ally is shaving them, and Lilli stands there tranced out, sick with love and longing.

This remote, working-class, tourist-town Australia suggests a corrupted frontier settlement. The view of the cliffs and the sea includes the rusted debris of the caravan dwellers; the Mermaid is like the seedy trailer parks on the outskirts of American towns, but with a more pervasive sense of rootlessness and movement. The men and women, in their faded denims and cheap pastels, blend with the blue of the water. These people survive by changing their occupations with the seasons; they work hard in small businesses that look as if they had been thrown up out of packing crates. You see the crumminess of the town in the big, garish joint where the Elvis act is put on, and where Bet sings. (All the entertainers hit the same high decibel level.) An aging cowboy headliner called Country Joe (Bob Purtell) performs there against a backdrop of a huge bull's skull, and you get a taste of matey entertainment at a smoker, where Lilli earns the money she needs by doing a strip. You also see some less coarse men: Colin Friels as a fisherman who responds to Lilli's wry half smiles and likes her too much to watch her at the smoker, and Mark Hembrow as a garage mechanic who takes a chance on her and lets her have her car. Gillian Armstrong's style is crisp, and the camera whizzes past the scenic wonders, often turning rocks and road lines into abstractions. The superb cinematographer Russell Boyd chose to be his own camera operator this time—so he could have the excitement of giving Armstrong the fast tracking movement she wanted, and she could concentrate on the performances.

Lilli and her young teen-age daughter match up; you feel that they're true kin—they belong with each other. But their scenes together are courtship dances that Lilli keeps pulling back from, terrified of taking on the responsibility of motherhood when she hasn't been able to make it alone. You may intuit that her having abandoned the child who was her only hold on life is the reason she has trashed herself. She doesn't look at her failures that kindly, though. And Bet—piggy-faced and broad in the beam—tells her she's riffraff. At first, Bet seems threatening. It isn't until she has spent a night with Country Joe, and her steady fellow (John Clayton) has used his truck to ram Country Joe's fancy car, that we fully appreciate what a frank, lusty bawd she is. She wins us over when she seeks assurance from Country

Joe that he feels the night with her was worth the damage to his car. Bet isn't a monster; she's simply the wrong person to be raising the slender, pensive Ally, whose emotions are hidden away, like her mother's. Even Bet's sensitivities are crude.

Jan Adele makes her film début as the overprotective Bet, but she's a former vaudevillian who has been in show biz since she was three, and has done everything from ballet in tent shows, through singing with bands, to TV comedy. All her experience informs her presence here; it's a real turn, and the fact that she acts in a totally different style from that of Judy Davis (and the fourteen-year-old Claudia Karvan) strengthens the movie. Jan Adele projects to the rafters; she hands you every emotion neatly tagged. She's marvellous at it; she gives you the sense that in this rough country Bet hasn't been exposed to much in the way of amenities, or subtleties, either. The drama is in our feeling that Lilli must not leave her daughter in the embrace of this raucous old trouper. Bet isn't in the spirit of the film.

Lilli is so overcast—so unsure of herself—that we feel a mystery in her, despite her level gaze. Tall, skinny, red-haired Judy Davis was only twenty-three when she played her first leading role onscreen—in *My Brilliant Career*, in 1979. She may never have looked as beautiful as she does here in a motel-room scene with Colin Friels: he's lying on the bed, and she's standing by the window with her wavy hair wet from the shower. She's like a sea goddess. The first time we see her in this movie, she's on the stage in a tawdry mermaid dress of sequins and ruffles. The first time we see Ally, she's in the water, floating in a tidal pool; then she gets on her father's old surfboard—surfing is her refuge from the noisy junkiness of life with Bet. And the sight of the sea is mucked up by what people have done to the coast.

Gillian Armstrong and her scenarist don't connect the dotted lines, and you don't want them to. I expected more to go on between Lilli and the Colin Friels character, maybe because Davis has a special serenity with Friels (he's her husband), but the script doesn't build on this accord. That's a small matter; so is Lilli's unnecessary waffling at the end. The movie's emotional suggestiveness may be off-putting to some people; they may be so trained to expect action that they'll complain that not enough is going on. But a great many young women are likely to feel that this is the movie they've wanted to make. (Some of them have already made pieces of it; the humiliation of the striptease has been the subject of many women film students' shorts.) The acute, well-written script acknowledges the basic ineffableness of some experiences, especially in a self-conscious scene toward the end where Lilli tries to explain to Ally why she deserted her. And it all goes together. It goes with the way Lilli looks when she's about to leave town and abandon her daughter for the second time; paying off the garage mechanic and thanking him, she's white as death. Judy Davis has been compared with Jeanne Moreau, and that's apt, but she's Moreau without the cultural swank, the high-fashion gloss. And there's no movieish gloss here, either. Men don't mistreat Lilli, and she doesn't mistreat them. She just screws herself over, and the film's only question is, Will she stop?

The New Yorker, February 22, 1988

BEETLEJUICE

Beetlejuice is a farce about what happens to us after death: it's a bugaboo farce. At the start, the camera seems to be flying over an idyllic New England town, but the town changes into a miniature town on a table, and Adam (Alec Baldwin), the hobbyist who has carved it, takes a spider off a little rooftop. Adam and his wife, Barbara (Geena Davis), are a devoted, though regretfully childless, young couple who have been happy in their cozy old barnlike house—an eccentric pile of angles and peaks—while fending off realtors who want to sell it for them. The two drive into town on an errand, passing through a picture-postcard covered wooden bridge, but on the way back, as they go through the bridge, Barbara swerves to avoid hitting a dog, and the director, Tim Burton, reveals his first great gag: the car hangs over the edge of the quaint red bridge, kept from plunging into the river by the weight of the dog on a loose plank. When the dog gets bored and trots off, the car falls.

The next we see of Adam and Barbara, they're ghosts—tame, sweet, home-loving ghosts, not very different from how they were in life. The movie doesn't really get going until a New York family (who are far more ghoulish) buy the house and start redecorating, turning it into a high-tech space to show off the slinky wife's huge works of sculpture (which are like petrified insects). Miffed, Adam and Barbara want to scare these intruders away, but they're too mild to do the job themselves, so they call upon the services of the rutty little demon Betelgeuse, pronounced Beetlejuice, who is played by Michael Keaton, and who rises from the graveyard in the table-top town. The movie had perked up when the New Yorkers arrived, because Delia the sculptor, the madwoman who's the new lady of the house, is played by the smudge-faced blond Catherine O'Hara, late of SCTV, and the possessor of the freakiest blue-eyed stare since early Gene Wilder. (She has sexy evil eyes.) Delia is too macabre and uppity to be fazed by ordinary apparitions. Even the decaying Beetlejuice himself—he might be a carnival attraction: This way to the exhumed hipster!—barely distracts her. But Keaton is like an exploding head. He isn't onscreen nearly enough—when he is, he shoots the film sky-high.

This is not the kind of spook show that gives you shivers; it gives you outré shocks. Adam and Barbara are like the juvenile and the ingénue singing their duets in the M-G-M Marx Brothers pictures while we wait for lewd,

1171

foxy Groucho to grab the girls' bottoms. Michael Keaton is the Groucho here, but fast and furious, like Robin Williams when he's speeding, or Bill Murray having a conniption fit. And maybe because of the slow start and the teasing visual design—the whole movie seems to take place in a hand-painted nowhere, with the "real" town and the toy town miscegenating—Keaton creates a lust for more hot licks. He appears here with a fringe of filthy hair, greenish rotting teeth—snaggled—and an ensemble of mucky rags. And he keeps varying in size (like the star Betelgeuse). When he's let loose and the transformations start, along with the gravity-defying stunts, I wanted more and more of them. I wanted the overstimulation of prepubescent play—a child's debauch. And that's what Tim Burton, who began in the animation department at Disney, and directed his first movie in 1985 (*Pee-wee's Big Adventure*), offers. He's still in his twenties, and he has a kid's delight in the homegrown surreal. The plot is just a formality. To enjoy the movie, you may have to be prepared to jump back into a jack-in-the-box universe. But it may work even better if it takes you unawares and you start laughing at a visually sophisticated form of the rabid-redneck kids' humor you haven't thought about in years—the kind of humor that features wormy skeletons and shrunken heads. Here the shrunken heads are still attached to full-sized bodies.

The end is subdued. The final scenes have a plot logic that you can't really fault, but logic isn't what you want, and you feel as if the comedy blitz is suddenly over without your having fully grasped that it was ending. The last part isn't very well directed, and neither are the scenes where O'Hara's Delia decides that having a haunted house will bring her some social cachet. Burton may not have found his storytelling skills yet, or his structure, either, but then he may never find them. This movie is something to see, even if it's a blossoming chaos and the jokes sometimes leave you behind. (When Burton picked Robert Goulet and Dick Cavett for small roles, he probably wanted them to make fun of their images, but they don't appear to know how, and the writers—Michael McDowell, Larry Wilson, and Warren Skaaren—haven't steered them.) Still, the best of W. C. Fields was often half gummed up, and that doesn't seem to matter fifty-five years later. With crazy comedy, you settle for the spurts of inspiration, and *Beetlejuice* has them. When Delia and her New York art-world guests are at the dinner table and, possessed, suddenly rise to sing the calypso banana-boat song "Day-O," it's a mighty moment—a haymaker. And you can't tell why. (If you could, it wouldn't be funny.) The satire of a waiting room in the social services bureaucracy of the afterlife (which is staffed by suicides) is like great early animation. It features a spectral effect linking cigarettes and death so creepily that the audience sucks in its breath and laughs: when a raspy-voiced social worker, played by Sylvia Sidney, lights up, she exhales smoke through her nose, her mouth, and her slit throat.

The movie, with its toy town, is like Red Grooms' cities: it's an art work that has no depth but jangles with energy. Tim Burton takes stabs into the

irrational, the incongruous, the plain nutty. And though a lot of his moves don't connect, enough of them do to make this spotty, dissonant movie a comedy classic. The story is bland—it involves the parental love that Adam and Barbara develop for the sculptor's stepdaughter (Winona Ryder)—but its blandness is edged with near-genius. Michael Keaton has never been so uninhibited a comic; his physical assurance really is demonic. He's a case of the beezie-weezies.

The New Yorker, April 18, 1988

WINGS OF DESIRE
ZONE POEM

Seen through the eyes of two angels who hover over the city blocks, Berlin is in tinted black-and-white. The image suggests metal, with a little of the lustre of old coins or tarnished silverware. And as the camera wafts in and out of airplanes, and into rooms high up in apartment buildings, and the angels observe the forlorn, dissociated lives of people who live in reverie, it's as if black-and-white itself had petered out—as if the movie image was exhausted. What you see has a bluish-green softness, and it's clear enough, but it feels at a remove; it's a reminder of an image. *Wings of Desire*—the original title of this Franco-German production is *Der Himmel über Berlin,* which means the heaven, or sky, over Berlin—has the look of a dupe of a dupe. That look is telling you that movies are now ghosts of themselves.

The director, Wim Wenders, who wrote the script with the collaboration of Peter Handke, has a theme: in an approximation of Rilke's words, "Joy has gone astray." We're told that "when the child was a child," stories held together. Now all we have is fragmentation, entropy. And a sad-faced old man called Homer (Curt Bois) wanders through the ruins of the old metropolis trying to keep its story alive; his thoughts trigger flashbacks to Nazi atrocities.

The two angels—Damiel (Bruno Ganz) and Cassiel (Otto Sander)—roam through the bleak concrete buildings of the divided city; its ugliness is almost abstract. Wearing suits and overcoats, the two observers look like civil servants, except for their ponytails. They pick up scraps of stories as they move unseen among desolate individuals, listening to what's in their minds—listening to the questions about existence that these people ask themselves. The angels have a poetic presence: they're antennae for the thoughts of anonymous Berliners who can't speak what they think. (There are no emotional outbursts; the people's interior dialogues are detailed, measured, accurate—as if they could describe something only by its exact di-

mensions.) The angel Damiel's face is infinitely compassionate, and the angel Cassiel knits his brow in worry; these two are in a muzzy state of empathy for everyone, everything. And they listen with the patience and concern of a seraphic, neutered uncle. Children can see them, and some grownups know when they're around—those who are childlike at heart (moviegoers, perhaps, and Americans), those who aren't split asunder, and still have the ability to feel things directly.

For about forty-five minutes, the mood of the opening shots is sustained. Our overhearing what the angels hear—the thoughts chanted on the track, all in even, quiet tones, as grayed out as the sunless skies—works on us like a tranquillizer. The dim whimsy, the recitations of prose poetry that recall the Beats—it all produces a blissed-out stupor that feels vaguely avant-garde. And this movie, which is dedicated to Ozu, Tarkovsky, and Truffaut, is full of charming (and almost charming) conceits, such as the angels' attentiveness to the murmur of thought in the modern, fluorescent-lighted state library building. (It suggests *Alphaville* with lead weights on the camera.) This is where solitary people—who look as if they were forgotten by the world—come to read and to walk among the books. (These walkers recall the book memorizers in *Fahrenheit 451*.)

The film can hatch conceits in viewers. The angels can make you feel as if you're walking around in the presence of an absent world, in the presence of people you've known. And when you see the angels listening to the people's thoughts you may miss someone to whisper your feelings about the movie to. You have plenty of time for musing while looking at this after-the-apocalypse city, scarred by the Wall—the dividing line of two powers, and the symbol of the divided souls.

Wings of Desire constantly articulates the impossibility of finding any meaning in anything. At the same time, it's a love-story message movie. The angels, in their apartness and in their distress over the spiritual emptiness of the people, are like the cliché kind of intellectuals. Then Damiel, drooping from the sameness of his everlasting rounds and the ennui of seeing in monochromatic tones, eavesdrops on the thoughts of Marion (Solveig Dommartin), a beautiful, lonely French aerialist who's dressed as an angel with feather wings, and performs in a tacky circus. (She recalls Merna Kennedy in Chaplin's *The Circus* and Nastassja Kinski in Coppola's *One from the Heart*.) She goes to a punk-rock club, and Damiel watches her there, dancing by herself, gyrating, her manner zombielike. When he sits among the children who are entranced by her trapeze work, this Chaplinesque girl awakens him to childish joy—of what it's like to believe in the magic of trapeze artists. He feels the stirrings of desire, and he sees her in color. He begins to long for the ordinary pleasures—to hold an apple in his hand, to drink a cup of hot coffee. When he turns in his wings—so to speak—and plunges to earth, he has a new spring in his walk. The film breaks into full color, and he goes to find his aerialist.

He searches the city for her, and she searches, too, for she knows not

whom, and they meet in the bar that adjoins the punk club. There, looking right at the camera, Marion speaks to Damiel for the first time, and it's an oration. She goes on and on, declaiming—giving voice to her romantic, enigmatic thoughts in the affectless tone that he found so fetching when he listened to the workings of her mind. (It's as if Merna Kennedy, at the end of the silent *The Circus,* started to speechify.) And she faces the audience and challenges us to take our voyages. *Gott im Himmel!*

A friend of mine says that he loved every second of this movie and he couldn't wait to leave. To put it simply, *Wings of Desire* has a visual fascination but no animating force—that's part of why it's being acclaimed as art. The film's lassitude—the way shots are held for small eternities, and the action seems to begin every three or four minutes—suggests some purpose beyond narrative, suggests that you're experiencing the psychic craving of the Berliners as they drift through their chilly days, searching to be whole again. It's a sluggish, weary-winged fable; it seems to be saying that if you're a grownup living in postwar Germany a reminder of childish joy is the most you can hope for. The halfhearted coming together of Damiel and Marion is a fairy tale that we're not quite meant to believe; the film's tone of high German woe certainly indicates that. Even if Wenders wants to believe it, his moviemaking betrays him: the color sections are tawdry compared with the spooky spirituality of the black-and-white passages. The film's meaning appears to be: We Germans recognize in ourselves a forever-to-be-unfulfilled wish for connectedness.

The only character with any pep is an American, played by Peter Falk, who is starring in a Nazi-period film that's being shot on the site of an actual Second World War bunker. Falk—he's called by his own name—enjoys the pleasures of simple sensory gratifications. With his big noggin and the gruff mischief in the way he plays along with the other characters, he's solidly American. (And he's a relief from Ganz's poignancy; there's so much of it that it gnaws at you.) Falk is the only free agent in the whole movie: when he takes a step, he really wants to go where he's heading. Even when he soliloquizes like the Berliners, his thoughts are practical; they have a funky warmth. (In interviews, Wenders says that Falk wrote this material himself.)

My guess is that the Falk subplot is in the picture mainly because Wenders loves American movies and the people connected with them. But, if I read Wenders right, he's also suggesting (as he has in the past) that movies are the American language, and that American movies (and rock) have colonized the Germans, causing another rift in their consciousness. He's saying, "How lucky the Americans are—they didn't suffer the way we did." He knows he can't make movies that race along, that are all narrative, studded with personalities. He's got his Rilke and that scar of castration, the Wall. The whole movie is saying, "If only I could express myself like a child or an American moviemaker! Then I could unify the divided German soul, or, at least, my own soul."

But, of course, Wenders doesn't get into the spirit of popular art. When he uses a pop form, it's lifeless—a simulation of ascetic high art. Marion is lovely, but on her last night with the circus, when she and one of the roustabouts at the outdoor farewell party sing together, Wenders seems to have just plopped them there. He names the circus for his celebrated cinematographer, Henri Alekan (and includes allusions to Cocteau's 1946 *Beauty and the Beast,* which Alekan shot), yet from the sound of the laughter of the children who are supposed to be showing their joy at the circus they've got infant doses of Weltschmerz. The punk-club scenes are so rhythmless and desolate that they're almost a parody of German anguish. And I have misgivings about Wenders' including actual atrocity pictures; it's as if he wanted to fortify his sense of defeat, his enervation. But then this is a movie with depressive angels—a notion worthy of Tarkovsky (for whom the whole universe was depressive).

Wenders films what makes him feel impotent. Yet he wants to inspire us: when Damiel and Marion embrace, Wenders wants to light a candle in our hearts, or, at least, half a candle. It's this torchbearer Wenders who uses such corny devices as having the children be able to see the angels; he even has a little crippled girl who smiles at Damiel. Sentimentality and meaninglessness: postmodern kitsch. It's enough to make moviegoers feel impotent.

The New Yorker, May 30, 1988

BIG BUSINESS

In 1938, when I was a student at Berkeley, I laughed so hard at Harry Ritz playing a hillbilly in *Kentucky Moonshine* that I fell off the theatre seat. (My date said he would take me to anything else but never to another movie. He became a judge.) I think I might have fallen off my seat again at *Big Business* when Bette Midler appeared as a hillbilly girl in a frilly short skirt and petticoats, milking a cow and yodelling, if the damn-fool moviemakers hadn't cut away in the middle of her song. Later in the movie, after Midler has come to New York City, she encounters a steel-drum band near Fifth Avenue and, ecstatic, begins to yodel again. Once more, the moviemakers cut to some stupid story point. Midler is far more free and inspired here than she was in *Outrageous Fortune* or *Ruthless People.* Every time she enters, she blows everything else away. But she has to do it in quick takes.

The movie is an elaboration of the intricate old farce about two sets of identical twins accidentally mismatched at birth; it comes to us from Plautus via *The Comedy of Errors* and from there to the thirties musical *The Boys from Syracuse* and on to the 1970 spoof of swashbucklers, *Start the Revolution Without Me,* with Gene Wilder and Donald Sutherland as mismatched pairs of peasants and aristocrats in eighteenth-century France. This time, it's Midler and Lily Tomlin as Sadie and Rose Ratliff, who live in a backwoods Southern town with one factory, which is about to be shut down by the heartless conglomerate Moramax. The Ratliffs go up north to New York City to protest to Moramax's stockholders and are mistaken for Sadie and Rose Shelton, who control the outfit. The four women and their various courtiers, flunkies, and love objects wind up spending the weekend at the Plaza Hotel. (Actually, it's a more spacious, vacuously glamorized Plaza—most of the interiors were constructed at the Disney Studios, in Burbank.)

The writers (Dori Pierson and Marc Rubel are credited) had a plan: Midler's hick Sadie Ratliff and Tomlin's rich Rose Shelton, who were raised by the wrong parents, feel out of place and fantasize about the life they feel they belong in. Hick Sadie longs to buy expensive clothes and throw money around; rich Rose, a bleeding-heart do-gooder, takes in stray animals and yearns for country living. And the costumer had a smart notion: Midler's two Sadies are drawn to the same styles in clothing, and Tomlin's two Roses are partial to pink. All sorts of good ideas float around in this movie, but the director, Jim Abrahams (he was a member of the trio that directed *Airplane!*, *Top Secret!*, and *Ruthless People*), doesn't have the knack of making the details click into place. Tomlin doesn't thrive. She keeps trying out things that don't add up to much; the effect is a bit dithering. And Abrahams shows no affection for the rural life that Rose Ratliff is trying to protect, or for Tomlin's acting style, which has its roots in that life. You're aware of an awful lot of mistaken-identity plot and aware of how imprecise most of it is. (The big stockholders' meeting is a complete muck-up.) Yet the picture moves along, spattering the air with throwaway gags, and a minute after something misfires you're laughing out loud.

Fred Ward, who plays hick Rose's down-home suitor (and comes on to rich Rose), manages to be both the essence of rube and a forthright, attractive fellow. Serenely unself-conscious, he takes over as the film's hero. And Midler breezes through, kicking one gong after another. Tomlin's two Roses have virtuous impulses, while Midler—as both Sadies—is pure appetite. Sadie Ratliff is the most recognizably human of comic creations—a supplicant abasing herself before the world's goodies. She watches *Dynasty* over and over, and dreams of being Alexis; her eyes dance when she looks in Cartier's window. Midler, who wrote a children's book about a little girl whose first word is "More!," makes Sadie Ratliff's hankering for luxuries palpable—it's her soul's need. Midler plays this scruffy Sadie as a warm-hearted chickabiddy, and she plays rich Sadie as a lusty shrew who has developed a taste for power. (Maybe it's only in a twins story that a performer gets the chance to be both sweetly money-hungry and monstrously money-hungry.)

Midler rescues scenes by using her clothes as props: when Sadie the mogul of Moramax flips up her collar, the gesture bespeaks perfect self-satisfaction. (Chaplin did this sort of thing, and he didn't do it better.) And her snooty asides are terrific: this gorgon keeps her best lines to herself. The film often looks third class, and the plot keeps conking out, but its climax—when the two sets of twins finally confront each other—is a visual brain-twister. (It's derived from *Duck Soup* and goes back to Max Linder, but it has its own kick.) And Midler is a classic figure—a grinning urchin out of *Volpone*. Her appetite is the audience's appetite. It's as if she and we were passing a flask of euphoria back and forth. More!

The New Yorker, June 27, 1988

PART ELEVEN

MOVIE LOVE

1991

TEQUILA SUNRISE

Michelle Pfeiffer tells Mel Gibson how sorry she is that she hurt his feelings. He replies, "C'mon, it didn't hurt that bad," pauses, and adds, "Just lookin' at you hurts more." If a moviegoer didn't already know that *Tequila Sunrise* was the work of a master romantic tantalizer, Gibson's line should clinch it. That's the kind of ritualized confession of love that gave a picture like *To Have and Have Not* its place in moviegoers' affections. What makes the line go ping is that Mel Gibson's blue eyes are wide with yearning as he says it, and Michelle Pfeiffer is so crystalline in her beauty that he seems to be speaking the simple truth. (If she weren't a vision, the picture would crash.) It's a line that Gary Cooper might have spoken to Marlene Dietrich in *Morocco;* it requires youth and innocence in the man and flowerlike perfection in the woman.

You have to be able to enjoy trashy shamelessness to enjoy old Hollywood and to enjoy *Tequila Sunrise.* Robert Towne, who wrote and directed, is soaked in the perfume of thirties and forties Hollywood romanticism. Chances are that while you're watching the triangular shuffle of Gibson and Pfeiffer and Kurt Russell, as Gibson's friend who also gets involved with Pfeiffer, you'll know you're being had but you'll love it. This old shell game can make you feel alert and happy—at least, it can when it's brought up to date with the seductive panache of a Robert Towne.

Tequila Sunrise is about flirtation; it's about Towne's wanting to give pleasure. Set in San Pedro and the other beach communities in and around

L.A., it has a golden, studied casualness; the cinematographer, Conrad Hall, feasts on the stars' faces, the three sets of blue eyes, the beachfront, the water washing through the scenes, the waves crashing over lovers. All this beauty—and it's about cops and robbers! And not even about that, exactly. Towne has the effrontery to offer us the wizened plot device of the two friends from school days—one (Gibson) has become a crook, the other (Russell) a cop—who are in love with the same girl. But the movie is much too derivative and vague to be a successful crime melodrama; it doesn't have the compression of a thriller. There's an emptiness at its center—a feeling of hurt and loneliness, a lesion of vitality.

Gibson's McKussic, a former drug dealer who's desperately trying to succeed in the irrigation business, is driven to make manic fun of how hard it has been to get out of the drug trade. He tells Pfeiffer's Jo Ann, "Nobody wants me to *quit*. The cops wanna *bust* me, the Colombians want my *connections*, my wife she wants my *money*, her lawyer agrees, and mine likes getting paid to argue with them. . . . I haven't even mentioned my customers. You *know* they don't want me to quit." This special pleading for McKussic's purity is right at the heart of the movie (and it gives Mel Gibson a warmer character than he has played before). Mac is like the Bogart heroes who have finer feelings than people understand, and his love for Jo Ann is a truer, deeper love than Russell's Nick Frescia offers. (Mac is also a prodigious cocksman.) It doesn't take long for a viewer to grasp that Mac is the writer-director's simplified and idealized version of himself. Besides, Towne has said that his legal troubles—a divorce, and litigation over a couple of movie projects—made him feel like a criminal, so that it was easy for him to identify with Mac. (And those who have read interviews with him won't have much trouble spotting drug dealing as a metaphor for script doctoring, a lucrative sideline that his associates wanted him to mainline—his rewrites were a convenience for directors and producers. Drug dealing can also serve as a tidy metaphor for the messier matter of drug use, which also makes you feel like a criminal.)

The movie has a lot of talk about friendship, and whether the bond between Mac and Nick, who's the head of the narcotics squad in L.A. County, can withstand the pressure from the Feds to bust Mac, or can withstand Nick's wily maneuvers to extract information about Mac from Jo Ann. But the characters aren't centered enough for their subterfuges to amount to much—they're just vagrant impulses that lead to romantic misunderstandings. Towne's actual legal troubles involved old, close friends, but in the movie he doesn't supply the injuries that have been done to Mac and doesn't pin them on anybody in particular. (Nick hasn't done any real harm to him, and even when they argue their voices have the rhythm of friends arguing.) Yet Mac is melancholy, as if betrayal were in the air he breathed. We do see that he's bled dry by his ex-wife (Ann Magnuson), who's out for everything she can get and won't let him see his son if he doesn't deliver his payments. But his grievances seem cosmic, and he longs for a decent, respectable life. His character is a victim fantasy.

The picture may have a special erotic appeal for women, because Mac is waiting for the true-heart woman, the woman whose love is limitless and unconditional, the woman whose only need is to be a helpmate. That's Jo Ann, a woman who never lies. (She's the opposite of Brigid in *The Maltese Falcon*.) Jo Ann, who, with her brother, operates an elegant Italian restaurant, is soft-spoken and refined—a lady. She has her own code of honor, her own gallantry. At the restaurant, she's a pro: she's thoroughly in command of seeming in command. And the film equates her smoothness with the best of traditional values. She isn't up to anything, so Mac can put himself in her hands. And she falls in love with him, supposedly, because she believes that he's been more truthful to her than Nick has been. It's a priggish, vacuous ideal-woman role, but Michelle Pfeiffer bursts right through it. She activates Towne's romantic dream of the good, kind woman.

Kurt Russell's worldly jokester Nick—a calculating charmer—gives the plot a little bit of motor, or, at least, an occasional push. And the movie badly needs Russell's brazenness and his slippery grin; it needs his sly, shiny eyes. Nick locates us in a wisecracking movie tradition, especially when he razzes the high-muck-a-muck from the federal Drug Enforcement Agency. (J. T. Walsh makes this clown villain the quintessential flatfoot; it's a classic turn.) But Russell's main function is as a contrast to Mac, who's the male ingénue here. Both Nick and Jo Ann want to protect Mac, because he's a-hurtin'. And because he's a saintly stud.

The movie is a confluence of fantasies, with a crime plot that often seems to be stalled, as if a projector had broken down. A good melodramatic structure should rhyme: we should hold our breath at the pacing as the pieces come together, and maybe smile at how neat the fit is. Here the pieces straggle, and by the end you're probably ignoring the plot points. Raul Julia, who turns up as the Mexican Comandante Escalante, has a big, likable, rumbling presence; his role recalls the Leo Carrillo parts in movies like *The Gay Desperado,* with a new aplomb. And for a few seconds here and there Raul Julia takes over; he's funny, and he detonates. (The character's lack of moral conflicts gives his scenes a giddy high.) Then the film's languor settles in again. An elaborate government sting operation waits while Mac and Escalante play Ping-Pong, and waits again while they sit in a boat and Mac talks drivel about bullfighting. (It's the worst dialogue in the film; for sheer inappropriateness it's matched only by Dave Grusin's aggressive, out-to-slay-you score.)

Most of the dialogue is sprightly—it's easy, everyday talk that actors can breathe to. But Towne's directing is, surprisingly, better than his construction—maybe because when he plans to direct he leaves things loose. He says, "I make the character fit the actor, I don't try to make the actor fit the character." That sounds as if he's highly variable, a modernist. But he isn't. He likes bits from old movies, such as having the cops who are planning to surprise Mac be so dumb that they leave peanut shells wherever they've been posted. The difference between the way Towne handles the peanut shells and the way a director of the thirties would have (and did) is that he doesn't sock the joke home; he glides over it. He wants the effect, yet he doesn't want to be crude about it, so he half does it. Almost everything in the action scenes of the last three-quarters of an hour is half done. Often he gives you the preparation for action and no follow-through; sometimes the reverse.

Towne's memory is stocked with movie tricks, but what he really treasures is the rhapsodic buzz of those moments when two stars hooked into each other's eyes. That's what saves *Tequila Sunrise*. His obsessions about friendship and betrayal don't mesh with the plot (which is off somewhere floating in cloudland), but his understanding of how movies work for audiences lightens this movie, keeps it happy. It's about a guy who wants to say, "I'm dying from loving you so much," and a girl who knows that in a hot tub he's "like a world champion." Traditionally, these feelings are disguised, or kidded, before they're presented in public. Robert Towne puts them right out on the table. (Both Mac and Nick approach Jo Ann through the pain her beauty causes them. Nick phones and tells her, "I'm going to die if I don't see you.") By rational standards the movie is flimsy and stupid, but by romantic standards it's delectable. The three talented stars are smashing, and the film's paranoid narcissism is dreamy and pretty. Hollywood glamour has a lot to do with a moviegoer's braving out the silliness that's part of it. This is a lusciously silly movie. It has an amorous shine.

The New Yorker, December 26, 1988

MISSISSIPPI BURNING

The director Alan Parker likes to operate in a wildly melodramatic universe of his own creation. In *Mississippi Burning*, which is set during the Freedom Summer of 1964, he treats Southerners the way he treated the Turks ten years ago in *Midnight Express*. And he twists facts here as he did there, with the same apparent objective: to come up with garish forms of violence. We see the white Southerners burning and beating and lynching, but Parker isn't content with that. He wants to give the audience violence it can cheer. A black F.B.I. man is introduced so he can threaten to castrate a white man, and the F.B.I. strings up a suspected Klansman to scare him into testifying against his buddies. Then, there are the inventions that jack up the plot. A deputy sheriff (Brad Dourif) brutally beats his tiny wife (Frances McDormand) while his K.K.K. pals watch to make sure he does a thorough job. She has succumbed to the overtures of an F.B.I. man (Gene

Hackman) and told him where the bodies of three missing civil-rights workers were to be found. (Actually, the F.B.I. informant was a man, and he was given a thirty-thousand-dollar reward for his help.) The entire movie hinges on the ploy that the F.B.I. couldn't stop the K.K.K. from its terrorism against blacks until it swung over to vigilante tactics. And we're put in the position of applauding the F.B.I.'s dirtiest forms of intimidation. This cheap gimmick undercuts the whole civil-rights subject; it validates the terrorist methods of the Klan.

When black people here are on a march, they look withdrawn, dead-eyed, blank; there's no elation or glory in their progress down the street. The Civil Rights Act had just been passed in the Senate, and during that Freedom Summer, when roughly a thousand students and activists arrived in Mississippi to set up schools and register blacks to vote, blacks themselves were busy in the fight for desegregation; they were holding rallies, staging protests, and forming picket lines. They were training themselves to take verbal and physical abuse without being provoked to violence. In the movie, the blacks are sheeplike and frightened; they seem totally unprepared. The events here took place eight and a half years after Rosa Parks refused to go to the back of the bus, but Alan Parker is essentially putting blacks at the back again. The picture opens with a fictionalized recreation of the murder of the three civil-rights workers—James Chaney, the local black who was working for CORE, and two young Jewish activists from up North, Andrew Goodman and Michael Schwerner—who were in their station wagon and were stopped by Ku Klux Klansmen and lawmen. Chaney was driving; in the movie, he has been replaced at the wheel by one of the whites. It's a small detail, but the details add up to a civil-rights movie in which blacks don't do much of anything except inspire pity and sympathy in the two F.B.I. men (Hackman and Willem Dafoe) who are the heroes.

Hackman's Anderson and Dafoe's Ward arrive in the small town where the three men were last seen; their mission is to find out what happened to them. Anderson is a burly, big Mississippian who grew up dirt poor and knows that for whites to feel that they're better than blacks may be the only point of pride they've got. He understands, but it disgusts him. He's a complicated, lonely man who no longer feels at home in the South yet isn't at home with Northerners, either. (Actually, Hackman, a Midwesterner, had never been in the Deep South before, but you wouldn't guess it from his performance.) The pale, bespectacled Ward, who is in charge of the investigation, looks small next to Anderson. He's formal, conscientious, and deeply courteous. A Harvard Law School man who was at the Department of Justice before joining the Bureau, he represents the idealism of the Kennedy era—he's brave and dedicated, but rigid. The man has no common sense. And he inadvertently sets off a brief war between the Bureau and the Klan.

When the local people, black and white alike, won't tell Ward anything, he thinks the answer is to bring in more agents, and after he's got a huge manhunt going and still has no results he brings in Naval Reserves. The K.K.K. fights the invasion by attacking black people and burning their churches. Anderson, who knows how to nose around town and pick up leads, keeps arguing with Ward, showing him that he's making the situation worse. At one point, they face off as if they were going to kill each other, and the movie turns into a bad imitation of a Western. But what's involved in the running battle between the two is the central cheat of the movie. Parker, working from a script by Chris Gerolmo (which he says he rewrote), sets up Dafoe's Ward as a high-principled official with no resourcefulness or flexibility or canniness, and says that he represents the only legal way to tackle the problems. The only alternative, according to Parker, is the illegal, underhanded methods that Anderson insists must be used. And, of course, Anderson—an uncommon common man, whom Hackman plays with humor and buried rage—is the man we identify with. Hackman draws us to him; he's the star here—he's vivid. And he's the spokesman for brutality. There isn't even a whisper of a suggestion that Anderson may get any undue satisfaction from the brutal methods that Ward, recognizing his own defeat, finally allows him to employ. No—they're employed righteously, for Biblical vengeance. (The common man knows what those gents from Harvard Law are too educated to understand.) Parker uses the civil-rights movement to make a wham-bam Charles Bronson movie, and, from his blithe public statements, he seems unaware that this could be thought morally repugnant.

He justifies his small inventions and his big, crude ones in terms of fiscal responsibility to his backers. Presumably, the audience needs a whomp in the gut every two minutes. But if it does, that's because whomping is Parker's basic way of reaching people, and he sets up a pattern. He pounds you, in scenes like the one of the K.K.K., armed with clubs, gathering outside a church in which black people are singing. He won't let go of effects like the lowing of cows in a barn that's been set on fire. (He takes the title very literally; the sets keep going up in flames.) Yet, despite the heaviness of *Mississippi Burning*, it doesn't necessarily stay with you—it's too mechanical, too inexpressive. (There are exceptions: a night shot of the station wagon, with the three young men, coming over a wavy, hilly road, followed by two cars and a truck with no lights; the lovely shades of regret in some of Hackman's scenes with Frances McDormand; the cheeriness of the actress Park Overall's remarks in the town beauty parlor.) Parker is a slicker—a man with talent and technique but without a sustaining sensibility. Each time I heard the pulsating music start working me up for the next bout of violence, I dreaded what was coming. The manipulation got to me, all right, but the only emotion I felt was hatred of the movie.

The New Yorker, December 26, 1988

DANGEROUS LIAISONS
THE COMEDY OF EVIL

In the prologue of *Dangerous Liaisons,* the Marquise de Merteuil (Glenn Close) and the Vicomte de Valmont (John Malkovich) are in their homes, with fleets of servants preparing them for the start of their daily social engagements. And as they're massaged and are given their facials and are made up and dressed and bejewelled it's as if they were being readied for a play—or a war. It's a wonderfully shrewd opening. The director, Stephen Frears, and the screenwriter, Christopher Hampton, who reworked his theatrical version of the Choderlos de Laclos novel *Les Liaisons Dangereuses,* take us right into a world of artifice—the customs and pleasures of French aristocrats in the late seventeen-seventies—and keep us so close to these people that we can examine their lace and their wigs and their skins. The novel, which was originally published in Paris in 1782, condemned in court in 1824, publicly burned, and banned for the rest of the nineteenth century, has a tone and a texture unlike those of any other novel. Written in the form of highly confidential letters, it is principally about the erotic power games played by the Marquise and Valmont, who were once lovers but are now allies and co-conspirators. Laclos, an artillery officer who eventually, under Napoleon, rose to be a general, shows these two aristocrats planning sexual conquests with the cunning and deviousness of military masters, and with far more cruelty, since their victims don't know that they have been made pawns in a campaign. The implication is that the depraved pair stand for their class (and for what after 1789 was to be known as the ancien régime). The success of the movie is that in taking you so far into the systematic debauchery it gets you to feel the emotions under the clever, petty calculations. (It's like uncovering the carnal roots of chess.) By the end, the artificiality has dissolved and something forceful and shocking has taken over.

All along, you see the duplicitousness under the Marquise's wholesome, open-faced, pink-and-creamy exterior. That's what gives the material its comic austerity: you see what's under her farm-fresh smile, you know the heart that beats under her charmingly freckled bosom. Lighted by the marvelous cinematographer Philippe Rousselot *(Diva, Hope and Glory),* she looks as "natural" as a Fragonard. But she's playacting when she makes herself the sympathetic confidante of the conventional-minded ladies of her circle; she feels utter contempt for them, and she twists and turns them to her purposes. The storytelling isn't clear enough at the start: it glides over the plan the Marquise outlines to Valmont. A recent lover who has deserted her is going to marry a rich virgin, the fifteen-year-old, convent-trained Cécile (Uma Thurman); to get back at him, the Marquise has hatched the idea that Valmont should seduce the girl. But Valmont isn't stimulated by the suggestion; he thinks the defloration so easy that it's unworthy of his talents. He takes Cécile on, but only as secondary to a more prestigious target he has chosen for himself: a devout young married woman who's a citadel of virtue—Mme. de Tourvel (Michelle Pfeiffer). Somehow, the Marquise's request of Valmont and the matter of their former relationship and current alliance aren't sufficiently weighted, and you're not fully drawn in; for a long time, you watch the movie as if it were a charmingly wicked marionette show. And that's how you watch it even after everything is lucid and you begin to be fascinated. The Marquise has a grandeur in her manipulativeness: she ruthlessly sets about destroying Cécile, whose mother (Swoosie Kurtz) is her close friend. The girl herself adores her; to the Marquise, this is simply an advantage to be used—she'll use anything to get back at the lover who rejected her.

There are times when the Marquise—a happy widow—sounds much like a modern, "liberated" woman. This is basically faithful to Laclos, who reads like a feminist if you don't pick up the nuances. Here is a passage from Letter 152, in which the Marquise reprimands Valmont for his "connubial" manner with her: "Do you know, Vicomte, why I never married again? It was certainly not for lack of advantageous matches: it was solely so that no one should have the right to object to anything I might do. It was not even for fear that I might no longer be able to have my way, for I should always have succeeded in that in the end: but I should have found it irksome if anyone had had so much as a right to complain. In short, I wished to lie only when I wanted to, not when I had to." In both novel and movie, the Marquise is liberated to lie and scheme, and her primary motive is vicious, vengeful jealousy. At the start, she wants to pay back the lover who prefers a virgin; near the end, she wants to destroy Valmont, because he has fallen in love with the pious prude he set out to amuse himself with. When he describes his ecstasy in bed with Mme. de Tourvel, the Marquise recognizes that he's in love, and the color drains from her face; she's a victim of her feelings, like the men and women she despises for their weakness. She's enraged; she feels left out.

The Marquise is actually the opposite of liberated: she is one of the most formidable examples of hell-hath-no-fury-like-a-woman-scorned in all literature. Childless, of course, she's woman the destroyer, and, despite her reserve and her control, and her superficial rationality, she pulls the lowest kind of "feminine" treachery: she cancels the game she has going with Valmont after he has won, and pins the blame on him. She's a power-hungry, castrating female as conceived by an eighteenth-century male writer. She's also a great character, in the way that Richard III is great. She's polished in her savagery, and the straight-backed Glenn Close, looking matriarchal and pure (even her teeth are perfect), gives a smooth performance that is by far her best work onscreen. She may lack the ravaged intensity that Jeanne Moreau brought to the role in the 1959 modern-dress version by Roger Vadim, and she's rather bland (though less so in the second half),

but she has terrific bearing, and her arch Marquise, with her immaculate simulation of propriety, provides a balance to Malkovich's outré Valmont.

Malkovich takes a little getting used to, because of his furtive eyes, his pursed lips, his slight speech impediment (is it a lisp?), and his little moues. Though he wears a powdered wig, he's weirdly far from the conventional movie image of a French nobleman of the pre-Revolutionary period. Some reptilian men are very successful sexually, but reptilian and fey make an odd combination. Still, off-putting as the casting of Malkovich is, it works cumulatively—even triumphantly. He brings the movie a clowning wit; this Valmont is a cutup and a boudoir farceur. (He uses a trace of effeminacy as an all-purpose lubricant for a tricky gesture or line reading.) And when his dark hair is long and loose it seems to propel him sexually; it helps you make sense of his conquests. When Gérard Philipe played the role, in the Vadim version, he was near death, and he didn't suggest the energy that Valmont requires, but he still had remnants of angelic good looks, and that helped explain women's attraction to him. (It's generally assumed that angelic-looking men can get away with plenty—that that's how the devil fools us.) With Malkovich in the role, Valmont's warped soul is on the outside. Yet Malkovich gives you the sense that Valmont is a priapic freak, and the movie needs that. The Vicomte is the freak who grows into a romantic. (Once he does, he's no good to the Marquise.) And, maybe because this Valmont's depravity is on the surface, along with his mocking humor, he's likable—he's funny, and his swinishness is fascinating. You can see before the Marquise does that he's in love with the serious-minded bourgeoise. And you can see that he's foolish enough, and vain enough, to try to live up to what the Marquise expects of him, in order to be thought irreproachably heartless. (He has a left-handed sense of honor.)

As Mme. de Tourvel, who clings to her conception of honor, the paradisially beautiful Michelle Pfeiffer is caught in frightened closeups. Stiff in her tight bodice and her crisp bonnets, this modest little wife, generous and philanthropic, seems almost plain. But when passion hits her it overpowers her. Her face is damp; she's sweaty—Valmont has set her on fire. And when he rejects her brutally (he just flat out lets her have it), and she breaks down crying, she's helplessly human, a real person caught in a maze of deception. This is when the movie comes together. Mme. de Tourvel's suffering cuts through the decorative formality; suddenly, the marionettes have blood in their veins. The comedy goes out of the game, and the viewer may feel slightly stunned at the impact the movie begins to have. Mme. de Tourvel's collapse is what all that choice cruelty was pointing toward. The transition is so affecting partly because of the traplike construction of the story and partly because Pfeiffer's performance is very simple—it feels true. She makes it totally convincing that the rake Valmont would experience ecstasy while releasing Mme. de Tourvel from her Puritan timidity, yet would be afraid of being laughed at for loving this woman from a different class—a woman without guile or wit.

From then on, everything that happens—and it happens bam, bam, bam—seems part of an unstoppable chain of events. Frears might almost be letting the story tell itself as he moves right through the Marquise's declaration of war, the casualties that follow, and on to the hooting scene (described in Letter 173). Frears' technique is remarkably unaffected. Using American actors (instead of following the Hollywood tradition of casting British actors as French aristocrats) gives the film a directness, an emotional immediacy. (Mildred Natwick is admirably straightforward as Valmont's aged aunt.) So do the speedy, encircling camera movements, and the ravishing closeups, with every facet of the women's earrings picking up light. This must be one of the least static costume films ever shot. (The play version has eighteen scenes; Hampton says the screenplay has two hundred.) But, then, by the end this doesn't feel like a costume film: though the locations include several châteaus near Paris, and the clothes are magnificent, *Dangerous Liaisons* is brisk and unsentimental. There's a minute of a Gluck opera in the background of two scenes, and when a pause is needed there's a brief, blissful interlude of singers at a musicale, but the movie has the let's-get-on-with-it quality that's Frears' signature.

Possibly there's no way to make a picture this fast (it was shot in ten weeks) and achieve something comparable in greatness to the elegant comedy of evil that Laclos left us. There are dismal clinkers in Hampton's dialogue; he strains to give the Marquise and Valmont witty dialogue to underline their perversity. (He's saying they're too clever by half.) And the scenes between the Marquise and Valmont miss out on sensual excitement: you don't feel an electrical current crackling between them. But the casting is still strong. (It's clear that the Marquise has poisoned her capacity to love, and that she has no means left to express her feelings for Valmont except by destroying him, the woman he cares for, and herself.) This is a first-rate piece of work by a director who's daring and agile. The unfussiness of Frears' approach is tonic. The movie gets at the important things and doesn't linger over them. It's heaven—alive in a way that movies of classics rarely are.

The New Yorker, January 9, 1989

RAIN MAN
STUNT

R*ain Man* is Dustin Hoffman humping one note on a piano for two hours and eleven minutes. It's his dream role. As the autistic savant Raymond Babbitt, he's impenetrable: he doesn't make eye contact or touch anyone or carry on a conversation; he doesn't care what anybody thinks of him.

Autistic means self-involved, and Raymond is withdrawn in his world of obsessive rituals. So Hoffman doesn't have to play off anybody; he gets to act all by himself. He can work on his trudging, mechanical walk and the tilt of his head and the irascible, nagging sameness of his inflections. Autistics aren't known to be jerky like this (they're more likely to move slowly and fluidly), but Hoffman's performance has an intricate consistency. Even his tight voice fits his conception.

In dramatic terms, what distinguishes autism from other behavioral syndromes is that you don't get a direct emotional response from an autistic person. Even after Raymond is kidnapped by his younger brother, the slimeball Charlie (Tom Cruise), who hopes to get hold of some of the three million dollars their father has left in trust for Raymond's care, Raymond shows no awareness of what's happening to him. Yet because of the way the director, Barry Levinson, sets up the situations there's nothing for you to do except watch Hoffman intently, microscopically, searching for clues to Raymond's feelings. And you may begin to think that you're reading him, that Levinson is bootlegging you teeny glimmers. What you definitely get is the zigzags of Raymond's head that suggest panic at the violation of his daily routines. And now and then he lets out a primal bleat or squawk that alerts you to his terror of a new situation.

The heads of autistics seem to be wired in a closed-off way, as if their brains were divided into little boxes—little worlds unto themselves. And this is especially puzzling in the small percentage who, like Raymond, have surreal talents; he's a wizard—a sci-fi computer mutant—at some mathematical-memory functions. Hoffman gets to play it all: a disconnected, pesky child with inexplicable powers. For close to an hour, it's an entertaining comic turn. Intuitively, Hoffman seems to understand that we'd enjoy identifying with Raymond's obstinacy—it's his way to win out over his crummy brother—and when the audience laughs at Raymond the laughs are always friendly. He's accepted as a harmless, endearing alien—E.T. in autistic drag. But then the performance has nowhere to go. It becomes a repetitive, boring feat, though the boringness can be construed as fidelity to the role (and masochists can regard it as great acting). Slightly stupefied as I left the theatre, I wondered for a second or two why the movie people didn't just have an autistic person play the part. (In the seventies, when Robert Wilson staged his *A Letter for Queen Victoria*, he used an actual autistic teen-ager in the show, with babbling trance-inducing music that seemed to evoke the fixations of an autistic child.) But with an actual autistic there would be no movie: this whole picture is Hoffman's stunt. It's an acting exercise—working out minuscule variations on his one note. It's no more than an exercise, because Hoffman doesn't challenge us: we're given no reason to change our attitude toward Raymond; we have the same view of him from the beginning of the movie to the end.

Hoffman's crabbed intensity worked marvellously when he played the paranoiac paroled robber in *Straight Time*, and it worked as nippy self-satire when he played the perfectionist actor in *Tootsie*. But it doesn't feel right here. This is the fanatic, uncompromising actor in *Tootsie* playing an autistic the way he played a tomato. (In his mind's eye he's always watching the audience watch him.) It's a determinedly external, locked-in performance (and Levinson makes no attempt, like Wilson's, to take us inside the character by Expressionist means). We're on the outside staring at this virtuoso apparatus. Hoffman doesn't allow Raymond a minute of simple relaxed sluggishness; he keeps you conscious of the buzzing of anxiety in Raymond's brain. He keeps his actor's engine chugging and upstages the movie.

The kidnap plot is no more than a barefaced contrivance to get the two brothers on the road together. *Rain Man* has to get outdoors, or it's just a TV sickness-of-the-week movie; it cinematizes a TV theme by moving the brothers from place to place. Their father has left Charlie a 1949 Buick Roadmaster convertible, and they travel in it, with many a stop, from Cincinnati to L.A. In the first days, the materialistic Charlie is tantrummy and almost insanely callous; he shouts crude insults at Raymond. Obviously these scenes are intended to show how self-centered Charlie is, and how far he has to go to become a sensitive, loving person; he's meant to be spiritually autistic. But, oddly, Charlie's jeering at Raymond doesn't cause you pain. Levinson's directing is too flaccid for you to feel the scenes sharply; there's no conviction in them. (This makes the movie easy to swallow, on a TV level.) And Cruise as a slimeball is just a sugarpuss in Italian tailoring. He doesn't even use his body in an expressive way. His performance here consists of not smiling too much—so as not to distract his fans from watching Hoffman. (This could be called "restraint.") Cruise is an actor in the same sense that Robert Taylor was an actor. He's patented: his knowing that a camera is on him produces nothing but fraudulence.

Charlie has felt sorry for himself for years. That's been his justification for his cheap huckstering; he runs a shady business in L.A., selling imported sports cars that don't quite meet American regulations. But during the trip—Charlie's voyage of self-discovery—he has no one to hustle, and (according to plot calculation) is forced back on himself. Levinson lays it out for the audience on a platter: Charlie has the capacity to change. In due course, after he vents his exasperation at Raymond's inflexibility, he begins to understand himself better and he learns to care about Raymond. And when the two brothers touch heads it's clear that the time they've spent together has affected them both. They've regained the bond they had when Charlie was a baby and Raymond sang to him. This heads-together image has its poetry. It also sums up the film's anti-sentimental sentimental bilge.

Rain Man is getting credit for treating autism "authentically," because Raymond isn't cured; in a simple transposition, it's Charlie who's cured. Actually, autism here is a dramatic gimmick that gives an offbeat tone to a conventional buddy movie. (*Rain Man* has parallels to several scenes in *Midnight Run* and *Twins*, but the standard buddy-movie tricks are so subdued that they may squeak by as "life.") The press has been full of accounts of the research into autism done by Hoffman and Levinson and the principal script-writer, Ronald Bass, but what's the use of all this research if then they rig the story and throw in a big sequence with Raymond using his whiz-bang memory to make a killing in Las Vegas that takes care of Charlie's money troubles? And what's the point of setting up Raymond's avoidance of being touched if Charlie is going to hold him while showing him how to dance and Charlie's warm-hearted Italian girlfriend (Valeria Golino) is going to teach him how to kiss? (Is that something Raymond is likely to be called on to do?) Everything in this movie is fudged ever so humanistically, in a perfunctory, low-pressure way. And the picture has its effectiveness: people are crying at it. Of course they're crying at it—it's a piece of wet kitsch.

Levinson—it's his temperament—stretches out the scenes until they yawn. You may sit there thinking "And more?" "And again?" and "We've already been here!" This is the kind of moviemaking in which you've been there before you get there.

In the context of a hit like *Rain Man*—it's the top box-office film in the country—it may seem almost naïve to suggest that if Raymond is the central character, and the given of the material is that he can't express his mental state, then it's up to the moviemakers to do it. Movies have often been at their most eloquent when the writers and directors and designers and composers used the possibilities of visual and aural stylization, of imagination and fantasy, to envision how the world might be perceived by disordered psyches. (Examples: just about any film noir you can think of, the 1981 M-G-M musical *Pennies from Heaven, Blue Velvet, Raising Arizona, Dreamchild, The Stepfather,* De Palma's *Carrie,* the BBC miniseries *The Singing Detective.*) If moviemakers don't risk shaking up audiences and making our nerves tingle, they're likely to fall back on hauling an autistic savant to Las Vegas, duding him up, and teaching him to kiss.

The New Yorker, February 6, 1989

ABOUT TERI GARR IN
OUT COLD

As Sunny, Teri Garr is slim and fast. She moves like a darting goldfish. And she's like a psychic in reverse: we can read the workings of her mind. We follow her slapdash, opportunistic scheming as clearly as if her thoughts were comic-strip captions.

Teri Garr plays her role with a savage, twinkling joy. Why doesn't her skill get more recognition? I think it's partly because she holds nothing back, and emotions so shallow yet so fully communicated belong to caricature, to sketches. She seems two-dimensional, crisp, weightless. That's why she's perfect for this movie. A few glints of Sunny's eyes and a slight nibble of her lip and it's clear just what she's up to. (When she wants something, she sends out rays.)

The New Yorker, March 6, 1989

LIFE LESSONS, FROM NEW YORK STORIES

As an artist in Martin Scorsese's *Life Lessons,* the first part of the anthology film *New York Stories,* Nick Nolte is more bricklayer than aesthete, and that's what's great about him. After the artist's girl tells him she's leaving him, he gets into a rhythm as he spreads bright colors on a huge horizontal canvas, and you can see that he has the energy to breathe life into it. This isn't a matter of physical size; it's his conviction, his sureness. Scorsese is a skinny little guy, but he's got this energy, too. And he uses Nolte's Lionel Dobie for good-humored self-satire. Still, Nolte's towering stockiness does help: he's a wonderful sculptural object—a loping, gray-bearded beast spattered with paint. He pads up and down in front of the canvas moving his brushstrokes to rock and roll, played loud enough to drown out distractions. Dobie works fast. Smiling, he's dancing with his brushes, painting to the music. Scorsese knows that painting to rock is a cliché, but he also knows that it's a good way for an Action painter to work. The music turned up high like that unifies Dobie's impulses. His sensuality is all working together, exciting him, keeping him going.

That sensuality is also the story's comic spirit: Scorsese is laughing at Dobie while identifying with him. That's what makes the little, forty-five-minute film so intensely enjoyable. Even Dobie's possessive love for Paulette (Rosanna Arquette), his assistant, who lives and works in an enclosure in the loft, is comic. She's just a slip of a girl. Roughly fifty, he's almost two and a half times her age; he's at least twice her size. And, though her eyes still shine when she watches him paint, she's fed up with him—with his slack belly, his slyness, his genius. She's ready to move on. (It's too bad that her work doesn't suggest his influence; if she painted wan imitation Dobies, her plight would have a bit more pungency.) Dobie is lucky: he's drawn to girls he can impress—he's drawn to groupies. And he's famous enough to attract an endless supply of them. But he can't let go. He's so sneakily determined to hang on to Paulette that, like Dostoyevski, whose life is the source of the screenplay that Scorsese sketched for the writer, Richard Price, Dobie solemnly pledges that if his protégée will go on living with him he won't touch her.

Dobie torments himself; he torments her. To some extent, he knows what he's doing: he needs to keep his turbulence up. He fetishizes every part of her, and especially her leg, with its fine gold-chain anklet, indolently extended on her bed. It's a perfect piece of erotic calendar art; he yearns to kiss that foot. He thinks that it's all he can think about; we laugh at his roiling frustration, because he somehow pours it into his work. He's a laboratory: he manufactures the tumult he needs for his painting. Appraising a possible replacement for Paulette, he tries to gauge whether he can fetishize this girl, too. She doesn't matter to him any more than Paulette does. We enjoy watching this ego furnace of his. (Staring at Paulette's foot, he remarks, "Nothing personal.") The girls aren't hurt by his manipulations: they're getting what they want—they're getting entrée into the big-time art world. And we enjoy the rich downtown impasto: the not-surprised-by-anything dealer (suave and grouchy Patrick O'Neal, with his parched voice), the performance artist (Steve Buscemi), the young painter (Jesse Borrego), the cops, the celebrities, the celebrity hounds. It isn't just Dobie's colors that are squeezed out straight from the tube (they land on his matted hair, his glasses, his Cartier watch, his belly); Nestor Almendros lights the crowds and parties so they have this same thick brilliance. No doubt Scorsese feels an affinity with the Abstract Expressionist idea that the canvas should be exciting all over; there's a visual buzz going on throughout the movie. This is the SoHo carnival as Scorsese sees it, zeroing in on objects the way the painter does. He keeps it all swarming to the (often parodying) music.

I was caught up in the passionate thrashing around that Scorsese did in *The Last Temptation of Christ*. His ambivalences and confusions became visible; they were right there on the screen. And he seemed to have gone straight through to the sources of his love of moviemaking. He told stories about a man (he looked like a Flemish Christ) who was perhaps a bit of a fool, and maybe a charlatan, and yet performed miracles, and such is the nature of movie-watching that (even if you're not a Christian) you wanted more and more miracles. You wanted him to show those doubters. Now it's as if Scorsese, having put his fanatic adolescent perplexities on the screen, had cleared his head. Maybe his films will no longer have to swing between passivity and violence.

Life Lessons is his most genial work: if jealousy and rejection fuel Dobie's art, happiness fuels it, too. Everything that keeps him jumping goes into it. The fun of the movie is in its not taking Dobie or his art too seriously. He's not a man of much depth, but the picture doesn't wring its hands about that. Scorsese has lightened up, and in a satisfying way. He's developed a sense of horseplay. We don't feel he's scoring off Dobie, because he's scoring off himself. He sees the comedy of his own compulsiveness in love and art, and he's able to sustain this vision.

Price's script is rather broad, but, given a halfway-good role, Nolte takes it all the way. He's a master of the inchoate, the deeply mixed up. He's like the man with a hoe: you can read his muscles. And he gives this little picture scale and heft. Dobie, preparing for a new show, stays up all night painting, aware that Paulette is entertaining a young lover in her partitioned mini-loft inside the huge loft. He lets up on the blaring rock and listens to Mario Del Monaco singing "Nessun dorma," from Puccini's *Turandot*. For a minute, his energy flags, and he sits bare-chested, spent—trying to come to terms with both his fatigue and the pulsating sensations that drive him on. The tenor lifts up his voice in the sweet anguish of "Nessun dorma"—no sleep, no sleep until he has possessed the woman who eludes him. And, with Nolte sitting there listening, you don't have to know what the words mean to roar with laughter.

The New Yorker, March 20, 1989

LET'S GET LOST

Since the beginning of movies, what has made a screen performer a star has usually been that he or she functioned as a dream love object for multitudes of people. There are other kinds of stars, of course, but the glamorous figures have been the lifeblood of the movies. (And possibly American films have been popular around the world because the figures we fetishized travelled so well: they fit right into the amorous longings of many other cultures.)

As a young man, in the nineteen-fifties, the cool jazz trumpeter and singer Chet Baker had the casual deviltry and the "Blame It on My Youth" handsomeness to become a screen idol. He looked like James Dean, with deep-set eyes and a Steve Canyon jaw, and he was slated to appear opposite Natalie Wood in an M-G-M movie based on his own rise to stardom in the West Coast jazz scene. But Baker, who was taking drugs at the age of twenty-four—he later acknowledged that his favorite high was speedballs of heroin and cocaine—was in so much trouble with the police by then that he skipped out to Europe. (Robert Wagner played the jazz-trumpeter role written for Baker; the movie, *All the Fine Young Cannibals,* came out in 1960.)

Baker was busted over and over; he served time in Italy, in the United States, and in Britain, and he managed to get himself deported from several countries. He also got beaten up, and on one momentous occasion, in San Francisco in 1968, his teeth were knocked out; it was three years (most of it "on public assistance") before he learned to blow his horn wearing dentures. But with his face caved in he still had his musicianship and his romantic glamour, though in the seventies and eighties it was the glamour of a ravaged dreamboat. In May, 1988, just a few months before *Let's Get Lost,* the documentary about him that Bruce Weber was preparing, was first shown, at a European film festival, he died, at age fifty-eight, after a fall from a second-floor window in an Amsterdam hotel near the drug dealers' section of town.

His road manager said, "It was a hot night. He was probably just sitting on the windowsill and nodded out. One time too many."

Let's Get Lost isn't primarily about Chet Baker the jazz musician; it's about Chet Baker the love object, the fetish. Weber, the photographer who does the advertising spreads for Calvin Klein featuring well-muscled male torsos, has a definite "type." His earlier, 1987 documentary, *Broken Noses*, centers on the theme of macho as it's exemplified by a lightweight boxer, Andy Minsker, who coached a club of kids ranging in age from ten to sixteen. But Minsker comes across as a lightweight in too many ways. Whatever Weber was trying to indicate about macho was elusive, and the footage becomes somewhat discomforting when the camera lingers on the little boys' beautiful scrawny chests. Near the start of the film, Minsker is said to look like a young Chet Baker, and he does—he's got the jawline and the build. But he doesn't have Baker's theatrical aura. And when Baker's languorous music—cool but with a pop sweetness—is heard on the track while Minsker and his brother roughhouse, you may feel that Weber is trying to eroticize footage that doesn't really have much kick. My guess is that by the time Weber finished *Broken Noses*, and dedicated it to Baker, he'd realized that it was a warmup, and that his real subject was the young trumpeter who had fascinated him since he was sixteen and bought his first Chet Baker record.

Weber proceeded to collect still photographs and film clips from Baker's early days in L.A. with Charlie Parker (in 1952), Gerry Mulligan (1952–53), and others; from TV appearances in the fifties and sixties; and from quickie movies that Baker acted in in Italy and Hollywood. These finds are intermingled with footage of Weber (off camera) hanging out with the older, ruined Baker and interviewing his friends and associates, his mother, his wives and children and lovers. (Sometimes Minsker turns up alongside Baker.) Behind it all is a soundtrack made up of Baker recordings that span more than three decades—the idealized essence of the man. And maybe because Weber, despite his lifelong fixation on this charmer, knew him only as a battered, treacherous wreck, in the two years before his death, *Let's Get Lost* is one of the most suggestive (and unresolved) films ever made. It's about love, but love with few illusions.

Self-destructive beauties like Chet Baker are attractive to us in ways we can't quite pin down. When we see him as he was in the early fifties, on the West Coast, he evokes terms like "Beat," "cool," "dangerous"—all of them tinged with doomy romanticism. And the Santa Monica palm trees, tall against dark skies, are a magical evocation of that smoky era. Weber's visual intuitions are as lyrical and right as Baker's melodic instincts. (I dug through my dusty pile of 45s and found ten Baker records; he doesn't sing on any of them, but you could almost swear you heard the words coming out of his horn.)

You see Chet Baker as a kid who was out for adolescent pleasures: convertibles, pretty girls, booze, drugs. He didn't have to goad himself to master the horn; it came easy to him—he was a natural. He was out for adolescent pleasures all his life. And you see how blank his beauty is and how corrupt he becomes. Weber documents his own obsession with a beauty who had turned into a sunken-eyed death's-head long before he met him. (The film recalls the scene in *Ugetsu* when the artist finds that his dream Lady is an evil wraith.)

The early photographs of the smooth-chested Baker holding his trumpet aren't by Weber, but they have something of the animal magnetism of the expressionless, athletic models in Weber's fashion layouts. Baker's soft voice can be heard on "Imagination [Is Funny]," and he sings in a glossy pastoral scene from an Italian movie, posed among youthful picnickers. In his later years, Baker was given to beating up on women (and he is said to have ratted on his friends to save himself from arrest). All this time, he was singing romantic songs.

Toward the end, there was an unmistakable whiff of Skid Row con artistry about him, even though he made two hundred thousand dollars his last year. We get to see what drew audiences. He went to the Cannes Film Festival in 1987, when *Broken Noses* was screened there, and his performance at Cannes, singing Elvis Costello's "Almost Blue," is part of *Let's Get Lost*. Wrapped in his romantic myth, he was always a jazz crooner—his voice was always small. Now it's a breathy murmur, yet his stoned, introverted tonelessness is oddly sensuous. He sings very slowly, and the effect is dreamy—the impeccable phrasing sounds like something remembered from the deep past (though the song is new). He does what he's been doing for more than thirty-five years, and the crowd is hushed. He's singing a torch song after the flame is gone; he's selling the romance of burnout. (It's a new kind of Dionysian image—not of frenzy but of oblivion.)

Weber included some rather undistinguished color sequences in *Broken Noses;* this time, working again with the cinematographer Jeff Preiss, in 16 mm., he sticks to black-and-white, and it's reticent yet expressive, impassioned. The film has its lapses, though. At one point, we hear Baker singing on the track while we see him, haggard and sinister (like a Jack Palance villain), in the Santa Monica sunshine bumping carnival cars. The scene is reminiscent of student films, and it sticks out, because Baker isn't being fetishized here—just pointlessly photographed. Toward the end, Weber throws in a collage of celebrities at Cannes (past and present) which doesn't belong here. It's padding and it wrecks the organization of the last half hour. (At two hours, the film is slightly long.)

There are also lapses in moral judgment: badgering the women being interviewed, and setting them against each other. When the singer Ruth Young, who's from a show-biz family, is questioned about her relationship with Baker, she's delighted to perform for the camera, and she's lively, witty, and tough. (When she sings, it's clear that she modelled her style on Baker's). But Carol, the Englishwoman who's the mother of three of his children, isn't part of show biz, and she feels awkward when she's asked similar questions. She doesn't want to bitch about her children's father, and she doesn't want to offend Baker's mother. (So she blames Ruth for everything that's gone wrong.) When Carol and also Baker's mother make it clear that they don't want to talk about certain matters, Weber keeps the camera on them while they plead for privacy. Is there perhaps an element of hostility in the way he presses the women? It's obvious that Baker has been hell on those close to him—why pry and compound their pain? Weber is an artist when he directs so that the imagery appears to be one with Baker's music. When he becomes more aggressive (and more petty), as he does with the women, the sequences are just skillful boorish cinéma vérité.

Weber spent his own money on *Let's Get Lost* (over a million dollars), and, of all movies made for obsessive reasons, this is one of the most naked. It's naked even in the way that this man in thrall to his "type" shows no bond of sympathy with the women who are similarly in thrall. Maybe it took a photographer-director to aestheticize his fetish to such a degree that it's impossible here to separate Chet Baker the scrupulously observed subject from Chet Baker the erotic dream. *Let's Get Lost* is shamelessly true to the (perhaps universal) experience of infatuation.

The New Yorker, May 1, 1989

THE RAINBOW
TRAMPLED

Describing the landscape where the heroine, Ursula Brangwen, walks toward the woods in *The Rainbow*, D. H. Lawrence wrote, "It was very splendid, free and chaotic." That's true of *The Rainbow* itself. It doesn't have the dramatic clarity (or the greatness) of its successor, *Women in Love*, but it's a passionately heated landmark novel about marriage. This chronicle of three generations of a farming family is an attempt to show how marriage worked in the Victorian and Edwardian periods and why it became subject to new strains in the industrial age. Ursula, who experiences those strains—and is aware of them—flails at everything around her. While still in her teens, she's in conflict between her drives and the repressive claims of conventional marriage. It isn't just sex she wants; she yearns for sexual and spiritual union. The novel, which was completed and published in 1915, was prosecuted for obscenity and ordered destroyed. It's not hard to understand why. The writing is intensely sensual and often ecstatic; it's potent—Lawrence makes you feel that the whole world is panting in rhythm with his language. And Ursula, trying to break free, challenges Christianity and colonialism, and questions the other ideas that her fiancé, Anton—an attractive man with a fine, slender body who's in the Royal Engineers—casually accepts. When she expresses her feelings, he hates her. Finally, he wants to marry her, he wants to kill her. The new movie version, by Ken Russell (who filmed *Women in Love* in 1969), doesn't impose an artificial pattern or plot on the material, but it isn't splendid. Amorphous and unsatisfying would be more accurate.

The pastoral locations are grassy vistas that seem to melt before your eyes. The Midlands look the way a reader wants them to look, and the images suggest that the material is being approached with humility and seriousness. This isn't one of Russell's lurid, campy pictures. But his underlying attitudes haven't really changed; the campiness is simply more restrained. The adaptation, which he did with his wife, Vivian, is a slapdash job—speeches are borrowed from one set of characters for another, and incidents are thrown in. So the themes don't cohere. It isn't clear what the story is about, besides the one theme that the "modern" woman's desire for independence leads to turmoil, and that there's hope in this turmoil. (If Ursula married the officer, who has no deep connections with her, she'd shrivel.) The movie's most powerful section is the treatment of Ursula's first job—when, at seventeen, she takes a teaching post at a school where the children of the poor are beaten into whining submission. Russell seems relieved to get away from the difficult, blind anger that's woven into the sexual experiences of Ursula (Sammi Davis) and Anton (Paul McGann). He plunges into the Dickensian miseries of the school, where the contending forces are clearer.

The ads for *The Rainbow* feature a banner line from the review in the *Times*: "Ken Russell is the purest interpreter D. H. Lawrence could have hoped for." In his worst nightmares. Russell's fidelity (to roughly the second half of the novel, the part that moves from the previous generations of the Brangwen family to concentrate on Ursula) is staggeringly superficial. The fault isn't just in the script; it's in how he has directed Sammi Davis, and how she plays the role. She made a smart, sunny impression in relatively small, teenager parts in *Mona Lisa, Hope and Glory, A Prayer for the Dying* (less sunny), and other movies; and, as the cunning little schemer—a starring role—in the BBC's Thomas Hardy adaptation, *The Day After the Fair,* she had an authentic horror. (But she didn't have to represent the consciousness of the Hardy material.) As Ursula, she has a scrappiness that works well in the school-teaching scenes, but in the rest of the movie nothing she says seems to have any substance: her rude, angry lines just pop into her mouth right out of the script. This Ursula is blank-faced and lightweight. It makes sense that she should seem surly and withdrawn to her family and the other characters, but she can't be merely that to us, or who's going to give us what is the glory of the novel—Lawrence's intuitive exploration of her feelings and her imagination? That's what's missing. One of the pioneering feminist heroines—a woman who represents an advance on previous generations, a woman on a quest—has been turned into a snippy, closed-off brat.

As if to make up for the passion that's omitted, Russell adds an episode in which Ursula (when she's still a schoolgirl) poses nude for a dirty-old-man painter (Dudley Sutton), who becomes furious when she won't let him beat her. And Russell adds such details as the headmaster maneuvering the young teacher Ursula into displaying her bottom for him. But Lawrence's material isn't about scruffy lechery; it's about sexuality and spirit. Russell's additions detract from the poetic intensity of what Lawrence was up to, and muddy the conflicts. Since it's Winifred, the teacher that the schoolgirl Ursula has a crush on, who dares Ursula to go to the painter's studio, without warning her about his kinks, Winifred seems callous and sadistic. The scenes involving Winifred (Amanda Donohoe) are fairly weird anyway, since Donohoe, who was the serpentlike fanged vampire in Russell's 1988 *The Lair of the White Worm,* retains some of her viperishness here. She's a leering mannish lesbian, who seduces Ursula with soft caresses and anti-male talk, and then turns about and marries Ursula's plump and prosperous mine-owner uncle, played with smiling finesse by David Hemmings. (You couldn't guess from the movie that in the novel Ursula is the matchmaker.)

Glenda Jackson and Christopher Gable are surprisingly relaxed as Ursula's parents, and (in small details) they show us how different their sexual life is from hers. The mother keeps having babies; the father is proud of being able to support his family, and finds his other joys at the church organ and in wood carving. The parents' lives are eventful yet peaceful in ways that Ursula will never know. But will anybody who hasn't read the novel be able to understand Ursula the dreamer? Or will they just think she's an impossibly petulant twerp?

Funny thing about this movie: Russell, notorious for overheating most of his pictures, has left the heat out of this one. He seems to be trying to serve the novel without recognizing what a blazing vision it is, how it stirs a reader. And he seems to have run out of bravura. (The climactic scene, in which Ursula is in danger of being trampled by horses—and perhaps by a marriage based merely on sexual attraction—is emotionally inert.) The most sensuous moment is very brief. Just after Ursula and Anton meet—when she isn't quite sixteen—they go into a church that's being restored. They're secluded there; he opens several of the miniature buttons on one of the gloves she's wearing, exposing a small bit of flesh, and kisses it. That's at least the beginning of something.

The New Yorker, May 29, 1989

ABOUT NICOLAS CAGE IN
VAMPIRE'S KISS

Uusually, when an actor plays a freak you can still spot the feet-on-the-ground professional. Nicolas Cage doesn't give you that rootedness. He's up there in the air, and when you watch him in *Raising Arizona* or

Moonstruck it's a little dizzying—you're not quite sure you understand what's going on. It could be that this kid—he's only twenty-four—is an actor before he's a human being. That would explain his having had two front teeth knocked out for his role as the mutilated Vietnam vet in *Birdy;* it would explain his eating a plump, wriggling cockroach in his new film *Vampire's Kiss.* These things may not seem very different from Robert De Niro's going from a hundred and forty-five pounds to two hundred and fifteen pounds to play the older Jake La Motta, and De Niro could also be said to be an actor before he's a human being, but they go in different directions. De Niro swells and thickens and sinks down; he walks heavy—he's formidable. Cage strips himself, he takes flight, he wings it. I don't mean to suggest that he's the actor De Niro is—only that, in his own daring, light-headed way, he's a prodigy. He does some of the way-out stuff that you love actors in silent movies for doing, and he makes it work with sound.

The New Yorker, June 12, 1989

BATMAN
THE CITY GONE PSYCHO

In *Batman,* the movement of the camera gives us the sensation of swerving (by radar) through the sinister nighttime canyons of Gotham City. We move swiftly among the forbidding, thickly clustered skyscrapers and dart around the girders and pillars of their cavelike underpinnings. This is the brutal city where crime festers—a city of alleys, not avenues. In one of these alleys, Bruce Wayne as a child watched, helpless, as his parents were mugged and senselessly shot down. Now a grown man and fabulously wealthy, Bruce (Michael Keaton) patrols the city from the rooftops. He has developed his physical strength to the utmost, and, disguised in body armor, a cowl, and a wide-winged cape, and with the aid of a high-tech arsenal, he scales buildings and swoops down on thugs and mobsters—Batman.

There's a primitive visual fascination in the idea of a princeling obsessed with vengeance who turns himself into a creature of the night, and the director, Tim Burton, has given the movie a look, a tone, an eerie intensity. Burton, who's thirty, has a macabre sensibility, with a cheerfulness that's infectious; his three films (*Pee-wee's Big Adventure* and *Beetlejuice* are the other two) get you laughing at your own fear of death.

Seen straight on, the armored Batman is as stiff and strong-jawed as a Wagnerian hero. His cowl-mask has straight-up sides that end in erect ears; he gives the impression of standing at attention all the time. (He's on guard duty.) But something else is going on, too. The eye slits reveal only the lower part of his eyes—you perceive strange, hooded flickers of anger. When

Batman is in motion, what you see can recall the movies, such as *The Mark of Zorro* and the 1930 mystery comedy *The Bat Whispers,* that the eighteen-year-old cartoonist Bob Kane had in mind when he concocted the comic-book hero, in 1939. Though the Tim Burton film is based on Kane's characters, it gets some of its funky, nihilistic charge from more recent "graphic novels" about Batman, like Frank Miller's 1986 *The Dark Knight Returns* and Alan Moore's 1988 *The Killing Joke.* This powerfully glamorous new *Batman,* with sets angled and lighted like film noir, goes beyond pulp; it gallops into the cocky unknown.

In the movie's absurdist vision, Batman's antagonist is the sniggering mobster Jack Napier (Jack Nicholson), who turns into the leering madman the Joker. Clearly, Batman and the Joker are intended to represent good and evil counterparts, or, at least, twin freaks, locked together in combat; it was Jack Napier who made an orphan of Bruce Wayne, and it was Batman who dropped Jack into the vat of toxic chemicals that disfigured him. That's the basic plan. But last year's writers' strike started just as the movie was set to go into production, and the promising script, by Sam Hamm (it reads beautifully), never got its final shaping; the touching up that Warren Skaaren (and uncredited others) gave it didn't develop the characters or provide the turning points that were needed. With the young hipster Keaton and the aging hipster Nicholson cast opposite each other, we expect an unholy taunting camaraderie—or certainly some recognition on Batman's part that he and the Joker have a similarity. And we do get a tease now and then: when the two meet, their actions have the formality of Kabuki theatre. But the underwritten movie slides right over the central conflict: good and evil hardly know each other.

At times, it's as if pages of the script had drifted away. The mob kingpin (Jack Palance, in a hearty, ripe performance) is toppled by Jack Napier, who moves to take control of the city, but we're not tipped to what new corruption he has in mind. We wait for the moment when the photo-journalist Vicki Vale (Kim Basinger), who's in love with Bruce Wayne and is drawn to Batman, will learn they're the same person. She's just about to when the scene (it's in her apartment) is interrupted by the Joker, who barges in with his henchmen—we expect him to carry her away. The revelation of Batman's identity is suspended (we never get to see it), and the Joker trots off without his prize. After this double non-whammy, a little air seems to leak out of the movie. And it's full of these missed moments; the director just lets them go. Vicki and Bruce, dining together, are seated at opposite ends of an immense banquet table in a baronial hall in Wayne Manor; two thousand years of show business have prepared us for a zinging payoff—we feel almost deprived when we don't get it. Yet these underplayed scenes have a pleasing suggestiveness. The dinner scene, for example, shows us that Bruce is flexible, despite his attraction to armor. (He collects it.) And Vicki quickly realizes that the Bruce Wayne–Batman identity is less important than the question Is he married only to his Batman compulsion or is he willing to share his life with her?

The movie has a dynamics of feeling; it has its own ache. Michael Keaton's poor-little-rich-boy hero is slightly dissociated, somewhat depressed, a fellow who can take his dream vehicle, the Batmobile, for granted. How do you play a guy who likes to go around in a bat costume? Keaton has thought out this fellow's hesitations, his peculiarity, his quietness. In some situations, the unarmed Bruce is once again a passive, helpless kid. (In a triste scene at night, he hangs by his ankles on gym equipment, rocking softly—trying to lull himself to sleep.) Keaton's Bruce-Batman is really the only human being in the movie; he gives it gravity and emotional coloring. This is a man whose mission has taken over his life. The plangent symphonic score, by Danny Elfman, might be the musical form of his thoughts; it's wonderfully morose superhero music.

When Nicholson's Joker appears for the first time, the movie lights up like a pinball machine: the devil has arrived. (Nicholson is playing the role Keaton played in *Beetlejuice*.) The Joker is marvellously dandified—a fashion plate. The great bohemian chapeaus and the playing-card zoot suits, in purple, green, orange, and aqua, that Bob Ringwood has designed for him have a harlequin chic. They're very like the outfits the illustrator Brian Boland gave the character in *The Killing Joke*, and Nicholson struts in them like a homicidal minstrel, dancing to hurdy-gurdy songs by Prince—the Joker's theme music. But the grin carved into the Joker's face doesn't have the horror of the one on Conrad Veidt's face in the 1927 *The Man Who Laughs* (where Bob Kane acknowledges he took it from). Veidt played a man who never forgot his mutilation. Nicholson's Jack Napier is too garish to suffer from having been turned into a clown; the mutilation doesn't cripple him, it fulfills him. And so his wanting to get back at Batman is just crazy spite.

This may work for the kids in the audience, and the Joker's face stirs up a child's confused fear of—and delight in—clowns. (They're like kids made hideous and laughed at.) But possibly the Joker's comic-book dazzle diminishes the film's streak of morbid grandeur—the streak that links this *Batman* to the reverbs that *The Phantom of the Opera* and *The Hunchback of Notre Dame* set off in us. When the adversaries have their final, moonlight encounter, among the gargoyles on the bell tower of Gotham's crumbling, abandoned cathedral, they could be like the Phantom of the Opera split in two, but there's pain in Keaton, there's no pain in Nicholson. The Joker may look a little like Olivier as the John Osborne vaudevillian, but he isn't human: he's all entertainer, a glinting-eyed cartoon—he's still springing gags after he's dead. This interpretation is too mechanical to be fully satisfying. And is Nicholson entertainer enough? He doesn't show the physical elegance and inventiveness we may hope for.

The master flake Tim Burton understands what there is about Batman that captures the moviegoer's imagination. The picture doesn't give us any help on the question of why Bruce Wayne, in creating an alternate identity, picked a pointy-eared, satanic-looking varmint. (Was it simply to gain a sense of menace and to intimidate his prey?) But Burton uses the fluttering Batman enigmatically, playfully. He provides potent, elusive images that draw us in (and our minds do the rest). There may be no more romantic flight of imagination in modern movies than the drive that Vicki and Batman take, by Batmobile, rocketing through a magical forest. Yet though we're watching a gothic variation of the lonely-superhero theme, we're never allowed to forget our hero's human limitations. He's a touchingly comic fellow. When he's all dressed up in his bat drag, he still thinks it necessary to identify himself by saying, in a confidential tone, "I'm Batman."

The movie's darkness is essential to its hold on us. The whole conception of Batman and Gotham City is a nighttime vision—a childlike fantasy of the big city that the muggers took over. The caped crusader who can find his way around in the miasmal dark is the only one who can root out the hoods. The good boy Batman has his shiny-toy weapons (the spiked gauntlets, the utility belt equipped with projectile launcher, even the magnificent Batwing fighter plane), but he's alone. The bad boys travel in packs: the Joker and his troupe of sociopaths break into the Flugelheim Museum, merrily slashing and defiling the paintings—the Joker sees himself as an artist of destruction.

Batman and the Joker are fighting for the soul of the city that spawned them. We see what shape things are in right from the opening scenes. Gotham City, with its jumble of buildings shooting miles and miles up into the dirty skies, is the product of uncontrolled greed. Without sunshine or greenery, the buildings look like derelicts. This is New York City deliberately taken just one step beyond the present; it's the city as you imagine it when you're really down on it. It's Manhattan gone psycho. But even when you're down on it you can get into your punk fantasies about how swollen it is, how blighted and yet horribly alive.

The designer, Anton Furst, seems to have got into that kind of jangled delight, putting together domes and spires, elongated tenements, a drab city hall with statues bowed down in despair, and streets and factories with the coal-mine glow of the castles and battlements in *Chimes at Midnight*. Gotham City has something of the sculptural fascination of the retro-future cities in *Blade Runner* and *Brazil*—it's like Fritz Lang's *Metropolis* corroded and cankered. If H. G. Wells' *Time Machine* took you there, you'd want to escape back to the present. Still, you revel in this scary Fascistic playground: the camera crawls voluptuously over the concrete and the sewers, and the city excites you—it has belly-laugh wit.

When Gotham City celebrates its two-hundredth birthday, the big parade balloons are filled with poison gas—an inspiration of the Joker's. (He rides on a float, jiggling to the music; his painted red grin has wing tips.) Paranoia and comic-book cheesiness don't defeat Tim Burton; he feels the kick in them—he likes their style. The cinematographer, Roger Pratt, brings theatrical artifice to just about every shot—a high gorgeousness, with pur-

ples and blacks that are like our dream of a terrific rock concert. The movie
even has giant spotlights (and the Batsignal from the original comic books).
This spectacle about an avenging angel trying to protect a city that's already
an apocalyptic mess is an American variant of *Wings of Desire*. It has a poetic
quality, but it moves pop fast. The masked man in the swirling, windblown
cape has become the hero of a comic opera that's mean and anarchic and
blissful. It has so many unpredictable spins that what's missing doesn't seem
to matter much. The images sing.

The New Yorker, July 10, 1989

CASUALTIES OF WAR
A WOUNDED APPARITION

Some movies—*Grand Illusion* and *Shoeshine* come to mind, and the two
Godfathers and *The Chant of Jimmie Blacksmith* and *The Night of the Shooting
Stars*—can affect us in more direct, emotional ways than simple entertainment movies. They have more imagination, more poetry, more intensity
than the usual fare; they have large themes, and a vision. They can leave us
feeling simultaneously elated and wiped out. Overwhelmed, we may experience a helpless anger if we hear people mock them or poke holes in them
in order to dismiss them. The new *Casualties of War* has this kind of purity.
If you meet people who are bored by movies you love such as *The Earrings
of Madame De . . .* or *The Unbearable Lightness of Being*, chances are you can
brush it off and think it's their loss. But this new film is the kind that makes
you feel protective. When you leave the theatre, you'll probably find that
you're not ready to talk about it. You may also find it hard to talk lightly
about anything.

   Casualties of War is based on a Vietnam incident of 1966 that was reported in *The New Yorker* by the late Daniel Lang, in the issue of October 18,
1969. (The article was reprinted as a book.) Lang gave a calm, emotionally
devastating account of a squad of five American soldiers who were sent on
a five-day reconnaissance mission; they kidnapped a Vietnamese village girl,
raped her, and then covered up their crime by killing her. The account
dealt with the kind of gangbang rape that the Vietnam War had in common
with virtually all wars, except that the rapists here, unable in general to distinguish Vietcong sympathizers from other Vietnamese, didn't care that the
girl wasn't Vietcong. This indifference to whether a candidate for rape is
friend or foe may not really be that much of an exception; it may be frequent in wartime. What's unusual here may simply be that a witness forced
the case into the open and it resulted in four court-martial convictions.

   A number of movie people hoped to make a film of the Lang article, and, though it was commercially risky, Warners bought the rights and announced that Jack Clayton would make the picture—an arrangement that fell apart. Plans involving John Schlesinger and other directors also collapsed, but the article may have been the (unofficial) taking-off point for one film that did get made: Elia Kazan's low-budget, 16-mm. *The Visitors,* of 1972, which Kazan himself financed. He used a prosecution for rape and murder as background material to explain why a couple of ex-servicemen released from Leavenworth on a technicality were out to get the former buddy who had testified against them. Eventually, in 1987, after Brian De Palma had a success with *The Untouchables,* he was able to persuade Paramount to pick up the rights to the Lang story, which he'd had in the back of his mind since 1969. A script was commissioned from the playwright David Rabe, the quondam Catholic and Vietnam vet who had written *Streamers* and other plays about the war (and had wanted to work on this material for some years), but, when De Palma was all set to film it in Thailand, Paramount pulled out. The picture finally got under way at Columbia—the first picture to be approved by the company's new president, Dawn Steel. Whatever else she does, she should be honored for that decision, because twenty years later this is still risky material.

■   ■   ■

Lang's factual narrative is based on conversations with Eriksson, the witness who testified against the other men, and on the court-martial records. (The names were changed to protect everyone's privacy.) Rabe's script follows it closely, except that Rabe dramatizes the story by creating several incidents to explain what led to the rape and what followed.

When Eriksson (Michael J. Fox), who has just arrived in Vietnam, is out in a jungle skirmish at night, a mortar explosion shifts the earth under him; he drops down, caught, his feet dangling in an enemy tunnel. De Palma photographs the scene as if it were an ant farm—he shows us aboveground and underground in the same shot. Eriksson yells for help, and in the instant that a Vietcong, who has been crawling toward the dangling legs, slashes at them with his knife, Sergeant Meserve (Sean Penn) pulls Eriksson out. A minute later, Meserve saves him again from that Vietcong, who has come out of the hole to get him.

In the morning, the soldiers enter a peaceful-looking village; they stand near the mud-and-bamboo huts and see a stream and bridges and, a little way in the distance, paddy fields where women and elderly men are working, under the shadow of harsh, steep mountains. The tiered compositions are pale, like Chinese ink paintings. Throughout the movie, everything that's beyond the understanding of the Americans seems to be visualized in layered images; this subtle landscape reaching to Heaven is the site of the random violence that leads to the rape.

Smiling and eager, Eriksson walks behind two water buffalo, helping an ancient farmer with his plowing. Brownie (Erik King), a large-spirited, joshing black soldier, who is Meserve's pal—they're both due to go home in less than a month—cautions Eriksson about his exposed position on the field and walks him back to where the Sarge is taking time out, with the other men. They're all relaxed in a clearing near this friendly village, but we become ominously aware that the villagers in the paddies are evaporating. Brownie is standing with an arm around Meserve when the pastoral scene is ruptured: bullets tear into Brownie from a V.C. across the stream. An instant later, a guerrilla who's dressed as a farmer runs toward the group and flings a grenade at them. Meserve spots him and warns Eriksson, who turns and fires his grenade launcher; by luck, he explodes the V.C.'s grenade. Then the screen is divided by a couple of split-focus effects: in one, Eriksson, in closeup, rejoices at his freak shot and is so excited that he lets the grenade-thrower slip away; in another, Eriksson is staring the wrong way while behind him a couple of women open a tunnel for a V.C., who disappears into it. Meanwhile, Meserve fires his M-16 rifle, and then, his face showing his agony, he uses his hand like a poultice on Brownie's wound. A soldier radios for medical help, and Meserve, never letting go of his friend, keeps reassuring him until he's loaded on a chopper.

■　■　■

In these early scenes, Meserve is skillful and resourceful. He's only twenty years old, and as Sean Penn plays him he has the reckless bravery of youth. He's genuinely heroic. But Brownie dies (as Meserve knew he would), and back at the base camp the men, who have readied themselves for a visit to a brothel, are stopped and told that the village adjoining the base has been declared off limits. It's too much for Meserve, who has been put in charge of the five-day mission to check out a mountain area for signs of Vietcong activity, and later that night he finishes briefing his men by telling them to be ready to leave an hour early, so they can detour to a village to "requisition" a girl. Eriksson half thinks the Sarge is kidding. It takes a while for him (and for us) to understand that Meserve is not the man he was; only a day has passed since his friend was killed, but he has become bitter and vindictive—a conscious trickster and sinner.

Has something in Meserve snapped? Paul Fussell writes in his new book *Wartime* that in the Second World War the American military "learned that men will inevitably go mad in battle and that no appeal to patriotism, manliness, or loyalty to the group will ultimately matter." So "in later wars things were arranged differently," he explains. "In Vietnam, it was understood that a man fulfilled his combat obligation and purchased his reprieve if he served a fixed term, 365 days, and not days in combat either but days in the theatre of war. The infantry was now treated somewhat like the Air Corps in the Second War: performance of a stated number of missions guaranteed escape." Meserve, who has led dozens of combat patrols, has reached his limit with only a few weeks to go; he turns into an outlaw with a smooth justification for anything. (The kidnapping is a matter of cool planning: the girl can be explained as a "V.C. whore" taken for interrogation.) When Meserve's five-man patrol, having set out before dawn, arrives at the village he selected in advance, he and Corporal Clark (Don Harvey) peer into one hut after another, shining a flashlight on the sleeping women until they find one to their taste—Oanh (Thuy Thu Le), a girl of eighteen or twenty.

The terrified girl clings to her family. Clark carries her out, and her mother and sister come rushing after him, pleading in words that are just jabber to the soldiers, who want to get moving before it's light. They've taken only a few steps when the mother desperately hands them the girl's scarf. It's a pitiful, ambiguous gesture. She seems to want Oanh to have the comfort of this scarf—perhaps it's new, perhaps it's the only token of love the mother can offer her daughter. Eriksson says "Oh Jesus God" when he sees the men's actions, even before the mother holds out the scarf. Then he mutters helplessly, "I'm sorry." He's sick with grief, and we in the audience may experience a surge of horror; we know we're watching something irrevocable. Clark, a crude, tall kid who suggests a young Lee Marvin, is irritated by the girl's crying and whimpering, and he stuffs the scarf into her mouth, to gag her.

■   ■   ■

The men climb high above the valleys and set up a temporary command post in an abandoned hut in the mountains; it's here that the sobbing, sniffling girl is brutalized. (Thereafter, she's referred to as "the whore" or "the bitch.") Eriksson refuses his turn to rape her, but he can't keep the others from tying her up, beating her, and violating her. He himself is assaulted when he tries to stop them from killing her. Eriksson is brave, but he's also inexperienced and unsure of himself. In the few minutes in which he's alone with the girl and could help her escape, he delays because he's afraid of being charged as a deserter. The opportunity passes, and we can see the misery in his eyes. Meserve sees it, too—sees that Eriksson finds him disgusting, indecent. And he begins to play up to Eriksson's view of him: he deliberately turns himself into a jeering, macho clown, taunting Eriksson, questioning his masculinity, threatening him. Meserve starts to act out his madness; that's the rationale for Penn's theatrical, heated-up performance. He brings off the early, quiet scenes, too. When Meserve shaves after learning of Brownie's death, we see that the hopefulness has drained out of him. Suddenly he's older; the radiance is gone. Soon he's all calculation. Although he was coarse before, it was good-humored coarseness; now there's cynical, low cunning in it. Fox, in contrast, uses a minimum of showmanship. He gives such an interior performance that it may be undervalued. To play a young American in Vietnam who's instinctively thoughtful and idealistic—who's uncorrupted—is excruciatingly difficult, yet Fox never lets the character come across as a prig. The two men act in totally different styles, and the styles match up.

And, whatever the soldiers say or do, there's the spectre of the dazed, battered girl ranting in an accusatory singsong. The movie is haunted by Oanh long before she's dead. The rapists think they've killed her, but she rises; in our minds, she rises again and again. On the basis of the actual soldiers' descriptions of the girl's refusal to accept death, Daniel Lang called her "a wounded apparition," and De Palma and his cinematographer, Stephen H. Burum, give us images that live up to those words—perhaps even go beyond them. Trying to escape along a railway trestle high up against the wall of a canyon, Oanh might be a Kabuki ghost. She goes past suffering into the realm of myth, which in this movie has its own music—a recurring melody played on the panflute.

That lonely music keeps reminding us of the despoiled girl, of the incomprehensible language, the tunnels, the hidden meanings, the sorrow. Eriksson can't forgive himself for his failure to save Oanh. The picture shows us how daringly far he would have had to go to prevent what happened; he would have had to be lucky as well as brave. This is basically the theme that De Palma worked with in his finest movie up until now, the political fantasy *Blow Out,* in which the protagonist, played by John Travolta, also failed to save a young woman's life. We in the audience are put in the man's position: we're made to feel the awfulness of being ineffectual. This lifelike defeat is central to the movie. (One hot day on my first trip to New York City, I walked past a group of men on a tenement stoop. One of them, in a sweaty sleeveless T-shirt, stood shouting at a screaming, weeping little boy perhaps eighteen months old. The man must have caught a glimpse of my stricken face, because he called out, "You don't like it, lady? Then how do you like this?" And he picked up a bottle of pink soda pop from the sidewalk and poured it on the baby's head. Wailing sounds, much louder than before, followed me down the street.)

Eriksson feels he must at least reveal what happened to Oanh and where her body lies. He's a dogged innocent trying to find out what to do; he goes to the higher-ups in the Army and gets a load of doubletalk and some straight talk, too. The gist of it is that in normal (i.e., peacetime) circumstances Meserve would not have buckled like this, and they want Eriksson to keep quiet about it. But he can't deal with their reasoning; he has to stick with the rules he grew up with. He moves through one layer of realization to the next; there's always another, hidden level. The longer Eriksson is in Vietnam, the more the ground opens up beneath him. He can't even go to the latrine without seeing below the floor slats a grenade that Clark has just put there, to kill him.

■　　■　　■

De Palma has mapped out every shot, yet the picture is alive and mysterious. When Meserve rapes Oanh, the horizon seems to twist into a crooked position; everything is bent away from us. Afterward, he goes outside in the rain and confronts Eriksson, who's standing guard. Meserve's relationship to the universe has changed; the images of nature have a different texture, and when he lifts his face to the sky you may think he's swapped souls with a werewolf. Eriksson is numb and demoralized, and the rain courses down his cheeks in slow motion. De Palma has such seductive, virtuosic control of film craft that he can express convulsions in the unconscious.

In the first use of the split-focus effect, Eriksson was so happy about having hit the grenade that he lost track of the enemy. In a later use of the split effect, Eriksson tries to save Oanh from execution by creating a gigantic diversion: he shoots his gun and draws enemy fire. What he doesn't know is that Clark, who is behind him, is stabbing her. He didn't know what was going on behind him after he was rescued from the tunnel, either. This is Vietnam, where you get fooled. It's also De Palmaland. There are more dimensions than you can keep track of, as the ant-farm shot tells you. And the protagonist who maps things out to protect the girl from other men (as Travolta did) will always be surprised. The theme has such personal meaning for the director that his technique—his own mapping out of the scenes—is itself a dramatization of the theme. His art is in controlling everything, but he still can't account for everything. He plans everything and discovers something more.

De Palma keeps you aware of the whole movie as a composition. Like Godard, he bounces you in and out of the assumptions about movies that you have brought with you to the theatre. He stretches time and distance, using techniques that he developed in horror-fantasy and suspense pictures, but without the pop overtones. He shifts from realism to hallucinatory Expressionism. When the wounded Brownie is flown out by helicopter, the movement of the yellow-green river running beneath him suggests being so close up against a painting that it's pure pigment. When Eriksson is flown out, it's at an angle you've never seen before: he looks up at the rotor blades as they darken the sky. These helicopters are on drugs.

■　■　■

Great movies are rarely perfect movies. David Rabe wrestles with the ugly side of male bonding; he's on to American men's bluster and showoff, and his scenes certainly have drive. But his dialogue is sometimes explicit in the grungy-poetic mode of "important" American theatre. The actual Eriksson was in fact (as he is in the movie) married and a Lutheran. He was also, as Daniel Lang reported, articulate. This is Eriksson talking to Lang:

> We all figured we might be dead in the next minute, so what difference did it make what we did? But the longer I was over there, the more I became convinced that it was the other way around that counted—that *because* we might not be around much longer, we had to take extra care how we behaved.

Rabe uses these remarks but places them maladroitly (as a response to something that has just happened), and he makes them sound like the stumbling thoughts of a folksy, subliterate fellow reaching for truth:

> I mean, just because each one of us might at any second be blown away, everybody's actin' like we can do anything, man, and it don't matter what we do—but I'm thinkin' maybe it's the other way around, maybe the main thing is just the opposite. Because we might be dead in the next split second, maybe we gotta be extra careful what we do—because maybe it matters more—Jesus, maybe it matters more than we even know.

This passage is the heaviest hammering in the movie (and the poorest piece of staging), but it's also a clear indication of Rabe's method. De Palma works directly on our emotions. Rabe's dialogue sometimes sounds like the work of a professional anti-war dramatist trying to make us think. Still, there's none of the ego satisfaction of moral indignation that is put into most Vietnam films and what De Palma does with the camera is so powerful that the few times you wince at the dialogue are almost breathers.

■　■　■

This movie about war and rape—De Palma's nineteenth film—is the culmination of his best work. In essence, it's feminist. I think that in his earlier movies De Palma was always involved in examining (and sometimes satirizing) victimization, but he was often accused of being a victimizer. Some moviegoers (women, especially) were offended by his thrillers; they thought there was something reprehensibly sadistic in his cleverness. He *was* clever. When people talk about their sex fantasies, their descriptions almost always sound like movies, and De Palma headed right for that linkage: he teased the audience about how susceptible it was to romantic manipulation. *Carrie* and *Dressed to Kill* are like lulling erotic reveries that keep getting broken into by scary jokes. He let you know that he was jerking you around and that it was for your amused, childish delight, but a lot of highly vocal people expressed shock. This time, De Palma touches on raw places in people's reactions to his earlier movies; he gets at the reality that may have made some moviegoers too fearful to enjoy themselves. He goes to the heart of sexual victimization, and he does it with a new authority. The way he makes movies now, it's as if he were saying, "What is getting older if it isn't learning more ways that you're vulnerable?"

■　■　■

Cruelty is not taken lightly in this movie. In the audience, we feel alone with the sounds that come out of Oanh's throat; we're alone with the sight of the blood clotting her nose. The director has isolated us from all distractions. There are no plot subterfuges; war is the only metaphor. The soldiers hate

Vietnam and the Vietnamese for their frustrations, their grievances, their fear, and they take their revenge on the girl. When Brownie is shot, Eriksson, like Meserve and the others, feels that they've come to fight for the defense of the villagers who knew about the hidden guerrillas and could have warned them. They feel betrayed. Could the villagers have warned them without being killed themselves? It's doubtful, but the soldiers are sure of it, and for most of them that's justification enough for what they do to Oanh. The movie doesn't give us the aftermath: Oanh's mother searched for her and got South Vietnamese troops to help in the search; the mother was then taken away by the Vietcong, accused of having led the troops to a V.C. munitions cache. De Palma simply concentrates on what happened and why.

Meserve and Clark and one of the other men feel like conquerors when they take Oanh with them. They act out their own war fantasy; they feel it's a soldier's right to seize women for his pleasure. Comradeship is about the only spiritual value these jungle fighters still recognize; they're fighting for each other, and they feel that a gangbang relieves their tensions and brings them closer together. When Clark slings Oanh over his shoulder and carries her out of her family's hut, he's the hero of his own comic strip. These men don't suffer from guilt—not in the way that Eriksson suffers for the few minutes of indecisiveness in which he might have saved Oanh's life. He's turned from a cheerful, forthright kid into a desolate loner.

At the end, the swelling sound of musical absolution seems to be saying that Eriksson must put his experiences in Vietnam behind him—that he has to accept that he did all he could, and go on without always blaming himself. De Palma may underestimate the passion of his images: we don't believe that Eriksson can put Oanh's death into any kind of sane perspective, because we've just felt the sting of what he lived through. He may tell himself that he did all he could, but he feels he should have been able to protect her. The doubt is there in his eyes. (I hear that baby's cries after almost fifty years.) What makes the movie so eerily affecting? Possibly it's Oanh's last moments of life—the needle-sharp presentation of her frailty and strength, and how they intertwine. When she falls to her death, the image is otherworldly, lacerating. It's the supreme violation.

The New Yorker, August 21, 1989

MY LEFT FOOT
SATYR

In the middle of *My Left Foot,* the movie about the Dubliner Christy [
a victim of cerebral palsy who became a painter and a writer,
(Daniel Day-Lewis) is in a restaurant, at a dinner party celebr

opening of an exhibition of the pictures he painted by holding a brush between his toes. For some time, he has been misinterpreting the friendly manner of the woman doctor who has been training him, and who arranged the show, and now, high on booze and success, he erupts. "I love you, Eileen," he says, and then, sharing his happiness with the others at the table, "I love you all." Eileen, not comprehending that his love for her is passionate and sexual, takes the occasion to announce that she's going to marry the gallery owner in six months. In his staccato, distorted speech, Christy spits out "Con-grat-u-la-tions" so that the syllables sound like slaps, and then he lashes her with "I'm glad you taught me to speak so I could say that, Eileen." The restaurant is suddenly quiet: everyone is watching his torment as he beats his head on the table and yanks the tablecloth off with his teeth.

It's all very fast, and it may be the most emotionally wrenching scene I've ever experienced at the movies. The greatness of Day-Lewis's performance is that he pulls you inside Christy Brown's frustration and rage (and his bottomless thirst). There's nothing soft or maudlin about this movie's view of Christy. Right from the first shot, it's clear that the Irish playwright-director Jim Sheridan, who wrote the superb screenplay, with another Irish playwright, Shane Connaughton, knows what he's doing. Christy's left foot is starting a record on his turntable; there's a scratchy stop, and the foot starts it up again—Mozart's *Così Fan Tutte.* A few toes wriggle to the music, and then in a sudden cut the bearded head of the man that the musical toes belong to jerks into the frame, and we see the tight pursed mouth, the tense face, and the twisted-upward, lolling head with slitted eyes peering down. He's anguished and locked in yet excitingly insolent. Day-Lewis seizes the viewer; he takes possession of you. His interpretation recalls Olivier's crook-backed, long-nosed Richard III; Day-Lewis's *Christy* Brown has the sexual seductiveness that was so startling in the Olivier Richard.

The defiance in Christy's glance carries over when the film flashes back from the acclaimed young author and artist in 1959 to the birth, in 1932, of the crippled, twitching child—the tenth of twenty-two children born to the Browns—who is thought to be a vegetable. The child actor (Hugh O'Conor) is a fine matchup with Day-Lewis and does wonderful work, but the small Christy might affect us as a Tiny Tim if we didn't have the image of the adult blending with him. Lying on the floor under the staircase like part of the furniture, Christy watches the crowded family life dominated by the violent, heavy-drinking bricklayer father (Ray McAnally), and bound together by the large, reassuring mother (Brenda Fricker). Despite what the doctors say and what the neighbors think, Christy's mother persists in believing that he has a mind. One day when he's alone in the house with her, he hears her fall; pregnant and near term, she's unconscious at the bottom of the stairs, lying near the front door. He squirms and writhes, flinging his way downstairs, and then banging his foot against the door until a neighbor hears the commotion, comes to the house, and sends her off in an ambulance. But when the neighbors gather they don't praise the boy.

don't realize that he summoned them. Seeing him there, they think his mother fell while carrying this moron downstairs. I don't know that any movie has ever given us so strong a feeling of an intelligence struggling to come out, to be recognized.

Finally one day, the boy, seeing a piece of chalk on the floor and desperate for some means of asserting himself, sticks out his left foot (he later described it as "the only key to the door of the prison I was in"), works the chalk between his toes, and makes a mark on his sister's slate with it. The family, awed, watches. After that, his mother teaches him the alphabet, and his brothers push him around outside in a broken-down old go-cart—it's like a wheelbarrow—so he can play with them. He speaks only in strangled grunts, but some members of the family understand him (his mother always does), and his father, who calls Christy's cart his "chariot," boasts of his accomplishments. It's a great day for all of them when this pale, gnarled kid takes chalk in his toes and, with a gruelling effort at control, writes "MOTHER" on the floor. (Astonishingly, even at that moment you don't feel manipulated; the directing is too plain, too fierce for sentimentality.)

Day-Lewis takes over when Christy is seventeen and, lying flat in the streets, is an accepted participant in his brothers' fast, roughneck games. As goalkeeper for a soccer match, he stops the ball with his head. The whack gives you a jolt. It gives him a savage satisfaction; it buoys him up. Out with his brothers, Christy's a hardheaded working-class cripple. At home, he paints watercolors. And though he can't feed himself or take care of his excretory functions or wash or dress himself, his life is one romantic infatuation after another—he courts the girls with pictures and poems. (In some ways, his story is a whirling satire of the Irishman as impetuous carnal dreamer.)

This is Jim Sheridan's first feature film, but he's an experienced man of the theatre, with a moviemaker's vision and a grownup's sense of integrity. There's no overacting and none of the wordiness that crept into Christy Brown's later books. His autobiography, *My Left Foot*, published when he was twenty-two, is a simple account (with perhaps a surfeit of creditable emotions). His best-known work, the semi-autobiographical novel *Down All the Days*, published when he was thirty-seven (and smitten with Thomas Wolfe), is the kind of prose-poetry that's generally described as roistering and irrepressible. It's a chore to get through. But what a life he lived! Sheridan and Connaughton know that their story is not the making of an artistic genius: it's the release of an imprisoned comic spirit. What makes Christy Brown such a zesty subject for a movie is that, with all his physical handicaps, he became a traveller, a pub crawler, a husband, a joker. He became a literary lion and made a pile of money; *Down All the Days*, a best-seller, was published in fifteen countries. The movie may tear you apart, but it's the story of a triumphantly tough guy who lived it up.

In a section of the film called "Hell," the father is laid off while the family has nothing to eat but porridge, and Christy can't paint there's no money for coal—he has to go to bed. (The boys sleep four to a bed, sardine style.) It isn't until Christy is nineteen that his mother is able to buy him the wheelchair that she's been saving for. She's tough, too: she won't touch the money even during the porridge days. (She has her own hell: nine of her children didn't survive infancy.) There's nothing frail about these people; they're strong, and they're uncannily intuitive. The mother, who has always understood what is going on in Christy, is aware of the danger that the woman doctor (Fiona Shaw) represents; the mother worries that the doctor has brought too much hope to Christy's voice.

The cinematographer (Jack Conroy) brings the family close to you, and the images of flesh—the broad-faced Juno-like mother, the sculptural pink jowliness of the father, the girls in their first experiments with makeup, the raw-faced boys—come at you the way they do in a Dreyer film. In one scene, a bulging vein divides Christy's bony forehead right down the middle; sometimes when he tries to talk, he drools spittle. There isn't a wasted shot in the movie. A Halloween fresco is instantly stored as something not to be forgotten. And there is a moment that is simply peerless when Mr. Brown, the head of the house, is laid low; he falls to the floor—to Christy's province—and Christy is face to face with his dead father. It's a mythic image. But it doesn't go on a second too long. Neither does the wake—a real Irish wake that ends in a brawl. A man there offends Christy, who uses his talented left foot to kick the glass smack out of the guy's hand. (Christy loves to drink so he can misbehave.)

Everything goes right with the movie—which probably means that Sheridan and Connaughton hit the right subject for them and surrounded Day-Lewis with just the right players. But probably none of it would have worked without him and his demonic eyes. (At times, Day-Lewis's Christy uses his eyes to speak wicked thoughts for him, as Olivier's Richard III did. They're flirts, these characters. As for the actors, when they're deformed they're free to be more themselves than ever.) Something central in Day-Lewis connects with what's central in Christy. You could say that they share a bawdy vitality, and they do, but it's much more than that. It's in the passion that Day-Lewis has for acting: he goes in to find (i.e., create) the spirit of the character so that he can release it. That's how he asserts himself. So he responds to Christy's need for self-assertion and his refusal to see himself as a victim. Christy Brown died, at forty-nine, in 1981; he choked on food at Sunday dinner. This great, exhilarating movie—a comedy about suffering—gives him new life as a legendary Irish hero.

The New Yorker, October 2, 1989

THE FABULOUS BAKER BOYS
WHOOPEE

In *The Fabulous Baker Boys* the twenty-nine-year-old writer-director Steve Kloves glides you through a romantic fantasy that has a forties-movie sultriness and an eighties movie-struck melancholy. Put them together and you have a movie in which eighties glamour is being defined. Kloves gets you to reminisce in a special way: you have your stored-up forties fantasies, and now you see morose people in bars and night clubs that look left over from those days, and everybody's shrug about things being run-down is part of the glamour. If this film has a specific progenitor, it might be *Shoot the Piano Player,* Truffaut's comedy about melancholia, in which the piano-player hero wants not to care anymore—to be out of it. (The heroine says, "Even when he's with somebody, he walks alone.") Kloves has a new New Wave vision. He trips you off, inviting you to laugh if you want to. You feel the heat even if you're laughing.

Kloves has written quick, slang dialogue; most of what's being said is unspoken. Beau and Jeff Bridges are Frank and Jack, the Baker brothers of Seattle—a team of pianists who have been working together for thirty-one years, the last fifteen in cocktail lounges. (Jack was a child prodigy when they got their start.) For round-faced Frank, the older brother (Beau), playing the piano is a livelihood—nothing more. A settled suburban family man in his early forties, he handles the business side, picks the music, does the patter onstage, and worries about his bald spot and Jack's longish hair and lack of grooming. (As Beau plays him, Frank is the human center of the movie.) Jack, who's in his late thirties and lives in a crummy tenderloin apartment, is so fed up with everything that he can barely stay awake during the performances. He seems depressed, surly, as if he might wander off at any moment, but he sits there and goes through the motions.

Their arrangements—pop classics, standards, and show tunes—sound dead, and they've been getting fewer dates, and those in tackier rooms, when Frank proposes that they take on a girl vocalist. They audition thirty-seven songbirds who can't carry a tune before Michelle Pfeiffer turns up, as Susie Diamond, a tough, honest floozy. Asked what kind of experience she's had, Susie answers that for the last couple of years she's been "on call for the Triple-A Escort Service." But when she sings (Pfeiffer does her own singing) she's a sexy dream—tender, nostalgic, just what's wanted of a lounge performer. Her interpretations of the standards are simple and natural in a way that cuts through the thick overlay of pop banality. Once she's part of the act and she and the Baker boys are on their way up, she says she doesn't want to sing "Feelings" or "Bali Ha'i" again, but Frank insists, and when we hear her on "Feelings" she cleans away the psychodrama, and it actually sounds relatively fresh.

Susie loves to perform, and she has a low-down impudence—she gives the picture its kick. She's a funny girl, not as innocent or farcical as the love-lorn pixie that Pfeiffer played in *Married to the Mob* but with something of that free personality. Susie has a fast, profane way of saying what she thinks, and it's disruptive. Without especially meaning to, she challenges the brothers' relationship. She challenges it more directly after she discovers that Jack plays jazz piano when he's playing for himself. (The picture calls what he plays jazz, but it's not different enough from his bland teamwork—just a little harsher and a lot showier. His jazz is dubbed by Dave Grusin; the runs sound like colored lights on waterfalls.) Seeing Jack in his secret jazz world, Susie knows that this is a different man from the almost pathologically laid-back pianist she's been working with—that he loves music the way she does—and she's drawn to him.

Frank senses what's going on and becomes more of a fuss-budget, nitpicking about Jack's hair and his smoking. The three of them are beginning to make real money, but Frank keeps crabbing—nobody's neat enough for him. When they're at an expensively tasteful resort hotel, booked for the Christmas holidays, Frank is indignant because Susie is keeping him up by listening to Ellington at two in the morning.

While the pressures build, you're free-associating with old movies and smiling in recognition. Pfeiffer's good-bad Susie recalls the grinning infectiousness of Carole Lombard, the radiance of the very young Lauren Bacall, and Pfeiffer herself in other movies (and in her eager, fluid performance in John O'Hara's *Natica Jackson* on PBS). Mostly, it's the emotional states of romantic melodramas that are recalled—the moments when the hero, hollowing his cheeks, looks like a god but, for reasons he can't explain, leaves the heroine out on a limb. Jeff Bridges has never been as glamorously beyond reach as he is here. As Jack, he can show affection only to a dejected child and an old, sick dog. In the first scene, Jack has risen from the bed of a woman who asks if she'll see him again, and she's told "No." As he's closing the door behind him, she says, "You've got great hands." Jack is tall, quiet, sensual—a love object who spreads his long fingers and caresses the keys of a piano. Even when he plays alone at a jazz joint his face seems sad, blurred, as if he were remembering what music used to mean to him. (That's the eighties side of the movie: this Sleeping Beauty may never fully wake up.)

Everyone has bluesy, narcissistic feelings, and that's what Steve Kloves is into. The movie is all fake blues, but the fakeness isn't offensive because it's recognized for what it is, and respected for the longings it calls up. Dennis Potter got it right when, in an interview, the critic Michael Sragow asked him, "Why do popular songs have so much power in your work?" He answered:

> Because I don't make the mistake that high-culture mongers
> do of assuming that because people like cheap art, their feelings
> are cheap, too. When people say, "Oh listen, they're playing our
> song," they don't mean "Our song, this little cheap, tinkling, syn-

copated piece of rubbish, is what we felt when we met." What they're saying is, "That song reminds us of that tremendous feeling we had when we met."

Essentially, at *The Fabulous Baker Boys* we're laughing together at the magnetism of popular music and the magnetism of commercial-movie emotions; they overlap so much they're practically the same thing. (The story line blends them.)

And we're laughing at the dazzling happiness that radiates from Michelle Pfeiffer as she sings eight songs, including "More Than You Know" and two by Rodgers and Hart—"Ten Cents a Dance" and "My Funny Valentine." We laugh the hardest when she writhes and thrashes about on top of Jack's grand piano in the ballroom of the resort hotel on New Year's Eve. Frank has been called away, and Susie finally has her shot at seducing Jack. She goes all out, while singing "Makin' Whoopee." Kloves and Dave Grusin blow the opportunity to make the song more of a communication between the piano and the vocalist, but with Pfeiffer in deep-red velvet crawling on the piano like a long-legged kitty-cat and sliding down to be closer to the pianist, something new has been achieved in torrid comedy. Pfeiffer's dress is red the way Rita Hayworth's dress in *Gilda* was black—as a statement. Hayworth hit a peak of comic voluptuousness in that gown, doing striptease movements to "Put the Blame on Mame," with Anita Ellis's voice coming out of her. Pfeiffer in red doesn't displace Hayworth; making love to Jack through her song, she matches her.

Kloves previously had a script produced that he wrote when he was twenty-two—*Racing with the Moon*. That movie was actually set in the forties, and it, too, had a moody, low-keyed texture and the kind of dialogue that allows the actors to find their way. But it was too much like a sensitive first novel. It didn't have Michelle Pfeiffer or anything like the swooniness that this demi-musical has. Kloves hasn't devised subplots that will pay off late in the story; he works with melodramatic atmosphere but not with melodrama, and he doesn't give the movie the boost that might be expected toward the end. It may seem to drift for a bit. Yet it has a look; the cinematographer, Michael Ballhaus, has given it a funky languor. By ordinary-movie standards, the pacing here could be snappier at times—more decisive—but it's of a piece with the bluesiness. The relaxed, nowhere-to-go atmosphere holds the film in a memory vise. The choice of songs, their placement, and the sound mix itself are extraordinary—so subtle they make fun of any fears of kitschy emotions. And there's a thrill in watching the three actors, because they seem perfect at what they're doing—newly minted icons.

The Bridges brothers don't have to act brotherhood; it takes care of itself. At one point, Frank is doing his usual inane, ingratiating patter about himself and his brother, to yank applause from the audience. Suddenly, the near-catatonic Jack says, "I love you, Frank," in a low, muffled voice. Is he just being hostile? Or are these true feelings that he had to express to cauterize the show-biz lies? Frank is so rattled that he needs to recover himself before going on with his routine. Kloves lets the two underplay their scenes together. They don't reach out to us; we reach out to them.

The New Yorker, October 16, 1989

HENRY V

Shakespeare's *Henry V,* written in 1599, or thereabouts, is perhaps the greatest jingo play ever conceived. It celebrates the victory of the underdogs—the English. At Agincourt, King Henry's valiant archers, outnumbered five to one and exhausted and fighting on foreign soil, destroy the expensively armored French. When the tally is handed to Henry, he reads it aloud to his men: the French have lost ten thousand men, the English just twenty-nine. Then the modest, devout Henry cautions his soldiers not to boast of this victory, and he orders the singing of "Non nobis domine" ("Not unto us, O Lord, not unto us, but unto thy name give glory"). But the play itself is far from modest. Written for an English audience, it tells us what great fighters we English are. And we're yeomen, naturally democratic; the French are sleek courtiers—an army of nobles, and a Dauphin who jeers at us.

Shakespeare is a jingo showman but he's no jingo fool. Along with the crowd-pleasing heroism the play offers doubts and complicated feelings. It suggests that what has led the Englishmen to Agincourt is military adventurism. Henry has allowed himself to believe the councillors who have told him he has a legitimate claim to the throne of France. Yet the arguments that convince him sound like monkeyshines; the English are out for conquest.

At the center of this ambivalent patriotic play is the twenty-seven-year-old king, who is steeling himself for the responsibilities of leadership, and has given up the disreputable pals of his carousing days. Our Henry isn't merely an ideal leader, a fair-minded, disciplined, man-to-man king; he's the ideal Englishman—honest, considerate, bluff—and so the ideal man. Yet can an audience be meant to love a man who "killed the heart" of Jack Falstaff with the words "I know thee not, old man," and orders the hanging of the petty thief Bardolph, his former drinking companion? King Henry is too judicious to be loved. But the role is a star turn: audiences can love an actor for bringing it off.

Laurence Olivier played the part on the screen forty-five years ago, in a *Henry V* that he directed, with the encouragement of the British government. Britain was under attack, and his film caught the mood of the moment. It was—and remains—a heart-lifting triumph; it has bright colors, trick perspectives, and the enormous charm of childhood tales of chivalry.

Olivier (he was thirty-six) brings a playful, bashful glamour to the role. His voice rings out thrillingly; you carry the sound with you forever. The new version, adapted and directed by its star, the young Shakespearean actor Kenneth Branagh (pronounced with the "g" silent), in no way replaces that first *Henry*, but it finds a niche of its own. Branagh's *Henry V* isn't exultant. His approach doesn't make possible the kind of patriotic triumph joined to an artistic triumph that Olivier had; the times don't make it possible, either. This new film reflects (or seems to reflect) Vietnam, and the Thatcher Government's Falklands War. Henry's archers with their longbows don't leap about in a way that suggests Robin Hood's men. The new battle at Agincourt is a slow-motion dance of bloody horror, and the victory is shallow and mournful.

Branagh—he was the confused, infatuated young man in the moonlit water with Jacqueline Bisset in *High Season,* and he was Mr. Tansley to Rosemary Harris's Mrs. Ramsay in the TV *To the Lighthouse* and Guy Pringle in the series *Fortunes of War*—was born into a Protestant working-class family in Belfast, in 1960. As Henry, he has the flyaway hair of a schoolboy, and, under his shiny dark-blond mop, his face is not what used to be called nobly proportioned. The burning blue eyes, the thin slash of a mouth, the big, determined chin, the trace of baby fat in the cheeks—none of them match. Together, though, they convey a suggestion of secret knowledge, and his head, overscaled for his short frame, rivets attention. He has something of James Cagney's confident Irishness; he's an intensely likable performer, with a straightforwardness that drives the whole film ahead.

Each of Henry's scenes with the gallant, intelligent French herald, Mountjoy (Christopher Ravenscroft), advances the plot by showing Mountjoy taking ever-larger measure of the king; their encounters are like signposts in a friendship. Once Henry is away from the dark palace, where high officials lurk in the shadows, and is out-of-doors, he becomes a different man—the brave, affable soldier king. (He'd rather be on his white horse than on his throne.) Part of the fun is in Henry's surprising everyone by his resourcefulness, and Branagh plays the same game with the audience. Just after Henry has learned that his troops—mud-soaked, ragged, and sick—will have to fight the fresh, finely accoutred French, he says, "We are in God's hand." Rain comes pouring down on him, and he raises weary, distrustful eyes to Heaven. (The touch of irony is Olivier-like, but not too much so.) And, at Agincourt, just after Henry has learned of the slaughter of the noncombatant page boys he listens to the compulsive chatter of the Welshman Fluellen (Ian Holm), a pedant on the subject of military discipline, and the man's nuttiness suddenly gets to him: with tears and blood still streaking his face, he breaks into laughter. (This daring release feels like pure, spontaneous Branagh.)

This actor's earthy, doughy presence is the wrapping for his beautiful, expressive voice. Emotion pours out of it with surprising ease; he's conversational without sacrificing the poetry. His readings are a source of true pleasure. Listening to him, you think, With an instrument like that, he can play anything.

Yet he puts a symphony orchestra under the great St. Crispin's Day speech (which Olivier delivered a cappella). The "Non nobis domine" is magnificent as a male chorus joins the soloist; we hear it over the last view of the carnage at Agincourt, as Henry walks across the field of corpses, carrying Falstaff's murdered boy (Christian Bale). But then Branagh thickens the emotion with the rising sound of the orchestra, and the effect is banalized. He's given to thickening other actors' emotions the same way.

Much of the film has been set at night, with fiery lighting. Flames and smoke from the siege of Harfleur outline Henry as he sits on his white horse and inspires his soldiers to "cry 'God for Harry, England, and Saint George!' " Campfires and torches illumine the bivouac on the night before battle. Flickering fires give a Rembrandt glow to the interior of the inn where Falstaff (Robbie Coltrane) lies on his deathbed. There's a little too much Rembrandt glow; it's like the lush underscoring—it's imitation art.

Branagh is not an overnight great moviemaker. His attempts at spectacular effects strain his inventiveness (and he doesn't come up with anything comparable to the first flight of the arrows in the Olivier film or to the battle in Welles' *Chimes at Midnight*). Olivier staged the play between brackets, moving from the stage of the Globe Theatre to a larger world of artifice; he used color and design anti-naturalistically. Branagh opens the play in a movie-studio soundstage and attempts a more realistic approach. It's rather basic, and it's overintense: closeups as a way to achieve immediacy, with many too many meaningful looks exchanged. (You may begin to fixate on the actors' trendy haircuts.) The battle scenes are powerful; shown very close in, the images of fighting and its aftermath are like details of a large—unseen—painting. But Branagh, like a clever gifted student, prolongs them, overworking his cadavers. He's a flamboyant realist. He has an appetite for theatrical excesses, as he shows in the deranged, Darth Vader entrance he gives himself. (He does everything but waggle a false nose at the camera.) He shows it, too, in some of Derek Jacobi's carrying-on as the chorus-narrator: Jacobi slithers about from place to place, and at times he's like a radio announcer at the racetrack trying to crank up the listeners' excitement. When the scenes require a light, stylized touch—Katherine of France (Emma Thompson) being given an English lesson by her companion (Geraldine McEwan); Henry wooing Katherine—Branagh echoes the Olivier version, but he can't quite find a rhythm. Since this fast-paced, fire-and-smoke movie lacks the formality that would give the courtship scene a tone, we don't know how to take it when Henry, having just met Katherine, says, "I love you."

Branagh's interpretation of *Henry V* emphasizes the price paid for war: the bloodshed. He's trying to make it into an anti-war film, an epic noir. But he can't quite dampen the play's rush of excitement—not with Henry delivering all those rousing words to his soldiers, calling them "we few, we happy few, we band of brothers." (Shakespeare shows how the English language it-self can be turned into a patriotic symbol.) In keeping with his generation's supposed disillusion with war, Branagh has minimized the play's glorifica-tion of the English fighting man. His conception of how to film the play is to look closely at the conniving, the misgivings, the ego wars. He doesn't in-dicate why the French lost at Agincourt. We hear the Constable of France (Richard Easton) smugly saying "I have the best armor in the world," but Branagh doesn't show that the French and their horses were fatally encum-bered by their armor and chain mail and other trappings; when the arrows hit—and obviously most of them would have hit the horses, whose bodies were more exposed—the riders fell into the water and mud, and were too weighed down to get up. They were massacred while they struggled like bee-tles on their backs. As Branagh stages the battle, with the two sides engaged in hand-to-hand combat, there's no way to understand why the English rather than the French won (except that God is with them).

But, scene by scene, there's always more than enough to take in. It's a company of stars: Judi Dench as Mistress Quickly, calling "Adieu" to her hus-band, Ancient Pistol (Robert Stephens); Paul Scofield as the melancholy French king whose face foretells the doom of his army; Brian Blessed as Exeter; Richard Briers as cherry-nosed Bardolph; Alec McCowen as Ely; and on and on. Branagh seems to have a special gift for bringing out great re-active moments: Ravenscroft's herald registering the probable consequences of the mistake the Dauphin has made in insulting this English king; the fear in the eyes of the English as they behold the hugeness of the approaching French army; Henry himself pretending not to be watching everyone watch him. Best of all, perhaps, is Ian Holm's Fluellen, too obsessed to gauge other people's reactions, his bright eyes flashing while he talks for his own satisfaction. The film's point of view leaves you without elation, but the ac-tors are so up that you feel their pride in working on true dramatic poetry.

The New Yorker, November 27, 1989

THE LITTLE MERMAID

Hans Christian Andersen's tear-stained *The Little Mermaid* is peerlessly mythic. It's the closest thing women have to a feminine Faust story. The Little Mermaid gives up her lovely voice—her means of expression—in exchange for legs, so she'll be able to walk on land and attract the man she loves. If she can win him in marriage, she will gain an immortal soul; if she can't, she'll be foam on the sea.

I didn't expect the new Disney *The Little Mermaid* to be Faust, but after reading the reviews ("everything an animated feature should be," "reclaims the movie house as a dream palace," and so on) I expected to see something more than a bland reworking of old Disney fairy tales, featuring a teen-age tootsie in a flirty seashell bra. This is a technologically sophisticated cartoon with just about all the simpering old Disney values in place. (The Faust theme acquires a wholesome family sub-theme.) The film does have a cheerful calypso number ("Under the Sea"), and the color is bright—at least, until the mermaid goes on land, when everything seems to dull out.

Are we trying to put kids into some sort of moral-aesthetic safe house? Parents seem desperate for harmless family entertainment. Probably they don't mind this movie's being vapid, because the whole family can share it, and no one is offended. We're caught in a culture warp. Our children are flushed with pleasure when we read them *Where the Wild Things Are* or Roald Dahl's sinister stories. Kids are ecstatic watching videos of *The Secret of* NIMH and *The Dark Crystal.* Yet here comes the press telling us that *The Little Mermaid* is "due for immortality." People are made to feel that this stale pastry is what they should be taking their kids to, that it's art for children. And when they see the movie they may believe it, because this *Mermaid* is just a slightly updated version of what their parents took them to. They've been imprinted with Disney-style kitsch.

The New Yorker, December 11, 1989

ENEMIES, A LOVE STORY
PULLING THE RUG OUT

Isaac Bashevis Singer sold his novel *Enemies, A Love Story,* a movie was made of it, and he still possesses it—that's a novelist's dream. Singer constructed a post-Holocaust sex farce with three passionately jealous women in love with a stealthy, guilt-ridden man. It's about refugees who are lost, who go on living in New York and chasing each other into bed after they've vanished from their lives. The director, Paul Mazursky, has gathered a superbly balanced cast and kept the action so smooth that the viewer is carried along on a tide of mystical slyness. It's overwhelming.

Ron Silver is quiet, self-effacing Herman Broder, a middle-class Polish Jewish intellectual who survived the Holocaust by hiding in a hayloft for three years; Yadwiga (Margaret Sophie Stein), a Gentile peasant who had been a servant in his family, risked her life to take care of him. When the war was over and he learned that his wife and children were dead, he married the sweet goose Yadwiga out of gratitude (and maybe a little lust) and brought her to New York with him. Now it's 1949. Herman and his devoted slavey Yadwiga live in Brooklyn, with a window overlooking the Wonder Wheel at Coney Island. He works as a ghostwriter, turning out sermons and books for a celebrity-lecturer rabbi, but he tells his wife he's a book sales-man; that gives him an excuse to be away from home. He keeps another res-idence, in the Bronx, with his hot-tempered mistress, Masha (Lena Olin), a survivor of the camps. Herman lives in fear; he's still hiding. But when he makes love to Masha he forgets the terrors of the past. It's the only time he forgets.

Herman invents dangers, and not only because he's anxiously trying to cover up his double domestic arrangements. The guardedness, the secrecy, the guile are all necessary to him; they're his strategy for survival. He was furtive even before he was traumatized by the Holocaust. It's part of Herman's passive nature to lie, rather than to risk showdowns. He can't make decisions; they have to be forced on him. He doesn't even initiate the almost constant sexual activity he's involved in; women keep jumping his bones, and he acquiesces. He doesn't want to give up his shining-eyed, pug-nosed Yadwiga, who looks after him as if he were a lord, and he certainly doesn't want to give up the wild, teasing Masha, whose sexy voice is enough to fog his senses. When she thinks she's pregnant and threatens to leave him if she has to have an abortion, he marries her, too. And when his first wife, Tamara (Anjelica Huston), who was shot and left in a pile of corpses but dragged herself to safety, and has been in a camp in Russia, arrives on Manhattan's Lower East Side, he doesn't want to give her up, either. He would like to remain a trigamist. Who can blame him? Ron Silver makes Herman's predicament understandable. And Herman is understandably ter-rified of hurting anybody.

Herman conceals basic information about himself from the rabbi who employs him; he conceals different things from each of the three women. Then, at a lavish party given by the rabbi, Herman's worlds collide, and he's confused about what he's hidden from whom. It's a situation out of a classic boudoir farce, but Herman and his three wives—Tamara, the witchlike, se-ductive mother figure, with black-dyed hair; Yadwiga, the natural-blond child; Masha, the lover, with thick, dark, reddish hair—are not the characters we're accustomed to seeing in Frenchy bedrooms.

It's a central joke in the material that Herman and his Jewish wives, Ta-mara and Masha, who all suffered as Jews, are intellectually sophisticated nonbelievers but are emotionally half-believers. (They abuse God the Sadist, who put them in the hands of the Nazis.) The only practicing Jew is the sim-ple Yadwiga, who has become a convert in order to be a dutiful, pious wife to Herman and bear his child. Yadwiga and her efforts to be Jewish are a source of amusement to Tamara and Masha. (In a moment of stress, Yadwiga forgets herself, and makes the sign of the cross.) Tamara and Masha can't help being Jewish. For them, it's not a matter of religious faith; it's a matter of memories, and of being lost. In their nightmares, they're still in Poland. When they wake up, they're in limbo.

Anjelica Huston's Tamara feels dead because her children are dead (though they return in her dreams and that invigorates her); she's a strong, capable woman, with an erotic aura, an accented, Garboesque voice, and knowing, sidelong glances. She takes over a shop specializing in Judaica—books, ornaments, ritual artifacts—and she holds Herman's life together. Lena Olin's Masha, who lives with her hyper-emotional mother (Judith Malina), quarrelling and making up, both of them constantly in a state of nerves, is diabolically willful. She lives on tea, cigarettes, and liquor, and keeps Herman in torment with her hysterical threats that she'll go away and he'll never see her again. Masha is educated and smart, but she works as a cashier in a cafeteria; she has no connection with her job, her environment. She barely notices what country she's in, yet she lives intensely in the present, and pulls Herman into it with her. She's all id; she's part Angel of Death.

Ron Silver's owl-faced Herman, with his wise, sneaky expressions, may seem an unlikely pivot for this sex comedy—he doesn't quite have the spoiled-Jewish-prince narcissism to attract these women—but the more you see of him the funnier and more likely he becomes. Herman has fear and irony in his face, and you can read his thoughts, if you ever get around to noticing him. If you lift up the brim of his brown fedora, there it all is. This ghostwriter to a rabbi (he's also the ghost of the scholars he's descended from) may sometimes pray, but he only believes in lust and hiding. Singer puts it simply:

> At moments when Herman fantasized about a new metaphysic,
> or even a new religion, he based everything on the attraction of
> the sexes. In the beginning was lust.

And following close upon that is his obsessive, prurient hunt for evidence of sexual betrayal; he can't bear the possibility that any of his three wives has ever been unfaithful to him—he schemes and wheedles to find out.

There's no special pleading or self-pity in Mazursky's view of the characters—not even in his view of ghostly Herman. These refugees who go on living after they've died retain their petty follies in an exacerbated form. When Herman first sees Tamara after the gap of years in which their children have been slaughtered, he says, "I didn't know you were alive," and she complains, "You never knew." The movie is full of jokes, such as the moment in a subway station when Herman, who has been commuting to the rabbi's place and from one domicile to another, can't trust his instincts and has to pause before mounting the steps to Brooklyn, the Bronx, or Manhattan. Herman's love life is a map of poor-Jewish New York, and when he goes to the rabbi's apartment, on Central Park West, he climbs the social ladder. The loud, big-hearted rabbi (Alan King) is the picture of happy assimilation. He would like to help Herman make his way in the city; he doesn't understand that Herman is a Jewish Bartleby the Scrivener and can't be helped—he has to recede, fade away, flee.

The plot suggests a tragicomic opera, yet Mazursky's tone is even-tempered, restrained. There's nothing aseptic about this restraint—it has its own deeply crazy turmoil. But restraint is not what we've come to expect from Mazursky. He has always adored the show-biz tradition of turning your own emotionality into something brazenly entertaining. Here he's warm and sensual without being showy; he seems fulfilled. The characters go in circles, getting themselves into sex in order to forget other things and then waking up back where they were. Mazursky pulls the rug out from under us, and we drop through the farce.

The movie is richly satisfying; it's an act of homage to a world-class comedian with a dirty mind of genius. Singer himself is a ghost who writes: *Enemies,* which came out in English in 1972, was his first novel set in America, and was, of course, written in the ghost language Yiddish. The minor characters—Malina as Masha's mother, Mazursky as the husband Masha must get rid of in order to marry Herman, Phil Leeds as Pesheles, the gnomish blabbermouth who reveals Herman's secrets at the party—seem to have folk roots in Singer's world. And Lena Olin gives Masha a feverish urgency. Olin's Masha has lowdown prettiness and transcendent beauty. The performance is conceived with a different kind of verve from that of Olin's bowler-hatted Sabina in *The Unbearable Lightness of Being.* Masha gives in to her impulses like a Dostoyevski heroine. Singer sums her up:

> Masha was the best argument Herman knew for Schopenhauer's thesis that intelligence is nothing more than a servant of blind will.

That's exactly how Olin plays her. Masha, with her irrational intelligence, is heated and bold in a way that gives the movie the demonism it needs. She and Tamara are both glinting-eyed sirens, but Masha is Herman's chief sexual enemy. She justifies his need to hide. The soundtrack features klezmer—a band with a clarinet (played here by Giora Feidman), trumpets, a snare drum, a bass drum, and a guitar or balalaika, performing a type of medieval Jewish party music. The sound has a whirling, brassy plangency. It's plaintive yet pitiless—it goes with the Wonder Wheel and Masha's tarty walk.

The New Yorker, December 25, 1989

DRIVING MISS DAISY

The surprise of the director Bruce Beresford's movie of Alfred Uhry's much honored play *Driving Miss Daisy* is that it's been "opened up" just enough to satisfy our curiosity and make things seem natural, without impairing the structure—which is still a series of two-character sketches.

There are a few dead spots at the beginning, when the camera loiters in Miss Daisy's house and we seem to be asked to observe how quiet life was for the tasteful rich in Atlanta in 1948, but after ten minutes or so the film finds its rhythm, and the spacious house, with its fine woodwork and interior archways, becomes a character—it has a presence. (And it helps to make Miss Daisy's economic security palpable.) I prefer the movie to the stage version, which felt too mild and sincere and messagey; it's an ingratiating play about race relations—what the theatre had been waiting for. Uhry, who did the screen adaptation, seems to have pared away a little flab. And the movie, by bringing the characters close up, creates a stronger emotional involvement. The material is full of manipulative bits—it's virtually all manipulative bits—but Beresford understands how to work them while cutting down on their obviousness. He gives them a light, airy texture; he sets them in the sun.

Jessica Tandy is tightfisted, suspicious Daisy Werthan, a Jewish widow of seventy-two who's determined to do things her own way. She drives her own way, and wrecks her shiny new Chrysler. No insurance company will give her coverage, so her son, Boolie (Dan Aykroyd), who runs the cotton mill started by his father and grandfather, suggests she hire a chauffeur to drive her new Hudson. She has a black housekeeper (Esther Rolle), whom she's been pleased with for many years, but she's outraged at the idea of adding to her household: she doesn't want her privacy invaded, and she regards servants as probable thieves. Seeing her trapped in her house by her contrariness, Boolie disregards her wishes and hires a black chauffeur, Hoke Colburn (Morgan Freeman), a widower about a decade younger than she is. Boolie arranges to pay Hoke's salary (in order to block her claim that a chauffeur would be a waste of her money) and sends him over. But Boolie, a relaxed Jewish good-old-boy Southerner, plump and content, can't persuade his mother to accept the driver as part of her household. It's up to Hoke to win acceptance. And so we have the entertainment of watching the dignified, shrewd Hoke use all his wiles on this anxious, straight-backed old biddy, courting her day after day. At first, she ignores him; then she rebuffs him. She spurns his efforts to make himself useful about the house and the garden. He's deferent and patient, saying "Yes'm" when she puts him down. (He says other things under his breath.) And finally, after six days, his well-mannered persistence wins out. She lets him drive her to the Piggly Wiggly (and pecks at him every inch of the way). That's only the first step in her acceptance of his services; he goes on courting her for twenty-five years.

The movie is the story of the companionship that develops between these two: the thrifty former schoolteacher, who grew up poor and still sees herself as poor, and the illiterate, proud, handsome Hoke. Their story is touched by the changes in Southern life during the years they spend together; the movie ends in 1973, covering the time of the civil-rights movement, and that's more than incidental. But the two are not representative figures. The movie is essentially about how Hoke changes Miss Daisy. Their

1228

relationship becomes closer and deeper, and as she ages and becomes more vulnerable and fearful she comes to accept him as her best friend.

The movie is really built. Uhry knows how to make the developments comic: he's got this huffy, ornery woman to play everything off. As Jessica Tandy's Miss Daisy becomes older and more dependent on Hoke, she seems to undergo a spiritual transformation: her skin becomes translucent, she looks poetically frail. But she doesn't go soft: she's as sharp-tongued and bossy as ever. I've seen Jessica Tandy in many movies, going back to her American début, in 1944, in *The Seventh Cross,* and she has never been as lovely and varied as she is here, at eighty, playing Miss Daisy, from seventy-two to ninety-seven. She's more subtly comic now, and she risks more; the very old Miss Daisy has the grin of a gamine. The role (based on Uhry's grandmother, with a few great-aunts thrown in) gives her a chance to show glimpses of what she's learned in a lifetime of acting, and she has the simple assurance to hold us in her palm. It's a crowning performance; Miss Daisy is convincingly likable and impossible.

As Daisy's son, Dan Aykroyd sounds more Southern than she does, and this feels right. By temperament she's not a relaxed drawler, like Boolie; she speaks like the prim schoolmarm she was. Aykroyd's Boolie is a man of great forbearance: he has to be, to get along with his mother and with his social-climbing, fanny-twitching wife, Florine (Patti LuPone, in a vital, funny caricature). Boolie is an easygoing onlooker; he enjoys watching Hoke break down his mother's stubbornness. This may be the first time Aykroyd has stayed within the limits of a screen character that wasn't shaped for his crazy-galoot style of comedy, and, with the help of a first-rate aging specialist, who thickens him, he handles the twenty-five-year span like a veteran charmer. He's quite wonderful as the humorous, unheroic Boolie; maybe the company he was in inspired him.

Morgan Freeman is a master of irony. The role of Hoke isn't written with the fullness that went into Daisy; chances are that Uhry didn't get to observe as many sides of his grandmother's chaffeur (on whom the character is modelled). But the Memphis-born Freeman—the one Southerner of the three (Tandy is from London, Aykroyd from Canada)—fills in the character from what he knows of Southern blacks' verbal styles of accommodation and of self-amusement. Tandy partners him flawlessly; their performances achieve a beautiful equilibrium. But it's his movie. We identify with Hoke—with his carefulness, his reserve. We feel the slight tension in his not being able to express himself directly. The speed and power that Freeman has shown in other roles are kept out of sight here; instead we get the low, resonant voice (with high notes when he's harried), the inflections of his "Yes'm," and wit in every line of his body. He's playing the most courtly and dependable of black servants of an earlier era, yet he keeps us aware that this man is never servile; Hoke is always measuring the distance between white Southerners and himself.

When Hoke has his job interview with Boolie, he tells him that he likes working for Jewish people, and gradually we see why. Miss Daisy is stiffly defensive on race issues; she claims to be free of prejudice. But she frequently senses her own vulnerability to insult, and she feels a bond with Hoke. (She detests her daughter-in-law, who doesn't know how to treat servants—i.e., doesn't understand what's due them.) The movie is about the love between blacks and whites (Jewish division) at a time when a wealthy Southern Jewish matron plays mahjongg, is addressed by her servants as Miss Daisy, and eats alone in the dining room even after she has become an advocate of civil rights. It's a time when a man like Hoke goes on weighing his words to the end of his days.

The movie gives us an insight into the author's background that we didn't get from the play, but it's still a rigged view of the past. The black man is made upright, considerate, human—he's made perfect—so that nothing will disturb our appreciation of the gentle, bittersweet reverie we're watching. Yet there's a memorable unstressed moment when the radio in the sunny house carries the sound of Gabriela Benackova singing the numinous "Song to the Moon," from Dvořák's opera *Rusalka,* and we get a sense of how lonely and empty Miss Daisy's life is. And, after the housekeeper dies (at work in the kitchen) Miss Daisy, Boolie, and Hoke sit together on a bench at the funeral; they listen to Indra A. Thomas and the Little Friendship Missionary Baptist Church Choir (of Decatur, Georgia), and maybe they're thinking, like you, that it's worth dying to have singing like that. The bursting forth of sensuality in that church, while Miss Daisy sits pale and pinched, is part of the (blessedly) unspoken meaning of the movie. *Driving Miss Daisy* retains its coziness and its slightness, but it has been filmed eloquently.

The New Yorker, December 25, 1989

BORN ON THE FOURTH OF JULY
POTENCY

Ron Kovic (Tom Cruise), the hero of *Born on the Fourth of July,* believes everything he hears at the Independence Day ceremonies in Massapequa, Long Island. Pure of heart and patriotic, he trusts in Mom, the Catholic Church, and the flag-waving values John Wayne stands for. Ron thinks war is glamorous; it's how he'll prove himself a man. And so he joins the Marine Corps, goes to Vietnam, and is shocked to discover brutality, dirt, and horror.

It's almost inconceivable that Ron Kovic was as innocent as the movie and the 1976 autobiography on which it's based make him out to be. Was this kid kept in a bubble? At some level, everybody knows about the ugliness of war. Didn't he ever read anything on the Civil War—not even *The Red Badge of Courage?* When he was growing up, kids were into black humor, sarcasm, and put-ons. If he was as vulnerable to media influences as the movie and the book indicate, wouldn't he have heard of *Catch-22* and *One Flew Over the Cuckoo's Nest?* Wouldn't he have looked at *Mad?* Ron seems to have blotted out everything that didn't conform to his priggish views. When his younger brother is singing "The Times They Are A-Changin'," it doesn't mean anything to him.

Born on the Fourth of July, directed by Oliver Stone, who wrote the script with Kovic, is committed to the idea of Ron's total naïveté. He's presented as a credulous boy whose country lied to him. Wherever you look in this movie, people are representative figures rather than people, and the falseness starts during the opening credits, with the dusty, emotionally charged Fourth of July celebration in 1956—Ronnie's tenth birthday. Massapequa is less than an hour from New York City on the Long Island Rail Road, but this set (constructed in Texas) looks like Oliver Stone's vision of Midwestern America in the fifties—clapboard picturesque. He uses slow motion to mythologize the drum majorettes. Even the kids' baseball game is a slo-mo elegy. A lyrical glow fuses sports and kids playing soldier and civic boosterism and imperialism. And John Williams' music is like a tidal wave. It comes beating down on you while you're trying to duck Robert Richardson's frenzied camera angles. So much rapture, so soon. I was suffering from pastoral overload before the credits were finished.

Of course Ronnie's country lied to him. Part of growing up is developing a bullshit detector, and kids usually do a pretty fair job of wising each other up. Ron Kovic's Candide-like innocence matches that hazy archetypal parade: they're both fantasies. But they make it easier for him (and the movie) to blame everybody for not stopping him when he wanted to be a hero. To Ron, the Marine recruiter (Tom Berenger) who comes to the Massapequa high school is like a god. Ron's virginal high-mindedness makes him the perfect patsy for a before-and-after movie. What's in between is Vietnam and the rise of the antiwar movement.

On Ron Kovic's second tour of duty, in 1968, when he was a twenty-one-year-old sergeant, his spine was severed, and he was left paralyzed from the chest down. The movie is a scream of rage at how he was betrayed, mutilated, neglected; it's also an uplifting account of how he boozed, quarrelled with everyone, and despaired until he stopped being contemptuous of the war protesters and became active in Vietnam Veterans Against the War. Kovic's book is simple and explicit; he states his case in plain, angry words. Stone's movie yells at you for two hours and twenty-five minutes. Stone tells you and he shows you at the same time; everything is swollen with meaning. The movie is constructed as a series of blackout episodes that suggest the Stations of the Cross; rising strings alert you to the heavy stuff. Then the finale—Resurrection—takes Ron into white light, and John Williams lays on the trumpets.

The central question that's raised is "Why did you tell me lies about what war would be like?" It's not "Why did you tell me lies about what the Vietnam War was about?"—although it shifts into that at times. Stone's most celebrated film, *Platoon*, culminated in the young hero's shooting the man who represented evil, but *Born on the Fourth of July* appears to be a pacifist movie, an indictment of all war, along the lines of Dalton Trumbo's 1939 protest novel *Johnny Got His Gun*. You can't be sure, because there's never a sequence where Ron figures out the war is wrong; we simply see him go from personal bitterness to a new faith. The morality of taking up arms in Vietnam (or anywhere else) isn't really what the movie is about anyway. The audience is carried along by Tom Cruise's Ronnie yelling that his penis will never be hard again. The core of the movie is Ron's emotional need to make people acknowledge what he has lost. There's a shrill, demanding child inside the activist—a child whose claims we can't deny. And Stone's visual rant slips by because this kid's outrage at losing his potency is more graphic and real to us than anything else. It affects us in a cruder, deeper way than Ron's sloganeering and his political denunciations of the war.

What we hear when Ron causes a commotion at the 1972 Republican Convention and shouts at Nixon is a kid who knows he has lost something and who is going to make an unholy fuss about it. He's going to be heard. Yes, he's expressing the rage of other disabled veterans who feel betrayed—wasted in a war we shouldn't have got into. But what really reaches us is that Ron finds his lost potency when the Convention cameras are on him. He finds it in forcing the country to recognize what it did to him and others like him. He's saying, "You owe me this," or, "Activism is all you've left me, and you can't take it away." And he's saying, "I paid for what I did over there, and I go on paying for it. You haven't paid—your shame is greater." He doesn't really say that, but it's what filmgoers hear and respond to. The movie, having presented him as the innocent Catholic boy going to war for the glory of God, now reaps the reward: the audience—some of the audience—experiences a breast-beating catharsis.

Almost everything else in this antiwar Fourth of July parade that spans twenty years is chaotic sensationalism. When Ron, in an argument with his mother, drunkenly pulls out his catheter and says, "It's what I've got instead of a penis," and she shrieks, "Don't say 'penis' in this house!" she becomes a comic-strip uptight mom. And when he gets back at her by yelling "Penis! Penis!" at the top of his lungs, so the whole neighborhood can hear him, it's a phony, easy scene. We're supposed to see that his mother denies the realities of war and every other kind of reality—that this repressive mom who told him the Communists had to be stopped was part of the system that deluded him. We're invited to jeer at her villainy.

A scraping-bottom scene that takes place on a roadside in the Mexican desert has a druggy, *El Topo* flavor. The burned-out, drunken Kovic brawls with another burned-out, drunken paraplegic (Willem Dafoe), and they spit in each other's faces, knock each other out of their wheelchairs, and go on wrestling. The two men, fighting over which one takes the prize for committing the worst atrocities in Vietnam, are like bugs screaming in the sand; they're right out of the theatre of the absurd—they've even got dry, rattlesnake sounds for accompaniment—and you have to laugh. But it's too showy, too style-conscious; it makes you aware of how overblown the whole movie is.

In Vietnam, Ron's platoon, thinking they're attacking Vietcong, massacre a group of village women and children. Then, during the confusion of a skirmish, Ron kills a nineteen-year-old soldier from Georgia, but can't fully accept it—it happened so fast. He tells his major about it, and the major doesn't want to hear it; he doesn't know how to handle Ron's confession, so Ron is stuck with the sickening guilt. After Ron is paralyzed and in a wheelchair, he makes a trip to Georgia to confess to the soldier's parents and young widow. That may relieve Ron's pain, but what about the pain he causes the others? (The father had been proud of the honor guard that came with the body.) The scene might be affecting if it were staged to show that Ron's need is so overpowering he can't consider the family's grief. Instead, it suggests that Stone thinks even blind self-expression is good. (In the book, there's no visit to Georgia. Maybe the trip took place, and Kovic left it out. But I remember the scene from an earlier movie, where after the war the protagonist went to the dead soldier's family and asked forgiveness; there, though, the dead soldier was part of the enemy forces, and the protagonist was offering the family solace.)

Oliver Stone has an instinct for the symbolism that stirs the public. He clung to the Ron Kovic story that he first worked on as a screenwriter more than ten years ago. But he must never have been able to think the material through. *Born on the Fourth of July* seems to ride on its own surface, as if moviemaking were a form of surfing. Kovic doesn't turn against the Vietnam War until long after he gets home, expecting to be welcomed as a hero, and is put in the rat-infested Bronx Veterans Hospital. What would have happened if people had been considerate and kind to Ron, and talked up his bravery? Would he have gone on being a war-mongering patriot? I didn't expect the movie to answer this kind of question, but I expected it to show enough about Ron's character for us to make some guesses for ourselves. We come out knowing nothing about him except that his self-righteousness—his will to complain and make a ruckus—is rather glorious. I don't think I've ever seen another epic about a bad loser; I wish Stone had recognized what he was on to, and shaped the conception. (In essence, *Born* is satire played straight. The impotent Ron Kovic holds the nation hostage.)

How is Tom Cruise? I forgot he was there. Cruise is on magazine covers. Of course he is—he's a cute kid and his face sells magazines. And magazine editors may justify their cover stories by claiming he's turning into a terrific actor. They may believe it, and moviegoers may assent. Moviegoers like to believe that those they have made stars are great actors. People used to say that Gary Cooper was a fine actor—probably because when they looked in his face they were ready to give him their power of attorney. Cruise has the right All-American-boy look for his role here, but you wait for something to emerge, and realize the look goes all the way through. He has a little-boy voice and no depth of emotion. (In Vietnam, when Ron barks orders to his squad there's no authority in his tone; he still has no authority when he goes in to speak, by invitation, at the Democratic Convention in 1976.) Cruise does have a manic streak, and Stone uses it for hysteria. (He might be a tennis pro falling to his knees and throwing his fists up in the air.) Cruise gets through Stone's noisy Stations of the Cross without disgracing himself, but he's negligible. Nothing he does is unexpected. He's likable in his boyish, quieter moments, but when those are over he disappears inside Ron Kovic's receding hairline, Fu Manchu mustache, and long, matted hair.

Oliver Stone has a taste for blood and fire, and for the anguish and disillusionment that follow. Everything is in capital letters. He flatters the audience with the myth that we believed in the war and then we woke up; like Ron Kovic, we're turned into generic Eagle Scouts. The counterculture is presented in a nostalgic, aesthetically reactionary way; it's made part of our certified popular memories. *Born on the Fourth of July* is like one of those commemorative issues of *Life*—this one covers 1956 to 1976. Stone plays bumper cars with the camera and uses cutting to jam you into the action, and you can't even enjoy his uncouthness, because it's put at the service of sanctimony.

The New Yorker, January 22, 1990

GOODFELLAS
TUMESCENCE AS STYLE

Martin Scorsese's *GoodFellas* has a lift. It's like *Raging Bull*, except that it's not domineering. It's like *Raging Bull* made in a jolly, festive frame of mind. It's about being a guy and guys getting high on being a guy. In the Nicholas Pileggi book *Wiseguy*, which this movie is based on, the Mafia-led mobsters are moral runts—and that was the joke of how John Huston showed them, from the Don on down, in *Prizzi's Honor*. But Scorsese, a rap artist keeping up the heat, doesn't go in for ironic detachment. He loves the Brooklyn gang milieu, because it's where distortion, hyperbole, and exuberance all commingle. His mobsters are high on having a wad of cash in their pockets. The movie is about being cock of the walk, with banners flying and crowds cheering.

Is it a great movie? I don't think so. But it's a triumphant piece of filmmaking—journalism presented with the brio of drama. Every frame is active and vivid, and you can feel the director's passionate delight in making these pictures move. When Henry Hill (Ray Liotta), the central character, crosses a Long Island street to beat up the man who tried to put the make on his girl, the dogwood is in bloom, and all through this movie we're aware of the ultra-greenness of the suburbs that the gangsters live in; these thieves are always negotiating their way through shrubs and hedges. Or they're preparing food, ceremonially, gregariously—stirring vats of sauce, slicing garlic razor thin. We see them in bars and restaurants, where they take preferential treatment as their due, and in the tacky interiors of their noisy homes. We see them hijacking, fencing stolen goods, fixing horse races, shaking down restaurant owners, committing arson, preparing cargo thefts at the airport, burying murder victims. And the different aspects of their lives are like operatic motifs.

What's missing? Well, there are no great voices. The script, by Pileggi and Scorsese, isn't really dramatized; instead, Scorsese raises the volume on the music, and the guys work themselves up, get hard, erupt. This isn't the kind of mindless movie that offers up brutality as entertainment, with good guys versus bad guys. Scorsese offers up brutal racketeering and says this is all there is to these men. Scorsese's Jake La Motta could do one thing: fight. These guys can do one thing: steal.

The book is an account of the life of the actual Henry Hill, as he told it to Pileggi after he entered the Federal Witness Protection Program, and the movie picks up his story in 1955, with the obliging eleven-year-old kid, half-Irish, half-Sicilian, working as an errand boy at the cabstand hangout of the Brooklyn neighborhood gang headed by Paulie (Paul Sorvino). As the gang's pet, Henry gets the approval he wants and plenty of spending money; by the time he's fourteen, he's on the payroll of a construction company and knows the ins and outs of the rackets. In the years ahead, crime is a romp for him. He gets a real charge out of pulling scams side by side with his older pals, Jimmy (Robert De Niro) and Tommy (Joe Pesci), and when he takes his Jewish girlfriend, Karen (Lorraine Bracco) to flashy, expensive places he hands out big tips and is greeted as a celebrity. (He's twenty-one.) Karen, who's no bimbo (she has a sense of her worth), likes the danger that emanates from him. His life has the look of a Puerto Rican Day parade crossed with a rock concert; she's excited when she sees his gun (the gun he slugged his rival with). In *Raging Bull,* the young male tries to ram his way through a brick wall; in *GoodFellas,* the young male finds a welcoming warm spot, first with Paulie and the gang, and soon with Jimmy and Tommy, and then with his wife—Karen—and a couple of kids, and a mistress set up in an apartment.

It's a little off key when Henry reacts to Tommy and Jimmy's acts of violence with puzzled revulsion. During a card game, Joe Pesci's Tommy, clowning around, shoots a teenager who's slow to serve him a drink. Incidents like this—they're terrifically well framed—appear to be pointing toward an awakening sensibility in Henry, but nothing comes of them, so they seem perfunctory, a sop to conventionality. (De Niro has a scene where he goes berserk, and that doesn't develop into anything, either.)

The movie's underpinnings could have been linked together: they suggest that the Mafia and other organized-crime gangs are continually being destroyed from within by raw male lawlessness. De Niro's Jimmy brings off the theft of a lifetime—the six-million-dollar Lufthansa heist, until then the biggest cash robbery in United States history—but he can't control his troops; they're so undisciplined, such small-timers at heart, that they start spending ostentatiously, and paranoiac Jimmy, who wants to keep all the dough anyway, takes it as a regretful necessity that he has to whack them—i.e., bump them off. (There were at least ten murders after the successful robbery.) Paulie has strict rules against drugs, because drugs turn men into informers who destroy the "family." But the family doesn't have the decency (or forethought) to support the wives and children of the men who are sent to prison, so when Henry is sent up, Karen becomes his partner, smuggling him dope that he deals inside—it's like a regular franchise. And he begins snorting cocaine. (The movie is about how swindling makes you feel alive, and that's what cocaine can keep you feeling.) By the time Henry is out of prison and is running a dealership from his Long Island home, he's a manic wreck, ready to sell out his mentor, Paulie, and every hood he knows. And he feels justified, because his closest pal, Jimmy, is ready to whack him and his wife, too.

But Scorsese doesn't weight the incidents dramatically; he leaves the themes, and even the story, lying there inert. In a hurried, not very shapely concluding sequence he ties up some threads and tells us about a few of the characters in final titles—omitting, though, a high-comic piece of information: Hill was so determinedly crooked he used the new identity given him by the Witness Protection Program to start up a new life of thievery and was thrown out of the program. But then we've learned so little about him. It's startling to read the title telling us that Henry and Karen separated after twenty-five years, because we realize we don't have any knowledge of what kept them together so long. The picture has scope rather than depth. We see Henry Hill only from the outside, and he has been made to seem slightly cut off from the mob life. He has been turned into a retread of the anxious, dutiful Harvey Keitel character in *Mean Streets*, when he needs to be a rat and the motor of the movie. *GoodFellas* is like the Howard Hawks *Scarface* without Scarface.

Paul Sorvino's Paulie comes through; reluctant to move his bulk, he basks in his power quietly, and never calls attention to himself. Though Lorraine Bracco's Karen doesn't get much screen time, she has a hot, bright vitality; she seems more sexual, more full of go, than her husband. She's in love with him even when she pulls a gun on him. And some of the minor players give the movie a frenzied, funny texture. Tony Darrow is comically desperate as a restaurant owner who's so exhausted by the mob's harassment that he pleads with Paulie to accept a partnership in the business.

Welker White brings a nip of assertiveness to her scenes as a Waspy drug courier who has to have her lucky hat to make a coke delivery. And all the mobsters and hangers-on and their women seem to belong to their settings. It's just the three major hoods, played by Liotta, De Niro, and Pesci, who don't have a strong enough presence.

Scorsese had a great critical success with *Raging Bull* (1980), selected by international polls of critics as the best film of the eighties—a picture in which he presented his central character as an icon of brutishness. This time, he wants the central characters to be realistically shallow. But what flattens the movie isn't that they're shallow sociopaths; it's that these sociopaths are conceived shallowly, the way they used to be in B pictures. (It wasn't just the low budgets that were evoked by the term "B picture"; it was also the unmemorable characters.) When Henry Hill is a child, he lives across the street from the Mafia cabstand and observes the sporty life of racketeers as they get in and out of limos; he wants to make it big like them. The life he watches is like the images on movie screens that Scorsese and the rest of us watched, but we're not invited to identify with his longings.

An actor can play a shallow hood and still be memorable if we're drawn in to understand the hood's motives and emotions. (Bogart used to take us pretty deeply into hoods.) But these actors seem too old for their parts, too settled in. They get to us only in isolated scary scenes: Pesci's Tommy demanding "What do you mean, I'm funny?," De Niro's Jimmy wearing an unnatural smile as he waves Karen into what might be a death trap.

Yet the moviemaking has such bravura that you respond as if you were at a live performance. It's Scorsese's performance. He came of age as a director in the early seventies, at a time when many film enthusiasts were caught up in the sixties idea that a good movie is always about its director. There's a streak of metaphoric truth in this, but here Scorsese puts the idea right up front.

The filmmaking process becomes the subject of the movie. All you want to talk about is the glorious whizzing camera, the freeze-frames and jump cuts. That may be why young film enthusiasts are so turned on by Scorsese's work: they don't just respond to his films, they want to be him. When Orson Welles made *Touch of Evil,* the filmmaking process just about took over—the movie was one flourish after another. But that was 1958, and making a thriller about your own wallowing love of the film medium was a thrilling stunt. And Welles didn't drain the characters; rather, he made them more baroque, to match his flourishes. He filled the screen with stars. In 1990, when a movie spans thirty years and runs to epic length, we may miss what big characters can do—what Nick Nolte's sly Lionel Dobie did for Scorsese's *Life Lessons,* in *New York Stories,* drawing everything together.

Scorsese the arousal junkie makes you feel you'd like to hang out with him and listen to him tell how he brought off the effects; he's a master. But this picture doesn't have the juice and richness that come with major performances. It has no arc, and doesn't climax; it just comes to a stop. Conceivably the abruptness could work, but I don't think it does. Will the lift of the moviemaking still carry some people aloft? Maybe, because watching the movie is like getting strung out on pure sensation. That's Scorsese's idea of a hood's life. It's also a young film enthusiast's dream of a director's life, and in Scorsese's case it's not far from the truth.

The New Yorker, September 24, 1990

ABOUT MERYL STREEP IN

POSTCARDS FROM THE EDGE

Meryl Streep just about always seems miscast. (She makes a career out of seeming to overcome being miscast.) In *Postcards from the Edge*, she's witty and resourceful, yet every expression is eerily off, not quite human. When she sings in a country-and-Western style, she's note-perfect, but it's like a diva singing jazz—you don't believe it. Streep has a genius for mimicry: she's imitating a country-and-Western singer singing. These were my musings to a friend, who put it more simply: "She's an android." Yes, and it's Streep's android quality that gives *Postcards* whatever interest it has.

This tale of a sorrowful, wisecracking starlet whose brassy, boozing former-star mother (Shirley MacLaine) started her on sleeping pills when she was nine is camp without the zest of camp. It's camp played borderline straight—a druggy-Cinderella movie about an unformed girl who has to go past despair to find herself. The director, Mike Nichols, is a parodist who feigns sincerity, and his tone keeps slipping around. What's clear is that we're meant to adore the daughter, who is wounded by her mother's cheap competitiveness. Nichols wants us to be enthralled by the daughter's radiant face, her refinement, her honesty. He keeps the camera on Streep as if to prove that he can make her a popular big star—a new Crawford or Bette Davis. (She remains distant, emotionally atonal.)

The New Yorker, October 22, 1990

THE GRIFTERS

Anjelica Huston has a mysterious presence. You can't tell what its sources are, but it seems related to the economy of her acting. In *Prizzi's Honor,* she used her Brooklyn accent to open up the character; in *Enemies, A Love Story,* the suggestion of pain gave force to each thing she did, especially when she made the pain comic. Huston is already past the age at which Garbo retired, and there's nothing youthful about her—but then there never was. (There wasn't much that was youthful about Garbo, either; being considered ageless often means looking older than you are.) Huston doesn't flaunt her androgyny or seem ashamed of it. Agelessness and androgyny are simply among her attributes. She's overpoweringly sexual; young men might find her frightening.

That makes casting her as Lilly Dillon in *The Grifters* an intuitive sneaky-right decision, because the core of the story is the refusal of Lilly's son, Roy (John Cusack), to have anything to do with her. He's paying her back. In his childhood, she was cold and miserly; she withheld any kindness. Now that he's twenty-five and has been on his own since he was seventeen, she shows up. Lilly is tough and she's seductive; she's the dominatrix as mother, and he's afraid of her getting her hooks in him.

The Grifters is based on one of the punchier pulp novels by Jim Thompson—a bitter, somewhat repellent book with a misanthropic integrity. Published in 1963, it's about three scam artists (Lilly, Roy, and Roy's bubbly bedmate Moira, played by Annette Bening)—people who never got a break and don't give anybody else a break. Each of these chisellers has his or her own methods and agenda; there's no yielding by any of them (and no redemption). The film retains Thompson's hardboiled pitilessness, and a tension is created by placing these fifties or early sixties characters in nineties L.A. locations; we feel piqued, jazzed up. Toying with L.A. film noir, the director, Stephen Frears, and the scriptwriter, Donald E. Westlake, do twisted, anomalous things. The Elmer Bernstein score tries for a tart, sour Kurt Weill effect, and doesn't quite bring it off, but Westlake keeps some of Thompson's slangy, compact dialogue and adds his own, which has a madcap edge. The movie starts with comic capers, then uses Thompson's class resentment and grim hopelessness to smack us with discord. We're watching a form of cabaret.

This criminal subculture doesn't come equipped with a detective as moral explorer. It's a void, where Roy, who holds a salesman's job as a cover, lives alone by rules he has devised for himself. A cautious, hard-eyed practitioner of the "short con"—fleecing cashiers by getting change for a twenty and slipping them a ten, or playing craps with trick dice—he doesn't have to worry about doing time in prison. Roy has repressed any signs of an identifiable personality, and he does nothing to attract attention; he won't let himself have friends—that's being a sucker. He makes himself colorless, and socks his money away. It's a horrible, grubby life—a mole's life—and he's an intelligent, handsome kid, who could have gone to college, who could have lived among people. It's his angry touchiness about his young mother (she was only fourteen when she had him) that keeps him in his miserable isolation. He's getting even with her by throwing his life away.

Frears introduces the three characters (in the sections of a vertically divided triple screen) as they arrive at the places where they're about to do their grifts. Each of the three is putting on the face that he or she presents to the world. We're formally meeting three false fronts. It's Lilly's dream that her son will go straight and be a loving comfort to her, but she herself works for the Baltimore syndicate: she travels, placing bets at the tracks. Annette Bening's Moira* is a sex fantasy come to luscious life. She's irrepressible—a real tootsie—and it takes a while for her adorable, kittenish perversity to make you apprehensive. Moira the smiler has been trained in big cons—scams that rake in bundles of money but can also land you in prison—and she's out to make Roy her partner. Roy likes Moira in his bed, but he was jerked around by his mother and he's not about to get jerked around again. He hates feeling that people might want to make something of him; he's not interested in becoming anything. Cusack suggests that Roy is cocky enough to think that he's something already, that he's living on his own terms.

Roy turns both women down, but he's an innocent compared with these two blondes—the killer mom and the tease—who are close to the same age. (It's perfect that Cusack gives his most memorable line reading to the word "Mom.") The two women battle over Roy's essence—the money that's hidden in the clown paintings in his apartment. In the structure of the film, it's Roy who's the clown.

There's nothing to fill out in a Jim Thompson novel; there's no room for characterization. It's socially conscious thin stuff. The three are stuck. You grasp the limits of what's available to them and how hard their dreams hit those limits, and you see them try to break through by using each other. Frears and Westlake are smart enough not to attempt to make a big thing of it. They keep it snappy, and heighten the sexual electricity.

Bening's two-faced little-girl quality is dazzling—just what film noir thrives on. When Moira blames Lilly for Roy's rejecting her proposition and turns treacherous, Bening makes the shift convincing; she's a stunning actress and a superb wiggler. And film noir is enriched by two competing femmes fatales. Huston's power as Lilly is astounding. This actress generally plays tightly controlled characters. (Her Gretta Conroy in *The Dead* was an exception.) Lilly is usually peremptory, displaying the authority of a woman who has worked for big-time mobsters for years; her whole existence is based on manipulation and control. She's a thief trying to outwit the thieves she works for. When she isn't sure she's succeeding, we can read the terror under the control. She's like a trapped animal when her boss (Pat Hingle), who thinks she has tricked him, shows up to punish her. Hingle, sucking on a big cigar, is chilling; as the power m.c. pulling the strings, he gives what's probably his best performance ever, and Huston matches him. The scene has a jangle; it's *Cabaret* moved from Berlin to L.A.

Actors are con artists, and our entertainment is in watching them get away with things. When Lilly, at the close, comes down in the elevator at

*In the movie, it's pronounced Myra.

Roy's apartment hotel, you may be reminded of Mary Astor in the elevator at the close of John Huston's *The Maltese Falcon,* and when, a little before that, Lilly pulls a maneuver on her son that's just about the ultimate con, you may recall John Huston in *Chinatown* saying, "Most people never have to face that at the right time and right place, they're capable of anything."

The leading characters' acceptance of brutality in Martin Scorsese's *GoodFellas* fails to scare us, and it doesn't haunt us afterward—perhaps it isn't meant to. But by the end of *The Grifters* (which Scorsese produced) Lilly's ruthless amorality is shocking—it has weight—and I think that's because Anjelica Huston is willing to be taken as monstrous; she contains this possibility as part of what she is. And when Lilly shows her willingness to do anything to survive she's a great character. At the end of John Huston's *The Treasure of the Sierra Madre,* the fortune is dispersed to the winds; here it's gathered up. Anjelica Huston's Lilly bites right through the film-noir pulp; the scene is paralyzing, and it won't go away.

The New Yorker, November 19, 1990

VINCENT & THEO

In *Vincent & Theo,* Vincent (Tim Roth) is slight, and has carrot-colored hair, jagged teeth, and workman's clothes smeared with paint; his tall, dark younger brother, the art dealer Theo (Paul Rhys), is turned out like a bourgeois aesthete. But when they're together and flare up, their words burst out impatiently, spasmodically. They have similar temperaments and a helpless inability to be calm and rational with each other. The director, Robert Altman, and the screenwriter, Julian Mitchell, know that we have some understanding of the basic Vincent van Gogh life story—the loneliness, the self-mutilation, the early death. What they've given us is an interpretation of the bond between the brothers—the bond that helps to keep Vincent alive while it tears Theo apart.

Vincent is obsessive about his painting; Theo is obsessive about Vincent and about his own inability to sell Vincent's work and help him—he can give him only a pittance. When Theo gets the telegram from Arles telling him that Vincent has cut off his earlobe, he takes a minute to be sick and then goes to him. In Arles, he touches the words that Vincent has written on the wall of his house: "I am the holy spirit. I am whole in spirit." Theo fits his hand flat against the handprint Vincent has left on the wall, and we know that Theo will never be whole in spirit.

At the hospital, Theo takes Vincent's hand. As he sits there bowed down, Vincent cops a look at him, and there's a suggestion that Vincent is checking to gauge the depth of Theo's agony. When Theo returns to Paris, his wife, meaning to comfort him, reaches for his hand; he pulls it away, refusing solace. Ill with syphilis, he has some of Vincent's reckless urgency; it's at war with his efforts to make an elegant conventional life for himself and his wife.

The two brothers' names hand-printed on top of swirls of thick ochre paint form the opening title, and then there's a flash-forward to the auction at Christie's where "Sunflowers" is sold for forty million dollars. This is the movie's taking-off place: an irony too obvious to be satirical and too obvious to be ignored. The film looks at it straight on. The auction is a union of the worlds the brothers are trapped in, a culmination of their yearnings and frustrations. Throughout the picture, Altman crosscuts between Theo's attempt to function as a businessman dealer and Vincent's plunging further into sun and light and crying out for the companionship he needs to stabilize him.

It has become standard practice to disparage Vincente Minnelli's 1956 *Lust for Life,* with Kirk Douglas as Vincent—principally, maybe, because it's a big Hollywood production. But it's an honorable big production, and Douglas and, in the relatively small part of Theo, James Donald are far from contemptible. What dates it is that Minnelli, following the dramatic conventions of his period, lays everything out for us, and, desperate not to be cheap or overblown, he's somewhat pedestrian. The Altman film is emotionally direct. When we first see Tim Roth's Vincent, he's lying on top of his bedcovers. The scene might be a still-life until he blinks and makes sudden, jerky movements with his pipe, moving it from his mouth to his hand and back again; Theo is in the room talking to him (about money, as always), and Vincent's reactions to him are so lightninglike they're almost subliminal. The brothers are inside each other's heads, and we have an extreme degree of empathy with Vincent. Without any overt "acting," Roth's Vincent simply gets to us, and we understand how he gets to Theo. Roth's acting is a form of kinetic discharge. It's 1879, and this is Vincent van Gogh taunting Theo with the announcement "I'm going to be a painter. What do you think of that?" Yet it's as if he were someone we'd grown up with—a self-amused, deracinated boy whose crooked, toothy smile drew us to him though he'd always alarmed us a little.

In the years that the movie spans—van Gogh's life as a painter, from 1879 to 1890—Vincent studies draftsmanship and tries to make the art scene, but he begins to be detached from the life going on around him. He takes part in it politely, but he's not there emotionally—he's only in his work. Vincent is a zealot about ways of seeing; then, as he becomes more isolated, his art becomes all about what he feels. And the film seems to pass beyond conventional sophistication and to see things from Vincent's point of view. Altman doesn't simply reproduce the scenes that van Gogh painted; rather, he brings out responses similar to the responses you have when you look at the paintings. He heads right for the sensuality, the intensity.

You feel that especially after Vincent has quarrelled with Paul Gauguin

(Wladimir Yordanoff): a field of sunflowers in the wind is like a sulfur storm overpowering the artist. The orchestral score, by Gabriel Yared, is soft and lyrical, but with an exciting overlay of electronic discord—of something deafening. Vincent smashes a canvas among the sunflowers—then uproots a few to take home. Whenever he's painting, he sticks his brushes in his mouth; now, carrying the storm back to his room, he licks the paint and muck off his table, finishes the last of his booze, and takes a swig of turpentine. He spits out a mouthful, cries out, and takes another swig. This time, he gets it down. His lifting a knife to his ear is just the next step. At the end of his life, you feel the way you do when someone you grew up with dies. You feel as you do coming out of O'Neill's *A Moon for the Misbegotten;* you know that the character couldn't go on any longer. Vincent ruptures the flesh; he ruptures the canvas.

Theo, who's all big, protruding eyes, can't go on much longer, either. Throughout, in the crosscut scenes, we've been steeped in his oppressive workplaces and cramped apartments. In one scene, he tiptoes among dozens of tiny, ornately framed pictures laid out on the floor. The walls, with patterned wallpapers (like Vuillard's) and paintings hung frame next to frame, always seem to be closing in. And when he rents a room to commemorate Vincent's paintings—an empty space where he's surrounded by them—and his wife, Jo (the remarkable young actress Johanna Ter Steege), and his brother-in-law (Hans Kesting) look at him as if he's lost his mind, he shuts the door on them. He has told them the truth—that this art is the most important thing in his life. With Vincent dead, it's clear that Vincent was what was pagan and alive in Theo. Alone, he crumples on the floor like a Schiele figure; he's got nothing left but his torment. The film moves from Theo in his shrine vanishing into Vincent's paintings to Theo naked in an institution vanishing into madness. (He survived Vincent by only six months.)

This double Passion-play movie is very different from the other Robert Altman movies (even allowing for how different they are from each other). The theme—the bitter entanglement of art and commerce—holds Altman in a vise of his choosing. He doesn't go at it glancingly here. This great theme is his lifelong theme, and, staying with it strictly in terms of the van Gogh brothers, he's able to release his own feelings about how an artist's frustrations lead him to acts of self-destructive fury—cutting off his ear to spite his face. It's a movie about two sensualists made by a sensualist, who understands that their bond of love of art is also a bond of shared rage at the world of commerce. Theo suddenly walks away from Vincent's funeral, where the glib, fatuous Dr. Gachet (Jean-Pierre Cassel)—a collector who keeps his paintings in a vault—is speaking; Theo can't listen to the pomposities an instant longer.

There isn't a high-flown minute in this movie. It has a simple, fluid tactility and a quick tempo. Julian Mitchell's dialogue is to the point, and the scenes aren't resolved; they're left just slightly askew. Near the beginning,

Vincent's prostitute-model Sien (Jip Wjingaarden) blows up at him because he goes on sketching her when she's on her break—when she isn't modelling, when she's herself. It's partly an issue of privacy, but it's also an issue of commerce; the breaks are *her* time. Vincent stops and apologizes, though it's when she is herself that she's a great subject. Perhaps he's just being politic. (Altman, famed for his spontaneity, his caught moments, allows for a faint ambiguousness.) Vincent takes the pregnant Sien and her small daughter to an exhibition of a three-hundred-and-sixty-degree painting, a diorama of a seascape that's like an ancestor of motion pictures, except that it's the spectators who move; the child goes into the seascape to pee. And there's a high-strung variation on the usual joyous repasts in the French countryside: Theo, Jo, Vincent, and others are gathered at Dr. Gachet's table listening to this self-congratulatory fellow shoot the breeze about Vincent's being cured and as sane as anybody. (When the Doctor is afraid that his daughter Marguerite, played by Bernadette Giraud, is becoming fond of Vincent, he says that Vincent is a hopeless case.)

Gauguin has an arrogant self-sufficiency that makes it clear he could never be the admiring friend Vincent longed for; Vincent was deluded about him. Vincent, trudging along with his backpack, has only Theo, and he obstinately pressures him, believing that Theo could sell his pictures if he just tried harder; he wants to believe that things are simpler than they are. After his experience with Gauguin, he gives up on humanity. But he still has flickering hopes. Like his brother, he's drawn to the wholesome, redemptive physicality of creamy-cheeked bourgeois women. Dr. Gachet's words about his condition close off this possibility.

This daring movie works on its own relentless, celebratory terms. The production design, by Stephen Altman (the director's son), and the cinematography, by Jean Lepine, are freshly thought out. With their help, the director gets images—such as the ones of Sien at the beach, staggering into the surf as she goes into labor—that have something comparable to the power of the paintings. Something devastating is achieved when Vincent in the wheat field where the crows are cawing sets a canvas on his easel. He draws a line on it, look toward what he's about to paint, but is too upset to make another mark, and enters the picture. The crows take wing.

The actors and the moviemakers have felt their way into the van Gogh passion and madness and come out with an austere movie. It doesn't flinch from the blunt banality of saying that there's no place for the artist's singleminded intensity in this commercial world. Which is true yet not quite true. Altman finds a sliver of an audience.

The New Yorker, November 19, 1990

DANCES WITH WOLVES

A friend of mine broke up with his woman friend after they went to see *Field of Dreams:* she liked it. As soon as I got home from *Dances with Wolves,* I ran to the phone and warned him not to go to it with his new woman friend. Set during the Civil War, this new big Indians-versus-Cavalry epic is about how the white men drove the Native Americans from their land. But Kevin Costner, who directed *Dances with Wolves* and stars in it, is not a man who lets himself be ripped apart by the violent cruelty of what happened. He's no extremist: it's a middle-of-the-road epic. Lieutenant Dunbar (Costner), a Union officer, sees that the Sioux have a superior culture—they're held up as models for the rest of us—and he changes sides. Costner must have heard Joseph Campbell on PBS advising people to "follow your bliss." This is a nature-boy movie, a kid's daydream of being an Indian. When Dunbar has become a Sioux named Dances with Wolves, he writes in his journal that he knows for the first time who he really is. Costner has feathers in his hair and feathers in his head.

Once our hero has become an Indian, we don't have to feel torn or divided. We can see that the white men are foulmouthed, dirty louts. The movie—Costner's début as a director—is childishly naïve. When Lieutenant Dunbar is alone with his pet wolf, he's like Robinson Crusoe on Mars. When he tries to get to know the Sioux, and he and they are feeling each other out, it's like a sci-fi film that has the hero trying to communicate with an alien race. But in this movie it's the white men who are the aliens: the smelly brutes are even killing each other, in the war between the North and the South. Luckily, we Indians are part of a harmonious community. Dances with Wolves has never seen people "so dedicated to their families." And he loves their humor.

At the beginning, there's a bizarre Civil War battle sequence with the wounded Lieutenant Dunbar riding on horseback between rows of Union and Confederate soldiers, his arms outstretched, welcoming bullets in a Christlike embrace, and throughout the movie he is brutalized, seems dead, but rises again. (Does getting beaten give Costner a self-righteous feeling? Even when it's as unconvincingly staged as it is here?) There's nothing really campy or shamelessly flamboyant after the opening. There isn't even anything with narrative power or bite to it. This Western is like a New Age social-studies lesson. It isn't really revisionist; it's the old stuff toned down and sensitized.

Costner and his friend Michael Blake, who worked up the material with him in mind and then wrote the novel and the screenplay, are full of good will. They're trying to show the last years of the Sioux as an independent nation from the Sioux point of view. And it's that sympathy for the Indians that (I think) the audience is responding to. But Costner and Blake are moviemaking novices. Instead of helping us understand the Sioux, they simply make the Sioux like genial versions of us. The film provides the groovy wisdom of the Sioux on the subjects of peace and togetherness: you never fight among yourselves—you negotiate. Each of the Indian characters is given a trait or two; they all come across as simpleminded, but so does the hero. Even the villains are endearingly dumb, the way they are in stories children write.

There's nothing affected about Costner's acting or directing. You hear his laid-back, surfer accent; you see his deliberate goofy faints and falls, and all the closeups of his handsomeness. This epic was made by a bland megalomaniac. (The Indians should have named him Plays with Camera.) You look at that untroubled face and know he can make everything lightweight. How is he as a director? Well, he has moments of competence. And the movie has an authentic vastness. The wide-screen cinematography, by Dean Semler, features the ridges, horizons, and golden sunsets of South Dakota; it's pictorial rather than emotionally expressive, but it's spacious and open at times, and there are fine images of buffalo pounding by.

Mostly, the action is sluggish and the scenes are poorly shaped. Crowds of moviegoers love the movie, though—maybe partly because the issues have been made so simple. As soon as you see the Indians, amused, watch the hero frolicking with his wolf, you know that the white men will kill it. Maybe, also, crowds love this epic because it's so innocent: Costner shows us his bare ass like a kid at camp feeling one with the great outdoors. He's the boyish man of the hour: the Sioux onscreen revere him, because he's heroic and modest, too. TV interviewers acclaim him for the same qualities. He's the Orson Welles that everybody wants—Orson Welles with no belly.

The New Yorker, December 17, 1990

THE SHELTERING SKY

It used to be said of the composer-writer Paul Bowles and his playwright-novelist wife, Jane, that he was afraid of nothing and she was afraid of everything. That was before he published his first novel, *The Sheltering Sky,* which seems an elaboration of the remark. The 1949 book was his semi-autobiographical account of their marriage—an account that fascinated readers by its Olympian closeted tone. Under the novel's vaporousness is a pop theme: what happens to a modern, dissatisfied woman—a New York artist-intellectual—if she's in the Sahara, her husband dies, and she's enslaved in a harem? She loves it and hates it; she goes mad. But this is not simply a male writer's version of a woman's harem-whore fantasy: the wife, Kit, seems to be fulfilling the nature and desires that the husband, Port, cannot fulfill for himself.

Bowles is so private he doesn't let you in on much. Reading the book, you can't tell who is who sexually; stonewalling is Bowles' literary art. But the novel attracted directors the way Malcolm Lowry's *Under the Volcano* did. Movie people talked about it with awe (Robert Aldrich, Nicolas Roeg, and Mick Jagger were among those who thought of filming it), and when Bernardo Bertolucci got caught up in it he must have been awed, too. His new *The Sheltering Sky* filters out the pop element that gives the book its bit of kicky horror.

Tall, blond Port (John Malkovich), powerfully built, has a creamy voice, a soft pout, and slightly weaving hips. It's the postwar era, and Kit (Debra Winger), his wife of ten years, wears her dark curly hair cropped but piled high on her forehead—she looks like a fashionable illustrator's idea of a spunky lesbian. They're so close a couple they're almost a single person, yet they're unhappy, petulant, snagged. They're one person, but they're also isolated from each other. Even on the rare occasions when they have sex together, there's no passion in it. Most days, they can only quarrel. Port feels that they'll never be in synch, that he wants them to reach the country of the unconscious but Kit holds back. So they go on journeys from the decaying known to the scary unknown with a third person along as a buffer. On the 1947 trip that the film covers, it's rich, handsome, dull Tunner (Campbell Scott). His attentions to Kit give some sexual edge and jealousy to the married pair, and his presence binds them closer; he doesn't have their style, and they treat him as a clod. They're a nasty, brittle pair, strangling in their style.

Crossing boundless landscapes, the three go from Oran, in Algeria, to remote villages in the Sahara, because Port believes in testing himself; he likes rigors and danger, likes the idea of fearlessness. (It's his special arrogance; it's part of his narcissism to see himself as an adventurer.) He takes long night walks in unlighted alleyways and (rather risibly) lets a pimp steer him to a thieving Arab girl in a tent. Kit, hugging her hotel rooms and looking at her luggage for reassurance, lets herself be seduced by Tunner. Sneakily, Port contrives to get rid of him, and the couple, alone, go farther into the boredom of the desert. We wait and wait for all this trekking by train and car and bus to start paying off, but what Bertolucci and his cinematographer, Vittorio Storaro, give us is flies, squalor, and dunes. (*The Sheltering Sky* won't do a lot for North African tourism.) Eventually, with Kit watching over him but helpless to save him, Port succumbs to typhoid.

In Bowles' account (as I make it out), Port dies giving birth to Kit's sexuality, and she becomes him. Fearlessly, fatalistically, she goes into the desert at night, joins a caravan of merchants, and is raped repeatedly by a crude, feudal old Tuareg tribesman and a younger Tuareg, who turns her into his chattel. Bowles' description appears to be his own fantasy of what the hypercivilized Kit—and Port—really want. Kit's (Port's) madness is a sexual version of the Heart of Darkness. The novel is a horror fantasy, like Bowles' most famous short story, the 1945 "A Distant Episode," about a French professor of linguistics who comes to North Africa to study desert dialects: nomads cut out his tongue, dress him in tin cans, and make him dance like a clown. In that story (which prefigures the novel), the professor goes mad—he becomes the nomads' clown. Bowles' *The Sheltering Sky* is high-toned sensationalism; by the end, it has turned into pulp exotica—the alienated intellectual's version of Valentino's *The Sheik*.

In the movie, all this is muffled. Bertolucci doesn't make any big alterations, but the attenuated story becomes even more attenuated, and after Port's death there's no suspense, no drama. When Kit goes farther into the desert, you may think the movie is about changing time zones, and, essentially, you're right. The older rapist is left out, and we don't feel the fullness of Kit's sexual release, or the fullness of her debasement when she's one of the women in the seraglio. She's never raped: the young Tuareg is a tender lover. What we get is too affectless to be a sex fantasy; affectlessness itself is the point.

In the novel, Kit becomes all about sex; the movie is about her giving over to another way of seeing. There may be nothing the matter with that, except as a viewing experience. The picture goes deep into monotony. Bertolucci has lost interest in pace and excitement and verve. He's up to something moral: he's looking outside Western culture, hoping for an erotic tranquility—something abstract, like Islamic art, that will keep you fixated, not moving.

Would I like the movie better if Bertolucci had put in the novel's cheap thrills? You bet I would. I might have laughed at the trashiness, but that's better than feeling apathetic. I don't respect his choice of this material, but, having chosen it, he might have tried to get at the high-risk desire to be overpowered, instead of filling the closet with sand and art. The whole thing has the impressively decadent look of an Armani ad. Storaro is Storaro. His cinematography is lovely but unsurprising—in truth, a little stale. (The graceful camels might be the same ones who posed for him in *Ishtar*.)

Port isn't simply a repressed homosexual; he's a repressed heterosexual. He's a furtive, skunky aesthete, a man of no generous impulses—our worst self-image of white civilization. Bertolucci and his co-scriptwriter, Mark Peploe, have given Port a gloating moment when, after his session with the Arab prostitute, he holds up the wallet that she thinks she has effectively made off with. He has been contentedly nuzzling her ripe melon breasts, but he has to show her he has outmaneuvered her, even though that gives her time to make the shrill, trilling cry that alerts her protectors. (Perhaps Port wants to be chased.) The ingenious Malkovich brings new character textures to the screen: Port is full of smug self-hatred.

Winger takes on a definite resemblance to the iconic photographs of Jane Bowles, but what's the point when the makeup and hairdo aren't attractive on her? (Most people will just think she's losing her looks.) Winger speaks as if she were reading; she never seems to get the hang of the character. (Maybe nobody could, or maybe it would take someone like the young Katharine Hepburn.) Except for a bit of derisive mimicry of Tunner, Winger seems to have nothing to play until Port is feverish and dying. Then she can show hysterical anxiety; it's as if she suddenly dipped into surplus emotions from earlier roles.

At the beginning of the picture, we see that Kit has packed *Nightwood* in her bag. That's about a woman who becomes a dog; here she becomes a zombie. When Kit joins the caravan, rides a camel, and is on her way to becoming a contented love slave, we gauge how long she's en route by the phases of the moon. Her movement into the desert night seems to be intended as a rebirth. (By the time the caravan reaches its destination, she looks like a winsome, dark-skinned Arab boy. Or is it Port who has come out as a homosexual?) The moon phases in the deep-blue desert sky are charmingly cartoonish, but probably the mocking tone isn't intended. (It may be something that happens when Bertolucci gets consciously poetic, as in his 1979 *Luna*.) Once Kit is part of the caravan, we're meant to feel that there has been a shift in her psyche. Bertolucci signals us that she has moved away from the verbal, from definitions and categories, by giving us a long, silent passage (though he keeps the trance music—the drums and flutes—going). She has achieved Port's goal: the country of the unconscious.

The picture never quickens your response to anything. Rather, it's a New Age way of viewing the desert and its inhabitants as primal. Rolling benignly on their camels' backs, the tribesmen are themselves New Agey. We're led to believe that they're not neurotic, like Port, or dull, like Tunner. (In this view, the nomads don't have to strive to be unconscious; it's their heritage.) The seventy-nine-year-old Bowles has been enlisted to play some sort of presiding expatriate sage; he's like the zombie master when he looks into Kit's gray-blue eyes and asks her, "Are you lost?" As I interpret the movie, the wandering Kit, thrown out of the seraglio, may be lost but she isn't mad: having been transmuted, she's drawn to anonymity and impersonality. You're left with the impression that she'd rather be a nameless whore in some Casbah than return to the New York heebie-jeebies.

Bertolucci thought about the Paul Bowles novel so much it disintegrated. If he had filmed "A Distant Episode," he might have presented the insane professor of linguistics (who remained in the desert) as having ma~~de~~ a sound political choice. I'm pushing it of course; I'm trying to in~~dicate~~ that the sensibilities of Bowles and Bertolucci simply don't fit t~~oget~~~~her~~.

Just as Bertolucci and his cowriter Peploe suggested in *T*~~he La~~*st Emperor* that forced reëducation—Communist brainwashing—had ~~na~~tural cleansing, ~~Pu Yi's soul,~~ so now they propose that Kit's blanking out is a form ~~ed pet: a dog?) is~~ and that her being used for nothing but sex (like ~~this movie, because if~~ ~~his~~ sexual liberation. I hope I'm wildly overinterp~~r~~ ~~Western intellectuals who~~ I'm not, Bertolucci has become a caricature ~~at he's telling us how deca-~~ reject Western values. And at the same ~~uous, sumptuous fantasy that~~ dent we are he's making this oversc~~ex life.~~ looks as if it's about Lawrence of

The New Yorker, December 17, 1990

Movie Love

What thou lovest well remains, the rest is dross
What thou lov'st well shall not be reft from thee
What thou lov'st well is thy true heritage . . .

POUND, CANTO LXXXI

These last years have not been a time of great moviemaking fervor. What has been sustaining is that there is so much to love in movies besides great moviemaking. The young writer Chuck Wilson reports that his earliest movie memory is of his mother and his aunt taking him, when he was six, to see *Funny Girl,* and as he recalls, "In the final scene, when Barbra Streisand, as Fanny Brice, sings, 'My Man,' it seems to me that I grew taller, yes, I leaned forward, some part of me rose up to meet the force coming from the screen. . . . I was rising to get close to the woman I saw there. But I also rose to get closer to my self."

An avidity for more is built into the love of movies. Something else is built in: you have to be open to the idea of getting drunk on movies. (Being able to talk about movies with someone—to share the giddy high excitement you feel—is enough for a friendship.)

Our emotions rise to meet the force coming from the screen, and they go on rising throughout our movie-going lives. When this happens in a popular art form—when it's an art experience that we discover for ourselves—it is sometimes disparaged as fannishness. But there's something there that goes deeper than connoisseurship or taste. It's a fusion of art and love.

in her bag. That's about a woman who becomes a dog; here she becomes a zombie. When Kit joins the caravan, rides a camel, and is on her way to becoming a contented love slave, we gauge how long she's en route by the phases of the moon. Her movement into the desert night seems to be intended as a rebirth. (By the time the caravan reaches its destination, she looks like a winsome, dark-skinned Arab boy. Or is it Port who has come out as a homosexual?) The moon phases in the deep-blue desert sky are charmingly cartoonish, but probably the mocking tone isn't intended. (It may be something that happens when Bertolucci gets consciously poetic, as in his 1979 *Luna*.) Once Kit is part of the caravan, we're meant to feel that there has been a shift in her psyche. Bertolucci signals us that she has moved away from the verbal, from definitions and categories, by giving us a long, silent passage (though he keeps the trance music—the drums and flutes—going). She has achieved Port's goal: the country of the unconscious.

The picture never quickens your response to anything. Rather, it's a New Age way of viewing the desert and its inhabitants as primal. Rolling benignly on their camels' backs, the tribesmen are themselves New Agey. We're led to believe that they're not neurotic, like Port, or dull, like Tunner. (In this view, the nomads don't have to strive to be unconscious; it's their heritage.) The seventy-nine-year-old Bowles has been enlisted to play some sort of presiding expatriate sage; he's like the zombie master when he looks into Kit's gray-blue eyes and asks her, "Are you lost?" As I interpret the movie, the wandering Kit, thrown out of the seraglio, may be lost but she isn't mad: having been transmuted, she's drawn to anonymity and impersonality. You're left with the impression that she'd rather be a nameless whore in some Casbah than return to the New York heebie-jeebies.

Bertolucci thought about the Paul Bowles novel so much it disintegrated. If he had filmed "A Distant Episode," he might have presented the insane professor of linguistics (who remained in the desert) as having made a sound political choice. I'm pushing it, of course; I'm trying to indicate that the sensibilities of Bowles and Bertolucci simply don't fit together.

Just as Bertolucci and his co-writer Peploe suggested in *The Last Emperor* that forced reëducation—Communist brainwashing—had saved Pu Yi's soul, so now they propose that Kit's blanking out is a form of cultural cleansing, and that her being used for nothing but sex (like a trained pet: a dog?) is sexual liberation. I hope I'm wildly overinterpreting this movie, because if I'm not, Bertolucci has become a caricature of the Western intellectuals who reject Western values. And at the same time that he's telling us how decadent we are he's making this overscaled, sensuous, sumptuous fantasy that looks as if it's about Lawrence of Arabia's sex life.

The New Yorker, December 17, 1990

Movie Love

)

What thou lovest well remains, the rest is dross
What thou lov'st well shall not be reft from thee
What thou lov'st well is thy true heritage . . .

POUND, CANTO LXXXI

These last years have not been a time of great moviemaking fervor. What has been sustaining is that there is so much to love in movies besides great moviemaking. The young writer Chuck Wilson reports that his earliest movie memory is of his mother and his aunt taking him, when he was six, to see *Funny Girl,* and as he recalls, "In the final scene, when Barbra Streisand, as Fanny Brice, sings, 'My Man,' it seems to me that I grew taller, yes, I leaned forward, some part of me rose up to meet the force coming from the screen. . . . I was rising to get close to the woman I saw there. But I also rose to get closer to my self."

An avidity for more is built into the love of movies. Something else is built in: you have to be open to the idea of getting drunk on movies. (Being able to talk about movies with someone—to share the giddy high excitement you feel—is enough for a friendship.)

Our emotions rise to meet the force coming from the screen, and they go on rising throughout our movie-going lives. When this happens in a popular art form—when it's an art experience that we discover for ourselves—it is sometimes disparaged as fannishness. But there's something there that goes deeper than connoisseurship or taste. It's a fusion of art and love.

INDEX

Asphalt Jungle, The, 666
Assassins et Voleurs, 462
Astaire, Fred, 5, 37, 124, 251, 291, 430, 471–75, 566, 621, 922
As the Twig Is Bent, 323
Astor, Mary, 1241
Atherton, William, 559, 560, 676
Atkinson, Brooks, 245
L'Atalante, 112, 455, 653
Atlantic City, 889–93
À Tout Prendre, 508
Attenborough, Richard, 967, 968, 969
At the Back of the North Wind, 941
Atwill, Lionel, 602
Auberjonois, René, 782
Aubrey, James, 434
Auden, W. H., 152, 517, 718
Audran, Stéphane, 463
Auer, Gregory M., 701
Auer, Mischa, 95
Aumont, Jean-Pierre, 654
Austen, Jane, 493
Auteuil, Daniel, 1145
Autobiography of Miss Jane Pittman, The, 571
Averback, Hy, 335
Avery, Margaret, 1091
L'Avventura, 28, 30, 50, 113, 387, 388, 456
Awful Truth, The, 286, 619, 622, 623, 624, 631, 632, 633, 641
Axelrod, George, 90, 205
Aykroyd, Dan, 1228, 1229

Babenco, Hector, 909–13, 1128
Babita, 657
Babylon Revisited (Fitzgerald), 387
Bacall, Lauren, 103, 153, 337, 389, 1218
Bach, Johann Sebastian, 480, 484, 1096
Bach, Steven, 1078–80
Bachelet, Jean, 114
Bachelor and the Bobby Soxer, The, 635, 637
Bachrach, Burt, 333
Bacon, Francis, 454
Bacon, Kevin, 931
Badalamenti, Angelo, 1112
Bad Company, 525, 721
Badham, John, 764
Bagneris, Vernel, 921
Bagnold, Enid, 468
Bail, Chuck, 844
Bailey, Charles W., II, 205
Bailey, John, 856
Baillie, Bruce, 85
Bainter, Fay, 389
Baker, Chet, 1196–99
Baker, Ian, 839
Baker, Joe Don, 549, 551–52
Baker, Kathy, 1134
Baker, Lenny, 678, 679
Baker, Stanley, 117
Baker's Wife, The, 1145

Balcony, The, 350
Baldwin, Alec, 1171
Bale, Christian, 1222
Balin, Mireille, 709
Ball, Lucille, 268
Ballad of Cable Hogue, The, 377
Ballard, Carroll, 85, 827, 939
Ballard, Lucien, 86, 669
Ballet Review, 473
Ballhaus, Michael, 1053, 1219
Balthazar, 179
Bananas, 390, 439, 532, 533, 534
Bancroft, Anne, 566, 676, 860, 1160
Bancroft, George, 247, 254
Band, Richard, 1087
Band, The, 781
Banderas, Antonio, 1131, 1132
Bandits of Orgosolo, 729
Band of Outsiders, 81–84, 89, 100, 148, 377
Band Wagon, The, 466
Banerjee, Victor, 1042, 1043, 1044, 1069, 1070
Bang the Drum Slowly, 508–509, 807
Bank Dick, The, 1139
Bankhead, Tallulah, 411, 622
Bannen, Ian, 968, 1148
Bara, Theda, 26
Barbarella, 188, 379, 455
Barbarosa, 1077
Barber, Samuel, 860, 1123
Barbieri, Gato, 455
Bardot, Brigitte, 100, 202, 387, 388, 761
Barefoot in the Park, 169, 219
Barker, The, 247
Barkin, Ellen, 930, 931, 982
Barnes, Howard, 280
Barr, Jean-Marc, 1148
Barr, Richard, 241, 297
Barrault, Marie-Christine, 697, 865
Barrett, Roy, 836
Barretts of Wimpole Street, The, 311
Barrie, George, 642
Barrie, J. M., 15
Barrow, Clyde, 142–57
Barry, John, 714
Barry, Julian, 586, 591
Barry, Philip, 243, 636–37
Barry Lyndon, 922
Barrymore, Drew, 941–42
Barrymore, Ethel, 638–39
Barrymore, John, 128, 130, 843, 956, 978
Barrymore, Lionel, 79, 199, 639
Barthelmess, Richard, 225
Bartkowiak, Andrzej, 1069
Bartók, Béla, 30
Barty, Billy, 615–16
Barwood, Hal, 560
Basic Training of Pavlo Hummel, The, 560
Basie, Count, 1096
Basinger, Kim, 1203

Blain, Gérard, 737, 738
Blair, Linda, 537, 539
Blaise, Pierre, 577, 580
Blake, Michael, 1245
Blake, Nicholas, 268
Blake, William, 42
Blakley, Ronee, 612
Blatty, William Peter, 536–39
Blauner, Peter, 1122
Blazing Saddles, 603, 715
Blessed, Brian, 1223
Blessed Event, 120, 254
Blier, Bertrand, 787–94, 1053
Blithedale Romance, The (Hawthorne), 1021, 1022
Block, Lawrence, 1102
Blondell, Joan, 218, 410, 649
Blood of a Poet, The, 403, 578, 669
Bloody Kids, 1099
Bloom, Claire, 1014
Blossom, Roberts, 741, 757
Blow Out, 900–904, 1210
Blow Up, 105–11, 222, 613, 694, 900, 901
Blue, James, 86
Blue, Robert, 1054
Blue Angel, The, 431
Blue Max, The, 714
Blue Movie (Southern), 450
Blue Velvet, 1109–15, 1193
Blume in Love, 503, 517, 679, 681
Bob & Carol & Ted & Alice, 334–39, 515, 679, 930
Bobby Deerfield, 732
Bock, Jerry, 400
Bode, Ralf D., 764, 833–34
Body and Soul, 875
Body Heat, 931
Boffety, Jean, 547
Bogarde, Dirk, 34, 116
Bogart Humphrey, 25, 103, 121, 125, 155, 214, 217, 371, 515, 516, 520, 548, 629, 667, 722, 723, 753, 1237
Bogdanovich, Peter, 500
Böhm, Karl, 662
La Bohème, 1163
Bohringer, Richard, 937
Bois, Curt, 210, 1173
Boland, Brian, 1204
Boland, Mary, 204, 251
Bolger, Ray, 795
Bologna, Joe, 955
Bombshell, 254, 495, 964
Bonanova, Fortunio, 293
Bond, Julian, 1061, 1063
Bondarchuk, Sergei, 743
Bonnie and Clyde, xix, 141–57, 178, 180, 211, 332, 495, 498, 544, 547, 601, 607, 608, 721, 778
Bonnie Parker Story, The, 143
Booke, Sorrell, 525

Book of Nonsense (Ray), 64
Boom!, 428
Boom Boom, 628
Boorman, John, 503, 776, 894–99, 1146–49
Boorman, Katrine, 897
Borges, Jorge Luis, 228
Borgnine, Ernest, 476
Bori, Lucrezia, 627
Born, Max, 354
Born Losers, 408
Born on the Fourth of July, 1230–34
Born to Win, 390, 439
Born Yesterday, 495
Borrego, Jesse, 1195
Bose, Lucia, 709
Boss' Son, The, 1054
Bostonians, The, 1021–25
Bostonians, The (James), 1021, 1025
Boswell, Connee, 920
Bottoms, Timothy, 413
Boudu Saved from Drowning, 111–12, 114, 688, 1092
Bound for Glory, 768
Bounty, The, 1100
Bouquet, Carole, 762
Bourke-White, Margaret, 968
Bouton, Jim, 518
Bovasso, Julie, 1066, 1163
Bow, Clara, 225, 247
Bowers, William, 599
Bowie, David, 693–94
Bowker, Judi, 1062
Bowles, Jane, 1246, 1248
Bowles, Paul, 1246–49
Bowman, Lee, 635
Boxcar Bertha, 510
Boyd, James, 277
Boyd, Russell, 1035, 1169
Boyden, Peter, 903
Boyer, Charles, 21, 126, 621, 624, 768, 943, 1001
Boyer, Myriam, 688
Boy Friend, The, 752
Boy in the Plastic Bubble, The, 765
Boyle, Peter, 601, 602, 682, 683
Boys from Brazil, The, 930
Boys from Syracuse, The, 430, 1176
Boys in the Band, The, 193
Bozzufi, Marcel, 345–46
Bracco, Lorraine, 1236
Brach, Gérard, 1145
Brackett, Charles, 246, 628
Brackett, Leigh, 518
Brady, Mathew, 173
Branagh, Kenneth, 1221–23
Brando, Jocelyn, 907
Brando, Marlon, 4, 6, 128, 130, 151, 167–68, 361–65, 436–37, 450–56, 564, 567, 595, 597, 667, 684, 765, 876, 877, 903, 1066
Brandt, Bill, 860

Duck Soup, 104, 249, 257, 324, 632, 1096, 1178
Duel, 559, 755
Duel at Diablo, 135
Duff, Howard, 720, 722
Duhamel, Antoine, 186
Dukakis, Olympia, 1163
Duke, Daryl, 485
Duke, Patty, 698
Dullea, Keir, 166
Dumarcay, Philippe, 790
Dumas, Alexander, 269
du Maurier, Daphne, 528, 529, 531
Dummar, Melvin, 848–49, 851, 852, 853–54
Dummy, The, 247
Dumont, José, 1129
Dumont, Margaret, 533
Dunaway, Faye, 150, 151, 152, 513, 702, 706, 781, 904–908
Duncan, Isadora, 244, 262, 323
Dundas, Jennie, 1034
Dune, 1112, 1113
Dunne, Dominick, 465
Dunne, Irene, 170, 221, 619, 620, 623, 632, 633, 634, 635, 636
Dunne, John Gregory, 465
Duprez, June, 638
Duran, Jorge, 910
Duras, Marguerite, 31, 724–27
Durbin, Deanna, 251
Durning, Charles, 676, 967
Duse, Eleonora, 198
Duvall, Robert, 437, 599–600, 671, 703, 811, 982, 983
Duvall, Shelley, 545, 547, 613, 1139
Duvivier, Julien, 112, 761
Dux, Pierre, 345
Dyer, Peter John, 8–9, 10, 12
Dzundza, George, 802, 807

Earhart, Amelia, 285, 406
Earrings of Madame de . . . , The, 20–23, 377, 607, 1001, 1206
Earth, 64, 745
Earthquake, 591–94
East, Sister Carol, 1115
East of Eden, 31, 124, 799
Easton, Richard, 1223
Eastwood, Clint, 211, 419, 420, 540–42, 552, 567, 717, 777, 801, 820
Easy Living, 210, 258, 964
Easy Rider, 329–30, 448, 498, 510, 1115
Ebb, Fred, 431–32
Eburne, Maude, 127
Ecstasy, 980
Eddy, Nelson, 251, 628
Ede, H. S., 468, 470
Eden, Anthony, 441
Edge of Darkness, 344
Edge of the City, 12

Edwards, Blake, 90–91
Edwards, Sebastian Rice, 1146, 1149
Egan, Michael, 679
Eiger Sanction, The, 718
8½, 69–72, 88, 110, 209, 222, 354, 355, 508, 610, 842–43, 862, 865
8 Million Ways to Die, 1102–03, 1122
Eisenstein, Sergei, 30, 64, 68–69, 88, 92, 133, 149, 154, 172, 173, 207, 361, 526, 527, 691, 696, 731, 743, 749, 781
El, 98
El Dorado, 138, 140–41
Eleni, 1088
Elephant Man, The, 858–62, 1113, 1123
Elfman, Danny, 1204
Elgar, Edward, 417
Elias, Alix, 742
Eliot, George, 493, 775
Eliot, T. S., 171, 230
Ellington, Duke, 460
Elliott, Denholm, 199, 1091
Ellis, Anita, 1219
Ellison, Harlan, 94
Ellsberg, Daniel, 394
Elmes, Frederick, 1113
El Topo, 401–406
Elvira Madigan, 178, 333
Elvis, 868
Elvis on Tour, 510
Emigrants, The, 450
Emmich, Cliff, 485
Empire Strikes Back, The, 818, 827, 833, 941, 984–86
Emshwiller, Ed, 570
Enchanted Cottage, The, 323
Enemies, A Love Story, 1224–27, 1238–39
Les Enfants Terribles, 26, 83, 163, 578
Enforcer, The, 717–18
Enjo, 28, 44
Enoch Arden (Tennyson), 634
Enriquez, René, 1011
Ensor, James, 431
Enter Laughing, 210, 335
Enter Madam, 622
Entertainer, The, 77, 112, 184, 718
Eraserhead, 858, 860, 861, 1113
Erections, Ejaculations, Exhibitions and General Tales of Ordinary Madness, 979
Ericson, Eric, 662
Ermey, Lee, 1141
Erwin, Stuart, 254
Escape Artist, The, 940, 941
E. T. The Extra-Terrestrial, 939–43
L'Etranger, 25
Euripides, 380–84
Eustache, Jean, 555, 556, 557–58, 739
Evans, Gene, 550
Evans, Walker, 146
Every Day Except Christmas (Anderson), 22
Every Girl Should Be Married, 636

Guinness, Alec, 111, 759, 987, 1042, 1043–44, 1075
Guitry, Sacha, 462–63, 792, 1136
Gulpilil, 812
Gumshoe, 1099
Gun Crazy, 143
Gunfighter, The, 60, 136
Gunga Din, 59, 632, 633–34, 638
Gunn, Moses, 525
Guns at Batasi, 714
"Gunsmoke," 670
Gunther, John, 322
Guss, Louis, 1163
Guthrie, Arlo, 333
Guttenberg, Steve, 930
Guys and Dolls, 430
Gwynne, Fred, 1041
Gwynne, Michael C., 485
Gypsy, 430

Haas, Lukas, 1046, 1047
Hack, Shelley, 1126
Hackman, Gene, 154, 391, 393, 475, 563, 602, 693, 1009, 1010, 1013, 1184–85
Hagegård, Håkan, 662
Hail the Conquering Hero, 560
Hair, 355, 586
Half a Sixpence, 205
Hall, Conrad, 333, 1182
Hall, James, 247
Hall, Porter, 127
Halsey, Richard, 485
Hambling, Gerry, 929
Hamill, Mark, 984
Hamilton, Edith, 384
Hamilton, Margaret, 699
Hamlet, 78, 270
Hamm, Sam, 1203
Hammerstein, Arthur, 628, 630
Hammerstein, Reggie, 628, 630
Hammerstein II, Oscar, 628, 630
Hammett, Dashiell, 517, 519, 732, 733, 734–35, 736
Hampton, Christopher, 1187
Hampton, Hope, 308
Hampton, Paul, 458
Handke, Peter, 1173
Handle with Care, 740–42
Hanft, Helen, 863
Hanks, Tom, 1020
Hanley, Gerald, 969
Hannah, Daryl, 947, 1138
Hannah and Her Sisters, 1095–97
Hannant, Brian, 953
Harbach, Otto, 628
Hard Day's Night, A, 220, 221
Harding, Ann, 632
Hard Times, 1009
Hardwick, Elizabeth, 117
Hardwick, Michael, 667

Hardy, Oliver, 176
Hardy, Robert, 1062, 1063
Hardy, Thomas, 359, 1200
Harlettes, the, 873
Harlow, 94
Harlow, Jean, 153, 254, 476, 492, 631, 875, 964
Harmon, Deborah, 871
Harnick, Sheldon, 400
Harold and Maude, 608
Harper, Jessica, 585, 865, 920, 923, 956
Harper, Tess, 982, 983
Harris, Ed, 1005, 1009, 1081, 1082, 1083
Harris, Frank, 468
Harris, Leonard, 683
Harris, Richard, 583
Harris, Rosalind, 398
Harris, Rosemary, 191, 1221
Harrison, George, 1160
Harrison, Jerry, 1031
Harrold, Kathryn, 1053
Harron, Robert, 225
Harry & Tonto, 590, 679
Hart, Moss, 243, 251, 254, 262, 272, 324, 570, 629, 637
Hart, William S., 409
Hartlip, Aline, 1063
Hartman, Elizabeth, 551
Harvest, 1145
Harvey, Anthony, 190
Harvey, Don, 1209
Harvey, Laurence, 360
Hasford, Gustav, 1141, 1143–44
Hatfield, Hurd, 1118
Hauer, Rutger, 948
Havers, Nigel, 1042
Having Wonderful Time, 766
Hawaii, 199
Hawks, Howard, 82, 103, 140–41, 153, 194, 285, 286, 317, 632–33, 634, 1003
Hawn, Goldie, 559, 560, 603, 605–606
Hawthorne, Nathaniel, 1021, 1022, 1139
Hayden, Sterling, 518, 744–45, 747, 749
Hayes, Billy, 796–800
Hayes, Helen, 191, 410, 632
Hayes, John Michael, 86
Hayes, Terry, 953
Hayman, David, 1147
Hayward, Leland, 306
Hayward, Susan, 32, 429, 457, 687
Hayworth, Rita, 72, 619, 1219
Head, Edith, 665
Healy, Ted, 393
Hearst, Millicent, 300, 309
Hearst, Patty, 705
Hearst, William Randolph, 235–325
Hearst, Lord of San Simeon, 313
Heartbreakers, 1052–56
Heart of Darkness, 268, 882
Heaven Can Wait, 774, 776–77, 779

Lyne, Adrian, 1149, 1150, 1151
Lynley, Carol, 476
Lyon, Sue, 42

McAlpine, Don, 1091
McAnally, Ray, 1214
MacArthur, Charles, 107, 236, 243, 254–55, 262–63, 286, 301, 633
Macbeth, 301, 358
MacBird, 156
McCabe & Mrs. Miller, 375–78, 439, 477, 544–45, 547, 605, 900, 1118, 1163
McCambridge, Mercedes, 402
McCann, Donal, 1156, 1159
McCarey, Leo, 632
McCarthy, Joseph, 205, 235, 259, 261, 344, 497
McCarthy, Kevin, 811
McCartney, Paul, 108
McCormick, Edith Rockefeller, 306–307
McCormick, Harold, 306–307
McCowen, Alec, 1223
McCrea, Joel, 251, 254, 414, 632, 673, 720, 1052
McCullers, Carson, 165, 168, 169
Macdonald, Dwight, 13, 30, 47, 60–61, 63, 65
MacDonald, George, 941
MacDonald, Jeanette, 251, 628, 629
McDormand, Frances, 1184, 1186
McDowall, Roddy, 476
McDowell, Malcolm, 415, 417
McDowell, Michael, 1172
McEwan, Geraldine, 1222
McGann, Paul, 1200
McGill, Bruce, 741
Macgill, Moyna, 210
McGillis, Kelly, 1046, 1047, 1107
McGovern, Elizabeth, 855, 1058
MacGraw, Ali, 780
McGuire, Don, 963
McKay, Louis, 458
McKean, Michael, 870
McKee, Lonette, 686, 687, 1038, 1039, 1040
McKeon, Doug, 916, 917
Mackie, Bob, 923, 924
McKinley, William, 296, 300
MacLachlan, Kyle, 1110, 1112
McLaglen, Andrew V., 138
McLaglen, Victor, 348, 633
MacLaine, Shirley, 188, 411, 419, 513, 971, 1238
McLaren, Hollis, 891, 892
McLiam, John, 525
McLuhan, Marshall, 369
McMartin, John, 901
MacMurray, Fred, 515–16
McMurtry, Larry, 10
Macnaughton, Robert, 941
McNeice, Ian, 1161

MacNicol, Peter, 970
McPherson, Aimee Semple, 269–70, 323
McQueen, Steve, 135, 217, 566, 567, 820
McRae, Frank, 870
Macy, Bill, 721, 955
Madame X, 79–81, 943
Mädchen in Uniform, 173
Made for Each Other, 439, 499
Madigan, Amy, 1082
Mad Love, 318, 319
Mad Max, 950, 1140
Mad Max 2 (The Road Warrior), 949–54, 977, 992, 1140
Magee, Patrick, 416
Magic Face, The, 552
Magic Flute, The, 660–63, 667
Magnani, Anna, 18–20, 113, 149, 396, 730, 889
Magnificent Ambersons, The, 66, 121, 129, 130, 241, 284, 302
Magnum Force, 540–44, 552, 717, 718, 801
Magnuson, Ann, 1182
Mahler, Gustav, 3
Mahogany, 654–56
Mahoney, John, 1163
Maidstone, 452
Mailer, Norman, xxi, 91, 92, 166, 192, 350, 366, 426, 452–53, 454, 491–98, 508, 666, 684, 979, 1105
Main, Marjorie, 155
Major Dundee, 86, 422
Makioka Sisters, The (Tanizaki), 1049
Malkovich, John, 1187, 1189, 1247
Malle, Louis, 385–89, 576–81, 889, 891, 892, 893, 961, 969
Malory, Sir Thomas, 896
Maltby, Jr., Richard, 764
Maltese Falcon, The, 91, 290, 666, 1183, 1241
Maltese Falcon, The (Hammett), 519
Mame, 635
Mamoulian, Rouben, 247
Man Alone, A, 552
Manchurian Candidate, The, 5, 61, 141, 143, 156, 205, 809
Mancuso, Nick, 1052, 1054
Mandingo, 705, 765
Manès, Gina, 886
Man Escaped, A, 386–87
Man for All Seasons, A, 145, 189, 213–14, 732, 735
Manhattan, 865, 866, 867–68, 970, 1095, 1097
Man I Love, The, 247
Mankiewicz, Don, 244
Mankiewicz, Frank, 244
Mankiewicz, Herman J., xx, 241–325
Mankiewicz, Johanna, 244
Mankiewicz, Joseph L., 121, 129, 243, 267, 298, 324

La Strada, 173
Spradlin, G. D., 600
Sragow, Michael, 873, 1218
Stagecoach, 136–37, 318, 549
Stakeout on Dope Street, 574
Stalin, Joseph, 259, 260, 261, 287
Stallings, Laurence, 252, 311
Stallone, Sylvester, 765, 1064, 1065
Stamp, Terence, 55, 1099
Stang, Arnold, 412
Stanley, Kim, 702, 706, 1003
Stanwyck, Barbara, 26, 410, 517, 585, 977
Stapleton, Maureen, 572, 784, 785, 786
Stapleton, Oliver, 1099
Star!, 395, 572
Stardust Memories, 862–68, 1096
Star Is Born, A (1954), 42
Star Is Born, A (1976), 781
Starstruck, 1036, 1168
Star Trek II: The Wrath of Khan, 943–44
Start the Revolution Without Me, 601, 1176
Star Wars, 756, 758, 759, 818, 894, 984, 985, 987
State of Siege, 526
Steagle, The, 390
Steegmuller, Francis, 895
Steel, Dawn, 1207
Steenburgen, Mary, 850
Stefanelli, Simonetta, 437
Steiger, Rod, 214, 215, 397, 413, 518
Stein, Gertrude, 46
Stein, Joe, 954
Stein, Joseph, 399
Stein, Margaret Sophie, 1224
Steinberg, Norman, 955
Steiner, Max, 714
Stella Dallas, 32, 1168
Stendhal, 75, 76
Stepfather, The, 1126–28, 1193
Stéphane, Nicole, 163, 578
Stephens, Robert, 1223
Sterling, Ford, 625
Stern, Bert, 491
Stern, Daniel, 930
Stern, Isaac, 396, 399
Stern, Sandor, 825
Sterne, Laurence, 1167
Stevens, Andrew, 771
Stevens, Ashton, 270
Stevens, George, 59, 632, 634, 731, 802, 950
Stevens, Leslie, 154
Stevens, Stella, 476
Stewart, Bill, 1013
Stewart, Donald Ogden, 243, 969
Stewart, James, 137, 207, 254, 517, 620, 621
Stine, Harold E., 349
Sting, The, 561, 563, 564, 570, 723
Stir Crazy, 934
Stockwell, Dean, 1113
Stoddard, Brandon, 572

Stokowski, Leopold, 460
Stoler, Shirley, 806
Stone, Oliver, 796, 1103, 1122–25, 1231, 1233, 1234
Stop Making Sense, 1030–32, 1115
Stoppa, Paolo, 999
Storaro, Vittorio, 455, 746, 1152, 1247
Story of Adèle H., The, 650–54
Story on Page One, The, 638
Straight, Beatrice, 703
Straight, Place, and Show, 103
Straight Time, 1191
Strange Ones, The, 26
Stranger, The, 165, 168–69
Strangers on a Train, 5, 737
Strasberg, Lee, 493, 496, 599
Stravinsky, Igor, 30, 384
Straw Dogs, 422–26, 439, 1009
Streep, Meryl, 803, 806, 970–71, 1238
Streetcar Named Desire, A, 6, 195
Streetcar Named Desire, A (Williams), 497
Street Smart, 1133–35
Streisand, Barbra, 182–84, 365–66, 414, 459, 477, 511–13, 619–20, 687, 699, 712, 872, 1015–20, 1250
Strick, Joseph, 349–52
Strindberg, August, 48, 456, 478, 481, 482, 581, 890
Stuart, Gloria, 957
Stulberg, Gordon, 594
Stunt Man, The, 840–47, 956
Sturges, John, 205
Sturges, Preston, 40, 121, 243, 246, 252, 262, 270, 271, 288, 290, 560, 629, 635, 851, 852, 862, 1152
Stuyck, Joris, 1063
Styron, William, 969–71
Subterraneans, The, 467
Sugarland Express, The, 559–61, 564, 605, 755
Sullavan, Margaret, 250, 306, 766
Sullivan, Ed, 147
Sullivan, Sean, 893
Sullivan's Travels, 862
Summer Interlude, 479
Summer Stock, 474
Sunday, Bloody Sunday, 438, 439
Sundays and Cybèle, 62
Sundowners, The, 214, 731
Sunset Boulevard, 174
Sunshine Boys, The, 922
Supremes, the, 460
Susann, Jacqueline, 570
Suspicion, 640, 831
Susskind, David, 209
Sutherland, Donald, 347, 348, 379, 528, 529, 530, 693, 747, 750, 752, 809, 810, 854, 857, 1155, 1176
Sutton, Dudley, 1200
Suzy, 631, 641
Swain, Mack, 625